BUSINESS

EIGHTH EDITION

William M. Pride
Texas A & M University

Robert J. Hughes
Dallas County Community College

Jack R. Kapoor
College of DuPage

HOUGHTON MIFFLIN COMPANY
Boston New York

Editor-in-Chief: George T. Hoffman
Associate Sponsoring Editor: Susan M. Kahn
Editorial Assistant: Kira Robinson-Keates
Senior Project Editor: Rachel D'Angelo Wimberly
Editorial Assistant: Sarah Cleary
Senior Production/Design Coordinator: Jill Haber
Senior Manufacturing Coordinator: Marie Barnes
Marketing Manager: Steven W. Mikels
Marketing Associate: Lisa E. Boden

Custom Publishing Editor: Dee Renfrow
Custom Publishing Production Manager: Kathleen McCourt
Project Coordinator: Anisha Sandhu

Cover Image: © Jennifer Roycroft, Roycroft Design

Printed in the United States of America.

ISBN: 0-618-53091-6
N03702

2 3 4 5 6 7 8 9 – DSG – 06 05

222 Berkeley Street • Boston, MA 02116

Address all correspondence and order information to the above address.

Brief Contents

Contents

5 Choosing a Form of Business Ownership 135

6 Small Business, Entrepreneurship, and Franchises 165

11 Motivating and Satisfying Employees 311

12 Enhancing Union-Management Relations 337

15 Wholesaling, Retailing, and Physical Distribution 433

16 Developing Integrated Marketing Communications 465

Part VI Information for Business Strategy and Decision Making 497

17 Acquiring, Organizing, and Using Information 498

18 Using Accounting Information 531

Part VII Finance and Investment 565

19 Understanding Money, Banking, and Credit 566

20 Mastering Financial Management 599

21 Understanding Securities Markets and Investments 629

Preface

CHANGE! No other word better describes the current business environment. Three years ago, when the seventh edition of Pride/Hughes/Kapoor was published, employment opportunities, investment opportunities, and career advancement opportunities had never been greater. Today, the economic picture looks much different. Consider just some of the changes that have occurred.

- There have been a large number of business failures—especially in the technology and information industries.
- The number of people unemployed has increased to approximately 6 percent of the nation's work force.
- There are fewer manufacturing jobs in the United States as business firms have begun producing more goods in foreign countries.

These important changes along with the tragic events of September 11, the war on terrorism, and many more are discussed in this new edition of *Business.* In fact, the primary reason behind this new edition is to provide students and instructors with the latest information available. We are especially proud of this edition because we wrote it with two goals in mind: *Achieving Student Success* and *Achieving Great Teaching.*

Special Note to Our Customers

Pride/Hughes/Kapoor *Business* is the best selling introduction to business textbook in the market. We thank you for your support. Certainly, comments and suggestions made by professors and reviewers like you who teach the course, our national advisory board, and students who take the course have helped to make each edition of *Business* better than the last. As authors, we encourage you to read the preface for an overview of how we have revised the new edition. We invite you to spend some time examining the text, features, illustrations, and cases. We hope you like what you see in this new, eighth edition of *Business*!

WMP, RJH, JRK

Achieving Student Success!

For many years, people assumed that business prosperity would continue. When the bubble burst, people were faced with the question: What do we do now? It is a difficult question to answer. Certainly, for a college student taking business courses or a new employee just starting a career, the question is particularly difficult to answer. And yet, there are still opportunities for people who are willing to work hard, continue to learn, and possess the ability to adapt to change. That's where the new Pride/Hughes/Kapoor *Business* learning package can help.

We believe that students deserve the most up-to-date, interesting, and relevant textbook and package. This edition begins with a thoroughly revised, beautifully designed full-color textbook that invites students into the study of business and helps them achieve success by providing the content coverage, real-world examples, pedagogical aids, and career-related information that is important in today's ever-changing business world.

When students purchase a new copy of the eighth edition of *Business,* they get more than a textbook. Shrink-wrapped with every new text is the *Business Bonus Pack: Your Guide to an "A"* that includes a variety of multimedia study aids and tips about how to use them to study more effectively and succeed in the course.

At the same time that we offer a thoroughly revised full-length text and the best learning package in the marketplace, students also get a great low price. The eighth edition of *Business,* available in convenient loose-leaf format that allows flexible use of the text, is priced ⅓ less than our full-length competitors.

Achieving Great Teaching!

Our objective has always been to provide both students and instructors with a textbook and package that is relevant and accurate, and is as interesting as business itself. To that end, we worked hard to make sure that this new edition of *Business* maintains our tradition of providing quality instructional materials based on our own classroom experiences. All three of us teach college level courses. Collectively, we have over 70 years of experience teaching Introduction to Business, including teaching multiple sections of Introduction to Business every semester. We revise the *Business* text and package based on our own experiences in the classroom and with the help of comments and suggestions from other professors, reviewers, our national advisory board members, students, and a very committed team of professionals at our publisher—Houghton Mifflin. Finally, we either write each component or are heavily involved in each component of our instructional package. We think that our classroom experience and personal involvement in the publishing process make a difference and help to create a package that enables both students and instructors to achieve success!

New to This Edition

Suggestions from both educators and students who have used previous editions have been incorporated into the eighth edition. Here are some of the new ways that we make business accessible and relevant.

- All text content is completely revised and provides a comprehensive survey of the major functional areas of business including management, marketing, accounting, finance, and information technology as well as core topics such as ethics and social responsibility, forms of ownership, small business, and international business.
- In addition to the above topics, this edition provides coverage of today's special hot topics such as the nation's economic problems, efforts to improve accounting standards and corporate credibility, the dot-com meltdown, entrepreneurial businesses, diversity, globalization, and the increasing use of technology and e-business.
- All of the *Inside Business* opening vignettes for each chapter in this edition are new. Examples of featured companies include The Container Store, Starbucks, MSN, and Google. *Return to Inside Business* at the end of each chapter provides additional information and questions to stimulate class discussion.
- All of the boxed features in this edition are new. Their themes are Adapting to Change, Examining Ethics, Exploring Business, Going Global, and Talking Technology.
- New video cases accompany every chapter. Examples of highlighted companies include Stonyfield Farms, JetBlue, Remington, and Merrill Lynch Direct.
- A new feature—"Running a Business"—is a continuing video case showcasing Finagle-A-Bagel, a real small business located in the Boston area. Appearing at the conclusion to each part of the text, this multi-part case allows students to integrate and apply their knowledge from each section of the text to a real business situation.
- A new feature—"Building a Business Plan"—helps students to choose a business they would like to start and then develop their own business plans. This series of exercises can be used as a semester-long project and can be completed individually or in teams.

Exciting Boxed Features

A variety of boxed features highlight today's important issues.

Adapting to Change

In today's business environment nothing is more certain than change. Business people must deal with both the benefits and challenges of these changes. The workplace changes on which we focus fall into several broad areas, including career information, cultural diversity, and changes in business practices. Sample topics include

- Keep Your Career Moving in the Right Direction (Chapter 1)
- South African Airways Navigates Nontariff Barriers (Chapter 3)
- What Makes a Great Leader? (Chapter 7)
- Labor Unions Play a Bigger Role in Corporate Governance (Chapter 12)
- Reality Accounting 101: Changes for the Better (Chapter 18)

Examining Ethics

Following up on the ethical coverage provided in Chapter 2, "Being Ethical and Socially Responsible," the Examining Ethics features are designed to develop students' abilities to think critically about typical ethical dilemmas that can arise in business. Questions are provided to encourage classroom discussion. Examples of topics discussed are

- Accounting Scandals: What Went Wrong (Chapter 1)
- Two Companies That Give Something Back (Chapter 5)
- Should Companies Fire 10 Percent of Their Employees Annually? (Chapter 10)
- Lying to Customers (Chapter 13)
- Should Executives Get Preferential IPO Treatment? (Chapter 20)

Exploring Business

The Exploring Business series examines a wide range of organizations and contemporary topics that include business trends, social issues, success stories, and personal applications for students. Sample topics include

- Big Mergers: Fast Track to Investor Wealth? (Chapter 5)
- Making Decisions Under Pressure (Chapter 7)
- Investing in People at Edward Jones (Chapter 10)
- What Companies Want in Sales Representatives (Chapter 16)
- Identity Theft: A Real Possibility (Chapter 19)

Going Global

This series of features, together with Chapter 3, "Exploring Global Business," is designed to enhance students' awareness of the globalization of the business world. Sample features include

- The World According to Wal-Mart (Chapter 5)
- Automakers Drive Productivity Higher (Chapter 9)
- Protecting Employees in Other Countries (Chapter 11)
- Harlem Globetrotters Bring Basketball Fun to the World (Chapter 13)
- China's Rise in Information Technology (Chapter 17)

Talking Technology

Both consumers and businesses are aware of the impact that technology has had on the way we do business. The topics covered in this feature describe some of the latest, state-of-the-art applications that promise to change the way we live. Selected topics include

- Do Privacy Policies Protect Internet Users? (Chapter 2)
- Easy as Dell (Chapter 4)
- How Does the Work Get Done at Motek? (Chapter 8)
- EDS: The Information Expert (Chapter 17)
- To Pick a Winning Investment, Get Help Online (Chapter 21)

Effective Pedagogical Aids

This business course doesn't have to be difficult! We have done everything possible to eliminate the problems that students typically encounter. We asked reviewers with years of teaching experience to discuss what tools are most effective. In addition business students were asked to critique each component. Based on this feedback, the text includes the following features.

Part Introductions

Each of the text's seven parts begins with a concise description of the materials to follow. From the outset of each part, students are exposed to upcoming content and develop a better understanding of the chapters' context within the text.

Learning Objectives

A student with a purpose will learn more effectively than a student wandering aimlessly. Each chapter of *Business* begins with clearly stated learning objectives signaling important concepts to be mastered. The learning objectives are reinforced as they appear in the margins within the chapter and serve as the chapter summary's organizing framework. To aid instructors, questions in the *Test Bank* are keyed to the learning objectives.

Inside Business

Chapter-opening Inside Business features introduce the theme of each chapter and focus on pertinent activities of real organizations. Sample topics include

- Coca-Cola Thinks Small to Capture Global Markets (Chapter 3)
- There Are No "Yah-Whos" at Yahoo! (Chapter 7)
- Workplace Reforms at Mitsubishi's Illinois Plant (Chapter 11)
- AutoTrader.com Revs Up an Exciting Promotion Mix (Chapter 16)
- Bank of America Banks on Online Banking (Chapter 19)

The decisions and activities of these organizations not only demonstrate what companies are actually doing, but also make the materials in each chapter relevant and absorbing. When students become involved in the chapter material, critical thinking and active participation replace passive acceptance, and real learning takes place.

Introductory Chapter Overview

The opening paragraphs of each chapter offer an informal chapter preview while also providing a smooth transition from the Inside Business section. When students are ready to review, each introductory paragraph also serves as a useful reminder of chapter content.

Margin Notes

Two types of margin notes help students understand and retain important concepts. First, each *learning objective* is positioned at the beginning of the section where it is discussed Second, to aid students in building a basic business vocabulary, the definition of each *key term* is placed in the margin near the introduction of the term in the text.

Stimulating Writing Style

One of our major objectives in *Business* is to communicate to students our enthusiasm for business in a direct, engaging manner. Throughout the book we have used a writing style that builds interest and facilitates students' understanding of the concepts discussed. To ensure that the text is stimulating and easy for students to use, we have given special attention to word choice, sentence structure, and the presentation of business language.

Real-World Examples and Illustrations

Numerous real-world examples drawn from familiar organizations and recognizable products are used in each chapter. Is Microsoft an illegal monopoly? How can diversity help an organization succeed? What is included on a personal balance sheet and personal income statement? Why do people invest in mutual funds? Contemporary examples such as these catch students' attention and enable them to apply the concepts and issues of each chapter to their personal lives. The *Spotlight* feature highlights up-to-date fun facts; the *Using the Internet* feature highlights useful websites related to particular topics; and the content-based photo captions provide continual, eye-catching examples that reinforce text material.

Return to Inside Business

The Return to Inside Business feature offers additional information about the organization profiled at the beginning of the chapter to reinforce the application of specific principles. Accompanying questions can be used for classroom discussion. Suggested answers are included in the *Instructor's Resource Manual.*

Complete End-of-Chapter Review Materials

We provide the practical applications that make a business course so valuable for students. Several activities are included at the end of each chapter.

- A summary, based on the chapter's learning objectives, that reviews important ideas presented within the chapter.
- A list of key terms with page references.
- A complete set of review questions that reinforce chapter definitions and concepts.
- Discussion questions that encourage careful consideration of selected issues by asking students to engage in critical thinking and writing about chapter topics.

Video Cases

A video case at the end of each chapter focuses on recognizable organizations. The cases offer descriptions of current business issues and activities, allowing students to consider the real-world implications associated with the concepts covered in the chapter. Related questions suitable for class discussion or individual assignment follow each case. Sample video cases include

- The Global Saga of Subway (Chapter 3)
- Entrepreneurial Spirit Pervades the Percy Inn (Chapter 6)
- Wheelworks Tries to Satisfy Employees and Customers (Chapter 11)
- Fun, Furniture, Movies, and More at Jordan's Furniture (Chapter 16)
- Financial Fusion Fuels Financial Services Transactions (Chapter 19)

Building Skills for Career Success

Each chapter ends with a section entitled "Building Skills for Career Success." The five exercises in this section are Exploring the Internet, Developing Critical Thinking Skills, Building Team Skills, Researching Different Careers, and Improving Communication Skills. Related questions and activities suitable for class discussion or individual assignments follow each exercise. Suggested answers or teaching tips are included in the *Instructor's Resource Manual.*

Glossary

A glossary of major business terms from the text appears at the end of the book. The glossary serves as a convenient reference tool to reinforce students' learning of basic business vocabulary.

Complete Package of Support Materials

Accompanying the eighth edition of *Business* is a support package that focuses on generating enthusiasm in your class, achieving student success, increasing the effectiveness of instructors, and helping students to learn and apply business concepts.

For Instructors to Plan, Present, and Assess More Effectively

Instructor's Resource Manual. The comprehensive *Instructor's Resource Manual,* written by the text's authors, features the following items for each chapter:

- Note from the authors
- Learning objectives
- Brief chapter outline
- Guide for using the transparency acetates
- Comprehensive lecture outline (including transparency cross references, suggestions on where video material can be used, suggested answers to Examining Ethics feature questions, and At Issue debate features for class discussion)
- Answers to the Return to Inside Business questions, review questions, discussion questions, and case questions
- Comments on the Building Skills for Career Success exercises
- Two chapter quizzes with answer keys
- Answer key for transparency class exercise and quizzes

In addition, the *Instructor's Resource Manual* provides a transition guide to the eighth edition, suggestions for planning the course, sample syllabi, and FAQs about teaching introduction to business. The materials in this section and the FAQs are especially useful for adjunct instructors who don't teach on a full-time basis.

Instructor's Activity Manual. New to this edition, this activity manual includes useful tips, tools, and exercises to enhance the classroom experience. This collection of materials comes from a variety of sources, including the text authors and instructors across the country who teach the introduction to business course.

Test Bank. Written and class-tested by the text's authors, the *Test Bank* contains over 4,000 items. Each chapter contains a variety of essay, true/false, and multiple-choice questions. An item-information column in the *Test Bank* specifies details about each question, such as learning objective tie-in, learning level (knowledge or application), answer, and text page reference. More specific information about different types of test questions appears in the introduction to the *Test Bank.*

***HMClassPrep with HMTesting* CD-ROM.** This instructor's CD provides a variety of teaching resources in electronic format allowing for easy customization to meet your specific instructional needs. Files included on the CD include PowerPoint, Word files from the *Instructor's Resource Manual,* and selected videos.

On the same CD for your convenience is the electronic version of the printed *Test Bank.* This program allows instructors to generate and change tests easily. The program includes an online testing feature by which instructors can administer tests via their local area network or over the Web. It also has a gradebook feature that lets users set up classes, record and track grades from tests or assignments, analyze grades, and produce class and individual statistics.

Instructor's Web Site. This password-protected site includes valuable tools to help instructors design and prepare for the course. The contents include the Pride/Hughes/Kapoor update service that provides real-world examples of current events that impact individual businesses, consumers, and the economy. Other materials included on the Instructor's Web Site include FAQs about teaching introduction to business, sample syllabi, PowerPoint slides that can be downloaded, Word files from the *Instructor's Resource Manual,* and more.

Online/Distance Learning Support. Instructors can create and customize online course materials to use in distance learning, distributed learning, or as a supplement to traditional classes. The *Blackboard* and *WebCT* course materials that accompany the text include a variety of study aids for students as well as course management tools for instructors.

New! *Master the Class* Game. Written by John Drea, Western Illinois University, this interactive game allows instructors to review key concepts with their students in a fun and engaging way.

PowerPoint Slide Presentations. PowerPoint slides have been specially developed for this edition of *Business.* We offer two separate versions to give you maximum flexibility. One version provides a complete outline of text content, including key figures and tables. Another version adds enhancements to the complete outline, including additional figures and in-class activities. Instructors can use these presentations as is, or may edit, delete, and add to them to suit their specific class needs.

Videos. There are seven new part-ending videos that relate to the Finagle-A-Bagel part-ending cases. In addition there are twenty-one video modules, one for each chapter, to help instructors bring lectures to life by providing thought-provoking insights into real-world companies, products, and issues. Each chapter module includes four segments: a chapter overview, two key concept segments, and a segment supporting the end-of-chapter video case. Special note: all end-of-chapter videos are new for this edition of *Business.* A complete description of the part ending-videos and each chapter's series of video segments is provided in the *Video Guide.* The videos are available on VHS and DVD.

Video Guide. This guide is designed to help instructors integrate text content with the video series. A video preview and description of each of the four segments (overview, two separate concept segments, and the video case) are provided for each chapter video. Similar information is provided for each part video. Multiple-choice questions that can be used for classroom discussion or testing are also provided.

Transparencies. The instructional package includes 300 color transparencies – some drawn from the text and over 150 from outside sources. Supplemental transparencies for each chapter include a chapter outline, a class exercise useful for stimulating class discussion, a debate issue excellent for generating fast-paced class interaction, and a multiple-choice chapter quiz. Additional transparencies for each chapter include definitions and figures not found in the text.

For Students to Enhance Knowledge and Application Skills

New! *Business Bonus Pack: Your Guide to an "A".* This comprehensive multimedia package of student support CDs accompanies every new copy of the textbook. A set of four Audio Review CDs with 10 to 12 minute summaries highlights key concepts and terms for each chapter. These are ideal for students who learn best by listening and students on the go. The new HM eStudy CD includes a variety of tools to help students study: learning objectives in essay-question format, glossaries, chapter summaries, brief chapter outlines that can be annotated with student notes, chapter previews with video overviews for selected chapters, self-test questions (different from those on the website and in the printed study guide), and Business Plan worksheets to accompany the new end-of-part business plan feature.

Student Web Site. This valuable resource includes online true/false and multiple-choice self tests that give students immediate feedback on their progress; career-related information and links; the end-of-chapter Exploring the Internet exercises with links to the assigned sites and any updates that are necessary to keep the exercises current; links to the companies highlighted in the Inside Business opening cases, boxed features, and end-of-chapter cases; downloadable brief chapter outlines that can be used for notetaking; interactive Flash Cards for studying key terms; and more.

Study Guide. Written by Kathryn Hegar of Mountain View College, the *Study Guide* is a self-help tool for students to use in learning definitions, concepts, and relationships in each chapter. Based on student feedback, the exercises and questions have been designed to be especially useful for self-evaluation and review purposes. For each chapter in the text, the *Study Guide* provides key terms, matching questions, true/false questions, multiple-choice questions, short answer and analytical questions, and an answer key.

It's Strictly Business Telecourse Guide, 4th edition. For those students enrolled in the It's Strictly Business Telecourse, this guide provides the necessary correlation between the video lessons and the textbook, including assignments, learning objectives, key terms, text focus points, video focus points, and practice tests.

***The Ultimate Job Hunter's Guidebook,* 4th Edition.** This practical, how-to handbook by Susan Greene (Greene Marketing and Advertising) and Melanie Martel (New Hampshire Technical Institute) is a concise manual containing abundant examples, practical advice, and exercises related to each of the job hunter's major tasks: conducting a self-assessment, preparing résumés and cover letters, targeting potential employers, obtaining letters of recommendation, filling out job applications, interviewing, and starting a new job. The guide also covers current topics of interest such as online job hunting, handling rejection, networking, evaluating job offers, negotiating salary, looking ahead to future opportunities, and strategies for long-term career development. It also includes numerous success stories to inspire students.

New! *Personal Finance Handbook: A Guide to Securing Your Financial Future.* Written by Ray Forgue (University of Kentucky) and Tom Garman (Virginia Tech University), this handbook is intended to be a reference for students to assist them in their financial planning. Figures, tables, boxes, and two sample budgets illustrate key concepts.

A Final Note to Students and Instructors

We have worked very hard to bring you a text and support package that is current and will successfully address a variety of needs. Since a text should always be evaluated by the students and instructors who use it, we would welcome and sincerely appreciate your comments and suggestions. Please feel free to contact us.

William M. Pride
Department of Marketing
Texas A & M University
College Station, TX 77843
w-pride@tamu.edu

Robert J. Hughes
Division of Business and Professions
Dallas County Community Colleges
12800 Abrams
Dallas, TX 75243
rjh8410@dcccd.edu

Jack R. Kapoor
Division of Business and Technology
College of DuPage
425 Fawell Blvd.
Glen Ellyn, IL 60137
kapoorj@cdnet.cod.edu

Acknowledgments

We thank Brahm Canzer at John Abbot College for helping us develop technology-related materials for the text and supplements. We thank Kathryn Hegar of Mountain View College for developing the *Study Guide*. We thank Peggy Borchardt of Richland College for providing the SCANS correlation. We thank John Drea at Western Illinois University for creating the "Master the Class" review game. We thank Mary C. Greene, MATESOL, UC Extension and San Jose State University, for her review of the text for accessibility to non-native speakers. We thank the R. Jan LeCroy Center for Educational Telecommunications of the Dallas County Community College District for the Telecourse partnership and providing the related student and instructor materials. Finally we thank the following people for technical assistance: Adele Lewis, Clarissa Sims, Mark Finch, Sejal Taneja, Niki Manning, Megan O'Leary, Lindsey Dunn, Marian Wood, Theresa Kapoor, David Pierce, Karen Guessford, Kathryn Thumme, Margaret Hill, Nathan Heller, and Karen Tucker.

A special Faculty Advisory Board assisted us in making decisions both large and small throughout the entire development process of the text and the instructional package. For being "on-call" and available to answer questions and make valuable suggestions, we are grateful to those who participated:

Susan Cremins
Westchester Community College
Sharon Dexter
Southeast Community College
Michael Drafke
College of DuPage
Janice Feldbauer
Austin Community College
Larry A. Flick
Three Rivers Community College
Karen Gore
Ivy Technical State College
Linda Hefferin
Elgin Community College
Dennis Shannon
Southwestern Illinois College
Cindy Simerly
Lakeland Community College
Lynette Teal
Ivy Technical State College
Frank Titlow
St. Petersburg College

For the generous gift of their time and for their thoughtful and useful comments and suggestions, we are indebted to the following reviewers of this and previous editions. Their suggestions have helped us improve and refine the text as well as the whole instructional package.

David V. Aiken
Hocking College
Phyllis C. Alderdice
Jefferson Community College
Marilyn Amaker
Orangeburg-Calhoun Technical College
Harold Amsbaugh
North Central Technical College
Carole Anderson
Clarion University
Lydia E. Anderson
Fresno City College
Maria Aria
Camden County College
James O. Armstrong, II
John Tyler Community College
Ed Atzenhoefer
Clark State Community College
Harold C. Babson
Columbus State Community College
Xenia P. Balabkins
Middlesex County College
Gloria Bemben
Finger Lakes Community College
Charles Bennett
Tyler Junior College
Robert W. Bitter
Southwest Missouri State University
Mary Jo Boehms
Jackson State Community College
Stewart Bonem
Cincinnati Technical College
James Boyle
Glendale Community College
Steve Bradley
Austin Community College
Lyle V. Brenna
Pikes Peak Community College
Tom Brinkman
Cincinnati Technical College
Robert Brinkmeyer
University of Cincinnati
Harvey S. Bronstein
Oakland Community College
Edward Brown
Franklin University
Joseph Brum
Fayetteville Technical Institute

Janice Bryan
Jacksonville College
Howard R. Budner
Manhattan Community College
Clara Buitenbos
Pan American University
C. Alan Burns
Lee College
Frank Busch
Louisiana Technical University
Joseph E. Cantrell
DeAnza College
Brahm Canzer
John Abbot College
Don Cappa
Chabot College
Robert Carrel
Vincennes University
Richard M. Chamberlain
Lorain County Community College
Bruce H. Charnov
Hofstra University
Lawrence Chase
Tompkins Cortland Community College
Felipe Chia
Harrisburg Area Community College
Michael Cicero
Highline Community College
William Clarey
Bradley University
Robert Coiro
LaGuardia Community College
Don Coppa
Chabot College
Robert J. Cox
Salt Lake Community College
Bruce Cudney
Middlesex Community College
Andrew Curran
Antonelli Institute of Art and Photography
Gary Cutler
Dyersburg State Community College
Rex R. Cutshall
Vincennes University
John Daily
St. Edward's University
Brian Davis
Weber State University
Gregory Davis
Georgia Southwestern State University
Helen M. Davis
Jefferson Community College
Harris D. Dean
Lansing Community College
Wayne H. Decker
Memphis State University
William M. Dickson
Green River Community College
M. Dougherty
Madison Area Technical College
Michael Drafke
College of DuPage
Richard Dugger
Kilgore College
Sam Dunbar
Delgado Community College
Robert Elk
Seminole Community College
Pat Ellebracht
Northeastern Missouri State University
John H. Espey
Cecil Community College
Carleton S. Everett
Des Moines Area Community College
Frank M. Falcetta
Middlesex County College
Thomas Falcone
Indiana University of Pennsylvania
Janice Feldbauer
Austin Community College
Coe Fields
Tarrant County Junior College
Carol Fischer
University of Wisconsin—Waukesha
Gregory F. Fox
Erie Community College
Michael Fritz
Portland Community College at Rock Creek
Fred Fry
Bradley University
Eduardo F. Garcia
Laredo Junior College
Arlen Gastineau
Valencia Community College
Carmine Paul Gibaldi
St. John's University
Edwin Giermak
College of DuPage
R. Gillingham
Vincennes University
Robert Googins
Shasta College
W. Michael Gough
DeAnza College
Cheryl Davisson Gracie
Washtenaw Community College
Joseph Gray
Nassau Community College
Michael Griffin
University of Massachusetts—Dartmouth
Ricky W. Griffin
Texas A & M University
Stephen W. Griffin
Tarrant County Junior College
Roy Grundy
College of DuPage
John Gubbay
Moraine Valley Community College
Rick Guidicessi
Des Moines Area Community College
Ronald Hadley
St. Petersburg Junior College
Carnella Hardin
Glendale Community College
Aristotle Haretos
Flagler College
Keith Harman
National-Louis University
Richard Hartley
Solano Community College
Richard Haskey
University of Wisconsin
Carolyn Hatton
Cincinnati State University
Sanford Helman
Middlesex County College
Victor B. Heltzer
Middlesex County College
Ronald L. Hensell
Mendocino College
Leonard Herzstein
Skyline College
Donald Hiebert
Northern Oklahoma College
Nathan Himelstein
Essex County College
L. Duke Hobbs
Texas A & M University
Charles Hobson
Indiana University Northwest
Marie R. Hodge
Bowling Green State University

Gerald Hollier
University of Texas—Brownsville
Jay S. Hollowell
Commonwealth College
Townsend Hopper
Joseph Hrebenak
Community College of Allegheny County—Allegheny
James L. Hyek
Los Angeles Valley College
James V. Isherwood
Community College of Rhode Island
Charleen S. Jaeb
Cuyahoga Community College
Sally Jefferson
Western Illinois University
Jenna Johannpeter
Belleville Area College
Gene E. A. Johnson
Clark College
Carol A. Jones
Cuyahoga Community College
Pat Jones
Eastern New Mexico University
Robert Kegel
Cypress College
Isaac W. J. Keim, III
Delta College
George Kelley
Erie Community College
Marshall Keyser
Moorpark College
Betty Ann Kirk
Tallahassee Community College
Edward Kirk
Vincennes University
Karl Kleiner
Ocean County College
Clyde Kobberdahl
Cincinnati Technical College
Connie Koehler
McHenry County College
Robert Kreitner
Arizona State University
Patrick Kroll
University of Minnesota, General College
Kenneth Lacho
University of New Orleans
John Lathrop
New Mexico Junior College
R. Michael Lebda
DeVry Institute of Technology
Martin Lecker
SUNY Rockland Community College
George Leonard
St. Petersburg Junior College
Marvin Levine
Orange County Community College
Chad Lewis
Everett Community College
Jianwen Liao
Robert Morris College
William M. Lindsay
Northern Kentucky University
Carl H. Lippold
Embry-Riddle Aeronautical University
Thomas Lloyd
Westmoreland County Community College
Paul James Londrigan
Mott Community College
Kathleen Lorencz
Oakland Community College
Fritz Lotz
Southwestern College
Robert C. Lowery
Brookdale Community College
Anthony Lucas
Community College of Allegheny County—Allegheny
Sheldon A. Mador
Los Angeles Trade and Technical College
Joan Mansfield
Central Missouri State University
Gayle J. Marco
Robert Morris College
John Martin
Mt. San Antonio Community College
Irving Mason
Herkimer County Community College
John F. McDonough
Menlo College
Catherine McElroy
Bucks County Community College
L. J. McGlamory
North Harris County College
Charles Meiser
Lake Superior State University
Ina Midkiff-Kennedy
Austin Community College—Northridge
Edwin Miner
Phoenix College
Linda Morable
Dallas County Community Colleges
Charles Morrow
Cuyahoga Community College
T. Mouzopoulos
American College of Greece
W. Gale Mueller
Spokane Community College
C. Mullery
Humboldt State University
Robert J. Mullin
Orange County Community College
Patricia Murray
Virginia Union University
Robert Nay
Stark Technical College
James Nead
Vincennes University
Jerry Novak
Alaska Pacific University
Grantley Nurse
Raritan Valley Community College
Gerald O'Bryan
Danville Area Community College
Larry Olanrewaju
Virginia Union University
David G. Oliver
Edison Community College
John R. Pappalardo
Keene State College
Dennis Pappas
Columbus Technical Institute
Roberta F. Passenant
Berkshire Community College
Clarissa M. H. Patterson
Bryant College
Kenneth Peissig
College of Menominee Nation
Constantine Petrides
Manhattan Community College
Donald Pettit
Suffolk County Community College
Norman Petty
Central Piedmont Community College
Joseph Platts
Miami-Dade Community College
Gloria D. Poplawsky
University Of Toledo
Greg Powell
Southern Utah University
Fred D. Pragasam
SUNY at Cobleskill

Peter Quinn
Commonwealth College
Kimberly Ray
North Carolina A & T State University
Robert Reinke
University of South Dakota
William Ritchie
Florida Gulf Coast University
Kenneth Robinson
Wesley College
John Roisch
Clark County Community College
Rick Rowray
Ball State University
Jill Russell
Camden County College
Karl C. Rutkowski
Pierce Junior College
Martin S. St. John
Westmoreland County Community College
Ben Sackmary
Buffalo State College
Eddie Sanders, Jr.
Chicago State University
P.L. Sandlin
East Los Angeles College
Nicholas Sarantakes
Austin Community College
Warren Schlesinger
Ithaca College
Marilyn Schwartz
College of Marin
Jon E. Seely
Tulsa Junior College
John E. Seitz
Oakton Community College
J. Gregory Service
Broward Community College—North Campus
Lynne M. Severance
Eastern Washington University
Dennis Shannon
Belleville Area College
Richard Shapiro
Cuyahoga Community College
Raymond Shea
Monroe Community College
Lynette Shishido
Santa Monica College
Anne Smevog
Cleveland Technical College
James Smith
Rocky Mountain College
David Sollars
Auburn University Montgomery
Carl Sonntag
Pikes Peak Community College
Russell W. Southhall
Laney College
John Spence
University of Southwestern Louisiana
Rieann Spence-Gale
Northern Virginia Community College
Nancy Z. Spillman
President, Economic Education Enterprises
Richard J. Stanish
Tulsa Junior College
Jeffrey Stauffer
Ventura College
Jim Steele
Chattanooga State Technical Community College
William A. Steiden
Jefferson Community College
E. George Stook
Anne Arundel Community College
W. Sidney Sugg
Lakeland Community College
Lynn Suksdorf
Salt Lake Community College
Richard L. Sutton
University of Nevada—Las Vegas
Robert E. Swindle
Glendale Community College
William A. Syvertsen
Fresno City College
Raymond D. Tewell
American River College
George Thomas
Johnston Technical College
Judy Thompson
Briar Cliff College
William C. Thompson
Foothill Community College
Karen Thomas
St. Cloud University
James B. Thurman
George Washington University
Patric S. Tillman
Grayson County College
Charles E. Tychsen
Northern Virginia Community College—Annandale
Ted Valvoda
Lakeland Community College
Robert H. Vaughn
Lakeland Community College
Frederick A. Viohl
Troy State University
C. Thomas Vogt
Allan Hancock College
Loren K. Waldman
Franklin University
Stephen R. Walsh
Providence College
Elizabeth Wark
Springfield College
John Warner
The University of New Mexico—Albuquerque
Randy Waterman
Dallas County Community Colleges
W. J. Waters, Jr.
Central Piedmont Community College
Philip A. Weatherford
Embry-Riddle Aeronautical University
Jerry E. Wheat
Indiana University, Southeast Campus
Elizabeth White
Orange County Community College
Benjamin Wieder
Queensborough Community College
Ralph Wilcox
Kirkwood Community College
Charlotte Williams
Jones County Junior College
Larry Williams
Palomar College
Paul Williams
Mott Community College
Steven Winter
Orange County Community College
Wallace Wirth
South Suburban College
Amy Wojciechowski
West Shore Community College
Nathaniel Woods
Columbus State Community College
Gregory J. Worosz
Schoolcraft College
Marilyn Young
Tulsa Junior College

Many talented professionals at Houghton Mifflin have contributed to the development of *Business*, Eighth Edition. We are especially grateful to Charlie Hartford, George Hoffman, Steve Mikels, Lisa Boden, Susan Kahn, Kira Robinson-Kates, Rachel D'Angelo Wimberly, Sarah Cleary, Jill Haber and Marie Barnes. Their inspiration, patience, support, and friendship are invaluable.

part I

The Environment of Business

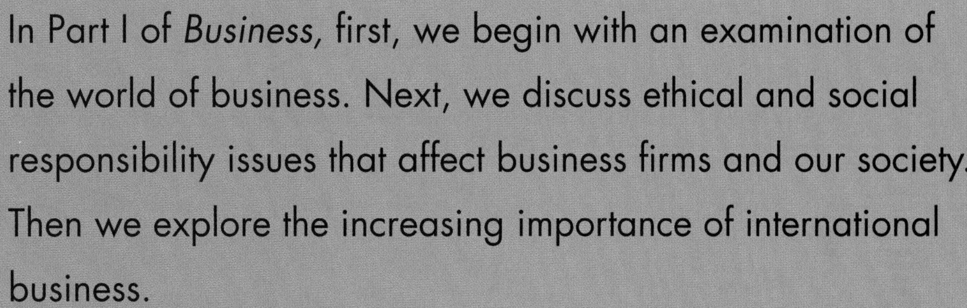

In Part I of *Business,* first, we begin with an examination of the world of business. Next, we discuss ethical and social responsibility issues that affect business firms and our society. Then we explore the increasing importance of international business.

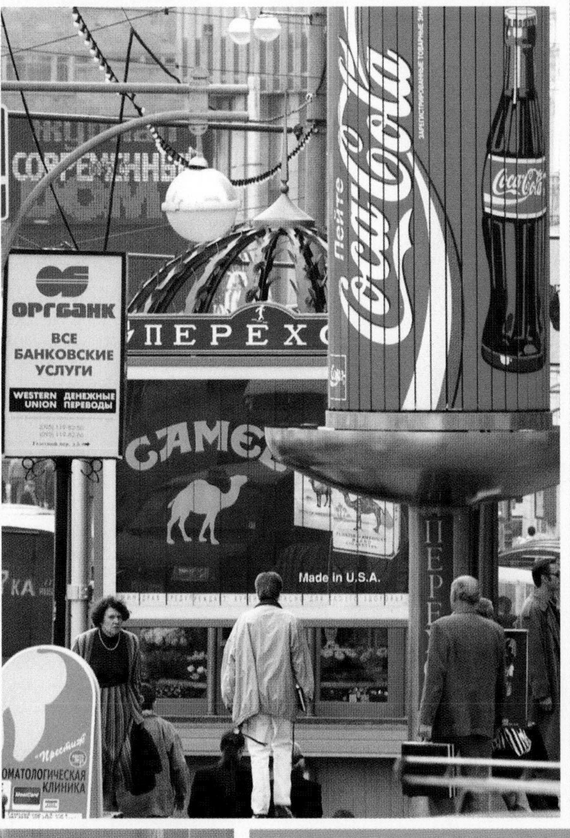

1 **Exploring the World of Business**

2 **Being Ethical and Socially Responsible**

3 **Exploring Global Business**

chapter

1

Exploring the World of Business

learning objectives

1 Discuss your future in the world of business.

2 Define *business,* and identify potential risks and rewards.

3 Describe the two types of economic systems: capitalism and command economy.

4 Identify the ways to measure economic performance.

5 Outline the four types of competition.

6 Summarize the development of America's business system.

7 Discuss the challenges that American businesses will encounter in the future.

The Container Store knows that even the most successful business must prove its worth to customers every day to thrive in the ever-changing world of business.

inside business

The Container Store: A Breed Apart from Ordinary Businesses

NEED A BOX, bottle, bucket, or basket? Whether you want to herd your dirty laundry into one handy hamper or store your spices in space-saving jars, you'll find all the containers you need at the Container Store. The Container Store is no ordinary retail business. In addition to stocking 10,000 storage products, the company's extraordinary customer service marks it as a breed apart from the typical retailer.

Cofounders Garrett Boone and Kip Tindell came up with the idea of the Container Store in 1978 after working for other retail companies. When they spotted some unusual but practical storage items at an industry show, the two friends decided to sell products that would help people organize their homes and home offices. However, locating suppliers was a challenge. At the time, manufacturers were accustomed to supplying storage items for commercial use but not for home use. Tindell remembers: "It was kind of embarrassing to convince people that you would open a store of empty boxes. It took a long time to get commercial manufacturers to sell these things to us."

The first Container Store in Dallas wound up pioneering a new retailing category: storage and organization products. Today the business rings up nearly $300 million in annual sales through twenty-nine stores in California, Georgia, Illinois, New York, Texas, and six other states. Home-improvement stores such as the Home Depot and Lowes now carry storage products, as do home products stores such as Bed, Bath, and Beyond. However, no competitor can duplicate the diverse array of practical and attractive storage products that customers can buy at the Container Store. These days, manufacturers eagerly line up to sell to the chain.

Just as important, applicants eagerly line up to work for the Container Store. In fact, the company has placed near the top of *Fortune* magazine's annual survey of the best U.S. companies to work for four consecutive years—and topped the list for two years in a row. Tindell and Boone only hire people who are genuinely enthusiastic and interested in helping customers. To attract the best employees, the company offers above-average salaries and generous benefits, as well as healthy raises for top performers. New employees receive 235 hours of training during their first year, far more than the average retailer offers, and 162 hours of additional training in successive years. The result is a knowledgeable, attentive sales staff who are ready and willing to help customers tackle even the toughest storage problems.

Thanks to an inspired business idea and a customer-oriented work force, the Container Store has enjoyed 20 percent sales growth year after year. Yet the cofounders realize that even the most successful business must prove its worth to customers every day to thrive in the ever-changing world of business.[1]

The world has changed! Since the last edition of *Business* was published three years ago, the economy has taken a nosedive, we have experienced the tragic events of September 11, the war on terrorism continues, and the stock market has lost roughly a third of its value. In fact, many employees and investors have even lost faith in the economic system that has in the past enabled people in the United States to enjoy prosperity and the highest standard of living in the world. And yet, make no mistake about it, our economic system will survive.

While it is hard to imagine that anything good could come out of the problems that we have experienced in the last three years, these problems have forced businesses to examine how they do *business*. Think for a moment about the Container Store—the corporation profiled in the Inside Business opening case for this chapter. This relatively young company has placed near the top of *Fortune* magazine's annual survey of the best U.S. companies to work for four consecutive years—and topped the list for two years in a row. While the company has enjoyed 20 percent sales growth year after year, it has continued to examine the *way* it does business and the way it treats both its customers and its employees. As a result of constantly working to improve the way it does business, the Container Store is an excellent example of what American business should be doing.

Our economic system provides an amazing amount of freedom that allows businesses that range in size from the small corner grocer to the Container Store and even larger corporations to adapt to changing business environments. Within certain limits, imposed mainly to ensure public safety, the owners of a business can produce any legal good or service they choose and attempt to sell it at the price they set. This system of business, in which individuals decide what to produce, how to produce it, and at what price to sell it, is called **free enterprise.** Our free-enterprise system ensures, for example, that Dell Computer can buy parts from Intel and software from Lotus and manufacture its own computers. Our system gives Dell's owners and stockholders the right to make a profit from the company's success; it gives Dell's management the right to compete with Hewlett Packard and IBM; and it gives computer buyers the right to choose.

free enterprise the system of business in which individuals are free to decide what to produce, how to produce it, and at what price to sell it

In this chapter we look briefly at what business is and how it got that way. First, we discuss your future in business and explore some important reasons for studying business. Then we define *business*, noting how business organizations satisfy needs and earn profits. Next, we examine how capitalism and command economies answer four basic economic questions. Then our focus shifts to how the nations of the world measure economic performance and the four types of competitive situations. Next, we go back into American history for a look at the events that helped shape today's business system. We conclude this chapter with a discussion of the challenges that businesses face.

Your Future in the Changing World of Business

learning objective

1 Discuss your future in the world of business.

The key word in this heading is *change*. For many years, people in business—both employees and managers—assumed that prosperity would continue. When the bubble burst, a large number of these same people then began to ask the question: What do we do now? Although a fair question, it is a difficult question to answer. Certainly, for a college student taking business courses or a beginning employee just starting a career, the question is even more difficult to answer. And yet there are still opportunities out there for people who are willing to work hard, continue to learn, and possess the ability to adapt to change. Let's begin our discussion in this section with three basic questions.

- What do you want?
- Why do you want it?
- Write it down!

During a segment on the Oprah Winfrey television show, Joe Dudley, one of the world's most successful black business owners, gave the preceding advice to anyone who wants to succeed in business. And his advice is an excellent way to begin our discussion of what free enterprise is all about. What is so amazing about Dudley's success is that he took $10 and started a manufacturing business in his own kitchen, with his wife and children serving as the new firm's only employees. He went on to develop his own line of hair-care products and open a chain of beauty schools and beauty supply stores. Today Mr. Dudley has built a $30 million dollar empire and is president of Dudley Products, Inc—one of the most successful minority-owned companies in the nation. Not only a successful business owner, he is also a winner of the Horatio Alger Award—an award given to outstanding individuals who have succeeded in the face of adversity.[2] While many people would say that Joe Dudley was just lucky or happened to be in the right place at the right time, the truth is that he became a success because he had a dream and worked hard to turn his dream into a reality. He would be the first to tell you that you have the same opportunities that he had.

Now more than ever before, people who are going to experience success must adapt to change in order to take advantage of the opportunities that are out there. Whether you want to obtain part-time employment to pay college and living expenses, begin your career as a full-time employee, or start a business, you must *bring something to the table* that makes you different from the next person. You must be able to rise to the occasion and meet the demands of an ever-changing business environment. Consider just some of the changes that have occurred since the previous edition of *Business* was published.

- There have been a large number of business failures—especially in the technology and information industries.
- The number of people unemployed has increased to approximately 6 percent of the nation's work force.
- There are fewer manufacturing jobs in the United States as business firms have begun producing more and more goods in foreign countries.

Even more important than these changes is the general feeling of frustration that people at all levels of business are experiencing. How long this feeling will prevail is anyone's guess, but it does point to one very important fact that affects you: Employers and our capitalistic economic system are more demanding than ever before. Ask yourself: What can I do that will make employers want to pay me a salary? What skills do I have that employers need? With these two questions in mind, we begin the next section with another basic question: Why study business?

Why Study Business?

The potential benefits of higher education are enormous. To begin with, there are economic benefits. Over their lifetimes, college graduates on the average earn much more than high school graduates.[3]

The nice feature of education and knowledge is that once you have it, no one can take it away. It is yours to use for a lifetime. In this section we explore what you may expect to get out of this business course and text. You will find at least four quite compelling reasons for studying business.

For Help in Choosing a Career What do you want to do with the rest of your life? Someplace, sometime, someone probably has asked you that same question. And like many people, you may find it a difficult question to answer. This business course will introduce you to a wide array of employment opportunities. In private enterprise, these range from small, local businesses

Using the Internet @

Your Internet connection to more business information and study tools begins at Houghton Mifflin's College Division website. Enter the URL **http://college.hmco.com/students/**. Go to the course area for business, and select the textbook website for Pride/Hughes/Kapoor *Business,* 8/e or one of the Resource Centers. You will find a wealth of information including text updates, ACE self-test questions, key term flashcards, links to companies featured in the textbook, a research center, careers information, and much more.

Spotlight

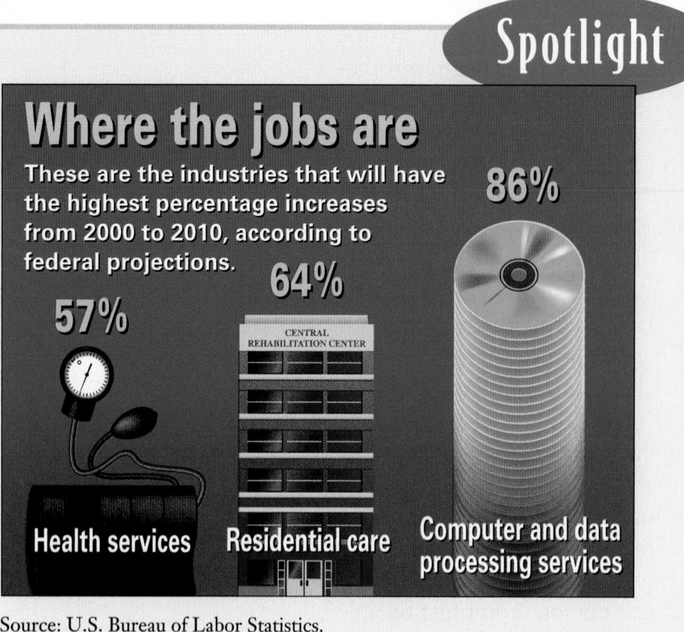

Source: U.S. Bureau of Labor Statistics.

owned by one individual to large companies like American Express and Marriott International that are owned by thousands of stockholders. There are also employment opportunities with federal, state, county, and local governments and with not-for-profit organizations like the Red Cross and Save the Children. For help in deciding what career might be right for you, read Appendix A: Careers in Business. Also, you might want to read information about researching a career and the steps necessary to perform a job search that appear on the Houghton Mifflin website. To view this information:

1. Make an Internet connection and go to **http://college.hmco.com/business/students.**
2. Scroll down and select the Careers Resource Center.
3. Click on the area that you want to view.

One thing to remember as you think about what your ideal career might be is that a person's choice of a career is ultimately just a reflection of what he or she values and holds most important. Because people have different values, they choose different careers; what will give one individual personal satisfaction may not satisfy another. For example, one person may dream of a career as a corporate executive and becoming a millionaire before the age of thirty. Another may choose a career that has more modest monetary rewards but that provides the opportunity to help others. One person may be willing to work long hours and seek additional responsibility in order to get promotions and pay raises. Someone else may prefer a less demanding job with little stress and more free time. What you choose to do with your life will be based on what you feel is most important.

To Be a Successful Employee Deciding on the type of career you want is only a first step. To get a job in your chosen field and to be successful at it, you will have to develop a plan, or road map, that ensures that you have the skills and knowledge the job requires. Today's employers are looking for job applicants who can *do something*, not just fill a spot on an organizational chart. You will be expected to have both the technical skills needed to accomplish a specific task and the ability to work well with many types of people in a culturally diverse work force. These skills, together with a working knowledge of the American business system, can give you an inside edge when you are interviewing with a prospective employer.

This course, your instructor, and all the resources available at your college or university can help you acquire the skills and knowledge you will need for a successful career. But don't underestimate your part in making your dream a reality. It will take hard work, dedication, perseverance, and time management to achieve your goals. Time management is especially important because it will help you to accomplish the tasks that you consider most important. As an added bonus, it is also a skill that employers value. Communication skills are also important. Today, most employers are looking for employees who can compose a business letter and get it in mailable form. They also want employees who can talk with customers and use e-mail to communicate with people within and outside the organization. Employers also will be interested in any work experience you may have had in cooperative work/school programs, during summer vacations, or in part-time jobs during the school year. These things can make a difference when it is time to apply for the job you really want. For more information on steps you can take to keep your career moving in the right direction once you find that first job, read Adapting to Change.

adapting to change

Keep Your Career Moving in the Right Direction

ONCE YOU'RE ON A COMPANY'S PAYROLL, what can you do to keep moving up, regardless of whether the economy is up or down? Even when companies are laying off workers or freezing raises, savvy career builders can thrive by making themselves more valuable to their employers. To advance from an entry-level job to a more responsible, better-paying position, consider the following advice from career development experts:

- *Prove your worth.* Help your company become more productive, solve a problem, or profit from a sudden opportunity. Karen Norris did this at Oracle, a software company, by deftly managing an internal website as a clearinghouse for pricing and licensing information. "People talk about it as being the single source of truth for our policies," her manager says. To spread the word, Norris began visiting other departments to discuss critical pricing and licensing issues. Her accomplishments caught the attention of her superiors and earned her three promotions in four years.
- *Showcase your achievements.* Not everyone can point to a website as evidence of achievement. To showcase your accomplishments, start assembling a file or portfolio of commendations, awards, and samples of your best work to go over during performance evaluations. Take this file with you when you try for a promotion or a transfer to a different department.
- *Continue learning.* New skills and knowledge will help you in your current position and prepare you for more responsibility in the next position. Keep learning by reading industry publications, attending seminars, taking courses, and staying in touch with colleagues in related fields as well as in your own area of expertise.
- *Know how to network.* Find a mentor, if possible, to help guide your career. Also build relationships with those above, below, and on your organizational level. You'll not only hear about new positions and projects from your sources, you'll also have the contacts you need to get things done as you move up.

A Final Word

Your career is your responsibility, so keep your eye on your long-term goals and be ready to prove your worth, showcase your achievements, continue learning, and network your way to a better position.

To Start Your Own Business Some people prefer to work for themselves, and they open their own businesses. To be successful, business owners must possess many of the same skills that successful employees have. And they must be willing to work hard and put in long hours.

It also helps if your small business can provide a product or service that customers want. For example, Mark Cuban started a small Internet company called Broadcast.com that now provides hundreds of live and on-demand audio and video programs ranging from rap music to sporting events to business events over the Internet. This new, high-tech start-up company quickly became a major player in electronic business or what many refer to as e-business. **e-Business** is the organized effort of individuals to produce and sell, for a profit, the products and services that satisfy society's needs *through the Internet*. When Cuban sold Broadcast.com to Yahoo! Inc., he became a billionaire. Today he is an expert on how the Internet and e-business will affect society in the future and believes that there is a real need for all companies, not just technology companies, to provide something that their customers want. If they do not do that, their company could very well fail.[4]

e-business the organized effort of individuals to produce and sell, for a profit, the products and services that satisfy society's needs through the Internet

Unfortunately, many small-business firms fail; 70 percent of them fail within the first five years. Typical reasons for business failures include undercapitalization, poor business location, poor customer service, unqualified or untrained employees, fraud, lack of a proper business plan, and failure to seek outside professional help.[5] The material in Chapter 6 and selected topics and examples throughout this text will help you to decide whether you want to open your own business. This material also will help you to overcome many of these problems.

A business owner with a future in the world of fashion design! Sixteen years ago, Marisol Deluna started her career as an employee working in the Garment District in New York. Today, she owns a successful fashion design business that creates handbags, scarves, ties, bridal accessories, and other clothing accessories. Her products are sold under the label Marisol Deluna New York in fashion boutiques in the United States, Canada, and Europe. Deluna's products are also sold on her website, **www.marisoldeluna.com**.

To Become a Better Informed Consumer and Investor The world of business surrounds us. You cannot buy a home, a new Grand Prix from the local Pontiac dealer, a Black & Decker sander at the Home Depot, a pair of jeans at the Gap, or a hot dog from a street vendor without entering a business transaction. These and thousands of similar transactions describe the true nature of the American business system.

Because you no doubt will engage in business transactions almost every day of your life, one very good reason for studying business is to become a more fully informed consumer. Your knowledge of business will enable you to make intelligent buying decisions and to spend your money more wisely. This same basic understanding of business also will make you a better-informed investor. Before proceeding to the next section, take a few minutes to familiarize yourself with the text by reading the following material.

Special Note to Students

It is important to begin reading this text with one thing in mind: *This business course does not have to be difficult.* In fact, we have done everything possible to eliminate the problems that students encounter in a typical class. All the features in each chapter have been evaluated and recommended by instructors with years of teaching experience. In addition, business students were asked to critique each chapter component. Based on this feedback, the text includes the following features:

- *Learning objectives* appear at the beginning of each chapter. All objectives signal important concepts to be mastered within the chapter.
- *Inside Business* is a chapter-opening case that highlights how successful companies do business on a day-to-day basis. These short cases were chosen to illustrate the key concepts and ideas described in each chapter.
- *Margin notes* are used throughout the text to reinforce both learning objectives and key terms.

- *Boxed features* highlight ethical behavior, changes in the workplace, global issues, and the impact of technology on business today. In addition, a boxed feature entitled Exploring Business highlights a wide range of contemporary business issues.
- *Spotlight* features highlight interesting facts about business and society and often provide a real-world example of an important concept within a chapter.
- *Using the Internet* features provide useful web addresses that relate to chapter material.
- *End-of-chapter materials* provide questions about the opening case, a chapter summary, a list of key terms, review and discussion questions, and a video case. The last section of every chapter is entitled Building Skills for Career Success and includes exercises devoted to exploring the Internet, developing critical-thinking skills, building team skills, researching different careers, and improving communication skills.
- *End-of-part materials* provide a continuing video case about the Finagle A Bagel Company that operates a chain of retail outlets in the northeastern section of the United States. Also, at the end of each major part is an exercise designed to help you develop the components that are included in a typical business plan.

In addition to the text, a number of student supplements will help you explore the world of business. We are especially proud of several items that are available with this edition of *Business*. The Student CD will help you to review important concepts with interactive practice tests and other study aids. The Audio Review CDs give a quick summary of each chapter allowing you to review material while you are on the go. We are also proud of the website that accompanies this edition. There you will find online study aids including many tools designed to help ensure your success in this course. If you want to take a look at the Internet support materials available for this edition of *Business*,

1. Make an Internet connection and go to **http://college.hmco.com/business/students.**
2. Under General Business, scroll down and click on Pride/Hughes/Kapoor, *Business*, 8e.
3. Then click on Go.

As authors, we realize that you are our customers. We want you to be successful. And we want you to appreciate business and how it affects your life as an employee and a consumer. Since a text always should be evaluated by the students and instructors who use it, we would welcome and sincerely appreciate your comments and suggestions. Please feel free to contact us by using one of the following e-mail addresses:

Bill Pride: **w-pride@tamu.edu**
Bob Hughes: **rjh8410@dcccd.edu**
Jack Kapoor: **kapoorj@cdnet.cod.edu**

Business: A Definition

learning objective

2 Define *business,* and identify potential risks and rewards.

Business is the organized effort of individuals to produce and sell, for a profit, the products and services that satisfy society's needs. The general term *business* refers to all such efforts within a society (as in "American business") or within an industry (as in "the steel business"). However, *a business* is a particular organization, such as Dudley Products, Inc., Kraft Foods, Inc., or Cracker Barrel Old Country Stores. To be successful, a business must perform three activities. It must be organized. It must satisfy needs. And it must earn a profit.

business the organized effort of individuals to produce and sell, for a profit, the products and services that satisfy society's needs

The Organized Effort of Individuals

For a business to be organized, it must combine four kinds of resources: material, human, financial, and informational. *Material* resources include the raw materials used in manufacturing processes, as well as buildings and machinery. For example, Sara Lee

figure 1.1

Combining Resources
A business must effectively combine all four resources to be successful.

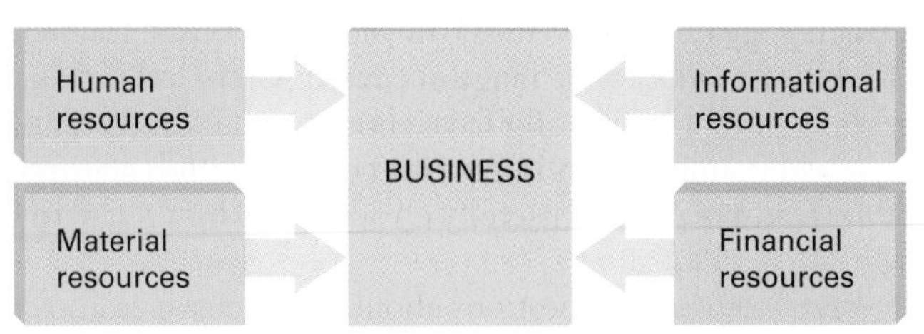

Corporation needs flour, sugar, butter, eggs, and other raw materials to produce the food products it sells worldwide. In addition, this Chicago-based company needs human, financial, and informational resources. *Human* resources are the people who furnish their labor to the business in return for wages. The *financial* resource is the money required to pay employees, purchase materials, and generally keep the business operating. And *information* is the resource that tells the managers of the business how effectively the other resources are being combined and used (see Figure 1.1).

Today, businesses usually are organized as one of three specific types. *Manufacturing businesses* process various materials into tangible goods, such as delivery trucks or towels. Intel, for example, produces computer chips that, in turn, are sold to companies that manufacture computers. *Service businesses* produce services, such as haircuts, legal advice, or tax preparation. And some firms called *marketing intermediaries* buy products from manufacturers and then resell them. Sony Corporation is a manufacturer that produces stereo equipment, among other things. These products may be sold to a marketing intermediary such as Best Buy or Circuit City, which then resells the manufactured goods to consumers in their retail stores.

One man's trash is another man's treasure. One sure way to build a successful business is to meet the needs of your customers. Brian Scudamore did just that when he started 1–800-GOT-JUNK back in 1989. Today, his company is the largest junk removal business in the United States. Depending on location, the company charges about $350 to haul away a truckload of trash. Then GOT JUNK donates anything salvageable to charity and disposes of the rest. With 36 franchisees in 25 cities, Scudamore's company will bring in $12 million this year.

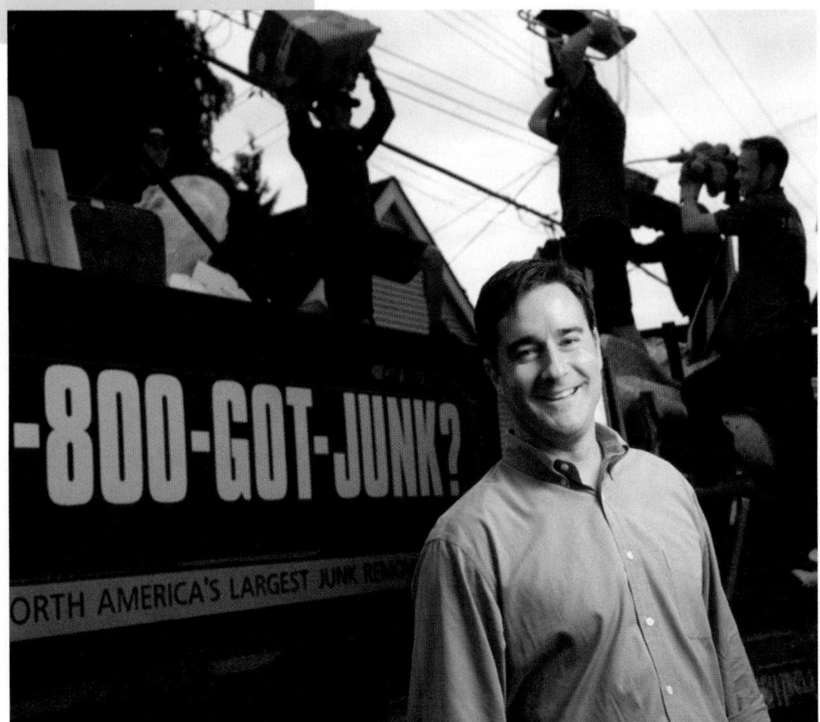

Satisfying Needs

The ultimate objective of every firm must be to satisfy the needs of its customers. People generally do not buy goods and services simply to own them; they buy products and services to satisfy particular needs. People rarely buy an automobile solely to store it in a garage; they do, however, buy automobiles to satisfy their need for transportation. Some of us may feel that this need is best satisfied by an air-conditioned BMW with stereo compact-disc player, automatic transmission, power seats and windows, and remote-control side mirrors. Others may believe that a Ford Focus with a stick shift and an AM radio will do just fine. Both products are available to those who want them, along with a wide variety of other products that satisfy the need for transportation.

When firms lose sight of their customers' needs, they are likely to find the going rough. However, when businesses understand their customers' needs and work to satisfy those needs, they are usually successful. Back in 1962, Sam Walton opened his first discount store in Rogers, Arkansas. Although the original store was quite different from the Wal-Mart Superstores you see today, the basic ideas of providing customer service and offering goods that satisfied needs at low prices are part of the reason why this firm has grown to become the largest retailer in the world.[6] Today, Wal-Mart provides its products and services to more than 100 million customers each week. Although it currently has more than 3200 retail stores in the United States and 1100 retail stores in nine different countries, this highly successful discount store organization continues to open new stores to meet the needs of its customers around the globe.[7]

Business Profit

A business receives money (sales revenue) from its customers in exchange for goods or services. It also must pay out money to cover the expenses involved in doing business. If the firm's sales revenues are greater than its expenses, it has earned a profit. More specifically, as shown in Figure 1.2, **profit** is what remains after all business expenses have been deducted from sales revenue. (A negative profit, which results when a firm's expenses are greater than its sales revenue, is called a *loss*.)

profit what remains after all business expenses have been deducted from sales revenue

The profit earned by a business becomes the property of its owners. Thus, in one sense, profit is the reward business owners receive for producing goods and services that consumers want. Profit is also the payment that business owners receive for assuming the considerable risks of ownership. One of these is the risk of not being paid. Everyone else—employees, suppliers, and lenders—must be paid before the owners. A second risk that owners run is the risk of losing whatever they have invested into the business.

A business that cannot earn a profit is very likely to fail, in which case the owners lose whatever money, effort, and time they have invested. Although there have been business failures in all industries in recent years, the high-tech industry and specifically dot-com companies have experienced a large number of failures. Simply put, here is what happened. In the 1990s, there were a large number of investors who wanted to cash in on the technology boom and often would provide initial financing for new high-tech start-up firms. These start-up firms used the money to expand their business operations, hoping that they could generate enough sales revenues to pay their expenses and eventually earn profits before they burned through their initial financing. For many of these firms, including Kozmo.com, Pets.com, Quokka Sports, and NBCi, bankruptcy, a merger, or absorption by a large corporation was the result of continually operating at a loss.[8] Today, even larger, more recognizable firms like Amazon.com, Lucent Technologies, and many other firms in high-tech industries are struggling to reduce losses and return to profitability.[9] Do not underestimate the importance of profits. In some cases, the pursuit of profits is so important for some corporate executives that they will "cook" the firm's books. To see what happens when profits become too important, read Examining Ethics (on p. 12).

To satisfy society's needs and make a profit, a business must operate within the parameters of a nation's economic system. In the next section we describe two different types of economic systems and how they affect not only businesses but also the people within a nation.

Sales revenue

Expenses	Profit

figure 1.2

The Relationship Between Sales Revenue and Profit

Profit is what remains after all business expenses have been deducted from sales revenue.

examining ethics

Accounting Scandals: What Went Wrong

PROFIT MAKES THE BUSINESS WORLD go around. And so strong is the pressure to report ever-higher profit that some companies have fudged their figures to avoid disappointing shareholders, directors, analysts, lenders, and other stakeholders. Energy giant Enron, for example, minimized its debt and losses through complicated accounting tricks involving partnerships and special-purpose entities that did not appear on its financial statements. As a result, Enron made its earnings look better and was able to announce impressive profit gains quarter after quarter, driving the stock price higher and earning its executives generous bonuses. The manipulations came to light after questions were raised about the company's accounting practices. Ultimately, Enron filed for bankruptcy, and one of its financial executives pled guilty to fraud. Although the company is attempting to reorganize, thousands of workers have been laid off, and the stock has lost all value, hurting the retirement savings of employees and the investment portfolio values of many investors.

Enron is hardly alone. WorldCom, an international telecommunications firm, has admitted boosting sales revenue by more than $7 billion through suspect accounting methods. Other companies making headlines for accounting scandals include Global Crossing, Adelphia Communications, and Xerox. Although the intention was to enhance the profit picture, these efforts backfired in a very public way and hurt both employees and investors.

In response to the accounting scandals, the U.S. Congress enacted the Sarbanes-Oxley Act. Under this law, the CEOs of public corporations must swear to the accuracy of the financial reports they submit to the Securities and Exchange Commission (SEC). If they do not, they may be prosecuted and imprisoned or heavily fined. Also, the legislation outlaws destroying or altering company files to obstruct investigation of potential fraud, and it requires lawyers to bring questionable activities to the attention of senior management or the company's board of directors. In addition, the SEC has created the Public Company Accounting Oversight Board to examine the accounting practices that public corporations use to produce their financial reports.

Issues to Consider

1. Why would the Sarbanes-Oxley Act specifically require lawyers to notify top managers or the company's board of directors about questionable accounting activities?
2. What additional legal and managerial changes would you suggest to prevent the use of accounting tricks to manipulate corporate earnings?

Types of Economic Systems

learning objective

3 Describe the two types of economic systems: capitalism and command economy.

economics the study of how wealth is created and distributed

economy the way in which people deal with the creation and distribution of wealth

factors of production land and natural resources, labor, capital, and entrepreneurship

Economics is the study of how wealth is created and distributed. By *wealth*, we mean "anything of value," including the products produced and sold by business. *How wealth is distributed* simply means "who gets what." The way in which people deal with the creation and distribution of wealth determines the kind of economic system, or **economy,** that a nation has.

Over the years, the economic systems of the world have differed in essentially two ways: (1) the ownership of the factors of production and (2) how they answer four basic economic questions that direct a nation's economic activity. **Factors of production** are the resources used to produce goods and services. There are four such factors:

- *Land and natural resources*—elements in their natural state that can be used in the production process. Typical examples include crude oil, forests, minerals, land, water, and even air.
- *Labor*—human resources such as managers and employees.
- *Capital*—money, facilities, equipment, and machines used in the operation of organizations. While most people think of capital as just money, it also can be the manufacturing equipment on a Ford automobile assembly line or a computer used in the corporate offices of Ace Hardware.

- *Entrepreneurship*—the willingness to take risks and the knowledge and ability to use the other factors of production efficiently. An **entrepreneur** is a person who risks his or her time, effort, and money to start and operate a business.

entrepreneur a person who risks time, effort, and money to start and operate a business

A nation's economic system significantly affects all the economic activities of its citizens and organizations. This far-reaching impact becomes more apparent when we consider that a country's economic system provides answers to four basic economic questions:

1. What goods and services—and how much of each—will be produced?
2. How will these goods and services be produced?
3. For whom will these goods and services be produced?
4. Who owns and who controls the major factors of production?

Capitalism

Capitalism is an economic system in which individuals own and operate the majority of businesses that provide goods and services. Capitalism stems from the theories of the eighteenth-century Scottish economist Adam Smith. In his book *Wealth of Nations*, published in 1776, Smith argued that a society's interests are best served when the individuals within that society are allowed to pursue their own self-interest.

capitalism an economic system in which individuals own and operate the majority of businesses that provide goods and services

Adam Smith's capitalism is based on four fundamental issues. First, Smith argued that the creation of wealth is properly the concern of private individuals, not of government. Second, private individuals must own the resources used to create wealth. Smith argued that the owners of resources should be free to determine how these resources are used. They also should be free to enjoy the income, profits, and other benefits they might derive from the ownership of these resources. Third, Smith contended that economic freedom ensures the existence of competitive markets that allow both sellers and buyers to enter and exit as they choose. This freedom to enter or leave a market at will has given rise to the term *market economy*. A **market economy** (sometimes referred to as a *free-market economy*) is an economic system in which businesses and individuals make the decisions about what to produce and what to buy, and the market determines how much is sold and at what prices. Finally, in Smith's view, the role of government should be limited to providing defense against foreign enemies, ensuring internal order, and furnishing public works and education. With regard to the economy, government should act only as rule maker and umpire.

market economy an economic system in which businesses and individuals decide what to produce and buy, and the market determines quantities sold and prices

In other words, Smith believed that each person should be allowed to work toward his or her *own* economic gain, without interference from government. The French term *laissez faire* describes Smith's capitalistic system and implies that there shall be no government interference in the economy. Loosely translated, it means "let them do" (as they see fit).

Who wants to watch a movie on a cell phone? How do you produce a product to meet this need? Today, people around the world regard their cell phones as much more than just a telephone. In fact, they are often referred to as miniature multimedia entertainment and information centers that allow users to play games, send and receive pictures, and even watch movies. And while it is obvious that there are customers who want these services, the products would not be available if it were not for the research and development efforts of companies like Qualcomm, Nokia, AT&T Wireless, Verizon, and others that operate in a capitalistic economic system.

Capitalism in the United States

mixed economy an economy that exhibits elements of both capitalism and socialism

Our economic system is rooted in the laissez-faire capitalism of Adam Smith. However, our real-world economy is not as laissez faire as Smith would have liked because government participates as more than umpire and rule maker. Ours is, in fact, a **mixed economy,** one that exhibits elements of both capitalism and socialism.

In today's economy, the four basic economic questions discussed at the beginning of this section are answered through the interaction of households, businesses, and governments. The interactions among these three groups are shown in Figure 1.3.

Households Households made up of individuals are the consumers of goods and services, as well as owners of some of the factors of production. As *resource owners,* the members of households provide businesses with labor, capital, and other resources. In return, businesses pay wages, rent, and dividends and interest, which households receive as income.

consumer products goods and services purchased by individuals for personal consumption

As *consumers,* household members use their income to purchase the goods and services produced by business. Today approximately two-thirds of our nation's total production consists of **consumer products**—goods and services purchased by individuals for personal consumption. (The remaining third is purchased by businesses and governments.[10]) This means that consumers, as a group, are the biggest customer of American business.

Businesses Like households, businesses are engaged in two different exchanges. They exchange money for natural resources, labor, and capital and use these resources to produce goods and services. Then they exchange their goods and services for sales revenue. This sales revenue, in turn, is exchanged for additional resources, which are used to produce and sell more goods and services. Thus the circular flow of Figure 1.3 is continuous.

Along the way, of course, business owners would like to remove something from the circular flow in the form of profits. And households try to retain some income as savings. But are profits and savings really removed from the flow? Usually not! When

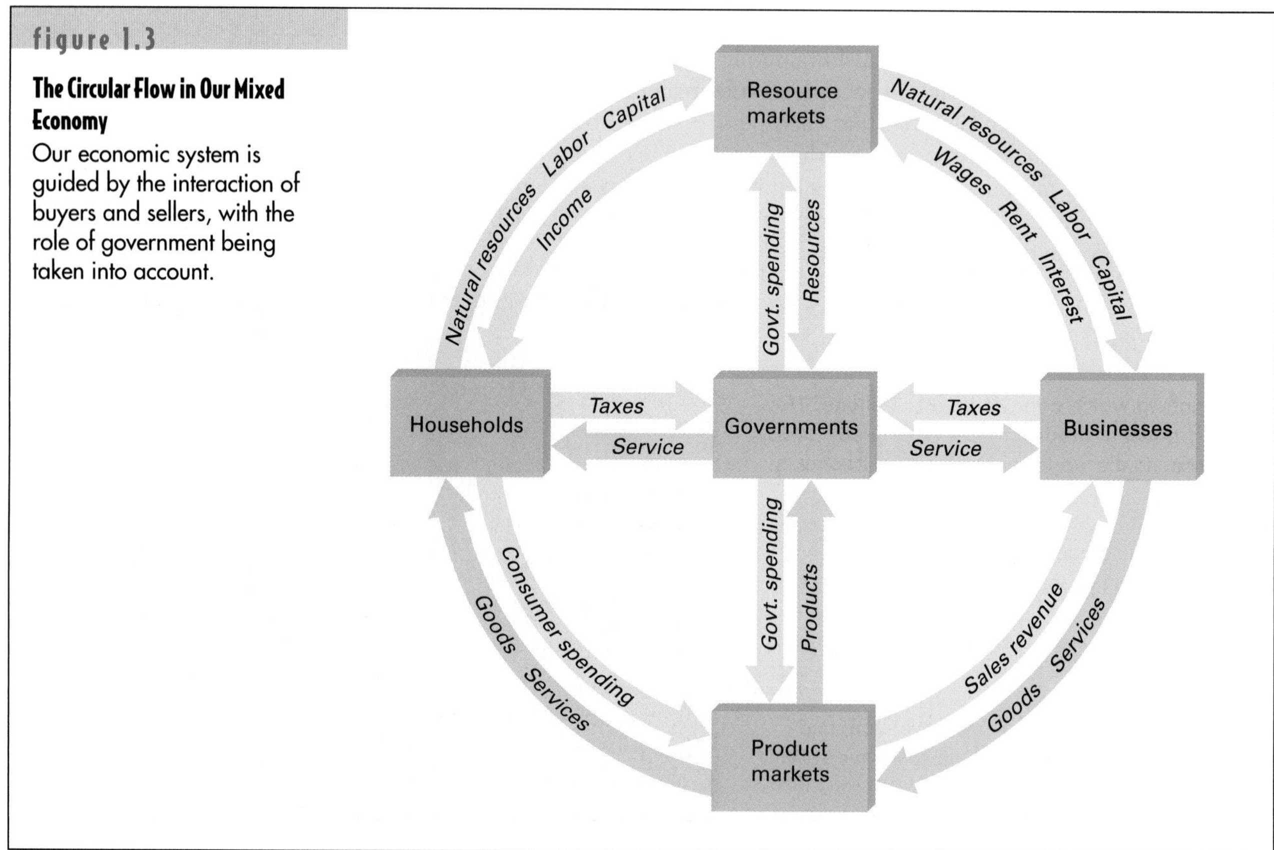

figure 1.3

The Circular Flow in Our Mixed Economy

Our economic system is guided by the interaction of buyers and sellers, with the role of government being taken into account.

the economy is running smoothly, households are willing to invest their savings in businesses. They can do so directly by buying stocks in businesses, by purchasing shares in mutual funds that purchase stocks in businesses, or by lending money to businesses. They also can invest indirectly by placing their savings in bank accounts; banks then invest these savings as part of their normal business operations. In either case, savings usually find their way back into the circular flow in order to finance business activities.

When business profits are distributed to business owners, these profits become household income. (Business owners are, after all, members of households.) And, as we saw, household income is retained in the circular flow as either consumer spending or invested savings. Thus business profits, too, are retained in the business system, and the circular flow is complete. How, then, does government fit in?

Governments The framers of our Constitution desired as little government interference with business as possible. At the same time, the Preamble to the Constitution sets forth the responsibility of government to protect and promote the public welfare. Local, state, and federal governments discharge this responsibility through regulation and the provision of services. Government regulations of business are discussed in detail in various chapters of this book. The numerous services are important but either (1) would not be produced by private business firms or (2) would be produced only for those who could afford them. Typical services include national defense, police and fire protection, education, and construction of roads and highways. To pay for all these services, governments collect a variety of taxes from households (such as personal income taxes and sales taxes) and from businesses (corporate income taxes).

Figure 1.3 shows this exchange of taxes for government services. It also shows government spending of tax dollars for resources and products required to provide these services.

Actually, with government included, our circular flow looks more like a combination of several flows. And in reality it is. The important point is that, together, the various flows make up a single unit—a complete economic system that effectively provides answers to the basic economic questions. Simply put, the system works.

Command Economies

Before we discuss how to measure a nation's economic performance, we look quickly at another economic system called a *command economy*. A **command economy** is an economic system in which the government decides what goods and services will be produced, how they will be produced, who gets available goods and services, and who owns and controls the major factors of production. The answers to all four basic economic questions are determined, at least to some degree, through centralized government planning. Today, two types of economic systems—*socialism* and *communism*—serve as examples of command economies.

command economy an economic system in which the government decides what will be produced, how it will be produced, who gets what is produced, and who owns and controls the major factors of production

Socialism In a *socialist* economy, the key industries are owned and controlled by the government. Such industries usually include transportation, utilities, communications, banking, and industries producing important materials such as steel. Land, buildings, and raw materials also may be the property of the state in a socialist economy. Depending on the country, private ownership of smaller businesses is permitted to varying degrees. People usually may choose their own occupations, but many work in state-owned industries.

What to produce and how to produce it are determined in accordance with national goals, which are based on projected needs and the availability of resources—at least for government-owned industries. The distribution of goods and services—who gets what—is also controlled by the state to the extent that it controls rents and wages. Among the professed aims of socialist countries are the equitable distribution of income, the elimination of poverty, the distribution of social services (such as medical care) to all who need them, and the elimination of the economic waste that supposedly accompanies capitalistic competition.

Britain, France, Sweden, and India are countries whose economies include a very visible degree of socialism. Other, more authoritarian countries actually may have socialist economies; however, we tend to think of them as communist because of their almost total lack of freedom.

Communism If Adam Smith was the father of capitalism, Karl Marx was the father of communism. In his writings during the mid-nineteenth century, Marx advocated a classless society whose citizens together owned all economic resources. All workers would then contribute to this *communist* society according to their ability and would receive benefits according to their need.

Since the breakup of the Soviet Union and economic reforms in China and most of the eastern European countries, the best remaining examples of communism are North Korea and Cuba. Today these so-called communist economies seem to practice a strictly controlled kind of socialism. Almost all economic resources are owned by the government. The basic economic questions are answered through centralized state planning, which sets prices and wages as well. Emphasis is placed on the production of goods the government needs rather than on the products that consumers might want, so there are frequent shortages of consumer goods. Workers have little choice of jobs, but special skills or talents seem to be rewarded with special privileges. Various groups of professionals (bureaucrats, university professors, and athletes, for example) fare much better than, say, factory workers.

Measuring Economic Performance

learning objective

4 Identify the ways to measure economic performance.

Today it is hard to turn on the radio, watch the news on television, or read the newspaper without hearing or seeing something about the economy. Unfortunately, for the last few years, most of the news describes a slowdown in the economy, higher unemployment rates, and even recession. But what do these terms really mean. How long will the economic downturn last? How does a depressed economy affect the typical business or the average person? While these questions are difficult to answer, the information in this section will help you to better understand what is really happening to our nation's economy.

Economic Indicators

productivity the average level of output per worker per hour

One way to measure a nation's economic performance is to assess its productivity. **Productivity** is the average level of output per worker per hour. An increase in productivity results in economic growth because a larger number of goods and services are produced by a given labor force. Although U.S. workers produce more than many workers in other countries, the *rate of productivity growth* has declined in the United States and has been surpassed in recent years by workers in Korea, Taiwan, and France.[11] There are a number of ways to improve a nation's productivity growth rate. And yet, reducing costs and enabling employees to work more efficiently are at the core of all attempts to improve productivity. For example, productivity in the United States is expected to improve dramatically as more economic activity is transferred onto the Internet, reducing costs for servicing customers and handling routine ordering functions between businesses. The resulting cost savings allow businesses to increase their profits and turn their efforts to other business opportunities. We discuss productivity in detail in Chapter 9.

gross domestic product (GDP) the total dollar value of all goods and services produced by all people within the boundaries of a country during a one-year period

In addition to productivity, a measure called *gross domestic product* can be used to measure the economic well being of a nation. **Gross domestic product (GDP)** is the total dollar value of all goods and services produced by all people within the boundaries of a country during a one-year period. For example, the value of automobiles produced by employees in both an American-owned General Motors plant and a Japanese-owned Toyota plant *in the United States* are both included in the GDP for the United States. The U.S. GDP was $10,442 billion in 2002.[12]

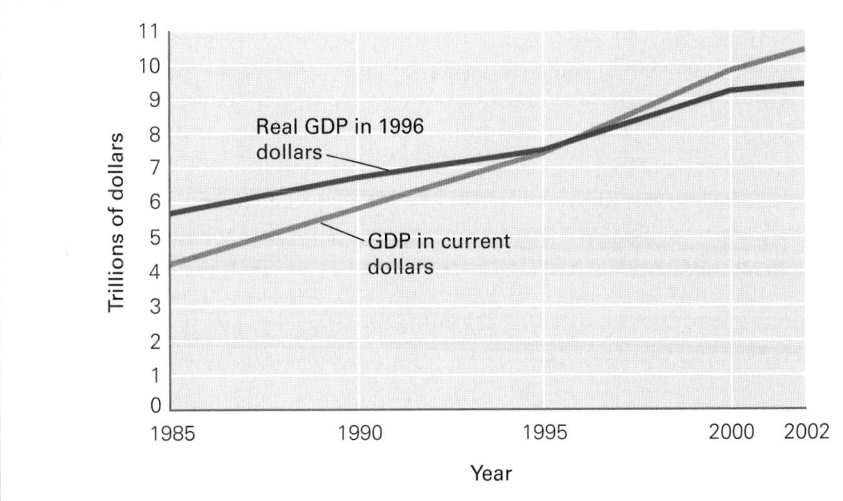

figure 1.4

GDP in Current Dollars and in Inflation-Adjusted Dollars
The changes in GDP and *real* GDP for the United States from one year to another year can be used to measure economic growth.

Source: U.S. Bureau of Economic Analysis website at **www.bea.gov**, February 1, 2003.

The GDP figure facilitates comparisons between the United States and other countries because it is the standard used in international guidelines for economic accounting. It is also possible to compare the GDP for one nation over several different time periods. This comparison allows observers to determine the extent to which a nation is experiencing economic growth. For example, government experts project that GDP will grow from $10,442 billion in 2002 to $12,835 billion by the year 2010.[13]

To make accurate comparisons of the GDP for different years, we must adjust the dollar amounts for inflation. **Inflation** is a general rise in the level of prices. By using inflation-adjusted figures, we are able to measure the *real* GDP for a nation. In effect, it is now possible to compare the products and services produced by a nation in constant dollars—dollars that will purchase the same amount of goods and services. Figure 1.4 depicts the GDP of the United States in current dollars and the *real* GDP in inflation-adjusted dollars. Note that between 1985 and 2002, America's *real* GDP grew from $5,717.1 billion to $9,436.1 billion.[14]

inflation a general rise in the level of prices

In addition to GDP and *real* GDP, there are other economic measures that can be used to evaluate a nation's economy. Some of the more significant terms are described in Table 1.1. Like the measures for GDP, these measures can be used to compare one economic statistic over different periods of time. For information about the current GDP and other statistical information about the economy, you may want to access the U.S. Bureau of Economic Analysis website at **www.bea.gov.**

table 1.1 Common Measures Used to Evaluate a Nation's Economic Health

Economic Measure	Description
1. Balance of trade	The total value of a nation's exports minus the total value of its imports over a specific period of time.
2. Consumer price index (CPI)	A monthly index that measures the changes in prices of a fixed basket of goods purchased by a typical consumer, including food, transportation, shelter, utilities, clothing, medical care, entertainment, and other items.
3. Inflation rate	An economic statistic that tracks the increase in prices of goods and services over a period of time. This measure is usually calculated on a monthly or annual basis.
4. Prime interest rate	The lowest interest rate that banks charge their most creditworthy customers.
5. Producer price index (PPI)	A monthly index that measures prices at the wholesale level.
6. Productivity rate	An economic measure that tracks the increase and decrease in the average level of output per worker.
7. Unemployment rate	The percentage of a nation's labor force that is unemployed at any time.

The Business Cycle

All industrialized nations of the world seek economic growth, full employment, and price stability. However, a nation's economy fluctuates rather than grows at a steady pace every year. In fact, if you were to graph the economic growth rate for a country such as the United States, it would resemble a roll coaster ride with peaks (high points) and troughs (low points). These fluctuations are generally referred to as the **business cycle,** that is, the recurrence of periods of growth and recession in a nation's economic activity. The changes that result from either growth or recession affect the amount of products and services that consumers are willing to purchase and, as a result, the amount of products and services produced. Generally, the business cycle consists of four states: the peak (sometimes referred to as *prosperity*), recession, the trough, and recovery.

business cycle the recurrence of periods of growth and recession in a nation's economic activity

During the *peak period*, unemployment is low, and total income is relatively high. As long as the economic outlook remains prosperous, consumers are willing to buy products and services. In fact, businesses often expand and offer new products and services during prosperity in order to take advantage of consumers' increased buying power.

Economists define a **recession** as two or more consecutive three-month periods of decline in a country's GDP. Because unemployment rises during a recession, total buying power declines. The pessimism that accompanies a recession often stifles both consumer and business spending. As buying power decreases, consumers tend to become more value-conscious and reluctant to purchase frivolous items. In response to a recession, many businesses focus on the products and services that provide the most value to their customers. Economists define a **depression** as a severe recession that lasts longer than a recession. A depression is characterized by extremely high unemployment rates, low wages, reduced purchasing power, lack of confidence in the economy, and a general decrease in business activity.

recession two or more consecutive three-month periods of decline in a country's gross domestic product

depression a severe recession that lasts longer than a recession

Economists refer to the third phase of the business cycle as the *trough*. The trough of a recession or depression is the phase in which a nation's output and employment bottom out and reach their lowest levels. To offset the effects of recession and depression, the federal government uses both monetary and fiscal policies. **Monetary policies** are the Federal Reserve's decisions that determine the size of the supply of money in the nation and the level of interest rates. Through **fiscal policy,** the government can influence the amount of savings and expenditures by altering the tax structure and changing the levels of government spending.

monetary policies Federal Reserve decisions that determine the size of the supply of money in the nation and the level of interest rates

fiscal policy government influence on the amount of savings and expenditures; accomplished by altering the tax structure and by changing the levels of government spending

Although the federal government collects over $2 trillion in annual revenues, the government often spends more than it receives, resulting in a **federal deficit.** For example, the government had a federal deficit for each year between 1980 and 1997. For each year between 1998 and 2001 (the last year that complete data are available), the federal government experienced a surplus and actually spent less than its annual revenues. The total of all federal deficits is called the **national debt.** Today, the U.S. national debt is about $5.6 trillion, or approximately $20,000 for every man, woman, and child in the United States.[15]

federal deficit a shortfall created when the federal government spends more in a fiscal year than it receives

national debt the total of all federal deficits

Some experts believe that effective use of monetary and fiscal policies can speed up recovery and reduce the amount of time the economy is in recession. *Recovery* is the movement of the economy from depression or recession to prosperity. High unemployment rates decline, income increases, and both the ability and the willingness to buy rise. Greater demand for products and services results in the recovery phase.

Types of Competition

learning objective

5 Outline the four types of competition.

Our capitalist system ensures that businesses make the decisions about what to produce, how to produce it, and what price to charge for the product. Mattel, Inc., for example, can introduce new versions of its famous Barbie doll, license the Barbie name, change the doll's price and method of distribution, and attempt to produce and market

Barbie in other countries or over the Internet at **www.mattel.com.** Our system also allows customers the right to choose between Mattel's products and those produced by competitors.

Competition like that between Mattel and other toy manufacturers is a necessary and extremely important by-product of capitalism. Because many individuals and groups can open businesses, business firms must compete with each other for sales. Business **competition,** then, is essentially a rivalry among businesses for sales to potential customers. In a capitalistic economy, competition also ensures that a firm will survive only if it serves its customers well. Economists recognize four different degrees of competition, ranging from ideal, complete competition to no competition at all. These are pure competition, monopolistic competition, oligopoly, and monopoly.

competition rivalry among businesses for sales to potential customers

Pure Competition

Pure competition is the market situation in which there are many buyers and sellers of a product, and no single buyer or seller is powerful enough to affect the price of that product. Note that this definition includes several important ideas. First, we are discussing the market for a single product, say, bushels of wheat. Second, all sellers offer essentially the same product for sale. Third, all buyers and sellers know everything there is to know about the market (including, in our example, the prices that all sellers are asking for their wheat). And fourth, the overall market is not affected by the actions of any one buyer or seller.

pure competition the market situation in which there are many buyers and sellers of a product, and no single buyer or seller is powerful enough to affect the price of that product

When pure competition exists, every seller should ask the same price that every other seller is asking. Why? Because if one seller wanted 50 cents more per bushel of wheat than all the others, that seller would not be able to sell a single bushel. Buyers could—and would—do better by purchasing wheat from the competition. On the other hand, a firm willing to sell below the going price would sell all its wheat quickly. But that seller would lose sales revenue (and profit) because buyers are actually willing to pay more.

In pure competition, then, sellers—and buyers as well—must accept the going price. However, who or what determines this price? Actually, everyone does. The price of each product is determined by the actions of *all buyers and all sellers together* through the forces of supply and demand.

The Basics of Supply and Demand

The **supply** of a particular product is the quantity of the product that *producers are willing to sell at each of various prices.* Producers are rational people, so we would expect them to offer more of a product for sale at higher prices and to offer less of the product at lower prices, as illustrated by the supply curve in Figure 1.5.

supply the quantity of a product that producers are willing to sell at each of various prices

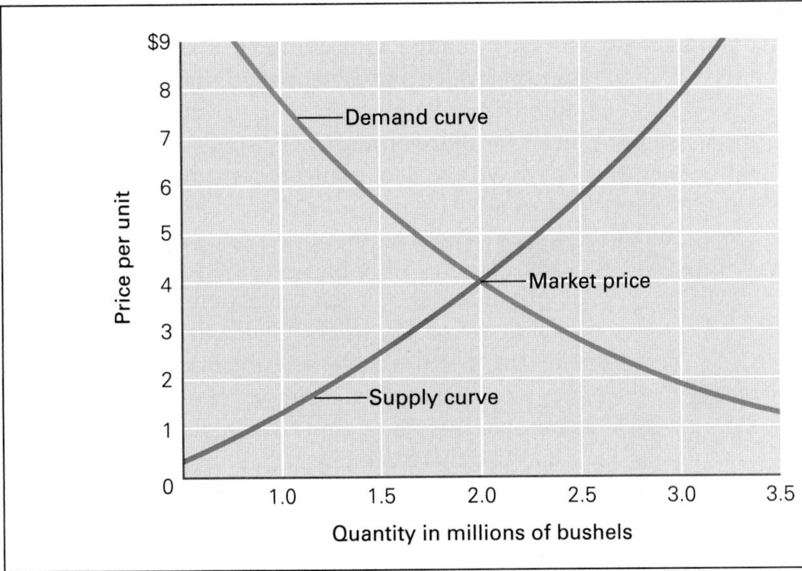

figure 1.5

Supply Curve and Demand Curve

The intersection of a supply curve and a demand curve is called the *equilibrium* or *market price.* This intersection indicates a single price and quantity at which suppliers will sell products and buyers will purchase them.

demand the quantity of a product that buyers are willing to purchase at each of various prices

The **demand** for a particular product is the quantity that *buyers are willing to purchase at each of various prices.* Buyers, too, are usually rational, so we would expect them—as a group—to buy more of a product when its price is low and to buy less of the product when its price is high, as depicted by the demand curve in Figure 1.5.

market price the price at which the quantity demanded is exactly equal to the quantity supplied

monopolistic competition a market situation in which there are many buyers along with a relatively large number of sellers who differentiate their products from the products of competitors

product differentiation the process of developing and promoting differences between one's products and all similar products

oligopoly a market (or industry) in which there are few sellers

The Equilibrium, or Market, Price There is always one certain price at which the demanded quantity of a product is exactly equal to the produced quantity of that product. Suppose that producers are willing to *supply* 2 million bushels of wheat at a price of \$4 per bushel and that buyers are willing to *purchase* 2 million bushels at a price of \$4 per bushel. In other words, supply and demand are in balance, or *in equilibrium,* at the price of \$4. Economists call this price the *market price.* The **market price** of any product is the price at which the quantity demanded is exactly equal to the quantity supplied. If suppliers produce 2 million bushels, then no one who is willing to pay \$4 per bushel will have to go without wheat, and no producer who is willing to sell at \$4 per bushel will be stuck with unsold wheat.

In theory and in the real world, market prices are affected by anything that affects supply and demand. The *demand* for wheat, for example, might change if researchers suddenly discovered that it offered a previously unknown health benefit. Then buyers would demand more wheat at every price. Or the *supply* of wheat might change if new technology permitted the production of greater quantities of wheat from the same amount of acreage. Other changes that can affect competitive prices are shifts in buyer tastes, the development of new products, fluctuations in income due to inflation or recession, or even changes in the weather that affect the production of wheat.

Pure competition is quite rare in today's world. Some specific markets (such as auctions of farm products) may come close, but no real market totally exhibits perfect competition. Many real markets, however, are examples of monopolistic competition.

Choice is good! Ever wonder why there are so many products that do the same thing? The answer to that question is one of the basic reasons why our economic system is successful. The fact that you have many choices even for common products like dishwashing detergents allows you to choose which one you like best. Simply put, if you don't like Joy, you can choose Dawn or Palmolive.

Monopolistic Competition

Monopolistic competition is a market situation in which there are many buyers along with a relatively large number of sellers. The various products available in a monopolistically competitive market are very similar in nature, and they are all intended to satisfy the same need. However, each seller attempts to make its product different from the others by providing unique product features, an attention-getting brand name, unique packaging, or services such as free delivery or a "lifetime" warranty.

Product differentiation is the process of developing and promoting differences between one's products and all similar products. It is a fact of life for the producers of many consumer goods, from soaps to clothing to furniture to personal computers. A furniture manufacturer such as Thomasville sees what looks like a mob of competitors, all trying to chip away at its market. By differentiating each of its products from all similar products, the producer obtains some limited control over the market price of its product. Under pure competition, the price of all furniture brands simply would be the market price of all similar furniture products.

Oligopoly

An **oligopoly** is a market situation (or industry) in which there are few sellers. Generally, these sellers are quite large, and sizable investments are required to enter into their market. Examples of oligopolies are the automobile, car rental, and farm implement industries.

Because there are few sellers in an oligopoly, the market actions of each seller can have a strong effect on competitors' sales. If General Motors, for example, reduces its automobile prices, Ford, Chrysler,

Toyota, and Nissan usually do the same to retain their market shares. As a result, similar products eventually have similar prices. In the absence of much price competition, product differentiation becomes the major competitive weapon; this is very evident in the advertising of the major auto manufacturers. For instance, when General Motors began offering low-interest financing for all its cars, Ford, Chrysler, and Toyota also launched competitive financing deals.

Monopoly

A **monopoly** is a market (or industry) with only one seller. Because only one firm is the supplier of a product, it would seem that it has complete control over price. However, no firm can set its price at some astronomical figure just because there is no competition; the firm would soon find it had no customers or sales revenue either. Instead, the firm in a monopoly position must consider the demand for its product and set the price at the most profitable level.

monopoly a market (or industry) with only one seller

Classic examples of monopolies in the United States are public utilities. Each utility firm operates in a **natural monopoly,** an industry that requires a huge investment in capital and within which any duplication of facilities would be wasteful. Natural monopolies are permitted to exist because the public interest is best served by their existence, but they operate under the scrutiny and control of various state and federal agencies. While many public utilities are still classified as natural monopolies, there is increased competition in many industries. For example, the breakup of AT&T has increased the amount of competition in the telecommunications industry. And there have been increased demands for consumer choice when choosing a company that provides electrical service to both homes and businesses.

natural monopoly an industry requiring huge investments in capital and within which duplication of facilities would be wasteful and thus not in the public interest

A legal monopoly—sometimes referred to as a *limited monopoly*—is created when the federal government issues a copyright, patent, or trademark. Each of these exists for a specific period of time and can be used to protect the owners of written materials, ideas, or product brands from unauthorized use by competitors that have not shared in the time, effort, and expense required for their development. Because Microsoft owns the copyright on its popular Windows software, it enjoys a limited-monopoly position. Competitors cannot take the Windows software, change the name, and sell it as their product without Microsoft's approval.

Except for natural monopolies and monopolies created by copyrights, patents, and trademarks, federal antitrust laws prohibit both monopolies and attempts to form monopolies. In fact, antitrust laws provided the legal basis for lawsuits by competitors, the federal government, and a number of individual states against Microsoft. Microsoft's opponents argue that the software giant has used unfair trade practices to systematically eliminate competitors. They also argue that Microsoft is too successful and takes advantage of its monopoly position by trying to stifle competition. Microsoft, on the other hand, argues that it has become one of the most successful companies in the world because it operates in a capitalistic society that encourages business firms to pursue excellence. According to Microsoft, it enjoys industry dominance because consumers choose its products voluntarily and that the court has no right to remove its proprietary right to continue selling its products that have contributed to American technological dominance in the personal computer (PC) field globally. At the time of publication, there were still numerous unresolved lawsuits against the software giant.

The Development of American Business

learning objective

6 Summarize the development of America's business system.

Our American business system has its roots in the knowledge, skills, and values that the earliest settlers brought to this country. Refer to Figure 1.6 (on p. 22) for an overall view of our nation's history, the development of our business system, and some major inventions that influenced the nation and our business system.

figure 1.6

Time Line of American Business
Throughout the history of the United States, invention and innovation have led naturally to change and a more industrialized economy.

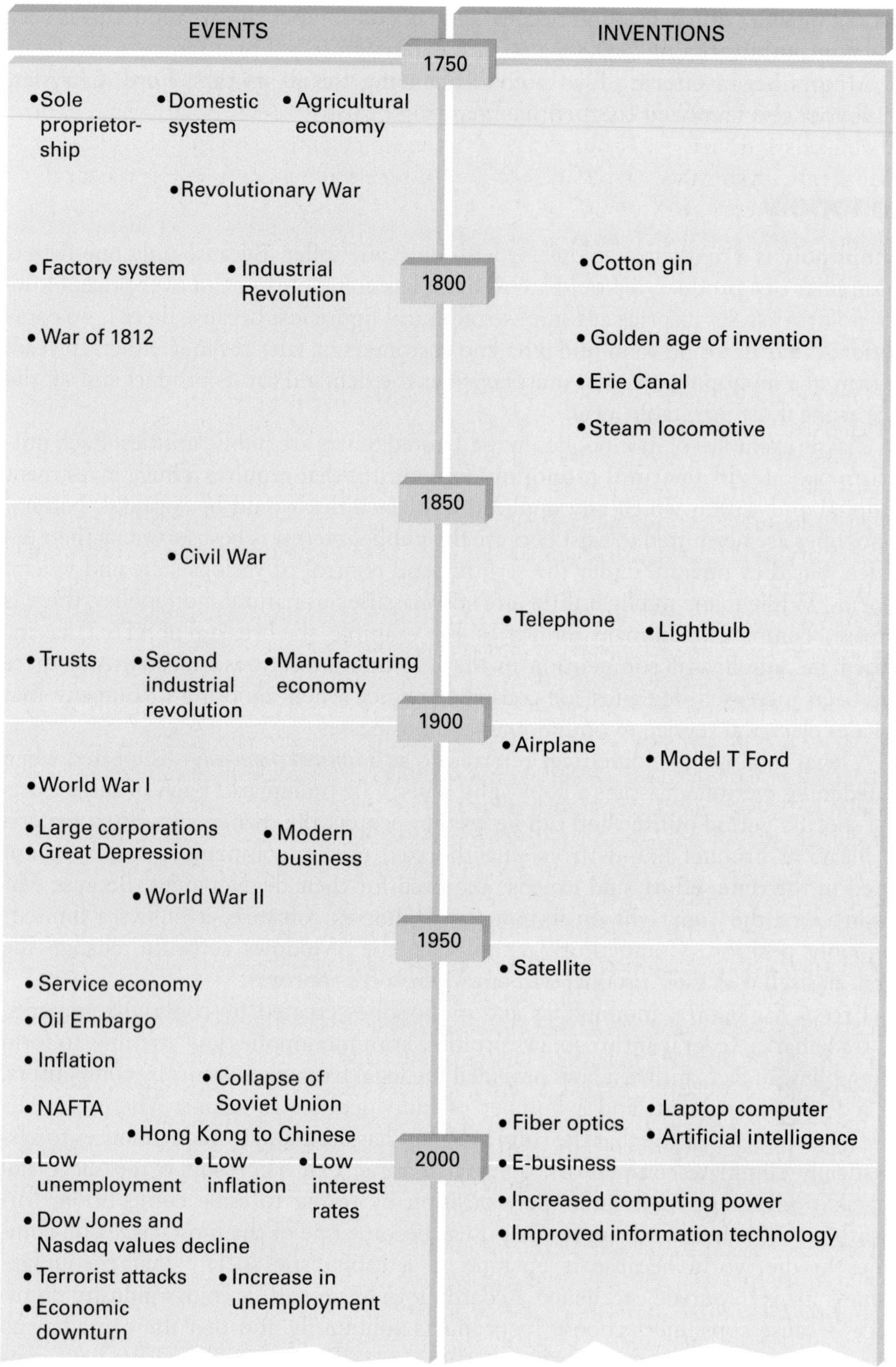

	EVENTS	INVENTIONS
1750	• Sole proprietorship • Domestic system • Agricultural economy • Revolutionary War	
1800	• Factory system • Industrial Revolution • War of 1812	• Cotton gin • Golden age of invention • Erie Canal • Steam locomotive
1850	• Civil War • Trusts • Second industrial revolution • Manufacturing economy	• Telephone • Lightbulb
1900	• World War I • Large corporations • Great Depression • Modern business • World War II	• Airplane • Model T Ford
1950	• Service economy • Oil Embargo • Inflation • Collapse of Soviet Union • NAFTA • Hong Kong to Chinese	• Satellite • Fiber optics • Laptop computer • Artificial intelligence
2000	• Low unemployment • Low inflation • Low interest rates • Dow Jones and Nasdaq values decline • Terrorist attacks • Increase in unemployment • Economic downturn	• E-business • Increased computing power • Improved information technology

The Colonial Period

The first settlers in the New World were concerned mainly with providing themselves with basic necessities—food, clothing, and shelter. Almost all families lived on farms, and the entire family worked at the business of surviving.

barter a system of exchange in which goods or services are traded directly for other goods and/or services without using money

The colonists did indeed survive, and eventually they were able to produce more than they consumed. They used their surplus for trading, mainly by barter, among themselves and with the English trading ships that called at the colonies. **Barter** is a system of exchange in which goods or services are traded directly for other goods and/or services—without using money. As this trade increased, small-scale business enterprises began to appear. Most of these businesses produced farm products. Other industries that had been founded by 1700 were shipbuilding, lumbering, fur trading, rum manufacturing, and fishing.

During the colonial period, 90 percent of the population was still living on farms and was engaged primarily in activities to meet their own needs. Some were able to use their skills and their excess time to work under the domestic system of production. The **domestic system** was a method of manufacturing in which an entrepreneur distributed raw materials to various homes, where families would process them into finished goods. The merchant entrepreneur then offered the goods for sale.

domestic system a method of manufacturing in which an entrepreneur distributes raw materials to various homes, where families would process them into finished goods to be offered for sale by the merchant entrepreneur

The Industrial Revolution

In 1790, a young English apprentice mechanic named Samuel Slater decided to sail to America. At this time, British law forbade the export of machinery, technology, and skilled workers. To get around the law, Slater painstakingly memorized the plans for Richard Arkwright's water-powered spinning machine, which had revolutionized the British textile industry, and left England disguised as a farmer. A year later he set up a textile factory in Pawtucket, Rhode Island, to spin raw cotton into thread. Slater's ingenuity resulted in America's first use of the **factory system** of manufacturing, in which all the materials, machinery, and workers required to manufacture a product are assembled in one place. The Industrial Revolution in America was born.

factory system a system of manufacturing in which all the materials, machinery, and workers required to manufacture a product are assembled in one place

The invention of the cotton gin in 1793 by Eli Whitney greatly increased the supply of cotton for the textile industry. And by 1814, Francis Cabot Lowell had established a factory in Waltham, Massachusetts, to spin, weave, and bleach cotton, all under one roof. In doing so, Lowell used a manufacturing technique called *specialization*. **Specialization** is the separation of a manufacturing process into distinct tasks and the assignment of different tasks to different individuals. The purpose of specialization is to increase the efficiency of industrial workers; Lowell's workers were able to produce 30 miles of cloth each day.

specialization the separation of a manufacturing process into distinct tasks and the assignment of different tasks to different individuals

The three decades from 1820 to 1850 were the golden age of invention and innovation in machinery. Elias Howe's sewing machine became available to convert materials into clothing. The agricultural machinery of John Deere and Cyrus McCormick revolutionized farm production. At the same time, new means of transportation greatly expanded the domestic markets for American products. The Erie Canal was opened in the 1820s. Soon afterward, thanks to Robert Fulton's engine, steamboats could move upstream against the current and use the rivers as highways for hauling bulk goods. During the 1830s and 1840s, the railroads began to extend the existing transportation system to the West, carrying goods and people much farther than was possible by waterways alone.

Many business historians view the period from 1870 to 1900 as the second industrial revolution; certainly, many characteristics of our modern business system took form during these three decades. In this period, for example, the nation shifted from a farm economy to a manufacturing economy. The developing coal and oil industries provided fuel for light, heat, and energy. During this time, the United States became not only an industrial giant but a leading world power as well.

Early Twentieth Century

Industrial growth and prosperity continued well into the twentieth century. Henry Ford's moving automotive assembly line, which brought the work to the worker, refined the concept of specialization and helped spur on the mass production of consumer goods. By the 1920s, the automobile industry had begun to influence the entire economy. The steel industry, which supplies materials to the auto industry, grew along with it. The oil and chemical industries grew just as fast. And the emerging airplane and airline industries promised convenient and faster transportation.

Fundamental changes occurred in business ownership and management as well. The largest businesses were no longer owned by one individual; instead, ownership was in the hands of thousands of corporate shareholders who were willing to invest in—but not to operate—a business.

Certain modern marketing techniques are products of this era, too. Large corporations developed new methods of advertising and selling. Time-payment plans made it possible for the average consumer to purchase costly durable goods such as automobiles, appliances, and home furnishings. Advertisements counseled the public to "buy now and pay later." Capitalism and our economy seemed strong and healthy, but it was not to last.

The human pain associated with unemployment and the Great Depression. During the Great Depression, unemployment rates in the United States were between 16 and 25 percent, forcing many would-be employees to wait in bread and soup lines just to get something to eat.

The Great Depression and Recovery

The Roaring Twenties ended with the sudden crash of the stock market in 1929 and the near collapse of the economy. The Great Depression that followed in the 1930s was a time of misery and human suffering. The unemployment rate varied between 16 and 25 percent in the years 1931 through 1939, and the value of goods and services produced in America fell by almost half. People lost their faith in business and its ability to satisfy the needs of society without government involvement.

After Franklin D. Roosevelt became president in 1933, the federal government devised a number of programs to get the economy moving again. In implementing these programs, the government got deeply involved in business for the first time. Many business people opposed this intervention, but they reluctantly accepted the new government regulations.

The economy was on the road to recovery when World War II broke out in Europe in 1939. The need for vast quantities of war materials—first for our allies and then for the American military as well—spurred business activity and technological development. This rapid economic pace continued after the war, and the 1950s and 1960s witnessed both increasing production and a rising standard of living. **Standard of living** is a loose, subjective measure of how well off an individual or a society is, mainly in terms of want satisfaction through goods and services.

standard of living a loose, subjective measure of how well off an individual or a society is mainly in terms of want satisfaction through goods and services

The Late Twentieth Century

In the mid-1970s, however, a shortage of crude oil led to a new set of problems for business. As the cost of petroleum products increased, a corresponding price increase took place in the cost of energy and the cost of goods and services. The result was inflation at a rate well over 10 percent per year during the early 1980s. Interest rates also increased dramatically, so both businesses and consumers reduced their borrowing. Business profits fell as the purchasing power of consumers was eroded by inflation and high interest rates. By the mid-1980s, many of these problem areas showed signs of improvement. Unfortunately, many managers now had something else to worry about—corporate mergers and takeovers. In addition, a large number of bank failures, coupled with an increasing number of bankruptcies, again made people uneasy about our business system.

By the early 1990s, the U.S. economy began to show signs of improvement and economic growth. Unemployment numbers, inflation, and interest—all factors that affect business—were now at record lows. In turn, business took advantage of this economic prosperity to invest in information technology, cut costs, and increase flexibility and efficiency. The Internet became a major force in the economy, with computer hardware, software, and Internet service providers taking advantage of the increased need for information. As further evidence of the financial health of the new economy, the stock market enjoyed the longest period of sustained economic growth in our history. Both the Dow Jones Industrial Average and the Nasdaq Stock Index—two measures that investors use to measure stock market performance—reached record highs. Unfortunately, by the last part of the twentieth century, a larger number of business failures and declining stock values were initial signs that larger economic problems were on the way.

The New Millennium

According to many economic experts, the first few years of the new millennium might be characterized as the best of times and the worst of times rolled into one package. On the plus side, technology became available at an affordable price. Both individuals and businesses could now access information with the click of a button. They also could buy and sell merchandise online. e-Business—a topic that we will continue to explore throughout this text—became an accepted method of conducting business. For more information on how e-business is changing, read Talking Technology.

In addition to information technology, the growth of service businesses and increasing opportunities for global trade also have changed the way American firms do business in the twenty-first century. Because they employ over three-fourths of the American work force, service businesses are a very important component of our economy.[16] As a result, service businesses must find ways to improve productivity and cut costs while at the same time providing jobs for even a larger portion of the work force. American businesses are also beginning to realize that to be successful, they must

talking technology

What B2B and B2C Really Mean

As the centerpiece of the New Economy, the Internet has spawned an alphabet soup of acronyms to describe various aspects of e-business. Business-to-business or B2B, for example, describes firms that conduct business with other businesses. Because business purchases tend to be much larger than consumer purchases, B2B accounts for most of today's e-business volume. Consider FreeMarkets, a B2B site that hosts online auctions where suppliers compete to sell goods and services to industrial and corporate buyers. FreeMarkets annually auctions more than $16 billion worth of B2B products.

In contrast, business-to-consumer or B2C describes firms that focus on conducting business with individual buyers. Online retail pioneer Amazon.com is a good example. Boldly advertising its competitive prices and huge selection of books, Amazon quickly became the Internet's dominant book retailer and later branched out into music, movies, toys, and many other products.

Although the transactions are digital, the traditional rules of business still apply to e-business. Some early B2B and B2C sites tried to lure customers with near-cost pricing, pricey advertising, and free shipping. Many burned through millions of dollars before closing down or selling out. B2C site Pets.com spent lavishly on television commercials featuring its sock puppet dog but never attracted enough loyal, paying customers to cover costs and turn a profit.

Why are FreeMarkets and Amazon flourishing? First, they offer all kinds of extras that please customers. FreeMarkets coaches businesses on how to use auctions to best advantage. It also screens suppliers, saving customers the trouble of doing such checks themselves. Amazon makes buying easy through one-click purchasing, and it tailors product recommendations to each customer's interests and buying patterns. Small wonder that customers buy from these sites again and again.

Second, successful B2B and B2C sites never stop innovating to compete more effectively. Amazon constantly adds products and features, promotional offers, and country-specific sites to maintain its lead over Barnesandnoble.com and other rivals.

Finally, they take a realistic view of market opportunities. Pets.com assumed that building a distinctive brand would automatically spark a tidal wave of sales. However, as popular as the sock puppet became, few people were interested in buying pet supplies on the web. As in the physical world of business, customers rule—B2B and B2C sites can sell only products that buyers are willing to buy.

enter the global marketplace. In short, American firms must meet the needs not only of American consumers but also of foreign consumers. And foreign firms are now selling record amounts of products and services to American consumers. Indeed, the world as far as business is concerned is becoming smaller. (Both our service economy and our place in the global marketplace are discussed more fully later in the text.)

On the negative side, as mentioned earlier in this chapter, it is hard to watch television, listen to the radio, or read the newspaper without hearing some news about the economy. Unfortunately, the news coverage often centers on economic problems rather than on solutions or success stories. Even though many of the economic indicators described in Table 1.1 on page 17 remain strong or show signs of improvement, there is still a certain amount of pessimism surrounding the economy. This *feeling*, coupled with a large number of business failures—especially in the high-tech industries—higher unemployment rates, factory closures, lower stock values, and other factors, has led many people to wonder how long before the economy turns the corner and begins to recover. To be sure, the tragic events of September 11 and the war on terrorism have contributed to this unrest and created new challenges as we continue the journey into the twenty-first century.

The Challenges Ahead

learning objective

7 Discuss the challenges that American businesses will encounter in the future.

There it is, the American business system in brief. When it works well, it provides jobs for those who are willing to work, a standard of living that few countries can match, and many opportunities for personal advancement. However, like every other system devised by humans, it is not perfect. Our business system may give us prosperity, but it also gave us the Great Depression of the 1930s and the economic problems of the 1970s, the late 1980s, and the first part of the twenty-first century.

Obviously, the system can be improved. It may need no more than a bit of fine-tuning, or it may require more extensive overhauling. Certainly there are plenty of people who are willing to tell us exactly what *they* think the American economy needs. But these people provide us only with conflicting opinions. Who is right and who is wrong? Even the experts cannot agree.

The experts do agree, however, that several key issues will challenge our economic system (and our nation) over the next decade. Some of the questions to be resolved include

- How can we encourage Iraq to establish a democratic and free society and resolve possible conflict with North Korea and other countries throughout the world?
- How can we create a more stable economy and create new jobs for those who want to work?
- How can we restore the public's trust in corporate financial matters?
- How can we meet the challenges of managing culturally diverse work forces to address the needs of a culturally diverse marketplace?
- How can we make American manufacturers more productive and more competitive with foreign producers who have lower labor costs?

Why diversity is important at Freddie Mac. For Freddie Mac employees like Anh Nguyen, diversity is about more than just hiring people with obvious cultural or racial differences. According to Nguyen, a diverse workgroup can share different points of view that can lead to solutions for complex problems in the home mortgage business.

- How can we encourage an entrepreneurial spirit in large, established corporations?
- How can we preserve the benefits of competition in our American economic system?
- How can we encourage economic growth and at the same time continue to conserve natural resources and protect our environment?
- How can we finance additional investment spending on information technology and replacement of obsolete machinery and equipment?
- How can we best market American-made products in foreign nations?
- How much government involvement in our economy is necessary for its continued well-being? In what areas should there be less involvement? In what areas, more?
- How can we evaluate the long-term economic costs and benefits of existing and proposed government programs?
- How can we meet the needs of the less fortunate?

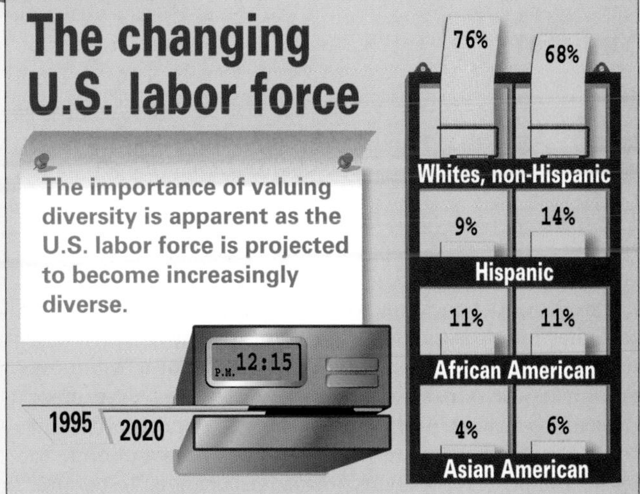

Source: Diversity Central, **www.diversityhotwire.com**, and *Workforce 2020*, Hudson Institute.

The answers to these questions are anything but simple. In the past, Americans have always been able to solve their economic problems through ingenuity and creativity. Now, as we continue the journey through the twenty-first century, we need that same ingenuity and creativity not only to solve our current problems but also to compete in the global marketplace.

According to economic experts, if we as a nation can become more competitive, we may solve many of our current domestic problems. As an added bonus, increased competitiveness also will enable us to meet the economic challenges posed by other industrialized nations of the world. The way we solve these problems will affect our own future, our children's future, and that of our nation. Within the American economic and political system, the answers are ours to provide.

The American business system is not perfect by any means, but it does work reasonably well. We discuss some of its problems in Chapter 2 as we examine the role of business as part of American society.

Return To inside business

The Container Store earns its success, day in and day out, by making customers the top priority. Despite increasing competitive pressures, changing customer tastes, and many other challenges, cofounders Garrett Boone and Kip Tindell and their work force remain dedicated to providing the highest quality service. Employees not only educate customers about different products, they also take the time to sketch specific plans showing how customers can use specific storage items to save space and simplify their lives.

Every company wants top-notch employees who care about their customers and look forward to developing their skills, just as every employee wants to work for a well-regarded company that educates and rewards its personnel. In the case of the Container Store, more than 19,000 people apply for positions every year, and only 8 percent of the work force leaves. Throughout the company's history, the cofounders and their management team have set the tone by letting their own enthusiasm shine through. "We all really love what we do, and that keeps us motivated," Tindell says. "We really enjoy going to work every day." And according to the *Fortune* surveys, the Container Store's employees feel exactly the same way.

Questions

1. The Container Store is often cited as an outstanding retail company. What factors have led to its success?
2. Would you want to work for a firm like the Container Store? Explain your answer.

Summary

Discuss your future in the world of business.

For many years, people in business—both employees and managers—assumed that prosperity would continue. When the bubble burst, a large number of these same people then began to ask the question: What do we do now? Although a fair question, it is a difficult question to answer. Certainly, for a college student taking business courses or a beginning employee just starting a career, the question is even more difficult to answer. And yet there are still opportunities out there for people who are willing to work hard, continue to learn, and possess the ability to adapt to change. To be sure, employers and our capitalistic economic system are more demanding than ever before. As you begin this course, ask yourself: What can I do that will make employers want to pay me a salary? What skills do I have that employers need? By introducing you to a wide range of employment opportunities, a business course also can help you to decide on a career. The kind of career you choose ultimately will depend on your own values and what you feel is most important in life. But deciding on the kind of career you want is only a first step. To get a job in your chosen field and to be successful at it, you will have to develop a plan, or road map, that ensures that you have the necessary skills and the knowledge the job requires to become a better employee. By studying business, you also may decide to start your own business and become a better consumer and investor.

Define *business,* and identify potential risks and rewards.

Business is the organized effort of individuals to produce and sell, for a profit, the products and services that satisfy society's needs. Four kinds of resources—material, human, financial, and informational—must be combined to start and operate a business. The three general types of businesses are manufacturers, service businesses, and marketing intermediaries. Profit is what remains after all business expenses are deducted from sales revenue. It is the payment that owners receive for assuming the risks of business—primarily the risks of not receiving payment and of losing whatever has been invested in the firm. Most often a business that is operated to satisfy its customers earns a reasonable profit.

Describe the two types of economic systems: capitalism and command economy.

Economics is the study of how wealth is created and distributed. An economy is a system through which a society decides those two issues. An economic system must answer four questions: What goods and services will be produced? How will they be produced? For whom will they be produced? Who owns and who controls the major factors of production? Capitalism (on which our economic system is based) is an economic system in which individuals own and operate the majority of businesses that provide goods and services. Capitalism stems from the theories of Adam Smith. Smith's pure laissez-faire capitalism is an economic system in which individuals and businesses answer these questions as they pursue their own self-interest. In a laissez-faire capitalist system, the factors of production are owned by private entities, and all individuals are free to use their resources as they see fit; prices are determined by the workings of supply and demand in competitive markets; and the economic role of government is limited to rule maker and umpire.

Our economic system today is a mixed economy. Although our present business system is essentially capitalist in nature, government takes part, along with households and businesses. In the circular flow that characterizes our business system (see Figure 1.3), households and businesses exchange resources for goods and services, using money as the medium of exchange. In a similar manner, government collects taxes from businesses and households and purchases products and resources with which to provide services.

In a command economy, government, rather than individuals, owns the factors of production and provides the answers to the three other economic questions. Socialist and communist economies are—at least in theory—command economies. In the real world, however, communists seem to practice a strictly controlled kind of socialism.

Identify the ways to measure economic performance.

One way to evaluate the performance of an economic system is to assess changes in productivity, which is the average level of output per worker per hour. Gross domestic product (GDP) also can be used to measure a nation's economic well-being and is the total dollar value of all goods and services produced by all people within the boundaries of a country during a one-year period. This figure facilitates comparisons between the United States and other countries because it is the standard used in international guidelines for economic accounting. It is also possible to adjust GDP for inflation and thus to measure *real* GDP. In addition to GDP, there are other economic indicators that can be used to measure a nation's economy. These include a nation's balance of trade, consumer price index, inflation rate, prime interest rate, producer price index, productivity rate, and unemployment rate.

A nation's economy fluctuates rather than grows at a steady pace every year. These fluctuations are generally referred to as the business cycle. Generally, the business cycle consists of four states: the peak (sometimes referred to as prosperity), recession, the trough, and recovery. Some experts believe that effective use of monetary policy (the Federal Reserve's decisions that determine the size of the supply of money and level of interest rates) and fiscal policies (the government's influence on the amount of savings and expenditures) can speed up recovery and even eliminate depressions for the business cycle.

Outline the four types of competition.

Competition is essentially a rivalry among businesses for sales to potential customers. In a capitalist economy, competition works to ensure the efficient and effective operation of business. Competition also ensures that a firm will survive only if it serves its customers well. Economists recognize four degrees of competition. Ranging from most to least competitive, the four degrees are pure competition, monopolistic competition, oligopoly, and monopoly. The factors of supply and demand generally influence the price that consumers pay producers for goods and services.

Summarize the development of America's business system.

Since its beginnings in the seventeenth century, American business has been based on private ownership of property and freedom of enterprise. And from this beginning, through the Industrial Revolution of the early nineteenth century, and to the phenomenal expansion of American industry in the nineteenth and early twentieth centuries, our government maintained an essentially laissez-faire attitude toward business. However, during the Great Depression of the 1930s, the federal government began to provide a number of social services to its citizens. Government's role in business has expanded considerably since that time.

During the 1970s, a shortage of crude oil led to higher prices and inflation. Business profits fell as the consumers' purchasing power was eroded by inflation and high interest rates. By the mid-1980s, corporate mergers and takeovers, bank failures, and an increasing number of bankruptcies made people uneasy about our business system. By the early 1990s, the U.S. economy began to show signs of improvement and economic growth. Unemployment numbers, inflation, and interest—all factors that affect business—were now at record lows. Fueled by investment in information technology, the stock market enjoyed the longest period of sustained economic growth in our history. Increased use of the Internet and e-business are now changing the way that firms do business. Other factors that affect the way firms do business include the increasing importance of services and global trade. Unfortunately, by the last part of the 1990s, a larger number of business failures and declining stock values were initial signs that more economic problems were on the way as we entered the twenty-first century.

Discuss the challenges that American businesses will encounter in the future.

Today, American businesses face a number of significant challenges. Among the issues to be contended with are the establishment of a democratic and free society in Iraq and possible conflict with North Korea and other countries; the creation of a stable economy and new jobs; restoring the public's trust in corporate financial matters; the effective management of cultural diversity in the workplace; the problem of encouraging the entrepreneurial spirit in large, established corporations; investment in information technology and replacement of obsolete machinery and equipment; and the extent of business's environmental and social responsibilities. If we as a nation can become more competitive, we may solve many of our domestic economic problems. As an added bonus, increased competitiveness will enable us to meet many of the challenges posed by foreign nations.

Key Terms

You should now be able to define and give an example relevant to each of the following terms.

free enterprise (4)
e-business (7)
business (9)
profit (11)
economics (12)
economy (12)
factors of production (12)
entrepreneur (13)
capitalism (13)
market economy (13)
mixed economy (14)
consumer products (14)
command economy (15)
productivity (16)
gross domestic product (GDP) (16)
inflation (17)
business cycle (18)
recession (18)
depression (18)
monetary policies (18)
fiscal policy (18)
federal deficit (18)
national debt (18)
competition (19)
pure competition (19)
supply (19)
demand (20)
market price (20)
monopolistic competition (20)
product differentiation (20)
oligopoly (20)
monopoly (21)
natural monopoly (21)
barter (22)
domestic system (23)
factory system (23)
specialization (23)
standard of living (24)

Review Questions

1. What reasons would you give if you were advising someone to study business?
2. What factors affect a person's choice of careers?
3. Describe the four resources that must be combined to organize and operate a business. How do they differ from the economist's factors of production?
4. What distinguishes consumers from other buyers of goods and services?
5. Describe the relationship among profit, business risk, and the satisfaction of customers' needs.
6. What are the four basic economic questions? How are they answered in a capitalist economy?
7. Describe the four fundamental issues required for a laissez-faire capitalist economy.
8. Why is the American economy called a mixed economy?
9. Based on Figure 1.3, outline the economic interactions between business and households in our business system.
10. How does capitalism differ from socialism and communism?
11. Define gross domestic product. Why is this economic measure significant?
12. Choose three of the economic measures described in Table 1.1 and describe why these indicators are important when measuring a nation's economy.
13. Identify and compare the four forms of competition.
14. Explain how the equilibrium, or market, price of a product is determined.
15. Trace the steps that led from farming for survival in the American colonial period to today's mass production.
16. What do you consider the most important challenges that will face people in the United States in the years ahead?

Discussion Questions

1. In what ways have the economic problems that the nation has experienced in the past three years affected business firms? In what ways have these problems affected employees?
2. What factors caused American business to develop into a mixed economic system rather than some other type of economic system?
3. Does an individual consumer really have a voice in answering the basic economic questions?
4. Is gross domestic product a reliable indicator of a nation's economic health? What might be a better indicator?
5. Discuss this statement: "Business competition encourages efficiency of production and leads to improved product quality."
6. In our business system, how is government involved in answering the four basic economic questions? Does government participate in the system or interfere with it?
7. Choose one of the challenges listed on pages 26–27 and describe possible ways that business and society could help solve or eliminate the problem in the future.

video case

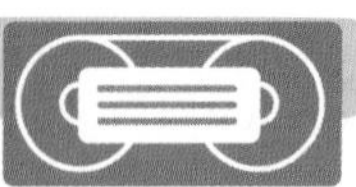

Stonyfield Farm's "Yogurt on a Mission"

Stonyfield Farm's "Yogurt on a mission" is changing the culture of at least one multinational corporation. Stonyfield Farm, founded in New Hampshire in 1983, began with three Jersey cows. Today it has grown into a 150-employee business churning out the third largest selling yogurt brand in America. The company's extensive line of organic foods includes refrigerated yogurts, ice cream, frozen yogurt, soft-serve yogurt, cultured soy snacks, and drinkable yogurts. All its products meet rigorous guidelines for organic certification because the ingredients are not produced with synthetic fertilizers or pesticides, antibiotics, and hormones. Although organic foods were not as popular when Stonyfield was established, they currently account for a whopping $9 billion in yearly sales.

Stonyfield is pursuing a five-part mission to (1) support family farmers, (2) be profitable, (3) offer quality products, (4) protect the environment, and (5) be a great place for employees to work. All of Stonyfield's decisions and actions reflect this ambitious multipronged mission. Managers are dedicated to using only the highest-quality ingredients to make all-natural food products that are both healthy and tasty. They use product packaging to educate customers about environmental causes such as global warming and recycling. They also are firmly committed to the family farms that supply organic milk for Stonyfield's products—paying a higher price so that the farmers can survive even when competing yogurt makers cut the amount they pay for milk. And they ensure that workplace conditions allow employees the opportunity to develop their skills and advance into new positions.

Following company policy to "reduce, reuse, recycle," Stonyfield's personnel always look for the most environmentally friendly ways to operate. For example, the company currently recycles 60 percent of its yogurt plant's waste. However, CEO Gary Hirshberg wants to increase that recycling level to 80 percent or higher. Even milk that does not meet the company's strict quality standards is not wasted—it goes to local farmers, who feed it to their pigs.

At the same time, Stonyfield proves that caring for the environment can be profitable. Using less energy or water actually lowers operating costs. Similarly, reducing or recycling waste lowers waste-removal costs. Just as important, communicating with customers about environmental issues creates a closer connection and builds sales by reinforcing brand loyalty. In fact, Stonyfield's sales have been growing rapidly, and it donates 10 percent of its profits to environmental causes every year.

In addition, Hirshberg is using his entrepreneurial talents to move beyond yogurt and soy into the lucrative world of fast food. The company recently opened O'Naturals in Maine, a restaurant serving healthy fast food in a comfortable, family-friendly setting—with environmental education as a side dish, of course. "We want to be McDonald's," the CEO states. "This is a billion-dollar brand idea."

Now Stonyfield is entering a new phase of its business life. In late 2001, France's Groupe Danone—maker of Dannon, the world's best-selling yogurt—acquired a 40 percent holding in Stonyfield. It has the option of becoming majority owner within a few years if Hirshberg approves. Under this agreement, Hirshberg retains management control of the company he built as long as it continues to achieve double-digit sales growth. And if he leaves, Groupe Danone has agreed to keep donating 10 percent of Stonyfield's profits to environmental causes for at least a decade afterward.

Can Stonyfield remain true to its roots even under new ownership? Groupe Danone's chairman says yes, explaining that Stonyfield is a model for doing business in the future. "We are driven by social values similar to Gary's," he notes. "We have to think not only in terms of economics, but also in terms of social responsibility." And Stonyfield is not the first socially responsible company to be swallowed up by a global giant. Ben & Jerry's is owned by Unilever, and Earth's Best baby food is owned by Hain Celestial Group (in which Heinz owns a small stake).

For his part, Hirshberg believes that Stonyfield is a "Trojan horse" that eventually will change Groupe Danone's approach to business. Because of Groupe Danone's international reach, it has the potential to substantially boost environmentalism by introducing many more organic products. This fits with Hirshberg's long-term view of socially responsible businesses and healthier customers: "If you make the right choices, then future generations will have a healthier planet and healthier, more enjoyable lives."[17]

Questions

1. As a business, what needs does Stonyfield satisfy for its customers?
2. Does the yogurt market reflect monopolistic competition or an oligopoly? Support your answer by discussing how Stonyfield's diverse line of organic foods helps the company to compete.
3. Why would a firm like Stonyfield embrace environmental causes and the concept of increasing sales and profits?
4. From the perspective of business profit, should Groupe Danone keep contributing to environmental causes for many years after Hirshberg leaves? Why?

Building Skills for Career Success

1. Exploring the Internet

The Internet is a global network of computers that can be accessed by anyone in the world. For example, your school or firm is most likely connected to the Web. You probably have private access through a commercial service provider like America Online, Prodigy, or a host of other smaller Internet service providers.

To familiarize you with the wealth of information available through the Internet and its usefulness to business students, this exercise focuses on information services available from a few popular "search engines" used to explore the web. Each of the remaining chapters in this text also contains an Internet exercise that is in some way associated with the topics covered in the chapter. After completing these exercises, not only will you be familiar with a variety of sources of business information, but you also will be better prepared to locate information you might need in the future.

To use one of these search engines, enter its *Internet address* in your web browser. The addresses of some popular search engines are

www.altavista.com
www.lycos.com
www.msn.com
www.yahoo.com

Visit the text web site for updates to this exercise.

Assignment

1. Examine the way in which two search engines present categories of information on their opening screens. Explore the articles in the business and economics categories. Which search engine was better to use, in your opinion? Why?
2. Think of a business topic that you would like to know more about, for example, careers, gross domestic product, or another concept introduced in this chapter. Using your preferred search engine, explore a few articles and

reports provided on your topic. Briefly summarize your findings.

2. Developing Critical Thinking Skills

Under capitalism, competition is a driving force that allows the market economy to work, affecting the supply of goods and services in the marketplace and the prices consumers pay for those goods and services. Let's see how competition works by pretending that you want to buy a new car.

Assignment

1. Brainstorm the following questions:
   a. Where would you go to get information about new cars?
   b. How will you decide on the make and model of car you want to buy, where to buy the car, and how to finance it?
   c. How is competition at work in this scenario?
   d. What are the pros and cons of competition as it affects the buyer?
2. Record your ideas.
3. Write a summary of the key points you learned about how competition works in the marketplace.

3. Building Team Skills

Over the past few years, employees have been expected to function as productive team members instead of working alone. People often believe that they can work effectively in teams, but many people find working with a group of people to be a challenge. Being an effective team member requires skills that encourage other members to participate in the team endeavor.

College classes that function as teams are more interesting and more fun to attend, and students generally learn more about the topics in the course. If your class is to function as a team, it is important to begin building the team early in the semester. One way to begin creating a team is to learn something about each student in the class. This helps team members feel comfortable with each other and fosters a sense of trust.

Assignment

1. Find a partner, preferably someone you do not know.
2. Each partner has two to three minutes to answer the following questions:
   a. What is your name, and where do you work?
   b. What interesting or unusual thing have you done in your life? (Do not talk about work or college; rather, focus on such things as hobbies, travel, family, and sports.)
   c. Why are you taking this course, and what do you expect to learn? (Satisfying a degree requirement is not an acceptable answer.)
3. Introduce your partner to the class. Use one to two minutes, depending on the size of the class.

4. Researching Different Careers

In this chapter, *entrepreneurship* is defined as the willingness to take risks and the knowledge and ability to use the other factors of production efficiently. An **entrepreneur** is a person who risks his or her time, effort, and money to start and operate a business. Often people believe that these terms apply only to small business operations, but recently, employees with entrepreneurial attitudes have advanced more rapidly in large companies.

Assignment

1. Go to the local library or use the Internet to research how large firms, especially corporations, are rewarding employees who have entrepreneurial skills.
2. Find answers to the following questions:
   a. Why is an entrepreneurial attitude important in corporations today?
   b. What makes an entrepreneurial employee different from other employees?
   c. How are these employees being rewarded, and are the rewards worth the effort?
3. Write a two-page report that summarizes your findings.

5. Improving Communication Skills

Most jobs today require good writing skills. Written communications in the workplace range from the simple task of jotting down telephone messages to the more complex tasks of writing memos, newspaper articles, policy manuals, and technical journals. Regardless of the type of communication, the writer must convey the correct information to the reader in a clear, concise, and courteous manner. This involves using effective writing skills, which can be improved through practice. You can begin improving your skills by writing in a journal on a regular basis.

Assignment

1. Each week during the semester, write your thoughts and ideas in a journal. Include business terms you learned during the week, and give an example of how each term is used in the business world. Also, do one of the following:
   a. Ask someone, preferably a person working in business, a question based on a topic in the class assignment for the week. Record the answers, and comment on your perceptions about the topic.
   b. Read a newspaper article relating to a topic covered in the class assignment for the week. Summarize your thoughts on the topic in your journal, specifically discussing what you learned.
2. Ask your instructor for guidelines and due dates for the completed journal and the summary you will prepare at the end of the semester.

chapter

2 Being Ethical and Socially Responsible

learning objectives

1 Understand what is meant by *business ethics*.

2 Identify the types of ethical concerns that arise in the business world.

3 Discuss the factors that affect the level of ethical behavior in organizations.

4 Explain how ethical decision making can be encouraged.

5 Describe how our current views on the social responsibility of business have evolved.

6 Explain the two views on the social responsibility of business and understand the arguments for and against increased social responsibility.

7 Discuss the factors that led to the consumer movement and list some of its results.

8 Analyze how present employment practices are being used to counteract past abuses.

9 Describe the major types of pollution, their causes, and their cures.

10 Identify the steps a business must take to implement a program of social responsibility.

Starbucks should be known for its social responsibility as much as its hearty lattes.

inside business

Starbucks Serves Up Social Responsibility

FROM SEATTLE TO SAUDI ARABIA AND BEYOND, Starbucks has built a $3 billion business by serving gourmet coffees in comfy surroundings. The company operates more than 4,200 stores in 42 states and another 1,200 stores throughout North America, Asia, Europe, and the Middle East. Its aggressive growth plans call for opening an additional 5,000 outlets worldwide within three years. Yet chairman Howard Schultz and his management team want Starbucks to be known for its social responsibility as much as for its hearty lattes and quality service.

Environmental protection is an integral part of Starbucks' agenda. With Conservation International, the company promotes environmentally friendly coffee farming practices in Mexico, Colombia, and other countries. Using these practices, hundreds of participating growers are able to preserve ecologically sensitive regions while selling more coffee at higher prices. At the store level, Starbucks' employees recycle a wide variety of materials and package used coffee grounds in used coffee bags for gardeners to use as compost material. "We try to find creative ways to contribute to a healthier environment," comments the firm's environmental affairs manager.

Starbucks also strives to be a good corporate citizen. The Starbucks Foundation provides funding for numerous community causes, and store employees are encouraged to volunteer their time for food drives, literacy programs, and other local projects. Every year, management details the previous year's accomplishments in a social responsibility report posted on the Starbucks' website.

Moreover, Starbucks emphasizes good relations with its work force. Unlike most companies, the firm offers health insurance coverage and other valuable benefits to part-time employees as well as full-time employees. In addition, it pays hourly employees slightly higher wages than competing chains pay. And based on the proportion of minority and female employees on its payroll, Starbucks has for several years been named to *Fortune* magazine's list of 100 best companies to work for.

As the fifth-largest buyer of coffee in the world, the company feels constant pressure to help farmers who are being squeezed by low coffee prices and rising production costs. In response, Starbucks now buys more coffee directly from farmers and farm cooperatives, often bypasses commodity markets to pay farmers more stable prices, and offers affordable loans to small growers. The company also works with TransFair to ensure that farmers receive a fair minimum price for high-quality beans sold to roasters. All these programs have contributed to Starbucks' reputation for social responsibility.[1]

Obviously, organizations like Starbucks want to be recognized as responsible corporate citizens. Such companies recognize the need to harmonize their operations with environmental demands and other vital social concerns. Not all firms, however, have taken steps to encourage a consideration of social responsibility and ethics in their decisions and day-to-day activities. Some managers still regard such business practices as a poor investment, in which the cost is not worth the return. Other managers—indeed, most managers—view the cost of these practices as a necessary business expense, similar to wages or rent.

Most managers today, like those at Starbucks, are finding ways of balancing a growing agenda of socially responsible activities with the drive to generate profits. This also happens to be a good way for a company to demonstrate its values and to attract like-minded employees, customers, and stockholders. In a highly competitive business environment, an increasing number of companies are, like Starbucks, seeking to set themselves apart by developing a reputation for ethical and socially responsible behavior.

We begin this chapter by defining *business ethics* and examining ethical issues. Next, we look at the standards of behavior in organizations and how ethical behavior can be encouraged. We then turn to the topic of social responsibility. We compare and contrast two present-day models of social responsibility and present arguments for and against increasing the social responsibility of business. After that, we examine the major elements of the consumer movement. We discuss how social responsibility in business has affected employment practices and environmental concerns. Finally, we consider the commitment, planning, and funding that go into a firm's program of social responsibility.

Business Ethics Defined

learning objective

1 Understand what is meant by *business ethics.*

Ethics is the study of right and wrong and of the morality of the choices individuals make. An ethical decision or action is one that is "right" according to some standard of behavior. **Business ethics** is the application of moral standards to business situations. Recent court cases involving unethical behavior have helped to make business ethics a matter of public concern. In one such case, Copley Pharmaceutical, Inc., pled guilty to federal criminal charges (and paid a $10.65 million fine) for falsifying drug manufacturers' reports to the Food and Drug Administration. In another much-publicized case, lawsuits against tobacco companies have led to $246 billion in settlements, although there has been only one class-action lawsuit filed on behalf of all smokers. That case, *Engle v. R. J. Reynolds*, could cost tobacco companies an estimated $500 billion. In another similar effort, recently twenty-eight cities and counties brought class-action suits against gun manufacturers. The suits seek to recover governments' expenses related to police protection, emergency services, and enforcement of local gun-control ordinances. Housing authorities around the country also are planning to file class-action suits against gun makers, holding them liable for unnecessary and preventable handgun violence.[2]

ethics the study of right and wrong and of the morality of the choices individuals make

business ethics the application of moral standards to business situations

Ethical Issues

learning objective

2 Identify the types of ethical concerns that arise in the business world.

Ethical issues often arise out of a business's relationship with investors, customers, employees, creditors, or competitors. Each of these groups has specific concerns and usually exerts pressure on the organization's managers. For example, investors want management to make sensible financial decisions that will boost sales, profits, and returns on their investments. Customers expect a firm's products to be safe, reliable, and reasonably priced. Employees demand to be treated fairly in hiring, promotion, and compensation decisions. Creditors require accounts to be paid on time and the accounting information furnished by the firm to be accurate. Competitors expect the firm's competitive practices to be fair and honest. Consider TAP Pharmaceutical Products, Inc., whose sales representatives offered every urologist in the United States a big-screen TV, computers, fax machines, and golf vacations if the doctors prescribed TAP's new prostate cancer drug, Lupron. Moreover, the sales representatives sold Lupron at cut-rate prices or gratis while defrauding Medicare. In 2001, the federal government won an $875 million judgment against TAP.[3]

Business people face ethical issues every day, and some of these issues can be difficult to assess. Although some types of issues arise infrequently, others occur regularly. Let's take a closer look at several ethical issues.

Fairness and Honesty

Fairness and honesty in business are two important ethical concerns. Besides obeying all laws and regulations, business people are expected to refrain from knowingly deceiving, misrepresenting, or intimidating others. The consequences of failing to do so can be expensive. Recently, for example, Missouri Secretary of State Matt Blunt has vocally objected to Merrill Lynch's proposed $100 million settlement with the state over charges that its analysts misled investors.[4]

talking technology

Do Privacy Policies Protect Internet Users?

PRIVACY HAS EMERGED as one of the key ethical issues in e-commerce. Privacy policies are supposed to let visitors know what a company plans to do with any information collected through its website. Yet privacy advocates worry that a site can change its privacy policy at any time—unilaterally deciding to share or act on users' personal data even if it had promised to keep information confidential in the past.

Consider what happened when Yahoo clarified its policy to explicitly reserve the right to communicate with users via mail, e-mail, and telephone. The Internet giant also announced that it would start sending users commercial messages from affiliates. Yahoo previously had allowed users to opt out of such contacts by clicking a few boxes. However, when the company announced its policy clarification, it wiped out any choices that users had already recorded. After notifying millions of users of the change, Yahoo allowed them sixty days to choose whether to receive phone calls, letters, and e-mail messages from the site and its affiliates.

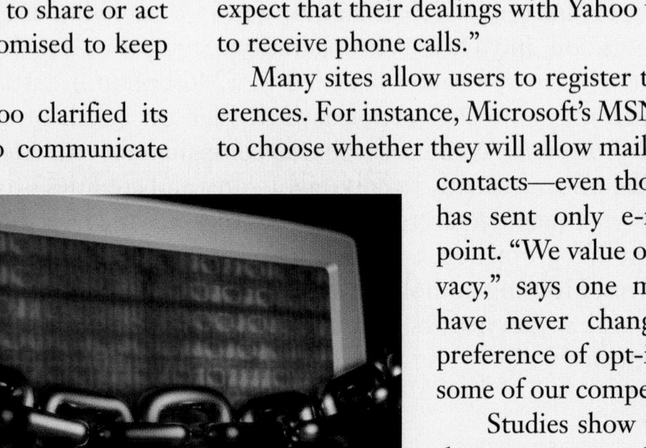

Yahoo believes that users will benefit from expanded communication. "We believe in the products and services we offer," says its editor-in-chief. "Our network has grown so much we want to tell users about them." However, the executive director of Electronic Privacy Information Center objects: "It's unfair. People thought they were going to get e-mail solicitations. They didn't expect that their dealings with Yahoo would cause them to receive phone calls."

Many sites allow users to register their contact preferences. For instance, Microsoft's MSN site invites users to choose whether they will allow mail, e-mail, or phone contacts—even though the company has sent only e-mails up to this point. "We value our customers' privacy," says one manager, "and we have never changed a customer's preference of opt-in or opt-out, like some of our competitors have done."

Studies show that less than half the users surveyed read the privacy policies of the sites they visit, and only a tiny percentage examine the policies in detail. Nonetheless, officials in the United States and Europe are addressing this ethical issue by preparing new rules to protect the privacy of Internet users.

In another case, a Florida Chevrolet dealer promised a "free four-day, three-night vacation to Acapulco" to anyone who bought a car or van. A customer purchased a van, but when the vacation voucher arrived, it was really a time-share sales promotion filled with numerous conditions and restrictions. The customer sued, and the jury awarded $1,768 in compensatory and $667,000 in punitive damages.[5]

Organizational Relationships

A business person may be tempted to place his or her personal welfare above the welfare of others or the welfare of the organization. For example, in late 2002, former CEO of Tyco International, Ltd., Leo Dennis Kozlowski was indicted for misappropriating $43 million in corporate funds to make philanthropic contributions in his own name, including $5 million to Seton Hall University, which named its new business school building Kozlowski Hall. Furthermore, according to Tyco, the former CEO took $61.7 million in interest-free relocation loans without the board's permission. He allegedly used the money to finance an opulent lifestyle and to buy properties that had nothing to do with corporate relocation.[6] Relationships with customers and coworkers often create ethical problems. Unethical behavior in these areas includes taking credit for others' ideas or work, not meeting one's commitments in a mutual agreement, and pressuring others to behave unethically.

Conflict of Interest

Conflict of interest results when a business person takes advantage of a situation for his or her own personal interest rather than for the employer's interest. Such conflict may occur when payments and gifts make their way into business deals. A wise rule to remember is that anything given to a person that might unfairly influence that person's business decision is a bribe, and all bribes are unethical.

For example, Nortel Networks Corporation does not permit its employees, officers, and directors to accept any gifts or to serve as directors or officers of any organization that might supply goods or services to Nortel Networks. However, Nortel employees may work part time with firms that are not competitors, suppliers, or customers. At AT&T, employees are instructed to discuss with their supervisors any investments that may seem improper. Verizon Communications forbids its employee and executives from holding a "significant" financial stake in vendors, suppliers, or customers.

Goodbye Joe Camel. Tobacco use is the single leading preventable cause of death in the United States. However, for years the tobacco companies misled consumers by showing healthy, active, and carefree people in smoking advertisements. Now we know better: even secondhand smoke is harmful and hazardous to one's health.

Communications

Business communications, especially advertising, can present ethical questions. False and misleading advertising is illegal and unethical, and it can infuriate customers. Sponsors of advertisements aimed at children must be especially careful to avoid misleading messages. Advertisers of health-related products also must take precautions to guard against deception when using such descriptive terms as *low fat*, *fat free*, and *light*. In fact, the Federal Trade Commission has issued guidelines on the use of these labels.

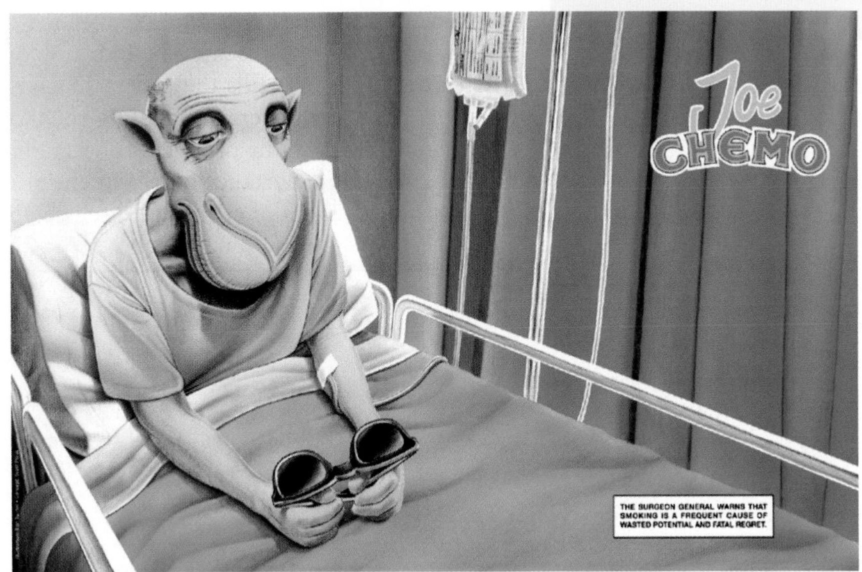

Factors Affecting Ethical Behavior

learning objective

3 Discuss the factors that affect the level of ethical behavior in organizations.

Is it possible for an individual with strong moral values to make ethically questionable decisions in a business setting? What factors affect a person's inclination to make either ethical or unethical decisions in a business organization? Although the answers to these questions are not entirely clear, three general sets of factors do appear to influence the standards of behavior in an organization. As shown in Figure 2.1, the sets consist of individual factors, social factors, and opportunity.

Several individual factors influence the level of ethical behavior in an organization. How much an individual knows about an issue is one factor: A decision maker with a greater amount of knowledge regarding a situation may take steps to avoid ethical problems, whereas a less-informed person may unknowingly take action that leads to an ethical quagmire. An individual's moral values and central, value-related attitudes also clearly influence his or her business behavior. Most people join organizations to accomplish personal goals. The types of personal goals an individual aspires to and the manner in which these goals are pursued have a significant impact on that individual's behavior in an organization.

A person's behavior in the workplace is, to some degree, determined by cultural norms, and these social factors vary from one culture to another. For example, in some countries it is acceptable and ethical for customs agents to receive gratuities for performing ordinary, legal tasks that are a part of their jobs, whereas in other countries these practices would be viewed as unethical and perhaps illegal. The actions and decisions of coworkers constitute another social factor believed to shape a person's sense of business ethics. For example, if your coworkers make long-distance telephone calls on company time and at company expense, you might view that behavior as acceptable and ethical because everyone does it. The moral values and attitudes of "significant others"—spouses, friends, and relatives, for instance—also can affect an employee's perception of what is ethical and unethical behavior in the workplace. Even the Internet presents new challenges for firms whose employees enjoy easy access to sites through convenient high-speed connections at work. An employee's behavior online can be viewed as offensive to coworkers and possibly lead to lawsuits against the firm if employees conduct unethical behavior on controversial websites not related to their job. As a result, research by Websense and the Center for Internet Studies reveals that nearly two out of three companies nationwide have disciplined employees and nearly one out of three have fired employees for Internet misuse in the workplace.[7]

Opportunity refers to the amount of freedom an organization gives an employee to behave unethically if he or she makes that choice. In some organizations, certain company policies and procedures reduce the opportunity to be unethical. For example, at some fast-food restaurants, one employee takes your order and receives your payment, and another fills the order. This procedure reduces the opportunity to be unethical because the person handling the money is not dispensing the product, and the person giving out the product is not handling the money. The existence of an ethical code and the importance management places on this code are other determinants of opportunity (codes of ethics are discussed in more detail in the next section). The

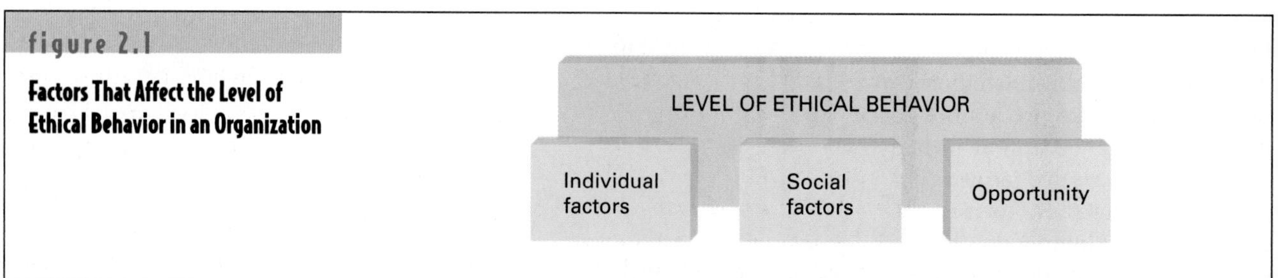

figure 2.1

Factors That Affect the Level of Ethical Behavior in an Organization

Source: Based on O. C. Ferrell and Larry Gresham, "A Contingency Framework for Understanding Ethical Decision Making in Marketing," *Journal of Marketing*, summer 1985, p. 89.

degree of enforcement of company policies, procedures, and ethical codes is a major force affecting opportunity. When violations are dealt with consistently and firmly, the opportunity to be unethical is reduced.

Now that we have considered some of the factors believed to influence the level of ethical behavior in the workplace, let's explore what can be done to encourage ethical behavior and to discourage unethical behavior.

Encouraging Ethical Behavior

learning objective

4 Explain how ethical decision making can be encouraged.

Most authorities agree that there is room for improvement in business ethics. A more problematic question is, Can business be made more ethical in the real world? The majority opinion on this issue suggests that government, trade associations, and individual firms can indeed establish acceptable levels of ethical behavior.

The government can encourage ethical behavior by legislating more stringent regulations. For example, the landmark Sarbanes-Oxley Act of 2002 gives those who report corporate misconduct sweeping new legal protection. At the signing ceremony, President George W. Bush stated, "The act adopts tough new provisions to deter and punish corporate and accounting fraud and corruption, ensure justice for wrongdoers, and protect the interests of workers and shareholders." Among other things, the law deals with corporate responsibility, conflicts of interest, and corporate accountability. However, rules require enforcement, and the unethical business person frequently seems to "slip something by" without getting caught. Increased regulation may help, but it surely cannot solve the entire ethics problem.

Trade associations can and often do provide ethical guidelines for their members. These organizations, which operate within particular industries, are in an excellent position to exert pressure on members who stoop to questionable business practices. For example, recently a pharmaceutical trade group adopted a new set of guidelines to halt the extravagant dinners and other gifts sales representatives often give to physicians. However, enforcement and authority vary from association to association. And because trade associations exist for the benefit of their members, harsh measures may be self-defeating.

Codes of ethics that companies provide to their employees are perhaps the most effective way to encourage ethical behavior. A **code of ethics** is a written guide to acceptable and ethical behavior as defined by an organization; it outlines uniform policies, standards, and punishments for violations. Because employees know what is expected of them and what will happen if they violate the rules, a code of ethics goes a long way toward encouraging ethical behavior. However, codes cannot possibly cover every situation. Companies also must create an environment in which employees recognize the importance of complying with the written code. Managers must provide direction by fostering communication, actively modeling and encouraging ethical decision making, and training employees to make ethical decisions.

code of ethics a guide to acceptable and ethical behavior as defined by the organization

During the 1980s, an increasing number of organizations created and implemented ethics codes. In a recent survey of *Fortune* 1000 firms, 93 percent of the companies that responded reported having a formal code of ethics. Some companies are now even taking steps to strengthen their codes. For example, to strengthen its accountability, the Healthcare Financial Management Association recently revised its code to designate contact persons who handle reports of ethics violations, to clarify how its board of directors should deal with violations of business ethics, and to guarantee a fair hearing process. S. C. Johnson & Son, makers of Pledge, Drano, Windex, and many other household products, is another firm that recognizes that it must behave in ways the public perceives as ethical; its code includes expectations for employees and its commitment to consumers, the community, and society in general. As shown in Figure 2.2,

Using the Internet

The International Business Ethics Institute (**http://www.business-ethics.org/**), a private nonprofit educational organization, promotes global business ethics and corporate responsibility. Its mission is to increase public awareness about international business ethics issues through the Round Table Discussion Series, the *International Business Ethics Review*, and this website. The institute assists firms in establishing effective ethics programs and disseminates information about corporate responsibility issues.

figure 2.2

Defining Acceptable Behavior: TI's Code of Ethics

Texas Instruments encourages ethical behavior through an extensive training program and a written code of ethics and shared values.

TEXAS INSTRUMENTS CODE OF ETHICS

"One of TI's greatest strengths is its values and ethics. We had some early leaders who set those values as the standard for how they lived their lives. And it is important that TI grew that way. It's something that we don't want to lose. At the same time, we must move more rapidly. But we don't want to confuse that with the fact that we're ethical and we're moral. We're very responsible, and we live up to what we say."

Tom Engibous, President and CEO
Texas Instruments, 1997

We Respect and Value People By:

Treating others as we want to be treated.

- Exercising the basic virtues of respect, dignity, kindness, courtesy and manners in all work relationships.
- Recognizing and avoiding behaviors that others may find offensive, including the manner in which we speak and relate to one another and the materials we bring into the workplace, both printed and electronically.
- Respecting the right and obligation of every TIer to resolve concerns relating to ethics questions in the course of our duties without retribution and retaliation.
- Giving all TIers the same opportunity to have their questions, issues and situations fairly considered while understanding that being treated fairly does not always mean that we will all be treated the same.
- Trusting one another to use sound judgment in our use of TI business and information systems.
- Understanding that even though TI has the obligation to monitor its business information systems activity, we will respect privacy by prohibiting random searches of individual TIers' communications.
- Recognizing that conduct socially and professionally acceptable in one culture and country may be viewed differently in another.

We Are Honest By:

Representing ourselves and our intentions truthfully.

- Offering full disclosure and withdrawing ourselves from discussions and decisions when our business judgment appears to be in conflict with a personal interest.
- Respecting the rights and property of others, including their intellectual property. Accepting confidential or trade secret information only after we clearly understand our obligations as defined in a nondisclosure agreement.
- Competing fairly without collusion or collaboration with competitors to divide markets, set prices, restrict production, allocate customers or otherwise restrain competition.
- Assuring that no payments or favors are offered to influence others to do something wrong.
- Keeping records that are accurate and include all payments and receipts.
- Exercising good judgment in the exchange of business courtesies, meals and entertainment by avoiding activities that could create even the appearance that our decisions could be compromised.
- Refusing to speculate in TI stock through frequent buying and selling or through other forms of speculative trading.

Source: Courtesy of Texas Instruments.

included in the ethics code of electronics giant Texas Instruments are issues relating to policies and procedures; laws and regulations; relationships with customers, suppliers, and competitors; conflicts of interest; handling of proprietary information; and code enforcement.

Assigning an ethics officer who coordinates ethical conduct gives employees someone to consult if they are not sure of the right thing to do. An ethics officer meets with employees and top management to provide ethical advice, establishes and maintains an anonymous confidential service to answer questions about ethical issues, and takes action on ethics code violations.

Sometimes, even employees who want to act ethically may find it difficult to do so. Unethical practices can become ingrained in an organization. Employees with high personal ethics may then take a controversial step called *whistle-blowing*. **Whistle-blowing** is informing the press or government officials about unethical practices within one's organization.

whistle-blowing informing the press or government officials about unethical practices within one's organization

The year 2002 was labeled as the "Year of the Whistle-blower." Consider Joe Speaker, a 40-year-old acting chief financial officer at Rite Aid Corp. in 1999. He discovered that inventories at Rite Aid had been overvalued and millions in expenses had not been properly reported. Further digging into Rite Aid's books revealed that $541 million in earnings over the previous two years were really $1.6 billion in losses. Mr. Speaker was a main government witness when former Rite Aid Corp. chairman and CEO Martin L. Grass went on trial. Mr. Speaker is among dozens of corporate managers who have blown the whistle. Enron Corporation's Sherron S. Watkins and WorldCom, Inc.'s Cynthia Cooper are now well known whistle-blowers and *Time* magazine's persons of the year 2002. According to Linda Chatman Thomsen, deputy director for enforcement at the Securities and Exchange Commission, "Whistle-blowers give us an insider's perspective and have advanced our investigation immeasurably." Stephen Meagher, a former federal prosecutor who represents whistle-blowers calls Watkins and Cooper national champions and says, "The business of whistle-blowing is booming."[8]

Whistle-blowing could have averted disaster and prevented needless deaths in the *Challenger* space shuttle disaster, for example. How could employees have known about life-threatening problems and let them pass? Whistle-blowing, on the other hand, can have serious repercussions for employees: Those who "blow whistles" sometimes lose their jobs. However, the Sarbanes-Oxley Act of 2002 protects the whistle-blowers who report corporate misconduct. Any executive who retaliates against a whistle-blower can be held criminally liable and imprisoned for up to 10 years.

When firms set up anonymous hotlines to handle ethically questionable situations, employees actually may be more likely to engage in whistle-blowing. When firms instead create an environment that educates employees and nurtures ethical behavior, fewer ethical problems arise, and ultimately, the need for whistle-blowing is greatly reduced.

It is difficult for an organization to develop ethics codes, policies, and procedures to deal with all relationships and every situation. When no company policy or procedures exists or applies, a quick test to determine if a behavior is ethical is to see if others—coworkers, customers, suppliers—approve of it. Ethical decisions always will withstand scrutiny. Openness and communication about choices often will build trust and strengthen business relationships. Table 2.1 provides some general guidelines for making ethical decisions.

Would you blow the whistle? Coleen Rowley of the FBI (shown here before testifying before the Senate Judiciary Committee), Cynthia Cooper of WorldCom, and Sherron Watkins of Enron couldn't take it anymore. These employees with high personal ethics blew the whistle on unethical practices in their organizations. For their bold stands, which had profound effects, Cooper, Rowley, and Watkins were featured on the cover of *Time* magazine as *Time*'s Persons of the Year.

table 2.1 Guidelines for Making Ethical Decisions

1. **Listen and learn.**	Recognize the problem or decision-making opportunity that confronts your company, team, or unit. Don't argue, criticize, or defend yourself—keep listening and reviewing until you are sure you understand others.
2. **Identify the ethical issues.**	Examine how coworkers and consumers are affected by the situation or decision at hand. Examine how you feel about the situation and understand the viewpoint of those involved in the decision or in the consequences of the decision.
3. **Create and analyze options.**	Try to put aside strong feelings such as anger or a desire for power and prestige and come up with as many alternatives as possible before developing an analysis. Ask everyone involved for ideas about which options offer the best long-term results for you and the company. Which option will increase your self-respect even if, in the long run, things don't work out the way you hope?
4. **Identify the best option from your point of view.**	Consider it and test it against some established criteria, such as respect, understanding, caring, fairness, honesty, and openness.
5. **Explain your decision and resolve any differences that arise.**	This may require neutral arbitration from a trusted manager or taking "time out" to reconsider, consult, or exchange written proposals before a decision is reached.

Source: Tom Rusk with D. Patrick Miller, "Doing the Right Thing," *Sky* Delta Airlines, Aug. 1993, pp. 18–22.

Social Responsibility

social responsibility the recognition that business activities have an impact on society and the consideration of that impact in business decision making

Social responsibility is the recognition that business activities have an impact on society and the consideration of that impact in business decision making. Obviously, social responsibility costs money. It is perhaps not so obvious—except in isolated cases—that social responsibility is also good business. Customers eventually find out which firms are acting responsibly and which are not. And just as easily as they cast their dollar votes for a product produced by a company that is socially responsible, they can vote against the firm that is not.

Consider the following examples of organizations that are attempting to be socially responsible:

- Social responsibility can take many forms—including flying lessons. Through Young Eagles, underwritten by S. C. Johnson, Phillips Petroleum, Lockheed Martin, Jaguar, and other corporations, 22,000 volunteer pilots have taken a half million youngsters on free flights designed to teach flying basics and inspire excitement about flying careers. Young Eagles is just one of the growing number of education projects undertaken by businesses building solid records as good corporate citizens.
- Recently, ExxonMobil Corporation contributed $126 million to nonprofit organizations for community projects. About $84 million in contributions were made in the United States and $42 million in more than seventy-five other countries. "When private companies invest in communities, they often do exceptional things," ExxonMobil Chairman Lee Raymond told the Chicago Executive Club. "We've built roads and schools, water lines and sewer systems, desalination plants, health clinics and community centers, and lots more," said Raymond. The company also encourages employees, retirees, and their families to contribute their own time and money to nonprofit organizations. For example, through the company's Volunteer Involvement Program alone, more than 300,000 hours of volunteer time were recorded in 2001.

ExxonMobil and its employees, retirees, dealers, and distributors around the world responded after the terrorist attacks on September 11. They contributed $21 million to organizations assisting surviving families and children of those killed in the attacks on New York and Washington. ExxonMobil donated $5 million directly and matched employee contributions three to one.

To meet its global social responsibility, the company contributed nearly $600,000 to earthquake relief efforts in El Salvador and India and to aid for the flood victims in Houston following tropical storm Allison.

Year 2001 marked the twenty-fifth anniversary of ExxonMobil's operation of a community health care services program for people living near the Arun gas field in Indonesia. The Civic Mission Clinic cares for as many as 500 people a day, with at least 2 million having received superior health services since the program began in 1976. Students at historically black colleges and universities receive financial assistance from ExxonMobil to complete their education. For example, in 2002, the company provided a $200,000 grant to the Tom Joyner Foundation. Tom Joyner is a nationally syndicated radio talk show host who is well known in the African-American community. Each month the foundation selects a college or university and sends the funds directly to the school's financial aid office, which awards scholarships to students based on financial need and academic achievement. The ExxonMobil grant benefited eleven schools and some forty students in 2002. "ExxonMobil's support has strengthened our impact significantly," said Joyner. "The grant allows students to complete their education, pay off their loans and enter the workforce successfully."[9]

- Motivated by the belief that amazing things happen when people are provided with the resources they need, Microsoft Corporation has been using technology to unlock the potential in individuals and communities since 1983. Recently, Microsoft and its employees contributed more than $246 million to 5,000 nonprofit organizations around the world to help communities. Microsoft is investing in youth throughout the world. For example, in Soweto, South Africa, students in two local high schools have been trained in computer literacy and subjects ranging from accounting to economics through the Microsoft and International Youth Foundation Initiative. Designed to equip young people with technology skills through education and training, the program has started projects in South Africa, Poland, and the Philippines. Additional sources from Microsoft expanded the program into Russia, other Asian countries, and Latin America.

  Microsoft provides kids with the technology tools they need. For example, Club Tech is a five-year, $100-million collaboration between Microsoft and Boys and Girls Clubs of America to "technology enable" every club by providing software and technology training. More than 700 clubs across the country are now part of Club Tech. Kids from Boston to Orlando to Phoenix are spending time using technology to connect with each other and to learn more about their world.

  How does Microsoft empower nonprofit organizations? The Microsoft & Npower National Partnership created nonprofit technology assistance organizations that provide low-cost and no-cost technology assistance to other nonprofit organizations, improving their ability to respond to issues in their communities. The $25-million Microsoft & Npower National Partnership established affiliates in

Philanthropy pays. Philanthropic programs—such as Revlon's Annual Run/Walk for Women to raise money to support research and treatment for women with cancer and their families—often link social responsibility with corporate self-interest. By supporting a cause that affects Revlon customers and attracting celebrity participants, Revlon increases awareness and presents a positive image for its products.

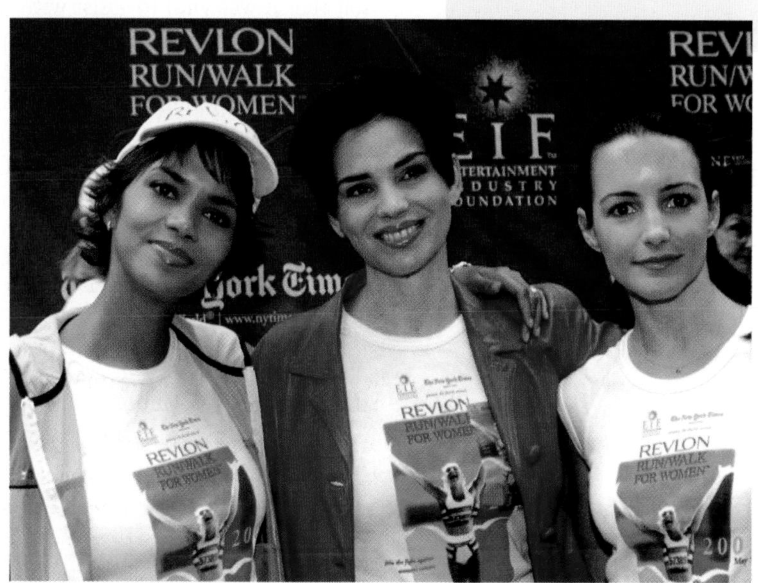

seven major cities across the United States in 2002 and five more affiliates in 2003. By providing much-needed funding and software to nonprofit organizations, libraries, and communities, Microsoft hopes to help bridge the "digital divide" that limits opportunities for success and prosperity.[10]

- Cisco Systems, Inc., believes that the most successful companies give back to their communities. Recently, Cisco sponsored the NetAid World Schoolhouse, helping thousands of children worldwide to have a better chance in life through education. In October 2002, the Cisco Networking Academy Program celebrated its fifth anniversary. Today, this program includes 9,900 academies worldwide, with more than 263,000 students learning to build the networks that ultimately will make greater opportunities available. Through another endeavor, Cisco Community Fellows Program, Cisco provides employees with opportunities to work for nonprofit organzations.[11]
- The General Mills Foundation is one of the nation's largest company-sponsored foundations. According to Chris Shea, president of General Mills Foundation and Community Action, "Now, more than ever, we need to focus on our responsibility to reach out and enrich the communities we serve—to discover the areas of greatest need and address them with breakthrough ideas, championship people, and financial resources." For example, recently General Mills donated over $20 million of its products to America's Second Harvest, the nation's largest domestic hunger-relief organization. Through a network of over 200 food banks and food-rescue programs, America's Second Harvest provides emergency food assistance to more than twenty-three million hungry Americans each year, eight million of whom are children.

  General Mills' employee and retiree contributions to United Way, matched dollar for dollar by the General Mills Foundation, contributed almost $9 million in the United States and Canada. Furthermore, General Mills plays a leadership role in support of education and arts and cultural organizations by matching employee and retiree contributions dollar for dollar. Recently, the foundation matched contributions of nearly $1.7 million to educational institutions and matched over $600,000 to arts and cultural organizations. General Mills' Box Tops for Education program continues to grow. At last count, there were over 70,000 K through 8 schools enrolled in the program—9,000 more than the previous year—and over twenty-two million households clipping box tops to earn money for their schools. In 2003, Box Tops for Education expects to give nearly $30 million to America's schools. In total, General Mills contributed over $66 million in 2002 to meet its social responsibility obligations.[12]
- Foot Locker, Inc., the world's leading retailer of athletic footwear and apparel, felt that it was vital to assist with the relief efforts after the horrific events of September 11, 2001. The company contributed thousands of garments to the rescue workers at Ground Zero. Additionally, the company and its employees pledged cash donations and contributed the profits from the sales of several hundred thousand specially designed T-shirts to the Twin Towers Fund. Foot Locker also established the Foot Locker Foundation to raise and donate additional funds to charitable causes such as the Twin Towers Fund. During December 2001, the foundation coordinated a charitable fund-raising event, On Our Feet, to unite the sports world to support this cause. About 1,400 members of the sporting community rallied and raised nearly $1 million for the families of victims of the World Trade Center disaster.[13]
- AT&T has built a tradition of supporting education, health and human services, the environment, public policy, and the arts in communities it serves since Alexander Graham Bell founded the company over a century ago. Since 1984, AT&T has invested more than $600 million in support of education. Currently, more than half the company's contribution dollars, employee volunteer time, and community-service activities are directed toward education. In 1995, AT&T created the AT&T Learning Network, a $150-million corporate commitment to support the education of children in schools across the nation by providing the

latest technology and cash grants to schools and communities. Recently, the AT&T Employee Matching Gifts Program contributed more than $4.4 million to thousands of nonprofit organizations, including nearly $900,000 to match employee contributions for September 11 disaster relief funds. Since 1911, AT&T has been a sponsor of the Telephone Pioneers of America, the world's largest industry-based volunteer organization consisting of nearly 750,000 employees and retirees from the telecommunications industry. Each year the Pioneers volunteer millions of hours and raise millions of dollars for health and human services and the environment.[14]

Spotlight

Charity begins at home
Households contribute to a variety of types of charitable institutions. These are the types of institutions that receive contributions from the largest percentage of U.S. households.
21%
27%
45%
Youth development
Human services
Religious organizations
(percentage of households)

Source: Independent Sector, "The Nonprofit Almanac in Brief."

- Dell Computer Corporation volunteers dedicated thousands of hours and personally donated millions of dollars to organizations such as the American Red Cross, Second Harvest, Capital Area Food Bank, March of Dimes, Juvenile Diabetes Research Foundation, and Milford Hospice. Following the tragic events of September 11, Dell and its employees contributed $3.5 million to relief efforts. During the year-end holidays, the company donated more than 34,000 pounds of food—feeding more than 7,000 families—and $50,000 worth of office equipment to more than thirty-seven nonprofit organizations. Dell continued its support of the E-quipping Youth student program through funding focused on health and human services, education and literacy, and technology access.

  In central Texas, Dell supported traditions such as the Martin Luther King celebration, the annual Trail of Lights holiday display, and arts programs such as the ballet and MEXICARTE Museum. Dell continued its partnership with the Round Rock Express baseball club by providing free tickets to local students in recognition of academic achievement. In central Tennessee, Dell supported the PENCIL Foundation and the E-Schools project and launched the Dell Student Technology Leaders program in partnership with Vanderbilt University and Lipscomb University. Dell was named Corporate Philanthropic Program of the Year by the Association of Fundraising Professionals in central Tennessee and received a KPMG Exemplar Award for commitment to the community.[15]

- The General Electric Company responded immediately to the September 11 tragedy. The GE family gave $25 million of aid in cash and services. The GE Fund contributed $10 million to the Twin Towers Fund, and 20,000 GE employees gave $2.5 million to the Red Cross, which was matched by the GE Fund. Since 1954, when the GE Fund began matching employee and retiree contributions, GE has donated more than $2 billion in matching gifts to colleges, universities, and other educational institutions. GE employees and retirees support United Way agencies by building playgrounds, collecting supplies for food banks, renovating homeless shelters, and serving as Big Brothers and Big Sisters. Furthermore, the GE Fund invented the corporate matching-gift program, now used by more than 1,000 corporations worldwide.

  GE Capital, one of GE's businesses, is also an involved corporate citizen because, "simply put, it's the right thing to do." "We bring good things to life" isn't just an advertising slogan. It's a multifaceted and ongoing commitment. For example, in fulfilling its global social responsibility, a GE Capital team rebuilt an orphanage in Thailand, refurbished playgrounds in London, provided entertainment at a home for children with disabilities in Mexico, hosted a "Happy Saturday" zoo field trip for inner-city children in the Czech Republic, and the list goes on. Through programs such as Global Community Days, employees participate in various projects. In one month alone, company volunteers were involved in more than fifty projects around the globe. Here at home, GE is building bridges between academia and business. Through an innovative multimillion-dollar investment in and partnership with the University of Connecticut, GE has developed a high-tech e-business lab where GE employees work with students and faculty on real e-business projects. The program adds state-of-the-art e-capacity to the UConn facility and curriculum while also helping the state of Connecticut to build a much needed information technology (IT) workforce. Through herSource.com, GE Medical Systems provides comprehensive breast cancer information helping women make more informed decisions, raise awareness, and drive home the importance of early detection.

GE and its employees have made a strong commitment to their communities. Whether it is volunteering over one million hours of annual service to young people, supporting innovative programs in education, or helping provide community service, the GE people are making a difference on a global scale. GE, its employees, the GE Fund, and GE Elfun (a global organization of GE employees and retirees) contribute more than $90 million annually to support education, the arts, the environment, and human service organizations worldwide.[16]

- Education programs often link social responsibility with corporate self-interest. For example, Bayer and Merck, two major pharmaceuticals firms, promote science education as a way to enlarge the pool of future employees. Students who visit the Bayer Science Forum in Elkhart, Indiana, work alongside scientists conducting a variety of experiments. And workshops created by the Merck Institute for Science Education show teachers how to put scientific principles into action through hands-on experiments.
- Computer giant Hewlett Packard promotes science and technology education by pairing students with employees who serve as mentors by e-mail for class projects. As many as 1,500 employees are corresponding with middle school and high school students to discuss projects as diverse as building a bicycle pump or investigating computer careers. "We are investing in our own future," comments Marsh Faber, Hewlett Packard's education marketing manager for general-purpose products. Whether they're teaching flying, science, or self-confidence, all these education projects are giving corporations the opportunity to showcase their commitment to social responsibility in a very tangible way.

These are just a few illustrations from the long list of companies that attempt to behave in socially responsible ways. In general, people are more likely to want to work for and buy from such organizations.

The Evolution of Social Responsibility in Business

learning objective

5 Describe how our current views on the social responsibility of business have evolved.

Business is far from perfect in many respects, but its record of social responsibility today is much better than in past decades. In fact, present demands for social responsibility have their roots in outraged reactions to the abusive business practices of the early 1900s.

During the first quarter of the twentieth century, businesses were free to operate pretty much as they chose. Government protection of workers and consumers was minimal. As a result, people either accepted what business had to offer or they did without. Working conditions were often deplorable by today's standards. The average work week in most industries exceeded sixty hours, no minimum-wage law existed, and employee benefits were almost nonexistent. Work areas were crowded and unsafe, and industrial accidents were the rule rather than the exception. To improve working conditions, employees organized and joined labor unions. During the early 1900s, however, businesses—with the help of government—were able to use court orders, brute force, and even the few existing antitrust laws to defeat union attempts to improve working conditions.

During this period, consumers generally were subject to the doctrine of **caveat emptor,** a Latin phrase meaning "let the buyer beware." In other words, "what you see is what you get," and if it is not what you expected, too bad. Although victims of unscrupulous business practices could take legal action, going to court was very expensive, and consumers rarely won their cases. Moreover, no consumer groups or government agencies existed to publicize their consumers' grievances or to hold sellers accountable for their actions.

caveat emptor a Latin phrase meaning "let the buyer beware"

Prior to the 1930s, most people believed that competition and the action of the marketplace would in time correct abuses. Government therefore became involved in day-to-day business activities only in cases of obvious abuse of the free-market system. Six of the more important business-related federal laws passed between 1887 and 1914 are described in Table 2.2. As you can see, these laws were aimed more at encouraging competition than at correcting abuses, although two of them did deal with the purity of food and drug products.

The collapse of the stock market on October 29, 1929, triggered the Great Depression and years of dire economic problems for the United States. Factory production fell by almost one-half, and up to 25 percent of the nation's work force was unemployed. Before long, public pressure mounted for government to "do something" about the economy and about worsening social conditions.

Soon after Franklin D. Roosevelt was inaugurated as president in 1933, he instituted programs to restore the economy and to improve social conditions. Laws were passed to correct what many viewed as the monopolistic abuses of big business, and various social services were provided for individuals. These massive federal programs became the foundation for increased government involvement in the dealings between business and society.

As government involvement has increased, so has everyone's awareness of the social responsibility of business. Today's business owners are concerned about the return on their investment, but at the same time most of them demand ethical behavior from employees. In addition, employees demand better working conditions, and consumers want safe, reliable products. Various advocacy groups echo these concerns and also call for careful consideration of our earth's delicate ecological balance. Managers therefore must operate in a complex business environment—one in which they are just as responsible for their managerial actions as for their actions as individual citizens. Interestingly, today's high-technology and Internet-based firms fare relatively

table 2.2 Early Government Regulations That Affected American Business

Government Regulation	Major Provisions
Interstate Commerce Act (1887)	First federal act to regulate business practices; provided regulation of railroads and shipping rates
Sherman Antitrust Act (1890)	Prevented monopolies or mergers where competition was endangered
Pure Food and Drug Act (1906)	Established limited supervision of interstate sale of food and drugs
Meat Inspection Act (1906)	Provided for limited supervision of interstate sale of meat and meat products
Federal Trade Commission Act (1914)	Created the Federal Trade Commission to investigate illegal trade practices
Clayton Antitrust Act (1914)	Eliminated many forms of price discrimination that gave large businesses a competitive advantage over smaller firms

MGM Mirage Bets on Global Internet Gambling

ONLINE BETTING is not yet legal in the United States, where gambling is one of the most highly regulated industries. However, 1,500 Internet casinos based in Great Britain, Costa Rica, and other nations—where such activities are legal—are attracting an estimated $4 billion in bets every year. Eyeing this fast-growing market, MGM Mirage has become the first U.S. gaming company to open an online casino, basing its headquarters on the Isle of Man, just off the British coast.

MGM is experienced in managing gambling operations through its ownership stakes in twelve Nevada casinos, including the MGM Grand and the Bellagio in Las Vegas. Like most casinos, MGM's Internet site features roulette, poker, blackjack, bingo, keno, slot machines, and other games. Anyone visiting the site can play some games without betting, but only gamblers who live in Ireland, Portugal, Spain, South Africa, New Zealand, and the United Kingdom are allowed to actually place bets.

To satisfy gambling regulations imposed by the Isle of Man, MGM maintains an extensive software system designed to verify each gambler's age and country of residence. However, Nevada regulators have no jurisdiction over this online casino and can take action only if the Isle of Man finds that MGM has violated local gambling regulations. Nonetheless, MGM sends Nevada regulators quarterly reports with updates on its Internet casino operations.

Despite federal and state laws outlawing online gambling, analysts estimate that more than half of the 4.5 million gamblers who place bets through Internet casinos live in the United States. From the perspective of social responsibility, the ease of gambling with a click of the mouse has addiction experts concerned. "The Internet is making the problem a thousand times worse because of its accessibility and increased ability to hide the problem behavior," says one psychologist. Now the New York attorney general and other officials are pressuring U.S. banks to block betting transactions charged on credit cards. On the other hand, some people want to legalize web betting so that U.S. regulators can exert more control. Watch for more heated debate as MGM and other gaming companies balance their interest in capturing a larger piece of this lucrative business with increased pressure for operating in a socially responsible manner.

well when it comes to environmental issues, worker conditions, the representation of minorities and women in upper management, animal testing, and charitable donations. According to the New York watch-group called the *Council on Economic Priorities*, which examines more than seven hundred of the country's largest companies annually, these new economy firms tend to rate better than average but are not immune from criticism.[17]

learning objective

6 Explain the two views on the social responsibility of business and understand the arguments for and against increased social responsibility.

Two Views of Social Responsibility

Government regulation and public awareness are *external* forces that have increased the social responsibility of business. But business decisions are made *within* the firm—and there, social responsibility begins with the attitude of management. Two contrasting philosophies, or models, define the range of management attitudes toward social responsibility.

The Economic Model

economic model of social responsibility the view that society will benefit most when business is left alone to produce and market profitable products that society needs

According to the traditional concept of business, a firm exists to produce quality goods and services, earn a reasonable profit, and provide jobs. In line with this concept, the **economic model of social responsibility** holds that society will benefit most when business is left alone to produce and market profitable products that society needs. The economic model has its origins in the eighteenth century, when businesses were owned primarily by entrepreneurs or owner-managers. Competition was vigorous among small firms, and short-run profits and survival were the primary concerns.

To the manager who adopts this traditional attitude, social responsibility is someone else's job. After all, stockholders invest in a corporation to earn a return on their investment, not because the firm is socially responsible, and the firm is legally obligated to act in the economic interest of its stockholders. Moreover, profitable firms pay federal, state, and local taxes that are used to meet the needs of society. Thus managers who concentrate on profit believe that they fulfill their social responsibility indirectly through the taxes paid by their firms. As a result, social responsibility becomes the problem of government, various environmental groups, charitable foundations, and similar organizations.

The Socioeconomic Model

In contrast, some managers believe that they have a responsibility not only to stockholders but also to customers, employees, suppliers, and the general public. This broader view is referred to as the **socioeconomic model of social responsibility.** It places emphasis not only on profits but also on the impact of business decisions on society.

socioeconomic model of social responsibility the concept that business should emphasize not only profits but also the impact of its decisions on society

Recently, increasing numbers of managers and firms have adopted the socioeconomic model, and they have done so for at least three reasons. First, business is dominated by the corporate form of ownership, and the corporation is a creation of society. If a corporation does not perform as a good citizen, society can and will demand changes. Second, many firms have begun to take pride in their social responsibility records, among them Starbucks Coffee, Hewlett Packard, Colgate-Palmolive, and Coca-Cola. Each of these companies is a winner of a Corporate Conscience Award in the areas of environmental concern, responsiveness to employees, equal opportunity, and community involvement. And of course, many other corporations are much more socially responsible today than they were ten years ago. Third, many business people believe that it is in their best interest to take the initiative in this area. The alternative may be legal action brought against the firm by some special-interest group; in such a situation, the firm may lose control of its activities.

The Pros and Cons of Social Responsibility

Business owners, managers, customers, and government officials have debated the pros and cons of the economic and socioeconomic models for years. Each side seems to have four major arguments to reinforce its viewpoint.

Arguments for Increased Social Responsibility Proponents of the socioeconomic model maintain that a business must do more than simply seek profits. To support their position, they offer the following arguments:

1. Because business is a part of our society, it cannot ignore social issues.
2. Business has the technical, financial, and managerial resources needed to tackle today's complex social issues.
3. By helping resolve social issues, business can create a more stable environment for long-term profitability.
4. Socially responsible decision making by firms can prevent increased government intervention, which would force businesses to do what they fail to do voluntarily.

These arguments are based on the assumption that a business has a responsibility not only to stockholders but also to customers, employees, suppliers, and the general public.

Arguments Against Increased Social Responsibility Opponents of the socioeconomic model argue that business should do what it does best: earn a profit by manufacturing and marketing products that people want. Those who support this position argue as follows:

1. Business managers are primarily responsible to stockholders, so management must be concerned with providing a return on owners' investments.

table 2.3 A Comparison of the Economic and Socioeconomic Models of Social Responsibility as Implemented in Business

Economic Model Primary Emphasis Is on			Socioeconomic Model Primary Emphasis Is on
1. Production	M	G	1. Quality of life
2. Exploitation of natural resources	I	R	2. Conservation of natural resources
3. Internal, market-based decisions	D	O	3. Market-based decisions, with some community controls
4. Economic return (profit)	D	U	4. Balance of economic return and social return
5. Firm's or manager's interest	L	N	5. Firm's and community's interests
6. Minor role for government	E	D	6. Active government

Source: Adapted from Keith Davis, William C. Frederick, and Robert L. Blomstron, *Business and Society: Concepts and Policy Issues* (New York: McGraw-Hill, 1980), p. 9. Used by permission of McGraw-Hill Book Company.

2. Corporate time, money, and talent should be used to maximize profits, not to solve society's problems.
3. Social problems affect society in general, so individual businesses should not be expected to solve these problems.
4. Social issues are the responsibility of government officials who are elected for that purpose and who are accountable to the voters for their decisions.

These arguments are obviously based on the assumption that the primary objective of business is to earn profits and that government and social institutions should deal with social problems.

Table 2.3 compares the economic and socioeconomic viewpoints in terms of business emphasis. Today few firms are either purely economic or purely socioeconomic in outlook; most have chosen some middle ground between the two extremes. However, our society generally seems to want—and even to expect—some degree of social responsibility from business. Thus, within this middle ground, businesses are leaning toward the socioeconomic view. In the next several sections we look at some results of this movement in four specific areas: consumerism, employment practices, concern for the environment, and implementation of social responsibility programs.

Consumerism

learning objective

7 Discuss the factors that led to the consumer movement and list some of its results.

consumerism all activities undertaken to protect the rights of consumers

Consumerism consists of all activities undertaken to protect the rights of consumers. The fundamental issues pursued by the consumer movement fall into three categories: environmental protection, product performance and safety, and information disclosure. Although consumerism has been with us to some extent since the early nineteenth century, the consumer movement became stronger in the 1960s. It was then that President John F. Kennedy declared that the consumer was entitled to a new "bill of rights."

The Six Basic Rights of Consumers

President Kennedy's consumer bill of rights asserted that consumers have a right to safety, to be informed, to choose, and to be heard. Two additional rights added in the last decade are the right to consumer education and the right to courteous service. These six rights are the basis of much of the consumer-oriented legislation that has been passed during the last forty years. These rights also provide an effective outline of the objectives and accomplishments of the consumer movement.

The Right to Safety The consumers' right to safety means that the products they purchase must be safe for their intended use, must include thorough and explicit directions for proper use, and must be tested by the manufacturer to ensure product quality and reliability. There are several reasons why American business firms must be concerned about product safety. Federal agencies such as the Food and Drug Administration and the Consumer Product Safety Commission have the power to force businesses that make or sell defective products to take corrective actions. Such actions include offering refunds, recalling defective products, issuing public warnings, and reimbursing consumers—all of which can be expensive. Business firms also should be aware that consumers and the government have been winning an increasing number of product-liability lawsuits against sellers of defective products. Moreover, the amount of the awards in these suits has been increasing steadily. Fearing the outcome of numerous lawsuits filed around the nation, tobacco giants Philip Morris and R. J. Reynolds, which for decades had denied that cigarettes cause illness, began negotiating in 1997 with state attorneys general, plaintiffs' lawyers, and antismoking activists. The tobacco giants proposed sweeping curbs on their sales and advertising practices and the payment of hundreds of billions of dollars in compensation. Yet another major reason for improving product safety is consumers' demand for safe products. People simply will stop buying a product they believe is unsafe or unreliable.

The Right to Be Informed The right to be informed means that consumers must have access to complete information about a product before they buy it. Detailed information about ingredients and nutrition must be provided on food containers, information about fabrics and laundering methods must be attached to clothing, and lenders must disclose the true cost of borrowing the money they make available to customers who purchase merchandise on credit.

examining ethics

Biking Video Game Wheels Out Controversy

IS IT ETHICAL to sell video games using live-action videos of nude women? Acclaim Entertainment is testing the boundaries with its Dave Mirra BMX XXX videogame, a biking videogame featuring topless characters and profanity. When players achieve certain levels of play, they gain access to video segments shot live at a New York strip club—the first video game to include such footage.

The Entertainment Software Rating Board, which rates video games, is labeling a growing number of products with a "mature" rating—denoting suitability for players aged 17 and older—because of extreme violence, profanity, nudity, and other content. One of the earliest mature-rated video games, Rockstar Games' Grand Theft Auto III, sold six million copies in its first nine months on the market. Violent mature-rated video games such as Resident Evil have sold up to twenty-two million copies.

Eyeing this potentially lucrative market, Acclaim Entertainment is marketing its BMX XXX videogame to men in the 17- to-35-year-old age group, using a $3-million advertising campaign with the slogan "Keep it dirty." Microsoft is offering the video game for its Xbox video game console, noting that parents can set the console to limit the video games their children play. However, the KB Toys chain refuses to carry the video game because the content is "not appropriate."

Video game executives stress that the rating system alerts parents to controversial content and helps retailers decide on options for displaying and selling items with a mature rating. At the same time, they say that players over age 17 want video games with more mature content. "We make mature topics available in books, magazines, film, and music," observes Vince Desi, CEO of the video game company Running With Scissors. "I think the rating system helps a lot, but the fact is, we are still a young industry. As more and more people get older who grew up playing video games, the social and political pressure will change." What are the ethics of using sex to sell video games?

Issues to Consider

1. Given the consumer's right to be informed, what ethical issues in communication might arise from Acclaim Entertainment's advertising campaign for the BMX XXX video game?
2. Given the consumer's right to choose, should retailers be responsible for ensuring that children under age 17 do not have access to mature-rated video games?

In addition, manufacturers must inform consumers about the potential dangers of using their products. Manufacturers that fail to provide such information can be held responsible for personal injuries suffered because of their products. For example, Maytag provides customers with a lengthy booklet that describes how they should use an automatic clothes washer. Sometimes such warnings seem excessive, but they are necessary if user injuries (and resulting lawsuits) are to be avoided.

The Right to Choose The right to choose means that consumers must have a choice of products, offered by different manufacturers and sellers, to satisfy a particular need. The government has done its part by encouraging competition through antitrust legislation. The greater the competition, the greater is the choice available to consumers.

Competition and the resulting freedom of choice provide additional benefits for customers by reducing prices. For example, when personal computers were introduced, they cost over $5,000. Thanks to intense competition and technological advancements, personal computers today can be purchased for less than $800.

The Right to Be Heard This fourth right means that someone will listen and take appropriate action when customers complain. Actually, management began to listen to consumers after World War II, when competition between businesses that manufactured and sold consumer goods increased. One way firms got a competitive edge was to listen to consumers and provide the products they said they wanted and needed. Today, businesses are listening even more attentively, and many larger firms have consumer relations departments that can be contacted easily via toll-free phone numbers. Other groups listen, too. Most large cities and some states have consumer affairs offices to act on citizens' complaints.

Additional Consumer Rights In 1975, President Gerald Ford added to the consumer bill of rights the right to consumer education, which entitles people to be fully informed about their rights as consumers. In 1994, President Bill Clinton added a sixth right, the right to service, which entitles consumers to convenience, courtesy, and responsiveness from manufacturers and sellers of consumer products.

Major Consumerism Forces

The major forces in consumerism are individual consumer advocates and organizations, consumer education programs, and consumer laws.

Consumer advocates, such as Ralph Nader, take it on themselves to protect the rights of consumers. They band together into consumer organizations, either independently or under government sponsorship. Some organizations, such as the National Consumers' League and the Consumer Federation of America, operate nationally, whereas others are active at state and local levels. They inform and organize other consumers, raise issues, help businesses develop consumer-oriented programs, and pressure lawmakers to enact consumer protection laws. Some consumer advocates and organizations encourage consumers to boycott products and businesses to which they have objections. Today the consumer movement has adopted corporate-style marketing and addresses a broad range of issues. Current campaigns include efforts (1) to curtail the use of animals for testing purposes, (2) to reduce liquor and cigarette billboard advertising in low-income, inner-city neighborhoods, and (3) to encourage recycling.

Educating consumers to make wiser purchasing decisions is perhaps one of the most far-reaching aspects of consumerism. Increasingly, consumer education is becoming a part of high school and college curricula and adult education programs. These programs cover many topics—for instance, what major factors should be considered when buying specific products, such as insurance, real estate, automobiles, appliances and furniture, clothes, and food; the provisions of certain consumer protection laws; and the sources of information that can help individuals become knowledgeable consumers.

table 2.4 Major Federal Legislation Protecting Consumers Since 1960

Legislation	Major Provisions
Federal Hazardous Substances Labeling Act (1960)	Required warning labels on household chemicals if they are highly toxic
Kefauver-Harris Drug Amendments (1962)	Established testing practices for drugs and required manufacturers to label drugs with generic names in addition to trade names
Cigarette Labeling Act (1965)	Required manufacturers to place standard warning labels on all cigarette packages and advertising
Fair Packaging and Labeling Act (1966)	Called for all products sold across state lines to be labeled with net weight, ingredients, and manufacturer's name and address
Motor Vehicle Safety Act (1966)	Established standards for safer cars
Wholesome Meat Act (1967)	Required states to inspect meat (but not poultry) sold within the state
Flammable Fabrics Act (1967)	Extended flammability standards for clothing to include children's sleepwear in sizes 0 to 6X
Truth in Lending Act (1968)	Required lenders and credit merchants to disclose the full cost of finance charges in both dollars and annual percentage rates
Child Protection and Toy Act (1969)	Banned toys with mechanical or electrical defects from interstate commerce
Credit Card Liability Act (1970)	Limited credit card holder's liability to $50 per card and stopped credit card companies from issuing unsolicited cards
Fair Credit Reporting Act (1971)	Required credit bureaus to provide credit reports to consumers regarding their own credit files; also provided for correction of incorrect information
Consumer Product Safety Commission Act (1972)	Established the Consumer Product Safety Commission
Trade Regulation Rule (1972)	Established a "cooling off" period of 72 hours for door-to-door sales
Fair Credit Billing Act (1974)	Amended the Truth in Lending Act to enable consumers to challenge billing errors
Equal Credit Opportunity Act (1974)	Provided equal credit opportunities for males and females and for married and single individuals
Magnuson-Moss Warranty-Federal Trade Commission Act (1975)	Provided for minimum disclosure standards for written consumer product warranties for products that cost more than $15
Amendments to Equal Credit Opportunity Act (1976, 1994)	Prevented discrimination based on race, creed, color, religion, age, and income when granting credit
Fair Debt Collection Practices Act (1977)	Outlawed abusive collection practices by third parties
Drug Price Competition and Patent Restoration Act (1984)	Established an abbreviated procedure for registering certain generic drugs
Orphan Drug Act (1985)	Amended the original 1983 Orphan Drug Act and extended tax incentives to encourage the development of drugs for rare diseases
Nutrition Labeling and Education Act (1990)	Required the Food and Drug Administration to review current food labeling and packaging focusing on nutrition label content, label format, ingredient labeling, food descriptors and standards, and health messages
Telephone Consumer Protection Act (1991)	Prohibited the use of automated dialing and prerecorded-voice calling equipment to make calls or deliver messages
Consumer Credit Reporting Reform Act (1997)	Placed more responsibility for accurate credit data on credit issuers; required creditors to verify that disputed data are accurate and to notify a consumer before reinstating the data
Children's Online Privacy Protection Act (2000)	Placed parents in control over what information is collected online from their children under age 13; required commercial website operators to maintain the confidentiality, security, and integrity of the personal information collected from children

Major advances in consumerism have come through federal legislation. Some laws enacted in the last forty-four years to protect your rights as a consumer are listed and described in Table 2.4. Most business people now realize that they ignore consumer issues only at their own peril. Managers know that improper handling of consumer complaints can result in lost sales, bad publicity, and lawsuits.

Employment Practices

learning objective

8 Analyze how present employment practices are being used to counteract past abuses.

minority a racial, religious, political, national, or other group regarded as different from the larger group of which it is a part and that is often singled out for unfavorable treatment

We have seen that managers who subscribe to the socioeconomic view of business's social responsibility, together with significant government legislation enacted to protect the buying public, have broadened the rights of consumers. The last four decades have seen similar progress in affirming the rights of employees to equal treatment in the workplace.

Everyone should have the opportunity to land a job for which he or she is qualified and to be rewarded on the basis of ability and performance. This is an important issue for society, and it also makes good business sense. Yet, over the years, this opportunity has been denied to members of various minority groups. A **minority** is a racial, religious, political, national, or other group regarded as different from the larger group of which it is a part and that is often singled out for unfavorable treatment.

The federal government responded to the outcry of minority groups during the 1960s and 1970s by passing a number of laws forbidding discrimination in the workplace. (These laws are discussed in Chapter 10 in the context of human resources management.) Now, forty-one years after passage of the first of these (the Civil Rights Act of 1964), abuses still exist. An example is the disparity in income levels for whites, blacks, and Hispanics, as illustrated in Figure 2.3. Lower incomes and higher unemployment rates also characterize Native Americans, handicapped persons, and women. Responsible managers have instituted a number of programs to counteract the results of discrimination. As part of his "Digital Divide" campaign tour, former President Clinton visited many communities to bring attention to the fact that a gap exists between Americans fortunate enough to be participating in Internet and high-technology industries and those who have been left out. He called on Silicon Valley business executives in the Palo Alto area of California in particular to accept the challenge and social responsibility to educate Americans rather than to import skilled workers to fill vacant jobs.[18]

Affirmative Action Programs

affirmative action program a plan designed to increase the number of minority employees at all levels within an organization

An **affirmative action program** is a plan designed to increase the number of minority employees at all levels within an organization. Employers with federal contracts of more than $50,000 per year must have written affirmative action plans. The objective of such programs is to ensure that minorities are represented within the organization in approximately the same proportion as in the surrounding community. If 25 percent of the electricians in a geographic area in which a company is located are black, then approximately 25 percent of the electricians it employs also should be black. Affirma-

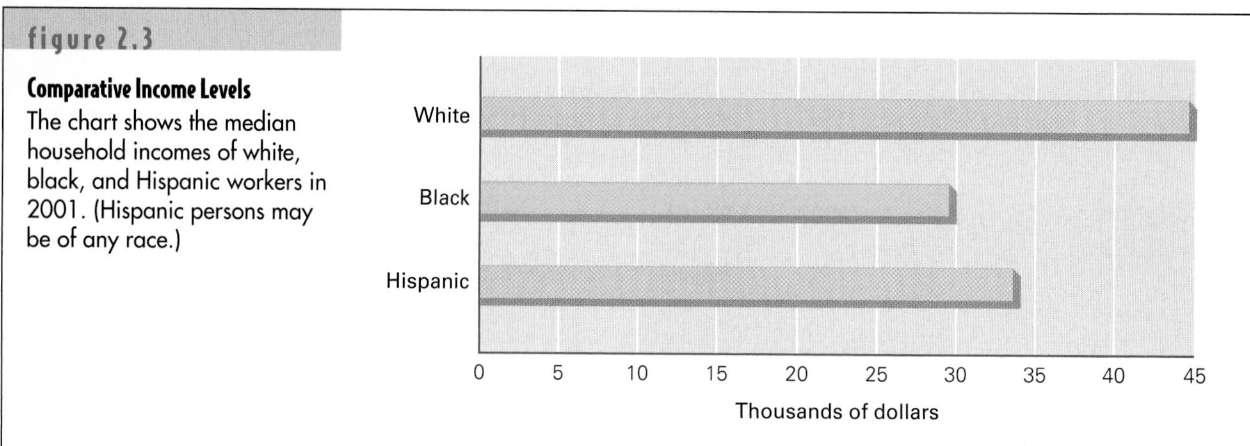

figure 2.3

Comparative Income Levels
The chart shows the median household incomes of white, black, and Hispanic workers in 2001. (Hispanic persons may be of any race.)

Source: U.S. Census Bureau, *Current Population Survey*, 1968 to 2002 Annual Demographic Supplements; **http://www.census.gov/hhes/www/img/incpov01/fig06.jpg**, accessed December 19, 2002.

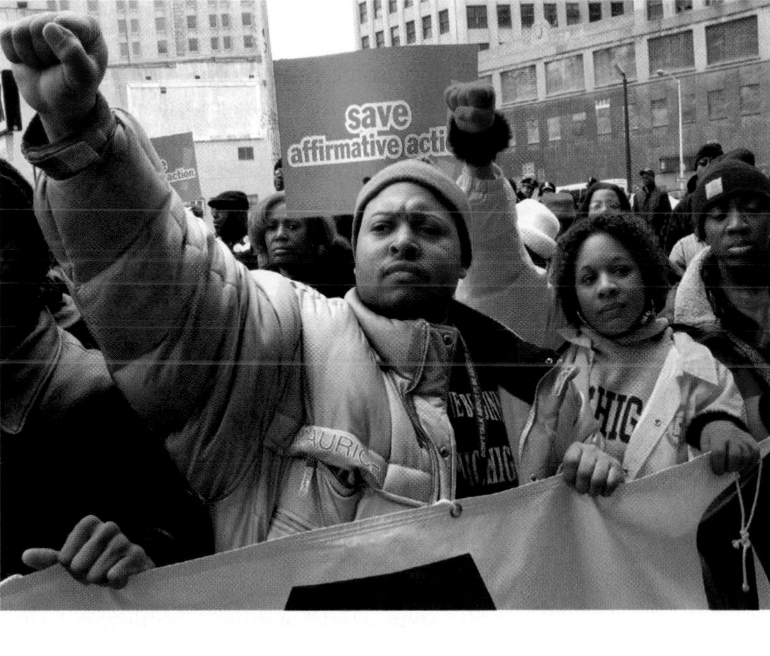

Strong opinions about affirmative action. Affirmative action programs ensure that minorities are represented within the organization in approximately the same proportion as in the surrounding community. But the courts have ruled that quotas are unconstitutional even though their purpose is commendable. Recently, in Detroit, Michigan, thousands marched in support of the University of Michigan's affirmative action programs. The U.S. Supreme Court later decided the university's basic affirmative-action policies are constitutional, but that its point system was not.

tive action plans encompass all areas of human resources management: recruiting, hiring, training, promotion, and pay.

Unfortunately, affirmative action programs have been plagued by two problems. The first involves quotas. In the beginning, many firms pledged to recruit and hire a certain number of minority members by a specific date. To achieve this goal, they were forced to consider only minority applicants for job openings; if they hired nonminority workers, they would be defeating their own purpose. However, the courts have ruled that such quotas are unconstitutional even though their purpose is commendable. They are, in fact, a form of discrimination called *reverse discrimination.*

The second problem is that although most such programs have been reasonably successful, not all business people are in favor of affirmative action programs. Managers not committed to these programs can "play the game" and still discriminate against workers. To help solve this problem, Congress created (and later strengthened) the **Equal Employment Opportunity Commission (EEOC),** a government agency with the power to investigate complaints of employment discrimination and sue firms that practice it.

Equal Employment Opportunity Commission (EEOC) a government agency with power to investigate complaints of employment discrimination and power to sue firms that practice it

The threat of legal action has persuaded some corporations to amend their hiring and promotional policies, but the discrepancy between men's and women's salaries still exists, as illustrated in Figure 2.4. For more than forty years, women have consistently earned only about 70 cents for each dollar earned by men.

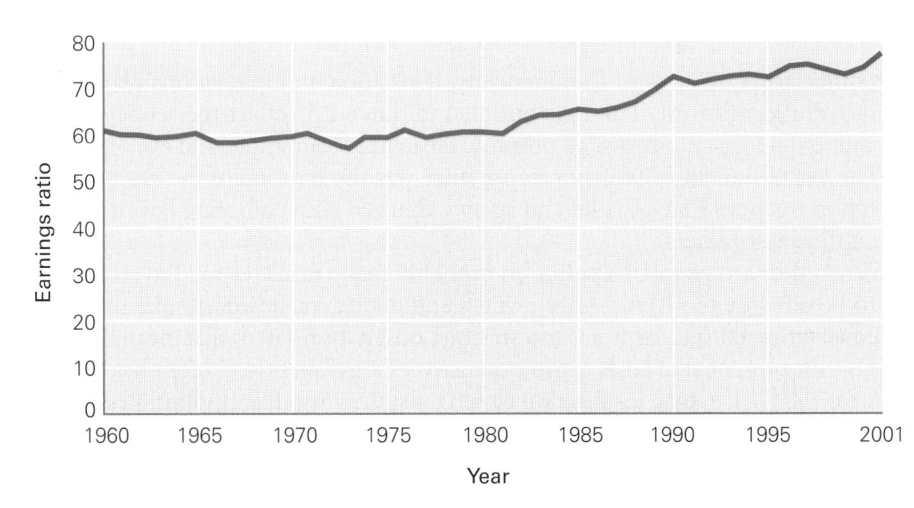

figure 2.4

Relative Earnings of Male and Female Workers

The ratio of women's to men's annual full-time earnings was 76 percent in 2001, a new all-time high, up from 74 percent first reached in 1996.

Source: U.S. Census Bureau, *Current Population Survey*, 1960 to 2002 Annual Demographic Supplements; **http://www.census.gov/hhes/www/img/incpov01/fig11.jpg,** accessed February 13, 2003.

Training Programs for the Hard-Core Unemployed

hard-core unemployed workers with little education or vocational training and a long history of unemployment

For some firms, social responsibility extends far beyond placing a help-wanted ad in the local newspaper. These firms have assumed the task of helping the **hard-core unemployed,** workers with little education or vocational training and a long history of unemployment. For example, a few years ago, General Mills helped establish Siyeza, a frozen soul-food processing plant in North Minneapolis. Through the years, Siyeza has provided stable, high-quality full-time jobs for a permanent core of eighty unemployed or underemployed minority inner-city residents. In addition, groups of up to a hundred temporary employees are called in when needed. Recently, Siyeza had a regular payroll of almost $1.9 million and is an example of the persistent commitment necessary to make positive changes in the community.[19] In the past, such workers often were turned down routinely by personnel managers, even for the most menial jobs.

National Alliance of Business (NAB) a joint business-government program to train the hard-core unemployed

Obviously, such workers require training; just as obviously, this training can be expensive and time-consuming. To share the costs, business and community leaders have joined together in a number of cooperative programs. One particularly successful partnership is the **National Alliance of Business (NAB).** The alliance's 5,000 members include companies of all sizes and industries, their CEOs and senior executives, as well as educators and community leaders. NAB, founded in 1968 by President Lyndon Johnson and Henry Ford II, is a major national business organization focusing on education and work force issues.

Concern for the Environment

learning objective

9 Describe the major types of pollution, their causes, and their cures.

The social consciousness of responsible business managers, the encouragement of a concerned government, and an increasing concern on the part of the public have led to a major effort to reduce environmental pollution, conserve natural resources, and reverse some of the worst effects of past negligence in this area.

pollution the contamination of water, air, or land through the actions of people in an industrialized society

Pollution is the contamination of water, air, or land through the actions of people in an industrialized society. For several decades, environmentalists have been warning us about the dangers of industrial pollution. Unfortunately, business and government leaders either ignored the problem or were not concerned about it until pollution became a threat to life and health in America. Today, Americans expect business and government leaders to take swift action to clean up our environment—and to keep it clean.

Effects of Environmental Legislation

As in other areas of concern to our society, legislation and regulations play a crucial role in pollution control. The laws outlined in Table 2.5 reflect the scope of current environmental legislation: laws to promote clean air, clean water, and even quiet work and living environments. Of major importance was the creation of the Environmental Protection Agency (EPA), the federal agency charged with enforcing laws designed to protect the environment.

When they are aware of a pollution problem, many firms respond to it rather than wait to be cited by the EPA. Other owners and managers, however, take the position that environmental standards are too strict. (Loosely translated, this means that compliance with present standards is too expensive.) Consequently, it often has been necessary for the EPA to take legal action to force firms to install antipollution equipment and to clean up waste storage areas.

Experience has shown that the combination of environmental legislation, voluntary compliance, and EPA action can succeed in cleaning up the environment and keeping it clean. However, much still remains to be done.

table 2.5 Summary of Major Environmental Laws

Legislation	Major Provisions
National Environmental Policy Act (1970)	Established the Environmental Protection Agency (EPA) to enforce federal laws that involve the environment
Clean Air Amendment (1970)	Provided stringent automotive, aircraft, and factory emission standards
Water Quality Improvement Act (1970)	Strengthened existing water pollution regulations and provided for large monetary fines against violators
Resource Recovery Act (1970)	Enlarged the solid-waste disposal program and provided for enforcement by the EPA
Water Pollution Control Act Amendment (1972)	Established standards for cleaning navigable streams and lakes and eliminating all harmful waste disposal by 1985
Noise Control Act (1972)	Established standards for major sources of noise and required the EPA to advise the Federal Aviation Administration on standards for airplanes
Clean Air Act Amendment (1977)	Established new deadlines for cleaning up polluted areas; also required review of existing air quality standards
Resource Conservation and Recovery Act (1984)	Amended the original 1976 act and required federal regulation of potentially dangerous solid-waste disposal
Clean Air Act Amendment (1987)	Established a national air quality standard for ozone
Oil Pollution Act (1990)	Expanded the nation's oil spill prevention and response activities; also established the Oil Spill Liability Trust Fund
Clean Air Act Amendments (1990)	Required that motor vehicles be equipped with onboard systems to control about 90 percent of refueling vapors

Water Pollution The Clean Water Act has been credited with greatly improving the condition of the waters in the United States. This success comes largely from the control of pollutant discharges from industrial and wastewater treatment plants. Although the quality of our nation's rivers, lakes, and streams has improved significantly in recent years, many of these surface waters remain severely polluted. Currently, one of the most serious water-quality problems results from the high level of toxic pollutants found in these waters.

Among the serious threats to people posed by water pollutants are respiratory irritation, cancer, kidney and liver damage, anemia, and heart failure. Toxic pollutants also damage fish and other forms of wildlife. In fish, they cause tumors or reproductive problems; shellfish and wildlife living in or drinking from toxin-infested waters also have suffered genetic defects.

A building that cares. From cutting pollution to using scrap materials, more companies are moving beyond governmental requirements to reap business benefits while safeguarding the environment. Visit the Chesapeake Bay Foundation headquarters in Annapolis, Maryland. Its offices are in the Phillip Merrill Environmental Center, which is equipped with solar panels that convert sunlight into electricity and boasts a holding tank that collects rain water for reuse in irrigation.

The task of water cleanup has proved to be extremely complicated and costly because of pollution runoff and toxic contamination. And yet improved water quality is not only necessary; it is also achievable. Consider Cleveland's Cuyahoga River. A few years ago the river was so contaminated by industrial wastes that it burst into flames one hot summer day! Now, after a sustained community cleanup effort, the river is pure enough for fish to thrive in.

Another serious issue is acid rain, which is contributing significantly to the deterioration of coastal waters, lakes, and marine life in the eastern United States. Acid rain forms when sulfur emitted by smokestacks in industrialized areas combines with moisture in the atmosphere to form acids that are spread by winds. The acids eventually fall to the earth in rain, which finds its way into streams, rivers, and lakes. The acid rain problem has spread rapidly in recent years, and experts fear that the situation will worsen if the nation begins to burn more coal to generate electricity. To solve the problem, investigators must first determine where the sulfur is being emitted. The expenses that this vital investigation and cleanup entail are going to be high. The human costs of having ignored the problem so long may be higher still.

Air Pollution Aviation emissions are a potentially significant and growing percentage of greenhouse gases that contribute to global warming. Aircraft emissions are potentially significant for several reasons. First, jet aircraft are the main source of human emissions deposited directly into the upper atmosphere, where they may have a greater warming effect than if they were released at the earth's surface. Second, carbon dioxide—the primary aircraft emission—is the main focus of international concern. For example, it survives in the atmosphere for nearly 100 years and contributes to global warming, according to the Intergovernmental Panel on Climate Change. The carbon dioxide emissions from worldwide aviation roughly equal those of some industrialized countries. Third, carbon dioxide emissions, combined with other gases and particles emitted by jet aircraft, could have two to four times as great an effect on the atmosphere as carbon dioxide alone. Fourth, the Intergovernmental Panel recently concluded that the rise in aviation emissions due to growing demand for air travel would not be fully offset by reductions in emissions achieved solely through technological improvements. Experts in the U.S. General Accounting Office interviewed, as well as the report of the Intergovernmental Panel, have cited several options for better understanding and mitigating the impact of aviation on the atmosphere as the industry grows. These options include (1) continuing research to improve the scientific understanding of aviation's effects on the global atmosphere as a basis for guiding the development of aircraft and engine technology to reduce them, (2) promoting more efficient air traffic operations through the introduction of new technologies and procedures, and (3) expanding the use of regulatory and economic measures to encourage reductions in emissions.[20]

Usually two or three factors combine to form air pollution in any given location. The first factor is large amounts of carbon monoxide and hydrocarbons emitted by motor vehicles concentrated in a relatively small area. The second is the smoke and other pollutants emitted by manufacturing facilities. These two factors can be partially eliminated through pollution-control devices on cars, trucks, and smokestacks.

A third factor that contributes to air pollution—one that cannot be changed—is the combination of weather and geography. The Los Angeles Basin, for example, combines just the right weather and geographic conditions for creating dense smog. Los Angeles has strict regulations regarding air pollution. Even so, Los Angeles still struggles with air pollution problems because of uncontrollable conditions.

How effective is air pollution control? The EPA estimates that the Clean Air Act and its amendments eventually will result in the removal of fifty-six billion pounds of pollution from the air each year, thus measurably reducing lung disease, cancer, and other serious health problems caused by air pollution. Other authorities note that we have already seen improvement in air quality. A number of cities have cleaner air today than they did thirty years ago. The latest evidence comes from the Foundation for Clean Air Progress, a nonprofit organization founded to educate the

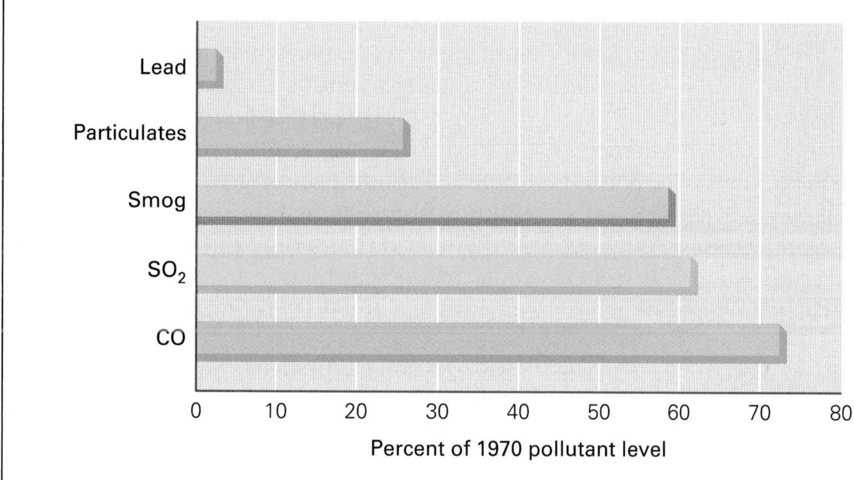

figure 2.5

Air Pollution Trends

A recent poll conducted by the Wirthlin research firm found that two-thirds of Americans believe that our air quality has been getting worse. However, in reality, lead, particulates, smog-causing compounds, sulfur dioxide, and carbon monoxide have dropped significantly during the last thirty-five years.

Source: Exxon Mobile Corporation, *The Lamp*, Spring 2002, p. 28. Data from Environmental Protection Agency. Reprinted by permission of The Exxon Mobil Corporation.

public about the nation's air quality. The Foundation examined U.S. government data over three decades and found extremely encouraging improvements. Here is what has gone up: energy consumption (41 percent), the U.S. population (38 percent), employment (70 percent), licensed drivers (71 percent), vehicles registrations (99 percent), vehicle miles traveled (148 percent), and inflation-adjusted growth in the economy (158 percent). However, during the same period, five of the six most important air quality measures have improved, as shown in Figure 2.5. While lead, particulates, smog-causing compounds, sulfur dioxide, and carbon monoxide have dropped significantly, only nitrogen oxides have risen. Even in southern California, bad air quality days have dropped to less than forty days a year, about 60 percent lower than just a decade ago. Other areas of the world, such as Europe, also have experienced dramatic improvements in air quality.[21] Numerous chemical companies have recognized that they must take responsibility for operating their plants in an environmentally safe manner; some now devote considerable capital to purchasing antipollution devices.

Critters don't like litter. Litter is just not natural. Land pollution is a serious problem in the United States and abroad. Here, the Virginia Department of Environmental Quality pleads with citizens to keep our land free of trash and other contaminants.

Land Pollution Air and water quality may be improving, but land pollution is still a serious problem in many areas. The fundamental issues are (1) how to restore damaged or contaminated land at a reasonable cost and (2) how to protect unpolluted land from future damage.

The land pollution problem has been worsening over the past few years because modern technology has continued to produce increasing amounts of chemical and radioactive waste. U.S. manufacturers produce an estimated forty to sixty million tons of contaminated oil, solvents, acids, and sludges each year. Service businesses, utility companies, hospitals, and other industries also dump vast amounts of wastes into the environment.

Individuals in the United States contribute to the waste-disposal problem, too. A shortage of landfills, owing to stricter regulations, makes garbage disposal a serious problem in some areas.

Spotlight

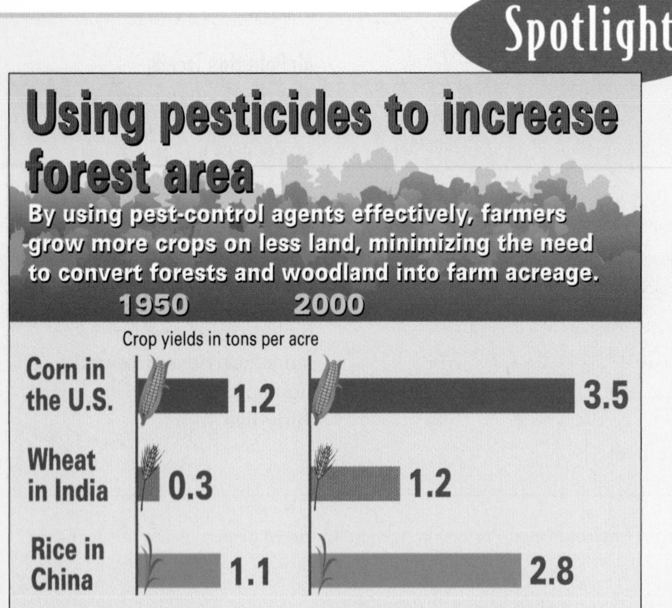

Source: Exxon Mobil, *The Lamp*, Spring 2002, p. 23. Data from Center for Global Food Issues.

Incinerators help solve the landfill-shortage problem, but they bring with them their own problems. They reduce the amount of garbage but also leave tons of ash to be buried—ash that often has a higher concentration of toxicity than the original garbage. Other causes of land pollution include strip-mining of coal, nonselective cutting of forests, and the development of agricultural land for housing and industry.

To help pay the enormous costs of cleaning up land polluted with chemicals and toxic wastes, Congress created a $1.6 billion Superfund in 1980. Originally, money was to flow into the Superfund from a tax paid by 800 oil and chemical companies that produce toxic waste. The EPA was to use the money in the Superfund to finance the cleanup of hazardous waste sites across the nation. To replenish the Superfund, the EPA had two options: It could sue companies guilty of dumping chemicals at specific waste sites, or it could negotiate with guilty companies and thus completely avoid the legal system. During the 1980s, officials at the EPA came under fire because they preferred negotiated settlements. Critics referred to these settlements as "sweetheart deals" with industry. They felt that the EPA should be much more aggressive in reducing land pollution. Of course, most corporate executives believe that cleanup efficiency and quality might be improved if companies were more involved in the process.

Since the Superfund was established, the EPA has spent about $17.7 billion, yet 42 percent of the nation's 1,400 most severely contaminated hazardous waste sites need cleanups.[22]

Noise Pollution Excessive noise caused by traffic, aircraft, and machinery can do physical harm to human beings. Research has shown that people who are exposed to loud noises for long periods of time can suffer permanent hearing loss. The Noise Control Act of 1972 established noise emission standards for aircraft and airports, railroads, and interstate motor carriers. The act also provided funding for noise research at state and local levels.

Noise levels can be reduced by two methods. The source of noise pollution can be isolated as much as possible. (Thus many metropolitan airports are located outside the cities.) And engineers can modify machinery and equipment to reduce noise levels. If it is impossible to reduce industrial noise to acceptable levels, workers should be required to wear earplugs to guard against permanent hearing damage.

Who Should Pay for a Clean Environment?

Governments and businesses are spending billions of dollars annually to reduce pollution—over $35 billion to control air pollution, $25 billion to control water pollution, and $12 billion to treat hazardous wastes.

To make matters worse, much of the money required to purify the environment is supposed to come from already depressed industries, such as the chemical industry. And a few firms have discovered that it is cheaper to pay a fine than to install expensive equipment for pollution control.

Who, then, will pay for the environmental cleanup? Many business leaders offer one answer—tax money should be used to clean up the environment and to keep it clean. They reason that business is not the only source of pollution, so business should not be forced to absorb the entire cost of the cleanup. Environmentalists disagree.

They believe that the cost of proper treatment and disposal of industrial wastes is an expense of doing business. In either case, consumers probably will pay a large part of the cost—either as taxes or in the form of higher prices for goods and services.

Implementing a Program of Social Responsibility

A firm's decision to be socially responsible is a step in the right direction—but only the first step. The firm must then develop and implement a program to reach this goal. The program will be affected by the firm's size, financial resources, past record in the area of social responsibility, and competition. Above all, however, the program must have the firm's total commitment or it will fail.

learning objective

10 Identify the steps a business must take to implement a program of social responsibility.

Developing a Program of Social Responsibility

An effective program for social responsibility takes time, money, and organization. In most cases, developing and implementing such a program will require four steps: securing the commitment of top executives, planning, appointing a director, and preparing a social audit.

Commitment of Top Executives Without the support of top executives, any program will soon falter and become ineffective. For example, the Boeing Company's Ethics and Business Conduct Committee is responsible for the ethics program. The committee is appointed by the Boeing Board of Directors, and its members include the company chairman and CEO, president and chief operating officer, presidents of the operating groups, and senior vice presidents. As evidence of their commitment to social responsibility, top managers should develop a policy statement that outlines key areas of concern. This statement sets a tone of positive support and later will serve as a guide for other employees as they become involved in the program.

Planning Next, a committee of managers should be appointed to plan the program. Whatever form their plan takes, it should deal with each of the issues described in the top managers' policy statement. If necessary, outside consultants can be hired to help develop the plan.

Appointment of a Director After the social responsibility plan is established, a top-level executive should be appointed to implement the organization's plan. This individual should be charged with recommending specific policies and helping individual departments understand and live up to the social responsibilities the firm has assumed. Depending on the size of the firm, the director may require a staff to handle the program on a day-to-day basis. For example, at the Boeing Company, the director of ethics and business conduct administers the ethics and business conduct program.

The Social Audit At specified intervals, the program director should prepare a social audit for the firm. A **social audit** is a comprehensive report of what an organization has done and is doing with regard to social issues that affect it. This document provides the information the firm needs to evaluate and revise its social responsibility program. Typical subject areas include human resources, community involvement, the quality and safety of products, business practices, and efforts to reduce pollution and improve the environment. The information included in a social audit should be as accurate and as quantitative as possible, and the audit should reveal both positive and negative aspects of the program.

social audit a comprehensive report of what an organization has done and is doing with regard to social issues that affect it

Today, many companies listen to concerned individuals within and outside the company. For example, the Boeing Ethics Line listens to and acts on concerns expressed by employees and others about possible violations of company policies, laws, or regulations, such as improper or unethical business practices, as well as health, safety, and environmental issues. Employees are encouraged to communicate their concerns, as well as ask questions about ethical issues. The Ethics Line is available to all Boeing employees, including Boeing subsidiaries. It is also available to concerned individuals outside the company.

Funding the Program

We have noted that social responsibility costs money. Thus, just like any other corporate undertaking, a program to improve social responsibility must be funded. Funding can come from three sources:

1. Management can pass the cost on to consumers in the form of higher prices.
2. The corporation may be forced to absorb the cost of the program if, for example, the competitive situation does not permit a price increase. In this case, the cost is treated as a business expense, and profit is reduced.
3. The federal government may pay for all or part of the cost through tax reductions or other incentives.

Return To inside business

Starbucks has worked hard to build a worldwide reputation for social responsibility. Despite its many programs, critics argue that such a large international corporation can and should do more. One high-profile issue is the company's relations with coffee farmers. A global glut of coffee beans has driven crop prices to historic lows while farming costs continue to rise. Even though lattes retail for $4 or more in some locations, many farmers are struggling to eke out a living. The fair-trade director for Global Exchange acknowledges that Starbucks built a health clinic in Guatemala, yet "it doesn't address the underlying poverty that is killing coffee farmers and their families."

Starbucks also has been criticized from within. Several years ago, store managers in California filed suit against the company, charging that they were required to work up to twenty extra hours weekly without overtime pay. Starbucks paid $18 million to settle the lawsuit, and it dropped the requirement. Looking ahead, Starbucks remains committed to a multifaceted program of social responsibility wherever it touches the lives of customers, suppliers, shareholders, employees, and other stakeholders.

Questions

1. Why would customers, employees, and shareholders prefer to be involved with a company such as Starbucks that puts special emphasis on social responsibility?
2. Considering Starbucks' social responsibility to consumers, should it raise its prices to be able to fund more programs to alleviate poverty among coffee farmers? Explain your answer.

chapter review

Summary

Understand what is meant by *business ethics.*

Ethics is the study of right and wrong and of the morality of choices. Business ethics is the application of moral standards to business situations.

Identify the types of ethical concerns that arise in the business world.

Ethical issues arise often in business situations out of relationships with investors, customers, employees, creditors, or competitors. Business people should make every effort to be fair, to consider the welfare of customers and others within the firm, to avoid conflicts of interest, and to communicate honestly.

Discuss the factors that affect the level of ethical behavior in organizations.

Individual, social, and opportunity factors all affect the level of ethical behavior in an organization. Individual factors include knowledge level, moral values and attitudes, and personal goals. Social factors include cultural norms and the actions and values of coworkers and significant others. Opportunity factors refer to the amount of leeway that exists in an organization for employees to behave unethically if they so choose.

Explain how ethical decision making can be encouraged.

Governments, trade associations, and individual firms can all establish guidelines for defining ethical behavior. Governments can pass stricter regulations. Trade associations provide ethical guidelines for their members. Companies provide codes of ethics—written guides to acceptable and ethical behavior as defined by an organization—and create an atmosphere in which ethical behavior is encouraged. An ethical employee working in an unethical environment may resort to whistle-blowing to bring a questionable practice to light.

Describe how our current views on the social responsibility of business have evolved.

In a socially responsible business, management realizes that its activities have an impact on society and considers that impact in the decision-making process. Before the 1930s, workers, consumers, and government had very little influence on business activities; as a result, business leaders gave little thought to social responsibility. All this changed with the Great Depression. Government regulations, employee demands, and consumer awareness combined to create a demand that businesses act in socially responsible ways.

Explain the two views on the social responsibility of business and understand the arguments for and against increased social responsibility.

The basic premise of the economic model of social responsibility is that society benefits most when business is left alone to produce profitable goods and services. According to the socioeconomic model, business has as much responsibility to society as it has to its owners. Most managers adopt a viewpoint somewhere between these two extremes.

Discuss the factors that led to the consumer movement and list some of its results.

Consumerism consists of all activities undertaken to protect the rights of consumers. The consumer movement generally has demanded—and received—attention from business in the areas of product safety, product information, product choices through competition, and the resolution of complaints about products and business practices. Although concerns over consumer rights have been around to some extent since the early nineteenth century, the movement became more powerful in the 1960s when President John F. Kennedy initiated the consumer "bill of rights." The six basic rights of consumers include the right to safety, the right to be informed, the right to choose, the right to be heard, and the rights to consumer education and courteous service.

Analyze how present employment practices are being used to counteract past abuses.

Legislation and public demand have prompted some businesses to correct past abuses in employment practices—mainly with regard to minority groups. Affirmative action and training of the hard-core unemployed are two types of programs that have been used successfully.

Describe the major types of pollution, their causes, and their cures.

Industry has contributed to the noise pollution and the pollution of our land and water through the dumping of wastes and to air pollution through vehicle and smokestack emissions. This contamination can be cleaned up and controlled, but the big question is, Who will pay? Present cleanup efforts are funded partly by government tax revenues, partly by business, and in the long run, by consumers.

Identify the steps a business must take to implement a program of social responsibility.

A program to implement social responsibility in a business begins with total commitment by top management. The program should be planned carefully, and a capable director should be appointed to implement it. Social audits should be prepared periodically as a means of evaluating and revising the program. Programs may be funded through price increases, reduction of profit, or federal incentives.

Key Terms

You should now be able to define and give an example relevant to each of the following terms:

ethics (35)
business ethics (35)
code of ethics (39)
whistle-blowing (41)
social responsibility (42)
caveat emptor (47)
economic model of social responsibility (48)
socioeconomic model of social responsibility (49)
consumerism (50)
minority (54)
affirmative action program (54)
Equal Employment Opportunity Commission (EEOC) (55)
hard-core unemployed (56)
National Alliance of Business (NAB) (56)
pollution (56)
social audit (61)

Review Questions

1. Why might an individual with high ethical standards act less ethically in business than in his or her personal life?
2. How would an organizational code of ethics help ensure ethical business behavior?
3. How and why did the American business environment change after the Great Depression?
4. What are the major differences between the economic model of social responsibility and the socioeconomic model?
5. What are the arguments for and against increasing the social responsibility of business?
6. Describe and give an example of each of the six basic rights of consumers.
7. There are more women than men in the United States. Why, then, are women considered a minority with regard to employment?
8. What is the goal of affirmative action programs? How is this goal achieved?
9. What is the primary function of the Equal Employment Opportunity Commission?
10. How do businesses contribute to each of the four forms of pollution? How can they avoid polluting the environment?
11. Our environment *can* be cleaned up and kept clean. Why haven't we simply done so?
12. Describe the steps involved in developing a social responsibility program within a large corporation.

Discussion Questions

1. When a company acts in an ethically questionable manner, what types of problems are caused for the organization and its customers?
2. How can an employee take an ethical stand regarding a business decision when his or her superior has already taken a different position?
3. Overall, would it be more profitable for a business to follow the economic model or the socioeconomic model of social responsibility?
4. Why should business take on the task of training the hard-core unemployed?
5. To what extent should the blame for vehicular air pollution be shared by manufacturers, consumers, and government?
6. Why is there so much government regulation involving social responsibility issues? Should there be less?

video case

Brewing Up Social Responsibility at New Belgium Brewing

New Belgium Brewing (NBB), America's first wind-powered brewery, aims to make both a better beer and a better society. Founded by husband-and-wife entrepreneurs Jeff Lebesch and Kim Jordan, the company offers European-style beers under intriguing brands such as Fat Tire and Sunshine Wheat. Lebesch hatched the idea for brewing his own beers after sipping local beers while touring Belgium on bicycle. Returning home with a special yeast strain, Lebesch experimented in his basement and came up with a beer he dubbed Fat Tire Amber Ale in honor of his bicycle trip.

By 1991, he and his wife were bottling and delivering five Belgian-style beers to liquor stores and other retailers in and around their home town of Fort Collins, Colorado. Within a few years, sales had grown so rapidly that NBB needed much more space. Lebesch and Jordan moved the operation into a former railroad depot and then moved again into a new state-of-the-art brewery.

Not only is the 80,000-square-foot facility highly automated for efficiency, it is also designed with the environment in mind. For example, sun tubes bring daylight to areas that lack windows, which reduces the brewery's energy requirements. As another energy-saving example, the brewery's kettles have steam condensers to capture and reuse hot water again and again. The biggest energy-conservation measure is a special cooling device that reduces the need for air conditioning in warm weather. In the office section, NBB employees reuse and recycle paper and as many other supplies as possible.

Soon after opening the new brewery, the entire staff voted to convert it to wind power, which is kinder to the environment because it does not pollute or require scarce fossil fuels. In addition to saving energy and natural resources, NBB is actually transforming the methane from its waste stream into energy through the process of cogeneration. It also has found ways to cut carbon dioxide emissions and reuse brewing by-products as cattle feed. Going further, NBB donates $1 to charitable causes for every barrel of beer it sells—which translates into more than $200,000 per year. Moreover, it donates the proceeds of its annual Tour de Fat biking event to nonprofit bicycling organizations.

Employee involvement is a key element of NBB's success. Lebesch and Jordan have unleashed the entrepreneurial spirit of the work force through employee ownership. Employees share in decisions, serve as taste testers, and receive detailed information about NBB's financial performance, including costs and profits. Being empowered as part owners not only motivates employees, it also gives them a great sense of pride in their work. And reminiscent of the bicycle trip that prompted Lebesch to brew his own beers, all employees receive a cruising bicycle on the first anniversary of joining the company.

Still, customers are most concerned with the taste of NBB's beers, which have won numerous awards and have attracted a large, loyal customer base in twelve states. In the last five years, Fat Tire's annual sales have grown from 0.9 million cases to 2.6 million cases. Many people become customers after hearing about the beer from long-time fans, and as its popularity grows, the word spreads even further. NBB does some advertising but its budget is tiny compared with deep-pocketed rivals such as Anheuser-Busch and Miller Brewing. Instead of glitzy commercials on national television, NBB uses a low-key approach to show customers that the company is comprised of "real people making real beer."

Today the company employs 140 people and is the sixth largest selling draft beer in America. Clearly, sales and profits are vital ingredients in NBB's long-term recipe, but they are not the only important elements. Jordan stresses that the company is not just about making beer—it is about creating what she calls "magic." Reflecting on her continued involvement in NBB, she says: "How do you support a community of people? How do you show up in the larger community? How do you strive to be a business role model? That's the part that keeps me really engaged here."

In fact, NBB has so successfully integrated social responsibility into its operations that it recently received an award from *Business Ethics* magazine. The award cited the company's "dedication to environmental excellence in every part of its innovative brewing process." Jordan, Lebesch, and all the NBB employee-owners can take pride in their efforts to build a better society as well as a better beer.[23]

Questions

1. What do you think Kim Jordan means when she talks about how New Belgium Brewing strives to be a "business role model," not just a beer maker?
2. Given New Belgium Brewing's emphasis on social responsibility, what would you suggest the company look at when preparing a social audit?
3. Should businesses charge more for products that are produced using more costly but environmentally friendly methods such as wind power? Should consumers pay more for products that are *not* produced using environmentally friendly methods because of the potential for costly environmental damage? Explain your answers.

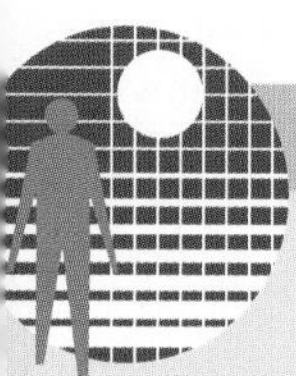

Building Skills for Career Success

1. Exploring the Internet

Socially responsible business behavior can be as simple as donating unneeded older computers to schools, mentoring interested learners in good business practice, or supplying public speakers to talk about career opportunities. Students, as part of the public at large, perceive a great deal of information about a company, its employees, and its owners by the positive social actions taken and perhaps even more by actions not taken. Microsoft donates millions of dollars of computers and software to educational institutions every year. Some consider this level of corporate giving insufficient given the scale of the wealth of the corporation. Others believe that firms have no obligation to give back any more than they wish and that recipients should be grateful. Visit the text website for updates to this exercise.

Assignment

1. Select any firm involved in high technology and the Internet such as Microsoft or IBM. Examine their website and report their corporate position on social responsibility and giving as they have stated it. What activities are they involved in? What programs do they support, and how do they support them?
2. Search the Internet for commentary on business social responsibility, form your own opinions, and then evaluate the social effort demonstrated by the firm you have selected. What more could the firm have done?

2. Developing Critical Thinking Skills

Recently an article entitled, "Employees Coming to Terms with Moral Issues on the Job" appeared in a big-city newspaper. It posed the following situations:

You are asked to work on a project you find morally wrong.

Important tasks are left undone because a coworker spends more time planning a social event than working on a proposal.

Your company is knowingly selling defective merchandise to customers.

Unfortunately, many employees currently are struggling with such issues. The moral dilemmas that arise when employees find their own ethical values incompatible with the work they do every day are causing a lot of stress in the workplace, and furthermore, these dilemmas are not being discussed. There exists an ethics gap. You may have already faced a similar situation in your workplace.

Assignment

1. In small groups with your classmates, discuss your answers to the following questions:
   a. If you were faced with any of the preceding situations, what would you do?
   b. Would you complete work you found morally unacceptable, or would you leave it undone and say nothing?
   c. If you spoke up, what would happen to you or your career? What would be the risk?
   d. What are your options?
   e. If you were a manager rather than a lower-level employee, would you feel differently and take a different approach to the issue? Why?
2. In a written report, summarize what you learned from this discussion.

3. Building Team Skills

A firm's code of ethics outlines the kind of behavior expected within the organization and serves as a guideline for encouraging ethical behavior in the workplace. It reflects the rights of the firm's workers, shareholders, and consumers.

Assignment

1. Working in a team of four, find a code of ethics for a business firm. Start the search by asking firms in your community for a copy of their codes, by visiting the library, or by searching and downloading information from the Internet.
2. Analyze the code of ethics you have chosen, and answer the following questions:
   a. What does the company's code of ethics say about the rights of its workers, shareholders, consumers, and suppliers? How does the code reflect the company's attitude toward competitors?
   b. How does this code of ethics resemble the information discussed in this chapter? How does it differ?
   c. As an employee in this company, how would you personally interpret the code of ethics? How might the code influence your behavior within the workplace? Give several examples.

4. Researching Different Careers

Business ethics has been at the heart of many discussions over the years and continues to trouble employees and shareholders. Stories about dishonesty and wrongful behavior in the workplace appear on a regular basis in newspapers and on the national news.

Assignment

Prepare a written report on the following:

1. Why can it be so difficult for people to do what is right?
2. What is your personal code of ethics? Prepare a code outlining what you believe is morally right. The document should include guidelines for your personal behavior.
3. How will your code of ethics affect your decisions about
   a. The types of questions you should ask in a job interview?
   b. Selecting a company in which to work?

5. Improving Communication Skills

Businesses with programs of social responsibility provide a wealth of services to groups in their communities, such as schools, libraries, city governments, and service and civic organizations. If you are not aware of the businesses in your community that are doing this, you might be surprised at what is happening.

Assignment

1. Identify several businesses in your community that are providing services to local institutions and organizations.
2. Prepare a table using the following columns to indicate what services they provide, what the impact of these services has been on your community, and in what ways they make a difference to the organization or institution receiving the services:

   Column 1: Name of company providing services
   Column 2: Types of services provided
   Column 3: Organizations or institutions receiving services
   Column 4: Impact in the community
   Column 5: Difference within the organization
3. Summarize your philosophy of business's social responsibility. As an employee, how would you feel about helping your company fulfill its social responsibility within the community? Why? Is that a fair job requirement? Explain.

chapter

3

Exploring Global Business

learning objectives

1 Explain the economic basis for international business.

2 Discuss the restrictions nations place on international trade, the objectives of these restrictions, and their results.

3 Outline the extent of international trade and identify the organizations working to foster it.

4 Define the methods by which a firm can organize for and enter into international markets.

5 Describe the various sources of export assistance.

6 Identify the institutions that help firms and nations finance international business.

Before it hit on a new strategy, Coca-Cola lost millions of dollars as it gained firsthand knowledge of the market in rural India.

inside business

Coca-Cola Thinks Small to Capture Global Markets

For Coca-Cola, two keys to building global profits are thinking small and saturating local markets with distribution points. The Atlanta-based company has been selling beverages for decades in nearly every country from Argentina to Zimbabwe. Recently, however, slower growth in worldwide sales volume has pushed Coca-Cola's senior managers to look more closely at markets that previously seemed less promising because of low income levels, high inflation, currency fluctuations, volatile political conditions, or other complications.

Few people in rural northern India, for example, can afford costly products such as kitchen appliances on the area's average monthly income of about $42. Even large-size soft drinks are out of reach for many. But after losing millions of dollars as it gained firsthand knowledge of the market, Coca-Cola hit on the dual strategy of adjusting the bottle size—to make its sodas more affordable for buyers—and putting its products in as many outlets as possible. Now Indians can buy a tiny 200-milliliter bottle of Coca-Cola for the equivalent of 12 cents at thousands of local bus-stop stands, neighborhood grocery stores, and food stalls. The deputy president of Coca-Cola India explains the company's outlet-by-outlet drive for distribution: "Our hands are firmly in the dust here. It's the only way we can capture this market."

Steve Heyer, Coca-Cola's marketing chief, is applying this strategy to improve sales and profits in Latin America, where sales have not met expectations. In Argentina, the gross domestic product has dropped by 15 percent, and the company faces considerable competition from inexpensive local beverages. Rather than compete on the basis of price alone, managers introduced a range of bottle sizes to accommodate different incomes and needs. They also began offering a higher number of returnable bottles to keep costs down and boost profits. As a result of these changes, Argentine buyers in a hurry can choose to pay roughly 33 cents for the convenience of a chilled single-serving bottle. Meanwhile, bargain hunters can opt to pay about 28 cents for a larger 1.25-liter unchilled bottle.

Building on this success in Argentina, Heyer has expanded the strategy to Brazil and other Latin American nations. Like their counterparts in India, local Coca-Cola managers are going store to store to arrange maximum distribution and ensure proper shelf placement for their products. After making the rounds with managers in Brazil, Argentina, and Mexico, Heyer concedes that this approach is more difficult to implement in Latin America than in the United States. "Marketing street to street . . . to different socio-economic levels adds a layer of complexity and execution you can't fully appreciate until you're staring at it," he says.[1]

Coca-Cola is just one of a growing number of U.S. companies, large and small, that are doing business with firms in other countries. Some companies, like Coca-Cola, sell to firms in other countries; others buy goods around the world to import into the United States. Whether they buy or sell products across national borders, these companies are all contributing to the volume of international trade that is fueling the global economy.

Theoretically, international trade is every bit as logical and worthwhile as interstate trade between, say, California and Washington. Yet nations tend to restrict the import of certain goods for a variety of reasons. For example, in the early 2000s, the United States restricted the import of Mexican fresh tomatoes because they were undercutting price levels of domestic fresh tomatoes.

Despite such restrictions, international trade has increased almost steadily since World War II. Many of the industrialized nations have signed trade agreements intended to eliminate problems in international business and to help less-developed nations participate in world trade. Individual firms around the world have seized the opportunity to compete in foreign markets by exporting products and increasing foreign production, as well as by other means.

In an international education policy statement in 2000, President Bill Clinton declared, "To continue to compete successfully in the global economy and to maintain our role as a world leader, the United States needs to ensure that its citizens develop a broad understanding of the world, proficiency in other languages, and knowledge of other cultures. America's leadership also depends on building ties with those who will guide the political, cultural, and economic development of their countries in the future."[2] Signing the Trade Act of 2002, President George W. Bush remarked, "Trade is an important source of good jobs for our workers and a source of higher growth for our economy. Free trade is also a proven strategy for building global prosperity and adding to the momentum of political freedom. Trade is an engine of economic growth. In our lifetime, trade has helped lift millions of people and whole nations out of poverty and put them on the path of prosperity."[3]

We describe international trade in this chapter in terms of modern specialization, whereby each country trades the surplus goods and services it produces most efficiently for products in short supply. We also explain the restrictions nations place on products and services from other countries and present some of the possible advantages and disadvantages of these restrictions. We then describe the extent of international trade and identify the organizations working to foster it. We describe several methods of entering international markets and the various sources of export assistance available from the federal government. Finally, we identify some of the institutions that provide the complex financing necessary for modern international trade.

The Basis for International Business

International business encompasses all business activities that involve exchanges across national boundaries. Thus a firm is engaged in international business when it buys some portion of its input from or sells some portion of its output to an organization located in a foreign country. (A small retail store may sell goods produced in some other country. However, because it purchases these goods from American distributors, it is not engaged in international trade.)

learning objective

1 Explain the economic basis for international business.

international business all business activities that involve exchanges across national boundaries

Absolute and Comparative Advantage

Some countries are better equipped than others to produce particular goods or services. The reason may be a country's natural resources, its labor supply, or even customs or a historical accident. Such a country would be best off if it could *specialize* in the production of such products because it can produce them most efficiently. The country could use what it needed of these products and then trade the surplus for products it could not produce efficiently on its own.

Saudi Arabia thus has specialized in the production of crude oil and petroleum products; South Africa, in diamonds; and Australia, in wool. Each of these countries is said to have an absolute advantage with regard to a particular product. An **absolute advantage** is the ability to produce a specific product more efficiently than any other nation.

absolute advantage the ability to produce a specific product more efficiently than any other nation

One country may have an absolute advantage with regard to several products, whereas another country may have no absolute advantage at all. Yet it is still worthwhile for these two countries to specialize and trade with each other. To see why this is so, imagine that you are the president of a successful manufacturing firm and that you can accurately type ninety words per minute. Your assistant can type eighty words per minute but would run the business poorly. You thus have an absolute advantage over your assistant in both typing and managing. However, you cannot afford to type your own letters because your time is better spent in managing the business. That is, you have a **comparative advantage** in managing. A comparative advantage is the ability to produce a specific product more efficiently than any other product.

comparative advantage the ability to produce a specific product more efficiently than any other product

Your assistant, on the other hand, has a comparative advantage in typing because he or she can do that better than managing the business. Thus you spend your time managing, and you leave the typing to your assistant. Overall, the business is run as efficiently as possible because you are each working in accordance with your own comparative advantage.

The same is true for nations. Goods and services are produced more efficiently when each country specializes in the products for which it has a comparative advantage. Moreover, by definition, every country has a comparative advantage in *some* product. The United States has many comparative advantages—in research and development, high-technology industries, and identifying new markets, for instance. California-based Yahoo, Inc., is considered a pioneer in the development of Internet search software. As growth in Internet usage accelerates globally, firms with experience and a proven product can exploit the comparative advantage they enjoy over local firms in foreign markets who might just be getting started in the commercial areas of the Internet. So far Yahoo has expanded operations to twenty countries worldwide.[4]

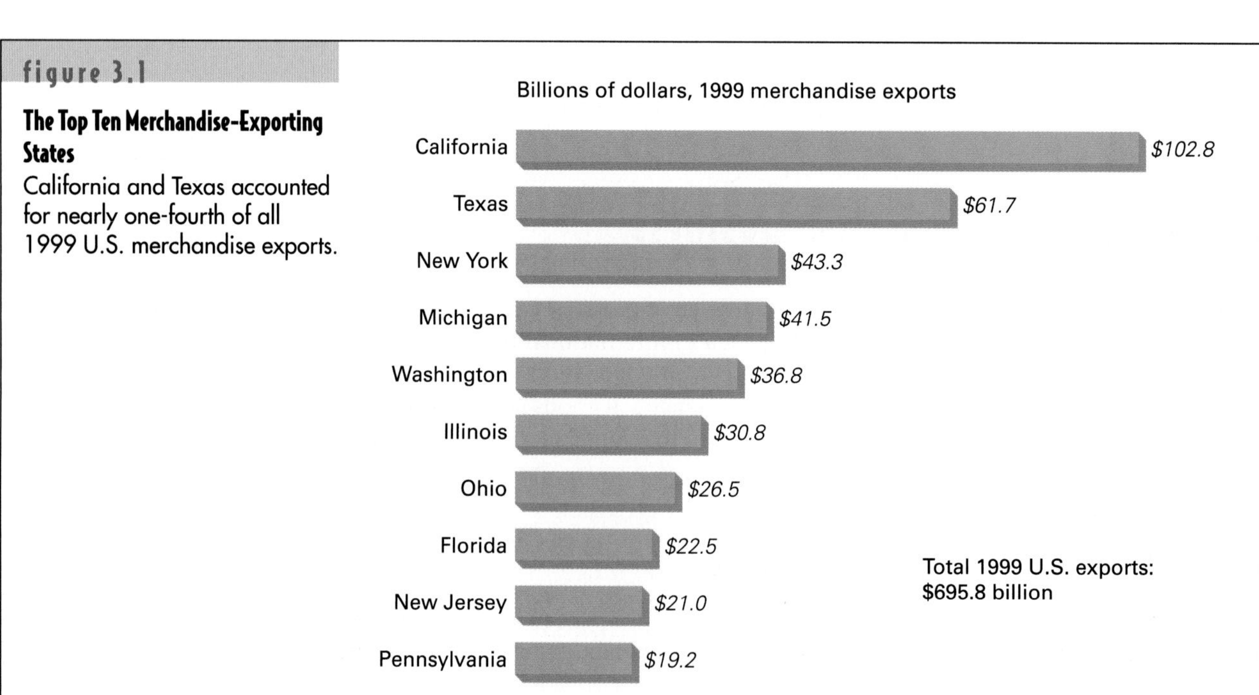

figure 3.1

The Top Ten Merchandise-Exporting States

California and Texas accounted for nearly one-fourth of all 1999 U.S. merchandise exports.

Source: **www.ita.gov**, accessed January 4, 2003.

Exporting and Importing

Suppose that the United States specializes in producing corn. It will then produce a surplus of corn, but perhaps it will have a shortage of wine. France, on the other hand, specializes in producing wine but experiences a shortage of corn. To satisfy both needs—for corn and for wine—the two countries should trade with each other. The United States should export corn and import wine. France should export wine and import corn.

Exporting is selling and shipping raw materials or products to other nations. The Boeing Company, for example, exports its airplanes to a number of countries for use by their airlines. Figure 3.1 (on the facing page) shows the top ten merchandise-exporting states in this country.

exporting selling and shipping raw materials or products to other nations

Importing is purchasing raw materials or products in other nations and bringing them into one's own country. Thus buyers for Macy's department stores may purchase rugs in India or raincoats in England and have them shipped back to the United States for resale.

importing purchasing raw materials or products in other nations and bringing them into one's own country

Importing and exporting are the principal activities in international trade. They give rise to an important concept called the *balance of trade.* A nation's **balance of trade** is the total value of its exports *minus* the total value of its imports over some period of time. If a country imports more than it exports, its balance of trade is negative and is said to be *unfavorable.* (A negative balance of trade is unfavorable because the country must export money to pay for its excess imports.) In 2001 the United States imported $1,146 billion worth of merchandise and exported $719 billion worth. It thus had a trade deficit of $427 billion. A **trade deficit** is a negative balance of trade (see Figure 3.2). However, as shown in Figure 3.3 (on p. 72), the United States has

balance of trade the total value of a nation's exports minus the total value of its imports over some period of time

trade deficit a negative balance of trade

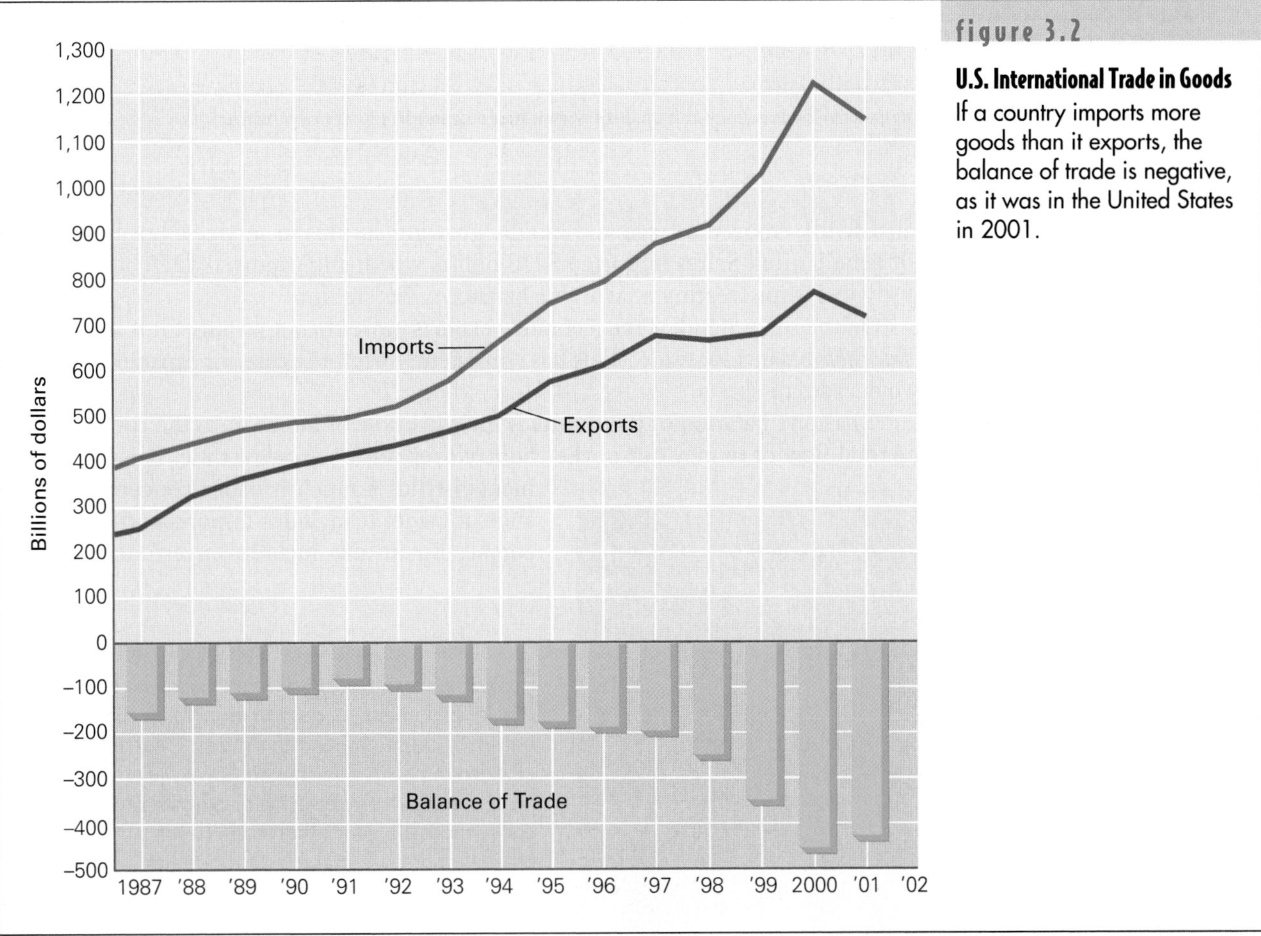

figure 3.2

U.S. International Trade in Goods

If a country imports more goods than it exports, the balance of trade is negative, as it was in the United States in 2001.

Source: U.S. Department of Commerce, International Trade Administration, **http://www.ita.doc.gov/td/industry/otea/usfth/aggregate/H99t01.txt,** accessed December 20, 2002.

figure 3.3

U.S. International Trade in Goods and Services and the Combined Balance

Even though the United States has a positive balance of trade in services, the combined effect is still a deficit in our balance of trade.

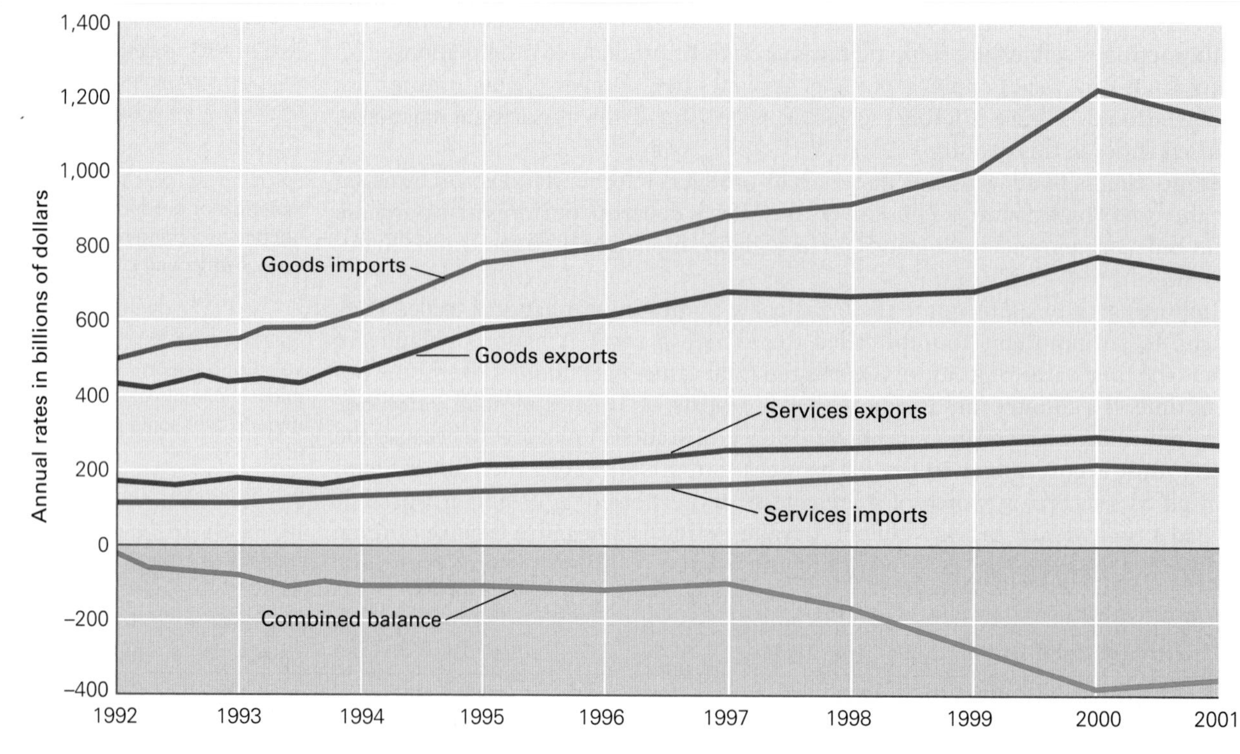

Source: U.S. Department of Commerce, International Trade Administration, **http://www.ita.doc.gov/td/industry/otea/usfth/aggregate/H99t02.txt,** accessed January 3, 2003.

consistently enjoyed a large and rapidly growing surplus in services. For example, in 2001 the United States imported $210 billion worth and exported $279 billion worth of services, thus creating a favorable balance of $69 billion.[5]

On the other hand, when a country exports more than it imports, it is said to have a *favorable* balance of trade. This has consistently been the case for Japan over the last two decades or so.

balance of payments the total flow of money into the country minus the total flow of money out of the country over some period of time

A nation's **balance of payments** is the total flow of money into the country *minus* the total flow of money out of the country over some period of time. Balance of payments is thus a much broader concept than balance of trade. It includes imports and exports, of course. But it also includes investments, money

Exploiting absolute advantage. Brazil has long specialized in the production of arabica coffee beans. Because of their natural resource, Brazil and other countries in Central and South America enjoy an absolute advantage—their ability to produce coffee more efficiently than countries in other parts of the world. Here in the Cerrado region in central Brazil, a farmer is growing high-quality arabica coffee plants under a canopy in a coffee nursery.

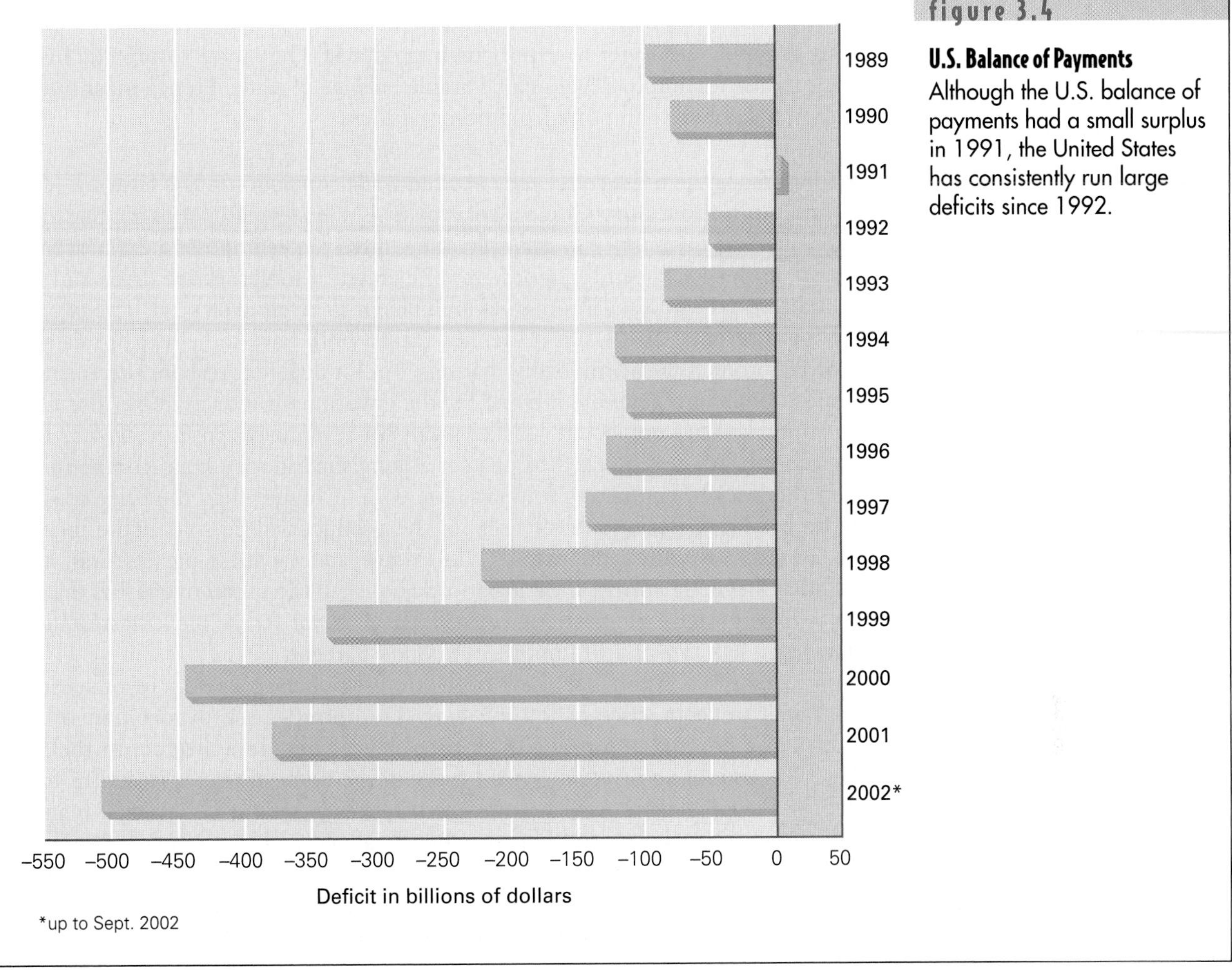

figure 3.4

U.S. Balance of Payments

Although the U.S. balance of payments had a small surplus in 1991, the United States has consistently run large deficits since 1992.

Source: U.S. Department of Commerce, Bureau of Economic Analysis, **http://www.bea.doc.gov/bea/di/bopa/bop1–2.htm**, accessed December 13, 2002.

spent by foreign tourists, payments by foreign governments, aid to foreign governments, and all other receipts and payments.

A continual deficit in a nation's balance of payments (a negative balance) can cause other nations to lose confidence in its economy. A continual surplus may indicate that the country encourages exports but limits imports by imposing trade restrictions. As Figure 3.4 shows, the United States has consistently suffered a deficit in its balance of payments since 1992. A bright spot for the U.S. global trade position is the stellar growth of worldwide Internet commerce, projected to reach $6.8 trillion in 2004 according to Forrester Research, Inc. Although North America currently represents the vast majority of activity, Asian-Pacific and western European countries are expected to make great strides in the race to catch up over the next few years.[6]

Restrictions to International Business

learning objective

2 Discuss the restrictions nations place on international trade, the objectives of these restrictions, and their results.

Specialization and international trade can result in the efficient production of want-satisfying goods and services on a worldwide basis. As we have noted, international business generally is increasing. Yet the nations of the world continue to erect barriers to free trade. They do so for reasons ranging from internal political and economic pressures to simple mistrust of other nations. We examine first the types of restrictions that are applied and then the arguments for and against trade restrictions.

Types of Trade Restrictions

Nations generally are eager to export their products. They want to provide markets for their industries and to develop a favorable balance of trade. Hence most trade restrictions are applied to imports from other nations.

import duty (tariff) a tax levied on a particular foreign product entering a country

Tariffs

Perhaps the most commonly applied trade restriction is the customs (or import) duty. An **import duty** (also called a **tariff**) is a tax levied on a particular foreign product entering a country. For example, the United States imposes a 2.2 percent import duty on fresh Chilean tomatoes, an 8.7 percent if tomatoes are dried and packaged, and nearly 12 percent if tomatoes are made into ketchup or salsa. The two types of tariffs are revenue tariffs and protective tariffs; both have the effect of raising the price of the product in the importing nations, but for different reasons. *Revenue tariffs* are imposed solely to generate income for the government. For example, the United States imposes a duty on Scotch whiskey solely for revenue purposes. *Protective tariffs*, on the other hand, are imposed to protect a domestic industry from competition by keeping the price of competing imports level with or higher than the price of similar domestic products. Because fewer units of the product will be sold at the increased price, fewer units will be imported. The French and Japanese agricultural sectors would both shrink drastically if their nations abolished the protective tariffs that keep the price of imported farm products high. Today U.S. tariffs are the lowest in history, with average tariff rates on all imports of under 4 percent.

dumping exportation of large quantities of a product at a price lower than that of the same product in the home market

Some countries rationalize their protectionist policies as a way of offsetting an international trade practice called *dumping*. **Dumping** is the exportation of large quantities of a product at a price lower than that of the same product in the home market. Thus dumping drives down the price of the domestic item. Recently, for example, the Pencil Makers Association, which represents eight U.S. pencil manufacturers, charged that low-priced pencils from Thailand and the People's Republic of China were being sold in the United States at less than fair value prices. Unable to compete with these inexpensive imports, several domestic manufacturers had to shut down. To protect themselves, domestic manufacturers can obtain an antidumping duty through the government to offset the advantage of the foreign product. Recently, for example, the U.S. Department of Commerce imposed preliminary antidumping duties on carbon steel products from the United Kingdom and hot-rolled steel products from Japan. Likewise, the European Union imposes antidumping duties on imports of cotton bed linens from India. In fact, during the first six months of 2002, seventeen nations had initiated 104 antidumping investigations against exports from a total of thirty-nine different countries.[7] According to Robert E. Litan, director of economic studies at the Brookings Institution, "Most economists think the antidumping laws are completely nuts, but I suspect that very few lawmakers even understand how they work. And now, the developing world is picking up on our bad example."[8]

nontariff barrier a nontax measure imposed by a government to favor domestic over foreign suppliers

Nontariff Barriers

A **nontariff barrier** is a nontax measure imposed by a government to favor domestic over foreign suppliers. Nontariff barriers create obstacles to the marketing of foreign goods in a country and increase costs for exporters. The following are a few examples of government-imposed nontariff barriers:

import quota a limit on the amount of a particular good that may be imported into a country during a given period of time

- An **import quota** is a limit on the amount of a particular good that may be imported into a country during a given period of time. The limit may be set in terms of either quantity (so many pounds of beef) or value (so many dollars' worth of shoes). Quotas also may be set on individual products imported from specific countries. Once an import quota has been reached, imports are halted until the specified time has elapsed.

embargo a complete halt to trading with a particular nation or in a particular product

- An **embargo** is a complete halt to trading with a particular nation or in a particular product. The embargo is used most often as a political weapon. At present, the United States has import embargoes against Cuba and North Korea—both as a result of extremely poor political relations.

adapting to change

South African Airways Navigates Nontariff Barriers

HOW CAN AN AIRLINE KEEP FLYING high in the face of restrictive government agreements and unpredictable currency fluctuations? These are key challenges confronting South African Airways (SAA), based in Johannesburg. Already a market leader serving twenty cities in the south of Africa—as well as twelve cities outside the continent—the airline is eager to satisfy the growing demand for reliable, regularly scheduled flights by establishing regional hubs to serve Nigeria, Angola, and other African nations.

However, long-term agreements between the governments currently restrict the number of weekly flights that each carrier could fly between certain countries. For instance, SAA is limited to just three weekly flights between Johannesburg, South Africa, and Luanda, Angola. Its Angolan-based competitor, TAAG, must operate under the same restrictions. Although SAA is eager to expand by offering daily flights to Luanda, Angolan officials have not approved the change out of concern for the effect that the increased competition would have on TAAG.

Despite an understanding among African nations to deregulate the airline industry starting in 1999, years have passed without significant change. One SAA executive recently lamented, "Until that gets implemented, growth opportunities will be much slower than they need to be." Soon an economic development initiative promoted by South Africa, Senegal, Algeria, and Nigeria may lower the barriers and allow SAA and other airlines to spread their wings over a broader area.

Because it crosses national borders, SAA also must address currency fluctuations. During one recent year, SAA based its financial projections on the value of 8 rand to $1. As the months went by, however, the foreign-exchange value changed until $1 was worth 11 rand. This was not a problem for SAA flights within South Africa, where tickets are priced in rand. However, tickets for pan-African flights—the most profitable routes—are priced in U.S. dollars, so the change hurt the company's bottom line. In response, management created several plans for shoring up finances in case the rand falls further, including cutting costs that are pegged to the dollar. Remaining ready to adapt to changes in governmental agreements and unpredictable currency fluctuations has helped SAA stay aloft while competitors struggle.

- A **foreign-exchange control** is a restriction on the amount of a particular foreign currency that can be purchased or sold. By limiting the amount of foreign currency importers can obtain, a government limits the amount of goods importers can purchase with that currency. This has the effect of limiting imports from the country whose foreign exchange is being controlled.

foreign-exchange control a restriction on the amount of a particular foreign currency that can be purchased or sold

- A nation can increase or decrease the value of its money relative to the currency of other nations. **Currency devaluation** is the reduction of the value of a nation's currency relative to the currencies of other countries.

  Devaluation increases the cost of foreign goods, while it decreases the cost of domestic goods to foreign firms. For example, suppose that the British pound is worth $2. Then an American-made $2,000 computer can be purchased for £1,000. However, if the United Kingdom devalues the pound so that it is worth only $1, that same computer will cost £2,000. The increased cost, in pounds, will reduce the import of American computers—and all foreign goods—into England.

  On the other hand, before devaluation, a £500 set of English bone china costs an American $1,000. After the devaluation, the set of china will cost only $500. The decreased cost will make the china—and all English goods—much more attractive to U.S. purchasers.

currency devaluation the reduction of the value of a nation's currency relative to the currencies of other countries

- Bureaucratic red tape is more subtle than the other forms of nontariff barriers. Yet it can be the most frustrating trade barrier of all. A few examples are unnecessarily restrictive application of standards and complex requirements related to product testing, labeling, and certification.

Another type of nontariff barrier is related to cultural attitudes. Cultural barriers can impede acceptance of products in foreign countries. For example, illustrations of feet are regarded as despicable in Thailand. When customers are unfamiliar with particular products from another country, their general perceptions of the country itself affect their attitude toward the product and help determine whether they will buy it. Because Mexican cars have not been viewed by the world as being quality products, Volkswagen, for example, may not want to advertise that some of its models sold in the United States are made in Mexico. Many retailers on the Internet have yet to come to grips with the task of designing an online shopping site that is attractive and functional for all global customers. According to a study by Forrester Research, 46 percent of all orders to U.S.-based sites placed by people living outside the United States went unfilled due to process failures. Given that the Forrester study suggests that the average website gets 30 percent of its traffic and 10 percent of its orders from non-U.S. customers, the results suggest that an enormous loss of potential export sales will continue until websites better reflect local buyer culture and behavior.[9]

Reasons for Trade Restrictions

Various reasons are advanced for trade restrictions either on the import of specific products or on trade with particular countries. We have noted that political considerations usually are involved in trade embargoes. Other frequently cited reasons for restricting trade include the following:

- *To equalize a nation's balance of payments.* This may be considered necessary to restore confidence in the country's monetary system and in its ability to repay its debts.
- *To protect new or weak industries.* A new, or *infant*, industry may not be strong enough to withstand foreign competition. Temporary trade restrictions may be used to give it a chance to grow and become self-sufficient. The problem is that once an industry is protected from foreign competition, it may refuse to grow, and "temporary" trade restrictions will become permanent. For example, a recent report by the General Accounting Office (GAO), the congressional investigative agency, has accused the federal government of routinely imposing quotas on foreign textiles without "demonstrating the threat of serious damage" to U.S. industry. The GAO said that the Committee for the Implementation of Textile Agreements sometimes applies quotas even though it cannot prove the textile industry's claims that American companies have been hurt or jobs eliminated.
- *To protect national security.* Restrictions in this category generally apply to technological products that must be kept out of the hands of potential enemies. For example, strategic and defense-related goods cannot be exported to unfriendly nations.

Protecting the life and health of citizens. The September 11, 2001 terrorist attacks changed the priorities of the Bureau of Customs and Border Protection (formerly the Customs Service). Before September 11 the Bureau's main purpose was to slow the flow of illegal drugs into the United States. Now the Bureau's main mission is to stop potential terrorist weapons from being smuggled into the country. The U.S. Customs officers at customs checkpoints, such as this Red Hook cargo terminal in Brooklyn, use the latest high-tech tools to fend off terrorism.

- *To protect the health of citizens.* Products may be embargoed because they are dangerous or unhealthy (for example, farm products contaminated with insecticides).
- *To retaliate for another nation's trade restrictions.* A country whose exports are taxed by another country may respond by imposing tariffs on imports from that country.
- *To protect domestic jobs.* By restricting imports, a nation can protect jobs in domestic industries. However, protecting these jobs can be expensive. For example, U.S. consumers spend about $25 billion a year to protect jobs in the textile and apparel industry—about $50,000 annually

per job.[10] And to protect 9,000 jobs in the U.S. carbon steel industry costs $6.8 billion, or $750,000 per job. In addition, Gary Hufbauer and Ben Goodrich, economists at the Institute for International Economics, estimate that the tariffs could temporarily save 3,500 jobs in the steel industry, but at an annual cost to steel users of $2 billion, or $584,000 per job saved. Yet recently the United States imposed tariffs of up to 30 percent on steel imported from Brazil, China, Japan, Russia, and the European Union.[11]

Reasons Against Trade Restrictions

Trade restrictions have immediate and long-term economic consequences—both within the restricting nation and in world trade patterns. These include

- *Higher prices for consumers.* Higher prices may result from the imposition of tariffs or the elimination of foreign competition, as described earlier. For example, imposing quota restrictions and import protections adds $25 billion annually to U.S. consumers' apparel costs by directly increasing costs for imported apparel.
- *Restriction of consumers' choices.* Again, this is a direct result of the elimination of some foreign products from the marketplace and of the artificially high prices that importers must charge for products that *are* still imported.
- *Misallocation of international resources.* The protection of weak industries results in the inefficient use of limited resources. The economies of both the restricting nation and other nations eventually suffer because of this waste.
- *Loss of jobs.* The restriction of imports by one nation must lead to cutbacks—and the loss of jobs—in the export-oriented industries of other nations. Furthermore, trade protection has a significant effect on the composition of employment. U.S. trade restrictions—whether on textiles, apparel, steel, or automobiles—benefit only a few industries while harming many others. The gains in employment accrue to the protected industries and their primary suppliers, and the losses are spread across all other industries. A few states gain employment, but many other states lose employment.

The Extent of International Business

Restrictions or not, international business is growing. Although the worldwide recessions of 1991 and 2001–2002 slowed the rate of growth, globalization is a reality of our time. Since the end of World War II, the proportion of trade as a share of global income has risen from 7 to 21 percent. In the United States, international trade now accounts for over one-fourth of gross domestic product (GDP). As trade barriers decrease, new competitors enter the global marketplace, creating more choices for consumers and new opportunities for job seekers. International business will grow along with the expansion of commercial use of the Internet.

learning objective

3 Outline the extent of international trade and identify the organizations working to foster it.

The World Economic Outlook for Trade

While the U.S. economy had been growing steadily until 2000 and recorded the longest peacetime expansion in the nation's history, the worldwide recession in 2001–2002 has slowed the rate of growth. This weakness of economies at home and overseas is the major reason behind the growth of our trade deficit in the last eight years. While the global economic recovery gradually continues, it will be weaker than earlier expected. International experts expected global economic growth of 3.5 percent in 2003 and 3.4 percent in 2004.[12] At this rate of growth, world production of goods and services will double by the year 2025. Figure 3.5 (on p. 78) shows the growth rate of world real GDP since 1970.

figure 3.5

Growth of World Real GDP Since 1970

Even though the economies of some of our major trading partners have been weak, with the new market-oriented economies in eastern Europe and Asia, the global economy is expected to grow at about 3 percent annually.

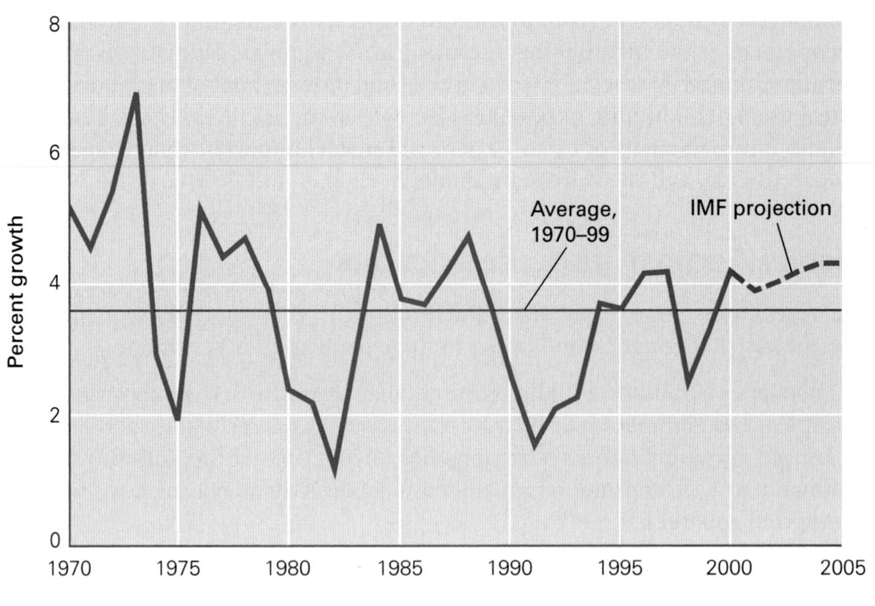

Source: From *The World Economic Outlook: The International Monetary Fund.* Reprinted with permission from the International Monetary Fund.

Perhaps even more impressive is that inflation has been falling in almost every major region of the world. For example, in South America, the declines have been spectacular. The International Monetary Fund (IMF), an international bank with more than 184 member nations, estimates that inflation rates in the developed industrial countries have fallen from 4.3 percent in 1991 to an estimated 1.7 percent in 2003. In the developing economies, the inflation slowdown has been even greater, from about 13 percent per year in 1991 to about 6 percent in 2003. Hence a favorable economic outlook for trade exists in the new millennium (see Figure 3.6).

figure 3.6

Annual Inflation Rates in Developing and Advanced Economies*

Inflation rate has been falling in almost every major region of the world and is expected to remain low in the near future.

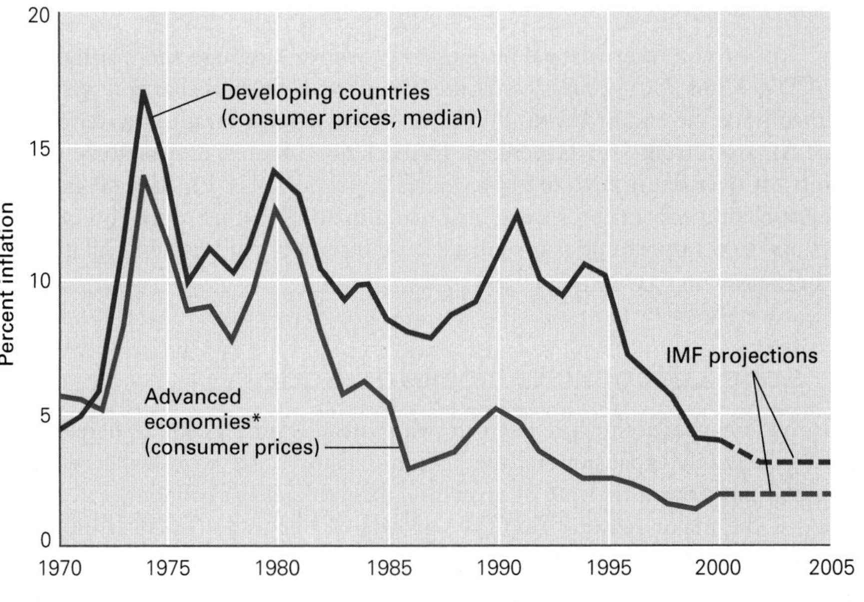

*Advanced economies include the United States, Japan, Germany, France, Italy, United Kingdom, and Canada. Developing economies include most countries in Africa, Asia, the Middle East, and South America.

Source: From *The World Economic Outlook: The International Monetary Fund.* Reprinted with permission from the International Monetary Fund.

Canada and Western Europe Our leading export-import partner, Canada, is projected to show the fastest growth. The inflation rate in Canada is about half the U.S. rate, and our exports to Canada are booming. However, economies in western Europe have been growing slowly. Only the United Kingdom enjoyed 1.9 percent economic growth in 2002 with the lowest level of unemployment in 20 years; the economies of Germany, Greece, Denmark, Switzerland, and Italy all grew less than 1.5 percent. Recent growth in Austria, Belgium, the Netherlands, and Portugal has been slow, whereas growth in Greece, Ireland and Spain has been stronger.

Mexico and South America Our second largest export-import partner, Mexico, suffered its sharpest recession ever in 1995, but its growth rate in 2003 was about 4.0 percent. In general, however, the Latin American economies declined more rapidly in 2002 than in the preceding two years. The economies of Argentina, Uruguay, Paraguay, Brazil, Venezuela, Ecuador, Peru, and a few other countries in that region have been sluggish due to political, economic, and financial market problems. A growth of about 3.0 percent is projected for the region.

Japan The recovery of the Japanese economy from three major recessions in a decade remains weak. After falling in 1997 and 1998, real GDP increased during the first half of 1999, but it declined by 4.0 percent again during the second half of the year. A growth of only 1 percent for 2003 and 1.6 percent for 2004 was projected.

Asia The economic recovery in Asia increased significantly in 2002. For example, in Korea and India, the GDP increased 6.3 and 5.0 percent, respectively. Even in the hardest-hit economies in the region, Singapore and Taiwan Province of China, the recovery continued in 2003. Growth in Korea is expected to moderate somewhat to about 5.9 percent and is expected to be between 4 and 5 percent in Singapore, Taiwan

going global

Yu-Gi-Oh Moves Beyond Japan

ALTHOUGH THE POKÉMON FAD HAS FADED, sales of trading cards and related products remain strong in Japan and in other countries. Just ask Konami, the Tokyo-based company seeking a larger share of the $300 million U.S. market for trading cards. Konami makes Yu-Gi-Oh (translation: "Game King") trading cards, which are based on a game featured in a successful Japanese comic book series. Whereas Pokémon players try to collect many different cards, Yu-Gi-Oh players use each card's unique power to design elaborate attack strategies.

At the peak of the Yu-Gi-Oh craze in Japan, Konami enjoyed profit margins exceeding 50 percent on sales of $500 million. The company released 2,000 cards over three years and widened the range of products under the Yu-Gi-Oh brand to include video games, television shows, clothing, and accessories. Promoting regional tournaments helped Konami boost the game's popularity and highlight the game's complexities, one of its appeals to boys aged 8 to 14.

The company changed Yu-Gi-Oh in a number of ways to suit the U.S. market. In addition to translating the text on each card, the company toned down the violence, eliminated nudity, and removed religious references. It selected Upper Deck—which has experience in marketing baseball cards—as its U.S. distributor and introduced the first of its trading cards just as interest in Pokémon began to flag. Airing an English-language version of the Yu-Gi-Oh television show on Kids WB further fueled demand. Within a few months, Yu-Gi-Oh replaced Pokémon as the top-selling card brand in many U.S. stores. Then sales surged higher after the Japanese publisher of the original comic book series launched a U.S. version.

To maintain momentum and prevent U.S. sales from falling off too quickly, Konami is working with Upper Deck to release a limited number of selected cards at regular intervals. At the same time, the company is expanding its international reach to spread Yu-Gi-Oh fever to Great Britain and other countries. If all goes well, Konami will be selling Yu-Gi-Oh products in many markets by the time the brand becomes old news in the United States.

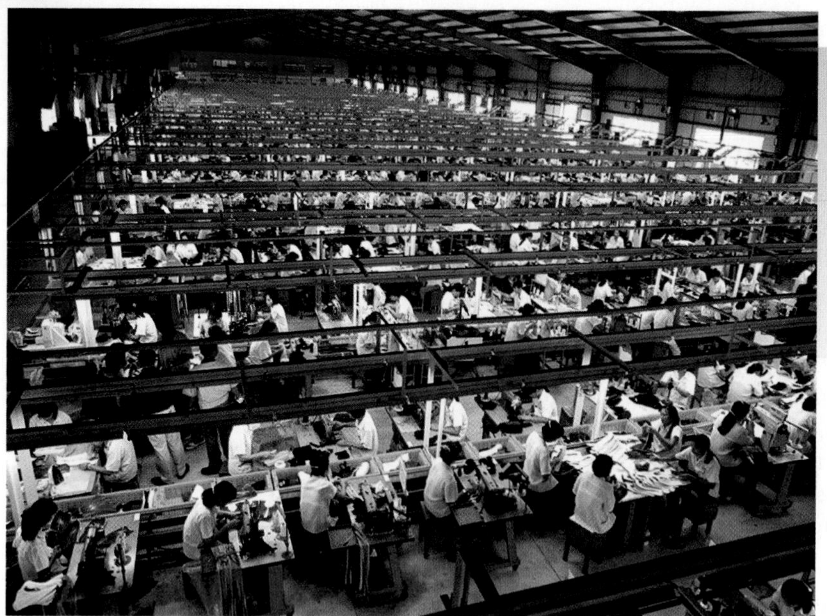

These shoes are made for walking. Nike's contractors and subcontractors are making Nike footwear at 68 factories in 12 countries including Taiwan, Korea, Indonesia, Thailand, mainland China, and Vietnam. According to Nike the company ensures that contractors' factories, like this one in Vietnam, comply with the firm's code of conduct.

Province of China, Indonesia, and Malaysia, whereas the economies of the Philippines and Thailand are projected to strengthen by 3 to 4 percent respectively.

Growing at an annual rate of 7.5 percent in 2002, the Chinese economy is by far the largest of the emerging Asian markets. China's inflation fell from an estimated 10 percent in 1996 to less than 1 percent in 2002: however, prices may increase marginally in 2003. Although inflation is down and economic growth continues, China faces several challenges. Perhaps the biggest will be tackling the inefficiency of China's state-owned enterprises. For example, Chinese oil giant SINOPEC requires 937,000 employees to generate $40 billion in revenues, whereas Exxon's 97,900 employees bring in $192 billion.[13] Many of these enterprises lose money every year, and reforming them will be politically difficult. Unemployment and underemployment are major problems in China, and state-run businesses employ millions. However, China's membership in the World Trade Organization is likely to add momentum to the structural reforms.

The two giant economies on the South Asian subcontinent, India and Pakistan, are expected to grow about 5.7 and 5 percent, respectively, in 2003. Economic growth in Australia and New Zealand is expected to be less than 4 percent.

Central and Eastern Europe and Russia After World War II, trade between the United States and the communist nations of central and eastern Europe was minimal. The United States maintained high tariff barriers on imports from most of these countries and also restricted its exports. However, since the disintegration of the Soviet Union and the collapse of communism, trade between the United States and central and eastern Europe has expanded substantially.

The countries that made the transition from communist to market economies quickly have recorded positive growth for several years—those that did not continue to struggle. Among the nations that have enjoyed several years of positive economic growth are the member countries of the Central European Free Trade Association (CEFTA): Hungary, the Czech Republic, Poland, Slovenia, and the Republic of Slovakia. An average growth of 3.3 percent is projected for this region.

Russia has been one of the countries whose transition to a market economy has been difficult. However, Russia's economic performance in 2002 was much better than expected. For example, GDP increased by 4.4 percent rather than remaining flat, and inflation was lower than anticipated. The reform efforts in Russia and most other countries of the former Soviet Union continue to lag behind schedule. In Ukraine and Belarus, economic growth remains slow, 4.8 and 3.5 percent, respectively, whereas in Kazakhstan the economy is growing at about 8 percent per year.

In central Europe and the Baltics, the economy is expanding. In Poland and Hungary, GDP is growing between 3 and 4 percent annually. Economies in the Slovak

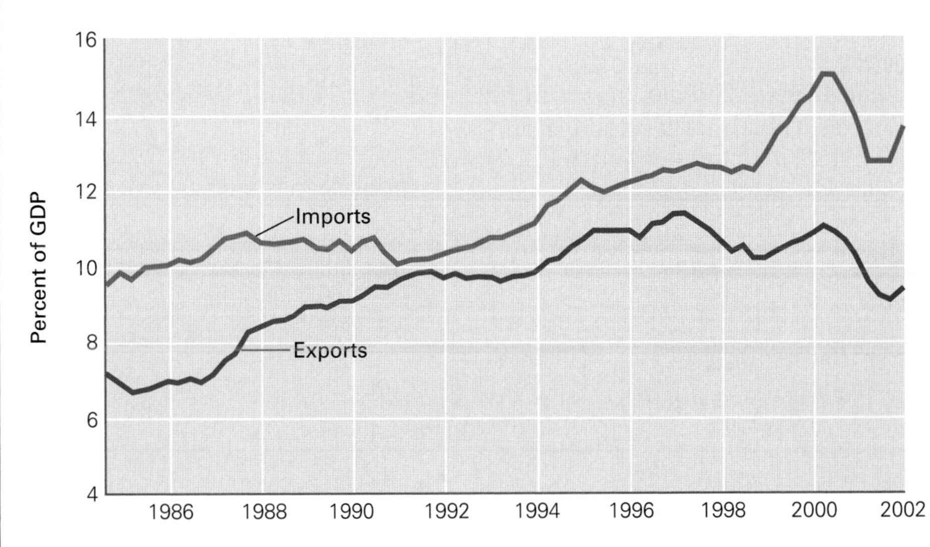

figure 3.7

Exports and Imports as Percentage of GDP

Exports as a percentage of U.S. GDP have increased from less than 7 percent in 1985 to about 10 percent today.

Source: *International Economic Trends*, The Federal Reserve Bank of St. Louis, November 2002, p. 80.

Republic, Estonia, Latvia, and Lithuania are expected to recover quite rapidly, 5 to 6 percent, in 2003.

U.S. exports to central and eastern Europe and Russia will increase, as will U.S. investment in these countries, as demand for capital goods and technology opens new markets for U.S. products. There already has been a substantial expansion in trade between the United States and the Czech Republic, the Slovak Federal Republic, Hungary, and Poland.

Exports and the U.S. Economy Globalization represents a huge opportunity for all countries—rich or poor. The fifteen-fold increase in trade volume over the past forty-five years has been one of the most important factors in the rise of living standards around the world. During this time, exports have become increasingly important to the U.S. economy. As Figure 3.7 shows, exports as a percentage of U.S. GDP have increased steadily since 1985, except in the 2001 recession. And our exports to developing and newly industrialized countries are on the rise. Table 3.1 shows the

table 3.1 Value of U.S. Merchandise Exports and Imports, 2001

Rank/Trading Partner	Exports ($ billions)	Rank/Trading Partner	Imports ($ billions)
1 Canada	163.4	1 Canada	216.3
2 Mexico	101.3	2 Mexico	131.3
3 Japan	57.5	3 Japan	126.5
4 United Kingdom	40.7	4 China	102.3
5 Germany	30.0	5 Germany	59.1
6 South Korea	22.2	6 United Kingdom	41.4
7 France	19.9	7 South Korea	35.2
8 Netherlands	19.5	8 Taiwan	33.4
9 China	19.2	9 France	30.4
10 Taiwan	18.1	10 Italy	23.8

Source: U.S. Department of Commerce, International Trade Administration, **http://www.ita.doc.gov/td/industry/otea/usfth/aggregate/H01T10.html,** August 12, 2002.

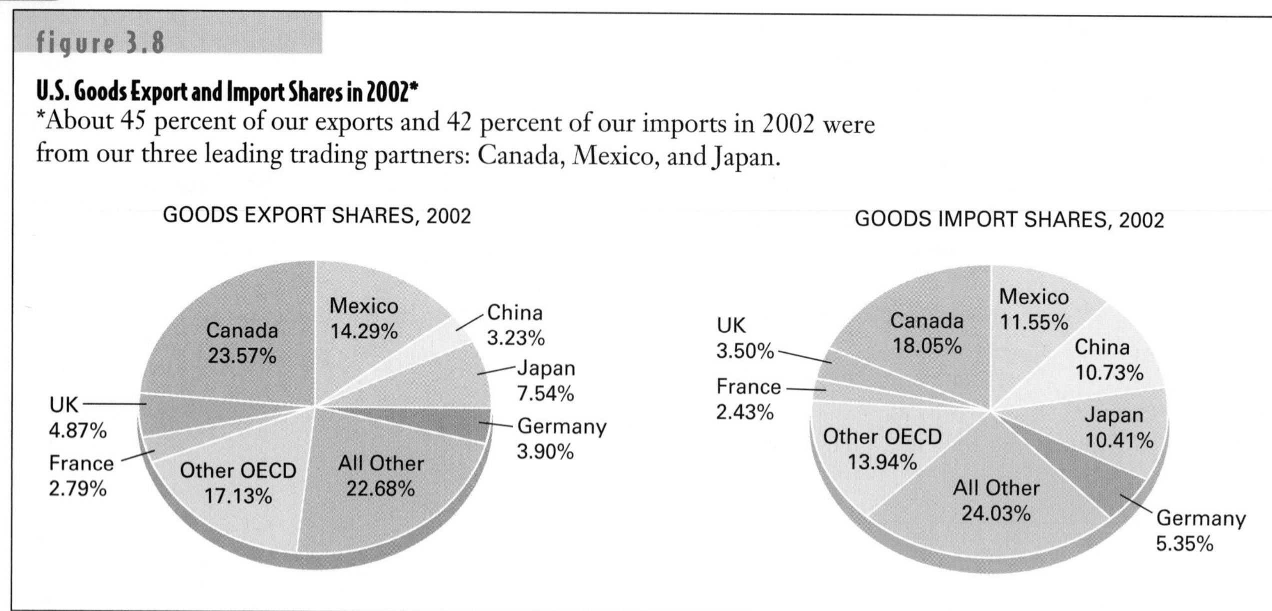

figure 3.8

U.S. Goods Export and Import Shares in 2002*

*About 45 percent of our exports and 42 percent of our imports in 2002 were from our three leading trading partners: Canada, Mexico, and Japan.

Source: The Federal Reserve Bank of St. Louis, *National Economic Trends*, February 2003, p. 18.

value of U.S. merchandise exports to and imports from each of the nation's ten major trading partners. Note that Canada and Mexico are our best partners for our exports and imports. Figure 3.8 shows the U.S. goods export and import shares in 2001. Major U.S. exports and imports are manufactured goods, agricultural products, and mineral fuels. Note again that approximately 46 percent of our exports and 43 percent of our imports were from the same three leading trading partners.

Many more U.S. firms need to take advantage of the almost limitless potential in exporting. At present, only one-third of all U.S. companies export. About fifty of these companies account for more than 40 percent of the country's exports. No industrial nation has greater potential for export expansion than the United States, and a mere 15 percent growth in export sales would put one million Americans to work.

The General Agreement on Tariffs and Trade and the World Trade Organization

General Agreement on Tariffs and Trade (GATT) an international organization of 132 nations dedicated to reducing or eliminating tariffs and other barriers to world trade

At the end of World War II, the United States and twenty-two other nations organized the body that came to be known as *GATT.* **The General Agreement on Tariffs and Trade (GATT)** was an international organization of 132 nations dedicated to reducing or eliminating tariffs and other barriers to world trade. These 132 nations accounted for 90 percent of the world's merchandise trade. GATT, headquartered in Geneva, Switzerland, provided a forum for tariff negotiations and a means for settling international trade disputes and problems. *Most-favored-nation status* (MFN) was the famous principle of GATT. It meant that each GATT member nation was to be treated equally by all contracting nations. MFN therefore ensured that any tariff reductions or other trade concessions were extended automatically to all GATT members. From 1947 to 1994, the body sponsored eight rounds of negotiations to reduce trade restrictions. Three of the most fruitful were the Kennedy Round, the Tokyo Round, and the Uruguay Round.

The Kennedy Round (1964–1967) In 1962 the U.S. Congress passed the Trade Expansion Act. This law gave President John F. Kennedy the authority to negotiate reciprocal trade agreements that could reduce U.S. tariffs by as much as 50 percent. Armed with this authority, which was granted for a period of five years, President Kennedy called for a round of negotiations through GATT.

These negotiations, which began in 1964, have since become known as the *Kennedy Round.* They were aimed at reducing tariffs and other barriers to trade in both industrial and agricultural products. The participants succeeded in reducing tariffs on these products by an average of more than 35 percent. They were less successful in removing other types of trade barriers.

Spotlight

The best and worst international partners?

Every year Transparency International conducts research to create the Corruption Perceptions Index.

10 = highly clean
0 = highly corrupt

Rank	Country	Score
1	Finland	9.7
2 (tie)	Denmark	9.5
2 (tie)	New Zealand	9.5
16	U.S.	7.7
101	Nigeria	1.6
102	Bangladesh	1.2

Source: Transparency International, 2002 Corruption Perceptions Index.

The Tokyo Round (1973–1979) In 1973 representatives of approximately one hundred nations gathered in Tokyo for another round of GATT negotiations. The *Tokyo Round* was completed in 1979. The participants negotiated tariff cuts of 30 to 35 percent, which were to be implemented over an eight-year period. In addition, they were able to remove or ease such nontariff barriers as import quotas, unrealistic quality standards for imports, and unnecessary red tape in customs procedures.

The Uruguay Round (1986–1993) In 1986 the *Uruguay Round* was launched to extend trade liberalization and to widen the GATT treaty to include textiles, agricultural products, business services, and intellectual-property rights. This most ambitious and comprehensive global commercial agreement in history concluded overall negotiations on December 15, 1993, with delegations on hand from 109 nations. Calling the 22,000-page agreement "truly momentous," U.S. Vice President Albert Gore said it will "bring the global trading system into the twenty-first century." Gore noted that in developed countries alone, the agreement could raise GDP as much as 3.5 percent in the coming decade. The agreement included provisions to lower tariffs by greater than one-third, to reform trade in agricultural goods, to write new rules of trade for intellectual property and services, and to strengthen the dispute-settlement process. These reforms were expected to expand the world economy by an estimated $200 billion annually.

The Uruguay Round also created the **World Trade Organization (WTO)** on January 1, 1995. The WTO was established by GATT to oversee the provisions of the Uruguay Round and resolve any resulting trade disputes. Membership of the WTO obliges 144 member nations to observe GATT rules. The WTO has judicial powers to mediate among members disputing the new rules. It incorporates trade in goods, services, and ideas and exerts more binding authority than GATT.

World Trade Organization (WTO) powerful successor to GATT that incorporates trade in goods, services, and ideas

The Doha Round (2001) On November 14, 2001 in Doha, Qatar, the WTO members agreed to further reduce trade barriers through multilateral trade negotiations over the next three years. This new round of negotiations will focus on industrial tariff and nontariff barriers, agriculture, services, and easing trade rules. U.S. exporters of industrial and agricultural goods and services should have improved access to overseas markets. The Doha Round has set the stage for WTO members to take an important step toward significant new multilateral trade liberalization. It is a difficult task, but the rewards—lower tariffs, more choices for consumers, and further integration of developing countries into the world trading system—are sure to be worth the effort.[14]

International Economic Communities

The primary objective of the WTO is to remove barriers to trade on a worldwide basis. On a smaller scale, an **economic community** is an organization of nations formed to promote the free movement of resources and products among its members

economic community an organization of nations formed to promote the free movement of resources and products among its members and to create common economic policies

examining ethics

Getting China to Crack Down on Counterfeits

Now that China is a WTO member, multinational companies are pushing for a crackdown on counterfeit products made in backstreet factories. Well-known companies such as Yamaha, Gillette, Shure, Levi Strauss, and Prada complain that Chinese counterfeiters are illegally copying their products right down to the packaging and product manuals. By Yamaha's estimate, as many as five of every six of its motorcycles in China are fake. Among Gillette's international brands, counterfeit Duracell batteries made in China are being sold in the United States, whereas bogus Sputnik razor blades made in China are being sold in Russia.

"They copy our packaging," notes the president of Shure, which makes microphones and related products. "They even copy the warranty return card to the letter. That's how blatant they are." Of course, buyers would have to be quite sophisticated to discern the difference between fake and real products by looks alone. "The counterfeiters or knockoff artists do a great job physically but a lousy job on the electronics. The product looks great but performs horribly," the Shure executive says. To stem the rising tide of fakes, the company has hired investigators to track pirated goods to their source. Not long ago, Shure worked with Chinese authorities to grab thousands of counterfeit microphones made in Shenzhen before they were sent to market in Russia and India. "We'll take our last penny and put it in this direction," Shure's president declares.

China has stated that it will quash counterfeiting, and it significantly increased the fines for convicted counterfeiters. Still, the international Agreement on Trade-Related Aspects of Intellectual Property, which governs such activities, is somewhat vague about what countries must do to deter fakes. Moreover, although local Chinese officials take action when multinational companies pay "case-handling fees" to expedite the process, they rarely turn the pirates over for prosecution. "They don't want to pass the case on to the police," says a Procter & Gamble spokesperson, "because they lose money." Apparently bribes to officials are a key lubricant, allowing counterfeiters to operate with minimal interference. Meanwhile, multinational companies say they lose tens of billions of dollars annually to counterfeiters—and they want China to move more forcefully against product pirates.

Issues to Consider

1. Who, specifically, is hurt by the manufacture and sale of bogus brand-name products?
2. How might a company such as Yamaha help consumers differentiate between a company-made motorcycle and a counterfeit with the Yamaha brand?

and to create common economic policies. A number of economic communities now exist. Table 3.2 lists the members of the four most familiar ones.

The *European Union* (EU), also known as the *European Economic Community* and the *Common Market,* was formed in 1958 by six countries—France, the Federal Republic of Germany, Italy, Belgium, the Netherlands, and Luxembourg. Its objective was freely conducted commerce among these nations and others that might later join. As shown in Table 3.2, nine more nations have joined the EU. (Cyprus, Poland, Hungary, the Czech Republic, Slovenia, and Estonia have begun formal negotiations to join the EU; Latvia, Lithuania, Slovakia, Romania, and Bulgaria have requested membership as well.)

Since January 2001, twelve member nations of the EU are participating in the new common currency, the euro. The euro is the single currency of the European Monetary Union nations.

A second community in Europe, the *European Economic Area* (EEA), became effective in January 1994. This pact consists of Iceland, Norway, and the fifteen member nations of the EU. The EEA, encompassing an area inhabited by more than 395 million people, allows for the free movement of goods throughout all seventeen countries.

The *North American Free Trade Agreement* (NAFTA) joined the United States with its first- and second-largest trading partners, Canada and Mexico. Implementation of NAFTA on January 1, 1994, created a market of over 416 million people. This market consists of Canada (population 31.3 million), the United States (284.8 million), and Mexico (100 million). Given the estimated annual output for this trade area of about

Connecting the European Union. The countries in the European Union are connected by more than agreements and a shared currency. They are physically connected by transportation such as the Eurostar, a high-speed train that takes business-people and tourists to London, Brussels, and Paris—fast.

$7 trillion, NAFTA has major implications for developing business opportunities in the United States.

NAFTA is built on the Canadian Free Trade Agreement (FTA), signed by the United States and Canada in 1989, and on the substantial trade and investment reforms undertaken by Mexico since the mid-1980s. Initiated by the Mexican government, formal negotiations on NAFTA began in June 1991 between the three governments. The

table 3.2 Members of Major International Economic Communities

European Union (EU)	North American Free Trade Agreement (NAFTA)	ASEAN Free Trade Area (AFTA)	Organization of Petroleum Exporting Countries (OPEC)
Austria*	United States	Brunei	Algeria
Belgium*	Canada	Burma	Indonesia
Denmark	Mexico	Cambodia	Iran
Finland*		Indonesia	Iraq
France*		Laos	Kuwait
Germany*		Malaysia	Libya
Greece*		Philippines	Nigeria
Ireland*		Singapore	Qatar
Italy*		Thailand	Saudi Arabia
Luxembourg*		Vietnam	United Arab Emirates
Netherlands*			Venezuela
Portugal*			
Spain*			
Sweden			
United Kingdom			

Note: EU and OPEC have been in existence for decades, but NAFTA and AFTA are newer international economic communities.
*Members of the European Monetary Union
Source: U.S. Department of Commerce, International Trade Administration, **http://www.ita.doc.gov/td/industry/otea/usfth/method,** October 10, 2002.

Spotlight

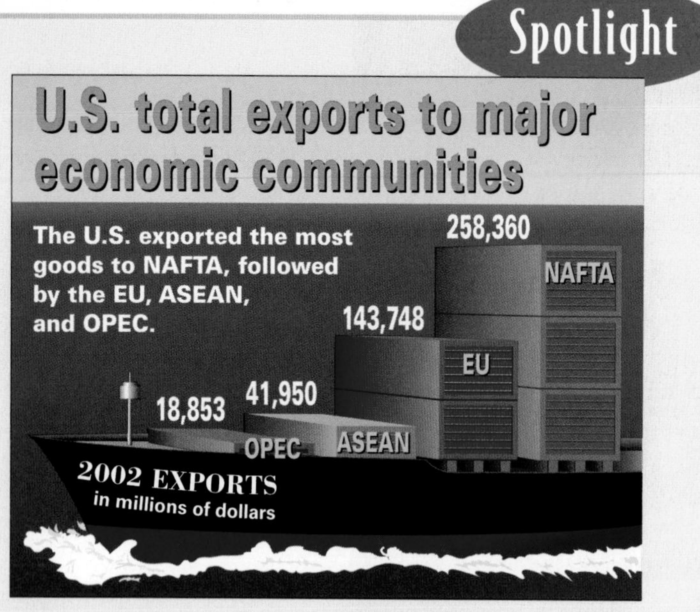

Source: U.S. Department of Commerce, International Trade Administration.

support of NAFTA by President Bill Clinton, past U.S. Presidents Ronald Reagan and Jimmy Carter, and Nobel Prize–winning economists provided the impetus for U.S. congressional ratification of NAFTA in November 1993. NAFTA will gradually eliminate all tariffs on goods produced and traded among Canada, Mexico, and the United States to provide for a totally free trade area by 2009. Chile is expected to become the fourth member of NAFTA, but political forces may delay its entry into the agreement for several years.

The *Association of Southeast Asian Nations* (ASEAN), with headquarters in Jakarta, Indonesia, was established in 1967 to promote political, economic, and social cooperation among its seven member countries: Indonesia, Malaysia, Philippines, Singapore, Thailand, Brunei, and Vietnam. In January 1992, ASEAN agreed to create a free trade area known as the ASEAN Free Trade Area (AFTA). AFTA countries have a population of more than 400 million people, and their trade totals $250 billion.

The *Pacific Rim*, referring to countries and economies bordering the Pacific Ocean, is an informal, flexible term generally regarded as a reference to East Asia, Canada, and the United States. At a minimum, the Pacific Rim includes Canada, Japan, the People's Republic of China, Taiwan, and the United States. It also may include Australia, Brunei, Cambodia, Hong Kong/Macau, Indonesia, Laos, North Korea, South Korea, Malaysia, New Zealand, the Pacific Islands, the Philippines, Russia (or the Commonwealth of Independent States), Singapore, Thailand, and Vietnam.

The *Commonwealth of Independent States* (CIS) was established in December 1991 as an association of eleven republics of the former Soviet Union: Russia, Ukraine, Belarus (formerly Byelorussia), Moldova (formerly Moldavia), Armenia, Azerbaijan, Uzbekistan, Turkmenistan, Tajikistan, Kazakhstan, and Kirgizstan (formerly Kirghiziya). The Baltic states did not join. Georgia maintained observer status before joining the CIS in November 1993.

In the western hemisphere, the *Caribbean Basin Initiative* (CBI) is an inter-American program led by the United States to give economic assistance and trade preferences to Caribbean and Central American countries. CBI provides duty-free access to the U.S. market for most products from the region and promotes private-sector development in member nations.

The *Common Market of the Southern Cone* (MERCOSUR) was established in 1991 under the Treaty of Asuncion to unite Argentina, Brazil, Paraguay, and Uruguay as a free trade alliance; Bolivia and Chile joined as associates in 1996. The alliance represents 215 million consumers—63 percent of South America's population—with a combined GDP of US$1.4 trillion, making it the third-largest trading bloc behind NAFTA and the EU. Like NAFTA, MERCOSUR promotes "the free circulation of goods, services and production factors among the countries" and established a common external tariff and commercial policy.[15]

The *Organization of Petroleum Exporting Countries* (OPEC) was founded in 1960 in response to reductions in the prices that oil companies were willing to pay for crude oil. The organization was conceived as a collective-bargaining unit to provide oil-producing nations with some control over oil prices.

Finally, the *Organization for Economic Cooperation and Development* (OECD) is a group of twenty-four industrialized market-economy countries of North America, Europe, the Far East, and the South Pacific. OECD, headquartered in Paris, was established in 1961 to promote economic development and international trade.

Methods of Entering International Business

A firm that has decided to enter international markets can do so in several ways. We shall discuss several different methods. These different approaches require varying degrees of involvement in international business. Typically, a firm begins its international operations at the simplest level. Then, depending on its goals, it may progress to higher levels of involvement.

learning objective

4 Define the methods by which a firm can organize for and enter into international markets.

Licensing

Licensing is a contractual agreement in which one firm permits another to produce and market its product and to use its brand name in return for a royalty or other compensation. For example, Yoplait yogurt is a French yogurt licensed for production in the United States. The Yoplait brand maintains an appealing French image, and in return, the U.S. producer pays the French firm a percentage of its income from sales of the product.

licensing a contractual agreement in which one firm permits another to produce and market its product and use its brand name in return for a royalty or other compensation

Licensing is especially advantageous for small manufacturers wanting to launch a well-known domestic brand internationally. For example, all Spalding sporting products are licensed worldwide. The licensor, the Questor Corporation, owns the Spalding name but produces no goods itself. The German firm of Lowenbrau has used licensing agreements, including one with Miller in the United States, to increase its beer sales worldwide without committing capital to building breweries.[16]

Licensing thus provides a simple method of expanding into a foreign market with virtually no investment. On the other hand, if the licensee does not maintain the licensor's product standards, the product's image may be damaged. Another possible disadvantage is that a licensing arrangement may not provide the original producer with any foreign marketing experience.

Exporting

A firm also may manufacture its products in its home country and export them for sale in foreign markets. Like licensing, exporting can be a relatively low-risk method of entering foreign markets. Unlike licensing, however, it is not a simple method; it opens up several levels of involvement to the exporting firm.

At the most basic level, the exporting firm may sell its products outright to an *export/import merchant*, which is essentially a merchant wholesaler. The merchant assumes all the risks of product ownership, distribution, and sale. It may even purchase the goods in the producer's home country and assume responsibility for exporting the goods. An important and practical issue for domestic firms dealing with foreign customers is securing payment. This is a two-sided issue that reflects the mutual concern rightly felt by both parties to the trade deal: The exporter would like to be paid before shipping the merchandise, whereas the importer would obviously prefer to know it has received the shipment before releasing any funds. Neither side wants to take the risk of fulfilling its part of the deal only later to discover that the other side has not. The result would lead to legal costs and complex, lengthy dealings wasteful of everyone's resources.

This mutual level of mistrust is in fact good business sense and has been around since the beginning of trade centuries ago. The solution then was as it still is today—for both parties to use a mutually trusted go-between who can ensure that the payment is held until the merchandise is in fact delivered according to the terms of the trade contract. The go-between representatives employed by the importer and exporter are still, as they were in

Using the Internet

"Our Mission: To Help U.S. Business Succeed, Globally." That's the stated goal for the International Trade Administration of the U.S. Department of Commerce, and given that one out of every ten Americans owes his or her job to exports, it is clear just how important trade is to America and why it is encouraged. You will find a variety of useful information related to international business and trade at the ITA website located at **http://www.ita.doc.gov/**. The site has links to statistics, industry analysis, trade laws, and answers to often-asked trade questions.

the past, the local domestic banks involved in international business.

Here is a simplified version of how it works. After signing contracts detailing the merchandise sold and terms for its delivery, an importer will ask its local bank to issue a **letter of credit** for the amount of money needed to pay for the merchandise. The letter of credit is issued "in favor of the exporter," meaning that the funds are tied specifically to the trade contract involved. The importer's bank forwards the letter of credit to the exporter's bank, which also normally deals in international transactions.

letter of credit issued by a bank on request of an importer stating that the bank will pay an amount of money to a stated beneficiary

The exporter's bank then notifies the exporter that a letter of credit has been received in its name, and the exporter can go ahead with the shipment. The carrier transporting the merchandise provides the exporter with evidence of the shipment in a document called a **bill of lading.** The exporter signs over title to the merchandise (now in transit) to its bank by delivering a signed copy of the bill of lading and letter of credit.

bill of lading issued by a transport carrier to an exporter to prove merchandise has been shipped

draft issued by the exporter's bank, ordering the importer's bank to pay for the merchandise, thus guaranteeing payment once accepted by the importer's bank

In exchange, the exporter issues a **draft** from the bank, which orders the importer's bank to pay for the merchandise. The draft, bill of lading, and letter of credit are sent from the exporter's bank to the importer's bank. Acceptance by the importer's bank leads to return of the draft and its sale by the exporter to its bank, meaning the exporter receives cash and the bank assumes the risk of collecting the funds from the foreign bank. The importer is obliged to pay its bank on delivery of the merchandise, and the deal is complete.

In most cases, the letter of credit is part of a lending arrangement between the importer and its bank, and of course, both banks earn fees for the issuing of letters of credit, drafts, and handling the import/export services for their clients. Furthermore, the process incorporates the fact that both importer and exporter will have different local currencies and might even negotiate their trade in a third currency. The banks look after all the necessary exchanges. For example, the vast majority of international business is negotiated in U.S. dollars, even though the trade may be between countries other than the United States. Thus, although the importer may end up paying for the merchandise in its local currency and the exporter may receive payment in another local currency, the banks involved will exchange all necessary foreign funds in order to allow the deal to take place.

The exporting firm may instead ship its products to an *export/import agent*, which for a commission or fee arranges the sale of the products to foreign intermediaries. The agent is an independent firm—like other agents—that sells and may perform other marketing functions for the exporter. The exporter, however, retains title to the products during shipment and until they are sold.

An exporting firm also may establish its own *sales offices*, or *branches*, in foreign countries. These installations are international extensions of the firm's distribution system. They represent a deeper involvement in international business than the other exporting techniques we have discussed—and thus they carry a greater risk. The exporting firm maintains control over sales, and it gains both experience and knowledge of foreign markets. Eventually, the firm also may develop its own sales force to operate in conjunction with foreign sales offices.

Joint Ventures

A *joint venture* is a partnership formed to achieve a specific goal or to operate for a specific period of time. A joint venture with an established firm in a foreign country provides immediate market knowledge and access, reduced risk, and control over product attributes. However, joint-venture agreements established across national borders can become extremely complex. As a result, joint-venture agreements generally require a very high level of commitment from all the parties involved.

A joint venture may be used to produce and market an existing product in a foreign nation or to develop an entirely new product. Recently, for example, Archer Daniels Midland Company (ADM), one of the world's leading food processors, entered into a joint venture with Gruma SA, Mexico's largest corn flour and tortilla company. Besides a 22 percent stake in Gruma, ADM also received stakes in other joint ventures operated by Gruma. One of them will combine both companies' U.S. corn flour operations, which account for about 25 percent of the U.S. market. ADM also has a 40 percent stake in a Mexican wheat flour mill. ADM's joint venture increased its participation in the growing Mexican economy, where ADM already produces corn syrup, fructose, starch, and wheat flour. And in order to share expertise, risk, and benefit from quicker development of new products in the fast-paced world of the Internet, iPlanet was formed as a joint venture between Sun Microsystems and Netscape Communications in March 1999 to develop e-commerce platforms. The alliance operates independently of the parent firms with its own management and goals.[17]

Venturing into a joint venture. A joint venture with established firm Hitachi Ltd. in Tokyo, Japan, provides the world's largest computer manufacturer IBM with immediate market knowledge and access, reduced risk, and control over product attributes. IBM and Hitachi executives formed an alliance in technology storage and set up a joint venture for hard disk drives to boost competitiveness.

Totally Owned Facilities

At a still deeper level of involvement in international business, a firm may develop *totally owned facilities*, that is, its own production and marketing facilities in one or more foreign nations. This *direct investment* provides complete control over operations, but it carries a greater risk than the joint venture. The firm is really establishing a subsidiary in a foreign country. Most firms do so only after they have acquired some knowledge of the host country's markets.

Direct investment may take either of two forms. In the first, the firm builds or purchases manufacturing and other facilities in the foreign country. It uses these facilities to produce its own established products and to market them in that country and perhaps in neighboring countries. Firms such as General Motors, Union Carbide, and Colgate-Palmolive are multinational companies with worldwide manufacturing facilities. Colgate-Palmolive factories are becoming *Eurofactories*, supplying neighboring countries as well as their own local markets.

A second form of direct investment in international business is the purchase of an existing firm in a foreign country under an arrangement that allows it to operate

Direct investment carries both opportunity and risk. Wal-Mart's direct investment in this totally-owned store in Shenzhen, China provides the world's largest retailer with complete control over operations. Direct ownership is the strongest commitment to international business and involves the greatest risk.

independently of the parent company. When Sony Corporation (a Japanese firm) decided to enter the motion-picture business in the United States, it chose to purchase Columbia Pictures Entertainment, Inc., rather than start a new motion-picture studio from scratch.

Strategic Alliances

strategic alliance a partnership formed to create competitive advantage on a worldwide basis

A **strategic alliance,** the newest form of international business structure, is a partnership formed to create competitive advantage on a worldwide basis. Strategic alliances are very similar to joint ventures. The number of strategic alliances is growing at an estimated rate of about 20 percent per year. In fact, in the automobile and computer industries, strategic alliances are becoming the predominant means of competing. International competition is so fierce and the costs of competing on a global basis are so high that few firms have all the resources needed to do it alone. Thus individual firms that lack the internal resources essential for international success may seek to collaborate with other companies.

An example of such an alliance is the New United Motor Manufacturing, Inc. (NUMMI), formed by Toyota and General Motors to make Chevrolet Novas and Toyota Tercels. This enterprise united the quality engineering of Japanese cars with the marketing expertise and market access of General Motors.[18]

Trading Companies

trading company provides a link between buyers and sellers in different countries

A **trading company** provides a link between buyers and sellers in different countries. A trading company, as its name implies, is not involved in manufacturing or owning assets related to manufacturing. It buys in one country at the lowest price consistent with quality and sells to buyers in another country. An important function of trading companies is taking title to products and performing all the activities necessary to move the products from the domestic country to a foreign country. For example, large grain-trading companies operating out of home offices both in the United States and overseas control a major portion of the world's trade in basic food commodities. These trading companies sell homogeneous agricultural commodities that can be stored and moved rapidly in response to market conditions. The best-known U.S. trading company is Sears World Trade, which specializes in consumer goods, light industrial items, and processed foods.[19]

Countertrade

countertrade an international barter transaction

In the early 1990s, many developing nations had major restrictions on converting domestic currency into foreign currency. Exporters therefore had to resort to barter agreements with importers. **Countertrade** is essentially an international barter transaction in which goods and services are exchanged for different goods and services. Examples include Saudi Arabia's purchase of ten 747 jets from Boeing with payment in crude oil, Philip Morris's sale of cigarettes to Russia in return for chemicals used to make fertilizers, and Iraq's barter of crude oil for warships from Italy.

The volume of countertrade is growing. Given the importance of countertrade as a means of financing world trade, prospective exporters undoubtedly will have to engage in this technique from time to time to gain access to international markets.

Multinational Firms

multinational enterprise a firm that operates on a worldwide scale without ties to any specific nation or region

A **multinational enterprise** is a firm that operates on a worldwide scale without ties to any specific nation or region. The multinational firm represents the highest level of involvement in international business. It is equally "at home" in most countries of the world. In fact, as far as the operations of the multinational enterprise are concerned,

table 3.3 The Ten Largest Multinational Corporations Outside the United States

2001 Rank	Company	Business	Country	Revenue ($ millions)
1	BP	Energy sources	United Kingdom	174,218
2	DaimlerChrysler	Automobiles	Germany	136,758
3	Royal Dutch/Shell Group	Energy sources	Netherlands/United Kingdom	135,211
4	Toyota Motor	Automobiles	Japan	120,731
5	Mitsubishi	Trading	Japan	105,741
6	Mitsui & Co	Trading	Japan	101,136
7	Total Fina Elf	Energy sources	France	94,243
8	Nippon T&T	Telecom	Japan	93,360
9	Itochu	Trading	Japan	91,114
10	Allianz Worldwide	Insurance	Germany	85,867

Source: "The International 500," *Forbes*, July 22, 2002, p. 129.

national boundaries exist only on maps. It is, however, organized under the laws of its home country.

Table 3.3 lists the ten largest multinational corporations outside the United States. Notice that five foreign-based multinational companies are located in Japan. Table 3.4 shows the ten largest foreign and U.S. public multinational companies; the ranking is based on a composite score reflecting each company's best three out of four rankings for sales, profits, assets, and market value. Table 3.5 (on p. 92) describes steps in entering international markets.

According to the chairman of the board of Dow Chemical Company, a multinational firm of U.S. origin, "The emergence of a world economy and of the multinational corporation has been accomplished hand in hand." He sees multinational enterprises moving toward what he calls the "anational company," a firm that has no nationality but belongs to all countries. In recognition of this movement, there have already been international conferences devoted to the question of how such enterprises would be controlled.

table 3.4 The Ten Largest Foreign and U.S. Multinational Corporations

2001 Rank	Company	Business	Country	Revenue ($ millions)
1	Wal-Mart Stores	General merchandiser	United States	219,812
2	ExxonMobil	Energy	United States	191,581
3	General Motors	Automobiles	United States	177,260
4	BP	Energy	United Kingdom	174,218
5	Ford Motor	Automobiles	United States	162,412
6	Enron*	Energy	United States	138,718
7	DaimlerChrysler	Automobiles	Germany	136,897
8	Royal Dutch/Shell Group	Energy	Netherlands/United Kingdom	135,211
9	General Electric	Electricity and electronics	United States	125,913
10	Toyota Motor	Automobiles	Japan	120,814

*Enron is bankrupt and disgraced, but *Fortune* does not disqualify it from the list of the world's biggest companies. The Global 500 measures revenues, not virtue.

Source: "Global 500: The World's Largest Corporations," *Fortune*, July 22, 2002, p. F-1, **www.fortune.com.**

table 3.5 Steps in Entering International Markets

Step	Activity	Marketing Tasks
1	Identify exportable products	Identify key selling features Identify needs that they satisfy Identify the selling constraints that are imposed
2	Identify key foreign markets for the products	Determine who the customers are Pinpoint what and when they will buy Do market research Establish priority, or "target," countries
3	Analyze how to sell in each priority market (methods will be affected by product characteristics and unique features of country/market)	Locate available government and private-sector resources Determine service and backup sales requirements
4	Set export prices and payment terms, methods, and techniques	Establish methods of export pricing Establish sales terms, quotations, invoices, and conditions of sale Determine methods of international payments, secured and unsecured
5	Estimate resource requirements and returns	Estimate financial requirements Estimate human resources requirements (full- or part-time export department or operation?) Estimate plant production capacity Determine necessary product adaptations
6	Establish overseas distribution network	Determine distribution agreement and other key marketing decisions (price, repair policies, returns, territory, performance, and termination) Know your customer (use U.S. Department of Commerce international marketing services)
7	Determine shipping, traffic, and documentation procedures and requirements	Determine methods of shipment (air or ocean freight, truck, rail) Finalize containerization Obtain validated export license Follow export-administration documentation procedures
8	Promote, sell, and be paid	Use international media, communications, advertising, trade shows, and exhibitions Determine the need for overseas travel (when, where, how often?) Initiate customer follow-up procedures
9	Continuously analyze current marketing, economic, and political situations	Recognize changing factors influencing marketing strategies Constantly reevaluate

Source: U.S. Department of Commerce, International Trade Administration, Washington, D.C.

Sources of Export Assistance

learning objective

5 Describe the various sources of export assistance.

In September 1993, President Bill Clinton announced the *National Export Strategy* (NES) to revitalize U.S. exports. Under the NES, the *Trade Promotion Coordinating Committee* (TPCC) assists U.S. firms in developing export-promotion programs. The export services and programs of the nineteen TPCC agencies can help American firms compete in foreign markets and create new jobs in the United States. An overview of selected export-assistance programs follows:

- *U.S. Export Assistance Centers (USEACs).* USEACs are federal export-assistance offices. They provide assistance in export marketing and trade finance by integrating in a single location the counselors and services of the U.S. and

Foreign Commercial Services of the Department of Commerce, the Export-Import Bank, the Small Business Administration, and the U.S. Agency for International Development: **http://www.sba.gov/oit/export/useac.html.**

- *International Trade Administration (ITA), U.S. Department of Commerce.* ITA offers assistance and information to exporters through its units, which include (1) domestic and overseas commercial officers, (2) country experts, and (3) industry experts. Each unit promotes products and offers services and programs for the U.S. exporting community: **http://www.ita.doc.gov.**
- *U.S. and Foreign Commercial Services (US&FCS).* To help U.S. firms compete more effectively in the global marketplace, the US&FCS has a network of trade specialists in sixty-seven countries worldwide. US&FCS offices provide information on foreign markets, agent/distributor location services, and trade leads, as well as counseling on business opportunities, trade barriers, and prospects abroad: **http://www.usatrade.gov/.**
- *Export Legal Assistance Network (ELAN).* ELAN is a nationwide group of attorneys with experience in international trade who provide free initial consultations to small businesses on export-related matters: **http://www.fita.org/elan/.**
- *Advocacy Center.* The Advocacy Center, established in November 1993, facilitates high-level U.S. official advocacy to assist U.S. firms competing for major projects and procurements worldwide. The center is directed by the Trade Promotion Coordinating Committee: **http://www.ita.doc.gov/advocacy.**
- *Trade Information Center (TIC).* This information center was established as a comprehensive source for U.S. companies seeking information on federal programs and activities that support U.S. exports, including information on overseas markets and industry trends. This center maintains a computerized calendar of U.S. government–sponsored domestic and overseas trade events: **http://www.ita.doc.gov/td/tic/.**
- *STATUSA/Internet (**http://www.stat-usa.gov**).* A comprehensive collection of business, economic, and trade information available on the web. Through this site, a firm can access the National Trade Data Bank (NTDB), daily trade leads and economic news, *Commerce Business Daily*, and the latest economic press releases and statistical series from the federal government. For more information on this low-cost service, call 1–800-STAT-USA (1–800–782–8872) or visit **http://www.stat-usa.gov/.**
- *TRADESTATS.* This is a comprehensive source for U.S. export and import data, both current and historical. Maintained by the Commerce Department's Office of Trade and Economic Analysis, this website contains total U.S. trade statistics by country and commodity, state and metropolitan area export data, and trade and industry statistics. Much of these data are downloadable: **http://www.ita.doc.gov/td/industry/otea/.**
- *Selected SBA market research-related general resources.* The Small Business Administration (SBA) publishes many helpful guides to assist small and medium-sized companies, including *Marketing for Small Business: An Overview*, *Researching Your Market*, and *Breaking into the Trade Game* or the videos *Marketing: Winning Customers with a Workable Plan* and *The Basics of Exporting*. Contact the Small Business Answer Desk at 1–800-UASK-SBA (1–800–827–5722) or visit **http://www.sba.gov/oit/.**
- *National Trade Data Bank (NTDB)*: The NTDB contains international economic and export-promotion information supplied by over twenty U.S. agencies. Data are updated daily on the Internet (**http://www.stat-usa.gov/tradtest.nsf**) and monthly on CD-ROM. The CD-ROM version is available for use at over 1,000 libraries throughout the country. The NTDB contains data from the Departments of Agriculture (Foreign Agriculture Service), Commerce (Bureau of Census, Bureau of Economic Analysis, International Trade Administration, and National Institute for Standards and Technology), Energy, and Labor (Bureau of Labor Statistics); the Central Intelligence Agency; the Export-Import

Bank; the Federal Reserve System; the U.S. International Trade Commission; the Overseas Private Investment Corporation; the Small Business Administration; and the U.S. Trade Representative.

These and other sources of export information enhance the business opportunities of U.S. firms seeking to enter expanding foreign markets. Another vital entry factor is financing.

Financing International Business

learning objective

6 Identify the institutions that help firms and nations finance international business.

International trade compounds the concerns of financial managers. Currency exchange rates, tariffs and foreign-exchange controls, and the tax structures of host nations all affect international operations and the flow of cash. In addition, financial managers must be concerned both with the financing of their international operations and with the means available to their customers to finance purchases.

Fortunately, along with business in general, a number of large banks have become international in scope. Many have established branches in major cities around the world. Thus, like firms in other industries, they are able to provide their services where and when they are needed. In addition, financial assistance is available from U.S. government and international sources.

Several of today's international financial organizations were founded many years ago to facilitate free trade and the exchange of currencies among nations. Some, such as the Inter-American Development Bank, are internationally supported and focus on developing countries. Others, such as the Export-Import Bank, are operated by one country but provide international financing.

The Export-Import Bank of the United States

Export-Import Bank of the United States
an independent agency of the U.S. government whose function it is to assist in financing the exports of American firms

The **Export-Import Bank of the United States,** created in 1934, is an independent agency of the U.S. government whose function it is to assist in financing the exports of American firms. *Eximbank*, as it is commonly called, extends and guarantees credit to overseas buyers of American goods and services and guarantees short-term financing for exports. It also cooperates with commercial banks in helping American exporters offer credit to their overseas customers. Recently, the Eximbank provided credit to Saudi Arabia in a $4 billion contract awarded to AT&T to update the Saudis' communication system. Since 1934, the Eximbank has supported over $300 billion in exports.

Multilateral Development Banks

multilateral development bank (MDB)
an internationally supported bank that provides loans to developing countries to help them grow

A **multilateral development bank (MDB)** is an internationally supported bank that provides loans to developing countries to help them grow. The most familiar is the World Bank, which operates worldwide. Four other MDBs operate primarily in Central and South America, Asia, Africa, and eastern and central Europe. All five are supported by the industrialized nations, including the United States.

The *Inter-American Development Bank* (IDB), the oldest and largest regional bank, was created in 1959 by ten Latin American countries and the United States. Forty-six member countries—twenty-six borrowing countries in Latin America and the Caribbean and twenty nonborrowing countries, including the United States, Japan, Canada, sixteen European countries, and Israel—now own the bank, which is headquartered in Washington, D.C. The IDB makes loans and provides technical advice and assistance to countries.

With sixty-one member nations, the *Asian Development Bank* (ADB), created in 1966, promotes economic and social progress in Asian and Pacific regions. The U.S. government is the second-largest contributor to the ADB's capital, after Japan. Recently, the ADB approved $5.4 billion for seventy-two loans in twenty-two countries; India received the largest loan of $1.5 billion, to be followed by China and Pakistan.[20]

The *African Development Bank* (AFDB) was established in 1964 with headquarters in Abidjan, Ivory Coast. Its members include fifty African and twenty-seven non-African countries. The AFDB's goal is to foster the economic and social development of its African members. The bank pursues this goal through loans, research, technical assistance, and the development of trade programs.

Established in 1991 to encourage reconstruction and development in the eastern and central European countries, the London-based *European Bank for Reconstruction and Development* (EBRD) is owned by sixty countries and two intergovernmental institutions. Its loans are geared toward developing market-oriented economies and promoting private enterprise.

The International Monetary Fund

The **International Monetary Fund (IMF)** is an international bank with more than 183 member nations that makes short-term loans to developing countries experiencing balance-of-payment deficits. This financing is contributed by member nations, and it must be repaid with interest. Loans are provided primarily to fund international trade.

International Monetary Fund (IMF) an international bank with more than 183 member nations that makes short-term loans to developing countries experiencing balance-of-payment deficits

Return To inside business

Steve Heyer, Coca-Cola's head of marketing, has traveled the globe to work with local managers in expanding distribution, adapting products, and adjusting prices to fit local market conditions. North American sales have been strong, but Latin American sales have grown more slowly. Therefore, Heyer has focused on ways to boost sales in countries such as Brazil, Argentina, and Venezuela, which are large and promising markets despite economic turmoil.

In addition, he has traveled to Africa to strategize with local Coca-Cola executives about increasing market share on that continent. Although runaway inflation is eroding Coca-Cola's profits in Zimbabwe and other countries, the company continues to lay the groundwork for long-term profitability by establishing a strong presence in numerous outlets. "We want to be everywhere, and will be there forever," says Alex Cummings, president of Coca-Cola's Africa operations.

Questions

1. Why might a country in Latin America or Africa resist Coca-Cola's efforts to expand local sales?
2. Was Coca-Cola a multinational firm the first time it entered the global marketplace decades ago? Is it a multinational firm today?

chapter review

Summary

Explain the economic basis for international business.

International business encompasses all business activities that involve exchanges across national boundaries. International trade is based on specialization, whereby each country produces those goods and services that it can produce more efficiently than any other goods and services. A nation is said to have a comparative advantage relative to these goods. International trade develops when each nation trades its surplus products for those in short supply.

A nation's balance of trade is the difference between the value of its exports and the value of its imports. Its balance of payments is the difference between the flow of money into and out of the nation. Generally, a negative balance of trade is considered unfavorable.

Discuss the restrictions nations place on international trade, the objectives of these restrictions, and their results.

Despite the benefits of world trade, nations tend to use tariffs and nontariff barriers (import quotas, embargoes, and other restrictions) to limit trade. These restrictions typically are justified as being needed to protect a nation's economy, industries, citizens, or security. They can result in the loss of jobs, higher prices, fewer choices in the marketplace, and the misallocation of resources.

Outline the extent of international trade and identify the organizations working to foster it.

World trade is generally increasing. Trade between the United States and other nations is increasing in dollar value but decreasing in terms of our share of the world market. The General Agreement on Tariffs and Trade (GATT) was formed to dismantle trade barriers and provide an environment in which international business can grow. Today the World Trade Organization (WTO) and various economic communities carry on that mission.

Define the methods by which a firm can organize for and enter into international markets.

A firm can enter international markets in several ways. It may license a foreign firm to produce and market its products. It may export its products and sell them through foreign intermediaries or its own sales organization abroad. Or it may sell its exports outright to an export/import merchant. It may enter into a joint venture with a foreign firm. It may establish its own foreign subsidiaries. Or it may develop into a multinational enterprise. Generally, each of these methods represents an increasingly deeper level of involvement in international business, with licensing being the simplest and the development of a multinational corporation the most involved.

Describe the various sources of export assistance.

Many government and international agencies provide export assistance to U.S. and foreign firms. The export services and programs of the nineteen agencies of the U.S. Trade Promotion Coordinating Committee (TPCC) can help U.S. firms compete in foreign markets and create new jobs in the United States. Sources of export assistance include U.S. Export Assistance Centers, the International Trade Administration, U.S. and Foreign Commercial Services, Export Legal Assistance Network, Advocacy Center, National Trade Data Bank, and other government and international agencies.

Identify the institutions that help firms and nations finance international business.

The financing of international trade is more complex than that of domestic trade. Institutions such as the Eximbank and the International Monetary Fund have been established to provide financing and ultimately to increase world trade for American and international firms.

Key Terms

You should now be able to define and give an example relevant to each of the following terms:

international business (69)
absolute advantage (70)
comparative advantage (70)
exporting (71)
importing (71)
balance of trade (71)
trade deficit (71)
balance of payments (72)
import duty (tariff) (74)
dumping (74)
nontariff barrier (74)
import quota (74)
embargo (74)
foreign-exchange control (75)
currency devaluation (75)
General Agreement on Tariffs and Trade (GATT) (82)
World Trade Organization (WTO) (83)
economic community (83)
licensing (87)
letter of credit (88)
bill of lading (88)
draft (88)
strategic alliance (90)
trading company (90)
countertrade (90)
multinational enterprise (90)
Export-Import Bank of the United States (94)
multilateral development bank (MDB) (94)
International Monetary Fund (IMF) (95)

Review Questions

1. Why do firms engage in international trade?
2. What is the difference between an absolute and a comparative advantage in international trade? How are both types of advantages related to the concept of specialization?
3. What is a favorable balance of trade? In what way is it "favorable"?
4. List and briefly describe the principal restrictions that may be applied to a nation's imports.
5. What reasons generally are given for imposing trade restrictions?
6. What are the general effects of import restrictions on trade?
7. Define and describe the major objectives of the World Trade Organization (WTO) and the international economic communities.
8. Which nations are the principal trading partners of the United States? What are the major U.S. imports and exports?

9. The methods of engaging in international business may be categorized as either direct or indirect. How would you classify each of the methods described in this chapter? Why?
10. In what ways is a multinational enterprise different from a large corporation that does business in several countries?
11. List some key sources of export assistance. How can these sources be useful to small business firms?
12. In what ways do Eximbank, multilateral development banks, and the IMF enhance international trade?

Discussion Questions

1. The United States restricts imports but, at the same time, supports the WTO and international banks whose objective is to enhance world trade. As a member of Congress, how would you justify this contradiction to your constituents?
2. What effects might the devaluation of a nation's currency have on its business firms? On its consumers? On the debts it owes to other nations?
3. Should imports to the United States be curtailed by, say, 20 percent to eliminate our trade deficit? What might happen if this was done?
4. When should a firm consider expanding from strictly domestic trade to international trade? When should it consider becoming further involved in international trade? What factors might affect the firm's decisions in each case?
5. How can a firm obtain the expertise needed to produce and market its products in, for example, the EU?

video case

The Global Saga of Subway

In 1965, when Dr. Peter Buck loaned 17-year-old Fred DeLuca $1,000 to open a sandwich shop in Bridgeport, Connecticut, he did not realize that they were launching what would become an immensely successful global business. At the time, DeLuca was thinking about earning money to pay for college, not creating a franchised organization that eventually would have its name on 16,000 restaurants in seventy-four countries. Today, Subway has more U.S. restaurants than McDonald's, and it is second only to McDonald's in the number of outlets worldwide. Nearly four decades after Subway's founding, its far-reaching growth and enthusiastic customer acceptance have made DeLuca a billionaire.

All Subway restaurants are individually owned and operated by franchisees. Each pays a $10,000 franchise fee to use the Subway name plus $65,000 to $175,000 to build a store, depending on location. Because Subway stores require much less space than many other fast-food restaurants, franchisees can choose high-traffic but nontraditional locations such as bus terminals, airports, hospitals, and military facilities. The company has been named the number one franchise opportunity on *Entrepreneur*'s Franchise 500 list—not just once but ten times—and also has won awards for its sandwiches and its advertising. Small wonder its annual revenues have skyrocketed past $5 billion, even as some competitors have struggled for profitability.

Subway franchisees have opened more than 2,500 restaurants outside the United States. Initially, DeLuca was not pushing for international expansion. However, when an entrepreneur from Bahrain approached Subway about opening a shop on the Persian Gulf island, management decided to accept the challenge of going global. Now Subway is making its name in all kinds of places.

For example, in Australia, where more than 300 Subway shops have opened since 1988, the company's goal is to make Subway the country's leading fast-food chain. Franchisees opened more than two dozen Subway shops in Germany within a few years as part of an intensive development program to boost countrywide sales. In addition to opening stores in Croatia, Finland, Poland, Oman, and many other countries, Subway is aiming to open thousands more restaurants across the United States, especially in areas where few currently exist.

Expanding a food venture into a foreign country involves many issues, such as finding good suppliers to provide quality sandwich ingredients. To ensure consistency from one store to another and one country to another, Subway insists on a "gold standard of quality" when adapting to international markets. Its franchisees run a cooperative that pools their collective buying power to obtain ingredients at advantageous prices. As part of the franchise arrangement, Subway trains new franchise owners, regardless of location. Initially, it trained international franchisees in England and the United States. Over time, it adapted to different languages and cultures, opening additional training facilities in Puerto Rico, Australia, and China.

When Subway enters a new market, it must build brand awareness while simultaneously learning about local eating preferences and customs. Rather than second-guessing cultural differences, the company attempts to adapt quickly to a new restaurant's immediate service area. In Israel, for example, Subway stores avoid violating religious dietary customs by keeping pork items off the menu. In countries where people are not accustomed to eating sandwiches, the company educates consumers about this uniquely American product.

Subway began promoting some of its menu items as health-conscious choices after learning about one customer's personal weight loss plan. Jared S. Fogle weighed 425 pounds when he put himself on a diet of lower-fat Subway sandwiches. Every day, Fogle would eat a six-inch turkey sandwich (no oil, mayo, condiments, or cheese) for lunch and a twelve-inch veggie sandwich (no condiments or cheese) for dinner. Within a year, he had lost 235 pounds. Fogle's story has become the focal point of a long-running campaign highlighting Subway's low-fat sandwiches. Subway has translated these commercials for key international markets and started airing commercials about other customers who lost weight in similar fashion.

Considering that a quarter-pound hamburger at one leading fast-food chain contains more than 62 grams of fat, Subway sandwiches with less than 10 grams of fat offer healthy alternatives that more people are choosing. These, along with quality ingredients, sandwiches to fit local tastes, and convenient locations, are helping Subway to build its brand all over the globe.[21]

Questions

1. Why has Subway been able to expand so quickly into international markets?
2. What are some advantages and disadvantages of Subway's method for expanding?
3. Do you agree with Subway's use of a health-conscious positioning to fuel its international expansion? Why or why not?

Building Skills for Career Success

1. Exploring the Internet

A popular question debated among firms actively involved on the Internet is whether or not there exists a truly global Internet-based customer, irrespective of any individual culture, linguistic, or nationality issues. Does this Internet-based universal customer see the Internet and products sold there in pretty much the same way? If so, then one model might fit all customers. For example, although Yahoo.com translates its web pages so that it is understood around the world, its look may be considered pretty much the same regardless of which international site you use. Is this good strategy, or should the sites reflect local customers differently? Visit the text website for updates to this exercise.

Assignment

1. Examine a website such as Yahoo's (**http://www.yahoo.com**) and its various international versions that operate in other languages around the world. Compare their similarities and differences as best you can, even if you do not understand the individual languages.
2. After making your comparison, do you now agree that there are indeed universal Internet products and customers? Explain your decision.

2. Developing Critical Thinking Skills

Suppose that you own and operate an electronics firm that manufactures transistors and integrated circuits. As foreign competitors enter the market and undercut your prices, you realize your high labor costs are hindering your ability to compete. You are concerned about what to do and are open for suggestions. Recently, you have been trying to decide whether to move your plant to Mexico where labor is cheaper.

Assignment

1. Questions you should consider in making this decision include the following:
   a. Would you be better off to build a new plant in Mexico or to buy an existing building?
   b. If you could find a Mexican electronics firm similar to yours, would it be wiser to try to buy it than to start your own operation?
   c. What are the risks involved in directly investing in your own facility in a foreign country?
   d. If you did decide to move your plant to Mexico, how would you go about it? Are there any government agencies that might offer you advice?
2. Prepare a two-page summary of your answers to these questions.

3. Building Team Skills

The North American Trade Agreement between the United States, Mexico, and Canada went into effect on January 1, 1994. It has made a difference in trade among the countries and has affected the lives of many people.

Assignment

1. Working in teams and using the resources of your library, investigate NAFTA. Answer the following questions:
   a. What are NAFTA's objectives?
   b. What are its benefits?
   c. What impact has NAFTA had on trade, jobs, and travel?

d. Some Americans were opposed to the implementation of NAFTA. What were their objections? Have any of these objections been justified?
e. Has NAFTA influenced your life? How?

2. Summarize your answers in a written report. Your team also should be prepared to give a class presentation.

4. Researching Different Careers

Today firms around the world need employees with special skills. In some countries such employees are not always available, and firms must then search abroad for qualified applicants. One way they can do this is through global work force databases. As business and trade operations continue to grow globally, you may one day find yourself working in a foreign country, perhaps for an American company doing business there or for a foreign company. In what foreign country would you like to work? What problems might you face?

Assignment

1. Choose a country in which you might like to work.
2. Research the country. The National Trade Data Bank (NTDA) is a good place to start. Find answers to the following questions:
   a. What language is spoken in this country? Are you proficient in it? What would you need to do if you are not proficient?
   b. What are the economic, social, and legal systems like in this nation?
   c. What is its history?
   d. What are its culture and social traditions like? How might they affect your work or your living arrangements?
3. Describe what you have found out about this country in a written report. Include an assessment of whether you would want to work there and the problems you might face if you did.

5. Improving Communication Skills

Working in a foreign country, even for a short time, can significantly affect your career. While there are benefits, there also may be many obstacles to overcome. How would you deal with the obstacles, and would it be worth the trouble? If you could work in another country for at least three years, how would it affect your career?

Assignment

1. Read newspaper articles and periodicals to find answers to the following questions:
   a. What would be the benefits of working in a foreign country for a three-year period? How might it advance your career?
   b. What obstacles might this experience present? How would you deal with them? Compare the benefits with the obstacles and record the findings in your journal.

The Rise of Finagle A Bagel

Would bagels sell in Hong Kong? Laura Beth Trust and Alan Litchman planned to find out. Trust was in Hong Kong working in the garment manufacturing industry, and Litchman was in real estate, but they were eager to start their own business. They were particularly interested in running a business where they would have direct customer contact and be able to get firsthand feedback about their products and services. And no matter what kind of business they started, it would be a family undertaking: The two entrepreneurs had recently decided to get married.

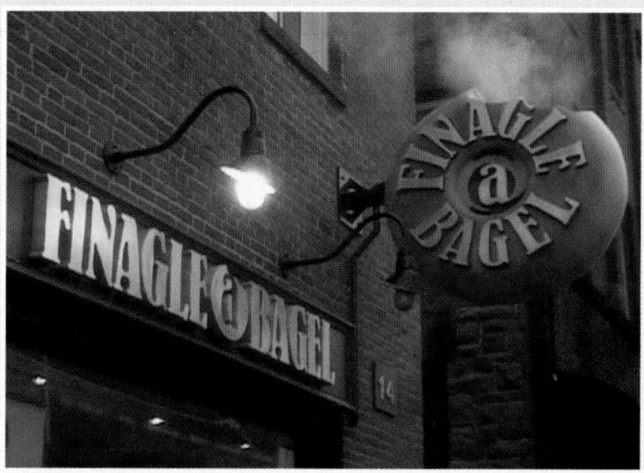

Looking around Hong Kong, Litchman and Trust noticed numerous Western-style food chains such as McDonald's, Pizza Hut, KFC, and Starbucks, but no bagel places. Yet they believed that Hong Kong's sophisticated, multicultural population would welcome authentic New York–style bagels. Although both the entrepreneurs had MBA degrees from the Sloan School of Management, neither had any restaurant experience or knew how to make a bagel. Still, because they sensed a profitable opportunity and possessed solid business skills, Trust and Litchman decided to move ahead. The two incorporated a company, found a partner, and then returned to the United States to investigate the bagel business. As part of their research, they approached two knowledgeable experts for advice.

One of the bagel experts was Larry Smith, who in 1982 had cofounded a tiny cheesecake store in Boston's historic Quincy Market. When business was slow, the store began selling bagels topped with leftover cream cheese. By the late 1980s, this sideline was doing so well that Smith and his partners changed their focus from cheesecakes to bagels and changed the store's name from Julian's Cheesecakes to Finagle A Bagel. They relocated the store from a cramped 63-square-foot storefront into a more spacious 922-square-foot space in the same busy market complex. Soon so many customers were lining up for bagels that the owners began opening additional Finagle A Bagel stores around downtown Boston.

New Ownership, New Growth

By the time Trust and Litchman met Smith, he was operating six successful bagel stores, was ringing up $10 million in annual sales, and was looking for a source of capital to open more stores. Therefore, instead of helping the entrepreneurs launch a business in Hong Kong, Smith suggested they stay and become involved in Finagle A Bagel. Because Litchman and Trust had roots in the Boston area, the opportunity to join a local bagel business was appealing both personally and professionally. Late in 1998, they bought a majority stake in Finagle A Bagel from Smith. The three owners agreed on how to divide management responsibilities and collaborated on plans for more aggressive expansion. Within a few years, Trust and Litchman completed a deal to buy the rest of the business and became the sole owners and copresidents.

Sales have increased nearly every year since the conversion to bagels, and today Finagle A Bagel operates seventeen stores, a corporate support center, and a dough-making factory. In addition to its eight downtown Boston stores, the company runs nine suburban stores stretching from thirty miles north in Beverly to thirty miles south in Norwell. On the drawing board are plans to open several more stores per year.

Branding the Bagel

Over time, the owners have introduced a wide range of bagels, sandwiches, and salads linked to the core bagel product. Bagels are baked fresh every day, and the stores receive daily deliveries of fresh salad fixings and other ingredients. Employees make each menu item to order while the customer watches. Some of the most popular offerings include a breakfast bagel pizza, salads with bagel-chip croutons, and BLT (bacon-lettuce-tomato) bagel sandwiches.

Finagle A Bagel is also boosting revenues by wholesaling its bagels to thousands of universities, hospitals, and corporate cafeterias. In addition, it sells several varieties of bagels under the Finagle A Bagel brand to the Shaw's Market grocery chain. Shaw's has been expanding in New England through mergers and acquisitions, opening new opportunities for its bagel supplier. "As they grow, we grow with them," comments Litchman. "More importantly, it gets our name into markets where we're not. And we can track the sales and see how we're doing." If a particular Shaw's supermarket registers unusually strong bagel sales, the copresidents will consider opening a store in or near that community.

The Bagel Economy

Although Finagle A Bagel competes with other bagel chains in and around Boston, its competition goes well beyond restaurants in that category. "You compete with a person selling a cup of coffee, you compete with a grocery store selling a salad," Litchman notes. "People only have so many 'dining dollars' and you need to convince them to spend those dining dollars in your store." Finagle A Bagel's competitive advantages are high-quality, fresh products, courteous and competent employees, and clean, attractive, and inviting restaurants.

Not long ago a recession following the terrorist attacks on New York and Washington, D.C., temporarily reduced Boston's tourist traffic and prompted corporate customers to cut back on catering orders from Finagle A Bagel. As a result, the company's sales revenues remained flat for about a year; then they began inching up as the economy moved toward recovery. Now Litchman and Trust expect their business to sell $25 million worth of bagels and related menu items in the coming year.

Social Responsibility Through Bagels

Social responsibility is an integral part of Finagle A Bagel's operations. Rather than simply throw away unsold bagels at the end of the day, the owners donate the bagels to schools, shelters, and other nonprofit organizations. When local nonprofit groups hold fund-raising events, the copresidents contribute bagels to feed the volunteers. Over the years, Finagle A Bagel has provided bagels to bicyclists raising money for St. Jude Children's Research Hospital, to swimmers raising money for breast cancer research, and to people building community playgrounds. Also, the copresidents are strongly committed to being fair to their customers by offering good value and a good experience. "Something that we need to remember and instill in our people all the time," Trust emphasizes, "is that customers are coming in and your responsibility is to give them the best that you can give them."

Even with 400-plus employees, the copresidents find that owning a business is a nonstop proposition. "Our typical day never ends," says Trust. They are constantly visiting stores, dealing with suppliers, reviewing financial results, and planning for the future. Despite all these responsibilities, this husband-and-wife entrepreneurial team enjoy applying their educational background and business experience to build a business that satisfies thousands of customers every day.

Questions

1. How has the business cycle affected Finagle A Bagel?
2. What is Finagle A Bagel doing to differentiate itself from competitors that want to a share of customers' dining dollars?
3. Why would Finagle A Bagel donate bagels to local charities rather than give them away to customers or employees?
4. If you wanted to open a bagel restaurant in Hong Kong, would you license the Finagle A Bagel brand? Why or why not?

Building a Business Plan Part I

A business plan is a carefully constructed guide for a person starting a business. The purpose of a well-prepared business plan is to show how practical and attainable the entrepreneur's goals are. It also serves as a concise document that potential investors can examine to see if they would like to invest or assist in financing a new venture. A business plan should include the following twelve components:

- Introduction
- Executive summary
- Benefits to the community
- Company and industry
- Management team
- Manufacturing and operations plan
- Labor force
- Marketing plan
- Financial plan
- Exit strategy
- Critical risks and assumptions
- Appendix

A brief description of each of these sections is provided in Chapter 6 (see also Table 6.3 on page 178).

This is the first of seven exercises that appear at the ends of each of the seven major parts in this textbook. The goal of these exercises is to help you work through the preceding components to create your own business plan. For example, in the exercise for this part you will make decisions and complete the research that will help you develop the introduction for your business plan and the benefits to the community that your business will provide. In the exercises for Parts II through VII you will add more components to your plan and eventually build a plan that actually could be used to start a business. The flowchart shown gives an overview of the steps you will be taking to prepare your business plan.

The First Step: Choosing Your Business

One of the first steps for starting your own business is to decide what type of business you want to start. Take some time to think about this decision. Before proceeding, answer the following questions:

- Why did you choose this type of business?
- Why do you think this business will be successful?
- Would you enjoy owning and operating this type of business?

Warning: Don't rush this step. This step often requires much thought, but it is well worth the time and effort. As an added bonus, you are more likely to develop a quality business plan if you really want to open this type of business.

Now that you have decided on a specific type of business, it is time to begin the planning process. The goal for this part is to complete the introduction and benefits to the community components of your business plan.

Before you begin, it is important to note that the business plan is not a document that is written and then set aside. It is a living document that an entrepreneur should refer to continuously in order to ensure that plans are being carried through appropriately. As the entrepreneur begins to execute the plan, he or she should monitor the business environment continuously and make changes to the plan to address any challenges or opportunities that were not foreseen originally.

Throughout this course you will, of course, be building your knowledge about business. Therefore, it will be appropriate for you to continually revisit parts of the plan that you have already written in order to refine them based on your more comprehensive knowledge. You will find that writing your plan is not a simple matter of starting at the beginning and moving chronologically through to the end. Instead, you probably will find yourself jumping around the various components, making refinements as you go. In fact, the second component—the executive summary—should be written last, but because of its comprehensive nature and its importance to potential investors, it appears after the introduction in the final business plan. By the end of this course, you should be able to put the finishing touches on your plan, making sure that all the parts create a comprehensive and sound whole so that you can present it for evaluation.

The Introduction Component

1.1. Start with the cover page. Provide the business name, street address, telephone number, web address (if any), name(s) of owner(s) of the business, and the date the plan is issued.

1.2. Next, provide background information on the company and include the general nature of the business: retailing, manufacturing, or service; what your product or service is; what is unique about it; and why you believe that your business will be successful.

1.3. Then include a summary statement of the business's financial needs, if any. You probably will need to revise your financial needs summary after

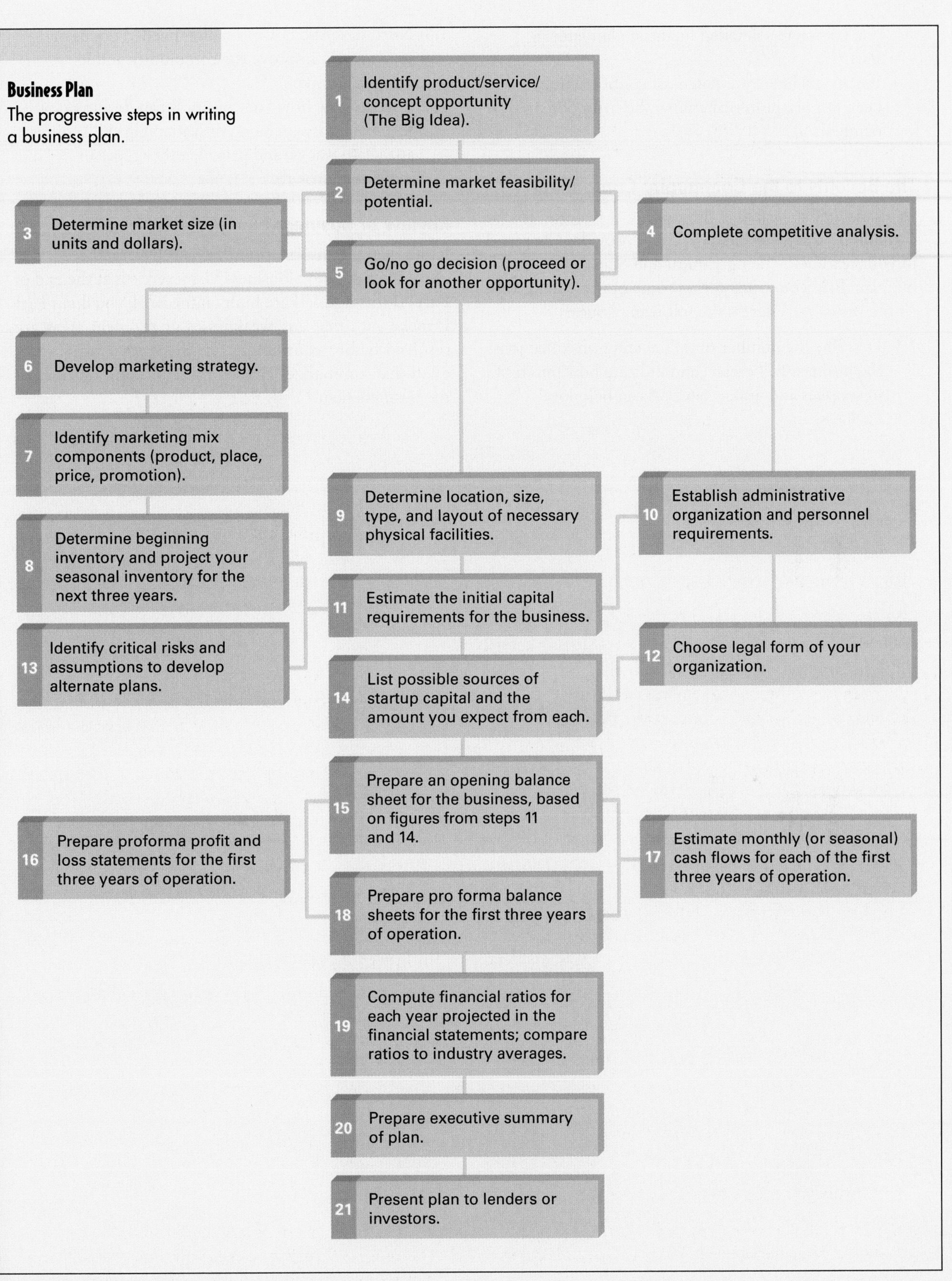

Business Plan
The progressive steps in writing a business plan.
1 Identify product/service/ concept opportunity (The Big Idea).
2 Determine market feasibility/ potential.
3 Determine market size (in units and dollars).
4 Complete competitive analysis.
5 Go/no go decision (proceed or look for another opportunity).
6 Develop marketing strategy.
7 Identify marketing mix components (product, place, price, promotion).
8 Determine beginning inventory and project your seasonal inventory for the next three years.
9 Determine location, size, type, and layout of necessary physical facilities.
10 Establish administrative organization and personnel requirements.
11 Estimate the initial capital requirements for the business.
12 Choose legal form of your organization.
13 Identify critical risks and assumptions to develop alternate plans.
14 List possible sources of startup capital and the amount you expect from each.
15 Prepare an opening balance sheet for the business, based on figures from steps 11 and 14.
16 Prepare proforma profit and loss statements for the first three years of operation.
17 Estimate monthly (or seasonal) cash flows for each of the first three years of operation.
18 Prepare pro forma balance sheets for the first three years of operation.
19 Compute financial ratios for each year projected in the financial statements; compare ratios to industry averages.
20 Prepare executive summary of plan.
21 Present plan to lenders or investors.

Source: Timothy S. Hatten, Small Business Management: Entrepreneurship and Beyond, 2d ed., p. 126. Copyright © 2003 by Houghton Mifflin Company. Used by permission of the Houghton Mifflin Company.

you complete a detailed financial plan later in Part VI.

1.4. Finally, include a statement of confidentiality to keep important information away from potential competitors.

The Benefits to the Community Component

In this section, describe the potential benefits to the community that your business could provide. Chapter 2 in your textbook, "Being Ethical and Socially Responsible," can help you in answering some of these questions. At the very least, address the following issues:

1.5. Describe the number of skilled and nonskilled jobs the business will create, and indicate how purchases of supplies and other materials can help local businesses.

1.6. Next, describe how providing needed goods or services will improve the community and its standard of living.

1.7. Finally, state how your business can develop new technical, management, or leadership skills; offer attractive wages; and provide other types of individual growth.

Review of Business Plan Activities

Read over the information that you have gathered. Because the Building a Business Plan exercises at the end of Parts II through VII are built on the work you do in Part I, make sure that any weaknesses or problem areas are resolved before continuing. Finally, write a brief statement that summarizes all the information for this part of the business plan.

part II

Trends in Business Today

In Part II of *Business* we look at several trends that influence how and where business is conducted. First, we investigate the exploding world of e-business. Then we move to a very practical aspect of business: How businesses are owned. Issues related to ownership are particularly interesting in today's world, where large global businesses coexist with small businesses. Finally, because the majority of businesses are small, we look at specific issues related to small business.

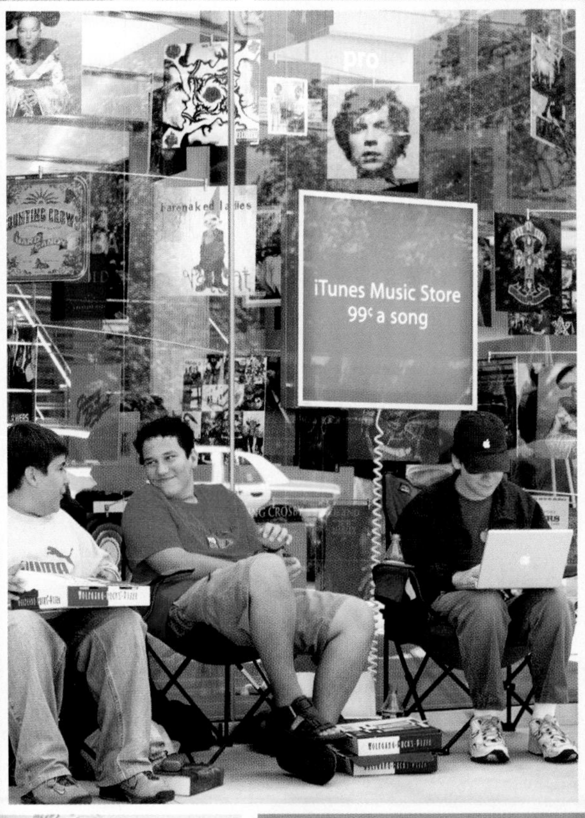

chapter

4 Navigating the World of e-Business

learning objectives

1 Define and explain the meaning of e-business.

2 Explore the basic framework of e-business.

3 Identify and explain fundamental models of e-business.

4 Understand the factors that influence an e-business plan.

5 Discuss the social and legal concerns of e-business.

6 Explore the growth, future opportunities, and challenges of e-business.

Even though the MSN network offers a dizzying array of options, customers can easily tailor the service to their personal preferences.

inside business

MSN: Gateway to the Internet

FOR ONLINE ACCESS to tickets, toys, and almost anything else, MSN is the gateway to the Internet for more than nine million people. Customers who pay $21.95 monthly for dial-up access over ordinary telephone lines (more for high-speed broadband access) can move with a click from MSN's home page to content and services provided by 10,000 other partners. Targeting families, MSN also has arranged a partnership to offer child-friendly Disney content and allow parents to check on their children's online activities.

As a unit of Microsoft, MSN can draw on the parent company's technology expertise and deal-making clout to fuel constant innovations from software upgrades to new services. Even though MSN offers a dizzying array of options, customers can easily tailor the service to their personal preferences. This means that investors can have the latest stock market news come up in a prominent position when they log onto MSN, for example, whereas sports fans can put current scores front and center. And MSN is increasingly international in scope, offering local content and services for thirty-four international markets, including Canada, China, Germany, and Japan.

Despite its growing popularity, MSN faces intense competition from rival America Online (AOL), which has thirty-five million customers and is the runaway leader in Internet access. Like MSN, AOL can use the connections of its powerful parent company—AOL Time Warner—to forge alliances and bring in business. And both companies face similar challenges in boosting the number of customers as well as squeezing more revenue from advertising and other sources. In the past, MSN lacked the flexibility to create media-rich advertisements, and it was not particularly responsive to its advertisers' needs. However, after recruiting a savvy magazine executive to direct advertising sales and beefing up its technical capabilities to run more sophisticated ads, MSN has been able to attract more advertising dollars, even during periods when online advertising was in a slump.

Can MSN overtake AOL's huge lead in the Internet access market? Not long ago MSN ran an advertising campaign encouraging AOL customers to switch to MSN. The campaign stressed the higher cost of AOL's dial-up service ($23.90 per month) and explained how easily AOL users could become MSN users. MSN was then drawing 6,000 new customers daily. "We've never been in a better situation to bring some heat to America Online," said an MSN vice president. AOL scoffed at MSN's competitive moves. "Last I checked, at its peak, eighteen people switched a day from AOL to MSN," said an AOL spokesperson. "Based on that, in the year 3000, they may well have caught up." But the battle for customers is far from over, and MSN clearly has the strength to be a formidable competitor over the long run.[1]

MSN is an example of a firm that can trace its history only as far back as the start of commercial activity on the Internet. Like other well-known e-business firms, such as Yahoo!, e-Bay, and Amazon, MSN owes its very existence to the Internet. Quite simply, without the Internet, there would be no MSN, Yahoo!, e-Bay, or Amazon.

Most firms, on the other hand, have developed or will develop an Internet presence by transferring some of their business practices to the Internet. This was the route taken by Disney, which found opportunities by placing some of its entertainment and information content online. For reasons we will examine more closely in this chapter, virtually all businesses eventually will find themselves conducting a growing proportion of their affairs on the Internet.

The fundamental division between businesses that invented themselves on the Internet, such as MSN, and previously established firms that have transferred only some of their activities to the Internet, such as the Gap, is a distinguishing characteristic of e-business. Firms with no history but the one defined on the Internet make their business decisions with a clear focus on the online world. There is no concern for interfering with other established business activity. On the other hand, firms such as the Gap are very concerned about how development on the Internet will affect their current retail store sales, costs, customer relations, and so forth.

This chapter examines the development of both types of businesses and provides a foundation for understanding how and why Internet activities will change the way businesses function in the future. We also take a closer look at how firms conduct business on the Internet and what growth opportunities may be available to both new and existing firms. Before exploring this new and exciting arena for business competition, however, let's begin by defining e-business.

Defining e-Business

learning objective

1 Define and explain the meaning of e-business.

e-business (electronic business) the organized effort of individuals to produce and sell, for a profit, the products and services that satisfy society's needs through the facilities available on the Internet

e-commerce buying and selling activities conducted online

In Chapter 1 we defined *business* as the organized effort of individuals to produce and sell, for a profit, the products and services that satisfy society's needs. In a simple sense then, **e-business,** or **electronic business,** can be defined as the organized effort of individuals to produce and sell, for a profit, the products and services that satisfy society's needs *through the facilities available on the Internet.* And just as we distinguished between any *individual business* and the general term *business,* which refers to all such efforts within a society, we recognize both the individual *e-business,* such as MSN, and the general concept of *e-business.* As you will see in the remainder of this chapter and throughout this book, e-business is transforming key business activities, such as buying and selling products and services, building better supplier and customer relationships, and improving general business operations.

Sometimes people use the term *e-commerce* instead of *e-business.* In a strict sense, *e-business* is used when one is speaking about all business activities and practices conducted on the Internet by an individual firm or industry. On the other hand, **e-commerce** is a part of e-business; the term refers only to buying and selling activities conducted online. These activities may include identifying suppliers, selecting products or services, making purchase commitments, completing financial transactions, and obtaining service.[2] We generally use the term *e-business* because of its broader definition and scope.

Organizing e-Business Resources

As noted in Chapter 1, to be organized, a business must combine *human, material, informational,* and *financial resources.* This is true of e-business, too (see Figure 4.1), but in this case the resources may be more specialized than in a typical business. For example, people who can design, create, and maintain websites are only a fraction of the specialized human resources required by businesses considering an Internet presence. Material resources must include specialized computers, sophisticated equipment and

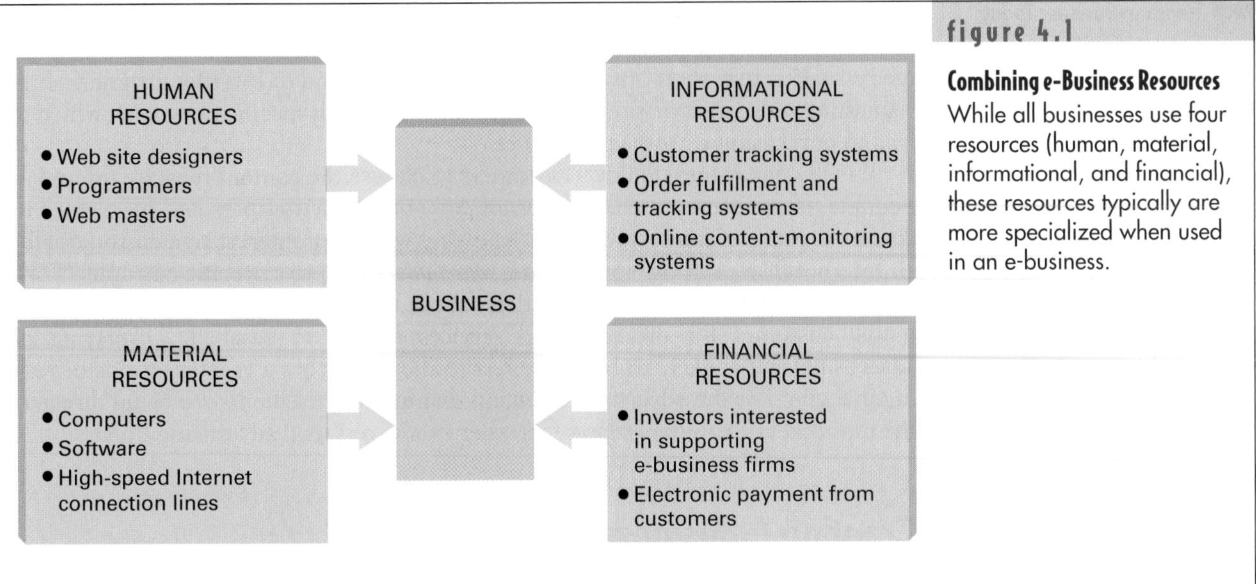

figure 4.1

Combining e-Business Resources
While all businesses use four resources (human, material, informational, and financial), these resources typically are more specialized when used in an e-business.

software, and high-speed Internet connection lines. Computer programs that track the number of customers to view a firm's website are generally among the specialized informational resources required. Financial resources, the money required to start and maintain the firm and allow it to grow, usually reflect greater participation by individual entrepreneurs and investors willing to invest in a high-tech firm instead of conventional financial sources such as banks.

Satisfying Needs Online

Let's start with two basic assumptions. First, the Internet has created some new customer needs that did not exist before the creation of the Internet. Second, e-businesses can satisfy those needs, as well as more traditional ones. For example, among the products and services AOL offers its customers are Internet access, browsers, chat rooms, databases, and exclusive Time Warner entertainment content. Amazon.com gives customers anywhere in the world access to the same virtual store of books, DVDs, and CDs. And at e-Bay's global auction site, customers can, for a small fee, buy and sell almost anything. In each of these examples, customers can use the Internet to meet a specific need.

Internet users also can access print media, such as newspapers and magazines, and radio and television programming at a time and place convenient to them. In addition to offering such a wide selection of content, the Internet provides the opportunity for *interaction*. In other words, communication is now an active two-way street between the online program and the viewer. CNN.com and other news-content sites encourage

Websites can be beautiful. While all businesses must satisfy the needs of their customers, some companies like 1–800-Flowers use 800 phone numbers and the Internet to sell their products. Is it successful? You bet! Last year, 1–800-Flowers sold product and services valued at $500 million.

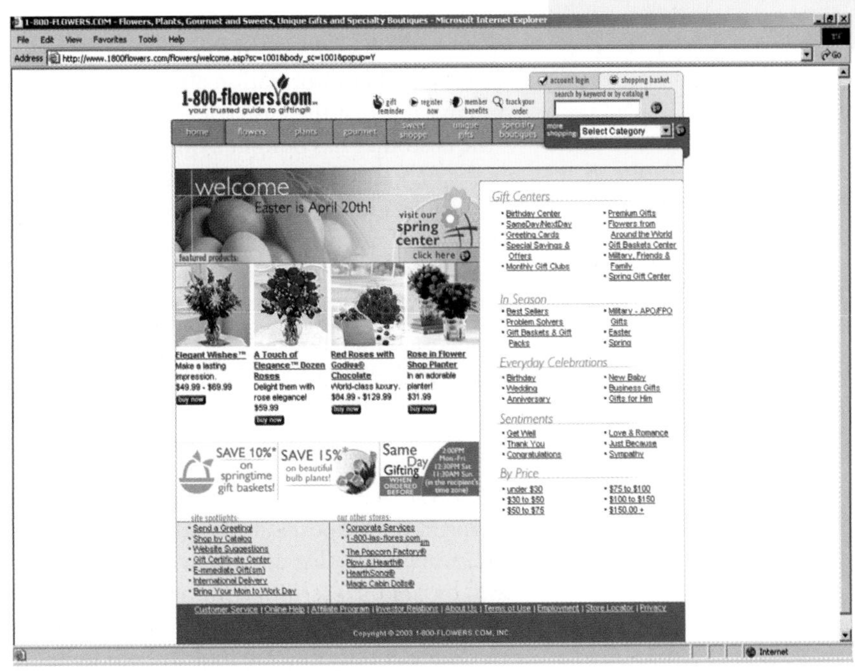

Source: Reprinted courtesy of 1800FLOWERS.com.

dialogue among viewers in chat rooms and exchanges with the writers of articles posted to the site. In contrast to the passive situation they encounter with traditional media such as television or radio, customers can respond to Internet programming by requesting more information about a product or posing specific questions, which may lead to purchasing a product or service.

Finally, the Internet allows customers to choose the content they are offered. For example, individuals can custom design daily online newspapers and magazines with articles that are of interest to them. Knowing what is of interest to a customer allows an Internet firm to direct appropriate, *smart advertising* to a specific customer. For example, someone wanting to read articles about the New York Yankees might be a potential customer for products and services related to baseball. Displaying only advertising that is likely to be of interest to the viewer has a greater chance of resulting in a sale. For the advertiser, knowing that its advertisements are being directed to the most likely customers represents a better way to spend advertising dollars.

Creating e-Business Profit

Firms can increase their profits either by increasing sales revenue or by reducing expenses through a variety of e-business activities.

revenue stream a source of revenue flowing into a firm

Revenue Growth Each source of revenue flowing into a firm is referred to as a **revenue stream**. Since revenue streams provide the dollars needed to operate the firm, identifying new sources of revenue is a major concern for any business. One way to increase revenues is to sell merchandise on the Internet. Online merchants can reach a global customer base twenty-four hours a day, seven days a week; the opportunity to shop on the Internet is virtually unrestricted. The removal of barriers that might keep customers from conventional stores is a major factor in increasing sales revenue potential for e-businesses, as firms like Amazon.com, Barnesandnoble.com, and Landsend.com have demonstrated. And yet the simple redirection of existing revenue to an online revenue stream is not desirable. For example, shifting revenues earned from customers inside a real store to revenues earned by those customers online does not create any real new revenue for a firm. The goal is to find new customers and generate new sales so that total revenues are increased. To see how Dell Computer increases revenues while helping customers get the "right" computer, read Talking Technology.

Intelligent informational systems also can help generate sales revenue for Internet firms. Such systems store information about each customer's purchases, along with a variety of other information about the buyer's preferences. Using this information, the system can assist the customer the next time he or she visits the website. For example, if the customer has bought a Shania Twain or Garth Brooks CD in the past, the system might suggest CDs by similar artists.

While some customers in certain situations may not make a purchase online, the existence of the firm's website and the services and information it provides may lead to increased sales in the firm's physical stores. For example, customers may use the Gap website simply to obtain product information about clothing but delay their actual purchases until they have had a chance to try on garments in a Gap retail store. Similarly, Toyota.com can provide basic comparative information for shoppers so that they are better prepared for their visit to an automobile showroom.

Typically, e-business revenue streams are created by the sale of products and services, by advertising placed on web pages, and by subscription fees charged for access to online services and content. For example, Hoover's Online (**www.hoovers.com**), a comprehensive source for company and industry information, makes some of its online content free for anyone who visits the site, but more detailed data are available only by paid subscription. In addition, it receives revenue from companies that are called *sponsors*, who advertise their products and services on Hoover's website.

Many Internet firms that distribute news, magazine and newspaper articles, and similar content generate revenue primarily from advertising sponsors and commissions earned from sellers of products linked to the site. Online shopping malls now provide groups of related vendors of electronic equipment, computer hardware and software, health foods, and fashion items with a new method of selling their products and services. And sites like Petco (**www.petco.com**) focus on the large market for pet supplies. WebMD (**www.webmd.com**) and other health-related sites provide information about remedies, diseases, and other health topics and issues. In many cases the vendors share online sales revenues with the site owners.

Expense Reduction Expense reduction is the other major way in which e-business can help increase profitability. Providing online access to information customers want can reduce the cost of dealing with customers. For example, most airlines provide updated scheduling and pricing information, as well as promotional material, on their websites. This reduces the costs of dealing with customers through a call center operated by employees and of mailing brochures, which may be outdated within weeks or easily misplaced by customers. SprintPCS (**www.sprintpcs.com**) is just one company that maintains an extensive website where potential customers can learn more about cell phone products and services, and current customers can access personal account information, send e-mail questions to customer service, and purchase additional products or services. With such extensive online services, SprintPCS does not have to maintain as many physical store locations as it would

Spotlight

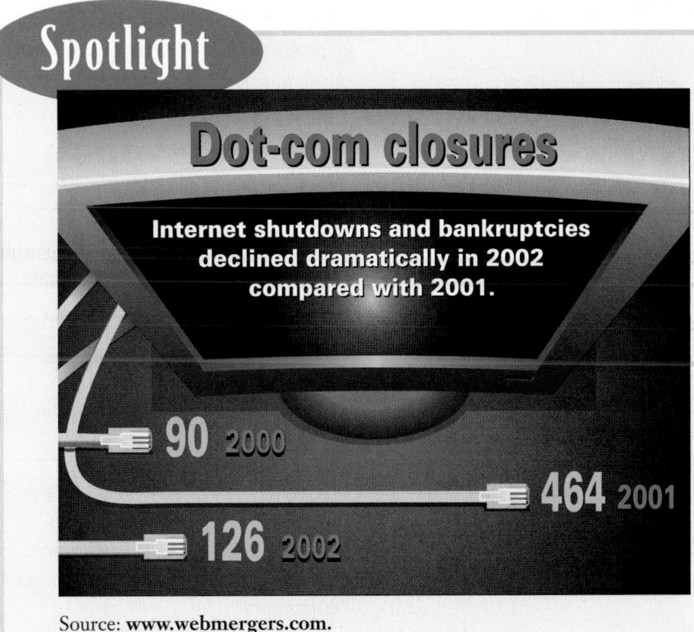

Source: **www.webmergers.com.**

talking technology

Easy as Dell

How does Dell do it? Competing against giant rivals such as IBM, the Austin-based computer company has captured a whopping 27 percent share of the U.S. personal computer market and 15 percent of the global market. The key to Dell's e-business success: using technology to customize products for each individual buyer.

Rather than building computers in advance and selling them as is, Dell invites customers to call a toll-free phone number or visit Dell.com and order computers built to their personal specifications. For example, Dell helped the information technology experts at the Bellagio Hotel in Las Vegas meet a tight deadline for installing high-speed servers built around a new computer chip. The tech experts had tested and decided on a chip that was not yet available commercially. They also liked Dell servers. So they talked with Dell, and as soon as the chip was in production, Dell put it into servers customized for the Bellagio's needs—the first manufacturer to use the new chip—and rushed the equipment to the hotel. Thanks to Dell's flexibility and responsiveness, the hotel met its schedule.

Dell's use of technology to customize products is a win-win situation. Individuals and corporate customers can order exactly the features and software they want and avoid paying for extras they cannot use. At the same time, making computers to order helps Dell gauge demand and plan accordingly—a valuable early-warning system to protect profits from sales fluctuations. When worldwide sales slowed not long ago, CEO Michael Dell observed that "we didn't get caught with inventory or the wrong cost structure." This technology also allows Dell to adapt to customer preferences around the world. In Japan, personal computer buyers like to try products before buying. Therefore, Dell set up a special website with detailed product information. It then put computer kiosks in local electronics stores so that customers could browse the website and follow up by testing the kiosk's demonstration computer before ordering. Although online buying is less popular in Japan than in the United States, Dell's Japanese website now sells $500,000 worth of computers every day—a testament to the company's e-business prowess.

table 4.1 Advantages and Disadvantages of e-Business

Advantages	Disadvantages
Increases productivity for both customers and employees by saving time and money	Requires specialized knowledge to use
Allows for communications at a more convenient place and time through e-mail and other software	User must have Internet access
Provides access to information anytime, anywhere	May be perceived as an undesirable means of communications compared with direct contact between people
Allows firms to profitably serve small markets	May result in lost customers or sales if online sales experience is unsatisfactory
Facilitates online shopping to geographically dispersed customers	Online promotional efforts such as e-mail and pop-up advertising may be annoying
Inexpensive methods to promote the firm and its products to current and potential customers	

without these online services. For more information on the advantages and disadvantages of e-business, look at Table 4.1.

We examine more examples of how e-business contributes to profitability throughout this chapter, especially as we focus on some of the business models for activity on the Internet.

A Framework for Understanding e-Business

learning objective

2 Explore the basic framework of e-business.

World Wide Web (the web) the Internet's multimedia environment of audio, visual, and text data

digitized data that have been converted to a type of signal that computers and telecommunications equipment that make up the Internet can understand

The Internet was conceived originally as an elaborate military communications network that would allow vital messages to be transmitted in the event of war. Before 1994, the U.S. National Science Foundation, the agency that funded and regulated use of the Internet, restricted its use to noncommercial activities, such as e-mail communication and the sharing of data among university researchers. However, as the potential commercial benefits of the Internet became increasingly obvious, a growing list of commercially interested groups demanded that the doors be opened to business activity. At about the same time, new technology emerged that simplified use of the Internet and allowed the addition of multimedia content. This multimedia environment of audio, visual, and text data came to be known as the **World Wide Web** (or more simply, **the web**).

The Internet can be envisioned as a large network of computers that pass small, standardized packets of electronic data from one station to another until they are delivered to their final destination. In a sense, the Internet is the equivalent of the telephone network that was created almost one hundred years ago. However, instead of transmitting just voice communications, the Internet can transfer a variety of multimedia data at high speed around the world. To be transferred over the Internet, data need to be **digitized**, which means converted to a type of signal that computers and telecommunications equipment that make up the Internet can understand.

Most firms involved in e-business today fall more or less into one of three primary groups as defined by their e-business activities (see Figure 4.2):

- Telecommunications and computer hardware manufacturers and Internet service providers
- Internet software producers
- Online sellers and content providers

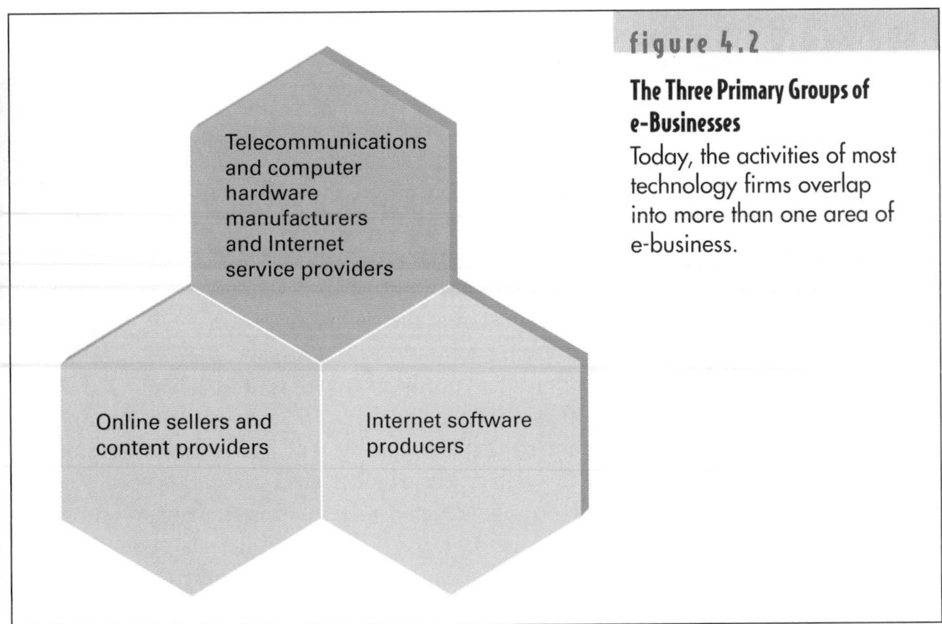

figure 4.2

The Three Primary Groups of e-Businesses
Today, the activities of most technology firms overlap into more than one area of e-business.

In this section we examine these three groups and also look at how e-business facilitates both global and small business operations.

Telecommunications and Computer Hardware Manufacturers and Internet Service Providers

The telecommunications and computer hardware manufacturers that helped build the Internet, together with Internet service providers, supply the physical infrastructure of the industry today. Lucent Technologies, Cisco Systems, and Nortel Networks produce most of the telecommunications hardware that allows the Internet to work. Companies such as IBM, Apple, Dell, Compaq, and Gateway produce many of the computers used by consumers, and companies such as Sun, IBM, and Hewlett Packard manufacture servers that control corporate computer networks. For more information about how computer hardware manufacturers use specialized components in their products, read Adapting to Change (on p. 114). **Internet service providers (ISPs),** which buy their technological capability from the makers of telecommunications and hardware manufacturers, provide customers with a connection to the Internet through various phone plugs and cables. This last link to the Internet is the shortest, but typically the slowest, in the global electronic network. As phone lines are replaced by high-speed Internet access, speed for home users will improve gradually to levels enjoyed by businesses in communities where the telecommunications infrastructure has already been upgraded. AOL is the largest and best-known ISP, whereas MSN is ranked second. And yet hundreds of smaller ISPs in both urban and rural areas also provide access to the Internet. Furthermore, recent developments in technologies using wireless networks within office buildings and small clusters of buildings such as college campuses are helping to create a more readily accessible Internet using a variety of communications devices.

Internet service providers (ISPs) provide customers with a connection to the Internet through various phone plugs and cables

Internet Software Producers

Producers of software that enable people to do things on the Internet are the second primary group of e-business firms. Searching the Internet, browsing websites, sending e-mail messages, shopping, and viewing multimedia content online are activities that require specialized computer programs. Browser software is the single most basic

adapting to change

Behind the Scenes with Semtech

DO YOU KNOW what a transient voltage suppressor is? Or a silicon rectifier? These are only two of the sophisticated products produced by Semtech, based in Camarillo, California. Neither the company's name nor its products may be familiar, but if you use a laptop computer, cell phone, or personal digital assistant, chances are it contains a Semtech component. In fact, the company plays a vital behind-the-scenes role in designing specialized semiconductors for computers, telecommunications devices, and many other consumer products.

A transient voltage suppressor protects an electronic system from being damaged by spikes in voltage. Manufacturers like Dell Computer, Cisco, IBM, Motorola, and Sony often incorporate such suppressors into their products. In addition, computer makers buy Semtech's semiconductors to regulate power supply and control touchpad and touch-screen input. However, the company was not always so focused on the commercial market.

When Semtech was founded in 1960, it specialized in electronic components for the growing military and aerospace markets. Because these customers set exacting standards for product performance and timely delivery, the company earned a reputation for both quality and reliability. Ten years ago, however, demand in these markets slowed. In response, Semtech began selling to the commercial market, which now accounts for most of its revenues. At the same time, the company continued offering military and aerospace customers older products such as the silicon rectifier, which changes alternating current to direct current so that the current will flow continuously one way through an electronic device.

To compete against Texas Instruments, National Semiconductor, and other high-tech companies, Semtech is constantly designing new semiconductors for unique functions. It is also diversifying by acquiring smaller tech firms experienced in serving particular segments of the commercial market, such as automated test equipment. The company rings up almost $200 million in annual sales and custom designs semiconductors for hundreds of products every year. Should sales begin to slow, Semtech can look to its past for clues about how to adapt for a successful future.

product for user interaction on the Internet. Currently, the dominant browser is Microsoft's Internet Explorer, followed well back by AOL's Netscape Communicator.

In addition to browser software, many people use search-engine software to find information on the Internet. Popular search engines include msn.com, yahoo.com, google.com, altavista.com, aol.com, lycos.com, netscape.com, and hundreds of lesser-known sites that enable users to search the Internet for needed information. By entering key words and phrases, users are guided to available online information that is ranked according to the search-engine rules for listing search results. For instance, some engines will list sites according to how often users have selected them after their search.

Today, e-mail is considered a standard communication software tool for all business people. Whether for internal or external communication, the low costs and benefits from using e-mail often make it the easiest Internet-based software solution to rationalize. More advanced and complex communications solutions might include customer relationship and supply-chain management software. Several large firms now sell complete **customer relationship management (CRM) software** solutions that incorporate a variety of methods that can be used to manage communication with customers and share important information with all of a firm's employees. And just as CRM software solutions help firms create more efficient relationships with their customers, **supply-chain management (SCM) software** solutions focus on ways to improve communication between the suppliers and users of materials and components. By providing their production requirements and planning information directly to their suppliers, manufacturers can reduce inventories, improve delivery schedules, and reduce costs, which can quickly show up as improved profitability. For example, Dell Computer's SCM software (**https://valuechain.dell.com**) virtually eliminates the need for the firm to maintain any inventory because suppliers are tied directly into Dell's new manufacturing facility in Round Rock, Texas. Manufacturing schedules and

customer relationship management (CRM) software software solutions that incorporate a variety of methods that can be used to manage communication with customers and share important information with all of the firm's employees

supply-chain management (SCM) software software solutions that focus on ways to improve communication between the suppliers and users of materials and components

parts orders are revised every two hours. Suppliers must keep an agreed-on level of inventory for Dell on hand at nearby local warehouses. As a result, 95 percent of Dell's PCs are built and shipped to customers within twelve hours of their orders being entered into the system. The new software has improved productivity by 160 percent and reduced errors in orders by 50 percent.[3]

Online Sellers and Content Providers

The third primary group of e-businesses consists of all the firms that customers actually interact with on websites. The Internet would still be limited to communication between individuals and among groups of special-interest researchers were it not for the activity of online sellers and content providers. In this area of e-business, we have just begun to see the development of strategies for reaching out to existing and new customers.

As noted earlier, some e-businesses, such as MSN and e-Bay, owe their existence to the Internet. They offer products and services that can be found only online. In contrast, other firms—among them the Gap, Nike, Restoration Hardware, and Gear—have moved only some of their business practices to the Internet. These firms use the Internet to sell merchandise, provide information to customers, and supplement their regular retail sales efforts and other traditional business activities.

Although the Internet is constantly changing, it is clear that both ISPs and businesses are scrambling to take advantage of the Internet's ability to provide customers with information. Time Warner's decision to merge with AOL is a case in point. By arranging for online distribution of interesting content that was formerly distributed through traditional magazines, radio, and television, Time Warner has found new opportunities for revenue growth. Similarly, traditional shopping behavior has been transferred to a virtual environment in which cyberspace retailers can provide more information to customers and have a greater degree of influence on the customer's decision.

The greatest opportunities for entrepreneurs on the Internet are in the production of a service or content. Anyone with a good idea that might appeal to a global audience stands a chance of successfully launching an e-business. As the short history of the Internet indicates, we are only at the beginning of new and exciting applications that can be delivered online. According to Timothy Draper, an insider in the world of e-business and the managing director of Draper Fisher Jurvetson, a West Coast venture capital firm, "The Internet has opened the world up, and that means everyone's now going to be part of the world economy."[4]

Online auctions: A new way to sell unique art objects. Three years ago, Glenn King, owner of Sacramento, California-based Exotica Art & Fashion, began using online auctions to reach new customers and boost sales of unique art items. Today, King, a former manager for Wal-Mart, Clorox, and Pepsi, says that online sales now account for forty percent of his firm's total revenue. In addition, contacts made as a result of his online art sales have enabled him to branch out into a line of imported clothing.

Global e-Business

All three primary groups of e-business firms are in a race to capture global business revenues. Telecommunications firms are competing to build the infrastructure in countries all over the world, and in many cases, they are skipping technological stepping-stones. For example, in poor countries where telephone poles have never existed ground-based wireless systems are now providing instant state-of-the-art communication. In many places ISPs and software producers such as AOL are competing against better-known local firms. And online sellers and content producers are selling their merchandise and services to customers all over the globe.

The ability to customize content for individual customer needs makes the Internet an adaptable tool for global enterprise. Consider Berlitz's website (**www.berlitz.com**) which allows anyone in the world to jump quickly to a website designed in the viewer's preferred language. By clicking on the appropriate icon, viewers can move forward to a website created to meet their needs in their own language. Once there, the viewer can examine Berlitz's wide range of products and services, including multimedia language-learning material, online translation services, and referrals to local Berlitz classroom-based instruction services. This global strategy, which reaches out to the world and yet allows for viewer customization, is at the heart of e-business.

Small e-Business

Based on early experience, the Internet will continue to be a powerful tool for small business. According to a report by Access Markets International (AMI) Partners and *Inc.* magazine, small-business online activity got off to a very quick start. Research showed that an estimated 400,000 U.S. small businesses sold their products and services on e-business sites in 1998, and this number jumped 50 percent to 600,000 in 1999. During the same period, the dollar amount of online transactions grew more than 1,000 percent, increasing from $2 billion to $25 billion. Interestingly, a significant number of small firms—six out of ten—were reluctant to sell their products online at the time because of security concerns, technology challenges, or the belief that their products were unsuited for online selling.[5]

However, despite these early concerns, online activity continues to grow. According to a recent American Express survey, 66 percent of small businesses had already integrated the Internet as a tool to help them run their businesses, using it for making travel plans; purchasing office supplies, equipment, or other business services; conducting industry or market research; marketing or advertising; networking with other entrepreneurs; purchasing goods from wholesalers; and managing accounts and making payments.[6]

Although large firms dominate e-business, the remarkable thing about the Internet is how accessible it is to small businesses. The relatively low cost of going online means that the Internet is open to thousands of small businesses seeking opportunities to sell their services or products internationally. In some cases, small firms have found a niche service or product to sell online. Special online shopping malls bring shoppers a wide selection of unique crafts and artistic creations from small businesses. And many small online magazines, or **e-zines,** as they are often called, have recently found their special audiences through the virtual world of online publishing. In fact, many small publications that began online have gone on to create print versions of their e-zines.

e-zines small online magazines

Writers like Stephen King and recording artists like Sarah McLachlan have discovered that they can earn higher profits by dealing directly with customers online rather than through conventional middlemen such as wholesalers and retail distributors. The Internet also has given unknown artists a new venue for finding an audience; after reading or listening to a sample of their work, newfound fans can order books or CDs directly or download and create their own copies. And software producers like MP3 and Napster were quick to provide users with the technology they could use to download copyrighted materials. Although both firms challenged the traditional methods of entertainment distribution, they also have been at the center of legal concerns over ownership of distribution rights to content on the Internet. More information about what firms in the publishing and music industries are doing about Internet-based distribution methods and protecting their property is provided later in this chapter.

Fundamental Models of e-Business

learning objective

3 Identify and explain fundamental models of e-business.

One way to get a better sense of how businesses are adapting to the opportunities available on the Internet is to identify e-business models. A **business model** represents a group of common characteristics and methods of doing business to generate sales revenues and reduce expenses. For example, all large food stores share a similar business model when it comes to their selection of merchandise, organizational structure, employee job requirements, and often, financing needs. Each of the models discussed below represents a primary e-business model. The models focus attention on the identity of a firm's customers.

business model represents a group of common characteristics and methods of doing business to generate sales revenues and reduce expenses

Business-to-Business (B2B) Model

Many e-businesses can be distinguished from others simply by their customer focus. For instance, some firms use the Internet mainly to conduct business with other businesses. These firms are generally referred to as having a **business-to-business**, or **B2B, model**. Currently, the vast majority of e-business is B2B in nature.

business-to-business (B2B) model firms that conduct business with other businesses

When examining B2B business firms, two clear types emerge. In the first type, the focus is simply on facilitating sales transactions between businesses. For example, Dell manufactures computers to specifications that customers enter on the Dell website. The vast majority of Dell's online orders are from corporate clients who are well informed about the products they need and are looking for fairly priced, high-quality computer products that will be delivered quickly. Basically, by building only what is ordered, Dell reduces storage and carrying costs and rarely is stuck with unsold inventory. By dealing directly with Dell, customers eliminate costs associated with wholesalers and retailers, thereby helping reduce the price they pay for equipment.

A second, more complex type of B2B model involves a company and its suppliers, which often are numerous, geographically dispersed, and difficult to manage. Although managing the activities between a firm and its suppliers is an established business strategy that existed before the Internet came along, it is a focal point of e-business activity for many firms. Today, suppliers use the Internet to bid on products and services they wish to sell to a customer, learn about the customer's rules and procedures that must be followed, and so forth. Likewise, firms seeking specific items can now ask

Whether your online business is treading water or riding a wave, Dell and Sprint can help! Because most small business owners do not have the expertise and time to deal with technology problems, they often turn to firms like Dell and Sprint for solutions that are affordable.

for bids on their websites and choose from available suppliers through the online system. For example, the online leader in the auto industry, Ford Motor Company, links 30,000 auto-parts suppliers and 6,900 dealers in its network, resulting in an estimated $8.9 billion savings each year on transaction costs, materials, and inventory. In addition, Ford expects to earn approximately $3 billion from the fees it charges for use of its supplier network.[7] Similarly, the Internet-based supplier system at General Motors is expected to eliminate the costs of processing more than 100,000 annual purchase orders, which average $125 each.[8]

Savings for both automobile manufacturers come primarily from the elimination of manual labor and the errors created by the repetitive entry of data by employees. For instance, under the old system, Ford might fax an order for parts to a supplier. The supplier would fill out another order form and send a copy to Ford for confirmation. The data would have to be entered in each company's computer system each step of the way. However, under the new system, the supplier has access to Ford's inventory of parts and can place bids for parts online. Ford eliminates the labor costs of data entry and much of the order-processing costs by connecting suppliers to the system.

Given the potential savings, it is no wonder that many other manufacturers and their suppliers are beginning to use the same kind of B2B systems that are used by Ford and General Motors. As an added bonus, manufacturers that use B2B systems can control their purchasing activities while allowing suppliers to become more involved in the production process.

Business-to-Consumer (B2C) Model

business-to-consumer (B2C) model firms that focus on conducting business with individual buyers

In contrast to the B2B model, firms like Amazon and e-Bay are clearly focused on individual buyers and so are referred to as having a **business-to-consumer**, or **B2C, model**. In a B2C situation, understanding how consumers behave online is critical to the firm's success. Typically, a business firm that uses a B2C model must answer the following questions:

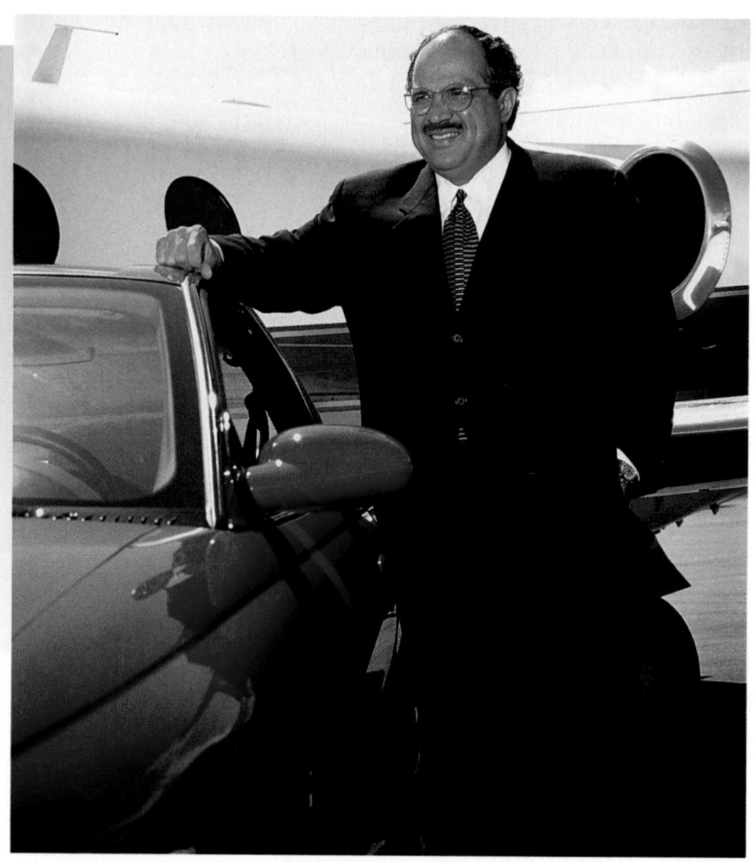

Using the Internet to increase sales. Cornelius Martin of Martin Automotive Group in Bowling Green, Kentucky sells a lot of automobiles. The owner of sixteen dealerships that generate annual sales revenues in excess of $350 million a year uses advertising, showrooms, salespeople, and the Internet to increase sales. Does it work? This year's sales are up an amazing 35 percent when compared to the previous year. According to Martin, a large part of the increase is the result of increased Internet activity that attracts customers to his dealerships.

- Will consumers use websites merely to simplify and speed up comparison shopping?
- Will customers purchase services and products online or end up buying at a traditional retail store?
- What sorts of products and services are best suited for online consumer shopping?
- Which products and services are simply not good choices at this stage of online development?

Although an enormous amount of research has been done to answer these and other questions about consumer shopping behavior in traditional stores, relatively little has been done to date about online consumer behavior. No doubt as more consumers make use of online environments, an increasing amount of research will help to explain how best to meet their needs. At the same time, the number and types of products and services sold online also will expand.

In addition to providing round-the-clock global access to all kinds of products and services, B2C firms often make a special effort to build long-term relationships with their customers. The rationale for this approach is that customers should be valued not only for the immediate sale but also for future sales if they become repeat customers. Often firms will make a special effort to make sure that the customer is satisfied and that problems, if any, are quickly solved. While a "little special attention" may increase the cost of doing business for a B2C firm, the customer's repeated purchases will repay the investment many times over. Specialized software also can help to build good customer relationships. Tracking the decisions and buying preferences as customers navigate a website, for instance, helps management make well-informed decisions about how best to serve such customers. This approach also can enhance inventory decisions, buying selections, and decisions in many other managerial areas. In essence, this is Amazon.com's selling approach. By tracking and analyzing customer data, Amazon can provide individualized service to its customers.

Today, B2B and B2C models are the most popular business models for e-business. And yet, there are other business models that perform specialized e-business activities to generate revenues. Most of the business models described in Table 4.2 are modified versions of the B2B and B2C models.

table 4.2 Other Business Models that Perform Specialized e-Business Activities

Although modified versions of B2B or B2C, the following business models perform specialized e-business activities to generate revenues.

Advertising e-business model	Advertisements that are displayed on a firm's website in return for a fee. Examples include pop-up and banner advertisements on search engines and other popular Internet sites.
Brokerage e-business model	Online marketplaces where buyers and sellers are brought together to facilitate exchange of goods and services. Examples include eBay (**www.ebay.com**), which provides a site for buying and selling virtually anything.
Consumer-to-consumer model	Peer-to-peer software that allows individuals to share information over the Internet. Examples include MP3 (**www.mp3.com**) and Morpheus (**www.morpheus.com**), which allow users to exchange audio, documents, photos, or video files.
Subscription and pay-per-view e-business models	Content that is available only to users who pay a fee to gain access to a website. Examples include investment information provided by Standard & Poor's (**www.standardandpoors.com**) or business research pro vided by Forrester Research, Inc. (**www.forrester.com**).

Creating an e-Business Plan

learning objective

4 Understand the factors that influence an e-business plan.

The approach taken to creating an e-business plan will depend on whether you are establishing a new Internet business or adding an online component to an existing business. In this section we consider some important factors that affect both situations.

Starting Up a New Internet Business from Scratch

For a new Internet business, a good e-business plan should provide detailed answers to basic questions. To begin, the planners need to determine if an Internet business will meet the needs of a group of customers. Furthermore, the planning process should provide planners with information that can help to identify and select groups of potential buyers, direct development of the online product or service, as well as the promotion, pricing, and distribution effort. The start-up planning also should indicate if the potential market will generate enough sales and profits to make the new venture worthwhile. The answers to these questions will determine what type of business model (B2B, B2C, or one of the specialized models described in Table 4.2) is appropriate for the new Internet business. Sometimes more than one business model is appropriate. For example, British children's author J. K. Rowling used the Internet to launch her international marketing effort for *Harry Potter and the Goblet of Fire*. The book launch became an event, with advance sales of 5.3 million copies.[9] Although mainly intended as a promotional effort to both bookstores and consumers, the website used both a B2B model and a B2C model. Eventually, many of these sales took place through Amazon.com and Barnesandnoble.com, as customers ordered online and had the books shipped as gifts to children for their summertime reading enjoyment. The website has grown since its inception and now serves as a site for ongoing marketing and advertising of new titles.

Building an Online Presence for an Existing Business

Today it is quite common for an existing business to add e-business activities. A business that already has a physical location and a customer base generally looks at e-business as a way to expand sales to current customers and to add new customers who are beyond the reach of the firm's geographic location. For example, retail firms such as Radio Shack, Sears, and many others have turned to the Internet to sell more products or to lead customers to physical stores in order to purchase products or services. Both customers who are seeking the convenience of shopping online and those who are simply using the website to view a retailer's catalog of merchandise and promotions before buying in a retail store can use the firm's website to satisfy their personal shopping needs. Although developing an online presence may seem like a logical extension of what a firm already does, there are important factors that must be considered before using the Internet to sell products or services or provide information to customers. To see how starting a new Internet business differs from building an online presence for an existing business, look at Figure 4.3. In the remainder of this section we examine how these factors can change the way an existing business firm develops an online presence.

Are Online Customers Really Different? For an existing business, one of the first concerns is how an online customer differs from a customer who walks into its physical stores. In some cases a firm may be reaching out to new markets that are geographically dispersed and quite different in a variety of ways from the customers the firm is used to dealing with in its physical stores. For example, customers who visit the J.C. Penney website may be different from customers who visit a department store located in a shopping mall in a large metropolitan area. The online customers may live

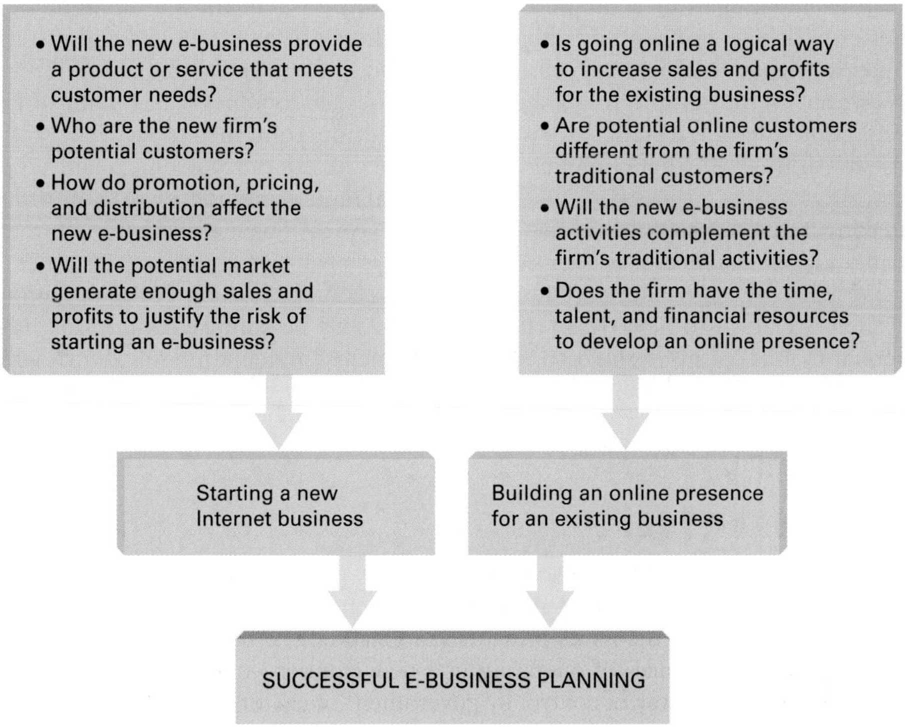

figure 4.3

Planning for a New Internet Business or Building an Online Presence for an Existing Business

The approach taken to creating an e-business plan will depend on whether you are establishing a new Internet business or adding an online component to an existing business.

- Will the new e-business provide a product or service that meets customer needs?
- Who are the new firm's potential customers?
- How do promotion, pricing, and distribution affect the new e-business?
- Will the potential market generate enough sales and profits to justify the risk of starting an e-business?

↓ Starting a new Internet business

- Is going online a logical way to increase sales and profits for the existing business?
- Are potential online customers different from the firm's traditional customers?
- Will the new e-business activities complement the firm's traditional activities?
- Does the firm have the time, talent, and financial resources to develop an online presence?

↓ Building an online presence for an existing business

↓ SUCCESSFUL E-BUSINESS PLANNING

in a rural area, earn more or less money, and have different needs when compared with shoppers in a metropolitan area. If the customers are different with different needs, the task of developing appropriate strategies to meet their needs is more complex. On the other hand, if both types of customers are similar with similar needs, many of the same methods used in the firm's physical stores can be transferred to the web. Advertising, pricing, and shipping methods, for instance, that are already in place can be used on the firm's website.

Generally, existing firms that want to sell products or services throughout the world face additional problems when going online. For instance, besides the obvious differences in language, a website selling a product such as clothing or footwear must provide standardized sizes that are used in different nations around the world. In fact, designing a website that can successfully communicate to individual customers in other nations can be a challenge for online vendors that is far greater than eliminating language barriers or simply ensuring the display of proper size references to customers.

Complementing Existing Non-Internet-Based Plans The development of a firm's e-business activities should be guided by one key objective: to complement the existing non-Internet-based business plan. The e-business plan must be in line with the firm's overall goals and objectives. If customer satisfaction, for example, is considered a weakness, providing information online and allowing customers to contact customer service employees by e-mail may reduce or eliminate the problem. But be warned: Developing e-business activities that can be used to solve or reduce a firm's problems can be a complex process that takes time. More information on how an e-business plan complements a firm's other planning activities is presented throughout the remainder of this book.

Complexity and Time Concerns Every business must be prepared to allow sufficient time for customers, suppliers, and staff to adapt to the new methods of operation necessitated by the installation of e-business activities. Online solutions such as introducing e-mail or a simple company website to help the staff communicate better with one another, customers, and suppliers can be developed and installed quickly without undue delay, cost, or disruption of current work responsibilities. However, as the complexity of the plan increases, so too does the amount of time required to design, install, and test the new solution—and then to train the staff to use it. All this is further complicated by the need to educate customers and suppliers, who will be expected to change to an unfamiliar method of placing orders, making requests for information, and other typical business activities. Internet banking, for instance, is growing in popularity, but it takes time for customers to get used to the procedures required to bank online. A strong customer support system is critical to help those customers who may be confused about the online screen menus, computer and connection problems, and anything else with which they may need assistance.

Social and Legal Concerns

learning objective

5 Discuss the social and legal concerns of e-business.

The social and legal concerns of an e-business extend beyond those shared by all businesses. In addition to the issues presented in Chapter 2, e-businesses must deal with the special circumstances of operating in a new frontier—one without borders and without much in the way of control by government or any organization.

Ethics and Social Responsibility

Socially responsible and ethical behavior by individuals and businesses on the Internet are major concerns. As discussed in Chapter 2, opportunity is a primary factor in determining whether people will behave unethically or illegally. Unfortunately, the Internet provides a shelter of anonymity and detachment for both individuals and firms. These factors may explain why certain behaviors have surfaced. For example, an ethically questionable practice in cyberspace is the unauthorized access and use of information discovered through computerized tracking of users once they are connected to the Internet. Essentially, a user may visit a web page and unknowingly receive a small piece of software code called a **cookie**. This connection may allow the sender to track where the user goes on the Internet and to measure how long the user stays at any particular website. Although a cookie may produce valuable customer information, it also can be viewed as an invasion of privacy, especially since users may not even be aware that their movements are being monitored.

cookie a small piece of software sent by a website that tracks an individual's Internet use

The special circumstances of social interaction in an online environment are also a matter of increasing concern. For example, in some cases, people engaging in online chat rooms will reveal personal information that they would never reveal in face-to-face settings. The online social environment, which encourages a false sense of privacy and security, tends to change an individual's behavior. People may buy things, say things, and do things they otherwise would not because of the effect of the virtual environment. But none of this should be surprising. People behave differently when they are on vacation, at a party, or watching a baseball game in a stadium. The environment has an effect on us, whether it is a physical environment or one created in cyberspace.

A number of issues about privacy and the distribution of questionable online content, such as pornographic and hate literature, will remain issues of concern in the foreseeable future. Most ISPs and browsers allow users to block out websites identified as adult in nature, and many chat rooms are supervised so that unacceptable language or behavior can be terminated. Nonetheless, given the openness of the Internet and the relative absence of regulation, online users will have to develop their own strategies for handling difficult ethical and social situations.

Privacy and Confidentiality Issues

Besides the unauthorized use of cookies on users' computers to track their online behavior, there are several other threats to users' privacy and confidentiality. According to research by the University of Denver's Privacy Foundation Workplace Surveillance Project, more than one-third of the forty million U.S. employees who work online—about fourteen million—are under continuous surveillance by their employers.[10]

Monitoring an employee's **log-file records,** which record the websites visited, may be intended to help employers police unauthorized Internet use on company time; however, the same records also can give a firm the opportunity to observe what otherwise might be considered private and confidential information. The Privacy Foundation study suggests that at the very least, employers need to disclose and publicize the level of surveillance to their employees and consider the corporate motivation for monitoring employees' behavior.[11]

log-file records files that store a record of the websites visited

Some firms also practice data mining. **Data mining** refers to the practice of searching through data records looking for useful information. Customer registration forms typically require a variety of information before a user is given access to a site. When this is combined with customer transaction records, data-mining analysis can provide what might be considered private and confidential information about individuals or groups. For example, suppose that a website offering free access to health information requires users to fill out a detailed registration form before they are granted a user identification and password. As a result of this voluntary disclosure, website operators can easily uncover correlations between users' demographic factors, such as age and gender, and the specific health topics and issues that interest them. The website operators could then conceivably sell this information to pharmaceutical firms. The information sold might suggest that there is a large group of potential customers over the age of 50 that have a high level of interest in a particular type of medication that the firm manufactures. Once this information is obtained, the pharmaceutical firm could begin a marketing campaign "to educate" potential customers about the benefits of their product.

data mining the practice of searching through data records looking for useful information

Advocates for better control of how information about users is collected and distributed to interested third parties such as businesses point to the potential misuse of information—intentionally or otherwise. If an individual, for instance, frequents a website that provides information about a life-threatening disease, an insurance company might refuse to insure this individual, thinking there is a higher risk associated with someone who wants more information about this disease.

The ability to collect and analyze personal data is critical for the industry if it is going to compete for advertisers' spending, and so it must learn to do this ethically. To help deal with this issue and to support industry self-regulation, the U.S. Federal Trade Commission (FTC) approved the formation of the Network Advertising Initiative (NAI) in 1999. The NAI, which is made up of over 90 percent of Internet advertisers, including the industry leaders DoubleClick and 24/7 Real Media, was established to set rules and guidelines for the collection and use of personal data. The NAI prohibits the collection of personal data from health and financial services websites that individuals are likely to visit. However, the NAI permits the cross-referencing of personal and web-collected data, provided that the user is informed that this is taking place and is allowed access to his or her records. By requiring the consent of users and making the process somewhat more open to scrutiny, the NAI has helped make online data collection more ethical than it used to be and lends support to the argument that the Internet can regulate itself without undue government interference.

Security Concerns and Cybercrime

Because the Internet today is often regarded as an unregulated frontier, both individual and business users must be particularly aware of online risks and dangers. According to research conducted by Computer Security Services, Inc., 85 percent of the firms surveyed had detected online security breaches during the previous year.[12]

Troops aboard the carrier Theodore Roosevelt send e-mails back home. The old adage that loose lips sink ships has a new meaning now that deployed troops can send e-mails to friends and relatives back home. Concerned that sensitive data might leak out, soldiers and sailors are told not to send detailed, operational information that could be used by an enemy.

Computer viruses, which can originate anywhere in the world, are software codes designed to disrupt normal computer operations. Their potentially devastating effects have given rise to a software security industry. Norton's antivirus program, distributed by Symantec (**www.symantec.com**), is only one of several well-known products that help to screen out incoming files containing unwanted viruses, such as the infamous "Love Bug." As long as undesirable data can be transmitted easily, viruses and other forms of online harassment will remain a security issue and a business opportunity for firms like Symantec, which must continuously revise its software to deal with newly issued viruses.

In addition to these risks, individual users and businesses must watch for criminal activities, including fraud and larceny. Because the Internet allows easy creation of websites, access from anywhere in the world, and anonymity for users, it is almost impossible to know with certainty that the website, organization, or individuals that you believe you are interacting with are what they seem. Just for a moment, consider how easy it is to use the Internet to defraud someone. A crook intent on defrauding someone can build a website that appears to be a legitimate charitable organization dedicated to raising funds for a worthy cause. Through various online promotional efforts such as e-mail campaigns and banner advertising, unsuspecting individuals may be enticed to make a quick donation to the cause by entering their credit card information in an online form that is conveniently displayed on the website or by putting a check in the mail, typically addressed to a post office box. If the individual uses the website to make a donation by credit card, the crooks can use credit card information to make unauthorized purchases. A second type of fraud occurs when a website offers to sell products at an unbelievably low price but never delivers the products, even though it collects the funds. By the time authorities are made aware of the fraud, the website operators usually have abandoned the site and set up a new website and repeated the process. These scenarios are similar to older-style mail fraud but are more complex and difficult to control because fraudulent websites can be set up anywhere in the world and often will be located in areas where the authorities are reluctant to interfere with the operators. As always, *caveat emptor* ("let the buyer beware") is good advice to follow, whether on the Internet or not.

computer viruses software codes that are designed to disrupt normal computer operations

To alleviate consumer concerns about online purchasing, the major credit card organizations such as MasterCard and Visa have instituted various programs to protect cardholders against fraudulent use of their cards on the Internet. For example, the **secure electronic transaction (SET)** encryption process, which was developed by MasterCard, Visa, IBM, Microsoft, and Netscape, prevents merchants from ever actually seeing any transaction data, including the customer's credit card number. The SET encryption process is described in more detail in Chapter 17.

secure electronic transaction (SET) an encryption process developed by MasterCard, Visa, IBM, Microsoft, and Netscape that prevents merchants from ever actually seeing any transaction data, including the customer's credit card number

Digital Property and Copyright Concerns

A major concern for businesses that use the Internet to distribute content is the legal right to control content ownership, commonly referred to as **copyright** laws. Most affected by this issue are the music and publishing industries. Both have had to deal with new technologies that have allowed individuals to make copies of their content.

copyright legal right to control content ownership

According to research conducted by Jupiter Media Metrix, the online music industry will be worth over $6 billion by 2006, suggesting that there is a huge market opportunity for both large and small competitors.[13] Now, with software provided by such firms as MP3 (**www.mp3.com**) and Kazaa (**www.kazaa.com**), any Internet user can create a file of a song online and then send it to someone else, without ever paying the copyright owner. As far as the music industry is concerned, every copy of a song passed along freely on the Internet represents lost sales revenue from a customer who otherwise would make a purchase. As a means of dealing with this problem, some music companies have begun to sign distribution contracts with firms such as MP3 in order to gain more control over the distribution of their content. Others have sought a solution by establishing a software mechanism of their own making that allows the distribution of music online but prevents its free distribution by those who are unauthorized. For example, MusicNet (**www.musicnet.com**), a service set up jointly by RealNetworks, AOL Time Warner, EMI Group, Bertelsmann AG's BMG, and Zomba, was established to control legal distribution of the firms' content.

In addition to problems in the music and publishing industries, available technology makes it quite easy to copy and use a company name or recognized trademark, such as McDonald's golden arches, without permission. Most firms post information about how their names and trademarks may be used legally and under what circumstances links to their sites can be made. However, there are many people who see the Internet as an open and unregulated environment and believe that no government or company should be able to control the distribution of information once it reaches the Internet. To combat this problem, most firms will take legal steps, if necessary, to protect their property, including brand names and trademarks, from unauthorized use.

Government Regulation and Taxation

For the most part, government regulators have come to view the Internet as just an extension of regular business activity of firms operating in their jurisdictions. To the extent that online business activities resemble traditional business activities, the same rules and regulations apply whether businesses exist entirely or only partially online. Therefore, when it comes to the collection of sales taxes on products and services sold online, you would think that online firms would be responsible for collecting sales taxes and then remitting them to local and state governments. This is not the case, and although state and local governments are working toward a uniform sales tax policy for online sales, online vendors are legally treated like mail-order companies, which collect sales taxes only if they have a physical presence in the customer's state. American buyers are expected to pay local *use* taxes on products bought in other states, but the responsibility for paying the use tax is the customer's, not the selling firm's.

Another area of concern is the sale and distribution of restricted products such as prescription drugs. In most areas, a person must present a doctor's prescription to a pharmacist to obtain restricted drugs. The Internet allows anyone to obtain medications online and, in some cases, with only a claim to a prescription and a credit card. It is, however, the legal responsibility of the online pharmacist to verify the validity of the order and to look for abusive patterns, such as doctors prescribing unusually large quantities of certain drugs for one patient. Nonetheless, the fact that prescription drugs can be bought online with relatively little difficulty opens the way for their being sold in the illicit drug market.

Although it should be emphasized that most firms attempt to ensure that their online activity is fair and legal, the Internet presents a great opportunity for illegal activity in which profit is a major motivator. In the absence of stricter government control, legal and ethical issues in the online environment will become even more pronounced as more firms move their traditional businesses to the Internet.

The Future of e-Business: Growth, Opportunities, and Challenges

learning objective

6 Explore the growth, future opportunities, and challenges of e-business.

Since the beginning of commercial activity on the Internet, developments in e-business have been rapid and formidable. Before the abrupt slowdown in e-business activity that began in 2000, Forrester Research, Inc., a research firm located in Cambridge, Massachusetts, had predicted that global Internet commerce would soar to $6.8 trillion by 2004, up substantially from earlier growth estimates.[14] However, by 2002, worldwide B2B e-commerce estimates were only at $823.4 billion for the year, with strong optimism for B2B trade to reach $2.4 trillion by 2004, according to eMarketer's "E-Commerce Trade and B2B Exchanges" report.[15] Clearly, the slowdown in e-business activity that began in 2000 continues to undermine confidence in such predictions. However, we can safely say that the long-term view held by the vast majority of analysts is that the Internet will continue to expand along with related technologies.

To date, only a small percentage of the potential global users have gone online. Current estimates suggest that perhaps between 400 to 500 million people use the web on a daily basis. However, according to research by Ipsos-Reid, Inc., even among the most developed Internet markets in the world, such as the United States, Canada, Sweden, and the Netherlands, about one-third of the people who could use the Internet choose not to do so. In fact, Ipsos-Reid found that only 6 percent of the world's six billion people are online, suggesting great opportunities for growth if more people can be persuaded that the benefits are worthwhile.[16]

Measurements of Growth

Measurements of e-business growth not only illustrate the magnitude and scope of how much has happened in just a few short years but also indicate trends for the future. According to research by Jupiter Media Metrix, by 2006 there will be about 210 million online users in the United States, up from the current level of about 157 million.[17] And research suggests that global Internet users spend an average of 7.6 hours online each month. Users from the United States and Canada spend the most time, with a combined average of nearly 13 hours per visitor per month, whereas users in Europe spend, on average, just over 5 hours a month on the Internet.[18] More indicative of Internet usage, however, are the data from Nielsen/NetRatings surveys showing that monthly average use was 13 hours online at home and 31 hours at work—suggesting the importance of the Internet as a work-related tool.[19]

The popularity of websites varies depending on the country and the research firm's methodology. Because users' preferences change over time, these ratings, like those of television and radio shows, are meaningful only if they are current. Up-to-date usage statistics, ratings, and rankings are available from firms that perform market research. For example, Jupiter Media Metrix reported that AOL was the most popular site in 2002, with about ninety-three million "unique visitors." (A *unique visitor* is a single person who visited at least once during the month; repeat visits by the same person are not counted.) Microsoft sites followed AOL, with eighty-four million unique visitors, and Yahoo! ranked third, with eighty million.[20]

Even with the economic downturn, the Internet will continue to offer great opportunities for growth. Firms that adapt existing business models to an online environment will continue to dominate development. Books, CDs, clothing, hotel accommodations, car rentals, and travel reservations are products and services well suited to online buying and selling. These products or services will continue to be sold in the tradi-

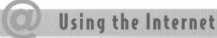

What do e-business players read to keep up to date on other people, ideas, and trends in the fast-paced world of e-business? Although there has been an information explosion due to the Internet, the answer is likely to include the following:

Wired: **www.wired.com**
Fast Company: **www.fastcompany.com**
Worth: **www.worth.com**
The Industry Standard: **www.thestandard.com**
CNET News: **www.news.com**
ZDNet: **www.zdnet.com**

tional way, as well as in a more cost-effective and efficient fashion over the Internet.

The most exciting prospect for businesses and customers is not the conversion of existing business activities to e-business activities but the creation of altogether new and unique products and services. While there are many examples of how the Internet can be used to distribute new and unique products, consider how the Internet is changing the music industry. As noted earlier, MP3 and Kazaa are only two of the firms providing software for the distribution of music directly to customers. Also now emerging are independent online music webcasters, which are presented to Internet users as online radio stations. Thus, in addition to enabling existing radio stations to find a global audience for their product, the technology exists for independent producers to set up their own unique radio webcasting stations. Netscape's webcast radio service (**http://radio.netscape.com**) provides information about how private and public webcasts can be created.

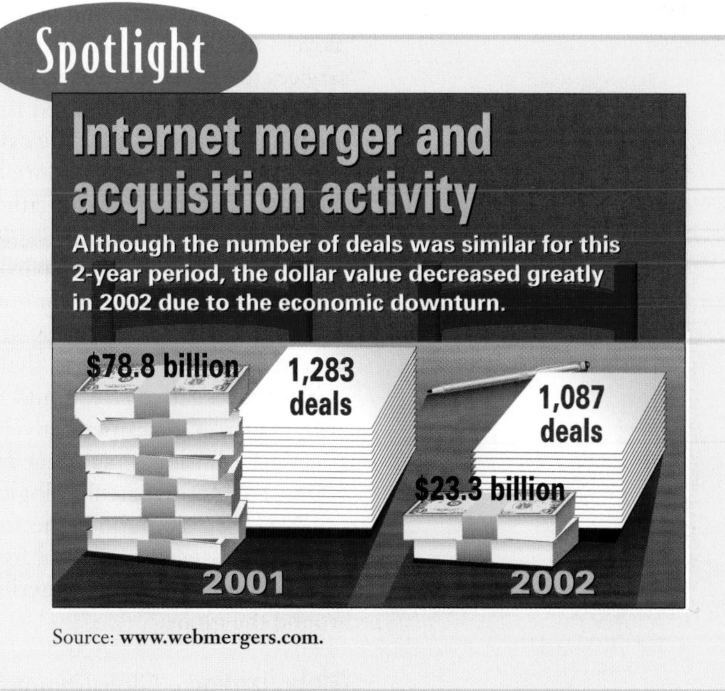

Spotlight
Internet merger and acquisition activity
Although the number of deals was similar for this 2-year period, the dollar value decreased greatly in 2002 due to the economic downturn.
$78.8 billion
1,283 deals
1,087 deals
$23.3 billion
2001
2002

Source: **www.webmergers.com.**

Environmental Forces Affecting e-Business

Although the environmental forces that are at work are complex, it is useful to think of them as either internal or external forces that affect an e-business. Internal environmental forces are those that are closely associated with the actions and decisions taking place within a firm. As shown in Figure 4.4, typical internal forces include the firm's planning activities, organization structure, human resources, management decisions,

External forces
Globalization
Legal issues
Demographic factors
Internal forces
Planning activities
Available financing
Organizational structure
Political forces
Successful e-business
Society
Information database
Human resources
Management decisions
Technology
The economy
Competition

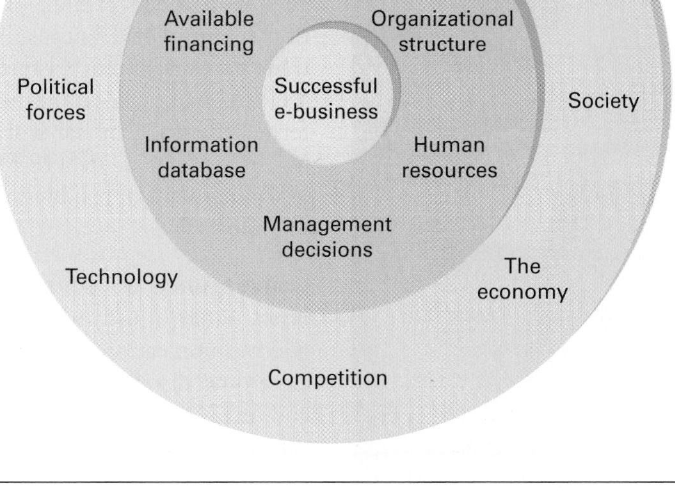

figure 4.4

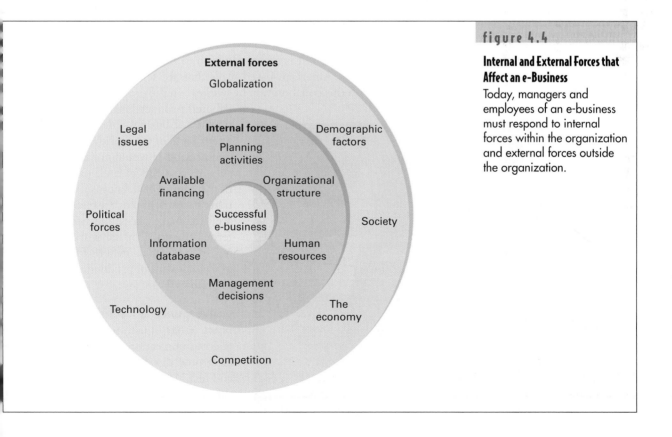

Internal and External Forces that Affect an e-Business

Today, managers and employees of an e-business must respond to internal forces within the organization and external forces outside the organization.

information database, and available financing. For example, a shortage of skilled employees needed for specialized project work can undermine a firm's ability to sell its services to clients. However, management might consider a particular project or client worthy of the effort required to recruit the needed staff from another country or pay premium salaries. Unlike the external environmental forces affecting the firm, internal forces such as this one are more likely to be under the direct control of management. In this case, management can either go out and hire the needed staff or choose to pass over a prospective project.

In contrast, external environmental forces are those factors affecting e-business planning that originate from outside the organization. These forces are unlikely to be controllable by an e-business firm. Instead, managers and employees of an e-business firm generally will react to these forces, attempting to shield the organization from any undue negative effects and finding ways to take advantage of opportunities in the ever-changing e-business environment. The primary external environmental forces affecting e-business planning include globalization, society, and demographic, economic, competitive, technological, and political and legal forces.

No discussion about the future of e-business would be complete without mentioning four specific external forces—globalization, convergence of technologies, online communities, and partnering online—that are already changing e-business firms around the globe.

Globalization Globalization is currently the focus of a great deal of discussion and debate—and with good reason. For many people, globalization is a positive force that is drawing the people of the world together to live under universally shared standards of culture, communication, technologies, and economics. To others, globalization represents a threat to their national cultures, identities, languages, and even their way of life.

Regardless of whether you think globalization is good or bad, it is highly associated with growth of the Internet, which helped speed the delivery of new ideas and information to people around the globe. Simply put, the Internet exemplifies globalization because a person with a computer and Internet access in North America, Europe, Africa, or Asia can access information and conduct business online with anyone with similar access anyplace in the world. The way one company—SAP—found to sell its software products in global markets is described in the Going Global boxed feature.

Because of globalization, it is not uncommon to find software engineers in India doing programming for American-based firms that are selling products to German customers. Along with this collaboration by workers on the production of globally distributed products and services comes the transfer of business methods used in different parts of the world. In addition, jobs that previously would not have been available to engineers in India or any other nation in the world because of geography, trade barriers, and other restrictive factors are now made accessible because the Internet creates a virtual workplace, allowing individuals anywhere to be part of a global network of production and marketing efforts.

The real thing: A new way to purchase Coca-Cola. Japan's top mobile carrier NTT DoCoMo and Coca-Cola have developed new technology that allows consumers to use their cell phones to purchase soft drinks from a vending machine. The system uses an infrared signal to turn the cell phone into a cash card that works with specially equipped vending machines.

Convergence of Technologies As webcast radio illustrates, the borders of telecommunications technologies for electronic distribution of sound, images, and text have become less clear. Today we can send and receive e-mail from pagers, interact with the Internet from a small

going global

SAP: Thirty Years in the Business of e-Business

SAP, BASED IN WALLDORF, GERMANY, has been giving companies an electronic boost since well before the term *e-business* became popular. Fast-food giant Burger King uses SAP software to share and analyze financial information worldwide. The Royal Dutch/Shell Group uses SAP software to make business information in centralized databases available to all 85,000 of its global employees. Although SAP was founded in 1972, it did not expand to serve customers beyond its home country until five years later. Today, more than 17,000 companies in fifty countries rely on SAP systems to bridge miles and time zones so that their employees, customers, and business partners can collaborate electronically.

When a company such as Burger King installs a web-based mySAP.com system, for example, its managers and employees can log onto the customized site from any location at any time. Once they enter their passwords, they can connect to shared documents, databases, programs, and analytical tools. If management chooses, trusted suppliers and partners also can be granted access to specific areas within the system. And the fast-food chain can have its mySAP.com system automatically send certain reports to particular employees, suppliers, or partners.

Companies install SAP's systems to improve productivity and speed decision making by electronically linking employees, customers, and partners regardless of location. They generally expect the systems to pay back in terms of better performance, in part because everyone shares the same up-to-date information and because the company can react more quickly to emerging opportunities. Customers also benefit from the company's increased efficiency and responsiveness. Although SAP's customer list includes many major corporations, a growing number of small and midsized firms use SAP's systems to standardize their information technology operations and support expansion strategies. Small wonder that the Internet age has made e-business even bigger business for SAP, which has a loyal following in Europe and North America and enjoys annual revenues exceeding $7 billion.

screen on a cell phone, and even have visually active telephone conversations. This phenomenon of overlapping capabilities and the merging of products and services into one fully integrated interactive system is referred to as the **convergence of technologies.** This convergence may well lead to interactive television programs, which would allow viewers to select their preferences in the way a program is presented. Viewers of a cooking show, for example, might be able to select whether they would prefer instructions for regular or nonfat cooking. The profile of the viewer's personal tastes and preferences could be maintained so that the next time the viewer watched the cooking show, the profile would be entered automatically and the appropriate data provided on the screen.

convergence of technologies the overlapping capabilities and the merging of products and services into one fully integrated interactive system

Online Communities **Online communities,** which are made up of groups of individuals or firms that want to exchange information, products, or services over the Internet, are a phenomenon that is likely to grow. One example of a thriving online community is iVillage.com, a commercial site for women. Other online communities include buyers' groups, such as OnVia.com, a site that helps small businesses secure government contracts online. Online learning communities continue to evolve as sites in a wide variety of fields, allowing people who share an interest or concern to communicate with each other. Geocities.com is only one portal to a huge selection of online communities.

online communities groups of individuals or firms that want to exchange information, products, or services over the Internet

Partnering Online While opportunities for independent e-business effort will continue, online partnerships, which can be of benefit to both large and small firms, are likely to be increasingly common. By playing a role within a larger entity, small firms can enjoy competitive advantage and access to marketable items, thereby increasing their rate of market penetration. A review of the major e-business sites, including those of IBM, Microsoft, and Oracle, indicates that the e-business approach taken by these firms involves local business firms.

Many Internet firms have been able to realize rapid growth through partnerships with smaller firms. For example, Amazon.com pays its website partners a commission on items bought by users whom the partners send to Amazon. Suppose that an online learning community made up of students of Spanish and small vendors of related products and services had a link on its web page that took viewers to Amazon.com. By connecting with Amazon.com, the site can earn revenue and at the same time satisfy users who might not find what they are looking for within the learning community's limited selection. The learning community's range of products is thus automatically extended to the wide selection carried by Amazon, and both Amazon and the learning community benefit.

This chapter has presented an overview of the fast-paced, emerging world of e-business. Throughout the book you will find more e-business references and examples as they apply to the different aspects of business, such as management, marketing, and finance. Chapter 17 covers the more technological side of e-business, focusing on such topics as web pages and standards for communications, software, and the communications system that makes up the Internet. In Chapters 5 and 6 we examine issues related to forms of business ownership and special considerations surrounding small business.

Return To inside business

In the battle for online dominance, MSN has a fighting chance to catch up with market leader AOL. MSN not only charges less for Internet access, its software also offers many convenient features such as easy photo editing and powerful parental controls. Eyeing the fast-growing market for Internet access on the go, MSN is also developing a version of its software for mobile devices such as web-enabled cell phones and handheld computers. MSN builds on its parent company's strengths by integrating Microsoft's highly popular Hotmail e-mail service and other Microsoft products.

What may tip the balance in MSN's favor is its lower-priced offer of broadband Internet access, designed to attract dial-up customers from AOL and other competitors. With MSN broadband, customers can stay connected to the web all the time and download or surf at much faster speeds than would be possible with an ordinary telephone connection. Analysts expect broadband to transform the way people access the Internet—as well as the competition between MSN and AOL. Stay tuned.

Questions

1. Clearly, MSN and its parent company, Microsoft, are major players in e-business. Is MSN using a B2B or a B2C model? Explain your answer.
2. Given that competition between AOL, MSN, and other ISPs is fierce, what would you do to help MSN attract and retain broadband customers?

chapter review

Summary

Define and explain the meaning of e-business.

e-Business, or electronic business, can be defined as the organized effort of individuals to produce and sell, for a profit, the products and services that satisfy society's needs *through the facilities available on the Internet*. The term *e-business* refers to all business activities and practices conducted on the Internet by an individual firm or the general concept of e-business. On the other hand, *e-commerce* is a part of e-business; the term refers only to online buying and selling activities, including identifying suppliers, selecting products or services, making purchase commitments, completing financial transactions, and obtaining service. The human, material, information, and financial resources that any business requires are highly specialized for e-business. Using e-business activities, it is possible to satisfy new customer needs created by the Internet as well as traditional ones in unique ways. Each source of revenue flowing into the firm is referred to as a *revenue stream.* By using a variety of e-business activities, firms can increase sales revenue and reduce expenses in order to increase profits.

Explore the basic framework of e-business.

Most firms involved in e-business fall more or less into one of three primary groups as defined by their e-business activities: (1) telecommunications and computer hardware manufacturers and Internet service providers, which together supply the physical infrastructure of the Internet; (2) producers of Internet software, which provide users with the ability to do things on the Internet; and (3) online sellers and content providers. The Internet would still be limited to communication between individuals and among groups of special-interest researchers were it not for the activity of online sellers and content producers. In this area of e-business we have just begun to see the development of online strategies for reaching out to existing and new customers. The special characteristics of e-business provide increased opportunity for firms to reach global markets and for small businesses to start up and grow.

Identify and explain fundamental models of e-business.

e-Business models focus attention on the identity of a firm's customers. Firms that use the Internet mainly to conduct business with other businesses are generally referred to as having a business-to-business, or B2B, model. Currently, the vast majority of e-business is B2B in nature. When examining B2B business firms, two clear types emerge. In the first type, the focus is simply on facilitating sales transactions between businesses. A second, more complex type of the B2B model involves a company and its suppliers. In contrast to the focus of the B2B model, firms such as Amazon and e-Bay are clearly focused on individual buyers and so are referred to as having a business-to-consumer, or B2C, model. In a B2C situation, understanding how consumers behave online is critical to the firm's success. And successful B2C firms often make a special effort to build long-term relationships with their customers. While B2B and B2C models are the most popular e-business models, there are other models that perform specialized e-business activities to generate revenues—see Table 4.2.

Understand the factors that influence an e-business plan.

The approach taken to creating an e-business plan will depend on whether you are establishing a new Internet business or adding an online component to an existing business. For a new Internet business, a good e-business plan should provide detailed answers to basic questions. Once the answers and initial research have been completed, it is time to choose a business model. Options include the business-to-business (B2B) model, the business-to-consumer (B2C) model, or one of the specialized models.

It is also quite common for an existing business to add e-business activities. A business that already has a physical location and a customer base generally looks at e-business as a way to expand sales to current customers and to add new customers who are beyond the reach of the firm's geographic location. Although developing an online presence may seem like a logical extension of what the firm already does, there are important factors that must be considered before using the Internet to sell products or services or provide information to customers. These factors include determining if online customers are really different from traditional customers, the degree to which e-business activities complement non-Internet-based activities, and complexity and time concerns when implementing new e-business activities.

Discuss the social and legal concerns of e-business.

The social and legal concerns of an e-business extend beyond those shared by all businesses. e-Businesses must deal with the special circumstances of operating in a new frontier—one without borders and with limited control by government or any other organization. As a result, consumers, businesses, and the government are all learning how to deal with issues related to ethics, social responsibility, privacy, confidentiality, security, cybercrimes, digital property and copyright concerns, and government regulation and taxation.

Explore the growth, future opportunities, and challenges of e-business.

Since the advent of commercial activity on the Internet, developments in e-business have been rapid and formidable. Clearly, the slowdown in e-business activity that began in 2000 continues to undermine confidence in predictions for Internet growth. However, we can safely say that the long-term view held by the vast majority of analysts is that the Internet will continue to expand along with related technologies. Although the environmental forces that are at work are complex, it is useful to think of them as either internal or external forces that affect an e-business. Internal environmental forces are those that are closely associated with the actions and decisions taking place within the firm. In contrast, external environmental forces are those factors affecting e-business planning that originate from outside the organization. No discussion about the future of e-business would be complete without mentioning four specific external forces—globalization, convergence of technologies, online communities, and partnering online—that are already changing e-business firms around the globe.

Key Terms

You should now be able to define and give an example relevant to each of the following terms:

e-business (electronic business) (108)
e-commerce (108)
revenue stream (110)
World Wide Web (the web) (112)
digitized (112)
Internet service providers (ISP) (113)
customer relationship management (CRM) software (114)
supply-chain management (SCM) software (114)
e-zines (116)
business model (117)
business-to-business (B2B) model (117)
business-to-consumer (B2C) model (118)
cookie (122)
log-file records (123)
data mining (123)
computer viruses (124)
secure electronic transaction (SET) (124)
copyright (124)
convergence of technologies (129)
online communities (129)

Review Questions

1. What are four major factors contained in the definition of e-business?
2. How does e-business differ from e-commerce?
3. How do e-businesses generate revenue streams?
4. What roles do telecommunications firms and Internet service providers play in e-business?
5. How do software producers contribute to e-business?
6. What does the term *content providers* mean?
7. Why does e-business represent a global opportunity to reach customers?
8. What are the two fundamental e-business models?
9. What concerns should be considered when creating an e-business plan?
10. Give an example of an unethical use of the Internet by a business or an individual.
11. What has been the general level of involvement of governments in e-business to date?
12. What is the difference between internal and external forces that affect an e-business? How do they change the way an e-business operates?
13. What does *convergence of technologies* mean?
14. What are online communities?
15. How can partnering with other e-businesses help firms compete on the Internet?

Discussion Questions

1. Can advertising provide enough revenue for an e-business to succeed in the long run?
2. How can small businesses compete against large-scale e-businesses?
3. What distinguishes the B2B and B2C e-business models?
4. How would planning differ for starting a new Internet business when compared with adding an e-business component to an existing business?
5. Pick two or three specific social, ethical, and legal issues facing e-business and discuss how they affect Internet users. From the standpoint of an e-business, how should these same issues be resolved?
6. Discuss the role of government and regulatory agencies in e-business.
7. Describe the growth of e-business since the start of commercial activities on the Internet. Do you think that the Internet will continue to grow as fast as it has in the past? Why?

video case

Absolute Quality Offers Multi-Lingual Support and More

How many customer service representatives can discuss products or answer technical questions in Italian or Swedish as well as English? e-Businesses that hire the Maryland-based company Absolute Quality to handle their customer support services get multilingual capabilities and much more. Founded in 1996, Absolute Quality maintains a state-of-the-art call center staffed by representatives who are ready to communicate with e-business's customers via e-mail, live online chat, telephone, or fax. Because e-commerce is global and customers may have questions or problems at any hour of the day, seven days a week, the company stands ready for round-the-clock customer service support.

e-Businesses are under increasing pressure to pay attention to customer service or risk losing customers to competitors on and off the Internet. However, e-business start-ups can be so busy that they let e-mail inquiries languish for days—if they answer them at all. Even established e-businesses may leave callers on hold for what seems like hours while their representatives are "busy helping other customers." Stephen Muirhead, Absolute Quality's president, points out that an e-business can easily spend millions buying and installing the necessary equipment and software. This investment does not include the expense of recruiting representatives and educating them about products. Moreover, a high-tech e-business must be ready to answer any kind of technical question its customers may pose.

Rather than stretch limited resources even thinner by trying to manage customer service internally, some e-businesses see outsourcing as a cost-effective alternative. Absolute Quality charges an initial setup fee when it first starts working for an e-business firm. After that, e-businesses pay only for actual customer service contacts. If twenty-five customers chat with Absolute Quality's representatives during the day, the e-business pays for twenty-five contacts, not for the overhead cost of maintaining a large call center and a trained staff capable of many more customer contacts. And the e-business can check Absolute Quality's online reports to determine how many customers requested service support during a particular day, what products they discussed, the length of their contact with reps, and the number of callers who hang up while waiting for service.

Not every e-business chooses to outsource its customer service function, however. For example, Lands' End, which sells apparel and merchandise for the home, has always handled its own customer service support. The company started with a catalog operation and added online sales and service during the Internet's early days. New e-businesses, however, may see Absolute Quality as a cost-effective way to give customers knowledgeable service without the headaches of starting a customer service department from scratch.

Of course, e-businesses that outsource customer service support worry about quality as much as cost. Thanks to Absolute Quality's advanced technology, its representatives can call up different databases when helping customers. For example, they can access records of a customer's previous service inquiries and follow up on resolutions in progress, research product details, and more. They can even schedule call-backs, if necessary, to suit each customer's convenience. Taking nothing for granted, Absolute Quality regularly monitors a sampling of each representative's customer contacts to be sure they are providing a high level of service. And representatives also receive feedback and training to improve their customer care skills. The goal is to answer customers' inquiries as fully and accurately as if the e-business's in-house personnel were doing the work. If Absolute Quality cannot provide *absolute quality*, the e-business will look bad.

Customer service outsourcing is only one of Absolute Quality's services. The company also tests educational software and video games for manufacturers on an outsourced basis. Its testers ensure that the products perform as the manufacturers promise. In addition, they log any glitches they find and check for complete compatibility with different computer systems. Even smaller firms now test their software and games to avoid disappointing or frustrating users.

Thanks to Absolute Quality's detailed reports, e-businesses not only can track their customer service expenses but also can analyze customers' inquiries and complaints as a way of planning future website and product improvements. As its business continues to increase year after year, Absolute Quality has responded to higher demand by expanding beyond Maryland to open facilities in California and Scotland. Its workforce of 250 employees can now handle both customer service support and software testing services in ten languages for e-businesses and technology firms in North America and Europe.[21]

Questions

1. Now that the Internet has opened new opportunities for satisfying customer needs, how does Absolute Quality satisfy its customers' needs and help them satisfy the needs of their customers?
2. If you were CEO of a company that needed to provide technical support to your customers, would you use in-house personnel or a firm like Absolute Quality? Explain your answer.
3. What privacy and security concerns might a company raise when considering whether to hire Absolute Quality to handle its online, e-mail, and telephone customer service contacts?

Building Skills for Career Success

1. Exploring the Internet

To thrive, all websites need visitors. Without the revenue that comes from firms that buy banner advertising on websites or the subscription fees paid by viewers, the necessary cash to create, maintain, and grow simply would not exist. What attracts viewers varies according to their lifestyles, age, gender, and information requirements. Many online communities focus on the interests of a selected target audience. MarthaStewart.com and iVillage.com are two well-known sites catering mostly to college-educated women interested in leisure, parenting, business, nutrition, and the like. However, these are only two sites in a sea of choices. Visit the text website for updates to this exercise.

Assignment

1. Identify and describe two or more websites with content that attracts you and keeps you returning on a regular basis.
2. How would you describe the target audience for these sites?
3. What advertisements are typically displayed?

2. Developing Critical Thinking Skills

Although the variety of products available to online shoppers is growing quickly, many people are reluctant to make purchases over the Internet. For a variety of reasons, some individuals are uncomfortable with using the Internet for this purpose, whereas others do so easily and often. The considerations involved in making a business-to-business purchase decision differ from those involved in making a personal purchase. However, the experience of buying office supplies from Staples.com for a business might influence an individual to visit other online sites to shop for personal items.

Assignment

1. Which sorts of products or services do you think would be easy to sell online? What kinds of things do you think would be difficult to purchase online? Explain your thinking.
2. Have you ever purchased anything over the Internet? Explain why you have or have not.
3. Explain how the considerations involved in buying office supplies from Staples.com for a business might differ from those involved in making a personal purchase.

3. Building Team Skills

An interesting approach taken by Yahoo.com and several other websites is to provide viewers with the tools needed to create a personal web page or community. Yahoo's GeoCities site (**http://geocities.yahoo.com**) provides simple instructions for creating a site and posting your own content, such as articles and photographs.

Assignment

1. Working in a group, examine some of the GeoCities communities and personal web pages. Discuss which sites you think work well and which do not. Explain your reasoning.
2. Develop an idea for your own website. Draw a sketch of how you would like the site to appear on the Internet. You may use ideas that look good on other personal pages.
3. Who is your target audience, and why do you think they will want to visit the site?

4. Researching Different Careers

The Internet offers a wide assortment of career opportunities in business, as well as in Internet-related technologies. As firms seek opportunities online, new e-businesses are springing up every day. In many cases these firms want people with a fresh outlook on how e-business can succeed, and they prefer individuals without preconceived notions about how to proceed. Website managers, designers, creative artists, and content specialists are just a few of the positions available. Many large online job sites, such as **Monster.com,** can help you find out about employment opportunities in e-business and the special skills required for various jobs.

Assignment

1. Summarize the positions that appear to be in high demand in e-business.
2. What are some of the special skills required to fill these jobs?
3. What salaries and benefits typically are associated with these positions?
4. Which job seems most appealing to you personally? Why?

5. Improving Communication Skills

Describing websites in summary form can be difficult because of the mix of information involved. A useful exercise is to create a table that can serve not only as an organizational tool for the information but also as a means of quick comparison.

Assignment

1. Create a table that will compare ten websites you have visited. Place the title of one type of information at the head of each column. For example, you might start with the firm's name in the first column, the type of product or service it sells online in the second column, and so forth.
2. Enter short descriptive data in each column.
3. Write a descriptive summary of the table you have prepared, identifying a few of the outstanding characteristics listed in the data.

chapter

5 Choosing a Form of Business Ownership

learning objectives

1 Describe the advantages and disadvantages of sole proprietorships.

2 Explain the different types of partners and the importance of partnership agreements.

3 Describe the advantages and disadvantages of partnerships.

4 Summarize how a corporation is formed.

5 Describe the advantages and disadvantages of a corporation.

6 Discuss the purpose of an S-corporation, limited-liability company, and other special forms of business ownership.

7 Explain how growth from within and growth through mergers can enable a business to expand.

To support aggressive growth, Procter & Gamble began acquiring other firms and products.

inside business

Procter & Gamble: A Company with a Rich History

William Procter owned a candle-making business; James Gamble owned a soap business. When the two young sole proprietors married sisters, their father-in-law convinced them to merge their businesses and form a partnership. He reasoned that a partnership would stand a much better chance of weathering the economic problems that small businesses were experiencing in the United States. In the grip of a financial panic, U.S. banks were closing, and people were concerned about the economic outlook. Thus, in 1837, with entrepreneurial optimism, the two formed a partnership called Procter & Gamble and set out to compete with fourteen other soap and candle makers in Cincinnati, Ohio. Twelve years later, their partnership was one of the largest companies in Cincinnati, with annual sales of $1 million and eighty employees.

The business continued to grow during the Civil War because Procter & Gamble won government contracts to supply soap and candles to the troops. After the war, soldiers brought their Procter & Gamble products home to their families, which helped build brand recognition. Then, in 1879, the company introduced Ivory, the "floating" soap. By 1890, Procter & Gamble had blossomed into a multimillion-dollar corporation selling more than thirty different products. Although the company phased out candles in the 1920s as the electric light bulb became commonplace, its research laboratory cranked out one innovative product after another. By the 1930s, Procter & Gamble was using radio advertising on nationally broadcast soap operas to strengthen its share of the market for consumer products.

As the 1990s came to an end, every American household used at least one Procter & Gamble product, such as Folgers coffee, Tide detergent, Crest toothpaste, Pampers disposable diapers, or Olay skin care products. However, corporate growth from within had slowed. Despite a steady stream of new products emerging from the company's legendary research facilities, such offerings as ThermaCare heat wraps and Swiffer mops were only moderately successful. To support more aggressive growth, the company had to move beyond its go-it-alone tradition and begin acquiring other firms and products.

Procter & Gamble's new era of growth started with the acquisition of Iams, maker of high-end pet foods, which it expanded into a billion-dollar business. Next, the company bought Clairol's hair care products, gaining such perennially popular items as Clairol Herbal Essences shampoo. In another departure from the past, Procter & Gamble gambled on the inventiveness of a small Cleveland start-up firm that had developed a low-cost battery-operated toothbrush. Within two years of this acquisition, Procter & Gamble was selling $200 million worth of Crest SpinBrush toothbrushes. Overall yearly sales now top $40 billion, thanks to the company's careful growth plans.[1]

Although Procter & Gamble began when William Procter (a sole proprietor) and James Gamble (a sole proprietor) formed a partnership, the company eventually became a global corporation. What's their secret of success? To answer this question, let's quickly review the definition of business given in Chapter 1. A *business* is the organized effort of individuals to produce and sell, for a profit, the products and services that satisfy society's needs. Procter & Gamble—or for that matter, any other successful business—is a practical example of this definition. The first and most important step for all businesses—sole proprietorships, partnerships, corporations, or some special forms of business ownership—is to produce products or services that their customers want.

Many people dream of opening a business, and one of the first decisions they must make is what form of ownership to choose. We begin this chapter by describing the three common forms of business ownership: sole proprietorships, partnerships, and corporations. We discuss how these types of businesses are formed and note the advantages and disadvantages of each. Next, we consider several types of business ownership usually chosen for special purposes, including S-corporations, limited-liability companies, government-owned corporations, not-for-profit corporations, cooperatives, joint ventures, and syndicates. We conclude the chapter with a discussion of how businesses can grow through internal expansion or through mergers with other companies.

Sole Proprietorships

learning objective

1 Describe the advantages and disadvantages of sole proprietorships.

A **sole proprietorship** is a business that is owned (and usually operated) by one person. Although a few sole proprietorships are large and have many employees, most are small. Sole proprietorship is the simplest form of business ownership and the easiest to start. In most instances, the owner (the *sole* proprietor) simply decides that he or she is in business and begins operations. Some of today's largest corporations, including Ford Motor Company, H. J. Heinz Company, and J.C. Penney Company, started out as tiny—and in many cases, struggling—sole proprietorships.

sole proprietorship a business that is owned (and usually operated) by one person

As you can see in Figure 5.1, there are more than 17.4 million sole proprietorships in the United States. They account for 72.2 percent of the country's business firms. Sole proprietorships are most common in retailing, service, and agriculture. Thus the clothing boutique, corner grocery, television repair shop down the street, and small, independent farmer are likely to be sole proprietorships. In addition to more traditional sole proprietorships, many entrepreneurs who possess computer and technology skills have started their own consulting services firms. Skilled Internet website designers, e-commerce programmers, software trainers, and many others have found that they are better off working for themselves as a sole proprietor. Not only can they pick and choose which job assignments to accept, but they also have found that they can earn more money by not working exclusively for one firm as a salaried employee.

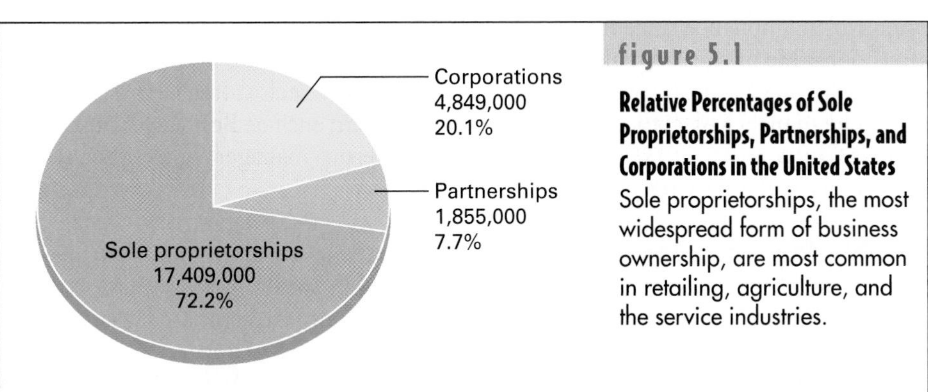

figure 5.1

Relative Percentages of Sole Proprietorships, Partnerships, and Corporations in the United States

Sole proprietorships, the most widespread form of business ownership, are most common in retailing, agriculture, and the service industries.

Source: U.S. Bureau of the Census website (**www.census.gov**), *Statistical Abstract of the United States*, 121st ed., Washington, D.C., 2001, p. 473.

Spotlight

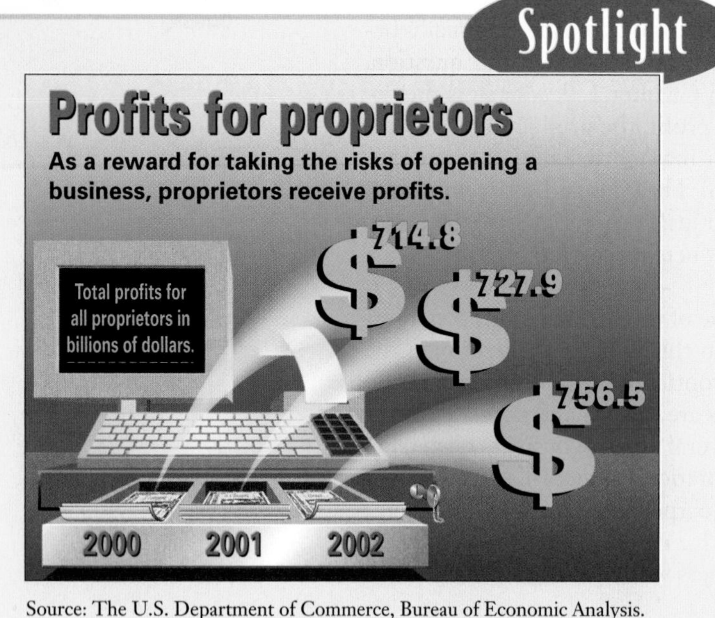

Source: The U.S. Department of Commerce, Bureau of Economic Analysis.

Advantages of Sole Proprietorships

Most of the advantages of sole proprietorships arise from the two main characteristics of this form of ownership: simplicity and individual control.

Ease of Start-Up Sole proprietorship is the simplest and cheapest way to start a business. Start-up requires no contracts, agreements, or other legal documents. Thus a sole proprietorship can be, and most often is, established without the services of an attorney. The legal requirements are often limited to registering the name of the business and purchasing any necessary licenses or permits. Beyond this, however, a sole proprietor pays no special start-up fees or taxes. Nor are there any minimum capital requirements.

If the enterprise does not succeed, the firm can be closed as easily as it was opened. Creditors must be paid, of course. But generally, the owner does not have to go through any legal procedure before hanging up an "Out of Business" sign.

Pride of Ownership A successful sole proprietor is often very proud of her or his accomplishments—and rightfully so. The amount of time and hard work that the owner invests in a sole proprietorship is substantial. In almost every case, the owner deserves a great deal of credit for assuming the risks and solving the day-to-day problems associated with operating sole proprietorships. Unfortunately, the reverse is also true. When the business fails, it is often the sole proprietor who is to blame.

Retention of All Profits Because all profits become the personal earnings of the owner, the owner has a strong incentive to succeed. This direct financial reward attracts many entrepreneurs to the sole proprietorship form of business and, if the business succeeds, is a source of great satisfaction.

Flexibility A sole proprietor is completely free to make decisions about the firm's operations. Without asking or waiting for anyone's approval, a sole proprietor can switch from retailing to wholesaling, move a shop's location, open a new store, or close an old one.

A sole proprietor also can respond to changes in market conditions much more quickly than the partnership and corporate forms of business. Suppose the sole proprietor of an appliance store finds that many customers now prefer to shop on Sunday afternoons. He or she can make an immediate change in business hours to take advantage of this information (provided that state laws allow such stores to open on Sunday). The manager of a store in a large corporate chain such as Best Buy Company or Circuit City may have to seek the approval of numerous managers and company officials before making such a change.

Possible Tax Advantages Profits earned by a sole proprietorship are taxed as the personal income of the owner. As a result, sole proprietors must report certain financial information on their personal tax returns and make estimated quarterly tax payments to the federal government. Thus a sole proprietorship does not pay the special state and federal income taxes that corporations pay. (As you will see later, a corporation's profits may be taxed twice. A sole proprietorship's profits are taxed only once.)

Disadvantages of Sole Proprietorships

The disadvantages of a sole proprietorship stem from the fact that these businesses are owned by one person. Some capable sole proprietors experience no problems. Individuals who start out with few management skills and little money are most at risk.

Unlimited Liability **Unlimited liability** is a legal concept that holds a business owner personally responsible for all the debts of the business. There is legally no difference between the debts of the business and the debts of the proprietor. If the business fails, or if the business is involved in a lawsuit and loses, the owner's personal property—including savings and other assets—can be seized (and sold if necessary) to pay creditors.

unlimited liability a legal concept that holds a business owner personally responsible for all the debts of the business

Unlimited liability is perhaps the major factor that tends to discourage would-be entrepreneurs with substantial personal wealth from using this form of business organization.

Lack of Continuity Legally, the sole proprietor *is* the business. If the owner retires, dies, or is declared legally incompetent, the business essentially ceases to exist. In many cases, however—especially when the business is a profitable enterprise—the owner's heirs take it over and either sell it or continue to operate it.

Lack of Money Banks, suppliers, and other lenders are usually unwilling to lend large sums of money to sole proprietorships. Only one person—the sole proprietor—can be held responsible for repaying such loans, and the assets of most sole proprietors are usually limited. Moreover, these assets may already have been used as the basis for personal borrowing (a home mortgage or car loan) or for short-term credit from suppliers. Lenders also worry about the lack of continuity of sole proprietorships: Who will repay a loan if the sole proprietor dies? Finally, many lenders are concerned about the large number of sole proprietorships that fail—a topic discussed in Chapter 6.

The limited ability to borrow money can prevent a sole proprietorship from growing. It is the main reason that many business owners, when in need of relatively large amounts of capital, change from the sole proprietorship to the partnership or corporate form of ownership.

Limited Management Skills The sole proprietor is often the sole manager—in addition to being the only salesperson, buyer, accountant, and on occasion, janitor. Even the most experienced business owner is unlikely to have expertise in all these areas. Consequently, unless he or she obtains the necessary expertise by hiring employees, assistants, or consultants, the business can suffer in the areas in which the owner is less knowledgeable. For the many sole proprietors who cannot hire the help they need, there just are not enough hours in the day to do everything that needs to be done. This usually means long hours each day, six-day or seven-day work weeks, few days off, and limited vacation time.

Difficulty in Hiring Employees The sole proprietor may find it hard to attract and keep competent help. Potential employees may feel that there is no room for advancement in a firm whose owner assumes all managerial responsibilities. And when those who *are* hired are ready to take on added responsibility, they may find that the only way to do so is to quit the sole proprietorship and go to work for a larger firm or start up their own businesses. The lure of higher salaries and increased benefits also may cause existing employees to change jobs.

His smile describes the satisfaction this entrepreneur feels. Derrick Angus, owner of Derrick's Jamaican Cuisine, learned it takes more than just good food if you are going to own and operate a profitable small business. Hard work, cost control, the right location, and even a little luck are needed if you are going to make it as a sole proprietor in the very competitive restaurant business.

Beyond the Sole Proprietorship

Like many others, you may decide that the major disadvantage of a sole proprietorship is the limited amount that one person can do in a workday. One way to reduce the effect of this disadvantage (and retain many of the advantages) is to have more than one owner.

Partnerships

learning objective

2 Explain the different types of partners and the importance of partnership agreements.

partnership a voluntary association of two or more persons to act as co-owners of a business for profit

A person who would not think of starting and running a business alone may enthusiastically seize the opportunity to enter into a business partnership. The U.S. Uniform Partnership Act defines a **partnership** as a voluntary association of two or more persons to act as co-owners of a business for profit. For example, in 1990, two young African-American entrepreneurs named Janet Smith and Gary Smith started Ivy Planning Group—a company that provides strategic planning and performance measurement for clients. Today the company has evolved into a multimillion-dollar company that has hired a diverse staff of employees and provides cultural diversity training for *Fortune* 500 firms and federal government agencies. In recognition of its efforts, Ivy Planning Group has been honored by *Black Enterprise* and *Working Woman* magazines. And Ms Smith was named “1 of 25 Most Influential Minority Women in Business” by Minority Business and Professionals Network.[2]

There are approximately 1.86 million partnerships in the United States. As shown in Figure 5.2, partnerships account for about $1,534 billion in receipts. Note, however, that this form of ownership is much less common than the sole proprietorship or the corporation. In fact, as Figure 5.1 shows, partnerships represent only about 8 percent of all American businesses. Although there is no legal maximum on the number of partners a partnership may have, most have only two. Large accounting, law, and advertising partnerships, however, are likely to have multiple partners. Regardless of the number of people involved, a partnership often represents a pooling of special managerial skills and talents; at other times, it is the result of a sole proprietor’s taking on a partner for the purpose of obtaining more capital.

Types of Partners

All partners are not necessarily equal. Some may be active in running the business, whereas others may have a limited role.

general partner a person who assumes full or shared responsibility for operating a business

General Partners A **general partner** is a person who assumes full or shared responsibility for operating a business. General partners are active in day-to-day business operations, and each partner can enter into contracts on behalf of the other

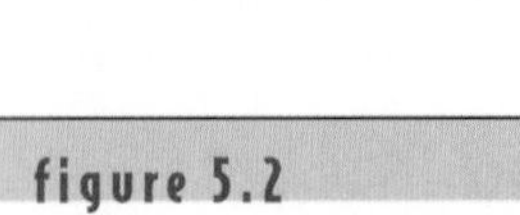

figure 5.2

Total Sales Receipts of American Businesses

Although corporations account for only 20.1 percent of U.S. businesses, they bring in 87.1 percent of the sales receipts.

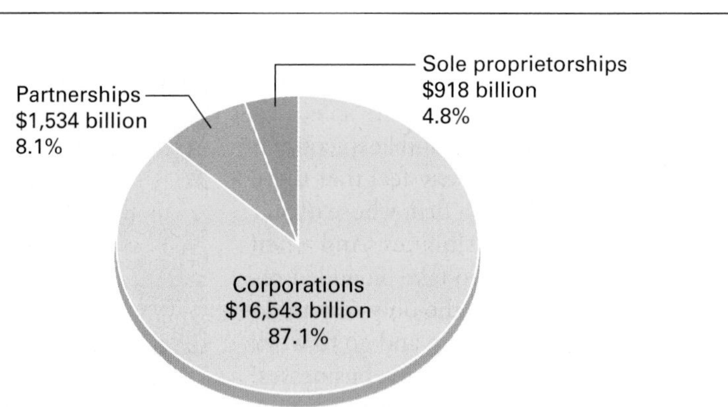

Source: U.S. Bureau of the Census website (**www.census.gov**), *Statistical Abstract of the United States*, 121st ed., Washington, D.C., 2001, p. 473.

A partnership that works: 8minuteDating.com and Tele-Publishing International. According to Tom Jaffee, founder of 8minuteDating.com, it only takes eight minutes to meet that special someone. True to his words, he found a business partner in just eight minutes. At a typical 8minuteDating.com event, Jaffee met Adam Segel, an executive with Tele-Publishing International. TPI runs the personal ads that appear in 550 newspapers across the U.S. When Segel was having dinner with his mother at the same restaurant hosting an 8minuteDating.com event, Jaffee introduced himself and they talked for just about 8 minutes. Each quickly described what he did, what his needs were, and what he could offer the other. The result: A partnership was formed. Today the businesses help each other by cross promoting their services to would-be customers.

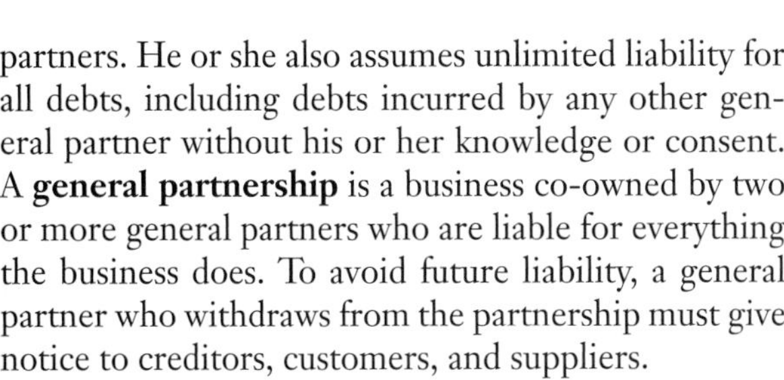

partners. He or she also assumes unlimited liability for all debts, including debts incurred by any other general partner without his or her knowledge or consent. A **general partnership** is a business co-owned by two or more general partners who are liable for everything the business does. To avoid future liability, a general partner who withdraws from the partnership must give notice to creditors, customers, and suppliers.

Limited Partners A **limited partner** is a person who contributes capital to a business but who has no management responsibility or liability for losses beyond his or her investment in the partnership. A **limited partnership** is a business co-owned by one or more general partners who manage the business and limited partners who invest money in it. Limited partnerships may be formed to finance real estate, oil and gas, motion-picture, and other business ventures. Typically, the general partner or partners collect management fees and receive a percentage of profits. Limited partners receive a portion of profits and tax benefits.

general partnership a business co-owned by two or more general partners who are liable for everything the business does

limited partner a person who contributes capital to a business but has no management responsibility or liability for losses beyond the amount he or she invested in the partnership

limited partnership a business co-owned by one or more general partners who manage the business and limited partners who invest money in it

Because of potential liability problems, special rules apply to limited partnerships. These rules are intended to protect customers and creditors who deal with limited partnerships. For example, prospective partners in a limited partnership must file a formal declaration, usually with the secretary of state or at their county courthouse, that describes the essential details of the partnership and the liability status of each partner involved in the business. At least one general partner must be responsible for the debts of the limited partnership. Also, some states prohibit the use of the limited partner's name in the partnership's name.

A special type of limited partnership is referred to as a *master limited partnership*. A **master limited partnership (MLP)** is a business partnership that is owned and managed like a corporation but taxed like a partnership. This special ownership arrangement has a major advantage when compared with the more traditional partnership and corporate forms of ownership. Units of ownership in MLPs can be sold to investors to raise capital and often are traded on organized security exchanges. Because MLP units can be traded on an exchange, investors can sell their units of ownership at any time, hopefully for a profit.

master limited partnership (MLP) a business partnership that is owned and managed like a corporation but taxed like a partnership

Originally, there were tax advantages to forming an MLP because profits from this special type of partnership were reported as personal income. MLPs thus avoided the double taxation paid on corporate income. Today, the Internal Revenue Service has limited many of the tax advantages of MLPs. Two MLPs you may recognize are the world-famous Boston Celtics basketball team and Bloomberg, the publisher of financial news.

The Partnership Agreement

Articles of partnership are an agreement listing and explaining the terms of the partnership. Although both oral and written partnership agreements are legal and can be enforced in the courts, a written agreement has an obvious advantage: It is not subject to lapses of memory.

Figure 5.3 shows a typical partnership agreement. The partnership agreement should state who will make the final decisions, what each partner's duties will be, and the investment each partner will make. The partnership agreement also should state how much profit or loss each partner receives or is responsible for. Finally, the partnership agreement should state what happens if a partner wants to dissolve the partnership or dies. The breakup of a partnership can be as complicated and traumatic as a divorce, and it is never too early to consider what could happen in the future. Although the people involved in a partnership can draft their own agreement, most experts recommend consulting an attorney.

When entering into a partnership agreement, partners would be wise to let a neutral third party—a consultant, an accountant, a lawyer, or a mutual friend—assist with any disputes that might arise. With no intense personal stake in the dispute, a third party can look beyond personal opinion and emotions to seek the best solution for the partnership. Each partner should agree to abide by the third party's decisions.

figure 5.3

Articles of Partnership

Articles of partnership is a written or oral agreement that lists and explains the terms of the partnership.

PARTNERSHIP AGREEMENT

Names of partners — This agreement, made June 20, 2004, between Penelope Wolfburg of 783A South Street, Hazelton, Idaho, and Ingrid Swenson of RR 5, Box 96, Hazelton, Idaho.

Nature, name, and address of business — 1. The above named persons have this day formed a partnership that shall operate under the name of W-S Jewelers, located at 85 Broad Street, Hazelton, Idaho 83335, and shall engage in jewelry sales and repairs.

Duration of partnership — 2. The duration of this agreement will be for a term of fifteen (15) years, beginning on June 20, 2004 or for a shorter term if agreed upon in writing by both partners.

Contribution of capital — 3. The initial investment by each partner will be as follows: Penelope Wolfburg, assets and liabilities of Wolfburg's Jewelry Store, valued at a capital investment of $40,000; Ingrid Swenson, cash of $20,000. These investments are partnership property.

Duties of each partner — 4. Each partner will give her time, skill, and attention to the operation of this partnership and will engage in no other business enterprise unless permission is granted in writing by the other partner.

Salaries, withdrawals, and distribution of profits — 5. The salary for each partner will be as follows: Penelope Wolfburg, $40,000 per year; Ingrid Swenson, $30,000 per year. Neither partner may withdraw cash or other assets from the business without express permission in writing from the other partner. All profits and losses of the business will be shared as follows: Penelope Wolfburg, 60 percent; Ingrid Swenson, 40 percent.

Termination — 6. Upon the dissolution of the partnership due to termination of this agreement, or to written permission by each of the partners, or to the death or incapacitation of one or both partners, a new contract may be entered into by the partners or the sole continuing partner has the option to purchase the other partner's interest in the business at a price that shall not exceed the balance in the terminating partner's capital account. The payment shall be made in cash in equal quarterly installments from the date of termination.

7. At the conclusion of this contract, unless it is agreed by both partners to continue the operation of the business under a new contract, the assets of the partnership, after the liabilities are paid, will be divided in proportion to the balance in each partner's capital account on that date.

Signatures — Penelope Wolfburg (signed) Penelope Wolfburg; Ingrid Swenson (signed) Ingrid Swenson

Date — June 20, 2004 Date; June 20, 2004 Date

Source: From Goldman and Sigismond, *Business Law*, 4th edition. Copyright © 1996, 2000 by Houghton Mifflin Company. Reprinted with permission.

Advantages of Partnerships

Partnerships have many advantages. The most important are described below.

learning objective

3 Describe the advantages and disadvantages of partnerships.

Ease of Start-Up Partnerships are relatively easy to form. Like a sole proprietorship, the legal requirements are often limited to registering the name of the business and purchasing any necessary licenses or permits. It may not even be necessary to prepare written articles of partnership, although doing so is generally a good idea.

Availability of Capital and Credit Because partners can pool their funds, a partnership usually has more capital available than a sole proprietorship does. This additional capital, coupled with the general partners' unlimited liability, can form the basis for a better credit rating. Banks and suppliers may be more willing to extend credit or grant larger loans to such a partnership than to a sole proprietor.

This does not mean that partnerships can borrow all the money they need. Many partnerships have found it hard to get long-term financing simply because lenders worry about the possibility of management disagreements and lack of continuity. In general, however, partnerships have greater assets and stand a better chance of obtaining the loans they need.

Retention of Profits As in a sole proprietorship, all profits belong to the owners of the partnership. The partners share directly in the financial rewards and therefore are highly motivated to do their best to make the firm succeed. As noted, the partnership agreement should state how much profit or loss each partner receives or is responsible for.

Personal Interest General partners are very concerned with the operation of the firm—perhaps even more so than sole proprietors. After all, they are responsible for the actions of all other general partners, as well as for their own.

Combined Business Skills and Knowledge Partners often have complementary skills. The weakness of one partner—in manufacturing, for example—may be offset by another partner's strength in that area. Moreover, the ability to discuss important decisions with another concerned individual often relieves some pressure and leads to more effective decision making.

Possible Tax Advantages Although a partnership pays no income tax, each partner is taxed on his or her share of the profit—in the same way a sole proprietor is taxed. They do not pay the special taxes (such as state and federal income taxes) imposed on corporations.

Disadvantages of Partnerships

Although partnerships have many advantages when compared with sole proprietorships and corporations, they also have some disadvantages, which anyone thinking of forming a partnership should consider.

Unlimited Liability As we have noted, each general partner has unlimited liability for all debts of the business. Each partner is legally and personally responsible for the debts and actions of any other partner, even if that partner did not incur those debts or do anything wrong. General partners thus run the risk of having to use their personal assets to pay creditors. Limited partners, however, risk only their original investment. Today, many states allow partners to form a limited-liability partnership (LLP) in which a partner in the LLP may have limited liability protection from legal action resulting from the malpractice of the other partners. Most states that allow LLPs restrict this type of ownership to certain types of professionals such as physicians, dentists, accountants, and attorneys. (Note the difference between a limited partnership and a limited-liability partnership. A limited partnership must have at least one general partner that has unlimited liability. On the other hand, all partners in a limited-liability partnership may have limited liability for the malpractice of the other partners.)

Lack of Continuity Partnerships are terminated if any one of the general partners dies, withdraws, or is declared legally incompetent. However, the remaining partners can purchase that partner's ownership share. For example, the partnership agreement may permit surviving partners to continue the business after buying a deceased partner's interest from his or her estate. However, if the partnership loses an owner whose specific management or technical skills cannot be replaced, it is not likely to survive.

Effects of Management Disagreements What happens to a partnership if one of the partners brings a spouse or a relative into the business? What happens if a partner wants to withdraw more money from the business? These questions describe only two problem areas that can lead to management disagreements. Notice that each of the preceding situations—and for that matter, most of the other problems that can develop in a partnership—involves one partner doing something that disturbs the other partner(s). This human factor is especially important because business partners—with egos, ambitions, and money on the line—are especially susceptible to friction. If the division of responsibilities among several partners is to be successful, and if partners are to work together as a team, they must have trust in each other. When partners begin to disagree about decisions, policies, or ethics, distrust may build and get worse as time passes—often to the point where it is impossible to operate the business successfully.

Frozen Investment It is easy to invest money in a partnership, but it is sometimes quite difficult to get it out. This is the case, for example, when remaining partners are unwilling to buy the share of the business that belongs to a partner who retires or wants to relocate to another city. To avoid such difficulties, the partnership agreement should include some procedure for buying out a partner.

In some cases, a partner must find someone outside the firm to buy his or her share. How easy or difficult it is to find an outsider depends on how successful the business is and how willing existing partners are to accept a new partner.

Beyond the Partnership

The main advantages of a partnership over a sole proprietorship are the added capital and management expertise of the partners. However, some of the basic disadvantages of the sole proprietorship also plague the general partnership. One disadvantage in particular—unlimited liability—can cause problems. A third form of business ownership, the corporation, overcomes this disadvantage.

Corporations

learning objective

4 Summarize how a corporation is formed.

corporation an artificial person created by law with most of the legal rights of a real person, including the rights to start and operate a business, to buy or sell property, to borrow money, to sue or be sued, and to enter into binding contracts

Perhaps the best definition of a corporation was given by Chief Justice John Marshall in a famous Supreme Court decision in 1819. A corporation, he said, "is an artificial being, invisible, intangible, and existing only in contemplation of the law." In other words, a **corporation** is an artificial person created by law, with most of the legal rights of a real person. These include the rights to start and operate a business, to buy or sell property, to borrow money, to sue or be sued, and to enter into binding contracts. Unlike a real person, however, a corporation exists only on paper.

There are 4.8 million corporations in the United States. They comprise only about 20 percent of all businesses, but they account for 87.1 percent of sales revenues. Table 5.1 lists the seven largest U.S. industrial corporations, ranked according to sales.

table 5.1 The Seven Largest U.S. Industrial Corporations, Ranked by Sales

Rank 2001	Rank 2000	Company	Sales ($ millions)	Profits ($ millions)	Assets ($ millions)
1	2	Wal-Mart Stores, Bentonville, Arkansas	219,812.0	6,671.0	83,375.0
2	1	EXXON Mobil, Irving, Texas	191,581.0	15,320.0	143,174.0
3	3	General Motors Detroit, Michigan	177,260.0	601.0	323,969.0
4	4	Ford Motor Company, Dearborn, Michigan	162,412.0	(5,453.0)	276,543.0
5	7	Enron, Houston, Texas	138,718.0	—	—
6	5	General Electric, Fairfield, Connecticut	125,913.0	13,684.0	495,023.0
7	6	Citigroup New York	112,022.0	14,126.0	1,050,000.0

Source: *Fortune 500*, © 2002 Time, Inc., April 15, 2002, p. F-1.

Corporate Ownership

The shares of ownership of a corporation are called **stock.** The people who own a corporation's stock—and thus own part of the corporation—are called **stockholders** or sometimes *shareholders*. Once a corporation has been formed, it may sell its stock to individuals or other companies that want to invest in the corporation. It also may issue stock as a reward to key employees in return for certain services or as a return to investors (in place of cash payments).

stock the shares of ownership of a corporation

stockholder a person who owns a corporation's stock

A **closed corporation** is a corporation whose stock is owned by relatively few people and is not sold to the general public. As an example, Mr. and Mrs. DeWitt Wallace owned virtually all the stock of Reader's Digest Association, making it one of the largest corporations of this kind. A person who wishes to sell the stock of a closed corporation generally arranges to sell it *privately* to another stockholder or a close acquaintance.

closed corporation a corporation whose stock is owned by relatively few people and is not sold to the general public

Although founded in 1922 as a closed corporation, the Reader's Digest Association became an open corporation when it sold stock to investors for the first time in 1990. An **open corporation** is one whose stock is bought and sold on security exchanges and can be purchased by any individual. General Motors Corporation is an example. Most large firms are open corporations, and their stockholders may number in the hundreds of thousands or even millions. For example, General Motors has almost one million and AT&T has about five million shareholders.

open corporation a corporation whose stock is bought and sold on security exchanges and can be purchased by any individual

incorporation the process of forming a corporation

Forming a Corporation

The process of forming a corporation is called **incorporation.** Although you may think that incorporating a business guarantees success, it does not. There is no special magic about placing the word *Incorporated* or the abbreviation *Inc.* after the name of a business. Unfortunately, like sole proprietorships or partnerships, incorporated businesses can go broke. The decision to incorporate a business therefore should be made only after carefully considering whether the corporate form of ownership suits your needs better than the sole proprietorship or partnership forms.

If you decide that the corporate form is the best form of organization for you, most experts recommend that you begin the incorporation process by consulting a lawyer to be sure that all legal requirements are met. While it may be possible to incorporate a business without legal help, it is well to keep in mind

Using the Internet @

Where can you find out more about starting and managing a business? The Small Business Administration website explores a number of business topics that are beneficial to new businesses as well as those currently in operation. Answers to typical questions such as which legal form is best and how to get financing are provided as well as the SBA answer desk where you can submit written questions about any specific concerns. Your gateway to the SBA is at **http://www.sbaonline.sba.gov/.**

table 5.2 Aspects of Business that May Require Legal Help

1. Choosing either the sole proprietorship, partnership, or corporate form of ownership
2. Constructing a partnership agreement
3. Establishing a corporation
4. Registering a corporation's stock
5. Obtaining a trademark, patent, or copyright
6. Filing for licenses or permits at the local, state, and federal levels
7. Purchasing an existing business or real estate
8. Leasing real estate or equipment
9. Hiring employees and independent contractors
10. Handling labor disputes and customer lawsuits
11. Extending credit and collecting debts
12. Handling bankruptcy and reorganization

Source: Adapted from Seth Godin (ed.), *1997 Business Almanac.* Copyright © 1996 by Houghton Mifflin Company, Boston.

domestic corporation a corporation in the state in which it is incorporated

foreign corporation a corporation in any state in which it does business except the one in which it is incorporated

the old saying, "A man who acts as his own attorney has a fool for a client." Unfortunately, this can be true for business owners when they start a business. Table 5.2 lists some aspects of starting and running a business that may require legal help.

Where to Incorporate A business is allowed to incorporate in any state that it chooses. Most small and medium-sized businesses are incorporated in the state where they do the most business. The founders of larger corporations or of those that will do business nationwide often compare the benefits that various states provide to corporations. Some states are more hospitable than others, and some offer fewer restrictions, lower taxes, and other benefits to attract new firms. Delaware offers the lowest organizational costs in the country. In fact, more than half the *Fortune* 500 companies are incorporated in Delaware, even though their corporate headquarters may be located in another state.[3]

An incorporated business is called a **domestic corporation** in the state in which it is incorporated. In all other states where it does business, it is called a **foreign corporation.** Sears, Roebuck, for example, is incorporated in New York, where it is a domestic corporation. In the remaining forty-nine states, Sears is a foreign corporation. Sears must register in all states where it does business and

A decision to incorporate doesn't have to be hard. Where can you go to get help incorporating a business? Most people turn to lawyers, accountants, consultants, the Internet, or a firm like The Company Corporation. The Company Corporation helps business owners make informed decisions about the choice of business ownership.

also pay taxes and annual fees to each state. A corporation chartered by a foreign government and conducting business in the United States is an **alien corporation.** Volkswagen, Sony Corporation, and the Royal Dutch/Shell Group are examples of alien corporations.

The Corporate Charter Once a home state has been chosen, the incorporator(s) submits *articles of incorporation* to the secretary of state. If the articles of incorporation are approved, they become the firm's corporate charter. A **corporate charter** is a contract between the corporation and the state in which the state recognizes the formation of the artificial person that is the corporation. Usually the charter (and thus the articles of incorporation) includes the following information:

- The firm's name and address
- The incorporators' names and addresses
- The purpose of the corporation
- The maximum amount of stock and types of stock to be issued
- The rights and privileges of stockholders
- The length of time the corporation is to exist

Spotlight

Dividends for stockholders

The dollar amounts below represent total dividend payments made by U.S. corporations to stockholders over a three-year period.

In billions

2000	$376.1
2001	$409.6
2002	$434.3

Source: The U.S. Department of Commerce, Bureau of Economic Analysis.

Each of these key details is the result of decisions the incorporators must make as they organize the firm—before they submit their articles of incorporation. To help you decide if the corporate form of organization is the right choice, you may want to review the material available on the Yahoo! Small Business website (**http://smallbusiness.yahoo.com**). In addition, before making a decision to organize your business as a corporation, you may want to consider two additional areas: stockholder's rights and the importance of the organizational meeting.

Stockholders' Rights There are two basic types of stock. Owners of **common stock** may vote on corporate matters. Generally, an owner of common stock has one vote for each share owned. The owners of **preferred stock** usually have no voting rights, but their claims on dividends are paid before those of common-stock owners.

Perhaps the most important right of owners of both common and preferred stock is to share in the profit earned by the corporation through the payment of dividends. A **dividend** is a distribution of earnings to the stockholders of a corporation. Other rights include receiving information about the corporation, voting on changes to the corporate charter, and attending the corporation's annual stockholders' meeting, where they may exercise their right to vote.

Because common stockholders usually live all over the nation, very few may actually attend a corporation's annual meeting. Instead, they vote by proxy. A **proxy** is a legal form listing issues to be decided and enabling stockholders to transfer their voting rights to some other individual or individuals. The stockholder can register a vote and transfer voting rights simply by signing and returning the form. And some corporations allow stockholders to exercise their right to vote by proxy by accessing the Internet or using a toll-free phone number.

Organizational Meeting As the last step in forming a corporation, the incorporators and original stockholders meet to elect their first board of directors. (Later, directors will be elected or reelected at the corporation's annual meetings.) The board members are directly responsible to the stockholders for the way they operate the firm.

alien corporation a corporation chartered by a foreign government and conducting business in the United States

corporate charter a contract between the corporation and the state in which the state recognizes the formation of the artificial person that is the corporation

common stock stock owned by individuals or firms who may vote on corporate matters but whose claims on profit and assets are subordinate to the claims of others

preferred stock stock owned by individuals or firms who usually do not have voting rights but whose claims on dividends are paid before those of common-stock owners

dividend a distribution of earnings to the stockholders of a corporation

proxy a legal form listing issues to be decided at a stockholders' meeting and enabling stockholders to transfer their voting rights to some other individual or individuals

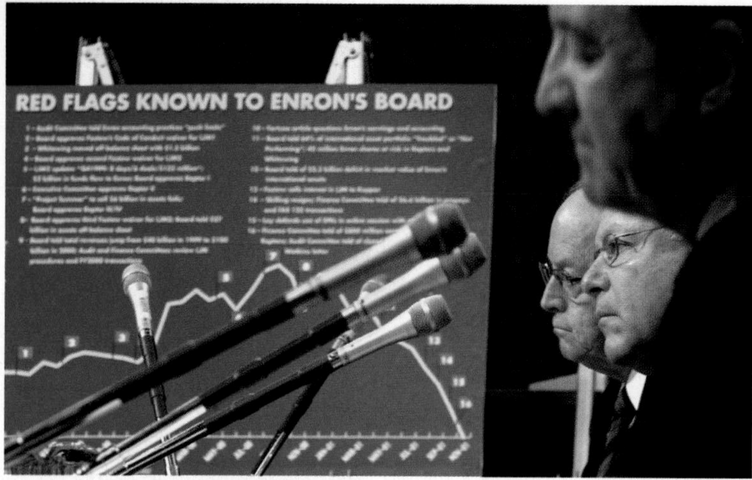

Difficult Questions for Enron's Board of Directors. When government officials learned of the accounting problems at Enron, a Senate committee demanded an explanation from the corporation's top governing body—its board of directors, who are responsible for a firm's overall operation. In this photo, three of Enron's board members are asked to explain how accounting problems at the world's largest energy-trading company led to bankruptcy and huge dollar losses for both employees and individuals who owned Enron stock.

Corporate Structure

The organizational structure of most corporations is more complicated than that of a sole proprietorship or partnership. This is especially true as the corporation begins to grow and expand. In a corporation, both the board of directors and the corporate officers are involved in management.

board of directors the top governing body of a corporation, the members of which are elected by the stockholders

Board of Directors

As an artificial person, a corporation can act only through its directors, who represent the corporation's stockholders. The **board of directors** is the top governing body of a corporation, and as we noted, directors are elected by the stockholders. Board members can be chosen from within the corporation or from outside it.

Directors who are elected from within the corporation are usually its top managers —the president and executive vice presidents, for example. Those elected from outside the corporation are generally experienced managers or entrepreneurs with proven leadership ability and/or specific talents the organization seems to need. In smaller corporations, majority stockholders usually serve as board members.

The major responsibilities of the board of directors are to set company goals and develop general plans (or strategies) for meeting those goals. The board also is responsible for the firm's overall operation.

corporate officers the chairman of the board, president, executive vice presidents, corporate secretary, treasurer, or any other top executive appointed by the board of directors

Corporate Officers

Corporate officers are appointed by the board of directors. The chairman of the board, president, executive vice presidents, corporate secretary, and treasurer are all corporate officers. They help the board to make plans, carry out strategies established by the board, hire employees, and manage day-to-day business activities. Periodically (usually each month), they report to the board of directors. And at the annual meeting, the directors report to the stockholders. In theory, then, the stockholders are able to control the activities of the entire corporation through its directors because they are the group that elects the board of directors (see Figure 5.4).

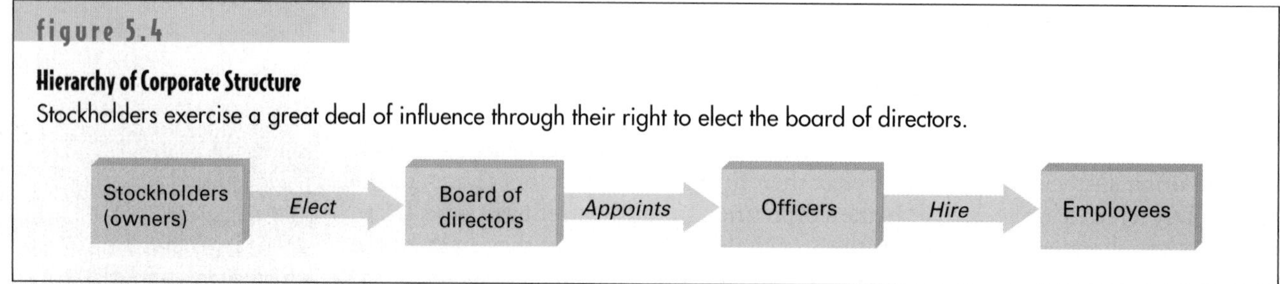

figure 5.4

Hierarchy of Corporate Structure

Stockholders exercise a great deal of influence through their right to elect the board of directors.

examining ethics

Two Companies That Give Something Back

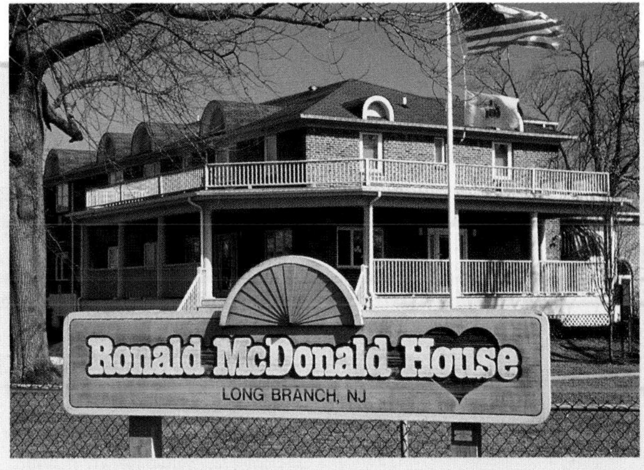

McDONALD'S AND TARGET do much more than create jobs and pay taxes in the communities where they operate. Both the fast-food chain and the discount retailer have earned a reputation for social responsibility and are especially active in projects for children. One of the best known is the Ronald McDonald House Charities, created by McDonald's to provide low-cost housing for families whose seriously ill children are being treated in area hospitals. Thousands of families have benefited from the home-like atmosphere and the support of other families while staying in Ronald McDonald Houses. In the course of a year, for example, the houses in Portland, Oregon, host 900 families, supported by McDonald's fundraisers and local contributions.

To celebrate World Children's Day, McDonald's donates a portion of one day's revenues to various children's aid programs around the world. In India, for instance, the chain has contributed funds to upgrade school facilities. It also donates generously to local relief efforts after natural disasters such as earthquakes. And because McDonald's operates more than 30,000 restaurants around the world, its recycling and environmental protection initiatives can make a significant difference.

Many of Target's social responsibility programs emphasize education. The retailer sponsors the Public Broadcasting System's Kids Share a Story literacy campaign and works with the Tiger Woods Foundation to educate children about career options and offer scholarships. It also donates to the Hispanic Scholarship Fund and the United Negro College Fund and contributes a small percentage of the value of purchases charged on Target Visa credit cards to buy supplies for schools across the United States.

Moreover, Target donates millions of dollars to St. Jude Children's Research Hospital and to Target House, a lodge where families of children receiving treatment at St. Jude's can stay for free. On a local level, many Target stores partner with nonprofit groups to meet the needs of families in their community. In Washington state, for example, local stores have teamed up with the United Way to give decorated Christmas trees to needy families. These are only some of the ways that Target and McDonald's—like many other corporations—give something back to their communities.

Issues to Consider

1. If you were a shareholder in McDonald's or Target, would you be willing to accept lower dividends so that the corporation could devote more money to social responsibility? Explain your answer.
2. How much say should employees and shareholders have in determining which causes Target or McDonald's will support?

Advantages of Corporations

learning objective

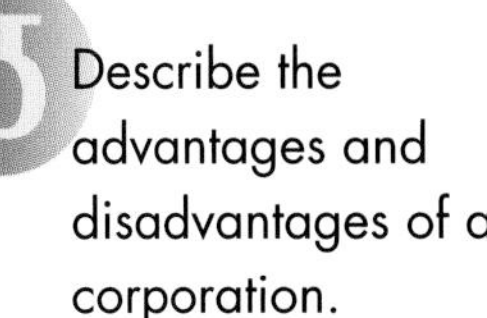

5 Describe the advantages and disadvantages of a corporation.

Back in October 2000, Manny Ruiz decided that it was time to start his own company. With the help of a team of media specialists, he founded Hispanic PR Wire, which became profitable within the first two years. In a business where hype is the name of the game, Hispanic PR Wire is the real thing and has established itself as the nation's leading news distribution service reaching U.S. Hispanic media and opinion leaders. Today the business continues to build on its early success.[4] Mr. Ruiz chose to incorporate his business because it provided a number of advantages that other forms of business ownership did not offer. Typical advantages include limited liability, ease of raising capital, ease of transfer of ownership, perpetual life, and specialized management.

limited liability a feature of corporate ownership that limits each owner's financial liability to the amount of money that he or she has paid for the corporation's stock

Limited Liability One of the most attractive features of corporate ownership is **limited liability.** With few exceptions, each owner's financial liability is limited to the amount of money he or she has paid for the corporation's stock. This feature arises from the fact that the corporation is itself a legal being, separate from its owners. If a corporation fails, creditors have a claim only on the corporation's assets, not on the owners' personal assets. Because it overcomes the problem of unlimited liability connected with sole proprietorships and general partnerships, limited liability is one of the chief reasons why entrepreneurs often choose the corporate form of organization.

Ease of Raising Capital The corporation is by far the most effective form of business ownership for raising capital. Like sole proprietorships and partnerships, corporations can borrow from lending institutions. However, they also can raise additional sums of money by selling stock. Individuals are more willing to invest in corporations than in other forms of business because their liability is limited, and they can sell their stock easily—hopefully for a profit. Information on the process a corporation uses to sell stock is provided in Chapter 20.

Ease of Transfer of Ownership A telephone call to a stockbroker is all that is required to put stock up for sale. Willing buyers are available for most stocks at the market price. Ownership is transferred when the sale is made, and practically no restrictions apply to the sale and purchase of stock issued by an open corporation. More information on the "mechanics" of buying and selling stock for investment purposes is provided in Chapter 21.

Perpetual Life Since it is essentially a legal "person," a corporation exists independently of its owners and survives them. Unless its charter specifies otherwise, a corporation has perpetual life. The withdrawal, death, or incompetence of a key executive or owner does not cause the corporation to be terminated. Sears, Roebuck, which started as a partnership in 1886 and incorporated in 1906, is one of the nation's largest retailing corporations, even though its original owners, Richard Sears and Alvah Roebuck, have been dead for decades.

Specialized Management Typically, corporations are able to recruit more skilled, knowledgeable, and talented managers than proprietorships and partnerships. This is so because they pay bigger salaries, offer excellent fringe benefits, and are large enough to offer considerable opportunity for advancement. Within the corporate structure, administration, human resources, finance, marketing, and operations are placed in the charge of experts in these fields.

Disadvantages of Corporations

Like its advantages, many of a corporation's disadvantages stem from its legal definition as an artificial person or legal entity. The most serious disadvantages are described below. (See Table 5.3 for a comparison of some of the advantages and disadvantages of a sole proprietorship, partnership, and corporation.)

table 5.3 Some Advantages and Disadvantages of a Sole Proprietorship, Partnership, and Corporation

	Sole Proprietorship	General Partnership	Regular Corporation
Protecting against liability for debts	Difficult	Difficult	Easy
Raising money	Difficult	Difficult	Easy
Ownership transfer	Difficult	Difficult	Easy
Preserving continuity	Difficult	Difficult	Easy
Government regulations	Few	Few	Many
Formation	Easy	Easy	Difficult
Income taxation	Once	Once	Twice

Difficulty and Expense of Formation Forming a corporation can be a relatively complex and costly process. The use of an attorney is usually necessary to complete the legal forms and apply to the state for a charter. Charter fees, attorney's fees, registration costs associated with selling stock, and other organizational costs can amount to thousands of dollars for even a medium-sized corporation. The costs of incorporating, in terms of both time and money, discourage many owners of smaller businesses from forming corporations.

Government Regulation A corporation must meet various government standards before it can sell its stock to the public. Then it must file many reports on its business operations and finances with local, state, and federal governments. In addition, the corporation must make periodic reports to its stockholders about various aspects of the business. In addition, its activities are restricted by law to those spelled out in its charter.

Double Taxation Unlike sole proprietorships and partnerships, corporations must pay a tax on their profits. In addition, stockholders must pay a personal income tax on profits received as dividends. Corporate profits are thus taxed twice—once as corporate income and a second time as the personal income of stockholders.

Lack of Secrecy Because open corporations are required to submit detailed reports to government agencies and to stockholders, they cannot keep their operations confidential. Competitors can study these corporate reports and then use the information to compete more effectively. In effect, every public corporation has to share some of its secrets with its competitors.

Other Types of Business Ownership

In addition to the sole proprietorship, partnership, and corporate form of organization, some entrepreneurs choose other forms of organization that meet their special needs. Additional organizational options include S-corporations, limited-liability companies, government-owned corporations, not-for-profit corporations, cooperatives, joint ventures, and syndicates.

learning objective

6 Discuss the purpose of an S-corporation, limited-liability company, and other special forms of business ownership.

S-Corporations

If a corporation meets certain requirements, its directors may apply to the Internal Revenue Service for status as an S-corporation. An **S-corporation** is a corporation that is taxed as though it were a partnership. In other words, the corporation's income is taxed only as the personal income of stockholders.

S-corporation a corporation that is taxed as though it were a partnership

Becoming an S-corporation can be an effective way to avoid double taxation while retaining the corporation's legal benefit of limited liability. Moreover, stockholders can personally claim their share of losses incurred by the corporation to offset their own personal income. To qualify for the special status of an S-corporation, a firm must meet the following criteria:

1. No more than seventy-five stockholders are allowed.
2. Stockholders must be individuals, estates, or certain trusts.
3. There can be only one class of outstanding stock.
4. The firm must be a domestic corporation.
5. There can be no nonresident alien stockholders.
6. All stockholders must agree to the decision to form an S-corporation.

Limited-Liability Companies

limited-liability company (LLC) a form of business ownership that provides limited-liability protection and is taxed like a partnership

In addition to the traditional forms of business ownership already covered, a new and promising form of ownership called a *limited-liability company* has been approved in all fifty states—although each state's laws may differ. A **limited-liability company (LLC)** is a form of business ownership that combines the benefits of a corporation and a partnership while avoiding some of the restrictions and disadvantages of those forms of ownership. Chief advantages of an LLC are

1. LLCs with at least two members are taxed like a partnership and thus avoid the double taxation imposed on most corporations. LLCs with just one member are taxed like a sole proprietorship.
2. Like a corporation, it provides limited-liability protection. An LLC thus extends the concept of personal-asset protection to small business owners.

Although many experts believe the LLC is nothing more than a variation of the S-corporation, there is a difference. An LLC is not restricted to seventy-five stockholders—a common drawback of the S-corporation. LLCs are also less restricted and have more flexibility than S-corporations in terms of who can become an owner and who can make management decisions. Although the owners of an LLC must file articles of organization with their state's secretary of state, they are not hampered by lots of Internal Revenue Service rules and government regulations that apply to corporations. As a result, experts are predicting that LLCs may become one of the most popular forms of business ownership available.

Government-Owned Corporations

government-owned corporation a corporation owned and operated by a local, state, or federal government

A **government-owned corporation** is owned and operated by a local, state, or federal government. The Tennessee Valley Authority (TVA), the National Aeronautics and Space Administration (NASA), and the Federal Deposit Insurance Corporation (FDIC) are all government-owned corporations. They are operated by the U.S. government. Most municipal bus lines and subways are run by city-owned corporations.

A government corporation usually provides a service the business sector is reluctant or unable to offer. Profit is secondary in such corporations. In fact, they may continually operate at a loss, particularly if they are involved in public transportation. Their main objective is to ensure that a particular service is available.

quasi-government corporation a business owned partly by the government and partly by private citizens or firms

In certain cases, a government will invite citizens or firms to invest in a government corporation as part owners. A business owned partly by the government and partly by private citizens or firms is called a **quasi-government corporation.** The Federal National Mortgage Association (Fannie Mae), the Federal Home Loan Mortgage Corporation (Freddie Mac), and Student Loan Marketing Association (Sallie Mae) are examples of businesses that were created as quasi-government corporations.

Not-for-Profit Corporations

not-for-profit corporation a corporation organized to provide a social, educational, religious, or other service rather than to earn a profit

A **not-for-profit corporation** is a corporation organized to provide a social, educational, religious, or other service rather than to earn a profit. Various charities, museums, private schools, and colleges are organized in this way, primarily to ensure limited liability. Habitat for Humanity is a not-for-profit corporation and was formed to provide homes for qualified low-income people who could not afford housing. Even though this corporation may receive more money than it spends, any surplus funds are "reinvested" in building activities to provide low-cost housing. It is a not-for-profit corporation because its primary purpose is to provide a social service. Other examples include the Public Broadcasting System (PBS), the Girl Scouts, and the Red Cross.

Occasionally, some not-for-profit organizations are inspired with entrepreneurial zeal. The New York Museum of Modern Art sold air rights in Manhattan for $17 million to allow the construction of a private forty-four-story residential tower. Tax-free income from the sale helped finance a new wing, doubling the size of the museum.

Do kids get in trouble when they hang out? Depends on where they hang out! David Edwards, a chemical engineer who started and later sold a very profitable company, felt strongly about giving something back to his Boston community. As a result, David and his wife formed the not-for-profit Cloud Foundation, established a $9 million endowment, and helped fund the acquisition of a three-story building that is used by 25 different community groups to help teenagers interested in art.

Cooperatives

A **cooperative** is an association of individuals or firms whose purpose is to perform some business function for its members. The cooperative can perform its function more effectively than any member could by acting alone. As a result, members benefit from its activities. For example, cooperatives purchase goods in bulk and distribute them to members; thus the unit cost is lower than it would be if each member bought the goods in a much smaller quantity.

cooperative an association of individuals or firms whose purpose is to perform some business function for its members

Although cooperatives are found in all segments of our economy, they are most prevalent in agriculture. Farmers use cooperatives to purchase supplies, to buy services such as trucking and storage, and to process and market their products. Ocean Spray Cranberries, Inc., for example, is a cooperative of some eight hundred cranberry growers and more than one hundred citrus growers spread throughout the country. Other examples of cooperatives include Missouri-based Farmland Industries and California-based Sunkist Growers.

Joint Ventures

A **joint venture** is an agreement between two or more groups to form a business entity in order to achieve a specific goal or to operate for a specific period of time. Both the scope of the joint venture and the liabilities of the people or businesses involved are usually limited to one project. Once the goal is reached, the period of time elapses, or the project is completed, the joint venture is dissolved.

joint venture an agreement between two or more groups to form a business entity in order to achieve a specific goal or to operate for a specific period of time

Corporations, as well as individuals, may enter into joint ventures. Major oil producers formed a number of joint ventures in the 1970s and 1980s to share the extremely high cost of exploring for offshore petroleum deposits. More recently, Walt Disney formed a joint venture with Pixar Animation Studios to create movies over the next ten years. Finally, Waltham Massachusetts–based E5 Systems has formed a joint venture with software-based Kingdee International Software Group to develop software for export.[5] While both companies are relatively small, they hope to grow and eventually help China to become a formidable rival for India—a country long known for its ability to produce quality software.

Syndicates

syndicate a temporary association of individuals or firms organized to perform a specific task that requires a large amount of capital

A **syndicate** is a temporary association of individuals or firms organized to perform a specific task that requires a large amount of capital. The syndicate is formed because no one person or firm is willing to put up the entire amount required for the undertaking. Like a joint venture, a syndicate is dissolved as soon as its purpose has been accomplished.

Syndicates are used most commonly to underwrite large insurance policies, loans, and investments. To share the risk of default, banks have formed syndicates to provide loans to developing countries. Stock brokerage firms usually join together in the same way to market a new issue of stock. For example, Morgan Stanley and other Wall Street firms formed a syndicate to sell shares of stock in United Parcel Service (UPS). The initial public offering was the largest in U.S. history—too large for Morgan Stanley to handle without help from other Wall Street firms. (An *initial public offering* is the term used to describe the first time a corporation sells stock to the general public.)

Corporate Growth

learning objective

7 Explain how growth from within and growth through mergers can enable a business to expand.

Growth seems to be a basic characteristic of business, at least for firms that can obtain the capital needed to finance growth. One reason for seeking growth has to do with profit: A larger firm generally has greater sales revenue and thus greater profit. Another reason is that in a growing economy, a business that does not grow is actually shrinking relative to the economy. A third reason is that business growth is a means by which some executives boost their power, prestige, and reputation.

Should all firms grow? Certainly not until they are ready. Growth poses new problems and requires additional resources that first must be available and then must be used effectively. The main ingredient in growth is capital—and as we have noted, capital is most readily available to corporations. Thus, to a great extent, business growth means corporate growth.

Growth from Within

Most corporations grow by expanding their present operations. Some introduce and sell new but related products. For example, Palm Computing handheld computing devices, Nintendo's electronic games, or Motorola's C330 cellular phone were improvements when compared with earlier models. Others expand the sale of present products to new geographic markets or to new groups of consumers in geographic markets already served. Currently, Wal-Mart has almost 3,000 stores in the United States, and Puerto Rico, and retail outlets in Argentina, Brazil, Canada, China, Germany, Korea, Mexico, and the United Kingdom and has long-range plans for expanding into additional international markets.

Growth from within, especially when carefully planned and controlled, can have relatively little adverse effect on a firm. For the most part, the firm continues to do what it has been doing, but on a larger scale. Because this type of growth is anticipated, it can be gradual, and the firm usually can adapt to it easily. For instance, Larry Ellison, chairman and CEO of Oracle Corporation of Redwood City, California, built the firm's annual revenues up from a mere $282 million in 1988 to an estimated $9.35 billion today. Much of that growth has taken place since 1994 as Oracle capitalized on its global leadership in information management software. Measuring growth in terms of employees and markets, Oracle now has more than 43,000 employees in more than 100 countries.[6]

going global

The World According to Wal-Mart

FIRST AMERICA, THEN THE WORLD. With more than 4,300 stores in the United States and eight other countries, Wal-Mart is by far the world's largest retailer. From its headquarters in Bentonville, Arkansas, the chain has expanded its low-price formula globally through a combination of growth from within, joint ventures, and growth through acquisitions.

Wal-Mart began its international expansion in 1991, when it opened a store in Mexico City through a joint venture with Cifra. Within a few years, Wal-Mart had acquired a majority stake in Cifra and soon afterward changed the corporate name to Wal-Mart de Mexico. Today the corporation runs 572 stores and restaurants across Mexico and rings up yearly sales of nearly $10 billion.

After opening stores in Puerto Rico, Wal-Mart next moved into Canada by acquiring more than 100 Woolco discount stores. The following year Wal-Mart entered the South American market, starting with a Sam's Club in Brazil and a Sam's Club in Argentina. Now thirty-three Wal-Mart discount stores employing 10,000 people operate in the two countries.

To tap the huge potential for retail sales in China, Wal-Mart formed a joint venture and opened a store in Shenzhen in 1996. China represents "the only overseas market where we can replicate the scale of our U.S. operations," says the president of Wal-Mart International, who plans to open thousands of stores within twenty years.

Less than two years after entering China, Wal-Mart acquired the Wertkauf retail chain to enter Germany, Europe's largest market. Within a few months, it also acquired the Interspar retail chain. Then Wal-Mart began renovating the existing stores and converting them to Supercenters as quickly as complex local rules would allow. However, intense competition and strict government regulations have slowed the company's expansion within Germany.

Next, Wal-Mart acquired a retailer in South Korea and opened additional units throughout the country. An even larger acquisition allowed Wal-Mart to move into the United Kingdom in 1999. ASDA was a well-known British food and apparel retailer with more than 250 stores when it was acquired by Wal-Mart. Today the stores, under the ASDA–Wal-Mart name, are a key component in Wal-Mart's $35 billion in non-U.S. revenues—with more sales to come through additional corporate growth.

Growth Through Mergers and Acquisitions

Another way a firm can grow is by purchasing another company. The purchase of one corporation by another is called a **merger.** An *acquisition* is essentially the same thing as a merger, but the term is usually used in reference to a large corporation's purchases of other corporations. Although most mergers and acquisitions are friendly, hostile takeovers also occur. A **hostile takeover** is a situation in which the management and board of directors of the firm targeted for acquisition disapprove of the merger, usually because their company will become a subsidiary of the purchasing firm and the acquired firm's management and board of directors will have to give up control.

merger the purchase of one corporation by another

hostile takeover a situation in which the management and board of directors of the firm targeted for acquisition disapprove of the merger

When a merger or acquisition becomes hostile, a corporate raider—another company or a wealthy investor—may make a tender offer or start a proxy fight to gain control of the target company. A **tender offer** is an offer to purchase the stock of a firm targeted for acquisition at a price just high enough to tempt stockholders to sell their shares. Corporate raiders also may initiate a proxy fight. A **proxy fight** is a technique used to gather enough stockholder votes to control the targeted company.

tender offer an offer to purchase the stock of a firm targeted for acquisition at a price just high enough to tempt stockholders to sell their shares

proxy fight a technique used to gather enough stockholder votes to control the targeted company

If the corporate raider is successful and takes over the targeted company, existing management is usually replaced. Faced with this probability, existing management may try the following techniques (sometimes referred to as "poison pills," "shark repellents," or "porcupine provisions") to maintain control of the firm and avoid the hostile takeover:

1. Issue a new class of preferred stock that gives stockholders the right to redeem their shares at a premium *after* the corporate raider assumes control of the company.
2. Allow existing stockholders to purchase new stock at a discounted price well below the market value of existing stock. This increases the number of

Sears and Lands' End: A merger that makes a lot of dollars and sense. When Sears acquired Lands' End, it was a match almost too good to be true. Both firms benefit from the merger. For Sears, Lands' End represented a great investment opportunity. For Lands' End, Sears represented a corporation with the financial resources to help the smaller company grow. As an added bonus, consumers benefit by being able to buy Lands' End merchandise in Sears stores.

outstanding shares and makes a hostile takeover more expensive for the corporate raider.

3. Give "golden parachute" contracts to top executives, thus ensuring that the corporate raider will find it very expensive to get rid of top management.
4. Adopt a supermajority provision, which requires at least a two-thirds or three-fourths majority of votes cast by stockholders to ratify a takeover by an outsider.
5. Create staggered terms for the corporation's board members. This makes it more difficult for the corporate raider to install a new board sympathetic to the takeover attempt.
6. Use leveraged recapitalization to make the company less attractive. *Leveraged recapitalization* means that the corporation obtains a large amount of debt capital and then makes large cash distributions to existing stockholders.
7. Find a "white knight"—a friendly corporation willing to take over the targeted company. Generally, the white knight agrees to keep existing management and allow the acquired firm to continue operating as an independent unit.

Whether mergers are friendly or hostile, they are generally classified as *horizontal, vertical,* or *conglomerate* (see Figure 5.5).

Horizontal Mergers A *horizontal merger* is a merger between firms that make and sell similar products or services in similar markets. The merger between Compaq and Hewlett Packard is an example of a horizontal merger because both firms are in the computer hardware industry. This type of merger tends to reduce the number of firms in an industry—and thus may reduce competition. For this reason, each merger may be reviewed carefully by federal agencies before it is permitted.

Vertical Mergers A *vertical merger* is a merger between firms that operate at different but related levels in the production and marketing of a product. Generally, one of the merging firms is either a supplier or a customer of the other. A vertical merger occurred when Lucent Technologies agreed to purchase Chromatis Networks. At the time, Lucent needed optical networking equipment to compete with Cisco and other networking firms. Rather than buy the equipment it needed, Lucent simply bought the company—Chromatis Networks—that produced the state-of-the-art equipment it needed to remain competitive in the ever-changing computer networking industry.

Conglomerate Mergers A *conglomerate merger* takes place between firms in completely different industries. One of the largest conglomerate mergers in recent history occurred when America Online (AOL) and Time Warner merged. AOL (an Internet service provider) purchased Time Warner (a firm rich in content). The AOL–Time Warner merger was friendly because it was beneficial for both firms. Simply put, combining the resources of both companies will result in different meth-

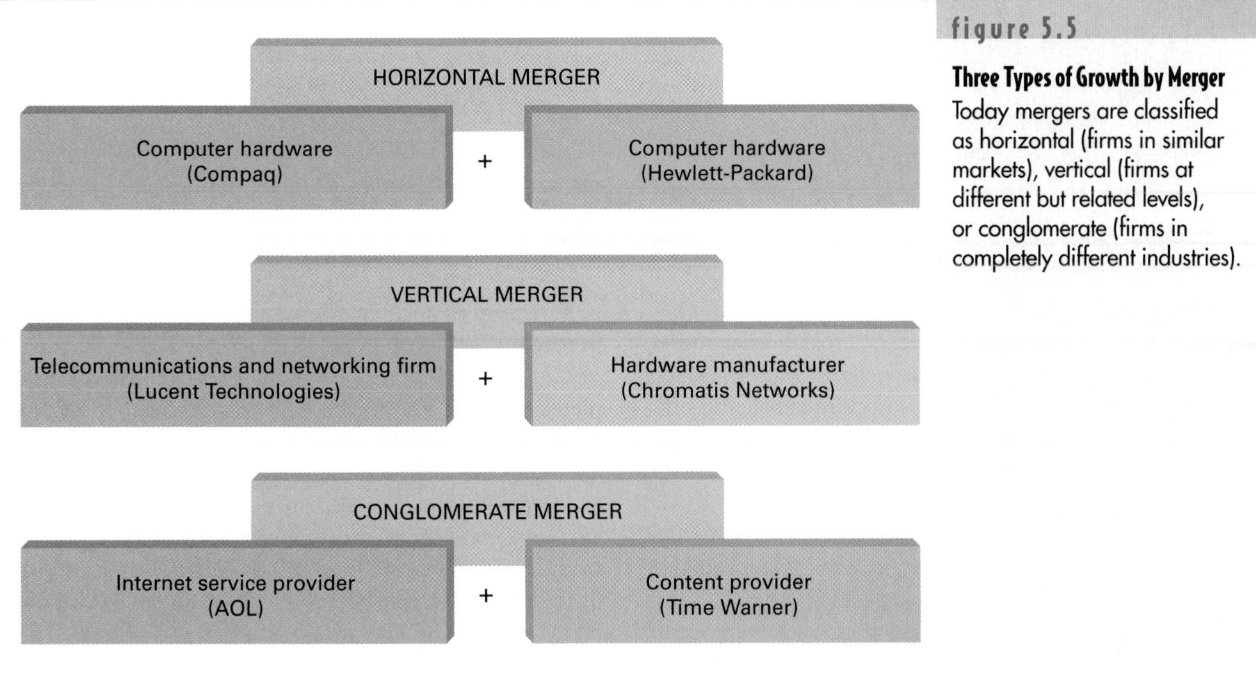

figure 5.5

Three Types of Growth by Merger
Today mergers are classified as horizontal (firms in similar markets), vertical (firms at different but related levels), or conglomerate (firms in completely different industries).

ods of packaging, distributing, and marketing of information and entertainment and create one very competitive *and* large corporation. As mentioned in Exploring Business (on p. 158) and at the time of publication, this huge conglomerate merger has not paid off for investors.

Current Merger Trends

Economists, financial analysts, corporate managers, and stockholders still hotly debate whether takeovers are good for the economy—or for individual companies—in the long run. One thing is clear, however: There are two sides to the takeover question. Takeover advocates argue that in companies that have been taken over, the purchasers have been able to make the company more profitable and productive by installing a new top management team and by forcing the company to concentrate on one main business. Takeover advocates also point out that proceeds from the sale of subsidiaries and divisions not aligned with the parent company's main business have been used either to pay off debt or to enhance the company.

Takeover opponents argue that takeovers do nothing to enhance corporate profitability or productivity. These critics argue that threats of takeovers have forced managers to devote valuable time to defending their companies from takeover, thus robbing time from new product development and other vital business activities. This, they believe, is why U.S. companies may be less competitive with companies in such countries as Japan, Germany, and South Korea, where takeovers rarely occur. Finally, the opposition argues that the only people who benefit from takeovers are investment bankers, brokerage firms, and takeover "artists," who receive financial rewards by manipulating U.S. corporations rather than by producing tangible products or services.

Most experts now predict that mergers and acquisitions during the first part of the twenty-first century will be the result of cash-rich companies looking to acquire businesses that will enhance their position in the marketplace. Analysts also anticipate more mergers that involve companies or investors from other countries. Regardless of the companies involved or where the companies are from, future mergers and acquisitions

exploring business

Big Mergers: Fast Track to Investor Wealth?

OVER THE YEARS, many corporations have had the urge to merge. One hundred years ago a wave of mergers combining smaller firms created regional and national manufacturing corporations on a scale never before seen. In recent years, cross-border mergers have brought together corporate giants seeking global growth opportunities and profit-enhancing efficiencies of scale. But do huge corporate mergers put the resulting behemoths on the fast track to investor wealth?

Business Week studied this issue by analyzing the pattern of megamergers for six recent years. According to the magazine's research, top management tended to pay too much for the acquired corporations, set overly optimistic goals for cost savings, and stumbled over integration efforts. When the corporations failed to live up to their lofty growth and profit plans, investors bailed out in droves. Thus the share price of many of the largest merged corporations barely kept up with that of industry peers—or even fell below, an outcome also confirmed by *Newsweek* research. In the end, the shareholders who did best were those who owned stock in the acquired company because they received a premium over market value for their shares.

High-tech mergers are especially tricky in part because such firms often have unusually strong corporate cultures that are difficult to blend. The highly touted merger between America Online and Time Warner is only one example of a titanic deal that had not paid off for investors even after two years. Still, executives continue to pursue major acquisitions.

One of the most closely watched high-tech mergers in recent years was Hewlett Packard's (HP's) acquisition of Compaq Computer. HP's CEO Carly Fiorina completed the $19 billion deal despite vigorous opposition from a son of one HP founder. In Fiorina's view, the acquisition gives HP the full range of products, services, and capabilities to compete with IBM. Cost cutting is also important if the combination is to succeed. Apart from laying off 15,000-plus employees, HP reduced its overall purchasing by $1 billion or more. However, many cultural and operations issues must be resolved to integrate the two companies into one. Meanwhile, HP's share price has moved both up and down since the acquisition. Will investors ultimately benefit? Only time will tell.

will be driven by solid business logic, the desire to compete in the international marketplace, and the explosion of information technology.

Experts also predict that less borrowed money (sometimes referred to as *debt capital*) will be used to pay for mergers and acquisitions. When considering possible merger deals, bankers and lenders today seem far more skeptical than they were in the 1980s and 1990s. In the old days, corporate raiders could borrow enough money to purchase the target company. They would then dismantle the company and sell off different parts—a process called **divestiture**—to make a quick profit or to raise cash to make loan payments.

divestiture the process of dismantling a company and selling off different parts

leveraged buyout (LBO) a purchase arrangement that allows a firm's managers and employees or a group of investors to purchase the company

Finally, experts predict more leveraged buyouts in the future. A **leveraged buyout (LBO)** is a purchase arrangement that allows a firm's managers and employees or a group of investors to purchase the company. (LBO activity is sometimes referred to as *taking a firm private.*) To gain control of a company, LBOs usually rely on borrowed money to purchase stock from existing stockholders. The borrowed money is later repaid through the company's earnings, sale of assets, or money obtained from selling more stock.

Whether they are sole proprietorships, partnerships, corporations, or some other form of business ownership, most U.S. businesses are small. In the next chapter we focus on these small businesses. We examine, among other things, the meaning of the word *small* as it applies to business and the place of small business in the American economy.

Return To inside business

Procter & Gamble has a rich history of innovation, starting in its partnership days and continuing under the corporate form of ownership. For decades, the company fueled growth from within by inventing all kinds of new products. In one recent year its research centers spent $1.7 billion in pursuit of imaginative product ideas. At the close of the twentieth century, however, growth had slowed, and the company began to look outside itself for expansion opportunities. In addition to acquiring established products and businesses, Procter & Gamble snapped up smaller firms that owned the rights to promising inventions—then used its marketing muscle to quickly build market share and sales.

Moreover, the company forged alliances with other companies to develop new products under prominent brand names. For example, in a joint venture with Clorox, Procter & Gamble applied its research expertise to the creation of new food-storage items to be marketed as Glad products. Although not every new product will be a blockbuster, the company remains committed to the kind of innovation that has fueled sales since the days of William Procter and James Gamble.

Questions

1. Procter & Gamble evolved from two separate sole proprietorships into a partnership and then into a corporation with stockholders, board members, managers, and 100,000 employees. Why do you think this form of ownership is appropriate for a company like Procter & Gamble?
2. Given its ability to acquire other businesses, why would a large corporation such as Procter & Gamble choose to grow by agreeing to a joint venture?

chapter review

Summary

Describe the advantages and disadvantages of sole proprietorships.

In a sole proprietorship, all business profits become the property of the owner, but the owner is also personally responsible for all business debts. A successful sole proprietorship can be a great source of pride for the owner. When comparing different types of business ownership, the sole proprietorship is the simplest form of business to enter, control, and leave. It also has possible tax advantages. Perhaps for these reasons, 72.2 percent of all American business firms are sole proprietorships. Sole proprietorships nevertheless have disadvantages, such as unlimited liability and limits on one person's ability to borrow or to be an expert in all fields.

Explain the different types of partners and the importance of partnership agreements.

Like sole proprietors, general partners are responsible for running the business and for all business debts. Limited partners receive a share of the profit in return for investing in the business. However, they are not responsible for business debts beyond the amount they have invested. It is also possible to form a master limited partnership (MLP) and sell units of ownership to raise capital. Regardless of the type of partnership, it is always a good idea to have a written agreement (or articles of partnership) setting forth the terms of a partnership.

Describe the advantages and disadvantages of partnerships.

Although partnership eliminates some of the disadvantages of sole proprietorship, it is the least popular of the major forms of business ownership. The major advantages of a partnership include ease of start-up, availability of capital and credit, retention of profits, personal interest, combined skills and knowledge, and possible tax advantages. The effects of management disagreements are one of the major disadvantages of a partnership. Other disadvantages include unlimited liability (in a general partnership), lack of continuity, and frozen investment. By forming a limited partnership, the disadvantage of unlimited liability may be eliminated for the limited partner(s). This same disadvantage may be eliminated for all partners that form a limited-liability partnership. Of course, special requirements must be met if partners form either the limited partnership or the limited-liability partnership.

Summarize how a corporation is formed.

A corporation is an artificial person created by law, with most of the legal rights of a real person, including the right to start and operate a business, to own property, and to enter into contracts. With the corporate form of ownership, stock can be sold to individuals to raise capital.

The process of forming a corporation is called incorporation. Most experts believe that the services of a lawyer are necessary when making decisions about where to incorporate and about obtaining a corporate charter, holding an organizational meeting, and all other legal details involved in incorporation. In theory, stockholders are able to control the activities of the corporation because they elect the board of directors who appoint the corporate officers.

Describe the advantages and disadvantages of a corporation.

Perhaps the major advantage of the corporate form is limited liability—stockholders are not liable for the corporation's debts beyond the amount they paid for its stock. Other important advantages include ease of raising capital, ease of transfer of ownership, perpetual life, and specialized management. A major disadvantage of the corporation is double taxation: All profits are taxed once as corporate income and again as personal income because stockholders must pay a personal income tax on the profits they receive as dividends. Other disadvantages include difficulty and expense of formation, government regulation, and lack of secrecy.

Discuss the purpose of an S-corporation, limited-liability company, and other special forms of business ownership.

S-corporations are corporations that are taxed as though they were partnerships but that enjoy the benefit of limited liability. To qualify as an S-corporation, a number of criteria must be met. A limited-liability company (LLC) is a form of business ownership that provides limited liability and has fewer restrictions. LLCs with at least two members are taxed like a partnership and thus avoid the double taxation imposed on most corporations. LLCs with just one member are taxed like a sole proprietorship. Government-owned corporations provide particular services, such as public transportation, to citizens. Not-for-profit corporations are formed to provide social services rather than to earn profits. Three additional forms of business ownership are the cooperative, joint venture, and syndicate. All are used by their owners to meet special needs, and each may be owned by either individuals or firms.

Explain how growth from within and growth through mergers can enable a business to expand.

A corporation may grow by expanding its present operations or through a merger or acquisition. Although most mergers are friendly, hostile takeovers also occur. A hostile takeover is a situation in which the management and board of directors of the firm targeted for acquisition disapprove of the merger. Mergers generally are classified as horizontal, vertical, or conglomerate mergers.

While economists, financial analysts, corporate managers, and stockholders debate the merits of mergers, some trends should be noted. First, experts predict that future mergers will be the result of cash-rich companies looking to acquire businesses that will enhance their position in the marketplace. Second, more mergers are likely to involve foreign companies or investors. Third, mergers will be driven by business logic, the desire to compete in the international marketplace, and the explosion of information technology. Fourth, there will be less debt financing. Finally, more leveraged buyouts are expected.

Key Terms

You should now be able to define and give an example relevant to each of the following terms:

sole proprietorship (137)
unlimited liability (139)
partnership (140)
general partner (140)
general partnership (141)
limited partner (141)
limited partnership (141)
master limited partnership (MLP) (141)
corporation (144)
stock (145)
stockholder (145)
closed corporation (145)
open corporation (145)
incorporation (145)
domestic corporation (146)
foreign corporation (146)
alien corporation (147)
corporate charter (147)
common stock (147)
preferred stock (147)
dividend (147)
proxy (147)
board of directors (148)
corporate officers (148)
limited liability (149)
S-corporation (151)
limited-liability company (LLC) (152)
government-owned corporation (152)
quasi-government corporation (152)
not-for-profit corporation (152)
cooperative (153)
joint venture (153)
syndicate (154)
merger (155)
hostile takeover (155)
tender offer (155)
proxy fight (155)
divestiture (158)
leveraged buyout (LBO) (158)

Review Questions

1. What is a sole proprietorship? What are the major advantages and disadvantages of this form of business ownership?
2. How does a partnership differ from a sole proprietorship? Which disadvantages of sole proprietorship does the partnership tend to eliminate or reduce?
3. What is the difference between a general partner and a limited partner?
4. What issues should be included in a partnership agreement? Why?
5. Explain the difference between
   a. An open corporation and a closed corporation
   b. A domestic corporation, a foreign corporation, and an alien corporation
6. Outline the incorporation process, and describe the basic corporate structure.
7. What rights do stockholders have?
8. What are the primary duties of a corporation's board of directors? How are directors elected?
9. What are the major advantages and disadvantages associated with the corporate form of business ownership?
10. How do an S-corporation and a limited-liability company differ?
11. Explain the difference between a government-owned corporation, a quasi-government corporation, and a not-for-profit corporation.
12. Why are cooperatives formed? Explain how they operate.
13. In what ways are joint ventures and syndicates alike? In what ways do they differ?
14. What is a hostile takeover? What can management do to prevent a hostile takeover?
15. Describe the three types of mergers.

Discussion Questions

1. If you were to start a business, which ownership form would you choose? What factors might affect your choice?
2. Why might an investor choose to become a partner in a limited-liability partnership business instead of purchasing the stock of an open corporation?
3. Discuss the following statement: "Corporations are not really run by their owners."
4. What kinds of services do government-owned corporations provide? How might such services be provided without government involvement?
5. Is growth a good thing for all firms? How does management know when a firm is ready to grow?
6. Assume that a corporate raider wants to purchase your firm, dismantle it, and sell the individual pieces. What could you do to avoid this hostile takeover?

video case

Bay Partners Sticks to Venture Capital Basics

All businesses—sole proprietorships, partnerships, and corporations—need money. And money is the business of Bay Partners, a venture-capital firm with headquarters in Cupertino, California. For more than 25 years, Bay Partners has been investing in up-and-coming high-tech companies connected with innovative goods and services. Its investments are typically in the range of $1 to $10 million. In addition, the partners of Bay Partners have been active participants in one or more technology start-ups over the years. Therefore, they have the knowledge and background to help each company in which they invest by serving as consultants, mentors, and financial advisors.

Not every company is a candidate for the funding and specialized assistance that the partners offer. As smart investors, they are extremely particular about which enterprises they choose to support. First, they look at the size of the market opportunity and how fast the market is growing. Ideally, Bay Partners would prefer to invest in entrepreneurial companies offering products for larger, faster-growing markets.

Next, Bay Partners looks at the managers who are running the company. Do these people have the expertise, experience, drive, and dedication to make the company successful? As the business grows, can they attract a

team of talented employees who are customer-oriented and flexible enough to adjust to the technology industry's rapid, often unexpected changes?

The product is another important part of the evaluation process. The partners consider whether the good or service will meet customers' needs and whether customers will have to drastically alter their behavior to use the product. Can the company communicate with customers about its innovation? What kind of competitive situation is the company likely to confront in the marketplace? The development process is also analyzed to be sure that the entrepreneurs have realistic plans and schedules for creating, testing, manufacturing, and introducing new products and technologies. Generally, Bay Partners invests in companies that are about to bring tested technologies to market rather than those with unproven ideas.

Finally, Bay Partners takes a good look at each company's business plan. Because the partners have been entrepreneurs, they understand the many challenges a company faces as it implements its business plan. Thus the partners do not focus exclusively on projected sales volume and revenue goals. In addition, they think about the plan as a whole. If it does not seem realistic, it is unlikely to be workable once the company is funded. This is critical because the partners do not make money unless the companies in which they invest make money.

Although venture capitalists rushed in to fund dot-com start-ups at the beginning of the Internet boom, many slashed their funding of web ventures when reality set in during the dot-com downturn. However, Bay Partners was not affected because it maintained its focus on investing in technology companies that were strong on business fundamentals and had fresh approaches to solving customers' problems.

The partners in Bay Partners like the excitement of working with new discoveries, of watching a business grow, and of helping entrepreneurs achieve their dreams. They do not invest in every company they analyze, but they do give entrepreneurs feedback on their ideas. In some cases, the partners will work with budding entrepreneurs to shape a promising concept into a business plan with potential. Currently, the venture-capital firm's portfolio of investments includes Sonicwall (which makes online security devices), Guidewire (transaction-processing software), NanoGram Devices (medical components), and SporTVision (media enhancements for sports broadcasting).

Despite their extensive analysis, the partners ar well aware of the risks—and the stress—they will en counter through their investments. Ultimately, whe the partners decide they are going to invest, they mak a long-term commitment of expertise as well as mone to help the business succeed. For example, three medi executives formed SporTVision as a corporation i 1998. Their plan was to enhance the viewers' experi ence of sports events aired on television and the wel Professional baseball, football, basketball, hocke golf, racing, and other sports have used SporTVision technology over the years. Even though the compan received venture-capital funding from Bay Partners number of years ago and is well beyond the start-u phase, at least one of the three founders talks with Bay Partners contact every week to discuss strateg hiring, and other operational matters.[7]

Questions

1. Imagine that you are a venture capitalist considerin whether to invest as a part owner in a start-up corpora tion with a promising but unproven technology. Yo know that owners have limited financial liability if th corporation fails. How would this affect your investmen decision?
2. The partners of Bay Partners are very particular abou which businesses they choose to support. What factor do they consider before making a decision to provid venture capital and management assistance to a start-u company?
3. Why would the partners at Bay Partners want to stay in volved in a start-up company once a decision is made t provide venture capital? From the entrepreneur's stand point, is this continued involvement good or bad? Ex plain your answer.

Building Skills for Career Success

1. Exploring the Internet

The arguments about mergers and acquisitions often come down to an evaluation of who benefits and by how much. Sometimes the benefits include access to new products, talented management, new customers, or new sources of capital. Often the debate is complicated by the involvement of firms based in different countries.

The Internet is a fertile environment for information and discussion about mergers. The firms involved will provide their view about who will benefit and why it is either a good thing or not. Journalists will report facts and offer commentary as to how they see the future result of any merger, and of course, chat rooms located on websites of many journals promote discussion about the issues. Visit the text website for updates to this exercise.

Assignment

1. Using an Internet search engine such as AltaVista or Yahoo!, locate two or three sites providing information about a recent merger (use a keyword like *merger*).
2. After examining these sites and reading journal articles, report information about the merger, such as the value, the reasons behind the action, and so forth.
3. Based on your assessment of the information you have read, do you think the merger is a good idea or not for the firms involved, the employees, the investors, the industry, and society as a whole? Explain your reasoning.

2. Developing Critical Thinking Skills

Suppose that you are a person who has always dreamed of owning a business but never had the money to open one. Since you were old enough to read a recipe, your mother allowed you to help in the kitchen. Most of all, you enjoyed baking and decorating cakes. You liked using your imagination to create cakes for special occasions. By the time you were in high school, you were baking and decorating wedding cakes for a fee. After high school, you started working full time as an adjuster for an insurance company. Your schedule now allows little time for baking and decorating cakes. Recently, you inherited $250,000, and changes at your job have created undue stress in your life. What should you do?

Assignment

1. Discuss the following points:
   a. What options are available to you?
   b. What specific factors must you consider in starting a business versus working for another firm?
   c. What form of ownership would be best for your business?
   d. What advantages and disadvantages apply to your preferred form of business ownership?
2. Prepare a two-page report summarizing your findings.

3. Building Team Skills

Using the scenario in Exercise 2, suppose that you have decided to quit your job as an insurance adjuster and open a bakery. Your business is now growing, and you have decided to add a full line of catering services. This means more work and responsibility. You will need someone to help you, but you are undecided about what to do. Should you hire an employee or find a partner? If you add a partner, how will you organize the business, and what will you need to do to create a legal partnership?

Assignment

1. In a group, discuss the following questions:
   a. What are the advantages and disadvantages of adding a partner versus hiring an employee?
   b. Assume that you have decided to form a partnership. What articles should be included in a partnership agreement?
   c. How would you go about finding a partner?
2. Summarize your group's answers to these questions, and present them to your class.
3. As a group, prepare an articles of partnership agreement. Be prepared to discuss the pros and cons of your group's agreement with other groups from your class, as well as to examine their agreements.

4. Researching Different Careers

Many people spend their entire lives working in jobs that they do not enjoy. Why is this so? Often it is because they have taken the first job they were offered without giving it much thought. How can you avoid having this happen to you? First, you should determine your "personal profile" by identifying and analyzing your own strengths, weaknesses, things you enjoy, and things you dislike. Second, you should identify the types of jobs that fit your profile. Third, you should identify and research the companies that offer those jobs.

Assignment

1. Take two sheets of paper and draw a line down the middle of each sheet, forming two columns on each page. Label column 1 "Things I Enjoy or Like to Do," column 2 "Things I Do Not Like Doing," column 3 "My Strengths," and column 4 "My Weaknesses."
2. Record data in each column over a period of at least one week. You may find it helpful to have a relative or friend give you input.
3. Summarize the data, and write a profile of yourself.
4. Prepare a list of jobs that fit your profile. Take your profile to a career counselor at your college or to the public library and ask for help in identifying jobs that fit your profile. Your college may offer testing to assess your skills and personality. The Strong-Campbell Interest Inventory and the Meyers-Briggs Personality Indicator can help you assess the kind of work you may enjoy. The Internet is another resource.
5. Research the companies that offer the types of jobs that fit your profile.
6. Write a report on your findings.

5. Improving Communication Skills

If businesses are to succeed, they must change continually. Change takes many forms. Every week newspapers report on companies taking steps to organize into larger units or to downsize into smaller units. This chapter has discussed several strategies that effect change in organizations. They include mergers and acquisitions, hostile takeovers, divestitures, and leveraged buyouts.

Assignment

1. Read articles illustrating how one or more of these strategies has caused an organization to change.
2. Write a two-page report covering the following:
   a. Explain in your own words what led up to this change.
   b. How will this change affect the company itself, its consumers, its employees, its investors, and its industry?
   c. What opportunities does this change create, and what problems do you forecast?

chapter

6 Small Business, Entrepreneurship, and Franchises

learning objectives

1. Define what a small business is and recognize the fields in which small businesses are concentrated.
2. Identify the people who start small businesses and the reasons why some succeed and many fail.
3. Assess the contributions of small businesses to our economy.
4. Judge the advantages and disadvantages of operating a small business.
5. Explain how the Small Business Administration helps small businesses.
6. Appraise the concept and types of franchising.
7. Analyze the growth of franchising and franchising's advantages and disadvantages.

Chris Madden launched a brand empire based on her name.

inside business

Chris Madden Builds a Home Decor Empire

STARTING WITH BOOKS and expanding into furniture and beyond, Chris Casson Madden is following her entrepreneurial instincts to build an empire that one day may rival the revenue and name recognition of Martha Stewart. Madden was a student at the Fashion Institute of Technology in New York and held a variety of publishing jobs before coauthoring her first book, *The Compleat Lemon* cookbook. Then she wrote a string of books about home design and decor that led Oprah Winfrey to appoint her as design correspondent.

The Madden brand really blossomed after the publication of her 1997 book, *A Room of Her Own: Women's Personal Spaces*, which showcased the special spaces of Winfrey, designer Jessica McClintock, actress Ali McGraw, and dozens of other busy American women. "There wasn't anyone speaking to women's personal needs for a sanctuary," Madden remembers. "Nor were there affordable, durable, stylish home furnishings available to make their homes a haven." The book struck a responsive chord with harried women seeking a quiet place to decompress at home. It sold 119,000 copies and put Madden on the best-seller lists—giving her the widespread exposure she needed to launch a brand empire based on her name.

When Bassett Furniture invited Madden to serve as its spokesperson, she wound up arranging for the company to license her brand for several lines of furniture. The company encouraged her to scrutinize every detail of the designs and materials. " 'You've got to get it right,' Rob Spilman, Bassett's president, told me at the outset," she explains. " 'It's got your name on it.' " Sales of the Madden-branded furniture collections doubled within two years, and the living room sets have become Bassett's top-selling products. Soon Madden branched out to license her name for a wider range of home-related products, including baby furniture for Babies "R" Us, rugs for Mohawk Home, candles for Austin International, and pillows for the Bed Bath & Beyond chain.

Whereas Madden's fifteen books have generated $1.3 million in royalty revenues over the years, her licensing arrangements—covering more than 163 products—have the potential to bring in many times that amount. The Bassett deal already contributes more than half of her firm's annual revenues. Although Madden is constantly bombarded with offers from companies who want to license her brand for everything from eyeglasses to gardening gloves, she is selective and rejects any products that do not fit her business plan. Now in her fifties, the entrepreneur serves as president, and her husband, Kevin Madden, serves as CEO of Madden, Inc. which also employs a public relations expert, a design director, and several other specialists. Looking ahead at her company's future, Madden observes, "The biggest challenge is going ahead in the right way for us. Not in being Martha."[1]

Just as Chris Madden's empire grew from writing one small lemon cookbook, most businesses start small. Unlike Madden's empire, most small businesses that survive usually stay small. They provide a solid foundation for our economy—as employers, as suppliers and purchasers of goods and services, and as taxpayers.

In this chapter we do not take small businesses for granted. Instead, we look closely at this important business sector—beginning with a definition of small business, a description of industries that often attract small businesses, and a profile of some of the people who start small businesses. Next, we consider the importance of small businesses in our economy. We also present the advantages and disadvantages of smallness in business. We then describe services provided by the Small Business Administration, a government agency formed to assist owners and managers of small businesses. We conclude the chapter with a discussion of the pros and cons of franchising, an approach to small-business ownership that has become very popular in the last thirty years.

Small Business: A Profile

learning objective

1 Define what a small business is and recognize the fields in which small businesses are concentrated.

The Small Business Administration (SBA) defines a **small business** as "one which is independently owned and operated for profit and is not dominant in its field." How small must a firm be not to dominate its field? That depends on the particular industry it is in. The SBA has developed the following specific "smallness" guidelines for the various industries.[2]

small business one that is independently owned and operated for profit and is not dominant in its field

- *Manufacturing*—a maximum of 500 to 1,500 employees, depending on the products manufactured
- *Wholesaling*—a maximum of 100 employees
- *Retailing*—maximum yearly sales or receipts ranging from $6 million to $24.5 million, depending on the industry
- *Mining*—a maximum of 500 employees
- *General construction*—average annual receipts ranging from $12 million to $28.5 million, depending on the industry
- *Special trade construction*—annual sales ranging up to $12 million
- *Agriculture*—maximum annual receipts of $0.75 million to $5 million
- *Services*—maximum annual receipts ranging from $6 million to $29 million, depending on the type of service

The SBA periodically revises and simplifies its small-business size regulations.

Annual sales in the millions of dollars may not seem very small. However, for many firms, profit is only a small percentage of total sales. Thus a firm may earn only $30,000 or $40,000 on yearly sales of $1 million—and that *is* small in comparison with the profits earned by most medium-sized and large firms. Moreover, most small firms have annual sales well below the maximum limits in the SBA guidelines.

The Small-Business Sector

A surprising number of Americans take advantage of their freedom to start a business. There are, in fact, about twenty-three million businesses in this country. Only just over 17,000 of these employ more than 500 workers—enough to be considered large.

Interest in owning or starting a small business has never been greater than it is today. During the last decade, the number of small businesses in the United States has increased 49 percent, and for the last few years, new business formation in the United States has broken successive records except during the 2001–2002 recession. Recently, nearly 580,000 new businesses were incorporated. Furthermore, part-time entrepreneurs have increased fivefold in recent years; they now account for one-third of all small businesses.[3]

Statistically, over 70 percent of new businesses can be expected to fail within their first five years.[4] The primary reason for these failures is mismanagement resulting from a lack of business know-how. The makeup of the small-business sector thus is constantly changing. Despite the high failure rate, many small businesses succeed modestly. Some, like Apple Computer, Inc., are extremely successful—to the point where they can no longer be considered small. Taken together, small businesses are also responsible for providing a high percentage of the jobs in the United States. According to some estimates, the figure is well over 50 percent.

Industries that Attract Small Businesses

Some industries, such as auto manufacturing, require huge investments in machinery and equipment. Businesses in such industries are big from the day they are started—if an entrepreneur or group of entrepreneurs can gather the capital required to start one.

By contrast, a number of other industries require only a low initial investment and some special skills or knowledge. It is these industries that tend to attract new businesses. Growing industries, such as outpatient care facilities, are attractive because of their profit potential. However, knowledgeable entrepreneurs choose areas with which they are familiar, and these are most often the more established industries. Table 6.1 shows the fastest growing industries in employment and the small-business shares of employment in those industries.

Small enterprise spans the gamut from corner newspaper vending to the development of optical fibers. The owners of small businesses sell gasoline, flowers, and coffee to go. They publish magazines, haul freight, teach languages, and program computers. They make wines, movies, and high-fashion clothes. They build new homes and restore old ones. They fix appliances, recycle metals, and sell used cars. They drive cabs and fly planes. They make us well when we are ill, and they sell us the products of corporate giants. The various kinds of businesses generally fall into three broad categories of industry: distribution, service, and production.

Got milk? His customers do. Small enterprise spans the gamut from corner hot-dog stand to delivering milk, butter, eggs, cottage cheese, yogurt, and ice cream. Here a Palo Alto, California milkman delivers dairy products in his white 1960 Ford milk truck to his customers in the San Francisco Bay Area.

Distribution Industries This category includes retailing, wholesaling, transportation, and communications—industries concerned with the movement of goods from producers to consumers. Distribution industries account for approximately 33 percent of all small businesses. Of these, almost three-quarters are involved in retailing, that is, the sale of goods directly to consumers. Clothing and jewelry stores, pet shops, bookstores, and grocery stores, for example, are all retailing firms. Slightly less than one-quarter of the small distribution firms are wholesalers. Wholesalers purchase products in quantity from manufacturers and then resell them to retailers.

Service Industries This category accounts for over 48 percent of all small businesses. Of these, about three-quarters provide such nonfinancial services as medical and dental care; watch, shoe, and TV repairs; haircutting and styling; restaurant meals; and dry cleaning. About 8 percent of the small service firms offer financial services, such as accounting, insurance, real estate, and investment counseling. An increasing number of self-employed Americans are running service businesses from home.

Production Industries This last category includes the construction, mining, and manufacturing industries. Only about 19 percent of all small businesses are in this group, mainly because these industries require relatively large initial investments. Small firms that do venture into production generally make parts and subassemblies for larger manufacturing firms or supply special skills to larger construction firms.

table 6.1 Fastest Growing Industries

This ranking is based on the percentage change (increase) in employment from 2001 to 2002. The small-business share of employment is greatest in landscape and horticultural services.

Industry	Annual Employment 2001	Percentage Increase from 2002	Percent Small Business
Oil and gas extraction	338,000	8.5	39.9
Pipelines, except natural gas	15,000	7.1	10.3
Landscape and horticultural services	560,200	5.9	84.0
Social services	3,056,900	5.4	80.5
Nondepository institutions*	720,200	4.7	34.9

*Includes personal and business credit institutions and mortgage and loan companies.
Source: Office of Advocacy, U.S. Small Business Administration, *Small Business Economic Indicators for 2002*, Table 12, p. 25, from data provided by the Bureau of Labor Statistics and the U.S. Census Bureau.

The People in Small Businesses: The Entrepreneurs

learning objective

2 Identify the people who start small businesses and the reasons why some succeed and many fail.

Small businesses typically are managed by the people who started and own them. Most of these people have held jobs with other firms and could still be so employed if they wanted. Yet owners of small businesses would rather take the risk of starting and operating their own firms, even if the money they make is less than the salaries they might otherwise earn.

Researchers have suggested a variety of personal factors as reasons why people go into business for themselves. One that is often cited is the "entrepreneurial spirit"—the desire to create a new business. For example, Nikki Olyai always knew she wanted to create and develop her own business. Her father, a successful businessman in Iran, was her role model. She came to the United States at the age of seventeen and lived with a host family in Salem, Oregon, attending high school there. Undergraduate and graduate degrees in computer science led her to start Innovision Technologies while she held two other jobs to keep the business going and took care of her 4-year-old son. In 2000, Nikki Olyai was honored by the Women's Business Enterprise National Council's "Salute to Women's Business Enterprises" as one of eleven top successful firms. Innovision Technologies specializes in information technology, systems analysis and assessment, project management, and quality assurance. In 1999 Olyai's firm was ranked 195 on the *Inc.* 500 list of America's fastest growing privately held companies. For three consecutive years her firm was selected as a "Future 50 of Greater Detroit Company."[5] Other factors, such as independence, the desire to determine one's own destiny, and the willingness to find and accept a challenge certainly play a part. Background may exert an influence as well. In particular, researchers think that people whose families have been in business (successfully or not) are most apt to start and run their own businesses. Those who start their own businesses also tend to cluster around certain ages—more than 70 percent are between 24 and 44 years of age[6] (see Figure 6.1 on p. 170).

The Internet has become a small-business on-ramp for teenaged entrepreneurs. Start-up costs are relatively small—a computer, a modem, a phone line, and an Internet domain name. Yet the rewards—and the opportunities—can be extremely large. Just ask Michael Furdyk, Michael Hayman, and Albert Lai. As teens, the three collaborated on MyDesktop.com, a website loaded with help tips for software and computer games. Within two years the site was drawing a million visitors monthly and bringing in $30,000 from ad revenues. The content and the traffic caught the eye of Internet.com, which bought the company for more than $1 million down, thousands of stock options, and additional cash payments based on growth. The entrepreneurs

How Old Is the Average Entrepreneur?
People in all age groups become entrepreneurs, but more than 70 percent are between 24 and 44 years of age.

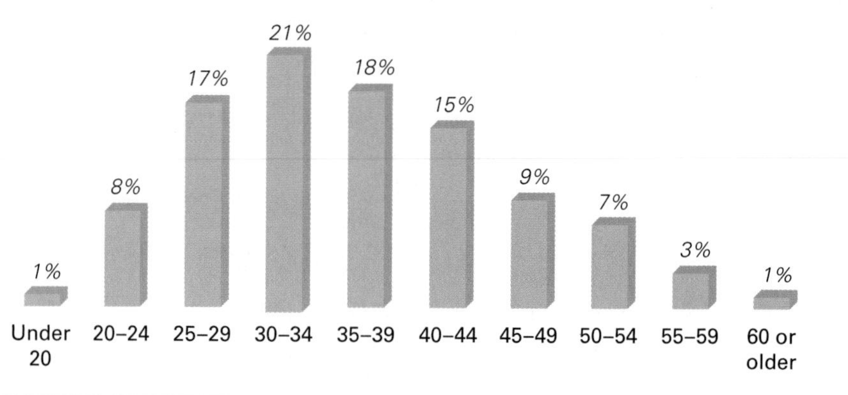

Source: Data developed and provided by the National Federation of Independent Business Foundation and sponsored by the American Express Travel Related Services Company, Inc.

immediately began working on a second web-based business, BuyBuddy.com. "It is an e-commerce site that we hope to make into a market player now that we have more experience and contacts," says Hayman. Or ask Cameron Johnson, the teen who started the SurfingPrizes.com site. Web surfers can earn money for every hour they are logged on to the site, which exposes them to ads from companies such as Discover Card, Ask Jeeves, Tickets.com, and Warner Brothers. More than 25,000 surfers have already signed up. What's Johnson's next move? "We will hopefully be able to file for an IPO [initial public offering] very shortly," he says, referring to plans to sell stock in the company.

High-tech teen entrepreneurship is definitely exploding. "There's not a period in history where we've seen such a plethora of young entrepreneurs," comments Nancy F. Koehn, associate professor of business administration at Harvard Business School. Still, teen entrepreneurs face unique pressures in juggling their schoolwork, their social life, and their high-tech workload. Some ultimately quit school, whereas others quit or cut back on their business activities. Melissa Sconyers, a web designer, chose to shrink her workload: "I had lost touch with my friends. I had to remember I am a teenager."[7]

Finally, there must be some motivation to start a business. A person may decide that he or she simply has "had enough" of working and earning a profit for someone else. Another may lose his or her job for some reason and decide to start the business he or she has always wanted rather than seek another job. Still another person may have an idea for a new product or a new way to sell an existing product. Or the opportunity to go into business may arise suddenly, perhaps as a result of a hobby, as was the case with Cheryl Strand. Strand started baking and decorating cakes from her home while working full time as a word processor at Clemson University. Her cakes became so popular that she soon found herself working through her lunch breaks and late into the night to meet customer demand.

After deciding to start her own business, Strand contacted the Clemson University Small Business Development Center. The center helped her prepare for the business start-up and develop a loan package—complete with a detailed business plan and financial statements for presentation at local banks. Strand obtained the $10,000 she needed. Since then, Cakes by Cheryl has doubled in size and increased sales by approximately 56 percent per year. It now offers fresh breads, deli sandwiches, a tempting line of baked goods, and catering and carry-out services.

Cheryl Strand is one of a growing number of women who are small-business owners. Women are 51 percent of the U.S. population, and according to the SBA, they owned at least 50 percent of all small businesses in 2002. Women already own 66 percent of the home-based businesses in this country, and the number of men in home-based businesses is growing rapidly.

According to the National Foundation for Women Business Owners, 9.1 million women-owned businesses in the United States provide over 27.5 million jobs and generate $3.6 trillion in sales annually.[8] Furthermore, women-owned businesses in the United States have proven that they are more successful; over 40 percent have been in business for twelve years or more. According to Dun and Bradstreet, women-owned businesses are financially sound and creditworthy, and their risk of failure is lower than average.

In some people, the motivation to start a business develops slowly as they gain the knowledge and ability required for success as a business owner. Knowledge and ability—especially management ability—are probably the most important factors involved. A new firm is very much built around the entrepreneur. The owner must be able to manage the firm's finances, its personnel (if there are any employees), and its day-to-day operations. He or she must handle sales, advertising, purchasing, pricing, and a variety of other business functions. The knowledge and ability to do so are acquired most often through experience working for other firms in the same area of business.

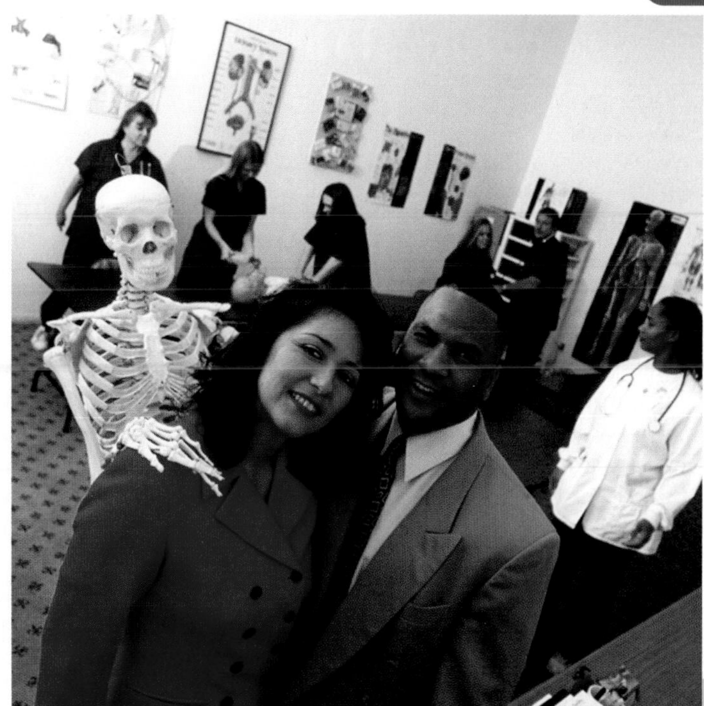

Entrepreneurs teach how to save lives. Husband and wife entrepreneurs Marco and Sandra Johnson founded Antelope Valley Medical College. The school employs ten full-time teachers who teach cardiopulmonary resuscitation (CPR) training, paramedic and emergency medical technician (EMT) training and certification, and re-certification to individual and corporate clients that include Boeing Co., Burger King, and employees of Lancaster, California, where the school is located. After saving lives as a firefighter but seeing too many people die because ordinary citizens did not know the basics about emergency medicine, Marco Johnson is happy to be able to save lives in a new way.

Why Small Businesses Fail

Small businesses are prone to failure. Capital, management, and planning are the key ingredients in the survival of a small business, as well as the most common reasons for failure. Businesses can experience a number of money-related problems. It may take several years before a business begins to show a profit. Entrepreneurs need to have not only the capital to open a business but also the money to operate it in its possibly lengthy start-up phase. One cash-flow obstacle often leads to others. And a series of cash-flow predicaments usually ends in a business failure. This scenario is played out all too often by small and not-so-small start-up Internet firms that fail to meet their financial backers' expectations and so are denied a second wave of investment dollars to continue their drive to establish a profitable online firm. For example, in one month alone Digital Entertainment Network shut its video streaming site, clothing distributor boo.com closed after spending more than $100 million in only six months of business, and healthshop.com shut its doors completely after failing to meet its investors' expectations.[9]

Many entrepreneurs lack the management skills required to run a business. Money, time, personnel, and inventory all need to be managed effectively if a small business is to succeed. Starting a small business requires much more than optimism and a good idea.

Success and expansion sometimes lead to problems. Frequently, entrepreneurs with successful small businesses make the mistake of overexpansion. Fast growth often results in dramatic changes in a business. Thus the entrepreneur must plan carefully and adjust competently to new and potentially disruptive situations.

Every day, and in every part of the country, people open new businesses. For example, recently, 580,000 new businesses opened their doors, but at the same time 544,000 businesses closed their business. Though many fail, others represent well-conceived ideas developed by entrepreneurs who have the expertise, resources, and determination to make their businesses succeed. As these well-prepared entrepreneurs pursue their individual goals, our society benefits in many ways from their work and creativity. Such billion-dollar companies as Apple Computer, McDonald's Corporation, and Procter & Gamble are all examples of small businesses that expanded into industry giants.

going global

Microloans Fuel Grass-Roots Entrepreneurs

A LOAN OF $25 IS ALL a first-time entrepreneur in Mexico needs to launch a small business. Just ask Constantino Lázaro, a carpenter who obtained a $25 loan from microlender Compartamos to buy an electric saw and start his furniture-making business. Just as Compartamos makes microloans to 112,000 entrepreneurs in Mexico, microlenders such as Grameen Bank in Bangladesh and Accion International in Latin America are offering tiny loans to help entrepreneurs in developing countries turn their small-business dreams into reality.

Compartamos, based in Mexico City, makes microloans ranging from $25 to as much as $5,000. However, not all loans go to individual borrowers. In some cases, a group of entrepreneurs—often women—start with one microloan and apportions the proceeds to members to use for small businesses such as pig farming. The group meets weekly to collect payments until the microloan is repaid. Then the members take out another microloan to continue building their businesses. Or one member of the group will use the microloan to start a business and repay the debt week by week. When she has repaid the debt, another member becomes eligible for the group's microloan.

Microlenders like lending to groups because peer pressure ensures high repayment rates of 98 percent or more. They also like lending to women because their business profits generally are used to support family members. Consider Pakmogda Zarata, an African entrepreneur who used microloans to open a small rice restaurant. As she repaid one microloan and borrowed a little more on the next one, she was able to buy more food at lower wholesale prices rather than paying higher retail prices. In this way, Zarata was able to increase her profits, expand by hiring employees, and pay school tuition for her children.

The microloan approach to funding small businesses is spreading around the world. An estimated 9,000 microlenders currently serve entrepreneurs who need $25 or more to start or grow their small businesses. Borrowers with home appliances or other collateral can qualify for larger loans. But even the smallest microloan has the potential to start an entrepreneur on the road to self-sufficiency.

The Importance of Small Businesses in Our Economy

learning objective

3 Assess the contributions of small businesses to our economy.

This country's economic history abounds with stories of ambitious men and women who turned their ideas into business dynasties. The Ford Motor Company started as a one-man operation with an innovative method for industrial production. L. L. Bean, Inc., can trace its beginnings to a basement shop in Freeport, Maine. Both Xerox and Polaroid began as small firms with a better way to do a job.

Providing Technical Innovation

Invention and innovation are part of the foundations of our economy. The increases in productivity that have characterized the past two hundred years of our history are all rooted in one principal source: new ways to do a job with less effort for less money. Studies show that the incidence of innovation among small-business workers is significantly higher than among workers in large businesses. Small firms produce two and a half times as many innovations as large firms relative to the number of persons employed.

According to the U.S. Office of Management and Budget, more than half the major technological advances of the twentieth century originated with individual inventors and small companies. Even just a sampling of those innovations is remarkable:

- Air conditioning
- Airplane
- Automatic transmission
- FM radio
- Heart valve

- Helicopter
- Instant camera
- Insulin
- Jet engine
- Penicillin
- Personal computer
- Power steering

Perhaps even more remarkable—and important—is that many of these inventions sparked major new U.S. industries or contributed to an established industry by adding some valuable service.

We may soon be seeing more innovations from small firms because of funding increases in the Small Business Innovation Research Program (SBIR). Under this program, federal agencies with large research and development (R&D) budgets must direct certain amounts of their R&D contracts to small businesses. Since the inception of the program in 1983, small firms have received over $6 billion in federal R&D awards.

An entrepreneur with a calling. More than half the major technological advances of the last century originated with individual inventors like Randice-Lisa Altschul. After inventing thousands of products, including board games for Miami Vice, The Simpsons and Teenage Mutant Ninja Turtles, the 42-year-old inventor is ready to launch her biggest invention—the Phone-Card-Phone, a disposable phone with a calling time limit—to be distributed by GE.

Providing Employment

Small firms traditionally have added more than their proportional share of new jobs to the economy. In 1998, the U.S. economy created over three million new jobs. Seven out of the ten industries that added the most new jobs were small-business-dominated industries. Small businesses creating the most new jobs in 1999 included business services, engineering and management services, and special trade contractors. Small firms hire a larger proportion of employees who are younger workers, older workers, women, or workers who prefer to work part time. Furthermore, small businesses provide 67 percent of workers with their first jobs and initial on-the-job training in basic skills. According to the SBA, small businesses represent about 99 percent of all employers, employ about 50 percent of the private work force, and provide about two-thirds of the net new jobs added to our economy.[10]

Small businesses thus contribute significantly to solving unemployment problems. Table 6.2 shows the industries that are generating the most new jobs and the small-business shares in those industries.

table 6.2 Industries Generating the Most Jobs

This ranking is based on the change (increase) in number of jobs from 2001 to 2002. The small-business share of new jobs is greatest in social services.

Industry	Annual Employment 2001	Increase from 2002	Percent Small Business
Health services	10,380,700	277,300	41.0
Social services	3,056,900	157,800	80.5
Engineering and management services	3,593,100	155,700	62.4
Eating and drinking places	8,256,900	112,900	64.5
Educational services	2,433,900	100,200	46.2

Source: Office of Advocacy, U.S. Small Business Administration, *Small Business Economic Indicators for 2002*, Table 12, p. 25, from data provided by the Bureau of Labor Statistics and the U.S. Census Bureau.

Providing Competition

Small businesses challenge larger, established firms in many ways, causing them to become more efficient and more responsive to consumer needs. A small business cannot, of course, compete with a large firm in all respects. But a number of small firms, each competing in its own particular area and its own particular way, together have the desired competitive effect. Thus several small janitorial companies together add up to reasonable competition for the no-longer-small ServiceMaster.

Filling Needs of Society and Other Businesses

By their nature, large firms must operate on a large scale. Many may be unwilling or unable to meet the special needs of smaller groups of consumers. Such groups create almost perfect markets for small companies, which can tailor their products to these groups and fill their needs profitably. A prime example is a firm that modifies automobile controls to accommodate handicapped drivers.

Small firms also provide a variety of goods and services to each other and to much larger firms. Sears, Roebuck purchases merchandise from approximately 12,000 suppliers—and most of them are small businesses. General Motors relies on more than 32,000 companies for parts and supplies and depends on more than 11,000 independent dealers to sell its automobiles and trucks. Large firms generally buy parts and assemblies from smaller firms for one very good reason: It is less expensive than manufacturing the parts in their own factories. This lower cost eventually is reflected in the price that consumers pay for their products.

It is clear that small businesses are a vital part of our economy and that, as consumers and as members of the labor force, we all benefit enormously from their existence. Now let us look at the situation from the viewpoint of the owners of small businesses.

The Pros and Cons of Smallness

learning objective

4 Judge the advantages and disadvantages of operating a small business.

Do most owners of small businesses dream that their firms will grow into giant corporations—managed by professionals—while they serve only on the board of directors? Or would they rather stay small, in a firm where they have the opportunity (and the responsibility) to do everything that needs to be done? The answers depend on the personal characteristics and motivations of the individual owners. For many, the advantages of remaining small far outweigh the disadvantages.

Advantages of Small Business

Small-business owners with limited resources often must struggle to enter competitive new markets. They also have to deal with increasing international competition. However, they enjoy several unique advantages.

Personal Relationships with Customers and Employees For those who like dealing with people, small business is the place to be. The owners of retail shops get to know many of their customers by name and deal with them on a personal basis. Through such relationships, small-business owners often become involved in the social, cultural, and political life of the community.

Relationships between owner-managers and employees also tend to be closer in smaller businesses. In many cases the owner is a friend and counselor as well as the boss.

These personal relationships provide an important business advantage. The personal service small businesses offer to customers is a major competitive weapon—one that larger firms try to match but often cannot. In addition, close relationships with

Getting personal. Not even one employee has left BitFlip Interactive Group—an interactive media developer—since its founding in 1997. What's the secret? According to co-founders Erin Jurew and Curt Middleton, it is ". . . respect for your employees. Realize you're not going to be in business without your employees—and show them loyalty."

employees often help the small-business owner keep effective workers who might earn more with a larger firm.

Ability to Adapt to Change Being his or her own boss, the owner-manager of a small business does not need anyone's permission to adapt to change. An owner may add or discontinue merchandise or services, change store hours, and experiment with various price strategies in response to changes in market conditions. And through personal relationships with customers, the owners of small businesses quickly become aware of changes in people's needs and interests, as well as in the activities of competing firms.

Simplified Recordkeeping Many small firms need only a simple set of records. Recordkeeping might consist of a checkbook, a cash-receipts journal in which to record all sales, and a cash-disbursements journal in which to record all amounts paid out. Obviously, enough records must be kept to allow for producing and filing accurate tax returns.

exploring business

YaYa Bike: A Cooperative Pedaling for Profits

JOIN A COOPERATIVE, PAY LOWER PRICES. That's the simple, bottom-line reason why more small businesses are banding together in purchasing cooperatives. Smaller firms placing individual orders frequently pay higher prices because they do not have the volume buying power of larger companies. In contrast, cooperatives use the combined buying power of all members to qualify for volume discounts, allowing members to lower their costs and price products to be competitive with larger rivals.

In the United States, an estimated 50,000 businesses are members of purchasing cooperatives. Local hardware retailers have long seen the advantages of joining a cooperative such as Ace Hardware or Do It Best to more effectively battle industry giants like Home Depot. Cooperatives usually levy a membership fee to help cover operating costs. In return, members are entitled to lower wholesale prices negotiated by the cooperative. Some cooperatives offer additional benefits, such as marketing assistance or exclusive product lines.

Consider the wheeling and dealing of YaYa Bike, a cooperative of small bicycle retailers. Bob Friedman, YaYa's president, signed up sixty-seven independent stores as members during the cooperative's first year, aiming for 1,000 members within five years. Members such as @The Hub Bicycles in Georgia and Kozy's Cyclery in Illinois pay $2,000 to join. Initially, they will share in rebates for buying from YaYa's roster of eighteen preferred suppliers. In the near future, YaYa plans to offer a proprietary line of bicycle products. Later, it may develop advertising campaigns for members' use.

One reason @The Hub Bicycles joined YaYa was to gain more bargaining power for dealing with suppliers. The Hawley Company, which distributes bicycle parts, became a YaYa preferred supplier to expand its customer base. Despite the potential benefits, experts suggest checking a cooperative's finances before joining to be sure that it can withstand tough times. Small-business owners also should determine whether membership will have a significant effect on their profits, whether other members have prospered through association with the cooperative, and whether the cooperative's management is active and informed.

Independence Small-business owners do not have to punch in and out, bid for vacation times, take orders from superiors, or worry about being fired or laid off. They are the masters of their own destinies—at least with regard to employment. For many people, this is the prime advantage of owning a small business.

Other Advantages According to the SBA, the most profitable companies in the United States are small firms that have been in business for more than ten years and employ fewer than twenty people. Small-business owners also enjoy all the advantages of sole proprietorships, which were discussed in Chapter 5. These include being able to keep all profits, the ease and low cost of going into business and (if necessary) going out of business, and being able to keep business information secret.

Disadvantages of Small Business

Personal contacts with customers, closer relationships with employees, being one's own boss, less cumbersome recordkeeping chores, and independence are the bright side of small business. In contrast, the dark side reflects problems unique to these firms.

Risk of Failure As we have noted, small businesses (especially new ones) run a heavy risk of going out of business—about two out of three close their doors within the first six years. Older, well-established small firms can be hit hard by a business recession, mainly because they do not have the financial resources to weather an extended difficult period.

Limited Potential Small businesses that survive do so with varying degrees of success. Many are simply the means of making a living for the owner and his or her family. The owner may have some technical skill—as a hair stylist or electrician, for example—and may have started a business to put this skill to work. Such a business is unlikely to grow into big business. Also, employees' potential for advancement is limited.

Limited Ability to Raise Capital Small businesses typically have a limited ability to obtain capital. Figure 6.2 shows that most small-business financing comes out of the owner's pocket. Personal loans from lending institutions provide only about one-fourth of the capital required by small businesses. About 70 percent of all new firms

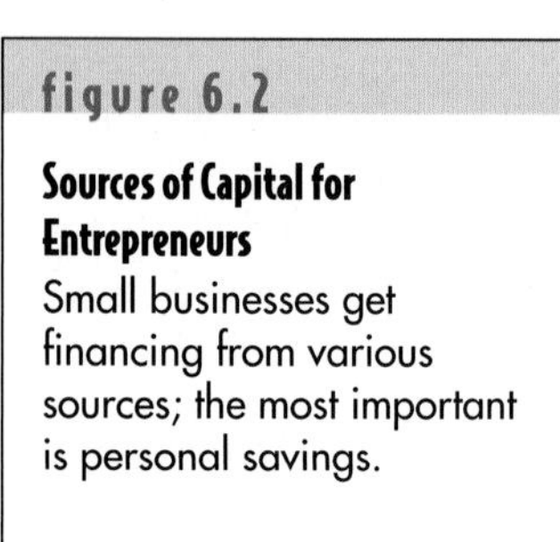
figure 6.2

Sources of Capital for Entrepreneurs
Small businesses get financing from various sources; the most important is personal savings.

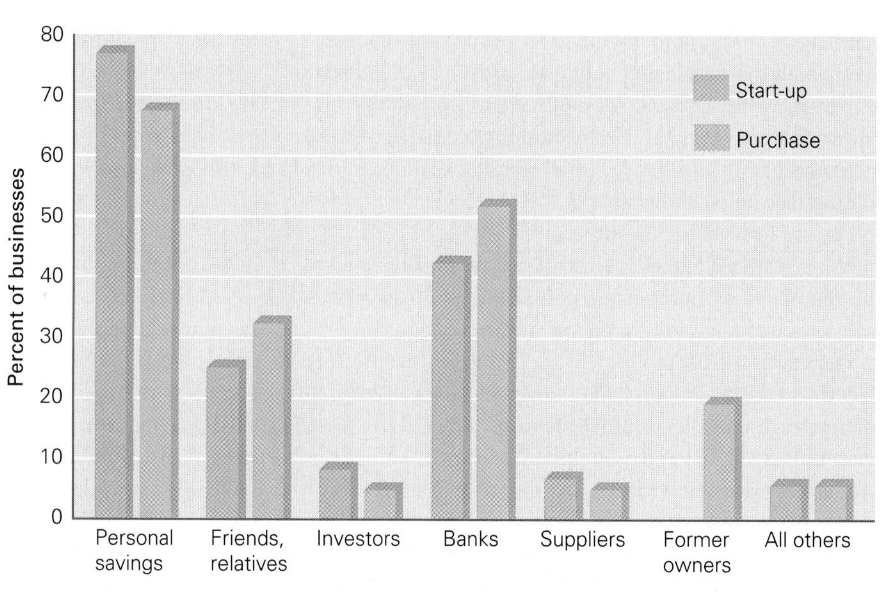

Source: Data developed and provided by the National Federation of Independent Business Foundation and sponsored by the American Express Travel Related Services Company, Inc.

begin with less than $20,000 in total capital, according to Census Bureau and Federal Reserve surveys. In fact, almost half of new firms begin with less than $10,000, usually provided by the owner or family members and friends.[11] Recognizing the opportunity to capitalize on the needs of small businesses with limited cash, firms like bigstep.com provide small businesses with the opportunity to create their own website for free, a service that generally would cost about $250 a month from other website service firms. Backed by partnerships with Sun Microsystems, the Washingtonpost.com, and Newsweek Interactive, bigstep.com makes its money from sponsorships and fees for optional services.[12] Fortunately for small businesses today, the Internet provides a powerful yet relatively inexpensive communication tool for reaching customers, suppliers, and employees. According to a recent study, about 88 percent of small businesses now have computers, and 39 percent have networks. Given the advantages of the Internet, it is not surprising that recently 53 percent of small businesses have a web page, as compared with 32 percent in 1998. More than 85 percent say that they use the Internet, up from 65 percent in 1998, to e-mail and research products. About 40 percent say that they use the Internet to purchase goods and services, and 23 percent say that they also sell products and services.[13]

Source: U.S. Census Bureau, U.S. Department of Labor, Employment and Training Administration, Administrative Office of the U.S. Courts, 2003.

talking technology

Travel Agencies Battle Internet Competition

HOW CAN SMALL STORE-FRONT travel agencies compete in today's wired world, where business travelers and vacationers can buy airline tickets, reserve hotel rooms, and book rental cars at the click of a mouse? The Internet hit small travel agencies hard in two ways. First, it allowed airlines to minimize commission payments by bypassing travel agents and selling directly to travelers through proprietary websites and industry sites such as Orbitz. In fact, Delta no longer pays any commissions to U.S. travel agents, and other airlines are following its lead, choking off a formerly steady income stream.

Second, the Internet brought competition from Expedia, Travelocity, and other sites that let customers compare prices and make travel arrangements online. Small wonder that over the past five years 18,000 small agencies have gone out of business. Many of the survivors cut their payrolls and began charging service fees for issuing tickets. They also found imaginative ways of adapting to this intensely competitive environment.

In Wichita, Kansas, family-owned Sunflower Travel has used the Internet to carve out a new niche in South Pacific tours. Drawing on her many trips through New Zealand and Australia, co-owner Barbara Hansen put together tours highlighting local wineries and horticultural events. She promotes these tours on a dedicated website linked to the New Zealand Tourist Office website. In addition, she drums up business by e-mailing tour information to garden clubs, florists, and wine retailers.

In contrast, Peggy's Travel in Bowie, Texas, chose to focus on building personal connections with customers. Owner Karen Casey runs an ongoing newspaper advertising campaign featuring photos of satisfied clients on vacation under the headline "Let Peggy's Travel Put YOU in the Picture." Each photo is accompanied by a brief explanation of that customer's trip. "The clients whose pictures appear in the paper feel honored, and they tell their friends about it," Casey says. "Now people ask us, 'If I book a trip [with you] and bring in the picture, will you put it in the paper?' " Thanks to this low-tech strategy, the agency increased its vacation travel business by 40 percent in just three years.

Although every person who considers starting a small business should be aware of the hazards and pitfalls we have noted, a well-conceived business plan may help to avoid the risk of failure. The U.S. government is also dedicated to helping small businesses make it. It expresses this aim most actively through the SBA.

Developing a Business Plan

business plan a carefully constructed guide for the person starting a business

Lack of planning can be as deadly as lack of money to a new small business. Planning is important to any business, large or small, and should never be overlooked or taken lightly. A **business plan** is a carefully constructed guide for the person starting a business. It also serves as a concise document that potential investors can examine to see if they would like to invest or assist in financing a new venture.

Table 6.3 shows the twelve sections a business plan should include. Each section is further explained at the end of each of the seven major parts in the text. The goal of each end-of-the part exercise is to help a business person create his or her own business plan. When constructing a business plan, the business person should strive to keep it easy to read, uncluttered, and complete. Like other busy executives, officials of financial institutions do not have the time to wade through pages of extraneous data.

table 6.3 Components of a Business Plan

1. **Introduction.** Basic information such as the name, address, and phone number of the business; the date the plan was issued; and a statement of confidentiality to keep important information away from potential competitors.
2. **Executive Summary.** A one- to two-page overview of the entire business plan, including a justification why the business will succeed.
3. **Benefits to the Community.** Information on how the business will have an impact on economic development, community development, and human development.
4. **Company and Industry.** The background of the company, choice of the legal business form, information on the products or services to be offered; and examination of the potential customers, current competitors, and the business's future.
5. **Management Team.** Discussion of skills, talents, and job descriptions of management team, managerial compensation, management training needs, and professional assistance requirements.
6. **Manufacturing and Operations Plan.** Discussion of facilities needed, space requirements, capital equipment, labor force, inventory control, and purchasing requirement.
7. **Labor Force.** Discussion of the quality of skilled workers available and the training, compensation, and motivation of workers.
8. **Marketing Plan.** Discussion of markets, market trends, competition, market share, pricing, promotion, distribution, and service policy.
9. **Financial Plan.** Summary of the investment needed, sales and cash-flow forecasts, breakeven analysis, and sources of funding.
10. **Exit Strategy.** Discussion of a succession plan or going public. Who will take over the business?
11. **Critical Risks and Assumptions.** Evaluation of the weaknesses of the business and how the company plans to deal with these and other business problems.
12. **Appendix.** Supplementary information crucial to the plan, such as résumés of owners and principal managers, advertising samples, organization chart, and any related information.

Source: Adapted from Timothy S. Hatten, *Small Business Management: Entrepreneurship and Beyond*, 2d ed. (Boston: Houghton Mifflin, 2003), pp. 113–127.

The business plan should answer the four questions banking officials and investors are most interested in: (1) What exactly is the nature and mission of the new venture? (2) Why is this new enterprise a good idea? (3) What are the business person's goals? (4) How much will the new venture cost?

The great amount of time and consideration that should go into creating a business plan probably will end up saving time later. For example, Sharon Burch, who was running a computer software business while earning a degree in business administration, had to write a business plan as part of one course. Burch has said, "I wish I'd taken the class before I started my business. I see a lot of things I could have done differently. But it has helped me since I've been using the business plan as a guide for my business."

Accuracy and realistic expectations are crucial to an effective business plan. It is unethical to deceive loan officers, and it is unwise to deceive yourself.

The Small Business Administration

learning objective

5 Explain how the Small Business Administration helps small businesses.

The **Small Business Administration (SBA),** created by Congress in 1953, is a governmental agency that assists, counsels, and protects the interests of small businesses in the United States. It helps people get into business and stay in business. The agency provides assistance to owners and managers of prospective, new, and established small businesses. Through more than one thousand offices and resource centers throughout the nation, the SBA provides both financial assistance and management counseling. It helps small firms bid for and obtain government contracts, and it helps them prepare to enter foreign markets.

Small Business Administration (SBA) a governmental agency that assists, counsels, and protects the interests of small businesses in the United States

SBA Management Assistance

Statistics show that most failures in small business are related to poor management. For this reason, the SBA places special emphasis on improving the management ability of the owners and managers of small businesses. The SBA's Management Assistance Program is extensive and diversified. It includes free individual counseling, courses, conferences, workshops, and a wide range of publications. Recently, the SBA provided management and technical assistance to nearly 850,000 small businesses through its 950 Small Business Development Centers and 13,000 volunteers from the Service Corps of Retired Executives.[14]

Management Courses and Workshops The management courses offered by the SBA cover all the functions, duties, and roles of managers. Instructors may be teachers from local colleges and universities or other professionals, such as management consultants, bankers, lawyers, and accountants. Fees for these courses are quite low. The most popular such course is a general survey of eight to ten different areas of business management. In follow-up studies, business people may concentrate in depth on one or more of these areas, depending on their particular strengths and weaknesses. The SBA occasionally offers one-day conferences. These conferences are aimed at keeping owner-managers up-to-date on new management developments, tax laws, and the like.

The SBA also invites prospective owners of small businesses to workshops at which management problems and good management practices are discussed. A major goal of these sessions is to emphasize the need for sufficient preparation before starting a new venture. Sometimes the sessions convince eager but poorly prepared entrepreneurs to slow down and wait until they are ready for the difficulties that lie ahead.

Using the Internet

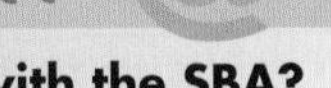

So How Do You Connect with the SBA?

The Internet is a great source of information for learning what assistance is available from the Small Business Administration. Do you want financial assistance or management counseling, do you want to bid for and obtain government contracts, do you want to enter foreign markets, or do you want to learn how to write a business plan? You can find answers to frequently asked questions at **http://www.sba.gov/advo/stats/sbfaq.html.**

Service Corps of Retired Executives (SCORE) a group of retired business people who volunteer their services to small businesses through SBA

SCORE The **Service Corps of Retired Executives (SCORE),** created in 1964, is a group of 13,000 retired business people including 2,070 women who volunteer their services to small businesses through the SBA. The collective experience of SCORE volunteers spans the full range of American enterprise. These volunteers have worked for such notable companies as Eastman Kodak, General Electric, IBM, and Procter & Gamble. Experts in areas of accounting, finance, marketing, engineering, and retailing provide counseling and mentoring to entrepreneurs.

A small-business owner who has a particular problem can request free counseling from SCORE. An assigned counselor visits the owner in his or her establishment and, through careful observation, analyzes the business situation and the problem. If the problem is complex, the counselor may call on other volunteer experts to assist. Finally, the counselor offers a plan for solving the problem and helping the owner through the critical period.

Consider the plight of Elizabeth Halvorsen, a mystery writer from Minneapolis. Her husband had built up the family advertising and graphic arts firm for seventeen years when he was called in 1991 to serve in the Persian Gulf War. The only one left behind who could run the business was Mrs. Halvorsen, who admittedly had no business experience. Enter SCORE. With a SCORE management expert at her side, she kept the business on track. Recently, SCORE volunteers served 4.5 million small-business people like Mrs. Halvorsen.[15]

Help for Minority-Owned Small Businesses Americans who are members of minority groups have had difficulty entering the nation's economic mainstream. Raising money is a nagging problem for minority business owners, who also may lack adequate training. Members of minority groups are, of course, eligible for all SBA programs, but the SBA makes a special effort to assist those who want to start small businesses or expand existing ones. For example, the Minority Business Development Agency awards grants to develop and increase business opportunities for members of racial and ethnic minorities.

Helping women become entrepreneurs is also a special goal of the SBA. Emily Harrington, one of nine children, was born in Manila, the Philippines. She arrived in the United States in 1972 as a foreign-exchange student. Convinced that there was a market for hard-working, dedicated minorities and women, she launched Qualified Resources, Inc. *Inc.* magazine selected her firm as one of "America's Fastest Growing Private Companies" just six years later. Harrington credits the U.S. Small Business Administration for giving her the technical support that made her first loan possible. Finding a SCORE counselor who worked directly with her, she refined her business plan until she got a bank loan. Before contacting the SBA, Harrington was turned down for business loans "by all the banks I approached," even though she worked as a manager of loan credit and collection for a bank. Later, Emily Harrington was SBA's year 2000 winner of the local, regional, and national Small Business Entrepreneurial Success Award for Rhode Island, the New England region, and the nation! For several years in a row, Qualified Resources, Inc., was named one of the fastest-growing private companies in Rhode Island.

small-business institute (SBI) a group of senior and graduate students in business administration who provide management counseling to small businesses

Small-Business Institutes A **small-business institute (SBI)** is a group of senior and graduate students in business administration who provide management counseling to small businesses. SBIs have been organized on almost 520 college campuses as another way to help business owners. The students work in small groups guided by faculty advisers and SBA management-assistance experts. Like SCORE volunteers, they analyze and help solve the problems of small-business owners at their business establishments.

small-business development center (SBDC) a university-based group that provides individual counseling and practical training to owners of small businesses

Small-Business Development Centers A **small-business development center (SBDC)** is a university-based group that provides individual counseling and practical training to owners of small businesses. SBDCs draw from the resources of local, state, and federal governments; private businesses; and universities. These groups can provide managerial and technical help, data from research studies, and other types of specialized assistance of value to small businesses. In 2003, there were over 1000 SBDC locations, primarily at colleges and universities.

SBA Publications The SBA issues management, marketing, and technical publications dealing with hundreds of topics of interest to present and prospective managers of small firms. Most of these publications are available from the SBA free of charge. Others can be obtained for a small fee from the U.S. Government Printing Office.

SBA Financial Assistance

Small businesses seem to be constantly in need of money. An owner may have enough capital to start and operate the business. But then he or she may require more money to finance increased operations during peak selling seasons, to pay for required pollution-control equipment, to finance an expansion, or to mop up after a natural disaster such as a flood or a terrorist attack. For example, the Supplemental Terrorist Activity Relief (STAR) program has made $2.4 billion in loans to 6,067 small businesses harmed or disrupted by the September 11 terrorist attacks. The SBA offers special financial-assistance programs that cover all these situations. However, its primary financial function is to guarantee loans to eligible businesses.

venture capital money that is invested in small (and sometimes struggling) firms that have the potential to become very successful

small-business investment companies (SBICs) privately owned firms that provide venture capital to small enterprises that meet their investment standards

Regular Business Loans Most of the SBA's business loans are actually made by private lenders such as banks, but repayment is partially guaranteed by the agency. That is, the SBA may guarantee that it will repay the lender up to 90 percent of the loan if the borrowing firm cannot repay it. Guaranteed loans approved on or after October 1, 2002, may be as large as $500,000 (this loan limit may be increased in the future). The average size of an SBA-guaranteed business loan is $208,000, and its average duration is about eight years. In 2002, the SBA approved approximately $25 billion in guaranteed loans.

Small-Business Investment Companies **Venture capital** is money that is invested in small (and sometimes struggling) firms that have the potential to become very successful. In many cases, only a lack of capital keeps these firms from rapid and solid growth. The people who invest in such firms expect that their investments will grow with the firms and become quite profitable.

The popularity of these investments has increased over the past twenty years, but most small firms still have difficulty in obtaining venture capital. To help such businesses, the SBA licenses, regulates, and provides financial assistance to **small-business investment companies (SBICs).** An SBIC is a privately owned firm that provides venture capital to small enterprises that meet its investment standards. SBICs are intended to be profit-making organizations. The aid the SBA offers allows them to invest in small businesses that otherwise would not attract venture capital. Since Congress created the program in 1958, SBICs have financed over 100,000 small businesses for a total of about $32.7 billion.

We have discussed the importance of the small-business segment of our economy. We have weighed the advantages and drawbacks of operating a small business as compared with a large one. But is there a way to achieve the best of both worlds? Can one preserve one's independence as a business owner and still enjoy some of the benefits of "bigness"? Let's take a close look at franchising.

Venturing capital. When the founders of Intelliseek Inc. Mahendra Vora (shown here) and his partner Sundar Kadayam needed financing for their firm, they found it in River Cities Capital Funds, a small business investment company located in Cincinnati, Ohio. Intelliseek Inc. provides software to capture, track, and analyze information for use in strategic planning, market research, product development, and brand marketing.

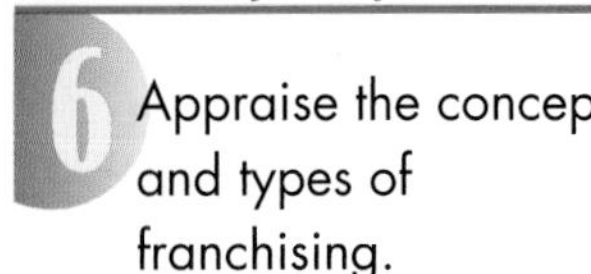

learning objective

6 Appraise the concept and types of franchising.

Franchising

franchise a license to operate an individually owned business as though it were part of a chain of outlets or stores

A **franchise** is a license to operate an individually owned business as if it were part of a chain of outlets or stores. Often the business itself is also called a *franchise.* Among the most familiar franchises are McDonald's, H & R Block, AAMCO Transmissions, GNC (General Nutrition Centers), and Dairy Queen. Many other franchises carry familiar names; this method of doing business has become very popular in the last thirty years or so. It is an attractive means of starting and operating a small business.

What Is Franchising?

franchising the actual granting of a franchise

franchisor an individual or organization granting a franchise

franchisee a person or organization purchasing a franchise

Franchising is the actual granting of a franchise. A **franchisor** is an individual or organization granting a franchise. A **franchisee** is a person or organization purchasing a franchise. The franchisor supplies a known and advertised business name, management skills, the required training and materials, and a method of doing business. The franchisee supplies labor and capital, operates the franchised business, and agrees to abide by the provisions of the franchise agreement. Table 6.4 lists some items that would be covered in a typical franchise agreement.

table 6.4 McDonald's Conventional Franchise Agreement as of January 2003

McDonald's (Franchisor) Provides	Individual (Franchisee) Supplies
1. Nationally recognized trademarks and an established reputation for quality	1. Total investment of approximately \$455,000 to \$768,500, which includes initial franchise fee of \$45,000
2. Designs and color schemes for restaurants, signs, and equipment	2. Approximate cash requirement of 25 to 40 percent of total investment; a minimum of \$175,000 of nonborrowed personal funds
3. Specifications for certain food products	3. Additional \$499,000 to \$740,000 if the building is purchased
4. Proven methods of inventory and operations control	4. A minimum of 4 percent of gross sales annually for marketing and advertising
5. Bookkeeping, accounting, and policies manuals specially geared toward a franchised restaurant	5. Payment of a service fee of 4 percent of monthly gross sales to McDonald's
6. A franchise term of up to twenty years	6. Payment of a variable rent percent of monthly gross sales to McDonald's based on McDonald's investment and/or sales
7. Formal training program completed on a part-time basis in approximately eighteen to twenty-four months in a McDonald's restaurant	7. Kitchen equipment, seating, decor, lighting, and signs in conformity with McDonald's standards (included in total investment figure)
8. Five weeks of classroom training, including two weeks at Hamburger University	8. Taxes, insurance, and maintenance costs on the restaurant building and land
9. Ongoing regional support services and field service staff	9. Commitment to ensuring high-quality standards and upholding the McDonald's reputation
10. Research and development of labor-saving equipment and methods	
11. Monthly bulletins, periodicals, or meetings to inform franchisees about management and marketing techniques	
12. Site selection (purchase or lease) and development, including building	

Source: "McDonald's Conventional Franchise Agreement as of January 2003," from *McDonald's Franchising,* McDonald's Corporation, Oak Brook, IL, **www.mcdonalds.com,** accessed January 12, 2003. Used with permission from McDonald's Corporation.

Franchising is not all fun and games. Franchising is designed to provide a tested formula for success, along with ongoing advice and training. The franchiser, such as the Learning Express, supplies a known and advertised business name, management skills, the required training and materials, and a method of doing business. Franchising, however, is not a guarantee of success for either franchisees or franchisors.

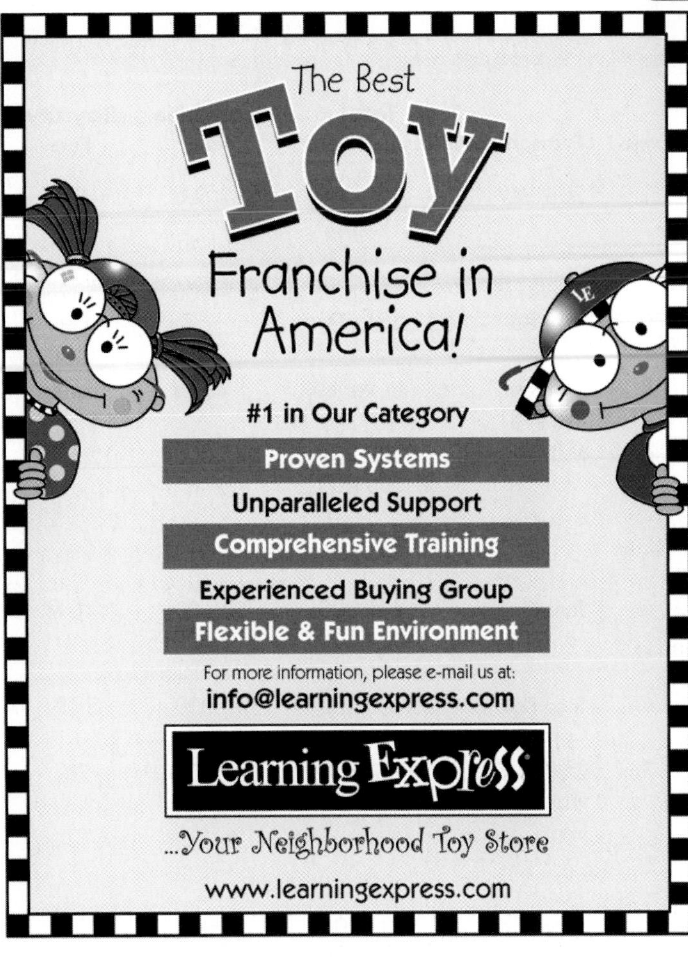

Types of Franchising Arrangements

Franchising arrangements fall into three general categories. In the first approach, a manufacturer authorizes a number of retail stores to sell a certain brand-name item. This franchising arrangement, one of the oldest, is prevalent in sales of passenger cars and trucks, farm equipment, shoes, paint, earth-moving equipment, and petroleum. About 90 percent of all gasoline is sold through franchised, independent retail service stations, and franchised dealers handle virtually all sales of new cars and trucks. In the second type of franchising arrangement, a producer licenses distributors to sell a given product to retailers. This arrangement is common in the soft-drink industry. Most national manufacturers of soft-drink syrups—the Coca-Cola Company, Dr. Pepper/Seven-Up Companies, PepsiCo, Royal Crown Companies, Inc.—franchise independent bottlers who then serve retailers. In a third form of franchising, a franchisor supplies brand names, techniques, or other services instead of a complete product. Although the franchisor may provide certain production and distribution services, its primary role is the careful development and control of marketing strategies. This approach to franchising, which is the most typical today, is used by Holiday Inns, the Howard Johnson Company, AAMCO Transmissions, McDonald's, Dairy Queen, Avis, Hertz Corporation, KFC (Kentucky Fried Chicken), and SUBWAY, to name but a few.

The Growth of Franchising

learning objective

7 Analyze the growth of franchising and franchising's advantages and disadvantages.

Franchising, which began in the United States around the time of the Civil War, was used originally by large firms, such as the Singer Sewing Company, to distribute their products. Franchising has been increasing steadily in popularity since the early 1900s, primarily for filling stations and car dealerships; however, this retailing strategy has experienced enormous growth since the mid-1970s. Recently, franchisers and franchisees generated $1 trillion in annual U.S. retail sales from 320,000 franchised small businesses in seventy-five industries. Franchising accounts for more than 40 percent of all U.S. retail sales and provides over eight million jobs. A new franchise opens every eight minutes somewhere in the United States.[16] The franchise proliferation generally has paralleled the expansion of the fast-food industry. As Table 6.5 (on p. 184) shows, five of *Entrepreneur* magazine's top-rated franchises for 2003 were in this category.

Of course, franchising is not limited to fast foods. Hair salons, tanning parlors, and dentists and lawyers are expected to participate in franchising arrangements in

table 6.5 *Entrepreneur's* **Top Ten Franchises in 2003**

Rank	Franchise	Total Investment	Franchise Fee	Royalty Fee	Net-Worth Requirement	Cash Requirement	Comments
1	SUBWAY	$52,000–$191,000	$12,500	8%	$30,000–$90,000	$30,000–$90,000	20-year renewable term
2	Curves for Women	$25,600–$31,100	$19,900	$395 per month	$20,000	$10,000	—
3	7-Eleven, Inc.	Varies	Varies	Varies	Varies	Varies	—
4	McDonald's	$489,900–$1,500,000	$45,000	12.5%+	N/A	$10,000	20-year renewable term; renewal fee $45,000
5	Jani-King	$11,300–$34,100	$8,600–$16,300+	10%	—	—	20-year renewable term
6	Taco Bell Corp.	$3,000,000	$45,000	5.5%	—	—	—
7	Quizno's Franchise Co.	$208,400–$243,800	$25,000	7%	$125,000	$60,000	15-year renewable term; renewal fee $1,000
8	Super 8 Motels, Inc.	$288,100–$2,300,000	Varies	5%	$1,000,000	$1,000,000	—
9	Jackson Hewitt Tax Service	$47,400–$75,200	$25,000	15%	$100,000–$200,000	$50,000	—
10	Sonic Drive In Restaurants	$621,300–$1,200,000	$30,000	1%–5%	$1,000,000	$300,000	—

Note: N/A = not available.
Source: *Entrepreneur* magazine's 2003 Franchise 500, **www.franchise500.com.**

growing numbers. Franchised health clubs, pest exterminators, and campgrounds are already widespread, as are franchised tax preparers and travel agencies. The real estate industry also has experienced a rapid increase in franchising.

Also, franchising is attracting more women and minority business owners in the United States than ever before. One reason is that special outreach programs designed to encourage franchisee diversity have developed. Franchisors such as Wendy's, McDonald's, Burger King, and Church's Chicken all have special corporate programs to attract minority and women franchisees. Just as important, successful women and minority franchisees are willing to get involved by offering advice and guidance to new franchisees.

Herman Petty, the first black McDonald's franchisee, remembers that the company provided a great deal of help while he worked to establish his first units. In turn, Petty traveled to help other black franchisees, and he invited new franchisees to gain hands-on experience in his Chicago restaurants before starting their own establishments. Petty also organized a support group, the National Black McDonald's Operators Association, to help black franchisees in other areas. Today this support group has

3 local chapters and more than 330 members across the country. "We are really concentrating on helping our operators to be successful both operationally and financially," says Craig Welburn, the McDonald's franchisee who leads the group.

Dual-branded franchises, in which two franchisors offer their products together, are a new small-business trend. For example, in 1993, pleased with the success of its first cobranded restaurant with Texaco in Beebe, Arkansas, McDonald's now has over 400 cobranded restaurants in the United States. In 2002, McDonald's planned to open 100 to 150 new restaurants.[17] Also, an agreement between franchisors Doctor's Associates, Inc., and TCBY Enterprises, Inc., now allows franchisees to sell SUBWAY sandwiches and TCBY yogurt in the same establishment.

Are Franchises Successful?

Franchising is designed to provide a tested formula for success, along with ongoing advice and training. The success rate for businesses owned and operated by franchisees is significantly higher than the success rate for other independently owned small businesses. In a recent nationwide Gallup poll of 944 franchise owners, 94 percent of franchisees indicated that they were very or somewhat successful, only 5 percent believed that they were very unsuccessful or somewhat unsuccessful, and 1 percent did not know. Despite these impressive statistics, franchising is not a guarantee of success for either franchisees or franchisors. Too rapid expansion, inadequate capital or management skills, and a host of other problems can cause failure for both franchisee and franchisor. Thus, for example, the Dizzy Dean's Beef and Burger franchise is no longer in business. Timothy Bates, a Wayne State University economist, warns that "Despite the hype that franchising is the safest way to go when starting a new business, the research just doesn't bear that out." Just consider Boston Chicken, which once had more than 1,200 restaurants before declaring bankruptcy in 1998.

Advantages of Franchising

Franchising plays a vital role in our economy and may soon become the dominant form of retailing. Why? Because franchising offers advantages to both the franchisor and the franchisee.

To the Franchisor The franchisor gains fast and well-controlled distribution of its products without incurring the high cost of constructing and operating its own outlets. The franchisor thus has more capital available to expand production and to use for advertising. At the same time, it can ensure, through the franchise agreement, that outlets are maintained and operated according to its own standards.

The franchisor also benefits from the fact that the franchisee—a sole proprietor in most cases—is likely to be very highly motivated to succeed. The success of the franchise means more sales, which translate into higher royalties for the franchisor.

To the Franchisee The franchisee gets the opportunity to start a business with limited capital and to make use of the business experience of others. Moreover, an outlet with a nationally advertised name, such as Radio Shack, McDonald's, or Century 21 Real Estate, has guaranteed customers as soon as it opens.

If business problems arise, the franchisor gives the franchisee guidance and advice. This counseling is primarily responsible for the very high degree of success enjoyed by franchises. In most cases, the franchisee does not pay for such help.

The franchisee also receives materials to use in local advertising and can take part in national promotional campaigns sponsored by the franchisor. McDonald's and its franchisees, for example, constitute one of the nation's top twenty purchasers of advertising. Finally, the franchisee may be able to minimize the cost of advertising, supplies, and various business necessities by purchasing them in cooperation with other franchisees.

Disadvantages of Franchising

The main disadvantage of franchising affects the franchisee, and it arises because th franchisor retains a great deal of control. The franchisor's contract can dictate eve aspect of the business: decor, design of employee uniforms, types of signs, and all th details of business operations. All Burger King french fries taste the same because a Burger King franchisees have to make them the same way.

Contract disputes are the cause of many lawsuits. For example, in 1997, Rekh Gabhawala, a Dunkin' Donuts franchisee in Milwaukee, alleged that the franchis was forcing her out of business so that the company could profit by reselling th downtown franchise to someone else; the company, on the other hand, alleged th Gabhawala breached the contract by not running the business according to compa standards.[18] In another 2002 case, Dunkin' Donuts sued Chris Romanias, its fra chisee in Pennsylvania, alleging that Romanias intentionally underreported gross sal to the company. Romanias, on the other hand, alleged that Dunkin' Donuts, Inc breached the contract because it failed to provide assistance in operating the fra chise.[19] Other franchisees claim that contracts are unfairly tilted toward the fra chisors. Yet others have charged that they lost their franchise and investment becau their franchisor would not approve the sale of the business when they found a buyer.

To arbitrate disputes between franchisors and franchisees, the National Franchis Mediation Program was established in 1993 by thirty member firms, including Burg King Corporation, McDonald's Corporation, and Wendy's International, Inc. Neg tiators have since resolved numerous cases through mediation. Recently, Carl's J brought in one of its largest franchisees to help set its system straight, making mo franchisees happy for the first time in years. The program also helped PepsiCo sett a long-term contract dispute and renegotiate its franchise agreements.

Because disagreements between franchisors and franchisees have increased in re cent years, many franchisees have been demanding government regulation of fra chising. In 1997, to avoid government regulation, some of the largest franchiso proposed a new self-policing plan to the Federal Trade Commission.

Franchise holders pay for their security, usually with a one-time franchise fee an continuing royalty and advertising fees, collected as a percentage of sales. As Table 6. (on p. 182) shows, a McDonald's franchisee pays an initial franchise fee of $45,000, a annual fee of 4 percent of gross sales (for advertising), and a monthly fee of 4 perce of gross sales. In Table 6.5 (on p. 184) you can see how much money a franchisee nee to start a new franchise for selected organizations. In some fields, franchise agreemen are not uniform. One franchisee may pay more than another for the same services.

Even success can cause problems. Sometimes a franchise is so successful that th franchisor opens its own outlet nearby, in direct competition—although franchise may fight back. For example, a court recently ruled that Burger King could not ente into direct competition with the franchisee because the contract was not specific o the issue. A spokesperson for one franchisor contends that the company "gives no ge ographical protection" to its franchise holders and thus is free to move in on them Franchise operators work hard. They often put in ten- and twelve-hour days, six day a week. The International Franchise Association advises prospective franchise pu chasers to investigate before investing and to approach buying a franchise cautiousl Franchises vary widely in approach as well as in products. Some, like Dunkin' Donu and Baskin-Robbins, demand long hours. Others, like Great Clips hair salons and A bert's Family Restaurants, are more appropriate for those who do not want to spen many hours at their stores.

Global Perspectives in Small Business

For small American businesses, the world is becoming smaller. National and interna tional economies are growing more and more interdependent as political leadershi and national economic directions change and trade barriers diminish or disappea

Globalization and instant worldwide communications are rapidly shrinking distances at the same time that they are expanding business opportunities. According to a recent study, the Internet is increasingly important to small-business strategic thinking, with more than 50 percent of those surveyed indicating that the Internet represented their most favored strategy for growth—a 17 percent increase from the year before. This was more than double the next favored choice, strategic alliances reflecting the opportunity to reach both global as well as domestic customers.[20]

The SBA offers help to the nation's small-business owners who want to enter the world markets. The SBA's efforts include counseling small firms on how and where to market overseas, matching U.S. small-business executives with potential overseas customers, and helping exporters secure financing. The agency brings small U.S. firms into direct contact with potential overseas buyers and partners. The U.S. Commercial Service, a Commerce Department division, aids small and medium-sized businesses in selling overseas. The division's global network includes 107 offices in the United States and 151 others in 83 countries around the world.[21]

Spotlight

Small doesn't mean local

Source: Timothy S. Hatten, *Small Business Management*, 2d ed. (Boston: Houghton Mifflin, 2003), p. 468.

International trade will become more important to small-business owners as they face unique challenges in the new century. Small businesses, which are expected to remain the dominant form of organization in this country, must be prepared to adapt to significant demographic and economic changes in the world marketplace.

This chapter ends our discussion of American business today. From here on we shall be looking closely at various aspects of business operations. We begin, in the next chapter, with a discussion of management—what management is, what managers do, and how they work to coordinate the basic economic resources within a business organization.

Return To inside business

Chris Madden works hard to keep her name in the public eye. In addition to writing books, she writes a lifestyle column that appears in 360 newspapers. She also has a weekly HGTV television program, "Interiors by Design," seen by fourteen million people per month. Also under consideration, says Kevin Madden, is a branded magazine. "A regular magazine would be a powerful tool to drive sales," he notes. Already people who want their homes to reflect the casual elegance showcased in the books and the television program can shop for Madden-branded furniture and accessories in hundreds of stores across the United States.

Still, Madden's business does not yet approach the size and scope of Martha Stewart's empire. Stewart employs 500 and rings up annual sales of nearly $300 million from licenses on 5,000 products. By comparison, Madden currently has only a handful of employees and earns licensing revenues of about $2 million. However, she continues to shape her company's future by signing profitable new licensing deals that will bring in millions of dollars in revenue over the coming years.

Questions

1. What entrepreneurial pitfalls should Chris and Kevin Madden watch for as they grow Madden, Inc., from a small business into a major brand empire?
2. If you were working on a business plan for Madden, Inc., what potential risks would you mention and how would you suggest the company deal with them?

Summary

Define what a small business is and recognize the fields in which small businesses are concentrated.

A small business is one that is independently owned and operated for profit and is not dominant in its field. There are about twenty-three million businesses in this country, and more than 90 percent of them are small businesses. Small businesses employ more than one-half of the nation's work force, even though about 70 percent of new businesses can be expected to fail within five years. More than half of all small businesses are in retailing and services.

Identify the people who start small businesses and the reasons why some succeed and many fail.

Such personal characteristics as independence, desire to create a new enterprise, and willingness to accept a challenge may encourage individuals to start small businesses. Various external circumstances, such as special expertise or even the loss of a job, also can supply the motivation to strike out on one's own. Poor planning and lack of capital and management experience are the major causes of small-business failures.

Assess the contributions of small businesses to our economy.

Small businesses have been responsible for a wide variety of inventions and innovations, some of which have given rise to new industries. Historically, small businesses have created the bulk of the nation's new jobs. Further, they have mounted effective competition to larger firms. They provide things that society needs, act as suppliers to larger firms, and serve as customers of other businesses, both large and small.

Judge the advantages and disadvantages of operating a small business.

The advantages of smallness in business include the opportunity to establish personal relationships with customers and employees, the ability to adapt to changes quickly, independence, and simplified recordkeeping. The major disadvantages are the high risk of failure, the limited potential for growth, and limited ability to raise capital.

Explain how the Small Business Administration helps small businesses.

The Small Business Administration (SBA) was created in 1953 to assist and counsel the nation's millions of small-business owners. The SBA offers management courses and workshops; managerial help, including one-to-one counseling through SCORE; various publications; and financial assistance through guaranteed loans and SBICs. It places special emphasis on aid to minority-owned businesses, including those owned by women.

Appraise the concept and types of franchising.

A franchise is a license to operate an individually owned business as though it were part of a chain. The franchisor provides a known business name, management skills, a method of doing business, and the training and required materials. The franchisee contributes labor and capital, operates the franchised business, and agrees to abide by the provisions of the franchise agreement. There are three major categories of franchise agreements.

Analyze the growth of franchising and franchising's advantages and disadvantages.

Franchising has grown tremendously since the mid-1970s. The franchisor's major advantage in franchising is fast and well-controlled distribution of products with minimal capital outlay. In return, the franchisee has the opportunity to open a business with limited capital, to make use of the business experience of others, and to sell to an existing clientele. For this, the franchisee usually must pay both an initial franchise fee and a continuing royalty based on sales. He or she also must follow the dictates of the franchise with regard to operation of the business.

Worldwide business opportunities are expanding for small businesses. The SBA assists small-business owners in penetrating foreign markets. The next century will present unique challenges and opportunities for small-business owners.

Key Terms

You should now be able to define and give an example relevant to each of the following terms:

small business (167)
business plan (178)
Small Business Administration (SBA) (179)
Service Corps of Retired Executives (SCORE) (180)
small-business institute (SBI) (180)
small-business development center (SBDC) (180)
venture capital (181)
small-business investment companies (SBICs) (181)
franchise (182)
franchising (182)
franchisor (182)
franchisee (182)

Review Questions

1. What information would you need to determine whether a particular business is small according to SBA guidelines?
2. Which two areas of business generally attract the most small businesses? Why are these areas attractive to small business?
3. Distinguish among service industries, distribution industries, and production industries.
4. What kinds of factors encourage certain people to start new businesses?
5. What are the major causes of small-business failure? Do these causes also apply to larger businesses?
6. Briefly describe four contributions of small business to the American economy.
7. What are the major advantages and disadvantages of smallness in business?
8. What are the major components of a business plan? Why should an individual develop a business plan?
9. Identify five ways in which the SBA provides management assistance to small businesses.
10. Identify two ways in which the SBA provides financial assistance to small businesses.
11. Why does the SBA concentrate on providing management and financial assistance to small businesses?
12. What is venture capital? How does the SBA help small businesses obtain it?
13. Explain the relationships among a franchise, the franchisor, and the franchisee.
14. What does the franchisor receive in a franchising agreement? What does the franchisee receive? What does each provide?
15. Cite one major benefit of franchising for the franchisor. Cite one major benefit of franchising for the franchisee.

Discussion Questions

1. Most people who start small businesses are aware of the high failure rate and the reasons for it. Why, then, do some take no steps to protect their firms from failure? What steps should they take?
2. Are the so-called advantages of small business really advantages? Wouldn't every small-business owner like his or her business to grow into a large firm?
3. Do average citizens benefit from the activities of the SBA, or is the SBA just another way to spend our tax money?
4. Would you rather own your own business independently or become a franchisee? Why?

video case

Entrepreneurial Spirit Pervades the Percy Inn

Maine native Dale Northrup traveled the world writing about hotels for almost twenty years before settling down to open his own bed and breakfast (B&B) inn. After visiting 23,000 hotels in seventy nations, he had a very definite idea of what a quaint New England inn should offer. Driven by entrepreneurial spirit, Northrup sold his home to finance the lengthy and expensive renovation of an 1830s apartment building in Portland's historic West End district.

Maine had long been a popular summer vacation destination, and B&Bs were thriving. In number of B&B inns, the state ranked fifth in the United States. Portland had been an active seaport in the late nineteenth century and now was a bustling city dotted with tourist shops. Northrup recognized that a period building such as his inn would be more appealing if it gave vacationers a nostalgic glimpse of the past. His goal was to create a cozy B&B, the Percy Inn, with character as well as modern conveniences.

When Northrup took possession, the building was dilapidated and needed a complete makeover. The would-be innkeeper rebuilt the walls, roof, plumbing, and electrical system. He added thick insulation between rooms for guest privacy and installed a sprinkler system for fire safety. He decorated the eight rooms in distinctly different styles, complete with private baths, queen-size beds, and unique touches such as handmade quilts. Each room was named for a well-known writer (such as Percy Shelley, Walt Whitman, and Dorothy Parker) or for its decor (Pine Suite I), adding to the atmosphere.

Remembering what he wished for when staying in hotels around the world, Northrup also put a phone, fax, and data port in each room. Planning ahead, he set up the wiring to accommodate other high-speed communication uses in the future. He also put CD players, TVs and VCRs, and refrigerators in every room (with kitchenettes in some) and assembled a video library for guests to browse.

Initially the would-be innkeeper wasn't sure that his urban B&B would attract enough visitors to be economically feasible. He took the precaution of wiring each room's utilities so that they could be metered individually if he had to rent them as apartments or convert the inn to a condominium. Northrup also arranged for eight off-street parking slots, solving a common problem that many B&Bs face at the height of the vacation season. And knowing that innkeepers usually work very long hours, he arranged for an assistant innkeeper, Phyllis Rogers, to help with reservations, breakfast, cleaning, greeting guests, and all the other details that keep a B&B running smoothly.

Contrary to Northrup's early fears, the Percy Inn was successful from the start. So many rooms were rented that the owner did not have to go back to freelance writing to supplement his income. However, he underestimated the challenge of laundry. The Percy Inn's eight rooms constantly generated a mountain of dirty sheets, pillowcases, and towels to be washed. Northrup and Rogers struggled to keep up with the laundry during the first year. In the second year Northrup bought two large washing machines and two large dryers so that he and his assistant could handle this time-consuming task more efficiently.

Like most small business owners, Northrup operated the Percy Inn on a tight budget. Rather than invest in paid advertising, he decided to set up an extensive website as his main marketing vehicle (**www.percyinn.com**). He included not only photos, rates, and descriptions of every guest room but also information about the neighborhood, local restaurants, driving directions, and raves about the inn from newspapers and magazines. Soon, 80 percent of the B&B's business was coming from this website. The other 20 percent was coming through referrals made by the local visitor's center and from the overflow of nearby inns.

Looking back, Northrup believes that having an assistant was vital to his success as a small business owner. He knew that he would be involved every hour of every day for at least the first two years, yet he knew he couldn't do everything himself. "Nobody runs a business like the owner," he observes, "but as long as you can direct, that's just as good." When Northrup isn't at the Percy Inn, Rogers is—and vice versa. As a team, they provide the kind of quality accommodations and personal service that brings guests back again and again.[22]

Questions

1. This chapter cites five advantages of small business. Which of these seem to apply to Dale Northrup's experience with the Percy Inn?
2. This chapter cites three disadvantages of small business. Based on what you know of the Percy Inn, which of these is likely to be the biggest problem for Northrup in the coming years?
3. Now that Northrup has the Percy Inn running smoothly, would you recommend that he open a second B&B to take advantage of rising tourism in Portland? Why or why not?

Building Skills for Career Success

1. Exploring the Internet

Perhaps the most challenging difficulty for small businesses is operating with scarce resources, especially people and money. To provide information and point small-business operators in the right direction, many Internet sites offer helpful products and services. Although most are sponsored by advertising and may be free of charge, some charge a fee, and others are a combination of both. The SBA within the U.S. Department of Commerce provides a wide array of free information and resources. You can find your way to the SBA through **http://www.sbaonline.sba.gov or http://www.sba.gov.** Visit the text website for updates to this exercise.

Assignment

1. Describe the various services provided by the SBA site.
2. What sources of funding are there?
3. What service would you like to see improved? How?

2. Developing Critical Thinking Skills

Small businesses play a vital role in our economy. They not only contribute to technological innovation and to the creation of many new jobs, but they also ensure that customers have an alternative to the products and services offered by large firms. In addition, by making parts for large firms at a cost lower than the large firms could make the parts themselves, they help keep the lid on consumer prices. Regardless of our need for them, many small businesses fail within their first five years. Why is this so?

Assignment

1. Identify several successful small businesses in your community.
2. Identify one small business that has failed.
3. Gather enough information about these businesses to answer the following questions:
   a. What role do small businesses play in your community?

b. Why are they important?
c. Why did the business fail?
d. What was the most important reason for its failure?
e. How might the business have survived?

4. Summarize what you have learned about the impact of small businesses on your community. Give the summary to your instructor.

3. Building Team Skills

A business plan is a written statement that documents the nature of a business and how that business intends to achieve its goals. Although entrepreneurs should prepare a business plan *before* starting a business, the plan also serves as an effective guide later on. The plan should concisely describe the business's mission, the amount of capital it requires, its target market, competition, resources, production plan, marketing plan, organizational plan, assessment of risk, and financial plan.

Assignment

1. Working in a team of four students, identify a company in your community that would benefit from using a business plan, or create a scenario in which a hypothetical entrepreneur wants to start a business.
2. Using the resources of the library or the Internet and/or interviews with business owners, write a business plan incorporating the information in Table 6.3
3. Present your business plan to the class.

4. Researching Different Careers

Many people dream of opening and operating their own businesses. Are you one of them? To be successful, entrepreneurs must have certain characteristics; their profiles generally differ from those of people who work for someone else. Do you know which personal characteristics make some entrepreneurs succeed and others fail? Do you fit the successful entrepreneur's profile? What is your potential for opening and operating a successful small business?

Assignment

1. Use the resources of the library or the Internet to establish what a successful entrepreneur's profile is and to determine whether your personal characteristics fit that profile. Internet addresses that can help you are **http://www.smartbiz.com/sbs/arts/ieb1.html** and **http://www.sba.gov** (see "Starting Your Business" and "FAQs"). These sites have quizzes online that can help you assess your personal characteristics. The SBA also has helpful brochures.
2. Interview several small-business owners. Ask them to describe the characteristics they think are necessary for being a successful entrepreneur.
3. Using your findings, write a report that includes the following:
   a. A profile of a successful small-business owner
   b. A comparison of your personal characteristics with the profile of the successful entrepreneur
   c. A discussion of your potential as a successful small-business owner

5. Improving Communication Skills

Franchising is a method of doing business that has grown steadily in popularity since the early 1900s. It offers entrepreneurs who want to start a business certain opportunities and advantages. If you started a business, would a franchise be an option?

Assignment

1. Choose a franchise business in your community, preferably one of those listed in Table 6.5.
2. Investigate the business by interviewing the franchise owner. Ask the following questions:
   a. Why did you decide to open a franchise business?
   b. What are the advantages or disadvantages of having a franchise agreement over opening a new business or buying an existing business?
   c. When you were deciding whether to become a franchisee, what were some of your major concerns? What type of research did you do?
   d. What key things does the franchisor provide for you? What are your obligations to the franchisor?
   e. What advice would you give a person who was thinking about becoming a franchisee?
3. Write a two-page report summarizing the information you have gathered.

Finagle A Bagel: A Fast-Growing Small Business

Finagle A Bagel, a fast-growing small business co-owned by Alan Litchman and Laura Trust, is at the forefront of one of the freshest concepts in the food-service business: fresh food. The stores bake a new batch of bagels every hour, and they receive new deliveries of cheeses, vegetables, and other ingredients every day. Rather than prepackage menu items, store employees make everything to order so that they can satisfy the specific needs of each *guest* (Finagle A Bagel's term for a customer). Customers like this arrangement because they get fresh food prepared to their exact preferences—whether it's extra cheese on a bagel pizza or no onions in a salad—along with prompt, friendly service.

"Every sandwich, every salad is built to order, so there's a lot of communication between the customers and the cashiers, the customers and the sandwich makers, the customers and the managers," explains Trust. As a result, Finagle A Bagel's store employees have ample opportunity to build customer relationships and encourage repeat business. Many, like Mirna Hernandez of the Tremont Street store in downtown Boston, are so familiar with what certain customers order that they spring into action when regulars enter the store. "We know what they want, and we just ring it in and take care of them," she says. Some employees even know their customers by name and make conversation as they create a sandwich or fill a coffee container.

Buying and Building the Business and Brand

The combination of a strong local following and favorable brand image is what attracted the entrepreneurs to Finagle A Bagel. Looking back, Litchman says that he and his wife recognized that building a small business would require more than good business sense. "It has a lot to do with having a great brand and having great food, and reinforcing the brand every day," he remembers. "That's one of the key things that we bought."

To further reinforce the brand and reward customer loyalty, Finagle A Bagel created the Frequent Finagler card. Cardholders receive one point for every dollar spent in a Finagle A Bagel store and can redeem accumulated points for coffee, juice, sandwiches, or a dozen bagels (actually a baker's dozen, meaning thirteen instead of twelve). To join, customers visit the company's website (**www.finagleabagel.com**) and complete a registration form asking for name, address, and other demographics. From then on, says Litchman, "It's a web-based program where customers can log on, check their points, and receive free gifts by mail. The Frequent Finagler is our big push right now to use technology as a means of generating store traffic."

Bagels Online?

Within a few years, Litchman expects to expand the website so that customers can order food and catering services directly online. Some food-service firms are already doing this. Starbucks, for example, invites customers to place coffee orders on its website for pickup at a local store. Unlike Starbucks, however, Finagle A Bagel has a more extensive menu, and its fresh-food concept is not as easily adapted to e-commerce. "In our stores, all the food is prepared fresh, and it is very customized," Litchman notes. "This entails a fair amount of interaction between employees and customers: 'What kind of croutons do you want? What kind of

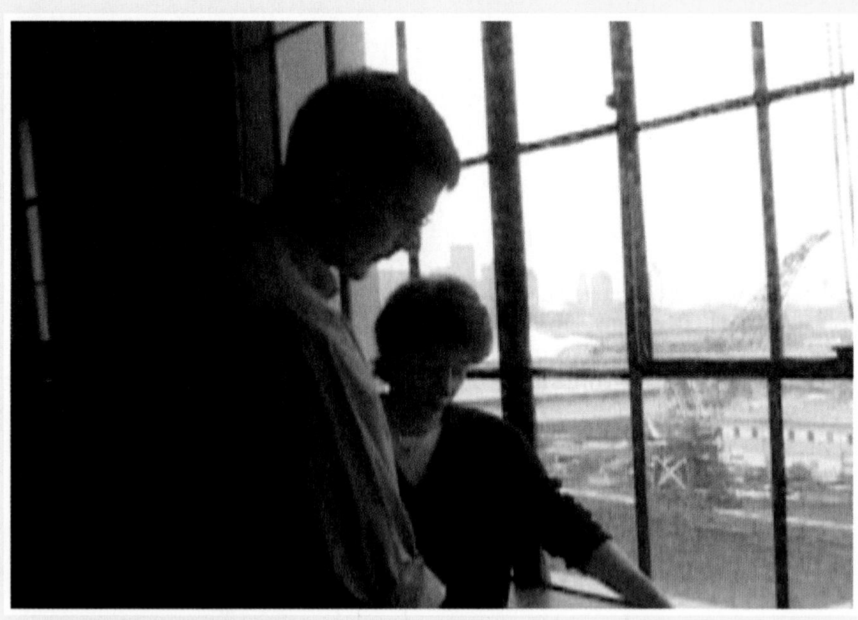

dressing? What kind of mustard?' When we're ready to go in that direction, it is going to be a fairly sizable technology venture for us to undertake."

Although Finagle A Bagel occasionally receives web or phone orders from customers hundreds or thousands of miles away, the copresidents have no immediate plans to expand outside the Boston metropolitan area. Pointing to regional food-service firms that have profited by opening dozens more stores in a wider geographic domain, Trust says, "We see that the most successful companies have really dominated their area first. Cheesecake Factory is an example of a company that's wildly successful right now, but they were a concept in California for decades before they moved beyond that area. In-and-Out Burger is an outstanding example of a food service company in the west that's done what we're trying to do. They had seventeen stores at one time, and now they have hundreds of stores. They're very successful, but they never left their backyard. That's kind of why we're staying where we are."

Growing a Small Business

Some small businesses achieve rapid growth through franchising. The entrepreneurs running Finagle A Bagel won't be going in that direction any time soon. "When you franchise, you gain a large influx of capital," says Trust, "but you begin to lose control over the people, the place, and the product. We are finding that our success comes from being on top of our stores, being able to control what happens." For years, the owners and their senior managers popped into different Finagle A Bagel stores every day. If franchisees were to open stores in Maine or New York, however, top management would be unable to check that the franchisees were upholding the brand image and providing excellent customer service.

As a corporation, Finagle a Bagel could, as some other small businesses do, raise money for growth through an initial public offering (IPO) of corporate stock. For now, however, the copresidents prefer not to transform their company into an open corporation. "Going public is very tricky in the food-service business," Trust observes. "Some people have done it very successfully; others have not." The copresidents want to maintain total control over the pace and direction of growth rather than feeling pressured to meet the growth expectations of securities analysts and shareholders. Running a fast-growing small business is their major challenge for now.

Questions

1. Why would Finagle A Bagel maintain a business-to-customer (B2C) website even though it is not yet set up to process online orders from individuals?
2. Under what conditions do you think Finagle A Bagel should consider franchising its fresh-food concept?
3. Although opening new stores and expanding the payroll is costly, the copresidents have chosen not to raise money through an IPO. Do you agree with this decision? Discuss the advantages and disadvantages.
4. If you were writing the executive summary of Finagle A Bagel's business plan to show to lenders, what key points would you stress?

Building a Business Plan Part II

After reading Part II, "Trends in Business Today," you should be ready to tackle the company and industry component of your business plan. In this section you will provide information about the background of the company, choice of the legal business form, information on the product or services to be offered, and descriptions of potential customers, current competitors, and the business's future. Chapter 5 in your textbook, "Choosing a Form of Business Ownership," and Chapter 6, "Small Business, Entrepreneurship, and Franchising," can help you to answer some of the questions in this part of the business plan.

The Company and Industry Component

The company and industry analysis should include the answers to at least the following questions:

2.1. What is the legal form of your business? Is your business a sole proprietorship, a partnership, or a corporation?

2.2. What licenses or permits you will need, if any?

2.3. Is your business a new independent business, a takeover, an expansion, or a franchise?

2.4. If you are dealing with an existing business, how did your company get to the point where it is today?

2.5. What does your business do, and how does it satisfy customers' needs?

2.6. How did you choose and develop the products or services to be sold, and how are they different from those currently on the market?

2.7. What industry do you operate in, and what are the industry-wide trends?

2.8. Who are the major competitors in your industry?

2.9. Have any businesses recently entered or exited? Why did they leave?

2.10. Why will your business be profitable, and what are your growth opportunities?

2.11. Does any part of your business involve e-business?

Review of Business Plan Activities

Make sure to check the information you have collected, make any changes, and correct any weaknesses before beginning Part III. *Reminder:* Review the answers to questions in the preceding part to make sure that all your answers are consistent throughout the business plan. Finally, write a summary statement that incorporates all the information for this part of the business plan.

part III

Management and Organization

This part of the book deals with the organization—the "thing" that is a business. We begin with a discussion of the management functions involved in developing and operating a business. Then we analyze the organization itself, to see what makes it tick. Next, we put the two together, to examine the part of a business that is directly concerned with manufacturing finished products.

chapter

7

Understanding the Management Process

learning objectives

1. Define what management is.
2. Describe the four basic management functions: planning, organizing, leading and motivating, and controlling.
3. Distinguish among the various kinds of managers in terms of both level and area of management.
4. Identify the key management skills and the managerial roles.
5. Explain the different types of leadership.
6. Discuss the steps in the managerial decision-making process.
7. Describe how organizations benefit from total quality management.
8. Summarize what it takes to become a successful manager today.

Yahoo!'s original mission was to grow as fast as you can and put things out there and see what works.

inside business

There Are No "Yah-Whos" at Yahoo!

WHAT BEGAN AS A SIMPLE LISTING of favorite websites has evolved into one of the world's best known and most successful e-businesses. Jerry Yang and David Filo were working on Ph.D. degrees at Stanford University when they first created their directory of interesting websites. Eyeing the business potential, the two wrote a business plan, registered the Yahoo! name, and obtained $1 million in venture capital funding to get underway. Next, the co-founders hired a high-tech executive to take the lead in planning and organizing the firm's activities as CEO. This allowed Filo to apply his technical skills to new technological advances, while Yang used his conceptual and interpersonal skills to serve as company strategist, spokesperson, lobbyist, and cheerleader.

In the early years, the business grew quickly as other companies paid handsomely to place ads on the highly popular Yahoo! site. Then a prolonged economic slump cut into advertising revenues just as the company had to battle more intense online competition. After the first CEO stepped down, he was replaced by Terry S. Semel, who used the skills and experiences from his studio management days at Warner Bros. to thoroughly analyze the company's situation. By this time, Yahoo! had 3,500 employees working in 44 separate business units. Semel spent considerable time asking each unit's managers about their operations and priorities. "I couldn't get my arms around something that had so many pieces and so many people running so many things, large and small," he remembers. "There was no specific strategy, no specific point of view." The chief operating officer confirms Semel's reaction. "Yahoo!'s original mission was to grow as fast as you can and put things out there and see what works," he says. "Nobody knew what would work."

This has all changed under Semel, who brought in a seasoned management team to pursue a bold new future for Yahoo!: "We're going to change the way people access the Internet," he stated. To start, Semel and his managers partnered with SBC Communications to deliver high-speed Internet service with special features customized for each user. In addition, they forged new business alliances and pursued acquisitions to expand the offerings for individual and corporate users. Finally, going against conventional wisdom, Semel added subscription fees for some well-liked services—a tough decision that paid off in higher profitability to fuel a brighter future for Yahoo![1]

The challenges at Yahoo! are proof that management can be one of the most exciting and rewarding professions available today. Managers of both small and large firms play an important part in shaping the world we live in. Depending on its size, a firm may employ a number of specialized managers who are responsible for particular areas of management, such as marketing, finance, and operations. That same organization also includes managers at several levels within the firm. For a company like Yahoo!, what is important is not the number of managers it employs, but the ability of these managers to achieve the organization's goals. As you will see in this chapter, today's managers wear many hats and perform a variety of different jobs.

In this chapter we define *management* and describe the four basic management functions of planning, organizing, leading and motivating, and controlling. Then we focus on the types of managers with respect to levels of responsibility and areas of expertise. Next, we focus on the skills of effective managers and the different roles managers must play. We examine several styles of leadership and explore the process by which managers make decisions. We also describe how total quality management can improve customer satisfaction. We conclude the chapter with a discussion of what it takes to be a successful manager today.

What Is Management?

learning objective

1 Define what management is.

management the process of coordinating people and other resources to achieve the goals of the organization

Management is the process of coordinating people and other resources to achieve the goals of the organization. As we saw in Chapter 1, most organizations make use of four kinds of resources: material, human, financial, and informational (see Figure 7.1).

Material resources are the tangible, physical resources an organization uses. For example, General Motors uses steel, glass, and fiberglass to produce cars and trucks on complex machine-driven assembly lines. A college or university uses books, classroom buildings, desks, and computers to educate students. And the Mayo Clinic uses beds, operating room equipment, and diagnostic machines to provide health care.

Perhaps the most important resources of any organization are its *human resources*—people. In fact, some firms live by the philosophy that their employees are their most important assets. One such firm is Southwest Airlines. Southwest treats its employees with the same respect and attention that it gives its passengers. Southwest selectively seeks employees with upbeat attitudes and promotes from within its own ranks 80 percent of the time. And when it is time for making decisions, everyone who will be affected is encouraged to get involved in the process. In an industry in which deregulation, extreme price competition, and fluctuating fuel costs have eliminated several major competitors Southwest keeps on growing and making a profit because of its valuable employees. Many experts would agree with Southwest's emphasis on employees. Evidence suggests that the way employees are developed and managed may have more impact on an organization than other vital components such as marketing, sound financial decisions about large expenditures, production, or use of technology.[4]

figure 7.1

The Four Main Resources of Management

Managers coordinate an organization's resources to achieve the goals of the organization.

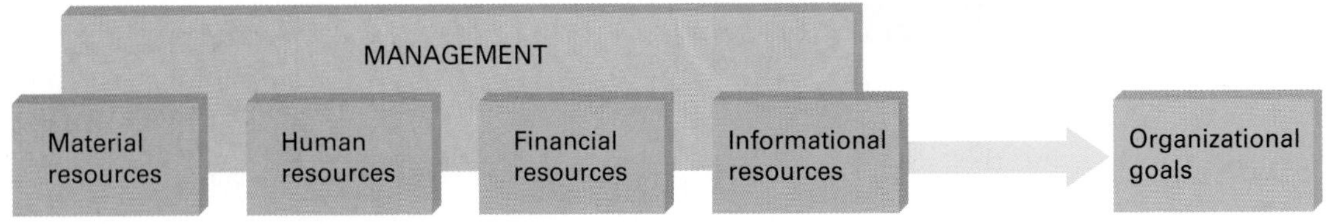

Financial resources are the funds the organization uses to meet its obligations to investors and creditors. A 7-Eleven convenience store obtains money from customers at the check-out counters and uses a portion of that money to pay its suppliers. Citicorp, a large New York bank, borrows and lends money. Your college obtains money in the form of tuition, income from its endowments, and state and federal grants. It uses the money to pay utility bills, insurance premiums, and professors' salaries.

Finally, many organizations increasingly find they cannot afford to ignore *information.* External environmental conditions—including the economy, consumer markets, technology, politics, and cultural forces—are all changing so rapidly that a business that does not adapt probably will not survive. And to adapt to change, the business must know what is changing and how it is changing. Most companies gather information about their competitors to increase their knowledge about changes in their particular industries and to learn from other companies' failures and successes.

It is important to realize that the four types of resources described earlier are only general categories of resources. Within each category are hundreds or thousands of more specific resources. It is this complex mix of specific resources—and not simply "some of each" of the four general categories—that managers must coordinate to produce goods and services.

Another interesting way to look at management is in terms of the different functions managers perform. These functions have been identified as planning, organizing, leading and motivating employees, and controlling. We look at each of these management functions in the next section.

Basic Management Functions

learning objective

2 Describe the four basic management functions: planning, organizing, leading and motivating, and controlling.

Gordon Bethune, a high school dropout who went on to become an airplane mechanic, took control of down-and-out Continental Airlines in 1994. When he arrived, he found a disjointed operation that had caused Continental to rank last in almost every Department of Transportation performance measure, such as on-time performance, lost baggage, and canceled flights. Using a combination of clever incentives and discussions with many employees, Bethune changed the attitudes and actions of workers, including the baggage handlers and gate agents. Today, as the fifth largest U.S. airline, 47,000 employees work together to board 44 million travelers annually onto 557 airplanes. Apparently, most employees are happy working for Continental in that it has recently appeared on *Fortune* magazine's list of the "100 Best Companies to Work For." By using many highly effective management skills, Bethune has dramatically turned Continental into a well-run, profitable, and congenial organization.[3]

Management functions such as those just described do not occur according to some rigid, preset timetable. Managers do not plan in January, organize in February, lead and motivate in March, and control in April. At any given time, managers may engage in a number of functions simultaneously. However, each function tends to lead naturally to others. Figure 7.2 provides a visual framework for a more detailed discussion of the four basic management functions. How well managers perform these key functions determines whether a business is successful.

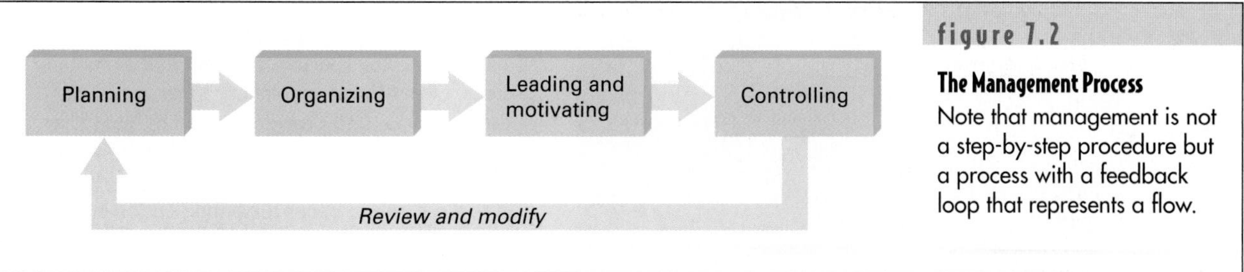

figure 7.2

The Management Process

Note that management is not a step-by-step procedure but a process with a feedback loop that represents a flow.

Planning

planning establishing organizational goals and deciding how to accomplish them

mission a statement of the basic purpose that makes an organization different from others

strategic planning the process of establishing an organization's major goals and objectives and allocating the resources to achieve them

goal an end result that an organization is expected to achieve over a one- to ten-year period

objective a specific statement detailing what an organization intends to accomplish over a shorter period of time

Planning, in its simplest form, is establishing organizational goals and deciding how to accomplish them. It is often referred to as the "first" management function because all other management functions depend on planning. Organizations such as Nissan, Houston Community Colleges, and the U.S. Secret Service begin the planning process by developing a mission statement.

An organization's **mission** is a statement of the basic purpose that makes this organization different from others. Yellow Freight Systems' mission statement is: "Pick it up on time, deliver it on time, and don't bust it."[4] Houston Community College System's mission is to provide an education for local citizens. The mission of the Secret Service is to protect the life of the president. Once an organization's mission has been described in a mission statement, the next step is to develop organizational goals and objectives, usually through strategic planning. **Strategic planning** is the process of establishing an organization's major goals and objectives and allocating the resources to achieve them.

Establishing Goals and Objectives

A **goal** is an end result that the organization is expected to achieve over a one- to ten-year period. For example, General Motors approved the introduction of the Hummer H2 with a goal of putting its militaristic vehicles on the road within two years.[5] Wal-Mart set goals of expanding from 3,400 U.S. stores to 5,000 within five years and having a 30 percent market share in every major business that it is in.[6] An **objective** is a specific statement detailing what the organization intends to accomplish over a shorter period of time compared with goals.

Goals and objectives can deal with a variety of factors, such as sales, company growth, costs, customer satisfaction, and employee morale. Whereas a small manufacturer may focus primarily on sales objectives for the next six months, a large firm may be more interested in goals for several years in the future. Phillips-Van Heusen for example, recently acquired Calvin Klein, and its executives see exciting growth opportunities for the combined company, with a goal of 15 to 20 percent annual earnings growth from 2005 through 2010. A related objective is to launch a new sportswear line for men that will produce $1 billion of revenue the first year.[7] Finally, goals are set at every level of an organization. Every member of an organization—the president of the company, the head of a department, and an operating employee at the lowest level—has a set of goals that he or she hopes to achieve.

The goals developed for these different levels must be consistent with one another. However, it is likely that some conflict will arise. A production department, for example, may have a goal of minimizing costs. One way to do this is to produce only one type of product and offer "no frills." Marketing, on the other hand, may have a goal of maximizing sales. And one way to implement this goal is to offer prospective customers a wide range of products with many options. As part of his or her

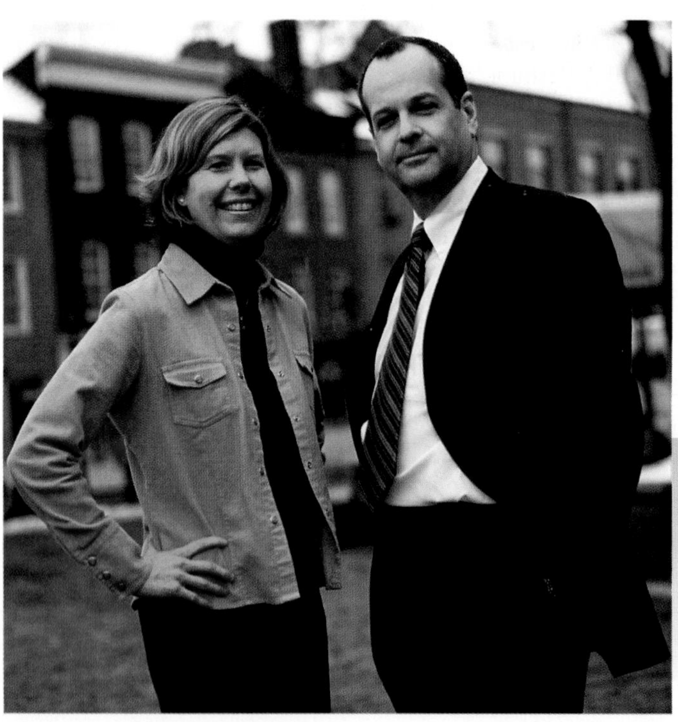

Planning may require specialists. Managers sometimes employ specialists to help in the planning process. Ellen Moore, an ethnographer, observes guests' behavior and provides research data to Ken Conklin, general manager of several hotels. Based on Moore's information, Conklin will develop plans that enable the hotels to better serve their customers.

own goal setting, the manager who is ultimately responsible for *both* departments must achieve some sort of balance between conflicting goals. This balancing process is called *optimization*.

The optimization of conflicting goals requires insight and ability. Faced with the marketing-versus-production conflict just described, most managers probably would not adopt either viewpoint completely. Instead, they might decide on a reasonably diverse product line offering only the most widely sought-after options. Such a compromise would seem to be best for the organization as a whole.

Establishing Plans to Accomplish Goals and Objectives Once goals and objectives have been set for the organization, managers must develop plans for achieving them. A **plan** is an outline of the actions by which the organization intends to accomplish its goals and objectives. Just as it has different goals and objectives, the organization also develops several types of plans. For example, the plan that General Motors developed to achieve its Hummer H2 goal mentioned previously included assembling a team of talented executives with automotive experience and negotiating an agreement with AM General to manufacture the vehicles. This plan became a reality, and sales of the Hummer H2 have exceeded the sales of Ford's Lincoln Navigator in recent months.[8]

plan an outline of the actions by which an organization intends to accomplish its goals and objectives

An organization's **strategy** is its broadest set of plans, developed as a guide for major policy setting and decision making. These plans are set by the board of directors and top management and generally are designed to achieve the long-term goals of the organization. Thus a firm's strategy defines what business the company is in or wants to be in and the kind of company it is or wants to be. When the U.S. Surgeon General issued a report linking smoking and cancer, top management at Philip Morris Companies recognized that the company's very survival was being threatened. Executives needed to develop a strategy to diversify into nontobacco products.

strategy an organization's broadest set of plans, developed as a guide for major policy setting and decision making

The Internet has challenged traditional strategic thinking that has worked well for a long time. For example, reluctant to move from a face-to-face sales approach to a less personal website approach, Allstate has created an Internet presence to support its established sales force.

In addition to strategies, most organizations also employ several narrower kinds of plans. A **tactical plan** is a smaller-scale plan developed to implement a strategy. Most tactical plans cover a one- to three-year period. If a strategic plan will take five years to complete, the firm may develop five tactical plans, one covering each year. Tactical plans may be updated periodically as conditions and experience dictate. Their more limited scope permits them to be changed more easily than strategies. In an attempt to fulfill its strategy of diversification, Philip Morris developed individual tactical plans to purchase several non-tobacco-related companies such as General Foods, Kraft Foods, and Miller Brewing.

tactical plan a smaller-scale plan developed to implement a strategy

An **operational plan** is a type of plan designed to implement tactical plans. Operational plans are usually established for one year or less and deal with how to accomplish the organization's specific objectives. Assume that after Philip Morris purchased Kraft Foods, managers adopted the objective of increasing sales of Kraft's Cheez Whiz by 5 percent during the first year. A sales increase of this size does not just happen, however. Management must develop an operational plan that describes certain activities the firm can undertake over the next year to bring about the increased sales. Specific components of the Kraft Cheez Whiz operational plan might include newspaper and television advertising, reduced prices, and coupon offers—all designed to increase consumer sales.

operational plan a type of plan designed to implement tactical plans

Regardless of how hard managers try, sometimes business activities do not go as planned. Today, most corporations also develop contingency plans along with strategies, tactical plans, and operational plans. A **contingency plan** is a plan that outlines alternative courses of action that may be taken if the organization's other plans are disrupted or become ineffective. Remember that one reason for Philip Morris's purchase of Kraft was to diversify into nontobacco products. If it became impossible to purchase Kraft, Philip Morris could fall back on contingency plans to purchase other nontobacco companies.

contingency plan a plan that outlines alternative courses of action that may be taken if an organization's other plans are disrupted or become ineffective

organizing the grouping of resources and activities to accomplish some end result in an efficient and effective manner

Organizing the Enterprise

After goal setting and planning, the second major function of the manager is organization. **Organizing** is the grouping of resources and activities to accomplish some end result in an efficient and effective manner. Consider the case of an inventor who creates a new product and goes into business to sell it. At first, he or she probably will do everything himself or herself—purchase raw materials, make the product, advertise it, sell it, and keep the business records up-to-date. Eventually, as business grows, the inventor will find that he or she needs help. To begin with, he or she might hire a professional sales representative and a part-time bookkeeper. Later, he or she might need to hire full-time sales staff, other people to assist with production, and an accountant. As the inventor hires new personnel, he or she must decide what each person will do, to whom that person will report, and generally how that person can best take part in the organization's activities. We discuss these and other facets of the organizing function in much more detail in Chapter 8.

leading the process of influencing people to work toward a common goal

motivating the process of providing reasons for people to work in the best interests of an organization

directing the combined processes of leading and motivating

controlling the process of evaluating and regulating ongoing activities to ensure that goals are achieved

Leading and Motivating

The leading and motivating function is concerned with the human resources within the organization. Specifically, **leading** is the process of influencing people to work toward a common goal. **Motivating** is the process of providing reasons for people to work in the best interests of the organization. Together, leading and motivating are often referred to as **directing.**

We have already noted the importance of an organization's human resources. Because of this importance, leading and motivating are critical activities. Obviously, different people do things for different reasons—that is, they have different *motivations*. Some are interested primarily in earning as much money as they can. Others may be spurred on by opportunities to get ahead in an organization. Part of the manager's job, then, is to determine what factors motivate workers and to try to provide those incentives in ways that encourage effective performance. For example, Nissan's CEO, Carlos Ghosn, has been successful at motivating his employees to give their best efforts for the company. His leadership style involves never punishing or giving orders to his employees. Through his leadership, Ghosn has helped Nissan to exceed its three-year Nissan Revival goals in just two years.[9]

Quite a bit of research has been done on both motivation and leadership. As you will see in Chapter 11, research on motivation has yielded very useful information. Research on leadership has been less successful. Despite decades of study, no one has discovered a general set of personal traits or characteristics that makes a good leader. Later in this chapter we discuss leadership in more detail.

Motivating employees can be fun! Some organizations attempt to create highly satisfying work environments to motivate employees. The founder of Burell Communications Group, Thomas Burrell, believes that meetings should be inspirational and fun.

Controlling Ongoing Activities

Controlling is the process of evaluating and regulating ongoing activities to ensure that goals are achieved. To see how controlling works, consider a rocket launched by NASA to place a satellite in orbit. Do NASA personnel simply fire the rocket and then check back in a few days to find out whether the satellite is in place? Of course not. The rocket is monitored constantly, and its course is regulated and adjusted as needed to get the satellite to its destination.

The control function includes three steps (see Figure 7.3). The first is *setting standards* with which performance can be compared. The second is *measuring actual performance* and comparing it with the standard. And the third is *taking corrective action* as necessary. Notice that the

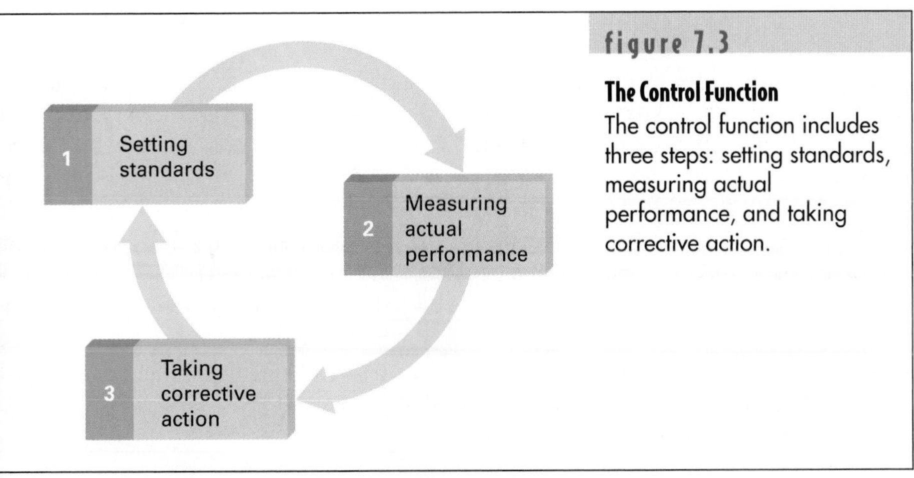

figure 7.3

The Control Function
The control function includes three steps: setting standards, measuring actual performance, and taking corrective action.

control function is circular in nature. The steps in the control function must be repeated periodically until the goal is achieved. For example, suppose that Southwest Airlines establishes a goal of increasing its profit by 12 percent next year. To ensure that this goal is reached, Southwest's management might monitor its profit on a monthly basis. After three months, if profit has increased by 3 percent, management might be able to assume that plans are going according to schedule. Probably no action will be taken. However, if profit has increased by only 1 percent after three months, some corrective action would be needed to get the firm on track. The particular action that is required depends on the reason for the small increase in profit.

Kinds of Managers

learning objective

3 Distinguish among the various kinds of managers in terms of both level and area of management.

Managers can be classified in two ways: according to their level within the organization, and according to their area of management. In this section we use both perspectives to explore the various types of managers.

Levels of Management

For the moment, think of an organization as a three-story structure (as illustrated in Figure 7.4). Each story corresponds to one of the three general levels of management: top managers, middle managers, and first-line managers.

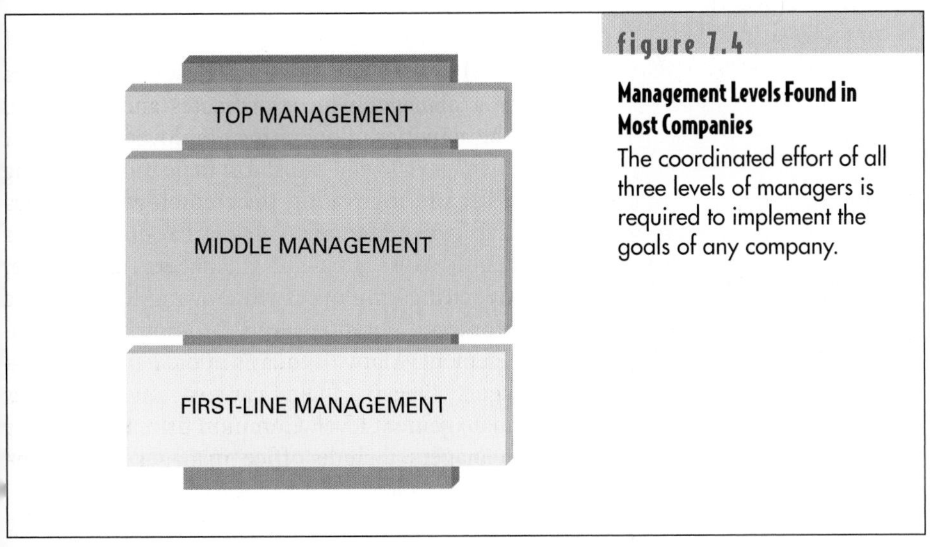

figure 7.4

Management Levels Found in Most Companies
The coordinated effort of all three levels of managers is required to implement the goals of any company.

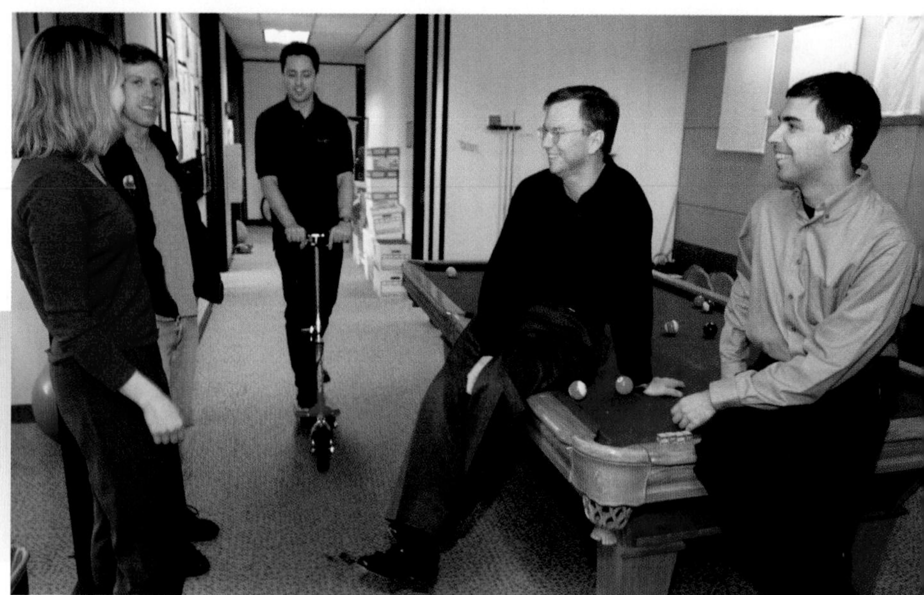

You don't have to be old to be a top manager. Dr. Eric E. Schmidt, Chairman and CEO of Google (second from right), holds an impromptu meeting with Google co-founders and staff members.

top manager an upper-level executive who guides and controls the overall fortunes of an organization

middle manager a manager who implements the strategy and major policies developed by top management

first-line manager a manager who coordinates and supervises the activities of operating employees

Top Managers A **top manager** is an upper-level executive who guides and control the overall fortunes of an organization. Top managers constitute a small group. In terms of planning, they are generally responsible for developing the organization' mission. They also determine the firm's strategy. Michael Dell, the founder of Del Computers, determined the need for a direct-to-consumer computer company. Many analysts attribute Michael Dell's long-term success to the significant amount of time he spends with customers that helps him make effective strategy and product decisions. Dell has continued to gain market share at a time when computer industry sales have decreased.[10] It takes years of hard work, long hours, and perseverance, as well as talent and no small share of good luck, to reach the ranks of top management in large companies. Common job titles associated with top managers are president, vice president, chief executive officer (CEO), and chief operating officer (COO).

Middle Managers Middle management probably comprises the largest group of managers in most organizations. A **middle manager** is a manager who implement the strategy developed by top managers. Middle managers develop tactical plans and operationa plans, and they coordinate and supervise the activities of first-line managers. Titles at the middle-management level include division manager, department head, plant manager, and operations manager.

Spotlight

Most important qualities for a CEO

Executives of *Fortune* 1,000 companies were asked: What do you believe is the most important quality for a CEO in tough times?

Effective communicator and motivator	47%
Decisiveness	31%
Being a visionary	15%

Source: *USA Today*, March 11, 2002, p. B1.

First-Line Managers A **first-line manager** is a manager who coordinates and supervises the activities of operating employees. First-line managers spend most of their time working with and motivating their employees, answering questions, and solving day-to-day problems. Most first-line managers are former operating employees who, owing to their hard work and potential, were promoted into management. Many of today's middle and top managers began their careers on this first management level. Common titles for first-line managers include office manager, supervisor and foreman.

figure 7.5

Areas of Management Specialization

Other areas may have to be added, depending on the nature of the firm and the industry.

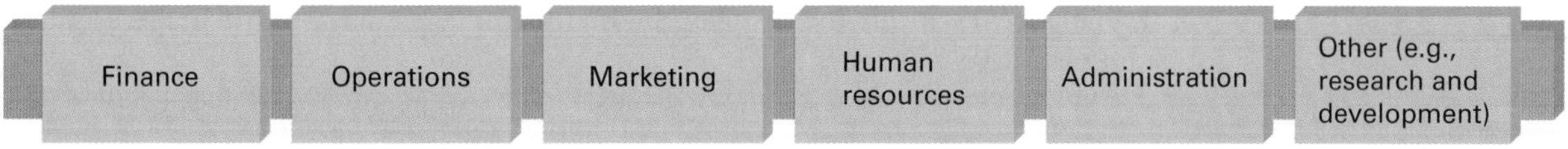

Finance | Operations | Marketing | Human resources | Administration | Other (e.g., research and development)

Areas of Management Specialization

Organizational structure also can be divided into areas of management specialization (see Figure 7.5). The most common areas are finance, operations, marketing, human resources, and administration. Depending on its mission, goals, and objectives, an organization may include other areas as well—research and development (R&D), for example.

Financial Managers A **financial manager** is primarily responsible for an organization's financial resources. Accounting and investment are specialized areas within financial management. Because financing affects the operation of the entire firm, many of the CEOs and presidents of this country's largest companies are people who got their "basic training" as financial managers.

financial manager a manager who is primarily responsible for an organization's financial resources

Operations Managers An **operations manager** manages the systems that convert resources into goods and services. Traditionally, operations management has been equated with manufacturing—the production of goods. However, in recent years, many of the techniques and procedures of operations management have been applied to the production of services and to a variety of nonbusiness activities. Like financial management, operations management has produced a large percentage of today's company CEOs and presidents.

operations manager a manager who manages the systems that convert resources into goods and services

Marketing Managers A **marketing manager** is responsible for facilitating the exchange of products between an organization and its customers or clients. Specific areas within marketing are marketing research, product management, advertising, promotion, sales, and distribution. A sizable number of today's company presidents have risen from the ranks of marketing management.

marketing manager a manager who is responsible for facilitating the exchange of products between an organization and its customers or clients

human resources manager a person charged with managing an organization's human resources programs

Human Resources Managers A **human resources manager** is charged with managing an organization's human resources programs. He or she engages in human resources planning; designs systems for hiring, training, and evaluating the performance of employees; and ensures that the organization follows government regulations concerning employment practices. Some human resources managers are making effective use of technology. For example, over one million job openings are posted on Monster.com, which attracts about eighteen million visitors monthly.[11]

The importance of human resources managers. Nancy Anderson is vice president of human resources management at DSM Pharmaceuticals. She played a major role in the transition from the previous CEO to the new one.

administrative manager a manager who is not associated with any specific functional area but who provides overall administrative guidance and leadership

Administrative Managers An **administrative manager** (also called a *general manager*) is not associated with any specific functional area but provides overall administrative guidance and leadership. A hospital administrator is an example of an administrative manager. He or she does not specialize in operations, finance, marketing, or human resources management but instead coordinates the activities of specialized managers in all these areas. In many respects, most top managers are really administrative managers.

Whatever their level in the organization and whatever area they specialize in, successful managers generally exhibit certain key skills and are able to play certain managerial roles. However, as we shall see, some skills are likely to be more critical at one level of management than at another.

What Makes Effective Managers?

learning objective

4 Identify the key management skills and the managerial roles.

In general, effective managers are those who (1) possess certain important skills and (2) are able to use those skills in a number of managerial roles. Probably no manager is called on to use any particular skill *constantly* or to play a particular role *all the time*. However, these skills and abilities must be available when they are needed.

Key Management Skills

The skills that typify effective managers tend to fall into three general categories: technical, conceptual, and interpersonal.

technical skill a specific skill needed to accomplish a specialized activity

Technical Skills A **technical skill** is a specific skill needed to accomplish a specialized activity. For example, the skills engineers and machinists need to do their jobs are technical skills. First-line managers (and, to a lesser extent, middle managers) need the technical skills relevant to the activities they manage. Although these managers may not have to perform the technical tasks themselves, they must be able to train subordinates, answer questions, and otherwise provide guidance and direction. A first-line manager in the accounting department of the Hyatt Corporation, for example, must be able to perform computerized accounting transactions *and* be able to help employees complete the same accounting task. In general, top managers do not rely on technical skills as heavily as do managers at other levels. Still, understanding the technical side of a business is an aid to effective management at every level.

conceptual skill the ability to think in abstract terms

Conceptual Skills **Conceptual skill** is the ability to think in abstract terms. Conceptual skill allows a manager to see the "big picture" and to understand how the various parts of an organization or an idea can fit together. These skills are useful in a wide range of situations, including the optimization of goals described earlier. They are usually more useful for top managers than for middle or first-line managers.

interpersonal skill the ability to deal effectively with other people

Interpersonal Skills An **interpersonal skill** is the ability to deal effectively with other people, both inside and outside an organization. Examples of interpersonal skills are the ability to relate to people, understand their needs and motives, and show genuine compassion. One reason why Mary Kay Ash, founder of Mary Kay Cosmetics, has been so successful is her ability to motivate her employees and to inspire their loyalty and devotion to her vision for the firm. And although it is obvious that a CEO like Mary Kay Ash must be able to work with employees throughout the organization, what is not so obvious is that middle and first-line managers also must possess interpersonal skills. For example, a first-line manager on an assembly line at Procter & Gamble must rely on employees to manufacture Tide laundry detergent. The better the manager's interpersonal skills, the more likely the manager will be able to lead and motivate those employees. When all other things are equal, the manager able to exhibit these skills will be more successful than the arrogant and brash manager who does not care about others. Interestingly enough, almost a fourth of America's 500 largest corporations' chief executives were members of fraternities in college. The social and interpersonal skills provided by that experience, along with the networking and contacts that resulted, seem to prepare members of fraternities and sororities to become successful managers. Beta Theta Pi leads the way with the most *Fortune* 500 CEOs.[12]

Spotlight

How quickly supervisors respond to employees

Office workers were asked how long it generally takes their boss to respond to them.

Within an hour or two 36%
Before closing that day 29%
Immediately 27%
I am lucky if they respond without several prompts 8%

Source: *USA Today*, March 27, 2002, p. A1.

Managerial Roles

Research suggests that managers must, from time to time, act in ten different roles if they are to be successful.[13] (By *role*, we mean a set of expectations that one must fulfill.) These ten roles can be grouped into three broad categories: decisional, interpersonal, and informational.

Decisional Roles As you might suspect, a **decisional role** is one that involves various aspects of management decision making. The decisional role can be subdivided into the following four specific managerial roles. In the role of *entrepreneur*, the manager is the voluntary initiator of change. For example, the CEO of DuPont decided to put more financial resources into its Experimental Station, a large R&D center, in order to create more new products. This entrepreneurial emphasis on R&D led to the creation of Sorona, a synthetic fiber similar to polyester that could be used for clothing, car upholstery, and carpeting. DuPont hopes that these decisions will pay great dividends in the long run.[14] A second role is that of *disturbance handler*. A manager who settles a strike is handling a disturbance. Third, the manager also occasionally plays the role of *resource allocator*. In this role, the manager might have to decide which departmental budgets to cut and which expenditure requests to approve. The fourth role is that of *negotiator*. Being a negotiator might involve settling a dispute between a manager and a worker assigned to the manager's work group.

decisional role a role that involves various aspects of management decision making

Interpersonal Roles Dealing with people is an integral part of the manager's job. An **interpersonal role** is one in which the manager deals with people. Like the decisional role, the interpersonal role can be broken down according to three managerial functions. The manager may be called on to serve as a *figurehead*, perhaps by attending a ribbon-cutting ceremony or taking an important client to dinner. The manager also may have to play the role of *liaison* by serving as a go-between for two different groups. As a liaison, a manager might represent his or her firm at meetings of an industry-wide trade organization. Finally, the manager often has to serve as a *leader*. Playing the role of leader includes being an example for others in the organization as well as developing the skills, abilities, and motivation of employees.

interpersonal role a role in which the manager deals with people

Informational Roles An **informational role** is one in which the manager either gathers or provides information. The informational role can be subdivided as follows: In the role of *monitor*, the manager actively seeks information that may be of value to the organization. For example, a manager who hears about a good business opportunity is engaging in the role of monitor. The second informational role is that of *disseminator*. In this role, the manager transmits key information to those who can use it. As a disseminator, the manager who heard about a good business opportunity would tell the appropriate marketing manager about it. The third informational role is that of *spokesperson*. In this role, the manager provides information to people outside the organization, such as the press, television reporters, and the public.

informational role a role in which the manager either gathers or provides information

Leadership

learning objective

5 Explain the different types of leadership.

leadership the ability to influence others

Leadership has been broadly defined as the ability to influence others. A leader has power and can use it to affect the behavior of others. Leadership is different from management in that a leader strives for voluntary cooperation, whereas a manager may have to depend on coercion to change employee behavior.

Formal and Informal Leadership

Some experts make a distinction between formal leadership and informal leadership. Formal leaders have legitimate power of position; that is, they have *authority* within an organization to influence others to work for the organization's objectives. Informal leaders usually have no such authority and may or may not exert their influence in support of the organization. Both formal and informal leaders make use of several kinds of power, including the ability to grant rewards or impose punishments, the possession of expert knowledge, and personal attraction or charisma. Informal leaders who identify with the organization's goals are a valuable asset to any organization. On the other hand, a business can be brought to its knees by informal leaders who turn work groups against management.

Styles of Leadership

For many years, leadership was viewed as a combination of personality traits, such as self-confidence, concern for people, intelligence, and dependability. Achieving a consensus on which traits were most important was difficult, however, and attention

adapting to change

What Makes a Great Leader?

IN TODAY'S FAST-CHANGING business environment, where new competitors can become instant threats and research breakthroughs can present immediate opportunities, companies need more than good management—they need great leaders. But what, exactly, makes a great leader?

Great leaders know how to communicate, an especially critical skill during tumultuous times. Although great leaders clearly articulate the organization's goals and strategies, they really earn the leadership mantle by connecting with people on an emotional level. In effect, great leaders provide the glue that binds an organization together. For example, after the terrorist attacks on the World Trade Center and the Pentagon, Pfizer's CEO announced a huge donation of medical supplies for the relief effort and sent frequent updates to keep the entire work force informed. The CEO's sensitive communications set an example for other Pfizer managers. "It made me feel inspired," remembers one vice president, "and showed the way for how to lead my own people."

Great leaders are also visionaries. By inspiring their employees to work toward a clear and compelling vision of the company's future, leaders create an excitement to achieve. Consider Richard Branson, whose vision of transforming the Virgin brand into a global powerhouse has energized employees and managers alike at the London-based Virgin Group. Traveling the world to visit company sites, Branson never misses a chance to reinforce this vision—and his enthusiasm spurs employees to even higher performance.

Great leaders welcome input. Whether a good idea comes from a senior executive or a new employee, a great leader wins loyalty and builds consensus by remaining open to different ideas and viewpoints. In the end, however, it is the leader who ultimately must make the tough decisions. "There will always be persuasive reasons not to take a risk," observes Professor Clayton Christensen of the Harvard Business School. "But if you only do what worked in the past, you will wake up one day and find that you've been passed by." Great leaders weigh the risks and the input and then make the many decisions, large and small, that keep their organizations moving ahead in the face of change.

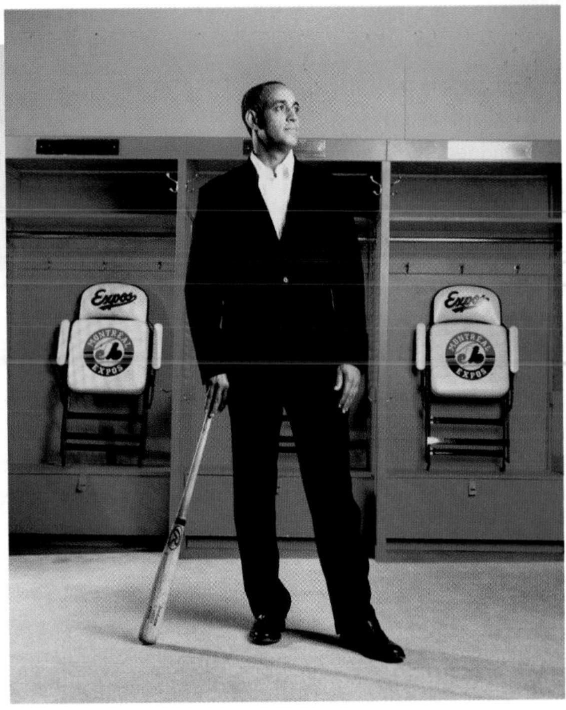

A highly effective leader joins the major league. When Omar Minaya became the general manager of the Montreal Expos baseball team, the team had averaged 95 losses per year over the previous three years. Through Minaya's highly effective leadership, the Expos have totally turned around and have become a highly competitive, successful organization.

turned to styles of leadership behavior. In the last few decades, several styles of leadership have been identified: authoritarian, laissez-faire, and democratic.[15] The **authoritarian leader** holds all authority and responsibility, with communication usually moving from top to bottom. This leader assigns workers to specific tasks and expects orderly, precise results. The leaders at United Parcel Service employ authoritarian leadership. At the other extreme is the **laissez-faire leader**, who gives authority to employees. With the laissez-faire style, subordinates are allowed to work as they choose with a minimum of interference. Communication flows horizontally among group members. Leaders at Apple Computer are known to employ a laissez-faire leadership style in order to give employees as much freedom as possible to develop new products. The **democratic leader** holds final responsibility but also delegates authority to others, who participate in determining work assignments. In this leadership style, communication is active both upward and downward. Employee commitment is high because of participation in the decision-making process. Managers for both Wal-Mart and Saturn have used the democratic leadership style to encourage employees to become more than just rank-and-file workers.

authoritarian leader one who holds all authority and responsibility, with communication usually moving from top to bottom

laissez-faire leader one who gives authority to employees and allows subordinates to work as they choose with a minimum of interference; communication flows horizontally among group members

democratic leader one who holds final responsibility but also delegates authority to others, who help determine work assignments; communication is active upward and downward

Which Managerial Leadership Style Is Best?

Today, most management experts agree that no one "best" managerial leadership style exists. Each of the styles described earlier—authoritarian, laissez faire, and democratic—has advantages and disadvantages. For example, democratic leadership can motivate employees to work effectively because they are implementing *their own* decisions. On the other hand, the decision-making process associated with democratic leadership takes time that subordinates could otherwise be devoting to the work itself.

Although hundreds of research studies have been conducted to prove which leadership style is best, there are still no definite conclusions. The "best" leadership seems to occur when the leader's style matches the situation. Actually, each of the three leadership styles can be effective in the right situation. The style that is *most* effective depends on the interaction among the employees, the characteristics of the work situation, and the manager's personality.

Managerial Decision Making

learning objective

6 Discuss the steps in the managerial decision-making process.

Decision making is the act of choosing one alternative from among a set of alternatives.[16] In ordinary, everyday situations, our decisions are made casually and informally. We encounter a problem, mull it over for a way out, settle on a likely solution, and go on. Managers, however, require a more systematic method for solving complex problems in a variety of situations. As shown in Figure 7.6 (on p. 210), managerial decision making involves four steps: (1) identifying the problem or opportunity, (2) generating alternatives, (3) selecting an alternative, and (4) implementing and evaluating the solution.

decision making the act of choosing one alternative from among a set of alternatives

figure 7.6

Major Steps in the Managerial Decision-Making Process

Managers require a systematic method for solving problems in a variety of situations.

Identifying the problem or opportunity → Generating alternatives → Selecting an alternative → Implementing and evaluating the solution

Identifying the Problem or Opportunity

problem the discrepancy between an actual condition and a desired condition

A **problem** is the discrepancy between an actual condition and a desired condition—the difference between what is occurring and what one wishes would occur. For example, a marketing manager at Campbell Soup Company has a problem if sales revenues for Campbell's Hungry Man frozen dinners are declining (the actual condition). To solve this problem, the marketing manager must take steps to increase sales revenues (desired condition). Most people consider a problem to be "negative"; however, a problem also can be "positive." A positive problem should be viewed as an "opportunity."

Although accurate identification of a problem is essential before the problem can be solved or turned into an opportunity, this stage of decision making creates many difficulties for managers. Sometimes managers' preconceptions of the problem prevent them from seeing the situation as it actually is. They produce an answer before

exploring business

Making Decisions Under Pressure

LIKE A FIREFIGHTER BATTLING A BLAZE or a military officer on a battlefield, you will have to make at least some decisions under pressure during your business career. Facing an unyielding deadline, you may have inadequate or even contradictory information about the problem, the alternatives, and the potential consequences of each option. Although most decisions will not be make-or-break decisions for your organization, you need to know how to make a decision when the heat is on.

When confronting a new problem, carefully examine the clues to tease out a pattern. If the pattern reminds you of a problem you resolved previously by following preset rules, you should be able to apply the appropriate rule (or a reasonable variation) to make a decision. A bank officer, for example, might use a modified version of the bank's debt-to-income guidelines to decide whether to approve or reject an unusual loan application.

If the problem seems more complicated, try to systematically and logically analyze the clues as well as the possible alternatives and outcomes. A manager facing customer complaints about service could, for example, diagram the company's service procedure as well as its competitors' procedures. This may bring out discrepancies or other hints to follow up in generating alternatives and making a decision.

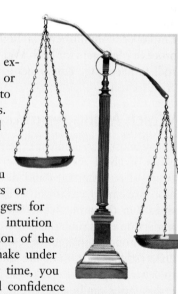

If the problem is extremely unpredictable or complex, be prepared to rely on your instincts. Keep an open mind and mull over the patterns you see emerging from whatever information you can gather. Ask experts or more experienced managers for input. Then let your intuition point you in the direction of the best decision you can make under the circumstances. Over time, you will gain experience and confidence that reinforce your intuition in such situations.

Tom Prichard, vice president for marketing at the educational toy company Leapfrog, does this when making decisions about new toys. When he and his staff instinctively believe a product will do well, they often push ahead even if their research does not entirely support the decision. "Other companies might walk away," Prichard says. "When we've got a great feeling about a product, we don't walk away." Intuition-based decisions have helped make Leapfrog's toys big hits with parents and children alike.

the proper question has ever been asked. In other cases, managers overlook truly significant issues by focusing on unimportant matters. Also, managers may mistakenly analyze problems in terms of symptoms rather than underlying causes. Sega, a player in the video game industry, faced a major problem as its Dreamcast game system drained the company's financial resources while trying to compete with Sony's PlayStation 2, Microsoft's X-box, and Nintendo's latest game machine. Managers evaluated this problem and decided to cut the company's losses and focus on producing games to be played on its competitors' systems. Sega continues to pursue this games-only opportunity against tough competitors such as Electronic Arts, Inc.[17]

Effective managers learn to look ahead so that they are prepared when decisions must be made. They clarify situations and examine the causes of problems, asking whether the presence or absence of certain variables alters a given situation. Finally, they consider how individual behaviors and values affect the way problems or opportunities are defined.

Generating Alternatives

After a problem has been suitably defined, the next task is to generate alternatives. Generally, the more important the decision, the more attention is devoted to this stage. Managers should be open to fresh, innovative ideas as well as to more obvious answers.

Certain techniques can aid in the generation of creative alternatives. Brainstorming, commonly used in group discussions, encourages participants to come up with as many new ideas as possible, no matter how outrageous. Other group members are not permitted to criticize or ridicule. Another approach to generating alternatives, developed by the U.S. Navy, is called "Blast! Then Refine." Group members tackle a recurring problem afresh, erasing from their minds all solutions and procedures tried in the past. The group then re-evaluates its original objectives, modifies them if necessary, and devises new solutions to the problem. Other techniques—including trial and error—are also useful in this stage of decision making.

Selecting an Alternative

A final decision is influenced by a number of considerations, including financial constraints, human and informational resources, time limits, legal obstacles, and political factors. Managers must select the alternative that will be most effective and practical under the circumstances. At times, two or more alternatives or some combination of alternatives will be equally appropriate. After considering several alternatives to become more competitive, IBM management decided to outsource the manufacturing of more products such as personal computers and disk drives and most recently decided to outsource low-end servers to Sanmina-SCI. This latest move was part of IBM's shift toward a focus on software and services. IBM believes that these decisions will save IBM millions and make it more competitive in a dynamic industry.[18]

Managers may choose solutions to problems on several levels. The word "satisfice" has been coined to describe solutions that are only adequate and not the best possible. When they lack time or information, managers often make decisions that "satisfice," even though this is not the optimal approach in the long run. Whenever possible, managers should try to investigate alternatives carefully and select the one that best solves the problem.

Implementing and Evaluating the Solution

Implementation of a decision requires time, planning, preparation of personnel, and evaluation of the results. Managers usually must deal with unforeseen consequences as well, even when they have carefully considered the alternatives.

The final step in managerial decision making entails evaluating the effectiveness of a decision. If the alternative that was chosen removes the difference between the actual condition and the desired condition, the decision is judged effective. If the problem still exists, managers may

- Decide to give the chosen alternative more time to work.
- Adopt a different alternative.
- Start the problem identification process all over again.

Failure to evaluate decisions adequately may have negative consequences. When Mattel introduced Lingerie Barbie, for example, there were some negative reactions from parents and social critics, even though Mattel indicated that Lingerie Barbie was aimed only at adult Barbie collectors.[19]

Managing Total Quality

learning objective

7 Describe how organizations benefit from total quality management.

total quality management (TQM) the coordination of efforts directed at improving customer satisfaction, increasing employee participation, strengthening supplier partnerships, and facilitating an organizational atmosphere of continuous quality improvement

The management of quality is a high priority in some organizations today. Major reasons for a greater focus on quality include foreign competition, more demanding customers, and poor financial performance resulting from reduced market shares and higher costs. Over the last few years, several U.S. firms have lost the dominant competitive positions they had held for decades.

Total quality management is a much broader concept than just controlling the quality of the product itself (which is discussed in Chapter 9). **Total quality management (TQM)** is the coordination of efforts directed at improving customer satisfaction, increasing employee participation, strengthening supplier partnerships, and facilitating an organizational atmosphere of continuous quality improvement. For TQM programs to be effective, management must address each of the following components:

- *Customer satisfaction.* Ways to improve customer satisfaction include producing higher-quality products, providing better customer service, and showing customers that the company really cares about them.
- *Employee participation.* Employee participation can be increased by allowing employees to contribute to decisions, to develop self-managed work teams, and to assume responsibility and accountability for improving the quality of their work.
- *Strengthening supplier partnerships.* Developing good working relationships with suppliers can help to ensure that the right supplies and materials will be delivered on time at a lower cost.
- *Continuous quality improvement.* This should not be viewed as achievable through one single program that has a target objective. A program based on continuous improvement has proven to be the most effective long-term approach.

Although many factors influence the effectiveness of a TQM program, two issues are crucial. First, top management must make a strong commitment to a TQM program by treating quality improvement as a top priority and giving it frequent attention. Firms that establish a TQM program but then focus on other priorities will find that their quality-improvement initiatives will fail. Second, management must coordinate the specific elements of a TQM program so that they work in harmony with each other.

Although not all U.S. companies have TQM programs, these programs provide many benefits. Overall financial benefits include lower operating costs, higher return on sales and on investments, and an improved ability to use premium pricing rather than competitive pricing. Additional benefits include faster development of innovations, improved ability to compete in global markets, higher levels of customer retention, an enhanced reputation, and a more productive and better satisfied work force.

talking technology

How to Manage a Successful Tech Company

EFFECTIVE MANAGEMENT makes all the difference between a technology company that flourishes and one that falters. One key to success is knowing how to enlist the participation of the tech experts who handle such critical tasks as developing software. The CEO of the networking-software firm Novell stresses that management must clarify what needs to be done without trying to control how the techies should do it. "You need to give them a problem or a set of objectives, provide them with a large amount of hardware, and then ask them to solve the problem," he says. Using this approach, Novell has improved its competitive position and pushed annual sales beyond $1 billion.

A second key to success is pressing for continuous improvement. Managers in the fast-paced technology industry know that they cannot afford to stop innovating. Consider Cree, a $155-million firm that makes lighting products based on technical breakthroughs with light-emitting diodes. Thanks to heavy investments in R&D, Cree is always expanding its product line to better serve customers. Now 70 percent of Cree's annual sales come from products the firm developed during the previous year.

A third key is to be prepared to change on a moment's notice. New technology, changes in customer needs, and new competition can leave a company behind if management is not ready, willing, and able to adjust. Managers at Novell, for example, observed that businesses were increasingly dependent on a multitude of software applications. As a result, systems administrators had to track employee passwords for accessing more than one program at a time—a nightmare for fast-growing companies that hire large numbers of new employees. Novell saw a lucrative opportunity for selling software that allows systems administrators to generate passwords so that new employees can log in once and gain access to all needed programs.

In exploiting this opportunity, Novell's managers forged alliances with two consulting firms that help corporate customers tighten systems security. This illustrates the fourth key to success for managing a tech company: Partner whenever possible. Managers at Novell and other tech firms work hard to develop mutually beneficial long-term relationships with suppliers, distributors, and other partners. Instead of going it alone, Novell can call on the support of its partner network when tackling new opportunities and challenges.

What It Takes to Become a Successful Manager Today

learning objective

8 Summarize what it takes to become a successful manager today.

Everyone hears stories about the corporate elite who make salaries in excess of $1 million a year, travel to and from work in chauffeur-driven limousines, and enjoy lucrative pension plans that provide for a luxurious lifestyle even after they retire. Although management obviously can be a very rewarding career, what is not so obvious is the amount of time and hard work that managers invest to achieve the impressive salaries and perks that may come with the job.

A Day in the Life of a Manager

Organizations do not pay managers to look good behind expensive wooden desks. Organizations pay for performance. As we already pointed out in this chapter, managers coordinate an organization's resources. They also perform the four basic management functions: planning, organizing, leading and motivating, and controlling. And managers make decisions and then implement and evaluate those decisions. This heavy workload requires that managers work long hours, and most do not get paid overtime for work in excess of forty hours a week. Typically, the number of hours increases as managers move up the corporate ladder.

Make no mistake about it: Today's managers work hard in tough, demanding jobs. The pace is hectic. Managers spend a great deal of time talking with people on an individual basis. The purpose of these conversations is usually to obtain information or to resolve problems. (Remember, a problem can be either negative or positive and is a discrepancy between an actual condition and a desired condition.) In addition to talking with individuals, a manager often spends a large part of the workday in meetings with other managers and employees. In most cases, the purpose of the meetings—some brief and some lengthy—is to resolve problems. And if the work is not completed by the end of the day, the manager usually packs unfinished tasks in a briefcase and totes them home to work on that night.

Personal Skills Required for Success

To be successful in today's competitive business environment, you must possess a number of different skills. Some of these skills—technical, conceptual, and interpersonal skills—were discussed earlier in this chapter. However, you also need to develop some "personal" skills in order to be successful. For starters, oral and written communication skills, computer skills, and critical-thinking skills may give you the edge in getting an entry-level management position.

- *Oral communication skills.* Because a large part of a manager's day is spent conversing with other managers and employees, the ability to speak *and* listen is critical for success. For example, oral communication skills are used when a manager must make sales presentations, conduct interviews, perform employee evaluations, and hold press conferences.
- *Written communication skills.* Managers must be able to write. The manager's ability to prepare letters, e-mails, memos, sales reports, and other written documents may spell the difference between success and failure.
- *Computer skills.* Today, many managers have a computer at their fingertips. Most employers do not expect you to be an expert computer programmer, but they do expect that you should know how to use a computer to prepare written and statistical reports and to communicate with other managers and employees in the organization.
- *Critical-thinking skills.* Employers expect managers to use the steps for effective managerial decision making that were described earlier in this chapter. They also expect managers to use their critical-thinking skills to ensure that they identify the problem correctly, generate reasonable alternatives, and select the "best" alternative to solve an organization's problem.

The Importance of Education and Experience

Although most experts agree that management skills must be learned on the job, the concepts that you learn in business courses lay the foundation for a successful career. In addition, successful completion of college courses or obtaining a degree can open doors to job interviews and career advancement.

Most applicants who enter the world of work do not have a wealth of work experience. And yet there are methods that you can use to "beef up" your résumé and to capitalize on the work experience you do have. First, obtain summer jobs that will provide opportunities to learn about the field you wish to enter when you finish your formal education. If you choose carefully, part-time jobs during the school year also can provide work experience that other job applicants may not have. (By the way, some colleges and universities sponsor cooperative work/school programs that give students college credit for job experience.) Even with a solid academic background and relevant work experience, many would-be managers still find it difficult to land the "right" job. Often they start in an entry-level position to gain more experience and eventually—after years on the job—reach that "ideal" job. Perseverance does pay!

Using the Internet

There is a tremendous amount of information available through innumerable sources today. As managers face growing demands on their time, CEOExpress **(http://www.ceoexpress.com)** aims to help managers work more productively by organizing the best resources on the web. The site filters and organizes content, presents links to valuable sites, and has added conveniences such as stock quotes, headline news, and customization.

Education counts. Having a significant amount of education and training will help most individuals advance to and be successful in managerial roles. These students are learning how to manage their own businesses at the Entrepreneurial School of Business at Clarkson University.

We include this practical advice not to frighten you but to provide a real-world view of what a manager's job is like. Once you know what is required of managers today—and how competitive the race is for the top jobs—you can decide whether a career in management is right for you.

In the next chapter we examine the organizing function of managers in some detail. We look specifically at various organizational forms that today's successful businesses use. Like many factors in management, how a business is organized depends on its goals, strategies, and personnel.

Return To inside business

Thanks to careful planning, organizing, leading, and controlling, Yahoo! has evolved beyond a simple list of websites to become one of the Internet's premier destinations. Although naysayers worried that CEO Terry Semel would drive people away by charging for some Yahoo! services, paying customers continue flocking to the company's game sites, match-making ads, and other subscription services. "Our objective is to provide our content on as many desktops as possible and get paid for it," explains a Yahoo! executive. This would give Yahoo! a more stable balance of advertising revenues and service fees and make the company less vulnerable to economic downturns and other uncontrollable forces.

Semel believes that Yahoo! must continue evolving to keep growing and generating profits. Although the company prospered early on by trying new things without a definite plan, the CEO notes that "times change; companies change. The company had to diversify and in order to diversify—to start building business—you have to have focus." Not only has Semel brought focus, he has brought a vivid vision of what Yahoo! can achieve: "We have a superb opportunity to be number one," the CEO states.

Questions

1. Which of the basic management functions are co-founders Filo and Yang emphasizing? Which functions are CEO Semel emphasizing?
2. Why is leadership especially important for a business such as Yahoo! that operates in a fast-changing technological industry?

Summary

Define what management is.

Management is the process of coordinating people and other resources to achieve the goals of the organization. Managers are concerned with four types of resources—material, human, financial, and informational.

Describe the four basic management functions: planning, organizing, leading and motivating, and controlling.

Managers perform four basic functions. Management functions do not occur according to some rigid, preset timetable, though. At any time, managers may engage in a number of functions simultaneously. However, each function tends to lead naturally to others. First, managers engage in planning—determining where the firm should be going and how best to get there. Three types of plans, from the broadest to the most specific, are strategies, tactical plans, and operational plans. Managers also organize resources and activities to accomplish results in an efficient and effective manner, and they lead and motivate others to work in the best interests of the organization. In addition, managers control ongoing activities to keep the organization on course. There are three steps in the control function: setting standards, measuring actual performance, and taking corrective action.

Distinguish among the various kinds of managers, in terms of both level and area of management.

Managers—or management positions—may be classified from two different perspectives. From the perspective of level within the organization, there are top managers, who control the fortunes of the organization; middle managers, who implement strategies and major policies; and first-line managers, who supervise the activities of operating employees. From the viewpoint of area of management, managers most often deal with the areas of finance, operations, marketing, human resources, and administration.

Identify the key management skills and the managerial roles.

Effective managers tend to possess a specific set of skills and to fill three basic managerial roles. Technical, conceptual, and interpersonal skills are all important, although the relative importance of each varies with the level of management within the organization. The primary managerial roles can be classified as decisional, interpersonal, or informational.

Explain the different types of leadership.

Managers' effectiveness often depends on their styles of leadership—that is, their ability to influence others, either formally or informally. Leadership styles include the authoritarian "do-it-my-way" style, the laissez-faire "do-it-your-way" style, and the democratic "let's-do-it-together" style.

Discuss the steps in the managerial decision-making process.

Decision making, an integral part of a manager's work, is the process of developing a set of possible alternative solutions to a problem and choosing one alternative from among the set. Managerial decision making involves four steps: Managers must accurately identify problems, generate several possible solutions, choose the solution that will be most effective under the circumstances, and implement and evaluate the chosen course of action.

Describe how organizations benefit from total quality management.

Total quality management (TQM) is the coordination of efforts directed at improving customer satisfaction, increasing employee participation, strengthening supplier partnerships, and facilitating an organizational atmosphere of continuous quality improvement. To have an effective TQM program, top management must make a strong, sustained commitment to the effort and must be able to coordinate all the program's elements so that they work in harmony. Overall financial benefits of TQM include lower operating costs, higher return on sales and investment, and an improved ability to use premium pricing rather than competitive pricing.

Summarize what it takes to become a successful manager today.

Organizations pay managers for their performance. Managers coordinate resources. They also plan, organize, lead, motivate, and control. They make decisions that can spell the difference between an organization's success and failure. To complete their tasks, managers work long hours at a hectic pace. To be successful, they need personal skills (oral and written communication skills, computer skills, and critical-thinking skills), an academic background that provides a foundation for a management career, and practical work experience.

Key Terms

You should now be able to define and give an example relevant to each of the following terms:

management (198)
planning (200)
mission (200)
strategic planning (200)
goal (200)
objective (200)
plan (201)
strategy (201)
tactical plan (201)
operational plan (201)
contingency plan (201)
organizing (202)
leading (202)
motivating (202)
directing (202)
controlling (202)
top manager (204)
middle manager (204)
first-line manager (204)
financial manager (205)
operations manager (205)
marketing manager (205)
human resources manager (205)
administrative manager (206)
technical skill (206)
conceptual skill (206)
interpersonal skill (206)
decisional role (207)
interpersonal role (207)
informational role (207)
leadership (208)
authoritarian leader (209)
laissez-faire leader (209)
democratic leader (209)
decision making (209)
problem (210)
total quality management (TQM) (212)

Review Questions

1. Define the term *manager* without using the word *management* in your definition.
2. What is the mission of a neighborhood restaurant? Of the Salvation Army? What might be reasonable objectives for these organizations?
3. What does the term *optimization* mean?
4. How do a strategy, a tactical plan, and an operational plan differ? What do they all have in common?
5. What exactly does a manager organize, and for what reason?
6. Why are leadership and motivation necessary in a business in which people are paid for their work?
7. Explain the steps involved in the control function.
8. How are the two perspectives on kinds of managers—that is, level and area—different from each other?
9. In what ways are management skills related to the roles managers play? Provide a specific example to support your answer.
10. Compare and contrast the major styles of leadership.
11. Discuss what happens during each of the four steps of the managerial decision-making process.
12. What are the major benefits of a total quality management program?
13. What personal skills should a manager possess in order to be successful?

Discussion Questions

1. Does a healthy firm (one that is doing well) have to worry about effective management? Explain.
2. Which of the management functions, skills, and roles do not apply to the owner-operator of a sole proprietorship?
3. Which leadership style might be best suited to each of the three general levels of management within an organization?
4. According to this chapter, the leadership style that is *most* effective depends on the interaction among the employees, the characteristics of the work situation, and the manager's personality. Do you agree or disagree? Explain your answer.
5. Do you think that people are really as important to an organization as this chapter seems to indicate?
6. As you learned in this chapter, managers often work long hours at a hectic pace. Would this type of career appeal to you? Explain your answer.

video case

VIPdesk Is at Your Service

Need restaurant reservations, home repairs, sports tickets, or a perfect gift for someone special? VIPdesk's expert team of concierges is on call at any hour of the day to help customers and employees of the companies it serves. CEO Mary Naylor created the company based on her years of experience providing on-site concierge services for the employees of corporations in major office complexes around metropolitan Washington, D.C. Recognizing the opportunity to cost-effectively serve a wider corporate customer base through the Internet, Naylor established her first concierge website in 1996 and then upgraded it to VIPdesk in 2000.

Today, VIPdesk handles concierge services for more than ten million users, and it is the leading provider of "live" web-based concierge services. Companies such as Van Kampen offer VIPdesk's services as a reward to outstanding employees. In addition, corporate clients such as MasterCard, Citibank, and Diner's Club offer VIPdesk's concierge services to select customers all over the United States.

When Naylor was planning VIPdesk, she knew that she might not get all the investment funding she needed to expand rapidly in the early years. Therefore, she developed several strategic plans with a range of goals and objectives, tactics, budgets, and performance measures. In fact, she received only one-third of the funding she originally wanted, so she implemented a slower-growth plan that required lower technology and marketing spending.

Naylor launched VIPdesk with six corporate customers and twenty-five managers and employees. As the business grew, she hired more employees to serve as concierges. Some worked in the Oregon call center; others worked from home on a part-time basis during periods of peak demand. These part-timers brought an in-depth knowledge of local resources they could tap to satisfy requests from users in their area, adding another dimension to the service. Over time, corporate customers began asking VIPdesk to coordinate additional services, such as travel rewards for their employees. Also, through customer surveys, Naylor and her managers identified new opportunities for increasing usage of VIPdesk's services. Soon the CEO hired a chief strategy officer with the conceptual skills to prepare long-term plans.

Interpersonal skills are extremely important for Naylor and other entrepreneurs because they personally deal with investors, employees, customers, suppliers, and many other people in the course of the working day. Although Naylor relies on skilled specialists to maintain the company's website and handle all other technical tasks, she has the vision to understand what technology can do for her business. This is why she offers access to her concierge services in many ways. Users who prefer to surf the web can log onto the VIPdesk site for information, to initiate a live text chat with a concierge, or to send e-mail messages requesting assistance. If they prefer, users can call a toll-free number for service, access customized information via web-enabled cell phones, or contact a concierge via a handheld computer such as a Palm.

No matter how users reach VIPdesk or what they request, they receive fast, free, professional help. Among the most common requests are help with travel arrangements, auto rentals, last-minute theater and sports tickets, personal shopping, and other errands. "In effect, what we provide to the customer is a virtual personal assistant," says the CEO.

Naylor works closely with her managers to plan for staffing when VIPdesk gets ready to sign a new corporate customer. First, they look at the number of users who will be covered under the contract. "Then we can look at how much usage we expect or how many requests will be placed from a population of a given size," she adds. Based on this information, she and her managers determine how many concierges might be needed to accommodate all the requests. Estimating the staffing level also helps management price services for new customers.

Competition is increasing all the time, but VIPdesk offers banks a reasonably priced way to reward people for carrying their credit cards. "It can cost less than a key chain or some token item that a corporation may give as a gift to a customer," Naylor observes. With so many banks trying to woo and win cardholders, VIPdesk should have a bright future ahead.[20]

Questions

1. At what management level would you expect a chief strategy officer to be positioned in VIPdesk's hierarchy?
2. Why would operations managers be particularly important in a business such as VIPdesk?
3. Based on what you know about VIPdesk, identify one potential threat for which you believe Naylor should have a contingency plan. Explain your answer.

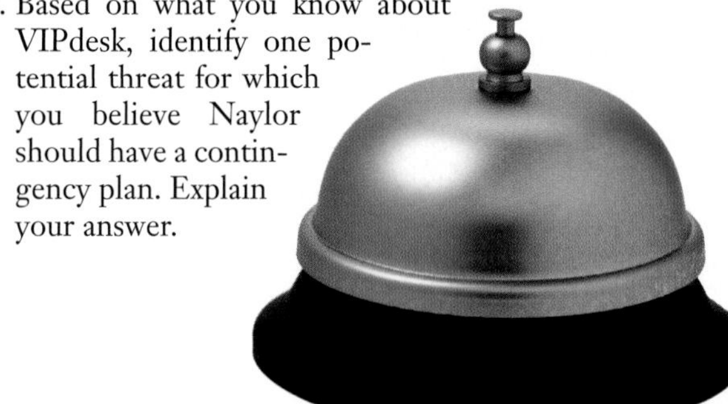

Building Skills for Career Success

1. Exploring the Internet

Most large companies at one time or another call on a management consulting firm for a variety of services, including employee training, help in the selection of an expensive purchase such as a computer system, recruitment of employees, and direction in reorganization and strategic planning.

Large consulting firms generally operate in the global marketplace and can provide information and assistance to companies considering entry into foreign countries or business alliances with foreign firms. They use their web pages, along with magazine-style articles, to celebrate their achievements and to present their credentials to clients. The business student can acquire an enormous amount of up-to-date information in the field of management by perusing these sites.

Assignment

1. Explore each of the following websites:

   Accenture: **http://www.accenture.com**

   BearingPoint (formerly KPMG Consulting): **http://www.bearingpoint.com**

   Cap Gemini Ernst & Young: **http://www.cgey.com**

   (Visit the text website for updates to this exercise.)
2. Judging from the articles and notices posted, what are the current areas of activities of one of these firms?
3. Explore one of these areas in more detail by comparing postings from each firm's site. For instance, if "global business opportunities" appears to be a popular area of management consulting, how has each firm distinguished itself in this area? Who would you call first for advice?
4. Given that consulting firms are always trying to fill positions for their clients and to meet their own recruitment needs, it is little wonder employment postings are a popular area on their sites. Examine these in detail. Based on your examination of the site and the registration format, what sort of recruit are they interested in?

2. Developing Critical Thinking Skills

As defined in the chapter, an organization's mission is a statement of the basic purpose that makes the organization different from others. Clearly, a mission statement, by indicating the purpose of a business, directly affects the company's employees, customers, and stockholders.

Assignment

1. Find the mission statements of three large corporations in different industries. The Internet is one source of mission statements. For example, you might search these sites:

   http://www.kodak.com

   http://www.benjerry.com

   http://www.usaa.com
2. Compare the mission statements on the basis of what each reflects about the philosophy of the company and its concern for employees, customers, and stockholders.
3. Which company would you like to work for and why?
4. Prepare a report on your findings.

3. Building Team Skills

Over the past few years, an increasing number of employees, stockholders, and customers have been demanding to know what their companies are about. As a result, more companies have been taking the time to analyze their operations and to prepare mission statements that focus on the purpose of the company. The mission statement is becoming a critical planning tool for successful companies. To make effective decisions, employees must understand the purpose of their company.

Assignment

1. Divide into teams and write a mission statement for one of the following types of businesses:

   Food service, restaurant
   Banking
   Airline
   Auto repair
   Cabinet manufacturing
2. Discuss your mission statement with other teams. How did the other teams interpret the purpose of your company? What is the mission statement saying about the company?
3. Write a one-page report on what you learned about developing mission statements.

4. Researching Different Careers

A successful career requires planning. Without a plan, or roadmap, you will find it very difficult, if not impossible, to reach your desired career destination. The first step in planning is to establish what your career goal is. You must then set objectives and develop plans for accomplishing those objectives. This kind of planning takes time, but it will pay off later.

Assignment

Complete the following statements:

1. My career goal is to __________________________.
   This statement should encapsulate what you want to accomplish over the long run. It may include the type of job you want and the type of business or industry you want to work in. Examples include
   - My career goal is to work as a top manager in the food industry.
   - My career goal is to supervise aircraft mechanics.
   - My career goal is to win the top achievement award in the advertising industry.
2. My career objectives are to ______________________.
   Objectives are benchmarks along the route to a career destination. They are more specific than a career goal. A statement about a career objective should specify what you want to accomplish, when you will complete it, and any other details that will serve as criteria against which you can measure your progress. Examples include
   - My objective is to be promoted to supervisor by January 1, 20xx.
   - My objective is to enroll in a management course at Main College in the spring semester 20xx.
   - My objective is to earn an A in the management course at Main College in the spring semester 20xx.
   - My objective is to prepare a status report by September 30 covering the last quarter's activities by asking Charlie in Quality Control to teach me the procedures.
3. Exchange your goal and objectives statements with another class member. Can your partner interpret your

objectives correctly? Are the objectives concise and complete? Do they include criteria against which you can measure your progress? If not, discuss the problem and rewrite the objective.

5. Improving Communication Skills

Being an efficient, productive employee in the workplace today requires certain personal and managerial skills. Without proficiency in these skills, promotions and other rewards are unlikely to be forthcoming. To be competitive, employees must periodically assess their skill levels and, when necessary, work to improve them. How do your personal and managerial skills measure up?

Assignment

1. Rate yourself and have at least two other people rate you on the skills listed in the following table.
2. Prepare a plan for improving your weak areas. The plan should specify exactly how, where, and by when you will accomplish your goal. It also should include criteria for measuring your level of improvement.

Skills Assessment

	Below average	**Average**	**Above average**	**Specific examples**
Personal skills				
Oral communication skills				
Written communication skills				
Computer skills				
Critical-thinking skills				
Managerial skills				
Conceptual skills				
Technical skills				
Interpersonal skills				
Decision-making skills				

chapter

8

Creating a Flexible Organization

Just as its customers' fashion and performance preferences change over time, so too must Nike's organization evolve.

learning objectives

1. Understand what an organization is and identify its characteristics.
2. Explain why job specialization is important.
3. Identify the various bases for departmentalization.
4. Explain how decentralization follows from delegation.
5. Understand how the span of management describes an organization.
6. Understand how the chain of command is established by using line and staff management.
7. Describe the four basic forms of organizational structure: bureaucratic, matrix, cluster, and network.
8. Summarize the use of corporate culture, intrapreneurship, committees, coordination techniques, informal groups, and the grapevine.

inside business

Nike Gets Organized

NIKE SELLS $10 billion worth of sports shoes and apparel every year, but it does not actually manufacture shoes. It employs numerous design specialists to develop dozens of new styles every year. It also keeps many specialists on the payroll to extensively research and creatively market its product lines. However, the company contracts with overseas factories to actually manufacture the products it designs and markets. This organizational structure has given Nike the flexibility to endure peaks and valleys in demand and profitability.

Still, just as its customers' fashion and performance preferences change over time, so too must Nike's organization continue to evolve. Its departments are structured mainly by type of product, such as soccer-related products and golf-related products. One of the newer departments, dubbed ACG for "all-conditions gear," was formed specifically to design and market clothing and footwear for participants in extreme sports such as snowboarding and skateboarding. Top management was eager for this unit to act more like a start-up rather than being constrained by Nike's traditional way of doing things. As a result, ACG's staff was housed in a building away from the other departments, and its managers were given the authority to put together a separate budget, organization chart, and marketing strategy. ACG also based more than a dozen designers in southern California, where they could observe the skateboarding culture at close range. As a result of these organizational steps, annual sales of ACG products are expected to increase by 20 percent per year.

In addition to organizing by product, Nike organizes some divisions according to customer. For example, the women's division is responsible for designing and marketing Nike products to women around the world—especially appropriate because the company is named for a Greek goddess. This division cuts across product lines, which makes it appealing for managers and employees who want to work on more than one type of product. Joining this division "was like having the blinders taken off," recalls one designer, who was enthusiastic about expanding beyond "always thinking just about running, or basketball, or soccer."

Another organizational change Nike made was to loosen top management's control on decision-making authority. For years, only very senior executives made all the important decisions. Now Nike allows certain teams drawn from different departments and different management levels to make decisions about broad new initiatives. This type of decentralization not only helps the company make decisions more quickly but also leads to more innovative strategies and sources of profitability. With Reebok, Adidas, and other competitors hot on Nike's heels, the company needs to stay nimble to sprint ahead in the global race for sales.[1]

To survive and to grow, companies like Nike must constantly look for ways to improve their methods of doing business. Managers at Nike, like those at many other organizations, deliberately reorganized the company to help it achieve its goals and objectives and to create satisfying products that will foster long-term customer relationships.

When firms are organized, or reorganized, the focus is sometimes on achieving low operating costs. In other cases, as in the case of Nike, the emphasis is on providing high-quality products to ensure customer satisfaction. The way a firm is organized influences its performance. Thus the issue of organization is important.

We begin this chapter by examining the business organization—what it is and how it functions in today's business environment. Next, we focus one by one on five characteristics that shape an organization's structure. We discuss job specialization within a company, the grouping of jobs into manageable units or departments, the delegation of power from management to workers, the span of management, and the establishment of a chain of command. Then we step back for an overall view of four approaches to organizational structure: the bureaucratic structure, the matrix structure, the cluster structure, and the network structure. Finally, we look at the network of social interactions—the informal organization—that operates within the formal business structure.

What Is an Organization?

learning objective

1 Understand what an organization is and identify its characteristics.

We used the term *organization* throughout Chapter 7 without really defining it mainly because its everyday meaning is close to its business meaning. Here, however, let us agree that an **organization** is a group of two or more people working together to achieve a common set of goals. A neighborhood dry cleaner owned and operated by a husband-and-wife team is an organization. IBM, Rubbermaid, and Home Depot, which employ thousands of workers worldwide, are also organizations in the very same sense. Although each corporation's organizational structure is vastly more complex than that of the dry-cleaning establishment, all must be organized if they are to achieve their goals.

organization a group of two or more people working together to achieve a common set of goals

Large and small organizations. All organizations—from small businesses like Michael Colca Furniture to large corporations like Xerox—must be organized to achieve their goals. Organization charts can help businesses to define positions and clarify reporting relationships.

figure 8.1

A Typical Corporate Organization Chart

A company's organization chart represents the positions and relationships within an organization and shows the managerial chains of command.

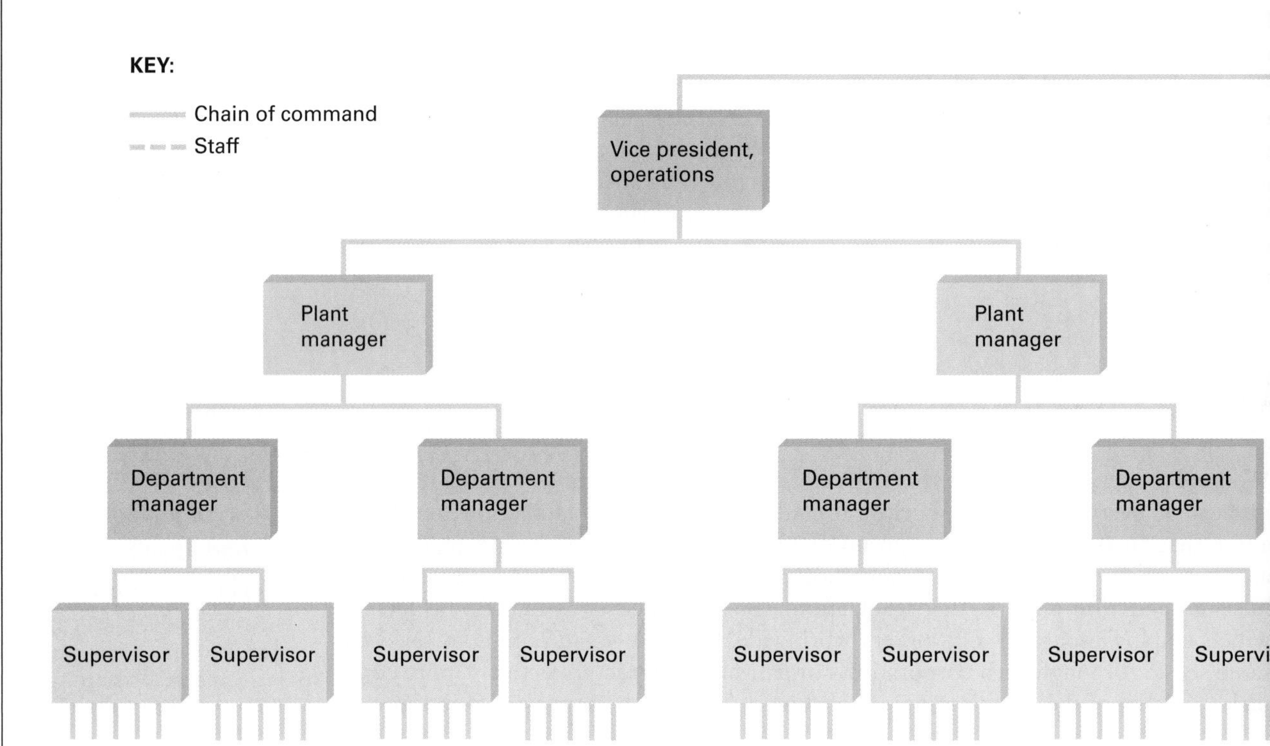

An inventor who goes into business to produce and market a new invention hires people, decides what each will do, determines who will report to whom, and so on. These activities are the essence of organizing, or creating, the organization. One way to create this "picture" is to create an organization chart.

Developing Organization Charts

organization chart a diagram that represents the positions and relationships within an organization

chain of command the line of authority that extends from the highest to the lowest levels of an organization

An **organization chart** is a diagram that represents the positions and relationships within an organization. An example of an organization chart is shown in Figure 8.1. What does it tell us? Each rectangle in the chart represents a particular position or person in the organization. At the top of the chart is the president; at the next level are the vice presidents. The solid vertical lines connecting the vice presidents to the president indicate that the vice presidents are in the chain of command. The **chain of command** is the line of authority that extends from the highest to the lowest levels of the organization. Moreover, each vice president reports directly to the president. Similarly, the plant managers, regional sales managers, and accounting department manager report directly to the vice presidents. The chain of command can be short or long. For example, at Royer's Roundtop Café, an independent restaurant in Roundtop, Texas, the chain of command is very short. Bud Royer, the owner, is responsible only to himself and can alter his hours or change his menu quickly. On the other hand, the chain of command at McDonald's is long. Before making certain types of changes,

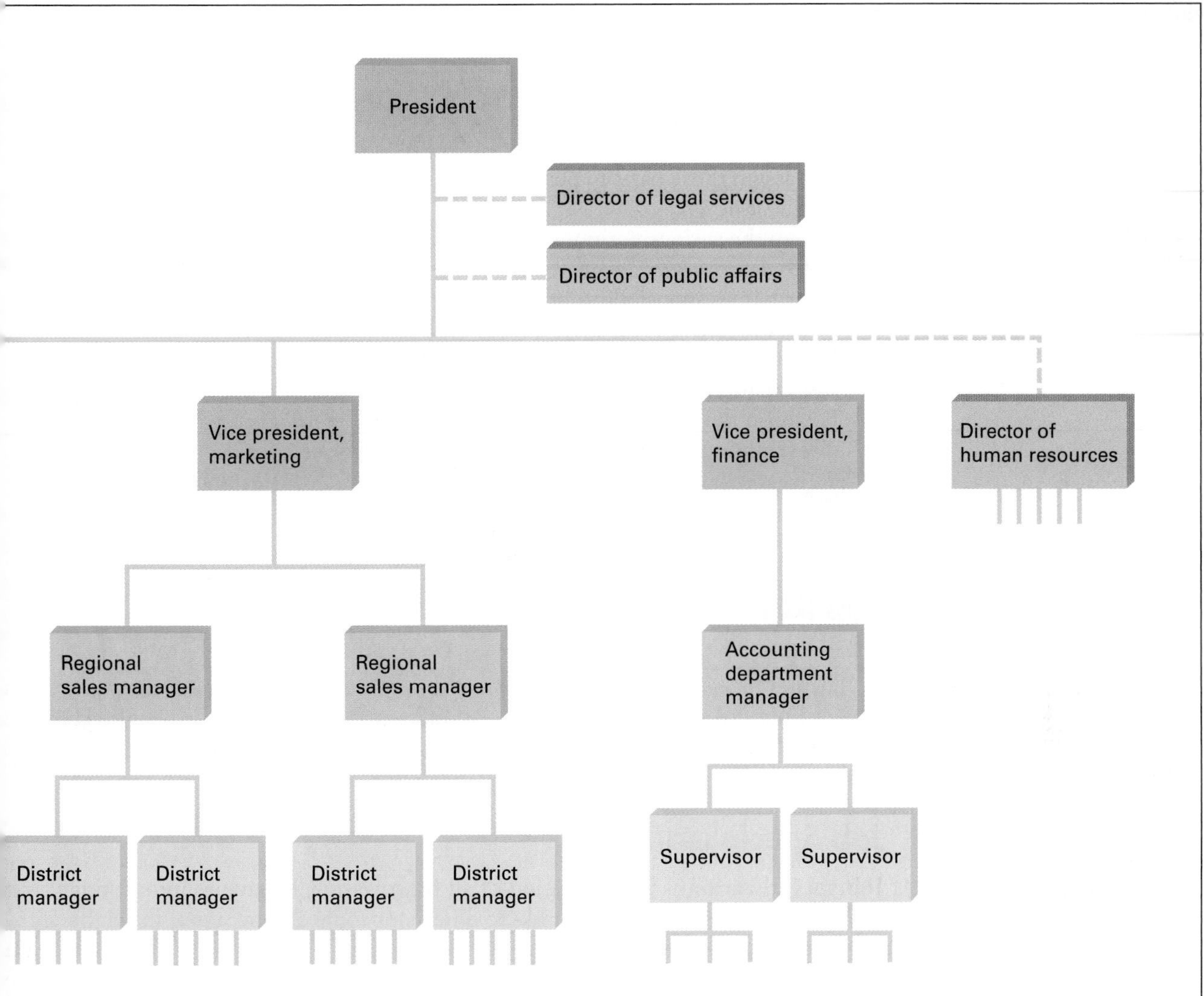

a McDonald's franchisee seeks permission from regional management, which, in turn, seeks approval from corporate headquarters.

Notice in the chart that the connections to the directors of legal services, public affairs, and human resources are shown as broken lines; these people are not part of the direct chain of command. Instead, they hold *advisory*, or *staff*, positions. This difference will be examined later in the chapter when we discuss line and staff positions.

Most smaller organizations find organization charts useful. They clarify positions and reporting relationships for everyone in the organization, and they help managers track growth and change in the organizational structure. For two reasons, however, many large organizations, such as ExxonMobil, Kellogg, and Procter & Gamble, do not maintain complete, detailed charts. First, it is difficult to accurately chart even a few dozen positions, much less the thousands that characterize larger firms. And second, larger organizations are almost always changing one part of their structure or another. An organization chart probably would be outdated before it was completed. However, organization must exist even if not in a formal chart in order for a business to be successful. 3M, the large, diversified company started in 1902, has about 75,000 employees and makes over 50,000 products and constantly works on developing more. 3M's organization chart was described recently as bewildering, which has caused financial analysts to complain about the difficulty of evaluating the company's performance. With a new CEO in place, changes are occurring, and now there is only one sales executive that handles large accounts such as Ford, Wal-Mart, and Procter & Gamble, whereas previously several different salespeople contacted the same customers due to a lack of internal organization.[2]

Five Steps for Organizing a Business

When a firm is started, management must decide how to organize the firm. These decisions are all part of five major steps that sum up the organizing process. The five steps are

1. Divide the work that is to be done by the entire organization into separate parts, and assign those parts to positions within the organization. This step is often called *job design*.
2. Group the various positions into manageable units, or departments. This step is called *departmentalization*.
3. Distribute responsibility and authority within the organization. This step is called *delegation*.
4. Determine the number of subordinates who will report to each manager. This step creates the firm's *span of management*.
5. Establish the organization's chain of command by designating the positions with direct authority and those that are support positions.

In the next several sections we discuss major issues associated with these steps.

Job Design

learning objective

2 Explain why job specialization is important.

In Chapter 1 we defined *specialization* as the separation of a manufacturing process into distinct tasks and the assignment of different tasks to different people. Here we are extending that concept to *all* the activities performed within an organization.

Job Specialization

job specialization the separation of all organizational activities into distinct tasks and the assignment of different tasks to different people

Job specialization is the separation of all organizational activities into distinct tasks and the assignment of different tasks to different people. Adam Smith, the eighteenth-century economist whose theories gave rise to capitalism, was the first to emphasize the power of specialization in his book *The Wealth of Nations*. According to Smith, the various tasks in a particular pin factory were arranged so that one worker drew the wire for the pins, another straightened the wire, a third cut it, a fourth ground the point, and a fifth attached the head. Using this method, Smith claimed, ten men were able to produce 48,000 pins per day. Before specialization, they could produce only 200 pins per day because each worker had to perform all five tasks!

Job specialization. Assembly line workers, such as the one at this GE refrigerator production facility, engage in job specialization, which in turn results in production efficiency.

The Rationale for Specialization

For a number of reasons, some job specialization is necessary in every organization. First and foremost is the simple fact that the "job" of most organizations is simply too large for one person to handle. In a firm such as Chrysler Corporation, thousands of people are needed to manufacture automobiles. Others are needed to sell the cars, to control the firm's finances, and so on.

Second, when a worker has to learn only a specific, highly specialized task, that individual should be able to learn to do it very efficiently. Third, the worker who is doing the same job over and over does not lose time changing from one operation to another, as the pin workers probably did when each was producing a complete pin. Fourth, the more specialized the job, the easier it may be to design specialized equipment for those who do it. And finally, the more specialized the job, the easier it is to train new employees when an employee quits or is absent from work.

Alternatives to Job Specialization

Unfortunately, specialization can have some negative consequences as well. The most significant drawback is the boredom and dissatisfaction many employees feel when they do the same job over and over. Monotony can be deadening. Bored employees may be absent from work frequently, may not put much effort into their work, and may even sabotage the company's efforts to produce quality products.

To combat these problems, managers often turn to job rotation. **Job rotation** is the systematic shifting of employees from one job to another. For example, a worker may be assigned to a different job every week for a four-week period and then return to the first job in the fifth week. The idea behind job rotation is to provide a variety of tasks so that workers are less likely to get bored and dissatisfied.

job rotation the systematic shifting of employees from one job to another

At Canadian Life, a life insurance company, job rotation is employed for senior management. Over 80 percent of senior managers are in different roles than they were four years ago. A spokesperson said that the company's job-rotation program is an essential part of the firm's positioning as a strong global competitor. Job rotation heightens employees' motivation and involvement, increases their career satisfaction and commitment to stay with a company, and gives them a better understanding of strategic issues.[3]

Two other approaches—job enlargement and job enrichment—also can provide solutions to the problems caused by job specialization. These topics, along with other methods used to motivate employees, are discussed in Chapter 11.

Departmentalization

learning objective

3 Identify the various bases for departmentalization.

After jobs are designed, they must be grouped together into "working units," or departments. This process is called *departmentalization.* More specifically, **departmentalization** is the process of grouping jobs into manageable units. Several departmentalization bases are commonly used. In fact, most firms use more than one. Today, the most common bases for organizing a business into effective departments are by function, by product, by location, and by type of customer.

departmentalization the process of grouping jobs into manageable units

By Function

Departmentalization by function groups jobs that relate to the same organizational activity. Under this scheme, all marketing personnel are grouped together in the marketing department, all production personnel in the production department, and so on.

departmentalization by function grouping jobs that relate to the same organizational activity

Most smaller and newer organizations base their departmentalization on function. Supervision is simplified because everyone is involved in the same kinds of activities, and coordination is fairly easy. The disadvantages of this method of grouping jobs are that it can lead to slow decision making and that it tends to emphasize the department rather than the organization as a whole.

By Product

departmentalization by product grouping activities related to a particular product or service

Departmentalization by product groups activities related to a particular good or service. This approach is used often by older and larger firms that produce and sell a variety of products. Each department handles its own marketing, production, financial management, and human resources activities.

Departmentalization by product makes decision making easier and provides for the integration of all activities associated with each product. However, it causes some duplication of specialized activities—such as finance—from department to department. And the emphasis is placed on the product rather than on the whole organization.

Microsoft frequently reorganizes its operations as technologies continue to change and expand. The latest business unit created by Microsoft is the Real Time Collaboration Group, which focuses on web-based conferencing and other types of communications products for businesses.[4]

By Location

departmentalization by location grouping activities according to the defined geographic area in which they are performed

Departmentalization by location groups activities according to the defined geographic area in which they are performed. Departmental areas may range from whole countries (for international firms) to regions within countries (for national firms) to areas of several city blocks (for police departments organized into precincts). Departmentalization by location allows the organization to respond readily to the unique demands or requirements of different locations. Nevertheless, a large administrative staff and an elaborate control system may be needed to coordinate operations in many locations.

By Customer

departmentalization by customer grouping activities according to the needs of various customer populations

Departmentalization by customer groups activities according to the needs of various customer populations. A local Chevrolet dealership, for example, may have one sales staff to deal with individual consumers and a different sales staff to work with corporate fleet buyers. The obvious advantage of this approach is that it allows the firm to deal efficiently with unique customers or customer groups. The biggest drawback is that a larger-than-usual administrative staff is needed.

Combinations of Bases

Many organizations use more than one of these departmentalization bases. For example, Hewlett Packard recently reorganized its operation prior to its acquisition of Compaq. The well-known CEO, Carly Fiorina, developed what she called "four quadrants." These four quadrants represent a combination of bases for departmentalization. Two sales and marketing groups are divided by customer, one for the mass market and one for large corporate clients, and two manufacturing and research groups are organized by product, with a division for computers and one for printing and imaging.[5]

Take a moment to examine Figure 8.2. Notice that departmentalization by customer is used to organize New-Wave Fashions, Inc., into three major divisions: men's clothing, women's clothing, and children's clothing. Then functional departmentalization is used to distinguish the firm's production and marketing activities. Finally, location is used to organize the firm's marketing efforts.

@ Using the Internet

Accenture is a leading consulting company that firms turn to for advice about reorganization of current structures and processes. A strategic alliance with Microsoft is driving the firm further into the specialized consulting services field of helping clients adapt to e-business. You can learn more about Accenture's activities as well as its clients' reorganization efforts in the new economy beginning at its home page **http://www.accenture.com/.**

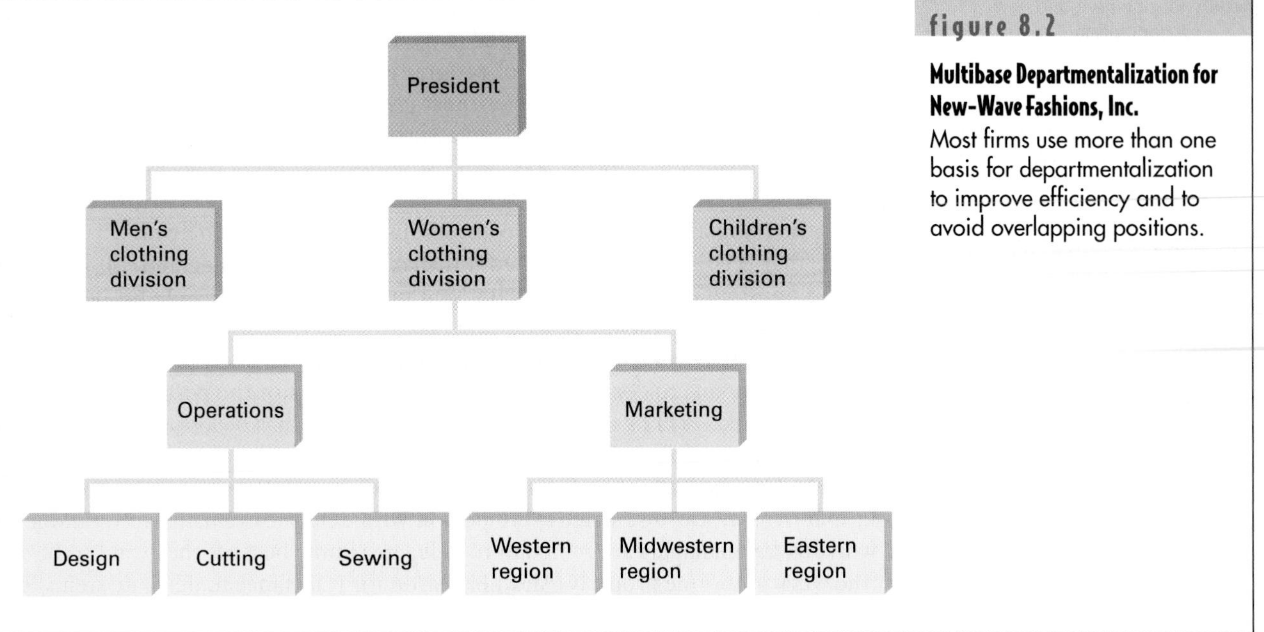

figure 8.2

Multibase Departmentalization for New-Wave Fashions, Inc.
Most firms use more than one basis for departmentalization to improve efficiency and to avoid overlapping positions.

Delegation, Decentralization, and Centralization

learning objective

4 Explain how decentralization follows from delegation.

The third major step in the organizing process is to distribute power in the organization. **Delegation** assigns part of a manager's work and power to other workers. The degree of centralization or decentralization of authority is determined by the overall pattern of delegation within the organization.

delegation assigning part of a manager's work and power to other workers

Delegation of Authority

Because no manager can do everything, delegation is vital to the completion of a manager's work. Delegation is also important in developing the skills and abilities of subordinates. It allows those who are being groomed for higher-level positions to play increasingly important roles in decision making.

Steps in Delegation The delegation process generally involves three steps (see Figure 8.3). First, the manager must *assign responsibility*. **Responsibility** is the duty to

responsibility the duty to do a job or perform a task

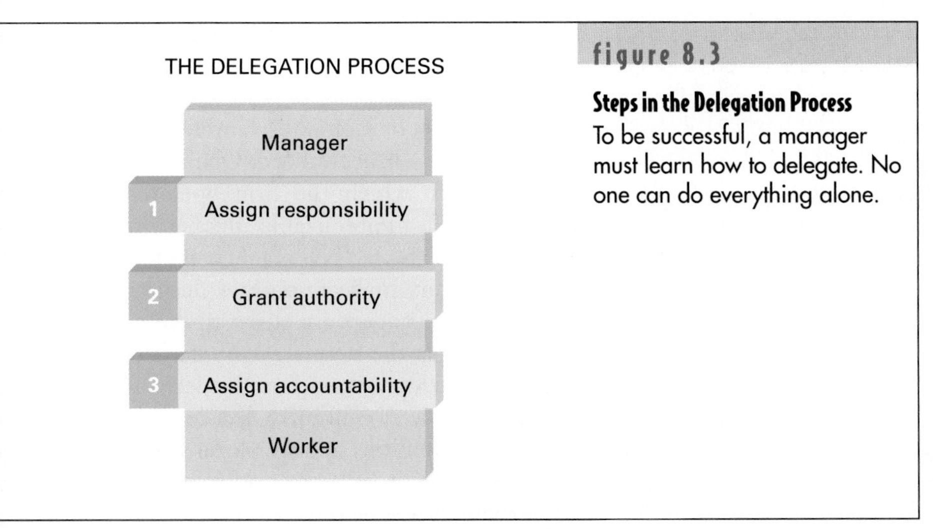

figure 8.3

Steps in the Delegation Process
To be successful, a manager must learn how to delegate. No one can do everything alone.

authority the power, within an organization, to accomplish an assigned job or task

accountability the obligation of a worker to accomplish an assigned job or task

do a job or perform a task. In most job settings, a manager simply gives the worker a job to do. Typical job assignments might range from having a worker prepare a report on the status of a new quality control program to placing the person in charge of a special task force. Second, the manager must *grant authority*. **Authority** is the power, within the organization, to accomplish an assigned job or task. This might include the power to obtain specific information, order supplies, authorize relevant expenditures, and make certain decisions. Finally, the manager must *create accountability*. **Accountability** is the obligation of a worker to accomplish an assigned job or task.

Note that accountability is created but that it cannot be delegated. Suppose that you are an operations manager for Delta Air Lines and are responsible for performing a specific task. You, in turn, delegate this task to someone else. You nonetheless remain accountable to your immediate supervisor for getting the task done properly. If the other person fails to complete the assignment, you—not the person to whom you delegated the task—will be called on to account for what has become *your* failure.

decentralized organization an organization in which management consciously attempts to spread authority widely in the lower levels of the organization

centralized organization an organization that systematically works to concentrate authority at the upper levels of the organization

Barriers to Delegation For several reasons, managers may be unwilling to delegate work. One reason was just stated—the person who delegates remains accountable for the work. Many managers are reluctant to delegate simply because they want to be sure that the work gets done properly. Another reason for reluctance to delegate stems from the opposite situation. The manager fears that the worker will do the work so well that he or she will attract the approving notice of higher-level managers and therefore will become a threat to the manager. Finally, some managers do not delegate because they are so disorganized they simply are not able to plan and assign work effectively.

Decentralization of Authority

The general pattern of delegation throughout an organization determines the extent to which that organization is decentralized or centralized. In a **decentralized organization**, management consciously attempts to spread authority widely across various organization levels. Coca-Cola has decentralized its global operations. A spokesperson said that Coke has to think local and act local. In the past, too many decisions had to be approved at the Atlanta headquarters, where precious time was lost. Now, more responsibility and accountability will be in the hands of local executives around the world.[6] A **centralized organization**, on the other hand, systematically works to concentrate authority at the upper levels. For example, many publishers of college-level textbooks are centralized organizations, with authority concentrated at the tops of these companies. Large organizations may have characteristics of both decentralized and centralized organizations. Wal-Mart centralizes its operations at headquarters in Bentonville, Arkansas, but usually permits tremendous independence in stocking the stores with items local customers want. The top management team in Bentonville focuses primarily on the top 20 percent and bottom 20 percent of its stores and tends to leave the rest alone.[7]

Decentralization leads to empowerment. Creating a decentralized organization means giving employees at all levels the authority to make numerous decisions. At the copier company Canon, workers in Japanese manufacturing plants, such as this one, are encouraged to come up with their own solutions. They work in small teams and resolve day-to-day issues by themselves.

A number of factors can influence the extent to which a firm is decentralized. One is the external environment in which the firm operates. The more complex and unpredictable this environment, the more likely it is that top management will let lower-level managers make important decisions. After all, lower-level managers are closer to the problems. Another factor is the nature of the decision itself. The riskier or the more important the decision, the greater is the tendency to centralize decision making. A third factor is the abilities of lower-level managers. If these managers do not have strong decision-making skills, top managers will be reluctant to decentralize. And, in

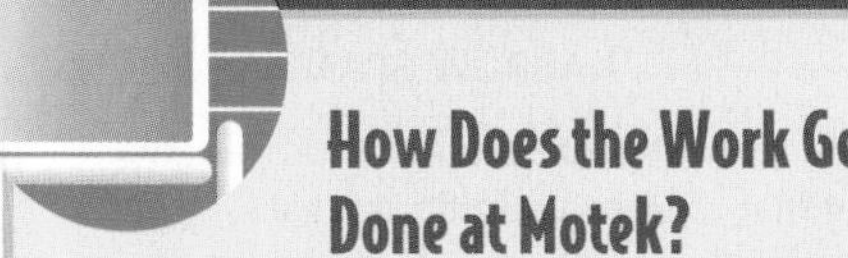

talking technology

How Does the Work Get Done at Motek?

DECENTRALIZATION AND DELEGATION are the driving forces behind the success of Motek, a software company located in Beverly Hills, California. Although some software firms allow software developers considerable freedom to make technical decisions, Motek founder Ann Price believes that all twenty-one employees should vote on virtually all company decisions. The majority rules on a wide range of issues such as work assignments, pay levels, vacation benefits, and even corporate debt.

Motek's chain of command is unusually short, even for a relatively small company. In fact, one project manager notes that "We don't really have bosses here." So how does the work actually get done without a hierarchy of managers constantly checking and rechecking progress?

When CEO Price established the company in 1989, she wanted to avoid the high-pressure work conditions that are commonplace in high-tech organizations. Reasoning that intelligent employees can make good decisions if they know what is going on inside the organization, she delegated authority to the lowest levels and opened the lines of communication. Now employees not only have individual accountability, but they also support each other in making sure that their teams' work gets done.

During Monday morning project meetings, for example, a team leader lists all the individual tasks that must be done. Employees then volunteer for different tasks and estimate how many hours during this work week they will need for each. By agreement, they will not start to tackle any task that they doubt can be completed by the end of the week. "We decide what happens," says one technician. "Things are rarely decreed from above."

As the week progresses, employees who discover they will not finish by Friday alert the team by Thursday afternoon in order to get extra help. Any task that is still too extensive gets carried over for completion during the following week. Interestingly, the company rewards employees who complete their tasks on time, as well as those who communicate that they cannot finish on time, with a $100 vacation travel voucher. This allows the team as a whole to make decisions about scheduling and shared responsibility so that even the most difficult projects move ahead steadily. It also reinforces Motek's ongoing commitment to decentralization.

contrast, strong lower-level decision-making skills encourage decentralization. Finally, a firm that traditionally has practiced centralization or decentralization is likely to maintain that posture in the future.

In principle, neither decentralization nor centralization is right or wrong. What works for one organization may or may not work for another. Kmart Corporation and McDonald's have both been very successful—and both practice centralization. By the same token, decentralization has worked very well for General Electric and Sears. Every organization must assess its own situation and then choose the level of centralization or decentralization that will work best.

The Span of Management

learning objective

5 Understand how the span of management describes an organization.

The fourth major step in organizing a business is establishing the **span of management** (or **span of control**), which is the number of workers who report directly to one manager. For hundreds of years, theorists have searched for an ideal span of management. When it became apparent that there is no perfect number of subordinates for a manager to supervise, they turned their attention to the more general issue of whether the span should be wide or narrow. This issue is complicated by the fact that the span of management may change from one department to another within the same organization. For example, the span of management at Federal Express varies within the company. Departments in which workers do the same tasks on a regular basis—customer service agents, handlers and sorters, couriers, and the like—usually have a span of management of fifteen to twenty employees per manager. Groups performing

span of management (or **span of control**) the number of workers who report directly to one manager

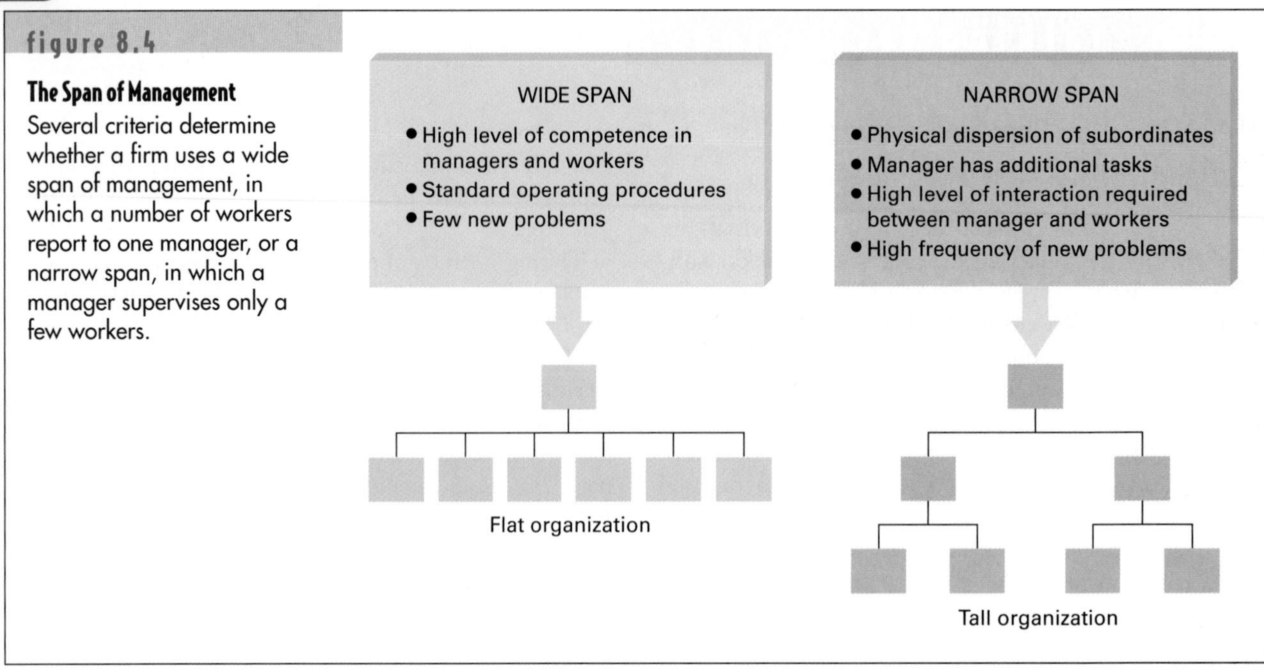
WIDE SPAN
• High level of competence in managers and workers
• Standard operating procedures
• Few new problems
Flat organization
NARROW SPAN
• Physical dispersion of subordinates
• Manager has additional tasks
• High level of interaction required between manager and workers
• High frequency of new problems
Tall organization

figure 8.4

The Span of Management
Several criteria determine whether a firm uses a wide span of management, in which a number of workers report to one manager, or a narrow span, in which a manager supervises only a few workers.

multiple and different tasks are more likely to have smaller spans of management consisting of five or six employees.[8] Thus Federal Express uses a wide span of control in some departments and a narrow span of control in others.

Wide and Narrow Spans of Control

A *wide* span of management exists when a manager has a larger number of subordinates. A *narrow* span exists when the manager has only a few subordinates. Several factors determine the span that is better for a particular manager (see Figure 8.4). Generally, the span of control may be wide when (1) the manager and the subordinates are very competent, (2) the organization has a well-established set of standard operating procedures, and (3) few new problems are expected to arise. The span should be narrow when (1) workers are physically located far from one another, (2) the manager has much work to do in addition to supervising workers, (3) a great deal of interaction is required between supervisor and workers, and (4) new problems arise frequently.

Organizational Height

organizational height the number of layers, or levels, of management in a firm

The span of management has an obvious impact on relations between managers and workers. It has a more subtle but equally important impact on the height of the organization. **Organizational height** is the number of layers, or levels, of management in a firm. The span of management plays a direct role in determining the height of the organization, as shown in Figure 8.4. If spans of management are wider, fewer levels are needed, and the organization is *flat*. If spans of management are generally narrow, more levels are needed, and the resulting organization is *tall*.

In a taller organization, administrative costs are higher because more managers are needed. And communication among levels may become distorted because information has to pass up and down through more people. When companies are looking to cut costs, one option is to decrease the organizational height in order to reduce the related administrative expenses. When Raytheon, a high-tech defense supplier, needed to reduce its enormous cost structure, the CEO decided to eliminate an entire layer of management, resulting in a flatter organization.[9] Although flat organizations avoid these problems, their managers may have to perform more administrative duties simply because there are fewer managers. Wide spans of management also may require managers to spend considerably more time supervising and working with subordinates.

Chain of Command: Line and Staff Management

learning objective

6 Understand how the chain of command is established by using line and staff management.

Establishing the chain of command is another step in organizing a business. It reaches from the highest to the lowest levels of management. A **line management position** is part of the chain of command; it is a position in which a person makes decisions and gives orders to subordinates to achieve the goals of the organization. A **staff management position,** by contrast, is a position created to provide support, advice, and expertise to someone in the chain of command. Staff managers are not part of the chain of command but do have authority over their assistants (see Figure 8.5).

line management position a position that is part of the chain of command and that includes direct responsibility for achieving the goals of the organization

staff management position a position created to provide support, advice, and expertise within an organization

Line and Staff Positions Compared

Both line and staff managers are needed for effective management, but the two kinds of positions differ in important ways. The basic difference is in terms of authority. Line managers have *line authority*, which means they can make decisions and issue directives that relate to the organization's goals.

Staff managers seldom have this kind of authority. Instead, they usually have either advisory authority or functional authority. *Advisory authority* is simply the expectation that line managers will consult the appropriate staff manager when making decisions. Functional authority is stronger, and in some ways it is like line authority. *Functional authority* is the authority of staff managers to make decisions and issue directives—but only about their own areas of expertise. For example, a legal adviser for Nike can decide whether to retain a particular clause in a contract but not what price to charge for a new product. Contracts are part of the legal adviser's area of expertise; pricing is not.

Line-Staff Conflict

For a variety of reasons, conflict between line managers and staff managers is fairly common in businesses. Staff managers often have more formal education and sometimes are younger (and perhaps more ambitious) than line managers. Line managers may perceive staff managers as a threat to their own authority and thus may resent them. For their part, staff managers may become annoyed or angry if their expert

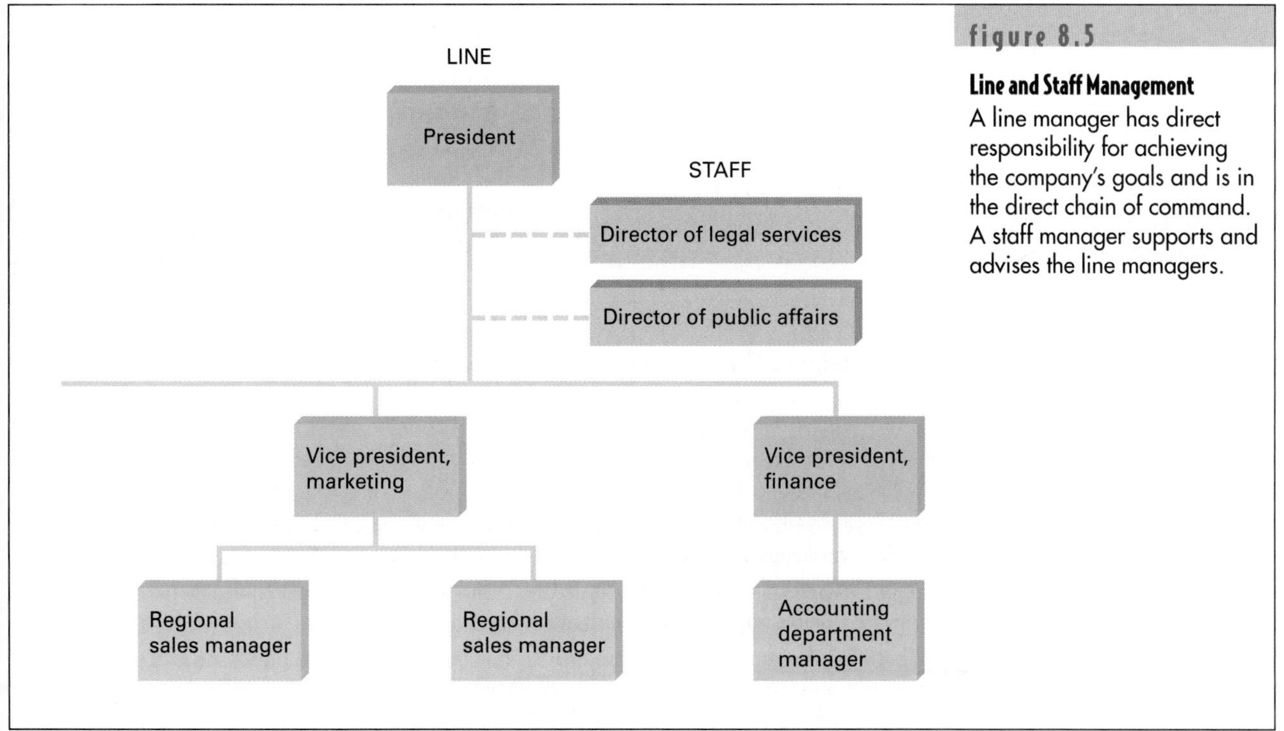

figure 8.5

Line and Staff Management
A line manager has direct responsibility for achieving the company's goals and is in the direct chain of command. A staff manager supports and advises the line managers.

adapting to change

Can Rightsizing the Organization Lead to Wrongsizing?

MILLIONS OF EMPLOYEES have lost their jobs in recent years as companies have adjusted to the ever-changing business environment. Sometimes companies downsize because they lack sufficient work for the entire work force. They also may lay off line and staff personnel when closing divisions or facilities, eliminating shifts, or eliminating nonessential jobs. But when does rightsizing become wrongsizing?

Rightsizing involves realigning an organization's human resources for a closer fit with overall strategy, goals, and financial resources. The intention is to become more competitive by redesigning the organizational structure and redefining both line and staff positions to focus on the most important activities and processes. However, some companies eliminate numerous positions without first determining which and how many are needed to accomplish vital tasks for organizational performance. The result is *wrongsizing*—the loss of key positions and personnel.

Management may have difficulty recruiting new managers and employees or persuading staff and line personnel to accept transfers if the company has endured rounds of layoffs punctuated by bursts of job growth. Taken to the extreme, cost-cutting layoffs can lead to *corporate anorexia*, in which the stripped-down work force is structured inappropriately or simply too dispirited to perform. Of course, layoffs to slash costs are the only way that embattled companies such as U.S. Airways have even a slim chance of survival.

All kinds of companies can use rightsizing to meet their goals. For example, consider a major retailer like Sears, whose sale revenue is subject to the whims of consumer purchasing patterns. Seeking higher profitability, Sears has learned to use rightsizing as a way to implement new strategies. "Most of the downsizing has been predominantly due to a shift in business model," says one official. "Our customer has told us that she's not willing to pay for a higher level of service. So we've changed our service level in the stores, moving more toward self-service in the smaller-ticket items." This meant thousands of layoffs as the chain revamped its stores and reduced the number of employees in certain departments. At the same time it put Sears in a more competitive position and supported its drive for improved profitability.

recommendations—in public relations or human resources management, for example—are not adopted by line management.

Fortunately, there are several ways to minimize the likelihood of such conflict. One way is to integrate line and staff managers into one team that works together. Another is to ensure that the areas of responsibility of line and staff managers are clearly defined. Finally, line and staff managers can both be held accountable for the results of their activities.

Before studying the next topic—forms of organizational structure—you may want to review the five organization-shaping characteristics that we have just discussed. See Table 8.1 for a summary.

table 8.1 Five Characteristics of Organizational Structure

Dimension	Purpose
Job design	To divide the work performed by an organization into parts and assign each part a position within the organization.
Departmentalization	To group various positions in an organization into manageable units. Departmentalization may be based on function, product, location, customer, or a combination of these bases.
Delegation	To distribute part of a manager's work and power to other workers. A deliberate concentration of authority at the upper levels of the organization creates a centralized structure. A wide distribution of authority into the lower levels of the organization creates a decentralized structure.
Span of management	To set the number of workers who report directly to one manager. A narrow span has only a few workers reporting to one manager. A wide span has a large number of workers reporting to one manager.
Line and staff management	To distinguish between those positions that are part of the chain of command and those that provide support, advice, or expertise to those in the chain of command.

Forms of Organizational Structure

learning objective

Describe the four basic forms of organizational structure: bureaucratic, matrix, cluster, and network.

Up to this point we have focused our attention on the major characteristics of organizational structure. In many ways this is like discussing the important parts of a jigsaw puzzle one by one. Now it is time to put the puzzle together. In particular, we discuss four basic forms of organizational structure: bureaucratic, matrix, cluster, and network.

The Bureaucratic Structure

The term *bureaucracy* is used often in an unfavorable context to suggest rigidity and red tape. This image may be negative, but it does capture some of the essence of the bureaucratic structure.

A **bureaucratic structure** is a management system based on a formal framework of authority that is outlined carefully and followed precisely. A bureaucracy is likely to have the following characteristics:

bureaucratic structure a management system based on a formal framework of authority that is outlined carefully and followed precisely

1. A high level of job specialization
2. Departmentalization by function
3. Formal patterns of delegation
4. A high degree of centralization
5. Narrow spans of management, resulting in a tall organization
6. Clearly defined line and staff positions with formal relationships between the two

Perhaps the best examples of contemporary bureaucracies are government agencies and colleges and universities. Consider the very rigid and formal college entrance and registration procedures. The reason for such procedures is to ensure that the organization is able to deal with large numbers of people in an equitable and fair manner. We may not enjoy them, but regulations and standard operating procedures pretty much guarantee uniform treatment.

Another example of a bureaucratic structure is the U.S. Postal Service. Like colleges and universities, the post office relies on procedures and rules to accomplish the organization's goals. However, the postal service has streamlined some of its procedures and initiated new services in order to compete with Federal Express, United Parcel Service, and other delivery services. As a result, customer satisfaction has begun to improve.

The biggest drawback to the bureaucratic structure is its lack of flexibility. A bureaucracy has trouble adjusting to change and coping with the unexpected. Because today's business environment is dynamic and complex, many firms have found that the bureaucratic structure is not an appropriate organizational structure. Interestingly, the Internet brings a new way of looking at the rigidity of bureaucratic structures. According to Eric Schmitt, an analyst at Forrester Research, Inc., organizations are in the midst of changing the way they do business as they adapt their corporate structure to an online presence based on Internet interaction with customers and suppliers. For example, Cisco Systems, Inc., uses the software of Ariba, Inc., to run its online purchasing system, which directs its 20,000 employees' interactions with more than 3,000 suppliers. Besides helping to standardize interaction processes, the result has been an estimated 10 to 20 percent savings.[10]

Have you ever worked at a bureaucratic structured organization? A frequent complaint about a bureaucratic structured organization, like the U.S. Patent and Trademark Office, is that the emphasis is on procedures and rules, rather than on productivity.

The Matrix Structure

matrix structure an organizational structure that combines vertical and horizontal lines of authority, usually by superimposing product departmentalization on a functionally departmentalized organization

cross-functional team a group of employees from different departments who work together on a specific project

The matrix structure is one of the more complex types of organizational structures. When the matrix structure is used, individuals report to more than one superior at the same time. The **matrix structure** combines vertical and horizontal lines of authority. The matrix structure occurs when product departmentalization is superimposed on a functionally departmentalized organization. In a matrix organization, authority flows both down and across.

To understand the structure of a matrix organization, first consider the usual functional arrangement, with people working in departments such as engineering, production, finance, and marketing. Now suppose that we assign people from these departments to a special group that is working on a new project as a team. This team is called a **cross-functional team.** Frequently, cross-functional teams are charged with the responsibility of developing new products. For example, Ford Motor Company assembled a special project team to design and manufacture its global cars. The manager in charge of a team is usually called a *project manager*. Any individual who is working with the team reports to *both* the project manager and the individual's superior in the functional department (see Figure 8.6).

Cross-functional team projects may be temporary, in which case the team is disbanded once the mission is accomplished, or they may be permanent. These teams are often empowered to make major decisions. Campbell Soup Company recently broadened its innovation group into a permanent cross-functional work team in charge of developing innovative new products and marketing techniques. Campbell's has encountered stiff competition in the soup industry and hopes that this team will create ways to increase the per capita soup consumption in the United States.[11] When a cross-functional team is employed, prospective team members may receive special training because effective teamwork can require skills different from those needed when working alone. For cross-functional teams to be successful, team members must be given specific information on the job each is required to perform. The team also must develop a sense of cohesiveness and maintain good communications among its members.

Matrix structures offer several advantages over other organizational forms. Added flexibility is probably the most obvious advantage. The matrix structure also can in-

figure 8.6

A Matrix Structure

A matrix is usually the result of combining product departmentalization with function departmentalization. It is a complex structure in which employees have more than one supervisor.

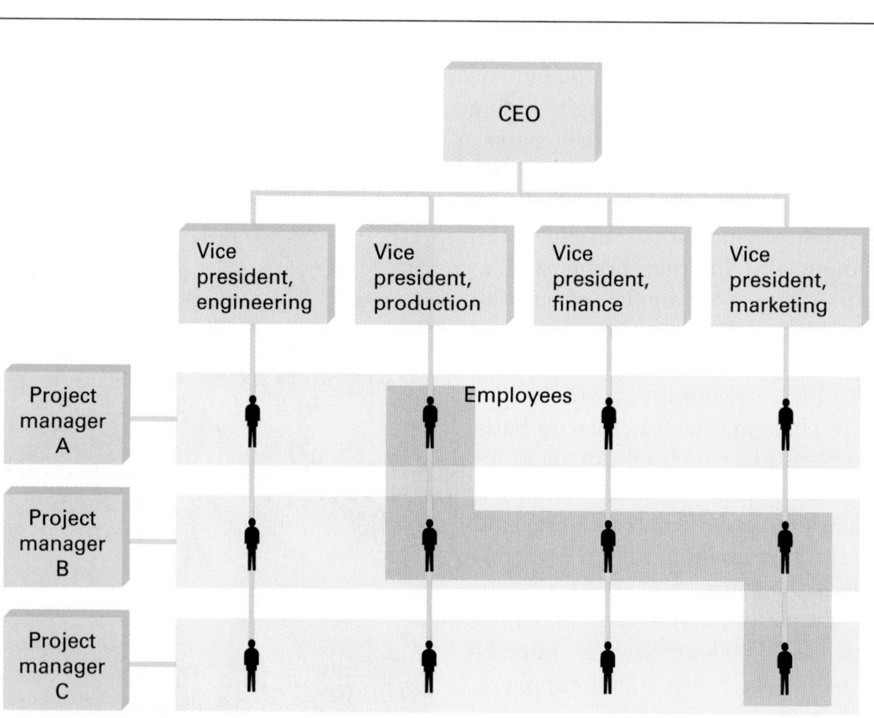

Source: *Management*, Sixth Edition by Ricky W. Griffin. Copyright © 1999 by Houghton Mifflin Company. Adapted with permission.

crease productivity, raise morale, and nurture creativity and innovation. In addition, employees experience personal development through doing a variety of jobs.

The matrix structure also has some disadvantages. Having employees report to more than one supervisor can cause confusion about who is in charge in various situations. Like committees, teams may take longer to resolve problems and issues than individuals working alone. Other difficulties include personality clashes, poor communication, undefined individual roles, unclear responsibilities, and finding ways to reward individual and team performance simultaneously. Because more managers and support staff may be needed, a matrix structure may be more expensive to maintain than other forms of organizational structure.

The Cluster Structure

A **cluster structure** is a type of business that consists primarily of teams with no or very few underlying departments. This type of structure is also called *team* or *collaborative*. In this type of organization, team members work together on a project until it is finished, and then the team may remain intact and be assigned another project, or team members may be reassigned to different teams, depending on their skills and the needs of the organization. In a cluster organization, the operating unit is the team and remains relatively small. If a team becomes too large, it can be split into multiple teams, or individuals can be assigned to other existing teams.

cluster structure an organization that consists primarily of teams with no or very few underlying departments

The cluster organizational structure has both strengths and weaknesses. Keeping the teams small provides the organization with the flexibility necessary to change directions quickly, to try new techniques, and to explore new ideas. Some employees in these types of organizations express concerns regarding job security and the increased amount of stress that arises due to the fact that changes occur rapidly.[12]

The Network Structure

In a **network structure** (sometimes called a *virtual organization*), administration is the primary function performed, and other functions such as engineering, production, marketing, and finance are contracted out to other organizations. Frequently, a network organization does not manufacture the products that it sells. This type of organization has only a few permanent employees consisting of top management and a few hourly clerical workers. Leased facilities and equipment, as well as temporary workers, are increased or decreased as the needs of the organization change. Thus there is rather limited formal structure associated with a network organization.

network structure an organization in which administration is the primary function and most other functions are contracted out to other firms

An obvious strength of a network structure is flexibility that allows the organization to adjust quickly to changes. Some of the challenges faced by managers in network-structured organizations include controlling the quality of work performed by other organizations, low morale and high turnover among hourly workers, and the vulnerability associated with relying on outside contractors.[13]

Additional Factors that Influence an Organization

learning objective 8

Summarize the use of corporate culture, intrapreneurship, committees, coordination techniques, informal groups, and the grapevine.

As you might expect, other factors in addition to those already covered in this chapter affect the way a large corporation operates on a day-to-day basis. To get a "true picture" of the organizational structure of a huge corporation like Marriott, for example, which employs over 140,500 people,[14] you need to consider the topics discussed in this section.

Corporate Culture

Managers do not perform their jobs in a vacuum. Most managers function within a corporate culture. A **corporate culture** is generally defined as the inner rites, rituals, heroes, and values of a firm. An organization's culture can have a powerful influence on how its

corporate culture the inner rites, rituals, heroes, and values of a firm

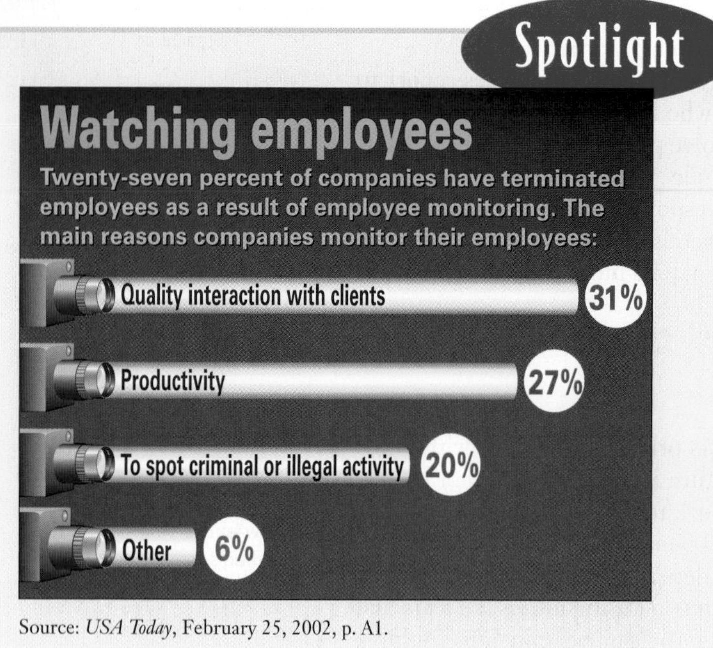
Spotlight
Watching employees
Twenty-seven percent of companies have terminated employees as a result of employee monitoring. The main reasons companies monitor their employees:
Quality interaction with clients
31%
Productivity
27%
To spot criminal or illegal activity
20%
Other
6%

Source: *USA Today*, February 25, 2002, p. A1.

employees think and act. It also can determine how the public perceives the organization.

Corporate culture generally is thought to have a very strong influence on a firm's performance over time. Hence it is useful to be able to assess a firm's corporate culture. Common indicators include the physical setting (building, office layouts, and so on), what the company itself says about its corporate culture (in its advertising and news releases, for example), how the company greets its guests (does it have formal or informal reception areas?), and how employees spend their time (working alone in an office most of the time or spending much of the day working with others).

Goffee and Jones have identified four distinct types of corporate cultures (see Figure 8.7). One is called the *networked culture*, characterized by a base of trust and friendship among employees, a strong commitment and feeling of loyalty to the organization, and a relaxed and informal environment. The *mercenary culture* embodies the feelings of passion, energy, sense of purpose, and excitement for one's work. The term *mercenary* does not imply that employees are motivated to work only for the money, but this is part of it. In this culture, employees are very intense, focused, and determined to win. In the *fragmented culture*, employees do not necessarily become friends, and they work "at" the organization, not "for" it. Employees have a high degree of autonomy, flexibility, and equality. The *communal culture* combines the positive traits of the networked culture and the mercenary culture—those of friendship, commitment, high focus on performance, and high energy. People's lives revolve around the product in this culture, and success by anyone in the organization is celebrated by all.[15]

Some experts believe that cultural change is needed when the company's environment is changing significantly, when the industry is becoming more competitive, when the company's performance is mediocre, when the company is growing rapidly, or when the company is about to become a truly large organization. For example, the personal computer (PC) industry has become highly competitive in recent years, especially as PC sales stagnated. Dell's top concern used to be handling its fast growth, but now Michael Dell and other top executives are focusing on developing the company's culture because sales growth has decreased. "The Soul of Dell" is the computer giant's guide to corporate culture and ethics, and management hopes that a strong culture will increase employee loyalty and the long-run success of the company.[16] Organizations of the future will look quite different from those of today. In particular, experts predict that tomorrow's business firms will be made up of small, task-oriented work groups, each with control over its own activities. These small groups will be coordinated through an elaborate computer network and held together by a strong corporate culture. Businesses operating in fast-changing industries will require leadership that supports trust and risk taking. Creating a culture of trust in an organization can lead to increases in growth, profit, productivity, and job satisfaction. A culture of trust can help retain the best people, inspire customer loyalty, develop new markets, and increase creativity.

Another specific area where corporate culture plays a vital role is in the integration of two or more companies. Business leaders often cite the role of corporate cultures in the integration process as one of the primary factors affecting the success of a merger or acquisition. Experts note that cor-

Creative corporate culture. At W.L. Gore, employees such as veteran salespeople Tom Erickson and John Cusick, decide who gets hired and how well their peers get paid. Every employee has a mentor, and work gets done by teams. All offices are the same size. At this company that makes the plastic used in everything from guitar strings to warm jackets, the unstructured work environment leads to creativity and success.

Buell

figure 8.7

Types of Corporate Cultures
Which corporate culture would you choose?

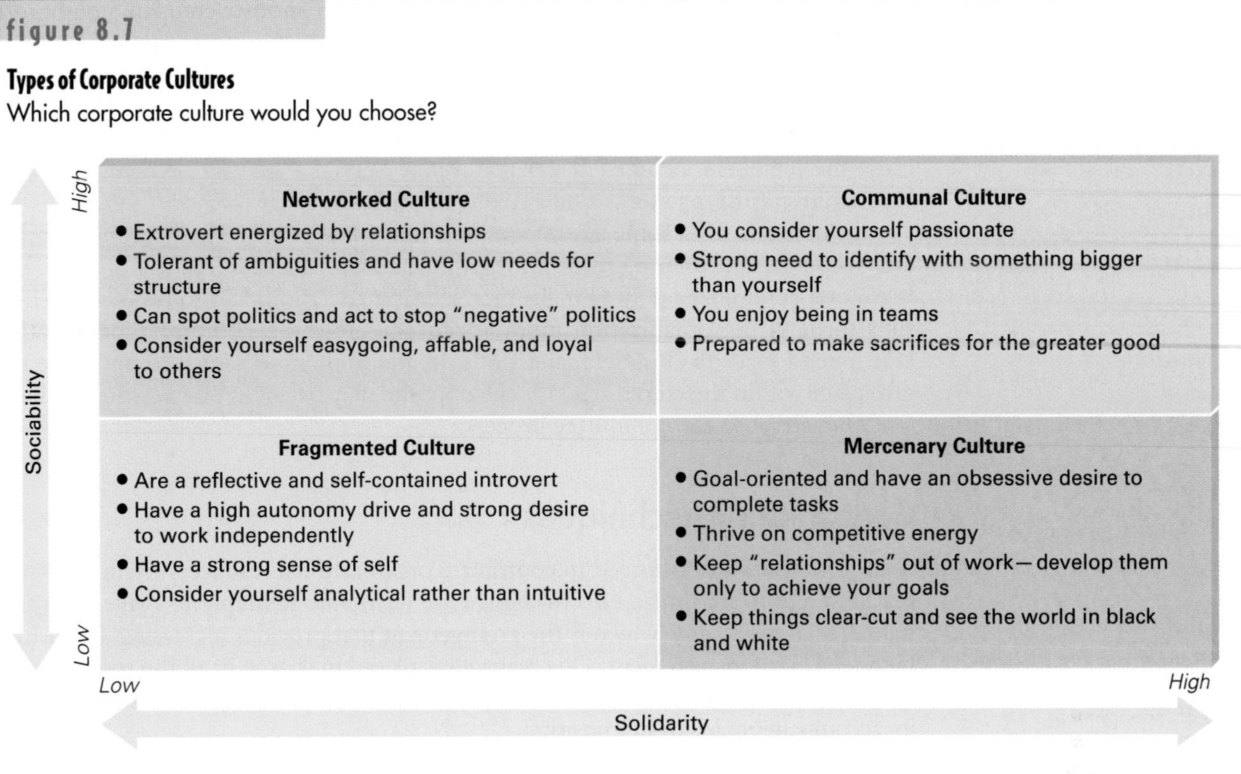

Source: "Types of Corporate Culture," from *The Character of a Corporation*, by Rob Goffee and Gareth Jones. Copyright © 1998 by Rob Goffee and Gareth Jones. Reprinted by permission of HarperCollins Publishers, Inc.

porate culture is a way of conducting business both within the company and externally as it interacts with customers. If the two merging companies do not address differences in corporate culture, they are setting themselves up for missed expectations and possibly failure.[17]

Intrapreneurship

Since innovations and new product development are important to companies, and since entrepreneurs are among the most innovative people around, it seems almost natural that an entrepreneurial character would surface prominently in many of today's larger organizations. An **intrapreneur** is an employee who takes responsibility for pushing an innovative idea, product, or process through an organization.[18] An intrapreneur possesses the confidence and drive of an entrepreneur but is allowed to use organizational resources for idea development. For example, Art Fry, inventor of the colorful Post-it-Notes that Americans can't live without, is a devoted advocate of intrapreneurship. Nurturing his notepad idea at Minnesota Mining and Manufacturing (3M) for years, Fry speaks highly of the intrapreneurial commitment at 3M. Fry indicates that an *intrapreneur* is an individual who does not have all the skills to get the job done and thus has to work within an organization, making use of its skills and attributes.

intrapreneur an employee who pushes an innovative idea, product, or process through an organization

Committees

Today, business firms use several types of committees that affect organizational structure. An **ad hoc committee** is created for a specific short-term purpose, such as reviewing the firm's employee benefits plan. Once its work is finished, the ad hoc committee disbands. A **standing committee** is a relatively permanent committee charged with performing a recurring task. A firm might establish a budget review committee, for example, to review departmental budget requests on an ongoing basis. Finally, a **task force** is a committee established to investigate a major problem or

ad hoc committee a committee created for a specific short-term purpose

standing committee a relatively permanent committee charged with performing some recurring task

task force a committee established to investigate a major problem or pending decision

pending decision. A firm contemplating a merger with another company might form a task force to assess the pros and cons of the merger. Governments also use task forces to deal with special problems and issues. Enron became the first company to ever have a government task force created specifically for investigating it, a public company. Of course, this was not the type of task force any company wants around because the members included Internal Revenue Service (IRS) and Federal Bureau of Investigation (FBI) agents as well as many attorneys.[19]

Committees offer some advantages over individual action. Their several members are, of course, able to bring more information and knowledge to the task at hand. Furthermore, committees tend to make more accurate decisions and to transmit their results through the organization more effectively. However, committee deliberations take much longer than individual actions. In addition, unnecessary compromise may take place within the committee. Or the opposite may occur, as one person dominates (and thus negates) the committee process.

Coordination Techniques

managerial hierarchy the arrangement that provides increasing authority at higher levels of management

A large organization is forced to coordinate organizational resources to minimize duplication and to maximize effectiveness. One technique is simply to make use of the **managerial hierarchy,** which is the arrangement that provides increasing authority at higher levels of management. One manager is placed in charge of all the resources that are to be coordinated. That person is able to coordinate them by virtue of the authority accompanying his or her position.

Resources also can be coordinated through rules and procedures. For example, a rule can govern how a firm's travel budget is to be allocated. This particular resource, then, would be coordinated in terms of that rule.

In complex situations, more sophisticated coordination techniques may be called for. One approach is to establish a liaison. A *liaison* is a go-between—a person who coordinates the activities of two groups. Suppose that General Motors is negotiating a complicated contract with a supplier of steering wheels. The supplier might appoint a liaison whose primary responsibility is to coordinate the contract negotiations. Finally, for *very*

exploring business

Celebrity CEOs: Is It All About Me?

Do companies benefit from celebrity CEOs? Look at high-profile CEOs such as Oracle's Larry Ellison and Virgin Group's Richard Branson. Whereas Ellison is well known for his aggressive approach to competition, Branson is game for almost any kind of corporate publicity stunt. Although both make headlines, they also use their unique management styles to shape corporate culture. Oracle's hard-charging culture, which reflects Ellison's leadership, helps the company battle archrival Microsoft. Similarly, Branson's try-anything manner inspires his employees to be more creative.

Although Ellison and Branson clearly have sparked enthusiastic performance within their organizations, celebrity CEOs are not always good for their companies. Professor Al Vicere of Penn State's Smeal College of Business observes that "their superstar status pushed the individual, not the organization, into the spotlight. It became about me, the CEO, and making my mark in the world." CEOs who focus more on making a name for themselves than on organizational priorities risk creating a "me first" culture. In such an atmosphere, managers and employees are more likely to make decisions for selfish reasons, not for the good of the company.

Certainly a dynamic, visionary CEO can make a huge difference by setting a positive tone, modeling the values of performance-oriented behavior, and keeping the organization on track toward its goals. Conversely, the CEO may be blamed when a company performs poorly, just as the coach may be blamed when a sports team performs poorly.

Still, experts such as Professor Rakesh Khurana of Harvard Business School stress that a company's performance cannot be attributed to only one person. Celebrity CEOs may get most of the credit, but even General Electric, often mentioned as America's best-managed company, could not succeed without the hard work of its 300,000 employees. Moreover, a backlash against luring big-name CEOs with big compensation packages has brought attention back to bottom-line performance as the bottom line.

complex coordination needs, a committee could be established. Suppose that General Motors is in the process of purchasing the steering-wheel supplier. In this case, a committee might be appointed to integrate the new firm into General Motors' larger organizational structure.

Source: *USA Today*, October 10, 2002, p. B1.

The Informal Organization

So far we have discussed the organization as a more or less formal structure consisting of interrelated positions. This is the organization that is shown on an organization chart. There is another kind of organization, however, that does not show up on any chart. We define this **informal organization** as the pattern of behavior and interaction that stems from personal rather than official relationships. Firmly embedded within every informal organization are informal groups and the notorious grapevine.

informal organization the pattern of behavior and interaction that stems from personal rather than official relationships

informal group a group created by the members themselves to accomplish goals that may or may not be relevant to an organization

Informal Groups An **informal group** is created by the group members themselves to accomplish goals that may or may not be relevant to the organization. Workers may create an informal group to go bowling, form a union, get a particular manager fired or transferred, or have lunch together every day. The group may last for several years or only a few hours.

Employees join informal groups for a variety of reasons. Perhaps the main reason is that people like to be with others who are similar to themselves. Or it may be that the goals of the group appeal to the individual. Others may join informal groups simply because they have a need to be with their associates and to be accepted by them.

Informal groups can be powerful forces in organizations. They can restrict output, or they can help managers through tight spots. They can cause disagreement and conflict, or they can help boost morale and job satisfaction. They can show new people how to contribute to the organization, or they can help people get away with substandard performance. Clearly, managers should be aware of these informal groups. Those who make the mistake of fighting the informal organization have a major obstacle to overcome.

grapevine the informal communications network within an organization

The Grapevine The **grapevine** is the informal communications network within an organization. It is completely separate from—and sometimes much faster than—the organization's formal channels of communication. Formal communications usually follow a path that parallels the organizational chain of command. By contrast, information can be transmitted through the grapevine in any direction—up, down, diagonally, or horizontally across the organizational structure. Subordinates may pass information to their bosses, an executive may relay something to a maintenance worker, or there may be an exchange of information between people who work in totally unrelated departments.

Grapevine information may be concerned with topics ranging from the latest management decisions, to the results of today's World Series game, to pure gossip. It can be important or of little interest. And it can be highly accurate or totally distorted.

How should managers treat the grapevine? Certainly they would be making a big mistake if they tried to eliminate it. People working together, day in and day out, are going to communicate. A more rational approach is to recognize the existence of the grapevine as a part—though an unofficial part—of the organization. For example, managers should respond promptly and aggressively to inaccurate grapevine information to minimize the damage that such mis-information might do. Moreover, the grapevine can come in handy when managers are on the receiving end of important communications from the informal organization.

In the next chapter we apply these and other management concepts to an extremely important business function: the production of goods and services.

Return To inside business

Nike never stands still in the global race for sales and profits. But with a flexible organization structure, the company can respond more effectively to changes in customer tastes, competitive pressures, and many other environmental elements. At the same time, Nike wants to ensure that the entire work force understands exactly what the company stands for. For this reason, it employs corporate storytellers to reinforce the culture by retelling stories from Nike's early days and hammering home the lessons to new employees.

"Our stories are not about extraordinary business plans or financial manipulations," stresses Nike's director of corporate education, who serves as chief storyteller. "They're about people getting things done." One often-told tale, illustrating the importance of innovation, is about how one of Nike's founders, coach Bill Bowerman, used a home waffle iron to make waffle-soled running shoes for his track team. "Every company has a history," comments another storyteller. "But we have a little bit more than a history. We have a heritage, something that's still relevant today. If we connect people to that, chances are that they won't view Nike as just another place to work."

Questions

1. How does Nike's women's division serve as an alternative to job specialization?
2. What is Nike doing to encourage intrapreneurship on the departmental level?

chapter review

Summary

Understand what an organization is and identify its characteristics.

An organization is a group of two or more people working together to achieve a common set of goals. The relationships among positions within an organization can be illustrated by means of an organization chart. Five specific characteristics—job design, departmentalization, delegation, span of management, and chain of command—help to determine what an organization chart and the organization itself look like.

Explain why job specialization is important.

Job specialization is the separation of all the activities within an organization into smaller components and the assignment of those different components to different people. Several factors combine to make specialization a useful technique for designing jobs, but high levels of specialization may cause employee dissatisfaction and boredom. One technique for overcoming these problems is job rotation.

3

Identify the various bases for departmentalization.

Departmentalization is the grouping of jobs into manageable units. Typical bases for departmentalization are by function, product, location, or customer. Because each of these bases provides particular advantages, most firms—especially larger ones—use a combination of different bases in different organizational situations.

Explain how decentralization follows from delegation.

Delegation is the assigning of part of a manager's work to other workers. It involves the following three steps: (a) assigning responsibility, (b) granting authority, and (c) creating accountability. A decentralized firm is one that delegates as much power as possible to people in the lower management levels. In a centralized firm, on the other hand, power is systematically retained at the upper levels.

Understand how the span of management describes an organization.

The span of management is the number of workers who report directly to a manager. Spans generally are characterized as wide (many workers per manager) or narrow (few workers per manager). Wide spans generally result in flat organizations (few layers of management); narrow spans generally result in tall organizations (many layers of management).

Understand how the chain of command is established by using line and staff management.

A line position is one that is in the organization's chain of command or line of authority. A manager in a line position makes decisions and gives orders to workers to achieve the goals of the organization. On the other hand, a manager in a staff position provides support, advice, and expertise to someone in the chain of command. Staff positions may carry some authority, but it usually applies only within staff areas of expertise.

Describe the four basic forms of organizational structure: bureaucratic, matrix, cluster, and network.

There are four basic forms of organizational structure. The bureaucratic structure is characterized by formality and rigidity. With the bureaucratic structure, rules and procedures are used to ensure uniformity. The matrix structure may be visualized as product departmentalization superimposed on functional departmentalization. With the matrix structure, an employee on a cross-functional team reports to both the project manager and the individual's supervisor in a functional department. A cluster structure is an organization that consists primarily of teams with very few underlying functional departments. In an organization with a network structure, the primary function performed internally is administration, and other functions are contracted out to other firms.

Summarize the use of corporate culture, intrapreneurship, committees, coordination techniques, informal groups, and the grapevine.

Corporate culture—the inner rites, rituals, heroes, and values of a firm—is thought to have a very strong influence on a firm's performance over time. An intrapreneur is an employee in an organizational environment who takes responsibility for pushing an innovative idea, product, or process through the organization. Additional elements that influence an organization include the use of committees and development of techniques for achieving coordination among various groups within the organization. Finally, both informal groups created by group members and an informal communication network called the grapevine may affect an organization and its performance.

Key Terms

You should now be able to define and give an example relevant to each of the following terms:

organization (223)
organization chart (224)
chain of command (224)
job specialization (226)
job rotation (227)
departmentalization (227)
departmentalization by function (227)
departmentalization by product (228)
departmentalization by location (228)
departmentalization by customer (228)
delegation (229)
responsibility (229)
authority (230)
accountability (230)
decentralized organization (230)
centralized organization (230)
span of management (or span of control) (231)
organizational height (232)
line management position (233)
staff management position (233)
bureaucratic structure (235)
matrix structure (236)
cross-functional team (236)
cluster structure (237)
network structure (237)
corporate culture (237)
intrapreneur (239)
ad hoc committee (239)
standing committee (239)
task force (239)
managerial hierarchy (240)
informal organization (241)
informal group (241)
grapevine (241)

Review Questions

1. In what way do organization charts create a picture of an organization?
2. What is the chain of command in an organization?
3. What determines the degree of specialization within an organization?
4. Describe how job rotation can be used to combat the problems caused by job specialization.
5. What are the major differences among the four departmentalization bases?
6. Why do most firms employ a combination of departmentalization bases?
7. What three steps are involved in delegation? Explain each.
8. How does a firm's top management influence its degree of centralization?
9. How is organizational height related to the span of management?
10. What are the key differences between line and staff positions?
11. Contrast the bureaucratic and matrix forms of organizational structure.
12. What are the differences between the cluster structure and the network structure?
13. What is corporate culture? Describe the major types.
14. Which form of organizational structure probably would lead to the strongest informal organization? Why?
15. How may the managerial hierarchy be used to coordinate the organization's resources?

Discussion Questions

1. Explain how the five steps of the organizing process determine the characteristics of the resulting organization. Which steps are most important?
2. Which kinds of firms probably would operate most effectively as centralized firms? As decentralized firms?
3. How do decisions concerning span of management the use of committees, and coordination techniques affect organizational structure?
4. How might a manager go about formalizing the informal organization?

Organizing for Success at Bakers' Best

When Michael Baker opened his Baker's Best take-out food store in 1984, every employee reported directly to him. He even handled a lot of the cooking. In the early days, the small business was known for its turkey sandwiches and was ringing up $200,000 in annual revenue from a tiny 500-square-foot storefront. Twenty years later Baker's Best is bringing in $7.5 million in annual revenue from four Boston-area business units: a daytime café, an evening restaurant, a full-service catering business, and a corporate catering business. The owner is still actively involved, but he no longer has to slice turkey or wrap sandwiches. Instead, he has put together an organization of skilled managers and employees to keep Baker's Best running smoothly.

An experienced operations manager who reports directly to Baker runs everything on a day-to-day basis. Under the operations manager are four managers, one for each of the business units. In turn, each business manager heads a fairly flat hierarchy of employees who specialize in particular tasks. For example, the full-service catering manager supervises four salespeople who sell catering jobs. She also hires, fires, and supervises a sizable crew of chefs, food servers, and bartenders, some of whom work part time for other catering companies, as well as for Baker's Best. On a smaller catering job, the chef manages the bartender and the on-site servers. On a larger catering job, however, a function manager supervises the chefs and all other on-site personnel and reports to the full-service catering manager. This organization allows the company to control both food and service quality and ensure customer satisfaction.

Unlike some entrepreneurs, Baker had no difficulty delegating authority as his business expanded. "I found someone for operations manager who is extraordinarily good at what he does," he explains. "He actually takes on a lot more responsibility than I do at this point. I used to think that my decisions were really good—and then I'd talk with him and realize that he might have made a better choice." The operations manager takes a hands-on approach to a wide variety of operational details, including the company's computer system. This leaves the owner free to deal with suppliers and keep a close watch on the bottom line. "We really complement one another," summarizes Baker.

Decentralizing authority also motivates managers and employees to do their best for Baker's Best. "When you open a business and can find someone who is better at certain things than you are, you have to let that person go ahead," the owner emphasizes. "If I micro-manage the people who work for me, I'm not going to keep the talent that I need."

Job specialization is traditional in a food operation, and Baker's Best is no exception. Food preparers are either on the "hot side" or the "cold side," and baking is an entirely separate specialization. At the same time, Baker increases the versatility of his work force by cross-training employees. For example, some of the employees began as dishwashers and then started learning to cook. "We always tell people that the more able they are, the more they're needed and can work in two or three different areas," Baker says. He and his managers encourage employees with talent to try new tasks, such as applying their creativity to assembling an attractive vegetable platter or using their sociability in customer-contact positions. Baker's Best strives to fill open positions from within, which means that good employees and managers can take advantage of opportunities for professional growth without changing employers.

One of the most important principles underlying the Baker's Best corporate culture is a high regard for employees. "We take really good care of the people who work here," says Baker. Employees receive generous bonuses, are eligible for health insurance and retirement accounts, receive tickets to sporting events, and get a cake and gift certificate on every birthday. The owner also throws a company party every year to show his appreciation for the hard work and dedication of the entire organization. His aim is to make Baker's Best a good environment in which to work so that he can attract and retain good employees. "Your employees are as important as your customers," the owner says. "If you lose sight of this, you have problem."[20]

Questions

1. What type of departmentalization basis is Baker's Best using? Explain your answer.
2. Why would an entrepreneur have difficulty learning to delegate authority as a small business grows bigger?
3. Why would a very small business, such as the early Baker's Best, have little need for staff positions?

Building Skills for Career Success

1. Exploring the Internet

After studying the various organizational structures described in this chapter and the reasons for employing them, you may be interested in learning about the organizational structures in place at large firms. As noted in the chapter, departmentalization is typically based on function, product, location, and customer. Many large firms successfully use a combination of these organizational strategies. You can gain a good sense of which organizational theme prevails in an industry by looking at several corporate sites.

Assignment

1. Explore the website of any large firm that you believe is representative of its industry, and find its organization chart or a description of its organization. Create a brief organization chart from the information you have found. (You may choose one of the consulting firms listed in the Internet exercise for Chapter 7).
2. Describe the bases on which this firm is departmentalized.

2. Developing Critical Thinking Skills

A firm's culture is a reflection of its most basic beliefs, values, customs, and rituals. Because it can have a powerful influence on how employees think and act, this culture also can have a powerful influence on a firm's performance. The influence may be for the better, of course, as in the case of Southwest Airlines, or it may be for the worse, as in the case of a bureaucratic organization whose employees feel hopelessly mired in red tape. When a company is concerned about mediocre performance and declining sales figures, its managers would do well to examine the cultural environment to see what might be in need of change.

Assignment

1. Analyze the cultural environment in which you work. (If you have no job, consider your school as your workplace and your instructor as your supervisor.) Ask yourself and your coworkers (or classmates) the following questions and record the answers:
   a. Do you feel that your supervisors welcome your ideas and respect them even when they may disagree with them? Do you take pride in your work? Do you feel that your work is appreciated? Do you think that the amount of work assigned to you is reasonable? Are you compensated adequately for your work?
   b. Are you proud to be associated with the company? Do you believe what the company says about itself in its advertisements? Are there any company policies or rules, written or unwritten, that you feel are unfair? Do you think that there is an opportunity for you to advance in this environment?
   c. How much independence do you have in carrying out your assignments? Are you ever allowed to act on your own, or do you feel that you have to consult with your supervisor on every detail?
   d. Do you enjoy the atmosphere in which you work? Is the physical setting pleasant? How often do you laugh in an average workday? How well do you get along with your supervisor and coworkers?
   e. Do you feel that the company cares about you? Will your supervisor give you time off when you have some pressing personal need? If the company had to downsize, how do you think you would be treated?
2. Using the responses to these questions, write a two-page paper describing how the culture of your workplace affects your performance and the overall performance of the firm. Point out the cultural factors that have the most beneficial and negative effects. Include your thoughts on how negative effects could be reversed.

3. Building Team Skills

An organization chart is a diagram showing how employees and tasks are grouped and how the lines of communication and authority flow within an organization. These charts can look very different depending on a number of factors, including the nature and size of the business, the way it is departmentalized, its patterns of delegating authority, and its span of management.

Assignment

1. Working in a team, use the following information to draw an organization chart: The KDS Design Center works closely with two home-construction companies, Amex and Highmass. KDS's role is to help customers select materials for their new homes and to ensure that their selections are communicated accurately to the builders. The company is also a retailer of wallpaper, blinds, and drapery. The retail department, the Amex accounts, and the Highmass accounts make up KDS's three departments. The company has the following positions:

   President
   Executive vice president
   Managers, 2
   Appointment coordinators, 2
   Amex coordinators, 2
   Highmass coordinators, 2
   Consultants/designers for the Amex and Highmass accounts, 15
   Retail positions, 4
   Payroll and billing personnel, 1

2. After your team has drawn the organization chart, discuss the following:
   a. What type of organizational structure does your chart depict? Is it a bureaucratic, matrix, cluster, or network structure? Why?

b. How does KDS use departmentalization?
c. To what extent is authority in the company centralized or decentralized?
d. What is the span of management within KDS?
e. Which positions are line positions and which are staff? Why?

3. Prepare a three-page report summarizing what the chart revealed about relationships and tasks at the KDS Design Center and what your team learned about the value of organization charts. Include your chart in your report.

4. Researching Different Careers

In the past, company loyalty and ability to assume increasing job responsibility usually ensured advancement within an organization. While the reasons for seeking advancement (the desire for a better-paying position, more prestige, and job satisfaction) have not changed, the qualifications for career advancement have. In today's business environment, climbing the corporate ladder requires packaging and marketing yourself. To be promoted within your company or to be considered for employment with another company, it is wise to improve your skills continually. By taking workshops and seminars or enrolling in community college courses, you can keep up with the changing technology in your industry. Networking with people in your business or community can help you find a new job. Most jobs are filled through personal contacts. Who you know can be important.

A list of your accomplishments on the job can reveal your strengths and weaknesses. Setting goals for improvement helps to increase your self-confidence.

Be sure to recognize the signs of job dissatisfaction. It may be time to move to another position or company.

Assignment

Are you prepared to climb the corporate ladder? Do a self-assessment by analyzing the following areas, and summarize the results in a two-page report.

1. Skills
   - What are your most valuable skills?
   - What skills do you lack?
   - Describe your plan for acquiring new skills and improving your skills.
2. Networking
   - How effectively are you using a mentor?
   - Are you a member of a professional organization?
   - In which community, civic, or church groups are you participating?
   - Whom have you added to your contact list in the last six weeks?
3. Accomplishments
   - What achievements have you reached in your job?
   - What would you like to accomplish? What will it take for you to reach your goal?
4. Promotion or new job
   - What is your likelihood for getting a promotion?
   - Are you ready for a change? What are you doing or willing to do to find another job?

5. Improving Communication Skills

Delegation of authority involves giving another person responsibility for performing a task and the authority or power needed to accomplish the task. The person doing the delegating, however, remains responsible, or accountable, for seeing that the job is done properly. Delegating work is important not only because it is often the only way a manager can accomplish everything that needs to be accomplished but also because it gives lower-level employees the opportunity to improve their skills. For a variety of reasons, managers sometimes fail to delegate authority. They may feel that their subordinates are not competent to perform the work properly, or they may feel that their subordinates are too competent, in which case they would pose a threat to the manager. And some managers are simply too disorganized to delegate their work.

Assignment

1. Arrange an interview with the manager of a business in your community. Prepare a list of questions you will ask in the interview. They should focus on the following topics:
   a. What is the general pattern of delegation in the company?
   b. To what extent is the organization centralized or decentralized?
   c. How much work does this manager delegate? What are the kinds of tasks delegated?
   d. What are the benefits of delegating work? What are the drawbacks?
   e. Does this manager experience any difficulties in delegating? If so, what are they? Has the manager thought of any ways to resolve them?
2. Write a two-page report on the results of your interview.

chapter

9

Producing Quality Goods and Services

learning objectives

1 Explain the nature of production.

2 Outline how the conversion process transforms raw materials, labor, and other resources into finished products or services.

3 Describe how research and development lead to new products and services.

4 Discuss the components involved in planning the production process.

5 Explain the four major areas of operations control: purchasing, inventory control, scheduling, and quality control.

6 Discuss the increasing role of computers, robotics, and flexible manufacturing in the production process.

7 Outline the reasons for recent trends in productivity.

Financier Wilbur L. Ross wants to rescue LTV and change the way the U.S. steel industry operates.

inside business

International Steel Group Forges Production Changes

CAN INTERNATIONAL STEEL GROUP (ISG) RISE from the ashes of twice-bankrupt LTV to make steel at a profit? LTV, Bethlehem Steel, and other steel manufacturers were once giants in America's smokestack industries. They fed raw iron ore into blast furnaces stoked by natural gas and coke to melt and reshape it into sheets and coils of steel for use in construction and in the commercial production of cars and other products. However, high costs have cut into Big Steel's profits in recent years. New equipment is expensive, and the price tag for relining existing furnaces—which must be done once a decade—can run more than $100 million. Furthermore, the traditional company hierarchy is top-heavy with layers of management, and unionized steel workers have contracts guaranteeing generous benefits into retirement.

Meanwhile, currency fluctuations have made steel from manufacturers in Japan, China, and Korea much less expensive than steel from U.S. manufacturers. Not surprisingly, American imports of foreign-made steel continue to rise, putting downward pricing pressure on U.S. steelmakers seeking to be competitive as they turn out more and more steel. In addition, newer minimills such as Nucor are using highly efficient, electrically powered manufacturing instead of smoke-belching blast furnaces to transform steel scrap into usable steel. The bottom line is a smaller bottom line for traditional steel mills and, in some cases, not enough profits to cover ongoing costs. While dozens of older steelmakers like LTV and Bethlehem have filed for bankruptcy, minimills are gaining ground and profitably producing nearly half of all steel made in America.

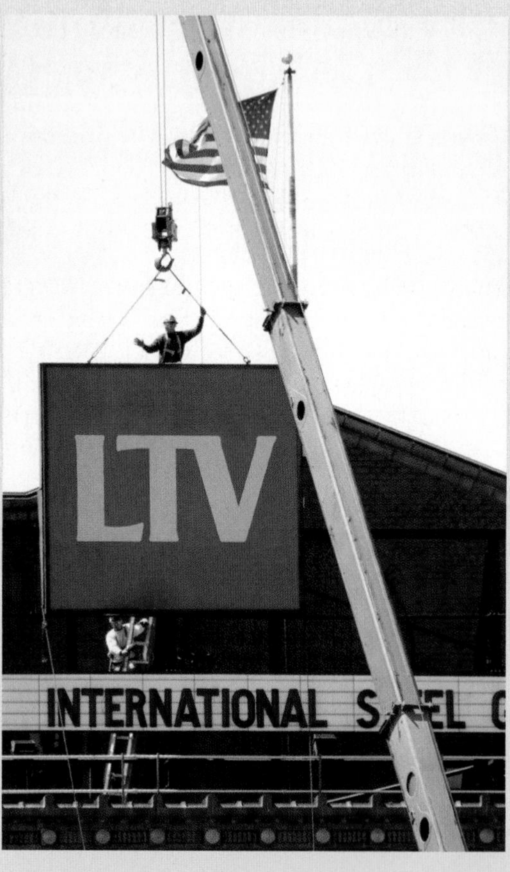

Now financier Wilbur L. Ross wants to rescue LTV and change the way the U.S. steel industry operates. Ross bought LTV's equipment and assets, as well as those of another bankrupt steelmaker, to form ISG. Because he did not buy these companies' actual operations, Ross did not assume their debts and contract liabilities—saving millions of dollars a year. This may not please creditors and retired LTV employees, who could lose company-paid pension and health-care benefits, but it does allow ISG to put 3,000 laid-off LTV employees back on the payroll.

Ross and ISG CEO Rodney Mott, a Nucor veteran, are reviewing every detail of the production process to minimize costs. More efficient work methods, more flexible scheduling, and leaner management ranks could reduce costs to the point where ISG would make a profit of $50 per ton at the market price of $320 per ton. The goal is to produce six million tons of steel per year, for a pretax profit of $300 million.[1]

Can ISG—the corporation profiled in the Inside Business opening case—succeed in a declining industry squeezed by international competition? While there are no guarantees, efficient work schedules, flexible scheduling, and leaner management can help ISG earn a profit and ultimately enable the firm to stay in business. In reality, no company illustrates this chapter's content—the production of quality goods and services—better than ISG. Companies like ISG take iron ore, steel scrap, natural gas, and electricity and other raw materials to produce steel that can be used to manufacture all kinds of finished products. While financier Wilbur Ross and ISG are trying to change the way the U.S. steel industry operates, it will not happen automatically. Both managers and employees must constantly look for ways to improve its methods of doing business. As a result, executives, managers, and workers continue to tinker with ISG's production system, make improvements where needed, and change the firm's operating procedures to become more competitive. Regardless of how the system is changed, however, the goal is still the same: Produce a product that people want.

We begin this chapter with an overview of operations management—the activities involved in the conversion of resources into products. In this section we also discuss competition in the global marketplace and careers in operations management. Next, we describe the conversion process that makes production possible and also note the growing role of services in our economy. Then we examine more closely three important aspects of operations management: developing ideas for new products, planning for production, and effectively controlling operations after production has begun. Next, we discuss changes in production as a result of automation, robotics, and computer-aided manufacturing. We close the chapter with a look at productivity trends and ways productivity can be improved.

What Is Production?

learning objective

1 Explain the nature of production.

Have you ever wondered where a new pair of Levi jeans comes from? Or a new Mitsubishi big-screen color television, Izod pullover sweater, or Uniroyal tire for your car? Even factory service on a Compaq notebook computer or a Maytag clothes dryer would be impossible if it weren't for the activities described in this chapter. In fact, these products and services and millions of others like them would not exist if it weren't for production activities.

Let's begin this chapter by reviewing what an operating manager does. In Chapter [1] we described an *operations manager* as a person who manages the systems that convert resources into goods and services. This area of management is usually referred to as **operations management;** it consists of all the activities managers engage in to produce goods and services.

operations management all activities managers engage in to produce goods and services

To produce a product or service successfully, a business must perform a number of specific activities. For example, suppose that an organization such as Toyota (the parent company of Lexus) has an idea for a new Lexus sport sedan called the IS 300, which will cost in excess of $30,000. Marketing research must determine not only if customers are willing to pay the price for this product but also what special features they want. Once it has been determined that there is a market for this type of automobile, Toyota's operations managers must turn the concept into reality.

Toyota's managers cannot just push the "start button" and immediately begin producing the new automobile. Production must be planned. As you will see, planning takes place both *before* anything is produced and *during* the production process.

Managers also must concern themselves with the control of operations to ensure that the organization's goals are achieved. For a product such as Toyota's Lexus IS 300 sport sedan, control of operations involves a number of important issues, including product quality, performance standards, the amount of inventory of both raw materials and finished products, and production costs.

We discuss each of the major activities of operations management later in this chapter. First, however, let's take a closer look at American manufacturers and how they compete in the global marketplace.

Fresh from the cow? Well, not exactly! Milk, like many products, must undergo a production process before you see it in the dairy department at your local supermarket or convenience store. The fact that no humans are shown in this photo is significant. For years, production experts have predicted more automation for all industries—even industries that have been around for a long time.

Competition in the Global Marketplace

After World War II, the United States became the most productive country in the world. For almost thirty years, until the late 1970s, its leadership was never threatened. By then, however, manufacturers in Japan, Germany, Great Britain, Italy, Korea, Sweden, and other industrialized nations were offering U.S. firms increasing competition. Once the leader in just about everything, U.S. firms lost market share in a number of vital industries, including steel, cement, building products, manufacturing equipment, farm machinery, and electronics. U.S. manufacturers quickly realized that "Made in the U.S.A." did not guarantee sales in the United States or foreign nations. Even to maintain market share, they would be forced to compete in an ever-smaller world to meet the needs of more demanding customers.

In an attempt to regain a competitive edge on foreign manufacturers, U.S. firms have taken another look at the importance of improving quality and meeting the needs of their customers. The most successful U.S. firms also have focused on the following:

1. Reducing production costs by selecting suppliers that offer higher-quality raw materials and components at reasonable prices
2. Replacing outdated equipment with state-of-the-art manufacturing equipment
3. Using computer-aided and flexible manufacturing systems that allow a higher degree of customization
4. Improving control procedures to help ensure lower manufacturing costs
5. Building new manufacturing facilities in foreign countries where labor costs are lower

Although competing in the global economy is a major challenge, it is a worthwhile pursuit. To see how automakers are improving productivity in order to compete in the global marketplace, read Going Global. For most firms, competing in the global marketplace is not only profitable; it is also an essential activity that requires the cooperation of everyone within the organization.

Careers in Operations Management

analytical process a process in operations management in which raw materials are broken into different component parts

Although it is hard to provide information about specific career opportunities in operations management, some generalizations do apply to this management area. First, you must appreciate the manufacturing process and the steps required to produce a product or service. A basic understanding of the difference between an analytical process and a synthetic process is essential. An **analytical process** breaks raw materials into different component parts. For example, a barrel of crude oil refined by Marathon Ashland Petroleum LLC—an Ohio-based oil and chemical refiner—can be broken down into

going global

Automakers Drive Productivity Higher

PRODUCTIVITY IS A CRITICAL ELEMENT in the auto industry's global competitive battle. Nissan, Honda, and Toyota all have opened U.S. assembly plants to serve the North American market. These manufacturers blend flexible manufacturing systems and worker ingenuity to boost productivity levels beyond those of their U.S. rivals.

Nissan, for example, can produce a vehicle in less than twenty-eight hours, compared with just over twenty-nine hours for Honda and just over thirty-one hours for Toyota. In contrast, Ford requires nearly forty hours to produce a vehicle—and General Motors and DaimlerChrysler take even longer. Improving productivity by even a few hours per vehicle can save time as well as labor. Productivity expert Ron Harbour estimates that DaimlerChrysler could assemble the same number of vehicles with 26,400 fewer employees if its productivity level equaled that of Nissan.

Just as important, Harbour notes that "the plants that have the highest quality are also the ones that are the most productive. That's because a good manufacturing process means guaranteeing quality at each point. You need a mechanism that says, 'If I put this together wrong, or if I forgot something in the process, it stops the [assembly] line.' That will make me fix it right there. And if you do that, you don't need all the repair, rework, and inspection people at the end of every assembly line." The result is higher productivity with higher quality built in.

Toyota is well known for its cutting-edge manufacturing systems. However, it also relies on its work force to increase productivity. Consider how it tackled a problem at one of its U.S. factories. Through inspection and customer complaints, the company learned that its radiator hoses sometimes leaked. Investigating, factory workers discovered that workers occasionally would forget to pull a pin from the radiator hose clamp, allowing coolant to leak out later. To solve this problem, they installed a spout with an electric eye to register each time a worker inserted a pin taken from a radiator hose. If a pin did not register every sixty seconds, the mechanism would stop the assembly line until the worker pulled off the pin. This boosted productivity by avoiding time-consuming, costly postproduction inspections and repairs—and it made customers happier.

gasoline, oil and lubricants, and many other petroleum by-products. A **synthetic process** is just the opposite of the analytical one; it combines raw materials or components to create a finished product. Black & Decker uses a synthetic system when it combines plastic, steel, rechargeable batteries, and other components to produce a cordless drill.

synthetic process a process in operations management in which raw materials or components are combined to create a finished product

Once you understand that operations managers are responsible for producing tangible products or services that customers want, you must determine how you fit into the production process. Today's successful operations managers must

1. be able to motivate and lead people.
2. understand how technology can make a manufacturer more productive and efficient.
3. appreciate the control processes that help lower production costs and improve product quality.
4. understand the relationship between the customer, the marketing of a product, and the production of a product.

If operations management seems like an area you might be interested in, why not do more career exploration? You could take an operations management course if your college or university offers one, or you could obtain a part-time job during the school year or a summer job in a manufacturing company.

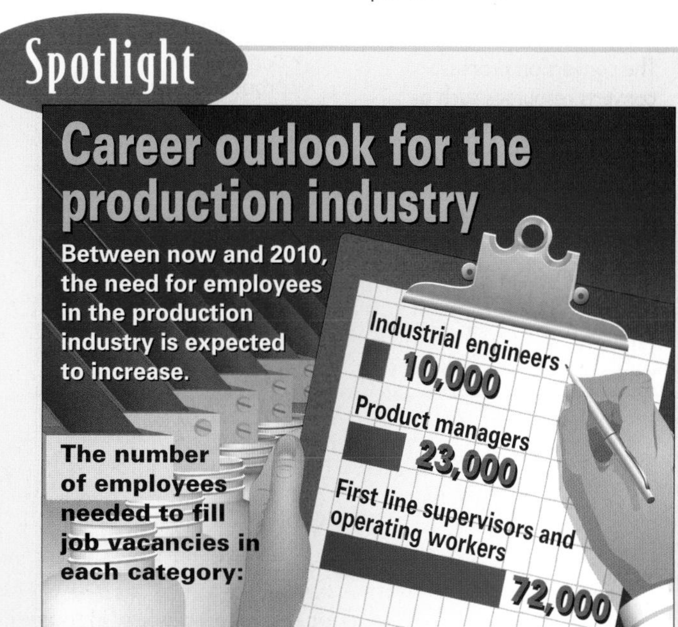

Spotlight
Career outlook for the production industry
Between now and 2010, the need for employees in the production industry is expected to increase.
The number of employees needed to fill job vacancies in each category:
Industrial engineers
10,000
Product managers
23,000
First line supervisors and operating workers
72,000

Source: "Occupational Report," U.S. Bureau of Labor Statistics (**www.bls.gov**).

learning objective

2 Outline how the conversion process transforms raw materials, labor, and other resources into finished products or services.

utility the ability of a good or service to satisfy a human need

form utility utility created by converting raw materials, people, finances, and information, into finished products

The Conversion Process

To have something to sell, a business must convert resources into goods and services. The resources are materials, finances, people, and information—the same resources discussed in Chapters 1 and 7. The goods and services are varied, ranging from heavy manufacturing equipment to fast food. The purpose of this conversion of resources into goods and services is to provide utility to customers. **Utility** is the ability of a good or service to satisfy a human need. Although there are four types of utility—form, place, time, and possession—operations management focuses primarily on form utility. **Form utility** is created by converting raw materials, people, finances, and information into finished products. The other types of utility—place, time, and possession—are discussed in Chapter 13.

But how does the conversion take place? How does Kellogg convert wheat, corn, sugar, salt, and other ingredients; money from previous sales and stockholders' investments; production workers and managers; and economic and marketing forecasts into cereal products? How does New York Life Insurance convert office buildings, insurance premiums, actuaries, and mortality tables into life insurance policies? They do so through the use of a conversion process like the one illustrated in Figure 9.1. As indicated by our New York Life Insurance example, the conversion process is not limited to manufacturing products. The conversion process also can be used to produce services.

The Nature of the Conversion

The conversion of resources into products and services can be described in several ways. We limit our discussion here to three: the focus or major resource used in the conversion process, its magnitude of change, and the number of production processes employed.

Focus By the *focus* of a conversion process we mean the resource or resources that comprise the major or most important *input*. For a bank such as Citibank, financial resources are the major resource used in the conversion process. A chemical and energy company such as ChevronTexaco concentrates on material resources. A college or university is concerned primarily with information. And a temporary employment service focuses on the use of human resources.

figure 9.1

The Conversion Process

The conversion process converts resources such as materials, finances, people, and information into useful goods, services, and ideas. It is a crucial step in the economic development of any nation.

INPUTS
- Concept for a new product or service
- Financing

CONVERSION
- Design and specifications
- Purchase of needed resources
- Hiring of employees

OUTPUTS
- Completed product or service

Magnitude of Change The *magnitude* of a conversion process is the degree to which the resources are physically changed. At one extreme lie such processes as the one by which the Glad Products Company, a subsidiary of the Clorox Corporation, produces Glad Cling Wrap. Various chemicals in liquid or powder form are combined to form long, thin sheets of plastic Glad Cling Wrap. Here the original resources are totally unrecognizable in the finished product. At the other extreme, Southwest Airlines produces *no* physical change in its original resources. The airline simply provides a service and transports people from one place to another.

Number of Production Processes A single firm may employ one production process or many. In general, larger firms that make a variety of products use multiple production processes. For example, General

Electric manufactures some of its own products, buys other merchandise from suppliers, and operates a credit division, an insurance company, and a medical equipment division. Smaller firms, by contrast, may use one production process or very few production processes. For example, Texas-based Advanced Cast Stone, Inc., manufactures one basic product: building materials made from concrete.

A sweet product from Smucker's. Form utility for Smucker's preserves, ice cream toppings, and breakfast syrups is created by employees using finances, information, and raw materials to produce a great tasting product. Since some of these products are sugar free, Smucker's must also use NutraSweet—an artificial sweetener—to obtain the taste that millions of customers expect when they purchase Smucker's products.

The Increasing Importance of Services

The application of the basic principles of operations management to the production of services has coincided with a dramatic growth in the number and diversity of service businesses. In 1900, only 28 percent of American workers were employed in service firms. By 1950, this figure had grown to 40 percent, and by the end of 2001, it had risen to 81 percent.[2] By any yardstick, service firms have become a dominant part of our economy. In fact, the American economy is now characterized as a **service economy** (see Figure 9.2). A service economy is one in which more effort is devoted to the production of services than to the production of goods.

This rapid growth is the primary reason for the increased use of production techniques in service firms. The managers of restaurants, laundries, real estate agencies, banks, movie theaters, airlines, travel bureaus, and other service firms have realized that they can benefit from the experience of manufacturers and construction firms. And yet the production of services is very different from the production of manufactured goods in the following four ways:

1. Services are consumed immediately and, unlike manufactured goods, cannot be stored. For example, a hair stylist cannot store completed haircuts like a manufacturer stores microwave ovens.
2. Services are provided when and where the customer desires the service. In many cases, customers will not travel as far to obtain a service as they would to purchase a manufactured product.
3. Services are usually labor intensive because the human resource is often the most important resource used in the production of services.
4. Services are intangible, and it is therefore more difficult to evaluate customer satisfaction.[3]

service economy an economy in which more effort is devoted to the production of services than to the production of goods

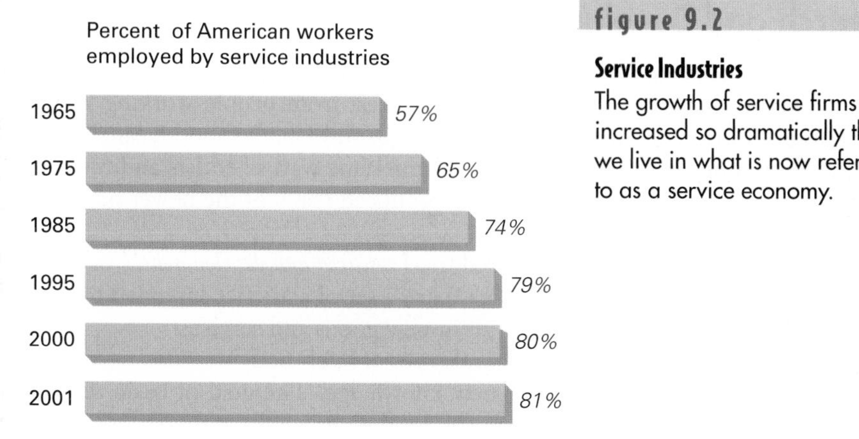

figure 9.2

Service Industries

The growth of service firms has increased so dramatically that we live in what is now referred to as a service economy.

Source: U.S. Bureau of Labor Statistics, *Monthly Labor Review*, August 2002, p. 72.

Although it is often more difficult to measure customer satisfaction, today's successful service firms work hard at providing the services customers want. Compared with manufacturers, service firms often listen more carefully to customers and respond more quickly to the market's changing needs. In an effort to meet increased demands for customer service, both manufacturers and traditional service businesses ranging from small mom-and-pop firms to large *Fortune* 500 companies are developing new ways to provide services and meet customer needs. For example, IBM is a well-known manufacturer of computer equipment. And yet IBM also must be concerned about providing service to its customers. Here's why—IBM operates in a very competitive industry. In order to be successful, it must gather as much information as possible about the customer in order to meet the needs of each individual customer. Want to buy a new IBM ThinkPad computer? All you have to do is to go to the IBM website and work through a series of questions designed to determine how the computer will be used. Still have questions? By using an 800 phone number, you can contact a customer service representative who will help you to make a decision. Service after the sale is also important because IBM maintains an ongoing dialogue with its customers to understand customer concerns and problems and identify customers who are ready to buy more of the firm's products.[4]

Now that we understand something about the production process that is used to transform resources into goods and services, we can consider three major activities involved in operations management. These are product development, planning for production, and operations control.

Where Do New Products and Services Come From?

learning objective

3 Describe how research and development lead to new products and services.

No firm can produce a product or service until it has an idea. In other words, someone must first come up with a new way to satisfy a need—a new product or an improvement in an existing product. Starbucks' milkshake-like coffee drink, Honda's ergonomically designed motorcycle, and Hewlett Packard's color printer all began as an idea. And the quest for new ideas that lead to new products goes on. Already there are companies that are developing new prescription medicines that hopefully will cure cancer, diabetes, and other terrible diseases. For more information about how one company—AstraZeneca—is using research and product development to create new prescription drugs, read Talking Technology (see p. 256). While no one can predict with 100 percent accuracy what types of products will be available in the next five years, it is safe to say that companies will continue to introduce new products that will change the way we take care of ourselves, interact with others, and find the information and services we need.

Research and Development

How did we get personal computers, CD players, and DVD players? We got them the same way we got light bulbs and automobile tires: from people working with new ideas. Thomas Edison created the first light bulb, and Charles Goodyear discovered the vulcanization process that led to tires. In the same way, scientists and researchers working in businesses and universities have produced many of the newer products we already take for granted.

research and development (R&D) a set of activities intended to identify new ideas that have the potential to result in new goods and services

These activities generally are referred to as *research and development.* For our purposes, **research and development (R&D)** are a set of activities intended to identify new ideas that have the potential to result in new goods and services.

Today, business firms use three general types of R&D activities. *Basic research* consists of activities aimed at uncovering new knowledge. The goal of basic research is scientific advancement, without regard for its potential use in the development of goods and services. *Applied research*, in contrast, consists of activities geared toward discovering new knowledge with some potential use. *Development and implementation* are research activities undertaken specifically to put new or existing knowledge to use in producing goods and services. The 3M Company has always been known for its development and implementation research activities. At the end of the twentieth century, the company had developed more than 50,000 products designed to make people's lives easier. Does a company like 3M quit innovating because it has developed successful products? No, not at all! Just recently, the 3M company used development and implementation when it combined its transdermal drug-delivery system with the drug nitroglycerin to create the smallest daily nitroglycerin patch in the world. This new product is called Minitran. For heart patients, this is a major breakthrough that makes their lives easier while enabling them to take the medicine they need to live a normal life.[5]

Corning's superglass for the next generation of computer chips. Unless you have been involved in the competitive research effort to develop the next generation of computer chips, you probably don't recognize the product shown in this photo. This photo illustrates the process used to slice calcium fluoride into "lens blanks," a critical component for producing the machines that will produce the next generation of computer chips. So, how important can a product that looks like a big hunk of cheese be? Lens blanks made from calcium fluoride are so important and the process so secretive that Corning won't even tell how many people work at the plant where this product is produced.

Product Extension and Refinement

When a brand-new product is first marketed, its sales are zero and slowly increase from that point. If the product is successful, annual sales increase more and more rapidly until they reach some peak. Then, as time passes, annual sales begin to decline, and they continue to decline until it is no longer profitable to manufacture the product. (This rise-and-decline pattern, called the *product life cycle*, is discussed in more detail in Chapter 14.)

If a firm sells only one product, when that product reaches the end of its life cycle, the firm will die too. To stay in business, the firm must, at the very least, find ways to refine or extend the want-satisfying capability of its product. Consider television sets. Since they were introduced in the late 1930s, television sets have been constantly *refined* so that they now provide clearer, sharper pictures with less dial adjusting. They are tuned electronically for better picture control and can even compensate for variations in room lighting and picture tube wear. During the same time, television sets also were *extended*. There are color as well as black-and-white sets, television-only sets, and others that include VCR and DVD players. There are even television sets that allow their owners to access the Internet. And the latest development—high-definition, or digital, televisions—is already available. Although initial prices are high, the improved picture will convince some consumers to bite the bullet and buy a new set.

Each refinement or extension results in an essentially "new" product whose sales make up for the declining sales of a product that was introduced earlier. When consumers discovered that the original five varieties of Campbell's Soup were of the highest quality, as well as inexpensive, the soups were an instant success. Although one of the most successful companies at the beginning of the 1900s, Campbell's had to continue to innovate, refine, and extend its product line. Today, the firm continues to focus on consumers' needs and listening to what customers say. For example, many consumers in the United States live in what is called an on-the-go society. To meet this need, Campbell's Soup has developed ready-to-serve products that can be popped into a microwave at work or school. In other countries, customer feedback is also used to adapt products to meet the needs of local customers. For example, Liebig Pur, a thick vegetable soup, is sold in cartons with a long shelf life in France.[6] In a similar fashion, Jell-O was introduced to the public in 1897 and was acquired by Kraft Foods in 1925. One of Kraft Foods' newer products, Jell-O Pudding Snacks, is still based on Jell-O and produces sales of more than $100 million annually.[7] For most firms, extension and refinement are expected results of their development and implementation effort. Most often they result from the application of new knowledge to existing products. For instance, improved technology affects the content companies can distribute on the Internet. The Disney Corporation currently has a clear advantage over competitors because much of its content is animation. Animation is the easiest content to transfer to the Internet, and the vast majority of Internet users only have access to

talking technology

Fighting Cancer One Pill at a Time

TECHNOLOGY AND DEEP POCKETS are helping London-based pharmaceutical giant AstraZeneca (AZ) find new prescription medicines to help in the war against cancer. The company invests millions of dollars every week in high-tech research and testing to develop and manufacture cancer-fighting drugs. The process is time consuming and labor intensive, as well as costly, and not every drug winds up being approved for its proposed use.

One success story is Arimidex, AZ's drug for treating breast cancer. Company scientists first used high-tech analysis to examine the characteristics of different types of cancer. Then, year after year, they tried different formulas in the laboratory, in animal tests, and in human trials to find the most effective combination. In 1996, the U.S. Food and Drug Administration (FDA) approved Arimidex for use against certain types of advanced breast cancer. After years of additional testing on 9,300 women worldwide, AZ's computerized analyses showed that the drug helped keep cancer from recurring in many users. Once the FDA approved the drug for use in more breast cancer situations, AZ geared up for higher production capacity.

Similarly, AZ's researchers worked for years on developing Casodex, a pill for treating prostate cancer. The potential market for this drug is relatively large because prostate cancer is second only to lung cancer in the number of diagnoses among men in Western countries. AZ's scientists conducted numerous tests and then used sophisticated equipment analyses to demonstrate that Casodex significantly reduced the risk of tumor growth in localized prostate cancers. After regulators in the United Kingdom, Greece, and other countries approved Casodex, AZ prepared its plants to manufacture the drug based on demand estimates.

On the other hand, AZ has faced some setbacks with its Iressa pill for lung cancer. Early animal and human trials went well. However, in two larger tests, the drug did not improve survival rates when used as part of the initial treatment for lung cancer (the largest market). Still, the FDA did recommend approving Iressa for use in treating patients whose tumors did not respond to other treatments (a much smaller market). Now AZ is analyzing the data to determine which patients respond best to Iressa so that it can get FDA approval and plan for additional manufacturing capacity.

narrow bandwidth, which delivers a reasonable-quality image of animation. As bandwidth access expands, Disney is expected to be ready with a vault full of prerecorded film and video content.[8]

Planning for Production

learning objective

4 Discuss the components involved in planning the production process.

Only a few of the many ideas for new products, refinements, and extensions ever reach the production stage. For those ideas that do, however, the next step is planning for production. Planning for production involves three major phases: design planning, facilities planning and site selection, and operational planning.

Design Planning

design planning the development of a plan for converting a product idea into an actual product

When the R&D staff at Compaq Computers recommended to top management that the firm produce and market an affordable notebook computer, the company could not simply swing into production the next day. Instead, a great deal of time and energy had to be invested in determining what the new computer would look like, where and how it would be produced, and what options would be included. These decisions are a part of design planning. **Design planning** is the development of a plan for converting a product idea into an actual product. The major decisions involved in design planning deal with product line, required capacity, and use of technology.

Product Line A **product line** is a group of similar products that differ only in relatively minor characteristics. During the design-planning stage, management must determine how many different product variations there will be. A computer manufacturer such as Compaq needs to determine how many different models to produce and what major options to offer. A restaurant chain such as Pizza Hut must decide how many menu items to offer.

product line a group of similar products that differ only in relatively minor characteristics

An important issue in deciding on the product line is to balance customer preferences and production requirements. For this reason, marketing managers play an important role in making product-line decisions. Once the product line has been determined, each distinct product within the product line must be designed. **Product design** is the process of creating a set of specifications from which the product can be produced. When designing a new product, specifications are extremely important. For example, product engineers for Whirlpool Corporation must make sure that a new frost-free refrigerator keeps food frozen in the freezer compartment. At the same time, they must make sure that lettuce and tomatoes do not freeze in the crisper section of the refrigerator. The need for a complete product design is fairly obvious; products that work cannot be manufactured without it. But services should be carefully designed as well—and *for the same reason.*

product design the process of creating a set of specifications from which a product can be produced

Required Capacity **Capacity** is the amount of products or services that an organization can produce in a given period of time. (The capacity of an automobile assembly plant, for instance, might be 300,000 cars per year.) Operations managers—again working with the firm's marketing managers—must determine the required capacity. This, in turn, determines the size of the production facility. Capacity of a production plant is vitally important. If the facility is built with too much capacity, valuable resources (plant, equipment, and money) will lie idle. If the facility offers insufficient capacity, additional capacity may have to be added later, when it is much more expensive than in the initial building stage.

capacity the amount of products or services that an organization can produce in a given time

Capacity means about the same thing to service businesses. For example, the capacity of a restaurant like the Hard Rock Cafe is the number of customers it can serve at one time. Like the manufacturing facility described earlier, if the restaurant is built with too much capacity—too many tables and chairs—valuable resources will be wasted. If the restaurant is too small, customers may have to wait for service; if the wait is too long, they may leave and choose another restaurant.

Use of Technology During the design-planning stage, management must determine the degree to which *automation* will be used to produce a product or service. Here, there is a tradeoff between high initial costs and low operating costs (for automation) and low initial costs and high operating costs (for human labor). Ultimately, management must choose between a labor-intensive technology and a capital-intensive technology. A **labor-intensive technology** is a process in which people must do most of the work. Housecleaning services and the New York Yankees baseball team, for example, are labor

labor-intensive technology a process in which people must do most of the work

What happened to this Jeep? Actually, the question should be, "What is going to happen to this Jeep?" Building a product as complex as an automobile requires many steps. This Jeep is in the middle of a journey through the new state-of-the-art high-tech DaimlerChrysler plant in Toledo, Ohio. Before the finished product can be driven off the assembly line, this Jeep Liberty will pass through more than 200 different workstations.

capital-intensive technology a process in which machines and equipment do most of the work

intensive. A **capital-intensive technology** is a process in which machines and equip-ment do most of the work. A Motorola automated assembly plant is capital intensive.

Facilities Planning and Site Selection

Once initial decisions have been made about a new product line, required capacity and the use of technology, it is time to determine where the products or services are going to be produced. Initially, managers must decide whether they will build a new plant or refurbish an existing factory. Generally, a business will choose to produce a new product in an existing factory as long as (1) the existing factory has enough capacity to handle customer demand for both the new product and established products and (2) the cost of refurbishing an existing factory is less than the cost of building a new one.

After exploring the capacity of existing factories, management may decide to build a new production facility. Once again, a number of decisions must be made. Should all the organization's production capacity be placed in one or two large facilities? Or should it be divided among several smaller facilities? In general, firms that market a wide variety of products find it more economical to have a number of smaller facilities. Firms that produce only a small number of products tend to have fewer but larger facilities.

In determining where to locate production facilities, management must consider a number of variables, including the following:

- Locations of major customers
- Transportation costs to deliver finished products to customers
- Geographic locations of suppliers of parts and raw materials
- Availability and cost of skilled and unskilled labor
- Quality of life for employees and management in the proposed location
- The cost of both land and construction required to build a new production facility
- Local and state taxes, environmental regulations, and zoning laws that could affect a new production facility
- The amount of financial support, if any, offered by local and state governments
- Special requirements, such as great amounts of energy or water used in the production process

Source: "Occupational Report," U.S. Bureau of Labor Statistics (**www.bls.gov**).

It may, of course, be impossible to find the perfect location for a production facility. In fact the choice of a location often involves balancing the most important variables for each production facility. Before making a final decision about where a proposed plant will be located and how it will be organized, two other factors—human resources and plant layout—should be examined.

Human Resources Several issues involved in facilities planning and site selection fall within the province of the human resources manager. Thus, at this stage, human resources and operations managers work closely together. For example, suppose that a U.S. firm such as Reebok International wants to lower labor costs by constructing a sophisticated production plant in China. The human resources manager will have to recruit managers and employees with the appropriate skills who are willing to relocate to a foreign country, or develop training programs for local Chinese workers, or do both. Human resources managers also can obtain and provide valuable information on the availability of skilled workers in various areas, wage rates, and other factors that may influence decisions concerning the use of technology and possible plant locations. To see how people help the 3M Corporation innovate and develop new products, read Adapting to Change.

Plant Layout **Plant layout** is the arrangement of machinery, equipment, and personnel within a production facility. Three general types of plant layout are used (see Figure 9.3 on p. 260).

plant layout the arrangement of machinery, equipment, and personnel within a production facility

The *process layout* is used when different operations are required for creating small batches of different products or working on different parts of a product. The plant is arranged so that each operation is performed in its own particular area. Once the task in one area is completed, the work in process is moved to another area. An auto repair facility at a local automobile dealership provides an example of a process layout. The various operations may be engine repair, body work, wheel alignment, and safety inspection. Each operation is performed in a different area. If you take your Lincoln Aviator for a wheel inspection, your car "visits" only the area where wheel alignments are performed.

A *product layout* (sometimes referred to as an *assembly line*) is used when all products undergo the same operations in the same sequence. Workstations are arranged to match the sequence of operations, and work flows from station to station. An assembly line is the best example of a product layout. For example, Pennsylvania-based Integrated Circuit Systems, Inc., uses a product layout to manufacture silicon timing devices for consumer and business electronic products.

A *fixed-position layout* is used when a very large product is produced. Aircraft manufacturers and shipbuilders apply this method because of the difficulty of moving a large product like an airliner or ship. The product remains stationary while people and machines are moved as needed to assemble the product. Boeing, for example, uses the fixed-position layout to build 777 jet aircraft at its Everett, Washington, manufac-

adapting to change

3M: Leading Through Innovation

FROM SCOTCH TAPE TO POST-IT-NOTES to Thinsulate insulation, 3M has been known as an innovator for more than a century. Part of the reason is its ongoing emphasis on R&D. The company budgets $1 billion annually for basic research, development, and implementation. Management gives 3M's 7,000 scientists considerable freedom to experiment with new ideas. At the same time, a committee of ten managers carefully weighs the potential of each innovation to determine which ideas merit further investment and in what order they should be developed. Over the years, the company has studied customer needs and developed 50,000 new products to meet those needs while also achieving sales and profit goals.

Consider 3M's health care division, where researchers have come up with a variety of products to solve medical problems. For example, 3M scientists recently focused on the common problem of removing a bandage without disturbing the wound or tearing out hairs. They tested various materials and finally put together a no-stick pad that protects the wound, surrounded by a stretchy band that holds even in water. Dubbed the Nexcare Ease-Off Bandage, this new product comes off without pain—an especially important consideration for kids with cuts.

The story behind the proliferation of Post-it-Notes illustrates another of 3M's strengths in innovation. Although a company scientist mixed up the formula for repositionable adhesive in 1968, years went by until new product development researcher Art Fry saw a potential use. The bookmarks he kept in his hymnal kept falling out—until Fry suddenly came up with the idea of backing them with repositionable adhesive so that they would stay put until he lifted them off. Still, many managers doubted the commercial value of what were essentially sticky scraps of paper. After two executives proved the product's value by selling it informally to businesses in Virginia, the company put Post-it-Notes into production in 1980. Since then, the basic idea has been refined for dozens of product extensions in a kaleidoscope of colors, sizes, and applications.

figure 9.3

Facilities Planning

The process layout is used when small batches of different products are created or worked on in a different operating sequence. The product layout (assembly line) is used when all products undergo the same operations in the same sequence. The fixed-position layout is used in producing a product too large to move.

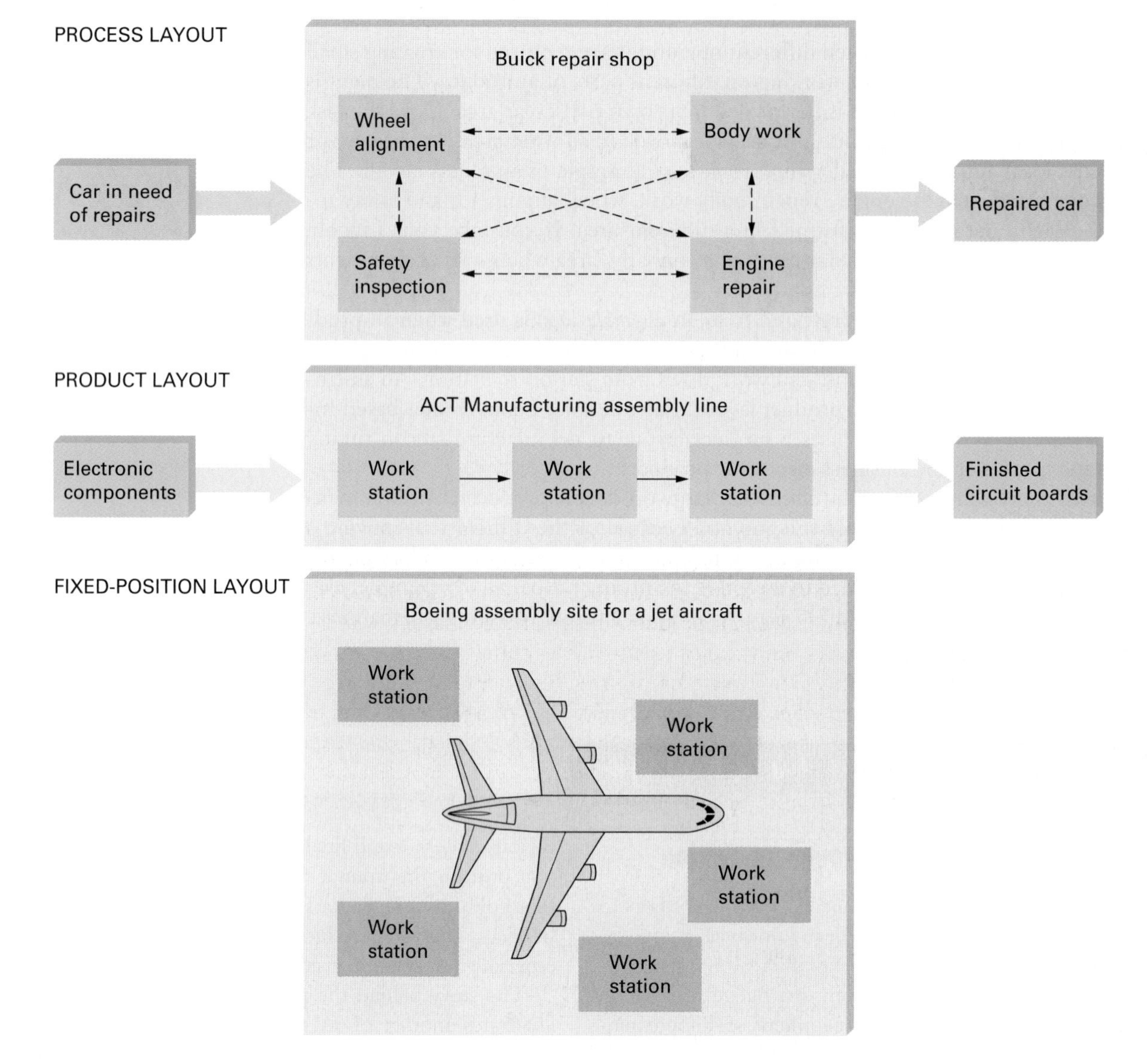

turing facility. When a fixed-position layout is used, it is much easier to move people and machines around the airliner than to move the plane during the production process.

Operational Planning

Once the product has been designed and a decision has been made to use an existing production facility or build a new one, operational plans must be developed. The objective of operational planning is to decide on the amount of products or services each facility will produce during a specific period of time. Four steps are required.

planning horizon the period during which a plan will be in effect

Step 1: Selecting a Planning Horizon A **planning horizon** is simply the time period during which a plan will be in effect. A common planning horizon for production plans is one year. Then, before each year is up, management must plan for the next.

A planning horizon of one year is generally long enough to average out seasonal increases and decreases in sales. At the same time, it is short enough for planners to adjust production to accommodate long-range sales trends. Firms that operate in a rapidly changing business environment with many competitors may find it best to select a shorter planning horizon to keep their production planning current.

Step 2: Estimating Market Demand The *market demand* for a product is the quantity that customers will purchase at the going price. This quantity must be estimated for the time period covered by the planning horizon. Sales projections developed by marketing managers are the basis for market-demand estimates.

Step 3: Comparing Market Demand with Capacity The third step in operational planning is to compare the estimated market demand with the facility's capacity to satisfy that demand. Again, demand and capacity must be compared for the same time period. One of three outcomes may result: Demand may exceed capacity, capacity may exceed demand, or capacity and demand may be equal. If they are equal, the facility should be operated at full capacity. However, if market demand and capacity are not equal, adjustments may be necessary.

Step 4: Adjusting Products or Services to Meet Demand Adjustments to production schedules are more common than most production managers would like. The biggest reason for changes to a firm's production schedule is changes in the amount of products or services that a company sells to its customers. For example, Indiana-based Berry Plastics uses an injection-molded manufacturing process to produce all kinds of plastic products. One particularly successful product line for Berry Plastics is drink cups that can be screen-printed to promote a company or the company's products or services.[9] If Berry Plastics obtains a large contract to provide promotional mugs to a large fast-food chain such as Whataburger or McDonald's, the company may need to work three shifts a day, seven days a week until the contract is fulfilled. Unfortunately, the reverse is also true. If the company's sales force does not generate new sales, there may only be enough work for the employees on one shift. It also may be necessary to reduce the number of days that those employees work to two or three days a week until new customers are found for the company's products. Specific suggestions used to adjust for increased or reduced demand for a company's products or services are described below.

When market demand exceeds capacity, several options are available to a firm. Production of products or services may be increased by operating the facility overtime with existing personnel or by starting a second or third work shift. For manufacturers, another response is to subcontract a portion of the work to other producers. If the excess demand is likely to be permanent, the firm may expand the current facility or build another facility.

Some firms occasionally pursue another option: Ignore the excess demand and allow it to remain unmet. For several years the Adolph Coors Company used this strategy. A mystique gradually developed around Coors beer because it was not available in many parts of the country. When the firm's brewing capacity was finally expanded, an eager market was waiting.

What happens when capacity exceeds market demand? Again, there are several options. To reduce output temporarily, workers may be laid off and part of the facility shut down. Or the facility may be operated on a shorter-than-normal work week for as long as the excess capacity persists. To adjust to a permanently decreased demand, management may shift the excess capacity of a manufacturing facility to the production of other goods or services. The most radical adjustment is to eliminate the excess capacity by selling unused facilities.

Operations Control

learning objective

5 Explain the four major areas of operations control: purchasing, inventory control, scheduling, and quality control.

purchasing all the activities involved in obtaining required materials, supplies, and parts from other firms

We have discussed the development of an idea for a product or service and the planning that translates that idea into the reality. Now we push the "start button" to begin the production process and examine four important areas of operations control: purchasing, inventory control, scheduling, and quality control (see Figure 9.4).

Purchasing

Purchasing consists of all the activities involved in obtaining required materials, supplies, and parts from other firms. Levi Strauss must purchase denim cloth, thread, and zippers before it can produce a single pair of jeans. Similarly, Nike, Inc., must purchase leather, rubber, cloth for linings, and laces before manufacturing a pair of athletic shoes. For all firms, the purchasing function is far from routine, and its importance should not be underestimated. For some products, purchased materials make up more than 50 percent of their wholesale costs. To improve their purchasing system, aerospace giants Boeing, BAE Systems, Lockheed Martin, and Raytheon jointly developed an online exchange that links more than 37,000 suppliers, hundreds of airlines, and national governments into a single web-based marketplace for parts estimated to be worth more than $400 billion in annual sales. It also reduces administrative costs and speeds procurement for the private and government aerospace and defense concerns worldwide.[10]

The objective of purchasing is to ensure that required materials are available when they are needed, in the proper amounts, and at minimum cost. To achieve this objective, management must select suppliers carefully. Generally, the company with purchasing needs and suppliers must develop a working relationship built on trust. For example, Harvard Technologies, a Hispanic-owned business in Texas; Cherokee Nation Industries, a Native American firm in Oklahoma; and Pacific Network Supply, an African-American-owned business in California formed a joint venture to market their products to SBC Communications and other large corporations. While you probably recognize SBC Communications as the telecommunications company that does business in nearly half of the United States, you may not recognize the three suppliers that formed the joint venture. All three firms were small companies that wanted to sell products and services to SBC. Each company found that SBC was reluctant to give large contracts to small companies because they did not have enough locations, inventory, and resources to meet the purchasing needs of a large corporation. However, when the three companies formed a joint venture named the Trilogy Partnership, SBC began buying telecommunications equipment from Trilogy. The joint venture is working, and sales for Harvard Technologies, Cherokee Nation Industries, and Pacific Network Supply have increased. At the same time, SBC Communications has found a supplier that can meet its purchasing needs.[11] Incidentally, SBC Communications won the National Minority Supplier Development Council's "Corporation of the Year" award for its efforts to do business with minorities.

Purchasing personnel should be on the lookout constantly for new or backup suppliers, even when their needs are being met by their present suppliers, because

figure 9.4

Four Aspects of Operations Control
Implementing the operations control system in any business requires the effective use of purchasing, inventory control, scheduling, and quality control.

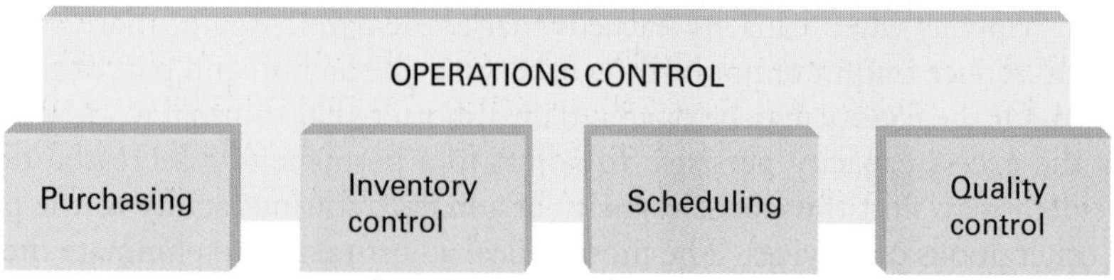

problems such as strikes and equipment breakdowns can cut off the flow of purchased materials from a primary supplier at any time.

The choice of suppliers should result from careful analysis of a number of factors. The following are especially critical:

- *Price.* Comparing prices offered by different suppliers are always an essential part of selecting a supplier. Even tiny differences in price add up to enormous sums when large quantities are purchased.
- *Quality.* Purchasing specialists are always challenged to find the "best" materials at the lowest price. Although the goal is not necessarily to find the highest quality available, purchasing specialists always try to buy materials at a level of quality in keeping with the type of product being manufactured. The minimum acceptable quality is usually specified by product designers.
- *Reliability.* An agreement to purchase high-quality materials at a low price is the purchaser's dream. But such an agreement becomes a nightmare if the supplier does not deliver. Purchasing personnel should check the reliability of potential suppliers, including their ability to meet delivery schedules.
- *Credit terms.* Purchasing specialists should determine if the supplier demands immediate payment or will extend credit. Also, does the supplier offer a cash discount or reduction in price for prompt payment?
- *Shipping costs.* One of the most overlooked factors in purchasing is the geographic location of the supplier. Low prices and favorable credit terms offered by a distant supplier can be wiped out when the buyer must pay the shipping costs. Above all, the question of who pays the shipping costs should be answered before any supplier is chosen.

Inventory Control

Can you imagine what would happen if a Coca-Cola manufacturing plant ran out of the company's familiar red and white aluminum cans? It would be impossible to complete the manufacturing process and ship the cases of Coke to retailers. Management would be forced to shut the assembly line down until the next shipment of cans arrived from a supplier. In reality, operations managers for Coca-Cola realize the disasters that a shortage of needed materials can cause and will avoid this type of problem if at all possible. The simple fact is that shutdowns are expensive because costs such as rent, wages, and insurance still must be paid.

Operations managers are concerned with three types of inventories. A *raw-materials inventory* consists of materials that will become part of the product during the production process. The *work-in-process inventory* consists of partially completed products. The *finished-goods inventory* consists of completed goods.

Associated with each type of inventory are a *holding cost*, or storage cost, and a *stock-out cost*, the cost of running out of inventory. **Inventory control** is the process of managing inventories in such a way as to minimize inventory costs, including both holding costs and potential stock-out costs. Today, computer systems are being used both to control inventory levels and to record costs. In both large and small firms, computer-based systems keep track of inventories, provide periodic inventory reports, and alert managers to impending stock-outs.

inventory control the process of managing inventories in such a way as to minimize inventory costs, including both holding costs and potential stock-out costs

One of the most sophisticated methods of inventory control used today is materials requirements planning. **Materials requirements planning (MRP)** is a computerized system that integrates production planning and inventory control. One of the great advantages of an MRP system is its ability to juggle delivery schedules and lead times effectively. For a complex product such as an automobile or airplane, it is virtually impossible for individual managers to oversee the hundreds of parts that go into the finished product. However, a manager using an MRP system can arrange both order and delivery schedules so that materials, parts, and supplies arrive when they are needed.

materials requirements planning (MRP) a computerized system that integrates production planning and inventory control

Two extensions of MRP are used by manufacturing firms today. The first is known as *manufacturing resource planning*, or simply *MRP II.* The primary difference between the two systems is that MRP involves just production and inventory personnel, whereas MRP II involves the entire organization. Thus MRP II provides a single common set of facts that can be used by all the organization's managers to make effective decisions. The second extension of MRP is known as *enterprise resource planning (ERP)*. The primary difference between ERP and the preceding methods of controlling inventory and production is that ERP software is more sophisticated and can monitor not only inventory and production processes but also quality, customer satisfaction, and even such variables as inventory at a supplier's location. While MRP and MRP II are used to monitor activities at one firm, ERP can be used to monitor activities at more than one firm. Today, ERP systems are expensive, but most large firms believe that the benefits are well worth the investment.

just-in-time inventory system a system designed to ensure that materials or supplies arrive at a facility just when they are needed so that storage and holding costs are minimized

Because large firms can incur huge inventory costs, much attention has been devoted to inventory control. The just-in-time system being used by some businesses is one result of all this attention. A **just-in-time inventory system** is designed to ensure that materials or supplies arrive at a facility just when they are needed so that storage and holding costs are minimized. The just-in-time system requires considerable cooperation between the supplier and the customer. The customer must specify what will be needed, when, and in what amounts. The supplier must be sure that the right supplies arrive at the agreed-on time and location.

Without proper inventory control, it is impossible for operations managers to schedule the work required to produce goods that can be sold to customers.

Scheduling

scheduling the process of ensuring that materials and other resources are at the right place at the right time

Scheduling is the process of ensuring that materials and other resources are at the right place at the right time. The materials and resources may be moved from a warehouse to the workstations, they may move from station to station along an assembly line, or they may arrive at workstations "just in time" to be made part of the work in process there. For finished goods, scheduling involves both movement into finished-goods inventory and shipment to customers to fill orders.

As our definition implies, both place and time are important to scheduling. (This is no different from, say, the scheduling of classes. You cannot attend your classes unless you know both where and when they are held.) The *routing* of materials is the sequence of workstations that the materials will follow. Assume that Drexel-Heritage —one of America's largest and oldest furniture manufacturers—is scheduling production of an oval coffee table made from cherry wood. Operations managers would route the needed materials (wood, screws, packaging materials, and so on) through a series of individual workstations along an assembly line. At each workstation, a specific task would be performed, and then the partially finished coffee table would move to the next workstation. Once all work is completed, Drexel can either store the completed coffee table in a warehouse or ship it to a retailer. When routing materials, operations managers are especially concerned with the sequence of each step of the production process. For the coffee table, the top and legs must be cut to specifications before the wood is finished. (If the wood were finished before being cut, the finish would be ruined, and the coffee table would have to be stained again.)

When scheduling production, managers also are concerned with timing. The *timing* function specifies when the materials will arrive at each station and how long they will remain there. For the cherry coffee table, it may take workers thirty minutes to cut the table top and legs and another thirty minutes to drill the holes and assemble the table. Before packaging the coffee table for shipment, it must be finished with cherry stain and allowed to dry. This last step may take as long as three days depending on weather conditions and humidity.

Whether or not the finished product requires a simple or complex production process, operations managers are responsible for monitoring schedules—called *follow-up*—to ensure that the work flows according to a timetable. For complex products, many operations managers prefer to use Gantt charts or the PERT technique.

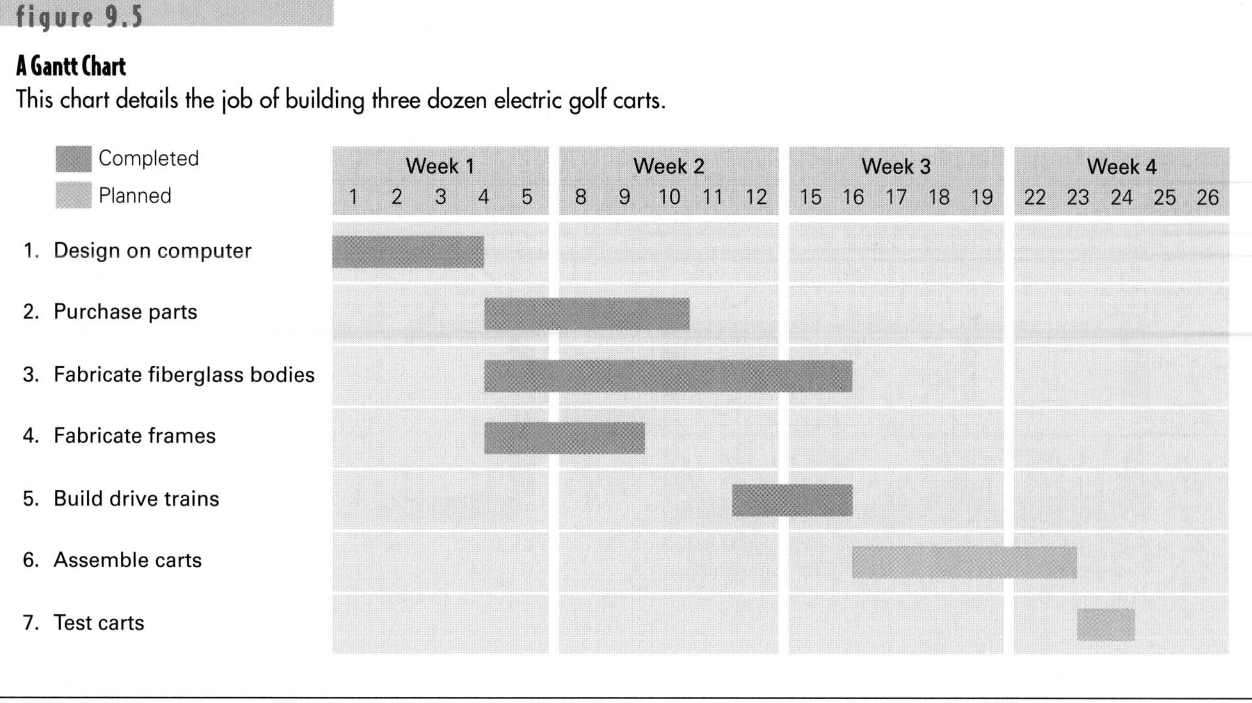

figure 9.5

A Gantt Chart

This chart details the job of building three dozen electric golf carts.

Source: Robert Kreitner, *Management*, Eighth Edition. Copyright © 2001 by Houghton Mifflin Company. Reprinted with permission.

Scheduling Through Gantt Charts Developed by Henry L. Gantt, a **Gantt chart** is a graphic scheduling device that displays the tasks to be performed on the vertical axis and the time required for each task on the horizontal axis. A Gantt chart that describes the activities required to build three dozen golf carts is illustrated in Figure 9.5. As you see in the figure, completed tasks also can be shown on a Gantt chart, so actual progress can be monitored against planned activities. Gantt charts are not particularly suitable for scheduling extremely complex situations. Nevertheless, using them forces a manager to plan the steps required to get a job done and to specify time requirements for each part of the job.

Gantt chart a graphic scheduling device that displays the tasks to be performed on the vertical axis and the time required for each task on the horizontal axis

Scheduling via PERT Another technique for scheduling a process or project and maintaining control of the schedule is **PERT (Program Evaluation and Review Technique).** To use PERT, we begin by identifying all the major *activities* involved in the project. For example, the activities involved in producing your textbook include editing the manuscript, designing the book, obtaining cost estimates, marking the manuscript for typesetting, setting type, and carrying out other activities. The completion of each of these activities is an *event.*

PERT (Program Evaluation and Review Technique) a scheduling technique that identifies the major activities necessary to complete a project and sequences them based on the time required to perform each one

Next, we arrange the events in a sequence. In doing so, we must be sure that an event that must occur before another event in the actual process also occurs before that event on the PERT chart. For example, the manuscript must be edited before the type is set. Therefore, in our sequence, the event "edit manuscript" must precede the event "set type."

Next, we use arrows to connect events that must occur in sequence. We then estimate the time required for each activity and mark it near the corresponding arrow. The sequence of production activities that take the longest time from start to finish is called the **critical path.** The activities on this path determine the minimum time in which the process can be completed. These activities are the ones that must be scheduled and controlled carefully. A delay in any one of them will cause a delay in completion of the project as a whole.

critical path the sequence of production activities that takes the longest time from start to finish

Figure 9.6 (on p. 266) is a PERT diagram for the production of this book. The critical path runs from event 1 to event 4 to event 5. It then runs through events 6, 8, and 9 to

figure 9.6

Simplified PERT Diagram for Producing this Book

A PERT diagram identifies the activities necessary to complete a given project and arranges the activities based on the total time required for each to become an event. The activities on the critical path determine the minimum time required.

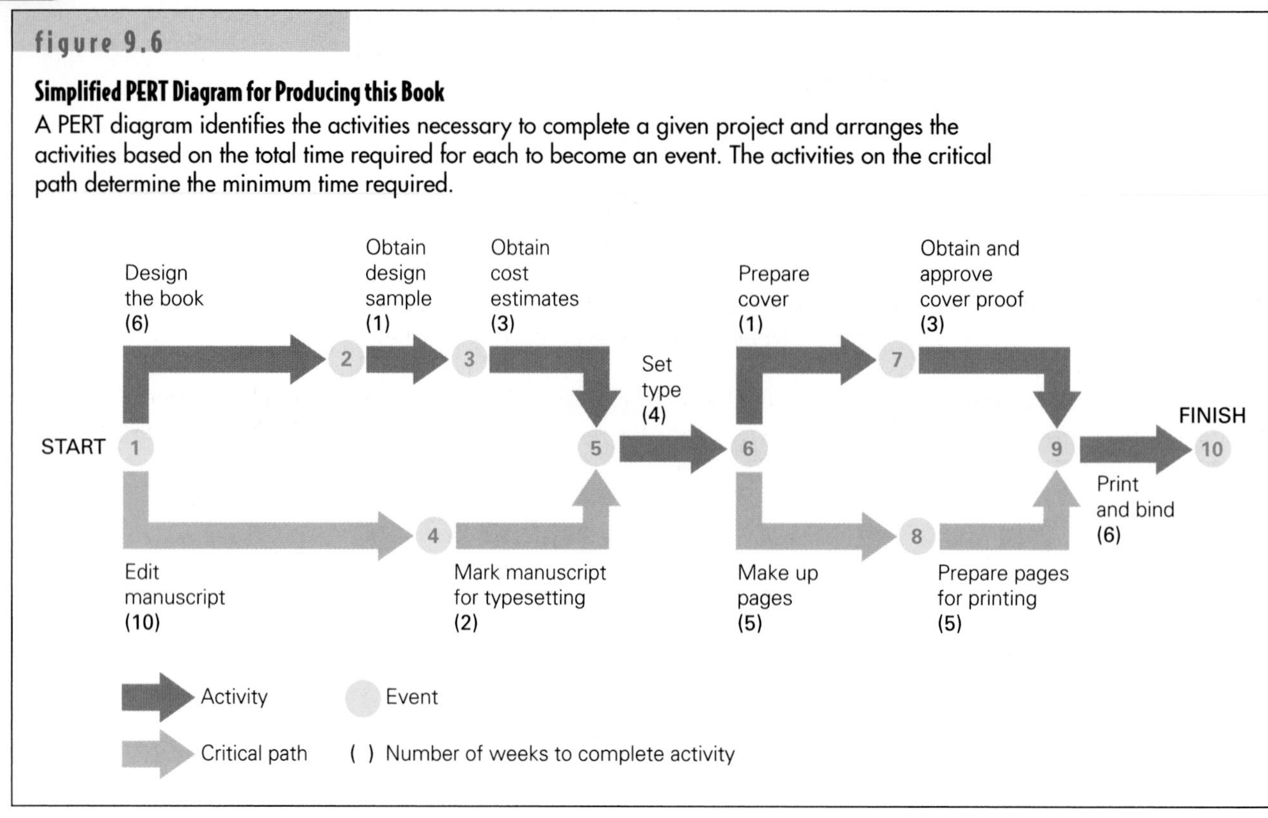

the finished book at event 10. Note that even a six-week delay in preparing the cover will not delay the production process. However, *any* delay in an activity on the critical path will hold up publication. Thus, if necessary, resources could be diverted from cover preparation to, say, making up of pages or preparing pages for printing.

Quality Control

quality control the process of ensuring that goods and services are produced in accordance with design specifications

statistical process control (SPC) a system that uses random sampling to obtain data that are plotted on control charts and graphs to see if the production process is operating as it should and to pinpoint problem areas

statistical quality control (SQC) a set of specific statistical techniques used to monitor all aspects of the production process to ensure that both work in progress and finished products meet the firm's quality standards

inspection the examination of the quality of work in process

Quality control is the process of ensuring that goods and services are produced in accordance with design specifications. The major objective of quality control is to see that the organization lives up to the standards it has set for itself on quality. Some firms, such as Mercedes-Benz and Neiman Marcus, have built their reputations on quality. Customers pay more for their products in return for assurances of high quality. Other firms adopt a strategy of emphasizing lower prices along with reasonable (but not particularly high) quality.

Many U.S. firms use two systems to gather statistical information about the quality of their products. **Statistical process control (SPC)** is a system that uses random sampling to obtain data that are plotted on control charts and graphs to see if the production process is operating as it should and pinpoint problem areas. **Statistical quality control (SQC),** a similar technique, is a set of specific statistical techniques used to monitor all aspects of the production process to ensure that both work in progress and finished products meet the firm's quality standards. A firm can use the information provided by both these to correct problems in the production process and to improve the quality of its products.

Increased effort is also being devoted to **inspection,** which is the examination of the quality of work in process. Inspections are performed at various times during production. Purchased materials may be inspected when they arrive at the production facility. Subassemblies and manufactured parts may be inspected before they become part of a finished product. And finished goods may be inspected before they are shipped to customers. Items that are within design specifications continue on their way. Those that are not within design specifications are removed from production.

The method of inspection depends on the item being examined. *Visual inspection* may be sufficient for products such as furniture or rug-cleaning services. General Electric may test one or two light bulbs from every hundred produced. At the other extreme, complete *x-ray inspection* may be required for the vital components of airplanes.

Improving Quality Through Employee Participation Historically, efforts to ensure quality increased the costs associated with making that good or service. For this reason, quality and productivity were viewed as conflicting: One was increased at the other's expense. Over the years, more and more managers have realized that quality is an essential "ingredient" of the good or service being provided. Viewed in this light, quality becomes an overall approach to doing business and is the concern of all members of an organization. This view of quality provides several benefits. The number of defects decreases, which causes profits to increase. Making products right the first time reduces many of the rejects and much of the rework. And making employees responsible for quality eliminates the need for inspection. An employee is indoctrinated to accept full responsibility for the quality of his or her work.

quality circle a group of employees who meet on company time to solve problems of product quality

Because of increased global competition, American manufacturers have adopted a goal that calls for better quality in their products. As noted in Chapter 7, a *total quality management (TQM)* program coordinates the efforts directed at improving customer satisfaction, increasing employee participation, strengthening supplier partnerships, and facilitating an organizational atmosphere of continuous quality improvement. Firms such as American Express, AT&T, Motorola, and Hewlett Packard have all used TQM to improve product quality and, ultimately, customer satisfaction.

The use of a **quality circle,** a group of employees who meet on company time to solve problems of product quality, is another way manufacturers are achieving better quality at the operations level. Quality circles have been used successfully in such companies as IBM, the Northrop Grumman Corporation, and Compaq Computers.

World Quality Standards: ISO 9000 and ISO 14000 Different companies have different perceptions of quality. Without a common standard of quality, however, customers may be at the mercy of manufacturers and vendors. As the number of companies competing in the world marketplace has increased, so has the seriousness of this problem. To deal with it, the International Organization for Standardization (a nonprofit organization in Geneva, Switzerland, with a membership of 140 countries) brought together a panel of quality experts to define what methods a company must use to produce a quality product.

In 1987, the panel published ISO 9000 (*iso* is Greek for "equal"), which sets the guidelines for quality management procedures that businesses must use to receive certification. This certification, issued by independent auditors, serves as evidence that a company meets the standards for quality control procedures in manufacturing design, production processes, product testing, training of employees, recordkeeping, and correction of defects.

Although certification is not a legal requirement to do business globally, the organization's 140 member countries have approved the ISO standards. In fact, ISO 9000 is so prevalent in the European Community that many customers refuse to do business with noncertified companies. As an added bonus, companies completing the certification process often discover new, cost-efficient ways to improve their existing quality control programs.

As a continuation of this standardization process, the International Organization for Standardization has

Wake up and smell the coffee! While it may look like this man is taking a coffee break, in reality he is performing a quality control check to make sure that Mexico-based Fomcafe's organic coffee not only smells like great coffee, but also tastes good. If the organic coffee passes this test and many more, then it is eventually shipped to the U.S. and Europe.

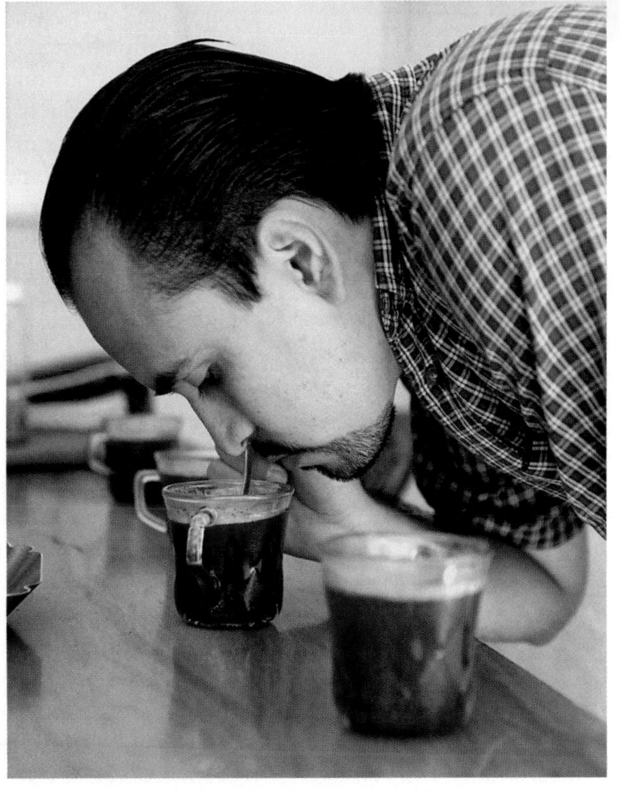

Using the Internet

There are several web-based gateway sources of information and journals devoted to quality management and production issues such as the National Association of Manufacturers (**www.nam.org**), *Quality Digest* (**www.qualitydigest.com**), and *Industry Week* (**http://www.iwgc.com/**).

developed ISO 14000. ISO 14000 is a series of international standards for incorporating environmental concerns into operations and product standards. As with ISO 9000 certification ISO 14000 requires that a company's procedures be documented by independent auditors. It also requires that a company develop an environmental management system that will help it to achieve environmental goals, objectives, and targets For many companies, certification is necessary because their competitors are certified or their customers refuse to do business with a firm that does not have ISO 14000 certification.

The Impact of Computers and Robotics on Production

learning objective

6 Discuss the increasing role of computers, robotics, and flexible manufacturing in the production process.

Automation, a development that has been revolutionizing the workplace, is the total or near-total use of machines to do work. The rapid increase in automated procedures has been made possible by the microprocessor, a silicon chip that led to the production of desktop computers. In factories, microprocessors are used in robotics and in computer manufacturing systems.

automation the total or near-total use of machines to do work

robotics the use of programmable machines to perform a variety of tasks by manipulating materials and tools

Robotics

Robotics is the use of programmable machines to perform a variety of tasks by manipulating materials and tools. Robots work quickly, accurately, and steadily. For example, Illumina, Inc., a San Diego company, uses robots to screen blood samples and identify DNA quirks that cause diseases. The information is then sold to some of the world's largest pharmaceutical companies, where it is used to alter existing prescription drugs, develop new drug therapies, and customize diagnoses and treatments for all kinds of serious diseases. As an added bonus, Illumina's robots can work 24 hours a day at much lower costs than if human lab workers performed the same tests.[12] Robots are especially effective in tedious, repetitive assembly-line jobs like this, as well as in handling hazardous materials. They are also useful as artificial "eyes" that can check the quality of products as they are being processed on the assembly lines. And miniature buglike robots can be used to inspect spaces too small for humans to enter.

To date, the automotive industry has made the most extensive use of robotics, but robots also have been used to mine coal, inspect the inner surfaces of pipes, assemble computer components, provide certain kinds of patient care in hospitals, and clean and guard buildings at night.

Computer Manufacturing Systems

People are quick to point out how computers have changed their everyday lives, but most people do not realize the impact computers have had on manufacturing. In simple terms, the factory of the future has already arrived. For most manufacturers, the changeover began with the use of computer-aided design and computer-aided manufacturing. **Computer-aided design (CAD)** is the use of computers to aid in the development of products. Using CAD, Ford speeds up car design, Canon designs new cameras and photocopiers, and American Greetings creates new birthday cards. **Computer-aided manufacturing (CAM)** is the use of computers to plan and control manufacturing processes. A well-designed CAM system allows manufacturers to become much more productive. Not only are a greater number of products produced, but speed and quality also increase. Toyota, Hasbro, Oneida, and Apple Computer all have used CAM to increase productivity.

computer-aided design (CAD) the use of computers to aid in the development of products

computer-aided manufacturing (CAM) the use of computers to plan and control manufacturing processes

If you are thinking that the next logical step is to combine the CAD and CAM computer systems, you are right. Today, the most successful manufacturers use CAD and CAM together to form a computer-integrated manufacturing system. Specifically, **computer-integrated manufacturing (CIM)** is a computer system that not only helps to design products but also controls the machinery needed to produce the finished product. For example, Liz Claiborne, Inc., uses CIM to design clothing, to establish patterns for new fashions, and then to cut the cloth needed to produce the finished product. Other advantages of using CIM include improved flexibility, more efficient scheduling, and higher product quality—all factors that make a production facility more competitive in today's global economy. Furthermore, specialized management software from firms such as Maxager.com enables factory managers to optimize plant operations by providing information about manufacturing costs. Instead of simply guessing which product lines are most profitable, the software uses machinery performance data to analyze profits, including the opportunity costs of the machinery used to produce the products. As a result, even though the cost is relative high, at 1 percent of revenues, client firms such as Motorola believe that paybacks in improved production schedules and the product selection process are well worth the investment.[13]

computer-integrated manufacturing (CIM) a computer system that not only helps to design products but also controls the machinery needed to produce the finished product

Flexible Manufacturing Systems

Manufacturers have known for a number of years that the old-style, traditional assembly lines used to manufacture products present a number of problems. For example, although traditional assembly lines turn out extremely large numbers of identical products economically, the system requires expensive, time-consuming retooling of equipment whenever a new product is to be manufactured. Now it is possible to use flexible manufacturing systems to solve such problems. A **flexible manufacturing system (FMS)** combines robotics and computer-integrated manufacturing in a single production system. Instead of having to spend vast amounts of time and effort to retool the traditional mechanical equipment on an assembly line for each new product, an FMS is rearranged simply by reprogramming electronic machines. Because FMSs require less time and expense to reprogram, manufacturers can produce smaller batches of a variety of products without raising the production cost.

flexible manufacturing system (FMS) a single production system that combines robotics and computer-integrated manufacturing

Advanced software and a flexible manufacturing system have enabled Dell Computer to change to a more customer-driven manufacturing process. The process starts when a customer phones a sales representative on a toll-free line or accesses Dell's website. Then the representative or the customer enters the specifications for the new product directly into a computer. The same computer processes the order to a nearby plant. Once the order is received, a team of employees with the help of a reprogrammable assembly line can build the product just the way the customer wants it. Products include desktops computers, notebook computers, and other Dell equipment.[14] Other firms that have used FMS include Goodyear, IBM, Levi Strauss, Motorola, and Andersen Windows. Although the costs of designing and installing an FMS like this are high, the electronic equipment is used more frequently and efficiently than the machinery on a traditional assembly line.

Technological Displacement

Automation is increasing productivity by cutting manufacturing time, reducing error, and simplifying retooling procedures. Many of the robots being developed for use in manufacturing will not replace human employees. Rather, these robots will work with employees in making their jobs safer and easier and help to prevent accidents. No one knows, however, what the effect will be on the work force. Some experts estimate that automation will bring changes to as many as 45 percent of all jobs within the next ten years. Total unemployment may not increase, but many workers will be faced with the choice of retraining for new jobs or seeking jobs in other sectors of the economy. Government, business, and education will have to cooperate to prepare workers for new roles in an automated workplace. For example, according to the

American Society of Travel Agents, the industry shift to Internet-based operations has been nothing short of catastrophic for small business travel operators. A Bear Stearns research report suggests that 25 percent or more of human agents are likely to be replaced by the online virtual services. Online operations are being transformed by firms such as Travelocity.com and Expedia.com, motivated by customers and industry vendors seeking ways to cut their respective costs.[15]

learning objective

7 Outline the reasons for recent trends in productivity.

Management of Productivity

productivity the average level of output per worker per hour

No coverage of production and operations management would be complete without a discussion of productivity. Productivity concerns all managers, but it is especially important to operations managers, the people who must oversee the creation of a firm's goods or services. We define **productivity** as the average level of output per worker per hour. Hence, if each worker at plant A produces seventy-five units per day and each worker at plant B produces only seventy units per day, the workers at plant A are more productive. If one bank teller serves twenty-five customers per hour and another serves twenty-eight per hour, the second teller is more productive.

Productivity Trends

U.S. manufacturing output per hour increased by 1.9 percent in 2001—the last year that complete results were available. Our productivity growth rate was ranked the fourth largest increase among the twelve countries for which comparable data are available—the United States, Canada, Japan, Korea, Taiwan, and seven European countries. Our *rate of productivity growth* is lagging behind the productivity growth rates of such countries as Korea, Taiwan, and France.[16] As you will see in the next section, there are a number of specific causes of productivity declines.

Causes of Productivity Declines

Several factors have been cited as possible causes of the reduction in America's productivity growth rate. First, the economic slowdown the United States has experienced since 1999 and the terrorist attacks that occurred on September 11 have caused many businesses to reduce the rate of investment in new equipment and technology. As workers have had to use increasingly outdated equipment, their productivity naturally has declined.

Ironically, some productivity experts have cited the use of technology as a reason for declining productivity rates. Although many businesses introduced new management information systems that were designed to provide employees with more up-to-date information that could be used to manage day-to-day business activities over the last decade, the amount of time required to implement and learn how to use these new management information systems and improved technology may have reduced productivity for some businesses. As employees and managers become more adept at using the new information technology, this downward influence on productivity trends will diminish.

Another important factor that has hurt U.S. productivity is the tremendous growth of the service sector in the United States. While this sector grew in the number of employees and economic importance, its productivity levels did not grow. Today, many economic experts agree that improving service-sector productivity is the next major hurdle facing U.S. business.

Finally, increased government regulation is frequently cited as a factor affecting productivity. Federal agencies such as the Occupational Safety and Health Administration (OSHA) and the Food and Drug Administration (FDA) are increasingly regulating business practices. The Goodyear Tire & Rubber Company generated 345,000 pages of computer printout weighing 3,200 pounds to comply with one new OSHA regulation! Furthermore, the company spends over $35 million each year solely to meet the requirements of six regulatory agencies.

When demand for your products is high, productivity becomes more important than ever. Hewlett-Packard spent $1 billion to reinvent its line of printers. The program was so important that HP's manufacturing facilities in different parts of the globe, including this production facility in Malaysia, were required to retool assembly lines and improve employee productivity. So was the program a success? You bet! The program helped HP regain lost market share in the competitive printer industry.

Improving Productivity

Several techniques and strategies have been suggested as possible cures for current productivity trends. For example, various government policies that may be hindering productivity could be eliminated or at least modified.

In addition, increased cooperation between management and labor could improve productivity. When unions and management work together, quite often the result is improved productivity. In a related area, many managers believe that increased employee motivation and participation can enhance productivity.

Still another potential solution to productivity problems is to change the incentives for work. Many firms simply pay employees for their time, regardless of how much or how little they produce. By changing the reward system so that people are paid for what they contribute rather than for the time they put in, it may be possible to motivate employees to produce at higher levels.

Finally, business must invest more money in facilities, equipment, and employee training. There is hard evidence that investments in technological innovations are linked to job growth, higher employee wages, new products, *and* increased productivity. While building a new factory or purchasing new equipment does not guarantee that a firm's productivity will increase, many companies such as Ford Motor Company, Honeywell International, Deere & Company, and IBM have experienced dramatic increases in productivity when employees can use state-of-the-art equipment. Once a business has made a commitment to invest in facilities and equipment, the next step is to train employees to use the new equipment. In turn, the employees' ability to use new equipment and new technology will increase productivity.

The next chapter treats a very important aspect of management—human resources management. In Chapter 10 we discuss a number of major components of human resources management, and we see how managers use various reward systems to boost motivation, productivity, and morale.

Return To inside business

At a time when many U.S. steelmaking plants are idle or being converted to new uses, International Steel Group (ISG) workers are chanting "Let's make steel!" The company wants to revamp operations for more efficiency—and more profit. If nonmill employees help out in the mill during peak production periods, the steelmaker can keep the overall work force to a manageable size while increasing productivity. Already ISG has increased the span of management to eliminate four layers and hundreds of executives, a major cost saving. It is also soliciting suggestions from workers about how to streamline any part of the production process.

ISG and other steelmakers have a little breathing room now that the U.S. government has imposed tariffs on imported steel. Still, ISG's future remains unclear. Hundreds of millions of dollars in investments are at stake, as are thousands of jobs and the livelihood of communities surrounding the plants. ISG will not have a second chance, warns CEO Rodney Mott: "If this plant fails again, we will never restart it." Can ISG make steel and profits?

Questions

1. How is global competition affecting ISG? What do you think about the government's use of tariffs to increase the price of imported steel?
2. Why is ISG so concerned about improving the productivity of its work force and its plants?

Summary

Explain the nature of production.

Operations management consists of all the activities that managers engage in to create goods and services. Operations are as relevant to service organizations as to manufacturing firms. Generally, three major activities are involved in producing goods or services: product development, planning for production, and operations control. Today, U.S. manufacturers are forced to compete in an ever-smaller world to meet the needs of more demanding customers. In an attempt to regain a competitive edge, they have taken another look at the importance of improving quality and meeting the needs of their customers. They also have reduced production costs, replaced outdated equipment, used computer-aided and flexible manufacturing systems, improved control procedures, and built new manufacturing facilities in foreign countries where labor costs are lower. Competing in the global economy is not only profitable; it is also an essential activity that requires the cooperation of everyone within an organization.

Outline how the conversion process transforms raw materials, labor, and other resources into finished products or services.

A business transforms resources into goods and services in order to provide utility to customers. Utility is the ability of a good or service to satisfy a human need. Form utility is created by converting raw materials, employees, finances, and information into finished products. Conversion processes vary in terms of the major resources used to produce goods and services (focus), the degree to which resources are changed (magnitude), and the number of production processes that a business uses. The application of the basic principles of operations management to the production of services has coincided with the growth of service businesses in the United States.

Describe how research and development lead to new products and services.

Operations management often begins with product research and development (R&D). The results of R&D may be entirely new products or extensions and refinements of existing products. R&D activities are classified as basic research (aimed at uncovering new knowledge), applied research (discovering new knowledge with some potential use), and development and implementation (using new or existing knowledge to produce goods and services).

Discuss the components involved in planning the production process.

Planning for production involves three major phases: design planning, facilities planning and site selection, and operational planning. First, design planning is undertaken to address questions related to the product line, required production capacity, and the use of technology. Production facilities, site selection, and human resources must then be considered. Operational planning focuses on the use of production facilities and resources. The steps for operational planning include (a) selecting a planning horizon, (b) estimating market demand, (c) comparing market demand with capacity, and (d) adjusting production of products or services to meet demand.

Explain the four major areas of operations control: purchasing, inventory control, scheduling, and quality control.

The major areas of operations control are purchasing, inventory control, scheduling, and quality control. Purchasing involves selecting suppliers. The choice of suppliers should result from careful analysis of a number of factors, including price, quality, reliability, credit terms, and shipping costs. Inventory control is the management of stocks of raw materials, work in process, and finished goods to minimize the total inventory cost. Today, most firms use a computerized system to maintain inventory records. In addition, many firms use a just-in-time inventory system, in which materials or supplies arrive at a facility just when they are needed so that storage and holding costs are minimized. Scheduling ensures that materials and other resources are at the right place at the right time—for use within the facility or for shipment to customers. Quality control guarantees that products meet the design specifications for those products. The major objective of quality control is to see that the organization lives up to the standards it has set for itself on quality. Some firms, such as Mercedes-Benz and Neiman Marcus, have built their reputations on quality. Customers pay more for their products in return for assurances of high quality. Other firms adopt a strategy of emphasizing lower prices along with reasonable (but not particularly high) quality.

Discuss the increasing role of computers, robotics, and flexible manufacturing in the production process.

Automation, the total or near-total use of machines to do work, has for some years been changing the way work is done in U.S. factories and offices. A growing number of industries are using programmable machines called robots to perform tasks that are tedious or hazardous to human beings. Computer-aided design, computer-aided manufacturing, and computer-integrated manufacturing use computers to help design and manufacture products. The flexible manufacturing system combines robotics and computer-integrated manufacturing to produce smaller batches of products more efficiently than on the traditional assembly line. Instead of having to spend vast amounts of time and effort to retool the traditional mechanical equipment on an assembly line for each new product, an FMS is rearranged simply by reprogramming electronic machines. Because FMSs require less time and expense to reprogram, manufacturers can produce smaller batches of a variety of products without raising the production cost.

Outline the reasons for recent trends in productivity.

The productivity growth rate in the United States has fallen behind the pace of growth in some of the other industrialized nations in recent years. Several factors have been cited as possible causes for this disturbing trend, and managers have begun to explore solutions for overcoming them. Possible solutions include less government regulation, increased cooperation between management and labor, increased employee motivation and participation, new incentives for work, and additional investment by business to fund new or renovated facilities, equipment, and employee training.

Key Terms

You should now be able to define and give an example relevant to each of the following terms:

operations management (249)
analytical process (250)
synthetic process (251)
utility (252)
form utility (252)
service economy (253)
research and development (R&D) (254)
design planning (256)
product line (257)
product design (257)
capacity (257)
labor-intensive technology (257)
capital-intensive technology (258)
plant layout (259)
planning horizon (261)
purchasing (262)
inventory control (263)
materials requirements planning (MRP) (263)
just-in-time inventory system (264)
scheduling (264)
Gantt chart (265)
PERT (Program Evaluation and Review Technique) (265)
critical path (265)
quality control (266)
statistical process control (SPC) (266)
statistical quality control (SQC) (266)
inspection (266)
quality circle (267)
automation (268)
robotics (268)
computer-aided design (CAD) (268)
computer-aided manufacturing (CAM) (268)
computer-integrated manufacturing (CIM) (269)
flexible manufacturing system (FMS) (269)
productivity (270)

Review Questions

1. List all the activities involved in operations management.
2. What is the difference between an analytical and a synthetic manufacturing process? Give an example of each type of process.
3. In terms of focus, magnitude, and number, characterize the production processes used by a local pizza parlor, a dry-cleaning establishment, and an auto repair shop.
4. Describe how research and development lead to new products.
5. What are the major elements of design planning?
6. What factors should be considered when selecting a site for a new manufacturing facility?
7. What is the objective of operational planning? What four steps are used to accomplish this objective?
8. If you were an operations manager, what would you do if market demand exceeded the production capacity of your manufacturing facility? What action would you take if the production capacity of your manufacturing facility exceeded market demand?
9. Why is selecting a supplier so important?
10. What costs must be balanced and minimized through inventory control?
11. How can materials requirements planning (MRP), manufacturing resource planning (MRP II), and enterprise resource planning (ERP) help control inventory and a company's production processes?
12. How does the just-in-time-inventory system help to reduce inventory costs?
13. Explain in what sense scheduling is a *control* function of operations managers.
14. How can management and employees use statistical process control, statistical quality control, and inspection to improve a firm's products?
15. How can CIM and FMS help a manufacturer produce products?
16. How might productivity be measured in a restaurant? In a department store? In a public school system?

Discussion Questions

1. Why would Rubbermaid—a successful U.S. company—need to expand and sell its products to customers in foreign countries?
2. Do certain kinds of firms need to stress particular areas of operations management? Explain.
3. Is it really necessary for service firms to engage in research and development? In planning for production planning and operations control?
4. How are the four areas of operations control interrelated?
5. In what ways can employees help to improve the quality of a firm's products?
6. Is operations management relevant to nonbusiness organizations such as colleges and hospitals? Why or why not?

video case

Remington Produces Cutting-Edge Shavers

Remington has been associated with many product "firsts." The company manufactured the first commercial typewriter in 1873, the first electric dry shaver in 1937, and the first cordless shaver in 1960. The company changed ownership, management, and focus a number of times during its history. In fact, one of the best-remembered ads of the 1980s featured then-owner Victor Kiam shaving with a Remington shaver while saying to the camera, "I liked the shaver so much, I bought the company." Despite all these changes, once the company began making shavers, it never stopped. Remington survived a difficult financial period in the 1990s and has since emerged with a more youthful image as a maker of personal care products for men and women.

Now based in Bridgeport, Connecticut, Remington offers a wide variety of electric shavers, hair trimmers, hair dryers, and other small appliances for personal grooming. Its main competitors are Norelco, Braun, Panasonic, and several other global makers of electric shaving products. Its products are sold in the United States, Europe, Australia, and New Zealand through drug, department, and discount stores, as well as online retailers. Remington also maintains seventy U.S. service stores and eleven U.K. service stores to sell and repair its products. Its website (**www.remington-products.com**) communicates product and service details for the global customer base.

Remington uses marketing research to gain an in-depth understanding of its customers' needs and to develop new technology and product designs to meet those needs. CEO Neil DeFeo notes that the company's products have changed over the years, but not men's beards. Yet what men and women are looking for in shavers has evolved over time. For example, women are under great time pressure today and are looking for products that help them to look and feel good in less time. In response, Remington has come up with innovative new appliances such as its hand waxer. Rather than spend time visiting a spa or salon, a woman can use the waxer to give herself a hand treatment at home, making her hands look and feel smoother and softer. In addition, Remington designed a special hair dryer to dry hair more quickly than ordinary dryers—another way to save time. Other trends affecting Remington's product lineup are changing lifestyles and an aging population.

New products, new technology, and new production methods are all helping Remington meet the needs of customers all over the world. In fact, new technology is just as important as product styling. Remington recently won a favorable ruling from the European Court of Justice in a battle over three-headed rotary razors. Philips trademarked the three-headed design in the 1960s. Decades later, it sued Remington for introducing a three-headed razor of its own, saying that three heads were part of the Philips brand. Remington won by arguing that a trademark cannot cover improved technical performance. In other words, although the hourglass Coca-Cola bottle does not improve the beverage's taste, the three-headed design does improve a razor's shaving ability.

Once Remington has completed a new design, the product is manufactured and assembled overseas. Some products may have up to a hundred components, which adds complexity to the production process. Nonetheless, the company continues to make the cutting parts in Connecticut so that it has tighter control over quality. Using specialized machinery, production workers punch blades out of steel and make cutters out of miles of aluminum coil. One shaver may require as many as seventy-five blades and three cutters, carefully manufactured, ground for sharpness, and tested before assembly.

To meet global demand for Remington shavers, the plant must turn out one million blades per day. Therefore, plant managers must plan in advance to buy and store supplies and materials, have everything in place when and where needed, and inspect the finished blades to ensure quality. Then the blades go to the foreign factories, where they are incorporated into shavers and trimmers.

After production is complete, Remington transports most of the finished products to its international network of independent distributors, which deliver them to retail outlets in eighty-five countries. The rest of the products go to company-owned facilities, where they are sold directly to retailers in Germany, New Zealand, and several other countries.[17]

Questions

1. Why would Remington choose to produce only blades in the United States rather than assembling entire shavers as well?
2. Which plant layout would you suggest that Remington use when making blades in its Connecticut factory? Why?
3. What is the focus of the conversion process in Remington's Connecticut factory?

Building Skills for Career Success

1. Exploring the Internet

Improvements in the quality of products and services is an ever-popular theme in business management. Besides the obvious increase to profitability to be gained by such improvements, a company's demonstration of its continuous search for ways to improve operations can be a powerful statement to customers, suppliers, and investors. Two of the larger schools of thought in this field are total quality management (TQM) and the European-based ISO 9000. Visit the text website for updates to this exercise.

Assignment

1. Use Internet search engines to find more information about each of these topics. The W. Edwards Deming Institute (**www.deming.org**) and the International Organization for Standardization (**www.iso.ch**) sites will be good places to begin.
2. From these web pages, can you tell whether there is any real difference between these two approaches?
3. Describe one success story of a firm that realized improvement by adopting either approach.

2. Developing Critical Thinking Skills

Plant layout—the arrangement of machinery, equipment, and personnel within a production facility—is a critical ingredient in a company's success. If the layout is inefficient, productivity and, ultimately, profits will suffer. The purpose of the business dictates the type of layout that will be most efficient. There are three general types: process layout, product layout, and fixed-position layout.

Assignment

1. For each of the following businesses, identify the best type of layout:

   One-hour dry cleaner
   Health club
   Auto repair shop
   Fast-food restaurant
   Shipyard that builds supertankers
   Automobile assembly plant

2. Prepare a two-page report explaining why you chose these layouts and why proper plant layout is important.

3. Building Team Skills

Suppose that you are planning to build a house in the country. It will be a brick, one-story structure of approximately 2,000 square feet, centrally heated and cooled. It will have three bedrooms, two bathrooms, a family room, a dining room, a kitchen with breakfast nook, a study, a utility room, an entry foyer, a two-car garage, a covered patio, and a fireplace. Appliances will operate on electricity and propane fuel. You have received approval and can be connected to the cooperative water system at any time. Public sewerage services are not available; therefore, you must rely on a septic system. You want to know how long it will take to build the house.

Assignment

1. Identify the major activities involved in the project. and sequence them in the proper order.
2. Estimate the time required for each activity, and establish the critical path.
3. Working in a group, prepare a PERT diagram to show the steps involved in building your house.
4. In a two-page report, summarize what you learned about using PERT as a planning and control tool.

4. Researching Different Careers

Because service businesses are now such a dominant part of our economy, job seekers sometimes overlook the employment opportunities available in production plants. Two positions often found in these plants are quality control inspector and purchasing agent.

Assignment

1. Using the *Occupational Outlook Handbook* at your local library or on the Internet (**http://www.bls.gov/oco/home.htm**), find the following information for the jobs of quality control inspector and purchasing agent:

   Job description, including main activities and responsibilities
   Employment outlook
   Earnings and working conditions
   Skills, training, and education required

2. Look for other production jobs that may interest you, and compile the same sort of information about them.
3. Summarize in a two-page report the key things you learned about jobs in production plants.

5. Improving Communication Skills

Total quality management (TQM) is a much broader concept than just controlling the quality of a single product. It is a philosophy that places quality at the center of everything a company does. In particular, TQM is aimed at improving customer satisfaction, increasing employee participation, strengthening supplier partnerships, and facilitating an organizational atmosphere of continuous quality improvement. For TQM to work successfully, it must start with a company's mission statement, be ingrained in the company's goals and objectives, and be implemented through the strategies that ultimately satisfy customer needs. Motorola and Hewlett Packard are two companies in which a concern for total quality is the driving force. How have these companies used TQM successfully? How will TQM influence their operations as they move into the next century and compete on a more global basis?

Assignment

1. Read articles or use the Internet to find out how Motorola and Hewlett Packard implement TQM.
2. Prepare a three-page report on your findings. The report should include answers to the following questions:
   a. Exactly how does each company focus on quality?
   b. How are the TQM programs of these two companies alike? How do they differ?
   c. How will TQM influence their operations in the twenty-first century?
   d. Using quality as a criterion, which company would you rather work for? Why?

Finagle A Bagel's Management, Organization, and Production Finesse

"We don't have a traditional corporate organizational chart," states Heather Robertson, Finagle A Bagel's director of marketing, human resources, and research and development. When she hires new employees, Robertson draws the usual type of organization chart showing the copresidents on the top and the store employees on the bottom. Then she turns it upside down, explaining: "The most important people in our stores are the crew members, and the store manager's role is to support those crew members. Middle management's role is to support the store managers. And the copresidents' responsibility is to support us," referring to herself and her middle-management colleagues.

In short, the copresidents and all the people in the Boston-based support center—as Finagle A Bagel terms its corporate headquarters—work as a team to help the seventeen general managers (who run the stores) and their crew members. Every store operates to achieve preset sales goals within budget guidelines. Higher-level managers are available to help any general manager whose store's performance falls outside the expected ranges. Moreover, each general manager is empowered to make decisions that will boost sales and make the most of opportunities to build positive relationships with local businesses and community organizations. "We want our general managers to view the store as their business," copresident Laura Trust emphasizes. "If a general manager wants to do something that will alleviate a store problem or increase sales, we give him the leeway to do it."

Many Bagels, One Factory

Although the copresidents decentralized authority for many store-level decisions, they achieved more efficiency by centralizing the authority and responsibility for food procurement and preparation. For example, the support center handles payroll, invoices, and many other time-consuming activities on behalf of all the stores. This reduces the paperwork burden on general managers and frees them to concentrate on managing store-level food service to satisfy customers.

Finagle A Bagel also maintains a production facility to mix bagel dough and organize the food and paper goods orders for each store. At present, the dough factory is running at roughly half its maximum capacity and can add extra shifts as needed. This centralized facility gathers whatever each store needs—raw dough, salad fixings, packages of condiments, or plastic bowls—and loads it on a truck for daily delivery.

Baking Bagels and More

Once the raw dough reaches a store, crew members follow the traditional New York–style method of boiling and baking bagels in various varieties, ranging from year-round favorites such as sesame to seasonal offerings such as pumpkin raisin. In line with Finagle A Bagel's fresh-food concept, the stores bake bagels every hour and tumble them into a line of bins near the front counter. Each store has a unique piece of equipment, dubbed the "bagel buzz saw," to slice and move bagels to the sandwich counter after customers

have placed their orders. This equipment not only helps prevent employee accidents and speeds food preparation, but it also entertains customers as they wait for their sandwiches.

Finagle A Bagel is constantly introducing new menu items to bring customers back throughout the day. One item the company has perfected is the bagel pizza. Earlier bagel pizzas turned out soggy, but the newest breakfast pizzas are both crunchy and tasty. The central production facility starts by mixing egg bagel dough, forms it into individual flat breads, grills the rounds, and ships them to the stores. There, a crew member tops each round with the customer's choice of ingredients, heats it, and serves it toasty fresh.

Managing a Bagel Restaurant

Finagle A Bagel's general managers stay busy from the early morning, when they open the store and help crew members to get ready for customers, to the time they close the store at night after one last look to see whether everything is in order for the next day. General managers like Paulo Pereira, who runs the Harvard Square Finagle A Bagel in Cambridge, must have the technical skills required to run a fast-paced food-service operation. They also need good conceptual skills so that they can look beyond each individual employee and task to see how everything should fit together. One way Pereira does this is by putting himself in the customer's shoes. He is constantly evaluating how customers would judge the in-store experience, from courteous, attentive counter service to availability of fresh foods, clean tables, and well-stocked condiment containers.

Just as important, Pereira—like other Finagle A Bagel general managers—must have excellent interpersonal skills to work effectively with customers, crew members, colleagues, and higher-level managers. A five-year veteran of Finagle A Bagel, Pereira knows that he can't be successful without being able to work well with other people, especially those he supervises. "You need to have a good crew behind you to help you every single hour of the day," he says. "Every employee needs to feel special and appreciated. I try to treat employees as fairly as possible, and I try to accommodate their needs."

Questions

1. What does Finagle A Bagel's upside-down organization chart suggest about the delegation of authority and coordination techniques within the company?
2. Is Finagle A Bagel a tall or flat organization? How do you know?
3. What values seem to permeate Finagle A Bagel's corporate culture?
4. Why would Finagle A Bagel build a dough factory that has much more capacity than the company needs to support its seventeen stores and its wholesale customers?

INC.

Building a Business Plan Part III

Now you should be ready to provide evidence that you have a management team with the necessary skills and experience to execute your business plan successfully. Only a competent management team can transform your vision into a successful business. You also should be able to describe your manufacturing and operations plans. The three chapters in Part III of your textbook, "Understanding the Management Process," "Creating a Flexible Organization," and "Producing Quality Goods and Services," should help you in answering some of the questions in this part of the business plan.

The Management Team Component

The management team component should include the answers to at least the following questions:

3.1. How is your team balanced in technical, conceptual, interpersonal, and other special skills needed in your business?
3.2. What will be your style of leadership?
3.3. How will your company be structured? Include a statement of the philosophy of management and company culture.
3.4. What are the key management positions, compensation, and key policies?
3.5. Include a job description for each management position and specify who will fill that position. *Note:* Prepare an organization chart and provide the résumé of each key manager for the appendix.
3.6. What other professionals, such as a lawyer, an insurance agent, a banker, and a certified public accountant, will you need for assistance?

The Manufacturing and Operations Plan Component

If you are in a manufacturing business, now is a good time to describe your manufacturing and operation plans, space requirements, equipment, labor force, inventory control, and purchasing requirements. Even if you are in a service-oriented business, many of these questions may still apply.

The manufacturing and operations plan component should include the answers to at least the following questions:

3.7. What are the advantages and disadvantages of your planned location in terms of

- Wage rates
- Unionization
- Labor pool
- Proximity to customers and suppliers
- Types of transportation available
- Tax rates
- Utility costs
- Zoning requirements

3.8. What facilities does your business require? Prepare a floor plan for the appendix. Will you rent, lease, or purchase the facilities?
3.9. Will you make or purchase component parts to be assembled into the finished product? Make sure to justify your "make-or-buy decision."
3.10. Who are your potential subcontractors and suppliers?
3.11. How will you control quality, inventory, and production? How will you measure your progress?
3.12. Is there a sufficient quantity of adequately skilled people in the local labor force to meet your needs?

Review of Business Plan Activities

Be sure to go over the information you have gathered. Check for any weaknesses and resolve them before beginning Part IV. Also review all the answers to the questions in Parts I, II, and III to be certain that all answers are consistent throughout the entire business plan. Finally, write a brief statement that summarizes all the information for this part of the business plan.

part IV

Human Resources

This part of *Business* is concerned with the most important and least predictable of all resources—people. We begin by examining the human resources efforts that organizations use to hire, develop, and retain their best employees. Then we discuss employee motivation and satisfaction. Finally, we look at organized labor and probe the sometimes controversial relationship between business management and labor unions.

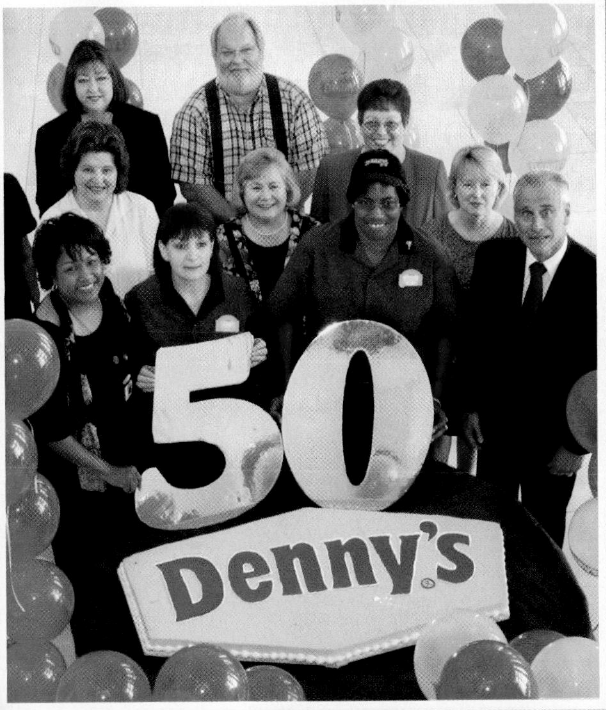

chapter

10 Attracting and Retaining the Best Employees

learning objectives

1. Describe the major components of human resources management.
2. Identify the steps in human resources planning.
3. Describe cultural diversity and understand some of the challenges and opportunities associated with it.
4. Explain the objectives and uses of job analysis.
5. Describe the processes of recruiting, employee selection, and orientation.
6. Discuss the primary elements of employee compensation and benefits.
7. Explain the purposes and techniques of employee training, development, and performance appraisal.
8. Outline the major legislation affecting human resources management.

Google attracts and retains talented, hard-working employees by making the workplace as comfortable and convenient as possible.

inside business

The Search Is On at Google

THE WORLD'S MOST POPULAR Internet search site is always searching for good employees. Google.com accounts for nearly half of all Web searches worldwide, processing 150 million queries every day in English and dozens of other languages. Not only is Google fast, it is amazingly accurate. Using sophisticated algorithms to evaluate the content and the number of links allows Google to identify the most relevant pages for each search request. More often than not, users who click the "I'm feeling lucky" link actually wind up at the best search results.

Co-founders Larry Page and Sergey Brin started Google as Ph.D. candidates at Stanford University (where Yahoo's co-founders also studied). By 1998, their experimental search site was attracting 10,000 searches per day. This convinced Page and Brin that the site could form the basis of a viable business. The two raised money and incorporated under the Google name (a play on the word *googol*, which stands for the number 1 followed by 100 zeroes). Within a few years, the company was earning annual revenues of $100 million from advertisers eager to reach the eyeballs of search customers.

Today, Google's California headquarters still bears traces of its dorm-room origin, with lava lamps, exercise balls, and video game consoles. Other unique features include a Google Café serving free lunches and dinners, free doctor's checkups, and a grand piano in the lobby. These are all part of the company's strategy to attract and retain talented, hard-working employees by making the workplace as comfortable and convenient as possible. "We wanted it to be the kind of place where you didn't have to leave and come back for dinner or for lunch, or you didn't have to take time off to go to the doctor's because you weren't keeping your posture good," explains Craig Silverstein, the director of technology. He stresses that Google wants "to make it a place where you're happy working."

Management is constantly recruiting to fill new positions, and its own site (**www.google.com**) is a rich source of résumés. The company offers testimonials from current employees, posts detailed descriptions of existing job openings, and discusses the corporate culture and benefits. Despite the mound of applications they receive, Google's managers are extremely particular about who they hire. "We are definitely growing slower than we would otherwise because of our stringent hiring standards," Silverstein says. Once hired, employees may find themselves working 10 hours a day or more when deadlines loom, but they also enjoy competitive pay, excellent benefits, and a collegial atmosphere. More important, they become part of a profitable business that encourages open communication, solicits new ideas from employees at all levels, and rewards good performance.[1]

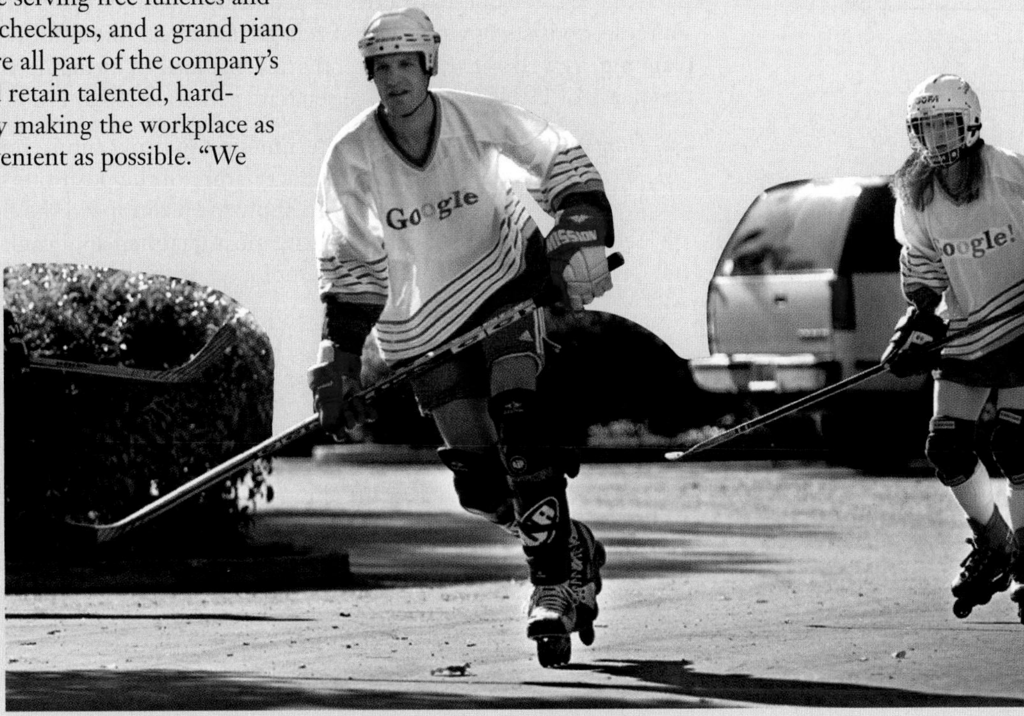

In recruiting skilled employees and retaining them in a highly competitive industr Google is able to recruit qualified employees because of its aggressive recruiting e: forts and its culture, management style, and employee benefits. For any compan these are very important factors in attracting, motivating, and retaining the appropr: ate mix of human resources.

We begin our study of human resources management (HRM) with an overview ‹ how businesses acquire, maintain, and develop their human resources. After listing th steps by which firms match their human resources needs with the supply available, w explore several dimensions of cultural diversity. Then we examine the concept of jo analysis. Next we focus on a firm's recruiting, selection, and orientation procedures : the means of acquiring employees. We also describe forms of employee compensatio that motivate employees to remain with a firm and to work effectively. Then we di: cuss methods of employee training, management development, and performance ap praisal. Finally we consider legislation that affects HRM practices.

learning objective

1 Describe the major components of human resources management.

Human Resources Management: An Overview

The human resource is not only unique and valuable; it is also an organization's mos important resource. It seems logical that an organization would expend a great deal ‹ effort to acquire and make full use of such a resource, and most organizations do. Thi effort is known as *human resources management* (HRM). It also has been called *staffin* and *personnel management*.

human resources management (HRM) all the activities involved in acquiring, maintaining, and developing an organization's human resources

Human resources management (HRM) consists of all the activities involved i acquiring, maintaining, and developing an organization's human resources. As th definition implies, HRM begins with acquisition—getting people to work for the or ganization. Next, steps must be taken to keep these valuable resources. (This is im portant; after all, they are the only business resources that can leave an organization : will.) Finally, the human resources should be developed to their full capacity to con tribute to the firm.

HRM Activities

Each of the three phases of HRM—acquiring, maintaining, and developing human re sources—consists of a number of related activities. Acquisition, for example, include planning, as well as the various activities that lead to hiring new personnel. Altogethe this phase of HRM includes five separate activities. They are

- *Human resources planning*—determining the firm's future human resources needs
- *Job analysis*—determining the exact nature of the positions to be filled
- *Recruiting*—attracting people to apply for positions in the firm
- *Selection*—choosing and hiring the most qualified applicants
- *Orientation*—acquainting new employees with the firm

Using the Internet

The Internet provides access to many excellent sources of both general information focusing on human resources, such as the Society for Human Resource Management **(http://www.shrm.org/)**, and more specialized areas, such as the American Society for Training and Development **(http://www.astd.org/)**.

Maintaining human resources consists primarily of encourag ing employees to remain with the firm and to work effectivel by using a variety of HRM programs, including

- *Employee relations*—increasing employee job satisfaction through satisfaction surveys, employee communication programs, exit interviews, and fair treatment
- *Compensation*—rewarding employee effort through monetary payments
- *Benefits*—providing rewards to ensure employee well-bein

The development phase of HRM is concerned with improvin employees' skills and expanding their capabilities. The two im portant activities within this phase are

- *Training and development*—teaching employees new skills, new jobs, and more effective ways of doing their present jobs
- *Performance appraisal*—assessing employees' current and potential performance levels

These activities are discussed in more detail shortly, when we have completed this overview of HRM.

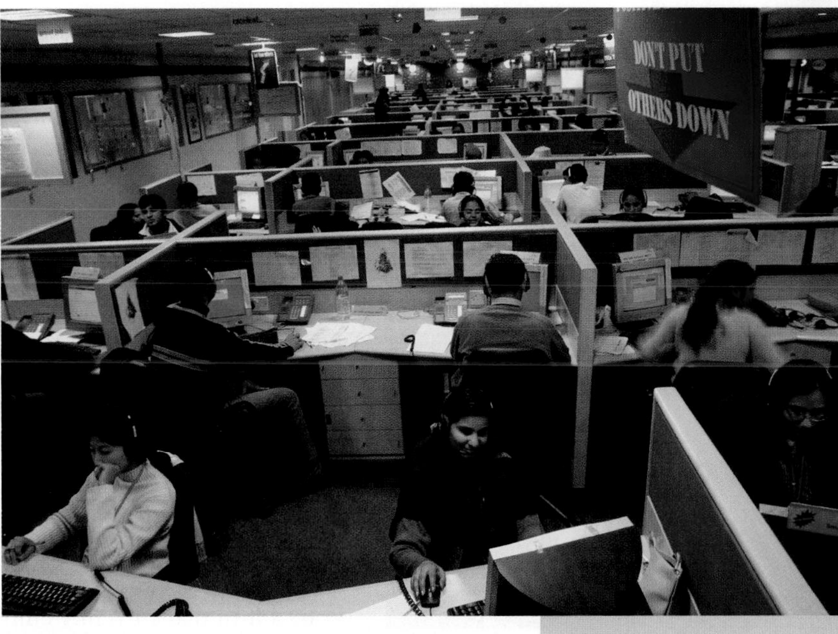

HRM activities: an on-going responsibility. Employees at Wipro Spectramind near New Delhi, India process claims for a major U.S. insurance company and provide help desk support for a large U.S. Internet service provider at about half the cost of U.S. employees. Wipro coaches these employees on how to speak American English to ensure that their U.S. customers receive the kind of service they need.

Responsibility for HRM

In general, HRM is a shared responsibility of line managers and staff HRM specialists. In very small organizations, the owner handles all or most HRM activities. As a firm grows in size, a human resources manager is hired to take over most of the staff responsibilities. As growth continues, additional staff positions are added as needed. In firms as large as, say, Disney, HRM activities tend to be very highly specialized. There may be separate groups to deal with compensation, benefits, training and development programs, and the other staff activities.

Specific HRM activities are assigned to those who are in the best position to perform them. Human resources planning and job analysis are usually done by staff specialists, with input from line managers. Similarly, recruiting and selection generally are handled by staff experts, although line managers are involved in the actual hiring decisions. Orientation programs usually are devised by staff specialists, and the orientation itself is carried out by both staff specialists and line managers. Compensation systems (including benefits) are most often developed and administered by the HRM staff. However, line managers recommend pay increases and promotions. Training and development activities usually are the joint responsibility of staff and line managers. Performance appraisal is the job of the line manager, although HRM staff personnel design the firm's appraisal system in many organizations.

Human Resources Planning

learning objective

2 Identify the steps in human resources planning.

Human resources planning is the development of strategies to meet a firm's future human resources needs. The starting point for this planning is the organization's overall strategic plan. From this, human resources planners can forecast the firm's future demand for human resources. Next, the planners must determine whether the needed human resources will be available; that is, they must anticipate the supply of human resources within the firm. Finally, they have to take steps to match supply with demand.

human resources planning the development of strategies to meet a firm's future human resources needs

Forecasting Human Resources Demand

Planners should base forecasts of the demand for human resources on as much relevant information as they can gather. The firm's overall strategic plan will provide information about future business ventures, new products, and projected expansions or contractions of particular product lines. Information on past staffing levels, evolving technologies, industry staffing practices, and projected economic trends also can be very helpful.

Forecasting human resources demand. Ifulfill.com is a company that ships nutritional supplements, videos, and other products for about 30 clients. Founder Paul Purdue must forecast human resources demands and adjust the size of his workforce quickly in order to meet seasonal fluctuations in his business. He relies on hiring temporary workers to meet part of his organization's demand for human resources.

HRM staff use all this information to determine both the number of employees the firm will require and their qualifications—including skills, experience, and knowledge. Planners use a wide range of methods to forecast specific personnel needs. For example, with one simple method, personnel requirements are projected to increase or decrease in the same proportion as sales revenue. Thus, if a 30 percent increase in sales volume is projected over the next two years, then up to a 30 percent increase in personnel requirements may be expected for the same period. (This method can be applied to specific positions as well as to the work force in general. It is not, however, a very precise forecasting method.) At the other extreme are elaborate, computer-based personnel planning models used by some large firms such as Exxon Corporation.

Forecasting Human Resources Supply

The forecast of the supply of human resources must take into account both the present work force and any changes or movements that may occur within it. For example, suppose that planners project that in five years a firm that currently employs 100 engineers will need to employ a total of 200 engineers. Planners cannot simply assume that they will have to hire 100 engineers over the next five years; during that period, some of the firm's present engineers are likely to be promoted, leave the firm, or move to other jobs within the firm. Thus planners may project the supply of engineers in five years at 87, which means that the firm will have to hire a total of 113 (or more) new engineers. When forecasting supply, planners should analyze the organization's existing employees to determine who can be retrained to perform the required tasks.

Two useful techniques for forecasting human resources supply are the replacement chart and the skills inventory. A **replacement chart** is a list of key personnel and their possible replacements within the firm. The chart is maintained to ensure that top management positions can be filled fairly quickly in the event of an unexpected death, resignation, or retirement. Some firms also provide additional training for employees who might eventually replace top managers.

replacement chart a list of key personnel and their possible replacements within a firm

skills inventory a computerized data bank containing information on the skills and experience of all present employees

A **skills inventory** is a computerized data bank containing information on the skills and experience of all present employees. It is used to search for candidates to fill new or newly available positions. For a special project, a manager may be seeking a current employee with specific information technology skills, at least six years of experience, and fluency in French. The skills inventory can quickly identify employees who possess such qualifications. Skill assessment tests can be administered inside an organization, or they can be provided by outside vendors. For example, SkillView Technologies, Inc., and Bookman Testing Services TeckChek are third-party information technology skill assessment providers. Furthermore, according to the Information Technology Association, there is a shortage of skilled knowledge workers, and this shortage is a driving force behind companies moving to outsourcing their computer system needs.[2] By using Internet-based hosts that provide all software and technical services for a monthly fee, firms can avoid staffing many highly specialized jobs.

Matching Supply with Demand

Once they have forecasts of both the demand for personnel and the firm's supply of personnel, planners can devise a course of action for matching the two. When demand is predicted to be greater than supply, plans must be made to recruit and select new employees. The timing of these actions depends on the types of positions to be filled. Suppose that we expect to open another plant in five years. Along with other employees, a plant manager and twenty-five maintenance workers will be needed. We probably can wait quite a while before we begin to recruit maintenance personnel. However, because the job of plant manager is so critical, we may start searching for the right person for that position immediately.

When supply is predicted to be greater than demand, the firm must take steps to reduce the size of its work force. Several methods are available, although none of them is especially pleasant for managers or discharged employees. When the oversupply is expected to be temporary, some employees may be *laid off*—dismissed from the work force until they are needed again.

Perhaps the most humane method for making personnel cutbacks is through attrition. *Attrition* is the normal reduction in the work force that occurs when employees leave a firm. If these employees are not replaced, the work force eventually shrinks to the point where supply matches demand. Of course, attrition may be a very slow process—often too slow to really help the firm. AutoNation, the U.S.'s largest new and used car retailer, recently achieved the desired cost cuts needed through employee attrition. Attrition reduced the work force by about 1,500 employees to bring its total employees base to about 30,000. Through the resulting cost reductions and measures to increase revenues, AutoNation was able to increase its earnings.[3]

Early retirement is another option. Under early retirement, people who are within a few years of retirement are permitted (or encouraged) to retire early with full benefits. Depending on the age makeup of the work force, this may or may not reduce the staff enough.

As a last resort, unneeded employees are sometimes simply *fired*. However, because of its negative impact, this method generally is used only when absolutely necessary.

Cultural Diversity in Human Resources

learning objective

3 Describe cultural diversity and understand some of the challenges and opportunities associated with it.

Today's work force is made up of many types of people. Firms can no longer safely assume that every employee walking in the door has similar beliefs or expectations. Whereas North American white males may believe in challenging authority, Asians tend to respect and defer to it. In Hispanic cultures, people often bring music, food, and family members to work, a custom that U.S. businesses traditionally have not allowed. A job applicant who will not make eye contact during an interview may be rejected for being unapproachable, when according to his or her culture, he or she was just being polite.

Since a larger number of women, minorities, and immigrants have entered the U.S. work force, the workplace is more diverse. It is estimated that women make up about 47 percent of the U.S. work force, and African Americans and Hispanics each account for about 11 percent.[4]

cultural (workplace) diversity differences among people in a work force due to race, ethnicity, and gender

Cultural (or **workplace) diversity** refers to the differences among people in a work force due to race, ethnicity, and gender. Increasing cultural diversity is forcing managers to learn to supervise and motivate people with a broader range of value systems. The flood of women into the work force, combined with a new emphasis on participative parenting by men, has brought many family-related issues to the workplace. Today's more educated employees also want greater independence and flexibility. In return for their efforts, they want both compensation and a better quality of life.

Although cultural diversity presents a challenge, managers should view it as an opportunity rather than a limitation. When managed properly, cultural diversity can provide competitive advantages for an organization. Table 10.1 (on p. 286) shows several benefits that creative management of cultural diversity can offer. A firm that manages diversity properly can develop cost advantages over firms that do not manage diversity

Spotlight

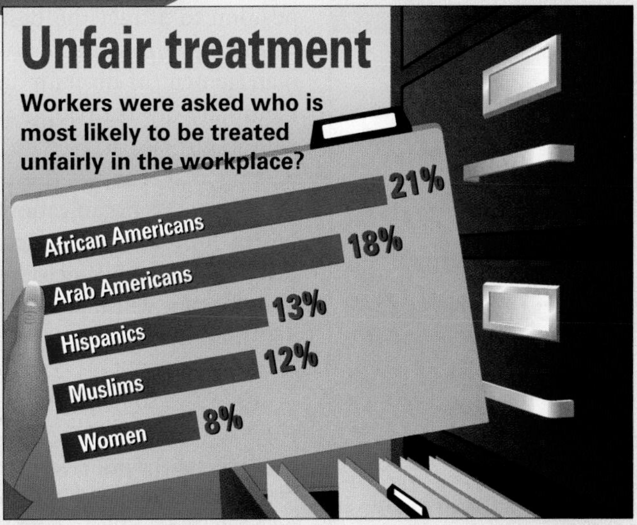

Unfair treatment

Workers were asked who is most likely to be treated unfairly in the workplace?

African Americans	21%
Arab Americans	18%
Hispanics	13%
Muslims	12%
Women	8%

Source: *USA Today*, April 10, 2002, p. B1.

table 10.1 Competitive Advantages of Cultural Diversity

Cost	As organizations become more diverse, the cost of a poor job in integrating workers will increase. Companies that handle this well can thus create cost advantages over those that do a poor job. In addition, companies also experience cost savings by hiring people with knowledge of various cultures as opposed to having to train Americans, for example, about how German people do business.
Resource acquisition	Companies develop reputations as being favorable or unfavorable prospective employers for women and ethnic minorities. Those with the best reputations for managing diversity will win the competition for the best personnel.
Marketing edge	For multinational organizations, the insight and cultural sensitivity that members with roots in other countries bring to the marketing effort should improve these efforts in important ways. The same rationale applies to marketing subpopulations domestically.
Flexibility	Culturally diverse employees often are open to a wider array of positions within a company and are more likely to move up the corporate ladder more rapidly, given excellent performance.
Creativity	Diversity of perspectives and less emphasis on conformity to norms of the past should improve the level of creativity.
Problem solving	Differences within decision-making and problem-solving groups potentially produce better decisions through a wider range of perspectives and more thorough critical analysis of issues.
Bilingual skills	Cultural diversity in the workplace brings with it bilingual and bicultural skills, which are very advantageous to the ever-growing global marketplace. Employees with knowledge about how other cultures work not only can speak to them in their language but also can prevent their company from making embarrassing moves due to lack of cultural sophistication. Thus companies seek job applicants with perhaps a background in cultures in which the company does business.

Sources: Taylor H. Cox and Stacy Blake, "Managing Cultural Diversity: Implications for Organizational Competitiveness," *Academy of Management Executive*, Vol. 5, No. 3, 1991, p. 46; Graciela Kenig, "Yo Soy Ingeniero: The Advantages of Being Bilingual in Technical Professions," *Diversity Monthly*, February 28, 1999, p. 13; and "Dialogue Skills in the Multicultural Workplace," *North American Post*, March 19, 1999, p. 2.

We

are dedicated
to diversity
for the
value

NEWTON-WELLESLEY
HOSPITAL
PARTNERS
For more information about employment opportunities, please visit our website at
www.nwh.org or call 617-243-6768

The value of cultural diversity. Organizations that are dedicated to diversity, like Newton-Wellesley Hospital, gain significant benefits from their efforts.

well. Moreover, organizations that manage diversity creatively are in a much better position to attract the best personnel. A culturally diverse organization may gain a marketing edge because it understands different cultural groups. Proper guidance and management of diversity in an organization also can improve the level of creativity. Culturally diverse people frequently are more flexible in the types of positions they will accept. Workers who bring fresh viewpoints to problem solving and decision making may enliven these processes substantially. Bilingual skills bring numerous benefits to an organization. Toyota, for example, recently decided to locate its sixth North American manufacturing facility in San Antonio, Texas, with one of the primary factors in the decision being the tremendous bilingual labor available in the area. This factory will manufacture Toyota trucks and will bring economic growth to the San Antonio area.[5]

Because cultural diversity creates challenges along with these advantages, it is important for an organization's employees to know how to cope with it. To accomplish this goal, numerous U.S. firms have taken action to train their managers to respect and manage diversity. Diversity training programs may include recruiting minorities, training minorities to be managers, training managers to view diversity positively, teaching English as a second language, providing mentoring programs, and facilitating support groups for immigrants. Many companies are realizing the necessity of having diversity training spanning beyond just racial issues. Eaton Corp., which manufactures engine parts for cars, has invested in diversity training and encourages its employees to consider religion, gender, and nationality in addition to race. Other companies add age, religious practices, weight, sexual orientation, and even hobbies to this list.[6] Due to the high quality of its cultural diversity program, Texas Instruments has received several awards for being one of the best places in America for minorities to work. Texas Instruments' cultural diversity program involves training and education, employee diversity groups, and corporate policies that support advancement of minorities in that organization. Thousands of managers, supervisors, and employees from all parts of the company have attended diversity training programs that have taught them to value the cultural differences in Texas Instruments. One of the reasons for this program's success is the strong commitment that senior management at Texas Instruments has made to this program.[7]

As is the case with many organizational goals, a diversity program will be successful only if it is systematic and ongoing and has a strong, sustained commitment from top leadership. Cultural diversity is here to stay. Its impact on organizations is widespread and will continue to grow within corporations. Management must learn to overcome the obstacles and capitalize on the advantages associated with the varying viewpoints and backgrounds of culturally diverse human resources.

Job Analysis

learning objective

4 Explain the objectives and uses of job analysis.

There is no sense in trying to hire people unless we know what we are hiring them for. In other words, we need to know the exact nature of a job before we can find the right person to do it.

Job analysis is a systematic procedure for studying jobs to determine their various elements and requirements. Consider the position of clerk, for example. In a large corporation, there may be fifty kinds of clerk positions. They all may be called "clerks," but each position may differ from the others in the activities to be performed, the level of proficiency required for each activity, and the particular set of qualifications that the position demands. These distinctions are the focus of job analysis.

job analysis a systematic procedure for studying jobs to determine their various elements and requirements

The job analysis for a particular position typically consists of two parts—a job description and a job specification. A **job description** is a list of the elements that make up a particular job. It includes the duties the jobholder must perform, the working conditions under which the job must be performed, the jobholder's responsibilities (including number and types of subordinates, if any), and the tools and equipment that must be used on the job (see Figure 10.1 on p. 288).

job description a list of the elements that make up a particular job

A **job specification** is a list of the qualifications required to perform a particular job. Included are the skills, abilities, education, and experience the jobholder must have. When attempting to hire a financial analyst, Bank of America used the following job specification: "Requires 8–10 years of financial experience, a broad based financial background, strong customer focus, the ability to work confidently with the client's management team, strong analytical skills. Must have strong Excel and Word skills. Personal characteristics should include strong desire to succeed, impact performer (individually and as a member of a team), positive attitude, high energy level and ability to influence others"[8]

job specification a list of the qualifications required to perform a particular job

The job analysis is not only the basis for recruiting and selecting new employees for either existing positions or new ones; it is also used in other areas of HRM, including evaluation and the determination of equitable compensation levels.

figure 10.1

Job Description and Job Specification

This job description explains the job of sales coordinator and lists the responsibilities of the position. The job specification is contained in the last paragraph.

HOUGHTON MIFFLIN COMPANY

JOB DESCRIPTION

TITLE:	Georgia Sales Coordinator	**DATE:**	3/25/05
DEPARTMENT:	College, Sales	**GRADE:**	12
REPORTS TO:	Regional Manager	**EXEMPT/NON-EXEMPT:**	Exempt

BRIEF SUMMARY:

Supervise one other Georgia-based sales representative to gain supervisory experience. Captain the 4 members of the outside sales rep team that are assigned to territories consisting of colleges and universities in Georgia. Oversee, coordinate, advise, and make decisions regarding Georgia sales activities. Based upon broad contact with customers across the state and communication with administrators of schools, the person will make recommendations regarding issues specific to the needs of higher education in the state of Georgia such as distance learning, conversion to the semester system, potential statewide adoptions, and faculty training.

PRINCIPLE ACCOUNTABILITIES:

1. Supervises/manages/trains one other Atlanta-based sales rep.
2. Advises two other sales reps regarding the Georgia schools in their territories.
3. Increases overall sales in Georgia as well as individual sales territory.
4. Assists regional manager in planning and coordinating regional meetings and Atlanta conferences.
5. Initiates a dialogue with campus administrators, particularly in the areas of the semester conversion, distance learning, and faculty development.

DIMENSIONS:

This position will have one direct report in addition to the leadership role played within the region. Revenue most directly impacted will be within the individually assigned territory, the supervised territory, and the overall sales for the state of Georgia.

KNOWLEDGE AND SKILLS:

Must have displayed a history of consistently outstanding sales in personal territory. Must demonstrate clear teamwork and leadership skills and be willing to extend beyond the individual territory goals. Should have a clear understanding of the company's systems and product offerings in order to train and lead other sales representatives. Must have the communication skills and presence to communicate articulately with higher education administrators and to serve as a bridge between the company and higher education in the state.

Source: Used with permission of Houghton Mifflin Company.

Recruiting, Selection, and Orientation

learning objective

5 Describe the processes of recruiting, employee selection, and orientation.

In an organization with jobs waiting to be filled, HRM personnel need to (1) find candidates for those jobs and (2) match the right candidate with each job. Three activities are involved: recruiting, selection, and (for new employees) orientation.

Recruiting

recruiting the process of attracting qualified job applicants

Recruiting is the process of attracting qualified job applicants. Because it is a vital link in a costly process (the cost of hiring an employee can be several thousand dollars), recruiting needs to be a systematic rather than a haphazard process. One goal of recruiters is to attract the "right number" of applicants. The right number is enough to allow a good match between applicants and open positions but not so many that matching them requires too much time and effort. For example, if there are five open positions and five applicants, the firm essentially has no choice. It must hire those five applicants (qualified or not), or the positions will remain open. At the other extreme, if several hundred job seekers apply for the five positions, HRM personnel will have to spend weeks processing their applications.

Tools for attracting job applicants. Some organizations use employment agencies, such as Monster.com, for recruiting purposes.

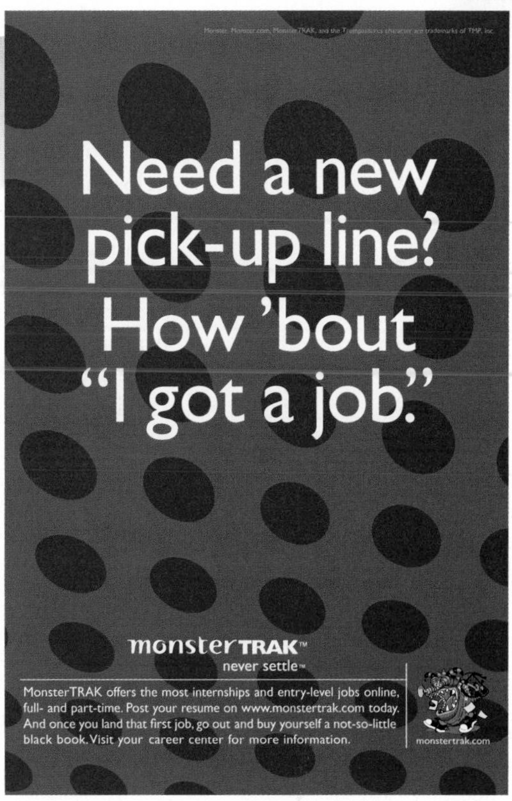

Recruiters may seek applicants outside the firm, within the firm, or both. The source used depends on the nature of the position, the situation within the firm, and sometimes the firm's established or traditional recruitment policies.

External Recruiting **External recruiting** is the attempt to attract job applicants from outside an organization. Among the means available for external recruiting are Internet websites, newspaper advertising, employment agencies, recruiting on college campuses and in union hiring halls, soliciting the recommendations of present employees, and conducting "open houses" in which potential employees are invited to visit the firm for a closer look. In addition, many people who are looking for work simply apply at the firm's employment office.

Clearly, it is best to match the recruiting means with the kind of applicant being sought. For example, private employment agencies most often handle professional people, whereas public employment agencies (operated by state or local governments) usually are more concerned with operations personnel. Hence we might approach a private agency if we were looking for a vice president, but we would be more inclined to contact a public agency if we wanted to hire a machinist.

external recruiting the attempt to attract job applicants from outside the organization

The primary advantage of external recruiting is that it enables the firm to bring in people with new perspectives and varied business backgrounds. It also may be the only way to attract applicants with the required skills and knowledge. A disadvantage of external recruiting is that it is often expensive, especially if private employment agencies must be used. External recruiting also may provoke resentment among present employees.

Recruiting at job fairs. At the largest job fair in Colorado, recruiters have an opportunity to meet numerous potential job applicants.

internal recruiting considering present employees as applicants for available positions

Internal Recruiting **Internal recruiting** means considering present employees as applicants for available positions. Generally, current employees are considered for *promotion* to higher-level positions. However, employees also may be considered for *transfer* from one position to another at the same level.

Promoting from within provides strong motivation for current employees and helps the firm retain quality personnel. General Electric, Exxon, and Eastman Kodak are companies dedicated to promoting from within. The practice of *job posting*, or informing current employees of upcoming openings, may be a company policy or be required by a union contract. The primary disadvantage of internal recruiting is that promoting a current employee leaves another position to be filled. Not only does the firm still incur recruiting and selection costs, but it also must now train two employees instead of one.

In many situations it may be impossible to recruit internally. For example, a new position may be such that no current employee is qualified to fill it. Or the firm may be growing so rapidly that there is no time to go through the re-assigning of positions that promotion or transfer requires.

Selection

selection the process of gathering information about applicants for a position and then using that information to choose the most appropriate applicant

Selection is the process of gathering information about applicants for a position and then using that information to choose the most appropriate applicant. Note the use of the word *appropriate*. In selection, the idea is not to hire the person with the *most* qualifications but rather to choose the applicant with the qualifications that are *most appropriate* for the job. The actual selection of an applicant often is made by one or more line managers who have responsibility for the position being filled. However, HRM personnel usually help the selection process by developing a pool of applicants and expediting the assessment of these applicants. Common means of obtaining information about applicants' qualifications are employment applications, tests, interviews, references, and assessment centers.

Employment Applications Just about everyone who applies for anything must submit an application. You probably filled one out to apply for admission to your school. An employment application is useful in collecting factual information on a candidate's education, work experience, and personal history (see Figure 10.2). The data obtained from applications usually are used for two purposes: to identify applicants who are worthy of further scrutiny and to familiarize interviewers with their backgrounds.

Many job candidates submit résumés to prospective employers, and some firms require them. A *résumé* is a one- or two-page summary of the candidate's background and qualifications. It may include a description of the type of job the applicant is seeking. A résumé may be sent to a firm to request consideration for available jobs, or it may be submitted along with an employment application.

To improve the usefulness of information gathered, HRM specialists ask current employees about the factors in their own backgrounds most strongly related to their current jobs. Then these factors are included on the applications and may be weighted more heavily when evaluating new applicants' qualifications.

Employment Tests Tests administered to job candidates usually focus on aptitudes, skills, abilities, or knowledge relevant to the jobs that are to be performed. Such tests (basic computer skills tests, for example) indicate how well the applicant will do on the job. Occasionally, companies use general intelligence or personality tests, but these are seldom helpful in predicting specific job performance. However, *Fortune* 500 companies as well as an increasing number of medium- and small-sized companies are using predictive-behavior personality tests as the cost to administer them decreases. Darden Restaurants, the company that includes The Olive Garden and Red Lobster, uses a work-style inventory in its hiring process for all positions in the company, whereas firms such as Disney and Hampton Inn use similar tests for management positions.[9]

figure 10.2

Typical Employment Application

Employers use applications to collect factual information on a candidate's education, work experience, and personal history.

3M Employment Application
Form 14650 - D

3M Staffing Resource Center
3M Center, Building 224-1W-02
P.O. Box 33224
St. Paul, MN 55133-3224

Name (Print or Type)

Personal Data (Print or Type) No. 109060

Name	Last	First	MI	Social Security Number
Present Address	Street Address			Home Telephone (Include Area Code) ( )
	City, State and Zip			Work Telephone (Include Area Code) ( )
	Internet e-mail Address			
Permanent Address	*Leave blank if same as above*	Street Address		Perm.
		City, State and Zip		Date of
Job Interest	Position applied for		Salary desired	Date
	Type of position applied for ☐ Regular ☐ Part-time ☐ Temporary ☐ Summer ☐			

Authorization to Work

It is unlawful for 3M to hire individuals that are not authorized to work in the United Sta citizens or aliens that are authorized to work in the United States. If you receive an offe offer, before you will be placed on the payroll, you will be required to document that yo that is authorized to work in the United States.

Are you a United States citizen or a lawful permanent resident? ☐ Yes ☐ No

If your answer is No, what type of Visa and employment authorization do you have?

Education History

Schools Attended (Last School First)	Attendance Dates Mo./Yr. From - To	Grad. Date	Degree Type
Name of School (City, State)	-		
	-		
	-		
	-		
High School or GED			

Additional Education Information

(If additional space is needed, attach separate page)

Faculty person who knows you best (name, telephone)

Memberships in professional or honorary societies and any other extracurricular activities

Post graduate research, title and description

Publications/Patents Issued

Please Open Folder and Complete Additional Information

Printed with soy inks on Torchglow Opaque (made of 50% recycled fiber, including 10%

General Information and Job Requirements

Are you willing to ➔ Work Shifts ☐ Yes ☐ No; Work overtime ☐ Yes ☐ No; Work a schedule other than M/F ☐ Yes ☐ No; Work a rotation work schedule ☐ Yes ☐ No

Travel ☐ Yes ___% ☐ No; List any restrictions regarding relocation; Are you willing to relocate? ☐ Yes ☐ No

If you wish to indicate that you were referred to 3M by any of the following, please check appropriate box and specify

☐ Employment advertisement (Name of publication) ☐ Employment agency (Name of agency) ☐ 3M Employee (Name) ☐ Other

Are you under 18? ☐ Yes ☐ No

Have you ever ☐ been employed by 3M or any 3M Subsidiary ☐ previously applied to 3M or any 3M Subsidiary

If so, please check appropriate box and specify location, date, employee number - (include last two 3M performance reviews if appropriate and available.)

Date/Employee Number

Employment Record

List most current or recent employer first, include periods of unemployment, include U.S. Military Service (show rank/rate at discharge, but not type of discharge). Include previous 3M experience (summer/part time jobs and Cooperative Education assignments and any volunteer experience which relates to the position you are applying for).

Employer (company name)	Immediate supervisor's name	Your job title
Street Address	Employment dates (mo. and yr.) From To	Salary Begin End
City, State, Zip Code	Reason for leaving or why do you want to leave?	
Company's Product or Service	Summarize your job duties	
Employer (company name)	Immediate supervisor's name	Your job title
Street Address	Employment dates (mo. and yr.) From To	Salary Begin End
City, State, Zip Code	Reason for leaving	
Company's Product or Service	Summarize your job duties	
Employer (company name)	Immediate supervisor's name	Your job title
Street Address	Employment dates (mo. and yr.) From To	Salary Begin End
City, State, Zip Code	Reason for leaving	
Company's Product or Service	Summarize your job duties	
Employer (company name)	Immediate supervisor's name	Your job title
Street Address	Employment dates (mo. and yr.) From To	Salary Begin End
City, State, Zip Code	Reason for leaving	
Company's Product or Service	Summarize your job duties	

Additional Information

(Please include any additional information you think might be helpful to use in considering you for employment, such as additional work experience, activities, accomplishments, etc.)

Source: Courtesy 3M.

At one time, a number of companies were criticized for using tests that were biased against members of certain minority groups—in particular, African Americans. The test results were, to a great extent, unrelated to job performance. Today a firm must be able to prove that a test is not discriminatory by demonstrating that it accurately measures one's ability to perform on the job. Applicants who believe that they have been discriminated against through an invalid test may file a complaint with the Equal Employment Opportunity Commission (EEOC).

Interviews The employment interview is perhaps the most widely used selection technique. Job candidates usually are interviewed by at least one member of the HRM staff and by the person for whom they will be working. Candidates for higher-level jobs also may meet with a department head or vice president and may have several additional interviews.

Interviews provide an opportunity for the applicant and the firm to learn more about each other. Interviewers can pose problems to test the candidate's abilities. They can probe employment history more deeply and learn something about the candidate's attitudes and motivation. The candidate, meanwhile, has a chance to find out more about the job and the people with whom he or she would be working.

Unfortunately, interviewing may be the stage at which discrimination enters the selection process. For example, suppose that a female applicant mentions that she is the mother of small children. Her interviewer may assume that she would not be available for job-related travel even though that may not be the case. In addition, interviewers may be unduly influenced by such factors as appearance. Or they may ask different questions of different applicants so that it becomes impossible to compare candidates' qualifications.

Some of these problems can be solved through better interviewer training and the use of structured interviews. In a *structured interview,* the interviewer asks only a prepared set of job-related questions. The firm also may consider using several different interviewers for each applicant, but this solution is likely to be a costly one.

References A job candidate generally is asked to furnish the names of references—people who can verify background information and provide personal evaluations of the candidate. Naturally, applicants tend to list only references who are likely to say good things about them. Thus personal evaluations obtained from references may not be of much value. However, references are often contacted to verify such information as previous job responsibilities and the reason an applicant chose to leave a former job.

adapting to change

How Do You Hire More Than a Million Employees?

HOW DOES THE WORLD'S LARGEST business employer hire more than a million employees? Wal-Mart's payroll already covers nearly 1.5 million associates (the company's term for employees), thanks to decades of growth. To staff new international stores, HRM personnel will need to hire 800,000 more employees during the next five years alone. In addition, because some employees inevitably leave (either voluntarily or due to poor performance), Wal-Mart must be ready to fill as many as 200,000 open positions in the coming years.

Hiring on such a massive scale is not easy. "The biggest challenge is the numbers," admits Coleman Peterson, Wal-Mart's executive vice president of people. "But the issue is no different than the one [founder] Sam Walton faced. We have to focus on one associate at a time." The stores themselves are a major source of applicants for entry-level positions. "Every time we open a Wal-Mart store or a Sam's Club, it's a recruiting post," Peterson says. Job applications are on prominent display in every store, ready to catch the eye of shoppers who pass by. Wal-Mart also relies heavily on internal recruiting to fill management positions. In fact, 70 percent of the company's managers started out as hourly workers on the sales floor or in the stock room and worked their way up.

The remainder of the management positions are filled through aggressive college recruiting. Every year Wal-Mart recruiters visit eighty campuses to hire graduates for slots in the company's management training program. Diversity is an important consideration. Nearly half of all management trainees are members of minority groups, and half are women. Moreover, human resources personnel have started inviting promising college students to enter the training program even before they graduate as a way to introduce them to the company and provide a taste of the fast-paced retail world.

Perhaps the biggest challenge is to preserve Wal-Mart's customer-centered culture despite its rapid international expansion. Human resources personnel must continue to recruit and train candidates willing to work hard and provide the kind of smiling customer service for which the company is known. Can the retailing giant find and retain one million employees who are committed to living those values every working day?

Assessment Centers An assessment center is used primarily to select current employees for promotion to higher-level management positions. Typically, a group of employees is sent to the center for two or three days. While there, they participate in activities designed to simulate the management environment and to predict managerial effectiveness. Trained observers (usually managers) make recommendations regarding promotion possibilities. Although this technique is gaining popularity, the expense involved limits its use to larger organizations.

Orientation

Once all the available information about job candidates has been collected and analyzed, those involved in the selection decide which candidate they would like to hire. A job offer is extended to the candidate. If it is accepted, the candidate becomes an employee and starts to work for the firm.

Soon after a candidate joins the firm, he or she goes through the firm's orientation program. **Orientation** is the process of acquainting new employees with the organization. Orientation topics range from such basic items as the location of the company cafeteria to concerns about various career paths within the firm. The orientation itself may consist of a half-hour informal presentation by a human resources manager. Or it may be an elaborate program involving dozens of people and lasting several days or weeks.

orientation the process of acquainting new employees with an organization

Compensation and Benefits

learning objective

6 Discuss the primary elements of employee compensation and benefits.

An effective employee reward system must (1) enable employees to satisfy their basic needs, (2) provide rewards comparable to those offered by other firms, (3) be distributed fairly within the organization, and (4) recognize that different people have different needs.

A firm's compensation system can be structured to meet the first three of these requirements. The fourth is more difficult in that it must take into account many variables among many people. Most firms offer a number of benefits that, taken together, generally help to provide for employees' varying needs.

Compensation Decisions

Compensation is the payment employees receive in return for their labor. Its importance to employees is obvious. And because compensation may account for up to 80 percent of a firm's operating costs, it is equally important to management. The firm's **compensation system—**the policies and strategies that determine employee compensation—therefore must be designed carefully to provide for employee needs while keeping labor costs within reasonable limits. For most firms, designing an effective compensation system requires three separate management decisions—about wage level, wage structure, and individual wages.

compensation the payment employees receive in return for their labor

compensation system the policies and strategies that determine employee compensation

Wage Level Management must first position the firm's general pay level relative to pay levels of comparable firms. In other words, will the firm pay its employees less than, more than, or about the same as similar organizations? Most firms choose a pay level near the industry average. A firm that is not in good financial shape may pay less than the going rate. Large, prosperous organizations, by contrast, may pay a little more than average to attract and retain the most capable employees.

To determine what the average is, the firm may use wage surveys. A **wage survey** is a collection of data on prevailing wage rates within an industry or a geographic area. Such surveys are compiled by industry associations, local governments, personnel associations, and (occasionally) individual firms.

wage survey a collection of data on prevailing wage rates within an industry or a geographic area

exploring business

Investing in People at Edward Jones

EVERY YEAR MORE THAN 100,000 people ask about working at a company that has purposely stayed far from its industry's central hub. The Edward Jones brokerage firm has not needed a fancy Wall Street headquarters to attract five million customers. In fact, the firm has always been based in St. Louis. Most of its brokers work out of small offices in suburban and rural locations, one broker to a branch. Edward Jones may not be one of America's highest-profile brokerages, but it has repeatedly been named one of the country's best companies to work for.

One reason so many applicants flock to Edward Jones is its compensation. Brokers work on commission based on how much money they invest for their customers. The typical broker with a decade of experience at Edward Jones can earn nearly $300,000 annually—and some bring in $1 million annually, including commissions, profit sharing, and bonuses.

A second reason is the company's comprehensive employee benefits. In addition to vacation pay, holiday pay, sick pay, and comprehensive life, accident, disability, and health insurance, the company reimburses employees for some tuition payments and some adoption expenses. Also, full-time employees participate in the company's flexible benefit plan and have the option of enrolling in special plans covering dental insurance, long-term care insurance, and retirement. And, depending on individual circumstances, some employees are allowed to work from home part of the time.

Edward Jones invests in its work force through months of paid training at the company's campus in Tempe, Arizona. New stockbrokers learn about investment opportunities as well as how to approach prospects and win new customers. Headquarters supplies detailed securities research, investment recommendations, and a computerized customer management system to support employees when they start in a branch.

Publicity about the company's employee-friendly values has brought even more inquiries from job-seekers—as many as 42,300 during a single month. True to the company's roots, the human resources staff handles this deluge by responding to everyone who submits a résumé. "It's reflective of who we are," notes the chief human resources officer. This kind of consideration is yet another reason why applicants flock to Edward Jones.

Wage Structure Next, management must decide on relative pay levels for all the positions within the firm. Will managers be paid more than secretaries? Will secretaries be paid more than custodians? The result of this set of decisions is often called the firm's *wage structure*.

The wage structure is almost always developed on the basis of a job evaluation. **Job evaluation** is the process of determining the relative worth of the various jobs within a firm. Most observers probably would agree that a secretary should make more money than a custodian, but how much more? Twice as much? One and one-half times as much? Job evaluation should provide the answers to such questions.

job evaluation the process of determining the relative worth of the various jobs within a firm

A number of techniques may be used to evaluate jobs. The simplest is to rank all the jobs within the firm according to their value to the firm. Of course, if there are more than a few jobs, this technique loses its simplicity very quickly. A more frequently used method is based on the job analysis. Points are allocated to each job for each of its elements and requirements, as set forth in the job analysis. For example, "college degree required" might be worth fifty points, whereas the need for a high school education might count for only twenty-five points. The more points a job is allocated, the more important it is presumed to be (and the higher its level in the firm's wage structure).

Individual Wages Finally, the specific payments individual employees will receive must be determined. Consider the case of two secretaries working side by side. Job evaluation has been used to determine the relative level of secretarial pay within the firm's wage structure. However, suppose that one secretary has fifteen years of experience and can accurately type eighty words per minute. The other has two years of experience and can type only fifty-five words per minute. In most firms these two people would not receive the same pay. Instead, a wage range would be established for the secretarial position. In this case, the range might be $7 to $9.50 per hour. The more experienced and proficient secretary would then be paid an amount near the top of the range (say, $8.90 per hour); the less experienced secretary would receive an amount that was lower but still within the range (say, $7.75 per hour).

Two wage decisions actually come into play here. First the employee's initial rate must be established. It is based on experience, other qualifications, and expected performance. Later, the employee may be given pay increases based on seniority and performance.

Comparable Worth

One reason women in the work force are paid less than men may be that a certain proportion of women occupy female-dominated jobs—nurses, secretaries, and medical records analysts, for example—that require education, skills, and training equal to higher-paid positions but that are undervalued by our economic system. **Comparable worth** is a concept that seeks equal compensation for jobs that require about the same level of education, training, and skills. Several states have enacted laws that require equal pay for comparable work in government positions. Critics of comparable worth argue that the market has determined the worth of these jobs and that laws should not be enacted to tamper with the pricing mechanism of the market. The Equal Pay Act, discussed later in this chapter, does not address the issue of comparable worth. Critics also argue that artificially inflating salaries for female-dominated occupations encourages women to keep these jobs rather than to seek out other higher-paying jobs.

comparable worth a concept that seeks equal compensation for jobs requiring about the same level of education, training, and skills

Types of Compensation

Compensation can be paid in a variety of forms. Most forms of compensation fall into the following categories: hourly wage, weekly or monthly salary, commissions, incentive payments, lump-sum salary increases, and profit sharing.

Hourly Wage An **hourly wage** is a specific amount of money paid for each hour of work. People who earn wages are paid their hourly wage for the first forty hours worked in any week. They are then paid one and one-half times their hourly wage for time worked in excess of forty hours. (That is, they are paid "time and a half" for overtime.) Workers in retailing and fast-food chains, on assembly lines, and in clerical positions usually are paid an hourly wage.

hourly wage a specific amount of money paid for each hour of work

Weekly or Monthly Salary A **salary** is a specific amount of money paid for an employee's work during a set calendar period, regardless of the actual number of hours worked. Salaried employees receive no overtime pay, but they do not lose pay when they are absent from work (within reasonable limits). Most professional and managerial positions are salaried.

salary a specific amount of money paid for an employee's work during a set calendar period, regardless of the actual number of hours worked

Commissions A **commission** is a payment that is a percentage of sales revenue. Sales representatives and sales managers often are paid entirely through commissions or through a combination of commissions and salary.

commission a payment that is a percentage of sales revenue

Incentive Payments An **incentive payment** is a payment in addition to wages, salary, or commissions. Incentive payments are really extra rewards for outstanding job performance. They may be distributed to all employees or only to certain employees within an organization. Some firms distribute incentive payments to all employees annually. The size of the payment depends on the firm's earnings and, at times, on the particular employee's length of service with the firm. Firms sometimes offer incentives to employees who exceed specific sales or production goals, a practice called *gain sharing*.

incentive payment a payment in addition to wages, salary, or commissions

To avoid yearly across-the-board salary increases, some organizations reward outstanding workers individually through *merit pay*. This pay-for-performance approach allows management to control labor costs while encouraging employees to work more efficiently. An employee's merit pay depends on his or her achievements relative to those of others.

Lump-Sum Salary Increases In traditional reward systems, an employee who receives an annual pay increase is given part of the increase in each pay period. For example, suppose that an employee on a monthly salary gets a 10 percent annual pay hike. He or she actually receives 10 percent of the former monthly salary added to each month's paycheck for a year. Companies that offer a **lump-sum salary increase** give the employee the option of taking the entire pay raise in one lump sum at the beginning of the year. The employee then draws his or her "regular" pay for the rest of the year. The lump-sum payment typically is treated as an interest-free loan that must be repaid if the employee leaves the firm during the year. B. F. Goodrich, Aetna Life and Casualty, and Timex all have offered variations of this plan.

lump-sum salary increase an entire pay raise taken in one lump sum

Profit Sharing **Profit sharing** is the distribution of a percentage of the firm's profit among its employees. The idea is to motivate employees to work effectively by giving them a stake in the company's financial success. Some firms—including Sears, Roebuck—have linked their profit-sharing plans to employee retirement programs; that is, employees receive their profit-sharing distributions, with interest, when they retire. For example, the profit-sharing plan at Pella, maker of doors and windows, results in a 15 percent contribution by the company to its employees' retirement programs.[10]

profit sharing the distribution of a percentage of the firm's profit among its employees

Employee Benefits

employee benefit a reward in addition to regular compensation that is provided indirectly to employees

An **employee benefit** is a reward in addition to regular compensation that is provided indirectly to employees. Employee benefits consist mainly of services (such as insurance) that are paid for partially or totally by employers and employee expenses (such as college tuition) that are reimbursed by employers. Currently, the average cost of these benefits is 28 percent of an employee's total compensation, which includes wages plus benefits. Thus a person who received total compensation (including benefits) of $40,000 a year earned $28,000 in wages and received an additional $11,200 in benefits.[11] A recent online survey conducted by TrueCareers found that 84 percent of employees would rather receive better benefits than higher salaries. These findings are significant to employers as they try to attract and retain good employees. Increased desire for benefits is partially the result of increasing health care insurance costs as copayments continue to rise.[12]

Provider of employee benefit programs. Numerous organizations, like CIGNA, help companies provide employee benefits such as retirement, health, life, and disability benefits.

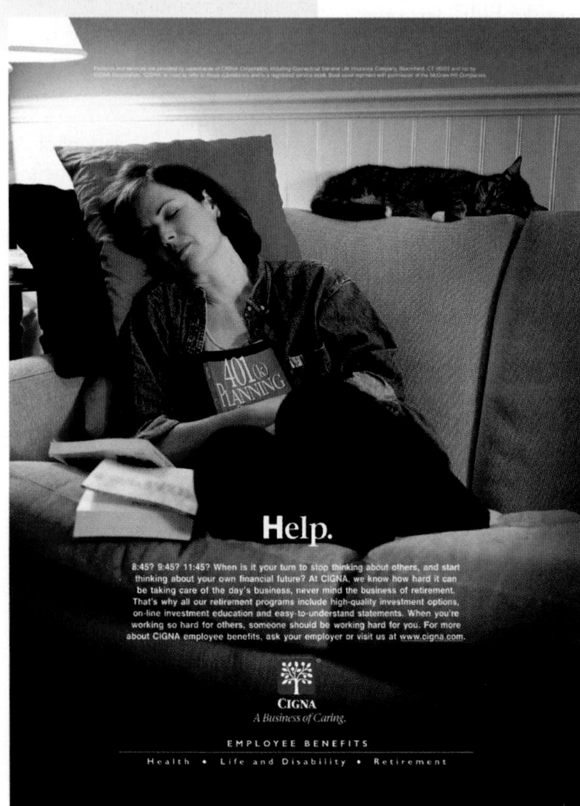

Types of Benefits Employee benefits take a variety of forms. *Pay for time not worked* covers such absences as vacation time, holidays, and sick leave. *Insurance packages* may include health, life, and dental insurance for employees and their families. Some firms pay the entire cost of the insurance package, and others share the cost with the employee. The costs of *pension and retirement programs* also may be borne entirely by the firm or shared with the employee.

Some benefits are required by law. For example, employers must maintain *workers' compensation insurance*, which pays medical bills for injuries that occur on the job and provides income for employees who are disabled by job-related injuries. Employers also must pay for *unemployment insurance* and contribute to each employee's federal *Social Security* account.

Other benefits provided by employers include tuition-reimbursement plans, credit unions, child care, company cafeterias that sell reduced-price meals, exercise rooms and other recreational facilities, and broad stock option plans that are available to all employees, not just top management. Some companies offer special benefits to U.S. military reservists who are called up for active duty. Due to world events such as the 9/11 terrorist attacks and continuing unrest in the Middle

East, many reservists have been called to duty out of their corporate offices. IBM offers to make up the difference between a reservist's military pay and his or her regular pay so that overall pay remains at the IBM level. In addition, normal benefits are still given when reservists are called, and employees can continue to contribute to their 401(k) and receive contributions from IBM. When reservists return from active duty, they come back to their same positions, and their active duty times counts toward their years of service with IBM.[13]

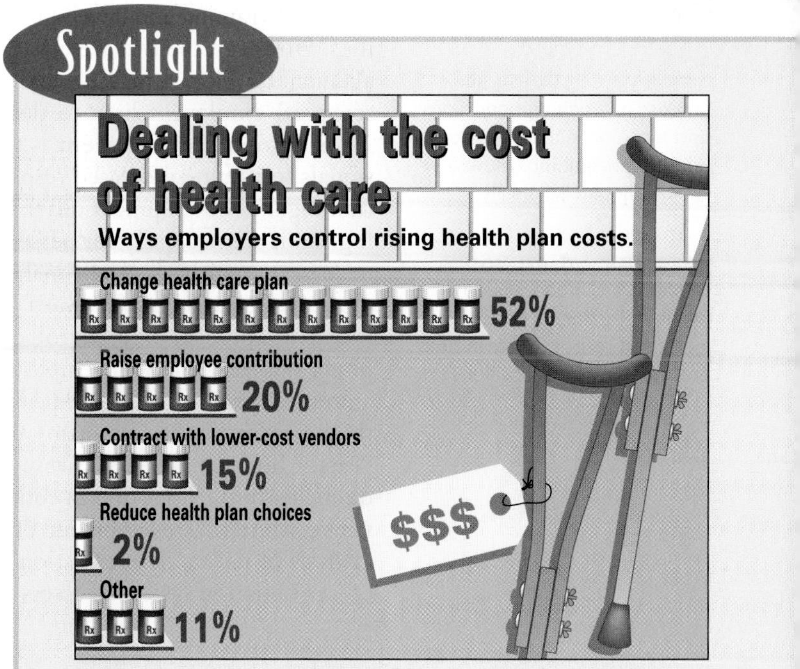

Some companies offer unusual benefits in order to attract and retain employees. DaimlerChrysler makes available to every salaried, non–United Auto Worker Union worker a one-time $4,000 work-family account that can be used for child care, adoption costs, elder care, college tuition, or extra retirement funds. Compuware Corporation, a software company, makes cheap meals available to workers to take home after a workout in the company gym. Dayton Hudson not only provides employees with discounts on airfares, rental cars, and hotels for vacations but also allows employees to customize weekly work schedules to fit their personal needs. Worthington Industries, a metal processing company located in Columbus, Ohio, offers employees on-site haircuts for just $3.00. At BP Exploration in Anchorage, Alaska, employees are given vacation allowances ($800 per family member) annually.[14]

Spotlight

Dealing with the cost of health care

Ways employers control rising health plan costs.

Change health care plan 52%

Raise employee contribution 20%

Contract with lower-cost vendors 15%

Reduce health plan choices 2%

Other 11%

$$$

Source: *USA Today*, August 14, 2002, p. B1.

Flexible Benefit Plans Through a **flexible benefit plan**, an employee receives a predetermined amount of benefit dollars and may allocate these dollars to various categories of benefits in the mix that best fits his or her needs. Some flexible benefit plans offer a broad array of benefit options, including health care, dental care, life insurance, accidental death and dismemberment coverage for both the worker and dependents, long-term disability coverage, vacation benefits, retirement savings, and dependent care benefits. Other firms offer limited options, primarily in health and life insurance and retirement plans.

flexible benefit plan compensation plan whereby an employee receives a predetermined amount of benefit dollars to spend on a package of benefits he or she has selected to meet individual needs

Although the cost of administering flexible plans is high, a number of organizations, including Quaker Oats and Coca-Cola, have implemented this option for several reasons. Because employees' needs are so diverse, flexible plans help firms to offer benefit packages that more specifically meet their employees' needs. Flexible plans can, in the long run, help a company contain costs because a specified amount is allocated to cover the benefits of each employee. Furthermore, organizations that offer flexible plans with many choices may be perceived as being employee-friendly. Thus they are in a better position to attract and retain qualified employees.

Training and Development

Training and development are extremely important at the Container Store. Because great customer service is so important, every first-year full-time salesperson receives about 185 hours of formal training as opposed to the industry standard, which is approximately 7 hours. Training and development continue throughout a person's career. Each store has a full-time trainer called the *super sales trainer* (SST). This trainer provides product training, sales training, and employee development training. Top management believes that the financial and human resources invested in training and development are well worth it.[15]

learning objective

7 Explain the purposes and techniques of employee training, development, and performance appraisal.

employee training the process of teaching operations and technical employees how to do their present jobs more effectively and efficiently

management development the process of preparing managers and other professionals to assume increased responsibility in both present and future positions

Both training and development are aimed at improving employees' skills and abilities. However, the two are usually differentiated as either employee training or management development. **Employee training** is the process of teaching operations and technical employees how to do their present jobs more effectively and efficiently. **Management development** is the process of preparing managers and other professionals to assume increased responsibility in both present and future positions. Thus training and development differ in who is being taught and the purpose of the teaching. Both are necessary for personal and organizational growth. Companies that hope to stay competitive typically make huge commitments to employee training and development. For example, Edward Jones, the stockbroker with nearly 8,000 branches, spends 3.8 percent of its payroll on training. These expenditures average out to be 146 hours per year for each employee, with new hires receiving about four times this amount of training. This dedication to its employees has helped Edward Jones claim the rating as the best company to work for by *Fortune* magazine for two consecutive years.[16] Internet-based e-learning is growing. Driven by cost, travel, and time savings, online learning alone and in conjunction with face-to-face situations is a strong alternative strategy. Development of a training program usually has three components: analysis of needs, determination of training and development methods, and creation of an evaluation system to assess the program's effectiveness.

Analysis of Training Needs

When thinking about developing a training program, managers must first determine if training is needed and, if so, what types of training needs exist. At times, what at first appears to be a need for training is actually, on assessment, a need for motivation. Training needs can vary considerably. For example, some employees may need training to improve their technical skills, or they may need training about organizational procedures. Training also may focus on business ethics, product information, or customer service. Because training is expensive, it is critical that the correct training needs be identified.

Training and Development Methods

A number of methods are available for employee training and management development. Some of these methods may be more suitable for one or the other, but most can be applied to both.

- *On-the-job methods.* The trainee learns by doing the work under the supervision of an experienced employee.
- *Simulations.* The work situation is simulated in a separate area so that learning takes place away from the day-to-day pressures of work.
- *Classroom teaching and lectures.* You probably already know these methods quite well.
- *Conferences and seminars.* Experts and learners meet to discuss problems and exchange ideas.
- *Role playing.* Participants act out the roles of others in the organization for better understanding of those roles (primarily a management development tool).

Evaluation of Training and Development

Training and development are very expensive. The training itself costs quite a bit, and employees are usually not working—or are working at a reduced load and pace—during training sessions. To ensure that training and development are cost-effective, the managers responsible should evaluate the company's efforts periodically.

A report prepared by the American Society for Training and Development (ASTD), an industry association that monitors and also promotes employee learning strategies, revealed the value of employee education programs. The report found that for an added $600 educational investment made by the firm in each employee, the firms surveyed experienced a 57 percent increase in sales per employee and 37 percent in gross profit. In dollar terms, the added investment returned $157,000 in net sales and $137,000 in gross profit per employee.[17] The starting point for this evaluation is a set of verifiable objectives that are developed *before* the training is undertaken. Suppose that a training program is expected to improve the skills of machinists. The objective of the program might be stated as follows: "At the end of the training period, each machinist should be able to process thirty parts per hour with no more than one defective part per ninety parts completed." This objective clearly specifies what is expected and how training results may be measured or verified. Evaluation then consists of measuring machinists' output and the ratio of defective parts produced after the training.

Training for emergencies. Even well-trained employees need additional training. This $200,000 computer controlled mannequin is used to simulate chemical injuries to train medical emergency staff members in procedures to treat terror-related medical emergencies.

The results of training evaluations should be made known to all those involved in the program—including trainees and upper management. For trainees, the results of evaluations can enhance motivation and learning. For upper management, the results may be the basis for making decisions about the training program itself.

Performance Appraisal

Performance appraisal is the evaluation of employees' current and potential levels of performance to allow managers to make objective human resources decisions. The process has three main objectives. First, managers use performance appraisals to let workers know how well they are doing and how they can do better in the future. Second, a performance appraisal provides an effective basis for distributing rewards, such as pay raises and promotions. Third, performance appraisal helps the organization monitor its employee selection, training, and development activities. If large numbers of employees continually perform below expectations, the firm may need to revise its selection process or strengthen its training and development activities.

performance appraisal the evaluation of employees' current and potential levels of performance to allow managers to make objective human resources decisions

Common Evaluation Techniques

The various techniques and methods for appraising employee performance are either objective or judgmental in nature.

Objective Methods Objective appraisal methods use some measurable quantity as the basis for assessing performance. Units of output, dollar volume of sales, number of defective products, and number of insurance claims processed are all objective, measurable quantities. Thus an employee who processes an average of twenty-six insurance claims per week is given a higher evaluation than one whose average is nineteen claims per week.

Such objective measures may require some adjustment for the work environment. Suppose that the first of our insurance-claims processors works in New York City and the second works in rural Iowa. Both must visit each client because they are processing homeowners' insurance claims. The difference in their average weekly output may be due entirely to the long distances the Iowan must travel to visit clients. In this case, the two workers may very well be equally competent and motivated. Thus a manager must take into account circumstances that may be hidden by a purely statistical measurement.

Judgmental Methods Judgmental appraisal methods are used much more frequently than objective methods. They require that the manager judge or estimate the employee's performance level. However, judgmental methods are not capricious. These methods are based on employee ranking or rating scales. When ranking is used, the manager ranks subordinates from best to worst. This approach has a number of drawbacks, including the lack of any absolute standard. Rating scales are the most popular judgmental appraisal technique. A *rating scale* consists of a number of statements; each employee is rated on the degree to which the statement applies (see Figure 10.3). For example, one statement might be, "This employee always does

figure 10.3

Performance Appraisal

Judgmental appraisal methods are used much more often than objective methods. Using judgmental methods requires that the manager estimates the employee's performance level relative to some standard.

3M **Contribution and Development Summary**
FORM 37450 - B

Employee Name | Employee Number | Job Title
Department | Location
Coach/Supervisor(s) Name(s) | Review Period From : To :

Major Job Responsibilities

Goals/Expectations | **Contributions/R**

Contribution (To be completed by coach/supervisor)

☐ **Good Level of Contribution for this year** ☐ **Exceptional L**
☐ **Unsatisfactory Level of Contribution for this year**

Development Summary

Areas of Strength | Development Priorities

Career Interests

Next job | Longer Range

Current Mobility

☐ **0** - Currently Unable to Relocate
☐ **1** - Position In Home Country Only (Use if Home Country is Outside U.S.)
☐ **2** - Position Within O.U.S. Region (e: Nordic, SEA...)
☐ **3** - Position Within O.U.S. Area (ex: Europe, Asia)
☐ **4** - Position In U.S.
☐ **5** - Position Anywhere In The World

Development

☐ **W** - Well placed. Development plans achievable in current role for at least the next year
☐ **C** - Ready now for a move to a different job for career broadening experience
☐ **I** - Ready now for a move to a different job involving increased responsibility
☐ **X** - Not well placed. Action required to resolve placement issues.

Comments on Development

Employee Comments

Coach/Supervisor Comments | **Other Supervisor (if applicable) and/or Reviewer**

Signatures

Coach/Supervisor Date | Other Coach/Supervisor or Reviewer Date
Employee Date

Source: Courtesy 3M.

high-quality work." The supervisor would give the employee a rating, from 5 down to 1, corresponding to gradations ranging from "strongly agree" to "strongly disagree." The ratings on all the statements are added to obtain the employee's total evaluation.

Avoiding Appraisal Errors Managers must be cautious if they are to avoid making mistakes when appraising employees. It is common to overuse one portion of an evaluation instrument, thus overemphasizing some issues and underemphasizing others. A manager must guard against allowing an employee's poor performance on one activity to influence his or her judgment of that subordinate's work on other activities. Similarly, putting too much weight on recent performance distorts an employee's evaluation. For example, if the employee is being rated on performance over the last year, a manager should not permit last month's disappointing performance to overshadow the quality of the work done in the first eleven months of the year. Finally, a manager must guard against discrimination on the basis of race, age, gender, religion, national origin, or sexual orientation.

examining ethics

Should Companies Fire 10 Percent of Their Employees Annually?

SHOULD COMPANIES USE A RIGID ranking system to label an employee's performance as either A, B, or C? General Electric has long used this method of appraising employee performance. Its managers are required to classify 20 percent of the work force in the top-performing A category, 70 percent in the middle-level B category, and 10 percent in the bottom-level C category. Employees in the A category receive raises and other rewards, whereas those in the C category lose their jobs. GE says that its purpose in ranking employees is to encourage better performance, not to cut staff.

However, some companies have met with legal challenges from employees who feel that such a rigid evaluation method is discriminatory. At one time the tire manufacturer Goodyear used a forced ranking system to evaluate salaried employees. Under this system, managers had to give an A rating to 10 percent of the personnel in their departments, a B rating to 80 percent, and a C rating to 10 percent. Those with C ratings received no merit raises and could be terminated or demoted if they repeatedly received C ratings. Then a group of employees in the C category filed an age-discrimination suit charging that a disproportionate number of employees receiving low rankings were older than age 40. The American Association of Retired People (AARP), an advocacy group for seniors, joined the lawsuit in support of the employees.

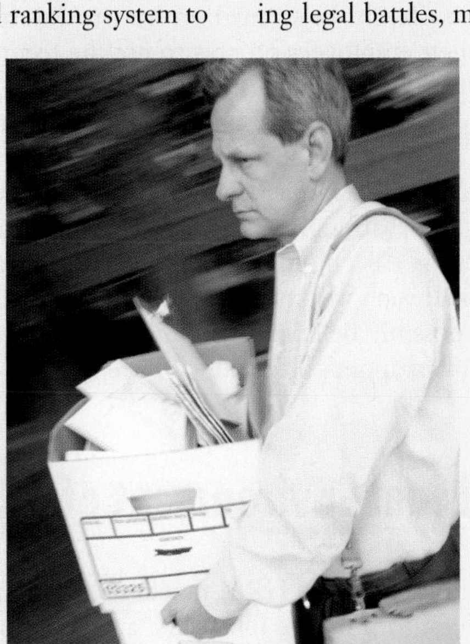

After using the forced ranking system for eighteen months, Goodyear announced a change, saying that internal feedback showed that "some modifications and clarifications were needed." Officials noted that ranking employees within individual work groups—instead of on a broader, company-wide basis—was problematic. Using the new system, managers now determine whether an employee's performance exceeds expectations, meets expectations, or is unsatisfactory.

Detroit-based automaker Ford went to court over its performance evaluation system not long ago, when hundreds of employees charged that the forced ranking method resulted in age discrimination. The AARP added its voice to that of the employees in this case as well. The company eventually settled the case by paying the employees $10.5 million. With other companies facing legal battles, more managers are taking a fresh look at the pros and cons of ABC ranking systems.

Issues to Consider

1. Is forced ranking under an ABC evaluation system an objective or a judgmental method of appraising employee performance? What are the implications for employees' attitudes toward this system?
2. A former General Electric CEO said that not terminating bottom-ranked employees is "a form of cruelty" because they would be fired at some point, quite possibly in the middle of their careers. Do you agree? Explain your answer.

Performance Feedback

No matter which appraisal technique is used, the results should be discussed with the employee soon after the evaluation is completed. The manager should explain the basis for present rewards and should let the employee know what he or she can do to be recognized as a better performer in the future. The information provided to an employee in such discussions is called a *performance feedback interview*.

There are three major approaches to performance feedback interviews: tell and sell, tell and listen, and problem solving. In a *tell-and-sell* feedback interview, the superior tells the employee how good or bad the employee's performance has been and then attempts to persuade the employee to accept this evaluation. Since the employee has no input into the evaluation, the tell-and-sell interview can lead to defensiveness, resentment, and frustration on the part of the subordinate. The employee may not accept the results of the interview and may not be committed to achieving the goals that are set.

With the *tell-and-listen* approach, the supervisor tells the employee what has been right and wrong with the employee's performance and then gives the employee a chance to respond. The subordinate simply may be given an opportunity to react to the supervisor's statements or may be permitted to offer a full self-appraisal, challenging the supervisor's assessment.

In the *problem-solving* approach, employees evaluate their own performances and set their own goals for future performance. The supervisor is more a colleague than a judge and offers comments and advice in a noncritical manner. An active and open dialogue ensues in which goals for improvement are mutually established. The problem-solving interview is more likely to result in the employee's commitment to the established goals.

To avoid some of the problems associated with the tell-and-sell interview, a mixed approach is sometimes used. The mixed interview uses the tell-and-sell approach to communicate administrative decisions and the problem-solving approach to discuss employee development issues and future performance goals.[18]

An appraisal approach that has become popular is called a *360-degree evaluation*. A 360-degree evaluation collects anonymous reviews about an employee from his or her peers, subordinates, and supervisors and then compiles these reviews into a feedback report that is given to the employee. Companies that invest significant resources in employee development efforts are especially likely to use 360-degree evaluations. An employee should not be given a feedback report without first having a one-on-one meeting with his or her supervisor. The most appropriate way to introduce a 360-degree evaluation system in a company is to begin with upper-level management. Then managers should be trained on how to interpret feedback reports so that they can coach their employees on how to use the feedback to achieve higher-level job-related skills and behaviors.[19]

Finally, we should note that many managers find it difficult to discuss the negative aspects of an appraisal. Unfortunately, they may ignore performance feedback altogether or provide it in a very weak and ineffectual manner. In truth, though, most employees have strengths that can be emphasized to soften the discussion of their weaknesses. An employee may not even be aware of weaknesses and their consequences. If such weaknesses are not pointed out through performance feedback, they cannot possibly be eliminated. Only through tactful, honest communication can the results of an appraisal be fully utilized.

learning objective

8 Outline the major legislation affecting human resources management.

The Legal Environment of HRM

Legislation regarding HRM practices has been passed mainly to protect the rights of employees, to promote job safety, and to eliminate discrimination in the workplace. The major federal laws affecting HRM are described in Table 10.2.

table 10.2 Federal Legislation Affecting Human Resources Management

Law	Purpose
National Labor Relations Act (1935)	Establishes a collective-bargaining process in labor-management relations as well as the National Labor Relations Board (NLRB)
Fair Labor Standards Act (1938)	Establishes a minimum wage and an overtime pay rate for employees working more than forty hours per week
Labor-Management Relations Act (1947)	Provides a balance between union power and management power; also known as the Taft-Hartley Act
Equal Pay Act (1963)	Specifies that men and women who do equal jobs must be paid the same wage
Title VII of the Civil Rights Act (1964)	Outlaws discrimination in employment practices based on sex, race, color, religion, or national origin
Age Discrimination in Employment Act (1967/1986)	Outlaws personnel practices that discriminate against people aged 40 and older; the 1986 amendment eliminates a mandatory retirement age
Occupational Safety and Health Act (1970)	Regulates the degree to which employees can be exposed to hazardous substances and specifies the safety equipment that the employer must provide
Employment Retirement Income Security Act (1974)	Regulates company retirement programs and provides a federal insurance program for retirement plans that go bankrupt
Worker Adjustment and Retraining Notification (WARN) Act (1988)	Requires employer to give employees sixty days notice regarding plant closure or layoff of fifty or more employees
Americans with Disabilities Act (1990)	Prohibits discrimination against qualified individuals with disabilities in all employment practices, including job application procedures, hiring, firing, advancement, compensation, training, and other terms, conditions, and privileges of employment
Civil Rights Act (1991)	Facilitates employees' suing employers for sexual discrimination and collecting punitive damages
Family and Medical Leave Act (1993)	Requires an organization with fifty or more employees to provide up to twelve weeks of leave without pay on the birth (or adoption) of an employee's child or if an employee or his or her spouse, child, or parent is seriously ill

National Labor Relations Act and Labor-Management Relations Act

These laws are concerned with dealings between business firms and labor unions. This general area is, in concept, a part of HRM. However, because of its importance, it is often treated as a separate set of activities. We discuss both labor-management relations and these two acts in detail in Chapter 12.

Fair Labor Standards Act

This act, passed in 1938 and amended many times since, applies primarily to wages. It established minimum wages and overtime pay rates. Many managers and other professionals, however, are exempt from this law. Managers, for example, seldom get paid overtime when they work more than forty hours a week.

Equal Pay Act

Passed in 1963, this law overlaps somewhat with Title VII of the Civil Rights Act (see below). The Equal Pay Act specifies that men and women who are doing equal jobs must be paid the same wage. Equal jobs are jobs that demand equal effort, skill, and responsibility and that are performed under the same conditions. Differences in pay are legal if they can be attributed to differences in seniority, qualifications, or performance. However, women cannot be paid less (or more) for the same work solely because they are women.

Civil Rights Acts

Title VII of the Civil Rights Act of 1964 applies directly to selection and promotion. It forbids organizations with fifteen or more employees to discriminate in those areas on the basis of sex, race, color, religion, or national origin. The purpose of Title VII is to ensure that employers make personnel decisions on the basis of employee qualifications only. As a result of this act, discrimination in employment (especially against African Americans) has been reduced in this country.

The Equal Employment Opportunity Commission (EEOC) is charged with enforcing Title VII. A person who believes that he or she has been discriminated against can file a complaint with the EEOC. The EEOC investigates the complaint, and if it finds that the person has, in fact, been the victim of discrimination, the commission can take legal action on his or her behalf.

The Civil Rights Act of 1991 facilitates an employee's suing and collecting punitive damages for sexual discrimination. Discriminatory promotion and termination decisions as well as on-the-job issues, such as sexual harassment, are covered by this act.

Age Discrimination in Employment Act

The general purpose of this act, which was passed in 1967 and amended in 1986, is the same as that of Title VII—to eliminate discrimination. However, as the name implies, the Age Discrimination in Employment Act is concerned only with discrimination based on age. It applies to companies with twenty or more employees. In particular, it outlaws personnel practices that discriminate against people aged forty or older. (No federal law forbids discrimination against people younger than age 40, but several states have adopted age discrimination laws that apply to a variety of age groups.) Also outlawed are company policies that specify a mandatory retirement age. Employers must base employment decisions on ability and not on a number. The EEOC recently settled an age discrimination suit with Foot Locker when it found evidence that older workers had been laid off and then quickly replaced with younger employees at Foot Locker. The EEOC determined that this discrimination was nationwide and ordered payment of $3.5 million to 678 former employees all age 40 or older.[20]

Protecting employees. When dealing with potentially hazardous substances, the Occupational Safety and Health Administration requires that workers wear protective gear. These workers are collecting and removing contaminated sand after an oil spill off the coast of California.

Occupational Safety and Health Act

Passed in 1970, this act is concerned mainly with issues of employee health and safety. For example, the act regulates the degree to which employees can be exposed to hazardous substances. It also specifies the safety equipment that the employer must provide.

The Occupational Safety and Health Administration (OSHA) was created to enforce this act. Inspectors from OSHA investigate employee complaints regarding unsafe working conditions. They also make spot checks on companies operating n particularly hazardous industries, such as chemicals and mining, to ensure compliance with the law. A firm found to be in violation of federal standards can be heavily fined or shut down. Many people feel that issuing OSHA violations is not enough to protect workers from harm. McWane Industries, a large manufacturer of pipes and other products, has been cited for nearly 1,000 safety and environmental violations since 1995. Yet it has still had nine employees killed in its plants during this time. Although the company has paid about $10 million in fines for violations and has three criminal convictions, safety continues to be a major concern. Workers at one of McWane's plants have been seen with bumper stickers saying, "Pray for me. I work at Kennedy Valve." Although OSHA has made much progress, workplace safety is still a major concern.[21]

Employee Retirement Income Security Act

This act was passed in 1974 to protect the retirement benefits of employees. It does not require that firms provide a retirement plan. However, it does specify that *if* a retirement plan is provided, it must be managed in such a way that the interests of employees are protected. It also provides federal insurance for retirement plans that go bankrupt.

Affirmative Action

Affirmative action is not one act but a series of executive orders issued by the president of the United States. These orders established the requirement for affirmative action in personnel practices. This stipulation applies to all employers with fifty or more employees holding federal contracts in excess of $50,000. It prescribes that such employers (1) actively encourage job applications from members of minority groups and (2) hire qualified employees from minority groups not fully represented in their organizations. Many firms that do not hold government contracts voluntarily take part in this affirmative action program.

Americans with Disabilities Act

The Americans with Disabilities Act (ADA) prohibits discrimination against qualified individuals with disabilities in all employment practices—including job application procedures, hiring, firing, advancement, compensation, training, and other terms and conditions of employment. All private employers and government agencies with fifteen or more employees are covered by the ADA. Defining who is a qualified individual with a disability is, of course, difficult. Depending on how "qualified individual with a disability" is interpreted, up to forty-three million Americans can be included under this law. This law also mandates that all businesses that serve the public must make their facilities accessible to people with disabilities.

Not only are individuals with obvious physical disabilities protected under the ADA, but also safeguarded are those with less visible conditions such as heart disease, diabetes, epilepsy, cancer, AIDS, and emotional illnesses. Because of this law, many organizations no longer require job applicants to pass physical examinations as a condition of employment. In 1998, there were about 42,000 civil complaints related to disability discrimination.[22]

Employers are required to provide disabled employees with reasonable accommodation. *Reasonable accommodation* is any modification or adjustment to a job or work environment that will enable a qualified employee with a disability to perform a central job function. Examples of reasonable accommodation include making existing facilities readily accessible to and usable by an individual confined to a wheelchair. Reasonable accommodation also might mean restructuring a job, modifying work schedules, acquiring or modifying equipment, providing qualified readers or interpreters, or changing training programs.

Return To inside business

Google started with two employees in 1998—its co-founders, Sergey Brin and Larry Page—and now employs more than 500 in the Googleplex headquarters outside San Francisco and in other offices. Executives say that the company would grow even faster if it could find enough qualified employees. And because Google is moving into many other countries, it needs an even more diverse work force to be competitive in every market.

Forecasting human resources demand can be difficult because Google expects to double its revenues every year. At the same time, the company's judicious approach to hiring keeps growth and expenses from ballooning out of control. Profitability is a priority when Google managers analyze the financial aspects of potential staffing levels. And when recruiting, they actively seek to attract applicants from a wide range of backgrounds. Only with the right people in the right positions can Google continue to wring profits from the world's most popular search site.

Questions

1. Considering Google's emphasis on profitability, would you recommend that the company cut back on free meals and other benefits if expenses become too high relative to revenues? Explain your answer.
2. In addition to recruiting through its website, how would you suggest that Google attract qualified applicants for open positions?

chapter review

Summary

Describe the major components of human resources management.

Human resources management (HRM) is the set of activities involved in acquiring, maintaining, and developing an organization's human resources. Responsibility for HRM is shared by specialized staff and line managers. HRM activities include human resources planning, job analysis, recruiting, selection, orientation, compensation, benefits, training and development, and performance appraisal.

Identify the steps in human resources planning.

Human resources planning consists of forecasting the human resources that a firm will need and those that it will have available and then planning a course of action to match supply with demand. Layoffs, attrition, early retirement, and (as a last resort) firing are ways to reduce the size of the work force. Supply is increased through hiring.

Describe cultural diversity and understand some of the challenges and opportunities associated with it.

Cultural diversity refers to the differences among people in a work force due to race, ethnicity, and gender. With an increasing number of women, minorities, and immigrants entering the U.S. work force, management is faced with both challenges and competitive advantages. Some organizations are implementing diversity-related training programs and working to make the most of cultural diversity. With the proper guidance and management, a culturally diverse organization can prove beneficial to all involved.

Explain the objectives and uses of job analysis.

Job analysis provides a job description and a job specification for each position within a firm. A job description is a list of the elements that make up a particular job. A job specification is a list of qualifications required to perform a particular job. Job analysis is used in evaluation and in determining compensation levels and serves as the basis for recruiting and selecting new employees.

Describe the processes of recruiting, employee selection, and orientation.

Recruiting is the process of attracting qualified job applicants. Candidates for open positions may be recruited from within or outside a firm. In the selection process, information about candidates is obtained from applications, résumés, tests, interviews, references, or assessment centers. This information is then used to select the most appropriate candidate for the job. Newly hired employees will then go through a formal or informal orientation program to acquaint them with the firm.

Discuss the primary elements of employee compensation and benefits.

Compensation is the payment employees receive in return for their labor. In developing a system for paying employees, management must decide on the firm's general wage level (relative to other firms), the wage structure within the firm, and individual wages. Wage surveys and job analyses are useful in making these decisions. Employees may be paid hourly wages, salaries, or commissions. They also may receive incentive payments, lump-sum salary increases, and profit-sharing payments. Employee benefits, which are nonmonetary rewards to employees, add about 28 percent to the cost of compensation.

Explain the purposes and techniques of employee training, development, and performance appraisal.

Employee training and management development programs enhance the ability of employees to contribute to a firm. When developing a training program, training needs should be analyzed. Then training methods should be selected. Because training is expensive, an organization should periodically evaluate the effectiveness of its training programs.

Performance appraisal, or evaluation, is used to provide employees with performance feedback, to serve as a basis for distributing rewards, and to monitor selection and training activities. Both objective and judgmental appraisal techniques are used. Their results are communicated to employees through three performance feedback approaches: tell and sell, tell and listen, and problem solving.

Outline the major legislation affecting human resources management.

A number of laws have been passed that affect HRM practices and that protect the rights and safety of employees. Some of these are the National Labor Relations Act of 1935, the Labor-Management Relations Act of 1947, the Fair Labor Standards Act of 1938, the Equal Pay Act of 1963, Title VII of the Civil Rights Act of 1964, the Age Discrimination in Employment Acts of 1967 and 1986, the Occupational Safety and Health Act of 1970, the Employment Retirement Income Security Act of 1974, the Worker Adjustment and Retraining Notification Act of 1988, the Americans with Disabilities Act of 1990, the Civil Rights Act of 1991, and the Family and Medical Leave Act of 1993.

Key Terms

You should now be able to define and give an example relevant to each of the following terms:

human resources management (HRM) (282)
human resources planning (283)
replacement chart (284)
skills inventory (284)
cultural (workplace) diversity (285)
job analysis (287)
job description (287)
job specification (287)
recruiting (288)
external recruiting (289)
internal recruiting (290)
selection (290)
orientation (293)
compensation (293)
compensation system (293)
wage survey (293)
job evaluation (294)
comparable worth (295)
hourly wage (295)
salary (295)
commission (295)
incentive payment (295)
lump-sum salary increase (296)
profit sharing (296)
employee benefit (296)
flexible benefit plan (297)
employee training (298)
management development (298)
performance appraisal (299)

Review Questions

1. List the three main HRM activities and their objectives.
2. In general, on what basis is responsibility for HRM divided between line and staff managers?
3. How is a forecast of human resources demand related to a firm's organizational planning?
4. How do human resources managers go about matching a firm's supply of workers with its demand for workers?
5. What are the major challenges and benefits associated with a culturally diverse work force?
6. How are a job analysis, job description, and job specification related?
7. What are the advantages and disadvantages of external recruiting? Of internal recruiting?
8. In your opinion, what are the two best techniques for gathering information about job candidates?
9. Why is orientation an important HRM activity?
10. Explain how the three wage-related decisions result in a compensation system.
11. How is a job analysis used in the process of job evaluation?
12. Suppose that you have just opened a new Ford sales showroom and repair shop. Which of your employees would be paid wages, which would receive salaries, and which would receive commissions?
13. What is the difference between the objective of employee training and the objective of management development?
14. Why is it so important to provide feedback after a performance appraisal?

Discussion Questions

1. How accurately can managers plan for future human resources needs?
2. How might an organization's recruiting and selection practices be affected by the general level of employment?
3. Are employee benefits really necessary? Why?
4. As a manager, what actions would you take if an operations employee with six years of experience on the job refused ongoing training and ignored performance feedback?
5. Why are there so many laws relating to HRM practices? Which are the most important laws, in your opinion?

video case

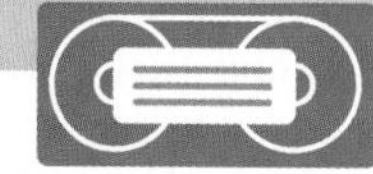

New England Aquarium's New Wave of Diversity

From sea turtles and seals to penguins and porpoises, the nonprofit New England Aquarium houses an incredibly diverse array of creatures. Its 200,000-gallon tank serves as an underwater microcosm of the world's sea life. The aquarium's official mission statement is "to present, promote, and protect the world of water." It also wants to appeal to the broadest possible audience and build a work force of paid and unpaid staff that reflects the diversity of the Boston community.

Volunteers are a major resource for the New England Aquarium. Its staff of 1,000 volunteers—one of the nonprofit world's largest—contributes 100,000 hours of service yearly, working with animals, exhibits, and more. Many high school and college students volunteer to try out possible career choices. Adults with and without specialized college degrees (in fields such as marine biology and environmental affairs) volunteer their time as well. And the New England Aquarium's internships offer college students and recent graduates hands-on experience in veterinary services, communications, and other key areas.

Maureen C. Hentz, director of volunteer programs, is a champion for workplace diversity. Most organizations "are good at putting diversity in their mission statements and talking about it, but not actually accomplishing it," she observes. In contrast, she and her New England Aquarium colleagues are aggressively reaching out to recruit volunteers, interns, and employees of different races, ethnicities, socioeconomic levels, physical abilities, and ages. In addition, they welcome people of diverse educational backgrounds, personalities, and viewpoints because of the new ideas these differences can bring to the organization's opportunities and challenges.

One reason the New England Aquarium needs to constantly recruit and train new volunteers (and employees) is that the number of visitors is increasing every year, thanks in part to the highly popular IMAX theater that opened in 2001. Another reason is that, like most nonprofits, the New England Aquarium has a very limited budget and must carefully manage its payroll expenses. Therefore, Hentz is always looking for volunteers to assist paid staff in various departments, including education, administration, and animal rescue.

The New England Aquarium must plan for employees, volunteers, or interns to handle certain tasks whenever the facility is open to visitors. For example, cashiers are needed to collect admission fees during daytime, evening, and weekend hours. Volunteers are often available to work during weekend hours, but the organization has difficulty filling some of the volunteer positions during daytime hours. This is another reason why Hentz and her staff are always attending community meetings and finding other ways to encourage volunteerism.

The web is an important and cost-effective recruiting tool for the New England Aquarium. Prospective volunteers can browse its website (**www.neaq.org**) to find open positions, read job descriptions and specifications, and download an application form to complete and submit. Hentz and her staff members read through all the applications and ask those who seem the most qualified to come in for a personal interview. Once the final selections are made, volunteers are notified about their assignments and working hours. They receive training in the organization's procedures and learn their specific duties before they start their jobs.

Candidates for internships must send a letter expressing interest in working as an intern and include a résumé plus two academic or professional references. Also, they must acknowledge in writing that they know they will not be paid and will receive no housing assistance if they serve as interns. As an option, candidates can send a letter of reference and a college transcript to support the application letter. After reviewing all the application materials, the New England Aquarium's internship coordinators interview the most promising candidates and make the final selections. Interns, like volunteers, gain valuable experience and can list their New England Aquarium positions on their résumés when looking for future employment.

The New England Aquarium is just as meticulous in hiring employees as it is in attracting unpaid workers. To recruit and retain a diverse and capable work force, the organization offers a broad package of benefits. Employees receive medical and dental insurance, disability and life insurance, paid holidays and sick days, paid vacation, a pension plan, tuition reimbursement, New England Aquarium discounts, subsidized transportation, and other perks. Just as important, they have an opportunity to be part of an organization that protects the underwater environment, educates the public, and saves the lives of whales and other marine life.[23]

Questions

1. Why would the New England Aquarium require people to apply in writing for unpaid volunteer and internship positions?
2. In addition to using the web and attending community meetings, what other external recruiting techniques would you suggest that Hentz use? Why?
3. Do you think that the New England Aquarium should periodically evaluate the performance of its volunteers? Support your answer.

Building Skills for Career Success

1. Exploring the Internet

Although you may believe that your formal learning will end when you graduate and enter the working world, it won't. Companies both large and small spend billions of dollars annually in training employees and updating their knowledge and skills. Besides supporting employees who attend accredited continuing-education programs, companies also may provide more specialized in-house course work on new technologies, products, and markets for strategic planning. The Internet is an excellent search tool to find out about course work offered by private training organizations as well as by traditional academic institutions. Learning online over the Internet is a fast-growing alternative, especially for busy employees requiring updates to skills in the information technology (IT) field, where software knowledge must be refreshed continuously. (Visit the text website for updates to this exercise.)

Assignment

1. Visit the websites of several academic institutions and examine their course work offerings. Also examine the offerings of some of the following private consulting firms:
   Learning Tree International: **http://www.learningtree.com**
   Accenture: **http://www.accenture.com**
   KPMG: **http://www.kpmg.com**
   Ernst & Young: **http://www.ey.com/global**
2. What professional continuing-education training and services are provided by one of the academic institutions whose site you visited?
3. What sort of training is offered by one of the preceding consulting firms?
4. From the company's point of view, what is the total real cost of a day's worth of employee training? What is the money value of one day of study for a full-time college student? Can you explain why firms are willing to pay higher starting salaries for employees with higher levels of education?
5. The American Society for Training and Development (**http://www.astd.org/**) and the Society for Human Resource Management (**http://www.shrm.org/**) are two good sources for information about online training programs. Describe what you found out at these and other sites providing online learning solutions.

2. Developing Critical Thinking Skills

Suppose that you are the manager of the six supervisors described in the following list. They have all just completed two years of service with you and are eligible for an annual raise. How will you determine who will receive a raise and how much each will receive?

- Joe Garcia has impressed you by his above-average performance on several difficult projects. Some of his subordinates, however, do not like the way he assigns jobs. You are aware that several family crises have left him short of cash.
- Sandy Vance meets her goals, but you feel that she could do better. She is single, likes to socialize, and at times arrives late for work. Several of her subordinates have low skill levels, but Sandy feels that she has adequately explained their duties to them. You believe that Sandy may care more about her friends than about coaching her subordinates. Her workers never complain and appear to be satisfied with their jobs.
- Paul Steiberg is not a good performer, and his work group does not feel that he is an effective leader. You also know his group is the toughest one to manage. The work is hard and dirty. You realize that it would be very difficult to replace him, and you therefore do not want to lose him.
- Anna Chen runs a tight ship. Her subordinates like her and feel that she is an excellent leader. She listens to them and supports them. Recently, her group won the TOP (The Outstanding Performance) Award. Anna's husband is CEO of a consulting firm, and as far as you know, she is not in financial need.
- Jill Foster has successfully completed every assignment. You are impressed by this, particularly since she has a very difficult job. You recently learned that she spends several hours every week on her own taking classes to improve her skills. Jill seems to be motivated more by recognition than by money.
- Fred Hammer is a jolly person who gets along with everyone. His subordinates like him, but you do not think that he is getting the job done to your expectations. He has missed a critical delivery date

twice, and this cost the firm over $5,000 each time. He recently divorced his wife and is having an extremely difficult time meeting his financial obligations.

Assignment

1. You have $25,000 available for raises. As you think about how you will allot the money, consider the following:
   a. What criteria will you use in making a fair distribution?
   b. Will you distribute the entire $25,000? If not, what will you do with the remainder?
2. Prepare a four-column table in the following manner:
   a. In column 1, write the name of the employee.
   b. In column 2, write the amount of the raise.
   c. In column 3, write the percentage of the $25,000 the employee will receive.
   d. In column 4, list the reasons for your decision.

3. Building Team Skills

The New Therapy Company is soliciting a contract to provide five nursing homes with physical, occupational, speech, and respiratory therapy. The therapists will float among the five nursing homes. The therapists have not yet been hired, but the nursing homes expect them to be fully trained and ready to go to work in three months. The previous therapy company lost its contract because of high staff turnover due to "burnout" (a common problem in this type of work), high costs, and low-quality care. The nursing homes want a plan specifying how the New Therapy Company will meet staffing needs, keep costs low, and provide high-quality care.

Assignment

1. Working in a group, discuss how the New Therapy Company can meet the three-month deadline and still ensure that the care its therapists provide is of high quality. Also discuss the following:
   a. How many of each type of therapist will the company need?
   b. How will it prevent therapists from "burning out"?
   c. How can it retain experienced staff and still limit costs?
   d. Are promotions available for any of the staff? What is the career ladder?
   e. How will the company manage therapists at five different locations? How will it keep in touch with them (computer, voice mail, monthly meetings)? Would it make more sense to have therapists work permanently at each location rather than rotate among them?
   f. How will the company justify the travel costs? What other expenses might it expect?
2. Prepare a plan for the New Therapy Company to present to the nursing homes.

4. Researching Different Careers

A résumé provides a summary of your skills, abilities, and achievements. It also may include a description of the type of job you want. A well-prepared résumé indicates that you know what your career objectives are, shows that you have given serious thought to your career, and tells a potential employer what you are qualified to do. The way a résumé is prepared can make a difference in whether you are considered for a job.

Assignment

1. Prepare a résumé for a job that you want using the information in Appendix A.
   a. First, determine what your skills are and decide which skills are needed to do this particular job.
   b. Decide which type of format—chronological or functional—would be most effective in presenting your skills and experience.
   c. Keep the résumé to one page, if possible (definitely no more than two pages). (Note that portfolio items may be attached for certain types of jobs, such as artwork.)
2. Have several people review the résumé for accuracy.
3. Ask your instructor to comment on your résumé.

5. Improving Communication Skills

Workplaces in the United States are becoming more culturally diverse. Employees from other countries bring their customs, traditions, values, and language with them to the workplace. It can be difficult for some employees who have worked in a business for a long time to adjust to the changes that accompany cultural diversity. The work environment may become tense and full of distrust and hostility as conflicts erupt among employees. This appears to be the situation at the Zire Company, which manufactures fence posts from recycled plastic. As the company's human resources manager, you are faced with the job of changing this environment into one that encourages cooperation, trust, and mutual respect among employees.

Assignment

1. Putting yourself in the role of the Zire Company's human resources manager, address the following questions:
   a. What are the issues and problems associated with cultural diversity in your company?
   b. What benefits and opportunities could this diversity have for your company?
   c. How can you encourage employees to be more understanding and have greater empathy toward workers who are different from themselves?
2. On the basis of your answers to these questions, prepare a plan for creating an environment that will foster cooperation, trust, and mutual respect among the employees of the Zire Company.

chapter

11 Motivating and Satisfying Employees

learning objectives

1 Explain what motivation is.

2 Understand some major historical perspectives on motivation.

3 Describe three contemporary views of motivation: equity theory, expectancy theory, and goal-setting theory.

4 Explain several techniques for increasing employee motivation.

Removing factory robots helped employees feel more secure in their jobs.

inside business

Workplace Reforms at Mitsubishi's Illinois Plant

ABNORMAL THINGS are happening in Normal, Illinois, home of Mitsubishi's only U.S. car factory. In 1998 the plant's productivity level was the lowest of all the car factories in America. Despite a highly automated factory with dozens of robots, the Normal plant could turn out only forty-two vehicles per hour. About 20 percent of the vehicles coming off the assembly line needed some kind of repair or adjustment. Just as bad, the plant wasted $30 worth of parts for each car produced, adding millions in costs that Mitsubishi could ill afford, considering that it had lost money in the U.S. market for ten consecutive years.

Senior Mitsubishi managers in Japan thought about closing the Normal plant. They knew that sales of other Japanese cars made in U.S. factories far outstripped those of American-made Mitsubishi models such as the Galant and the Montero. They also realized that cars made in the Normal plant lacked the world-class quality for which rivals Honda and Toyota were renowned. And the company had just settled an Equal Employment Opportunity Commission sexual harassment lawsuit by paying $34 million. Not surprisingly, widespread publicity about the lawsuit had hurt worker morale.

Instead of shutting down the Normal plant, Mitsubishi hired Richard Gilligan, a former Ford factory manager, to revamp it. Gilligan soon discovered that some robots actually hurt productivity by inadvertently breaking car parts that employees then had to stop and repair. He ordered more than thirty robots removed and allowed workers to tackle the tasks—which they accomplished more efficiently. This change not only helped employees feel more secure in their jobs; it also showed that their efforts could improve productivity. "I wanted the people here to be in charge of the processes and have the discipline to make it all work right," Gilligan said later.

For this reason, Gilligan put employees, not engineers, in charge of fixing quality glitches. One key problem they solved was water leakage in the Eclipse model. Dealers were replacing windshields when customers complained about leaks after driving in the rain. Employees at the Normal plant figured out that water leaked in because the engine compartment wall had too many bolt holes. They quickly changed the drilling procedure, which solved the problem and reduced Mitsubishi's costs.

In addition, employees formed cross-functional teams to review product quality weekly. "We want to hear the report when something goes wrong, but we also have to know when something's getting better," observes one manager. "We want to know exactly why it's getting better." In fact, both quality and productivity are getting better. Almost 90 percent of the vehicles coming off the assembly line need no repairs, and plant output is up dramatically, to sixty-five cars per hour.[1]

To achieve its goals, any organization—whether it's Mitsubishi, Starbucks, IBM, or a local convenience store—must be sure that its employees have more than the right raw materials, adequate facilities, and equipment that works. The organization also must ensure that its employees are *motivated*. To some extent, a high level of employee motivation derives from effective management practices.

In this chapter, after first explaining what motivation is, we present several views of motivation that have influenced management practices over the years: Taylor's ideas of scientific management, Mayo's Hawthorne Studies, Maslow's hierarchy of needs, Herzberg's motivation-hygiene theory, McGregor's Theory X and Theory Y, Ouchi's Theory Z, and reinforcement theory. Then, turning our attention to contemporary ideas, we examine equity theory, expectancy theory, and goal-setting theory. Finally, we discuss specific techniques managers can use to foster employee motivation and satisfaction.

What Is Motivation?

learning objective

1 Explain what motivation is.

A *motive* is something that causes a person to act. A successful athlete is said to be "highly motivated." A student who avoids work is said to be "unmotivated." We define **motivation** as the individual internal process that energizes, directs, and sustains behavior. It is the personal "force" that causes you or me to act in a particular way. For example, job rotation may increase your job satisfaction and your enthusiasm for your work so that you devote more energy to it, but perhaps job rotation would not have the same impact on me.

motivation the individual internal process that energizes, directs, and sustains behavior; the personal "force" that causes us to behave in a particular way

Morale is an employee's attitude or feelings about the job, about superiors, and about the firm itself. To achieve organizational goals effectively, employees need more than the right raw materials, adequate facilities, and equipment that works. High morale results mainly from the satisfaction of needs on the job or as a result of the job. One need that might be satisfied on the job is the need *to be recognized* as an important contributor to the organization. A need satisfied as a result of the job is the

morale an employee's feelings about his or her job and superiors and about the firm itself

What is motivation?
Ed Foreman, Motivational Specialist, attempts to rev up Albertsons employees. Albertsons is currently in a major competitive battle with Wal-Mart, which is gaining market share in the grocery business. Foreman was hired by Albertsons chief executive Lawrence R. Johnston, who believes that a positive attitude leads to positive actions, which result in business success.

Spotlight

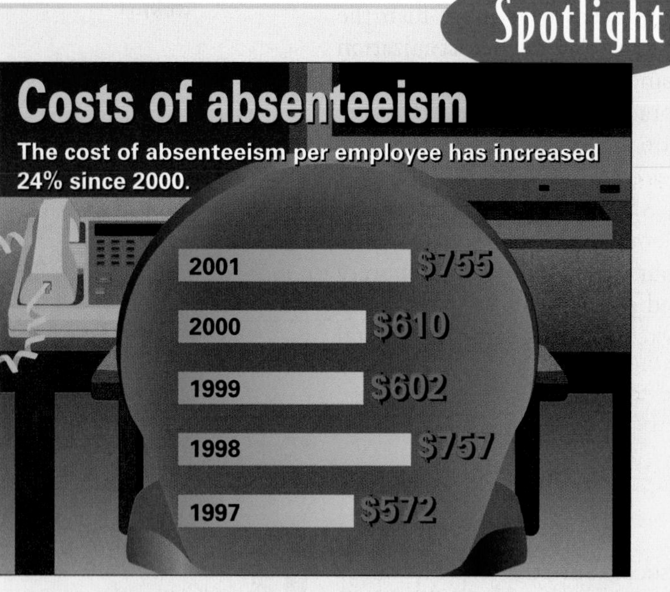

Source: *USA Today*, January 3, 2002, p. B2.

need for *financial security*. High morale, in turn leads to dedication and loyalty, as well as to the desire to do the job well. Low morale can lead to shoddy work, absenteeism, and high turnover rates as employees leave to seek more satisfying jobs with other firms. Executives at Sun Microsystems say that employee morale has suffered along with the decrease in the company's stock price from a high of around $60 to a low of less than $2.50 per share. The stock market view of Sun has affected more than just the value of employees' stock options. Sometimes creative solutions are needed to motivate people and boost morale. This is especially true where barriers to change are deeply rooted in cultural stereotypes of the job and in the industry. For example, to break down these barriers and enhance their creative development skills, clients of famed comedy house Second City, including Nortel Networks, AT&T, and PricewaterhouseCoopers, provide corporate sessions using improvisation to change managers' behavior.[3]

Motivation, morale, and the satisfaction of employees' needs are thus intertwined. Along with productivity, they have been the subject of much study since the end of the nineteenth century. We continue our discussion of motivation by outlining some landmarks of that early research.

exploring business

Using Uncommon Tactics to Get Hired

WHAT CAN MOTIVATED APPLICANTS do to stand out from the crowd, get interviewed, and get hired in bad times, when good jobs are scarce? Knowing that companies may receive hundreds of résumés for each open position, creative job seekers have tried a variety of attention-getting tactics. One submitted lottery tickets with her résumé, whereas another ordered Chinese food for the recruiter, complete with a fortune cookie containing his name and phone number. An applicant even handcuffed himself to the desk during a job interview.

In many cases applicants try such nontraditional techniques after months of fruitlessly applying for jobs. "We're seeing people who have been without work for six months to a year and are just getting by on their savings," explains an employment specialist. "So, many believe that they have nothing to lose" by using more imaginative methods to connect with hiring managers.

For example, after Tiffany Fox graduated with a masters degree, she spent three months searching for a job without success. Finally, she dressed in business attire and stood on bustling Houston street corners holding a sign saying "Hire me." When people stopped to chat, she gave them brief résumés and her phone number. As a result, Fox fielded 150 phone calls and went to 10 job interviews before landing a sales position with a telecommunications firm.

Despite Fox's success, experts warn that outlandish tactics actually can backfire. A Boston-area employment executive stresses that seeking attention by trying "very unusual things can hurt an individual's chances" of being considered for the job. On the other hand, as the director of human resources for the Boston Beer Company notes, "Creativity is a bonus if a person has the skill sets." She cites a job seeker who sent in his résumé along with a home video about marketing the company's Sam Adams beer. Thanks to this unconventional but job-appropriate approach, the applicant was invited to interview—and got hired for the company's marketing department.

Historical Perspectives on Motivation

learning objective

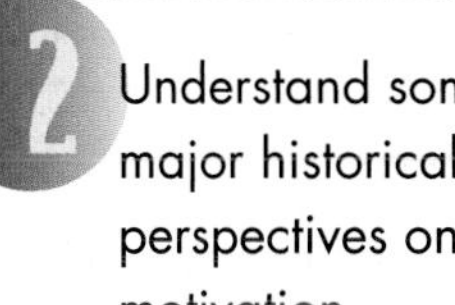

Understand some major historical perspectives on motivation.

Researchers often begin a study with a fairly narrow goal in mind. After they develop an understanding of their subject, however, they realize that both their goal and their research should be broadened. This is exactly what happened when early research into productivity blossomed into the more modern study of employee motivation.

Scientific Management

Toward the end of the nineteenth century, Frederick W. Taylor became interested in improving the efficiency of individual workers. This interest stemmed from his own experiences in manufacturing plants. It eventually led to **scientific management**, the application of scientific principles to management of work and workers.

scientific management the application of scientific principles to management of work and workers

One of Taylor's first jobs was with the Midvale Steel Company in Philadelphia, where he developed a strong distaste for waste and inefficiency. He also observed a practice he called "soldiering." Workers soldiered, or worked slowly, because they feared that if they worked faster, they would run out of work and lose their jobs. Taylor realized that managers were not aware of this practice because they had no idea what the workers' productivity levels *should* be.

Taylor later left Midvale and spent several years at Bethlehem Steel. It was there that he made his most significant contribution. In particular, he suggested that each job should be broken down into separate tasks. Then management should determine (1) the best way to perform these tasks and (2) the job output to expect when the tasks were performed properly. Next, management should carefully choose the best person for each job and train that person to do the job properly. Finally, management should cooperate with workers to ensure that jobs were performed as planned.

Taylor also developed the idea that most people work only to earn money. He therefore reasoned that pay should be tied directly to output. The more a person produced, the more he or she should be paid. This gave rise to the **piece-rate system**, under which employees are paid a certain amount for each unit of output they produce. Under Taylor's piece-rate system, each employee was assigned an output quota. Those exceeding the quota were paid a higher per-unit rate for *all* units they produced (see Figure 11.1). Today the piece-rate system is still used by some manufacturers and by farmers who grow crops that are harvested by farm laborers.

piece-rate system a compensation system under which employees are paid a certain amount for each unit of output they produce

When Taylor's system was put into practice at Bethlehem Steel, the results were dramatic. Average earnings per day for steel handlers rose from $1.15 to $1.88. (Don't let the low wages that prevailed at the time obscure the fact that this was an increase of better than 60 percent!) The average amount of steel handled per day increased from sixteen to fifty-seven tons.

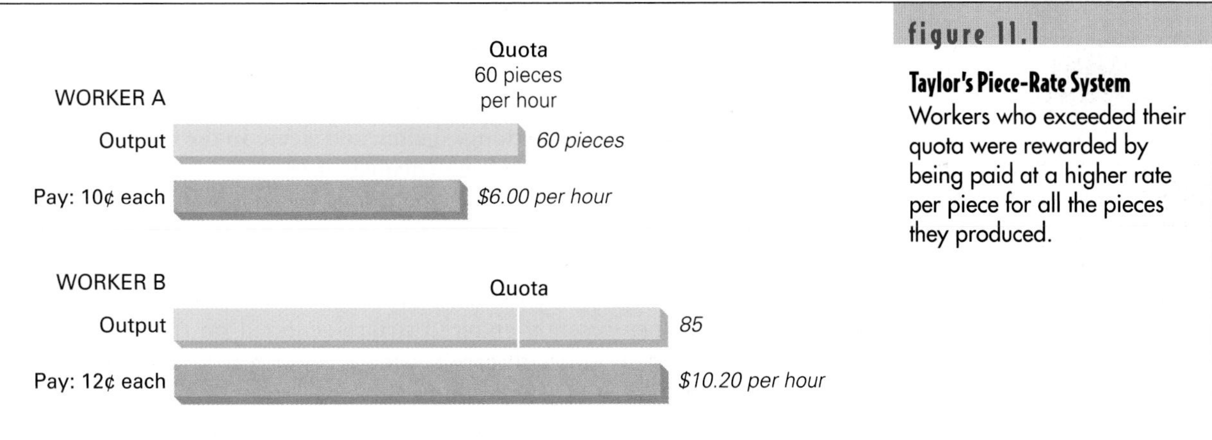

figure 11.1

Taylor's Piece-Rate System
Workers who exceeded their quota were rewarded by being paid at a higher rate per piece for all the pieces they produced.

Taylor's revolutionary ideas had a profound impact on management practice. However, his view of motivation was soon recognized as overly simplistic and narrow. It is true that most people expect to be paid for their work, but it is also true that people work for a variety of reasons other than pay. Simply increasing a person's pay may not increase that person's motivation or productivity.

The Hawthorne Studies

Between 1927 and 1932, Elton Mayo conducted two experiments at the Hawthorne plant of the Western Electric Company in Chicago. The original objective of these studies, now referred to as the Hawthorne Studies, was to determine the effects of the work environment on employee productivity.

In the first set of experiments, lighting in the workplace was varied for one group of workers but not for a second group. Then the productivity of both groups was measured to determine the effect of the light. To the amazement of the researchers, productivity increased for *both* groups. And for the group whose lighting was varied, productivity remained high until the light was reduced to the level of moonlight!

The second set of experiments focused on the effectiveness of the piece-rate system in increasing the output of *groups* of workers. Researchers expected that output would increase because faster workers would put pressure on slower workers to produce more. Again, the results were not as expected. Output remained constant, no matter what "standard" rates management set.

The researchers came to the conclusion that *human factors* were responsible for the results of the two experiments. In the lighting experiments, researchers had given both groups of workers a *sense of involvement* in their jobs merely by asking them to participate in the research. These workers—perhaps for the first time—felt as though they were an important part of the organization. In the piece-rate experiments, each group of workers informally set the acceptable rate of output for the group. To gain or retain the *social acceptance* of the group, each worker had to produce at that rate. Slower or faster workers were pressured to maintain the group's pace.

The Hawthorne Studies showed that such human factors are at least as important to motivation as pay rates. From these and other studies, the *human relations movement* in management was born. Its premise was simple: Employees who are happy and satisfied with their work are motivated to perform better. Hence management would do best to provide a work environment that maximizes employee satisfaction.

Maslow's Hierarchy of Needs

need a personal requirement

Maslow's hierarchy of needs a sequence of human needs in the order of their importance

physiological needs the things we require for survival

safety needs the things we require for physical and emotional security

Abraham Maslow, an American psychologist whose best-known works were published in the 1960s and 1970s, developed a theory of motivation based on a hierarchy of needs. A **need** is a personal requirement. Maslow assumed that humans are "wanting" beings who seek to fulfill a variety of needs. He observed that these needs can be arranged according to their importance in a sequence now known as **Maslow's hierarchy of needs** (see Figure 11.2).

At the most basic level are **physiological needs**, the things we require to survive. They include food and water, clothing, shelter, and sleep. In the employment context, these needs are usually satisfied through adequate wages.

At the next level are **safety needs**, the things we require for physical and emotional security. Safety needs may be satisfied through job security, health insurance, pension plans, and safe working conditions. During a time of falling corporate profits, many companies are facing increasing insurance premiums for employee health care. Both GE and Hershey recently endured strikes centered on the issue of increased health care costs. Reduced health care coverage is a threat to employees' needs for safety. Some companies are trying to find unique solutions. For example, SAS, a software company, maintains its own health care center that offers free physical examinations, emergency treatment, immunizations, and care for chronic illnesses.[4]

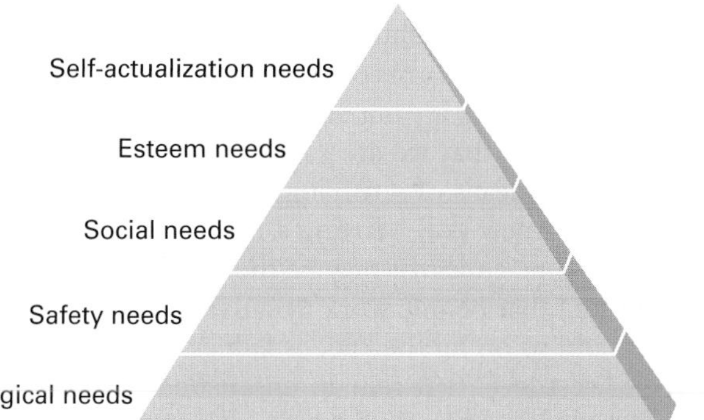

figure 11.2

Maslow's Hierarchy of Needs
Maslow believed that people act to fulfill five categories of needs.

Next are the **social needs**, the human requirements for love and affection and a sense of belonging. To an extent, these needs can be satisfied through relationships in the work environment and the informal organization. However, social networks beyond the workplace—with family and friends, for example—are usually needed too. Casino operator Isle of Capri Casinos, Inc., uses unique methods to help employees meet their social needs. The company holds an annual retreat for managers that is fun and exciting. The latest retreat was called "Isle Survive" and featured a "Survivor"-like game where employees were teamed up and given money and other resources and sent on a sort of scavenger hunt. This is just one of the ways Isle of Capri motivates its workers, and the company seems to be successful in meeting its employees' needs, as evidenced by the lowest employee turnover in the industry.[5]

social needs
our requirements for love and affection and a sense of belonging

going global

Protecting Employees in Other Countries

KEN KRUSENSTERNA, OWNER of a Dallas trucking company, had driven across the border into Mexico for business reasons every week for five years without mishap. The trip was simply part of his routine—until the day he was kidnapped, beaten, and held for ransom. Although he was rescued after two weeks, Krusensterna sold his company rather than return to Mexico on business again.

Kidnapping and robbery are relatively remote but real dangers for multinational firms' employees and managers who work in or travel to other countries. Kidnappers in parts of Mexico, Brazil, Argentina, Colombia, and other developing nations sometimes target foreign business people whose employers seem able to pay ransoms totaling thousands or millions of dollars. Thieves also may assault and rob foreign business people. Now companies are taking a number of precautions to keep their personnel safe.

Many firms educate their employees about the risks of working and traveling abroad through seminars and frequent updates. Nova Chemicals, based in Canada, sends out regular e-mail warnings about problem areas so that employees know what to expect when they travel. Employees of Nortel Networks know to check the company's intranet for comprehensive safety information before and during an international business trip. Nortel also gives its employees a toll-free phone number to call from any country, at any hour, if they run into trouble and need emergency assistance.

Other multinationals go even further. For example, Japanese companies with operations near Tijuana often require transferred executives to live in southern California and travel to their factories on buses protected by armed guards. Some companies hire security specialists to teach their business travelers how to survive if they are attacked or kidnapped, even conducting mock kidnappings to reinforce the skills. At a minimum, experts say that employees who work or travel in other nations should not call attention to themselves. They also should avoid flashing cash in public and keep corporate logos hidden. Finally, varying the daily routine will make it more difficult for criminals to plan a kidnapping or robbery.

esteem needs our need for respect, recognition, and a sense of our own accomplishment and worth

self-actualization needs the need to grow and develop and to become all that we are capable of being

At the level of **esteem needs** we require respect and recognition from others and a sense of our own accomplishment and worth (self-esteem). These needs may be satisfied through personal accomplishment, promotion to more responsible jobs, various honors and awards, and other forms of recognition.

At the top of the hierarchy are our **self-actualization needs**, the needs to grow and develop and to become all that we are capable of being. These are the most difficult needs to satisfy, and the means of satisfying them tend to vary with the individual. For some people, learning a new skill, starting a new career after retirement, or becoming "the best there is" at some endeavor may be the way to realize self-actualization.

Maslow suggested that people work to satisfy their physiological needs first, then their safety needs, and so on up the "needs ladder." In general, they are motivated by the needs at the lowest level that remain unsatisfied. However, needs at one level do not have to be satisfied completely before needs at the next-higher level come into play. If the majority of a person's physiological and safety needs are satisfied, that person will be motivated primarily by social needs. But any physiological and safety needs that remain unsatisfied also will be important.

Maslow's hierarchy of needs provides a useful way of viewing employee motivation, as well as a guide for management. By and large, American business has been able to satisfy workers' basic needs, but the higher-order needs present more of a challenge. These needs are not satisfied in a simple manner, and the means of satisfaction vary from one employee to another.

Herzberg's Motivation-Hygiene Theory

In the late 1950s, Frederick Herzberg interviewed approximately two hundred accountants and engineers in Pittsburgh. During the interviews, he asked them to think of a time when they had felt especially good about their jobs and their work. Then, he asked them to describe the factor or factors that had caused them to feel that way. Next, he did the same regarding a time when they had felt especially bad about their work. He was surprised to find that feeling good and feeling bad resulted from entirely different sets of factors; that is, low pay may have made a particular person feel bad, but it was not high pay that had made that person feel good. Instead, it was some completely different factor.

Satisfaction and Dissatisfaction Before Herzberg's interviews, the general assumption was that employee satisfaction and dissatisfaction lay at opposite ends of the same scale. People felt satisfied, dissatisfied, or somewhere in between. But Herzberg's interviews convinced him that satisfaction and dissatisfaction may be different dimensions altogether. One dimension might range from satisfaction to no satisfaction, and the other might range from dissatisfaction to no dissatisfaction. In other words, the opposite of satisfaction is not dissatisfaction. The idea that satisfaction and dissatisfaction are separate and distinct dimensions is referred to as the **motivation-hygiene theory** (see Figure 11.3).

motivation-hygiene theory the idea that satisfaction and dissatisfaction are separate and distinct dimensions

motivation factors job factors that increase motivation but whose absence does not necessarily result in dissatisfaction

hygiene factors job factors that reduce dissatisfaction when present to an acceptable degree but that do not necessarily result in high levels of motivation

The job factors that Herzberg found most frequently associated with satisfaction are achievement, recognition, responsibility, advancement, growth, and the work itself. These factors generally are referred to as **motivation factors** because their presence increases motivation. However, their absence does not necessarily result in feelings of dissatisfaction. When motivation factors are present, they act as *satisfiers*.

Job factors cited as causing dissatisfaction are supervision, working conditions, interpersonal relationships, pay, job security, and company policies and administration. These factors, called **hygiene factors**, reduce dissatisfaction when they are present to an acceptable degree. However, they do not necessarily result in high levels of motivation. When hygiene factors are absent, they act as *dissatisfiers*. For example, the level of dissatisfaction in Silicon Valley and especially among employees at dot-com start-ups is a growing reality as many people working long hours, often without much social contact outside of the workplace, have decided that career advancement is not offset by the absence of a personal life.[6]

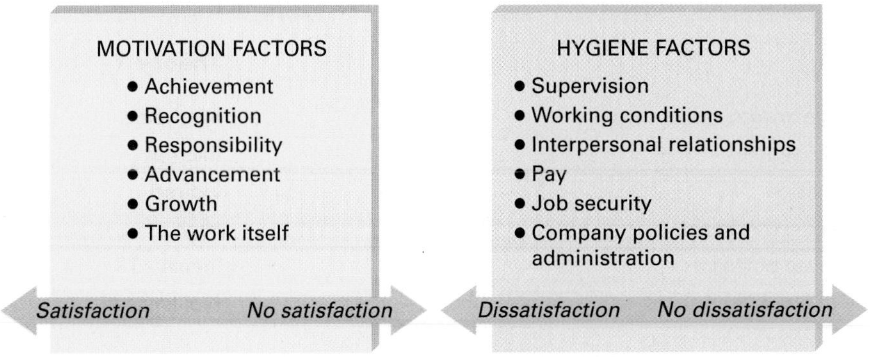

figure 11.3

Herzberg's Motivation-Hygiene Theory

Herzberg's theory takes into account that there are different dimensions to job satisfaction and dissatisfaction and that these factors do not overlap.

MOTIVATION FACTORS
- Achievement
- Recognition
- Responsibility
- Advancement
- Growth
- The work itself

Satisfaction ↔ *No satisfaction*

HYGIENE FACTORS
- Supervision
- Working conditions
- Interpersonal relationships
- Pay
- Job security
- Company policies and administration

Dissatisfaction ↔ *No dissatisfaction*

Using Herzberg's Motivation-Hygiene Theory Herzberg provides explicit guidelines for using the motivation-hygiene theory of employee motivation. He suggests that the hygiene factors must be present to ensure that a worker can function comfortably. He warns, however, that a state of *no dissatisfaction* never exists. In any situation, people will always be dissatisfied with something.

According to Herzberg, managers should make hygiene as positive as possible but should then expect only short-term, not long-term, improvement in motivation. Managers must focus instead on providing those motivation factors that presumably *will* enhance motivation and long-term effort.

We should note that employee pay has more effect than Herzberg's theory indicates. He suggests that pay provides only short-term change and not true motivation. Yet, in many organizations, pay constitutes a form of recognition and reward for achievement—and recognition and achievement are both motivation factors. The effect of pay may depend on how it is distributed. If a pay increase does not depend on performance (as in across-the-board or cost-of-living raises), it may not motivate people. However, if pay is increased as a form of recognition (as in bonuses or incentives), it may play a powerful role in motivating employees to higher performance.

Theory X and Theory Y

The concepts of Theory X and Theory Y were advanced by Douglas McGregor in his book *The Human Side of Enterprise*.[7] They are, in essence, sets of assumptions that underlie management's attitudes and beliefs regarding worker behavior.

Theory X is a concept of employee motivation generally consistent with Taylor's scientific management. Theory X assumes that employees dislike work and will function effectively only in a highly controlled work environment. According to Theory X,

Theory X a concept of employee motivation generally consistent with Taylor's scientific management; assumes that employees dislike work and will function only in a highly controlled work environment

1. people dislike work and try to avoid it.
2. because people dislike work, managers must coerce, control, and frequently threaten employees to achieve organizational goals.
3. people generally must be led because they have little ambition and will not seek responsibility; they are concerned mainly with security.

The logical outcome of such assumptions will be a highly controlled work environment—one in which managers make all the decisions and employees take all the orders.

On the other hand, **Theory Y** is a concept of employee motivation generally consistent with the ideas of the human relations movement. Theory Y assumes that employees accept responsibility and work toward organizational goals if by so doing they also achieve personal rewards. According to Theory Y,

Theory Y a concept of employee motivation generally consistent with the ideas of the human relations movement; assumes that employees accept responsibility and work toward organizational goals if by so doing they also achieve personal rewards

1. people do not naturally dislike work; in fact, work is an important part of their lives.

table 11.1 Theory X and Theory Y Contrasted

Area	Theory X	Theory Y
Attitude toward work	Dislike	Involvement
Control systems	External	Internal
Supervision	Direct	Indirect
Level of commitment	Low	High
Employee potential	Ignored	Identified
Use of human resources	Limited	Not limited

2. people will work toward goals to which they are committed.
3. people become committed to goals when it is clear that accomplishing the goals will bring personal rewards.
4. people often seek out and willingly accept responsibility.
5. employees have the potential to help accomplish organizational goals.
6. organizations generally do not make full use of their human resources.

Obviously, this view is quite different from—and much more positive than—that of Theory X. McGregor argued that most managers behave in accordance with Theory X. But he maintained that Theory Y is more appropriate and effective as a guide for managerial action (see Table 11.1).

The human relations movement and Theories X and Y increased managers' awareness of the importance of social factors in the workplace. However, human motivation is a complex and dynamic process to which there is no simple key. Neither money nor social factors alone can provide the answer. Rather, a variety of factors must be considered in any attempt to increase motivation.

Theory Z

William Ouchi, a management professor at UCLA, studied business practices in American and Japanese firms. He concluded that different types of management systems dominate in these two countries.[8] In Japan, Ouchi found what he calls *type J* firms. They are characterized by lifetime employment for employees, collective (or group) decision making, collective responsibility for the outcomes of decisions, slow evaluation and promotion, implied control mechanisms, nonspecialized career paths, and a holistic concern for employees as people.

American industry is dominated by what Ouchi calls *type A* firms, which follow a different pattern. They emphasize short-term employment, individual decision making, individual responsibility for the outcomes of decisions, rapid evaluation and promotion, explicit control mechanisms, specialized career paths, and a segmented concern for employees only as employees.

A few very successful American firms represent a blend of the type J and type A patterns. These firms, called *type Z* organizations, emphasize long-term employment, collective decision making, individual responsibility for the outcomes of decisions, slow evaluation and promotion, informal control along with some formalized measures, moderately specialized career paths, and a holistic concern for employees.

Theory Z the belief that some middle ground between Ouchi's type A and type J practices is best for American business

Ouchi's **Theory Z** is the belief that some middle ground between his type A and type J practices is best for American business (see Figure 11.4). A major part of Theory Z is the emphasis on participative decision making. The focus is on "we" rather than on "us versus them." Theory Z employees and managers view the organization as a family. This participative spirit fosters cooperation and the dissemination of information and organizational values.

figure 11.4

The Features of Theory Z

The best aspects of Japanese and American management theories combine to form the nucleus of Theory Z.

Reinforcement Theory

reinforcement theory a theory of motivation based on the premise that behavior that is rewarded is likely to be repeated, whereas behavior that is punished is less likely to recur

Reinforcement theory is based on the premise that behavior that is rewarded is likely to be repeated, whereas behavior that is punished is less likely to recur. A *reinforcement* is an action that follows directly from a particular behavior. It may be a pay raise following a particularly large sale to a new customer or a reprimand for coming to work late.

Reinforcements can take a variety of forms and can be used in a number of ways. A *positive reinforcement* is one that strengthens desired behavior by providing a reward. For example, many employees respond well to praise; recognition from their supervisors for a job well done increases (strengthens) their willingness to perform well in the future. A *negative reinforcement* strengthens desired behavior by eliminating an undesirable task or situation. Suppose that a machine shop must be cleaned thoroughly every month—a dirty, miserable task. During one particular month when the workers do a less-than-satisfactory job at their normal work assignments, the boss requires the workers to clean the factory rather than bringing in the usual private maintenance service. The employees will be motivated to work harder the next month to avoid the unpleasant cleanup duty again.

Punishment is an undesired consequence of undesirable behavior. Common forms of punishment used in organizations include reprimands, reduced pay, disciplinary layoffs, and termination (firing). Punishment often does more harm than good. It tends to create an unpleasant environment, fosters hostility and resentment, and suppresses undesirable behavior only until the supervisor's back is turned.

Managers who rely on *extinction* hope to eliminate undesirable behavior by not responding to it. The idea is that the behavior eventually will become "extinct." Suppose, for example, that an employee has the habit of writing memo after memo to his or her manager about insignificant events. If the manager does not respond to any of these memos, the employee probably will stop writing them, and the behavior will have been squelched.

The effectiveness of reinforcement depends on which type is used and how it is timed. One approach may work best under certain conditions, but some situations lend themselves to the use of more than one approach. Generally, positive reinforcement is considered the most effective, and it is recommended when the manager has a choice.

Continual reinforcement can become tedious for both managers and employees, especially when the same behavior is being reinforced over and over in the same way.

At the start, it may be necessary to reinforce a desired behavior every time it occurs. However, once a desired behavior has become more or less established, occasional reinforcement seems to be most effective.

Contemporary Views on Motivation

learning objective

3 Describe three contemporary views of motivation: equity theory, expectancy theory, and goal-setting theory.

Maslow's hierarchy of needs and Herzberg's motivation-hygiene theory are popular and widely known theories of motivation. Each is also a significant step up from the relatively narrow views of scientific management and Theories X and Y. But they do have one weakness: Each attempts to specify *what* motivates people, but neither explains *why* or *how* motivation develops or is sustained over time. In recent years managers have begun to explore three other models that take a more dynamic view of motivation. These are equity theory, expectancy theory, and goal-setting theory.

Equity Theory

equity theory a theory of motivation based on the premise that people are motivated to obtain and preserve equitable treatment for themselves

The **equity theory** of motivation is based on the premise that people are motivated to obtain and preserve equitable treatment for themselves. As used here, *equity* is the distribution of rewards in direct proportion to the contribution of each employee to the organization. Everyone need not receive the *same* rewards, but the rewards should be in accordance with individual contributions.

According to this theory, we tend to implement the idea of equity in the following way. First, we develop our own input-to-outcome ratio. *Inputs* are the time, effort, skills, education, experience, and so on that we contribute to the organization. *Outcomes* are the rewards we get from the organization, such as pay, benefits, recognition, and promotions. Next, we compare this ratio with what we perceive as the input-to-outcome ratio for some other person. It might be a co-worker, a friend who works for another firm, or even an average of all the people in our organization. This person is called the *comparison other*. Note that our perception of this person's input-to-outcome ratio may be absolutely correct or completely wrong. However, we believe that it is correct.

If the two ratios are roughly the same, we feel that the organization is treating us equitably. In this case we are motivated to leave things as they are. However, if our ratio is the higher of the two, we feel under-rewarded and are motivated to make changes. We may (1) decrease our own inputs by not working so hard, (2) try to increase our total outcome by asking for a raise in pay, (3) try to get the comparison other to increase some inputs or receive decreased outcomes, (4) leave the work situation, or (5) do a new comparison with a different comparison other.

Equity theory is most relevant to pay as an outcome. Because pay is a very real measure of a person's worth to an organization, comparisons involving pay are a natural part of organizational life. Managers can try to avoid problems arising from inequity by making sure that rewards are distributed on the basis of performance and that everyone clearly understands the basis for his or her own pay.

Understanding motivation. Fujio Mitarai, President and CEO of Canon, Inc. understands the importance of motivating employees by encouraging them to have a strong sense of their individual responsibility and future goals. Having independent initiative and an ambitious spirit in one's work is also a strong part of Canon's philosophy.

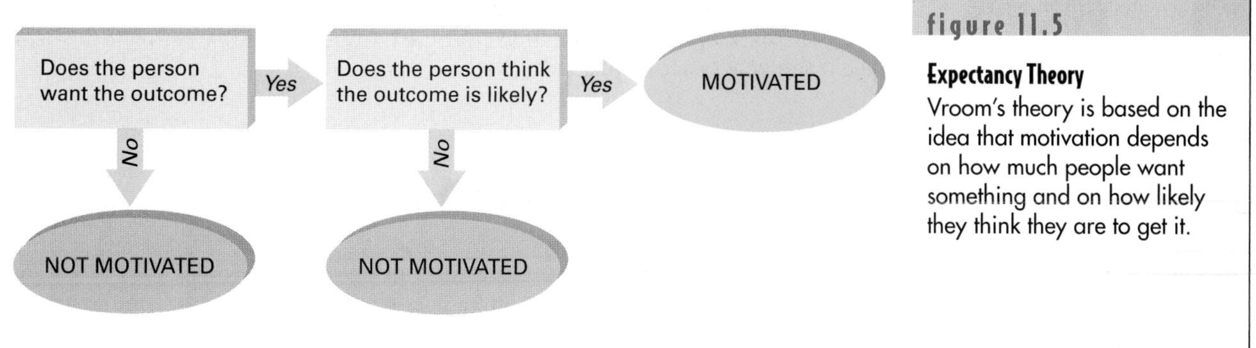

figure 11.5

Expectancy Theory
Vroom's theory is based on the idea that motivation depends on how much people want something and on how likely they think they are to get it.

Expectancy Theory

Expectancy theory, developed by Victor Vroom, is a very complex model of motivation based on a deceptively simple assumption. According to expectancy theory, motivation depends on how much we want something and on how likely we think we are to get it (see Figure 11.5). Consider, for example, the case of three sales representatives who are candidates for promotion to one sales manager's job. Bill has had a very good sales year and always gets good performance evaluations. However, he isn't sure he wants the job because it involves a great deal of travel, long working hours, and much stress and pressure. Paul wants the job badly but doesn't think he has much chance of getting it. He has had a terrible sales year and gets only mediocre performance evaluations from his present boss. Susan wants the job as much as Paul, and she thinks that she has a pretty good shot at it. Her sales have improved significantly this past year, and her evaluations are the best in the company.

expectancy theory a model of motivation based on the assumption that motivation depends on how much we want something and on how likely we think we are to get it

Expectancy theory would predict that Bill and Paul are not very motivated to seek the promotion. Bill doesn't really want it, and Paul doesn't think he has much of a chance of getting it. Susan, however, is very motivated to seek the promotion because she wants it *and* thinks that she can get it.

Expectancy theory is complex because each action we take is likely to lead to several different outcomes; some we may want, and others we may not want. For example, a person who works hard and puts in many extra hours may get a pay raise, be promoted, and gain valuable new job skills. However, that person also may be forced to spend less time with his or her family and be forced to cut back on social life.

For one person, the promotion may be paramount, the pay raise and new skills fairly important, and the loss of family and social life of negligible importance. For someone else, the family and social life may be the most important, the pay raise of moderate importance, the new skills unimportant, and the promotion undesirable because of the additional hours it would require. The first person would be motivated to work hard and put in the extra hours, whereas the second person would not be at all motivated to do so. In other words, it is the entire bundle of outcomes—and the individual's evaluation of the importance of each outcome—that determines motivation.

Expectancy theory is difficult to apply, but it does provide several useful guidelines for managers. It suggests that managers must recognize that (1) employees work for a variety of reasons, (2) these reasons, or expected outcomes, may change over time, and (3) it is necessary to clearly show employees how they can attain the outcomes they desire.

Goal-Setting Theory

Goal-setting theory suggests that employees are motivated to achieve goals that they and their managers establish together. The goal should be very specific, moderately difficult, and one the employee will be committed to achieve.[9] Rewards should be tied directly to goal achievement. Using goal-setting theory, a manager can design rewards that fit employee needs, clarify expectations, maintain equity, and provide

goal-setting theory a theory of motivation suggesting that employees are motivated to achieve goals they and their managers establish together

reinforcement. A major benefit of this theory is that it provides a good understanding of the goal the employee is to achieve and the rewards that will accrue to the employee if the goal is accomplished.

Key Motivation Techniques

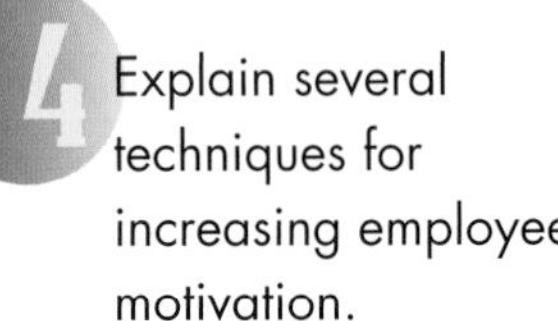

learning objective

4 Explain several techniques for increasing employee motivation.

Today it takes more than a generous salary to motivate employees. Increasingly, companies are trying to provide motivation by satisfying employees' less tangible needs. In this section we discuss several specific—and somewhat more orthodox—techniques that help managers to boost employee motivation and job satisfaction.

Management by Objectives

management by objectives (MBO) a motivation technique in which managers and employees collaborate in setting goals

Management by objectives (MBO) is a motivation technique in which managers and employees collaborate in setting goals. The primary purpose of MBO is to clarify the roles employees are expected to play in reaching the organization's goals. By allowing individuals to participate in goal setting and performance evaluation, MBO increases their motivation. Most MBO programs consist of a series of five steps, as shown in Figure 11.6.

The first step in setting up an MBO program is to secure the acceptance of top management. It is essential that top managers endorse and participate in the program if others in the firm are to accept it. The commitment of top management also provides a natural starting point for educating employees about the purposes and mechanics of MBO.

Next, preliminary goals must be established. Top management also plays a major role in this activity because the preliminary goals reflect the firm's mission and strategy. The intent of an MBO program is to have these goals filter down through the organization.

The third step, which actually consists of several smaller steps, is the heart of MBO:

figure 11.6

The Five Steps of an Effective MBO Program

An MBO program clarifies the roles employees are expected to play in reaching the organization's goals and allows employees to participate in goal setting and performance evaluation.

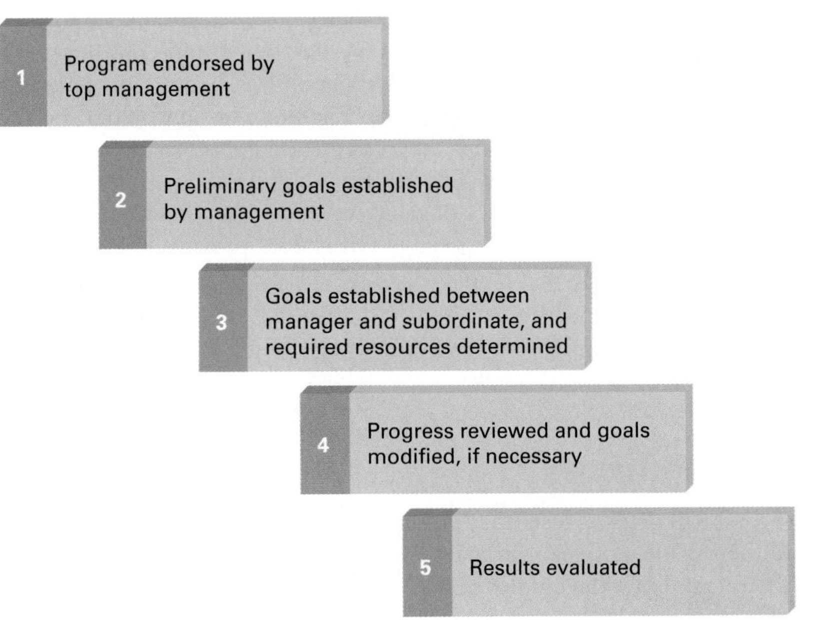

1. The manager explains to each employee that he or she has accepted certain goals for the group (the manager as well as the employees) and asks the individual to think about how he or she can help to achieve these goals.
2. The manager later meets with each employee individually. Together they establish goals for the employee. Whenever possible, the goals should be measurable and should specify the time frame for completion (usually one year).
3. The manager and the employee decide what resources the employee will need to accomplish his or her goals.

As the fourth step, the manager and each employee meet periodically to review the employee's progress. They may agree to modify certain goals during these meetings if circumstances have changed. For example, a sales representative may have accepted a goal of increasing sales by 20 percent. However, an aggressive competitor may have entered the marketplace, making this goal unattainable. In light of this circumstance, the goal may be revised downward to 10 or 15 percent.

The fifth step in the MBO process is evaluation. At the end of the designated time period, the manager and each employee meet again to determine which of the individual's goals were met, which were not met, and why. The employee's reward (in the form of a pay raise, praise, or promotion) is based primarily on the degree of goal attainment.

Like every other management method, MBO has advantages and disadvantages. MBO can motivate employees by involving them actively in the life of the firm. The collaboration on goal setting and performance appraisal improves communication and

adapting to change

Can Napping on the Job Improve Productivity and Satisfaction?

A BRIEF NAP is nothing unusual for employees working at Sprint's operations center in Phoenix. In fact, Sprint not only tolerates napping, it encourages it. The Federal Aviation Administration actually requires the pilot and copilot to nap (not at the same time) during rest periods on long-distance flights so that they will be more alert for the landing sequence. Yet almost all U.S. employers take the opposite view: They do not tolerate napping on the job.

However, some research has confirmed the work benefits of power napping. A Harvard University study found that after napping on the job for an hour, an employee can perform nearly as well at the end of the work day as at the beginning. The employee feels better—enhancing satisfaction—and is more productive for more of the day. An earlier study in Japan reported that a twenty-minute nap improves employee self-confidence and performance.

On the other hand, lack of sleep takes a high toll. According to the National Sleep Foundation, it can lead to higher error and accident rates, higher absenteeism, and higher turnover on the job. Moreover, weary employees who are not allowed to nap may snap at colleagues, mistreat customers, forget important tasks, and cause other disruptions that take away from the organization's performance.

Although employers who want to encourage workplace napping could provide cots, pillows, and alarm clocks, many have little floor space to spare. Instead, they can distribute some of the current crop of ergonomically correct adjustable office chairs so that employees can recline comfortably or even stretch out horizontally without leaving their desks.

Dr. William Anthony, author of *Napping at Work*, believes that more employers should wake up to the power of power napping on the job. "Workplace napping is a natural, no-cost way to increase productivity," he stresses. Harvard researcher Sarah Mednick agrees: "My advice to employers is if you really want people to be working well, you would give them the benefit of a nap to make them even more productive."

makes employees feel that they are an important part of the organization. Periodic review of progress also enhances control within an organization. A major problem with MBO is that it does not work unless the process begins at the top of an organization. In some cases MBO results in excessive paperwork. In addition, some managers have difficulty sitting down and working out goals with their employees and may instead just assign them goals.[10] Finally, MBO programs prove difficult to implement unless goals are quantifiable.

MBO has proved to be an effective motivational tool in many organizations. Tenneco, Black & Decker, Du Pont, General Foods, and General Motors all have reported success with MBO. Like any management technique, however, it must be applied with caution and in the right spirit if it is to work.

Job Enrichment

job enrichment a motivation technique that provides employees with more variety and responsibility in their jobs

Job enrichment is a method of motivating employees by providing them with variety in their tasks while giving them some responsibility for, and control over, their jobs. At the same time, employees gain new skills and acquire a broader perspective about how their individual work contributes to the goals of the organization. Earlier in this chapter we noted that Herzberg's motivation-hygiene theory is one rationale for the use of job enrichment; that is, the added responsibility and control that job enrichment confers on employees increases their satisfaction and motivation. Employees at 3M get to spend 15 percent of their time at work on whatever projects they choose regardless of the relationship of these "pet projects" to the employees' regular duties. This type of enrichment can motivate employees and create a variety of benefits for the company.[11] At times, **job enlargement**—expanding a worker's assignments to include additional but similar tasks—can lead to job enrichment. Job enlargement might mean that a worker on an assembly line who used to connect three wires to components moving down the line now connects five wires. Unfortunately, the added tasks are often just as routine as those the worker performed before the change. In such cases, enlargement may not be effective. AT&T, IBM, and Maytag Corporation all have experimented with job enlargement.

job enlargement expanding a worker's assignments to include additional but similar tasks

Whereas job enlargement does not really change the routine and monotonous nature of jobs, job enrichment does. Job enrichment requires that added tasks give an employee more responsibility for what he or she does. It provides workers with both more tasks to do and more control over how they perform them. In particular, job enrichment removes many controls from jobs, gives workers more authority, and assigns work in complete, natural units. Moreover, employees frequently are given fresh and challenging job assignments. By blending more planning and decision making into jobs, job enrichment gives work more depth and complexity.

job redesign a type of job enrichment in which work is restructured to cultivate the worker-job match

Job redesign is a type of job enrichment in which work is restructured in ways that cultivate the worker-job match. Job redesign can be achieved by combining tasks, forming work groups, or establishing closer customer relationships. Employees often are more motivated when jobs are combined because the increased variety of tasks presents more challenge and therefore more reward. Work groups motivate employees by showing them how their jobs fit within the organization as a whole and how they contribute to its success. Establishing client relationships allows employees to interact directly with customers. Not only does this type of redesign add a personal dimension to employment, but it also provides workers with immediate and relevant feedback about how they are doing their jobs.

Among the companies that have used job enrichment successfully are General Foods, Texas Instruments, and Chevron Corporation. Chevron's program focuses on employees' career development and on helping them enhance their effectiveness and job satisfaction. The company's career-enrichment process, now serving as a model for many other organizations, follows a step-by-step procedure that includes preparation, joint planning, plan review, implementation, and end-of-period review.

Job enrichment works best when employees seek more challenging work. Of course, not all workers respond positively to job-enrichment programs. Employees must desire personal growth and have the skills and knowledge to perform enriched jobs. Lack of self-confidence, fear of failure, or distrust of management's intentions are likely to lead to ineffective performance on enriched jobs. In addition, some workers do not view their jobs as routine and boring, and others even prefer routine jobs because they find them satisfying. Companies that use job enrichment as an alternative to specialization also face extra expenses, such as the cost of retraining. Another motivation for job redesign is to reduce employees' stress at work. A job redesign that carefully matches worker to job can prevent stress-related injuries, which constitute about 60 to 80 percent of all work-related injuries. The reduced stress also creates greater motivation.[12]

Spotlight

Causes of job stress

Seven out of ten employees say they feel "moderate" to "great" stress on the job.

Demands of the job	54%
Co-workers	20%
The boss	10%
Layoff fears	8%

The four top causes of stress

Source: *USA Today*, October 29, 2002, p. A1.

Behavior Modification

Behavior modification is a systematic program of reinforcement to encourage desirable behavior. Behavior modification involves both rewards to encourage desirable actions and punishments to discourage undesirable actions. However, studies have shown that rewards, such as compliments and expressions of appreciation, are much more effective behavior modifiers than punishments, such as reprimands and scorn.

behavior modification a systematic program of reinforcement to encourage desirable behavior

When applied to management, behavior modification strives to encourage desirable organizational behavior. Use of this technique begins with the identification of a *target behavior*—the behavior that is to be changed. (It might be low production levels or a high rate of absenteeism, for example.) Existing levels of this behavior are then measured. Next, managers provide positive reinforcement in the form of a reward when employees exhibit the *desired behavior* (such as increased production or less absenteeism). The reward might be praise or a more tangible form of recognition, such as a gift, meal, or trip. Finally, the levels of the target behavior are measured again to determine whether the desired changes have been achieved. If they have, the reinforcement is maintained. However, if the target behavior has not changed significantly in the desired direction, the reward system must be changed to one that is likely to be more effective. The key is to devise effective rewards that not only will modify employees' behavior in desired ways but also will motivate them. To this end, experts suggest that management should reward quality, loyalty, and productivity.

Flextime

To most people, a work schedule means the standard nine-to-five, forty-hour workweek. In reality, though, many people have work schedules that are quite different from this. Police officers, firefighters, restaurant personnel, airline employees, and medical personnel usually have work schedules that are far from standard. Some manufacturers also rotate personnel from shift to shift. And many professional people—such as managers, artists, and lawyers—need more than forty hours each week to get their work done.

The needs and lifestyles of today's work force are changing. Dual-income families make up a much larger share of the work force than ever before, and women are one of its fastest-growing sectors. And more employees are responsible for the care of elderly relatives. Recognizing that these changes increase the demand for family time, many employers are offering flexible work schedules that not only help employees manage their time better but also increase employee motivation and job satisfaction.

Being employee friendly with flexible schedules. Duane Ruh at Little Log Co., manufacturer of bird houses and bird feeders, is concerned that his employees have satisfying personal lives. To that end, he allows his employees to build flexibility into their work schedules.

Flextime is a system in which employees set their own work hours within certain limits determined by employers. Typically the firm establishes two bands of time: the *core time*, when all employees must be at work, and the *flexible time*, when employees may choose whether to be at work. The only condition is that every employee must work a total of eight hours each day. For example, the hours between 9 and 11 a.m. and 1 and 3 p.m. might be core time, and the hours between 6 and 9 a.m., between 11 a.m. and 1 p.m., and between 3 and 6 p.m. might be flexible time. This would give employees the option of coming in early and getting off early, coming in later and leaving later, or taking an extralong lunch break. But flextime also ensures that everyone is present at certain times, when conferences with supervisors and department meetings can be scheduled. Another type of flextime allows employees to work a forty-hour work week in four days instead of five. Workers who put in ten hours a day instead of eight get an extra day off each week. According to a survey conducted by the Society for Human Resource Management, the percentage of firms offering flextime has increased from 56 to 64 percent over the past five years. The largest increase comes from small firms, who often can attract and retain employees with more flexible conditions when they cannot match the salary and insurance benefits of larger firms.[13]

flextime a system in which employees set their own work hours within employer-determined limits

The sense of independence and autonomy employees gain from having a say in what hours they work can be a motivating factor. In addition, employees who have enough time to deal with nonwork issues often work more productively and with greater satisfaction when they are on the job. Approximately 29 percent of U.S. workers participate in determining their own work schedules, thus experiencing some form of flextime.[14] Two common problems associated with using flextime are (1) supervisors sometimes find their jobs complicated by having employees who come and go at different times, and (2) employees without flextime sometimes resent coworkers who have it.

Part-Time Work and Job Sharing

part-time work permanent employment in which individuals work less than a standard work week

Part-time work is permanent employment in which individuals work less than a standard work week. The specific number of hours worked varies, but part-time jobs are structured so that all responsibilities can be completed in the number of hours an employee works. Part-time work is of special interest to parents who want more time with their children and people who simply desire more leisure time. One disadvantage of part-time work is that it often does not provide the benefits that come with a full-time position. This is not, however, the case at Starbucks, where approximately 80 percent of its employees work part time. Starbucks does not treat its part-time employees any differently from its full-time employees; all receive the same access to numerous benefits, which even includes a free pound of coffee every week.[15]

job sharing an arrangement whereby two people share one full-time position

Job sharing (sometimes referred to as *work sharing*) is an arrangement whereby two people share one full-time position. One job sharer may work from 8 a.m. to noon, and the other may work from 1 to 5 p.m., or they may alternate work days. For example, at the BBC, two women share the same job. By communicating daily through telephone, voice mail, and fax machines, these announcers are able to handle a challenging administrative position and still have time for their families. Through their partnership at work, they have been able to share a position for more than six years.[16] Job sharing combines the security of a full-time position with the flexibility of a part-time job. Among the "100 Best Companies for Working Mothers," 94 offer job sharing because it allows these companies to retain highly talented professionals.[17]

Part-time work. Liz Vanzura gave up a high-pressure full-time position as director of marketing for Volkswagen for a part-time job as ad director for GM's newly acquired Hummer division in order to have a more fulfilling and satisfying personal life. Her new boss at GM, Mike DiGiovanni knew that this special work arrangement was the perfect lure to bring the highly-valued Vanzura to his team.

For firms, job sharing provides a unique opportunity to attract highly skilled employees who might not be available on a full-time basis. In addition, companies can save on expenses by reducing the cost of benefits and avoiding the disruptions of employee turnover. For employees, opting for the flexibility of job sharing may mean giving up some of the benefits received for full-time work. In addition, job sharing is difficult if tasks are not easily divisible or if two people do not work or communicate well with one another.

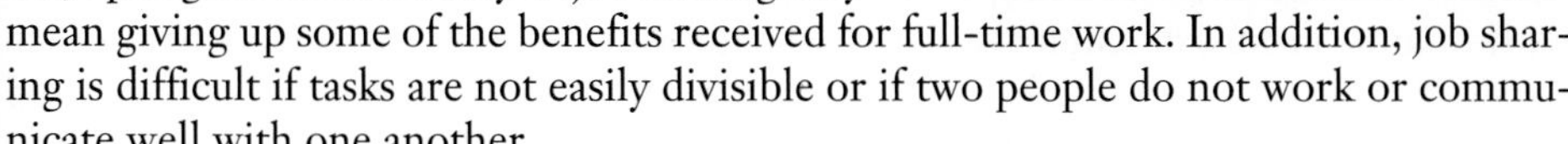

Telecommuting

A growing number of companies allow **telecommuting**—working at home all the time or for a portion of the work week. Personal computers, modems, fax machines, voice mail, cellular phones, and overnight couriers all facilitate the work-at-home trend. Working at home means that individuals can set their own hours and have more time with their families. Even the federal government is recognizing the benefits of telecommuting in that 90 percent of the U.S. Treasury Inspector General for Tax Administration (TIGTA) workers and over 100 lawyers for the U.S. Trademark Office telecommute at least three days a week.[18]

telecommuting working at home all the time or for a portion of the work week

Companies that allow telecommuting experience several benefits, including increased productivity, lower real estate and travel costs, reduced employee absenteeism and turnover, increased work/life balance and improved morale, and access to additional labor pools. Pitney Bowes reports that an additional benefit gained when employees work from home is the company's image as a good corporate citizen because the program helps to decrease pollution and traffic congestion.[19] Among the disadvantages to telecommuting are feelings of isolation, putting in longer hours, and being distracted by family or household responsibilities. In addition, some supervisors have difficulty monitoring productivity.

At IBM, about 25 percent of its 320,000 employees worldwide engage in telecommuting, which saves IBM about $700 million in real estate costs annually. IBM also benefits from higher productivity and employee satisfaction.[20]

Using the Internet @

Home offices, mobile offices, and telecommuting are growing in popularity. The Internet is a great source of personal and professional services the mobile worker can call on whenever assistance away from the office is needed. A few online service firms such as Bungo.com, MyEvents.com, and Staples.com can provide calendar functions, printing, and secretarial services, to mention just a few.

Employee Empowerment

Many companies are increasing employee motivation and satisfaction through the use of empowerment. **Empowerment** means making employees more involved in their jobs and in the operations of the organization by increasing their participation in decision making. With empowerment, control no longer flows exclusively from the top levels of the organization downward. Empowered employees have a voice in what they

empowerment making employees more involved in their jobs by increasing their participation in decision making

do and how and when they do it. In some organizations, employees' input is restricted to individual choices, such as when to take breaks. In other companies, their responsibilities may encompass more far-reaching issues. At Ritz-Carlton Hotels, empowerment frequently requires people skills, such as conflict resolution. When a guest has a complaint, the employee who receives the complaint is considered to "own" it and must immediately and independently figure out how to address it. Employees empowered to solve such problems often become good candidates for promotion. Employee turnover at Ritz-Carlton is only one-fifth the hotel industry average.[21]

For empowerment to work effectively, management must be involved. Managers should set expectations, communicate standards, institute periodic evaluations, and guarantee follow-up. Effectively implemented, empowerment can lead to increased job satisfaction, improved job performance, higher-self esteem, and increased organizational commitment. Obstacles to empowerment include resistance on the part of management, distrust of management on the part of workers, insufficient training, and poor communication between management and employees.

Self-Managed Work Teams

self-managed work teams groups of employees with the authority and skills to manage themselves

Another method for increasing employee motivation is to introduce **self-managed work teams,** groups of employees with the authority and skills to manage themselves. Experts suggest that workers on self-managed teams are more motivated and satisfied because they have more task variety and more job control. On many work teams, members rotate through all the jobs for which the team is responsible. Some organizations cross-train the entire team so that everyone can perform everyone else's job. In a traditional business structure, management is responsible for hiring and firing employees, establishing budgets, purchasing supplies, conducting performance reviews, and disciplining team members. When teams are in place, they take over some or all of these management functions.

To make the most effective use of teams, organizations must be committed to the team approach, team objectives must be clear, training and education must be ongoing, and there must be a system for compensating the accomplishment of team-based goals. One such compensation system is *gain sharing*, in which employee bonuses are tied to achievement of team goals, such as increased sales or productivity or improved customer satisfaction.

When implemented correctly, use of work teams can lead to higher employee morale, increased productivity, and often innovation. Both Xerox and Procter & Gamble have successfully implemented the self-directed team strategy. At its factory, Ferrari uses work teams designed to let each team perform a variety of tasks for about an hour and a half before the vehicle moves on to the next team. Employees learn more job skills, are more interested in their work, and develop a greater sense of pride in and loyalty for Ferrari.[22] Smaller organizations also can benefit. For example, Allina, a company that operates nonprofit hospitals in Minnesota, has had excellent results since creating management-union teams. One of these teams saved the company $200,000 annually by improving the procedure for equipment maintenance.

Is there a pig in the house? To increase employee satisfaction, some organizations allow their workers to bring their pets to work for an occasional "Pet Day." Some companies even welcome employees' pets on a regular basis.

Although the work-team strategy is increasingly popular, it is not without its

problems. Lack of support from managers and supervisors and insufficient training in the team approach can minimize or eliminate benefits. In addition, companies must be prepared for the initial costs of training and implementation. For example, Whirlpool recently implemented a strategy using self-managed work teams that were charged with developing innovative new products. These teams, called "skunk works," had an initial budget of $50 million, but Whirlpool vowed to increase their budget because the company recently launched the new Gladiator brand of garage storage units and appliances as a direct result of a skunk works team. The launch of this line showed employees that their ideas are taken seriously no matter what their status is in the organization.[23]

Employee Ownership

Some organizations are discovering that a highly effective technique for motivating employees is **employee ownership**—that is, employees own the company they work for by virtue of being stockholders. Employee-owned businesses directly reward employees for success. When the company enjoys increased sales or lower costs, employees benefit directly. The National Center for Employee Ownership, an organization that studies employee-owned American businesses, reports that employee stock ownership plans (ESOPs) provide considerable employee incentive and increase employee involvement and commitment. In the United States today, about 8.5 million employees participate in 11,000 ESOPs and stock bonus plans.[24] As a means to motivate top executives and, frequently, middle-ranking managers who are working long days for what are generally considered poor salaries, some firms provide stock options as part of the employee compensation package. The option is simply the right to buy shares of the firm within a prescribed time at a set price. If the firm does well and its stock price rises past the set price (presumably because of all the work being done by the employee), the employee can exercise the option and immediately sell the stock and cash in on the company's success.

employee ownership a situation in which employees own the company they work for by virtue of being stockholders

The difficulties of such companies as United Airlines have damaged the idea of employee ownership. United's ESOP has failed to solve problems between employees and management. In addition, Lowe's, the home-improvement retailer, recently stopped its long-running and mostly successful ESOP and transferred remaining money into 401(k) plans.[25]

Return To inside business

Richard Gilligan found a number of ways to motivate the dispirited work force of the Mitsubishi plant in Normal, Illinois. Bucking the trend toward increased plant automation, he replaced some robots with skilled employees who could handle certain tasks more carefully and more productively. He also used job enrichment to expand workers' responsibilities into the realm of quality and empowered them to uncover problems and recommend solutions. Yet another way Gilligan boosted morale was by supporting plant workers who suggested a new mission statement in which respect for people was the top priority (followed by quality and productivity).

These changes motivated the Normal work force and fueled the plant's amazing turnaround. Productivity is 41 percent higher, waste has been reduced to less than $5 per vehicle, and workers need fewer than twenty-one hours to produce a car, compared with thirty-seven hours in 1998. Mitsubishi management was so pleased that Normal was assigned to manufacture additional models as part of an expansion plan to boost American sales. Workplace reforms are clearly paying off in higher motivation—and dollars and cents—in Normal, Illinois.

Questions

1. Does the Normal plant follow Theory X or Theory Y for employee motivation? Explain your answer.
2. Which of the need categories in Maslow's hierarchy might workers have difficulty satisfying if they experience sexual harassment or racial discrimination in the workplace? What are the implications for motivation?

chapter review

Summary

Explain what motivation is.

Motivation is the individual internal process that energizes, directs, and sustains behavior. Motivation is affected by employee morale—that is, the employee's feelings about the job, superiors, and the firm itself. Motivation, morale, and job satisfaction are closely related.

Understand some major historical perspectives on motivation.

One of the first approaches to employee motivation was Frederick Taylor's scientific management, the application of scientific principles to the management of work and workers. Taylor believed that employees work only for money and that they must be closely supervised and managed. This thinking led to the piece-rate system, under which employees are paid a certain amount for each unit they produce. The Hawthorne Studies attempted to determine the effects of the work environment on productivity. Results of these studies indicated that human factors affect productivity more than do physical aspects of the workplace.

Maslow's hierarchy of needs suggests that people are motivated by five sets of needs. In ascending order of importance, these motivators are physiological, safety, social, esteem, and self-actualization needs. People are motivated by the lowest set of needs that remains unfulfilled. As needs at one level are satisfied, people try to satisfy needs at the next level.

Frederick Herzberg found that job satisfaction and dissatisfaction are influenced by two distinct sets of factors. Motivation factors, including recognition and responsibility, affect an employee's degree of satisfaction, but their absence does not necessarily cause dissatisfaction. Hygiene factors, including pay and working conditions, affect an employee's degree of dissatisfaction but do not affect satisfaction.

Theory X is a concept of motivation that assumes that employees dislike work and will function effectively only in a highly controlled work environment. Thus, to achieve an organization's goals, managers must coerce, control, and threaten employees. This theory is generally consistent with Taylor's scientific management. Theory Y is more in keeping with the results of the Hawthorne Studies and the human relations movement. It suggests that employees can be motivated to behave as responsible members of the organization. Theory Z emphasizes long-term employment, collective decision making, individual responsibility for the outcomes of decisions, informal control, and a holistic concern for employees. Reinforcement theory is based on the idea that people will repeat behavior that is rewarded and will avoid behavior that is punished.

Describe three contemporary views of motivation: equity theory, expectancy theory, and goal-setting theory.

Equity theory maintains that people are motivated to obtain and preserve equitable treatment for themselves. Expectancy theory suggests that our motivation depends on how much we want something and how likely we think we are to get it. Goal-setting theory suggests that employees are motivated to achieve a goal that they and their managers establish together.

Explain several techniques for increasing employee motivation.

Management by objectives (MBO) is a motivation technique in which managers and employees collaborate in setting goals. MBO motivates employees by getting them more involved in their jobs and in the organization as a whole. Job enrichment seeks to motivate employees by varying their tasks and giving them more responsibility for and control over their jobs. Job enlargement, expanding a worker's assignments to include additional tasks, is one aspect of job enrichment. Job redesign is a type of job enrichment in which work is restructured to improve the worker-job match.

Behavior modification uses reinforcement to encourage desirable behavior. Rewards for productivity, quality, and loyalty change employees' behavior in desired ways and also increase motivation.

Allowing employees to work more flexible hours is another way to build motivation and job satisfaction. Flextime is a system of work scheduling that allows workers to set their own hours as long as they fall within limits established by employers. Part-time work is permanent employment in which individuals work less than a standard work week. Job sharing is an arrangement whereby two people share one full-time position. Telecommuting allows employees to work at home all or part of the work week. All these types of work arrangements give employees more time outside the workplace to deal with family responsibilities or to enjoy free time.

Employee empowerment, self-managed work teams, and employee ownership are also techniques that boost employee motivation. Empowerment increases employees' involvement in their jobs by increasing their decision-making authority. Self-managed work teams are groups of employees with the authority and skills to manage themselves. When employees participate in ownership programs such as employee stock ownership plans (ESOPs), they have more incentive to make the company succeed and therefore work more effectively.

Key Terms

You should now be able to define and give an example relevant to each of the following terms:

motivation (313)
morale (313)
scientific management (315)
piece-rate system (315)
need (316)
Maslow's hierarchy of needs (316)
physiological needs (316)
safety needs (316)
social needs (317)
esteem needs (318)
self-actualization needs (318)
motivation-hygiene theory (318)
motivation factors (318)
hygiene factors (318)
Theory X (319)
Theory Y (319)
Theory Z (320)
reinforcement theory (321)
equity theory (322)
expectancy theory (323)
goal-setting theory (323)
management by objectives (MBO) (324)
job enrichment (326)
job enlargement (326)
job redesign (326)
behavior modification (327)
flextime (328)
part-time work (328)
job sharing (328)
telecommuting (329)
empowerment (329)
self-managed work teams (330)
employee ownership (331)

Review Questions

1. How do scientific management and Theory X differ from the human relations movement and Theory Y?
2. How did the results of the Hawthorne Studies influence researchers' thinking about employee motivation?
3. What are the five sets of needs in Maslow's hierarchy? How are a person's needs related to motivation?
4. What are the two dimensions in Herzberg's theory? What kinds of elements affect each dimension?
5. What is the fundamental premise of reinforcement theory?
6. According to equity theory, how does an employee determine whether he or she is being treated equitably?
7. According to expectancy theory, what two variables determine motivation?
8. Identify and describe the major techniques for motivating employees.
9. Describe the steps involved in the MBO process.
10. What are the objectives of MBO? What do you think might be its disadvantages?
11. How does employee participation increase motivation?
12. Describe the steps in the process of behavior modification.
13. What are the major benefits and most common problems associated with the use of self-managed work teams?

Discussion Questions

1. How might managers make use of Maslow's hierarchy of needs in motivating employees? What problems would they encounter?
2. Do the various theories of motivation contradict each other or complement each other? Explain.
3. What combination of motivational techniques do you think would result in the best overall motivation and reward system?
4. Reinforcement theory and behavior modification have been called demeaning because they tend to treat people "like mice in a maze." Do you agree?

video case

Wheelworks Tries to Satisfy Employees and Customers

From mountain bikes to tandems, Wheelworks' employees are motivated to sell just about every kind of bicycle. Founded in 1977, the Wheelworks three-store chain in suburban Boston has been named one of the top ten U.S. bicycle retailers for more than a decade. Each store displays dozens of LeMond, Trek, and other brand-name bicycles for mountain biking, triathlon, cyclocross, touring, fitness, and other cycling activities. The chain currently markets more than 10,000 bicycles and brings in $10.5 million in annual sales revenue every year. It maintains a year-round staff of forty-five full-time employees and hires fifty-five additional employees to handle seasonal sales spikes. It also has built its reputation within New England by sponsoring races and rides as well as cycling teams.

When customers visit one of the Wheelworks locations, they can talk cycling with salespeople who understand bicycles and enjoy sharing what they know. Many employees participate in racing activities and local cycling groups and were recruited originally through those connections. Others were hired after replying to job openings posted on the Wheelworks website (**www.wheelworks.com**). All are passionate about cycling and eager to help novice and expert bicyclists alike.

New sales employees hired for the main store receive formal training about the company's policies and products. At the two branch stores, experienced employees act as mentors to new hires in an informal buddy system that supplements on-the-job training. All the firm's employees are invited to examine new bicycles and accessories and to ask questions when manufacturers' representatives visit the stores. Sales personnel also attend up to five in-store training clinics every month, each focusing on a particular product, product category, or manufacturer. Gaining such in-depth knowledge is an extra incentive for a work force excited about the world of cycling. So is being recognized by having their photos, biographies, and bicycling background publicized on the company's website.

During good-weather months, all Wheelworks' stores must be fully staffed to sell and service bicycles. On the other hand, employees are more likely to want time off during that period because they want to train, ride, or race. Wheelworks keeps its work force satisfied by being flexible about working hours. The company offers competitive retail wages and benefits such as health insurance coverage, vacation and sick pay, and profit sharing. It also rewards sales employees with seasonal bonuses tied to achieving company sales goals rather than to individual sales records. This compensation method gives employees the freedom to sell the right product for each customer's needs rather than trying to earn a special reward by selling an item that is not right for the customer. Employees prefer this approach because customers will see them as specialists with expert knowledge rather than as pushy salespeople. Still, the sales manager occasionally appeals to his team's competitive spirit by urging them to match or exceed each other's sales accomplishments.

Each salesperson sets goals for personal development as well as for store sales contributions. Store managers sit down to formally evaluate the performance of new salespeople six months after they are hired and then on an annual basis. However, sales personnel do not have to wait months to find out how they are doing. Because Wheelworks is not a huge organization, managers and peers constantly provide informal feedback and support. And salespeople who turn out to be stronger or more interested in nonsales activities can transfer easily to another job within he company, such as bicycle repair.

Seasonal employees who perform well are invited to join the year-round staff when jobs become open. Employees also can branch out to handle a variety of tasks in addition to their regular duties. Mechanics, for example, can teach bicycle repair classes sponsored by the store. And employees can get involved in one of the socially responsible events supported by Wheelworks, such as bike tours to raise funds for AIDS prevention programs.

Because Wheelworks' stores are known for their extensive inventory and expert staff, customers buy bicycles and then return for service, advice, and better or more updated models. For their part, the employees get paid for doing what they love—working with bicycles and with other cycling enthusiasts—in a professional yet fun environment.[26]

Questions

1. Which of the personal needs in Maslow's hierarchy do mentors and new employees fulfill through Wheelworks' mentoring program?
2. Which of Herzberg's motivation factors are in evidence at Wheelworks?
3. Why would Wheelworks' employees be motivated by striving to meet professional development goals as well as sales goals?

Building Skills for Career Success

1. Exploring the Internet

There are few employee incentives as motivating as owning "a piece of the action." Either through profit sharing or equity, many firms realize that the opportunity to share in the wealth generated by their effort is a primary force to drive employees toward better performance and a sense of ownership. The Foundation for Enterprise Development (**http://www.fed.org/**) is a nonprofit organization dedicated to helping entrepreneurs and executives use employee ownership and equity compensation as a fair and effective means of motivating the work force and improving corporate performance. You can learn more about this approach at the foundation's website. Visit the text website for updates to this exercise.

Assignment

1. Describe the content and services provided by the Foundation for Enterprise Development through its website.
2. Do you agree with this orientation toward motivation of employees/owners, or does it seem contrived to you? Discuss.
3. How else might employees be motivated to improve their performance?

2. Developing Critical Thinking Skills

This chapter has described several theories managers can use as guidelines in motivating employees to do the best job possible for the company. Among these theories are Maslow's hierarchy of needs, equity theory, expectancy theory, and goal-setting theory. How effective would each of these theories be in motivating you to be a more productive employee?

Assignment

1. Identify five job needs that are important to you.
2. Determine which of the theories mentioned above would work best to satisfy your job needs.
3. Prepare a two-page report explaining how you reached these conclusions.

3. Building Team Skills

By increasing employees' participation in decision making, empowerment makes workers feel more involved in their jobs and the operations of the organization. While empowerment may seem like a commonsense idea, it is a concept not universally found in the workplace. If you had empowerment in your job, how would you describe it?

Assignment

1. Use brainstorming to explore the concept of empowerment.
   a. Write each letter of the word *empowerment* in a vertical column on a sheet of paper or on the classroom chalkboard.
   b. Think of several words that begin with each letter.
   c. Write the words next to the appropriate letter.
2. Formulate a statement by choosing one word from each letter that best describes what empowerment means to you.
3. Analyze the statement.
   a. How relevant is the statement for you in terms of empowerment? Or empowerment in your workplace?
   b. What changes must occur in your workplace for you to have empowerment?
   c. How would you describe yourself as an empowered employee?
   d. What opportunities would empowerment give to you in your workplace?
4. Prepare a report of your findings.

4. Researching Different Careers

Because a manager's job varies from department to department within firms, as well as among firms, it is virtually impossible to write a generic description of a manager's job. If you are contemplating becoming a manager, you may find it very helpful to spend time on the job with several managers learning firsthand what they do.

Assignment

1. Make an appointment with managers in three firms, preferably firms of different sizes. When you make the appointments, request a tour of the facilities.
2. Ask the managers the following questions:
   a. What do you do in your job?
   b. What do you like most and least about your job? Why?
   c. What skills do you need in your job?
   d. How much education does your job require?
   e. What advice do you have for someone thinking about pursuing a career in management?
3. Summarize your findings in a two-page report. Include answers to these questions:
   a. Is management a realistic field of study for you? Why?
   b. What might be a better career choice? Why?

5. Improving Communication Skills

Suppose that you and a friend went into the auto repair business some years ago. You had the technical expertise, and he had the business knowledge. Although funds were tight for the first three years, your customer base grew, and you were able to hire extra help and expand business hours. Your business is now six years old and very successful. You have five people working under you. Henry, your most productive employee, wants to be promoted to a supervisory position. However, two other employees, Jack and Fred, have seniority over Henry, and you anticipate much dissension and poor morale if you go ahead and promote Henry. Henry clearly deserves the supervisory position because of his hard work and superior skills, but you stand to lose the other two employees if you promote him.

Assignment

1. Analyze the scenario, and answer these questions:
   a. Will you promote Henry? If so, why?
   b. How can you motivate Jack and Fred to stay with you if you promote Henry?
2. Refer to specific motivational techniques or theories to explain your reasoning in resolving the situation with Henry, Jack, and Fred.
3. Prepare a three-page report outlining and justifying your decision.

chapter

12

Enhancing Union-Management Relations

learning objectives

1 Explain how and why labor unions came into being.

2 Discuss the sources of unions' negotiating power and trends in union membership.

3 Identify the main focus of several major pieces of labor-management legislation.

4 Enumerate the steps involved in forming a union and show how the National Labor Relations Board is involved in the process.

5 Describe the basic elements in the collective-bargaining process.

6 Identify the major issues covered in a union-management contract.

7 Explain the primary bargaining tools available to unions and management.

If United Airlines could not win concessions from all five unions, it would have great difficulty emerging from bankruptcy.

inside business

United Airlines Flies into More Labor Turbulence

Relations between labor and management were already bumpy when United Airlines threatened to file for bankruptcy in 2002. Although the airline employed more than 80,000 people and operated 1,900 flights daily, its financial picture was grim. Airfares were at the lowest level in fifteen years, squeezing profits. Just as bad, the combination of recession and public fear following the terrorist attacks on the World Trade Center and the Pentagon meant that fewer travelers were flying, which reduced revenues.

United's executives asked the unions for salary concessions to reduce the carrier's payroll so that it would be more competitive with lower-cost rivals. The unions were reluctant to agree. They remembered when management had asked for contract concessions during a financial crisis eight years earlier. At the time, the International Association of Machinists and the Air Line Pilots Association agreed, in exchange for an ownership stake and seats on the board of directors. United's financial situation had been up and down since then. If United now filed for bankruptcy protection, the unions stood to lose their 55 percent stake and their board seats.

After months of talks, a group of five unions representing United employees accepted cost-cutting measures totaling billions of dollars. (Senior company managers also took pay cuts of 11 percent.) Four unions came to an agreement over exactly how much of the total cuts each would bear, but the mechanics in the machinists' union balked.

United's executives finally put the airline into bankruptcy in December 2002. This gave management new leverage because a bankruptcy judge has the power to alter union contracts. By the end of the year, management had again worked out short-term cost-cutting deals with four unions. The pilots took salary cuts of 29 percent. The meteorologists and flight dispatchers took cuts of 13 percent, and the flight attendants took cuts of 9 percent. The machinists' union still refused to take salary cuts.

If United could not win concessions from all five unions, it would have great difficulty obtaining the financing to eventually emerge from bankruptcy. Management therefore asked the bankruptcy court to order cuts for members of the machinists' union. Agreeing, the judge mandated a 14 percent salary reduction for the next five months to keep United flying and prevent "irreparable damage."

With this concession, United would save $70 million in monthly payroll costs for several months. The airline also would qualify for the loans it needed to operate while going through the bankruptcy reorganization process. However, United's management still had to negotiate longer-term concessions with its unions to bring costs down for a more competitive position in the future. Given the history of the airline's relations between management and labor, this would not be easy.[1]

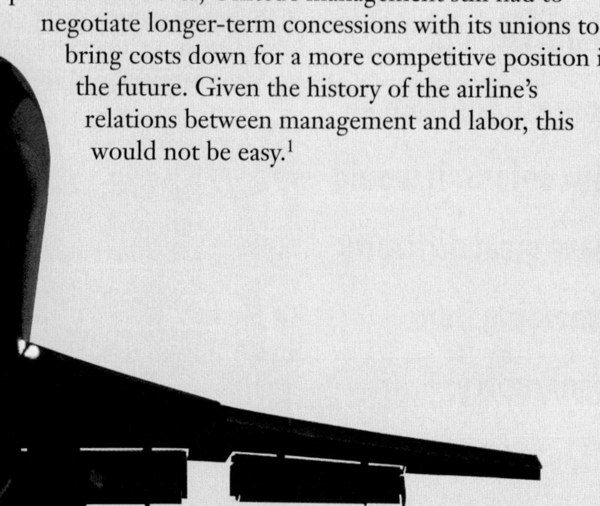

Some companies like United Airlines have been unionized for years and have experienced ups and downs for both management and the unions. Many businesses today have highly cooperative relationships with labor unions. A **labor union** is an organization of workers acting together to negotiate their wages and working conditions with employers. In the United States, nonmanagement employees have the legal right to form unions and to bargain, as a group, with management. The result of the bargaining process is a *labor contract*, a written agreement that is in force for a set period of time (usually one to three years). The dealings between labor unions and business management, both in the bargaining process and beyond it, are called **union-management relations** or, more simply, **labor relations.**

labor union an organization of workers acting together to negotiate their wages and working conditions with employers

union-management (labor) relations the dealings between labor unions and business management, both in the bargaining process and beyond it

Because labor and management have different goals, they tend to be at odds with each other. However, these goals must be attained by the same means—through the production of goods and services. At contract bargaining sessions, the two groups must work together to attain their goals. Perhaps mainly for this reason, antagonism now seems to be giving way to cooperation in union-management relations.

We open this chapter by reviewing the history of labor unions in this country. Then we turn our attention to organized labor today, noting current membership trends and union-management partnerships and summarizing important labor-relations laws. We discuss the unionization process, why employees join unions, how a union is formed, and what the National Labor Relations Board does. Collective-bargaining procedures are then explained. Next, we consider issues in union-management contracts, including employee pay, working hours, security, management rights, and grievance procedures. We close with a discussion of various labor and management negotiating techniques: strikes, slowdowns and boycotts, lockouts, mediation, and arbitration.

The Historical Development of Unions

learning objective

1 Explain how and why labor unions came into being.

Until the middle of the nineteenth century, there was very little organization of labor in this country. Groups of workers did occasionally form a **craft union,** an organization of skilled workers in a single craft or trade. These alliances usually were limited to a single city, and they often lasted only a short time. In 1786, the first known strike in the United States involved a group of Philadelphia printers who stopped working over demands for higher wages. When the employers granted the printers a pay increase, the group disbanded.

craft union an organization of skilled workers in a single craft or trade

Early History

In the mid-1800s, improved transportation opened new markets for manufactured goods. Improved manufacturing methods made it possible to supply those markets, and American industry began to grow. The Civil War and the continued growth of the railroads after the war led to further industrial expansion.

Large-scale production required more and more skilled industrial workers. As the skilled labor force grew, craft unions emerged in the more industrialized areas. From these craft unions, three significant labor organizations evolved. (See Figure 12.1 on p. 340 for a historical overview of unions and their patterns of membership.)

Knights of Labor The first significant national labor organization to emerge was the Knights of Labor, which was formed as a secret society in 1869 by Uriah Stephens, a utopian reformer and abolitionist from Philadelphia. Membership reached approximately 700,000 by 1886. One major goal of the Knights was to eliminate the depersonalization of the worker that resulted from mass-production technology. Another was to improve the moral standards of both employees and society. To the detriment of the group, its leaders concentrated so intently on social and economic change that they did not recognize the effects of technological change. Moreover, they assumed

figure 12.1

Historical Overview of Unions

The total number of members for all unions generally rose between 1869, when the first truly national union was organized, and 1975. The dates of major events in the history of labor unions are singled out along the line of membership change.

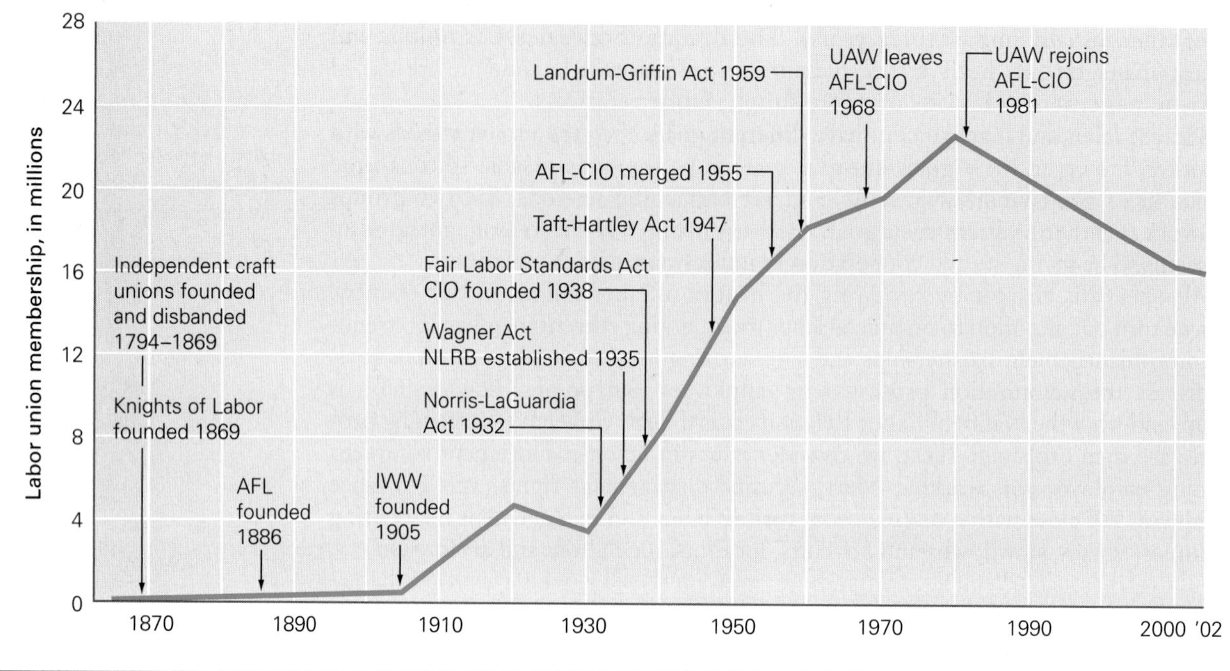

Sources: U.S. Bureau of Labor Statistics, *Dictionary of U.S. Labor Organizations*, 1986–1987; **www.aflcio.org;** *Statistical Abstract of the United States, 2001.*

that all employees had the same goals as the Knights' leaders—social and moral reform. The major reason for the demise of the Knights was the Haymarket riot of 1886. At a rally (called to demand a reduction in the length of a work day from ten to eight hours) in Chicago's Haymarket Square, a bomb exploded. Several police officers and civilians were killed or wounded. The Knights were not implicated directly, but they quickly lost public favor.

American Federation of Labor In 1886, several leaders of the Knights joined with independent craft unions to form the *American Federation of Labor* (AFL). Samuel Gompers, one of the AFL's founders, became its first president. Gompers believed that the goals of the union should be those of its members rather than those

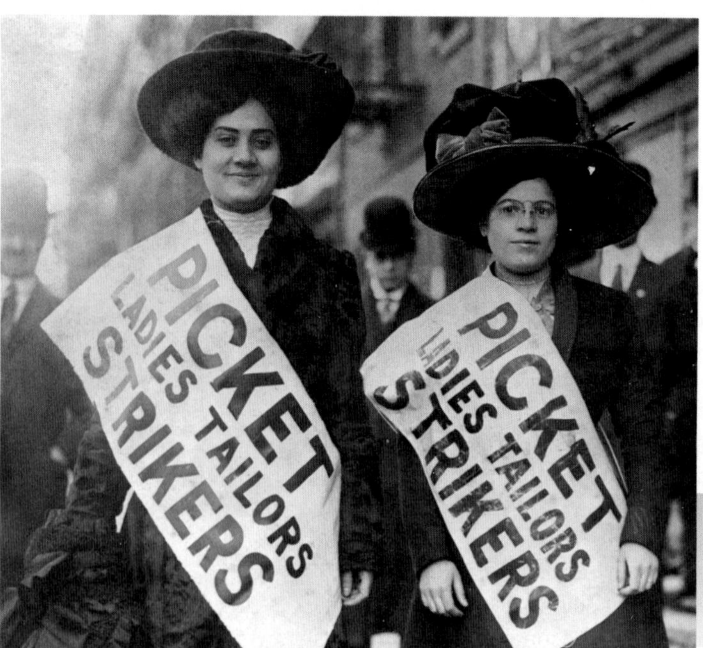

Protesting for better work conditions. These women picket during the 1910 Ladies Tailors strike in New York.

of its leaders. The AFL did not seek to change the existing business system, as the Knights of Labor had. Instead, its goal was to improve its members' living standards within that system.

Another major difference between the Knights of Labor and the AFL was in their positions regarding strikes. A **strike** is a temporary work stoppage by employees, calculated to add force to their demands. The Knights did not favor the use of strikes, whereas the AFL strongly believed that striking was an effective labor weapon. The AFL also believed that organized labor should play a major role in politics. As we will see, the AFL is still very much a part of the American labor scene.

strike a temporary work stoppage by employees, calculated to add force to their demands

Industrial Workers of the World The *Industrial Workers of the World* (IWW) was created in 1905 as a radical alternative to the AFL. Among its goals was the overthrow of capitalism. This revolutionary stance prevented the IWW from gaining much of a foothold. Perhaps its major accomplishment was to make the AFL seem, by comparison, less threatening to the general public and to business leaders.

Evolution of Contemporary Labor Organizations

Between 1900 and 1920, both business and government attempted to keep labor unions from growing. This period was plagued by strikes and violent confrontations between management and unions. In steelworks, garment factories, and auto plants, clashes took place in which striking union members fought bitterly against nonunion workers, police, and private security guards.

The AFL continued to be the major force in organized labor. By 1920 its membership included 75 percent of all those who had joined unions. Throughout its existence, however, the AFL had been unsure of the best way to deal with unskilled and semiskilled workers. Most of its members were skilled workers in specific crafts or trades. However, technological changes during World War I had brought about a significant increase in the number of unskilled and semiskilled employees in the work force. These people sought to join the AFL, but they were not well received by its established membership.

Some unions within the AFL did recognize the need to organize unskilled and semiskilled workers, and they began to penetrate the automotive and steel industries. The type of union they formed was an **industrial union,** an organization of both skilled and unskilled workers in a single industry. Soon workers in the rubber, mining, newspaper, and communications industries also were organized into unions. Eventually, these unions left the AFL and formed the *Congress of Industrial Organizations* (CIO).

industrial union an organization of both skilled and unskilled workers in a single industry

During this same time (the late 1930s), there was a major upswing in rank-and-file membership in the AFL, the CIO, and independent unions. Strong union leadership, the development of effective negotiating tactics, and favorable legislation combined to increase total union membership to nine million in 1940. At this point the CIO began to rival the AFL in size and influence. There was another bitter rivalry: The AFL and CIO often clashed over which of them had the right to organize and represent particular groups of employees.

Since World War II, the labor scene has gone through a number of changes. For one thing, during and after the war years there was a downturn in public opinion regarding unions. A few isolated but very visible strikes during the war caused public sentiment to shift against unionism. Perhaps the most significant occurrence, however, was the merger of the AFL and the CIO. After years of bickering, the two groups recognized that they were wasting effort and resources by fighting each other and that a merger would greatly increase the strength of both. The merger took place on December 5, 1955. The resulting organization, called the *AFL-CIO*, had a membership of as many as sixteen million workers, which made it the largest labor organization of its kind in the world. Its first president was George Meany, who served until 1979.

Organized Labor Today

learning objective

2 Discuss the sources of unions' negotiating power and trends in union membership.

The power of unions to negotiate effectively with management is derived from two sources. The first is their membership. The more workers a union represents within an industry, the greater is its clout in dealing with firms operating in that industry. The second source of union power is the group of laws that guarantee unions the right to negotiate and, at the same time, regulate the negotiating process.

Union Membership

At present, union members account for a relatively small portion of the American work force: Approximately 14.5 percent of the nation's workers belong to unions. Union membership is concentrated in a few industries and job categories. Within these industries, though, unions wield considerable power.

The AFL-CIO is still the largest union organization in this country, boasting approximately thirteen million members. Those represented by the AFL-CIO include actors, barbers, construction workers, carpenters, retail clerks, musicians, teachers, postal workers, painters, steel and iron workers, firefighters, bricklayers, and newspaper reporters. Figure 12.2 shows the organization of the AFL-CIO.

One of the largest unions not associated directly with the AFL-CIO is the *Teamsters Union.* The Teamsters were originally part of the AFL-CIO, but in 1957 they were expelled for corrupt and illegal practices. The union started out as an organization of professional drivers, but it has begun recently to recruit employees in a wide variety of jobs. Current membership is about 1.3 million workers.

The *United Auto Workers* (UAW) represents employees in the automobile industry. The UAW, too, originally was part of the AFL-CIO, but it left the parent union—of its own accord—in 1968. Currently, the UAW has about 748,000 members. For a while, the Teamsters and the UAW formed a semi-structured partnership called the *Alliance for Labor Action.* This partnership eventually was dissolved, and the UAW again became part of the AFL-CIO in 1981.

Membership Trends

The proportion of union members relative to the size of the nation's work force has declined over the last thirty years. Moreover, total union membership has dropped since 1980 despite steadily increasing membership in earlier years (see Figure 12.1). To a great extent, this decline in membership is caused by changing trends in business, such as the following:

- Heavily unionized industries have either been decreasing in size or have not been growing as fast as non-unionized industries. For example, cutbacks in the steel industry have tended to reduce union membership. At the same time, the growth of high-tech industries has increased the ranks of nonunion workers.
- Many firms have moved from the heavily unionized Northeast and Great Lakes regions to the less unionized Southeast and Southwest—the so-called Sunbelt. At the relocated plants, formerly unionized firms tend to hire nonunion workers.
- The largest growth in employment is occurring in the service industries, and these industries typically are not unionized.

Union membership trends today. In the face of declining union membership, John J. Sweeney, president of the AFL-CIO, has encouraged the unions that are part of AFL-CIO to increase membership through aggressive recruitment.

figure 12.2

AFL-CIO Organization Chart

Like a big corporation, the AFL-CIO has organized its chain of command to best attain its goals as well as the goals of the various unions it represents.

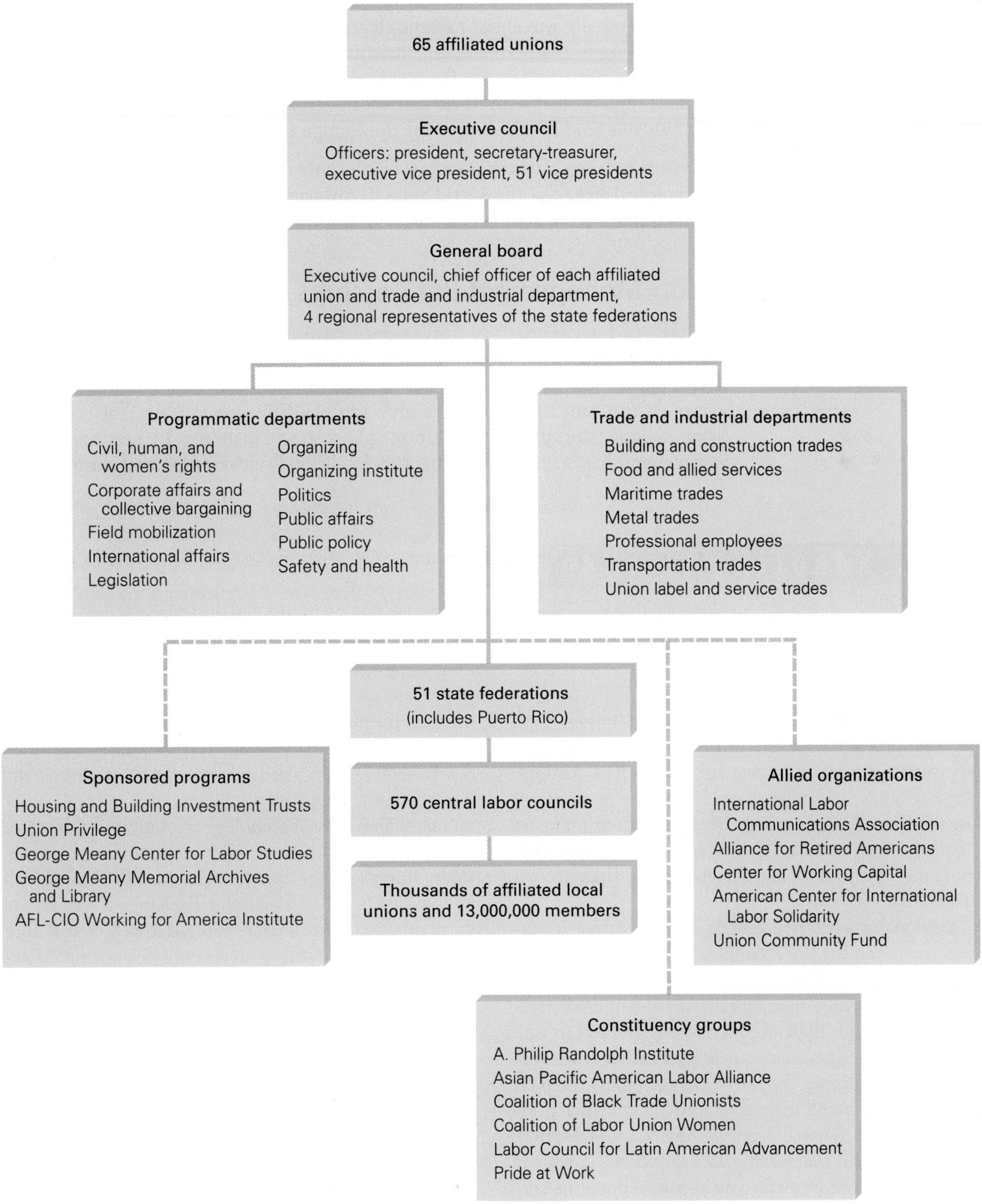

Source: Adapted from **www.aflcio.org/aboutaflcio/about/howworks/index.cfm** and **www.aflcio.org/aboutaflcio/about/howworks/organizationchart.cfm,** 2003.

- Some U.S. companies have moved their manufacturing operations to other countries where less unionized labor is employed.
- Management is providing benefits that tend to reduce employees' need for unionization. Increased employee participation and better wages and working conditions are goals of unions. When these benefits are already supplied by management, workers are less likely to join existing unions or start new ones. The number of elections to vote on forming new unions has declined. The unions usually win about half the elections.
- According to Alan Greenspan, chairman of the Federal Reserve, American labor laws and culture allow for the quicker displacement of unneeded workers and their replacement with those that are in demand, whereas labor laws in other countries tend to take longer for the change to take place.

It remains to be seen whether unions will be able to regain the prominence and power they enjoyed between the world wars and during the 1950s. There is little doubt, however, that they will remain a powerful force in particular industries.

Union-Management Partnerships

For most of the twentieth century, unions have represented workers with respect to wages and working conditions. To obtain rights for workers and recognition for themselves, unions have engaged in often-antagonistic collective-bargaining sessions and strikes. At the same time, management traditionally has protected its own rights of decision making, workplace organization, and strategic planning. Increasingly, however, management has become aware that this traditionally adversarial relationship does not

adapting to change

Labor Unions Play a Bigger Role in Corporate Governance

DURING THE PAST DECADE, unions have become increasingly active in the battle to reform the way public corporations manage themselves. Unions' pension funds hold more than $3 trillion in shares of large and small corporations. Because of their immense clout, they are successfully forcing corporations to become more responsive and accountable to shareholders in a number of ways.

One major issue is executive compensation. Teamsters' management, for example, was concerned about corporate executives receiving excessively high severance packages. The union therefore drafted a shareholder resolution calling for Bank of America shareholders to vote on any severance payments totaling more than twice the executive's annual pay. The bank's shareholders voted on the resolution, and a majority approved it. Labor pressure also has prompted Bank of America and Norfolk Southern to limit the use of *golden parachutes*, lavish pay packages for executives who may be forced out if the corporation is acquired.

Another issue is the relationship between accounting firms and the corporations whose financial statements they audit. Unions and many governance experts want to prevent corporations from hiring the same accounting firm for consulting and auditing projects because of the potential conflict of interest. Because they own nearly $100 million worth of shares in Walt Disney, the United Association of Plumbers and several other unions submitted a shareholder resolution to this effect for consideration at the corporation's annual meeting. Walt Disney's management fought the move, unsuccessfully asking the Securities and Exchange Commission for permission to keep the resolution from a vote. Before the meeting took place, however, a rising tide of accounting scandals at other corporations convinced Walt Disney to proactively announce that it would stop buying consulting services from its auditor. After unions submitted similar resolutions at thirty-three other companies, more than a dozen agreed to new restrictions on relations with accounting firms.

The AFL-CIO created an Office of Investment in 1997 to protect the interests of its unions' mammoth stock holdings. Other unions are joining the fight as well. Year by year, labor is stepping up the pace and scope of its initiatives, filing hundreds of resolutions to reform corporate governance for the benefit of all shareholders.

result in the kind of high-performance workplace and empowered work force necessary to succeed in today's highly competitive markets. For their part, unions and their members acknowledge that most major strikes result in failures that cost members thousands of jobs and reduce the union's credibility. Today, instead of maintaining an "us versus them" mentality, many unions are becoming partners with management, cooperating to enhance the workplace, empower workers, increase production, improve quality, and reduce costs. According to the Department of Labor, the number of union-management partnerships in the United States is increasing.

Union-management partnerships can be initiated by union leaders, employees, or management. *Limited partnerships* center on accomplishing one specific task or project, such as the introduction of teams or the design of training programs. For example, Levi Strauss formed a limited partnership with its employees who are members of the Amalgamated Clothing and Textile Workers Union to help the company in setting up team operations in its nonunion plants. *Long-range strategic partnerships* focus on sharing decision-making power for a whole range of workplace and business issues. Long-range partnerships sometimes begin as limited ones and develop slowly over time.

Although strategic union-management partnerships vary, most of them have several characteristics in common. First, strategic partnerships focus on developing cooperative relationships between unions and management instead of arguing over contractual rights. Second, partners work toward mutual gain, in which the organization becomes more competitive, employees are better off, and unions are stronger as a result of the partnership. Finally, as already noted, strategic partners engage in joint decision making on a broad array of issues.[2] These issues include performance expectations, organizational structure, strategic alliances, new technology, pay and benefits, employee security and involvement, union-management roles, product development, and education and training.

Good labor-management relations can help everyone to deal with new and difficult labor issues as they develop. For example, many companies hope that their union-management partnerships will be strong enough to deal with the critical issue of rising health care costs. Unions work hard to protect their members from having to pay an increased percentage of health care costs, and they have experienced some success, in that an average union worker pays about 18 percent of his or her health care costs compared to a nonunion worker's contribution of about 23 percent. Strong union-management partnerships will play a vital role in resolving health care issues.[3]

Union-management partnerships have many potential benefits for management, workers, and unions. For management, partnerships can result in lower costs, increased revenue, improved product quality, and greater customer satisfaction. For workers, benefits may include increased response to their needs, more decision-making opportunities, less supervision, more responsibility, and increased job security. Unions can gain credibility, strength, and increased membership.

Among the many organizations that have found union-management partnerships beneficial is Saturn. The labor-management partnership between the Saturn Corporation and the UAW is one of the boldest experiments in U.S. industrial relations today. It was created through a joint design effort that included the UAW as a full partner in decisions regarding product, technology, suppliers, retailers, site selection, business planning, training, quality systems, job design, and manufacturing systems. This partnership has resulted in a dense communications network throughout the company's management system as well as improvement in quality performance.[4]

Labor-Management Legislation

learning objective

3 Identify the main focus of several major pieces of labor-management legislation.

As we have noted, business opposed early efforts to organize labor. The federal government generally supported anti-union efforts through the court system, and in some cases federal troops were used to end strikes. Gradually, however, the government began to correct this imbalance through the legislative process.

Norris-LaGuardia Act

The first major piece of legislation to secure rights for unions, the *Norris-LaGuardia Act* of 1932, was considered a landmark in labor-management relations. This act made it difficult for businesses to obtain court orders that banned strikes, picketing, or union membership drives. Previously, courts had issued such orders readily as a means of curbing these activities.

National Labor Relations Act

The *National Labor Relations Act*, also known as the *Wagner Act*, was passed by Congress in 1935. It established procedures by which employees decide whether they want to be represented by a union. If workers choose to be represented, the Wagner Act requires management to negotiate with union representatives. Before this law was passed, union efforts sometimes were interpreted as violating the Sherman Act (1890) because they were viewed as attempts to monopolize. The Wagner Act also forbids certain unfair labor practices on the part of management, such as firing or punishing workers because they are pro-union, spying on union meetings, and bribing employees to vote against unionization.

National Labor Relations Board (NLRB) the federal agency that enforces the provisions of the Wagner Act

Finally, the Wagner Act established the **National Labor Relations Board (NLRB)** to enforce the provisions of the law. The NLRB is primarily concerned with (1) overseeing the elections in which employees decide whether they will be represented by a union and (2) investigating complaints lodged by unions or employees. For example, several employees at bulletproof vest manufacturer Point Blank Body Armor claimed that they were fired for leading a union organizing campaign at the company. The NLRB was concerned about the length of time a thorough investigation into the matter would take and ordered the company to rehire the workers.[5] In another recent action, the NLRB denied Allstate Insurance agents the right to form a union because the agents officially were classified as independent contractors. Independent contractors basically act as entrepreneurs and are not covered by the Wagner Act.[6]

Fair Labor Standards Act

In 1938, Congress enacted the *Fair Labor Standards Act*. One major provision of this act permits the federal government to set a minimum wage. The first minimum wage, which was set in the late 1930s and did not include farm workers and retail employees, was $0.25 an hour. Today the minimum wage is $5.15 an hour. Some employees, such as farm workers, are still exempt from the minimum-wage provisions. The act also requires that employees be paid overtime rates for work in excess of forty hours a week. Finally, it prohibits the use of child labor.

Labor-Management Relations Act

The legislation of the 1930s sought to discourage unfair practices on the part of employers. Recall from Figure 12.1 that union membership grew from approximately two million in 1910 to almost twelve million by 1945. Unions represented over 35 percent of all non-agricultural employees in 1945. As union membership and power grew, however, the federal government began to examine the practices of labor. Several long and bitter strikes, mainly in the coal mining and trucking industries, in the early 1940s led to a demand for legislative restraint on unions. As a result, in 1947 Congress passed the *Labor-Management Relations Act*, also known as the *Taft-Hartley Act*, over President Harry Truman's veto.

@ Using the Internet

The U.S. Department of Labor website (**http://www.dol.gov/**) provides a good overview of the major issues concerning labor news, legislation, and statistics. There are also links to other websites focusing on labor issues.

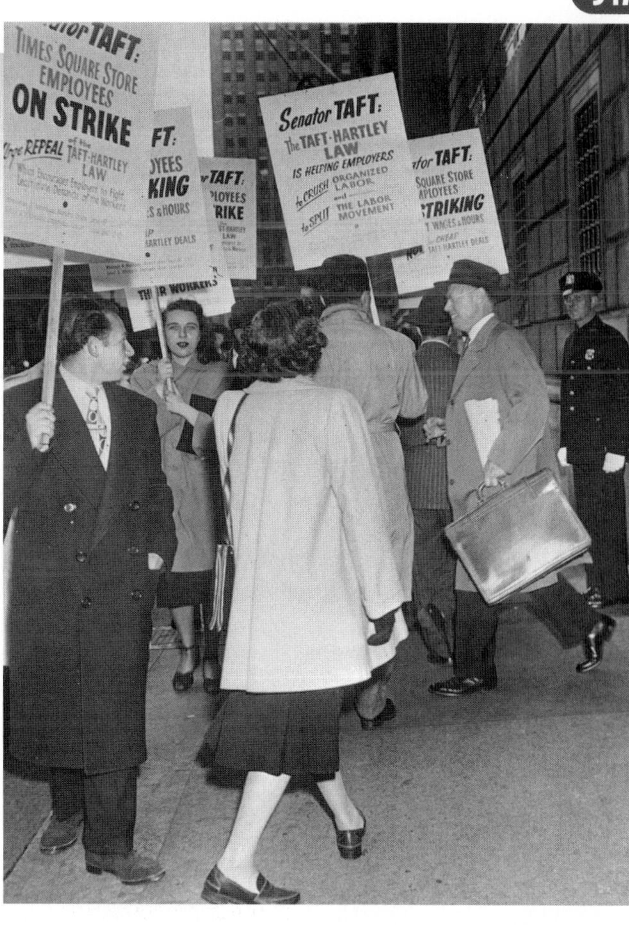

Protesting the Taft-Hartley Act. In 1949 Senator Robert Taft walked through a picket line that denounced the Taft-Hartley Act and called for its repeal.

The objective of the Taft-Hartley Act is to provide a balance between union power and management authority. It lists unfair labor practices that unions are forbidden to use. These include refusal to bargain with management in good faith, charging excessive membership dues, harassing non-union workers, and using various means of coercion against employers.

The Taft-Hartley Act also gives management more rights during union organizing campaigns. For example, management may outline for employees the advantages and disadvantages of union membership, as long as the information it presents is accurate. The act gives the president of the United States the power to obtain a temporary injunction to prevent or stop a strike that endangers national health and safety. An **injunction** is a court order requiring a person or group either to perform some act or to refrain from performing some act. President George W. Bush invoked the Taft-Hartley Act when union representatives could not reach an agreement with the Pacific Maritime Association. This ten-day shut-down delayed more than $12 billion worth of goods at a critical time for most retailers preparing for the holiday season. President Bush was the first to issue an injunction under this law since 1978.[7] Finally, the Taft-Hartley Act authorized states to enact laws to allow employees to work in a unionized firm without joining the union. About twenty states (many in the South) have passed such *right-to-work laws*.

injunction a court order requiring a person or group either to perform some act or to refrain from performing some act

Landrum-Griffin Act

In the 1950s, Senate investigations and hearings exposed racketeering in unions and uncovered cases of bribery, extortion, and embezzlement among union leaders. It was discovered that a few union leaders had taken union funds for personal use and accepted payoffs from employers for union protection. Some were involved in arson, blackmail, and murder. Public pressure for reform resulted in the 1959 *Landrum-Griffin Act*.

This law was designed to regulate the internal functioning of labor unions. Provisions of the law require unions to file annual reports with the U.S. Department of Labor regarding their finances, elections, and various decisions made by union officers. The Landrum-Griffin Act also ensures that each union member has the right to seek, nominate, and vote for each elected position in his or her union. It provides safeguards governing union funds, and it requires management and unions to report the lending of management funds to union officers, union members, or local unions.

The various pieces of legislation we have reviewed here effectively regulate much of the relationship between labor and management after a union has been established. The next section demonstrates that forming a union is also a carefully regulated process.

The Unionization Process

learning objective

4 Enumerate the steps involved in forming a union and show how the National Labor Relations Board is involved in the process.

For a union to be formed at a particular firm, some employees of the firm first must be interested in being represented by a union. Then they must take a number of steps to formally declare their desire for a union. To ensure fairness, most of the steps in this unionization process are supervised by the NLRB.

Why Some Employees Join Unions

Obviously, employees start or join a union for a variety of reasons. One commonly cited reason is to combat alienation. Some employees—especially those whose jobs are dull and repetitive—may perceive themselves as merely parts of a machine. They may feel that they lose their individual or social identity at work. Union membership is one way to establish contact with others in a firm.

Another common reason for joining a union is the perception that union membership increases job security. No one wants to live in fear of arbitrary or capricious dismissal from a job. Unions actually have only limited ability to guarantee a member's job, but they can help increase job security by enforcing seniority rules.

Employees also may join a union because of dissatisfaction with one or more elements of their jobs. If they are unhappy with their pay, benefits, or working conditions, they may look to a union to correct the perceived deficiencies.

Some people join unions because of their personal backgrounds. For example, a person whose parents are strong believers in unions might be inclined to feel just as positive about union membership.

examining ethics

UAW Tries to Organize Auto Parts Suppliers

UNION MEMBERSHIP in the U.S. auto parts industry has been on a roller-coaster ride. During the 1970s, 80 percent of the companies supplying auto parts to domestic automakers were unionized. Over the years, however, union membership dropped to 15 percent of suppliers. Now the UAW is working to reverse the downward trend through organizing campaigns at Johnson Controls, Intier Automotive, Metaldyne, and other suppliers.

Part of the UAW's strategy involves drawing Ford, General Motors, and DaimlerChrysler into the fray. Johnson Controls, for example, supplies instrument panels and other interior parts to all three U.S. automakers. Roughly 20 percent of the company's employees were already union members when the UAW called a two-day strike at four plants that make parts for the Chevy Trailblazer and Jeep Liberty SUVs. Because General Motors and DaimlerChrysler depend on Johnson to deliver parts on a very tight schedule, the strike disrupted production of the two fast-selling vehicles.

Therefore, say insiders, the two automakers worked behind the scenes to persuade Johnson to quickly settle the strike. Johnson's management decided to increase union workers' hourly wages and allow organizers to distribute authorization cards to 8,000 employees at twenty-six plants. The company also agreed to recognize the union if more than half the employees signed the cards rather than requiring a formal election. Two other suppliers, Metaldyne and Intier Automotive, also agreed to allow UAW organizing efforts at many plants. Unlike Johnson and Metaldyne, which both agreed to recognize the union if a majority of employees signed authorization cards, Intier insisted on a formal secret-ballot election.

On the positive side, industry publication *Automotive News* observes that employees at plants with poor working conditions and low wages will benefit from unionization. However, it also notes that the suppliers went along because they feared that a UAW strike could hurt them financially and threaten good relations with their customers, the automakers. The UAW's president says, "We're not a strike-happy union, but we're also not afraid to use a point of leverage to support workers who want UAW representation."

Issues to Consider

1. Is it ethical to use such pressure, even if employees benefit? Other than strike or threaten to strike, what do you think the UAW can and should do to unionize more plants?
2. Do you think that Ford, General Motors, and DaimlerChrysler should get involved in the UAW's attempt to organize auto parts workers? Explain your answer.

In some situations, employees *must* join a union to keep their jobs. Many unions try, through their labor contracts, to require that a firm's new employees join the union after a specified probationary period. Under the Taft-Hartley Act, states may pass right-to-work laws prohibiting this practice.

Spotlight

Union advantages

The AFL-CIO presents statistics showing advantages to union workers over nonunion workers. Workers who get...

Workers who get...	Union	Nonunion
Guaranteed pension	69%	14%
Health benefits	75%	49%
Short-term disability coverage	69%	30%
Life insurance coverage	82%	51%

Source: **www.aflcio.org/aboutunions/joinunions/whyjoin/uniondifference.**

Steps in Forming a Union

The first step in forming a union is the *organizing campaign* (see Figure 12.3). Its primary objective is to develop widespread employee interest in having a union. To kick off the campaign, a national union may send organizers to the firm to stir this interest. Alternatively, the employees themselves may decide that they want a union. Then they contact the appropriate national union and ask for organizing assistance.

The organizing campaign can be quite emotional, and it may lead to conflict between employees and management. On the one hand, the employees who want the union will be dedicated to its creation. On the other hand, management will be extremely sensitive to what it sees as a potential threat to its power and control.

At some point during the organizing campaign, employees are asked to sign *authorization cards* (see Figure 12.4 on p. 350) to indicate—in writing—their support for the union. Because of various NLRB rules and regulations, both union organizers and company management must be very careful in their behavior during this authorization drive. For example, employees cannot be asked to sign the cards when they are supposed to be working. And management may not indicate in any way that employees' jobs or job security will be in jeopardy if they *do* sign the cards.

If at least 30 percent of the eligible employees sign authorization cards, the organizers generally request that the firm recognize the union as the employees' bargaining representative. Usually the firm rejects this request, and a *formal election* is held to decide whether to have a union. This election usually involves secret ballots and is conducted by the NLRB. The outcome of the election is determined by a simple majority of eligible employees who choose to vote.

If the union obtains a majority, it becomes the official bargaining agent for its members, and the final step, *NLRB certification*, takes place. The union may immediately begin the process of negotiating a labor contract with management. If the union is voted down, the NLRB will not allow another election for one year.

Several factors can complicate the unionization process. For example, the **bargaining unit**, which is the specific group of employees that the union is to represent, must be defined. Union organizers may want to represent all hourly employees at a particular site (such as all workers at a manufacturing plant). Or they may wish to represent only a specific group of employees (such as all electricians in a large manufacturing plant).

Another issue that may have to be resolved is that of **jurisdiction,** which is the right of a particular union to organize particular groups of workers (such as nurses). When jurisdictions overlap or are unclear, the employees themselves may decide who will represent them. In some cases, two or more unions may be trying to organize some or all of the employees of a firm. Then the election choices may be union A, union B, or no union at all. A merger was proposed recently to combine two unions, the Screen Actors Guild and the American Federation of Television and Radio Artists. The combined union would have about 150,000 members and would be able to avoid some jurisdictional issues previously encountered by having more authority to represent actors, recording artists, and broadcasters.[8]

figure 12.3

Steps in Forming a Union

The unionization process consists of a campaign, signing of authorization cards, a formal election, and certification of the election by the National Labor Relations Board.

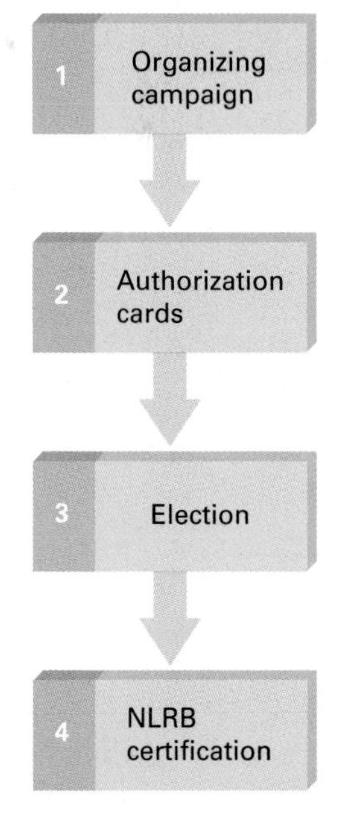

bargaining unit the specific group of employees represented by a union

jurisdiction the right of a particular union to organize particular workers

figure 12.4

Sample Authorization Card
Unions must have written authorization to represent employees.

OBLIGATION OF

"I ______________________ (PLEASE PRINT NAME), in the presence of members of the ______________________ promise and agree to conform to and abide by the Constitution and laws of the __________ and its Local Unions. I will further the purpose for which the __________ is instituted. I will bear true allegiance to it and will not sacrifice its interest in any manner."

____
(TO BE SIGNED BY APPLICANT — PLEASE DO NOT PRINT)

PRINT OR TYPE IN BLACK INK ONLY

SEX – MALE ☐ FEMALE ☐

LAST NAME FIRST INITIAL	SOCIAL SECURITY NO.
ADDRESS (STREET & NUMBER)	DATE OF BIRTH
CITY & STATE (OR PROVINCE) POSTAL CODE	TELEPHONE NO.
PRESENT EMPLOYER	DATE HIRED
CLASSIFICATION	DATE OF THIS APPLICATION

Have you ever been a member of ? YES ☐ NO ☐ If so, where? LOCAL NO. STATE

PORTION BELOW TO BE FILLED IN BY L.U. SECRETARY

LOCAL UNION NO.	DATE OF INITIATION	TYPE OF MEMBERSHIP	CARD NO.

The Role of the NLRB

As we have demonstrated, the NLRB is heavily involved in the unionization process. Generally, the NLRB is responsible for overseeing the organizing campaign, conducting the election (if one is warranted), and certifying the election results.

During the organizing campaign, both employers and union organizers can take steps to educate employees regarding the advantages and disadvantages of having a union. However, neither is allowed to use underhanded tactics or to distort the truth. If violations occur, the NLRB can stop the questionable behavior, postpone the election, or set aside the results of an election that has already taken place.

The NLRB usually conducts the election within forty-five days of receiving the required number of signed authorization cards from the organizers. A very high percentage of the eligible voters generally participates in the election, and it is held at the workplace during normal working hours. In certain cases, however, a mail ballot or other form of election may be called for.

Certification of the election involves counting the votes and considering challenges to the election. After the election results are announced, management and the union organizers have five days in which to challenge the election. The basis for a challenge might be improper conduct prior to the election or participation by an ineligible voter. After considering any challenges, the NLRB passes final judgment on the election results.

When union representation is established, union and management get down to the serious business of contract negotiations.

Collective Bargaining

learning objective

5 Describe the basic elements in the collective-bargaining process.

Once certified by the NLRB, a new union's first task is to establish its own identity and structure. It immediately signs up as many members as possible. Then, in an internal election, members choose officers and representatives. A negotiating committee is also chosen to begin **collective bargaining,** the process of negotiating a labor contract with management.

collective bargaining the process of negotiating a labor contract with management

The First Contract

To prepare for its first contract session with management, the negotiating committee decides on its position on the various contract issues and determines the issues that are most important to the union's members. For example, the two most pressing concerns might be a general wage increase and an improved benefits package.

The union then informs management that it is ready to begin negotiations, and the two parties agree on a time and location. Both sides continue to prepare for the session up to the actual date of the negotiations.

Negotiations occasionally are held on company premises, but it is more common for the parties to meet away from the workplace—perhaps in a local hotel. The union typically is represented by the negotiating committee and one or more officials from the regional or national union office. The firm normally is represented by managers from the industrial-relations, operations, HRM, and legal departments. Each side is required by law to negotiate in good faith and not to stall or attempt to extend the bargaining proceedings unnecessarily.

The union normally presents its contract demands first. Management then responds to the demands, often with a counter-proposal. The bargaining may move back and forth, from proposal to counter-proposal, over a number of meetings. Throughout the process, union representatives constantly keep their members informed of what is going on and how the negotiating committee feels about the various proposals and counter-proposals.

Each side clearly tries to "get its own way" as much as possible, but each also recognizes the need for compromise. For example, the union may begin the negotiations by demanding a wage increase of $1 per hour but may be willing to accept 60 cents per hour. Management initially may offer 40 cents but may be willing to pay 75 cents.

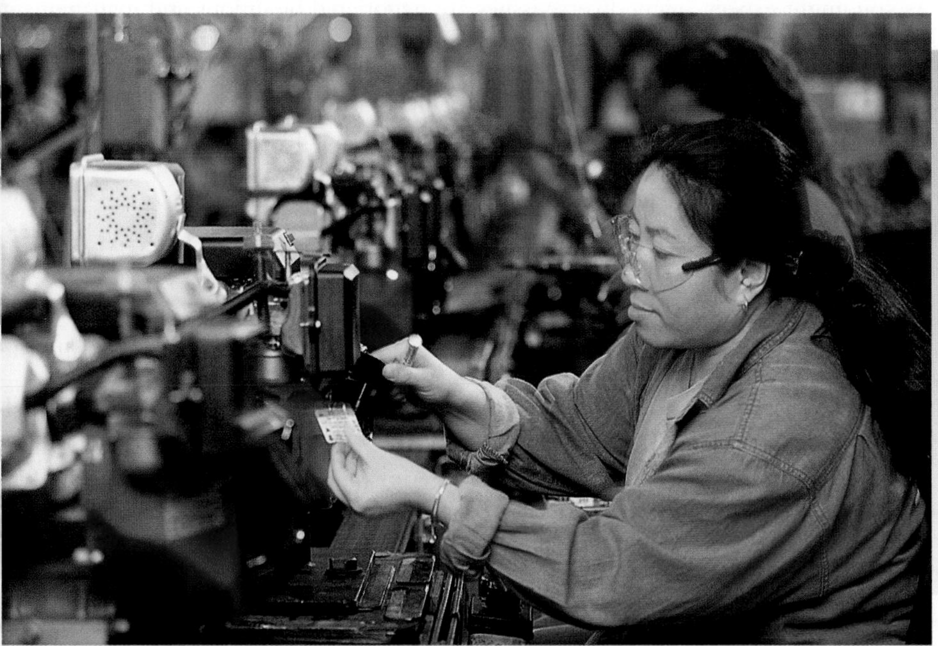

Will collective bargaining occur? To take advantage of lower cost, non-union labor, Briggs and Stratton—manufacturer of small gasoline-powered engines—moved its production operations from a single, enormous production facility in Milwaukee, to six considerably smaller plants in the South. Because the new facilities are considerably smaller and highly automated with a smaller number of workers, it is less likely that its workers will join unions.

Eventually, the two sides will agree on a wage increase of between 60 and 75 cents per hour.

If an agreement cannot be reached, the union may strike. Strikes are rare during a union's first contract negotiations. In most cases, the negotiating teams are able to agree on an initial contract without recourse to a strike.

ratification approval of a labor contract by a vote of the union membership

The final step in collective bargaining is **ratification,** which is approval of the contract by a vote of the union membership. If the membership accepts the terms of the contract, it is signed and becomes a legally binding agreement. If the contract is not ratified, the negotiators must go back and try to iron out a more acceptable agreement.

Later Contracts

A labor contract may cover a period of one to three years or more, but every contract has an expiration date. As that date approaches, both management and the union begin to prepare for new contract negotiations. Now, however, the entire process is likely to be much thornier than the first negotiation.

For one thing, the union and the firm have "lived with each other" for several years, during which some difficulties may have emerged. Each side may see certain issues as being of critical importance—issues that provoke a great deal of emotion at the bargaining table and often are difficult to resolve. For another thing, each side has learned from the earlier negotiations. Each may take a harder line on certain issues and be less willing to compromise.

The contract deadline itself also produces tension. As the expiration date of the existing contract draws near, each side feels pressure—real or imagined—to reach an agreement. This pressure may nudge the negotiators toward agreement, but it also can have the opposite effect, making an accord more difficult to reach. Moreover, at some point during the negotiations, union leaders are likely to take a *strike vote*. This vote reveals whether union members are willing to strike in the event that a new contract is not negotiated before the old one expires. In almost all cases this vote supports a strike. Thus the threat of a strike may add to the pressure mounting on both sides as they go about the business of negotiating.

Union-Management Contract Issues

learning objective

6 Identify the major issues covered in a union-management contract.

As you might expect, many diverse issues are negotiated by unions and management and are incorporated into a labor contract. Unions tend to emphasize issues related to members' income, their standard of living, and the strength of the union. Management's primary goals are to retain as much control as possible over the firm's operations and to maximize its strength relative to that of the union. The balance of power between union and management varies from firm to firm.

Employee Pay

An area of bargaining central to union-management relations is employee pay. Three separate issues usually are involved: the forms of pay, the magnitude of pay, and the means by which the magnitude of pay will be determined.

Forms of Pay The primary form of pay is direct compensation—the wage or salary and benefits an employee receives in exchange for his or her contribution to the organization. Because direct compensation is a fairly straightforward issue, negotiators often spend much more of their time developing a benefits package for employees. And as the range of benefits and their costs have escalated over the years, this element of pay has become increasingly important and complex.

We discussed the various employee benefits in Chapter 10. Of these, health, life, disability, and dental insurance are important benefits that unions try to obtain for heir members. As the costs of health care continue to increase, insurance benefits are costing employers more, and many are trying to pass a portion of this increased cost on to their employees. Unions do not take these increased burdens lightly, and health care benefits recently led to the first General Electric strike in over thirty years. Many large companies such as General Motors, Ford, Lucent, and Goodyear will face these issues as they negotiate new union contracts in the near future.[9] Deferred compensation, in the form of pension or retirement programs, is also a common focal point. Decisions about deferred compensation can have a long-lasting impact on a company. General Motors is still suffering from the hefty compensation payments that it agreed to back in 1990 to appease the UAW. These payments add an extra $1,350 in costs to every car General Motors manufactures compared with a Japanese car built at a nonunion U.S. plant. General Motors will spend many years and billions of dollars paying these retired UAW employees.[10]

Other benefits commonly dealt with in the bargaining process include paid vacation time, holidays, and a policy on paid sick leave. Obviously, unions argue for as much paid vacation and holiday time as possible and for liberal sick-leave policies. Management naturally takes the opposite position.

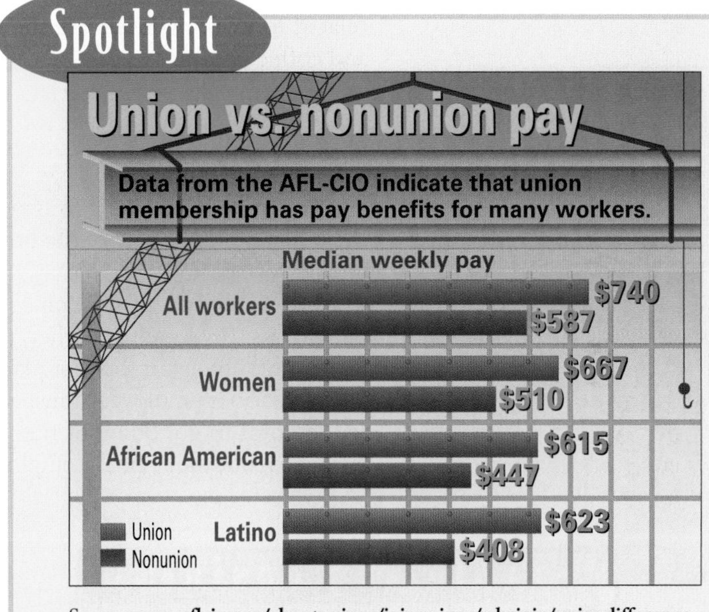

Source: www.aflcio.org/aboutunions/joinunions/whyjoin/uniondifference.

Magnitude of Pay Of considerable importance is the *magnitude*, or amount, of pay that employees receive as both direct and indirect compensation. The union attempts to ensure that pay is on par with that received by other employees in the same or similar industries, both locally and nationally. The union also attempts to include in the contract clauses that provide pay increases over the life of the agreement. The most common is the *cost-of-living clause*, which ties periodic pay increases to increases in the cost of living, as defined by various economic statistics or indicators.

Of course, the magnitude of pay is also affected by the organization's ability to pay. If the firm has posted large profits recently, the union may expect large pay increases for its members. If the firm has not been very profitable, the union may agree to smaller pay hikes or even to a pay freeze. In an extreme situation (e.g., when the firm is bordering on bankruptcy), the union may agree to pay cuts. Very stringent conditions usually are included in any agreement to a pay cut.

Bargaining with regard to magnitude also revolves around employee benefits. At one extreme, unions seek a wide range of benefits, entirely or largely paid for by the firm. At the other extreme, management may be willing to offer the benefits package but may want its employees to bear most of the cost. Again, factors such as equity (with similar firms and jobs) and ability to pay enter into the final agreement.

Pay Determinants Negotiators also address the question of how individual pay will be determined. For management, the ideal arrangement is to tie wages to each employee's productivity. As we saw, this method of payment tends to motivate and reward effort. Unions, on the other hand, feel that this arrangement can create unnecessary competition among employees. They generally argue that employees should be paid—at least in part—according to seniority. **Seniority** is the length of time an employee has worked for the organization.

seniority the length of time an employee has worked for an organization

Determinants regarding benefits also are negotiated. For example, management may want to provide profit-sharing benefits only to employees who have worked for the firm for a specified number of years. The union may want these benefits provided to all employees.

Working Hours

overtime time worked in excess of forty hours in one week; under some union contracts, time worked in excess of eight hours in a single day

Working hours are another important issue in contract negotiations. The matter of overtime is of special interest. Federal law defines **overtime** as time worked in excess of forty hours in one week. And it specifies that overtime pay must be at least one and one-half times the normal hourly wage. Unions may attempt to negotiate overtime rates for all hours worked beyond eight hours in a single day. Similarly, the union may attempt to obtain higher overtime rates (say, twice the normal hourly wage) for weekend or holiday work. Still another issue is an upper limit to overtime, beyond which employees can refuse to work.

In firms with two or more work shifts, workers on less desirable shifts are paid a premium for their time. Both the amount of the premium and the manner in which workers are chosen for (or choose) particular shifts are negotiable issues. Other issues related to working hours are the work starting times and the length of lunch periods and coffee breaks.

Security

Security actually covers two issues. One is the job security of the individual worker; the other is the security of the union as the bargaining representative of the firm's employees.

job security protection against the loss of employment

Job security is protection against the loss of employment. It is a major concern of individuals. As we noted earlier, the desire for increased job security is a major reason for joining unions in the first place. In the typical labor contract, job security is based on seniority. If employees must be laid off or dismissed, those with the least seniority are the first to go. Some of the more senior employees may have to move to lower-level jobs, but they remain employed.

exploring business

Will Strikes Score or Strike Out?

BASEBALL PLAYERS walking the picket line? Hockey players locked out of their arenas? Welcome to the major leagues, where relations between the unionized players and the team owners have not always been cordial. In 1994, the Players Association called a strike against the Major League Baseball owners that lasted so long the World Series was canceled. In the winter of 1994–1995, National Hockey League (NHL) team owners locked out members of the Player's Association for 104 days, resulting in a shortened forty-eight-game season. Even the Women's National Basketball Association has seen labor strife between the Players Association and the team owners.

Salary limits are a key issue for both sides in nearly every sport. To provide more financial stability, the owners want to institute or maintain caps to keep salaries from spiraling out of control. Players in the National Football League and the National Basketball Association already face salary caps, but baseball and hockey players want to avoid the imposition of salary caps.

Big money is at stake. In the NHL, players earn an average annual salary of approximately $1.7 million—more than twice the average salary players received before the 1994 lockout. Professional baseball players earn an average annual salary of $2.4 million, nearly double the average before the 1994 strike. Superstars such as Alex Rodriguez can negotiate considerably more. Rodriguez, for example, negotiated a $252-million ten-year contract with the Texas Rangers. On the other hand, after the baseball union and owners agreed on a pact in 2002, many owners sought to minimize their labor costs by offering shorter-term contracts and lower salaries to players not considered stars.

Because many players enjoy supersized salaries and owners generally are wealthy, fans are often far less sympathetic to sports labor disputes than they are to other labor disputes. Baseball lost a large number of fans after the 1994 strike, a fact that players and owners kept in mind as they successfully resolved their differences in 2002 without disrupting any games. Ultimately, fans are likely to continue as an invisible but important influence on sports as the players and the owners negotiate collective-bargaining agreements in the future.

Union security is protection of the union's position as the employees' bargaining agent. Union security is frequently a more volatile issue than job security. Unions strive for as much security as possible, but management tends to see an increase in union security as an erosion of its control.

union security protection of the union's position as the employees' bargaining agent

Union security arises directly from its membership. The greater the ratio of union employees to nonunion employees, the more secure the union is. In contract negotiations, unions thus attempt to establish various union membership conditions. The most restrictive of these is the **closed shop,** in which workers must join the union before they are hired. This condition was outlawed by the Taft-Hartley Act, but several other arrangements, including the following, are subject to negotiation:

closed shop a workplace in which workers must join the union before they are hired; outlawed by the Taft-Hartley Act

- The **union shop,** in which new employees must join the union after a specified probationary period
- The **agency shop,** in which employees can choose not to join the union but must pay dues to the union anyway (The idea is that nonunion employees benefit from union activities and should help to support them.)
- The **maintenance shop,** in which an employee who joins the union must remain a union member as long as he or she is employed by the firm

union shop a workplace in which new employees must join the union after a specified probationary period

agency shop a workplace in which employees can choose not to join the union but must pay dues to the union anyway

maintenance shop a workplace in which an employee who joins the union must remain a union member as long as he or she is employed by the firm

Management Rights

Of particular interest to the firm are those rights and privileges that are to be retained by management. For example, the firm wants as much control as possible over whom it hires, how work is scheduled, and how discipline is handled. The union, in contrast, would like some control over these and other matters affecting its members. It is interesting that some unions are making progress toward their goal of playing a more direct role in corporate governance. Some union executives have, in fact, been given seats on corporate boards of directors.

Grievance Procedures

A **grievance procedure** is a formally established course of action for resolving employee complaints against management. Virtually every labor contract contains a grievance procedure. Procedures vary in scope and detail, but they may involve all four steps described below (see Figure 12.5 on p. 356).

grievance procedure a formally established course of action for resolving employee complaints against management

Original Grievance The process begins with an employee who believes that he or she has been treated unfairly, in violation of the labor contract. For example, an employee may be entitled to a formal performance review after six months on the job. If no such review is conducted, the employee may file a grievance. To do so, the employee explains the grievance to a **shop steward,** an employee elected by union members to serve as their representative. The employee and the steward then discuss the grievance with the employee's immediate supervisor. Both the grievance and the supervisor's response are put in writing.

shop steward an employee elected by union members to serve as their representative

Broader Discussion In most cases the problem is resolved during the initial discussion with the supervisor. If it is not, a second discussion is held. Now the participants include the original parties (employee, supervisor, and steward), a representative from the union's grievance committee, and the firm's industrial-relations representative. Again, a record is kept of the discussion and its results.

Full-Scale Discussion If the grievance is still not resolved, a full-scale discussion is arranged. This discussion includes everyone involved in the broader discussion, as well as all remaining members of the union's grievance committee and another high-level manager. As usual, all proceedings are put in writing. All participants are careful not to violate the labor contract during this attempt to resolve the complaint.

figure 12.5

Steps in Resolving a Grievance

The employee grievance procedure for most organizations consists of four steps. Each ensuing step involves all the personnel from the preceding step plus at least one higher-level person. The final step is to go to a neutral third party, the arbitrator.

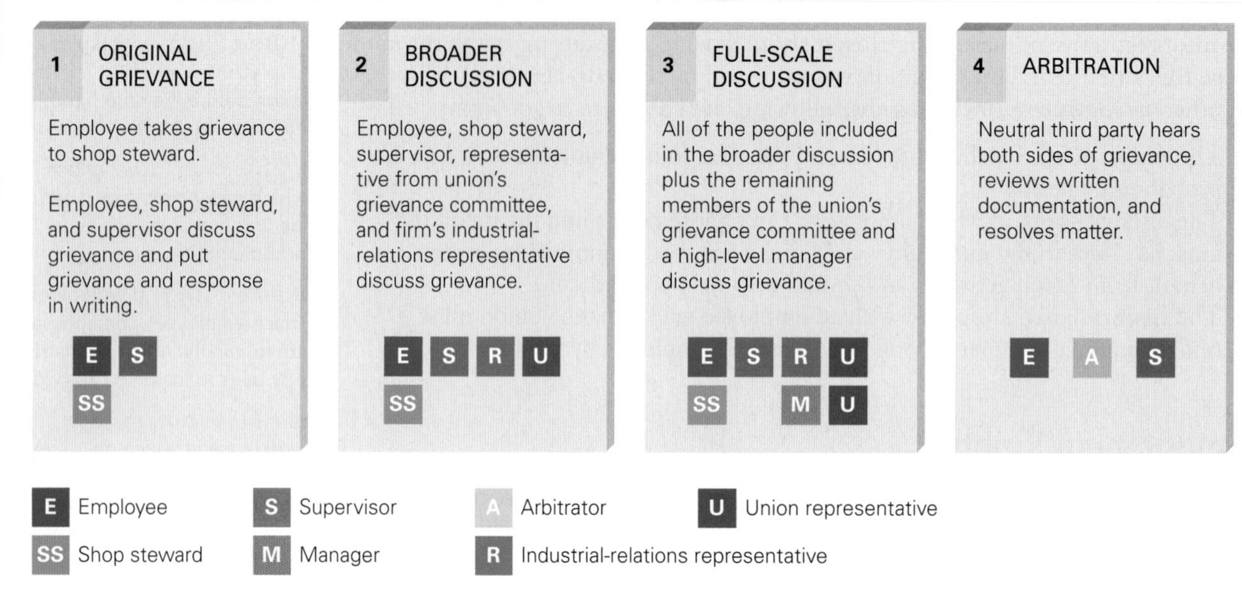
1 ORIGINAL GRIEVANCE
Employee takes grievance to shop steward.
Employee, shop steward, and supervisor discuss grievance and put grievance and response in writing.
E S
SS
2 BROADER DISCUSSION
Employee, shop steward, supervisor, representative from union's grievance committee, and firm's industrial-relations representative discuss grievance.
E S R U
SS
3 FULL-SCALE DISCUSSION
All of the people included in the broader discussion plus the remaining members of the union's grievance committee and a high-level manager discuss grievance.
E S R U
SS M U
4 ARBITRATION
Neutral third party hears both sides of grievance, reviews written documentation, and resolves matter.
E A S
E Employee
S Supervisor
A Arbitrator
U Union representative
SS Shop steward
M Manager
R Industrial-relations representative

arbitration the step in a grievance procedure in which a neutral third party hears the two sides of a dispute and renders a decision

Arbitration The final step in a grievance procedure is **arbitration,** in which a neutral third party hears the grievance and renders a binding decision. As in a court hearing, each side presents its case and has the right to cross-examine witnesses. In addition, the arbitrator reviews the written documentation of all previous steps in the grievance procedure. Both sides may then give summary arguments and/or present briefs. The arbitrator then decides whether a provision of the labor contract has been violated and proposes a remedy. The arbitrator cannot make any decision that would add to, detract from, or modify the terms of the contract. If it can be proved that the arbitrator exceeded the scope of his or her authority, either party may appeal the decision to the courts.

What actually happens when union and management "lock horns" over all the issues we have mentioned? We can answer this question by looking now at the negotiating tools each side can wield.

Union and Management Negotiating Tools

learning objective 7 Explain the primary bargaining tools available to unions and management.

Management and unions can draw on certain tools to influence each other during contract negotiations. Both sides may use advertising and publicity to gain support for their respective positions. The most extreme tools are strikes and lockouts, but there are other, milder techniques as well.

Strikes

Unions go out on strike only in a very few instances and almost always only after an existing labor contract has expired. (In 2001, there were only twenty-four major strikes in the private sector—*major* meaning those involving over 1,000 workers.[11])

Even then, if new contract negotiations seem to be proceeding smoothly, a union does not actually start a strike. The union does take a strike vote, but the vote may be used primarily to show members' commitment to a strike if negotiations fail.

The main objective of a strike is to put financial pressure on the company to encourage management to meet unions' demands. When union members do go out on strike, it is usually because negotiations seem to be stalled. A strike is simply a work stoppage: The employees do not report for work. In addition, striking workers engage in **picketing,** marching back and forth in front of their place of employment with signs informing the public that a strike is in progress. In doing so, they hope that (1) the public will be sympathetic to the strikers and will not patronize the struck firm, (2) nonstriking employees of the firm will honor the picket line and not report to work either, and (3) members of other unions will not cross the picket line (e.g., to make deliveries) and thus will further restrict the operations of the struck firm. Unions also may engage in informational picketing to let companies know of their dissatisfaction. For example, American Eagle pilots who are members of the Air Line Pilots Association International (ALPA), held an informational picketing at two international airports to protest management's recent decisions about the company's future. With 66,000 members, ALPA is the largest and oldest pilot union in the world.[12]

Using a strike to negotiate. A strike can increase public support for the union's cause and decrease the firm's ability to operate effectively. These employees at General Electric are using the strike as a negotiating tool to protest rising health costs.

Obviously, strikes are expensive to both the firm and the strikers. The firm loses business and earnings during the strike, and the striking workers lose the wages they would have earned if they had been at their jobs. During a strike, unions try to provide their members with as much support as possible. Larger unions are able to put a portion of their members' dues into a *strike fund.* The fund is used to provide financial support for striking union members. At times, workers may go out on a **wildcat strike,** which is a strike that has not been approved by the union. In this situation, union leaders typically work with management to convince the strikers to return to work.

picketing marching back and forth in front of a place of employment with signs informing the public that a strike is in progress

wildcat strike a strike not approved by the strikers' union

Slowdowns and Boycotts

Almost every labor contract contains a clause that prohibits strikes during the life of the contract. (This is why strikes, if they occur, usually take place after a contract has expired.) However, a union may strike a firm while the contract is in force if members believe that management has violated its terms. Workers also may engage in a **slowdown,** a technique whereby workers report to their jobs but work at a pace that is slower than normal.

slowdown a technique whereby workers report to their jobs but work at a slower pace than normal

boycott a refusal to do business with a particular firm

A **boycott** is a refusal to do business with a particular firm. Unions occasionally bring this strategy to bear by urging members (and sympathizers) not to purchase the products of a firm with which they are having a dispute. The AFL-CIO and the Paper, Allied-Industrial, Chemical and Energy Workers Union (PACE) launched a boycott against Graphic Packaging Corporation (GPC) and its controlling owner, Coors Brewing Company, urging union members and sympathizers not to purchase Coors Beer or other products sold in GPC packaging. This boycott is the union's response to GPC's demands for employees to work extended hours and on their scheduled days off including weekends and holidays.[13] A *primary boycott,* aimed at the employer directly involved in the dispute, can be a powerful weapon. A *secondary boycott*, aimed at a firm doing business with the employer, is prohibited by the Taft-Hartley Act. Cesar Chavez, a migrant worker who founded the United Farm Workers Union, used boycotts to draw attention to the low pay and awful conditions endured by produce pickers.

Lockouts and Strikebreakers

lockout a firm's refusal to allow employees to enter the workplace

Management's most potent weapon is the lockout. In a **lockout,** the firm refuses to allow employees to enter the workplace. Like strikes, lockouts are expensive for both the firm and its employees. For this reason, they are used rarely and then only in certain circumstances. A firm that produces perishable goods, for example, may use a lockout if management believes that its employees will soon go on strike. The idea is to stop production in time to ensure minimal spoilage of finished goods or work in process.

strikebreaker a nonunion employee who performs the job of a striking union member

Management also may attempt to hire strikebreakers. A **strikebreaker** is a nonunion employee who performs the job of a striking union member. Hiring strikebreakers can result in violence when picketing employees confront the nonunion workers at the entrance to the struck facility. The firm also faces the problem of finding qualified replacements for the striking workers. Sometimes management personnel take over the jobs of strikers. Managers at telephone companies have handled the switchboards on more than one occasion.

Mediation and Arbitration

Strikes and strikebreaking and lockouts and boycotts all pit one side against the other. Ultimately, one side "wins" and the other "loses." Unfortunately, the negative effects of such actions—including resentment, fear, and distrust—may linger for months or years after a dispute has been resolved.

More productive techniques that are being used increasingly are mediation and arbitration. Either one may come into play before a labor contract expires or after some other strategy, such as a strike, has proved ineffective.

mediation the use of a neutral third party to assist management and the union during their negotiations

Mediation is the use of a neutral third party to assist management and the union during their negotiations. This third party (the mediator) listens to both sides, trying to find common ground for agreement. The mediator also tries to facilitate communication between the two sides, to promote compromise, and generally to keep the negotiations moving. At first the mediator may meet privately with each side. Eventually, however, his or her goal is to get the two to settle their differences at the bargaining table. UPS uses a form of mediation in its negotiations between its union members and management. The method involves both the Independent Pilots Union and UPS identifying problem areas and developing solutions under the guidance of the National Mediation Board. This mediation approach has reduced the time and conflict involved in negotiating contracts.[14]

Unlike mediation, the *arbitration* step is a formal hearing. Just as it may be the final step in a grievance procedure, it also may be used in contract negotiations (perhaps after mediation attempts) when the two sides cannot agree on one or more issues. Here, the arbitrator hears the formal positions of both parties on outstanding, unresolved issues. The arbitrator then analyzes these positions and makes a decision on the possible resolution of the issues. If both sides have agreed in advance that the arbitration will be *binding*, they must accept the arbitrator's decision.

If mediation and arbitration are unsuccessful, then, under the provisions of the Taft-Hartley Act, the president of the United States can obtain a temporary injunction to prevent or stop a strike if it would jeopardize national health or security.

This chapter ends our discussion of human resources. Next, we examine the marketing function of business. We begin, in Chapter 13, by discussing the meaning of the term *marketing* and the various markets for products and services.

Return To inside business

Tensions were running high between management and labor at United Airlines even before the carrier filed for bankruptcy. Management had demanded and received contract concessions from the unions in the past, and other disputes had stirred up ill feelings on both sides. After the bankruptcy filing, the judge's order to cut pay for the 35,000 members of the machinists' union did not improve the situation.

Union officials and members expressed concern that management had not been completely candid in discussing possible solutions to the carrier's problems. A United mechanic in California told the *New York Times* that "we're disappointed the company has not negotiated with us and not come up with a good business plan." This view was echoed by a spokesperson for the pilots' union, who noted that "the pilots are doing their fair share for the company to meet its financing goals. But the company has to do more for [the union] in terms of being transparent and talking to us about what their long-term goals are." If not, he warned, "There's a point where the level of frustration will boil over." United might be grounded forever if relations between labor and management did not improve.

Questions

1. If you had been heading the machinists' union, what negotiating tools would you have used to influence management before and after United's bankruptcy filing? Why?
2. If you had joined United's management team after the bankruptcy filing, what would you have suggested to improve relations with all five unions?

chapter review

Summary

Explain how and why labor unions came into being.

A labor union is an organization of workers who act together to negotiate wages and working conditions with their employers. Labor relations are the dealings between labor unions and business management.

The first major union in the United States was the Knights of Labor, formed in 1869 to eliminate the depersonalization of workers. The Knights were followed in 1886 by the American Federation of Labor (AFL). The goal of the AFL was to improve its members' living standards without changing the business system. In 1905 the radical Industrial Workers of the World (IWW) was formed; its goal was the overthrow of capitalism. Of these three, only the AFL remained when the Congress of Industrial Organizations (CIO) was founded as a body of industrial unions between World War I and World War II. After years of competing, the AFL and CIO merged in 1955. The largest union not affiliated with the AFL-CIO is the Teamsters Union.

Discuss the sources of unions' negotiating power and trends in union membership.

The power of unions to negotiate with management comes from two sources. The first is the size of their membership. The second source is the groups of laws that guarantee unions the right to negotiate and that regulate the negotiation process. At present, union membership accounts for less than 15 percent of the American work force, and it seems to be decreasing for various reasons. Nonetheless, unions wield considerable power in many industries—those in which their members comprise a large proportion of the work force.

Many unions today are entering into partnerships with management rather than maintaining their traditional adversarial position. Unions and management cooperate to increase production, improve quality, lower costs, empower workers, and enhance the workplace. Limited partnerships center on accomplishing one specific task or project. Long-range strategic partnerships focus on sharing decision-making power for a range of workplace and business matters.

Identify the main focus of several major pieces of labor-management legislation.

Important laws that affect union power are the Norris-LaGuardia Act (limits management's ability to obtain injunctions against unions), the Wagner Act (forbids certain unfair labor practices by management), the Fair Labor Standards Act (allows the federal government to set the minimum wage and to mandate overtime rates), the Taft-Hartley Act (forbids certain unfair practices by unions), and the Landrum-Griffin Act (regulates the internal functioning of labor unions). The National Labor Relations Board (NLRB), a federal agency that oversees union-management relations, was created by the Wagner Act.

Enumerate the steps involved in forming a union and show how the National Labor Relations Board is involved in the process.

Attempts to form a union within a firm begin with an organizing campaign to develop widespread employee interest in having a union. Next, employees sign authorization cards indicating in writing their support for the union. The third step is to hold a formal election to decide whether to have a union. Finally, if the union obtains a majority, it receives NLRB certification, making it the official bargaining agent for its members. The entire process is supervised by the NLRB, which oversees the organizing campaign, conducts the election, and certifies the election results.

Describe the basic elements in the collective-bargaining process.

Once a union is established, it may negotiate a labor contract with management through the process of collective bargaining. First, the negotiating committee decides on its position on the various contract issues. The union informs management that it is ready to begin negotiations, and a time and place are set. The union is represented by the negotiating committee, and the organization is represented by managers from several departments in the company. Each side is required to negotiate in good faith and not to stall or attempt to extend the bargaining unnecessarily. The final step is ratification, which is approval of the contract by a vote of the union membership.

Identify the major issues covered in a union-management contract.

As the expiration date of an existing contract approaches, management and the union begin to negotiate a new contract. Contract issues include employee pay and benefits, working hours, job and union security, management rights, and grievance procedures.

Explain the primary bargaining tools available to unions and management.

Management and unions can use certain tools to sway one another—and public opinion—during contract negotiations. Advertising and publicity help each side gain support. When contract negotiations do not run smoothly, unions may apply pressure on management through strikes, slowdowns, or boycotts. Management may counter by imposing lockouts or hiring strikebreakers. Less drastic techniques for breaking contract deadlocks are mediation and arbitration. In both, a neutral third party is involved in the negotiations.

Key Terms

You should now be able to define and give an example relevant to each of the following terms:

labor union (339)
union-management (labor) relations (339)
craft union (339)
strike (341)
industrial union (341)
National Labor Relations Board (NLRB) (346)
injunction (347)
bargaining unit (349)
jurisdiction (349)
collective bargaining (351)
ratification (352)
seniority (353)
overtime (354)
job security (354)
union security (355)
closed shop (355)
union shop (355)
agency shop (355)
maintenance shop (355)
grievance procedure (355)
shop steward (355)
arbitration (356)
picketing (357)
wildcat strike (357)
slowdown (357)
boycott (357)
lockout (358)
strikebreaker (358)
mediation (358)

Review Questions

1. Briefly describe the history of unions in the United States.
2. Describe the three characteristics common to most union-management partnerships. Discuss the benefits of union-management partnerships to management, unions, and workers.
3. How has government regulation of union-management relations evolved during this century?
4. For what reasons do employees start or join unions?
5. Describe the process of forming a union, and explain the role of the National Labor Relations Board (NLRB) in that process.
6. List the major areas that are negotiated in a labor contract.
7. Explain the three issues involved in negotiations concerning employee pay.
8. What is the difference between job security and union security? How do unions attempt to enhance union security?
9. What is a grievance? Describe the typical grievance procedure.
10. What steps are involved in collective bargaining?

11. For what reasons are strikes and lockouts relatively rare nowadays?
12. What are the objectives of picketing?
13. In what ways do the techniques of mediation and arbitration differ?

Discussion Questions

1. Do unions really derive their power mainly from their membership and labor legislation? What are some other sources of union power?
2. Which labor contract issues are likely to be the easiest to resolve? Which are likely to be the most difficult?
3. Discuss the following statement: Union security means job security for union members.
4. How would you prepare for labor contract negotiations as a member of management? As head of the union negotiating committee?
5. Under what circumstances are strikes and lockouts justified in place of mediation or arbitration?

video case

Is Wal-Mart Waging War on Its Workers?

Wal-Mart, the world's largest private employer, is also one of organized labor's largest unionization targets. The retailer maintains a global work force of 1.3 million employees, and it hires thousands of employees every month as it continues to open new Wal-Mart and Sam's Club stores. The United Food and Commercial Workers Union (UFCW) says that Wal-Mart's employees would benefit from collective bargaining, citing the retailer's low wages, inadequate benefits, huge profits, and anti-union attitudes. However, Wal-Mart's management says that its associates (the company's term for employees) are treated well and need no outside representation to communicate with the company. Its associates voted the company onto *Fortune* magazine's list of "the Top 100 Companies to Work For" in at least four recent years. The clash between the UFCW and Wal-Mart management is fueling a bitter store-by-store, state-by-state battle over unionization.

The UFCW uses pro-union literature, meetings, and media releases to fuel organizing campaigns among Wal-Mart employees in Michigan, Ohio, Texas, Nevada, and many other states. "Americans can't live on a Wal-Mart paycheck," states Greg Denier, the UFCW's communications director. "Yet it's the dominant employer, and what they pay will be the future of working America." The union charges that Wal-Mart brainwashes its employees into believing that they can speak up without union help. The union also says that Wal-Mart uses surveillance, interrogation, intimidation, and termination to keep it stores union-free.

Some current and former employees and managers are supporting the UFCW campaign by publicly discussing their experiences. Gretchen Adams, a former Wal-Mart co-manager, stresses that many employees complained about the unaffordably high premiums for health insurance available through the retailer's benefit plan. Linda Gruen was so upset about the quality and expense of the insurance that she left her job as a Sam's Club cashier to become a UFCW organizer.

Former store manager Jon Lehman says that managers were to phone a special union hotline if they spotted organizing efforts in a store. After such a call, labor experts from Wal-Mart headquarters would come to the store and show employees anti-union training videos. According to union officials, these meetings, along with strategically placed surveillance cameras and termination threats, intimidated employees and strongly discouraged pro-union sentiment.

Wal-Mart strongly denies the UFCW's allegations. "It's our approach with our associates to treat them right and have a genuine partnership with them," responds Wal-Mart spokesperson Bill Wertz. "We need a lot of people to conduct our business and fill our existing stores. We couldn't do that if we mistreated our people." In fact, Wertz says, "The question our people have is what the unions' real intent is. It doesn't seem like a genuine membership drive. It seems like more of an effort to discredit the company and protect those companies that do employ union members." Wal-Mart has long offered benefits such as health insurance, retirement plans, incentive bonuses, stock purchase plans, and merchandise discounts. It is also known for promotion from within. More than half its managers started as hourly employees.

Since the days when founder Sam Walton personally ran the company, Wal-Mart has sought to keep unions at bay. Whenever an organizing campaign surfaces in a store, management repeats one key message: Employees can speak for themselves without the assistance of any outsiders. "Wal-Mart doesn't need a union," agrees Loretta Hartgrave, a department manager with twenty-seven years of experience with the company. "Why do we need someone to talk for us when we can talk for ourselves?"

Legally, Wal-Mart is allowed to call employees together for anti-union meetings, show them anti-union videos, and distribute anti-union literature. According to an academic study, 92 percent of companies use anti-union meetings, and 70 percent send workers anti-union literature when faced with an organizing campaign. The use of anti-union experts is widespread as well. The executive vice president of Wal-Mart's People Division says that it uses labor experts to "educate associates about how these [union election] processes work." On the other hand, according to former Wal-Mart "people" manager Stan Fortune, the actions he took years ago as a self-described company "union buster" were not legal.

In fact, Wal-Mart has had to defend itself against twenty-eight NLRB complaints in a sixteen-month period, charging the company with illegal actions such as threatening, disciplining, or interrogating union organizers. The company is also defending against a California lawsuit claiming sexual discrimination against women employees. In addition, an Oregon jury recently found the company guilty of forcing employees in that state's stores to work overtime without pay. Similar lawsuits have been filed in Texas, Ohio, and Louisiana.

Whatever the outcome of these legal actions, Wal-Mart's staunchly nonunion stance will keep it at odds with the UFCW. Is Wal-Mart waging war on its workers, as the UFCW asserts? Or is the union using rhetoric to stir up pro-union feelings among Wal-Mart's work force?[15]

Questions

1. Why does the UFCW want to unionize and represent Wal-Mart employees? What types of obstacles does the UFCW union face in this effort?
2. Why do companies like Wal-Mart that have acceptable benefit plans (and have even won awards) also have to engage in strong anti-union activities?
3. Do you think that Wal-Mart store employees would vote for or against unionization? Explain your answer.

Building Skills for Career Success

1. Exploring the Internet

Union websites provide a wealth of information about union activities and concerns. Just as a corporate home page gives a firm the opportunity to describe its mission and goals and present its image to the world, so too does a website allow a union to speak to its membership as well as to the public at large. Visit the text website for updates to this exercise.

Assignment

1. Visit the following websites:

   AFL-CIO: **http://www.aflcio.com**

   United Auto Workers: **http://www.uaw.org**
2. What are the mission statements of these unions?
3. Briefly describe your impression of the areas of interest to union members.
4. What is your impression of the tone of these websites? Do they differ in any way from a typical business website?

2. Developing Critical Thinking Skills

Recently, while on its final approach to an airport in Lubbock, Texas, a commercial airliner encountered a flock of ducks. The flight crew believed that one or more of the ducks hit the aircraft and were ingested into the plane's main engine. The aircraft landed safely and taxied to the terminal. The flight crew advised the maintenance and operations crews of the incident. Operations grounded the plane until it could be inspected, but because of the time of day, maintenance personnel available to perform the inspection were in short supply. The airline had to call in two off-duty mechanics. A supervisor, calling from an overtime list, made calls until contacting two available mechanics. They worked on overtime pay to perform the inspection and return the aircraft to a safe flying status. Several days after the inspection, a mechanic on the overtime list who was not home when the supervisor called complained that she had been denied overtime. This union member believed that the company owed her overtime pay for the same number of hours worked by a mechanic who performed the actual inspection. The company disagreed. What options are available to resolve this conflict?

Assignment

1. Using the following questions as guidelines, determine how this dispute can be resolved.
   a. What options are available to the unhappy mechanic? What process must she pursue? How does this process work?
   b. Do you believe that the mechanic should receive pay for time she did not work? Justify your answer.
   c. What do you think was the final outcome of this conflict?
2. Prepare a report describing how you would resolve this situation.

3. Building Team Skills

For more than a century American unions have played an important role in the workplace, striving to improve the working conditions and quality of life of employees. Today, federal laws cover many of the workers' rights that unions first championed. For this reason, some people believe that unions are no longer necessary. According to some experts, however, as technology changes the workplace and as cultural diversity and the number of part-time workers increase, unions will increase their memberships and become stronger as we enter the next century. What do you think?

Assignment

1. Form a "pro" group and a "con" group and join one of them.
2. Debate whether unions will be stronger or weaker in the next century.

3. Record the key points for each side.
4. Summarize in a report what you learned about unions and their usefulness, and state your position on the debated issue.

4. Researching Different Careers

When applying for a job, whether mailing or faxing in your résumé, you should always include a letter of application, or a cover letter, as it is often called. A well-prepared cover letter should convince the prospective employer to read your résumé and to phone you for an interview. The letter should describe the job you want and your qualifications for the job. It also should let the firm know where you can be reached to set up an appointment for an interview.

Assignment

1. Prepare a letter of application to use with the résumé you prepared in Chapter 10. (An example appears in Appendix A.)
2. After having several friends review your letter, edit it carefully.
3. Ask your instructor to comment on your letter.

5. Improving Communication Skills

A union contract is an agreement between a company and its employees who are union members. The contract sets forth the procedures that both parties must use to resolve disputes. Sometimes, however, the disputed issues become so complex that they cannot be resolved easily by union and management. At this point, mediators usually step in to help move both sides closer to resolving their issues. At times, even this measure is not enough, and the union calls a strike.

Assignment

1. Read recent newspaper articles about issues that divide a firm's management and its union employees.
2. Find answers to the following questions:
   a. What are the disputed issues?
   b. Which issues are the most difficult to resolve? Why?
   c. Where does each party stand on the issues?
   d. How are the issues being resolved, or if they are already resolved, how were they resolved?
   e. What might be the effect of this dispute on union-management relations?
3. Summarize your findings and what you learned about unions in a report.

Inside the People Business at Finagle A Bagel

People are a vital ingredient in Finagle A Bagel's recipe for success. As a quick-serve business, the company strives for high turnover in food, not employees. In fact, careful attention to HRM has enabled Finagle A Bagel to continue expanding its market share without spending money on advertising. Low work force turnover means less money and time spent on recruiting and training—an important financial consideration for a fast-growing business. It also means that Finagle A Bagel has the human resources strength to combine super service with fresh food for a distinctive competitive advantage in a crowded marketplace.

The Right People in the Right Place

"We depend on our crew at the store level—who are interacting with our guests every day—to know their jobs, to understand the company mission, and to communicate with the guests," says Heather Robertson, who directs the company's marketing, human resources, and research and development. "And once we get them on board, people don't leave our company. They just stay. They realize that it can be a career for them."

A sizable number of Finagle A Bagel's managers and employees (including Robertson) were hired years ago and became so excited about the product, the company, and the customers that they simply stayed. Many remain with Finagle A Bagel because they prefer the more personal atmosphere of a 400-employee business over the relatively faceless anonymity of a gigantic corporation. "It's really unusual to have one-on-one interaction on a daily basis with the president of the company or any senior executive member of the company," Robertson states. "Our cashiers, our café attendants, our bakers, and our managers know they can pick up the phone at any point and call anybody here and say, 'Here's my problem. How do I fix it?' or 'I need your help.' The size of our company allows us to do that, and the culture of the company encourages that."

Because bagels are an integral part of every menu item, employees who join Finagle A Bagel must "love" bagels, regardless of any other skills or experiences they bring to their jobs. When Robertson advertises to fill an open position in Finagle A Bagel's support center, for example, she always mentions this requirement. As résumés come in, she sorts them according to whether the candidates indicate a fondness for bagels. Those who fail to mention it are automatically disqualified from consideration.

Different Kinds of Managers for Different Locations

Alan Litchman, Finagle A Bagel's co-president, says that selecting a candidate to manage one of the Boston stores is easier than selecting one for a suburban store. Given the inner-city location of the company's support center, he or another executive can get to the Boston stores more quickly if a problem arises. Moreover, the city stores compete by providing speedy, accurate service to busy customers who have little time to waste waiting in line. Paulo Pereira, general manager of the Harvard Square store in Cambridge, has become an expert in squeezing inefficiencies from the city stores so that customers are in and out more quickly. By increasing the number of customers served each day and slashing the number of bagels left over at closing, Pereira boosts both sales revenues and profits.

When selecting a manager for a suburban store, Litchman looks for people with an "owner-operator mentality" who have the drive, initiative, and know-how to build business locally. His message to a potential general manager is "If you want to be a franchisee but don't have the capital, or if you want to own your own business, we're going to put you in business. You don't have to give us any money to do that. And if your store achieves more than a certain level of sales or profits, we'll start splitting the bottom line with you in a bonus program." Consider Nick Cochran, who worked his way up from assistant manager to general manager of the store in Wayland, an affluent Boston suburb. Cochran's enthusiasm for quality and service has drawn a highly loyal customer following and contributed to the Wayland store's success.

Hiring and Motivating Store Personnel

General managers such as Cochran and Pereira are responsible for recruiting, interviewing, hiring, training, motivating, and evaluating store-level personnel. They assign job responsibilities according to the skills and strengths of each manager and employee, but they also expect everyone to work as a team during extremely busy periods. In addition to motivating general managers by offering bonuses based on meeting revenue and profit goals, Finagle A Bagel encourages crew members to take advantage of extra training and internal promotions.

"In a company our size," stresses co-president Laura Trust, "there is always opportunity. You just have to find the right fit for the individual." In fact, says her husband, "The best supervisors, coordinators, assistant managers, or managers in any unit—by far—are the ones who have started with us at a lower level and worked their way up."

Diverse Work Force, Family Business

Finagle A Bagel has an extremely diverse work force made up of people originally from Latin America, Europe, western Africa, and many other areas. Over the years, the company has served as a sponsor for new Americans who need government-issued work permits so they can legally remain in the United States for work reasons. Despite diversity's

many advantages—including creativity, flexibility, and the ability to relate to a broader customer base—it can also create communication challenges when English is not an employee's native language. To avoid confusion, Litchman and Trust insist that employees speak only in English when addressing customers.

As a small, family-run business, Finagle A Bagel sees its workforce as a group of unique individuals, not interchangeable cogs in an impersonal corporate machine. Trust feels strongly that "there's a responsibility that you have to your employees and to your colleagues. These people work for you—they work hard to try and move your company forward—and their efforts need to be recognized." Because the business is still small, she adds "the people who have become a part of the management team are very much like a family to Alan and me. If you run your company that way, then you'll be successful because everybody believes that you care about not only the work they do but everything they do, and every part of their lives affects their job."

Questions

1. What affect has diversity had on Finagle A Bagel?
2. If you were the general manager of a downtown Finagle A Bagel store, what job description and job specification would you prepare for a cashier? Based on these, what kinds of questions would you ask when interviewing candidates for this position?
3. Which of Herzberg's motivation factors are Trust and Litchman emphasizing for general managers?
4. Would it be feasible for Finagle A Bagel to apply the concept of flextime to store employees? To senior managers at the support center? Explain.

Building a Business Plan Part IV

In this section of your business plan you will expand on the type and quantity of employees that will be required to operate the business. Your human resource requirements are determined by the type of business and by the size and scale of your operation. From the preceding section, you should have a good idea of how many people you will need. And Part IV of your textbook, "Human Resources," especially Chapters 10 and 11, should help you in answering some of the questions in this part of the business plan.

The Human Resources Component

To ensure successful performance by employees, you must inform workers of their specific job requirements. Employees must know what is expected on the job, and they are entitled to expect regular feedback on their work. It is vital to have a formal job description and job specification for every position in your business. Also, you should establish procedures for evaluating performance.

The labor force component should include the answers to at least the following questions:

4.1. How many employees will you require, and what are their qualifications—including skills, experience, and knowledge? How many jobs will be full time? Part time?

4.2. Will you have written job descriptions for each position?

4.3. Have you prepared a job application form? Do you know what can legally be included in it?

4.4. What criteria will you use in selecting employees?

4.5. Have you made plans for the orientation process?

4.6. Who will do the training?

4.7. What can you afford to pay in wages and salaries? Is this in line with the going rate in your region and industry?

4.8. Who will evaluate your employees?

4.9. Will you delegate any authority to employees?

4.10. Have you developed a set of disciplinary rules?

4.11. Do you plan to interview employees when they resign?

Review of Business Plan Activities

Remember that your employees are the most valuable and important resource. Therefore, make sure that you expend a great deal of effort to acquire and make full use of this resource. Check and resolve any issues in this component of your business plan before beginning Part V. Again, make sure that your answers to the questions in each part are consistent with the entire business plan. Finally, write a brief statement that summarizes all the information for this part of the business plan.

part V

Marketing

The business activities that make up a firm's marketing efforts are those most directly concerned with satisfying customers' needs. In this part we explore these activities in some detail. Initially, we discuss markets, marketing mix and environment, marketing plans, and buying behavior. Then, in turn, we discuss the four elements that together make up a marketing mix: product, price, distribution, and promotion.

chapter

13

Building Customer Relationships Through Effective Marketing

learning objectives

1. Understand the meaning of *marketing* and explain how it creates utility for purchasers of products.
2. Trace the development of the marketing concept and understand how it is implemented.
3. Understand what markets are and how they are classified.
4. Identify the four elements of the marketing mix and be aware of their importance in developing a marketing strategy.
5. Explain how the marketing environment affects strategic market planning.
6. Understand the major components of a marketing plan.
7. Describe how market measurement and sales forecasting are used.
8. Distinguish between a marketing information system and marketing research.
9. Identify the major steps in the consumer buying decision process and the sets of factors that may influence this process.
10. Describe three ways of measuring consumer income.

Enthusiasm runs so high for Harley-Davidson that experts frequently cite the brand among America's best known.

inside business

Harley-Davidson Throttles Up for Its Second Century

HARLEY-DAVIDSON HAS ROARED up and down the fast track since founders William Harley and Arthur Davidson built their first motorcycle in 1903. Now in its second century of satisfying customers, the company annually sells more than 260,000 motorcycles in the United States, Japan, and Europe. Although quality slipped in the 1970s and 1980s during a period of rapid expansion, Harley-Davidson rekindled customer interest by cutting back on manufacturing output, focusing on quality, and redesigning its products.

Soon the company was well on the road to reclaiming its market dominance in the United States and beating back competition from Yamaha, Honda, Suzuki, and Kawasaki. Despite higher demand, management learned from the past and increased production only slightly from year to year to maintain quality. As a result, enthusiasts sometimes waited one or two years for popular models and even paid more than the regular price when a bike became available. During its centennial year, Harley-Davidson created special limited-edition birthday models that pushed demand higher still. Enthusiasm runs so high that experts frequently cite the brand, along with Coca-Cola and Disney, as among America's best known.

How does the company determine what its customers want? To start, nearly half of its 8,000 employees own a Harley-Davidson motorcycle. Because they must buy from dealers, employees find out firsthand how their products are sold and how dealers treat customers. They also participate in business simulations designed to offer a taste of what dealers face in working to satisfy customers. In addition, hundreds of Harley-Davidson employees attend cycling rallies to mingle with customers and observe their preferences and habits. For instance, after observing how riders personalized their bikes with unusual handlebars and unique paint jobs, the company launched a line of custom bikes with special accessories. These motorcycles sell for around $25,000 and earn more profit than regular models, which fetch $8,000 to $17,000 or more.

The road ahead may be bumpy. Research shows that the company's customers are getting older. In the mid-1980s, the average age of a Harley-Davidson buyer was 35. Now the average age is 46. Meanwhile, younger customers are attracted to the sportier, higher-performance models made by competitors. To compete, Harley-Davidson has developed sleek new cruising motorcycles with liquid-cooled engines, some capable of reaching 140 miles per hour. Through its Buell subsidiary, the company is also luring younger customers with starter motorcycles priced at just over $4,000.

CEO Jeff Bleustein is well aware that every market changes over time, which means that Harley-Davidson must continue to update its product line and mix year after year. "The only thing that can stop us is if we get complacent," he states. "Even though we've been successful, we can't stand still."[1]

table 13.1 Major Marketing Functions

Exchange Functions: All companies—manufacturers, wholesalers, and retailers—buy and sell to market their merchandise.

1. **Buying** includes obtaining raw materials to make products, knowing how much merchandise to keep on hand, and selecting suppliers.
2. **Selling** creates possession utility by transferring the title of a product from seller to customer.

Physical Distribution Functions: These functions involve the flow of goods from producers to customers. Transportation and storage provide time utility and place utility and require careful management of inventory.

3. **Transporting** involves selecting a mode of transport that provides an acceptable delivery schedule at an acceptable price.
4. **Storing** goods is often necessary to sell them at the best selling time.

Facilitating Functions: These functions help the other functions take place.

5. **Financing** helps at all stages of marketing. To buy raw materials, manufacturers often borrow from banks or receive credit from suppliers. Wholesalers may be financed by manufacturers, and retailers may receive financing from the wholesaler or manufacturer. Finally, retailers often provide financing to customers.
6. **Standardizing** sets uniform specifications for products or services. **Grading** classifies products by size and quality, usually through a sorting process. Together, standardization and grading facilitate production, transportation, storage, and selling.
7. **Risk taking**—even though competent management and insurance can minimize risks—is a constant reality of marketing because of such losses as bad-debt expense, obsolescence of products, theft by employees, and product-liability lawsuits.
8. **Gathering market information** is necessary for making all marketing decisions.

marketing the process of planning and executing the conception, pricing, promotion, and distribution of ideas, goods, and services to create exchanges that satisfy individual and organizational objectives

At Harley-Davidson, marketing efforts are directed at providing customer satisfaction. Although marketing encompasses a diverse set of decisions and activities performed by individuals and by both business and nonbusiness organizations, marketing always begins and ends with the customer. The American Marketing Association defines **marketing** as "the process of planning and executing the conception, pricing, promotion, and distribution of ideas, goods, and services to create exchanges that satisfy individual and organizational objectives." The marketing process involves eight major functions and numerous related activities (see Table 13.1). All these functions are essential if the marketing process is to be effective.

In this chapter we examine marketing activities that add value to products. We trace the evolution of the marketing concept and describe how organizations practice it. Next, our focus shifts to market classifications and marketing strategy. We analyze the four elements of a marketing mix and also discuss uncontrollable factors in the marketing environment. Then, we examine the major components of a marketing plan. We consider tools for strategic market planning, including market measurement, sales forecasts, marketing information systems, and marketing research. Last, we look at the forces that influence consumer and organizational buying behavior.

learning objective

1 Understand the meaning of *marketing* and explain how it creates utility for purchasers of products.

utility the ability of a good or service to satisfy a human need

Utility: The Value Added by Marketing

As defined in Chapter 9, **utility** is the ability of a good or service to satisfy a human need. A lunch at a Pizza Hut, an overnight stay at a Holiday Inn, and a Mercedes S500L all satisfy human needs. Thus each possesses utility. There are four kinds of utility.

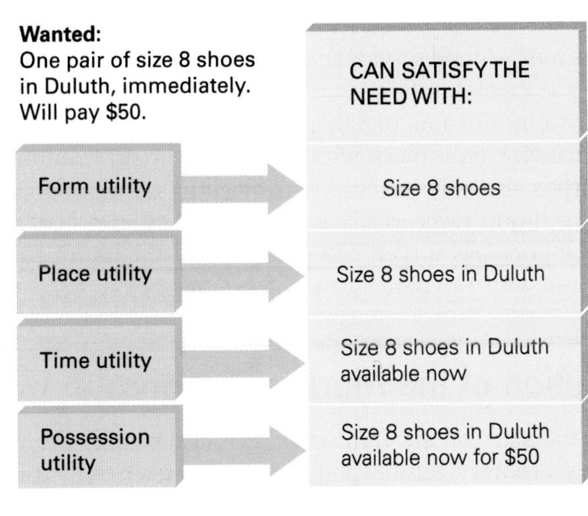

figure 13.1

Types of Utility

Form utility is created by the production process, but marketing creates place, time, and possession utility.

Form utility is created by converting production inputs into finished products. Marketing efforts may influence form utility indirectly because the data gathered as part of marketing research are frequently used to determine the size, shape, and features of a product.

form utility utility created by converting production inputs into finished products

The three kinds of utility that are created directly by marketing are place, time, and possession utility. **Place utility** is created by making a product available at a location where customers wish to purchase it. A pair of shoes is given place utility when it is shipped from a factory to a department store.

place utility utility created by making a product available at a location where customers wish to purchase it

Time utility is created by making a product available when customers wish to purchase it. For example, Halloween costumes may be manufactured in April but not displayed until late September, when consumers start buying them. By storing the costumes until they are wanted, the manufacturer or retailer provides time utility.

time utility utility created by making a product available when customers wish to purchase it

Possession utility is created by transferring title (or ownership) of a product to the buyer. For a product as simple as a pair of shoes, ownership usually is transferred by means of a sales slip or receipt. For such products as automobiles and homes, the transfer of title is a more complex process. Along with the title to its products, the seller transfers the right to use that product to satisfy a need (see Figure 13.1).

possession utility utility created by transferring title (or ownership) of a product to the buyer

Place, time, and possession utility have real value in terms of both money and convenience. This value is created and added to goods and services through a wide variety of marketing activities—from research indicating what customers want to product warranties ensuring that customers get what they pay for. Overall, these marketing activities account for about half of every dollar spent by consumers. When they are part of an integrated marketing program that delivers maximum utility to the customer, many would agree that they are worth the cost.

Place, time, and possession utility are only the most fundamental applications of marketing activities. In recent years, marketing activities have been influenced by a broad business philosophy known as the *marketing concept*.

The Marketing Concept

learning objective

2 Trace the development of the marketing concept and understand how it is implemented.

The process that leads any business to success seems simple. First, the firm must talk to its potential customers to assess their needs for its goods or services. Then the firm must develop a good or service to satisfy those needs. Finally, the firm must continue to seek ways to provide customer satisfaction. This process is an application of the marketing concept, or marketing orientation. As reasonable and logical as it appears to be, American business has been slow to accept it, but it is making some progress. An example of an organization that is implementing the marketing concept is Commerce

Yes, as a matter of fact, it is all about you, you, you.
Bank First. Be First.
When was the last time you felt like the center of attention?
When as the last time you stopped by First Bank? 1.800.760.BANK.
FIRST BANK
Member FDIC

Using the marketing concept. Like many organizations, FirstBank is attempting to practice the marketing concept by telling customers that the focus is on them.

Bancorp, located in New Jersey, Delaware, and Pennsylvania. Commerce Bancorp has ascertained what retail banking customers want—good service and low fees. Commerce offers its customers free checking, free money orders, weekday teller service from 7:30 a.m. to 8:00 p.m., and weekend teller hours. By providing customers with what they want, Commerce Bancorp is also able to achieve its objectives. Its earnings are growing almost twice as fast as those of the average bank, and its stock price has surged 278 percent over the last five years compared with 118 percent for the average bank stock.[2]

Evolution of the Marketing Concept

From the start of the Industrial Revolution until the early twentieth century, business effort was directed mainly toward the production of goods. Consumer demand for manufactured products was so great that manufacturers could almost bank on selling everything they produced. Business had a strong *production orientation*, in which emphasis was placed on increased output and production efficiency. Marketing was limited to taking orders and distributing finished goods.

In the 1920s, production caught up with and began to exceed demand. Now producers had to direct their efforts toward selling goods rather than just producing goods that consumers readily bought. This new *sales orientation* was characterized by increased advertising, enlarged sales forces, and occasionally, high-pressure selling techniques. Manufacturers produced the goods they expected consumers to want, and marketing consisted primarily of promoting products through personal selling and advertising, taking orders, and delivering goods.

During the 1950s, however, business people started to realize that even enormous advertising expenditures and the most thoroughly proven sales techniques were not enough. Something else was needed if products were to sell as well as expected. It was then that business managers recognized they were not primarily producers or sellers but rather were in the business of satisfying customers' needs. Marketers realized that the best approach was to adopt a customer orientation—in other words, the organization had to first determine what customers need and then develop goods and services to fill those particular needs (see Table 13.2).

marketing concept a business philosophy that involves the entire organization in the process of satisfying customers' needs while achieving the organization's goals

This **marketing concept** is a business philosophy that involves the entire organization in the process of satisfying customers' needs while achieving the organization's goals. All functional areas—research and development (R&D), production, finance, human resources, and of course, marketing—are viewed as playing a role in providing customer satisfaction. Based on the marketing concept, some organizations today are

table 13.2 Evolution of Customer Orientation

Business managers recognized that they were not primarily producers or sellers but rather were in the business of satisfying customers' wants.

Production Orientation	Sales Orientation	Customer Orientation
Take orders	Increase advertising	Determine customer needs
Distribute goods	Enlarge sales force	Develop products to fill these needs
	Intensify sales techniques	Achieve the organization's goals

employing **relationship marketing**, which involves developing mutually beneficial long-term partnerships with customers to enhance customer satisfaction and to stimulate long-term customer loyalty. Frequency programs that reward customer loyalty are one way of fostering long-term customer relationships. For example, Marriott Rewards gives its members three frequent-flyer miles per dollar spent at Marriott, Renaissance, Marriott Vacation Club International, and Marriott Conference Centers. This program also awards one mile per dollar spent at Courtyard, Fairfield Inn, and Residence Inn.[3]

relationship marketing developing mutually beneficial long-term partnerships with customers to enhance customer satisfaction and to stimulate long-term customer loyalty

Implementing the Marketing Concept

The marketing concept has been adopted by many of the most successful business firms. Some firms, such as Ford Motor Company and Apple Computer, have gone through minor or major reorganizations in the process. Because the marketing concept is essentially a business philosophy, anyone can say, "I believe in it." To make it work, however, management must fully adopt and then implement it.

For example, the managers and employees at Pike Place Fish, a fish market in Seattle, are striving to be truly great with customers. The company's objective is to make a difference in the lives of its customers. Thus managers and employees attempt to give each customer the experience of having been well served and appreciated whether or not the customer actually buys fish. At Pike Place Fish, managers and employees are committed to the belief that they can improve the quality of life for customers.[4]

examining ethics

Lying to Customers

LYING TO CUSTOMERS is a tactic not found in any marketing plan but unfortunately practiced by a surprising number of employees and companies. Research by *Sales and Marketing Management* magazine found that 45 percent of the managers surveyed had heard their company's salespeople lie about product delivery times. Twenty percent had heard their salespeople lie about the company's service. And more than 77 percent said that a competitor was spreading lies about their companies.

Employees who misrepresent products, prices, or some other element often do so to clinch a sale. They may be earning higher commissions or simply trying to keep their jobs by meeting sales quotas. Whatever the motivation, the effect is the same: These employees fail to tell customers the whole truth and nothing but the truth.

When employees lie, they not only act unethically, but they also hurt their companies' reputations. Not long ago six salespeople and the general manager of a Los Angeles car dealership were indicted for lying about pricing. They did not disclose certain costs and overcharged more than 1,000 buyers. Although the salespeople and general manager no longer work there, what kind of image does such an incident project for the dealership?

Lying also can be costly, as Household International found out. This financial services firm owns mortgage lending operations that target home owners who have imperfect credit histories. After officials in twenty states found that Household employees had not disclosed certain costs and had overcharged customers, the firm agreed to pay $484 million in restitution. It also agreed to limits on the fees it can charge and is required to accurately disclose all pricing—with an independent monitor enforcing these rules.

Finally, lying is poor business. Customers who realize that they have been misled rarely buy from that employee or company again. "In relationship selling you cannot lie—if you mess up, you'll never hear from the client again," stresses Professor Andy Zoltners of the Kellogg School of Management. By telling the truth, employees build trust and encourage customer loyalty. Still, for their own protection, customers always should remember the old adage of *caveat emptor*—"Let the buyer beware."

Issues to Consider

1. How does lying to customers contradict the marketing concept?
2. Under what circumstances might customers not question employees too closely about what seem to be unusually low or high prices?

To implement the marketing concept, a firm must first obtain information about its present and potential customers. The firm must determine not only what customers' needs are but also how well those needs are being satisfied by products currently on the market—both its own products and those of competitors. It must ascertain how its products might be improved and what opinions customers have about the firm and its marketing efforts.

The firm must then use this information to pinpoint the specific needs and potential customers toward which it will direct its marketing activities and resources. (Obviously, no firm can expect to satisfy all needs. And not every individual or firm can be considered a potential customer for every product manufactured or sold by a firm.) Next, the firm must mobilize its marketing resources to (1) provide a product that will satisfy its customers, (2) price the product at a level that is acceptable to buyers and that will yield an acceptable profit, (3) promote the product so that potential customers will be aware of its existence and its ability to satisfy their needs, and (4) ensure that the product is distributed so that it is available to customers where and when needed.

Finally, the firm must again obtain marketing information—this time regarding the effectiveness of its efforts. Can the product be improved? Is it being promoted properly? Is it being distributed efficiently? Is the price too high or too low? The firm must be ready to modify any or all of its marketing activities based on information about its customers and competitors. For example, UPS realized that it had the technology and expertise to do much more for its customers than just deliver packages, including the potential to save them millions of dollars a year. Research showed that customers trust the people in the brown trucks and uniforms characteristic of UPS. The company has built on this image to promote new services such as financing and logistics management. Using the ad campaign, "What can Brown do for you?" UPS seems to be effective in its efforts as it continues to experience significant growth in its non-package-delivery revenues.[5]

learning objective

3 Understand what markets are and how they are classified.

market a group of individuals or organizations, or both, that need products in a given category and that have the ability, willingness, and authority to purchase such products

Markets and Their Classification

A **market** is a group of individuals or organizations, or both, that need products in a given category and that have the ability, willingness, and authority to purchase such products. The people or organizations must want the product. They must be able to purchase the product by exchanging money, goods, or services for it. They must be willing to use their buying power. Finally, they must be socially and legally authorized to purchase the product.

Markets are broadly classified as consumer or business-to-business markets. These classifications are based on the characteristics of the individuals and organizations within each market. Because marketing efforts vary depending on the intended market, marketers should understand the general characteristics of these two groups.

Consumer markets consist of purchasers and/or household members who intend to consume or benefit from the purchased products and who do not buy products to make profits.

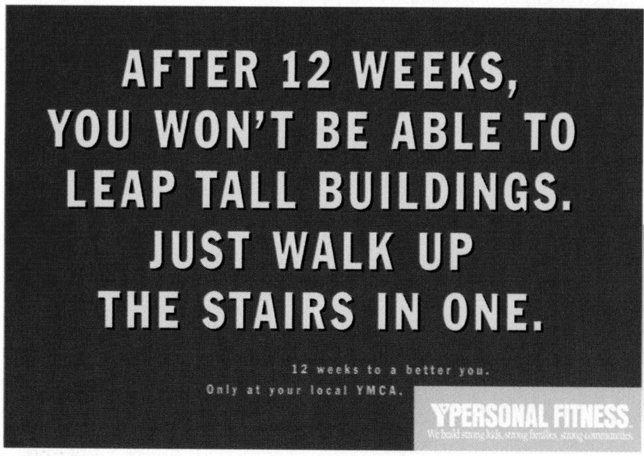

AFTER 12 WEEKS, YOU WON'T BE ABLE TO LEAP TALL BUILDINGS. JUST WALK UP THE STAIRS IN ONE.

12 weeks to a better you. Only at your local YMCA.

Y PERSONAL FITNESS

We build strong kids, strong families, strong communities.

How would you classify this organization? Not-for-profit organizations such as the YMCA, are a part of institutional markets. Their goals are different from typical business goals such as profit.

Business-to-business markets, also called *industrial markets,* are grouped broadly into producer, reseller, governmental, and institutional categories. These markets purchase specific kinds of products for use in making other products for resale or for day-to-day operations. *Producer markets* consist of individuals and business organizations that buy certain products to use in the manufacture of other products. *Reseller markets* consist of intermediaries such as wholesalers and retailers that buy finished products and sell them for a profit. *Governmental markets* consist of federal, state, county, and local governments. They buy goods and services to maintain internal operations and to provide citizens with such products as highways, education, water, energy, and national defense. Governmental purchases total billions of dollars each year. *Institutional markets* include churches, not-for-profit private schools and hospitals, civic clubs, fraternities and sororities, charitable organizations, and foundations. Their goals are different from such typical business goals as profit, market share, or return on investment.

Source: *USA Today*, October 18, 2001, p. B1.

Developing Marketing Strategies

A **marketing strategy** is a plan that will enable an organization to make the best use of its resources and advantages to meet its objectives. A marketing strategy consists of (1) the selection and analysis of a target market and (2) the creation and maintenance of an appropriate **marketing mix**, a combination of product, price, distribution, and promotion developed to satisfy a particular target market.

marketing strategy a plan that will enable an organization to make the best use of its resources and advantages to meet its objectives

marketing mix a combination of product, price, distribution, and promotion developed to satisfy a particular target market

Target Market Selection and Evaluation

A **target market** is a group of individuals, organizations, or both for which a firm develops and maintains a marketing mix suitable for the specific needs and preferences of that group. In selecting a target market, marketing managers examine potential markets for their possible effects on the firm's sales, costs, and profits. The managers attempt to determine whether the organization has the resources to produce a marketing mix that meets the needs of a particular target market and whether satisfying those needs is consistent with the firm's overall objectives. They also analyze the strengths and numbers of competitors already marketing to people in this target market. For example, Lego, the producer of well-known building blocks, traditionally has targeted boys with its products. The company has identified girls as a target market with enormous potential and no strong competitors for craft building-type products. Lego introduced its Clickits line, which contains jewelry, hair accessories, picture frames, and other kits that girls can use to build related items. The company spent heavily on promotion and on partnerships with Limited Too in order to introduce Clickits.[6] When selecting a target market, marketing managers generally take either the undifferentiated approach or the market segmentation approach.

target market a group of individuals or organizations, or both, for which a firm develops and maintains a marketing mix suitable for the specific needs and preferences of that group

Undifferentiated Approach A company that designs a single marketing mix and directs it at the entire market for a particular product is using an **undifferentiated approach** (see Figure 13.2 on p. 376). This approach assumes that individual customers

undifferentiated approach directing a single marketing mix at the entire market for a particular product

figure 13.2

General Approaches for Selecting Target Markets

The undifferentiated approach assumes that individual customers have similar needs and that most customers can be satisfied with a single marketing mix. When customers' needs vary, the market segmentation approach—either concentrated or differentiated—should be used.

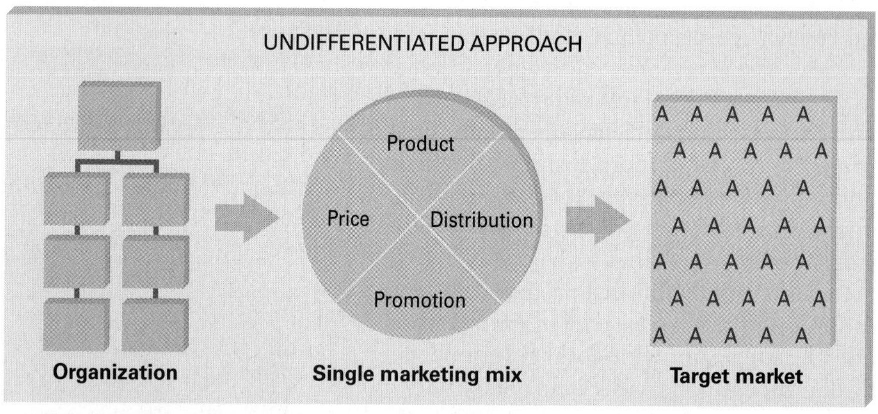

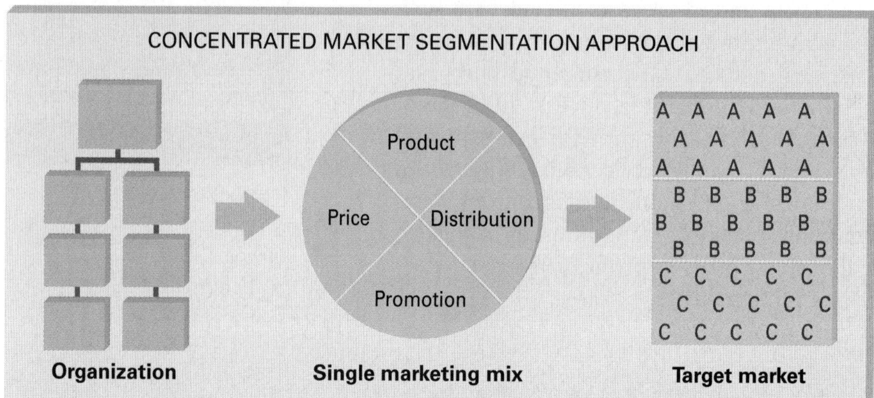

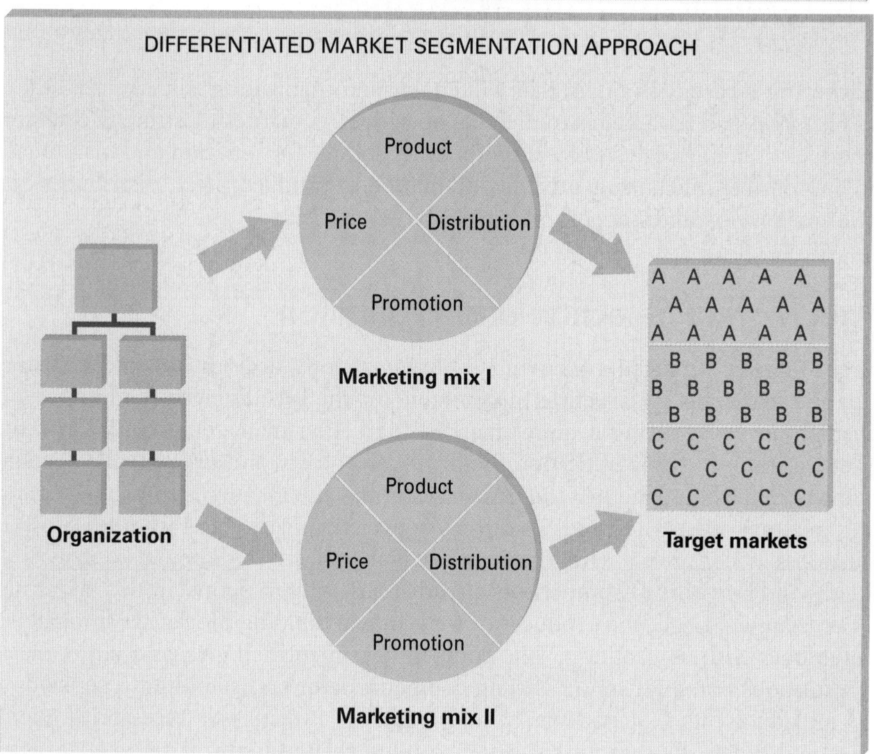

NOTE: The letters in each target market represent potential customers. Customers that have the same letters have similar characteristics and similar product needs.

Source: William M. Pride and O. C. Ferrell, *Marketing: Concepts and Strategies*, 12th ed. Copyright © 2003 by Houghton Mifflin Company. Adapted with permission.

n the target market for a specific kind of product have similar needs and that the organization therefore can satisfy most customers with a single marketing mix. This single marketing mix consists of one type of product with little or no variation, one price, one promotional program aimed at everyone, and one distribution system to reach all customers in the total market. Products that can be marketed successfully with the undifferentiated approach include staple food items, such as sugar and salt, and certain kinds of farm produce. An undifferentiated approach is useful in only a limited number of situations because for most product categories, buyers have different needs. When customers' needs vary, a company should use the market segmentation approach.

Market Segmentation Approach A firm that is marketing forty-foot yachts would not direct its marketing effort toward every person in the total boat market. Some might want a sailboat or a canoe. Others might want a speedboat or an outboard-powered fishing boat. Still others might be looking for something resembling a small ocean liner. Marketing efforts directed toward these boat buyers would be wasted.

Instead, the firm would direct its attention toward a particular portion, or *segment*, of the total market for boats. A **market segment** is a group of individuals or organizations within a market that shares one or more common characteristics. The process of dividing a market into segments is called **market segmentation**. As shown in Figure 13.2, there are two types of market segmentation approaches: concentrated and differentiated. When an organization uses *concentrated* market segmentation, a single marketing mix is directed at a single market segment. If *differentiated* market segmentation is employed, multiple marketing mixes are focused on multiple market segments.

market segment a group of individuals or organizations within a market that share one or more common characteristics

market segmentation the process of dividing a market into segments and directing a marketing mix at a particular segment or segments rather than at the total market

In our boat example, one common characteristic, or *basis*, for segmentation might be "end use of a boat." The firm would be interested primarily in that market segment whose uses for a boat could lead to the purchase of a forty-foot yacht. Another basis for segmentation might be income; still another might be geographic location. Each of these variables can affect the type of boat an individual might purchase. When choosing a basis for segmentation, it is important to select a characteristic that relates to differences in people's needs for a product. The yacht producer, for example, would not use religion to segment the boat market because people's needs for boats do not vary based on religion.

Marketers use a wide variety of segmentation bases. Those bases most commonly applied to consumer markets are shown in Table 13.3. Each may be used as a single basis for market segmentation or in combination with other bases. For example,

table 13.3 Common Bases of Market Segmentation

Demographic	Psychographic	Geographic	Behavioristic
Age	Personality attributes	Region	Volume usage
Gender	Motives	Urban, suburban, rural	End use
Race	Lifestyles	Market density	Benefit expectations
Ethnicity		Climate	Brand loyalty
Income		Terrain	Price sensitivity
Education		City size	
Occupation		County size	
Family size		State size	
Family life cycle			
Religion			
Social class			

Source: William M. Pride and O. C. Ferrell, *Marketing: Concepts and Strategies*, 12th ed. Copyright © 2003 by Houghton Mifflin Company. Adapted with permission.

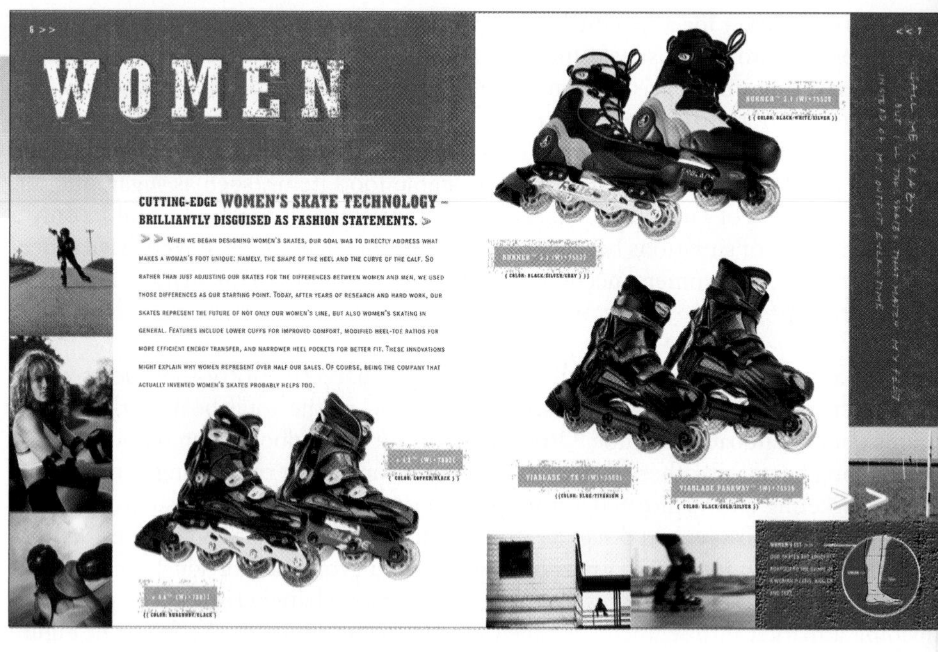

Gender-Based Segmentation. The skates in this catalog are designed for and market to women.

Vertu, a part of mobile phone maker Nokia, has segmented the market for cellular phones and is using a concentrated targeting strategy. The segment Vertu is after is very wealthy customers who want luxurious, social-status possessions. The company's mobile phones are made from precious materials, including gold, platinum, and sapphire crystal. The phones include a button that connects the owner to a personal assistant twenty-four hours a day. To reach its wealthy target market, Vertu sells its phones in private suites in select large cities (e.g., New York, London, Paris, Tokyo, and of course, Beverly Hills) and at Nieman Marcus department stores for a price ranging from just under $5,000 to almost $20,000 per phone. Such stars as Gwyneth Paltrow and Madonna are some of Vertu's customers.[7]

Creating a Marketing Mix

learning objective

4 Identify the four elements of the marketing mix and be aware of their importance in developing a marketing strategy.

A business firm controls four important elements of marketing that it combines in a way that reaches the firm's target market. These are the *product* itself, the *price* of the product, the means chosen for its *distribution*, and the *promotion* of the product. When combined, these four elements form a marketing mix (see Figure 13.3).

A firm can vary its marketing mix by changing any one or more of these ingredients. Thus a firm may use one marketing mix to reach one target market and a second, somewhat different marketing mix to reach another target market. For example, most automakers produce several different types and models of vehicles and aim them at different market segments based on age, income, and other factors.

For example, as the number of babies in Japan decreased, baby-food producers needed to find new ways to boost revenues. They discovered that the same qualities characteristic of baby food, such as softness, small bite size, and low salt content, also appealed to the growing senior population. Through the creation of new marketing mixes (including different promotion and product labels such as "Food for Ages 1–100"), the companies are now successfully selling products to seniors that are not all that different from baby food.[8]

The *product* ingredient of the marketing mix includes decisions about the product's design, brand name, packaging, warranties, and the like. When McDonald's decides on brand names, package designs, sizes of orders, flavors of sauces, and recipes, these choices are all part of the product ingredient.

The *pricing* ingredient is concerned with both base prices and discounts of various kinds. Pricing decisions are intended to achieve particular goals, such as to maximize profit or even to make room for new models. The rebates offered by automobile man-

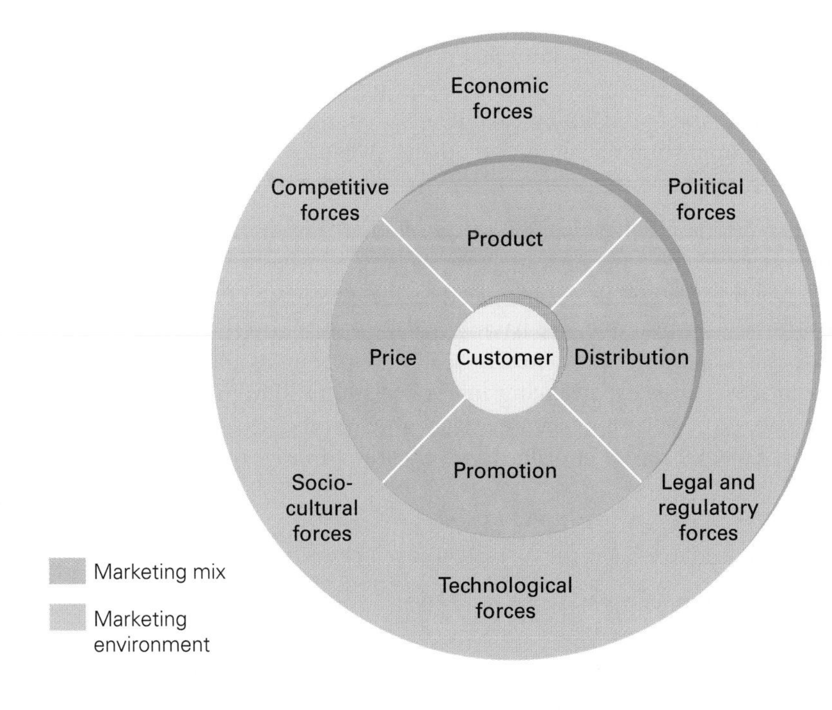

figure 13.3

The Marketing Mix and the Marketing Environment

The marketing mix consists of elements that the firm controls—product, price, distribution, and promotion. The firm generally has no control over forces in the marketing environment.

Source: William M. Pride and O. C. Ferrell, *Marketing: Concepts and Strategies*, 12th ed. Copyright © 2003 by Houghton Mifflin Company. Adapted with permission.

ufacturers are a pricing strategy developed to boost low auto sales. Product and pricing are discussed in detail in Chapter 14.

The *distribution* ingredient involves not only transportation and storage but also the selection of intermediaries. How many levels of intermediaries should be used in the distribution of a particular product? Should the product be distributed as widely as possible? Or should distribution be restricted to a few specialized outlets in each area? These and other questions related to distribution are considered in Chapter 15.

The *promotion* ingredient focuses on providing information to target markets. The major forms of promotion are advertising, personal selling, sales promotion, and public relations. These four forms are discussed in Chapter 16.

These ingredients of the marketing mix are controllable elements. A firm can vary each of them to suit its organizational goals, marketing goals, and target markets. As we extend our discussion of marketing strategy, we will see that the marketing environment includes a number of *uncontrollable* elements.

Marketing Strategy and the Marketing Environment

learning objective

5 Explain how the marketing environment affects strategic market planning.

The marketing mix consists of elements that a firm controls and uses to reach its target market. In addition, the firm has control over such organizational resources as finances and information. These resources, too, may be used to accomplish marketing goals. However, the firm's marketing activities are also affected by a number of external—and generally uncontrollable—forces. As Figure 13.3 illustrates, the forces that make up the external *marketing environment* are

- *Economic forces*—the effects of economic conditions on customers' ability and willingness to buy
- *Sociocultural forces*—influences in a society and its culture that result in changes in attitudes, beliefs, norms, customs, and lifestyles
- *Political forces*—influences that arise through the actions of elected and appointed officials

- *Competitive forces*—the actions of competitors, who are in the process of implementing their own marketing plans
- *Legal and regulatory forces*—laws that protect consumers and competition and government regulations that affect marketing
- *Technological forces*—technological changes that, on the one hand, can create new marketing opportunities or, on the other, can cause products to become obsolete almost overnight

These forces influence decisions about marketing mix ingredients. Changes in the environment can have a major impact on existing marketing strategies. In addition, changes in environmental forces may lead to abrupt shifts in customers' needs. Technological forces, for example, are having a major impact on the music industry, forcing giant's such as Sony to cut nearly 1,000 jobs from its music department in an effort to cut costs after experiencing losses of $140 million in a nine-month period. Sony and other music companies must continue to react to piracy, CD burners, and other environmental forces in order to reverse the three-year global decline in music sales.[9]

Developing a Marketing Plan

learning objective

6 Understand the major components of a marketing plan.

marketing plan a written document that specifies an organization's resources, objectives, strategy, and implementation and control efforts to be used in marketing a specific product or product group

A **marketing plan** is a written document that specifies an organization's resources, objectives, marketing strategy, and implementation and control efforts to be used in marketing a specific product or product group. The marketing plan describes the firm's current position or situation, establishes marketing objectives for the product, and specifies how the organization will attempt to achieve these objectives. Marketing plans vary with respect to the time period involved. Short-range plans are for one year or less, medium-range plans cover from over one year up to five years, and long-range plans cover periods of more than five years.

Although time-consuming, developing a clear, well-written marketing plan is important. The plan will be used for communication among the firm's employees. It covers the assignment of responsibilities, tasks, and schedules for implementation. It specifies how resources are to be allocated to achieve marketing objectives. It helps marketing managers monitor and evaluate the performance of the marketing strategy. Because the forces of the marketing environment are subject to change, marketing plans have to be updated frequently. Disney, for example, recently made changes to its marketing plans by combining all activities and licensing associated with the Power Rangers, Winnie the Pooh, and Disney Princess into one marketing plan with a $500-million budget. The primary goal is to send consistent messages about branding to customers. As the new marketing plan is implemented, Disney will have to respond quickly to customers' reactions and make adjustments to the plan.[10] The major components of a marketing plan are shown in Table 13.4.

Market Measurement and Sales Forecasting

learning objective

7 Describe how market measurement and sales forecasting are used.

Measuring the sales potential of specific types of market segments helps an organization make some important decisions. It can evaluate the feasibility of entering new segments. The organization also can decide how best to allocate its marketing resources and activities among market segments in which it is already active. All such estimates should identify the relevant time frame. Like marketing plans, these estimates may be short-range, covering periods of less than one year; medium-range, covering one to five years; and long-range, covering more than five years. The estimates also should define the geographic boundaries of the forecast. For example, sales potential

table 13.4 Components of a Marketing Plan

Executive Summary

This short statement summarizing the entire report is sometimes easier to write *after* the marketing plan has been developed.

Environmental Analysis

This consists of current information about the environment in which a company will market its product, the target market, and performance objectives.

Assessing the *marketing environment* includes

1. Looking at forces affecting marketing—competitive, legal, political, economic, technological, and sociocultural.
2. Assessing the organization's marketing resources—availability of human resources, capacity of equipment, and financial resources.

Assessing the *target market* includes asking

1. What are the current needs of each target market?
2. What changes in these needs are anticipated?
3. How well are the company's products meeting these needs?
4. What are the relevant aspects of consumer behavior and product use?

Evaluating the firm's *current marketing objectives and performance* includes

1. Making sure that the firm's objectives are consistent with the marketing environment.
2. Analyzing the company's sales volume, market share, and profitability.

Strengths and Weaknesses

Here the focus is on the advantages and disadvantages that an organization has in meeting the target market's needs.

- *Example of a strength:* The company has a highly trained and capable sales force.
- *Example of a weakness*: The company's products have a low-quality image even though the actual quality is equal to or exceeds the quality of the major competitor's products.

Opportunities and Threats

This section covers factors that exist outside and independent of the company but that nonetheless can affect operations.

- *Opportunity*: Favorable conditions in the environment that could produce rewards for the company if acted on—for example, consumers have less leisure time and demand more convenience products.
- *Threat*: Conditions that may prevent the company from achieving its objectives unless acted on—for example, more women are working outside the home, which means that the company's door-to-door sales are suffering.

Marketing Objectives

This section states what the marketing activities are designed to accomplish. Forms of marketing objectives include

- Product introduction, improvement, or innovation
- Sales or market share
- Profitability
- Pricing
- Distribution
- Advertising

Marketing objectives must

- Be expressed in clear, simple terms.
- Be written so that they can be measured accurately.
- Give a time frame for achieving objectives.
- Be consistent with the company's overall marketing strategy.

Marketing Strategies

Marketing strategy includes selecting the target market and developing the marketing mix.

- *Selecting a target market*: Describe the target market in terms of demographic, geographic, psychographic, and product usage characteristics.
- *Determining the marketing mix*: Decide how product distribution, promotion, and price will satisfy customer needs.

Marketing Implementation

This section describes the process of putting the marketing strategies into action and answers

- What specific actions will we take?
- How will we perform these activities?
- Who is responsible for completing the activities?
- How much will these activities cost?

Evaluation and Control

How will the results of the marketing plan be measured and evaluated? Factors to be considered include

- *Performance standards*: How will the product's performance be judged?
- *Financial controls*: How will the company assess whether the marketing plan is working?
- *Monitoring procedures*: How will the cause of any problems be pinpointed?

Source: From Pride/Ferrell, *Marketing*.

Using the Internet

An excellent online resource for marketing information is the American Marketing Association's website (**http://www.marketingpower.com**). The site also provides access to a host of specialized marketing publications such as *Marketing News, Marketing Management, Marketing Research*, and the *Journal of Marketing*, to list but a few.

can be estimated for a city, county, state, or group of nations. Finally, analysts should indicate whether their estimates are for a specific product item, a product line, or an entire product category.

A **sales forecast** is an estimate of the amount of a product that an organization expects to sell during a certain period of time, based on a specified level of marketing effort. Managers in different divisions of an organization rely on sales forecasts when they purchase raw materials, schedule production, secure financial resources, consider plant or equipment purchases, hire personnel, and plan inventory levels. Because the accuracy of a sales forecast is so important, organizations often use several forecasting methods, including executive judgments, surveys of buyers or sales personnel, time-series analyses, correlation analyses, and market tests. The specific methods used depend on the costs involved, type of product, characteristics of the market, time span of the forecast, purposes for which the forecast is used, stability of historical sales data, availability of the required information, and expertise and experience of forecasters.

sales forecast an estimate of the amount of a product that an organization expects to sell during a certain period of time based on a specified level of marketing effort

learning objective

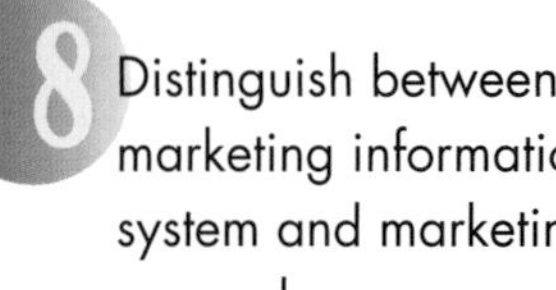

8 Distinguish between a marketing information system and marketing research.

Marketing Information

The availability and use of accurate and timely information are critical to making effective marketing decisions. A wealth of marketing information is obtainable. There are two general ways to obtain it: through a marketing information system and through marketing research.

marketing information system a system for managing marketing information that is gathered continually from internal and external sources

Marketing Information Systems

A **marketing information system** is a framework for managing marketing information that is gathered continually from internal and external sources. Most such systems are computer-based because of the amount of data the system must accept, store, sort, and retrieve. *Continual* collection of data is essential if the system is to incorporate the most up-to-date information.

In concept, the operation of a marketing information system is not complex. Data from a variety of sources are fed into the system. Data from *internal* sources include sales figures, product and marketing costs, inventory levels, and activities of the sales force. Data from *external* sources relate to the organization's suppliers, intermediaries, and customers; competitors' marketing activities; and economic conditions. All these data are stored and processed within the marketing information system. Its output is a flow of information in the form that is most useful for making marketing decisions. This information might include daily sales

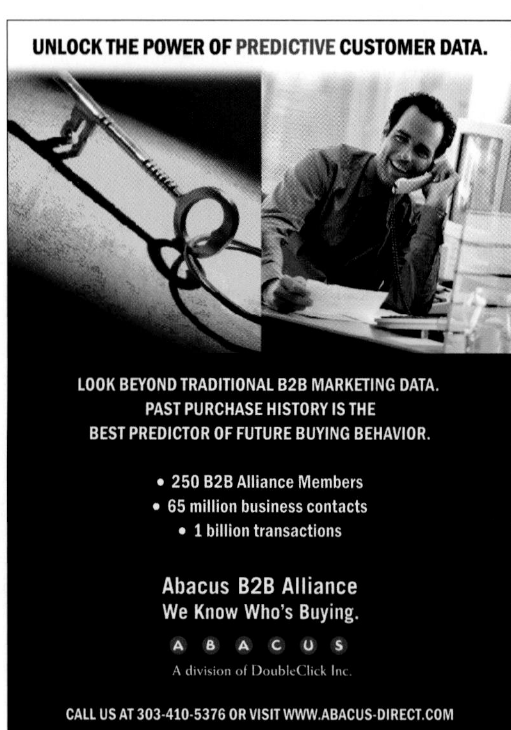

Marketing information provider. Many organizations, such as Abacus, a division of DoubleClick Inc., provide information to help marketers develop, implement, and manage marketing strategies. effectively.

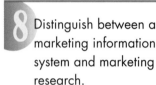

reports by territory and product, forecasts of sales or buying trends, and reports on changes in market share for the major brands in a specific industry. Both the information outputs and their form depend on the requirements of the personnel in the organization.

Marketing Research

Marketing research is the process of systematically gathering, recording, and analyzing data concerning a particular marketing problem. Thus marketing research is used in specific situations to obtain information not otherwise available to decision makers. It is an intermittent, rather than a continual, source of marketing information. A new software company, There, Inc., used marketing research to determine whether or not online gamers would be willing to spend actual dollars to buy virtual goods for their online characters. The CEO of There was astonished to learn that about 16 to 20 percent of those tested were willing to trade real money for "Therebucks" in order to dress their created cyberspace characters with virtual Nikes and Levis.[11]

marketing research the process of systematically gathering, recording, and analyzing data concerning a particular marketing problem

Table 13.5 outlines a six-step procedure for conducting marketing research. This procedure is particularly well suited to testing new products, determining various characteristics of consumer markets, and evaluating promotional activities. Food-processing companies, such as Kraft General Foods and Kellogg's, use a variety of marketing research methods to avoid costly mistakes in introducing the wrong products or products in the wrong way or at the wrong time. They have been particularly interested in using marketing research to learn more about the African-American and Hispanic markets. Understanding of the food preferences, loyalties, and purchase motivators of these groups enables these companies to serve them better.

table 13.5 The Six Steps of Marketing Research

Step	Description
1. Define the problem	In this step the problem is clearly and accurately stated to determine what issues are involved in the research, what questions to ask, and what types of solutions are needed. This is a crucial step that should not be rushed.
2. Make a preliminary investigation	The objective of preliminary investigation is to develop both a sharper definition of the problem and a set of tentative answers. The tentative answers are developed by examining internal information and published data and by talking with persons who have some experience with the problem. These answers will be tested by further research.
3. Plan the research	At this stage researchers know what facts are needed to resolve the identified problem and what facts are available. They make plans on how to gather needed but missing data.
4. Gather factual information	Once the basic research plan has been completed, the needed information can be collected by mail, telephone, or personal interviews; by observation; or from commercial or government data sources. The choice depends on the plan and the available sources of information.
5. Interpret the information	Facts by themselves do not always provide a sound solution to a marketing problem. They must be interpreted and analyzed to determine the choices available to management.
6. Reach a conclusion	Sometimes the conclusion or recommendation becomes obvious when the facts are interpreted. However, in other cases, reaching a conclusion may not be so easy because of gaps in the information or intangible factors that are difficult to evaluate. If and when the evidence is less than complete, it is important to say so.

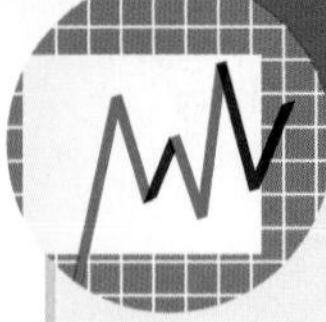

exploring business

Observing Customers in Their Native Habitats

THE PROBLEM: How to find out what consumers really want when they buy or use a product. The solution: *Ethnography*, observing and interviewing consumers in action at home or in stores. Surveys and other techniques are extremely valuable marketing research techniques. However, consumers are not always able to express their needs, nor do they always behave as they tell researchers they do. Through ethnography, marketers can learn more about underlying needs, design products to meet those needs, and create an appropriate marketing mix for each targeted segment. This is why more marketers are acting like anthropologists by using ethnography to study consumer behavior in everyday settings.

For example, the U.K. footwear manufacturer Clarks recently used ethnography when it designed new boots targeting the "active walker" segment. Rather than guess at these consumers' expectations and buying habits, the company commissioned ethnographic research to study the consumers in this segment at home and then walking and hiking. The researchers also observed consumers shopping for walking boots in different stores.

On the basis of all this information, Clarks created a new boot with an improved sole, better shock absorption, and a simplified lacing pattern. The company also provided retailers with point-of-sale presentation ideas to help sell the new product. Thanks to the insights gleaned from ethnography, Clarks successfully launched its Active Mover boot as the cornerstone of a new product line for active walkers.

A growing number of marketers are using ethnography to catch customers in the act of shopping. For example, a Minneapolis advertising agency operates a small store called Once Famous. The store carries a highly eclectic merchandise mix because at any one time the agency may be testing shopper reaction to baby clothes, candles, furniture, and more. To avoid invading shoppers' privacy, the store has a prominent sign notifying consumers that they will be videotaped if they enter. Inside, trained interviewers also ask shoppers about their choices to understand their preferences and motivations—information that can help companies do an even better job of serving their customers.

Using Technology to Gather and Analyze Marketing Information

Technology is making information for marketing decisions increasingly accessible. The ability of firms to electronically track the purchase behaviors of customers and to better determine what they want is changing the nature of marketing. The integration of telecommunications with computing technology provides marketers with access to accurate information not only about customers and competitors but also about industry forecasts and business trends. Among the communication tools that are radically changing the way marketers obtain and use information are databases, online information services, and the Internet.

A *database* is a collection of information arranged for easy access and retrieval. Using databases, marketers tap into internal sales reports, newspaper articles, company news releases, government economic reports, bibliographies, and more. Many marketers use commercial databases, such as LEXIS-NEXIS, to obtain useful information for marketing decisions. Many of these commercial databases are available in printed form (for a fee), online (for a fee), or on purchasable CD-ROMs. Others develop their own databases in-house. Some firms sell their databases to other organizations. *Reader's Digest*, for example, markets a database that provides information on 100 million households. Dunn & Bradstreet markets a database that includes information on the addresses, phone numbers, and contacts of businesses located in specific areas.

Information provided by a single firm on household demographics, purchases, television viewing behavior, and responses to promotions such as coupons and free samples is called *single-source data*. For example, Behavior Scan, offered by Information Resources, Inc., screens about 60,000 households in twenty-six U.S. markets.

This single-source information service monitors household televisions and records he programs and commercials viewed. When buyers from these households shop in tores equipped with scanning registers, they present Hotline cards (similar to credit ards) to cashiers. This enables each customer's identification to be electronically oded so that the firm can track each product purchased and store the information in database.

Online information services offer subscribers access to e-mail, websites, files for downloading (such as with Acrobat Reader), news, databases, and research materials. By subscribing to mailing lists, marketers can receive electronic newsletters and par-icipate in online discussions with other network users. This ability to communicate nline with customers, suppliers, and employees improves the capability of a firm's marketing information system and helps the company track its customers' changing desires and buying habits.

The *Internet* has evolved as a powerful communication medium, linking cus-omers and companies around the world via computer networks with e-mail, forums, veb pages, and more. Growth in Internet use, and especially the World Wide Web, nas given rise to an entire industry that makes marketing information easily accessible o both companies and customers. The web organizes a great deal of the information available on the Internet into a series of interconnected "pages." Among the many veb pages useful for marketing research are the home pages of Nielsen marketing re-search and *Advertising Age*. While most web home pages are open to all Internet users, some companies, such as U.S. West and Turner Broadcasting System, also maintain nternal web pages, called *intranets*, that allow employees to access internal data and acilitate communication among departments.

Table 13.6 lists a number of websites that may serve as valuable resources for mar-keting research. The Bureau of the Census, for example, uses the World Wide Web to

table 13.6 Internet Sources of Marketing Information

Source	Website
Government Sources	
U.S. Census Bureau	**www.census.gov**
U.S. Department of State	**www.state.gov**
FedWorld	**www.fedworld.gov**
Commercial Sources	
A. C. Nielsen	**www.acnielsen.com**
Information Resources, Inc.	**www.infores.com**
Gallup	**www.gallup.com**
Arbitron	**www.arbitron.com**
Chamber of Commerce	**chamber-of-commerce.com**
Periodicals and Books	
American Demographics	**www.americandemographics.com**
Advertising Age	**www.adage.com**
Sales & Marketing Management	**www.salesandmarketing.com**
Fortune	**www.fortune.com/fortune**
Inc.	**www.inc.com/home**
Business Week	**www.businessweek.com**
Bloomberg Report	**www.bloomberg.com**

Source: From Pride/Ferrell, *Marketing*. Copyright © 2003 by Houghton Mifflin Company. Reprinted with permission.

disseminate information that may be useful to marketing researchers, particularly through the *Statistical Abstract of the United States* and data from the most recent Census. The "Census Lookup" option allows marketing researchers to create their own customized information. With this online tool, researchers can select tables by clicking boxes to select a state and then, within the state, the county, place, and urbanized area or metropolitan statistical area to be examined.

buying behavior the decisions and actions of people involved in buying and using products

consumer buying behavior the purchasing of products for personal or household use, not for business purposes

business buying behavior the purchasing of products by producers, resellers, governmental units, and institutions

Types of Buying Behavior

Buying behavior may be defined as the decisions and actions of people involved in buying and using products.[12] **Consumer buying behavior** refers to the purchasing of products for personal or household use, not for business purposes. **Business buying behavior** is the purchasing of products by producers, resellers, governmental units, and institutions. Since a firm's success depends greatly on buyers' reactions to a particular marketing strategy, it is important to understand buying behavior. Marketing managers are better able to predict customer responses to marketing strategies and to develop a satisfying marketing mix if they are aware of the factors that affect buying behavior.

learning objective

9 Identify the major steps in the consumer buying decision process and the sets of factors that may influence this process.

Consumer Buying Behavior

Consumers' buying behaviors differ when they buy different types of products. For frequently purchased low-cost items, a consumer employs routine response behavior involving very little search or decision-making effort. The buyer uses limited decision making for purchases made occasionally or when more information is needed about an unknown product in a well-known product category. When buying an unfamiliar, expensive item or one that is seldom purchased, the consumer engages in extensive decision making.

A person deciding on a purchase goes through some or all of the steps shown in Figure 13.4. First, the consumer acknowledges that a problem exists. A problem is usually the lack of a product or service that is desired or needed. Then the buyer looks for information, which may include brand names, product characteristics, warranties, and other features. Next, the buyer weighs the various alternatives he or she has discovered and then finally makes a choice and acquires the item. In the after-purchase stage, the consumer evaluates the suitability of the product. This judgment will affect future purchases. As Figure 13.4 shows, the buying process is influenced by situational factors (physical surroundings, social surroundings, time, purchase reason, and buyer's mood and condition), psychological factors (perception, motives, learning, attitudes, personality, and lifestyle), and social factors (family, roles, peer groups, social class, culture, and subculture).

Routine response purchase behavior. When purchasing gum and candy bars, most consumers will employ routine response behavior. That is, they do not put much effort into deciding which low-cost product to buy.

Business Buying Behavior

Business buyers consider a product's quality, its price, and the service provided by suppliers. Marketers at GraniteRock Company understand the value of customer service and thus concentrate their efforts on on-time delivery to distinguish GraniteRock from its competitors.[13] Business buyers usually are better informed than consumers about products and

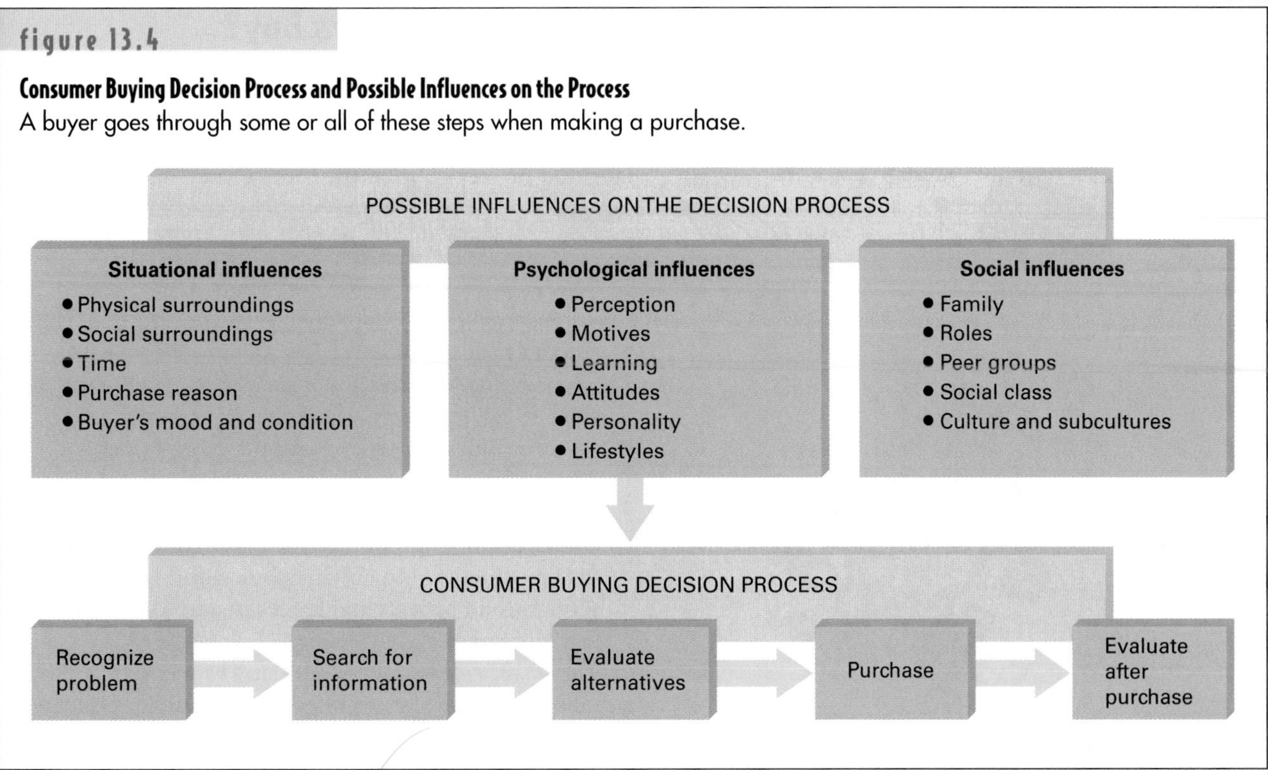

Source: William M. Pride and O. C. Ferrell, *Marketing: Concepts and Strategies*, 12th ed. Copyright © 2003 by Houghton Mifflin Company. Adapted with permission.

generally buy in larger quantities. In a business, a committee or group of people, rather than single individuals, often decides on purchases. Committee members must consider the organization's objectives, purchasing policies, resources, and personnel. Business buying occurs through description, inspection, sampling, or negotiation. A number of organizations buy a variety of products online. School districts save 10 to 20 percent on school supplies and receive their orders in two days instead of seven days.[14]

The American Consumer

In this section we examine several measures of consumer income, a major source of buying power. By looking at why, what, where, and when consumers buy, we gain a better understanding of how this income is spent.

learning objective

10 Describe three ways of measuring consumer income.

Consumer Income

Purchasing power is created by income. However, as every taxpayer knows, not all income is available for spending. For this reason, marketers consider income in three different ways. **Personal income** is the income an individual receives from all sources *less* the Social Security taxes the individual must pay. **Disposable income** is personal income *less* all additional personal taxes. These taxes include income, estate, gift, and property taxes levied by local, state, and federal governments. About 3 percent of all disposable income is saved. **Discretionary income** is disposable income *less* savings and expenditures on food, clothing, and housing. Discretionary income is of particular interest to marketers because consumers have the most choice in spending it. Consumers use their discretionary income to purchase items ranging from automobiles and vacations to movies and pet food.

personal income the income an individual receives from all sources *less* the Social Security taxes the individual must pay

disposable income personal income *less* all additional personal taxes

discretionary income disposable income *less* savings and expenditures on food, clothing, and housing

Can you identify with the problem this product will solve? Marketers sometimes employ advertising to encourage problem recognition, the first stage of the consumer buying decision process. Once consumers realize they have a need or a use for a product, they are on their way to purchasing it.

Why Do Consumers Buy?

Consumers buy with the hope of getting a large amount of current and future satisfaction relative to their buying power. They buy because they would rather have a particular good or service than the money they have to spend to buy it. Here are major reasons why consumers choose to buy some specific products:

1. *They have a use for the product.* Many items fill an immediate "use" need. A family needs pots and pans; a student needs books.
2. *They like the convenience a product offers.* Such items as electric can openers and cordless telephones are not essential, but they offer convenience and thus satisfaction.
3. *They believe the purchase will enhance their wealth.* People collect antiques or gold coins as investments as well as for enjoyment. Homeowners buy paint, landscape services, and ornamental fences to add to the value of their property.
4. *They take pride in ownership.* Many consumers purchase items such as Rolex watches because such products provide status and pride of ownership as well as utility.
5. *They buy for safety.* Consumers buy health, life, and fire insurance to protect themselves and their families. Smoke detectors, burglar alarms, traveler's checks, and similar products also provide safety and protection.

What Do Consumers Buy?

Figure 13.5 shows how consumer spending is divided among various categories of goods and services. The average American household spent $38,045 in 2000, according to the latest available data from the Bureau of Labor Statistics. The greatest proportion of disposable income was spent on food, clothing, and shelter. The largest share—$12,319—went toward housing and related expenses, such as supplies, utilities, and furnishings. The second-largest expense was transportation, with families spending an average of $7,417 on cars and other vehicles, insurance, repairs, and public transportation. The average household spent $5,158 on food, including $3,021 to eat at home. Clothing and related services, such as dry cleaning, used up $1,856. Another $1,863 went toward entertainment, and slightly more than $2,066 was spent on health care.[15]

Consumers are changing their spending patterns. They are spending more money on goods and services that they think will keep them healthy, mobile, and informed. Over the last year, participation in selected sport and fitness activities has changed. Engaged couples are showing a preference for experiences and activities over possessions; many skip registering at stores that sell traditional wedding gifts such as china and silver and instead request gifts such as sporting goods, camping

Spotlight

Few college students spend big bucks for Valentine's Day

When asked how much they thought they'd spend on Valentine's Day, here's how college-age men and women replied:

More than $100	Between $50–$100	Less than $50	Nothing
4%	10%	30%	55%

Source: *USA Today*, February 12, 2002, p. A1.

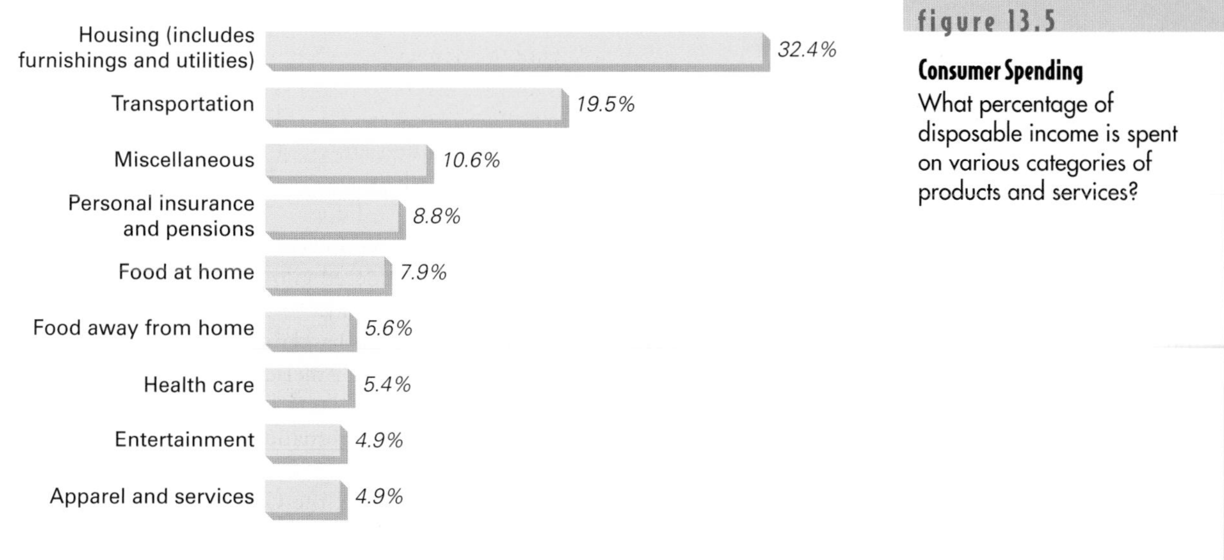

figure 13.5

Consumer Spending
What percentage of disposable income is spent on various categories of products and services?

ource: "Consumer Expenditures in 2002," Bureau of Labor Statistics, April 2002.

quipment, and tools. Spending on computers and educational toys is also on the ise. Parents may scrimp in other areas but buy educational toys because they believe hose toys are "an investment" in their children's future. Working parents also place igh value on scarce family time, thus spending more of their budgets on family va- ations and outings. The top 1 percent of wealthier Americans shun luxury items, uch as furs and jewelry, in favor of spending money on their children or investing for etirement.[16]

Vhere Do Consumers Buy?

robably the most important influence on a consumer's decision about where to buy particular product is his or her perception of the store. Consumers' general im- ressions of an establishment's products, prices, and sales personnel can mean the

Does your dog tell you where to shop? Customers decide where to buy based on their perceptions of stores as well as on location, product assortment, price, and service availability. Animal lovers know that PETsMART stores welcome four-legged customers and that they offer high-quality products at reasonable prices.

Harlem Globetrotters Bring Basketball Fun to the World

THE HARLEM GLOBETROTTERS have been entertaining audiences with their unique brand of basketball fun for more than seventy-five years. The team got its start when promoter Abe Saperstein, who lived on the north side of Chicago, organized a group of African-American players from the south side in 1926. The team played excellent basketball for thirteen years, rarely losing a game. Then, after a defeat in their first professional basketball championship series, the Globetrotters started fooling around on the court. The audience was delighted, which encouraged the players to clown around even more—and a new form of entertainment was born, melding the best of basketball and humor.

All Globetrotters had top athletic skills. Three set height records for vertical slam dunks, including Michael "Wild Thing" Wilson, who completed a twelve-foot dunk (the regulation basket height is ten feet). Some players went on to become National Basketball Association stars, including Wilt Chamberlain and Connie Hawkins, among others. But comedic flair was just as important. Once the team began emphasizing entertainment, Globetrotter Inman Jackson established the "Clown Prince" of basketball, a role that Meadowlark Lemon and others embellished over the years. Reece "Goose" Tatum created many of the hilarious routines considered Globetrotters classics today.

Fifty years ago basketball was still primarily an American sport. However, the team successfully built an international following by marketing both athleticism and good-natured hijinks. In time, the Globetrotters became global basketball ambassadors. Recently, they were admitted to the Basketball Hall of Fame. This continued popularity has prompted Burger King, Fubu, and other companies to forge marketing alliances linking specific products and promotions with the well-known Globetrotters brand.

By now the team has entertained more than 120 million fans in 117 countries. What accounts for its worldwide appeal? "Comedy's an art form, and I think the fact that we could make people laugh and have access to the hearts and minds of generations and cultures by the way the Globetrotters did what they did was a tremendous asset," observes former player Mannie Jackson, who now owns the team.

difference between repeat sales and lost business. Consumers distinguish among various types of retail outlets (such as specialty shops, department stores, and discount outlets), and they choose particular types of stores for specific purchases. Many retail outlets go to a great deal of trouble to build and maintain a particular image, and they carry only those products that fit the image. Consumers also select the businesses they patronize on the basis of location, product assortment, and such services as credit terms, return privileges, and free delivery.

People buy online, too. A recent survey shows that the top two sites for both men and women are Amazon.com and Barnes&Noble.com. For women, the most often purchased products bought online are books, CDs, computers, health and beauty products, toys, and clothing. Men's online purchases focus on computers, CDs, books, small consumer electronics, videos, and air travel. Because of the convenience, speed, and efficiency offered, men prefer to shop at online malls. However, women prefer to shop at brick-and-mortar malls.[17] More and more consumers are choosing to shop on the Internet or to seek information to enable a purchase at a later time. According to Nielsen/NetRatings there are an estimated 15 million websites today. However, people tend to visit their favorite top ten sites repeatedly. When they do venture onto a new site for the first time, they usually do not stay very long. According to NetSmart America, 87 percent of viewers quickly abandon a new site due to the frustration they experience navigating unfamiliar content. If building web traffic is a serious goal, the message for site designers is clear: Keep it simple.[18]

When Do Consumers Buy?

In general, consumers buy when buying is most convenient. Certain business hours have long been standard for establishments that sell consumer products. However, many of these establishments have stretched their hours to include evenings, holidays, and Sundays. Also, many catalog and online companies are accessible twenty-four hours a day, seven days a week. Ultimately, customers control when they do their buying.

In the next chapter we discuss two elements of the marketing mix: product and price. Our emphasis will be on product development and pricing within a marketing strategy.

Return To inside business

Harley-Davidson is marketing more than just casual two-wheeled transportation—it is clearly marketing a lifestyle choice that customers consciously make. In addition to buying Harley-Davidson motorcycles, many customers wear branded apparel, and a few show off tattoos of the famous winged brand mark. They also connect with each other and the brand through the Harley Owners Group—640,000 members strong—which sponsors events such as cross-country tours benefiting charities.

Still, Harley-Davidson's future depends on bringing the next generation of customers into the fold. To that end, it has established the Rider's Edge program to teach first-timers how to ride and care for their motorcycles. The company website also has a special section devoted to the basics of motorcycling. Although 90 percent of Harley-Davidson's customers are male, the number of female customers has doubled in the past decade—a trend that company marketers want to encourage. To stay on the road to higher sales and profits, Harley-Davidson will have to stay attuned to all its customers' needs and watch the rearview mirror for signs of aggressive competitors.

Questions

1. Why would Harley-Davidson prefer to introduce a starter motorcycle selling for about $4,000 under its subsidiary's brand name?
2. Which type of utility is Harley-Davidson providing through its dealership network? Which type of utility is it providing by marketing different motorcycle models?

chapter review

Summary

Understand the meaning of *marketing* and explain how it creates utility for purchasers of products.

Marketing is the process of planning and executing the conception, pricing, promotion, and distribution of ideas, goods, and services to create exchanges that satisfy individual and organizational objectives. Marketing adds value in the form of utility or the power of a product or service to satisfy a need. It creates place utility by making products available where customers want them, time utility by making products available when customers want them, and possession utility by transferring the ownership of products to buyers.

Trace the development of the marketing concept and understand how it is implemented.

From the Industrial Revolution until the early twentieth century, business people focused on the production of goods; from the 1920s to the 1950s, the emphasis moved to the selling of goods. During the 1950s, however, business people recognized that their enterprises involved not only producing and selling products but also satisfying customers' needs. They began to implement the marketing concept, a business philosophy that involves the entire organization in the dual processes of meeting the customers' needs and achieving the organization's goals.

Implementation of the marketing concept begins and ends with customers—first to determine what customers' needs are and later to evaluate how well the firm is meeting those needs.

Understand what markets are and how they are classified.

A market consists of people with needs, the ability to buy, and the desire and authority to purchase. Markets are classified as consumer and industrial (producer, reseller, governmental, and institutional) markets.

Identify the four elements of the marketing mix and be aware of their importance in developing a marketing strategy.

A marketing strategy is a plan for the best use of an organization's resources to meet its objectives. Developing a marketing strategy involves selecting and analyzing a target market and creating and maintaining a marketing mix that will satisfy that target market. A target market is chosen through either the undifferentiated approach or the market segmentation approach. A market segment is a group of individuals or organizations within a market that have similar characteristics and needs. Businesses that use an undifferentiated approach design a single marketing mix and direct it at the entire market for a particular product. The market segmentation approach directs a marketing mix at a segment of a market.

The four elements of a firm's marketing mix are product, price, distribution, and promotion. The product ingredient includes decisions about the product's design, brand name, packaging, and warranties. The pricing ingredient is concerned with both base prices and various types of discounts. Distribution involves not only transportation and storage but also the selection of intermediaries. Promotion focuses on providing information to target markets. The elements of the marketing mix can be varied to suit broad organizational goals, marketing objectives, and target markets.

Explain how the marketing environment affects strategic market planning.

To achieve a firm's marketing objectives, marketing mix strategies must begin with an assessment of the marketing environment, which in turn will influence decisions about marketing mix ingredients. Marketing activities are affected by a number of external forces that make up the marketing environment. These forces include economic forces, sociocultural forces, political forces, competitive forces, legal and regulatory forces, and technological forces. Economic forces affect customers' ability and willingness to buy. Sociocultural forces are societal and cultural factors, such as attitudes, beliefs, and lifestyles, that affect customers' buying choices. Political forces and legal and regulatory forces influence marketing planning through laws that protect consumers and regulate competition. Competitive forces are the actions of competitors who are implementing their own marketing plans. Technological forces can create new marketing opportunities or quickly cause a product to become obsolete.

Understand the major components of a marketing plan.

A marketing plan is a written document that specifies an organization's resources, objectives, strategy, and implementation and control efforts to be used in marketing a specific product or product group. The marketing plan describes a firm's current position, establishes marketing objectives, and specifies the methods the organization will use to achieve these objectives. Marketing plans can be short-range, covering one year or less; medium-range, covering two to five years; and long-range, covering periods of more than five years.

Describe how market measurement and sales forecasting are used.

Market measurement and sales forecasting are used to estimate sales potential and predict product sales in specific market segments.

Distinguish between a marketing information system and marketing research.

Strategies are monitored and evaluated through marketing research and the marketing information system that stores and processes internal and external data in a form that aids marketing decision making. A marketing information system is a system for managing marketing information that is gathered continually from internal and external sources. Marketing research is the process of systematically gathering, recording, and analyzing data concerning a particular marketing problem. It is an intermittent, rather than a continual, source of marketing information. Technology is making information for marketing decisions more accessible. Electronic communication tools can be very useful for accumulating accurate information with minimal customer interaction. Information technologies that are changing the way marketers obtain and use information are databases, online information services, and the Internet.

Identify the major steps in the consumer buying decision process and the sets of factors that may influence this process.

Buying behavior consists of the decisions and actions of people involved in buying and using products. Consumer buying behavior refers to the purchase of products for personal or household use. Organizational buying behavior is the purchase of products by producers, resellers, governments, and institutions. Understanding buying behavior helps marketers predict how buyers will respond to marketing strategies. The consumer buying decision process consists of five steps, including recognizing the problem, searching for information, evaluating alternatives, purchasing, and evaluating after purchase. Factors affecting the consumer buying decision process fall into three categories: situational influences, psychological influences, and social influences.

Describe three ways of measuring consumer income.

Personal income is the income an individual receives, less the Social Security taxes he or she must pay. Disposable income is personal income minus all other taxes. Discretionary income is what remains of disposable income after savings and expenditures for necessities. Consumers use discretionary income to buy goods and services that best satisfy their needs.

Key Terms

You should now be able to define and give an example relevant to each of the following terms:

marketing (370)
utility (370)
form utility (371)
place utility (371)
time utility (371)
possession utility (371)
marketing concept (372)
relationship marketing (373)
market (374)
marketing strategy (375)
marketing mix (375)
target market (375)
undifferentiated approach (375)
market segment (377)
market segmentation (377)
marketing plan (380)
sales forecast (382)
marketing information system (382)
marketing research (383)
buying behavior (386)
consumer buying behavior (386)
business buying behavior (386)
personal income (387)
disposable income (387)
discretionary income (387)

Review Questions

1. How, specifically, does marketing create place, time, and possession utility?
2. How is a marketing-oriented firm different from a production-oriented firm or a sales-oriented firm?
3. What are the major requirements for a group of individuals and organizations to be a market? How does a consumer market differ from a business-to-business market?
4. What are the major components of a marketing strategy?
5. What is the purpose of market segmentation? What is the relationship between market segmentation and the selection of target markets?
6. What are the four elements of the marketing mix? In what sense are they "controllable"?
7. Describe the forces in the marketing environment that affect an organization's marketing decisions.
8. What is a marketing plan, and what are its major components?
9. What major issues should be specified before conducting a sales forecast?
10. What is the difference between a marketing information system and a marketing research project? How might the two be related?
11. What new information technologies are changing the ways that marketers keep track of business trends and customers?
12. Why do marketers need to understand buying behavior?
13. How are personal income, disposable income, and discretionary income related? Which is the best indicator of consumer purchasing power?
14. List five reasons why consumers make purchases. What need is satisfied in each case?

Discussion Questions

1. In what way is each of the following a marketing activity?
   a. The provision of sufficient parking space for customers at a suburban shopping mall
   b. The purchase by a clothing store of seven dozen sweaters in assorted sizes and colors
   c. The inclusion of a longer and more comprehensive warranty on an automobile
2. How might adoption of the marketing concept benefit a firm? How might it benefit the firm's customers?
3. Is marketing information as important to small firms as it is to larger firms? Explain.
4. How does the marketing environment affect a firm's marketing strategy?

video case

Building Memories and More at Build-A-Bear

How many retail empires are built by chief executive bears (CEBs)—especially CEBs with a keen sense of marketing? So far just one: the Build-A-Bear Workshop, a retailer that turns the buying process into a hands-on, interactive experience its customers will long remember.

The CEB behind Build-A-Bear is Maxine Clark, who spent twenty-five years as an executive with May Department Stores before leaving the corporate world to become an entrepreneur in 1997. Thinking back to her much-loved teddy bear and to the magic she remembered in special shopping trips as a child, Clark decided that her business would combine entertainment and retailing to please children of all ages. Today her idea has blossomed into a nationwide chain of more than 100 stores ringing up $107 million in annual sales.

When Clark started planning her business, she was determined to make memories, not simply sell an everyday, off-the-shelf product. Thus she devised a store-based workshop environment and invited customers to participate in crafting their own stuffed animals. Master Bear Builders (store employees) help customers choose the types of animals they want. Bears, bunnies, dogs, ponies, and frogs, available in small or large sizes, are just some of the choices. Next, customers select the fake-fur color and the amount of stuffing and then carefully insert the heart. To add a voice, they can insert a prerecorded sound chip or record a personalized sound chip. Then customers help stitch the seams, gently fluff the fur, and name their new friends. If they wish, they can pick out clothing and accessories such as angel wings or miniature cowboy gear. The result is a one-of-a-kind stuffed animal that goes home in a house-shaped package.

As part of the buying procedure, customers enter their animal's names and their own names and addresses, e-mail addresses, gender, and birth dates at computer stations in each store. Build-A-Bear uses this information to generate each toy's birth certificate, signed by Clark as CEB. Then the information is pooled with sales data and other details, carefully analyzed, and used to plan newsletters and other promotional efforts. In addition, because each animal contains a unique bar-coded tag, the company can return lost toys by consulting the database to determine ownership. So far the company has used the system to reunite fifty lost animals with their owners.

Before opening the first Build-A-Bear store in St. Louis, Missouri, Clark tested the idea on a friend's 10-year-old daughter, who was enthusiastic about the concept. As the chain grows, she continues to stay in touch with changes in her market's needs and behavior through a Cub Advisory Board of twenty children ages 6 to 14. The group meets quarterly to discuss new promotional programs and proposals for new products. Between meetings, Clark requests the board's feedback on specific questions via mail and e-mail. She also reads customer letters and e-mail messages to find out about the market's likes and dislikes.

Creating memorable in-store buying experiences requires lots of behind-the-scenes planning. Build-A-Bear's retail employees must complete a three-week training course at World Bearquarters before they start work in a store. They learn not only how to put the animals together but also how to work with a customer base that ranges from toddlers to grandparents. In the highly competitive retail industry, the personal touch differentiates Build-A-Bear from the typical mall store. It also transforms the buying experience into a special event that customers enjoy and want to repeat. And the stores themselves are geared to special events in their customers' lives. For example, parents can arrange for children's birthday parties at local Build-A-Bear stores during which each participant makes a customized toy.

Although Build-A-Bear began as a one-store business, it has quickly grown into a bear-sized success story. With stores in thirty states, the chain is now looking to expand to Canada, Australia, and Japan. Prices for a basic toy body start at about $12, but apparel, hats, and other accessories bring the average sale to more than $30. It is small wonder that the average Build-A-Bear store records sales of $700 per square foot, double the average for U.S. mall stores. Looking ahead, Clark is thinking about expanding into entertainment products such as books, television programs, and movies. This entrepreneur's special twist of combining entertainment with retailing to build customer relationships has made the teddy bear—now more than 100 years old—more popular than ever.[19]

Questions

1. Is there evidence that Build-A-Bear is trying to use the marketing concept? Explain.
2. Has Build-A-Bear used an undifferentiated approach, a concentrated approach, or a differentiated approach to segmenting a target market?
3. How has Build-A-Bear used its knowledge of consumer buying to attract customers?

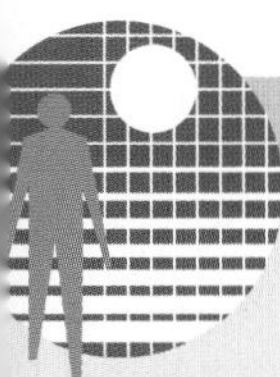

Building Skills for Career Success

1. Exploring the Internet

Consumer products companies with a variety of famous brand names known around the world are making their presence known on the Internet through websites and online banner advertising. The giants in consumer products include U.S.-based Procter & Gamble (**http://www.pg.com/**), Swiss-based Nestlé (**http://www.nestle.com/**), and British-based Unilever (**http://www.unilever.com/**).

According to a spokesperson for the Unilever Interactive Brand Center in New York, the firm is committed to making the Internet part of its marketing strategy. The center carries out R&D and serves as a model for others now in operation in the Netherlands and Singapore. Information is shared with interactive marketers assigned to specific business units. Eventually, centers will be established globally, reflecting the fact that most of Unilever's $52 billion of sales takes place in about 100 countries around the world.

Unilever's view that online consumer product sales are the way of the future was indicated by online alliances established with Microsoft Network, America Online, and NetGrocer.com. Creating an online dialogue with consumers on a global scale is no simple task. Cultural differences are often subtle and difficult to explain but nonetheless are perceived by the viewers interacting with a site. Unilever's website, which is its connection to customers all over the world, has a global feel to it. The question is whether or not it is satisfactory to each target audience.[20] Visit the text website for updates to this exercise.

Assignment

1. Examine the Unilever, Procter & Gamble, and Nestlé sites and describe the features that you think would be most interesting to consumers.
2. Describe those features you do not like and explain why.
3. Do you think that the sites can contribute to better consumer buyer behavior? Explain your thinking.

2. Developing Critical Thinking Skills

Market segmentation is the process of breaking down a larger target market into smaller segments. One common base of market segmentation is demographics. Demographics for the consumer market, which consists of individuals and household members who buy goods for their own use, include such criteria as age, gender, race, religion, income, family size, occupation, education, social class, and marital status. Liz Claiborne, Inc., retailer of women's apparel, uses demographics to target a market it calls *Liz Lady*. The company knows Liz Lady's age, income range, professional status, and family status, and it uses this profile to make marketing decisions.

Assignment

1. Identify a company that markets to the consumer.
2. Identify the company's major product.
3. Determine the demographics of one of the company's markets.
   a. From the list that follows, choose the demographics that apply to this market. (Remember that the demographics chosen must relate to the interest, need, and ability of the customer to purchase the product.)
   b. Briefly describe each demographic characteristic.

Consumer Market	*Description*
Age ___	___________
Income ___	___________
Gender ___	___________
Race ___	___________
Ethnicity ___	___________
Income ___	___________
Occupation ___	___________
Family size ___	___________
Education ___	___________
Religion ___	___________
Homeowner ___	___________
Marital status ___	___________
Social class ___	___________

4. Summarize your findings in a statement that describes the target market for the company's product.

3. Building Team Skills

Review the text definitions of *market* and *target market*. Markets can be classified as consumer or industrial. Buyer behavior consists of the decisions and actions of those involved in buying and using products or services. By examining aspects of a company's products, you can usually determine the company's target market and the characteristics important to members of that target market.

Assignment

1. Working in teams of three to five, identify a company and its major products.
2. List and discuss characteristics that customers may find important. These factors may include price, quality, brand name, variety of services, salespeople, customer service, special offers, promotional campaign, packaging, convenience of use, convenience of purchase, location, guarantees, store/office decor, and payment terms.

3. Write a description of the company's primary customer (target market).

4. Researching Different Careers

Before interviewing for a job, you should learn all you can about the company. With this information, you will be prepared to ask meaningful questions about the firm during the interview, and the interviewer will no doubt be impressed with your knowledge of the business and your interest in it. To find out about a company, you can conduct some market research.

Assignment

1. Choose at least two local companies for which you might like to work.
2. Contact your local Chamber of Commerce. (The Chamber of Commerce collects information about local businesses, and most of its services are free.) Ask for information about the companies.
3. Call the Better Business Bureau in your community and ask if there are any complaints against the companies.
4. Prepare a report summarizing your findings.

5. Improving Communication Skills

Each year *Sales and Marketing Management* magazine publishes an issue called "Survey of Buying Power." It contains data on every county in the United States and cities with populations over 10,000. Included are

- Total population
- Number of households
- Median cash income per household
- Population percentage breakdown by income
- Total retail sales for each of the following businesses: automotive, drug, food, furniture, general merchandise, and household appliances

Assignment

1. Choose one of the businesses whose total retail sales are given in *Sales and Marketing Management* magazine's annual "Survey of Buying Power."
2. Use the magazine to evaluate trends in the industry. Is demand for the product increasing or decreasing?
3. Report to the class on total retail sales and potential demand.
4. Summarize your findings in a report.

chapter

14

Creating and Pricing Products that Satisfy Customers

Blockbuster can earn profit margins of 70 percent on DVD rentals, compared with 60 percent on VHS rentals.

learning objectives

1 Explain what a product is and how products are classified.

2 Discuss the product life cycle and how it leads to new product development.

3 Define *product line* and *product mix* and distinguish between the two.

4 Identify the methods available for changing a product mix.

5 Explain the uses and importance of branding, packaging, and labeling.

6 Describe the economic basis of pricing and the means by which sellers can control prices and buyers' perceptions of prices.

7 Identify the major pricing objectives used by businesses.

8 Examine the three major pricing methods that firms employ.

9 Explain the different strategies available to companies for setting prices.

10 Describe three major types of pricing associated with business products.

inside business

Priced to Rent or Sell at Blockbuster

CAN SALES OF ENTERTAINMENT products help Blockbuster double its annual revenues to $8 billion within the next few years? The chain operates 5,400 stores across the United States plus thousands of stores in other countries, serving nearly 50 million customers. During the 1990s, Blockbuster grew to become the market leader in VHS movie rentals. Now CEO John Antioco is pursuing higher profits by stressing both sales and rentals of DVD movies, video games, and video game consoles.

Costs and product availability are two key factors in Blockbuster's rental pricing. Since 1997, the company has benefited from deals with the major U.S. movie studios to obtain a larger quantity of VHS movies at a much lower cost. In exchange for paying less upfront, Blockbuster shares 40 percent of the VHS rental fees with the studios. This has slashed the company's costs from about $65 to about $23 per VHS movie while expanding the selection for customers.

The economics of DVD rentals are even better for Blockbuster. The company buys DVDs outright from the studios for about $17 each and keeps all the rental revenues it earns. It can earn profit margins of 70 percent on DVD rentals, compared with profit margins of 60 percent on VHS rentals. Small wonder that the company has been clearing room for more DVDs by shrinking the shelf space devoted to VHS movies.

Blockbuster is also giving video games, consoles, and accessories more exposure in its stores to boost both rentals and sales. Already the chain has captured 50 percent of the video game rental market, but management sees much higher future demand. In part, rising demand is due to plummeting console prices. Another factor is the trend toward tying video games to popular action and fantasy movies. When the movies are released on DVD, they include brief samplers of the related video games, driving customers to Blockbuster and other stores to rent or buy.

Studies reveal that most customers prefer to try a video game before they buy it. Accordingly, Blockbuster has lengthened the video game rental period to give gamers more opportunity to play before they buy. It also has launched a "Rent it! Like it! Buy it!" program offering a steep discount if renters buy previously rented games. (The company offers a similar discount for buying DVD movies after renting.) These changes have helped Blockbuster boost revenue from video game rentals and sales quarter after quarter.

Now others are using pricing strategies to challenge Blockbuster. Netflix, an Internet-based company, rents DVD movies by mail for a flat monthly fee. And retailers such as Wal-Mart and Best Buy offer price promotions to build customer traffic and sell DVDs. Still, Blockbuster will be counting on pricing to support its growth initiatives by boosting both sales and rentals.[1]

learning objective

1 Explain what a product is and how products are classified.

A **product** is everything one receives in an exchange, including all tangible and intangible attributes and expected benefits. A DVD purchased at Blockbuster, for example, includes not only the DVD itself but also a protective case, instructions, and a warranty. A car includes a warranty, an owner's manual, and perhaps free emergency road service for a year. Some of the intangibles that may go with an automobile include the status associated with ownership and the memories generated from past rides. Developing and managing products effectively are crucial to an organization's ability to maintain successful marketing mixes.

product everything one receives in an exchange, including all tangible and intangible attributes and expected benefits; it may be a good, service, or idea

A product may be a good, a service, or an idea. A *good* is a real, physical thing that we can touch, such as a Classic Sport football. A *service* is the result of applying human or mechanical effort to a person or thing. Basically, a service is a change we pay others to make for us. A real estate agent's services result in a change in the ownership of real property. A barber's services result in a change in your appearance. An *idea* may take the form of philosophies, lessons, concepts, or advice. Often ideas are included with a good or service. Thus we might buy a book (a good) that provides ideas on how to lose weight. Or we might join Weight Watchers for ideas on how to lose weight and for help (services) in doing so.

Our definition of the term *product* is based on the concept of an exchange. In a purchase, the product is exchanged for money—an amount of money equal to the *price* of the product. When the product is a good, the price may include such services as delivery, installation, warranties, and training. A good *with* such services is not the same product as the good *without* such services. In other words, sellers set a price for a particular "package" of goods, services, and ideas. When the makeup of that package changes, the price should change as well.

We look first in this chapter at products. We examine product classifications and describe the four stages, or life cycle, through which every product moves. Next, we illustrate how firms manage products effectively by modifying or deleting existing products and by developing new products. We also discuss branding, packaging, and labeling of products. Then our focus shifts to pricing. We explain competitive factors that influence sellers' pricing decisions and also explore buyers' perceptions of prices. After considering organizational objectives that can be accomplished through pricing, we outline several methods for setting prices. Finally, we describe pricing strategies by which sellers can reach target markets successfully.

Classification of Products

Different classes of products are directed at particular target markets. A product's classification largely determines what kinds of distribution, promotion, and pricing are appropriate in marketing the product.

Products can be grouped into two general categories: consumer and business (also called *business-to-business* or *industrial products*). A product purchased to satisfy personal and family needs is a **consumer product**. A product bought for resale, for making other products, or for use in a firm's operations is a **business product**. The buyer's use of the product determines the classification of an item. Note that a single item can be both a consumer and a business product. A broom is a consumer product if you use it in your home. However, the same broom is a business product if you use it in the maintenance of your business. After a product is classified as a consumer or business product, it can be further categorized as a particular type of consumer or business product.

consumer product a product purchased to satisfy personal and family needs

business product a product bought for resale, for making other products, or for use in a firm's operations

Consumer Product Classifications

The traditional and most widely accepted system of classifying consumer products consists of three categories: convenience, shopping, and specialty products. These groupings are based primarily on characteristics of buyers' purchasing behavior.

Occasionally, mushrooms can be combined with something other than sausage & extra cheese.
Inspire your cooking with authentic flavors from around the world. One box of Near East can take dinner to completely new places.
Your way to inspired cooking.
Near East
RICE PILAF

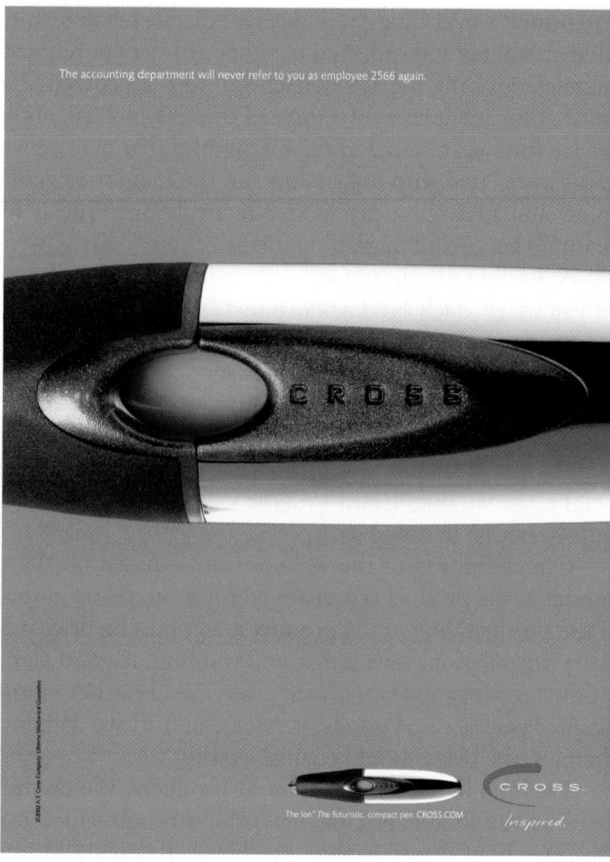

The Ion? The futuristic, compact pen. CROSS.COM

Convenience and shopping products. Most grocery items, such as Near East rice, are convenience products. Upper-end writing instruments, such as Cross Pens, are typically classified as shopping products.

convenience product a relatively inexpensive, frequently purchased item for which buyers want to exert only minimal effort

shopping product an item for which buyers are willing to expend considerable effort on planning and making the purchase

specialty product an item that possesses one or more unique characteristics for which a significant group of buyers is willing to expend considerable purchasing effort

A **convenience product** is a relatively inexpensive, frequently purchased item for which buyers want to exert only minimal effort. Examples include bread, gasoline, newspapers, soft drinks, and chewing gum. The buyer spends little time in planning the purchase of a convenience item or in comparing available brands or sellers.

A **shopping product** is an item for which buyers are willing to expend considerable effort on planning and making the purchase. Buyers allocate ample time for comparing stores and brands with respect to prices, product features, qualities, services, and perhaps warranties. Appliances, upholstered furniture, men's suits, bicycles, and cellular phones are examples of shopping products. These products are expected to last for a fairly long time and thus are purchased less frequently than convenience items.

A **specialty product** possesses one or more unique characteristics for which a group of buyers is willing to expend considerable purchasing effort. Buyers actually plan the purchase of a specialty product; they know exactly what they want and will not accept a substitute. In searching for specialty products, purchasers do not compare alternatives. Examples include unique sports cars, a specific type of antique dining table, a rare imported beer, or perhaps special handcrafted stereo speakers.

One problem with this approach to classification is that buyers may behave differently when purchasing a specific type of product. Thus a single product can fit into more than one category. To minimize this problem, marketers think in terms of how buyers are most likely to behave when purchasing a specific item.

Business Product Classifications

Based on their characteristics and intended uses, business products can be classified into the following categories: raw materials, major equipment, accessory equipment, component parts, process materials, supplies, and services.

Provider of business products. Xerox is a provider of imaging products and related services to other businesses.

A **raw material** is a basic material that actually becomes part of a physical product. It usually comes from mines, forests, oceans, or recycled solid wastes. Raw materials usually are bought and sold according to grades and specifications.

Major equipment includes large tools and machines used for production purposes. Examples of major equipment are lathes, cranes, and stamping machines. Some major equipment is custom-made for a particular organization, but other items are standardized products that perform one or several tasks for many types of organizations.

Accessory equipment is standardized equipment used in a firm's production or office activities. Examples include hand tools, typewriters, fractional-horsepower motors, and calculators. Compared with major equipment, accessory items are usually much less expensive and are purchased routinely with less negotiation.

A **component part** becomes part of a physical product and is either a finished item ready for assembly or a product that needs little processing before assembly. Although it becomes part of a larger product, a component part often can be identified easily. Clocks, tires, computer chips, and switches are examples of component parts.

A **process material** is used directly in the production of another product. Unlike a component part, however, a process material is not readily identifiable in the finished product. Like component parts, process materials are purchased according to industry standards or to the specifications of the individual purchaser. Examples include industrial glue and food preservatives.

A **supply** facilitates production and operations, but it does not become part of the finished product. Paper, pencils, oils, and cleaning agents are examples.

A **business service** is an intangible product that an organization uses in its operations. Examples include financial, legal, online, janitorial, and marketing research services. Purchasers must decide whether to provide their own services internally or to hire them from outside the organization.

raw material a basic material that actually becomes part of a physical product; usually comes from mines, forests, oceans, or recycled solid wastes

major equipment large tools and machines used for production purposes

accessory equipment standardized equipment used in a firm's production or office activities

component part an item that becomes part of a physical product and is either a finished item ready for assembly or a product that needs little processing before assembly

process material a material that is used directly in the production of another product but is not readily identifiable in the finished product

supply an item that facilitates production and operations but does not become part of the finished product

business service an intangible product that an organization uses in its operations

learning objective

2 Discuss the product life cycle and how it leads to new product development.

product life cycle a series of stages in which a product's sales revenue and profit increase, reach a peak, and then decline

The Product Life Cycle

In a way, products are like people. They are born, they live, and they die. Every product progresses through a **product life cycle,** a series of stages in which its sales revenue and profit increase, reach a peak, and then decline. A firm must be able to launch, modify, and delete products from its offering of products in response to changes in product life cycles. Otherwise, the firm's profits will disappear, and the firm will fail. Depending on the product, life-cycle stages will vary in length. In this section we discuss the stages of the life cycle and how marketers can use this information.

Stages of the Product Life Cycle

Generally, the product life cycle is assumed to be composed of four stages—introduction, growth, maturity, and decline—as shown in Figure 14.1. Some products progress through these stages rapidly, in a few weeks or months. Others may take years to go through each stage. The Rubik's Cube had a relatively short life cycle. Parker Brothers' Monopoly game, which was introduced over sixty years ago, is still going strong.

Introduction In the *introduction stage,* customer awareness and acceptance of the product are low. Sales rise gradually as a result of promotion and distribution activities, but initially, high development and marketing costs result in low profit or even in a loss. There are relatively few competitors. The price is sometimes high, and purchasers are primarily people who want to be "the first" to own the new product. The marketing challenge at this stage is to make potential customers aware of the product's existence and its features, benefits, and uses.

A new product is seldom an immediate success. Marketers must watch early buying patterns carefully and be prepared to modify the new product promptly if necessary. The product should be priced to attract the particular market segment that has the greatest desire and ability to buy the product. Plans for distribution and promotion should suit the targeted market segment. As with the product itself, the initial price, distribution channels, and promotional efforts may need to be adjusted quickly to maintain sales growth during the introduction stage.

figure 14.1

Product Life Cycle

The graph shows sales volume and profits during the life cycle of a product.

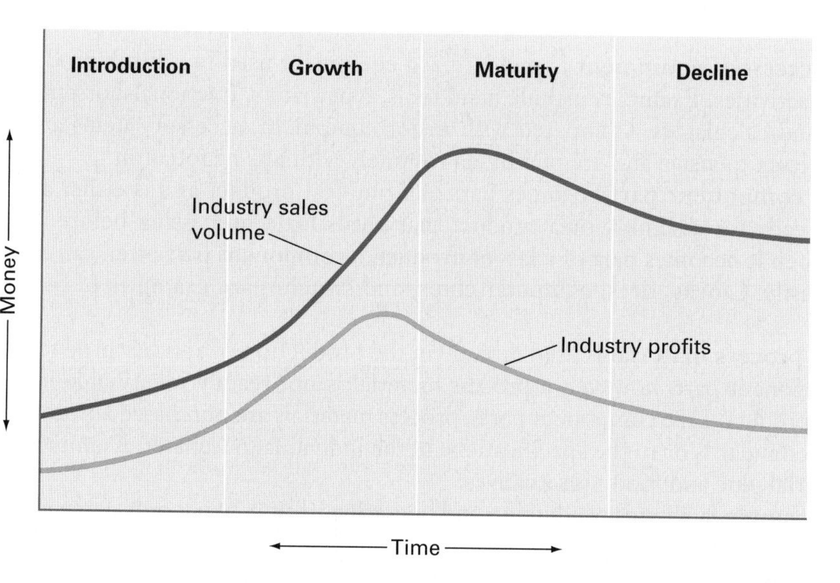

Source: William M. Pride and O. C. Ferrell, *Marketing: Concepts and Strategies,* 12th ed. Copyright © 2003 by Houghton Mifflin Company. Adapted with permission.

Growth In the *growth stage*, sales increase rapidly as the product becomes well known. Other firms probably have begun to market competing products. The competition and lower unit costs (due to mass production) result in a lower price, which reduces the profit per unit. Note that industry profits reach a peak and begin to decline during this stage. To meet the needs of the growing market, the originating firm offers modified versions of its product and expands its distribution. The 3M Company, the maker of Post-it Notes, has developed a variety of sizes, colors, and designs.

Cell phones are nearly everywhere. Cell phones are in the growth stage of the product life cycle. Several firms are introducing cell phones with new features. Here Chinese models in Shanghai are introducing new Motorola phones that can take and transmit photos.

Management's goal in the growth stage is to stabilize and strengthen the product's position by encouraging brand loyalty. To beat the competition, the company may further improve the product or expand the product line to appeal to specialized market segments. Management also may compete by lowering prices if increased production efficiency has resulted in savings for the company. As the product becomes more widely accepted, marketers may be able to broaden the network of distributors. Marketers also can emphasize customer service and prompt credit for defective products. During this period, promotional efforts attempt to build brand loyalty among customers.

The Internet has been a boon for digital photography, which is in the growth stage. According to Info Trends Research Group of Boston, by 2006, consumers will spend about $10 billion annually on digital cameras.[2] Part of this growth will be driven by Zing.com. Zing allows digital photographers to upload their pictures to free personal websites. Within their reserved area, users can edit, create albums, and e-mail images over the Internet.

Maturity Sales are still increasing at the beginning of the *maturity stage*, but the rate of increase has slowed. Later in this stage the sales curve peaks and begins to decline. Industry profits decline throughout this stage. Product lines are simplified, markets are segmented more carefully, and price competition increases. The increased competition forces weaker competitors to leave the industry. Refinements and extensions of the original product continue to appear on the market.

During a product's maturity stage, its market share may be strengthened by redesigned packaging or style changes. Also, consumers may be encouraged to use the product more often or in new ways. Pricing strategies are flexible during this stage. Markdowns and price incentives are not uncommon, although price increases may work to offset production and distribution costs. Marketers may offer incentives and assistance of various kinds to dealers to encourage them to support mature products, especially in the face of competition from private-label brands. New promotional efforts and aggressive personal selling may be necessary during this period of intense competition.

Decline During the *decline stage*, sales volume decreases sharply. Profits continue to fall. The number of competing firms declines, and the only survivors in the marketplace are firms that specialize in marketing the product. Production and marketing costs become the most important determinant of profit.

When a product adds to the success of the overall product line, the company may retain it; otherwise, management must determine when to eliminate the product. A product usually declines because of technological advances or environmental factors or because consumers have switched to competing brands. Therefore, few changes are made in the product itself during this stage. Instead, management may raise the price to cover costs, reprice to maintain market share, or lower the price to reduce inventory. Similarly, management will narrow distribution of the declining product to the most profitable existing markets. During this period, the company probably will not spend heavily on promotion, although it may use some advertising and sales incentives t slow the product's decline. The company may choose to eliminate less profitable ver sions of the product from the product line or may decide to drop the product entirely

Using the Product Life Cycle

Marketers should be aware of the life-cycle stage of each product for which they ar responsible. And they should try to estimate how long the product is expected to re main in that stage. Both must be taken into account in making decisions about th marketing strategy for a product. If a product is expected to remain in the maturit stage for a long time, a replacement product might be introduced later in the maturit stage. If the maturity stage is expected to be short, however, a new product should b introduced much earlier. For Example, Logitech, the world's leading manufacturer o computer mice, faces a short product life cycle with its technology-driven accessories In an industry with powerful competitors such as Microsoft, Logitech must frequentl introduce new products with the current trend toward everything wireless. The com pany has made strides against the competition with significant growth in sales over the past four years.[3] In some cases a firm may be willing to take the chance of speeding up the decline of existing products. In other situations a company will attempt to extend a product's life cycle. For example, General Mills has extended the life of Bisquick baking mix (launched in the mid-1930s) by significantly improving the product's formulation and creating and promoting a variety of uses.

examining ethics

What's Ahead for TiVo and Television?

TIVO PUTS TELEVISION viewers in control. Using the company's personal video recorder system, customers can automatically record all their favorite programs and then watch later without commercial interruptions simply by pressing a button. Customers also can plan what to record by subscribing to TiVo's extensive programming schedule, which covers two weeks of television listings, for a monthly fee. Although TiVo attracted fewer than one million subscribers in the three years following the product's introduction, more sign on each day. Yet, as the product settles into its growth stage, its features and usage raise a number of ethical issues.

For example, company research shows that 80 percent of users do use the product to skip the commercials in recorded programs. However, other research suggests that most television viewers avoid commercials with or without the use of TiVo. Still, should TiVo make it so easy for customers to circumvent the advertising that keeps programs on the air?

Clearly, someone has to cover the cost of airing television programs. Because of advertisers' sponsorship, viewers pay less to see cable programs or pay nothing to see broadcast programs. However, if TiVo's customers can easily skip commercials, what are the long-term implications if the product becomes more widely accepted? Might advertisers decide that they are not likely to reach their targeted audiences and therefore stop sponsoring programs? Would some programs disappear from broadcast television because they lack sponsorship? Would cable charges rise for viewers because the channels need to replace lost revenue?

TiVo is also developing a new product that allows customers to transfer their recorded television programs to DVDs. Should TiVo make it so easy for customers to potentially violate copyright laws by recording and then copying and selling programs? Finally, the company has arranged to place a "Best Buy" advertising box on its primary schedule screen. When customers click on the box, they see a thirty-second commercial followed by a special music video and a contest. Should TiVo put advertising in front of its viewers, knowing that most prefer not to watch commercials? What's ahead for TiVo and television?

Issues to Consider

1. Research indicates that 71 percent of TiVo users will watch a commercial if it is entertaining or if they are interested in the product. What are the implications for advertisers?
2. If you were a TiVo user, how would you react to seeing a "Best Buy" advertising box on the programming screen?

Product Line and Product Mix

learning objective

3 Define *product line* and *product mix* and distinguish between the two.

A **product line** is a group of similar products that differ only in relatively minor characteristics. Generally, the products within a product line are related to each other in the way they are produced, marketed, or used. Procter & Gamble, for example, manufactures and markets several shampoos, including Prell, Head & Shoulders, Pert Plus, and Ivory.

product line a group of similar products that differ only in relatively minor characteristics

product mix all the products a firm offers for sale

Many organizations tend to introduce new products within existing product lines. This permits them to apply the experience and knowledge they have acquired to the production and marketing of new products. Other firms develop entirely new product lines.

An organization's **product mix** consists of all the products the firm offers for sale. Two "dimensions" are often applied to a firm's product mix. The *width* of the mix is the number of product lines it contains. The *depth* of the mix is the average number of individual products within each line. These are general measures; we speak of a *broad* or a *narrow* mix rather than a mix of exactly three or five product lines. Some organizations provide broad product mixes to be competitive. For example, GE Financial Network (GEFN), a comprehensive Internet-based consumer-friendly financial services resource, provides an extensive product mix of financial services including home mortgages, mutual funds, stock price quotes, annuities, life insurance, auto insurance, long-term care insurance, credit cards, and auto warranty plans.[4]

Many firms seek new products to broaden their product mix, just as Eastman Kodak has done with digital cameras. By developing new product lines, firms gain additional experience and expertise. Moreover, they achieve stability by operating within several different markets. Problems in one particular market do not affect a multi-line firm nearly as much as they would affect a firm that depended entirely on a single product line.

Managing the Product Mix

learning objective

4 Identify the methods available for changing a product mix.

To provide products that satisfy people in a firm's target market or markets and that also achieve the organization's objectives, a marketer must develop, adjust, and maintain an effective product mix. Seldom can the same product mix be effective for long. Because customers' product preferences and attitudes change, their desire for a product may diminish or grow. In some cases a firm needs to alter its product mix to adapt to competition. A marketer may have to eliminate a product from the mix because one or more competitors dominate that product's specific market segment. Similarly, an organization may have to introduce a new product or modify an existing one to compete more effectively. For example, restaurants have found that consumers are demanding better food, so restaurants are more intensely managing their product mixes. Pizza Hut, one of Yum Brands' major chains, recently launched the Chicago Dish pizza and priced it at around $13. At Taco Bell, another Yum Brand, the $3.50 Southwest Steak Border Bowl is also designed to increase dine-in business and meet the needs of the consumer demanding better quality.[5] A marketer may expand the firm's product mix to take advantage of excess marketing and production capacity. For whatever reason a product mix is altered, the product mix must be managed to bring about improvements in the mix. There are three major ways to improve a product mix: change an existing product, delete a product, or develop a new product.

Changing Existing Products

Product modification refers to changing one or more of a product's characteristics. For this approach to be effective, several conditions must be met. First, the product must be modifiable. Second, existing customers must be able to perceive that a modification has been made, assuming that the modified item is still directed at the same

product modification the process of changing one or more of a product's characteristics

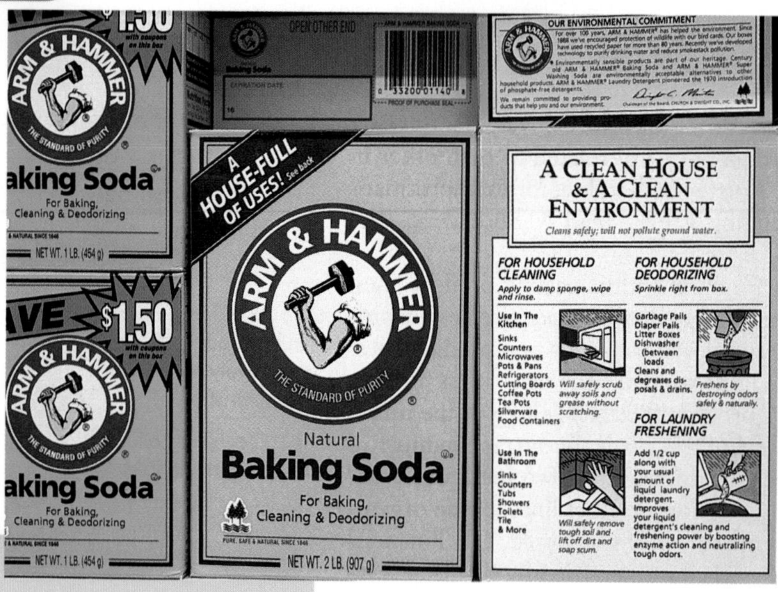

Managing the product mix. Marketers at Arm & Hammer have engaged in highly effective product management by finding and promoting new uses for its products.

target market. Third, the modification should make the product more consistent with customers' desires so that it provides greater satisfaction. For example, Ford modified its popular F-150 pickup by adding more interior room, better safety features, and an optional DVD player built in. The company designed these modifications for 80 percent of its F-150 customers who use the truck as family transportation.[6]

Existing products can be altered in three primary ways: in quality, function, and aesthetics. *Quality modifications* are changes that relate to a product's dependability and durability and usually are achieved by alterations in the materials or production process. *Functional modifications* affect a product's versatility, effectiveness, convenience, or safety; they usually require redesign of the product. Typical product categories that have undergone extensive functional modifications include home appliances, office and farm equipment, and consumer electronics. *Aesthetic modifications* are directed at changing the sensory appeal of a product by altering its taste, texture, sound, smell, or visual characteristics. Because a buyer's purchasing decision is affected by how a product looks, smells, tastes, feels, or sounds, an aesthetic modification may have a definite impact on purchases. Through aesthetic modifications, a firm can differentiate its product from competing brands and perhaps gain a sizable market share if customers find the modified product more appealing.

talking technology

Helping Beer Drinkers Cut the Carbs

COMPANIES GENERALLY use technology to add something to a product, such as more speed or more capabilities. Anheuser-Busch recently developed the technology for taking something away. Company marketers got the idea for a new product when they noticed that a growing number of weight-conscious consumers following low-carbohydrate diets were paying closer attention to their food's nutritional composition. In response, Anheuser-Busch's brewmeisters brewed up a special technology to reduce the carbohydrate content of Michelob beer to create Michelob Ultra.

The recipe called for water, pale two-row and Munich six-row barley, certain grains, imported hops, and cultured yeast. But the secret ingredient was the technology for extending the mashing process three times longer than usual, which "breaks down the carbs, but doesn't get rid of the taste," an Anheuser-Busch executive says.

Michelob Ultra (as in "ultralight") contains only 2.9 grams of carbohydrates, compared with 13 grams in ordinary beers. Despite this low carbohydrate level, the beer still delivers nearly 100 calories per bottle. Moreover, people with diabetes cannot drink bottle after bottle as if the beer had no carbohydrate content. Still, the product offers a way for dieters to enjoy one or two bottles even when they are restricting their daily carbohydrate intake.

Michelob Ultra is not the world's first low-carbohydrate beer. Some connoisseurs may recall Gablinger's Beer, a no-carbohydrate beer of the 1960s. Its marketing slogan insisted that the beer "didn't fill you up." However, the beer apparently had very little flavor and did not survive.

Now Anheuser-Busch is marketing Michelob Ultra as a good way for dieters to enjoy the beer taste without as many carbohydrates. The company makes no health claims but notes that its target market "transcends all demographics," including "people from 21 to 71, as long as they're still leading a healthy lifestyle." Miller Lite, which has 3.2 grams of carbohydrates, is also reaching out to the weight-conscious segment. Will dieters drink Michelob Ultra rather than give up beer altogether or drink Miller Lite? Anheuser-Busch's marketing experts continue working hard to make the beer a favorite of carbo-cutting dieters.

·eleting Products

) maintain an effective product mix, an organization often has to eliminate some oducts. This is called **product deletion**. A weak product costs a firm time, money, ıd resources that could be used to modify other products or develop new ones. Also, hen a weak product generates an unfavorable image among customers, the negative ıage may rub off on other products sold by the firm.

product deletion the elimination of one or more products from a product line

Most organizations find it difficult to delete a product. Some firms drop weak ·oducts only after they have become severe financial burdens. A better approach is ›me form of systematic review of the product's impact on the overall effectiveness of firm's product mix. Such a review should analyze a product's contribution to a comıny's sales for a given period. It should include estimates of future sales, costs, and ·ofits associated with the product and a consideration of whether changes in the mar-ȝting strategy could improve the product's performance.

A product deletion program definitely can improve a firm's performance. For exnple, Unilever recently launched a program to delete niche, marginal, and nonrategic brands to provide more room and resources for its core brands. Prior to the eletion program, Unilever had 1,800 products in sixty-seven product categories. fter implementing the deletion program, Unilever now participates in fourteen roduct categories. Unilever is putting more energy into its big brands because these ave the highest growth potential.[7]

)eveloping New Products

)eveloping and introducing new products is frequently time-consuming, expensive, nd risky. Thousands of new products are introduced annually. Depending on how 'e define it, the failure rate for new products ranges between 60 and 75 percent. Alıough developing new products is risky, failing to introduce new products can be ıst as hazardous. Kellogg, for example, was slow to introduce new products during ıe 1990s. By 2000, General Mills had become the number one cereal producer in ıe United States, putting Kellogg in second place.[8] New products generally are rouped into three categories on the basis of their degree of similarity to existing roducts. *Imitations* are products designed to be similar to—and to compete with— xisting products of other firms. Examples are the various brands of whitening tooth-›astes that were developed to compete with Rembrandt. *Adaptations* are variations of xisting products that are intended for an established market. For example, with inreasing concerns nationwide about health issues such as diabetes and obesity, Herhey decided to introduce product adaptations with the launching of its sugar-free ersions of twenty-four of its major chocolate brands in conjunction with a partnerhip with the American Diabetes Association. Instead of sugar, these candy bars conain Splenda.[9] Product refinements and extensions are most often considered daptations, although imitative products also may include some refinement and exension. Polaroid, for example, has introduced inexpensive digital cameras for the nass market and has become the number one digital camera seller in the United ›tates.[10] *Innovations* are entirely new products. They may give rise to a new industry ›r revolutionize an existing one. The introduction of CDs, for example, has brought najor changes to the recording industry. Innovative products take considerable time, ·ffort, and money to develop. They are therefore less common than adaptations and mitations. As shown in Figure 14.2, the process of developing a new product consists)f seven phases.

dea Generation Idea generation involves looking for product ideas that will help ı firm achieve its objectives. Although some organizations get their ideas almost by ·hance, firms trying to maximize product mix effectiveness usually develop systematic ›pproaches for generating new product ideas. Ideas may come from managers, re-ȝearchers, engineers, competitors, advertising agencies, management consultants, pri-'ate research organizations, customers, salespersons, or top executives.

figure 14.2

Phases of New Product Development
Generally, marketers follow these seven steps to develop a new product.

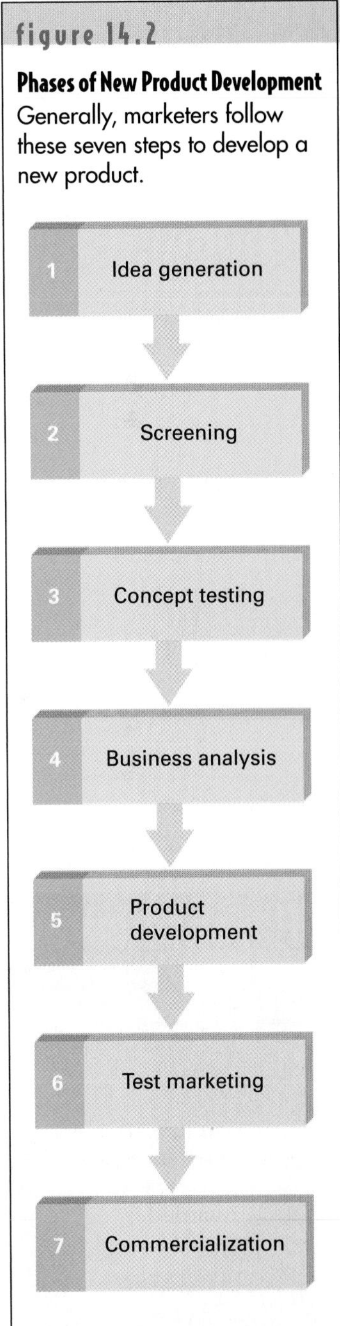

Source: William M. Pride and O. C. Ferrell, *Marketing: Concepts and Strategies*. 12th ed. Copyright © 2003 by Houghton Mifflin Company. Adapted with permission.

Screening During screening, ideas that do not match organizational resources a objectives are rejected. In this phase, a firm's managers consider whether the organ zation has personnel with the expertise to develop and market the proposed produc Management may reject a good idea because the company lacks the necessary ski and abilities. The largest number of product ideas are rejected during the screenir phase.

Concept Testing Concept testing is a phase in which a product idea is presented a small sample of potential buyers through a written or oral description (and perha a few drawings) to determine their attitudes and initial buying intentions regardir the product. For a single product idea, an organization can test one or several co cepts of the same product. Concept testing is a low-cost means for an organization determine consumers' initial reactions to a product idea before investing considerab resources in product research and development (R&D). Product development perso nel can use the results of concept testing to improve product attributes and produ benefits that are most important to potential customers. The types of questions aske vary considerably depending on the type of product idea being tested. The followin are typical questions:

- Which benefits of the proposed product are especially attractive to you?
- Which features are of little or no interest to you?
- What are the primary advantages of the proposed product over the one you currently use?
- If this product were available at an appropriate price, how often would you buy it?
- How could this proposed product be improved?

Business Analysis Business analysis provides tentative ideas about a potenti product's financial performance, including its probable profitability. During this stag the firm considers how the new product, if it were introduced, would affect the firm sales, costs, and profits. Marketing personnel usually work up preliminary sales an cost projections at this point, with the help of R&D and production managers.

Product Development In the product development phase, the company must fin out first if it is technically feasible to produce the product and then if the product ca be made at costs low enough to justify a reasonable price. If a product idea makes it t this point, it is transformed into a workin model, or *prototype*.

Test Marketing Test marketing is the limite introduction of a product in several towns o cities chosen to be representative of the intende target market. Its aim is to determine buyers probable reactions. The product is left in the tes markets long enough to give buyers a chance t repurchase the product if they are so inclined Marketers can experiment with advertising, pric ing, and packaging in different test areas and ca measure the extent of brand awareness, bran switching, and repeat purchases that result fro alterations in the marketing mix.

Commercialization During commercializa tion, plans for full-scale manufacturing an marketing must be refined and completed, an budgets for the project must be prepared. In th early part of the commercialization phase, mar keting management analyzes the results of tes

Table 14.1 Examples of Product Failures

Company	Product
3M	Floptical storage disk
IncrEdibles Breakaway Foods	Push n' Eat
General Mills	Betty Crocker MicroRave Singles
Adams(Pfizer)	Body Smarts nutritional bars
General Motors Corp.	Cadillac Allante luxury sedan
Anheuser-Busch Companies	Bud Dry and Michelob Dry beer
Coca-Cola	Surge Citrus drink
Heinz	Ketchup Salsa
Noxema	Noxema Skin Fitness

Sources: **www.newproductworks.com;** accessed January 17, 2003; Robert M. McMath, "Copycat Cupcakes Don't Cut It," *American Demographics*, January 1997, p. 60; and Eric Berggren and Thomas Nacher, "Why Good Ideas Go Bust," *Management Review*, February 2000, pp. 32–36.

marketing to find out what changes in the marketing mix are needed before the product is introduced. The results of test marketing may tell the marketers, for example, to change one or more of the product's physical attributes, to modify the distribution plans to include more retail outlets, to alter promotional efforts, or to change the product's price. Products usually are not introduced nationwide overnight. Most new products are marketed in stages, beginning in selected geographic areas and expanding into adjacent areas over a period of time.

Why Do Products Fail? Despite this rigorous process for developing product ideas, most new products end up as failures. In fact, many well-known companies have produced market failures (see Table 14.1).

Why does a new product fail? Mainly because the product and its marketing program are not planned and tested as completely as they should be. For example, to save on development costs, a firm may market-test its product but not its entire marketing mix. Or a firm may market a new product before all the "bugs" have been worked out. Or, when problems show up in the testing stage, a firm may try to recover its product development costs by pushing ahead with full-scale marketing anyway. Finally, some firms try to market new products with inadequate financing.

Branding, Packaging, and Labeling

learning objective 5 Explain the uses and importance of branding, packaging, and labeling.

Three important features of a product (particularly a consumer product) are its brand, package, and label. These features may be used to associate a product with a successful product line or to distinguish it from existing products. They may be designed to attract customers at the point of sale or to provide information to potential purchasers. Because the brand, package, and label are very real parts of the product, they deserve careful attention during product planning.

What Is a Brand?

brand a name, term, symbol, design, or any combination of these that identifies a seller's products as distinct from those of other sellers

brand name the part of a brand that can be spoken

brand mark the part of a brand that is a symbol or distinctive design

A **brand** is a name, term, symbol, design, or any combination of these that identifies a seller's products as distinct from those of other sellers.[11] A **brand name** is the part of a brand that can be spoken. It may include letters, words, numbers, or pronounceable symbols, such as the ampersand in *Procter & Gamble*. A **brand mark,** on the other hand, is the part of a brand that is a symbol or distinctive design, such as the Nike

exploring business

Creating Effective Brand Mascots

WHO ARE RED AND YELLOW? M&M lovers may not know these names, but they know what brand the animated candies represent. The list of well-known brand mascots goes on and on, from the AFLAC duck (promoting insurance) and the Ronald McDonald clown to Snap, Crackle, and Pop (promoting Kellogg's Rice Krispies cereal).

To be effective, a mascot should symbolize the brand's strengths while evoking positive feelings. Consider Maytag's dilemma. Customers buy dishwashers and other appliances on the basis of reliability and performance, but advertisements conveying these attributes through statistics would be dull and unappealing. Instead, the company's advertising agency came up with the idea for Ol' Lonely, a likable Maytag appliance repairman who never sees customers because of the brand's reliability. "Our consumer research shows time and again the character humanizes our brand, and that's a huge point for us," stresses Maytag's brand manager.

Another important principle is to update mascots over time so that they remain relevant. For example, the Buddy Lee kewpie doll first appeared in Lee Jeans advertisements several decades ago. When the company's advertising experts began planning a new campaign in the late 1990s, they thought about the mascot. By researching the target market of 18- to 24-year-olds, the experts learned that the mascot needed to be updated with "a new archetype of coolness" for today's jeans buyers. The update worked: Sales among this target market rose more than 20 percent in the campaign's first year.

Finally, give the brand mascot the right amount of exposure. Red Dog beer ads originally featured the Red Dog mascot talking about individuality. The dog became such a big hit in its own right that it popped up on clothing, key chains, and many other products, threatening the brand's individuality message.

In contrast, some companies give their mascots time off or lend them to other marketers. Ol' Lonely appeared in a Chevrolet Impala commercial, reinforcing how much free time the repairman has. Kellogg replaced its traditional mascots for a summer with Cartoon Network characters such as the Power Puff Girls. The idea was to refresh connections with children by building on the cartoon characters' popularity. Afterward, the reappearance of Kellogg's familiar mascots attracted children's attention as well.

trademark a brand name or brand mark that is registered with the U.S. Patent and Trademark Office and is thus legally protected from use by anyone except its owner

trade name the complete and legal name of an organization

manufacturer (or producer) brand a brand that is owned by a manufacturer

store (or private) brand a brand that is owned by an individual wholesaler or retailer

"swoosh." A **trademark** is a brand name or brand mark that is registered with the U.S Patent and Trademark Office and thus is legally protected from use by anyone excep its owner. A **trade name** is the complete and legal name of an organization, such a Pizza Hut or Houghton Mifflin Company (the publisher of this text).

Types of Brands

Brands often are classified according to who owns them: manufacturers or stores. A **manufacturer** (or **producer**) **brand**, as the name implies, is a brand that is owned b a manufacturer. Many foods (Frosted Flakes), major appliances (Whirlpool), gasoline (Exxon), automobiles (Honda), and clothing (Levis) are sold as manufacturers' brand Some consumers prefer manufacturer brands because they usually are nationall known, offer consistent quality, and are widely available.

A **store** (or **private**) **brand** is one that is owned by an individual wholesaler or retailer. Among the better-known store brands are Kenmore and Craftsman, both owned by Sears, Roebuck. Owners of store brands claim that they can offer lowe prices, earn greater profits, and improve customer loyalty with their own brands Some companies that manufacture private brands also produce their own manufacturer brands. They often find such operations profitable because they can use exces capacity and at the same time avoid most marketing costs. Many private-branded grocery products are produced by companies that specialize in making private-label products. About 20 percent of products sold in supermarkets are private-branded items.[12]

Consumer confidence is the most important element in the success of a brande product, whether the brand is owned by a producer or by a retailer. Because brandin identifies each product completely, customers can easily repurchase products that provide satisfaction, performance, and quality. And they can just as easily avoid or ignor products that do not. In supermarkets, the products most likely to keep their shelf space are the brands with large market shares and strong customer loyalty.

A **generic product** (sometimes called a **generic brand**) is a product with no brand at all. Its plain package carries only the name of the product—applesauce, peanut butter, potato chips, or whatever. Generic products, available in supermarkets since 1977, sometimes are made by the major producers that manufacture name brands. Even though generic brands may have accounted for as much as 10 percent of all grocery sales several years ago, they currently represent less than one-half of 1 percent.

generic product (or **brand**) a product with no brand at all

Benefits of Branding

Both buyers and sellers benefit from branding. Because brands are easily recognizable, they reduce the amount of time buyers must spend shopping; buyers can quickly identify the brands they prefer. Choosing particular brands, such as Tommy Hilfiger, Polo, Nautica, and Nike, can be a way of expressing oneself. When buyers are unable to evaluate a product's characteristics, brands can help them judge the quality of the product. For example, most buyers are not able to judge the quality of stereo components but may be guided by a well-respected brand name. Brands can symbolize a certain quality level to a customer, allowing that perception of quality to represent the actual quality of the item. Brands thus help to reduce a buyer's perceived risk of purchase. Finally, customers may receive a psychological reward that comes from owning a brand that symbolizes status. The Lexus brand is an example.

brand loyalty extent to which a customer is favorable toward buying a specific brand

Because buyers are already familiar with a firm's existing brands, branding helps a firm introduce a new product that carries the same brand name. For example, Unilever, the company that produces the Dove brand as well as many others, has continued to expand its Dove product line. Originally, Dove made bar soap and then extended to deodorant, facial cleansing products, and body soap. The latest additions are Dove shampoos and conditioners. Unilever hopes to quickly gain market share because of customers' favorable perceptions of Dove products.[13] Branding aids sellers in their promotional efforts because promotion of each branded product indirectly promotes other products of the same brand. H. G. Heinz, for example, markets many products with the Heinz brand name, such as ketchup, vinegar, vegetarian beans, gravies, barbecue sauce, and steak sauce. Promotion of one Heinz product indirectly promotes the others.

Protecting the brand. The maker of Tabasco brand pepper sauce employs the term "brand" when its name is used in order to keep the name Tabasco from becoming a generic term for the pepper sauce product category.

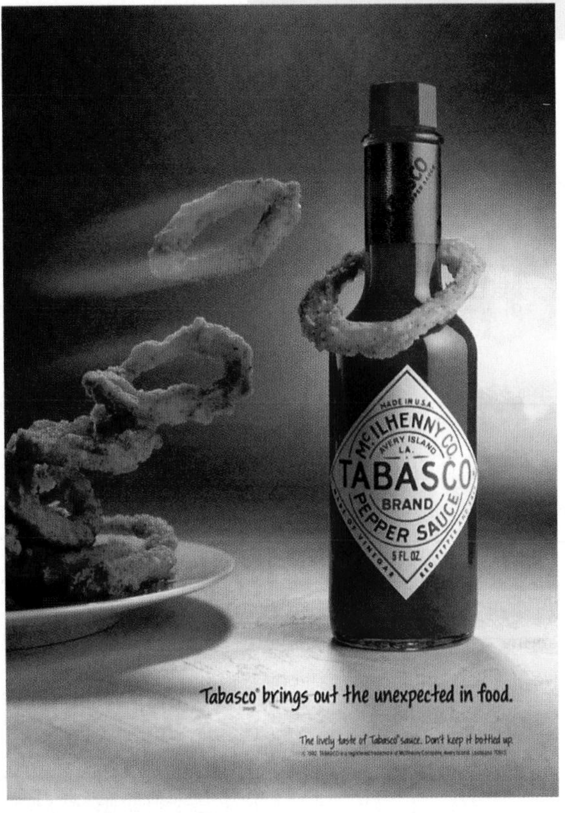
MADE IN U.S.A.
McILHENNY CO.
AVERY ISLAND LA.
TABASCO
BRAND
PEPPER SAUCE
5 FL OZ
Tabasco® brings out the unexpected in food.
The lively taste of Tabasco® sauce. Don't keep it bottled up.

One chief benefit of branding is the creation of **brand loyalty,** the extent to which a customer is favorable toward buying a specific brand. The stronger the brand loyalty, the greater is the likelihood that buyers will consistently choose the brand. There are three levels of brand loyalty: recognition, preference, and insistence. Brand recognition is the level of loyalty at which customers are aware that the brand exists and will purchase it if their preferred brands are unavailable or if they are unfamiliar with available brands. This is the weakest form of brand loyalty. Brand preference is the level of brand loyalty at which a customer prefers one brand over competing brands. However, if the preferred brand is unavailable, the customer is willing to substitute another brand. Brand insistence is the strongest level of brand loyalty. Brand-insistent customers strongly prefer a specific brand and will not buy substitutes. Brand insistence is the least common type of brand loyalty. Partly due to marketers' increased dependence on discounted prices, coupons, and other short-term promotions, and partly because of the enormous array of new products with similar characteristics, brand loyalty in general seems to be declining.

brand equity marketing and financial value associated with a brand's strength in a market

Brand equity is the marketing and financial value associated with a brand's strength in a market. Although difficult to measure, brand equity represents the value of a brand to an organization. Some of the world's most valuable brands include Coca-Cola, Microsoft, IBM, General Electric, and Intel.[14] The four major factors that contribute to brand equity are brand name awareness, brand associations, perceived brand quality, and brand loyalty. Brand awareness leads to brand familiarity, and buyers are more likely to select a familiar brand than an unfamiliar one. The associations linked to a brand can connect a personality type or lifestyle with a particular brand. For example, consumers may associate De Beers diamonds with loving, long-lasting relationships. When consumers are unable to judge for themselves the quality of a product, they may rely on their perception of the quality of the product's brand. Finally, brand loyalty is a valued element of brand equity because it reduces both a brand's vulnerability to competitors and the need to spend tremendous resources to attract new customers; it also provides brand visibility and encourages retailers to carry the brand. New companies, for example, have much work to do in establishing new brands to compete with well-known brands. For example, China's Beijing Li Ning Sports Goods Company, started by the gymnastic gold medalist Li Ning, is establishing itself as a rival brand to Nike in shoes and sporting goods. Building brand equity will take both time and large investments of capital. Currently, Li Ning spends 11 percent of its revenues on marketing efforts to increase brand recognition and loyalty. The company is expanding internationally, and its "L" logo that resembles a wavy check mark is set up to rival the Nike swoosh in China and beyond.[15]

Marketing on the Internet sometimes is best done in collaboration with a better-known web brand. For instance, Unilever's joint effort with web portal Excite@Home, a better-known web brand than Unilever or any of its 1,000 individual brands, scored results that Unilever's site would never have been able to achieve independently. By distributing Recipe Secrets on Excite@Home's site, consumers were able to see practical demonstrations of Unilever products and effectively view cooking lessons online. The Recipe Secrets banner advertisement prompted 8 percent of consumers who saw it to visit the site; of those consumers, 62 percent obtained a recipe. The fact that about 11 percent of visitors to the site were further motivated to actually buy a Recipe Secrets product at their grocery store, is testimony to the success of the joint effort.[16]

Choosing and Protecting a Brand

A number of issues should be considered when selecting a brand name. The name should be easy for customers to say, spell, and recall. Short, one-syllable names such as *Tide* often satisfy this requirement. The brand name should suggest, in a positive way, the product's uses, special characteristics, and major benefits and should be distinctive enough to set it apart from competing brands. Choosing the right brand name has become a challenge because many obvious product names have already been used.

It is important that a firm select a brand that can be protected through registration, reserving it for exclusive use by that firm. Some brands, because of their designs, are more easily infringed on than others. Although registration protects trademarks domestically for ten years and can be renewed indefinitely, a firm should develop a system for ensuring that its trademarks will be renewed as needed. To protect its exclusive right to the brand, the company must ensure that the selected brand will not be considered an infringement on any existing brand already registered with the U.S. Patent and Trademark Office. This task may be complicated by the fact that infringement is determined by the courts, which base their decisions on whether a brand causes consumers to be confused, mistaken, or deceived about the source of the product. Starbucks, the Seattle-based coffee company, recently took legal action against companies using similar brand names, including Sambuck's Coffeehouse, Black Bear's Charbucks Blend, and A&D Cafe's Warbucks coffee.[17]

@ Using the Internet

The U.S. government gateways to consumer information about products, safety, pricing, fraud, and many other issues of interest are available through a variety of online publications and links at **http://www.pueblo.gsa.gov/** and **http://www.consumer.gov.**

A firm must guard against a brand name's becoming a generic term that refers to general product category. Generic terms cannot be legally protected as exclusive brand names. For example, names such as *yo-yo, aspirin, escalator*, and *thermos*—all exclusively brand names at one time—eventually were declared generic terms that refer to product categories. As such, they could no longer be protected. To ensure that a brand name does not become a generic term, the firm should spell the name with a capital letter and use it as an adjective to modify the name of the general product class, as in Jell-O Brand Gelatin. An organization can deal directly with this problem by advertising that its brand is a trademark and should not be used generically. Firms also can use the registered trademark symbol ® to indicate that the brand is trademarked.

Branding Strategies

The basic branding decision for any firm is whether to brand its products. A producer may market its products under its own brands, private brands, or both. A retail store may carry only producer brands, its own brands, or both. Once either type of firm decides to brand, it chooses one of two branding strategies: individual branding or family branding.

Individual branding is the strategy in which a firm uses a different brand for each of its products. For example, Procter & Gamble uses individual branding for its line of bar soaps, which includes Ivory, Camay, Zest, Safeguard, Coast, and Oil of Olay. Individual branding offers two major advantages. A problem with one product will not affect the good name of the firm's other products. And the different brands can be directed toward different market segments. For example, Marriotts' Fairfield Inns are directed toward budget-minded travelers and Marriott Hotels toward upscale customers.

individual branding the strategy in which a firm uses a different brand for each of its products

Family branding is the strategy in which a firm uses the same brand for all or most of its products. Sony, Dell, IBM, and Xerox use family branding for their entire product mixes. A major advantage of family branding is that the promotion of any one item that carries the family brand tends to help all other products with the same brand name. In addition, a new product has a head start when its brand name is already known and accepted by customers.

family branding the strategy in which a firm uses the same brand for all or most of its products

Packaging

Packaging consists of all the activities involved in developing and providing a container with graphics for a product. The package is a vital part of the product. It can make the product more versatile, safer, or easier to use. Through its shape, appearance, and printed message, a package can influence purchasing decisions.

packaging all the activities involved in developing and providing a container with graphics for a product

Packaging Functions Effective packaging means more than simply putting products in containers and covering them with wrappers. The basic function of packaging materials is to protect the product and maintain its functional form. Fluids such as milk, orange juice, and hair spray need packages that preserve and protect them; the packaging should prevent damage that could affect the product's usefulness and increase costs. Since product tampering has become a problem for marketers of many types of goods, several packaging techniques have been developed to counter this danger. Some packages are also designed to foil shoplifting.

Another function of packaging is to offer consumer convenience. For example, small, aseptic packages—individual-serving boxes or plastic bags that contain liquids and do not require refrigeration—appeal strongly to children and to young adults with active lifestyles. The size or shape of a package may relate to the product's storage, convenience of use, or replacement rate. Small, single-serving cans of vegetables, for instance, may prevent waste and make storage easier. A third function of packaging is to promote a product by communicating its features, uses, benefits, and image. Sometimes a firm develops a reusable package to make its product more desirable. For example, the Cool Whip package doubles as a food-storage container.

Packaging design can be fun and useful. This Heinz ketchup package is designed to make the product more convenient to use.

Package Design Considerations Many factors must be weighed when developing packages. Obviously, one major consideration is cost. Although a number of packaging materials, processes, and designs are available, some are rather expensive. While U.S. buyers have shown a willingness to pay more for improved packaging, there are limits.

Marketers also must decide whether to package the product in single or multiple units. Multiple-unit packaging can increase demand by increasing the amount of the product available at the point of consumption (in the home, for example). However, multiple-unit packaging does not work for infrequently used products because buyers do not like to tie up their dollars in an excess supply or to store these products for a long time. However, multiple-unit packaging can make storage and handling easier (as in the case of six-packs used for soft drinks); it also can facilitate special price offers, such as two-for-one sales. In addition, multiple-unit packaging may increase consumer acceptance of a product by encouraging the buyer to try it several times. On the other hand, customers may hesitate to try the product at all if they do not have the option to buy just one.

Marketers should consider how much consistency is desirable among an organization's package designs. To promote an overall company image, a firm may decide that all packages must be similar or include one major element of the design. This approach, called *family packaging*, is sometimes used only for lines of products, as with Campbell's soups, Weight Watchers entrees, and Planters nuts. The best policy is sometimes no consistency, especially if a firm's products are unrelated or aimed at vastly different target markets.

Packages also play an important promotional role. Through verbal and nonverbal symbols, the package can inform potential buyers about the product's content, uses, features, advantages, and hazards. Firms can create desirable images and associations by choosing particular colors, designs, shapes, and textures. Many cosmetics manufacturers, for example, design their packages to create impressions of richness, luxury, and exclusiveness. The package performs another promotional function when it is designed to be safer or more convenient to use if such features help stimulate demand.

Packaging also must meet the needs of intermediaries. Wholesalers and retailers consider whether a package facilitates transportation, handling, and storage. Resellers may refuse to carry certain products if their packages are cumbersome.

Finally, firms must consider the issue of environmental responsibility when developing packages. Companies must balance consumers' desires for convenience against the need to preserve the environment. About one-half of all garbage consists of discarded plastic packaging, such as plastic soft drink bottles and carryout bags. Plastic packaging material is not biodegradable, and paper necessitates destruction of valuable forest lands. Consequently, many companies are exploring packaging alternatives and recycling more materials.

Labeling

labeling the presentation of information on a product or its package

Labeling is the presentation of information on a product or its package. The *label* is the part that contains the information. This information may include the brand name and mark, the registered trademark symbol ®, the package size and contents, product claims, directions for use and safety precautions, a list of ingredients, the name and address of the manufacturer, and the Universal Product Code symbol, which is used for automated checkout and inventory control.

A number of federal regulations specify information that *must* be included in the labeling for certain products. For example,

- Garments must be labeled with the name of the manufacturer, country of manufacture, fabric content, and cleaning instructions.

- Any food product for which a nutritional claim is made must have nutrition labeling that follows a standard format.
- Food product labels must state the number of servings per container, the serving size, the number of calories per serving, the number of calories derived from fat, and amounts of specific nutrients.
- Non-edible items such as shampoos and detergents must carry safety precautions as well as instructions for their use.

Such regulations are aimed at protecting customers from both misleading product claims and the improper (and thus unsafe) use of products.

Labels also may carry the details of written or express warranties. An **express warranty** is a written explanation of the responsibilities of the producer in the event that the product is found to be defective or otherwise unsatisfactory. As a result of consumer discontent (along with some federal legislation), firms have begun to simplify the wording of warranties and to extend their duration. The L. L. Bean warranty states, "Our products are guaranteed to give 100 percent satisfaction in every way. Return anything purchased from us at any time if it proves otherwise. We will replace it, refund your purchase price or credit your credit card, as you wish."

express warranty a written explanation of the responsibilities of the producer in the event that the product is found to be defective or otherwise unsatisfactory

Pricing Products

A product is a set of attributes and benefits that has been carefully designed to satisfy its market while earning a profit for its seller. No matter how well a product is designed, however, it cannot help an organization achieve its goals if it is priced incorrectly. Few people will purchase a product with too high a price, and a product with too low a price will earn little or no profit. Somewhere between too high and too low there is a "proper," effective price for each product. Let's take a closer look at how businesses go about determining a product's right price.

learning objective

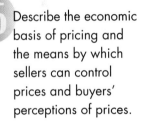

6 Describe the economic basis of pricing and the means by which sellers can control prices and buyers' perceptions of prices.

The Meaning and Use of Price

The **price** of a product is the amount of money a seller is willing to accept in exchange for the product at a given time and under given circumstances. At times, the price results from negotiations between buyer and seller. In many business situations, however, the price is fixed by the seller. Suppose that a seller sets a price of $10 for a particular product. In essence, the seller is saying, "Anyone who wants this product can have it here and now in exchange for $10."

price the amount of money a seller is willing to accept in exchange for a product at a given time and under given circumstances

Each interested buyer then makes a personal judgment regarding the utility of the product, often in terms of some dollar value. A particular person who feels that he or she will get at least $10 worth of want satisfaction (or value) from the product is likely to buy it. But if that person can get more want satisfaction by spending $10 in some other way, he or she will not buy it.

Price thus serves the function of *allocator*. First, it allocates goods and services among those who are willing and able to buy them. (As we noted in Chapter 1, the answer to the economic question "For whom to produce?" depends primarily on prices.) Second, price allocates financial resources (sales revenue) among producers according to how well they satisfy customers' needs. And third, price helps customers to allocate their own financial resources among various want-satisfying products.

Can Firms Control Their Prices?

To focus on the extent to which firms can control their prices, we must take another look at the forces of supply and demand and the actions of firms in a real economy.

figure 14.3

Supply and Demand Curves
Supply curve *(left)*: The upward slope means that producers will supply more jeans at higher prices. **Demand curve** *(center)*: The downward slope (to the right) means that buyers will purchase fewer jeans at higher prices. **Supply and demand curves together** *(right)*: Point *E* indicates equilibrium in quantity and price for both sellers and buyers.

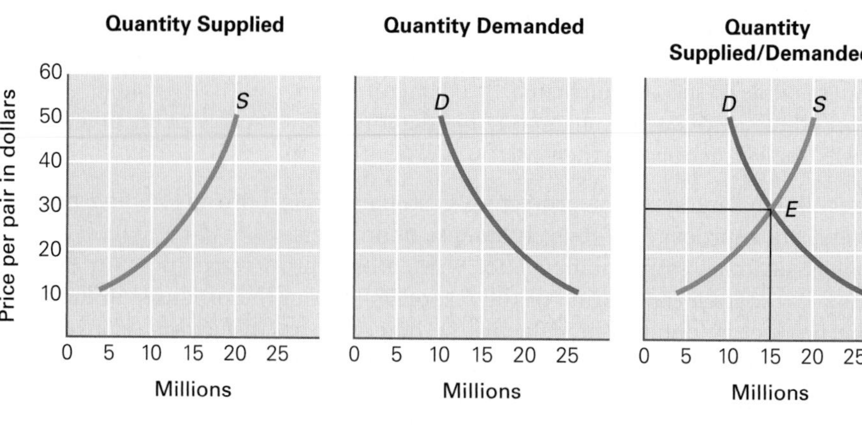

supply the quantity of a product that producers are willing to sell at each of various prices

demand the quantity of a product that buyers are willing to purchase at each of various prices

Supply and Demand—Once Again In Chapter 1 we defined the **supply** of a product as the quantity of the product that producers are willing to sell at each of various prices. We can draw a graph of the supply relationship for a particular product say, jeans (see the left graph in Figure 14.3). Note that the quantity supplied by producers *increases* as the price increases along this *supply curve*.

As defined in Chapter 1, the **demand** for a product is the quantity that buyers are willing to purchase at each of various prices. We also can draw a graph of the demand relationship (see the middle graph in Figure 14.3). Note that the quantity demanded by purchasers *increases* as the price decreases along the *demand curve*. The buyers and sellers of a product interact in the marketplace. We can show this interaction by superimposing the supply curve onto the demand curve for our product, as shown in the right graph in Figure 14.3. The two curves intersect at point *E*, which represents a quantity of fifteen million pairs of jeans and a price of $30 per pair. Point *E* is on the *supply curve*; thus producers are willing to supply fifteen million pairs at $30 each. Point *E* is also on the demand curve; thus buyers are willing to purchase fifteen million pairs at $30 each. Point *E* represents *equilibrium*. If fifteen million pairs are produced and priced at $30, they will all be sold. And everyone who is willing to pay $30 will be able to buy a pair of jeans.

Prices in the Real Economy In a (largely theoretical) system of pure competition, no producer has control over the price of its product. All producers must accept the equilibrium price. If they charge a higher price, they will not sell their products. If they charge a lower price, they will lose sales revenue and profits. In addition, the products of the various producers are indistinguishable from each other when a system of pure competition exists. Every bushel of wheat, for example, is exactly like every other bushel of wheat.

product differentiation the process of developing and promoting differences between one's product and all similar products

In the real economy, however, producers try to gain some control over price by differentiating their products from similar products. **Product differentiation** is the process of developing and promoting differences between one's product and all similar products. The idea behind product differentiation is to create a specific demand for the firm's product—to take the product out of competition with all similar products. Then, in its own little "submarket," the firm can control price to some degree. Jeans with certain designer labels are a result of product differentiation.

Firms also attempt to gain some control over price through advertising. If the advertising is effective, it will increase the quantity demanded. This may permit a firm to increase the price at which it sells its particular output.

In a real market, firms may reduce prices to obtain a competitive edge. A firm may hope to sell more units at a lower price, thereby increasing its total sales revenue. Although each unit earns less profit, total profit may rise.

Finally, the few large sellers in an oligopoly (an industry in which there are few sellers) have considerable control over price mainly because each controls a large proportion of the total supply of its product. However, as we pointed out in Chapter 1, this control of price is diluted by each firm's wariness of its competitors.

Overall, then, firms in the real economy do exert some control over prices. How they use this control depends on their pricing goals and their production and marketing costs, as well as on the workings of supply and demand in competitive markets.

Price and Nonprice Competition

Before the price of a product can be set, an organization must decide on the basis on which it will compete—on the basis of price alone or some combination of factors. The choice influences pricing decisions as well as other marketing mix variables.

price competition an emphasis on setting a price equal to or lower than competitors' prices to gain sales or market share

nonprice competition competition based on factors other than price

Price competition occurs when a seller emphasizes the low price of a product and sets a price that equals or beats competitors' prices. To use this approach most effectively, a seller must have the flexibility to change prices often and must do so rapidly and aggressively whenever competitors change their prices. Price competition allows a marketer to set prices based on demand for the product or in response to changes in the firm's finances. Competitors can do likewise, however, which is a major drawback of price competition. They, too, can quickly match or outdo an organization's price cuts. In addition, if circumstances force a seller to raise prices, competing firms may be able to maintain their lower prices.

The Internet makes price comparison relatively easy for users. This ease of price comparison helps to drive competition. Examples of websites where customers can compare prices include mysimon.com, pricescan.com, bizrate.com, and pricegrabber.com.

Nonprice competition is based on factors other than price. It is used most effectively when a seller can make its product stand out from the competition by distinctive product quality, customer service, promotion, packaging, or other features. Buyers must be able to perceive these distinguishing characteristics and consider them desirable. Once customers have chosen a brand for nonprice reasons, they may not be attracted as easily to competing firms and brands. In this way, a seller can build customer loyalty to its brand. For example, Petsmart competes on value rather than price. The store has variety, 12,000 items in stock and another 80,000 available for order. And it offers service right in the store, including pet grooming, a veterinary clinic, and a pet adoption center. All these features add to the total experience of shopping at Petsmart and are part of its nonprice competition with other pet supply stores.[18]

Price competition. Airlines typically engage in price competition.

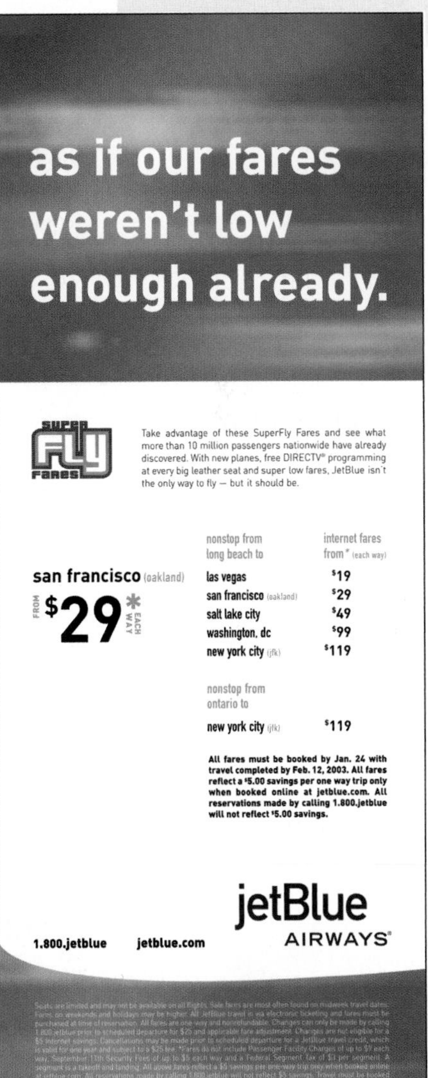

Buyers' Perceptions of Price

In setting prices, managers should consider the price sensitivity of people in the target market. How important is price to them? Is it always "very important"? Members of one market segment may be more influenced by price than members of another. For a particular product, the price may be a bigger factor to some buyers than to others. For example, buyers may be more sensitive to price when purchasing gasoline than when purchasing running shoes.

Buyers will accept different ranges of prices for different products; that is, they will tolerate a narrow range for certain items and a wider range for others. Consider the wide range of prices that consumers pay for soft drinks—from 10 cents per ounce at the movies down to 1.5 cents per ounce on sale at the grocery store. Management should be aware of these limits of acceptability and the products to which they apply. The firm also should take note of buyers' perceptions of a given product in relation to competing products. A premium price may be appropriate if a

Bistro.
Isn't that French for "extortion?"
HACIENDA
MEXICAN RESTAURANTS
Real. Good. Mexican.

Buyers' perception of price. Hacienda Mexican Restaurants employs advertising to influence customers' perceptions of price. This company wants customers to perceive that Hacienda Mexican Restaurants provides high quality Mexican food at moderate prices.

product is considered superior to others in its category or if the product has inspired strong brand loyalty. On the other hand, if buyers have even a hint of a negative view of a product, a lower price may be necessary.

Sometimes buyers relate price to quality. They may consider a higher price to be an indicator of higher quality. Managers involved in pricing decisions should determine whether this outlook is widespread in the target market. If it is, a higher price may improve the image of a product and, in turn, make the product more desirable. For example, German automobile manufacturer Porsche has always worked to keep its quality and image as a luxury sports car maker. In addition to its traditional 911 model and more recently the Boxster model, Porsche recently added a new model called the Cayenne. Porsche hopes this SUV-like vehicle will be very desirable to customers, equally for those who are willing to pay the $88,900.[19]

Pricing Objectives

learning objective

7 Identify the major pricing objectives used by businesses.

Before setting prices for a firm's products, management must decide what it expects to accomplish through pricing. That is, management must set pricing objectives that are in line with both organizational and marketing objectives. Of course, one objective of pricing is to make a profit, but this may not be a firm's primary objective. One or more of the following factors may be just as important.

Survival

A firm may have to price its products to survive—either as an organization or as a player in a particular market. This usually means that the firm will cut its price to attract customers, even if it then must operate at a loss. Obviously, such a goal can hardly be pursued on a long-term basis, for consistent losses would cause the business to fail.

Profit Maximization

Many firms may state that their goal is to maximize profit, but this goal is impossible to define (and thus impossible to achieve). What, exactly, is the *maximum* profit? How does a firm know when it has been reached? Firms that wish to set profit goals should express them as either specific dollar amounts or percentage increases over previous profits.

Target Return on Investment

The *return on investment* (ROI) is the amount earned as a result of that investment. Some firms set an annual percentage ROI as their pricing goal. ConAgra, the company that produces Healthy Choice meals and a multitude of other products, has a target after-tax ROI of 20 percent.

Spotlight

How much would you pay for a textbook?

Depending on a person's evaluation of price, he or she may be willing to spend across a broad range of prices for the same textbook.

Used book purchased from another student	$52.00
Used book from bookstore	$74.00
New book purchased online	$87.00
New book purchased from bookstore	$105.00

Source: *USA Today*, January 13, 2003, p. A1.

Market-Share Goals

A firm's *market share* is its proportion of total industry sales. Some firms attempt, through pricing, to maintain or increase their share of the market. To gain market share, AOL priced three hours of service for $4.95.[20]

Status-Quo Pricing

In pricing their products, some firms are guided by a desire to avoid "making waves," or to maintain the status quo. This is especially true in industries that depend on price stability. If such a firm can maintain its profit or market share simply by meeting the competition—charging about the same price as competitors for similar products—then it will do so.

Pricing Methods

learning objective

8 Examine the three major pricing methods that firms employ.

Once a firm has developed its pricing objectives, it must select a pricing method to reach that goal. Two factors are important to every firm engaged in setting prices. The first is recognition that the market, and not the firm's costs, ultimately determines the price at which a product will sell. The second is awareness that costs and expected sales can be used only to establish some sort of *price floor*, the minimum price at which the firm can sell its product without incurring a loss. In this section we look at three kinds of pricing methods: cost-based, demand-based, and competition-based pricing.

Cost-Based Pricing

Using the simplest method of pricing, *cost-based pricing*, the seller first determines the total cost of producing (or purchasing) one unit of the product. The seller then adds an amount to cover additional costs (such as insurance or interest) and profit. The amount that is added is called the **markup.** The total of the cost plus the markup is the selling price of the product.

markup the amount a seller adds to the cost of a product to determine its basic selling price

A firm's management can calculate markup as a percentage of its total costs. Suppose, for example, that the total cost of manufacturing and marketing 1,000 portable stereos is $100,000, or $100 per unit. If the manufacturer wants a markup that is 20 percent above its costs, the selling price will be $100 plus 20 percent of $100, or $120 per unit.

Markup pricing is easy to apply, and it is used by many businesses (mostly retailers and wholesalers). However, it has two major flaws. The first is the difficulty of determining an effective markup percentage. If this percentage is too high, the product may be overpriced for its market; then too few units may be sold to return the total cost of producing and marketing the product. In contrast, if the markup percentage is too low, the seller is "giving away" profit it could have earned simply by assigning a higher price. In other words, the markup percentage needs to be set to account for the workings of the market, and that is very difficult to do.

The second problem with markup pricing is that it separates pricing from other business functions. The product is priced *after* production quantities are determined, *after* costs are incurred, and almost without regard for the market or the marketing mix. To be most effective, the various business functions should be integrated. *Each* should have an impact on *all* marketing decisions.

breakeven quantity the number of units that must be sold for the total revenue (from all units sold) to equal the total cost (of all units sold)

total revenue the total amount received from sales of a product

fixed cost a cost incurred no matter how many units of a product are produced or sold

variable cost a cost that depends on the number of units produced

total cost the sum of the fixed costs and the variable costs attributed to a product

Cost-based pricing also can be facilitated through the use of breakeven analysis. For any product, the **breakeven quantity** is the number of units that must be sold for the total revenue (from all units sold) to equal the total cost (of all units sold). **Total revenue** is the total amount received from the sales of a product. We can estimate projected total revenue as the selling price multiplied by the number of units sold.

The costs involved in operating a business can be broadly classified as either fixed or variable costs. A **fixed cost** is a cost incurred no matter how many units of a product are produced or sold. Rent, for example, is a fixed cost; it remains the same whether 1 unit or 1,000 are produced. A **variable cost** is a cost that depends on the number of units produced. The cost of fabricating parts for a stereo receiver is a variable cost. The more units produced, the higher is the cost of parts. The **total cost** of producing a certain number of units is the sum of the fixed costs and the variable costs attributed to those units.

If we assume a particular selling price, we can find the breakeven quantity either graphically or by using a formula. Figure 14.4 graphs the total revenue earned and the total cost incurred by the sale of various quantities of a hypothetical product. With fixed costs of $40,000, variable costs of $60 per unit, and a selling price of $120, the breakeven quantity is 667 units. To find the breakeven quantity, first deduct the variable cost from the selling price to determine how much money the sale of one unit contributes to offsetting fixed costs. Then divide that contribution into the total fixed costs to arrive at the breakeven quantity. (The breakeven quantity in Figure 14.4 is the quantity represented by the intersection of the total revenue and total cost axes.) If the firm sells more than 667 units at $120 each, it will earn a profit. If it sells fewer units, it will suffer a loss.

figure 14.4

Breakeven Analysis

Breakeven analysis answers the question, What is the lowest level of production and sales at which a company can break even on a particular product?

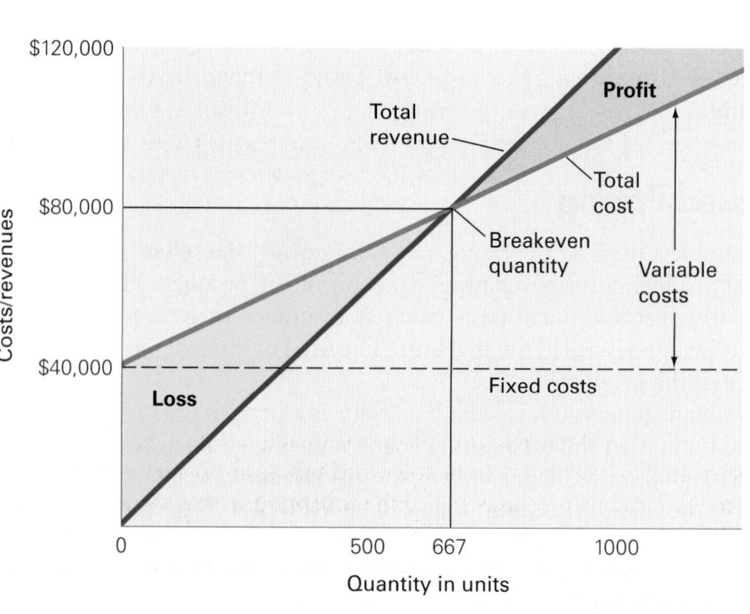

Demand-Based Pricing

Rather than basing the price of a product on its cost, companies sometimes use a pricing method based on the level of demand for the product: *demand-based pricing*. This method results in a high price when product demand is strong and a low price when demand is weak. Some long-distance telephone companies use demand-based pricing. Buyers of new cars that are in high demand, such as Hummer H2, Ford Mustang SVT Cobra, Mazda RX8, and BMW Z8, pay sticker prices plus a premium. To use this method, a marketer estimates the amount of a product that customers will demand at different prices and then chooses the price that generates the highest total revenue. Obviously, the effectiveness of this method depends on the firm's ability to estimate demand accurately.

A firm may favor a demand-based pricing method called *price differentiation* if it wants to use more than one price in the marketing of a specific product. Price differentiation can be based on such considerations as time of the purchase, type of customer, or type of distribution channel. For example, Florida hotel accommodations are more expensive in winter than in summer; a homeowner pays more for air-conditioner filters than does an apartment complex owner purchasing the same size filters in greater quantity; and Christmas tree ornaments are usually cheaper on December 26 than on December 16. For price differentiation to work correctly, the company must first be able to segment a market on the basis of different strengths of demand and then to keep the segments separate enough so that segment members who buy at lower prices cannot sell to buyers in segments that are charged a higher price. This isolation could be accomplished, for example, by selling to geographically separated segments.

Compared with cost-based pricing, demand-based pricing places a firm in a better position to attain higher profit levels, assuming that buyers value the product at levels sufficiently above the product's cost. To use demand-based pricing, however, management must be able to estimate demand at different price levels, which may be difficult to do accurately.

Competition-Based Pricing

In using *competition-based pricing*, an organization considers costs and revenue secondary to competitors' prices. The importance of this method increases if competing products are quite similar and the organization is serving markets in which price is the crucial variable of the marketing strategy. A firm that uses competition-based pricing may choose to be below competitors' prices, slightly above competitors' prices, or at the same level. The price that your bookstore paid to the publishing company of this text was determined using competition-based pricing. Competition-based pricing can help attain a pricing objective to increase sales or market share. Competition-based pricing may be combined with other cost approaches to arrive at profitable levels.

Pricing Strategies

learning objective

Explain the different strategies available to companies for setting prices.

A pricing strategy is a course of action designed to achieve pricing objectives. Generally, pricing strategies help marketers solve the practical problems of setting prices. The extent to which a business uses any of the following strategies depends on its pricing and marketing objectives, the markets for its products, the degree of product differentiation, the life-cycle stage of the product, and other factors. Figure 14.5 (on p. 422) contains a list of the major types of pricing strategies. We discuss these strategies in the remainder of this section.

figure 14.5

Types of Pricing Strategies

Companies have a variety of pricing strategies available to them.

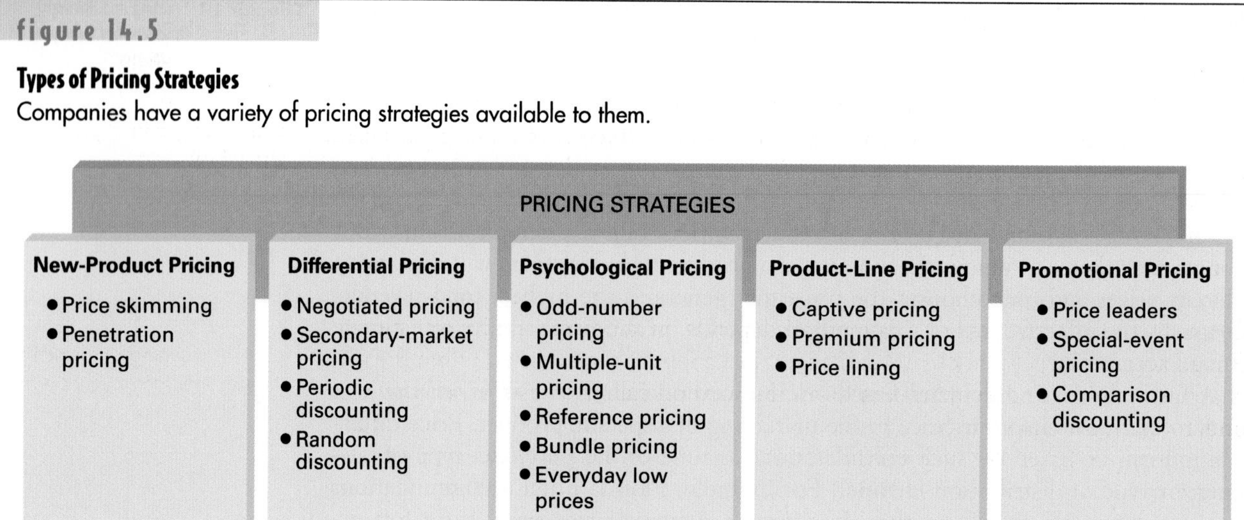

PRICING STRATEGIES
New-Product Pricing
• Price skimming
• Penetration pricing
Differential Pricing
• Negotiated pricing
• Secondary-market pricing
• Periodic discounting
• Random discounting
Psychological Pricing
• Odd-number pricing
• Multiple-unit pricing
• Reference pricing
• Bundle pricing
• Everyday low prices
• Customary pricing
Product-Line Pricing
• Captive pricing
• Premium pricing
• Price lining
Promotional Pricing
• Price leaders
• Special-event pricing
• Comparison discounting

New Product Strategies

The two primary types of new product pricing strategies are price skimming and penetration pricing. An organization can use either one or even both over a period of time.

price skimming the strategy of charging the highest possible price for a product during the introduction stage of its life cycle

Price Skimming Some consumers are willing to pay a high price for an innovative product either because of its novelty or because of the prestige or status that ownership confers. **Price skimming** is the strategy of charging the highest possible price for a product during the introduction stage of its life cycle. The seller essentially "skims the cream" off the market, which helps to recover the high costs of R&D more quickly. Also, a skimming policy may hold down demand for the product, which is helpful if the firm's production capacity is limited during the introduction stage. The greatest disadvantage is that a skimming price may make the product appear lucrative to potential competitors, who may then attempt to enter that market.

penetration pricing the strategy of setting a low price for a new product

Penetration Pricing At the opposite extreme, **penetration pricing** is the strategy of setting a low price for a new product. The main purpose of setting a low price is to build market share for the product quickly. The seller hopes that the building of a large market share quickly will discourage competitors from entering the market. If the low price stimulates sales, the firm also may be able to order longer production runs, which result in lower production costs per unit. A disadvantage of penetration pricing is that it places a firm in a less flexible position. It is more difficult to raise prices significantly than it is to lower them.

Differential Pricing

An important issue in pricing decisions is whether to use a single price or different prices for the same product. A single price is easily understood by both employees and customers, and since many salespeople and customers do not like having to negotiate a price, it reduces the chance of a marketer developing an adversarial relationship with a customer.

Differential pricing means charging different prices to different buyers for the same quality and quantity of product. For differential pricing to be effective, the market must consist of multiple segments with different price sensitivities. When this method is employed, caution should be used to avoid confusing or antagonizing customers. Differential pricing can occur in several ways, including negotiated pricing, secondary-market pricing, periodic discounting, and random discounting.

Negotiated Pricing **Negotiated pricing** occurs when the final price is established through bargaining between the seller and the customer. Negotiated pricing occurs in a number of industries and at all levels of distribution. Even when there is a predetermined stated price or a price list, manufacturers, wholesalers, and retailers may still negotiate to establish the final sales price. Consumers commonly negotiate prices for houses, cars, and used equipment.

negotiated pricing establishing a final price through bargaining

Secondary-Market Pricing **Secondary-market pricing** means setting one price for the primary target market and a different price for another market. Often the price charged in the secondary market is lower. However, when the costs of serving a secondary market are higher than normal, secondary-market customers may have to pay a higher price. Examples of secondary markets include a geographically isolated domestic market, a market in a foreign country, and a segment willing to purchase a product during off-peak times (such as "early bird" diners at restaurants and off-peak users of cellular phones).

secondary-market pricing setting one price for the primary target market and a different price for another market

Periodic Discounting **Periodic discounting** is the temporary reduction of prices on a patterned or systematic basis. For example, many retailers have annual holiday sales, and some women's apparel stores have two seasonal sales each year—a winter sale in the last two weeks of January and a summer sale in the first two weeks of July. From the marketer's point of view, a major problem with periodic discounting is that customers can predict when the reductions will occur and may delay their purchases until they can take advantage of the lower prices.

periodic discounting temporary reduction of prices on a patterned or systematic basis

Random Discounting To alleviate the problem of customers' knowing when discounting will occur, some organizations employ **random discounting**. That is, they temporarily reduce their prices on an nonsystematic basis. When price reductions of a product occur randomly, current users of that brand are not likely to be able to predict when the reductions will occur and so will not delay their purchases in anticipation of buying the product at a lower price. Marketers also use random discounting to attract new customers. With the increasing use of deals such as 0 percent financing from many automobile manufacturers, random discounting has nearly become continuous discounting. However, Ford has been working on a system of yield management based on marketing research involving previous car sales. This has allowed Ford to determine which of its special offers it should make on specific models. For example, Ford found that Explorer customers prefer low-rate or 0 percent financing, whereas Focus and Crown Victoria customers respond better to cash rebates. This pricing policy led Ford to a 4 percent increase in revenue per vehicle during the same quarter when General Motors' revenue per vehicle declined by 7 percent.[21]

random discounting temporary reduction of prices on an unsystematic basis

Psychological Pricing Strategies

Psychological pricing strategies encourage purchases based on emotional responses rather than on economically rational responses. These strategies are used primarily for consumer products rather than business products.

Odd-Number Pricing Many retailers believe that consumers respond more positively to odd-number prices such as $4.99 than to whole-dollar prices such as $5. **Odd-number pricing** is the strategy of setting prices using odd numbers that are slightly below whole-dollar amounts. Nine and five are the most popular ending figures for odd-number prices.

odd-number pricing the strategy of setting prices using odd numbers that are slightly below whole-dollar amounts

Sellers who use this strategy believe that odd-number prices increase sales. The strategy is not limited to low-priced items. Auto manufacturers may set the price of a car at $11,999 rather than $12,000. Odd-number pricing has been the subject of various psychological studies, but the results have been inconclusive.

multiple-unit pricing the strategy of setting a single price for two or more units

Multiple-Unit Pricing

Many retailers (and especially supermarkets) practice **multiple-unit pricing**, setting a single price for two or more units, such as two cans for 99 cents rather than 50 cents per can. Especially for frequently purchased products, this strategy can increase sales. Customers who see the single price and who expect eventually to use more than one unit of the product regularly purchase multiple units to save money.

reference pricing pricing a product at a moderate level and positioning it next to a more expensive model or brand

Reference Pricing

Reference pricing means pricing a product at a moderate level and positioning it next to a more expensive model or brand in the hope that the customer will use the higher price as a reference price (i.e., a comparison price). Because of the comparison, the customer is expected to view the moderate price favorably. When you go to Sears to buy a VCR, a moderately priced VCR may appear especially attractive because it offers most of the important attributes of the more expensive alternatives on display and at a lower price.

bundle pricing packaging together two or more complementary products and selling them for a single price

Bundle Pricing

Bundle pricing is the packaging together of two or more products, usually of a complementary nature, to be sold for a single price. To be attractive to customers, the single price is usually considerably less than the sum of the prices of the individual products. Being able to buy the bundled combination of products in a single transaction may be of value to the customer as well. Bundle pricing is used commonly for banking and travel services, computers, and automobiles with option packages. Bundle pricing can help to increase customer satisfaction. Bundling slow-moving products with ones with a higher turnover, an organization can stimulate sales and increase its revenues. Selling products as a package rather than individually also may result in cost savings. As regulations in the telecommunications industry continue to evolve, many experts agree that telecom services will be provided together using bundled pricing in the near future. The new term *all-distance* has emerged, but the bundling of services goes beyond just combined pricing for local and long-distance services. Verizon, for example, is offering the "Veriations" plan that gives customers unlimited local, long-distance, wireless, and DSL for a bundled price of about $150 per month.[22]

everyday low prices (EDLPs) setting a low price for products on a consistent basis

Everyday Low Prices (EDLPs)

To reduce or eliminate the use of frequent short-term price reductions, some organizations use an approach referred to as **everyday low prices (EDLPs)**. When EDLPs are used, a marketer sets a low price for its products on a consistent basis rather than setting higher prices and frequently discounting them. EDLPs, though not deeply discounted, are set far enough below competitors' prices to make customers feel confident that they are receiving a fair price. EDLPs are employed by retailers such as Wal-Mart and by manufacturers such as Procter & Gamble. A company that uses EDLPs benefits from reduced promotional costs, reduced losses from frequent mark downs, and more stability in its sales. A major problem with this approach is that customers have mixed responses to it. In some instances, customers simply do not believe that EDLPs are what they say they are but are instead a marketing gimmick.

Everyday low prices. Wal-Mart employs everyday low prices as its primary pricing strategy.

Customary Pricing In **customary pricing**, certain goods are priced primarily on the basis of tradition. Examples of customary, or traditional, prices would be those set for candy bars and chewing gum.

customary pricing pricing on the basis of tradition

Product-Line Pricing

Rather than considering products on an item-by-item basis when determining pricing strategies, some marketers employ product-line pricing. *Product-line pricing* means establishing and adjusting the prices of multiple products within a product line. Product-line pricing can provide marketers with flexibility in price setting. For example, marketers can set prices so that one product is quite profitable while another increases market share by virtue of having a lower price than competing products.

When marketers employ product-line pricing, they have several strategies from which to choose. These include captive pricing, premium pricing, and price lining.

Captive Pricing When **captive pricing** is used, the basic product in a product line is priced low, but the price on the items required to operate or enhance it can be at a higher level. For example, a manufacturer of cameras and film may price a camera at a low level to attract customers but price the film at a relatively high price because customers must continue to purchase film in order to use their cameras.

captive pricing pricing the basic product in a product line low, but pricing related items at a higher level

Premium Pricing **Premium pricing** occurs when the highest quality product or the most versatile version of similar products in a product line is given the highest price. Other products in the line are priced to appeal to price-sensitive shoppers or to those who seek product-specific features. Marketers that use premium pricing often realize a significant portion of their profits from premium-priced products. Examples of product categories in which premium pricing is common are small kitchen appliances, beer, ice cream, and television cable service.

premium pricing pricing the highest quality or most versatile products higher than other models in the product line

Price Lining **Price lining** is the strategy of selling goods only at certain predetermined prices that reflect definite price breaks. For example, a shop may sell men's ties only at $22 and $37. This strategy is used widely in clothing and accessory stores. It eliminates minor price differences from the buying decision—both for customers and for managers who buy merchandise to sell in these stores.

price lining setting a limited number of prices for selected groups or lines of merchandise

Promotional Pricing

Price, as an ingredient in the marketing mix, is often coordinated with promotion. The two variables sometimes are so interrelated that the pricing policy is promotion-oriented. Examples of promotional pricing include price leaders, special-event pricing, and comparison discounting.

Price Leaders Sometimes a firm prices a few products below the usual markup, near cost, or below cost, which results in prices known as **price leaders**. This type of pricing is used most often in supermarkets and restaurants to attract customers by giving them especially low prices on a few items. Management hopes that sales of regularly priced products will more than offset the reduced revenues from the price leaders.

price leaders products priced below the usual markup, near cost, or below cost

Special-Event Pricing To increase sales volume, many organizations coordinate price with advertising or sales promotions for seasonal or special situations. **Special-event pricing** involves advertised sales or price cutting linked to a holiday, season, or event. If the pricing objective is survival, then special sales events may be designed to generate the necessary operating capital.

special-event pricing advertised sales or price cutting linked to a holiday, season, or event

Comparison Discounting **Comparison discounting** sets the price of a product at a specific level and simultaneously compares it with a higher price. The higher price may be the product's previous price, the price of a competing brand, the product's

comparison discounting setting a price at a specific level and comparing it with a higher price

price at another retail outlet, or a manufacturer's suggested retail price. Customers may find comparative discounting informative, and it can have a significant impact on them. However, because this pricing strategy on occasion has led to deceptive pricing practices, the Federal Trade Commission has established guidelines for comparison discounting. If the higher price against which the comparison is made is the price formerly charged for the product, sellers must have made the previous price available to customers for a reasonable period of time. If sellers present the higher price as the one charged by other retailers in the same trade area, they must be able to demonstrate that this claim is true. When they present the higher price as the manufacturer's suggested retail price, then the higher price must be similar to the price at which a reasonable proportion of the product was sold. Some manufacturers' suggested retail prices are so high that very few products are actually sold at those prices. In such cases, it would be deceptive to use comparison discounting.

Pricing Business Products

learning objective

10 Describe three major types of pricing associated with business products.

Many of the pricing issues discussed thus far in this chapter deal with pricing in general. Setting prices for business products can be different from setting prices for consumer products due to several factors such as size of purchases, transportation considerations, and geographic issues. We examine three types of pricing associated with business products, including geographic pricing, transfer pricing, and discounting.

Geographic Pricing

Geographic pricing strategies deal with delivery costs. The pricing strategy that requires the buyer to pay the delivery costs is called *FOB origin pricing*. It stands for "free on board at the point of origin," which means that the price does not include freight charges, and thus the buyer must pay the transportation costs from the seller's warehouse to the buyer's place of business. *FOB destination* indicates that the price does include freight charges, and thus the seller pays these charges.

Transfer Pricing

transfer pricing prices charged in sales between an organization's units

When one unit in an organization sells a product to another unit, **transfer pricing** occurs. The price is determined by calculating the cost of the product. A transfer price can vary depending on the types of costs included in the calculations. The choice of the costs to include when calculating the transfer price depends on the company's management strategy and the nature of the units' interaction. An organization also must ensure that transfer pricing is fair to all units involved in the purchases.

Discounting

discount a deduction from the price of an item

A **discount** is a deduction from the price of an item. Producers and sellers offer a wide variety of discounts to their customers, including the following:

- *Trade discounts* are discounts from the list prices that are offered to marketing intermediaries, or middlemen. A furniture retailer, for example, may receive a 40 percent discount from the manufacturer. The retailer would then pay $60 for a lamp carrying a list price of $100. Intermediaries, discussed in Chapter 15, perform various marketing activities in return for trade discounts.
- *Quantity discounts* are discounts given to customers who buy in large quantities. The seller's per-unit selling cost is lower for larger purchases. The quantity discount is a way of passing part of these savings on to the buyer.

- *Cash discounts* are discounts offered for prompt payment. A seller may offer a discount of "2/10, net 30," meaning that the buyer may take a 2 percent discount if the bill is paid within ten days and that the bill must be paid in full within thirty days.
- A *seasonal discount* is a price reduction to buyers who purchase out of season. This discount lets the seller maintain steadier production during the year. For example, automobile rental agencies offer seasonal discounts in winter and early spring to encourage firms to use automobiles during the slow months of the automobile rental business.
- An *allowance* is a reduction in price to achieve a desired goal. Trade-in allowances, for example, are price reductions granted for turning in used equipment when purchasing new equipment. This type of discount is popular in the aircraft industry. Another example is a promotional allowance, which is a price reduction granted to dealers for participating in advertising and sales-support programs intended to increase sales of a particular item.

In this chapter we discussed two ingredients of the marketing mix—product and pricing. Chapter 15 is devoted to a third marketing mix element—distribution. As that chapter shows, distribution includes not only the physical movement of products but also the organizations that facilitate exchanges among the producers and users of products.

Return To inside business

Blockbuster is pushing sales as well as rentals of a broader range of entertainment products these days. Some offers link both revenue sources. For example, each customer who buys a new DVD receives one free movie rental. In addition, the company has added high-profit snacks, soft drinks, and other products that encourage impulse purchasing. It also has created special departments featuring Spanish-language movies, magazines, and other items in areas with high Latino populations, such as Houston and San Diego.

Still, Blockbuster's rental revenues are likely to remain much higher than its sales revenues well into the future. "How many movies are most consumers going to want to pay about $20 to own?" the CEO asks. "The reality of the economics—$20 versus a $4 rental—is that the rental market will be predominant for a long, long time." The company has been testing other pricing approaches, such as a flat monthly fee for thirty days of movie rentals.

Questions

1. What are Blockbuster's primary pricing objectives?
2. Would you recommend that Blockbuster use price skimming for new DVD releases of hugely popular movies? Explain your answer.

chapter review

Summary

Explain what a product is and how products are classified.

A product is everything one receives in an exchange, including all attributes and expected benefits. The product may be a manufactured item, a service, an idea, or some combination of these.

Products are classified according to their ultimate use. Classification affects a product's distribution, promotion, and pricing. Consumer products, which include convenience, shopping, and specialty products, are purchased to satisfy personal and family needs. Business products are purchased for resale, for making other products, or for use in a firm's operations. Business products can be classified as raw materials, major equipment, accessory equipment, component parts, process materials, supplies, and services.

Discuss the product life cycle and how it leads to new product development.

Every product moves through a series of four stages—introduction, growth, maturity, and decline—which together form the product life cycle. As the product progresses through these stages, its sales and profitability increase, peak, and then decline. Marketers keep track of the life-cycle stage of products in order to estimate when a new product should be introduced to replace a declining one.

Define *product line* and *product mix* and distinguish between the two.

A product line is a group of similar products marketed by a firm. The products in a product line are related to each other in the way they are produced, marketed, and used. The firm's product mix includes all the products it offers for sale. The width of a mix is the number of product lines it contains. The depth of the mix is the average number of individual products within each line.

Identify the methods available for changing a product mix.

Customer satisfaction and organizational objectives require marketers to develop, adjust, and maintain an effective product mix. Marketers may improve a product mix by changing existing products, deleting products, and developing new products.

New products are developed through a series of seven steps. The first step, idea generation, involves the accumulation of a pool of possible product ideas. Screening, the second step, removes from consideration those product ideas that do not mesh with organizational goals or resources. Concept testing, the third step, is a phase in which a small sample of potential buyers is exposed to a proposed product through a written or oral description in order to determine their initial reaction and buying intentions. The fourth step, business analysis, generates information about the potential sales, costs, and profits. During the development step, the product idea is transformed into mock-ups and actual prototypes to determine if the product is technically feasible to build and can be produced at reasonable costs. Test marketing is an actual launch of the product in several selected cities. Finally, during commercialization, plans for full-scale production and marketing are refined and implemented. Most product failures result from inadequate product planning and development.

Explain the uses and importance of branding, packaging, and labeling.

A brand is a name, term, symbol, design, or any combination of these that identifies a seller's products as distinct from those of other sellers. Brands can be classified as manufacturer brands, store brands, or generic brands. A firm can choose between two branding strategies—individual branding or family branding. Branding strategies are used to associate (or *not* associate) particular products with existing products, producers, or intermediaries. Packaging protects goods, offers consumer convenience, and enhances marketing efforts by communicating product features, uses, benefits, and image. Labeling provides customers with product information, some of which is required by law.

Describe the economic basis of pricing and the means by which sellers can control prices and buyers' perceptions of prices.

Under the ideal conditions of pure competition, an individual seller has no control over the price of its products. Prices are determined by the workings of supply and demand. In our real economy, however, sellers do exert some control, primarily through product differentiation. Product differentiation is the process of developing and promoting differences between one's product and all similar products. Firms also attempt to gain some control over pricing through advertising. A few large sellers have considerable control over prices because each controls a large proportion of the total supply of the product. Firms must consider the relative importance of price to buyers in the target market before setting prices. Buyers' perceptions of prices are affected by the importance of the product to them, the range of prices they consider acceptable, their perceptions of competing products, and their association of quality with price.

Identify the major pricing objectives used by businesses.

Objectives of pricing include survival, profit maximization, target return on investment, achieving market goals, and maintaining the status quo. Firms sometimes have to price products to survive, which usually requires cutting prices to attract customers. Return on investment (ROI) is the amount earned as a result of the investment in developing and marketing the product. The firm sets an annual percentage ROI as the pricing goal. Some firms use pricing to maintain or increase their market share. And in industries in which price stability is important, firms often price their products by charging about the same as competitors.

Examine the three major pricing methods that firms employ.

The three major pricing methods are cost-based pricing, demand-based pricing, and competition-based pricing. When cost-based pricing is employed, a proportion of the cost is added to the total cost to determine the selling price. When demand-based pricing is used, the price will be higher when demand is higher, and the price will be lower when demand is lower. A firm that uses competition-based pricing may choose to price below competitors' prices, at the same level as competitors' prices, or slightly above competitors' prices.

Explain the different strategies available to companies for setting prices.

Pricing strategies fall into five categories: new product pricing, differential pricing, psychological pricing, product-line pricing, and promotional pricing. Price skimming and penetration pricing are two strategies used for pricing new products. Differential pricing can be accomplished through negotiated pricing, secondary-market pricing, periodic discounting, and random discounting. The types of psychological pricing strategies are odd-number pricing, multiple-unit pricing, reference pricing, bundle pricing, everyday low prices, and customary pricing. Product-line pricing can be achieved through captive pricing, premium pricing, and price lining. The major types of promotional pricing are price-leader pricing, special-event pricing, and comparison discounting.

Describe three major types of pricing associated with business products.

Setting prices for business products can be different from setting prices for consumer products as a result of several factors, such as size of purchases, transportation considerations, and geographic issues. The three types of pricing associated with the pricing of business products are geographic pricing, transfer pricing, and discounting.

Key Terms

You should now be able to define and give an example relevant to each of the following terms:

product (399)
consumer product (399)
business product (399)
convenience product (400)
shopping product (400)
specialty product (400)
raw material (401)
major equipment (401)
accessory equipment (401)
component part (401)
process material (401)
supply (401)
business service (401)
product life cycle (402)
product line (405)
product mix (405)
product modification (405)
product deletion (407)
brand (409)
brand name (409)
brand mark (409)
trademark (410)
trade name (410)
manufacturer (or producer) brand (410)
store (or private) brand (410)
generic product (or brand) (411)
brand loyalty (411)
brand equity (412)
individual branding (413)
family branding (413)
packaging (413)
labeling (414)
express warranty (415)
price (415)
supply (416)
demand (416)
product differentiation (416)
price competition (417)
nonprice competition (417)
markup (419)
breakeven quantity (420)
total revenue (420)
fixed cost (420)
variable cost (420)
total cost (420)
price skimming (422)
penetration pricing (422)
negotiated pricing (423)
secondary-market pricing (423)
periodic discounting (423)
random discounting (423)
odd-number pricing (423)
multiple-unit pricing (424)
reference pricing (424)
bundle pricing (424)
everyday low prices (EDLPs) (424)
customary pricing (425)
captive pricing (425)
premium pricing (425)
price lining (425)
price leaders (425)
special-event pricing (425)
comparison discounting (425)
transfer pricing (426)
discount (426)

Review Questions

1. What does the purchaser of a product obtain besides the good, service, or idea itself?
2. What are the products of (a) a bank, (b) an insurance company, and (c) a university?
3. What major factor determines whether a product is a consumer or a business product?
4. Describe each of the classifications of business products.
5. What are the four stages of the product life cycle? How can a firm determine which stage a particular product is in?
6. What is the difference between a product line and a product mix? Give an example of each.
7. Under what conditions does product modification work best?

8. Why do products have to be deleted from a product mix?
9. Why must firms introduce new products?
10. Briefly describe the seven new product development stages.
11. What is the difference between manufacturer brands and store brands? Between family branding and individual branding?
12. How can packaging be used to enhance marketing activities?
13. For what purposes is labeling used?
14. What is the primary function of prices in our economy?
15. Compare and contrast the characteristics of price and nonprice competition.
16. How might buyers' perceptions of price influence pricing decisions?
17. List and briefly describe the five major pricing objectives.
18. What are the differences among markup pricing, pricing by breakeven analysis, and competition-based pricing?
19. In what way is demand-based pricing more realistic than markup pricing?
20. Why would a firm use competition-based pricing?
21. What are the five major categories of pricing strategies? Give at least two examples of specific strategies that fall into each category.
22. Identify and describe the main types of discounts that are used in the pricing of business products.

Discussion Questions

1. Why is it important to understand how products are classified?
2. What factors might determine how long a product remains in each stage of the product life cycle? What can a firm do to prolong each stage?
3. Some firms do not delete products until they become financially threatening. What problems may result from relying on this practice?
4. Which steps in the evolution of new products are most important? Which are least important? Defend your choices.
5. Do branding, packaging, and labeling really benefit consumers? Explain.
6. To what extent can a firm control its prices in our market economy? What factors limit such control?
7. Under what conditions would a firm be most likely to use nonprice competition?
8. Can a firm have more than one pricing objective? Can it use more than one of the pricing methods discussed in this chapter? Explain.
9. What are the major disadvantages of price skimming?
10. What is an "effective" price?
11. Under what conditions would a business most likely decide to employ one of the differential pricing strategies?
12. For what types of products are psychological pricing strategies most likely to be used?

video case

JetBlue Is a Rare Bird: Flight Plan for Profitability

Which U.S. airline has the highest profit margin? Not industry giant American Airlines—and not even the perennially profitable Southwest Airlines. The answer is JetBlue, a customer-friendly, low-fare airline started by serial entrepreneur David Neeleman. During one recent three-month period, JetBlue's profit margin was 17.5 percent, more than four times higher than Southwest's profit margin of 3.9 percent. How does JetBlue do it?

When Neeleman sold his Utah-based airline to Southwest Airlines in 1994, he signed a contract agreeing not to compete in the airline industry for five years. While mulling over plans for a new airline, he started and sold a reservation management system and served on the board of a low-fare Canadian airline. By 1999, the entrepreneur had created a new flight plan for his full-throttle return to the skies with JetBlue.

CEO Neeleman and his management team decided to base the start-up airline in New York City after thoroughly analyzing the area's air travel patterns. They found that "low-quality, high-fare airlines" were the only choices for New York travelers. They also found that travelers had to contend with crowds and delays at nearby La Guardia Airport unless they were willing to venture eight miles farther to fly from John F. Kennedy International Airport. JFK was not a regional hub for major airlines or for low-fare carriers such as Southwest. Seizing an opportunity to trade off a slightly less convenient location for less competition and better on-time performance, Neeleman secured more than seventy takeoff and landing slots at JFK Airport.

His plan called for flying routes that attracted a high volume of travelers, such as New York to Florida. At the same time, he avoided congested, competitive routes such as New York to Chicago. "We wanted to go where we could make money," the CEO states. Recognizing that price is one of the top considerations for travelers, he set JetBlue's ticket prices to attract vacationers as well as business travelers.

Major carriers typically quote dozens of fares for each flight, depending on time of day, purchase timing, seat location, and other factors. By comparison, JetBlue's pricing structure is far simpler, with one ticket price per flight based on demand and equalizing passenger loads so that no jets take off empty while others are completely full. Thus tickets for Sunday-night flights are priced higher because of higher demand, whereas tickets for Tuesday-night flights are often priced lower due to lower demand.

Between JetBlue's everyday low fares and the occasional promotional fares it charges for new routes, the airline has attracted a sizable and loyal customer base. Half its passengers are repeat customers, and 20 percent of its passengers account for half of JetBlue's ticket revenue. More passengers per flight means a higher profit margin. On average, the airline fills 80 percent of its seats, higher than the overall industry average, which is in the low 70 percent range.

Just as important, Neeleman has kept costs low without sacrificing customer comfort. All the airline's jets are new, with leather seats set wider apart for more legroom and a seat-back personal video screen showing free satellite television programming. The new jets burn less fuel than older jets, so JetBlue's costs are lower because of higher fuel efficiency. New jets come with a five-year warranty, a money-saver because the airline has to budget only for routine maintenance service. Payroll costs eat up about 25 percent of revenue, much less than Southwest's 33 percent of revenue and Delta's 44 percent of revenue. And half the airline's ticket sales come through the Internet at a cost of about 50 cents per ticket, a considerable savings over selling through travel agents and airline reservationists.

All these cost-shaving measures keep JetBlue's total costs well below those of Southwest and other leading airlines. In turn, low costs allow Neeleman to charge low prices while getting customers to their destinations in comfort. Responding to customer requests, the airline now offers a frequent-flyer program to reward repeat customers and asks customers to fill out feedback forms any time their JetBlue flight is delayed or has other problems. The CEO is so involved in the airline's operations that he gets a pager message whenever one of the flights is more than one minute late taking off or landing. Says Neeleman: "You can be efficient and effective and deliver a great experience at the same time." [23]

Questions

1. How would you use the airplane and other physical aspects of the business to build the JetBlue brand?
2. In an industry where pricing has driven many firms out of business or into bankruptcy protection, why does JetBlue compete so successfully on the basis of price?
3. How does JetBlue use pricing to deal with demand fluctuations?

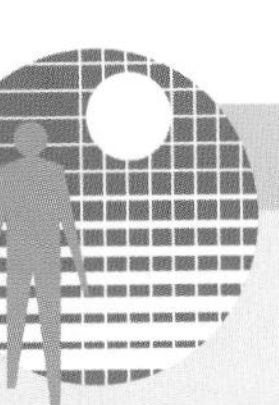

Building Skills for Career Success

1. Exploring the Internet

The Internet has quickly taken comparison shopping to a new level. Several websites such as bizrate.com, pricescan.com, and mysimon.com have emerged boasting that they can find the consumer the best deal on any product. From computers to watches, these sites offer unbiased price and product information to compare virtually any product. Users may read reviews about products as well as provide their own input from personal experience. Some of these sites also offer special promotions and incentives in exchange for user information. Visit the text website for updates to this exercise.

Assignment

1. Search all three of the websites listed above for the same product.
2. Did you notice any significant differences between the sites and the information they provide?
3. What percentage of searches do you think lead to purchases as opposed to browsing? Explain your answer.
4. Which site are you most likely to use on a regular basis? Why?
5. In what ways do these websites contribute to price competition?

2. Developing Critical Thinking Skills

A feature is a characteristic of a product or service that enables it to perform its function. Benefits are the results a person receives from using a product or service. For example, a toothpaste's stain-removing formula is a feature; the benefit to the user is whiter teeth. While features are valuable and enhance a product, benefits motivate people to buy. The customer is more interested in how the product can help (the benefits) than in the details of the product (the features).

Assignment

1. Choose a product and identify its features and benefits.
2. Divide a sheet of paper into two columns. In one column, list the features of the product. In the other column, list the benefits each feature yields to the buyer.
3. Prepare a statement that would motivate you to buy this product.

3. Building Team Skills

In his book, *The Post-Industrial Society*, Peter Drucker wrote:

> Society, community, and family are all conserving institutions. They try to maintain stability and to prevent, or at least slow down, change. But the organization of the post-capitalist society of organizations is a destabilizer. Because its function is to put knowledge to work—on tools, processes, and products; on work; on knowledge itself—it must be organized for constant change. It must be organized for innovation.

New product development is important in this process of systematically abandoning the past and building a future. Current customers can be sources of ideas for new products and services and ways of improving existing ones.

Assignment

1. Working in teams of five to seven, brainstorm ideas for new products or services for your college.
2. Construct questions to ask currently enrolled students (your customers). Sample questions might include
   a. Why did you choose this college?
   b. How can this college be improved?
   c. What products or services do you wish were available?
3. Conduct the survey and review the results.
4. Prepare a list of improvements and/or new products or services for your college.

4. Researching Different Careers

Standard & Poor's Industry Surveys, designed for investors, provides insight into various industries and the companies that compete within those industries. The "Basic Analysis" section gives overviews of industry trends and issues. The other sections define some basic industry terms, report the latest revenues and earnings of more than 1,000 companies, and occasionally list major reference books and trade associations.

Assignment

1. Identify an industry in which you might like to work.
2. Find the industry in *Standard & Poor's. (Note: Standard & Poor's* uses broad categories of industry. For example, an apparel or home furnishings store would be included under "Retail" or "Textiles.")
3. Identify the following:
   a. Trends and issues in the industry.
   b. Opportunities and/or problems that might arise in the industry in the next five years.
   c. Major competitors within the industry. (These companies are your potential employers.)
4. Prepare a report of your findings.

5. Improving Communication Skills

One often-overlooked source of business information is the Yellow Pages of the local telephone directory. The Yellow Pages can give you insight into the nature and scope of local companies.

Assignment

1. Choose a product and look it up in the Yellow Pages.
2. Telephone three companies that provide the product and ask for directions from your campus.
3. Evaluate the quality of the directions given and your impression of each company's service.
4. Report on your findings.

chapter

15 Wholesaling, Retailing, and Physical Distribution

learning objectives

1. Identify the various channels of distribution that are used for consumer and industrial products.
2. Explain the concept of market coverage.
3. Understand how supply-chain management facilitates partnering among channel members.
4. Describe what a vertical marketing system is and identify the types of vertical marketing systems.
5. Discuss the need for wholesalers and describe the services they provide to retailers and manufacturers.
6. Identify and describe the major types of wholesalers.
7. Distinguish among the major types of retailers.
8. Explain the wheel of retailing hypothesis.
9. Identify the categories of shopping centers and the factors that determine how shopping centers are classified.
10. Explain the five most important physical distribution activities.

Dollar General continues to expand regardless of whether the economy is improving or deteriorating.

inside business

Dollar General Draws Customers with Convenience and Low Prices

DOLLAR GENERAL STORES has built a loyal customer base by offering both convenience and low prices. Based in Tennessee, Dollar General rings up more than $5.3 billion in annual sales through 6,000 stores in twenty-seven states. Unlike the huge stores in the Wal-Mart chain, the average Dollar General Store occupies just 7,000 square feet. Because the stores are small, customers can easily pop in, locate what they need, and be on their way within a few minutes.

The chain targets families with yearly household incomes of $30,000 and retirees living on fixed monthly incomes. Its pricing policies are geared specifically to the needs and behavior of customers in its target market. Prices start at $1 and range up to $20, with most items priced lower than $10. Despite these low price points, each store sells, on average, nearly $1 million worth of merchandise annually.

Although Dollar General Stores lack the frills of department stores, they are filled with basic items that draw customers back again and again. In fact, 64 percent of revenue comes from sales of everyday products such as paper goods, food and beverages, household cleaners, and health and beauty aids. The smallest category, family clothing, accounts for only 10 percent of the chain's retail sales. By emphasizing fast-selling products and strictly controlling inventory, the retailer has been able to improve cost efficiency and keep prices low.

Discount giant Wal-Mart is a long-time competitor. In addition, Dollar General faces strong competition from dollar retailers such as Family Dollar Stores, Dollar Tree Stores, Fred's, and Bill's. Like Dollar General, these chains open stores near low-income neighborhoods and stock ordinary household products that customers buy frequently. Dollar General and its rivals also must contend with competition from supermarkets selling similar products. Yet research shows that customers are visiting dollar stores more often these days—making approximately eleven shopping trips per year. By comparison, the number of visits to grocery stores has been going down in recent years.

Given its competitive situation, Dollar General is paying even closer attention to costs and operations. The company shuns media advertising in favor of targeted direct-mail campaigns to support new store openings. It is also building new distribution centers to fuel an aggressive growth strategy. During tight economic times, upscale retailers with higher-quality merchandise, more services, and fancier stores struggle for sales. However, Dollar General continues to expand regardless of whether the economy is improving or deteriorating. The company knows that its customers appreciate everyday low prices, which make their dollars stretch even farther, in good times and in bad times.[1]

More than two million firms in the United States help move products from producers to consumers. Of all marketers, retail firms that sell directly to consumers are the most visible. Store chains such as Dollar General Stores, Starbucks, Sears, and Wal-Mart operate retail outlets where consumers make purchases. Some retailers, such as Avon Products and Amway, send their salespeople to the homes of customers. Other retailers, such as Lands' End and L.L. Bean, sell through catalogs or through both catalogs and stores. Still others, such as Amazon, sell online to customers.

In addition, there are more than half a million wholesalers that sell merchandise to other firms. Most consumers know little about these firms, which work "behind the scenes" and rarely sell directly to consumers. These and other intermediaries are concerned with the transfer of both products and ownership. They thus help to create the time, place, and possession utilities that are critical to marketing. As we will see, they also perform a number of services for their suppliers and their customers.

In this chapter we initially examine various channels of distribution that products follow as they move from producer to ultimate user. Then we discuss wholesalers and retailers within these channels. Next, we examine the types of shopping centers. Finally, we explore the physical distribution function and the major modes of transportation that are used to move goods.

Channels of Distribution

learning objective

1 Identify the various channels of distribution that are used for consumer and industrial products.

A **channel of distribution**, or **marketing channel**, is a sequence of marketing organizations that directs a product from the producer to the ultimate user. Every marketing channel begins with the producer and ends with either the consumer or the business user.

A marketing organization that links a producer and user within a marketing channel is called a **middleman**, or **marketing intermediary.** For the most part, middlemen are concerned with the transfer of *ownership* of products. A **merchant middleman** (or, more simply, a *merchant*) is a middleman that actually takes title to products by buying them. A **functional middleman**, on the other hand, helps in the transfer of ownership of products but does not take title to the products.

Different channels of distribution generally are used to move consumer and business products. The six most commonly used channels are illustrated in Figure 15.1 (on p. 436).

channel of distribution (or **marketing channel**) a sequence of marketing organizations that directs a product from the producer to the ultimate user

middleman (or **marketing intermediary**) a marketing organization that links a producer and user within a marketing channel

merchant middleman a middleman that actually takes title to products by buying them

functional middleman a middleman that helps in the transfer of ownership of products but does not take title to the products

retailer a middleman that buys from producers or other middlemen and sells to consumers

Channels for Consumer Products

Producer to Consumer This channel, often called the *direct channel*, includes no marketing intermediaries. Practically all services and a few consumer goods are distributed through a direct channel. Examples of marketers that sell goods directly to consumers include Dell Computer, Mary Kay Cosmetics, Spiegel, and Avon Products.

Producers sell directly to consumers for several reasons. They can better control the quality and price of their products. They do not have to pay (through discounts) for the services of intermediaries. And they can maintain closer ties with customers.

Producer to Retailer to Consumer A **retailer** is a middleman that buys from producers or other middlemen and sells to consumers. Producers sell directly to retailers when retailers (such as Wal-Mart) can buy in large quantities. This channel is used most often for products that are bulky, such as furniture and automobiles, for which additional handling would increase selling costs. It is also the usual channel for perishable products, such as fruits and vegetables, and for high-fashion products that must reach the consumer in the shortest possible time.

Producer to Wholesaler to Retailer to Consumer This channel is known as the *traditional channel* because many consumer goods (especially convenience goods) pass

figure 15.1

Distribution Channels

Producers use various channels to distribute their products.

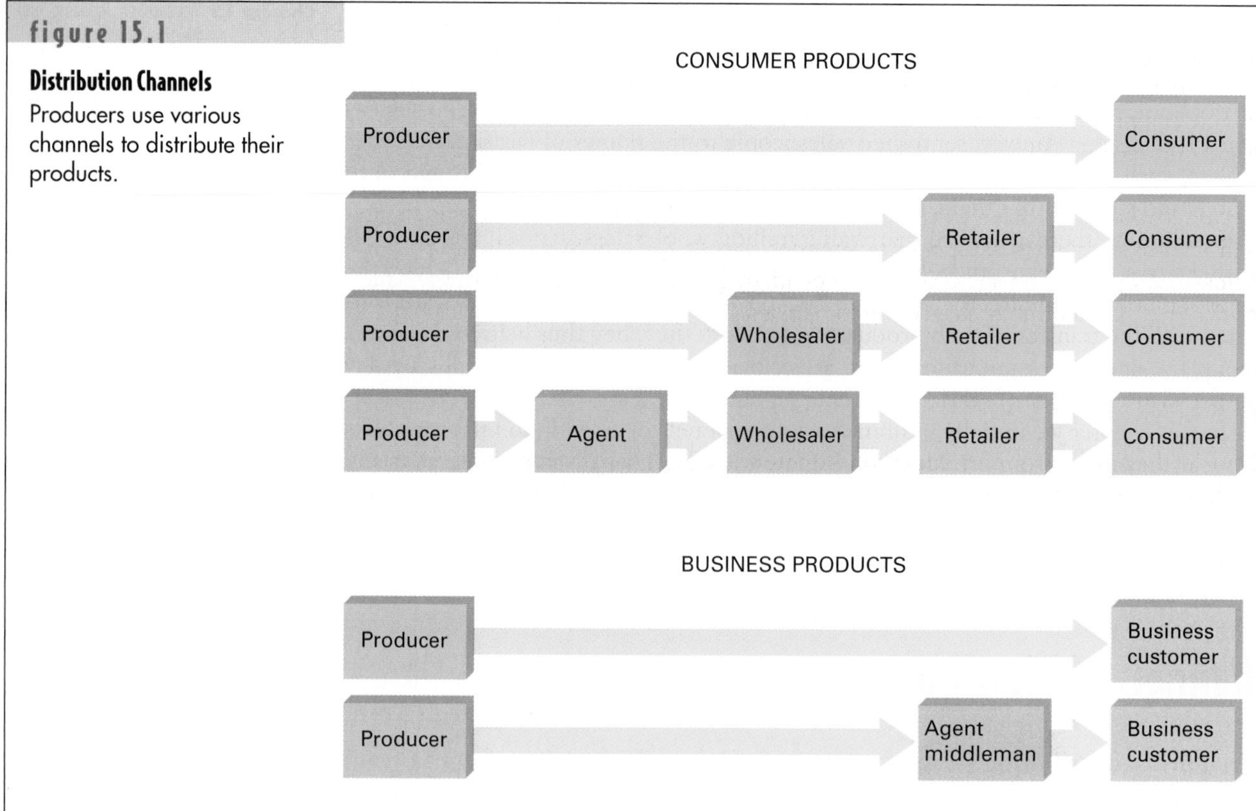

wholesaler a middleman that sells products to other firms

through wholesalers to retailers. A **wholesaler** is a middleman that sells products to other firms. These firms may be retailers, industrial users, or other wholesalers. A producer uses wholesalers when its products are carried by so many retailers that the producer cannot deal with all of them. For example, the maker of Wrigley's gum uses this type of channel.

Producer to Agent to Wholesaler to Retailer to Consumer Producers may use agents to reach wholesalers. Agents are functional middlemen that do not take title to products and that are compensated by commissions paid by producers. Often these products are inexpensive, frequently purchased items. For example, to reach a large number of potential customers, a small manufacturer of gas-powered lawn edgers might choose to use agents to market its product to wholesalers, which in turn sell the lawn edgers to a large number of retailers. This channel is also used for highly seasonal products (such as Christmas tree ornaments) and by producers that do not have their own sales forces.

Multiple Channels for Consumer Products Often a manufacturer uses different distribution channels to reach different market segments. A manufacturer uses multiple channels, for example, when the same product is sold to consumers and business customers. Multiple channels are also used to increase sales or to capture a larger share of the market. With the goal of selling as much merchandise as possible, Firestone markets its tires through its own retail outlets as well as through independent dealers.

Channels for Business Products

Producers of business products generally tend to use short channels. We will outline the two that are used most commonly.

Producer to Business User In this direct channel, the manufacturer's own sales force sells directly to business users. Heavy machinery, airplanes, and major equipment usually are distributed in this way. The very short channel allows the producer to provide customers with expert and timely services, such as delivery, machinery installation, and repairs.

Producer to Agent Middleman to Business User Manufacturers use this channel to distribute such items as operating supplies, accessory equipment, small tools, and standardized parts. The agent is an independent intermediary between the producer and the user. Generally, agents represent sellers.

Market Coverage

learning objective

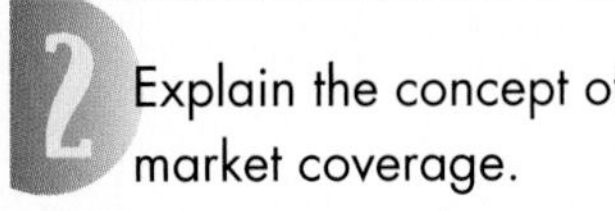

Explain the concept of market coverage.

How does a producer decide which distribution channels (and which particular intermediaries) to use? Like every other marketing decision, this one should be based on all relevant factors. These include the firm's production capabilities and marketing resources, the target market and buying patterns of potential customers, and the product itself. After evaluating these factors, the producer can choose a particular *intensity of market coverage*. Then the producer selects channels and intermediaries to implement that coverage (see Figure 15.2).

intensive distribution the use of all available outlets for a product

Intensive distribution is the use of all available outlets for a product. The producer that wants to give its product the widest possible exposure in the marketplace chooses intensive distribution. The manufacturer saturates the market by selling to any intermediary of good financial standing that is willing to stock and sell the product. For the consumer, intensive distribution means being able to shop at a convenient store and spend minimum time buying the product. Many convenience goods, including candy, gum, and soft drinks, are distributed intensively. In fact, PepsiCo, with its soft drinks and Frito Lay snack foods, traditionally focused its intensive distribution on convenience stores and supermarkets. Experts believe that the future success for PepsiCo's use of intensive distribution will include greater focus on outlets such as Blockbuster, Auto Zone, Starbucks, and Dollar General Stores.[2]

selective distribution the use of only a portion of the available outlets for a product in each geographic area

Selective distribution is the use of only a portion of the available outlets for a product in each geographic area. Manufacturers of goods such as furniture, major home appliances, and clothing typically prefer selective distribution. Franchisors also

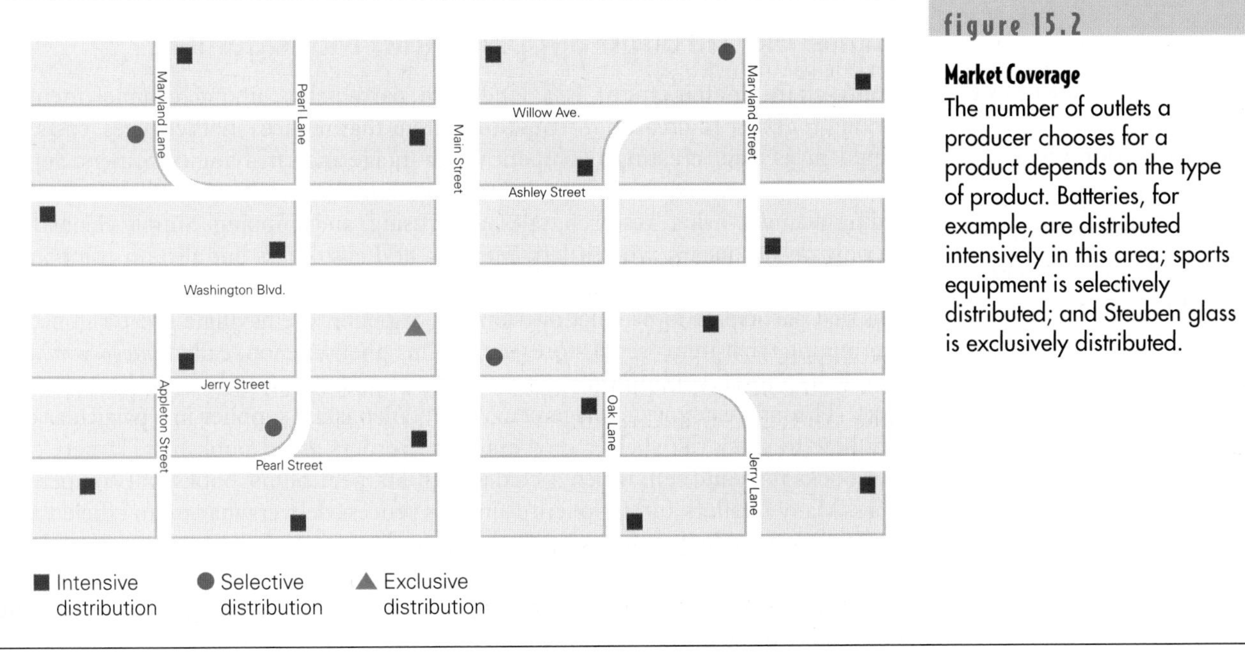

figure 15.2

Market Coverage

The number of outlets a producer chooses for a product depends on the type of product. Batteries, for example, are distributed intensively in this area; sports equipment is selectively distributed; and Steuben glass is exclusively distributed.

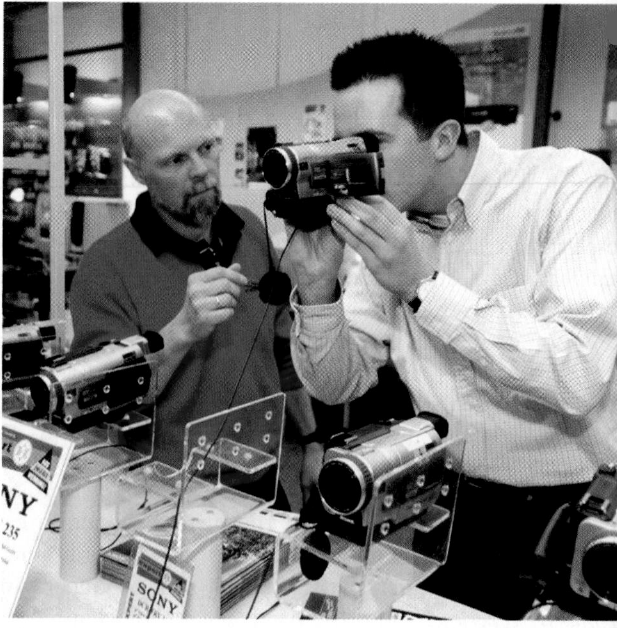

Intensive and selective distribution. Soda is distributed through intensive distribution. Most digital cameras are sold through selective distribution.

use selective distribution in granting franchises for the sale of their goods and services in a specific geographic area. Levi Strauss, like most clothing companies, uses selective distribution to get its products to consumers. The company recently decided to expand the distribution of its denim products beyond its usual choices of department and specialty stores. It launched its new Type One jeans for its regular distribution outlets and is expanding through the introduction of its Levi Strauss Signature line in Wal-Mart stores. Levi is counting on this less selective approach to distribution to boost its sales significantly. Some executives are concerned about the effect this tactic will have on sales of Levi's higher-priced department store denim products.[3]

exclusive distribution the use of only a single retail outlet for a product in a large geographic area

Exclusive distribution is the use of only a single retail outlet for a product in a large geographic area. Exclusive distribution is usually limited to very prestigious products. It is appropriate, for instance, for specialty goods such as upscale pianos, fine china, and expensive jewelry. The producer usually places many requirements (inventory levels, sales training, service quality, warranty procedures) on exclusive dealers.

Partnering Through Supply-Chain Management

learning objective

3 Understand how supply-chain management facilitates partnering among channel members.

supply-chain management long-term partnership among channel members working together to create a distribution system that reduces inefficiencies, costs, and redundancies while creating a competitive advantage and satisfying customers

Supply-chain management is a long-term partnership among channel members working together to create a distribution system that reduces inefficiencies, costs, and redundancies while creating a competitive advantage and satisfying customers. Supply-chain management requires cooperation throughout the entire marketing channel, including manufacturing, research, sales, advertising, and shipping. Supply chains focus not only on producers, wholesalers, retailers, and customers but also on component-parts suppliers, shipping companies, communication companies, and other organizations that participate in product distribution. Suppliers are having a greater impact on determining what items retail stores carry. This phenomenon, called *category management*, is becoming common for mass merchandisers, supermarkets, and convenience stores. Through category management, the retailer asks a supplier in a particular category how to stock the shelves. For example, Borders asked publisher HarperCollins what books it should sell, which includes both HarperCollins' books and competitors' books. Many retailers and suppliers claim this process delivers maximum efficiency.[4]

Traditionally, buyers and sellers have been adversarial when negotiating purchases. Supply-chain management, however, encourages cooperation in reducing the costs of inventory, transportation, administration, and handling; in speeding order-cycle times; and in increasing profits for all channel members. When buyers, sellers, marketing termediaries, and facilitating agencies work together, cus-mers' needs regarding delivery, scheduling, packaging, and her requirements are better met. Home Depot, North Amer-a's largest home-improvement retailer, is working to help its ppliers improve productivity and thereby supply Home epot with better-quality products at lower costs. The com-ny has even suggested a cooperative partnership with its mpetitors so that regional trucking companies making deliv-ies to all these organizations can provide faster, more efficient livery.

Technology has enhanced the implementation of supply-ain management significantly. Through computerized inte-ated information sharing, channel members reduce costs d improve customer service. At Wal-Mart, for example, pply-chain management has almost eliminated the occur-nce of out-of-stock items. Using bar-code and electronic ta interchange (EDI) technology, stores, warehouses, and ppliers communicate quickly and easily to keep Wal-Mart's elves stocked with items customers want. Furthermore, ere are currently about four hundred electronic trading mmunities made up of businesses selling to other businesses, cluding auctions, exchanges, e-procurement hubs, and mul-supplier online catalogs. As many major industries transform eir processes over the next five to ten years, the end results ill be increased productivity by reducing inventory, shortening cycle time, and moving wasted human effort.

Supply chain management. Menlo promotes its supply chain management capabilities.

exploring business

Partnering with Channel Members

PARTNERING IS A MAJOR TREND in distribution today. Seeking to do a better job of reaching and satisfying customers through improved channel efficiencies, many companies are forging closer partnerships with key channel members. As in any relationship, the companies and channel members must choose their partners carefully, communicate clearly, and agree on the expectations and obligations of both sides.

"Channel partners are an extension of your company," says the channel manager for Hoffman Enclosures, which manufactures industrial equipment. This is why Hoffman is extremely picky about its channel partners, seeking out distributors that demonstrate in-depth product knowledge and provide top-notch customer service.

Companies that do business on a global scale face the challenge of partnering with hundreds or even thousands of channel members, sometimes spread across immense distances. Consider Microsoft, which sells its software products in virtually every country. Channel partnerships are vital to Microsoft's success because many business customers and consumers depend on retailers and computer specialists to recommend software, install it, and provide training. Therefore, the software giant has a staff of hundreds and spends millions of dollars annually to maintain relations with the 800,000 channel partners who service its worldwide customer base. Microsoft knows that its channel partners need training and support as well as good products to sell. "If we think we've engineered something well for the customer," says CEO Steve Ballmer, "but blow it up with the partner and it never sees the light of day at the customer end, we've screwed it up."

Channel management executives at Computer Associates, which provides information technology services, work hard to explain the company's role and the role they want channel partners to play. "Too many times you recruit channel partners and promise the world, and then the expectations are far different from reality," says Mark Milford, general manager of its North American channel group. To prevent misunderstandings, Computer Associates delineates the training and assistance it will provide and asks channel partners to submit plans showing the actions they will take to generate agreed-on revenue levels. Then, if a channel relationship does not work out, Milford believes "it was a bad job of setting expectations upfront."

learning objective

4 Describe what a vertical marketing system is and identify the types of vertical marketing systems.

vertical channel integration the combining of two or more stages of a distribution channel under a single firm's management

vertical marketing system (VMS) a centrally managed distribution channel resulting from vertical channel integration

Vertical Marketing Systems

Vertical channel integration occurs when two or more stages of a distribution channel are combined and managed by one firm. A **vertical marketing system (VMS)** is a centrally managed distribution channel resulting from vertical channel integration. This merging eliminates the need for certain intermediaries. One member of a marketing channel may assume the responsibilities of another member, or it actually may purchase the operations of that member. For example, a large-volume discount retailer that ships and warehouses its own stock directly from manufacturers does not need a wholesaler. Total vertical integration occurs when a single management controls all operations from production to final sale. Oil companies that own wells, transportation facilities, refineries, terminals, and service stations exemplify total vertical integration.

There are three types of VMSs: administered, contractual, and corporate. In an *administered VMS*, one of the channel members dominates the other members, perhaps because of its large size. Under its influence, the channel members collaborate on production and distribution. A powerful manufacturer, such as Procter & Gamble, receives a great deal of cooperation from intermediaries that carry its brands. Although the goals of the entire system are considered when decisions are made, control rests with individual channel members, as in conventional marketing channels. Under a *contractual VMS*, cooperative arrangements and the rights and obligations of channel members are defined by contracts or other legal measures. In a *corporate VMS*, actual ownership is the vehicle by which production and distribution are joined. For example, Benetton manufactures clothing, which it then ships to its own retail outlets. Most vertical marketing systems are organized to improve distribution by combining individual operations.

Marketing Intermediaries: Wholesalers

learning objective

5 Discuss the need for wholesalers and describe the services they provide to retailers and manufacturers.

Wholesalers may be the most misunderstood of marketing intermediaries. Producers sometimes try to eliminate them from distribution channels by dealing directly with retailers or consumers. Yet wholesalers provide a variety of essential marketing services. Although wholesalers can be eliminated, their functions cannot be eliminated; these functions *must* be performed by other channel members or by the consumer or ultimate user. Eliminating a wholesaler may or may not cut distribution costs.

Justifications for Marketing Intermediaries

The press, consumers, public officials, and other marketers often charge wholesalers, at least in principle, with inefficiency and parasitism. Consumers in particular feel strongly that the distribution channel should be made as short as possible. They assume that the fewer the intermediaries in a distribution channel, the lower the price of the product will be.

Those who believe that the elimination of wholesalers would bring about lower prices, however, do not recognize that the services wholesalers perform would still be needed. Those services simply would be provided by other means, and consumers would still bear the costs. Moreover, all manufacturers would have to keep extensive records and employ enough personnel to deal with a multitude of retailers individually. Even with direct distribution, products might be considerably more expensive because prices would reflect the costs of producers' inefficiencies. Figure 15.3 shows that sixteen contacts could result from the efforts of four buyers purchasing the products of four producers. With the assistance of an intermediary, only eight contacts would be necessary.

To illustrate further the useful role of wholesalers in the marketing system, assume that all wholesalers in the candy industry were abolished. With thousands of

figure 15.3

Efficiency Provided by an Intermediary

The services of an intermediary reduce the number of contacts, or exchanges, between producers and buyers, thereby increasing efficiency.

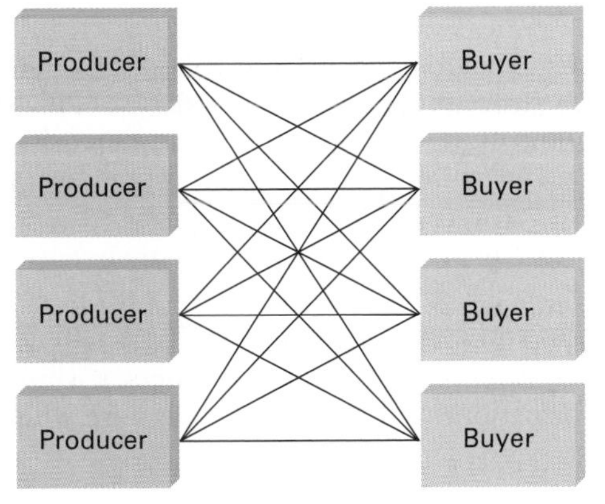

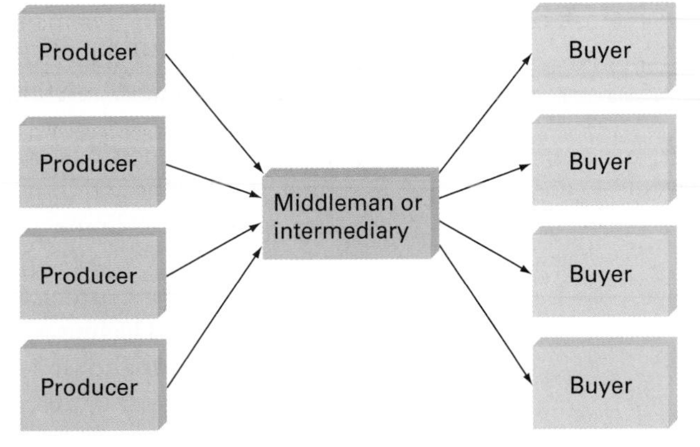

ource: William M. Pride and O. C. Ferrell, *Marketing: Concepts and Strategies*, 12th ed. Copyright © 2003 by Ioughton Mifflin Company. Adapted with permission.

andy retailers to contact, candy manufacturers would be making an extremely large umber of sales calls just to maintain the present level of product visibility. Hershey 'oods, for example, would have to set up warehouses all over the country, organize a leet of trucks, purchase and maintain thousands of vending machines, and deliver all ts own candy. Sales and distribution costs for candy would soar. Candy producers vould be contacting and shipping products to thousands of small businesses instead of o a limited number of large wholesalers and retailers. The outrageous costs of this inefficiency would be passed on to consumers. Candy bars would be more expensive and likely vailable through fewer retailers.

Wholesalers often are more efficient and economical not only for manufacturers but also or consumers. Because pressure to eliminate hem comes from both ends of the marketing hannel, wholesalers should perform only hose functions that are genuinely in demand. To stay in business, wholesalers also should ake care to be efficient and productive and to provide high-quality services to other channel nembers.

Wholesalers' Services to Retailers

Wholesalers help retailers by buying in large quantities and then selling to retailers in maller quantities and by delivering goods to etailers. They also stock—in one place—the variety of goods that retailers otherwise would have to buy from many producers. And wholesalers provide assistance in three other vital areas: promotion, market information, and financial aid.

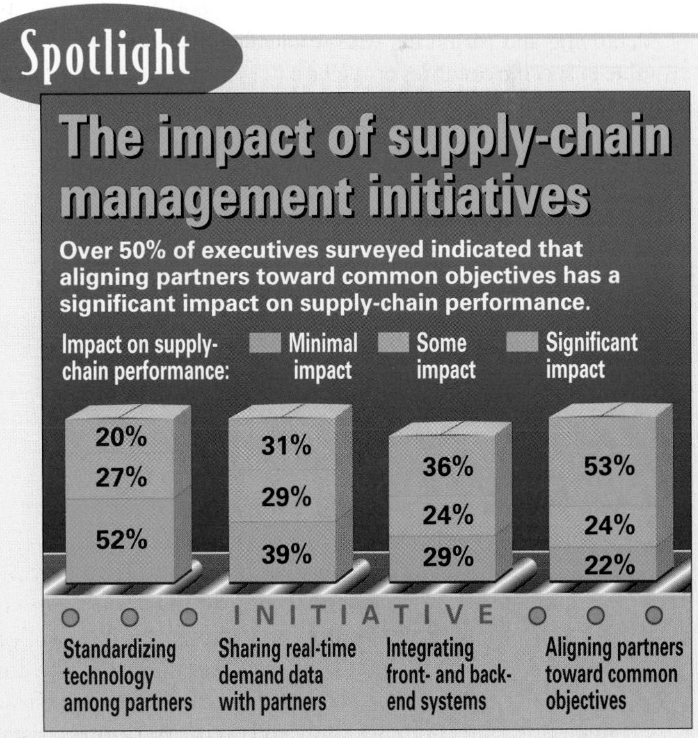

Source: Tim Stevens, "View from on High," *Industry Week*, November 1, 2001; accessed from IndustryWeek.com, June 7, 2002.

Promotion Some wholesalers help to promote the products they sell to retailer These services are usually either free or performed at cost. Wholesalers, for exampl are major sources of display materials designed to stimulate impulse buying. They als may help retailers to build effective window, counter, and shelf displays; they may eve assign their own employees to work on the retail sales floor during special promo tions.

Market Information Wholesalers are a constant source of market informatio Wholesalers have numerous contacts with local businesses and distant suppliers. I the course of these dealings, they accumulate information about consumer deman prices, supply conditions, new developments within the trade, and even industry per sonnel. This information may be relayed to retailers informally through the whole saler's sales force. Some wholesalers also provide information to their custome through websites.

Information regarding industry sales and competitive prices is especially impo tant to all firms. Dealing with a number of suppliers and many retailers, a wholesal is a natural clearinghouse for such information. And most wholesalers are willing t pass information on to their customers.

Financial Aid Most wholesalers provide a type of financial aid that retaile often take for granted. By making prompt and frequent deliveries, wholesalers en

going global

Selecting Wholesalers for Global Markets

COMPANIES THAT HAVE DECIDED to go global face the crucial decision of selecting local wholesalers to distribute their products. Experts offer these guidelines for identifying and partnering with wholesalers that can add value in specific countries or regions:

- *Screen distributors carefully.* Loctite, a Connecticut-based adhesives manufacturer, originally worked with international wholesalers that handled similar products. The firm eventually found this arrangement to be unsatisfactory because the wholesalers "represent the market's status quo, and we are selling a replacement technology and attempting to change the market," says a Loctite executive. Now the company screens wholesalers on the basis of training, commitment, support, and willingness to partner for mutual success.
- *Understand each wholesaler's strengths.* Next, a company should understand how each wholesaler's strengths fit with the product strategy in each market. For example, food companies seeking to market a wide product mix in South America and Southeast Asia might choose a wholesaler such as Makro. This wholesaler operates warehouses where buyers for small hotels, restaurants, and catering firms can conveniently buy foods as needed.
- *Identify value-added services.* Find out what each wholesaler can do to add value to the relationship. For example, many European wholesalers are willing to affix price tags or provide special product packaging for different markets or end users. A growing number of wholesalers offer to use their distribution savvy to more efficiently manage other parts of the supply chain for companies.
- *Build a long-term relationship.* Producers that show they are interested in long-term distribution relationships give their wholesalers more incentive to work together in developing the market. Producers may even want to invest in their international wholesalers to smooth the way for influencing local distribution activities.
- *Examine detailed data.* Rather than taking a hands-off position, producers working with global wholesalers should request in-depth financial and channel data for each market. This helps management learn about local market conditions and ensures that wholesale pricing and other details are in line with the producer's strategies and goals.
- *Think regional.* Organizing regional distribution councils or networks allows producers to encourage ongoing coordination of wholesaling strategies for its products in multiple markets.

able retailers to keep their own inventory investments small in relation to sales. Such indirect financial aid reduces the amount of operating capital that retailers need.

In some industries, wholesalers extend direct financial assistance through long-term loans. Most wholesalers also provide help through delayed billing, giving customers thirty to ninety days *after delivery* to pay for merchandise. Wholesalers of seasonal merchandise may offer even longer payment periods. For example, a wholesaler of lawn and garden supplies may deliver seed to retailers in January but not bill them for it until May.

Wholesalers' Services to Manufacturers

Some of the services that wholesalers perform for producers are similar to those they provide to retailers. Others are quite different.

Providing an Instant Sales Force A wholesaler provides its producers with an instant sales force so that producers' sales representatives need not call on retailers. This can result in enormous savings for producers. For example, Lever Brothers and General Foods would have to spend millions of dollars each year to field a sales force large enough to call on all the retailers that sell their numerous products. Instead, these producers rely on wholesalers to sell and distribute their products to many retailers. These producers do have sales forces, though, that call on wholesalers and large retailers.

Reducing Inventory Costs Wholesalers purchase goods in sizable quantities from manufacturers and store these goods for resale. By doing so, they reduce the amount of finished-goods inventory that producers must hold and thereby reduce the cost of carrying inventories.

Assuming Credit Risks When producers sell through wholesalers, it is the wholesalers who extend credit to retailers, make collections from retailers, and assume the risks of nonpayment. These services reduce the producers' cost of extending credit to customers and the resulting bad-debt expense.

Furnishing Market Information Just as they do for retailers, wholesalers supply market information to the producers they serve. Valuable information accumulated by wholesalers may concern consumer demand, the producers' competition, and buying trends.

Types of Wholesalers

learning objective

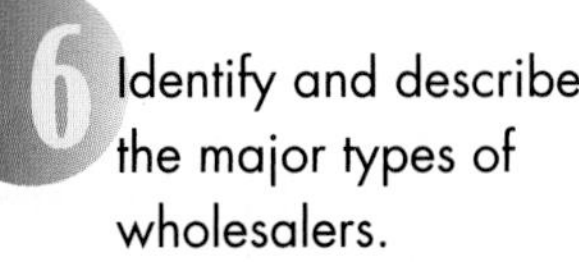

Identify and describe the major types of wholesalers.

Wholesalers generally fall into three categories: merchant wholesalers; commission merchants, agents, and brokers; and manufacturers' sales branches and sales offices. Of these, merchant wholesalers constitute the largest portion. They account for about four-fifths of all wholesale establishments and employees.

merchant wholesaler a middleman that purchases goods in large quantities and then sells them to other wholesalers or retailers and to institutional, farm, government, professional, or industrial users

Merchant Wholesalers A **merchant wholesaler** is a middleman that purchases goods in large quantities and then sells them to other wholesalers or retailers and to institutional, farm, government, professional, or industrial users. Merchant wholesalers usually operate one or more warehouses at which they receive, take title to, and store goods. These wholesalers are sometimes called *distributors* or *jobbers*.

Most merchant wholesalers are businesses composed of salespeople, order takers, receiving and shipping clerks, inventory managers, and office personnel. The successful merchant wholesaler must analyze available products and market needs. It must be able to adapt the type, variety, and quality of its products to changing market conditions.

Merchant wholesalers may be classified as full-service or limited-service wholesalers depending on the number of services they provide. A **full-service wholesaler** performs the entire range of wholesaler functions described earlier in this section. These functions include delivering goods, supplying warehousing, arranging for credit, supporting promotional activities, and providing general customer assistance.

full-service wholesaler a middleman that performs the entire range of wholesaler functions

Under this broad heading are the general merchandise wholesaler, limited-line wholesaler, and specialty-line wholesaler. A **general merchandise wholesaler** deals in a wide variety of products, such as drugs, hardware, nonperishable foods, cosmetics, detergents, and tobacco. A **limited-line wholesaler** stocks only a few product lines but carries numerous product items within each line. A **specialty-line wholesaler** carries a select group of products within a single line. Food delicacies such as shellfish represent the kind of product handled by this wholesaler.

general merchandise wholesaler a middleman that deals in a wide variety of products

limited-line wholesaler a middleman that stocks only a few product lines but carries numerous product items within each line

specialty-line wholesaler a middleman that carries a select group of products within a single line

In contrast to a full-service wholesaler, a **limited-service wholesaler** assumes responsibility for a few wholesale services only. Other marketing tasks are left to other channel members or consumers. This category includes cash-and-carry wholesalers, truck wholesalers, drop shippers, and mail-order wholesalers.

limited-service wholesaler a middleman that assumes responsibility for a few wholesale services only

Commission Merchants, Agents, and Brokers Commission merchants, agents, and brokers are functional middlemen. Functional middlemen do not take title to products. They perform a small number of marketing activities and are paid a commission that is a percentage of the sales price.

A **commission merchant** usually carries merchandise and negotiates sales for manufacturers. In most cases commission merchants have the power to set the prices and terms of sales. After a sale is made, they either arrange for delivery or provide transportation services.

commission merchant a middleman that carries merchandise and negotiates sales for manufacturers

An **agent** is a middleman that expedites exchanges, represents a buyer or a seller, and often is hired permanently on a commission basis. When agents represent producers, they are known as *sales agents* or *manufacturer's agents*. As long as the products represented do not compete, a sales agent may represent one or several manufacturers on a commission basis. The agent solicits orders for the manufacturers within a specific territory. As a rule, the manufacturers ship the merchandise and bill the customers directly. The manufacturers also set the prices and other conditions of the sales. What do the manufacturers gain by using a sales agent? The sales agent provides immediate entry into a territory, regular calls on customers, selling experience, and a known, predetermined selling expense (a commission that is a percentage of sales revenue).

agent a middleman that expedites exchanges, represents a buyer or a seller, and often is hired permanently on a commission basis

A **broker** is a middleman that specializes in a particular commodity, represents either a buyer *or* a seller, and is likely to be hired on a temporary basis. However, food brokers, which sell grocery products to resellers, generally have long-term relationships with their clients. Brokers may perform only the selling function or both buying and selling, using established contacts or special knowledge of their fields.

broker a middleman that specializes in a particular commodity, represents either a buyer or a seller, and is likely to be hired on a temporary basis

Manufacturers' Sales Branches and Sales Offices A **manufacturer's sales branch** is, in essence, a merchant wholesaler that is owned by a manufacturer. Sales branches carry inventory, extend credit, deliver goods, and offer help in promoting products. Their customers are retailers, other wholesalers, and industrial purchasers.

manufacturer's sales branch essentially a merchant wholesaler that is owned by a manufacturer

manufacturer's sales office essentially a sales agent owned by a manufacturer

Because sales branches are owned by producers, they stock primarily the goods manufactured by their own firms. Selling policies and terms usually are established centrally and then transmitted to branch managers for implementation.

A **manufacturer's sales office** is essentially a sales agent owned by a manufacturer. Sales offices may sell goods manufactured by their own firms and also certain products of other manufacturers that complement their own product lines. For example, Hiram Walker & Sons imports wine from Spain to increase the number of products its sales offices can offer to customers.

Using the Internet

The National Retail Federation (**http://www.nrf.com/**) and the American Wholesale Marketers Association (**http://www.awmanet.org/**) are two industry gateways for information about their respective distribution channels. Each site provides access to online journals and links to related websites of interest to retailers and wholesalers.

1arketing Intermediaries: Retailers

learning objective

7 Distinguish among the major types of retailers.

:etailers are the final link between producers and consumers. Retailers may buy from ither wholesalers or producers. They sell not only goods but also such services as auto epairs, haircuts, and dry cleaning. Some retailers sell both. Sears, Roebuck sells conumer goods, financial services, and repair services for home appliances bought at Sears.

Of approximately 2.6 million retail firms in the United States, about 90 percent ave annual sales of less than $1 million. On the other hand, some large retail organiations realize well over $1 million in sales revenue per day. Table 15.1 lists the twenty argest retail organizations and their approximate sales revenues and yearly profits. 'igure 15.4 (on p. 446) shows retail sales categorized by major merchandise type and he percentage of total sales for each type.

lasses of In-Store Retailers

independent retailer a firm that operates only one retail outlet

chain retailer a company that operates more than one retail outlet

)ne way to classify retailers is by the number of stores owned and operated by the irm. An **independent retailer** is a firm that operates only one retail outlet. Approxiately three-fourths of retailers are independent. One-store operators, like all small usinesses, generally provide personal service and a convenient location.

A **chain retailer** is a company that operates more than one retail outlet. By dding outlets, chain retailers attempt to reach new geographic markets. As sales in-

table 15.1 The Twenty Largest Retail Firms in the United States

Rank	Company	Annual Sales (in millions)	Annual Profits (in millions)	Number of Stores
1	Wal-Mart, Inc.	$219,812,000	$6,671,000	4,414
2	The Home Depot	53,553,000	3,044,000	1,348
3	Kroger	50,098,000	1,042,000	3,534
4	Sears	41,078,000	735,000	2,960
5	Target	39,362,000	1,368,000	1,381
6	Albertsons	37,931,000	501,000	2,400
7	K-Mart	37,028,000	(244,000)	2,150
8	Costco	34,797,037	602,089	369
9	Safeway	34,301,000	1,284,400	1,773
10	J.C. Penney	32,004,000	98,000	3,770
11	Walgreens	24,623,000	885,600	3,520
12	Ahold USA*	23,200,000	1,300,000	1,325
13	CVS Corp.	22,241,000	398,500	4,191
14	Lowe's Cos.	22,111,108	1,023,262	744
15	Best Buy	19,597,000	570,000	1,900
16	Federated Dept. Stores	15,651,000	(276,000)	450
17	Publix Super Market	15,300,000	530,400	697
18	Rite Aid	13,869,000	(827,681)	3,500
19	Delhaize America	14,900,000	155,486	1,420
20	May Dept. Stores	14,175,000	703,000	839

*U.S. retail operations only; operating income reported + continuing operations.
Source: *Chain Drug Review*, October 14, 2002.

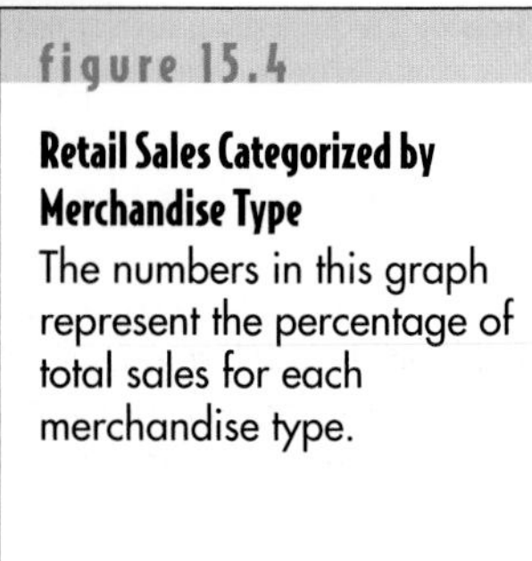

figure 15.4

Retail Sales Categorized by Merchandise Type
The numbers in this graph represent the percentage of total sales for each merchandise type.

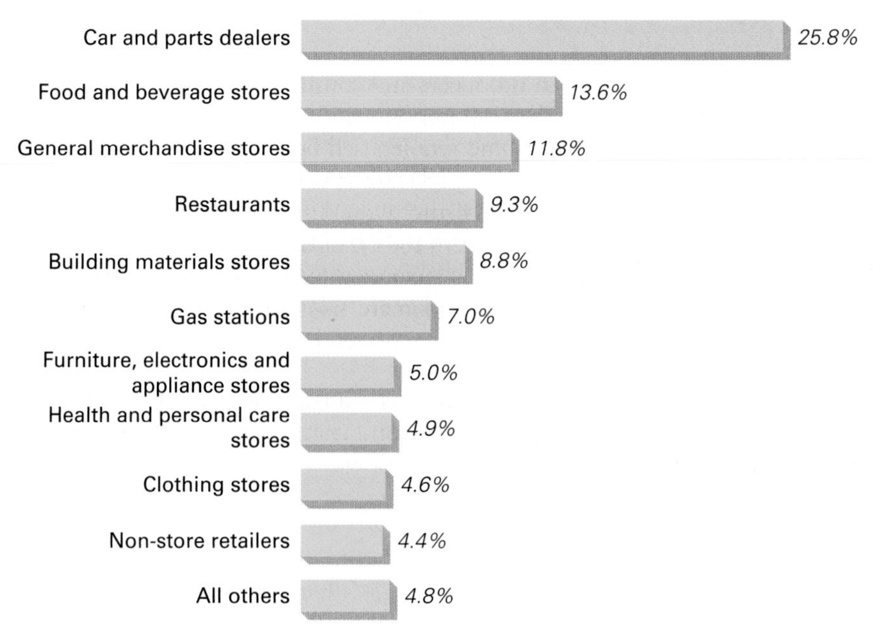

Source: U.S. Bureau of the Census, *Monthly Retail Trade: Sales and Inventories*, January 14, 2003, **www.census.gov.**

crease, chains usually buy merchandise in larger quantities and thus take advantage c quantity discounts. They also wield more power in their dealings with supplier About one-fourth of retail organizations operate chains.

Another way to classify in-store retailers is by store size and the kind and numbe of products carried. Let's take a closer look at store types based on these dimensions.

department store a retail store that (1) employs twenty-five or more persons and (2) sells at least home furnishings, appliances, family apparel, and household linens and dry goods, each in a different part of the store

Department Stores These large retail establishments consist of several sections, o departments, that sell a wide assortment of products. According to the U.S. Bureau c the Census, a **department store** is a retail store that (1) employs twenty-five or mor persons and (2) sells at least home furnishings, appliances, family apparel, and house hold linens and dry goods, each in a different part of the store. Marshall Field's i Chicago (and several other cities), Harrods in London, and Au Printemps in Paris ar examples of large department stores. Sears, Roebuck and J.C. Penney are also depart ment stores. Traditionally, department stores have been service-oriented. Along wit the goods they sell, these retailers provide credit, delivery, personal assistance, liber return policies, and pleasant shopping atmospheres.

discount store a self-service general merchandise outlet that sells products at lower-than-usual prices

Discount Stores A **discount store** is a self-service, general merchandise outlet tha sells products at lower-than-usual prices. These stores can offer lower prices by oper ating on smaller markups, by locating large retail showrooms in low-rent areas, and b offering minimal customer services. To keep prices low, discount stores operate on th basic principle of high turnover of such items as appliances, toys, clothing, automotiv products, and sports equipment. To attract customers, many discount stores also offe some food and household items at low prices. Popular discount stores include Kmar Wal-Mart, Dollar General, and Target.

As competition among discount stores has increased, some discounters have im proved their services, store environments, and locations. As a consequence, many c the better-known discount stores have assumed the characteristics of departmen stores. This upgrading has boosted their prices and blurred the distinction betwee some discount stores and department stores.[5]

catalog showroom a retail outlet that displays well-known brands and sells them at discount prices through catalogs within the store

Catalog and Warehouse Showrooms A **catalog showroom** is a retail outlet tha displays well-known brands and sells them at discount prices through catalogs withi the store. Colorful catalogs are available in the showroom (and sometimes by mail). The customer selects the merchandise, either from the catalog or from the showroom display. The customer fills out an order form provided by the store and hands the form to a clerk. The clerk retrieves the merchandise from a warehouse room that is adjacent to the selling area. Service Merchandise is a catalog showroom.

Warehouse showrooms are retail facilities with five basic characteristics: (1) large, low-cost buildings, (2) warehouse materials-handling technology, (3) vertical merchandise displays, (4) large on-premises inventories, and (5) minimal service. Some of the best-known showrooms are operated by big furniture retailers. These operations employ few personnel and offer few services. Most customers carry away purchases in the manufacturer's carton, although some warehouse showrooms will deliver for a fee.

warehouse showroom a retail facility in a large, low-cost building with large on-premises inventories and minimal service

Convenience Stores A **convenience store** is a small food store that sells a limited variety of products but remains open well beyond normal business hours. Almost 70 percent of convenience store customers live within a mile of the store. White Hen Pantry, 7-Eleven, Circle K, and Open Pantry stores, for example, are found in some areas, as are independent convenience stores. There are over 124,000 convenience stores in the United States, and two-thirds of Americans visit at least one of these locations every month. Convenience stores are the fastest growing category of retailer, with a 10 percent growth in sales over the past year compared with an 8 percent decline in overall retail sales.[6] Their limited product mixes and higher prices keep convenience stores from becoming a major threat to other grocery retailers.

convenience store a small food store that sells a limited variety of products but remains open well beyond normal business hours

Supermarkets A **supermarket** is a large self-service store that sells primarily food and household products. It stocks canned, fresh, frozen, and processed foods; paper products; and cleaning supplies. Supermarkets also may sell such items as housewares, toiletries, toys and games, drugs, stationery, books and magazines, plants and flowers, and a few clothing items.

supermarket a large self-service store that sells primarily food and household products

Supermarkets are large-scale operations that emphasize low prices and one-stop shopping for household needs. The first self-service food market opened over sixty years ago; it grossed only $5,000 per week, with an average sale of just $1.31.[7] Today a supermarket has annual sales of at least $2 million. Current top-ranking supermarkets include Kroger, Albertson's, Safeway, Winn-Dixie, and A&P. Many of these supermarket chains are finding it difficult to compete with superstores such as Wal-Mart Supercenters and are experiencing minuscule profit margins. Albertsons, Safeway, and Ahold's divisions including BI-LO and Giant are choosing to use funds set aside for expansion to remodel existing stores instead. They are emphasizing a neighborhood theme designed to meet the unique needs of local shoppers and to differentiate these supermarkets from superstores.[8]

Superstores A **superstore** is a large retail store that carries not only food and nonfood products ordinarily found in supermarkets but also additional product lines—housewares, hardware, small appliances, clothing, personal-care products, garden products, and automotive merchandise. Superstores also provide a number of services to entice customers. Typically, these include automotive repair, snack bars and restaurants, film developing, and banking.

superstore a large retail store that carries not only food and nonfood products ordinarily found in supermarkets but also additional product lines

Warehouse Clubs The **warehouse club** is a large-scale members-only establishment that combines cash-and-carry wholesaling features with discount retailing. For a nominal annual fee (about $25), small retailers may purchase products at wholesale prices for business use or for resale. Warehouse clubs also sell to ultimate consumers. Instead of paying a membership fee, individual consumers pay about 5 percent more on each item than do small-business owners. Individual purchasers usually can choose to pay yearly dues for membership cards that allow them to avoid the 5 percent additional charge.

warehouse club a large-scale members-only establishment that combines features of cash-and-carry wholesaling with discount retailing

Warehouse clubs offer the same types of products offered by discount stores but in a limited range of sizes and styles. Because their product lines are shallow and sales

Warehouse clubs. Sam's Club is an example of a warehouse club. To make purchases at Sam's Club, customers must be members and pay annual membership fees.

volumes are high, warehouse clubs can offer a broa range of merchandise, including perishable and non perishable foods, beverages, books, appliances, house wares, automotive parts, hardware, furniture, an sundries. The sales volume of most warehouse clubs i four to five times that of a typical department stor With stock turning over at an average rate of eightee times each year, warehouse clubs sell their goods be fore manufacturers' payment periods are up, thus re ducing their need for capital.

To keep their prices 20 to 40 percent lower than those of supermarkets and dis count stores, warehouse clubs provide few services. They generally advertise onl through direct mail. Their facilities often have concrete floors and aisles wide enoug for forklifts. Merchandise is stacked on pallets or displayed on pipe racks. Usually cus tomers must transport purchases themselves. Although at one time there were abou twenty competing warehouse clubs, only two major competitors remain: Sam's Clu and Costco.

traditional specialty store a store that carries a narrow product mix with deep product lines

Traditional Specialty Stores A **traditional specialty store** carries a narrow prod uct mix with deep product lines. Traditional specialty stores are sometimes calle *limited-line retailers*. If they carry depth in one particular product category, they ma be called *single-line retailers*. Specialty stores usually sell such products as clothing jewelry, sporting goods, fabrics, computers, flowers, baked goods, books, and pe supplies. Examples of specialty stores include the Gap, Radio Shack, Bath and Bod Works, and Foot Locker.

Specialty stores usually offer deeper product mixes than department stores. The attract customers by emphasizing service, atmosphere, and location. Consumers wh are dissatisfied with the impersonal atmosphere of large retailers often find the atten tion offered by small specialty stores appealing.

off-price retailer a store that buys manufacturers' seconds, overruns, returns, and off-season merchandise for resale to consumers at deep discounts

Off-Price Retailers An **off-price retailer** is a store that buys manufacturers' sec onds, overruns, returns, and off-season merchandise at below-wholesale prices and sell them to consumers at deep discounts. Off-price retailers sell limited lines of nationa brand and designer merchandise, usually clothing, shoes, or housewares. Examples c off-price retailers include T.J. Maxx, Burlington Coat Factory, and Marshalls. Off-pric stores charge up to 50 percent less than department stores do for comparable mer chandise but offer few customer services. They often include community dressin rooms and central checkout counters, and some off-price retailers have a no-returns no-exchanges policy.

category killer a very large specialty store that concentrates on a single product line and competes on the basis of low prices and product availability

Category Killers A **category killer** is a very large specialty store that concentrate on a single product line and competes by offering low prices and an enormous numbe of products. These stores are called *category killers* because they take business awa from smaller, high-cost retail stores. Examples of category killers include Hom Depot (building materials), Office Depot (office supplies and equipment), and Toy "R" Us. Category killers, due to the size of their product offerings and low prices, ma attract large numbers of customers. For example, IKEA, the Swedish furniture re tailer, attracted over 265,000 customers to its new store just outside of Moscow durin the first two weeks it was opened. IKEA management estimated that approximately 3 percent of these customers made purchases.[9]

Traditional specialty stores. Both Old Navy and Brooks Brothers are examples of traditional specialty stores.

Kinds of Nonstore Retailing

Nonstore retailing is selling that does not take place in conventional store facilities; consumers purchase products without visiting a store. Nonstore retailers use direct selling, direct marketing, and vending machines.

nonstore retailing a type of retailing whereby consumers purchase products without visiting a store

direct selling the marketing of products to ultimate consumers through face-to-face sales presentations at home or in the workplace

Direct Selling **Direct selling** is the marketing of products to customers through face-to-face sales presentations at home or in the workplace. Traditionally called *door-to-door selling*, direct selling generates about $77 billion in sales annually worldwide.[10] Instead of the door-to-door approach, many companies today—such as Mary Kay, Amway, and Avon—identify customers by mail, telephone, or at shopping malls and then make appointments. The "party plan" method of direct selling takes place in homes or in the workplace. Customers act as hosts and invite friends or coworkers to view products. A salesperson conducts the "party" and demonstrates products. Companies that rely on the party plan are Tupperware, Stanley Home Products, and Sarah Coventry.

Benefits of direct selling include product demonstration, personal attention, and convenience. In fact, personal attention is the foundation on which some direct sellers base their companies. The primary disadvantage of direct selling is that it is the most expensive form of retailing. Overall costs of direct selling are high because of high salesperson commissions and efforts required to locate prospects. In addition, some people view direct selling negatively, and some communities have enacted local ordinances regulating or even banning direct selling.

direct marketing the use of computers, telephones, and nonpersonal media to show products to customers, who can then purchase them by mail, telephone, or online

catalog marketing marketing in which an organization provides a catalog from which customers make selections and place orders by mail or telephone

Direct Marketing **Direct marketing** is the use of computers, telephones, and nonpersonal media to communicate product and organizational information to customers, who can then buy products by mail, telephone, or online. Catalog marketing, direct-response marketing, telemarketing, television home shopping, and online marketing are all types of direct marketing.

With **catalog marketing**, an organization provides a catalog from which customers make selections and place orders by mail or telephone. Some companies, such as Spiegel and J.C. Penney, offer a wide range of products. Other catalog companies, such as L.L. Bean and Lands' End, offer one major line of products. Certain catalog companies specialize in only a few products, such as educational toys or specialty foods. Many customers find catalog marketing efficient and convenient. Retailers do not have to invest in expensive store fixtures, and personal selling and operating expenses are significantly reduced. However, catalog marketing provides limited service and is most effective for only certain types of products. Some catalog retailers have reputations for excellent service. However, some catalog customers complain about product quality, delivery times, and shipment errors.

direct-response marketing marketing that occurs when a retailer advertises a product and makes it available through mail or telephone orders

Direct-response marketing occurs when a retailer advertises a product and makes it available through mail or telephone orders. Customers usually use a credit card to make purchases. Examples of direct-response marketing are a television commercial promoting a set of knives available through a toll-free number and a magazine ad for a series of cookbooks available by completing and mailing an order form. Sending letters, samples, brochures, or booklets to prospects on a mailing list are also forms of direct-response marketing.

telemarketing the performance of marketing-related activities by telephone

Telemarketing is using the telephone to perform marketing-related activities. Companies that use telemarketing to supplement other marketing methods include Merrill Lynch, Allstate Insurance, Avis, General Motors, MCI, and American Express. Some organizations use a prepared list of customers, and others rely on names from telephone directories and data banks. Advantages of telemarketing include generating sales leads, improving customer service, speeding up payment on past-due accounts, raising funds for nonprofit organizations, and gathering marketing information.

One problem with telemarketing is employee turnover. To attract and retain employees at its call center, Boston Communications Group designed the physical environment so that people would perceive this organization to be a good place to work. The company invested heavily to make the facility very comfortable for workers. The pay scale for these workers is on the upper end. Boston Communications is developing a child-care center adjacent to its facility so that employees' children can be in day care in close proximity to their parents. In addition, this company provides workers with highly flexible hours. Boston Communications' employee turnover rate is considerably lower than the average for call centers.[11]

adapting to change

PETsMART Reemphasizes In-Store Retailing

PETsMART IS RETURNING to its retailing roots. Jim and Janice Dougherty founded the Pet Food Warehouse in 1987 as a category killer store selling pet food and other pet supplies. Soon after expanding the Phoenix-based chain to seven stores, the founders left and were replaced by supermarket executive Sam Parker. Under Parker, the renamed PETsMART chain redesigned store interiors, opened dozens of new stores, and acquired other retailers in the United States and Canada.

By the late 1990s, PETsMART was selling roughly $2 billion worth of pet supplies per year. However, it faced competition from Internet-based pet supply retailers such as Pets.com (promoted by an outspoken sock puppet) and Petopia.com. "In late 1999, we all heard how the Web was going to wipe out retail stores," remembers Phil Francis, PETsMART's CEO. "It didn't quite happen that way."

Although the newcomers offered product giveaways, free or low-cost shipping, and other promotions to lure customers, they generated lower revenues than expected. Expenses continued to mount, fueled by expensive marketing campaigns and the high cost of shipping gigantic bags of pet food. Then the dot-com bubble burst, and Pets.com went under. PETsMART bought the firm's web address (but not the sock puppet) in 2001 to supplement its own website (**www.petsmart.com**).

Learning from the mistakes of its online rivals, PETsMART does not discount shipping charges on Internet purchases, nor does it push pet food online. Instead, its website features products that would tie up too much space and inventory investment to stock in every store, such as large fish tanks. The retailer also encourages customers to visit the website when they want to locate nearby PETsMART locations, saving countless phone calls to local stores.

Returning to its retail roots, the company is updating the oldest of its 570 stores and continuing to advertise the chain's broad merchandise assortment and low prices. Yet the website remains a solid, although tiny, portion of the business, bringing in about 2 percent of its $2.6 billion in annual sales. This accounts for nearly 25 percent of all U.S. pet supplies sold online—enough to make PETsMART the top dog in this niche.

Another problem for telemarketers is the push by the Federal Trade Commission (FTC) to forbid calling consumers who do not want to receive telemarketing calls. Although telemarketing has been restricted by call screening, caller ID, and other innovations, the FTC is pushing for a "do not call" list in order to protect consumers from being disturbed by telemarketers. Some states have already implemented programs involving do not call lists.[12]

Television home shopping displays products to television viewers, who can then order them by calling a toll-free number and paying by credit card. There are several home shopping cable channels. The most common products sold through television home shopping are electronics, clothing, housewares, and jewelry. Benefits of home shopping include time for thorough product demonstration and customer convenience.

Online retailing makes the presentation and sale of products possible through computer connections. Customers purchase products by ordering them through their terminals or by telephone. The phenomenal growth of the World Wide Web and of online information service providers, such as America Online (AOL), has created new retailing opportunities. Although some retailers with websites are currently using them primarily to promote products, a number of companies sell their goods online. Some online retailers such as Amazon and AOL began as online sellers and have remained exclusively as online sellers, whereas others began as traditional retail stores and later became online retailers as well. Examples include Barnes and Noble, Office Max, and Toys "R" Us. Consumers can purchase hard-to-find items such as Pez candy dispensers and Elvis memorabilia at e-Bay, The Internet is becoming a popular way to purchase personal and sexually oriented products such as hemorrhoid cream, condoms, and ovulation timers. Drugstore.com, which was founded in 1998, recently launched a new website at sexualwellbeing.com that focuses on specialty-type items related to sex. Drugstore.com's revenue has increased rapidly in recent years, and the company hopes the new website will further increase its growth.[13]

Spotlight

Top Internet shopping sites

Visitors per week to sites (excluding travel sites) in millions.

Site	Visitors (millions)
Wal-Mart Stores	2.8
MSN Shopping	3.1
Yahoo Shopping	7.4
Amazon	10.2
eBay	12.0

Source: *USA Today*, December 17, 2002, p. A1.

television home shopping selling in which products are displayed to television viewers, who can then order them by calling a toll-free number and paying by credit card

online retailing presenting and selling products through computer connections

Banks and brokerage firms have established websites to give their customers direct access to manage their accounts and to enable them to trade online. California-based Encirq.com has developed a new approach to gathering customer information and guarding the privacy of online customers at the same time. In association with a bank credit card program, online banking customers can choose to opt in or out of the Encirq's Illuminated Statement function at any time—free of charge. For those who participate, there are benefits. To begin with, their bank's customer service site presents a colorful, easy-to-read version of their credit card statement that may include logos of the companies on their statement, links to merchants' websites, and special promotions. By clicking on an item in the statement, consumers also can see more detailed information about the transaction. Encirq generates its revenues by selling advertising on the statement. Personal information remains secure on the customer's computer and will only be engaged to help direct the customer's purchasing if he or she wants it to. Those links are with merchants the customer has already bought from, and so, logically, the customer should feel more relaxed about associating in this manner.[14] With advances such as this in computer technology and consumers continuing to be pressed for time, online retailing will only escalate.

Automatic Vending **Automatic vending** is the use of machines to dispense products. Although vending machines only account for 2 percent of all retail sales, they are widely popular, with about 1,000 different types. They sell items that require little or

automatic vending the use of machines to dispense products

no thought before making the decision to buy, such as candy, cigarettes, newspapers, postage stamps, chewing gum, soft drinks, and coffee. These are goods that people will purchase at the nearest possible location. This category of vending also includes such machines as video game machines and automatic teller machines, which satisfy needs other than tangible products. Machines in areas of heavy traffic provide efficient and continuous services to consumers. Such high-volume areas may have more diverse product availability—for example, hot and cold sandwiches, as well as soups.

Automatic vending is one of the most impersonal forms of retailing. Machines do not require sales personnel, they permit twenty-four-hour service, and they do not require much space. Thus they can be placed in convenient locations in office buildings, educational institutions, motels and hotels, shopping malls, and service stations. However, these advantages are partly offset by the high costs of equipment and frequent servicing and repairs.

learning objective

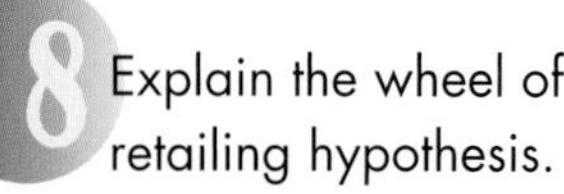

Explain the wheel of retailing hypothesis.

wheel of retailing a hypothesis that suggests that new retail operations usually begin at the bottom—in price, profits, and prestige—and gradually move up the cost/price scale, competing with newer businesses that are evolving in the same way

The Wheel of Retailing

Newly developing retail businesses strive for a secure position in the ever-changing retailing environment. One theory attempts to explain how types of retail stores originate and develop. The **wheel of retailing** hypothesis (see Figure 15.5) suggests that new retail operations usually begin at the bottom—in price, profits, and prestige. In time, their facilities become more elaborate, their investments increase, and their

figure 15.5

The Wheel of Retailing

If the "wheel" is considered to be turning slowly in the direction of the arrow, then the department stores around 1900 and the discounters of later years can be viewed as coming on the scene in the lower part of the wheel. As it slowly turns, they move with it, becoming higher-priced operations and, at the same time, leaving room for lower-priced types of firms to gain entry at the low end of the wheel.

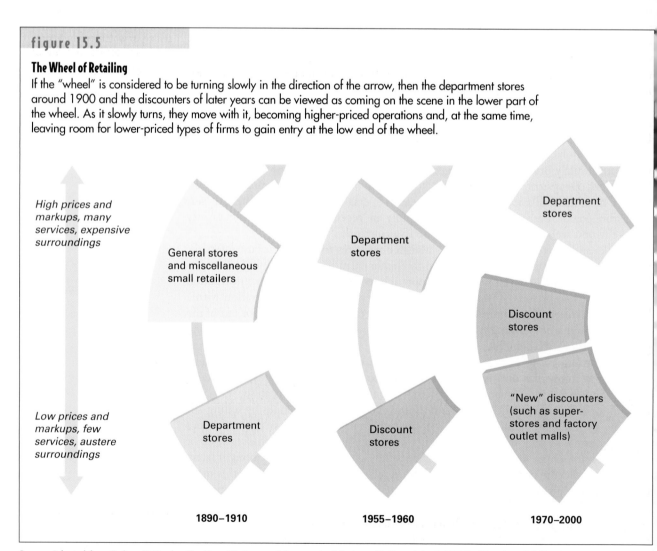

Source: Adapted from Robert F. Hartley, *Retailing: Challenge and Opportunity*, 3d ed., p. 42. Copyright © 1984 by Houghton Mifflin Company. Used by permission.

operating costs go up. Finally, the retailers emerge at the top of the cost/price scale, competing with newer businesses that are evolving in the same way.[15]

In Figure 15.5 the wheel of retailing illustrates the development of department and discount stores. Department stores such as Sears were originally high-volume, low-cost retailers competing with general stores and other small businesses. As the costs of services rose in department stores, discount stores began to fill the low-price retailing niche. Now many discount stores, in turn, are following the pattern by expanding services, improving locations, upgrading inventories, and raising prices.

Like most hypotheses, the wheel of retailing may not be universally applicable. The theory cannot predict what new retailing developments will occur or when, for example. In industrialized, expanding economies, however, the hypothesis does help to explain retailing patterns.

Planned Shopping Centers

learning objective

9 Identify the categories of shopping centers and the factors that determine how shopping centers are classified.

The planned shopping center is a self-contained retail facility constructed by independent owners and consisting of various stores. Shopping centers are designed and promoted to serve diverse groups of customers with widely differing needs. The management of a shopping center strives for a coordinated mix of stores, a comfortable atmosphere, adequate parking, pleasant landscaping, and special events to attract customers. The convenience of shopping for most family and household needs in a single location is an important part of shopping-center appeal.

A planned shopping center is one of three types: neighborhood, community, or regional. Although shopping centers vary, each offers a complementary mix of stores for the purpose of generating consumer traffic.

Neighborhood Shopping Centers

neighborhood shopping center a planned shopping center consisting of several small convenience and specialty stores

A **neighborhood shopping center** typically consists of several small convenience and specialty stores. Businesses in neighborhood shopping centers might include small grocery stores, drugstores, gas stations, and fast-food restaurants. These retailers serve consumers who live less than ten minutes away, usually within a two- to three-mile radius of the stores. Because most purchases in the neighborhood shopping center are based on convenience or personal contact, these retailers generally make only limited efforts to coordinate promotional activities among stores in the shopping center.

Community Shopping Centers

community shopping center a planned shopping center that includes one or two department stores and some specialty stores, along with convenience stores

A **community shopping center** includes one or two department stores and some specialty stores, along with convenience stores. It attracts consumers from a wider geographic area who will drive longer distances to find products and specialty items unavailable in neighborhood shopping centers. Community shopping centers, which are carefully planned and coordinated, generate traffic with special events such as art exhibits, automobile shows, and sidewalk sales. The management of a community shopping center maintains a balance of tenants so that the center can offer wide product mixes and deep product lines.

Regional Shopping Centers

regional shopping center a planned shopping center containing large department stores, numerous specialty stores, restaurants, movie theaters, and sometimes even hotels

A **regional shopping center** usually has large department stores, numerous specialty stores, restaurants, movie theaters, and sometimes even hotels. It carries most of the merchandise offered by a downtown shopping district. Downtown merchants, in fact, often have renovated their stores and enlarged their parking facilities to meet the

Planned shopping center. The mix of retailers in a planned shopping center is managed in such as way as to attract numerous shoppers and to effectively satisfy their needs with respect to the products offered by these retailers. This shopping center, Horton Plaza, is located in downtown San Diego.

competition of successful regional shopping centers. Urban expressways and improved public transportation also have helped many downtown shopping areas to remain vigorous.

Regional shopping centers carefully coordinate management and marketing activities to reach the 150,000 or more customers in their target market. These large centers usually advertise, hold special events, and provide transportation to certain groups of customers. They also maintain a suitable mix of stores. National chain stores can gain leases in regional shopping centers more easily than small independent stores because they are better able to meet the centers' financial requirements.

learning objective

10 Explain the five most important physical distribution activities.

Physical Distribution

physical distribution all those activities concerned with the efficient movement of products from the producer to the ultimate user

Physical distribution is all those activities concerned with the efficient movement of products from the producer to the ultimate user. Physical distribution is thus the movement of the products themselves—both goods and services—through their channels of distribution. It is a combination of several interrelated business functions. The most important of these are inventory management, order processing, warehousing, materials handling, and transportation.

Not too long ago each of these functions was considered distinct from all the others. In a fairly large firm, one group or department would handle each function. Each of these groups would work to minimize its own costs and to maximize its own effectiveness, but the result was usually high physical distribution costs.

Various studies of the problem emphasized both the interrelationships among the physical distribution functions *and* the relationships between physical distribution and other marketing functions. Long production runs may reduce per-unit product costs, but they can cause inventory-control and warehousing costs to skyrocket. A new automated warehouse may reduce materials-handling costs, but if the warehouse is not located properly, transportation time and costs may increase substantially. Because of such interrelationships, marketers now view physical distribution as an integrated effort that provides important marketing functions: getting the right product to the right place at the right time and at minimal *overall* cost.

Inventory Management

In Chapter 9 we discussed inventory management from the standpoint of operations. We defined **inventory management** as the process of managing inventories in such a way as to minimize inventory costs, including both holding costs and potential stock-out costs. Both the definition and the objective of inventory control apply here as well.

inventory management the process of managing inventories in such a way as to minimize inventory costs, including both holding costs and potential stock-out costs

Holding costs are the costs of storing products until they are purchased or shipped to customers. *Stock-out costs* are the costs of sales lost when items are not in inventory. Of course, holding costs can be reduced by minimizing inventories, but then stock-out costs could be financially threatening to the organization. And stock-out costs can be minimized by carrying very large inventories, but then holding costs would be enormous.

Inventory management is thus a sort of balancing act between stock-out costs and holding costs. The latter include the cost of money invested in inventory, the cost of storage space, insurance costs, and inventory taxes. Often, even a relatively small reduction in inventory investment can provide a relatively large increase in working capital. And sometimes this reduction can best be accomplished through a willingness to incur a reasonable level of stock-out costs. Best Buy, along with software company Retek, Inc., developed an inventory management system that provides Best Buy employees with information about the inventory of any of its stores in the region. Employees can share this information with customers and use it to facilitate the transfer of items from one retail location to another in an attempt to minimize both holding and stock-out costs. The companies will offer this software to other retailers as well.[16]

Order Processing

Order processing consists of activities involved in receiving and filling customers' purchase orders. It may include not only the means by which customers order products but also procedures for billing and for granting credit.

order processing activities involved in receiving and filling customers' purchase orders

Fast, efficient order processing is an important marketing service—one that can provide a dramatic competitive edge. The people who purchase goods for intermediaries are especially concerned with their suppliers' promptness and reliability in order processing. To them, promptness and reliability mean minimal inventory costs as well as the ability to order goods when they are needed rather than weeks in advance. The Internet is providing new opportunities for improving services associated with order processing.

Warehousing

Warehousing is the set of activities involved in receiving and storing goods and preparing them for reshipment. Goods are stored to create time utility; that is, they are held until they are needed for use or sale. Warehousing includes the following activities:

warehousing the set of activities involved in receiving and storing goods and preparing them for reshipment

- *Receiving goods*—The warehouse accepts delivered goods and assumes responsibility for them.
- *Identifying goods*—Records are made of the quantity of each item received. Items may be marked, coded, or tagged for identification.
- *Sorting goods*—Delivered goods may have to be sorted before being stored.
- *Dispatching goods to storage*—Items must be moved to specific storage areas, where they can be found later.
- *Holding goods*—The goods are kept in storage under proper protection until needed.
- *Recalling, picking, and assembling goods*—Items that are to leave the warehouse must be efficiently selected from storage and assembled.
- *Dispatching shipments*—Each shipment is packaged suitably and directed to the proper transport vehicle. Shipping and accounting documents are prepared.

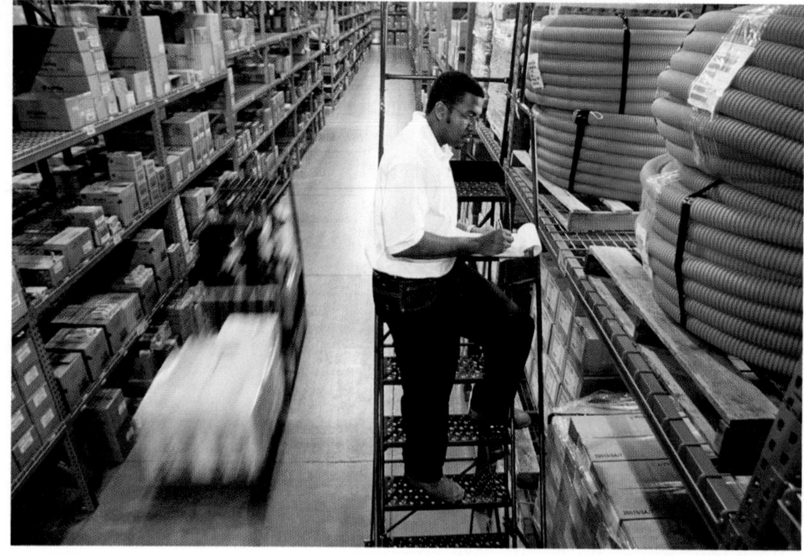

Warehousing. Some warehouses are highly automated while others are not.

A firm may use its own warehouses or rent space in public warehouses. A *private warehouse*, owned and operated by a particular firm, can be designed to serve the firm's specific needs. However, the organization must take on the task of financing the facility, determining the best location for it, and ensuring that it is used fully. Generally, only companies that deal in large quantities of goods can justify private warehouses.

Public warehouses offer their services to all individuals and firms. Most are huge, one-story structures on the outskirts of cities, where rail and truck transportation are easily available. They provide storage facilities, areas for sorting and assembling shipments, and office and display spaces for wholesalers and retailers. Public warehouses also will hold—and issue receipts for—goods used as collateral for borrowed funds.

Many organizations locate and design their warehouses not only to be cost efficient but also to provide excellent customer service. Fast delivery is a particularly important competitive requirement for Internet-based companies. Hewlett Packard's online marketing division (**www.hpshopping.com**), for example, maintains a warehouse close to the FedEx facility in Memphis. This allows the firm to take customer orders later in the evening and still guarantee next-day delivery.[17]

Materials Handling

materials handling the actual physical handling of goods, in warehousing as well as during transportation

Materials handling is the actual physical handling of goods—in warehouses as well as during transportation. Proper materials-handling procedures and techniques can increase the usable capacity of a warehouse or that of any means of transportation. Proper handling can reduce breakage and spoilage as well.

Modern materials handling attempts to reduce the number of times a product is handled. One method is called *unit loading*. Several smaller cartons, barrels, or boxes are combined into a single standard-size load that can be handled efficiently by forklift, conveyer, or truck.

Transportation

transportation the shipment of products to customers

carrier a firm that offers transportation services

As a part of physical distribution, **transportation** is simply the shipment of products to customers. The greater the distance between seller and purchaser, the more important is the choice of the means of transportation and the particular carrier.

A firm that offers transportation services is called a **carrier.** A *common carrier* is a transportation firm whose services are available to all shippers. Railroads, airlines, and most long-distance trucking firms are common carriers. A *contract carrier* is available for hire by one or several shippers. Contract carriers do not serve the general public. Moreover, the number of firms they can handle at any one time is limited by law. A *private carrier* is owned and operated by the shipper.

In addition, a shipper can hire agents called *freight forwarders* to handle its transportation. Freight forwarders pick up shipments from the shipper, ensure that the goods are loaded on selected carriers, and assume responsibility for safe delivery of the

table 15.2 Relative Ratings of Transportation Modes by Selection Criteria

	Selection Criteria					
Mode	**Cost**	**Speed**	**Dependability**	**Load Flexibility**	**Accessibility**	**Frequency**
Railroads	Moderate	Average	Average	High	High	Low
Trucks	High	Fast	High	Average	Very high	High
Airplanes	Very high	Very fast	High	Low	Average	Average
Waterways	Very low	Very slow	Average	Very high	Limited	Very low
Pipelines	Low	Slow	High	Very low	Very limited	Very high

shipments to their destinations. Freight forwarders often can group a number of small shipments into one large load (which is carried at a lower rate). This, of course, saves money for shippers.

The U.S. Postal Service offers *parcel post* delivery, which is widely used by mail-order houses. The post office provides complete geographic coverage at the lowest rates, but it limits the size and weight of the shipments it will accept. United Parcel Service, a privately owned firm, also provides small-parcel services for shippers. Other privately owned carriers, such as Federal Express, DHL, and Airborne, offer fast—often overnight—parcel delivery both within and outside the United States. There are also many local parcel carriers, including specialized delivery services for various time-sensitive industries, such as publishing.

The six major criteria used for selecting transportation modes are compared in Table 15.2. Obviously, the cost of a transportation mode is important to marketers. At times, marketers choose higher-cost modes of transportation because of the benefits they provide. Speed is measured by the total time that a carrier possesses the products, including time required for pickup and delivery, handling, and movement between point of origin and destination. Usually there is a direct relationship between cost and speed; that is, faster modes of transportation are more expensive. A transportation mode's dependability is determined by the consistency of service provided by that mode. Load flexibility is the degree to which a transportation mode can provide appropriate equipment and conditions for moving specific kinds of products and can be adapted for moving other kinds of products. For example, certain types of products may need controlled temperatures or humidity levels. Accessibility refers to a transportation mode's ability to move goods over a specific route or network. Frequency refers to how often a marketer can ship products by a specific transportation mode. Whereas pipelines provide continuous shipments, railroads and waterways follow specific schedules for moving products from one location to another. In Table 15.2, each transportation mode is rated on a relative basis for these six selection criteria. Figure 15.6 (on p. 458) shows recent trends and a breakdown by use of the five different modes of transportation.

Railroads In terms of total freight carried, railroads are America's most important mode of transportation. They are also the least expensive for many products.

Multi-modal transportation. Bax-It, like several other organizations, specializes in multi-modal transportation. In other words, this organization has the capabilities to employ more than one mode of transportation for a customer.

Need multi-modal shipping to any point worldwide?
BAX-iT.
With BAXSuite Transportation Solutions.
Whether your supply chain stretches across a continent or around the world, BAX Global can offer you a multi-modal shipping solution that delivers a more efficient JIT schedule up and down the supply chain, thus keeping inventories low, and making you more cost competitive in this ever growing global marketplace. Call us. One of our supply chain experts will be happy to outline a program for you. Then all you need to say is, BAX-iT.
BAX GLOBAL
1 800 CALL BAX
OR OUTSIDE THE U.S.: 602-458-6200

figure 15.6

Changes in Ton-Miles for Various Transportation Modes

Between 1980 and 2000, ton-miles for airlines, railroads, and trucks increased significantly, whereas pipeline and waterway usage remained steady. Examples of typical products carried by the various modes are shown here.

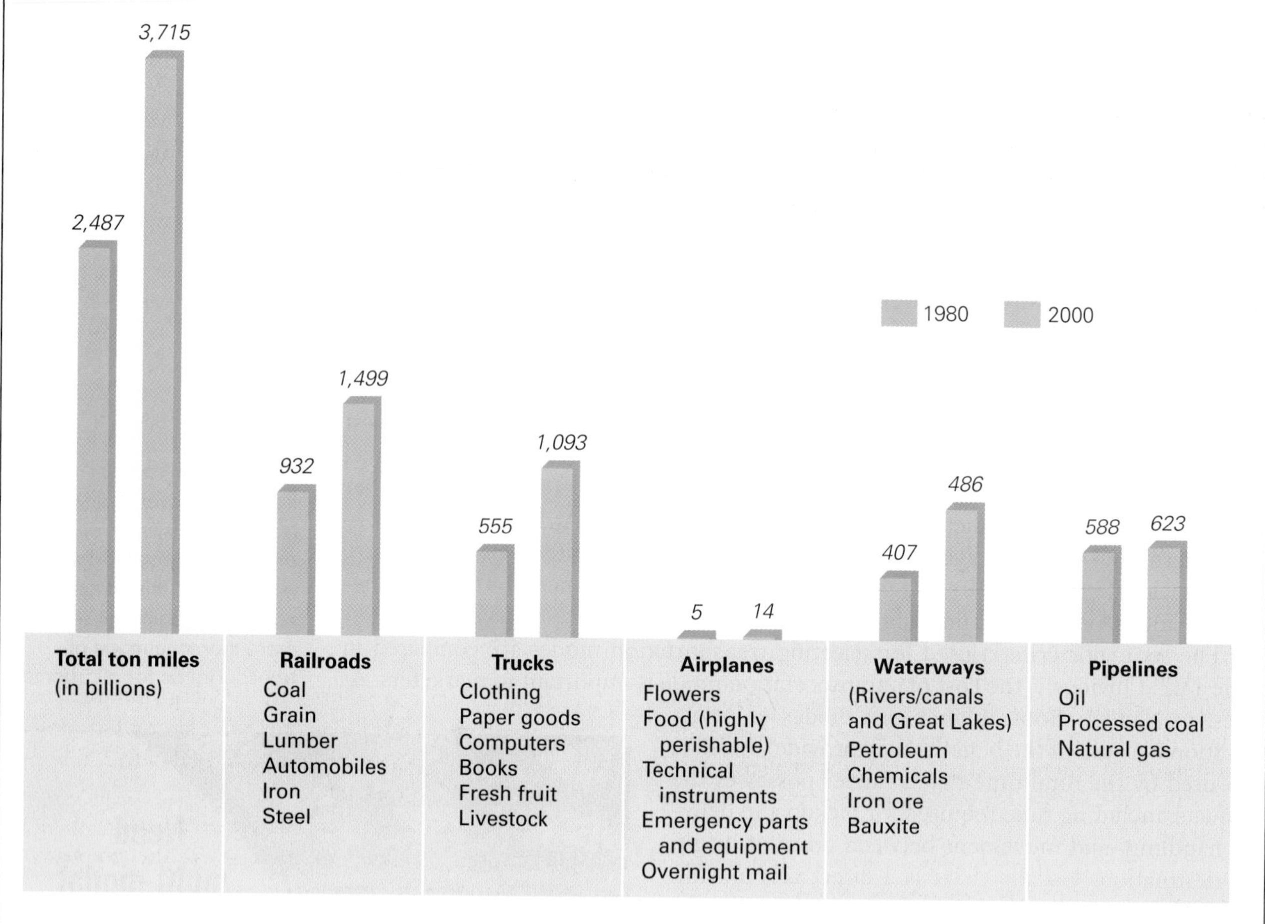

Source: U.S. Bureau of Transportation Statistics, *National Transportation Statistics 1999*, and *Statistical Abstract of the United States, 2001*.

Almost all railroads are common carriers, although a few coal-mining companies operate their own lines.

Many commodities carried by railroads could not be transported easily by any other means. They include a wide range of foodstuffs, raw materials, and manufactured goods. Coal ranks first by a considerable margin. Other major commodities carried by railroads include grain, paper and pulp products, liquids in tank-car loads, heavy equipment, and lumber.

Trucks The trucking industry consists of common, contract, and private carriers. It has undergone tremendous expansion since the creation of a national highway system in the 1920s. Trucks can move goods to suburban and rural areas not served by railroads. They can handle freight quickly and economically, and they carry a wide range of shipments. Many shippers favor this mode of transportation because it offers door-to-door service, less stringent packaging requirements than ships and airplanes, and flexible delivery schedules.

Railroad and truck carriers have teamed up to provide a form of transportation called *piggyback*. Truck trailers are carried from city to city on specially equipped railroad flatcars. Within each city, the trailers are then pulled in the usual way by truck tractors.

Airplanes Air transport is the fastest but most expensive means of transportation. All certified airlines are common carriers. Supplemental or charter lines are contract carriers.

Because of the high cost, lack of airport facilities in many areas, and reliance on weather conditions, airlines carry less than 1 percent of all intercity freight. Only high-value or perishable items, such as flowers, aircraft parts, and pharmaceuticals or goods that are needed immediately, are usually shipped by air.

Waterways Cargo ships and barges offer the least expensive but slowest form of transportation. They are used mainly for bulky nonperishable goods such as iron ore, bulk wheat, motor vehicles, and agricultural implements. Of course, shipment by water is limited to cities located on navigable waterways. But ships and barges account for about 13 percent of all intercity freight hauling.

Pipelines Pipelines are a highly specialized mode of transportation. They are used primarily to carry petroleum and natural gas. Pipelines have become more important as the nation's need for petroleum products has increased. Such products as semiliquid coal and wood chips also can be shipped through pipelines continuously, reliably, and with minimal handling.

In the next chapter we discuss the fourth element of the marketing mix—promotion.

Return To inside business

Dollar General's strategy for retail success combines conveniently located stores with low-priced merchandise. Still, Dollar General has had its share of challenges. Not long ago the company found accounting inaccuracies that resulted in profits being overstated by $100 million over three years. It also paid $162 million to settle stockholder lawsuits related to the inaccuracies. Soon afterward the founder's grandson gave up the CEO position (but remained involved as chairman of the board). The seasoned retailing executive who stepped in as acting CEO put a high priority on reducing operating expenses to boost the chain's profit margin.

Despite these challenges, Dollar General has logged double-digit sales gains in recent years and is putting even more pressure on competitors by opening hundreds of new stores every year. It is one of the five largest U.S. dollar retailers that together account for a total of $12 billion in annual sales. As the market leader, however, Dollar General makes up 44 percent of the top-five total sales—a proportion that is likely to increase as the company presses ahead with its expansion plans.

Questions

1. Why would Dollar General deliberately expand its stock of everyday household items and offer only a limited selection of clothing items?
2. Why is physical distribution so important to Dollar General's competitive situation?

chapter review

Summary

Identify the various channels of distribution that are used for consumer and industrial products.

A marketing channel is a sequence of marketing organizations that directs a product from producer to ultimate user. The marketing channel for a particular product is concerned with the transfer of ownership of that product. Merchant middlemen (merchants) actually take title to products, whereas functional middlemen simply aid in the transfer of title.

The channels used for consumer products include the direct channel from producer to consumer; the channel from producer to retailer to consumer; the channel from producer to wholesaler to retailer to consumer; and the channel from producer to agent to wholesaler to retailer to consumer. There are two major channels of industrial products: (1) producer to user and (2) producer to agent middleman to user.

Explain the concept of market coverage.

Channels and intermediaries are chosen to implement a given level of market coverage. Intensive distribution is the use of all available outlets for a product, providing the widest market coverage. Selective distribution uses only a portion of the available outlets in an area. Exclusive distribution uses only a single retail outlet for a product in a large geographic area.

Understand how supply-chain management facilitates partnering among channel members.

Supply-chain management is a long-term partnership among channel members working together to create a distribution system that reduces inefficiencies, costs, and redundancies while creating a competitive advantage and satisfying customers. Cooperation is required among all channel members, including manufacturing, research, sales, advertising, and shipping. When all channel partners work together, delivery, scheduling, packaging, and other customer requirements are better met. Technology, such as bar coding and electronic data exchange (EDI), makes supply-chain management easier to implement.

Describe what a vertical marketing system is and identify the types of vertical marketing systems.

A vertical marketing system (VMS) is a centrally managed system. It results when two or more channel members from different levels combine under one management. Administered, contractual, and corporate systems represent the three major types of VMSs.

Discuss the need for wholesalers and describe the services they provide to retailers and manufacturers.

Wholesalers are intermediaries that purchase from producers or other intermediaries and sell to industrial users, retailers, or other wholesalers. Wholesalers perform many functions in a distribution channel. If they are eliminated, other channel members—such as the producer or retailers—must perform these functions. Wholesalers provide retailers with help in promoting products, collecting information, and financing. They provide manufacturers with sales help, reduce their inventory costs, furnish market information, and extend credit to retailers.

Identify and describe the major types of wholesalers.

Merchant wholesalers buy and then sell products. Commission merchants and brokers are essentially agents and do not take title to the goods they distribute. Sales branches and offices are owned by the manufacturers they represent and resemble merchant wholesalers and agents, respectively.

Distinguish among the major types of retailers.

Retailers are intermediaries that buy from producers or wholesalers and sell to consumers. In-store retailers include department stores, discount stores, catalog and warehouse showrooms, convenience stores, supermarkets, superstores, warehouse clubs, traditional specialty stores, off-price retailers, and category killers. Nonstore retailers do not sell in conventional store facilities. Instead, they use direct selling, direct marketing, and automatic vending. Types of direct marketing include catalog marketing, direct-response marketing, telemarketing, television home shopping, and online retailing.

Explain the wheel of retailing hypothesis.

The wheel of retailing hypothesis states that retailers begin as low-status, low-margin, low-priced stores and over time evolve into high-cost, high-priced operations.

Identify the categories of shopping centers and the factors that determine how shopping centers are classified.

There are three major types of shopping centers: neighborhood, community, and regional. A center fits one of these categories based on its mix of stores and the size of the geographic area it serves.

Explain the five most important physical distribution activities.

Physical distribution consists of activities designed to move products from producers to ultimate users. Its five major functions are inventory management, order processing, warehousing, materials handling, and transportation. These interrelated functions are integrated into the marketing effort.

Key Terms

You should now be able to define and give an example relevant to each of the following terms:

channel of distribution (or marketing channel) (435)
middleman (or marketing intermediary) (435)
merchant middleman (435)
functional middleman (435)
retailer (435)
wholesaler (436)
intensive distribution (437)
selective distribution (437)
exclusive distribution (438)
supply-chain management (438)
vertical channel integration (440)
vertical marketing system (VMS) (440)
merchant wholesaler (443)
full-service wholesaler (444)
general merchandise wholesaler (444)
limited-line wholesaler (444)
specialty-line wholesaler (444)
limited-service wholesaler (444)
commission merchant (444)
agent (444)
broker (444)
manufacturer's sales branch (444)
manufacturer's sales office (444)
independent retailer (445)
chain retailer (445)
department store (446)
discount store (446)
catalog showroom (446)
warehouse showroom (447)
convenience store (447)
supermarket (447)
superstore (447)
warehouse club (447)
traditional specialty store (448)
off-price retailer (448)
category killer (448)
nonstore retailing (449)
direct selling (449)
direct marketing (449)
catalog marketing (449)
direct-response marketing (450)
telemarketing (450)
television home shopping (451)
online retailing (451)
automatic vending (451)
wheel of retailing (452)
neighborhood shopping center (453)
community shopping center (453)
regional shopping center (453)
physical distribution (454)
inventory management (455)
order processing (455)
warehousing (455)
materials handling (456)
transportation (456)
carrier (456)

Review Questions

1. In what ways is a channel of distribution different from the path taken by a product during physical distribution?
2. What are the most common marketing channels for consumer products? For industrial products?
3. What are the three general approaches to market coverage? What types of products are each used for?
4. What is a vertical marketing system? Identify examples of the three types of VMSs.
5. List the services performed by wholesalers. For whom is each service performed?
6. What is the basic difference between a merchant wholesaler and an agent?
7. Identify three kinds of full-service wholesalers. What factors are used to classify wholesalers into one of these categories?
8. Distinguish between (a) commission merchants and agents and (b) manufacturers' sales branches and manufacturers' sales offices.
9. What is the basic difference between wholesalers and retailers?
10. What is the difference between a department store and a discount store with regard to selling orientation and philosophy?
11. How do (a) convenience stores, (b) traditional specialty stores, and (c) category killers compete with other retail outlets?
12. What can nonstore retailers offer their customers that in-store retailers cannot?
13. What does the wheel of retailing hypothesis suggest about new retail operations?
14. Compare and contrast community shopping centers and regional shopping centers.
15. What is physical distribution? Which major functions does it include?
16. What activities besides storage are included in warehousing?
17. List the primary modes of transportation and cite at least one advantage of each.

Discussion Questions

1. Which distribution channels would producers of services be most likely to use? Why?
2. Many producers sell to consumers both directly and through middlemen. How can such a producer justify competing with its own middlemen?
3. In what situations might a producer use agents or commission merchants rather than its own sales offices or branches?
4. If a middleman is eliminated from a marketing channel, under what conditions will costs decrease? Under what conditions will costs increase? Will the middleman's functions be eliminated? Explain.
5. Which types of retail outlets are best suited to intensive distribution? To selective distribution? To exclusive distribution? Explain your answer in each case.
6. How are the various physical distribution functions related to each other? To the other elements of the marketing mix?

video case

Smarter Retailing at SmarterKids

Category killers such as Toys "R" Us stuff tens of thousands of products into their stores, many times the inventory level that a small local store could afford to stock. SmarterKids, headquartered near Boston, has a smarter way to retail toys. It carefully tests thousands of toys, games, books, software, and movies—but only stocks the approximately 4,000 items that meet its extremely demanding criteria. Parents log onto the SmarterKids website (**www.smarterkids.com**) to fill out surveys and checklists so that the retailer can recommend appropriate products for each child. Then, instead of pushing a cumbersome shopping cart through endless miles of cramped aisles, customers simply point and click to browse and buy.

CEO David Blohn has spent a lot of time studying his market. He knows that parents have limited time and do not want to wander through stores looking at a dizzying array of toys that may or may not be right for their children. Ideally, parents want to buy toys that their children will enjoy for more than a few days. And they want to buy toys that will help children to develop their skills and build their knowledge. Customers may well be impressed by the number of toys a retailer stocks. However, many will be motivated to buy from a retailer that helps narrow the choices to a manageable subset of toys that make sense for a particular child.

This is where SmarterKids comes in. Rather than compete on the basis of an extensive inventory, SmarterKids narrows the choices by having a team of teachers individually test each product. The teachers even watch every video and play every computer game being considered for the website. Then they rate the products using hundreds of criteria, including ease of use, creativity, and educational approach. The result is a smaller but more focused selection of products for newborns to 15-year-olds.

Testing is only one way that SmarterKids saves customers time. If parents complete a series of online surveys and checklists about each child, the site can automatically prepare a listing of appropriate product recommendations. For example, the Early Development Checklists help parents identify the progress that infants, toddlers, and preschool children have made in developing language skills, motor skills, and three other areas. The Learning Styles Survey helps parents determine how their preschool and elementary-school children prefer to learn. SmarterKids also sells a CD-ROM of tests for parents to use at home in assessing a child's vocabulary, reading comprehension, math computation, and other academic skills.

Based on the outcome of these tests, the retailer sets up a password-protected, personalized page entitled, "My Kid's Store," showing toys that are appropriate for each child. Parents also can access special sections of the website to learn more about products for special-needs children and for gifted and talented children. For more general parenting information, they can follow links to the Family Resources Center.

SmarterKids asks the customers who use its site ("designed for adult use") to register and provide information such as name and e-mail address. Only if customers take the optional step of filling out questionnaires and submitting data such as the child's age and gender can the retailer offer precisely tailored recommendations. Yet privacy is a primary concern for many customers who buy online. In response, the SmarterKids privacy policy reassures customers that the retailer will not sell or rent personal data. It also explains why it must place a cookie on each customer's site to store the individual details needed for personalization.

Not every customer will invest the time to register and submit data. But SmarterKids has found through research that customers who take advantage of the site's assessment capabilities wind up purchasing twice as much as those who do not. More data means that the retailer can do a better job of offering customized recommendations and planning e-mail newsletters and other targeted promotions. The idea is to establish and strengthen connections with customers by showing that SmarterKids is dedicated to satisfying their needs and the needs of their children. Big stores may have bigger inventories, but SmarterKids believes that its retailing strategy is smarter for long-term customer loyalty. "If you are able to develop a trusting relationship with consumers, they're going to come back time and time again," says the CEO.[18]

Questions

1. If you headed a toy manufacturing firm, would you be just as interested in having SmarterKids stock your products as having Toys "R" Us stock your products? Explain.
2. Some toys are sold through the direct selling "party plan." Would you recommend that SmarterKids use this retailing method? Why or why not?
3. What are the arguments for and against SmarterKids opening a store near its Boston headquarters to supplement its website?

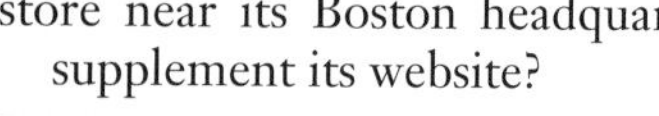

Building Skills for Career Success

1. Exploring the Internet

One reason the Internet has generated so much excitement and interest among both buyers and distributors of products is that it is a highly effective method of direct marketing. Already a multibillion dollar industry, electronic commerce is growing as more businesses recognize the power of the Internet to reach customers twenty-four hours a day anywhere in the world. In addition to using the Internet to provide product information to potential customers, businesses can use it to process orders and accept payment from customers. Quick delivery from warehouses or stores by couriers such as UPS and FedEx adds to the convenience of Internet shopping.

Businesses whose products traditionally have sold well through catalogs are clear leaders in the electronic marketplace. Books, CDs, clothing, and other frequently purchased, relatively low-cost items sell well through both the Internet and catalogs. As a result, many successful catalog companies are including the Internet as a means of communicating about products. And many of their customers are finding that they prefer the more dynamic online versions of the catalogs.

Assignment

1. Explore the websites listed below, or just enter "shopping" on one of the web search engines—then stand back! Also visit the text website for updates to this exercise.

   http://www.llbean.com
   http://www.jcpenney.com
   http://www.sears.com
   http://www.landsend.com
   http://www.barnesandnoble.com
   http://www.amazon.com
2. Which website does the best job of marketing merchandise? Explain your answer.
3. Find a product that you would be willing to buy over the Internet and explain why you would buy it. Name the website and describe the product.
4. Find a product that you would be unwilling to buy over the Internet and, again, explain your reasoning. Name the website and describe the product.

2. Developing Critical Thinking Skills

According to the wheel of retailing hypothesis, retail businesses begin as low-margin, low-priced, low-status operations. As they successfully challenge established retailers for market share, they upgrade their facilities and offer more services. This raises their costs and forces them to increase their prices so that eventually they become like the conventional retailers they replaced. As they move up from the low end of the wheel, new firms with lower costs and prices move in to take their place. For example, Kmart started as a low-priced operation that competed with department stores. Over time, it upgraded its facilities and products; big Kmart stores now offer such exclusive merchandise as Martha Stewart's bed-and-bath collection, full-service pharmacies, café areas, and "Pantry" areas stocked with frequently bought grocery items, including milk, eggs, and bread. In consequence, Kmart has become a higher-cost, higher-priced operation and, as such, is vulnerable to lower-priced firms entering at the low end of the wheel.

Assignment

1. Investigate the operations of a local retailer.
2. Use Figure 15.5 to explain how this retailer is evolving on the wheel of retailing.
3. Prepare a report on your findings.

3. Building Team Skills

Surveys are a commonly used tool in marketing research. The information they provide can reduce business risk and facilitate decision making. Retail outlets often survey their customers' wants and needs by distributing comment cards or questionnaires. The customer survey (on p. 464) is an example of a survey that a local photography shop might distribute to its customers.

Assignment

1. Working in teams of three to five, choose a local retailer.
2. Classify the retailer according to the major types of retailers.
3. Design a survey to help the retailer improve customer service. (You may find it beneficial to work with the retailer and actually administer the survey to the retailer's customers. Prepare a report of the survey results for the retailer.)
4. Present your findings to the class.

4. Researching Different Careers

When you are looking for a job, the people closest to you can be extremely helpful. Family members and friends may be able to answer your questions directly or put you in touch with someone else who can. This type of "networking" can lead to an "informational interview," in which you can meet with someone who will answer your questions about a career or a company and who also can provide inside information on related fields and other helpful hints.

Customer Survey

To help us serve you better please take a few minutes while your photographs are being developed to answer the following questions. Your opinions are important to us.

1. Do you live/work in the area? (Circle one or both if they apply.)
2. Why did you choose us? (Circle all that apply.)

   Close to home
   Close to work
   Convenience
   Good service
   Quality
   Full-service photography shop
   Other
3. How did you learn about us? (Circle one.)

   Newspaper
   Flyer/coupon
   Passing by
   Recommended by someone
   Other
4. How frequently do you have film developed? (Please estimate.)

   ________ Times per month
   ________ Times per year
5. Which aspects of our photography shop do you think need improvement?
6. Our operating hours are from 8:00 A.M. to 7:00 P.M. weekdays and Saturdays from 9:30 A.M. to 6:00 P.M. We are closed on Sundays and legal holidays. If changes in our operating hours would serve you better please specify how you would like them changed.
7. Age (Circle one.)

   Under 25
   26–89
   40–59
   Over 60

Comments:

Assignment

1. Choose a retailer or wholesaler and a position within the company that interests you.
2. Call the company and ask to speak to the person in that particular position. Explain that you are a college student interested in the position and ask to set up an "informational interview."
3. Prepare a list of questions to ask in the interview. The questions should focus on
   a. The type of training recommended for the position
   b. How the person entered the position and advanced in it
   c. What he or she likes and dislikes about the work
4. Present your findings to the class.

5. Improving Communication Skills

As the first step in finding a home, an increasing number of people are turning to the Internet rather than a realtor. The National Association of Realtors (NAR) lists over one million homes each month. However, over the past five years, the NAR has lost 100,000 members, a 12.2 percent decline. In addition, the total value of mortgages initiated online is expected to rise from $217 million at the end of 1996 to $25.5 billion by 2001. Home buyers can search the Internet for demographic information about a particular town or region, including school quality, crime rates, and income level, and can use relocation calculators, which estimate how much the cost of living differs from one region to another.

Assignment

1. Compare shopping for a home over the Internet with the traditional experience of shopping for a home with a realtor. (Be sure to consider the time required to gather information on housing, prices, order processing, and payment methods.)
2. Prepare a brief position paper entitled, "A Perspective: Nonstore Retailers Are/Are Not a Threat to Traditional Retailers."

chapter

16 Developing Integrated Marketing Communications

learning objectives

1 Describe integrated marketing communications.

2 Understand the role of promotion.

3 Explain the purposes of the three types of advertising.

4 Describe the advantages and disadvantages of the major advertising media.

5 Identify the major steps in developing an advertising campaign.

6 Recognize the various kinds of salespersons, the steps in the personal-selling process, and the major sales management tasks.

7 Describe sales promotion objectives and methods.

8 Understand the types and uses of public relations.

9 Identify the factors that influence the selection of promotion mix ingredients.

Rather than merely entertaining the audience, AutoTrader's commercials showed how to use the website to simplify car shopping.

inside business

AutoTrader.com Revs Up an Exciting Promotion Mix

SEE THE COMMERCIAL, play the game, shop for a car. Since its founding in 1997, AutoTrader.com has brought car buyers and sellers to its website through several integrated promotional efforts, including television commercials, interactive online games, and targeted e-mail messages.

The AutoTrader website (**www.autotrader.com**) features classified ads for more than two million new and used cars. Buyers and sellers—both individuals and dealers—make contact through the site to negotiate the final terms for sales. They also can choose to buy or sell through online car auctions, an increasingly popular alternative to traditional car-buying methods.

When AutoTrader first opened for business, few people had ever bought or sold a vehicle on the Internet. Therefore, the company faced the challenge of introducing its main target market—25- to 49-year-old men—to an unfamiliar process. The company's solution was practical and effective. Rather than merely entertaining the audience, like many early dot-com commercials, AutoTrader's informative commercials showed step by step how to use the site to simplify car shopping. As a result, the site was soon drawing more than 5.5 million visitors every month.

Next, AutoTrader's executives decided to target a slightly younger market of 18- to 24-year-olds, because this group of first-time car buyers accounts for a significant percentage of used-car purchases. They hired a video-game firm to adapt the look of the fast-paced television commercials to an online promotion entitled "Slide into Your Ride." Players could win prizes instantly for correctly lining up three cars by matching their colors. They also were eligible for a top sweepstakes prize of a $25,000 shopping spree on the AutoTrader site plus car stereo components and other prizes.

Knowing that students typically search for used cars before heading off for college in the fall, AutoTrader scheduled this promotional game for August and September. To attract players, it placed banner ads on the Ask Jeeves search engine and other popular sites. It also sent e-mail announcements to the site's online newsletter list and to people on a selected *Sports Illustrated* list.

For a total cost of $1 million, AutoTrader's promotional efforts boosted brand awareness and drew an additional 500,000 visitors to its site during the first month alone. More than half the visitors who played the game were women, and about one-third of the players were in the 18- to 24-year-old age group. More than 60 percent of the players signed up for AutoTrader's monthly online newsletter. Most important, several hundred thousand players searched for used cars on the AutoTrader site during the promotional period.[1]

Marketers at AutoTrader.com employ multiple promotional methods to create very favorable company and product images in the minds of customers. Skillful use of promotion is of great benefit to AutoTrader.com.

Promotion is communication about an organization and its products that is intended to inform, persuade, or remind target market members. The promotion with which we are most familiar—advertising—is intended to inform, persuade, or remind us to buy particular products. But there is more to promotion than advertising, and it is used for other purposes as well. Charities use promotion to inform us of their need for donations, to persuade us to give, and to remind us to do so in case we have forgotten. Even the Internal Revenue Service uses promotion (in the form of publicity) to remind us of its April 15 deadline for filing tax returns.

promotion communication about an organization and its products that is intended to inform, persuade, or remind target market members

A **promotion mix** (sometimes called a *marketing communications mix*) is the particular combination of promotional methods a firm uses to reach a target market. The makeup of a mix depends on many factors, including the firm's promotional resources and objectives, the nature of the target market, the product characteristics, and the feasibility of various promotional methods.

promotion mix the particular combination of promotion methods a firm uses to reach a target market

In this chapter we introduce four promotional methods and describe how they are used in an organization's marketing plans. First, we examine the role of advertising in the promotion mix. We discuss different types of advertising, the process of developing an advertising campaign, and social and legal concerns in advertising. Next, we consider several categories of personal selling, noting the importance of effective sales management. We also look at sales promotion—why firms use it and which sales promotion techniques are most effective. Then, we explain how public relations can be used to promote an organization and its products. Finally, we illustrate how these four promotional methods are combined in an effective promotion mix.

What Is Integrated Marketing Communications?

learning objective

1 Describe integrated marketing communications.

Integrated marketing communications is the coordination of promotion efforts to ensure the maximum informational and persuasive impact on customers. A major goal of integrated marketing communications is to send a consistent message to customers. Integrated marketing communications provides an organization with a way to coordinate and manage its promotional efforts to ensure that customers do receive consistent messages. This approach fosters not only long-term customer relationships but also the efficient use of promotional resources.

integrated marketing communications coordination of promotion efforts for maximum informational and persuasive impact on customers

The concept of integrated marketing communications has been increasingly accepted for several reasons. Mass-media advertising, a very popular promotional method in the past, is used less today because of its high costs and less predictable audience sizes. Marketers can now take advantage of more precisely targeted promotional tools, such as cable TV, direct mail, CD-ROMs, the Internet, special-interest magazines, and voice broadcasts. Database marketing is also allowing marketers to be more precise in targeting individual customers. Until recently, suppliers of marketing communications were specialists. Advertising agencies provided advertising campaigns, sales promotion companies provided sales promotion activities and materials, and public relations

Promotion comes in many different forms. Pepsi promotional skaters at a beach area in Rio De Janiero, Brazil, help to remind customers of this well-established brand. Efforts such as this may influence customers to think of the Pepsi brand when they are thirsty.

organizations engaged in public relations efforts. Today, a number of promotion-related companies provide one-stop shopping to the client seeking advertising, sales promotion, and public relations, thus reducing coordination problems for the sponsoring company. Because the overall cost of marketing communications has risen significantly upper management demands systematic evaluations of communications efforts to ensure that promotional resources are being used efficiently.[2] Although the fundamental role of promotion is not changing, the specific communication vehicles employed and the precision with which they are used are changing.

The Role of Promotion

learning objective

2 Understand the role of promotion.

Promotion is commonly the object of two misconceptions. Often people take note of highly visible promotional activities, such as advertising and personal selling, and conclude that these make up the entire field of marketing. People also sometimes consider promotional activities to be unnecessary, expensive, and the cause of higher prices. Neither view is accurate.

The role of promotion is to facilitate exchanges directly or indirectly by informing individuals, groups, or organizations and influencing them to accept a firm's products or to have more positive feelings about the firm. To expedite changes directly, marketers convey information about a firm's goods, services, and ideas to particular market segments. To bring about exchanges indirectly, marketers address interest groups (such as environmental and consumer groups), regulatory agencies, investors, and the general public concerning a company and its products. The broader role of promotion, therefore, is to maintain positive relationships between a company and various groups in the marketing environment.

Marketers frequently design promotional communications, such as advertisements, for specific groups, although some may be directed at wider audiences. Several different messages may be communicated simultaneously to different market segments. For example, Exxon Mobil Corporation may address customers about a new motor oil, inform investors about the firm's financial performance, and update the general public on the firm's environmental efforts.

Marketers must carefully plan, implement, and coordinate promotional communications to make the best use of them. The effectiveness of promotional activities depends greatly on the quality and quantity of information available to marketers about the organization's marketing environment (see Figure 16.1). If a marketer wants to influence customers to buy a certain product, for example, the firm must know who these customers are and how they make purchase decisions for that type of product. Marketers must gather and use information about particular audiences to communicate successfully with them. At times, two or more firms partner in joint promotional efforts. For example, Taco Bell carefully coordinated the promotion of its Monterey Chicken Quesadilla with Match.com. The quesadilla contains spicy pepper jack cheese and mild Monterey, and the two companies created a sweepstakes called "Monterey Match Up" in which one "spicy" couple and one "mild" couple win vacations to Monterey, California. To stick with the dating theme, related Taco Bell commercials aired on such shows as "The Bachelorette" and "Joe Millionaire."[3]

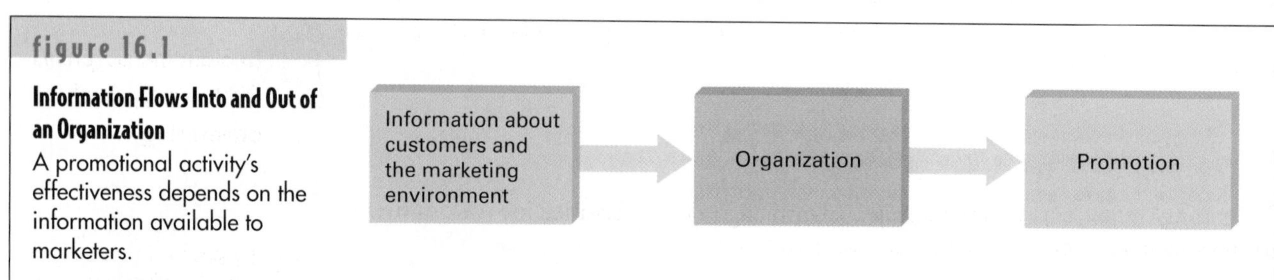

figure 16.1

Information Flows Into and Out of an Organization

A promotional activity's effectiveness depends on the information available to marketers.

Source: William M. Pride and O. C. Ferrell, *Marketing: Concepts and Strategies*, 12th ed. Copyright © 2003 by Houghton Mifflin Company. Adapted with permission.

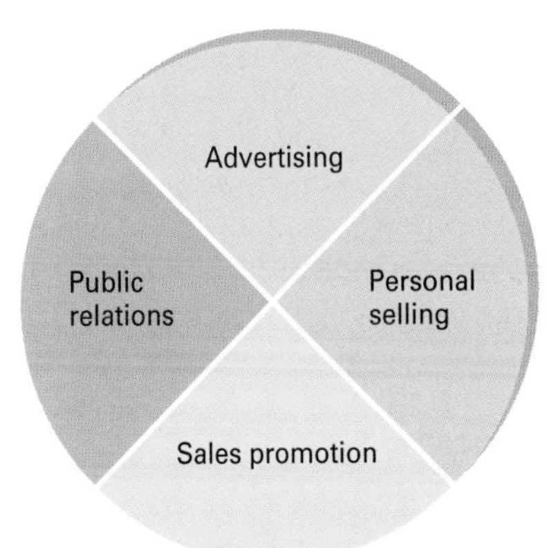

figure 16.2

Possible Ingredients of a Promotion Mix

Depending on the type of product and target market involved, one or more of these ingredients are used in a promotion mix.

ource: William M. Pride and O. C. Ferrell, *Marketing: Concepts and Strategies*, 12th ed. Copyright © 2003 y Houghton Mifflin Company. Adapted with permission.

The Promotion Mix: An Overview

Marketers can use several promotional methods to communicate with individuals, groups, and organizations. The methods that are combined to promote a particular product make up the promotion mix for that item.

Advertising, personal selling, sales promotion, and public relations are the four major elements in an organization's promotion mix (see Figure 16.2). While it is possible that one ingredient may be used, it is likely that two, three, or four of these ingredients will be used in a promotion mix depending on the type of product and target market involved.

Advertising is a paid nonpersonal message communicated to a select audience through a mass medium. Advertising is flexible enough that it can reach a very large target group or a small, carefully chosen one. **Personal selling** is personal communication aimed at informing customers and persuading them to buy a firm's products. It is more expensive to reach a consumer through personal selling than through advertising, but this method provides immediate feedback and is often more persuasive than advertising. **Sales promotion** is the use of activities or materials as direct inducements to customers or salespersons. It adds extra value to the product or increases the customer's incentive to buy the product. **Public relations** is a broad set of communication activities used to create and maintain favorable relationships between an organization and various public groups, both internal and external. Public relations activities are numerous and varied and can be a very effective form of promotion.

advertising a paid nonpersonal message communicated to a select audience through a mass medium

personal selling personal communication aimed at informing customers and persuading them to buy a firm's products

sales promotion the use of activities or materials as direct inducements to customers or salespersons

public relations communication activities used to create and maintain favorable relations between an organization and various public groups, both internal and external

Advertising

In 2001, organizations spent $231 billion on advertising in the United States.[4] Figure 16.3 (on p. 470) shows how advertising expenditures and employment in advertising have increased since 1977.

learning objective

3 Explain the purposes of the three types of advertising.

Types of Advertising by Purpose

Depending on its purpose and message, advertising may be classified into one of three groups: primary demand, selective demand, or institutional.

Primary-Demand Advertising **Primary-demand advertising** is advertising aimed at increasing the demand for *all* brands of a product within a specific industry.

primary-demand advertising advertising whose purpose is to increase the demand for *all* brands of a product within a specific industry

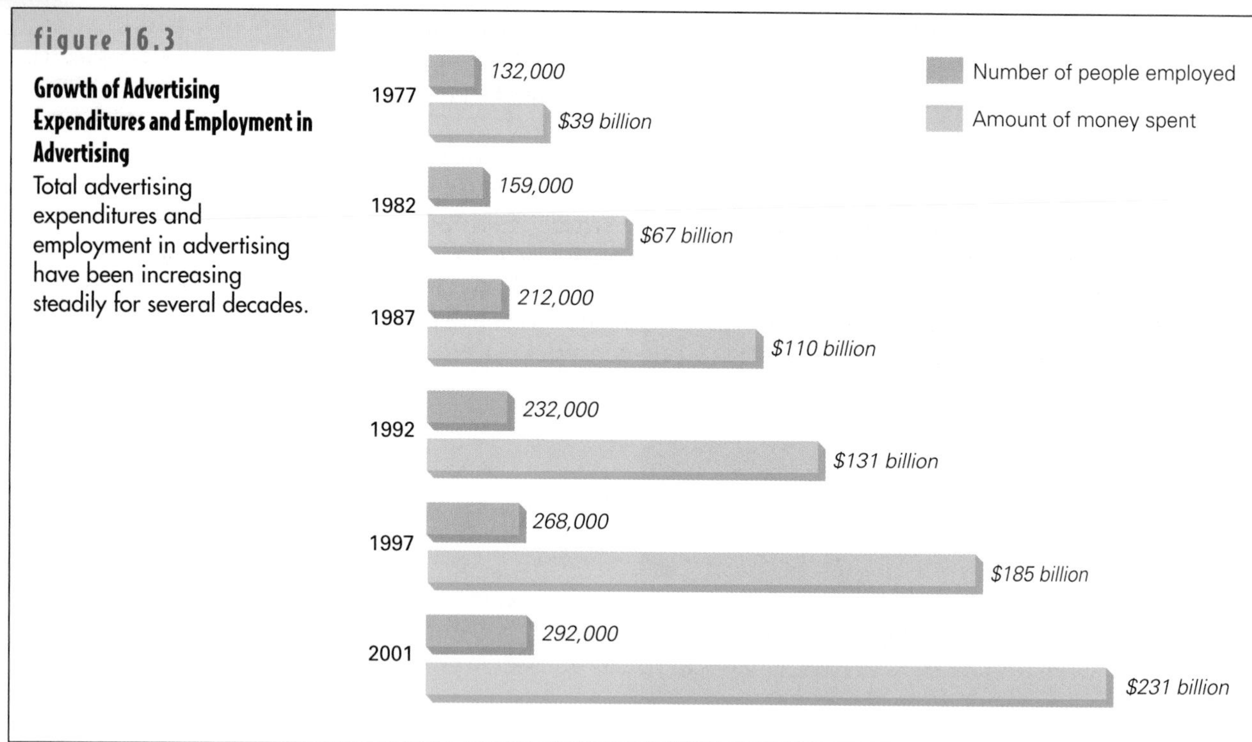

figure 16.3

Growth of Advertising Expenditures and Employment in Advertising
Total advertising expenditures and employment in advertising have been increasing steadily for several decades.

Source: *Advertising Age*, May 13, 2002; and U.S. Department of Labor, Bureau of Labor Statistics, *Employment and Earnings*, April 2002.

Trade and industry associations, such as the California Milk Processor Board ("Got Milk?"), are the major users of primary-demand advertising. Their advertisements promote broad product categories, such as beef, milk, pork, potatoes, and prunes, without mentioning specific brands.

selective-demand (or **brand**) **advertising** advertising that is used to sell a particular brand of product

Selective-Demand Advertising **Selective-demand** (or **brand**) **advertising** is advertising that is used to sell a particular brand of product. It is by far the most common type of advertising, and it accounts for the lion's share of advertising expenditures. Producers use brand-oriented advertising to convince us to buy everything from Bubble Yum to Buicks.

Selective advertising that aims at persuading consumers to make purchases within a short time is called *immediate-response advertising*. Most local advertising is of this type. Often local advertisers promote products with immediate appeal. Selective advertising aimed at keeping a firm's name or product before the public is called *reminder advertising*.

Comparative advertising, which has become more popular over the last three decades, compares specific characteristics of two or more identified brands. Of course, the comparison shows the advertiser's brand to be as good as or better than the other identified competing brands. Comparisons often are based on

Make ours doubles.
My sister and I hate to lose–nutrients, that is.
So we drink milk. It has 9 essential nutrients active bodies need.
You might say it's the only thing we serve.
got milk?

Generating primary demand. Several milk industry associations promote milk to stimulate primary demand. Rather than promoting a specific brand, the familiar "milk mustache" and "Got Milk?" ad campaigns are aimed at increasing demand for milk in general.

he outcome of surveys or research studies. Although competing firms act as effective vatchdogs against each other's advertising claims, consumers themselves sometimes ecome rather guarded concerning claims based on "scientific studies" and various tatistical manipulations. Comparative advertising is unacceptable or illegal in a numer of other countries.

nstitutional Advertising **Institutional advertising** is advertising designed to enance a firm's image or reputation. Many public utilities and larger firms, such as T&T and the major oil companies, use part of their advertising dollars to build oodwill rather than to stimulate sales directly. A positive public image helps an organization attract not only customers but also employees and investors.

institutional advertising advertising designed to enhance a firm's image or reputation

Advertising Media

The **advertising media** are the various forms of communication through which advertising reaches its audience. The major media are newspapers, magazines, direct nail, yellow pages, out-of-home, television, radio, and the Internet. Figure 16.4 hows how organizations allocate their advertising expenditures among the various nedia. Note that television and radio account for less than one-third of all media expenditures.

learning objective

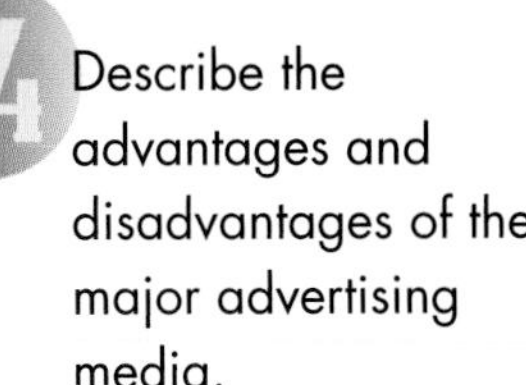

Describe the advantages and disadvantages of the major advertising media.

advertising media the various forms of communication through which advertising reaches its audience

Newspapers Newspaper advertising accounts for about 19 percent of all advertisng expenditures. Approximately 85 percent is purchased by local retailers. Retailers ise newspaper advertising extensively because it is relatively inexpensive compared vith other media. Moreover, since most newspapers provide local coverage, advertisng dollars are not wasted in reaching people outside the organization's market area. It s also timely. Ads usually can be placed just a few days before they are to appear.

There are some drawbacks, however, to newspaper advertising. It has a short life span; newspapers generally are read through once and then discarded. Color reproluction in newspapers is usually not high quality; thus most ads are run in black and white. Finally, marketers cannot target specific demographic groups through newspaer ads because newspapers are read by such a broad spectrum of people.

Magazines The advertising revenues of magazines have been almost flat over the ast few years. In 2001 they reached $11.1 billion, or about 4.8 percent of all advertisng expenditures.

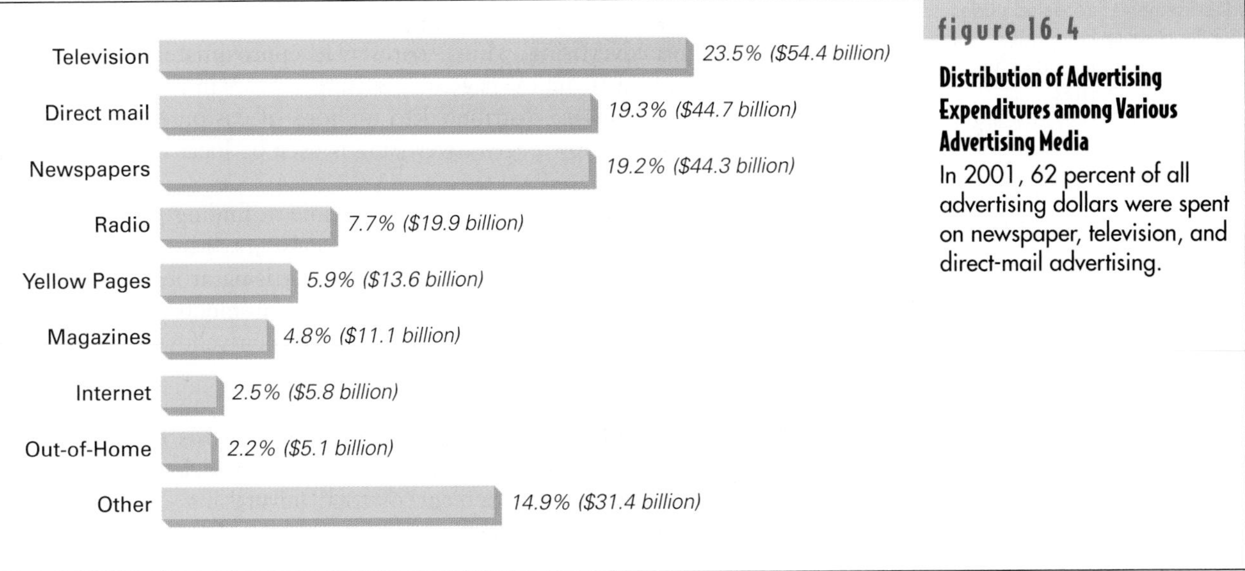

figure 16.4

Distribution of Advertising Expenditures among Various Advertising Media

In 2001, 62 percent of all advertising dollars were spent on newspaper, television, and direct-mail advertising.

Source: "Coen's Spending Totals for 2001," **www.adage.com/datacenter.cms**, May 13, 2002.

Advertisers can reach very specific market segments through ads in special interest magazines. A boat manufacturer has a ready-made consumer audience in subscribers to *Yachting* or *Sail*. Producers of photographic equipment advertise in *Travel & Leisure* or *Popular Photography*. A number of magazines such as *Time* and *Cosmopolitan* publish regional editions, which provide advertisers with geographic flexibility as well.

Magazine advertising is more prestigious than newspaper advertising, and it allows for high-quality color reproduction. In addition, magazine advertisements have a longer life span than those in other media. Issues of *National Geographic*, for example, may be kept for months or years, and the ads they contain may be viewed repeatedly.

The major disadvantages of magazine advertising are high cost and lack of timeliness. Because magazine ads normally must be prepared two to three months in advance, they cannot be adjusted to reflect the latest market conditions. Magazine ads—especially full-color ads—are also expensive. Although the cost of reaching a thousand people may compare favorably with that of other media, the cost of a full-page four-color ad can be very high—$183,000 in *Time*.

Using the Internet

Advertising Age **(http://www.adage.com/)** is the industry's preeminent source of marketing, advertising, and media news, information, and analysis. The website provides a variety of information about the advertising industry and online advertising in particular. Articles from various trade publications, as well as links to advertising agencies and samples of advertising, are among the many useful features presented.

direct-mail advertising promotional material mailed directly to individuals

Direct Mail **Direct-mail advertising** is promotional material mailed directly to individuals. Direct mail is the most selective medium; mailing lists are available (or can be compiled) to reach almost any target audience, from airplane enthusiasts to zoologists. The effectiveness of direct-mail advertising can be measured because the advertiser has a record of who received the advertisements and can track who responds to the ads.

Some organizations are using direct e-mail. To avoid customers receiving unwanted e-mail, a firm should ask customers to complete a request form in order to receive promotional e-mail from the company. For example, Lands' End's weekly e-mail newsletter, "What's New," goes to over 200,000 subscribers. Each has completed a subscription form on the company website.[5]

The success of direct-mail advertising depends to some extent on appropriate and current mailing lists. A direct-mail campaign may fail if the mailing list is outdated and the mailing does not reach the right people. In addition, this medium is relatively costly. Direct-mail advertising expenditures in 2001 amounted to more than $44 billion, almost 20 percent of the total.

yellow pages advertising simple listings or display advertisements presented under specific product categories appearing in print and online telephone directories

Yellow Pages Advertising **Yellow pages advertising**, appearing in print and online telephone directories, is presented under specific product categories and may appear as simple listings or as display advertisements. In 2001, advertisers spent $13.6 billion on yellow pages advertising, which represented approximately 5.9 percent of total advertising expenditures. Yellow pages advertising appears in over 6,000 editions of telephone directories that are distributed to millions of customers annually. Approximately 85 percent of yellow pages advertising is used by local advertisers as opposed to national advertisers.

Customers use yellow pages advertising to save time in finding products, to find information quickly, and to learn about products and marketers. It is estimated that approximately 60 percent of adults read yellow pages advertising at least once a week. Unlike other types of advertising media, yellow pages advertisements are purchased for one year and cannot be changed. Advertisers often pay for their yellow pages advertisements through monthly charges on their telephone statements.

out-of-home advertising short promotional messages on billboards, posters, signs, and transportation vehicles

Out-of-Home Advertising **Out-of-home advertising** consists of short promotional messages on billboards, posters, signs, and transportation vehicles. In 2001, advertisers spent $5.1 billion, or 2.5 percent of total advertising expenditures, on out-of-home advertising.

Sign and billboard advertising allows the marketer to focus on a particular geographic area; it is also fairly inexpensive. However, because most outdoor promotion is directed toward a mobile audience, the message must be limited to a few words. The medium is especially suitable for products that lend themselves to pictorial display.

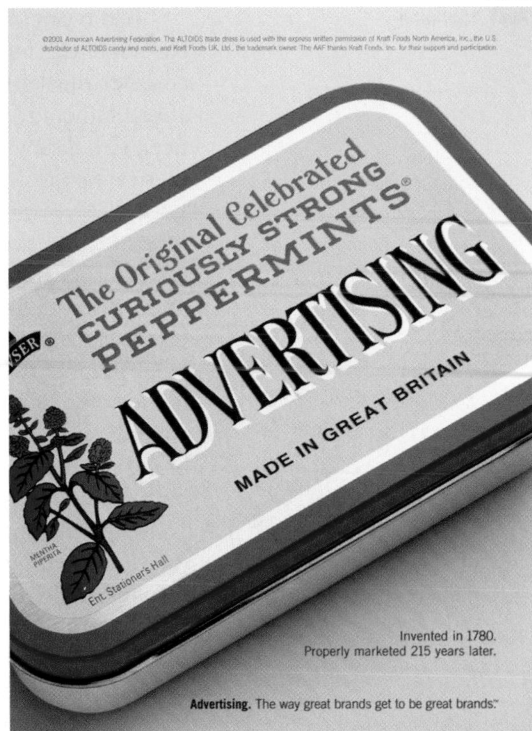

Brand building advertising. The maker of Altoids gave permission for the American Advertising Federation to modify its logo for use in the Great Brand Campaign. This integrated marketing communications program was launched by AAF to reinforce the essential strategic importance of advertising. Ad space was donated by numerous national newspapers and trade and consumer magazines to run this and similar ads.

Television Television ranks number one in total advertising revenue. In 2001, almost one-fourth of all advertising expenditures, about $55 billion, went to television. Approximately 99 percent of American homes have at least one television set that is watched an average of seven and one-half hours each day. The average U.S. household can receive twenty-eight TV channels, including cable and pay stations, and about 80 percent of households receive basic cable/satellite television. Television obviously provides advertisers with considerable access to consumers.

Television advertising is the primary medium for larger firms whose objective is to reach national or regional markets. A national advertiser may buy *network time*, which means that its message usually will be broadcast by hundreds of local stations affiliated with the network. However, the opportunity to reach extremely large television audiences has been reduced by the increased availability and popularity of cable channels and home videos. Both national and local firms may buy *local time* on a single station that covers a particular geographic area.

Advertisers may *sponsor* an entire show, participate with other sponsors of a show, or buy *spot time* for a single 10-, 20-, 30-, or 60-second commercial during or between programs. To an extent, they may select their audience by choosing the day of the week and the approximate time of day their ads will be shown. Anheuser-Busch advertises Budweiser Beer during TV football games because the majority of viewers are men, who are likely to buy beer. Another variation of television advertising is the commercial-free network show that works advertisers' products into news or variety segments during the actual show. The Warner Brothers Network has secured partners such as Visa USA and PepsiCo for this innovative television advertising.[6]

Another option available to television advertisers is the infomercial. An **infomercial** is a program-length televised commercial message resembling an entertainment or consumer affairs program. Infomercials for products such as exercise equipment tell customers why they need the product, what benefits it provides, in what ways it outperforms its competitors, and how much it costs. The "Crouching Tiger, Rising Mattress" infomercials were effective in the marketing of Aero Products' Raised Aerobed. Aero ran the infomercials on national cable, including MSNBC and CNN, and spent about $1 million a month.[7] Although infomercials initially were aired primarily over cable television, today they are becoming more common on other types of television. Currently, infomercials are responsible for marketing over $1 billion worth of products annually. Even some Fortune 500 companies are now using them.

infomercial a program-length televised commercial message resembling an entertainment or consumer affairs program

Television advertising rates are based on the number of people expected to be watching when the commercial is aired. In 2003, the average cost of a 30-second Superbowl commercial was $2.1 million.[8] Advertisers spend over $500,000 for a 30-second television commercial during a top-rated prime-time program.

Unlike magazine advertising, television advertising has a short life. If a viewer misses a commercial, it is missed forever. Viewers also may become indifferent to commercial messages. Or they may use the commercial time as a break from viewing, thus missing the message altogether. Remote-control devices make it especially easy to avoid television commercials.

Radio Advertisers spent $19.9 billion, or 7.7 percent of total expenditures, on radio advertising in 2001. Like magazine advertising, radio advertising offers selectivity. Radio stations develop programming for—and are tuned in by—specific groups of listeners. There are almost half a billion radios in the United States (about six per household), which makes radio the most accessible medium.

Radio can be less expensive than other media. Actual rates depend on geographic coverage, the number of commercials contracted for, the time period specified, and whether the station broadcasts on AM, FM, or both. Even small retailers are able to afford radio advertising. A radio advertiser can schedule and change ads on short notice. The disadvantages of using radio are the absence of visual images and (because there are so many stations) the small audience size.

Internet The newest advertising medium, and one that is increasing in popularity, is the Internet. In 2001, U.S. advertisers spent $5.8 billion on Internet advertising, approximately 2.5 percent of total advertising expenditures. Internet advertising can take various forms. The most common type of Internet ad is the banner ad, a rectangular graphic that appears at the top of a consumer website. Advertisers can use animation and interactive capabilities in their banner ads. Another type of Internet advertisement is the button ad, a small squarish ad containing only a corporate or brand name and usually appearing at the bottom of a web page. By clicking on the button, viewers go directly to a corporate website. For example, by clicking on a Netscape button, Internet users are taken directly to the Netscape website, where they can download Navigator browser software. The third type of Internet advertisement is sponsorship (or co-branded) ads. These ads integrate a company's brand with editorial content. The goal of this type of advertisement is to get users to strongly identify the advertiser with the site's mission. Keyword ads are another type of Internet advertisement. Featured primarily on web search engines such as Yahoo! and Excite, advertisers can link a specific ad to text or subject matter that an information seeker may enter. For example, Miller Brewing bought the word *beer* on Yahoo! so that every time someone conducts a search using that word, an ad for Miller Genuine Draft Beer pops up. Finally, there are interstitial ads, also known as "in-your-face ads." When viewers

adapting to change

Advergames: Promoting Products Through Fun and Games

ADVERTISERS REALIZE that people often ignore or switch stations during television commercials. They know that many Internet users delete commercial e-mail messages and click to close pop-up ads. Now a growing number of advertisers such as Honda, Fox Sports, and Walt Disney are taking a fresh approach by promoting their products through online "advergames." A cross between advertising and video games, advergames create a positive, interactive experience with the advertised brands and retain the audience's attention for longer periods.

Honda, for example, recently hired an advergame company to develop a web-based racing game featuring its cars. With eye-catching graphics, instant replays, and multiplayer capabilities, this advergame is reminiscent of classic racing arcade games. However, visitors to the Honda website have to answer a few questions (about age, address, occupation, and hobbies) before playing. This gives the automaker valuable data about who is interested in its vehicles. In exchange, Honda enters players in a drawing for a new Honda CR-V. Once the race begins, participants play for more than four minutes, on average. This advergame may not actually sell a car, but Honda's advertising agency believes that it is a cost-effective promotion. "Customers spend longer with your product than they do with a 30-second commercial," says an agency manager.

The most engaging advergames are so interesting that people play over and over. One Fox Sports baseball game invited players to try batting against major league pitchers Randy Johnson and Curt Schilling. More than 100,000 people remained on the site for an average of 30 minutes while playing.

Some marketers that target children use advergames to build awareness and encourage positive product attitudes. Nabisco, for example, encourages children to play candy-related games on Nabiscoworld (**www.nabiscoworld.com**). Walt Disney has posted movie-specific games on popular children's sites such as NeoPets (**www.neopets.com**), where children also may find advergames featuring Oral-B toothbrushes and Frito-Lay's snacks.

Advertisers may pay as much as $500,000 to create and post advergames. However, this is lower than the typical cost of producing and airing television commercials—for ads that bring in marketing data and leave players smiling.

click on a website, a window pops up to display a product ad. For example, when web users click on a nutrition site such as Phys.com, a full-screen animated ad for Procter & Gamble's Sunny Delight drink appears first.

Although the cost per thousand persons reached (CPM) of Internet advertising is higher than that of advertising on television, there are benefits of Internet advertising that experts say outweigh the expense. First, the number of people using the Internet continues to rise, which increases the potential size of the advertising audience. Second, online advertising can be more precise in targeting specific customers than most other media. In addition to expense, however, there are other problems associated with advertising on the Internet. First, many web ads are crude by comparison with television commercials. Second, there is no hard evidence that net browsers pay more attention to the ads they see there than they do to ads anywhere else.

Major Steps in Developing an Advertising Campaign

learning objective

5 Identify the major steps in developing an advertising campaign.

An advertising campaign is developed in several stages. These stages may vary in number and the order in which they are implemented depending on the company's resources, products, and audiences. The development of a campaign in any organization, however, will include the following steps in some form.

1. Identify and Analyze the Target Audience The target audience is the group of people toward which a firm's advertisements are directed. To pinpoint the organization's target audience and develop an effective campaign, marketers must analyze such information as the geographic distribution of potential customers; their age, sex, race, income, and education; and their attitudes toward both the advertiser's product and competing products. How marketers use this information will be influenced by the features of the product to be advertised and the nature of the competition. Precise identification of the target audience is crucial to the proper development of subsequent stages and, ultimately, to the success of the campaign itself.

2. Define the Advertising Objectives The goals of an advertising campaign should be stated precisely and in measurable terms. The objectives should include the current position of the firm, indicate how far and in what direction from that original reference point the company wishes to move, and specify a definite period of time for the achievement of the goals. Advertising objectives that focus on sales will stress increasing sales by a certain percentage or dollar amount or expanding the firm's market share. Communication objectives will emphasize increasing product or brand awareness, improving consumer attitudes, or conveying product information.

3. Create the Advertising Platform An advertising platform includes the important selling points or features that an advertiser wishes to incorporate into the advertising campaign. These features should be important to customers in their selection and use of a product, and if possible, they should be features that competing products lack. Although research into what consumers view as important issues is expensive, it is the most productive way to determine which issues to include in an advertising platform.

4. Determine the Advertising Appropriation The advertising appropriation is the total amount of

Target audience. Generally, advertisements are not aimed at everyone. Who is the target audience for this advertisement?

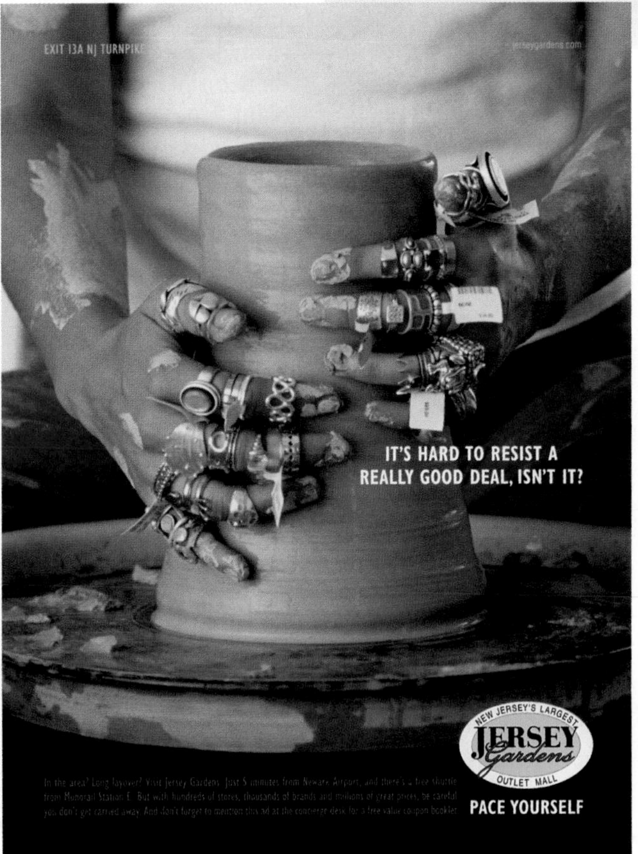

EXIT 13A NJ TURNPIKE
jerseygardens.com
IT'S HARD TO RESIST A REALLY GOOD DEAL, ISN'T IT?
NEW JERSEY'S LARGEST
JERSEY Gardens
OUTLET MALL
PACE YOURSELF

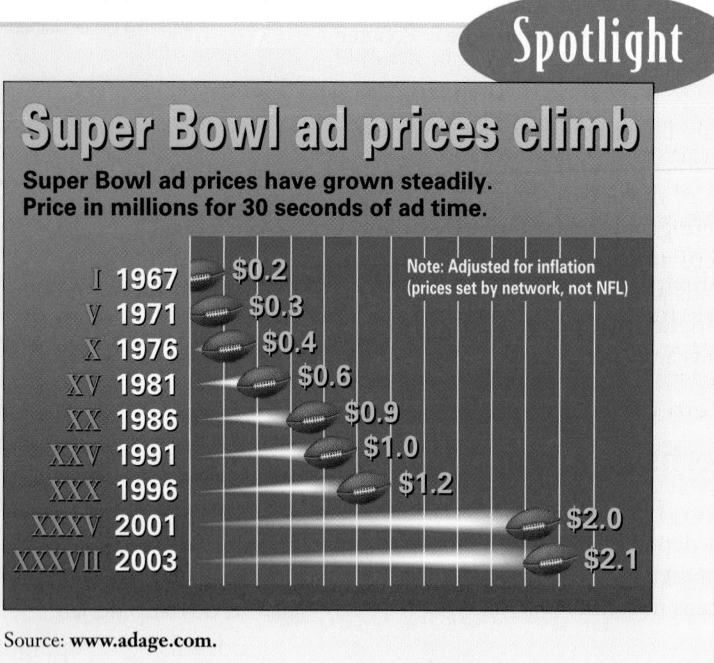

Source: **www.adage.com.**

money designated for advertising in a given period. This stage is critical to the success of the campaign because advertising efforts based on an inadequate budget will understimulate customer demand, and a budget too large will waste a company's resources. Advertising appropriations may be based on last year's (or next year's forecasted) sales, on what competitors spend on advertising, or on executive judgment.

5. Develop the Media Plan A media plan specifies exactly which media will be used in the campaign and when advertisements will appear. Although cost-effectiveness is not easy to measure, the primary concern of the media planner is to reach the largest possible number of persons in the target audience for each dollar spent. In addition to cost, media planners must consider the location and demographics of people in the advertising target, the content of the message, and the characteristics of the audiences reached by various media. The media planner begins with general media decisions, selects subclasses within each medium, and finally chooses particular media vehicles for the campaign.

6. Create the Advertising Message The content and form of a message are influenced by the product's features, the characteristics of people in the target audience, the objectives of the campaign, and the choice of media. An advertiser must consider these factors to choose words and illustrations that will be meaningful and appealing to persons in the advertising target. The copy, or words, of an advertisement will vary depending on the media choice but should attempt to move the audience through attention, interest, desire, and action. Artwork and visuals should complement copy by attracting the audience's attention and communicating an idea quickly. Coca-Cola recently followed the approach of PepsiCo by developing its advertising message around celebrities. Coke believes the new "Coca-Cola Real" slogan combined with stars such as Penelope Cruz, Lance Armstrong, and Courtney Cox-Arquette, will attract audiences' attention and bolster its declining sales.[9]

7. Execute the Campaign Execution of an advertising campaign requires extensive planning, scheduling, and coordinating because many tasks must be completed on time. The efforts of many people and firms are involved. Production companies, research organizations, media firms, printers, photoengravers, and commercial artists are just a few of the people and firms that may contribute to a campaign. Advertising managers must constantly assess the quality of the work and take corrective action when necessary. In some instances, advertisers make changes during the campaign to meet objectives more effectively.

8. Evaluate Advertising Effectiveness A campaign's success should be measured in terms of its original objectives before, during, and/or after the campaign. An advertiser should at least be able to estimate whether sales or market share went up because of the campaign or whether any change occurred in customer attitudes or brand awareness. Data from past and current sales, responses to coupon offers, and customer surveys administered by research organizations are some of the ways in which advertising effectiveness can be evaluated.

Advertising Agencies

Advertisers can plan and produce their own advertising with help from media personnel, or they can hire advertising agencies. An **advertising agency** is an independent firm that plans, produces, and places advertising for its clients. Many large ad agencies offer help with sales promotion and public relations as well. The media usually pay a commission of 15 percent to advertising agencies. Thus the cost to the agency's client can be quite moderate. The client may be asked to pay for selected services that the agency performs. Other methods for compensating agencies are also used.

advertising agency an independent firm that plans, produces, and places advertising for its clients

Firms that do a lot of advertising may use both an in-house advertising department and an independent agency. This approach gives the firm the advantage of being able to call on the agency's expertise in particular areas of advertising. An agency also can bring a fresh viewpoint to a firm's products and advertising plans.

Table 16.1 lists the nation's twenty leading advertisers in all media. In 2001, the number one spot went to General Motors.

Social and Legal Considerations in Advertising

Critics of U.S. advertising have two main complaints—that it is wasteful and that it can be deceptive. Although advertising (like any other activity) can be performed inefficiently, it is far from wasteful. Let's look at the evidence:

- Advertising is the most effective and least expensive means of communicating product information to a large number of individuals and organizations.

table 16.1 Advertising Expenditures and Sales Volume for the Top Twenty National Advertisers

Rank	Company	Advertising Expenditures (in millions)	Sales (in millions)	Advertising Expenditures as Percentage of Sales
1	General Motors Corp.	$3,374	$132,399	2.55
2	Procter & Gamble Co.	2,541	20,334	12.50
3	Ford Motor Co.	2,408	108,296	2.22
4	PepsiCo	2,210	18,215	12.13
5	Pfizer	2,189	19,932	10.98
6	DaimlerChrysler	1,985	72,708	2.73
7	AOL Time Warner	1,885	32,676	5.77
8	Philip Morris Cos.	1,816	52,098	3.49
9	Walt Disney Co.	1,757	20,970	8.38
10	Johnson & Johnson	1,618	20,204	8.00
11	Unilever	1,484	11,315	13.12
12	Sears Roebuck & Co.	1,480	36,753	4.02
13	Verizon Communications	1,462	64,649	2.26
14	Toyota Motor Corp.	1,399	46,529	3.00
15	A&T Corp.	1,372	52,550	2.61
16	Sony Corp.	1,310	21,127	6.20
17	Viacom	1,283	19,466	6.59
18	McDonald's Corp.	1,195	5,396	22.15
19	Diageo	1,181	9,231	12.79
20	Sprint Corp.	1,160	25,000	4.64

Source: Reprinted with permission from the June 24, 2002 issue of *Advertising Age*. Copyright © Crain Communications, Inc., 2002.

- Advertising encourages competition and is, in fact, a means of competition. It thus leads to the development of new and improved products, wider product choices, and lower prices.
- Advertising revenues support our mass communications media—newspapers, magazines, radio, and television. This means that advertising pays for much of our news coverage and entertainment programming.
- Advertising provides job opportunities in fields ranging from sales to film production.

Along with pure fact, advertising tends to include some exaggeration and occasiona deception. Consumers usually spot such distortion in short order. Also, various gov ernment and private agencies scrutinize advertising for false or misleading claims o offers. At the national level, the Federal Trade Commission (FTC), the Food an Drug Administration (FDA), and the Federal Communications Commission (FCC oversee advertising practices. The FDA recently conducted a survey of doctors abou the impact of direct-to-consumer advertising for prescription drugs and found that 9 percent could recall a patient initiating conversation about a drug they had seen ad vertised. A controversial type of advertising, direct-to-consumer prescription ad make patients more aware of potential treatments according to 72 percent of th physicians surveyed, and it also caused 47 percent of these doctors to feel pressure into prescribing a particular drug.[10] Advertising also may be monitored by state an local agencies, Better Business Bureaus, and industry associations. These organiza tions have varying degrees of control over advertising, but their overall effect has bee a positive one.

Personal Selling

Personal selling is the most adaptable of all promotional methods because the perso who is presenting the message can modify it to suit the individual buyer. Howeve personal selling is also the most expensive method of promotion.

Most successful salespeople are able to communicate with others on a one-to-on basis and are strongly motivated. They strive to have a thorough knowledge of th products they offer for sale. And they are willing and able to deal with the details in volved in handling and processing orders. Sales managers tend to emphasize thes qualities when recruiting and hiring.

Many selling situations demand the face-to-face contact and adaptability of per sonal selling. This is especially true of industrial sales, in which a single purchase ma amount to millions of dollars. Obviously, sales of that size must be based on carefull planned sales presentations, personal contact with customers, and thorough negotia tions.

learning objective

6 Recognize the various kinds of salespersons, the steps in the personal-selling process, and the major sales management tasks.

Kinds of Salespersons

Because most businesses employ different salespersons to perform different functions marketing managers must select the kinds of sales personnel that will be most effectiv in selling the firm's products. Salespersons may be identified as order getters, orde takers, and support personnel. A single individual can, and often does, perform a three functions.

order getter a salesperson who is responsible for selling a firm's products to new customers and increasing sales to present customers

creative selling selling products to new customers and increasing sales to present customers

Order Getters An **order getter** is responsible for what is sometimes called **creativ selling**: selling a firm's products to new customers and increasing sales to current cus tomers. An order getter must perceive buyers' needs, supply customers with informa tion about the firm's product, and persuade them to buy the product. Order-gettin activities may be separated into two groups. In current-customer sales, salespeopl concentrate on obtaining additional sales or leads for prospective sales from customer who have purchased the firm's products at least once. In new-business sales, sales per sonnel seek out new prospects and convince them to make an initial purchase of th

exploring business

What Companies Want in Sales Representatives

COMPANIES WANT SALES representatives with drive and positive attitudes, but what other characteristics do they look for? Knowing that salespeople must be able to make connections with prospects and customers, Enterprise Rent-A-Car looks for excellent communications skills when hiring college graduates for sales positions. The car-rental company also probes to find out whether applicants care about providing good service, which will keep customers loyal.

Flexibility is another key asset. Jennifer Tsonas, director of sales for New York's Sofitel Hotel, hires salespeople who are aggressive and capable of adapting to ever-changing conditions. She and her sales team must be ready to respond creatively when corporate customers make unexpected requests or when emergencies strike. For example, after terrorists attacked the World Trade Center, a telecommunications firm that had contracted to use the Sofitel wavered about bringing its employees to New York. Tsonas' sales team saved the deal by ripping up the contract, offering lower rates, and throwing in free office space for the firm's employees while they visited New York. Now the firm regularly holds meetings at the Sofitel, thanks to the sales staff's flexibility.

Steve Howe, who heads sales and marketing for a data storage firm, looks for salespeople flexible enough to handle both internal and external changes. Howe's company, Datalink, has kept pace with technological developments by completely overhauling its strategy three times in twelve years. As a result, he explains, "Our salespeople have had to reinvent themselves every time."

Also, Enterprise and many other companies seek out sales candidates with leadership potential. Why? Because they can count on these candidates to make decisions when necessary and rally to help colleagues solve customers' problems. In time, these representatives are likely to form the backbone of the company's sales management team—or move even higher in the hierarchy.

Hiring sales representatives who turn out to be irresponsible, insincere, or insensitive can be a costly mistake with potentially damaging consequences. In addition to paying for recruiting, training, and compensation, companies risk losing customers and weakening their competitive positions. This is why Enterprise, the Sofitel Hotel, Datalink, and so many other businesses take the time to identify candidates who have the characteristics needed for sales success.

irm's product. The real estate, insurance, appliance, heavy industrial machinery, and utomobile industries in particular depend on new-business sales.

Order Takers An **order taker** handles repeat sales in ways that maintain positive elationships with customers. An order taker sees that customers have products when nd where they are needed and in the proper amounts. *Inside order takers* receive incoming mail and telephone orders in some businesses; salespersons in retail stores are lso inside order takers. *Outside* (or *field*) *order takers* travel to customers. Often the uyer and the field salesperson develop a mutually beneficial relationship of placing, eceiving, and delivering orders. Both inside and outside order takers are active salesersons and often produce most of their companies' sales.

order taker a salesperson who handles repeat sales in ways that maintain positive relationships with customers

upport Personnel **Sales support personnel** aid in selling but are more involved n locating *prospects* (likely first-time customers), educating customers, building goodwill for the firm, and providing follow-up service. The most common categories of upport personnel are missionary, trade, and technical salespersons.

sales support personnel employees who aid in selling but are more involved in locating prospects, educating customers, building goodwill for the firm, and providing follow-up service

A **missionary salesperson,** who usually works for a manufacturer, visits retailers o persuade them to buy the manufacturer's products. If the retailers agree, they buy he products from wholesalers, who are the manufacturer's actual customers. Missionry salespersons often are employed by producers of medical supplies and pharmaceuicals to promote these products to retail druggists, physicians, and hospitals.

missionary salesperson a salesperson—generally employed by a manufacturer—who visits retailers to persuade them to buy the manufacturer's products

A **trade salesperson,** who generally works for a food producer or processor, assists customers in promoting products, especially in retail stores. A trade salesperson nay obtain additional shelf space for the products, restock shelves, set up displays, and istribute samples. Because trade salespersons are usually order takers as well, they are ot strictly support personnel.

trade salesperson a salesperson—generally employed by a food producer or processor—who assists customers in promoting products, especially in retail stores

technical salesperson a salesperson who assists a company's current customers in technical matters

A **technical salesperson** assists the company's current customers in technic matters. He or she may explain how to use a product, how it is made, how to install i or how a system is designed. A technical salesperson should be formally educated i science or engineering. Computers, steel, and chemicals are some of the produc handled by technical salespeople.

Marketers usually need sales personnel from several of these categories. Facto that affect hiring and other personnel decisions include the number of customers ar their characteristics; the product's attributes, complexity, and price; the distributic channels used by the company; and the company's approach to advertising.

figure 16.5

The Six Steps of the Personal-Selling Process

Personal selling is not only the most adaptable of all promotional methods but also the most expensive.

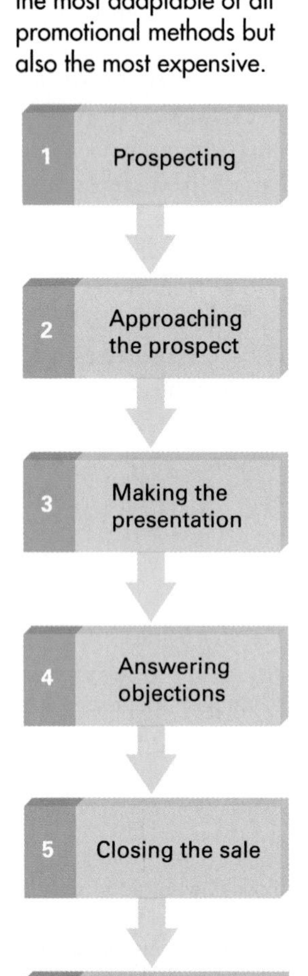

Source: William M. Pride and O. C. Ferrell, *Marketing: Concepts and Strategies*, 12th ed. Copyright © 2003 by Houghton Mifflin Company. Adapted with permission.

The Personal-Selling Process

No two selling situations are exactly alike, and no two salespeople perform their jol in exactly the same way. Most salespeople, however, follow the six-step procedure i lustrated in Figure 16.5.

Prospecting The first step in personal selling is to research potential buyers an choose the most likely customers, or prospects. Sources of prospects include busine associates and customers, public records, telephone and trade-association directorie and company files. The salesperson concentrates on those prospects who have the f nancial resources, willingness, and authority to buy the product.

Approaching the Prospect First impressions are often lasting impressions. Th the salesperson's first contact with the prospect is crucial to successful selling. Th best approach is one based on knowledge of the product, of the prospect's needs, ar of how the product can meet those needs. Salespeople who understand each cu tomer's particular situation are likely to make a good first impression—and to make sale.

Making the Presentation The next step is the actual delivery of the sales present tion. In many cases this includes demonstrating the product. The salesperson poin out the product's features, its benefits, and how it is superior to competitors' me chandise. If the product has been used successfully by other firms, the salesperson ma mention this as part of the presentation.

During a demonstration, the salesperson may suggest that the prospect try out th product personally. The demonstration and product trial should underscore specif points made during the presentation.

Answering Objections The prospect is likely to raise objections or ask questio at any time. This gives the salesperson a chance to eliminate objections that migl prevent a sale, to point out additional features, or to mention special services the con pany offers.

Closing the Sale To close the sale, the salesperson asks the prospect to buy th product. This is considered the critical point in the selling process. Many experience salespeople make use of a *trial closing*, in which they ask questions based on the a sumption that the customer is going to buy the product. The questions "When woul you want delivery?" and "Do you want the standard model or the one with the speci options package?" are typical of trial closings. They allow the reluctant prospect make a purchase without having to say, "I'll take it."

Following Up The salesperson must follow up after the sale to ensure that the pro uct is delivered on time, in the right quantity, and in proper operating condition. Durin follow-up, the salesperson also makes it clear that he or she is available in case problen develop. Follow-up leaves a good impression and eases the way toward future sale Hence it is essential to the selling process. The salesperson's job does not end with a sal It continues as long as the seller and the customer maintain a working relationship.

Managing Personal Selling

A firm's success often hinges on the competent management of its sales force. Although some companies operate efficiently without a sales force, most firms rely on a strong sales force—and the sales revenue it brings in—for their success.

Sales managers have responsibilities in a number of areas. They must set sales objectives in concrete, quantifiable terms and specifying a certain period of time and a certain geographic area. They must adjust the size of the sales force to meet changes in the firm's marketing plan and the marketing environment. Some sales forces such as those of The Hartford, Conseco, American General, and Citigroup exceed 100,000 people.[11] Sales managers must attract and hire effective salespersons. They must develop a training program and decide where, when, how, and for whom to conduct the training. They must formulate a fair and adequate compensation plan to keep qualified employees. They must motivate salespersons to boost their productivity.

Spotlight

Does your sales force need monitoring?

A recent survey of sales executives revealed these primary reasons they would use surveillance, such as video or electronic monitoring, to keep tabs on their salespeople:

To ensure productivity	26.5%
To ensure quality interaction with clients	30.7%
To ensure no criminal or illegal activity is occuring	20.4%
Other	5.9%
I would never monitor salespeople's activities	44.2%

Source: *Sales and Marketing Management*, February 2002, p. 34.

examining ethics

Is It Ethical to Buy Business From Your Customers?

WHEN DOES A GIFT become a bribe to buy a customer's business? Sales representatives and sales managers want to build goodwill, educate customers, and ensure that customers buy or recommend their products. Therefore, many give small gifts such as pens and pencils to keep their brand names in front of customers. However, giving more expensive gifts may be construed as crossing the line into bribery. Still, more than 23 percent of the sales managers and representatives responding to a survey by *Sales and Marketing Management* had felt pressured to give a gift worth more than $100 in exchange for a customer's business. Moreover, 88 percent of them said that they actually had given such gifts.

The line between gift and bribe is becoming clearer in the pharmaceuticals industry, where new drugs cost millions of dollars to develop. Companies want sales personnel to stimulate prescriptions by discussing the drugs with doctors. Traditionally, many representatives gave doctors concert tickets, golf bags with logos, steak dinners, and even cash, in addition to free drug samples. At one point drug companies were spending a total of $8 billion annually on all kinds of doctors' perks.

All this gift giving attracted the attention of industry leaders and government officials. To clarify which gifts are appropriate and when, the Pharmaceutical Research and Manufacturers of America recently adopted a voluntary ethics code. Representatives can buy meals for doctors in educational settings, but they cannot give golf bags with logos, tickets, cash, or other lavish gifts in exchange for an agreement to prescribe medications.

On the government side, Vermont now requires pharmaceutical firms to report gifts valued at $25 or more. Also, the U.S. Office of the Inspector General has announced that pharmaceutical firms may face legal action for giving lavish gifts, for paying doctors to switch patients to their drugs, or for paying doctors to participate in marketing efforts.

Experts emphasize that buying business is ineffective in the long run. "It really diminishes what you're doing," says one sales consultant. "Even people accepting such perks will start to figure that your service or pricing must not be very good if you have to resort to such things."

Issues to Consider

1. What guidelines would you recommend to prevent your company's sales personnel from buying business?
2. What guidelines would you recommend to prevent your company's buying personnel from accepting lavish gifts?

They must define sales territories and determine scheduling and routing of the sales force. Finally, sales managers must evaluate the operation as a whole through sales reports, communications with customers, and invoices.

Sales Promotion

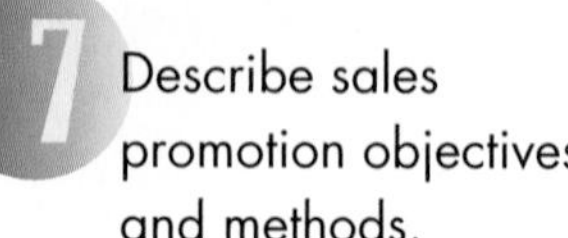

learning objective

7 Describe sales promotion objectives and methods.

Sales promotion consists of activities or materials that are direct inducements to customers or salespersons. Are you a member of an airline frequent-flyer program? Did you recently receive a free sample in the mail or at a supermarket? Did you or someone that you know get a Beanie Baby at McDonald's? Have you recently received a rebate from a manufacturer? Do you use coupons? All these are examples of sales promotion efforts. Sales promotion techniques often are used to enhance and supplement other promotional methods. They can have a significant impact on sales.

The dramatic increase in spending for sales promotion shows that marketers have recognized the potential of this promotional method. Many firms now include numerous sales promotion efforts as part of their overall promotion mix.

Sales Promotion Objectives

Sales promotion activities may be used singly or in combination, both offensively and defensively, to achieve one goal or a set of goals. Marketers use sales promotion activities and materials for a number of purposes, including

1. To attract new customers
2. To encourage trial of a new product
3. To invigorate the sales of a mature brand
4. To boost sales to current customers
5. To reinforce advertising
6. To increase traffic in retail stores
7. To steady irregular sales patterns
8. To build up reseller inventories
9. To neutralize competitive promotional efforts
10. To improve shelf space and displays[12]

Any sales promotion objectives should be consistent with the organization's general goals and with its marketing and promotional objectives.

Sales Promotion Methods

consumer sales promotion method a sales promotion method designed to attract consumers to particular retail stores and to motivate them to purchase certain new or established products

trade sales promotion method a sales promotion method designed to encourage wholesalers and retailers to stock and actively promote a manufacturer's product

Most sales promotion methods can be classified as promotional techniques for either consumer sales or trade sales. A **consumer sales promotion method** attracts consumers to particular retail stores and motivates them to purchase certain new or established products. A **trade sales promotion method** encourages wholesalers and retailers to stock and actively promote a manufacturer's product. Incentives such as money, merchandise, marketing assistance, and gifts are commonly awarded to resellers who buy products or respond positively in other ways. Of the combined dollars spent on sales promotion and advertising last year, about one-half was spent on trade promotions, one-fourth on consumer promotions, and one-fourth on advertising.

A number of factors enter into marketing decisions about which and how many sales promotion methods to use. Of greatest importance are the objectives of the promotional effort. Product characteristics—size, weight, cost, durability, uses, features, and hazards—and target market profiles—age, gender, income, location, density, usage rate, and buying patterns—likewise must be considered. Distribution channels and availability of appropriate resellers also influence the choice of sales promotion methods, as do the competitive and regulatory forces in the environment. Let's now discuss a few important sales promotion methods.

Rebates A **rebate** is a return of part of the purchase price of a product. Usually the refund is offered by the producer to consumers who send in a coupon along with a specific proof of purchase. Rebating is a relatively low-cost promotional method. Once used mainly to help launch new product items, it is now applied to a wide variety of products. Many automobile companies offer rebates on their vehicles. Ford has found that Explorers sell better, for example, at $36,000 with a $1,500 rebate than they do at a straight price of $34,500. General Motors has even started offering rebates on its Saturn vehicles, which are famed for their fixed, no haggle prices.[13] One problem with rebates is that many people perceive the redemption process as too complicated. Only about half of individuals who purchase rebated products actually apply for the rebates.[14]

rebate a return of part of the purchase price of a product

Coupons A **coupon** reduces the retail price of a particular item by a stated amount at the time of purchase. Coupons may be worth anywhere from a few cents to a few dollars. They are made available to customers through newspapers, magazines, direct mail, online, and shelf dispensers in stores. Some coupons are precisely targeted at customers. For Example, Nubella, a service created by Matthew Combs, works with grocery store scanners and grocery club cards to target coupons at selected consumers. Nubella compares what consumers buy with the U.S. Department of Agriculture's Recommended Daily Allowances (RDAs). It then detects nutritional deficiencies and mails coupons for foods containing the vitamins and minerals necessary to fill each consumer's nutritional gap.[15] Billions of coupons are distributed annually. Of these, just under 2 percent are redeemed by consumers. About 58 percent of consumers use at least one coupon per month. The largest number of coupons distributed are for household cleaners, condiments, frozen foods, medications and health aids, and paper products. Stores in some areas even deduct double or triple the value of manufacturers' coupons from the purchase price as a sales promotion technique of their own. Coupons also may offer free merchandise, either with or without an additional purchase of the product.

coupon reduces the retail price of a particular item by a stated amount at the time of purchase

Samples A **sample** is a free product given to customers to encourage trial. Samples may be offered via online coupons, direct mail, or in stores. It is the most expensive sales promotion technique, and while it is often used to promote new products, it can

sample a free product given to customers to encourage trial

Sampling the product. The maker of Snapple juices and teas attempts to induce product trial by providing free samples to consumers.

be used to promote established brands, too. Cosmetics companies often use samples to lure customers. Revlon teamed with Paramount Pictures in the movie *How to Lose a Guy in 10 Days*, starring Kate Hudson and Matthew McConaughey. Kate Hudson's character gives a goody bag of Revlon samples to a friend who recently suffered from a bad breakup, and in conjunction with the movie promotion, Revlon distributed samples of its cosmetics.[16]

Distribution of free samples through websites such as StartSampling.com and FreeSamples.com is growing. Consumers choose the free samples they would like to receive and request delivery. The online company manages the packaging and distribution of the samples. NSI, manufacturer of coffee flavorings called Flavour Creations, used a StartSampling online sample program to promote its products and expand their distribution. The owner of NSI was very impressed with consumer response to the StartSampling campaign. He said, "We have never had a response like this. People liked our product, and they called us and asked where they could buy it."[17]

premium a gift that a producer offers the customer in return for buying its product

Premiums A **premium** is a gift that a producer offers the customer in return for buying its product. A producer of packaged foods may, for instance, offer consumers a cookbook as a premium. Premiums can be attached to or enclosed inside packages. Examples would include a free car wash with a fill-up and a free toothbrush with a tube of toothpaste.

frequent-user incentive a program developed to reward customers who engage in repeat (frequent) purchases

Frequent-User Incentives A **frequent-user incentive** is a program developed to reward customers who engage in repeat (frequent) purchases. Such programs are used commonly by service businesses such as hotels and auto rental agencies. Frequent-user incentives build customer loyalty. Examples of successful frequent-user incentives include airline frequent-flyer programs and Subway's Sub Club Cards. Subway gives customers card stamps with each purchase and free sandwiches when they turn in cards with the requisite number of stamps. There are several online organizations such as Netcentives, MyPoints, and RealTime Media that provide businesses with customer-loyalty incentive programs. Customers of businesses that use these programs are rewarded in several ways, including cash, points for prizes, and airline miles.[18]

point-of-purchase display promotional material placed within a retail store

trade show an industry-wide exhibit at which many sellers display their products

Point-of-Purchase Displays A **point-of-purchase display** is promotional material placed within a retail store. The display is usually located near the product being promoted. It actually may hold merchandise (as do L'eggs hosiery displays) or inform customers about what the product offers and encourage them to buy it. Most point-of-purchase displays are prepared and set up by manufacturers and wholesalers.

Trade Shows A **trade show** is an industry-wide exhibit at which many sellers display their products. Some trade shows are organized exclusively

Auto show. The Detroit Auto Show is an example of a trade show. Some trade shows are open only to dealers whereas others are open to the general public. Here, Robert Lutz, GM Vice Chairman of Product Development presents a new concept car at the auto show.

for dealers—to permit manufacturers and wholesalers to show their latest lines to retailers. Others are promotions designed to stimulate consumer awareness and interest. Among the latter are boat shows, home shows, and flower shows put on each year in large cities. About 14 percent of total promotional dollars is spent on trade shows.[19]

Buying Allowances A **buying allowance** is a temporary price reduction to resellers for purchasing specified quantities of a product. For example, a laundry detergent manufacturer might give retailers $1 for each case of detergent purchased. A buying allowance may serve as an incentive to resellers to handle new products and may stimulate purchase of items in large quantities. While the buying allowance is simple, straightforward, and easily administered, competitors can respond quickly by offering a better buying allowance.

buying allowance a temporary price reduction to resellers for purchasing specified quantities of a product

Cooperative Advertising **Cooperative advertising** is an arrangement whereby a manufacturer agrees to pay a certain amount of the retailer's media cost for advertising the manufacturer's products. To be reimbursed, a retailer must show proof that the advertisements actually did appear. A large percentage of all cooperative advertising dollars are spent on newspaper advertisements. Not all retailers take advantage of available cooperative advertising offers because they cannot afford to advertise or do not choose to do so.

cooperative advertising an arrangement whereby a manufacturer agrees to pay a certain amount of the retailer's media cost for advertising the manufacturer's product

Public Relations

As noted earlier, public relations is a broad set of communication activities used to create and maintain favorable relationships between an organization and various public groups, both internal and external. These groups can include customers, employees, stockholders, suppliers, educators, the media, government officials, and society in general.

learning objective

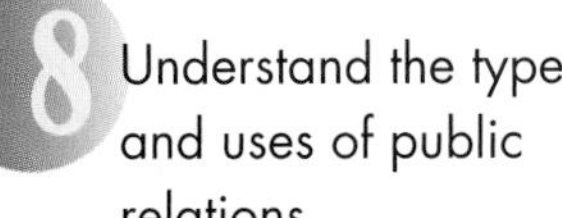

8 Understand the types and uses of public relations.

Types of Public Relations Tools

Organizations use a variety of public relations tools to convey messages and to create images. Public relations professionals prepare written materials such as brochures, newsletters, company magazines, annual reports, and news releases. They also create corporate-identity materials such as logos, business cards, signs, and stationery. Speeches are another public relations tool. Speeches can affect an organization's image and must therefore convey the desired message clearly.

Another public relations tool is event sponsorship, in which a company pays for all or part of a special event such as a concert, sports competition, festival, or play. Sponsoring special events is an effective way for organizations to increase brand recognition and receive media coverage with comparatively little investment. Eastman Kodak's sponsorship of the Olympic games and Evian's sponsorship of a convention for gourmet food lovers are examples of event sponsorship, as is Ben and Jerry's sponsorship of the "Pint for Pint" program that helped the American Red Cross boost blood donations. Ben and Jerry's sent its Scoop Truck to twenty-six college campuses and offered a free pint of ice cream to blood donors.[20]

Some public relations tools traditionally have been associated specifically with publicity, which is a part of public relations. **Publicity** is communication in news-story form about an organization, its products, or both. Publicity is transmitted through a mass medium, such as newspapers or radio, at no charge. Organizations use publicity to provide information about products; to announce new product launches, expansions, or research; and to strengthen the company's image. Public relations personnel sometimes organize events, such as grand openings with prizes and celebrities, to create news stories about the company.

publicity communication in news-story form about an organization, its products, or both

table 16.2 Possible Issues for News Releases

Use of new information technology	Packaging changes
Support of a social cause	New products
Improved warranties	Creation of new software
Reports on industry conditions	Research developments
New uses for established products	Company's history and development
Product endorsements	Launching of new website
Winning of quality awards	Award of contracts
Company name changes	Opening of new markets
Interviews with company officials	Improvements in financial position
Improved distribution policies	Opening of an exhibit
Global business initiatives	History of a brand
Sponsorship of athletic events	Winners of company contests
Visits by celebrities	Logo changes
Reports of new discoveries	Speeches of top management
Innovative marketing activities	Merit awards to the organization
Economic forecasts	Anniversaries of inventions

news release a typed page of about 300 words provided by an organization to the media as a form of publicity

feature article a piece (of up to 3,000 words) prepared by an organization for inclusion in a particular publication

captioned photograph a picture accompanied by a brief explanation

press conference a meeting at which invited media personnel hear important news announcements and receive supplementary textual materials and photographs

The most widely used type of publicity is the **news release.** It is generally one typed page of about 300 words provided by an organization to the media. The release includes the firm's name, address, phone number, and contact person. Table 16.2 lists some of the issues news releases can address. There are also several other kinds of publicity-based public relations tools. A **feature article,** which may run as long as 3,000 words, is usually written for inclusion in a particular publication. For example, a software firm might send an article about its new product to a computer magazine. A **captioned photograph,** a picture accompanied by a brief explanation, is an effective way to illustrate a new or improved product. A **press conference** allows invited media personnel to hear important news announcements and to receive supplementary textual materials and photographs. Finally, letters to the editor, special newspaper or magazine editorials, films, and tapes may be prepared and distributed to appropriate media for possible use.

At times, a single public relations tool will be adequate for a promotion mix. At other times, multiple public relations tools will be used in a mix. The specific types of public relations tools chosen depend on the composition of the target audience, the response of media personnel, the significance of the news item, and the nature and quantity of information to be communicated.

The Uses of Public Relations

Public relations can be used to promote people, places, activities, ideas, and even countries. Public relations focuses on enhancing the reputation of the total organization by making people aware of a company's products, brands, or activities and by creating specific company images such as innovativeness or dependability. For example, ice-cream maker Ben and Jerry's uses news stories and other public relations efforts to reinforce its reputation as a socially responsible company. By getting the media to report on a firm's accomplishments, public relations helps a company maintain positive public visibility. Effective management of public relations efforts also can reduce the unfavorable effects of negative events.

Promotion Planning

A **promotional campaign** is a plan for combining and using the four promotional methods—advertising, personal selling, sales promotion, and public relations—in a particular promotion mix to achieve one or more marketing goals. When selecting promotional methods to include in promotion mixes, it is important to coordinate promotional elements to maximize total informational and promotional impact on customers. Integrated marketing communication requires a marketer to look at the broad perspective when planning promotional programs and coordinating the total set of communication functions.

learning objective

9 Identify the factors that influence the selection of promotion mix ingredients.

In planning a promotional campaign, marketers must answer these two questions:

- What will be the role of promotion in the overall marketing mix?
- To what extent will each promotional method be used in the promotion mix?

promotional campaign a plan for combining and using the four promotional methods—advertising, personal selling, sales promotion, and publicity—in a particular promotion mix to achieve one or more marketing goals

The answer to the first question depends on the firm's marketing objectives, since the role of each element of the marketing mix—product, price, distribution, and promotion—depends on these detailed versions of the firm's marketing goals. The answer to the second question depends on the answer to the first, as well as on the target market.

Promotion and Marketing Objectives

Promotion is naturally better suited to certain marketing objectives than to others. For example, promotion can do little to further a marketing objective such as "reduce delivery time by one-third." It can, however, be used to inform customers that delivery is faster. Let's consider some objectives that *would* require the use of promotion as a primary ingredient of the marketing mix.

Providing Information This is, of course, the main function of promotion. It may be used to communicate to target markets the availability of new products or product features. It may alert them to special offers or give the locations of retailers that carry the firm's products. In other words, promotion can be used to enhance the effectiveness of each of the other ingredients of the marketing mix. For example, as H&R Block continues to expand beyond tax preparation services, it attempts to inform potential customers of its additional offerings. H&R Block also offers mortgages, investment advising, and other financial services and has nearly doubled it advertising budget in order to communicate the availability of all its services.[21]

Increasing Market Share Promotion can be used to convince new customers to try a product while maintaining the product loyalty of established customers. Comparative advertising, for example, is directed mainly at those who might—but presently do not—use a particular product. Advertising that emphasizes the product's features also assures those who *do* use the product that they have made a smart choice.

Positioning the Product The sales of a product depend, to a great extent, on its competition. The stronger the competition, the more difficult it is to maintain or increase sales. For this reason, many firms go to great lengths to position their products in the marketplace. **Positioning** is the development of a product image in buyers' minds relative to the images they have of competing products.

positioning the development of a product image in buyers' minds relative to the images they have of competing products

Promotion is the prime positioning tool. A marketer can use promotion to position a brand away from competitors to avoid competition. For example, Hardee's, the nation's sixth largest hamburger chain, is seeking to position itself as the place to go for big beef. Its new approach includes dropping about forty items from its menu and offering more Thickburgers ranging from one-third to two-thirds pound of beef per burger. This positioning is designed to avoid the value menu wars of McDonald's and Burger King. The new positioning was launched with a promotional campaign that actually pokes fun at Hardee's.[22] Promotion also may be used to position one product directly against another product. For example, Coca-Cola and Pepsi position their products to compete head-to-head against each other.

Stabilizing Sales Special promotional efforts can be used to increase sales during slack periods, such as the "off season" for certain sports equipment. By stabilizing sales in this way, a firm can use its production facilities more effectively and reduce both capital costs and inventory costs. Promotion is also often used to increase the sales of products that are in the declining stage of their life cycle. The objective is to keep them going for a little while longer.

Developing the Promotion Mix

Once the role of promotion is established, the various methods of promotion may be combined in a promotional campaign. As in so many other areas of business, promotion planning begins with a set of specific objectives. The promotion mix is then designed to accomplish these objectives.

Marketers often use several promotion mixes simultaneously if a firm sells multiple products. The selection of promotion mix ingredients and the degree to which they are used depend on the organization's resources and objectives, the nature of the target market, the characteristics of the product, and the feasibility of various promotional methods.

The amount of promotional resources available in an organization influences the number and intensity of promotional methods that marketers can use. A firm with a limited budget for promotion probably will rely on personal selling because the effectiveness of personal selling can be measured more easily than that of advertising. An organization's objectives also have an effect on its promotional activities. A company wishing to make a wide audience familiar with a new convenience item probably will depend heavily on advertising and sales promotion. If a company's objective is to communicate information to consumers—on the features of countertop appliances, for example—then the company may develop a promotion mix that includes some advertising, some sales promotion to attract consumers to stores, and much personal selling.

The size, geographic distribution, and socioeconomic characteristics of the target market play a part in the composition of a product's promotion mix. If the market is small, personal selling probably will be the most important element in the promotion mix. This is true of organizations that sell to small industrial markets and businesses that use only a few wholesalers to market their products. Companies that need to contact millions of potential customers, however, will emphasize sales promotion and advertising because these methods are relatively inexpensive. The age, income, and education of the target market also will influence the choice of promotion techniques. For example, with less-educated consumers, personal selling may be more effective than ads in newspapers or magazines.

In general, industrial products require a considerable amount of personal selling, whereas consumer goods depend on advertising. This is not true in every case, however. The price of the product also influences the composition of the promotion mix. Because consumers often want the advice of a salesperson on an expensive product, high-priced consumer goods may call for more personal selling. Similarly, advertising and sales promotion may be more crucial to marketers of seasonal items because having a year-round sales force is not always appropriate.

The cost and availability of promotional methods are important factors in the development of a promotion mix. Although national advertising and sales promotion activities are expensive, the cost per customer may be quite small if the campaign succeeds in reaching large numbers of people. In addition, local advertising outlets—newspapers, magazines, radio and television stations, and outdoor displays—may not be that costly for a small local business. In some situations, a firm may find that no available advertising medium reaches the target market effectively.

This chapter concludes our discussion of marketing. In the next chapter we begin our examination of information for business by discussing management information and computers.

Return To inside business

AutoTrader.com relies on an exciting promotion mix to build brand recognition and attract car buyers and sellers to its website. Continuing its strategy of targeting men, the company buys time to air its commercials during certain televised sporting events. For example, its racing-themed commercials appear during televised NASCAR events. The company also draws extra audience attention by sponsoring a special feature during televised races, known as the "AutoTrader.com Move of the Race."

These commercials and sponsorships coordinate with other promotional efforts. For example, the company's U.K. site recently used a racing game to expand awareness of the site's latest services. The site e-mailed the game to 700,000 customers who had registered to receive communications. In turn, the customers were invited to forward the game to their friends, spreading the word about AutoTrader to an even wider audience. Not only are such games cost-effective, they also encourage customers to become actively involved with the brand—setting the stage for future car purchases or sales through AutoTrader.

Questions

1. Now that customers are more familiar with online car shopping, should AutoTrader use selective-demand advertising or institutional advertising? Explain your answer.
2. How might AutoTrader measure the effectiveness of its e-mail campaigns? Of its television commercials?

chapter review

Summary

Describe integrated marketing communications.

Integrated marketing communications is the coordination of promotion efforts to achieve maximum informational and persuasive impact on customers.

Understand the role of promotion.

Promotion is communication about an organization and its products that is intended to inform, persuade, or remind target market members. The major ingredients of a promotion mix are advertising, personal selling, sales promotion, and public relations. The role of promotion is to facilitate exchanges directly or indirectly and to help an organization maintain favorable relationships with groups in the marketing environment.

Explain the purposes of the three types of advertising.

Advertising is a paid nonpersonal message communicated to a specific audience through a mass medium. Primary-demand advertising promotes the products of an entire industry rather than just a single brand. Selective-demand advertising promotes a particular brand of product. Institutional advertising is image-building advertising for a firm.

Describe the advantages and disadvantages of the major advertising media.

The major advertising media are newspapers, magazines, direct mail, outdoor displays, television, radio, and the Internet. Television accounts for the largest share of advertising expenditures, with newspapers running a close second. Newspapers are relatively inexpensive compared with other media, reach only people in the market area, and are timely. Disadvantages include a short life span, poor color reproduction, and an inability to target specific demographic groups. Magazine advertising can be quite prestigious. In addition, it can reach very specific market segments, can provide high-quality color reproduction, and has a relatively long life span. Major disadvantages are high cost and lack of timeliness. Direct mail is the most selective medium, and its effectiveness is measured easily. The disadvantage of direct mail is that if the mailing list is outdated and the advertisement does not reach the right people, then the campaign cannot be successful. An advantage of yellow pages advertising is that customers use it to save time in finding products, to find information quickly, and to learn about products and marketers. Unlike other types of advertising media, yellow-pages advertisements are purchased for one year and cannot be changed. Out-of-home advertising allows marketers to focus on a particular geographic area and is relatively inexpensive. Messages, though, must be limited to a few words because the audience is usually moving. Television offers marketers the opportunity to broadcast a firm's message nationwide. However, television advertising can be very expensive and has a short life span, and the advent of cable channels and home videos has reduced the likelihood of reaching extremely large audiences. Radio advertising offers selectivity, can be less expensive than other media, and is flexible for scheduling purposes. Radio's limitations include no visual presentation and fragmented, small audiences. Benefits of using the Internet as an advertising medium include the growing number of people using the Internet, which means a growing audience, and the ability to precisely target specific customers. Disadvantages include the relatively simplistic nature of the ads that can be produced, especially in comparison with television, and the lack of evidence that net browsers actually pay attention to the ads.

Identify the major steps in developing an advertising campaign.

An advertising campaign is developed in several stages. A firm's first task is to identify and analyze its advertising target. The goals of the campaign also must be clearly defined. Then the firm must develop the advertising platform, or statement of important selling points, and determine the size of the advertising budget. The next steps are to develop a media plan, to create the advertising message, and to execute the campaign. Finally, promotion managers must evaluate the effectiveness of the advertising efforts before, during, and/or after the campaign.

Recognize the various kinds of salespersons, the steps in the personal-selling process, and the major sales management tasks.

Personal selling is personal communication aimed at informing customers and persuading them to buy a firm's products. It is the most adaptable promotional method because the salesperson can modify the message to fit each buyer. Three major kinds of salepersons are order getters, order takers, and support personnel. The six steps in the personal-selling process are prospecting, approaching the prospect, making the presentation, answering objections, closing the sale, and following up. Sales managers are involved directly in setting sales force objectives; recruiting, selecting, and training salespersons; compensating and motivating sales personnel; creating sales territories; and evaluating sales performance.

Describe sales promotion objectives and methods.

Sales promotion is the use of activities and materials as direct inducements to customers and salespersons. The primary objective of sales promotion methods is to enhance and supplement other promotional methods. Methods of sales promotion include rebates, coupons, samples, premiums, frequent-user incentives, point-of-purchase displays, trade shows, buying allowances, and cooperative advertising.

Understand the types and uses of public relations.

Public relations is a broad set of communication activities used to create and maintain favorable relationships between an organization and various public groups, both internal and external. Organizations use a variety of public relations tools to convey messages and create images. Brochures, newsletters, company magazines, and annual reports are written public relations tools. Speeches, event sponsorship, and publicity are other public relations tools. Publicity is communication in news-story form about an organization, its products, or both. Types of publicity include news releases, feature articles, captioned photographs, and press conferences. Public relations can be used to promote people, places, activities, ideas, and even countries. It can be used to enhance the reputation of an organization and also to reduce the unfavorable effects of negative events.

Identify the factors that influence the selection of promotion mix ingredients.

A promotional campaign is a plan for combining and using advertising, personal selling, sales promotion, and publicity to achieve one or more marketing goals. Campaign objectives are developed from marketing objectives. Then the promotion mix is developed based on the organization's promotional resources and objectives, the nature of the target market, the product characteristics, and the feasibility of various promotional methods.

Key Terms

You should now be able to define and give an example relevant to each of the following terms:

promotion (467)
promotion mix (467)
integrated marketing communications (467)
advertising (469)
personal selling (469)
sales promotion (469)
public relations (469)
primary-demand advertising (469)
selective-demand (or brand) advertising (470)
institutional advertising (471)
advertising media (471)
direct-mail advertising (472)
yellow pages advertising (472)
out-of-home advertising (472)
infomercial (473)
advertising agency (477)
order getter (478)
creative selling (478)
order taker (479)
sales support personnel (479)
missionary salesperson (479)
trade salesperson (479)
technical salesperson (480)
consumer sales promotion method (482)

trade sales promotion method (482)
rebate (483)
coupon (483)
sample (483)
premium (484)
frequent-user incentive (484)
point-of-purchase display (484)
trade show (484)
buying allowance (485)
cooperative advertising (485)
publicity (485)
news release (486)
feature article (486)
captioned photograph (486)
press conference (486)
promotional campaign (487)
positioning (487)

Review Questions

1. What is integrated marketing communications, and why is it becoming increasingly accepted?
2. Identify and describe the major ingredients of a promotion mix.
3. What is the major role of promotion?
4. How are selective, institutional, and primary-demand advertising different from one another? Give an example of each.
5. List the four major print media, and give an advantage and a disadvantage of each.
6. What types of firms use each of the two electronic media?
7. Outline the main steps involved in developing an advertising campaign.
8. Why would a firm with its own advertising department use an ad agency?
9. Identify and give examples of the three major types of salespersons.
10. Explain how each step in the personal-selling process leads to the next step.
11. What are the major tasks involved in managing a sales force?
12. What are the major differences between consumer and trade sales promotion methods? Give examples of each.
13. What is cooperative advertising? What sorts of firms use it?
14. What is the difference between publicity and public relations? What is the purpose of each?
15. Why is promotion particularly effective in positioning a product? In stabilizing or increasing sales?
16. What factors determine the specific promotion mix that a firm should use?

Discussion Questions

1. Discuss the pros and cons of comparative advertising from the viewpoint of (a) the advertiser, (b) the advertiser's competitors, and (c) the target market.
2. Which kinds of advertising—in which media—influence you most? Why?
3. Which kinds of retail outlets or products require mainly order taking by salespeople?
4. A number of companies have shifted a portion of their promotion dollars from advertising to trade sales promotion methods? Why?
5. Why would a producer offer refunds or cents-off coupons rather than simply lowering the price of its products?
6. How can public relations efforts aimed at the general public help an organization?
7. Why do firms use event sponsorship?
8. What kind of promotion mix might be used to extend the life of a product that has entered the declining stage of its product life cycle?

video case

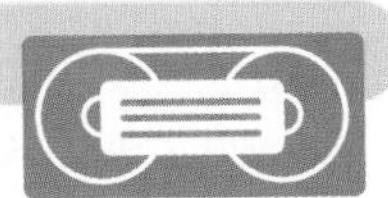

Fun, Furniture, Movies, and More at Jordan's Furniture

Brothers and co-presidents Barry and Eliot Tatelman run a unique retail chain. In fact, every one of their Jordan's Furniture stores is unique. The original store in downtown Waltham, Massachusetts, is as traditional as the sleek store in Nashua, New Hampshire, is contemporary. The store in Natick, Massachusetts, evokes the festive spirit of Bourbon Street in New Orleans, complete with steamboat. One section of the store holds a 262-seat IMAX 3D theater, popcorn and all. Anyone who has ever yearned to fly can experience a flight-simulation movie inside the store in Avon, Massachusetts. And by the way, every one of the four (soon to be five) stores also features a huge inventory of furniture.

The company's history stretches back to 1918, when Samuel Tatelman opened a small furniture store in Waltham. During the 1970s, his grandsons Barry and Eliot jointly assumed responsibility for running the store, which had eight employees. They made several decisions that dramatically altered the future course of the business. First, instead of trying to market to everyone, they narrowed their focus to a target market of 18- to 34-year-olds. This was an attractive market because people need furniture when they settle down and start families.

Second, the Tatelmans resolved to make the business fun for themselves, their customers, and their employees by injecting humor into the company's marketing efforts. Whereas many furniture stores were trumpeting promotional prices for selected items, Jordan's Furniture's ads would make customers smile—and remember the brand—rather than pushing price or trying to sell something specific. Yet the brothers also realized that this approach could backfire by making the brand seem tacky if they pushed the fun too far. Third, they decided to emphasize radio and television advertising because these media were popular with the target market and allowed the ads to reach a large regional audience quickly and efficiently.

Over the years, Jordan's Furniture has aired clever ads gently spoofing many aspects of popular culture. One television commercial mimicked a well-known commercial from The Gap featuring swing music and khaki-clad dancers. In another, the co-presidents painted their faces red in a wacky takeoff on the long-running Blue Man Group show in Boston (in which bald, blue-painted men play percussion). The two also have poked fun at baseball and the Boston Red Sox in a number of commercials.

Furniture stores typically budget up to 10 percent of their annual revenue for advertising. Although Jordan's Furniture budgets only about 1 percent of its revenue for advertising, it is able to saturate New England with commercials on fourteen radio stations and nine television stations. Week in and week out, the chain always has a campaign running to keep the brand in the public eye. It also invites customers to look at furniture on its website (**www.jordansfurniture.com**).

In addition to advertising, the Tatelman brothers use public relations and sales promotion to attract customers to their stores. For example, they gained enormous media coverage when they spent more than $4 million to open the IMAX theater inside their Natick store. Donating furniture to charities, sponsoring hunger walks, and giving gifts to Head Start children also have garnered positive media attention. Each store has its own twist on sales promotion to draw shoppers, from live music and multimedia special-effects shows to free balloons, cookies, and hotdogs.

Ordinarily, customers shop for furniture only to fill a particular need. The Tatelmans are out to change that behavior by making Jordan's Furniture an entertaining destination for the entire family. When their children ask to visit the in-store IMAX theater, for instance, the parents may spot an entertainment unit or a chair they want to buy. "People come in here for fun," observes Eliot Tatelman. "They wind up having fun but also buying." In essence, says Barry Tatelman, "We've made furniture an impulse item."

The chain's success attracted the eye of Warren Buffet, the head of Berkshire Hathaway who is famous for his astute investments. Buffet bought the company a few years ago and left the Tatelmans in charge to continue their winning ways. Today Jordan's Furniture brings in almost $300 million in annual revenue (an average of $950 per square foot) and employs more than 1,200. Who or what will the brothers spoof in their next campaign? Stay tuned.[23]

Questions

1. Why would the Tatelmans choose not to mention prices in their advertising?
2. Would you suggest that Jordan's Furniture tailor the opening page of its website to the theme of each new advertising campaign? Explain your answer.
3. When customers buy from Jordan's Furniture, they deal with salespeople. How do the chain's advertising and in-store attractions facilitate the personal-selling process?

Building Skills for Career Success

1. Exploring the Internet

As a promotional tool, the Internet stands alone among all media for cost-effectiveness and variety. A well-designed company website can enhance most of the promotional strategies discussed in this chapter. It can provide consumers with advertising copy and sales representatives with personal-selling support services and information anytime on demand. In addition, many companies use the Internet for sales promotion. For instance, most newspapers and magazines provide sample articles in the hope that interested readers eventually will become subscribers. And virtually all software companies present demonstration editions of their products for potential customers to explore and test.

Assignment

1. Visit two of the following websites and examine the promotional activities taking place there. Note the sort of promotion being used and its location within the site. Also visit the text website for updates to this exercise.

   http://www.wsj.com

   http://www.businessweek.com

   http://www.forbes.com

2. Describe the promotional tools exhibited on one of these sites.
3. What would you recommend the company do to improve the site?

2. Developing Critical Thinking Skills

Obviously, salespeople must know the products they are selling, but to give successful sales presentations, they also must know their competition. Armed with information about competing products, they are better able to field prospective customers' questions and objectives regarding their own products.

Assignment

1. Choose a product or service offered by one company and gather samples of the competitors' sales literature.

2. After examining the competitors' sales literature, answer the following questions:
   a. What type of literature do the competitors use to advertise their product or service? Do they use full-color brochures?
   b. Do they use videotapes?
   c. Do they offer giveaways or special discounts?
3. Compare the product or service you chose with what the competition is selling.
4. Compile a list of all the strengths and weaknesses you have discovered.

3. Building Team Skills

The cost of promotional methods is an important factor in a promotional campaign. Representatives who sell advertising space for magazines, newspapers, radio stations, and television stations can quote the price of the medium to the advertiser. The advertiser can then use cost per thousand persons reached (CPM) to compare the cost efficiency of vehicles in the same medium.

Assignment

1. Working in teams of five to seven, choose one of these media: local television stations, newspapers, or radio stations. You can choose magazines if your library has a copy of *Standard Rate and Data Service*.
2. Using the following equation, compare the CPM of advertising in whatever local medium you chose:

$$\text{CPM} = \frac{\text{price of the medium to the advertiser} \times 1000}{\text{circulation}}$$

3. To compare different newspapers' rates, use the milline rate (the cost of a unit of advertising copy):

$$\text{Milline} = \frac{1{,}000{,}000 \times \text{line rate}}{\text{circulation}}$$

4. Report your team's findings to the class.

4. Researching Different Careers

Most public libraries maintain relatively up-to-date collections of occupational or career materials. Begin your library search by looking at the computer listings under "vocations" or "careers" and then under specific fields. Check the library's periodicals section, where you will find trade and professional magazines and journals about specific occupations and industries. (*Business Periodicals Index*, published by H. W. Wilson, is an index to articles in major business publications. Arranged alphabetically, it is easy to use.) Familiarize yourself with the concerns and activities of potential employers by skimming their annual reports and other information they distribute to the public. You also can find occupational information on videocassettes, in kits, and through computerized information systems.

Assignment

1. Choose a specific occupation.
2. Conduct a library search of the occupation.
3. Prepare an annotated bibliography for the occupation.

5. Improving Communication Skills

The basis for a sales presentation is the prospect's needs. Successful salespeople divide their presentations into components, each of which is an important element in making the sale. Sales presentations typically include an introduction, definition of the need, benefits of the product or service, and the cost of the product or service. One of the most important components of the sales presentation is the demonstration. Commonly used presentation aids include the product itself, videotapes, slides, overheads, flip charts, and computers. A well-planned presentation turns prospects into customers.

Assignment

1. Choose a product that you can demonstrate.
2. Select the audiovisuals most appropriate for the demonstration.
3. Acting the part of a salesperson, explain step-by-step how the product works. Ask a classmate to play a skeptical customer who questions the reliability of the product. (This presentation may be videotaped or conducted before your classmates.)
4. Summarize what you learned about being a salesperson.

Finagle A Bagel's Approach to Marketing

Round, flat, seeded, plain, crowned with cheese, or cut into croutons, bagels form the basis of every menu item at Finagle A Bagel. "So many other shops will just grab onto whatever is hot, whatever is trendy, in a 'me-too' strategy," observes Heather Robertson, the director of marketing, human resources, and research and development. In contrast, she says, "We do bagels—that's what we do best. And any menu item in our stores really needs to reaffirm that as our core concept." That's the first of Finagle A Bagel's marketing rules.

In addition to its retailing activities, the company wholesales its bagels in bulk to hospitals, schools, and other organizations. It also wholesales a line of Finagle A Bagel–branded bagels for resale in Shaw's Market stores. Whether selling wholesale or retail, the company is always hunting for new product ideas involving bagels.

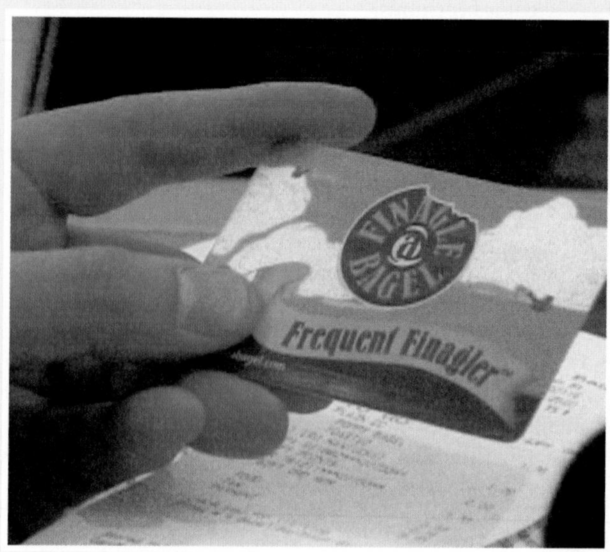

Product Development: Mix, Bake, Bite, and Try Again

To identify a new product idea, Robertson and her colleagues conduct informal research by talking with both customers and employees. They also browse food magazines and cookbooks for ideas about out-of-the-ordinary flavors, taste combinations, and preparation methods. When developing a new bagel variety, for example, Robertson says that she looks for ideas that are uncommon and innovative, yet appealing: "If someone else has a sun-dried tomato bagel, that's all the more reason for me not to do it. People look at Finagle A Bagel as kind of the trendsetter."

Once the marketing staff comes up with a promising idea, the next step is to write up a formula or recipe, walk downstairs to the dough factory, and mix up a test batch. Through trial and error, they refine the idea until they like the way the bagel or sandwich looks and tastes. Occasionally, Finagle A Bagel has to put an idea on hold until it can find just the right ingredients.

For example, when Robertson was working on a new bagel with jalapeno peppers and Cheddar cheese, she had difficulty finding a cheese that would melt during baking but not dissolve and disappear into the batter. Ultimately, she found a supplier willing to cook up cheese formulas especially for Finagle A Bagel. The supplier would send a batch of cheese overnight for Robertson to incorporate into the next day's test batch of bagels. After baking, Robertson would send some of the bagels overnight to the supplier so that the two of them could discuss the flavor, consistency, and other details.

The cheeses and bagels flew back and forth for eight months until Finagle A Bagel hit on a recipe that worked well. Then, says Robertson, "When we finally got it done, we shipped test batches to our stores, three stores at a time. And we just gave the product away. We'd make several batches during the week, and guess who would come back wanting to buy dozens of these bagels?" That's when she knew the new product was going to be a hit.

Samples and Coupons Spark Word-of-Mouth Communication

The story of the jalapeno-and-cheese bagel illustrates another of Finagle A Bagel's marketing rules: Spend nothing on advertising. Many quick-serve food companies use television and radio commercials, newspaper advertisements, and other mass-media messages to build brand awareness, promote products, and attract customers. However, Robertson and her colleagues believe that the best way to build the Finagle A Bagel brand and whet customers' appetites for a new menu item is to give them a free taste.

Consider what happened when Finagle A Bagel used samples and coupons to build lunchtime sales by promoting bagel sandwiches in one of the suburban stores. Instead of placing an ad in the local newspaper, Robertson and her staff went to the store and prepared 100 bagel sandwiches. They cut each in half and wrapped the halves individually. Then they set up 200 Finagle A Bagel bags, put a half-sandwich into each, and added a coupon for a free bagel sandwich without any risk. They piled all the bags into a big basket, attached a sign reading, "Free Bagel Sandwiches," and headed to a large intersection just a block from the store.

"Every time the light turned red, we would run out into the middle of the street and throw a bag through someone's car window," Robertson recalls. "We got a lot of strange looks. A few people would roll up their car windows . . . but a lot of people just thought it was hysterically funny.

They would be motioning, waving us over, saying, 'What have you got?' And then they'd go back to their office and tell their coworkers, 'Hey, you know what happened to me today? Some crazy lady threw a bagel through my car window, and it was great. You should check it out.' " The entire effort cost $100—and convinced a large number of customers to look around the store, try a sandwich risk-free, and talk up the experience to colleagues, friends, and family.

Buy a Branded Bagel—Again and Again

Although some restaurant companies want each unit to look distinctly different, Finagle A Bagel uses consistency to reinforce the brand image—another of its marketing rules. "We believe the stores should have a very similar look and feel so that you can walk into any Finagle A Bagel and know what to expect," says copresident Alan Litchman. For example, every Finagle A Bagel store sports an eye-catching burgundy-and-yellow sign featuring an oversized bagel with a few bites taken out. This bagel icon is repeated on posters highlighting menu items as well as on other store decorations.

Still, the suburban stores are not exactly like the downtown stores. Many of the suburban stores have children's furniture and cushiony chairs so that families can sit and relax. Free weekly concerts by the "Music Man"—a local musician—make these stores decidedly family friendly. The city stores have no children's furniture because they cater to busy working people who want to be in and out in a hurry. The Harvard Square store is unique: It has a liquor license and attracts a large student crowd, which means it is busier on weekends than on weekdays.

One of the most effective sales promotion techniques the company uses is the Frequent Finagler loyalty card, which rewards customers for making repeat purchases. For every dollar customers spend on bagels or other menu items, they receive Frequent Finagler points that can be redeemed for free coffee, free bagels, and so on. Customers are pleased because they receive extra value for the money they spend—and Finagle A Bagel is pleased because its average sale to loyal customers is higher.

Pricing a Bagel

Pricing is an important consideration in the competitive world of quick-serve food. This is where another of Finagle A Bagel's marketing rules comes in. Regardless of cost, the company will not compromise quality. Therefore, the first step in pricing a new product is to find the best possible ingredients and then examine the costs and calculate an approximate retail price. After thinking about what a customer might expect to pay for such a menu item, shopping the competition, and talking with some customers, the company settles on a price that represents "a great product for a fair value," says Robertson.

Although Finagle A Bagel's rental costs vary, the copresidents price menu items the same in higher-rent stores as in lower-rent stores. "We have considered adjusting prices based upon the location of the store, but we haven't done it because it can backfire in a very significant way," copresident Laura Trust explains. "People expect to be treated fairly, regardless of where they live."

Questions

1. Does Finagle A Bagel apply all seven phases of the new product development process when working on a new menu item such as the jalapeno-and-cheese bagel? Explain.
2. Do you agree with Laura Trust's assessment that adjusting prices based on store location can backfire? What arguments can you offer for and against Finagle A Bagel raising prices in higher-rent stores?
3. Finagle A Bagel is both a wholesaler and a retailer. Which of these two marketing intermediary roles do you think the company should develop more aggressively in the next few years? Why?
4. Should Finagle A Bagel continue to spend nothing on media advertising and rely instead primarily on sales promotion techniques such as samples and coupons?

Building a Business Plan Part V

INC.

This section is one of the most important components of your business plan. In this section you will present the facts that you have gathered on the size and nature of your market(s). State market size in dollars and units. How many units and what is the dollar value of the products you expect to sell in a given time period? Indicate your primary and secondary sources of data and the methods you used to estimate total market size and your market share. Part V of your textbook covers all marketing-related topics. These chapters should help you to answer the questions in this part of the business plan.

The Marketing Plan Component

The marketing plan component is and should be unique to your business. Many assumptions or projections used in the analysis may turn out differently; therefore, this component should be flexible enough to be adjusted as needed. The marketing plan should include answers to at least the following questions:

5.1. What are your target markets, and what common identifiable need(s) can you satisfy?

5.2. What are the competitive, legal, political, economic, technological, and sociocultural factors affecting your marketing efforts?

5.3. What are the current needs of each target market? Describe the target market in terms of demographic, geographic, psychographic, and product usage characteristics. What changes in the target market are anticipated?

5.4. What advantages and disadvantages do you have in meeting the target market's needs?

5.5. How will your product distribution, promotion, and price satisfy customer needs?

5.6. How effectively will your products meet these needs?

5.7. What are the relevant aspects of consumer behavior and product use?

5.8. What are your company's projected sales volume, market share, and profitability?

5.9. What are your marketing objectives? Include the following in your marketing objectives:

- Product introduction, improvement, or innovation
- Sales or market share
- Profitability
- Pricing
- Distribution
- Advertising (Prepare advertising samples for the Appendix.)

Make sure that your marketing objectives are clearly written, measurable, and consistent with your overall marketing strategy.

5.10. How will the results of your marketing plan be measured and evaluated?

Review of Business Plan Activities

Remember that even though it will be time-consuming, developing a clear, well-written marketing plan is important. Therefore, make sure that you have checked the plan for any weaknesses or problems before proceeding to Part VI. Also make certain that all your answers to the questions in this and other parts are consistent throughout the business plan. Finally, write a brief statement that summarizes all the information for this part of the business plan.

part VI

Information for Business Strategy and Decision Making

In this part of the book we focus on information, one of the four essential resources on which all businesses rely. First, we discuss the different kinds of information necessary for effective decision making, where it can be found, how it is organized, and how it can be used throughout an organization by those who need it. We then examine the role of accounting and how financial information is collected, stored, processed, presented, and used to better control managerial decision making.

chapter

17 Acquiring, Organizing, and Using Information

learning objectives

1 Understand how information is organized to help people make decisions.

2 Describe how business research is conducted.

3 Discuss management's information requirements.

4 Describe the five functions of an information system.

5 Explain how the Internet, intranet, standards for communications, and web pages affect business today.

6 Discuss how the Internet helps employees communicate, assists a firm's sales force, trains and recruits employees, and conducts financial activities.

7 Understand how business applications software can be used to collect and distribute information.

PeopleSoft's executives never forget that the point of their products is to help managers run their organizations and make decisions.

inside business

PeopleSoft Software Helps Managers Manage

PEOPLESOFT'S EXECUTIVES never forget that the point of their products is to help managers do a better job of running their organizations and making decisions. The California-based company's name comes from its original software products, designed in the late 1980s for automating such essential human resources tasks as calculating and issuing payroll checks. Over time, PeopleSoft has built a reputation for innovation by developing a wider range of applications for companies and government agencies to use in gathering and analyzing work force, customer, and financial data. Now managers in 4,700 companies around the world use PeopleSoft's applications to get detailed information in usable form when and where they need it.

Consider how companies can use PeopleSoft's customer relationship management software. This application can suggest additional products for sales personnel to sell to specific customers and monitor the results of these and other sales initiatives. It also allows front-line personnel access to detailed customer and transaction data for planning, sales, and service activities. Customer service, for example, can use this software to examine when each customer placed orders, what was ordered, when products were shipped, special requests, and other specifics. They can use its built-in e-mail and instant-messaging capabilities to communicate with colleagues and customers—simultaneously, if necessary—while resolving service inquiries.

In the past, organizations had to install PeopleSoft's software on each individual computer and then reinstall upgraded versions as they became available. However, when Craig Conway became CEO in 1999, he assigned nearly all of his 2,000 programmers and spent $500 million rewriting 138 PeopleSoft applications so that they would run smoothly over the Internet. Conway expected that this radical change would shave the high costs that companies typically incur to maintain applications on so many computers. As an added bonus, customers found that PeopleSoft's revised data-processing programs were much more convenient to use. Conway's radical change paid off. More than 1,500 customers have started using the web-based software, boosting PeopleSoft's revenue and profits.

Today PeopleSoft holds an estimated 50 percent of the market for human resources management software. In the overall market for organizational software, it competes with Oracle, another California software firm, and SAP, headquartered in Germany. To remain competitive, PeopleSoft has developed new products on its own and has acquired other businesses to expand its product line. For example, the acquisition of Vantive, a major supplier of customer relationship management software, strengthened PeopleSoft's plans for entering that part of the market. PeopleSoft also has forged alliances with IBM and other companies that provide information technology systems and services for organizational use. For its accomplishments, PeopleSoft has received numerous awards, including being named to *Fortune* magazine's list of the most admired U.S. technology companies.[1]

PeopleSoft operates in a very competitive industry. And yet this California-based firm has built a reputation for providing software that transforms data into information for managers and employees in 4,700 companies around the world. The firm's customer relationship management software, human resources management software, and organizational software enable users to operate more efficiently and at the same time reduce operating expenses. PeopleSoft's success is built on two important factors. First, the firm continues to innovate and develop new products to meet customers' information needs. Second, the need for information in today's business world has never been greater!

In this chapter we first examine the nature of information and how it is related to decision making and risk. Next, we look at business research and methods used to acquire information. Then we look at how information is organized and distributed within a firm. Finally, we examine the way the Internet and communications technologies allow a firm to both acquire and distribute information globally to both employees and outsiders interested in the company.

The Nature of Information

As we noted in Chapter 1, information is one of the four major resources (along with material, human, and financial resources) managers must have to operate a business. While a successful business uses all four resources efficiently, it is information that helps managers reduce risk when making a decision.

Information and Risk

The more information a manager has, the less risk there is that a decision will be incorrect; theoretically, with accurate and complete information, there is no risk whatsoever. On the other hand, a decision made without any information is a gamble. These two extreme situations are rare in business. For the most part, business decision makers see themselves located someplace between either extreme. As illustrated in Figure 17.1, when the amount of available information is high, there is less risk; when the amount of available information is low, there is more risk.

For example, suppose that a marketing manager for Procter & Gamble responsible for the promotion of a well-known shampoo such as Pantene Pro-V has called a meeting of her department team to consider the selection of a new magazine advertisement. The company's advertising agency has submitted two new advertisements in sealed envelopes. Neither the manager nor any of her team has seen them before. Only one selection will be made for the new advertising campaign. Which advertisement should be chosen?

Without any further information available to the group, any selection is equally risky, and the team might as well make the decision by flipping a coin. If, however,

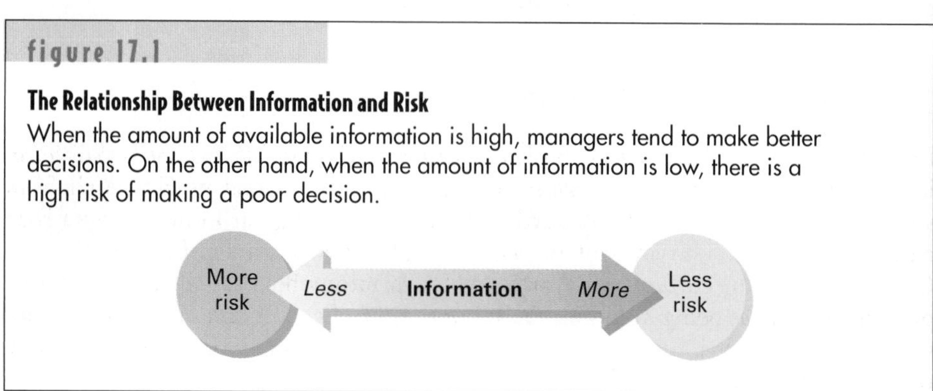

figure 17.1

The Relationship Between Information and Risk
When the amount of available information is high, managers tend to make better decisions. On the other hand, when the amount of information is low, there is a high risk of making a poor decision.

Would Microsoft snoop? Only with the permission of these computer users. Anthropologists employed by Microsoft systematically observe and collect data about how families use their computers. Then they turn the raw data into information that helps the software giant improve computer programs to meet the needs of their customers.

eam members were allowed to open the envelopes nd examine the advertisements, they would have nore information with which to form an opinion and hereby make an informed recommendation. If in addition to allowing them to examine the advertisements, the marketing manager circulated a report containing the reaction of a group of target consumers toward each of the two advertisements, the team would have even more information with which to work.

Information, when understood properly, produces knowledge and empowers nanagers and employees to make better decisions. To know what to do in a particular situation, people need information to guide their behavior. Without correct and timely information, individual performance will be undermined and, consequently, so will the performance of the entire organization.

Information Rules

learning objective

1 Understand how information is organized to help people make decisions.

Business research continues to show that discounts influence almost all car buyers. Simply put, if dealers lower their prices, they will sell more cars. This relationship between buyer behavior and price can be thought of as an *information rule*, which usually will guide the marketing manager correctly. A rule such as this emerges when business research confirms the same results each time that it studies the same or a similar set of circumstances. The experienced business person often makes decisions using information rules to quicken and simplify all kinds of tasks. Because of the volume of information they receive each day and their need to make decisions on a daily basis, business people try to accumulate information rules to shorten the time they spend analyzing choices.

Similarly, consumers use information rules to help them to make purchasing decisions. Research on consumer behavior suggests that buyers will attempt to simplify a complex decision-making process by considering only a few critical determining factors. The decision to purchase a new refrigerator can be greatly simplified by only considering the factors of brand name of the product, the warranty, and perhaps the price.

Information rules are the "great simplifiers" for all decision makers. Business research is continuously on the lookout for new rules that can be put to good use and discrediting old ones that are no longer valid. This ongoing process is necessary because business conditions rarely stay the same for very long.

The Difference Between Data and Information

Many people use the terms *data* and *information* interchangeably, but the two differ in important ways. **Data** are numerical or verbal descriptions that usually result from some sort of measurement. (The word *data* is plural; the singular form is *datum*.) Your current wage level, the amount of last year's after-tax profit for Hewlett Packard Computers, and the current retail prices of Honda automobiles are all data. Most people think of data as being numerical only, but they can be nonnumerical as well. A description of an individual as a "tall, athletic person with short, dark hair" certainly would qualify as data.

data numerical or verbal descriptions that usually result from some sort of measurement

figure 17.2

Data versus Information

Data are numerical or verbal descriptions that usually result from measurements; information is data presented in a form that is useful for a specific purpose. Thus the computer printout of every employee's wages is data, whereas the graph that compares average wages year by year is information.

	Jan	Feb	March	April	May	June	July	Aug	Sept	Oct	Nov	Dec	Totals
Female Employees													
Employee 1	1,150	1,150	1,150	1,150	1,150	1,150	1,200	1,200	1,200	1,200	1,200	1,300	$14,200
Employee 2	1,400	1,400	1,400	1,400	1,400	1,400	1,400	1,400	1,400	1,400	1,400	1,400	$16,800
Employee 3	1,600	1,600	1,600	1,600	1,800	1,800	1,800	1,800	1,800	1,900	1,900	1,900	$21,100
Employee 4	1,200	1,200	1,200	1,200	1,200	1,200	1,250	1,250	1,250	1,250	1,250	1,250	$14,700
Male Employees													
Employee 5	1,800	1,800	1,800	1,800	1,800	1,800	1,800	1,800	1,800	1,800	1,800	1,800	$21,600
Employee 6	2,000	2,000	2,000	2,000	2,000	2,000	2,100	2,100	2,100	2,100	2,100	2,100	$24,600
Employee 7	1,900	1,900	1,900	1,900	1,900	1,900	1,950	1,950	1,950	1,950	2,000	2,000	$23,200
Employee 8	2,400	2,400	2,400	2,400	2,400	2,400	2,500	2,500	2,500	2,500	2,500	2,500	$29,400

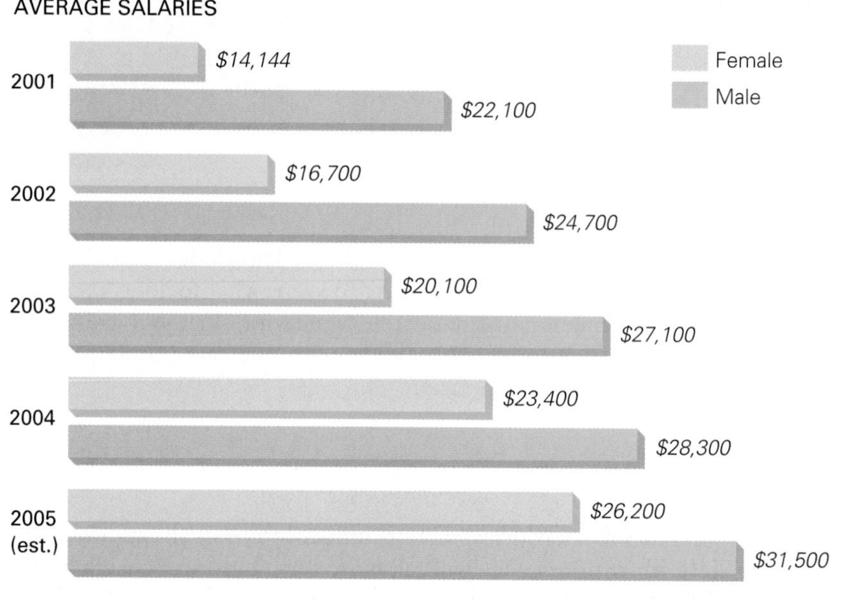

information data presented in a form that is useful for a specific purpose

Information is data presented in a form useful for a specific purpose. Suppose that a human resources manager wants to compare the wages paid to male and female employees over a period of five years. The manager might begin with a stack of computer printouts listing every person employed by the firm, along with each employee's current and past wages. The manager would be hard-pressed to make any sense of all the names and numbers. Such printouts consist of data rather than information.

Now suppose that the manager uses a computer to graph the average wages paid to men and to women in each of the five years. As Figure 17.2 shows, the result is information because the manager can use it for the purpose at hand—to compare wages paid to men with those paid to women over the five-year period. When summarized in the graph, the wage data from the printouts become information.

Large sets of data often must be summarized if they are to be useful, but this is not always the case. If the manager in our example had wanted to know only the wage history of a specific employee, that information would be contained in the original computer printout. That is, the data (the employee's name and wage history) already would be in the most useful form for the manager's purpose; they would need no further processing.

database a single collection of data stored in one place that can be used by people throughout an organization to make decisions

The average company maintains a great deal of data that can be transformed into information. Typical data include records pertaining to personnel, inventory, sales, and accounting. Often each type of data is stored in individual departments within an organization. However, the data can be used more effectively when they are organized into a database. A **database** is a single collection of data stored in one place that can be used by people throughout an organization to make decisions. Today, most companies have several different types of databases. Often the data and information necessary to form a firm's databases are the result of business research activities.

usiness Research

learning objective

Describe how business research is conducted.

or information about important issues that affect their ability to make decisions, usiness people read trade journals and professional publications, attend conferences, nd talk to experts both inside and outside their firms. Gathering information in this ay is referred to as *secondary research* because someone else did the original research. or example, a business decision maker may read articles published in *Fortune* magaine, the *Wall Street Journal*, or *BusinessWeek*. When secondary sources do not provide usiness people with sufficient information to make decisions with acceptable levels of isk, they may conduct their own *primary research*. In business, primary research emloys two fundamentally different approaches to information gathering and analysis: *ualitative* and *quantitative research*. Table 17.1 lists three popular methods generally ssociated with each category. It should be noted that each method may be employed n the other category as well. For instance, observation can be used to gather both uantitative and qualitative data.

ualitative Research

qualitative research a process that involves the descriptive or subjective reporting of information discovered by a researcher

ualitative research involves the descriptive or subjective reporting of information iscovered by a researcher. Generally, qualitative research is conducted in one of three ays: observation, interviews, or focus groups. For example, *observation* may be used o better understand retail shoppers' levels of satisfaction. The researcher simply may alk around a J.C. Penney department store observing the facial expressions and manerisms of shoppers. Several researchers also may study the behavior of the same roup of subjects so that a consensus of opinion can develop. The researchers then reate a formal report detailing each researcher's observations.

Business researchers also conduct *interviews* with individual subjects as well as roup interviews. The latter, which usually involve six to ten subjects, are called *focus roups*. A researcher for Dell Computer, for instance, may form a focus group to discuss features that should be incorporated in a new laptop computer. By posing quesions to the focus group and then recording their responses and concerns, the esearcher gathers information that can be used to "fine tune" the product. Based on he information provided by this and other focus groups, Dell can manufacture a roduct that more closely meets the needs of its customers. As an added bonus, valuble information often emerges from group interaction and dialogue. Ideas that the esearcher would never have thought to ask about in the first place also can arise.

table 17.1 Methods Used by Business Researchers

A number of different methods can be used to conduct qualitative and quantitative research

Qualitative Research Methods	Quantitative Research Methods
1. *Observation.* The act of noting or recording something, such as the facial expressions of shoppers in a retail store.	1. *Survey.* A research method that relies on asking the same questions to a large number of people to elicit responses and information.
2. *Interview.* A conversation conducted by a researcher with an individual to elicit responses and information to different research variables.	2. *Experiment.* A research method that involves the use of two or more groups of people to determine how people in each group react.
3. *Focus group.* A conversation conducted by a researcher with a small group of people to elicit responses and information.	3. *Content analysis.* A research method that involves measuring particular items in a written publication, television program, or radio program.

The basic problem with qualitative research is that it is only as good as the ability of the researcher to "read" the situation under study. Given that two people observing the same event may interpret the event quite differently, it is little wonder that some researchers are hesitant to place too great a value on qualitative research without knowing the credentials of the researchers involved. Even then, many are reluctant to place too much confidence in the "reading" of behavior.

Quantitative Research

quantitative research a process that involves the collection of numerical data for analysis through a survey, experiment, or content analysis

Quantitative research involves the collection of numerical data for analysis through *survey*, *experiment*, or *content analysis*. Many researchers believe that the statistical information that results from analysis of numerical data represents a more objective and unbiased picture than the subjective interpretation used in qualitative research. To gather numerical data through a *survey*, a researcher might approach shoppers in a Target discount store with a list of questions to determine their degree of satisfaction with store service, personnel, and the store's prices. A response scale often is used to simplify this process. For example, the researcher might ask customers to rank the following statements on a scale of 1 to 5, 5 indicating strong agreement with the statement; 4 indicating agreement; 3, indecision; 2, disagreement; and 1, strong disagreement:

1. The store personnel are friendly and courteous.
2. The store personnel are informed about their merchandise.
3. The store's prices are competitive with prices charged by other retailers in the same area.

A trained researcher walking around with a clipboard can easily ask such questions and record customers' responses. However, validity is a concern with this method, too. Some people might not want to speak to a stranger walking about with a clipboard; this may be especially true of customers who are strongly dissatisfied with store personnel. If this is the case, the data will be heavily biased. To avoid bias, researchers should use several different methods to test the validity of their data. Consistency among the test results can help alleviate management's concerns about the accuracy and validity of the research.

Experiments typically involve comparison studies of two or more groups of people. Suppose that managers at Southwest Airlines want to know which of three television advertisements is the best choice for the company's target market. Researchers might select three groups of people believed to be representative of the target market. Each group would be shown a film of only one advertisement, and a variety of measurements would be taken after they finished watching it. If the managers were interested in knowing the level of "brand awareness" among the target market, and the level of brand awareness was significantly higher among one group than among the other two, they would likely select the advertisement that was shown to that group. Researchers also might measure brand preferences *before* each group watched the advertisement and then immediately *after*. In this way, the effect of watching the advertisement would be more clearly evident.

Content analysis is a simple technique that involves measuring particular items in a written publication, television program, or radio program. For instance, suppose that footwear manufacturer Adidas wants to know the extent to which its competitors use a specific sports magazine to advertise their products. If the magazine is a popular choice among competitors, a marketing manager at Adidas might think that it is appropriate to use the same magazine to reach the same type of customer. To determine how much competing manufacturers use the magazine, researchers would examine back issues of the magazine over the last twelve months and count the number and size of advertisements bought by competitors. Based on how much competitors are using the magazine, Adidas might decide to begin an advertising campaign in the same magazine.

@ Using the Internet

Perhaps one of the best known pollsters and research firms, the Gallup Organization has been conducting public opinion surveys and providing other management consulting services since 1935. The company is frequently asked to survey the public about political issues—especially during election campaigns—as well as business and economic issues, social issues, and lifestyle topics. To view the company's latest survey results, visit **http://www.gallup.com/.**

Information you can use. Business researchers use Hoover's Online to gather information about millions of public and private companies. And Hoover's Online makes it easy to obtain the latest information about companies by providing frequent updates to its online database. For more information, go to www.hoovers.com.

9:30 a.m. Boss requests competitive report.

— 9:40 a.m. Log in to Hoover's Pro account. Get to work.

— 10:25 a.m. Finish competitive research.

— 11:15 a.m. Deliver report to CEO.

— 12:10 p.m. Look like hero. Join CEO for lunch.

Get instant access to up-to-date business prospecting and competitive information with a Hoover's Online Subscription.

- Focused: In-depth information on businesses, industries and people
- Fresh & Accurate: Real-time database updates
- Fair & Impartial: 70 dedicated, full-time business researchers
- Fast: Time-saving tools & easy-to-use Web site
- Far-Reaching: Millions of public and private companies
- Affordable: Just $1.09 per person* per day

www.hoovers.com

HOOVER'S ONLINE

The Business Information Authority™

Which Research Method to Choose

The decision about which research method or methods to use is often based on a combination of factors, including limitations on time and money and the need for accuracy and validity. In general, managers rely on the results of proven research methods until those methods no longer work well.

Nielsen Media Research, for example, traditionally has led the research industry in measuring the viewing behavior of television audiences. The firm uses a variety of techniques, including "people meters" placed in 5,000 households for nationwide audience measurement. The meter measures three things—when and how long a television is turned on, what station is being viewed, and who is watching. Who is watching television is measured by the "people" part of the people meter. Each member of the household is assigned a personal viewing button. These personal buttons allow Nielsen Media Research to determine which family member is watching which program. Once the data are collected, Nielsen then sells the information to advertisers who want to know when their target audience watches television and, in particular, which programs they watch. The people meter technique is a relatively recent response to the problems associated with earlier methods, such as the diary reports written by people paid to record their television viewing habits.

The Information System

Never in the history of the world has there been so much information available to individuals, business firms, and the government. Just for a moment, think back to the terrorist attacks on September 11. Everyone was watching their television sets, listening to the radio, or reading news stories on the Internet in order to obtain the information they needed to determine what was going on and what to expect. Now, years after the terrorist attacks, a new federal Department of Homeland Security uses information to track terrorist activities and hopefully prevent future attacks that have the potential to kill and destroy. Where does the information come from? In many organizations, including the government and business firms, the answer lies in a management information system (MIS). A **management information system (MIS)** is a system that provides managers and employees with the information they need to perform their jobs as effectively as possible (see Figure 17.3 on p. 506).

The purpose of an MIS (sometimes referred to as an *information technology system* or simply *IT system*) is to distribute timely and useful information from both internal and external sources to the managers and employees who need it. Today, most medium-sized to large business firms have an information technology officer. An **information technology officer** is a manager at the executive level who is responsible for ensuring that the firm has the equipment necessary to provide the information the firm's employees and managers need to make effective decisions.

management information system (MIS) a system that provides managers and employees with the information they need to perform their jobs as effectively as possible

information technology officer a manager at the executive level who is responsible for ensuring that a firm has the equipment necessary to provide the information the firm's employees and managers need to make effective decisions

figure 17.3

Management Information System (MIS)
After an MIS is installed, a user can get information directly from the MIS without having to go through other people in the organization.

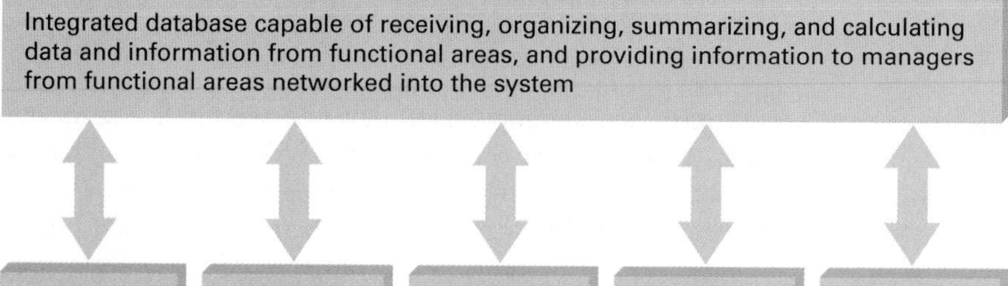
MANAGEMENT INFORMATION SYSTEM
Integrated database capable of receiving, organizing, summarizing, and calculating data and information from functional areas, and providing information to managers from functional areas networked into the system
Finance
Operations
Marketing
Human resources
Administration

Source: *Management*, 8th ed., by Ricky W. Griffin. Copyright © 2005 by Houghton Mifflin Company. Adapted with permission.

From simple e-mail to large, well-structured, user-friendly, and easily queried databases, today's typical MIS is built around a computerized system of recordkeeping and communications software. In many firms, the MIS is combined with a marketing information system (discussed in Chapter 13) so that it can provide information based on a wide variety of data. In fact, it makes little sense to have separate information systems for the various functional areas within a business. After all, the goal is to provide needed information to all managers and employees.

Managers' Information Requirements

learning objective

3 Discuss management's information requirements.

Managers have to plan for the future, implement their plans in the present, and evaluate results against what has been accomplished in the past. Thus they need access to information that summarizes future possibilities, the present situation, and past performance. Of course, the specific types of information they need depend on their area of management and on their level within the firm.

In Chapter 7 we identified five areas of management: finance, operations, marketing, human resources, and administration. Financial managers are obviously most concerned with their firm's finances. They study its debts and receivables, cash flow, future capitalization needs, financial statements, and other accounting information. Of equal importance to financial managers is information about the present state of the economy, interest rates, and predictions of business conditions in the future.

Operations managers are concerned with present and future sales levels, current inventory levels of work in process and finished goods, and the availability and cost of the resources required to produce products and services. And they are involved with new product planning. They also must keep abreast of any innovative production technology that might be useful to their firm.

Marketing managers need to have detailed information about their firm's product mix and the products offered by competitors. Such information includes prices and pricing strategies, new promotional campaigns, and products that competitors are test marketing. Information concerning target markets, current and projected market share, new and pending product legislation, and developments within channels of distribution is also important to marketing managers.

Human resources managers must be aware of anything that pertains to their firm's employees. Key examples include current wage levels and benefits packages both within their firm and in firms that compete for valuable employees, current legislation and court decisions that affect employment practices; union activities; and their firm's plans for growth, expansion, or mergers.

Administrative managers are responsible for the overall management of their organization. Thus they are concerned with the coordination of information—just as they are concerned with the coordination of material, human, and financial resources. First, administrators must ensure that all employees have access to the information they need to do their jobs. And second, they must ensure that the information is used in a consistent manner throughout the firm. Suppose, for example, that the operations group at General Electric (GE) is designing a plant that will open in five years and be devoted to manufacturing consumer electronic products. GE's management will want answers to many questions: Is the capacity of the plant consistent with marketing plans based on sales projections? Will human resources managers be able to staff the plant on the basis of employment forecasts? And do sales projections indicate enough income to cover the expected cost of the plant?

Administrative managers also must make sure that all managers and employees are able to use the information technology that is available. Certainly this requires that all employees receive the skills training required to use the firm's MIS. Finally, administrative managers also must commit to the costs of updating the firm's MIS and providing additional training when necessary.

Size and Complexity of the System

An MIS must be tailored to the needs of the organization it serves. In some firms, a tendency to save on initial costs may result in a system that is too small or overly simple. Such a system generally ends up serving only one or two management levels or a single department—the one that gets its data into the system first. Managers in other departments "give up" on the system as soon as they find that it cannot accept or process their data. Often they look elsewhere for information, process their own data, or simply do without.

Almost as bad is an MIS that is too large or too complex for the organization. Unused capacity and complexity do nothing but increase the cost of owning and operating the system. In addition, a system that is difficult to use probably will not be used at all. Managers may find that it is easier to maintain their own system of gathering information. Or again, they may try to operate without information that could be helpful when making decisions.

Today, there are many companies and countries that are involved in the high-tech information industry. To see how China is both developing and using high-tech products, read the Going Global (on p. 508) feature. Obviously, much is expected of an effective MIS system. Let's examine the functions an MIS system must perform to provide the information managers need.

A sweet tooth and management information: a perfect match! Although many consumers assume that products magically appear on store shelves, of course it is more complicated than that. For example, Ben & Jerry's information system tracks each pint of ice cream from the start of production to when it is sold in the store. Ben & Jerry's financial, operations, marketing, human resources, and administrative managers use information provided by the firm's management information system to make sure that you get ice cream at the right place and right time.

going global

China's Rise in Information Technology

THE FAST-PACED WORLD of information technology is looking East, where China is on the brink of becoming a major player. Building on earlier successes in electronic toys, computer chips, telecommunications devices, and software, the nation is now emerging as a major player in the high-tech world and a rival to firms in California's Silicon Valley.

One factor fueling China's rise is the availability of well-educated engineers, scientists, and technical experts working at far lower pay levels than their American counterparts. Whereas an engineer in China earns about $15,000 in annual salary and benefits, a Silicon Valley engineer earns up to ten times that amount. A second factor is China's policy of encouraging domestic firms to work with foreign firms. For example, Germany's Infineon Technologies is sharing its computer chip expertise with China's Semiconductor Manufacturing International Corporation. In exchange, the Chinese company is Infineon's exclusive supplier of certain memory chips. Another German company, Siemens, is working with Chinese companies to come up with wireless web access standards.

Still another factor that has led to China's expansion in the high-tech industry is that Chinese companies are successfully marketing their high-tech products in other countries. Ever heard of Huawei Technologies? Not nearly as well known as its U.S.-based rival Cisco Systems, Huawei originally made low-cost, high-quality versions of similar equipment manufactured by some of the leaders in the technology industry, including Cisco. Based on its early success, Huawei is now developing products with inventive technology twists. As a result, the company already rings up $240 million in annual sales outside China, a figure that could triple through distribution deals with wholesalers in Europe and America.

Meanwhile, many Western companies are opening research facilities in China, buying locally produced goods, and selling products to local customers. America's General Electric, for example, is opening a research center in Shanghai, as is Japan's Matsushita. And U.S.-based Cisco Systems is selling networking equipment and services to Shanghai Telecom and China Telecom. Clearly, China is well on its way toward developing and attracting the world's best information technology.

Functions of a Management Information System

learning objective

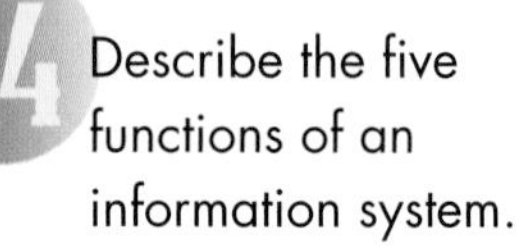

4 Describe the five functions of an information system.

To provide information, an MIS must perform five specific functions. It must collect data, store the data, update the data, process the data into information, and present information to users (see Figure 17.4).

Collecting Data

A firm's employees, with the help of an MIS system, must gather the data needed to establish the firm's *data bank*. The data bank should include all past and current data that may be useful in managing the firm. Because of the abundance of information available today, only useful information should be entered into the data bank. Data that serve no useful purpose must be filtered out. Even after the filtering process, experts estimate that 28 percent of data available today are read only once.[2] Clearly, the data entered into the system must be *relevant* to the needs of the firm's managers. And perhaps most important, the data must be *accurate*. Irrelevant data are simply useless; inaccurate data can be disastrous. The data can be obtained from within the firm and from outside sources.

Internal Sources of Data Typically, most of the data gathered for an MIS comes from internal sources. The most common internal sources of information are managers and employees, company records and reports, and minutes of meetings.

Past and present accounting data also can provide information about the firm's customers, creditors, and suppliers. Sales reports are a source of data on sales, pricing strategies, and the effectiveness of promotional campaigns. Human resources records are useful as a source of data on wage and benefits levels, hiring patterns, employee turnover, and other personnel variables.

Present and past production forecasts also should be included in the firm's data bank, along with data indicating how well these forecasts predicted actual events. Similarly, specific plans and management decisions—regarding capital expansion and new product development, for example—should be incorporated into the MIS system.

External Sources of Data External sources of data include customers, suppliers, bankers, trade and financial publications, industry conferences, online computer services, and firms that specialize in gathering data for organizations. Like internal data, data from external sources take various forms depending on the requirements of the firm and its managers and employees.

A marketing research company may acquire forecasts pertaining to product demand, consumer tastes, and other marketing variables. Suppliers are an excellent source of information about the future availability and costs of raw materials and component parts. Bankers often can provide valuable economic insights and projections. And the information furnished by trade publications and industry conferences usually is concerned as much with future projections as with present conditions.

Legal issues and court decisions that may affect a firm are discussed occasionally in local newspapers and, more often, in specialized publications such as the *Wall Street Journal*, *Fortune*, and *BusinessWeek*. Government publications such as the *Monthly Labor Review* and the *Federal Reserve Bulletin* are also quite useful as sources of external data, as are a number of online computer services.

Cautions in Collecting Data Three cautions should be observed in collecting data for a firm's data bank. First, the cost of obtaining data from some external sources, such as marketing research firms, can be quite high. In all cases—whether the data come from internal or external sources—the cost of obtaining data should be weighed against the potential benefits that having the data will confer on the firm.

Second, although computers generally do not make mistakes, the people who use them can make or cause errors. Simply by pushing the wrong key on a computer keyboard, you can change an entire set of data, along with the information it contains. The old adage "garbage in, garbage out" is worth remembering when using data or information generated by a computer to make decisions. When data (or information) and your judgment disagree, always check the data.

figure 17.4

Five Management Information System Functions

Every MIS must be tailored to the organization it serves and must perform five functions.

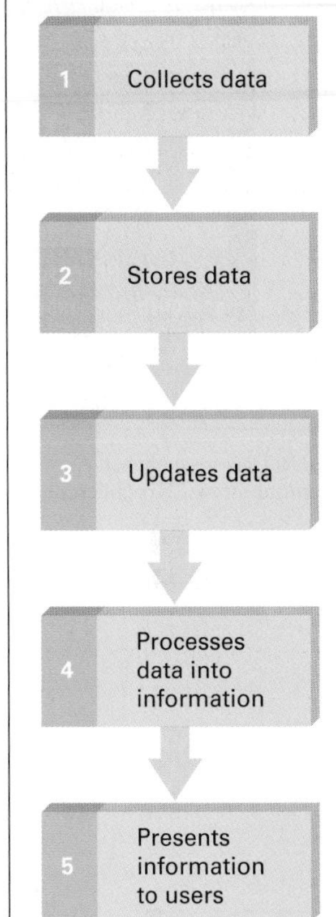

Find it. Faster.

You just got a request for a list of grocery stores in a three-state area with more than 20 employees.

You could search through dozens of reference sources to create that list. Or, you could call *Reference*USA, a division of *info*USA.

We offer the country's most extensive databases of business and residential information. And, you choose the format you want: print, CD-ROM or via the Internet.

Want more information? Call us today at **1-800-808-1113** or e-mail **reference@infoUSA.com.**

Your search is over.

"*Reference*USA offers superb depth, breadth, and currency in a very well-designed web interface. Recommended for all libraries serving business needs."
— Library Journal October 1, 2002

Friends of Libraries U.S.A.

5711 S. 86th Circle · P.O. Box 27347 · Omaha, NE 68127
Phone: (402) 593-4523 · Fax: (402) 596-7688 · www.referenceUSA.com

23163

Looking for a needle in a haystack? Even for the most experienced researchers, collecting data from external sources can be a time consuming and frustrating activity. That's when a company like ReferenceUSA can help. Because it provides the country's most extensive databases of business and residential information, ReferenceUSA, a division of infoUSA, can reduce the frustration and help you find just the information you need.

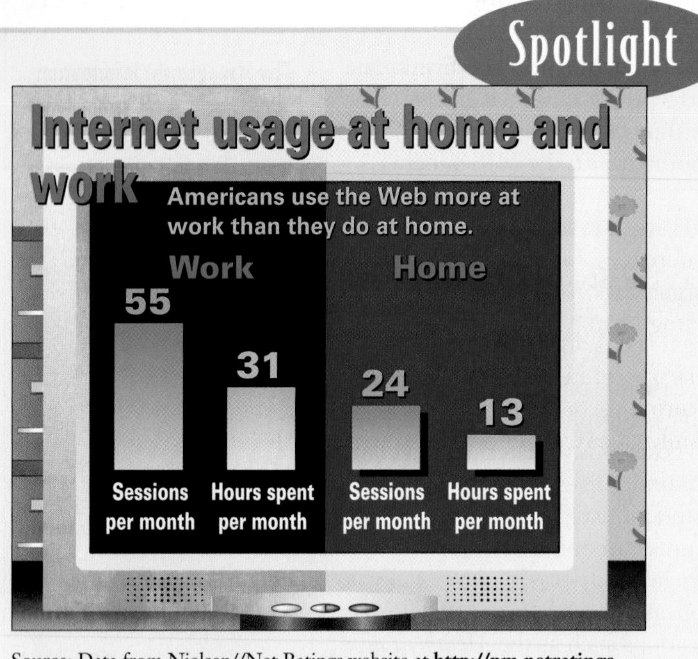

Source: Data from Nielsen//Net Ratings website at **http://pm.netratings.com/nnpm/owa/Nrpublicreports.usagemonthly**, March 21, 2003.

Third, outdated or incomplete data usuall yield inaccurate information. Data collection an ongoing process. New data must be added t the data bank either as they are obtained or i regularly scheduled updates.

Storing Data

An MIS must be capable of storing data unt they are needed. Options for storage of dat include

- Magnetic tape
- Hard disk drives
- Floppy disks
- CD-ROMs

Typically, the method chosen to store data de pends on the size of the organization. Sma businesses may enter data and then store ther directly on the hard drive inside an employee computer. Floppy disks and CD-ROMs als can be used to make copies of important infor mation or to move data and information fror one computer to another.

Generally, medium-sized to large businesses store data in a larger computer sys tem and provide access to employees through a computer network. In the early, com puterized MIS systems, a large mainframe computer served a network of user Mainframes are still in place in many firms that do large-scale data processing. How ever, they have been joined over the years by progressively smaller, faster, and less ex pensive desktop and laptop computers. Today, networks take on many configuration and are designed by specialists who work with a firm's information technology per sonnel to decide on what's best for the company.

Updating Data

Until businesses began using computers twenty-five or thirty years ago, informatio systems were manual affairs. Clerical personnel were responsible for typing the com pany's records, storing them in file cabinets, and retrieving the data when needed The manager who needed the information did any manipulation to transform th data contained in each file folder into useful information. Today, an MIS must be abl to update stored data regularly to ensure that the information presented to manager and employees is accurate, complete, and up-to-date. Operations managers a Goodyear Tire & Rubber Company, for instance, cannot produce finished good with last week's work-in-process inventory. They need to know what is availabl today.

The frequency with which data are updated depends on how fast they chang and how often they are used. When it is vital to have current data, updating ma occur as soon as the new data are available. Consider what happens when you deposi money in your checking account. As soon as the bank teller enters the appropriat data and depresses the computer's enter key, the bank's main computer "knows" tha you have made a deposit and adds the amount to your checking account balance. I addition to banking, retail merchants often use automatic updating in order to pro vide up-to-date information to managers and employees. For example, Giant Food, Maryland-based grocery-store chain, has cash registers that automatically transmi data on each item sold to a central computer. The computer adjusts the store's inven tory records accordingly. At any time of the day, a manager can get precise, up-to the-minute information on the inventory of every item the store sells. In som ystems the computer may even be programmed to reorder items whose inventories ll below some specified level.

Data and information also may be updated according to a predetermined time chedule. Data on paper documents, for instance, may be entered into the firm's data ank at certain intervals—every 24 hours, weekly, or monthly.

rocessing Data

)ata are collected, stored in an MIS, and updated under the assumption that they will e of use to managers and employees. Some data are used in the form in which they re stored. This is especially true of verbal data—a legal opinion, for example. Other ata require processing to extract, highlight, or summarize the information they conain. **Data processing** is the transformation of data into a form useful for a specific urpose. For verbal data, this processing consists mainly of extracting the pertinent naterial from storage and combining it into a report.

data processing the transformation of data into a form useful for a specific purpose

Most business data, however, are in the form of numbers—large groups of numers, such as daily sales totals or annual earnings of workers in a particular city. Such roups of numbers are difficult to handle and to comprehend, but their contents can e summarized through the use of statistics.

tatistics as Summaries A **statistic** is a measure that summarizes a particular charcteristic of an entire group of numbers. In this section we discuss the most commonly sed statistics, using the data given in Figure 17.5. This figure contains only eleven tems of data, which simplifies our discussion, but most business situations involve undreds or even thousands of items. Fortunately, computers can be programmed to rocess such large volumes of numbers quickly. Managers are free to concern themelves mainly with the information that results.

statistic a measure that summarizes a particular characteristic of an entire group of numbers

Developing a frequency distribution can reduce the number of items in a set of ata. A **frequency distribution** is a listing of the number of times each value appears n the set of data. For the data in Figure 17.5, the frequency distribution is as follows:

frequency distribution a listing of the number of times each value appears in a set of data

Monthly Salary	Frequency
$3,500	2
3,000	3
2,800	1
2,500	1
2,400	1
2,000	2
1,800	1

t is also possible to obtain a grouped frequency istribution:

Salary Range	Frequency
$3,000–3,500	5
2,500–2,999	2
2,000–2,499	3
1,500–1,999	1

Note that summarizing the data into a grouped requency distribution has reduced the number of lata items by approximately 65 percent.

figure 17.5

Statistics

Managers often examine statistics that describe trends in employee compensation.

Rondex Corporation

Employee Salaries for April 2004

Employee	Monthly Salary
Thomas P. Ouimet	$ 3,500
Marina Ruiz	3,500
Ronald F. Washington	3,000
Sarah H. Abrams	3,000
Kathleen L. Norton	3,000
Martin C. Hess	2,800
Jane Chang	2,500
Margaret S. Fernandez	2,400
John F. O'Malley	2,000
Robert Miller	2,000
William G. Dorfmann	1,800
Total	$29,500

Measures of Size and Dispersion The arithnetic mean, median, and mode are statistical neasures used to describe the size of numerical values in a set of data. Perhaps the most familiar statistic is the arithmetic mean, com monly called the *average*.

arithmetic mean the sum of all the values of a set of data divided by the number of items in the set

median the value at the exact middle of a set of data when the data are arranged in order

mode the value that appears most frequently in a set of data

The **arithmetic mean** of a set of data is the sum of all the data values divided b the number of items in the set. The sum of employee salaries given in Figure 17.5 $29,500. The average (arithmetic mean) of employee salaries is $2,681.82 ($29,500 11 = $2,681.82).

The **median** of a set of data is the value at the exact middle of the data when the are arranged in order. The data in Figure 17.5 are already arranged from the highe value to the lowest value. Their median is thus $2,800, which is exactly halfway be tween the top and bottom values.

The **mode** of a set of data is the value that appears most frequently in the set. I Figure 17.5, the $3,000 monthly salary appears three times, more often than any othe salary amount appears. Thus $3,000 is the mode for this set of data.

Although the arithmetic mean, or average, is the most commonly used statistic measure of size, it may be distorted by a few extremely small or large values in the se of data. In this case a manager may want to rely on the median or mode, or both, t describe the values in the data set. Managers often use the median to describe dolla values or income levels when the arithmetic mean for the same numbers is distorte In a similar fashion, marketers often use the mode to describe a firm's most successfu or popular product when average sales amounts for a group of products would be in accurate or misleading.

range the difference between the highest value and the lowest value in a set of data

Another characteristic of the items within a set of values is the dispersion, c spread. The simplest measure of dispersion is the **range,** which is the difference be tween the highest value and the lowest value in a set of data. The range of the data i Figure 17.5 is $3,500 − $1,800 = $1,700.

The smaller the range of the numbers in a set of data, the closer the values are t the mean—and thus the more effective the mean is as a measure of those values. Othe measures of dispersion used to describe business data are the *variance* and the *standar deviation*. These are somewhat more complicated than the range, and we shall not de fine or calculate them here. However, you should remember that larger values of bot the variance and the standard deviation indicate a greater spread among the values c the data.

With the proper software, a computer can provide these and other statistic measures almost as fast as a user can ask for them. How they are used is then up to th manager. Although statistics provide information in a more manageable form tha raw data, they can be interpreted incorrectly. Note, for example, that the average c the employee salaries given in Figure 17.5 is $2,681.82, yet not one of the employe salaries is exactly equal to this amount. This distinction between actual data and th statistics that describe them is an important one that you should never disregard.

Presenting Information

An MIS must be capable of presenting information in a usable form. That is, th method of presentation—reports, tables, graphs, or charts, for example—must be ap propriate for the information itself and for the uses to which it will be put.

Verbal information may be presented in list or paragraph form. Employees ofte are asked to prepare formal business reports. A typical business report includes (1) a introduction, (2) the body of the report, (3) the conclusions, and (4) the recommen dations.

The *introduction*, which sets the stage for the remainder of the report, describe the problem to be studied in the report, identifies the research techniques that wer used, and previews the material that will be presented in the report. The *body of the re port* should objectively describe the facts that were discovered in the process of com pleting the report. The body also should provide a foundation for the conclusions an the recommendations. The *conclusions* are statements of fact that describe the finding contained in the report. They should be specific, practical, and based on the evidenc contained in the report. The *recommendations* section presents suggestions on how th problem might be solved. Like the conclusions, the recommendations should be specific, practical, and based on the evidence.

Visual and tabular displays may be necessary in a formal business report. For example, numerical information and combinations of numerical and verbal information may be easier to understand if presented in charts and tables.

Visual Displays A *visual display* is a diagram that represents several items of information in a manner that makes comparison easier. The most accurate visual display is a *graph*, in which values are plotted to scale on a set of axes. Graphs are most effective for presenting information about one variable that changes with time (such as variations in sales figures for a business over a five- or ten-year period). Graphs tend to emphasize trends as well as peaks and low points in the value of the variable. Figure 17.6 illustrates examples of visual displays generated by a computer.

In a *bar chart*, each value is represented as a vertical or horizontal bar. The longer the bar, the greater is the value. This type of display is useful for presenting values that are to be compared. The eye can quickly pick out the longest or shortest bar or even those that seem to be of average size.

A *pie chart* is a circle ("pie") divided into "slices," each of which represents a different item. The circle represents the whole—for example, total sales. The size of each slice shows the contribution of that item to the whole. By their nature, pie charts are most effective in displaying the relative size or importance of various items of information.

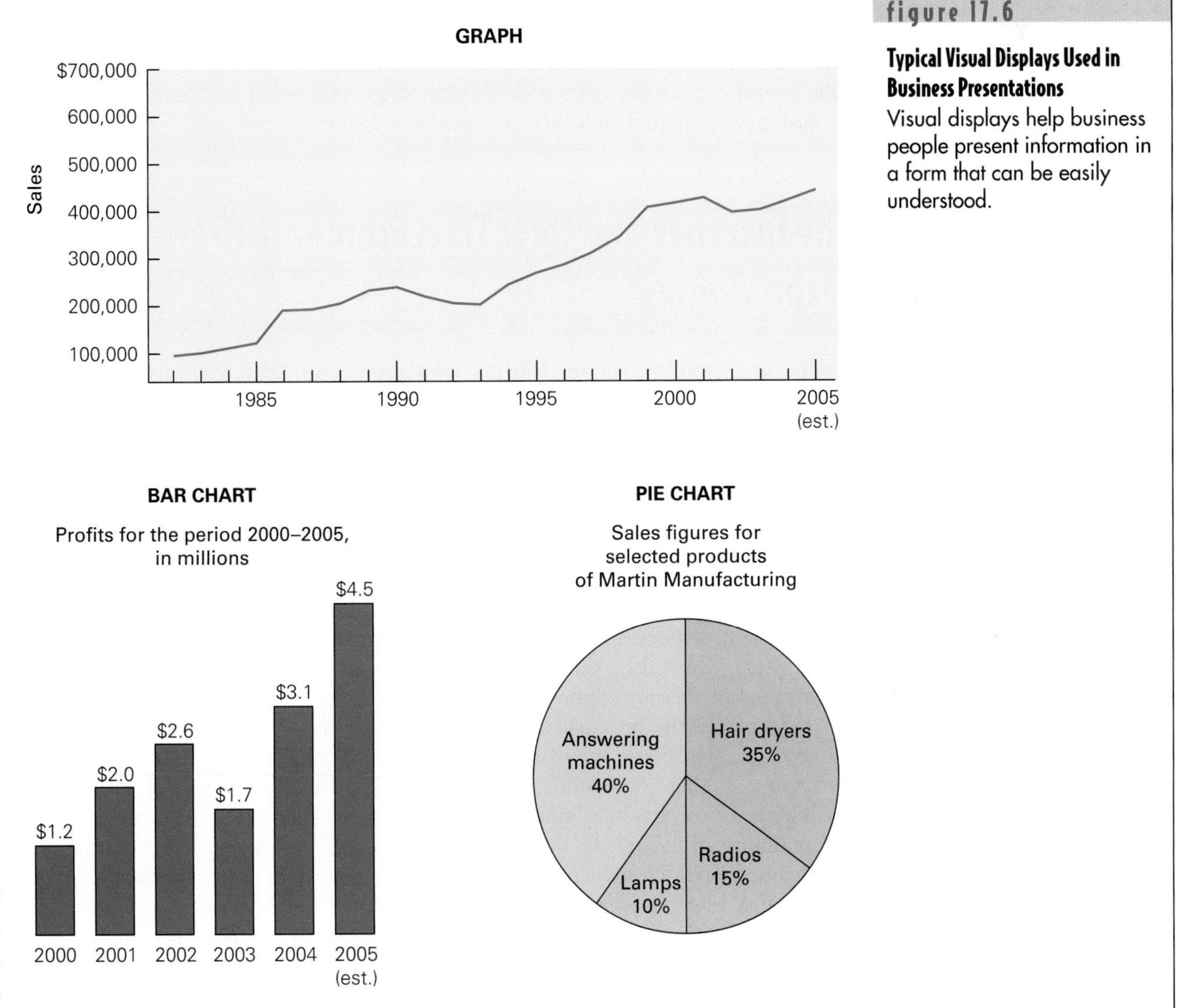

figure 17.6

Typical Visual Displays Used in Business Presentations

Visual displays help business people present information in a form that can be easily understood.

table 17.2 Typical Three-Column Table Used in Business Presentations

Tables are most useful for displaying information about two or more variables.

All-Star Technology

Projected Sales

Section of the Country	Number of Salespeople	Consumer Products	Industrial Products
Eastern territory	15	$1,500,000	$ 3,500,000
Midwestern territory	20	$2,000,000	$ 5,000,000
Western territory	10	$1,000,000	$ 4,000,000
TOTALS	45	$4,500,000	$12,500,000

Tabular Displays A tabular display is used to present verbal or numerical information in columns and rows. It is most useful in presenting information about two or more related variables. A table, for example, can be used to illustrate the number of salespeople in each category, sales volume for individual products, and total sales for all products (see Table 17.2). And information that is to be manipulated—for example, to calculate loan payments—also is usually displayed in tabular form.

Tabular displays generally have less impact than visual displays. Moreover, the data contained in most two-column tables (such as Figure 17.5) can be displayed visually. However, displaying the information that could be contained in a three-column table would require several bar or pie charts. In such cases, the items of information are easier to compare when they are presented in a table.

The Internet and New Telecommunication Technologies

learning objective 5

Explain how the Internet, intranet, standards for communications, and web pages affect business today.

information society
a society in which large groups of employees generate or depend on information to perform their jobs

We live in a rapidly changing **information society—**that is, a society in which large groups of employees generate or depend on information to perform their jobs. The need for more and better information will only continue to grow. Most experts predict that in the future computers will affect every aspect of our lives. Computers are already installed in cars, toys, and appliances. Musicians and engineers, artists and bank tellers, students and teachers use them. In fact, it would be very difficult to find a person not affected in some way by a computer or the information generated by a computer. To see how Intuit is developing software products that help both businesses and individuals, read Adapting to Change.

Today businesses are using the Internet to find and distribute information to global users. Currently, the primary business use of the Internet is e-business. In Chapter 4 *e-business* was defined as the organized effort of individuals to produce and sell, for a profit, the products and services that satisfy society's needs through the facilities available on the Internet. IDC, a respected market and technology research firm, forecasts that goods and services purchased through some sort of e-business will reach $5.8 trillion by 2006, up from $870 billion in 2002.[3] The Internet is also used for communicating between the firm's employees and its customers. e-Mail and file attachments are reducing the need for phone calls, faxes, and overnight document delivery. Finally, businesses use the Internet to gather information about competitors' products, prices, and other business strategies readily available on corporate websites and through online publications such as Bloomberg.com. And business use of the Internet is expected to increase dramatically in the next five to ten years. Clearly, the Internet is here to stay.

adapting to change

Intuit: A New Beginning

DURING THE DOT-COM CRAZE of the late 1990s, Intuit used profits from its successful software products to invest in a variety of online businesses. When Stephen M. Bennett became CEO, however, he got rid of unprofitable Internet activities such as an insurance website and a bill-payment service. Then he made a new beginning by refocusing the company on the lucrative business of providing software for small businesses. Today, small businesses mean big business for Intuit. Its QuickBooks product has locked up a whopping 85 percent of the market for small business accounting software. The California-based company also makes two popular products for individuals: Quicken personal finance software and TurboTax income tax software.

The original QuickBooks software was designed for companies with fewer than twenty employees, a $280-million market. Bennett put Intuit on the trail of even larger markets within the small business world. The company developed a variation of QuickBooks for small businesses employing 20 to 250 employees. It also acquired companies that make specialized software for small and medium-sized businesses in selected industries such as construction and (of course) accounting. It continues to serve the needs of its customers by spending hundreds of millions of dollars to introduce new software and update existing software every year.

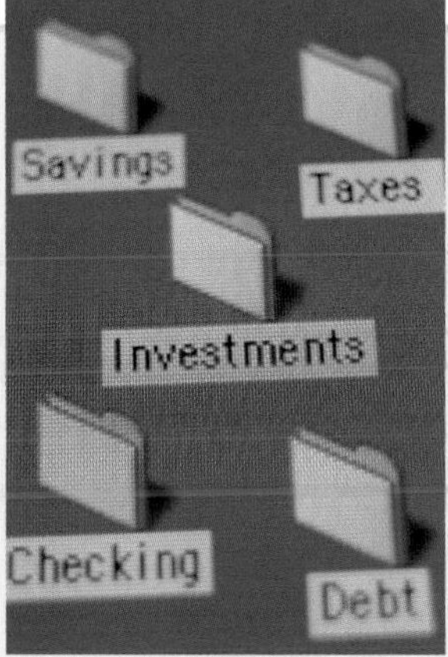

Bennett's emphasis on small business software has pushed Intuit's annual sales beyond $1.4 billion, even as many software companies have stumbled or failed. The CEO has even more ambitious plans for boosting the company's profit margin and improving software quality in the coming years. Quality improvement has already shaved $10 million from Intuit's costs, enhancing its bottom line.

Still, Intuit will face formidable competition from Microsoft and other software giants if it launches products for larger business customers. Even now Microsoft is invading Intuit's turf by acquiring software makers that serve the small business market. For his part, Bennett is enthusiastic about Intuit's competitive position. He believes that his company should restrict itself to markets where it can be one of the top two competitors. Intuit is already number one in accounting software for the smallest businesses. Can it be number one with larger businesses? Time will tell!

The Internet and the Intranet

Internet a worldwide network of computers linked through telecommunications

The **Internet** is a worldwide network of computers linked through telecommunications. Enabling users around the world to talk with each other electronically, the Internet provides access to a huge array of information sources. Originally an elaborate military project to ensure that national communications would continue in case of war, the network now has grown to over 700 million users worldwide.[4]

The Internet's most commonly used network for finding information is the *World Wide Web*. The web contains numerous *sites*—documents whose pages include text, graphics, and sound. To get on the Internet, you need a computer, a modem, and an *Internet service provider* (ISP), such as America Online, AT&T, SBC Communications, or other companies that provide a connection to the World Wide Web. In fact, there are more than 1,000 ISPs worldwide.[5] Today, connections to the Internet include simple telephone lines or faster digital subscriber lines (DSLs) and cabled broadband that carry larger amounts of data at quicker transfer speeds. And with new wireless technology it is possible to access the Internet by using your cellular phone.

As tools such as cellular telephones, pagers, and fax machines have converged with computer technology, inexpensive telecommunications services have become the norm in business. Consider the tools a salesperson for a clothing manufacturer might use during a typical sales call to a nationwide retailer such as the Gap. After discussing the customer's needs, the salesperson opens his or her portable laptop computer and, using his or her own personal cellular phone or a convenient phone jack in the office, dials the local phone number of his or her ISP. Once the salesperson is on the Internet, his or her *web browser*—software that helps users navigate and move around the World Wide Web—automatically connects him or her to his or her firm's own website.

The screen on the site's *home page* (first page) offers the salesperson severa choices, including access to the firm's MIS. By clicking on the appropriate icons, o graphic symbols, the salesperson is able to see invoicing records, the present status o outstanding orders, inventory at warehouses located around the globe, and photo graphs of all available products. Although the salesperson brought a few samples wit him or her to show the client the quality of the workmanship and fabrics, he or she ca generate images on his or her computer screen showing the color, pattern, and fabri of any of the firm's products. Furthermore, the latest fashion accessories are flashed o the side of the screen for the customer and sales representative to consider.

As the salesperson enters the items and quantities of the order into the computer a new icon appears on his or her screen indicating that the volume of buying entere thus far requires a credit check before the sale can be closed. While he or she completes the sales presentation, the firm's *decision-support system* (DSS) automatically calculates the allowable credit limit for the customer and provides credit authorization.

Because the Internet provides a relatively inexpensive way to advertise their products, take orders, and obtain information about customers for research purposes, companies have taken to the web in droves. Consider the following examples:

- Traditional catalog shoppers at L.L. Bean and J.C. Penney can browse through photographs of an array of consumer products on these companies' websites, place their orders, and select delivery dates.
- Federal Express distributes communications software to customers that allows them to schedule their own pickups and trace their shipments.
- Dell Computer provides a user-friendly screen on which customers can select the configuration specifications for their computer. After completing the order, the customer's information is automatically transferred to the manufacturing plant where production of the computer is begun.

In addition to corporate sites, the World Wide Web has a wide array of governmen and institutional sites that provide information to the public. There are also onlin sites available for most of the popular business periodicals. See Table 17.3 for a listin of favorite websites for business.

intranet a smaller version of the Internet for use within a firm

An **intranet** is a smaller version of the Internet for use within a firm. Using a series of customized web pages, employees can quickly find information about their firm as well as connect to external sources. For instance, an employee might use the intranet to access the firm's policy documents on customer warranties or even take a company-designed course on new products and how to introduce them to customers.

A nice job perk: online investment advice. One of the benefits that Hallmark Cards, Inc. offers its employees is online investment advice provided by Financial Engines. This picture shows a group of Hallmark employees at a demonstration learning how to use the online service to manage their retirement accounts.

table 17.3 Favorite Websites Used by Managers and Employees to Obtain Information about Business and the Economy

Sponsor and Description	Web Address
1. ***Bureau of Labor Statistics*** The Bureau of Labor Statistics provides statistical information about all facets of the economy.	**www.bls.gov**
2. ***Department of Commerce*** The Department of Commerce is the primary source of government-generated business information.	**www.commerce.gov**
3. ***Federal Reserve Bank of New York*** The Federal Reserve Bank of New York provides information about banking and the economy.	**www.ny.frb.org**
4. ***American Marketing Association*** The association uses its site to provide marketing information and services useful both to its members and to the general public.	**www.marketingpower.com**
5. ***BusinessWeek Online*** This site provides articles about business, finance, and economic issues that affect businesses and investors.	**www.businessweek.com**
6. ***Fortune Magazine Online*** This site provides articles about business, finance, and economic issues that affect businesses and investors.	**www.fortune.com**
7. ***Wall Street Journal Online*** This site provides current business news along with detailed coverage of the financial markets.	**www.wsj.com**
8. ***CEOExpress*** This site provides an exhaustive collection of well-organized links to a wide variety of business websites.	**www.ceoexpress.com**

Internet Standards for Communications

What is standardization? **Standardization** is defined as the guidelines that let products, services, materials, and processes achieve their purposes. Standardization allows computers to interact with other computers. Establishing standards is vital to ensure that an IBM computer in McPherson, Kansas, can "talk" with a Dell computer in San Francisco, California. It is just as important for software to be standardized if businesses and individuals are going to use computers to communicate and conduct business activities through the Internet.

standardization the guidelines that let products, services, materials, and processes achieve their purposes

To permit communication between different components of the Internet, a common standard language or protocol has emerged that is called *TCP/IP*. TCP/IP stands for Transmission Control Protocols and Internet Protocols. These protocols allow computers from all over the world to communicate with each other. Because all Internet users use these protocols, they have allowed the Internet to grow rapidly and provide access to all.

Website Addresses Every website on the Internet is identified by its *Uniform Resource Locator (URL)*, which acts as its address. To connect to a site, you enter its URL in your web browser. The URLs of most corporate sites are similar to the organizations' real names. For instance, you can reach IBM by entering **http://www.ibm.com.**

The first part of the entry, "http," sets the software protocols for proper transfer of information between your computer and the one at the site to which you are connecting. "http" stands for *hypertext transfer protocol. Hypertext* refers to words or phrases highlighted or underlined on a web page; when you select these, they link you to other websites.

Web Search Engines To find a particular website, you can take advantage of several free search programs available on the web, such as Yahoo!, Alta Vista, Google, and Ask Jeeves. While many Internet users are annoyed by the pop-up ads and advertising banners that are common on most search engines, the services provided by search engines are free of charge because advertisers buy space on their screens. Thus the services provided by a search engine are paid for in much the same way advertisements pay for television and radio broadcasts. To locate a search engine, enter its URL in your browser. Some URLs for popular search engines are

www.altavista.com
www.google.com
www.ask.com
www.lycos.com
www.netscape.com
www.yahoo.com

The home page for most search engines provides a short list of primary topic divisions, such as *business and economics*, *news and media*, and *reference*, as well as a search window where you can enter the particular topic you are looking for. Each site provides instructions and suggestions for finding what you want. With practice, you will get a general sense of how search engines function.

Spotlight

Popular search engines

The most popular search sites in the U.S.

Google	29.5%
Yahoo	28.9%
MSN	27.6%
AOL	18.4%

Source: Danny Sullivan, "Nielsen//Net Ratings Search Engine Ratings," **www.searchenginewatch.com/reports/netratings.html**, February 25, 2003.

Software for Creating Web Pages

Although it is possible to write a computer program to develop a web page, it is often easier to use a commercially available program such as Microsoft's FrontPage (**www.microsoft.com/frontpage/**) that requires a minimal amount of user programming knowledge. Generally, once a *template* or structure for the web page has been created, content such as text or images can be inserted or changed readily, allowing the site to remain current.

The design of a firm's website should be carefully thought out. The web page is, after all, the global image distributed to customers, suppliers, and other parties interested in knowing more about the firm and possibly doing business with the firm. What the website says about a company is important and should be developed carefully to portray the "right" image. Therefore, it is understandable that a firm without the internal human resources to design and launch its website will turn to the talents of creative experts available through web consulting firms.

Once a website is established, most companies prefer to manage their websites on their own computers. An alternative approach is to pay a hosting service that often will provide guaranteed user accessibility, e-commerce shopping software, site-updating services, and other specialized operational products and services. The company often can benefit by outsourcing these specialized web activities to firms that have the expertise to provide faster access to customers while maintaining a higher degree of security and lower operational costs.

Managing Internet Activities

learning objective

6 Discuss how the Internet helps employees communicate, assists a firm's sales force, trains and recruits employees, and conducts financial activities.

Today many employees use the Internet to conduct research, improve productivity and performance, and communicate with other employees while at the office or away from the office. In this section we examine several solutions to problems created when a firm or its employees use the Internet. In each case a solution is always evaluated in terms of its costs and compared with the benefits a firm receives, generally referred to as a *cost/benefit analysis*. Typical areas of concern for a business using the Internet include communications, sales, training and recruiting, and accounting and finance. Before reading the material below, take a look at the Talking Technology boxed feature to see how Electronic Data Systems (EDS) works to solve problems for customers.

Helping Employees Communicate

One of the first business applications of computer technology was e-mail. Once software was chosen and employees trained, communications could be carried out globally within and outside the firm at any time, twenty-four hours a day, seven days a week. The firm's cost for software, training, and Internet connection services were small when compared with the benefits of being able to communicate with all the firm's employees without having to use traditional pencil-and-paper methods or the telephone. And because e-mail provides an efficient means for people in various locations to work on a common project, there is less need for meetings, and travel expenses can be reduced while still providing an effective method of communication.

groupware one of the latest types of software that facilitates the management of large projects among geographically dispersed employees as well as such group activities as problem solving and brainstorming

Groupware is the latest type of software that facilitates the management of large projects among geographically dispersed employees, as well as such group activities as

talking technology

EDS: The Information Expert

When Bank of America's top executives decided to turn over responsibility for its international information technology operations to an outside company, they chose Electronic Data Systems (EDS). Based in Plano, Texas, EDS serves as an information expert for companies of all sizes, including the U.S. Navy, Continental Airlines, 7-Eleven, and many other organizations. Each organization's needs are unique and require a specialized information solution. For example, EDS runs the huge computer network that handles accounting, payroll, and flight reservations for Continental Airlines. It also runs the management information system and customized intranet ordering system for the 5,200 convenience stores in the 7-Eleven chain. To meet these and all the other information needs of its customers, EDS employs 138,000 employees in sixty nations.

One of EDS's key tools for managing customer relationships is its web-based Service Excellence Dashboard. The dashboard shows at a glance whether the company is meeting each customer's expectations for timely response and other service standards. A green light on the dashboard indicates excellent performance, but a red light indicates unacceptable performance. The idea behind the dashboard is to alert EDS's management to serious problems with a customer's information technology systems—problems that require immediate, high-level attention.

Consider what happened when the ordering system that EDS operates for 7-Eleven failed to work correctly. Because of problems with the equipment and software, individual stores could not consistently access the 7-Eleven's intranet to place orders. Even when a store actually connected with the firm's intranet, it couldn't always get its orders to the right suppliers—causing major problems. "If we can't process our orders, we can't get product into the stores," remembers one 7-Eleven official. "And if we don't have product in the stores, we don't have sales."

After the retailer's CEO contacted EDS's management about the problem, the dashboard section for 7-Eleven displayed a red light. EDS quickly assembled a cross-functional team of specialists to collaborate with 7-Eleven's technical specialists in finding the cause and fixing the problem. Then EDS completely redesigned the system, tested it, and installed it permanently. Only after 7-Eleven was satisfied did EDS change the dashboard light from red to green.

problem solving and brainstorming. By using groupware, a firm with thousands of employees linked together through its computer system can be thought of as a large-scale "thinking unit" with expertise and information available to anyone connected to the system. For example, suppose that the home office of a software development firm in a major city has been hired to prepare customized software for a client in another city. The project team leader uses the software to establish guidelines for the project, check availability of employees around the world, give individuals specific work assignments, and set up a schedule for work completion, testing, and final installation on the client's computer. As work progresses, the program automatically signals team members for their input. The team leader is also able to monitor work progress and may intervene if asked or if problems develop. Questions or details required by design engineers may be routed electronically to others in the group as well. When needed, people from various locations, possessing an array of knowledge and skills, can be called to the "workspace" created on the computer system for their contribution. When the work is finally completed, it can be forwarded to the client's computer and installed.

Besides being useful in project management, groupware provides an opportunity for establishing a collaborative learning system to help solve a specific problem. A **collaborative learning system** is a work environment that allows problem-solving participation by all team members. By posting a question or problem on the groupware's conference site, the team leader invites members, who may be located anywhere in the world, to submit messages that can help move the group toward a solution. If the conference site lists both successful and unsuccessful solutions to problems, members can learn from each other and presumably improve their performance in the future.

collaborative learning system a work environment that allows problem-solving participation by all team members

Today, e-mail solutions are available to firms of all sizes and are used for more than just communicating within a company. e-Mail is being used as a direct link between business and customer. When investment bank Putnell Lovell Securities, for example, sent research reports to clients by e-mail instead of printing, packaging, and shipping the reports, the firm saved over $500,000 a year.[6] No wonder that the research firm IDC projects that there will be sixty billion e-mails per day by 2006.[7]

Communications software programs are also a major source of sales revenue for such companies as Microsoft (NetMeeting and MSN's Messenger Service) and America On-Line (Instant Messenger).

Assisting the Firm's Sales Force

In addition to general communications programs that may be used by all of a firm's employees, there are also Internet-based software application programs sometimes referred to as customer-relationship management (CRM) programs that focus on the special informational needs of sales personnel. For example, sales force automation programs support sales representatives with organized databases of information such as names of clients, status of pending orders, and sales leads and opportunities, as well as any related advice or recommendations from other company personnel. Consider what happens when a sales representative for a pharmaceutical company such as Johnson & Johnson is planning to visit doctors, health care providers, and hospitals in the Chicago area. A sales force automation software program can help map out which clients should be visited by providing useful information such as how long it has been since they were last contacted. The software also can provide information about how clients were approached, what the results were of the last contacts, who else in the pharmaceutical firm has interacted with the client, and previous purchases the client has made.

In large organizations such as pharmaceutical firms, it is not uncommon to have several sales representatives dealing with different customers in various departments of a hospital or a large medical clinic. Sales force automation systems can prevent embarrassment for sales representatives who work in their own specialized areas and may not be aware of the bigger picture with respect to their firm's total sales efforts with the prospective customer. As sales representatives complete their visits, information about what was learned should be entered into the sales force automation system as soon as possible so that everyone can use the latest information. For instance, a sales representative might learn from an individual within the client's organization that another department is seeking information about a product that could provide a sales opportunity. Although the sales representative may not be involved directly in that field, the information can be entered into the firm's database of information. At the same time, a message can be sent to the sales manager or sales representative in the appropriate department that a new opportunity has been identified. Then a sales representative in the appropriate department can provide information to the potential customer and ultimately increase sales of the firm's products or services.

The industry-leading sales force automation software programs are distributed by PeopleSoft (**www.peoplesoft.com**), Siebel Systems (**www.siebel.com**), and eSales from Relavis Corporation (**www.relavis.com**).

Training Employees

Large and midsize companies spend a great deal of money on educational and training programs for employees. By distributing information about the firm, the organization, products and services, new procedures, and general information to employees through the Internet for reading and study at convenient times and places, firms can reduce training costs dramatically. For example, new employees generally are required to attend an intensive training program in which a wide variety of information about the firm is presented in a classroom setting. Online training may then be used on a variety of topics to provide additional information and keep both new and experienced employees up-to-date on the latest information about the firm and its products and services.

Information on a wide range of topics ranging from ethical behavior to sexual harassment to discrimination also can be distributed to a firm's employees. Often these sites may be needed only on rare occasions; however, it is important that employees know that the information exists and where it is. Furthermore, revision and distribution of important changes to this type of information are much easier if the information is provided on the company's website. Important announcements about changes to policies and procedures can be e-mailed and linked to the appropriate document that is maintained on the website.

Recruiting Employees

A common icon on most corporate websites is a link to "careers" or "employment opportunities." Firms looking for people with specialized skills can post their employee needs on their websites and reach potential candidates from around the globe. This is an extremely important method of recruiting employees for positions where labor shortages are common and individuals with the *right* skills are in high demand.

Furthermore, software programs can help large firms such as General Electric, ExxonMobil, and Citigroup establish a database of potential employees. This is an especially important function for a firm that receives thousands of unsolicited employment applications from people all over the world. The cost of organizing and processing this information is high, but software can reduce this expense when compared with a paper-based system. As a bonus, the software can organize data in a way most useful to the firm. Critical

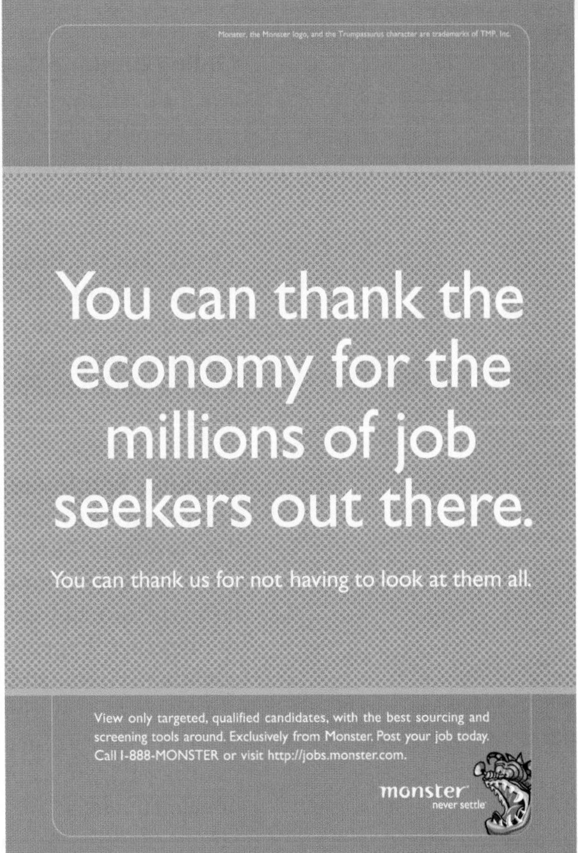

Finding the right employee can be a monster of a job. Monster.com provides a clearinghouse for job seekers and employers. Prospective employees use Monster.com to identify employers that have job openings. And according to many employers, Monster.com provides the best employee screening tools that can be used to identify qualified candidates.

data, such as an applicant's knowledge about IBM's pSeries 690 computer, for example, may be identified quickly by managers using the database.

In addition to individual corporate websites, would-be employees also can access online recruiting websites that can help to match up job seekers with businesses seeking to hire additional employees. Perhaps the best known of these is Monster.com (**www.monster.com**), which recognized the advantages of providing a clearinghouse for job seekers and employers. This type of online service helps resolve the problems that a person living in one city encounters when searching for employment in another city. On the other hand, this type of online service also can help employers attract job applicants who presently reside in other cities or countries.

Conducting Financial Activities

The banking and financial services industries were quick to recognize the advantages of using the Internet. Now other businesses are using the Internet to process e-business transactions, bank online, and track employee expenses. Each of these activities is important for a business that wants to compete in today's technological world.

Completing e-Business Transactions Today, theft of credit card information is a common concern for online shoppers. And to avoid losing potential online sales, businesses must make it easy for customers to pay for purchases online while ensuring that transactions are secure. To provide a sense of security, many businesses use the *secure electronic transaction* (SET) encryption process, which prevents merchants from actually seeing transaction data, including the customer's credit card number. (More information on this topic can be found at **www.setco.org.**) Other options include offering shoppers the choice of calling in their orders over the phone and speaking to an operator. Still another option is the use of a separate online-use bank card, such as Visa's NextCard. Finally, it is possible for a customer to bill their purchase through third parties. Acting like a bank, they process credit card transactions for merchants and assume the responsibility for collection.

Online Banking Services Today, online banking and financial services are available to businesses as well as consumers. Financial institutions can provide direct access to both checking and savings accounts, allowing clients to make payments, transfer funds between accounts, apply for loans, and obtain financial information. For both businesses and consumers, online banking is fast and easy, with many transactions completed with a click of the mouse any time of the day or night, seven days a week. For the financial institution, online banking is often cheaper than traditional banking activities because of the savings that occur when processing large numbers of transactions online. For both customer and financial institution, these systems provide an added measure of security. Many transactions can be handled without human intermediaries and paper documents, thus reducing potential mistakes and the risk of theft.

Tracking Employee Expenses The use of expense-tracking software provides an opportunity for firms to improve the way they process employee expense requests. Two products—Boomerang and NavigatER—available from Necho Systems Corporation (**www.necho.com**) allow employees such as sales representatives, who regularly pay for many expenses that are part of their job, to report their expenses through the Internet. Expenses are then charged to the appropriate accounts in the firm's accounting system, and sales representatives are issued a refund. Because Necho's software uses the Internet, sales representatives can input data whenever they want and wherever they happen to be in the world. The information they input will be securely transferred to appropriate company personnel, and once expenses are approved, reimbursement checks may be issued quickly. Clients, such as Procter & Gamble, PepsiCo, Honda, and Bayer, Inc., have been able to reduce expenses while simplifying expense accounting and reducing internal financial management costs by using Necho software.[8]

Business Applications Software

learning objective

7 Understand how business applications software can be used to collect and distribute information.

Early software typically performed a single function. Today, however, *integrated software* combines many functions in a single package. Integrated packages allow for the easy *linking* of text, numerical data, graphs, photos, and even audiovisual clips. A business report prepared using the Microsoft Office package, for instance, can include all these components, and the report may then be disseminated electronically through the firm's MIS or the Internet or printed and delivered through more traditional channels, including the U.S. Postal Service or messenger.

Integration offers at least two other benefits. Once data have been entered into an application in an integrated package, the data can be used in another integrated package without having to reenter the data again. Also, once a user learns one application, it is much easier to learn another application in an integrated package.

Current Business Applications

Software has been developed to satisfy almost every business need. Today the most common types of software for business applications focus on the following functions:

- Database management
- Graphics
- Spreadsheets
- Word processing
- Desktop publishing
- Accounting

From a career standpoint, you should realize that firms will assume that you possess, or will possess after training, a high degree of working comfort with several of these programs, particularly word processing, spreadsheets, and graphics.

Database Management As noted earlier, a database is a single collection of data stored in one place and used by people throughout an organization to make decisions. A **database management program** allows users to electronically store large amounts of data and to transform the data into information. Data can be sorted by different criteria. For example, a firm's personnel department may sort by each worker's gender, salary, and years of service. If management needs to know the names of workers who have at least fifteen years of experience, an employee using database management software can print a list of such employees in a matter of minutes. The same type of manipulation of data for other departments within a business is possible with database management software. In addition to building its own database, a company can subscribe to online computer services that enable users to access large external databases.

database management program software that allows users to electronically store large amounts of data and to transform the data into information

Graphics Whether you are playing a video game or watching the computerized scoreboard at a football stadium, you are viewing computer-generated graphics. A **graphics program** enables users to display and print pictures, drawings, charts, and diagrams. In business, graphics are used for oral or written presentations of financial analyses, budgets, sales projections, and the like.

graphics program software that enables users to display and print pictures, drawings, charts, and diagrams

Although visual aids have always been available, their use was restricted because someone had to take the time to draw them. With the aid of a graphics program, the computer can generate drawings in seconds. Typically, graphics software allows the user to select a type of visual aid from a menu of options. The user enters the numerical data, such as sales figures, to be illustrated. The computer program then converts the data into a graph, bar chart, or pie chart.

Spreadsheets A **spreadsheet program** is a software package that allows the user to organize numerical data into a grid of rows and columns. Among the popular spreadsheet programs are Microsoft Excel and Lotus 1-2-3. With a spreadsheet, the computer performs mathematical calculations automatically. For example, a manager

spreadsheet program a software package that allows users to organize numerical data into a grid of rows and columns

at Dallas-based Malone's Cost-Plus Grocery Stores may want to project sales and expenses for the next three-month period. The manager enters numerical data for both sales and expenses, and the spreadsheet software calculates the dollar amount of profit or loss based on the data. Spreadsheet software also can be used to answer "what if" questions. By changing data to match new assumptions, the manager can see how the change will affect other data in the spreadsheet. If the manager wanted to calculate the firm's profits based on projections that sales will increase by 5, 10, and 15 percent, three additional spreadsheets could be prepared based on each set of assumptions. In fact, a spreadsheet user can change any variable and, within seconds, have new information to aid in the decision-making process.

word-processing program software that allows a user to prepare and edit written documents and to store them in the computer or on a disk

Word Processing A **word-processing program** allows the user to prepare and edit letters, memos, reports, and other written documents and to store them in the computer or on a disk. Text revision is greatly simplified because the user can make changes where necessary without having to retype the entire document. In addition, word-processing programs can be used to send personalized copies of form letters. For example, most firms use a standard collection letter to urge prompt payment of past-due amounts. With a word-processing program, the letter can be personalized by adding an individual's name and address to each letter that is sent to all customers with overdue accounts. To appeal to customers, mail-order firms and direct-mail marketing firms make extensive of word-processing programs to personalize their sales letters. Thousands of letters—each addressed to a particular individual—can be prepared from one master document.

desktop publishing program a software package that enables users to combine text and graphics in reports, newsletters, and pamphlets

Desktop Publishing A **desktop publishing program** is a software package that enables users to combine text and graphics in reports, newsletters, and pamphlets. Most desktop publishing programs go beyond word-processing programs to give the user more control over complex designs and page layout. With the aid of a state-of-the-art printer, the user can prepare documents almost as professional looking as those produced by a printing company.

accounting program a software package that enables users to record and report financial information

Accounting An **accounting program** is a software package that enables the user to record, process, and report financial information. Almost all commercially available accounting packages contain three basic modules: general ledger and financial reporting, accounts receivable, and accounts payable. The general ledger and financial reporting module processes routine, daily accounting entries. This module also should prepare financial statements at the end of each accounting period. The accounts receivable module prepares customer invoices, maintains customer balances, allows different payment terms to different customers, and generates past-due notices to slow-paying customers. The accounts payable module records and monitors invoices from a firm's suppliers. It also should take advantage of cash discounts offered by suppliers for prompt payment. The better accounting packages also prepare checks to pay suppliers, vendors, and employees.

Other Business Applications

Although it is impossible to describe all the software business firms use today, three programs described in Chapter 9 deserve special mention here. Computer-aided design (CAD) programs use computers to aid in the development of products. Computer-aided manufacturing (CAM) programs use computers to plan and control manufacturing processes. And computer-integrated manufacturing (CIM) not only helps design products but also controls the machinery needed to produce finished products. Each of these programs streamlines the manufacturing process and ultimately makes a manufacturer more productive. As a result, programs such as these have become an integral part of business firms involved in manufacturing.

In this chapter we have explored some of the functions and requirements of a business firm's MIS and how a computer and the Internet can help people obtain the information they need to be effective employees. In Chapter 18 we examine the accounting process, which is a major source of information for business.

Return To inside business

Since developing its first human resources management software in 1988, PeopleSoft has expanded into software for other organizational functions, including distribution, financial reporting, manufacturing, purchasing, and customer relationship management. The company constantly adds new features to streamline the process that managers use to transform data into information that can be used to help managers and employees make decisions.

For example, PeopleSoft is developing enhanced reporting capabilities so that managers can analyze mounds of data—such as months of purchase orders—to produce meaningful results in a short time. Soon to be introduced are new software programs that will help decision makers predict trends in sales and other areas based on sophisticated analyses of historical data. In addition, the company is working on software that will help managers anticipate customers' needs by using previous customer behavior to "model" future customer behavior. Instead of trying to make sense of raw data, managers will be able to obtain timely, detailed information with only a few keystrokes.

Questions

1. Back in 1999, PeopleSoft made a commitment of $500 million to rewrite its software so that each of its programs would run smoothly over the Internet. Was this a good decision? Explain your answer.
2. How is this information likely to improve decision making and reduce the risk of making poor decisions once managers can use PeopleSoft software to predict trends and anticipate customers' needs?

chapter review

Summary

Understand how information is organized to help people make decisions.

The more information a manager has, the less risk there is that a decision will be incorrect. Information produces knowledge and empowers managers and employees to make better decisions. Without correct and timely information, individual performance will be undermined and, consequently, so will the performance of the entire organization. Because of the volume of information they receive each day and their need to make decisions on a daily basis, business people use information rules to shorten the time spent analyzing choices. Information rules emerge when business research confirms the same results each time it studies the same or a similar set of circumstances. Although many people use the terms *data* and *information* interchangeably, there is a difference. Data are numerical or verbal descriptions that usually result from some sort of measurement. Information is data presented in a form that is useful for a specific purpose. A database is a single collection of data stored in one place that can be used by people throughout an organization to make decisions.

Describe how business research is conducted.

When secondary sources do not provide business people with sufficient information to make decisions with acceptable levels of risk, they may undertake primary research. Primary research in business employs two fundamentally different approaches to information gathering and analysis. Qualitative research involves the descriptive or subjective reporting of information discovered by research. Generally, qualitative research is conducted in one of three ways: observation, interviews, or focus groups. Quantitative research involves the collection of numerical data for analysis through a survey, experiment, or content analysis. The decision about which research method to use is often based on a combination of factors, including limitations on time and money and the need or concern for accuracy and validity. In general, managers rely on the results of proven research methods until those methods no longer work well.

Discuss management's information requirements.

A management information system (MIS) is a means of providing managers with the information they need to perform their jobs as effectively as possible. The purpose of an MIS system is to distribute timely and useful information from both internal and external sources to the decision makers who need it. The specific types of information managers need depend on their area of management and level within the firm. An MIS system must be tailored to the information needs of the organization it serves.

Describe the five functions of an information system.

The five functions performed by an MIS system are collecting data, storing data, updating data, processing data into information, and presenting information to users. Data may be collected from such internal sources as company records, reports, and minutes of meetings, as well as from the firm's managers. External sources include customers, suppliers, bankers, trade and financial publications, industry conferences, online computer services, and information-gathering organizations. An MIS system must be able to store data until they are needed and to update them regularly to ensure that the information presented to managers is accurate, complete, and timely. Data processing is the MIS function that transforms stored data into a form useful for a specific purpose. Large groups of numerical data usually are processed into summary numbers called statistics. The most commonly used statistics are the arithmetic mean, median, and mode. Other statistics are the frequency distribution and the range, which is a measure of the dispersion, or spread, of data values. Finally, the processed data (which can now be called information) must be presented for use. Verbal information generally is presented in the form of a report. Numerical information most often is displayed in graphs, charts, or tables.

Explain how the Internet, intranet, standards for communications, and web pages affect business today.

We live in an information society—one in which large groups of employees generate or depend on information to perform their jobs. To find needed information, many businesses and individuals use the Internet. The Internet is a worldwide network of computers linked through telecommunications. Firms also can use an intranet to distribute information within the firm. To permit communication, a common standard language or protocol has emerged that allows computers to communicate with other computers. Because all Internet users use the same protocols, the Internet has grown rapidly and provides access to all users. By using the Internet to access websites, search engines, and web pages, users can obtain a wealth of information with the click of a computer's mouse.

Discuss how the Internet helps employees communicate, assists a firm's sales force, trains and recruits employees, and conducts financial activities.

Today, many employees use the Internet to conduct research, improve productivity and performance, and communicate with other employees while at the office or away from the office. One of the first computer applications in the workplace was electronic mail or simply e-mail, which provides for communication within and outside the firm at any time, twenty-four hours a day, seven days a week. An extension of e-mail is groupware, which is software that facilitates the management of large projects among geographically dispersed employees as well as such group activities as problem solving and brainstorming. The Internet and a sales force automation software program can provide a database of information that can be used to assist a sales representative. The Internet also can be used to improve employee training and recruitment while lowering costs. Finally, the Internet can help firms complete e-business transactions, bank online, and track employee expenses.

Understand how business applications software can be used to collect and distribute information.

Software has been developed to satisfy almost every business need. The most common programs for business applications include database management, graphics, spreadsheets, word processing, desktop publishing, and accounting. Although it is impossible to describe all the software business firms use today, computer-aided design (CAD), computer-aided manufacturing (CAM), and computer-integrated manufacturing (CIM) should be mentioned because they are used to help manufacture the products a firm sells in the marketplace. Each of these programs streamlines the manufacturing process and ultimately makes a manufacturer more productive. As a result, programs such as these have become an integral part of business. From a career standpoint, you should realize that firms will assume that you possess, or will possess after training, a high degree of working comfort with several of these programs, particularly word processing, spreadsheets, and graphics.

Key Terms

You should now be able to define and give an example relevant to each of the following terms:

data (501)
information (502)
database (502)
qualitative research (503)
quantitative research (504)
management information system (MIS) (505)
information technology officer (505)
data processing (511)
statistic (511)
frequency distribution (511)
arithmetic mean (512)
median (512)
mode (512)
range (512)
information society (514)
Internet (515)
intranet (516)
standardization (517)
groupware (519)
collaborative learning system (520)
database management program (523)
graphics program (523)
spreadsheet program (523)
word-processing program (524)
desktop publishing program (524)
accounting program (524)

Review Questions

1. In your own words, describe how information reduces risk when you make a personal or work-related decision.
2. What are information rules? How do they simplify the process of making decisions?
3. What is the difference between data and information? Give one example of accounting data and one example of accounting information.
4. What is the difference between qualitative research and quantitative research?
5. Describe the methods used to conduct qualitative research and quantitative research.
6. How do the information requirements of managers differ by management area?
7. Why must a management information system (MIS) be tailored to the needs of the organization it serves?
8. List five functions of an MIS.
9. What are the differences among the mean, median, and mode of a set of data? How can a few extremely small or large numbers affect the mean?
10. What are the components of a typical business report?
11. Explain the differences between the Internet and an intranet. What types of information does each of these networks provide?
12. Why is a common language or protocol necessary for the Internet to operate properly?
13. How can a web search engine such as Yahoo!, Alta Vista, or Google help you to find information on a business topic such as interest rates or the consumer price index?
14. What factors should be considered when a firm is developing a web page?
15. How do business firms use groupware to encourage collaborative learning systems?
16. Describe how the Internet and software can help a firm assist sales representatives, train and recruit employees, and track expenses.
17. Describe how businesses use database management programs, graphics programs, spreadsheet programs, word-processing programs, desktop publishing programs, and accounting programs.

Discussion Questions

1. How can confidential data and information (such as the wages of individual employees) be kept confidential and yet still be available to managers who need them?
2. Do managers really need all the kinds of information discussed in this chapter? If not, which kinds can they do without?
3. Why are computers so well suited to management information systems (MISs)? What are some things computers *cannot* do in dealing with data and information?
4. Assume that you have been out of college for ten years, are unemployed, and your computer skills are seriously outdated. How would you go about updating your computer skills?
5. How could the Internet help you to find information about employment opportunities at Coca-Cola, Johnson & Johnson, or Microsoft? Describe the process you would use to access this information.

video case

Bang Networks Banks on Web-Based Data Delivery

Up-to-the-minute information is the lifeblood of the financial world. Stock and bond prices are constantly fluctuating as securities are traded around the clock and around the world. Therefore, financial services firms need the very latest market information to make profitable decisions about buying, selling, or holding securities for customers and themselves.

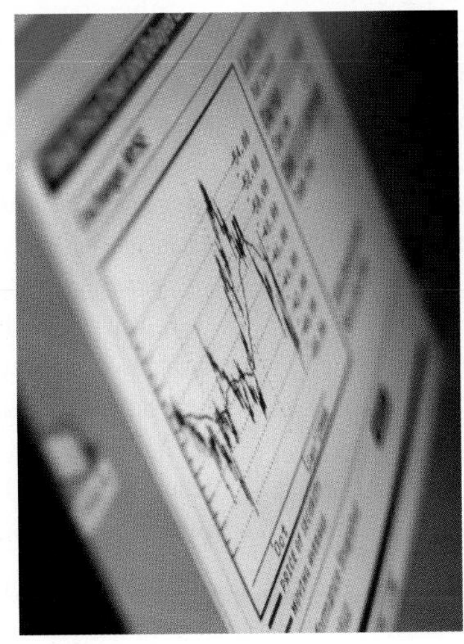

Until recently, however, bankers, securities traders, and many other decision makers had to use costly private networks and leased telecommunication lines to check the most current prices for stocks, bonds, and other financial instruments. Those without private networks or leased lines would have to wait a few moments—or refresh the page—to get updated prices because of slight delays caused by data transmission.

Now Bang Networks has invented a unique system of object routers to provide secure, web-based delivery of vital financial information. This system offers banks and other institutions a cost-effective way to eliminate transmission delays and receive or distribute financial market information live and in real time—the instant it is available. Users can see any update on their screens as it occurs, not one minute or even ten seconds later. Moreover, customers can save money by eliminating expensive leased lines and relying instead on high-speed Internet connections to receive updated information through the Bang Networks system.

Although Bang Networks is a high-tech firm, it recognizes that customers do not buy technology; they buy cost-effective information solutions to problems such as transmission delays and interruptions. The company's vision statement notes that its commitment "goes well beyond pure technology and products" to help customers make the most of technology to build their businesses. Bang Networks focuses only on financial information and the financial services industry, where its technology is especially valued because of the urgent demand for timely data. Its customer list includes the Federal Reserve Bank of New York, the Bank of New York, Dow Jones Newswires, GovPX, and IronPlanet.

GovPX, for example, distributes information about government bond pricing to 50,000 customers worldwide who buy and sell securities, evaluate the risk and worth of portfolios, and price other financial instruments according to bond values. In the past, GovPX—located in New York City—used dedicated leased lines to transmit information to each individual customer. The company had already begun talking with Bang Networks, headquartered in San Francisco, about its system. Then terrorists attacked New York's World Trade Center, severing nearly all of GovPX's telecommunication connections and disrupting transmissions to customers. GovPX had to act quickly to get back into full operation and resume feeding information to its customers. It called on Bang Networks, which immediately started setting up an Internet-based system using one of the few remaining phone lines available to GovPX. Within 48 hours, GovPX was again transmitting detailed bond pricing information to customers via the web.

Next, GovPX decided to hire Bang Networks to operate a backup system for the connections needed to funnel additional financial market information to customers. If one of the numerous information sources feeding information to GovPX lost its connection, it would be able to restore transmission by switching to the Bang Networks system. Just as important, GovPX was in a better position to add new customers at a much lower communications cost by transmitting via the Internet.

IronPlanet, another customer, turned to Bang Networks to support its rapid-fire online auctions of used construction equipment. This is big business: At any one time, hundreds of bidders might be vying for a $100,000 excavator. Auctions last only 30 minutes, so bidders must act quickly. If they cannot see the most recent bid, they may offer too much or too little—a problem either way for cost-conscious buyers and sellers. With the Bang Networks system, however, buyers can enter bids knowing that their screens reflect up-to-the-second information.

As an added bonus, Bang Networks offers secure transmission of data and information. Safeguarding sensitive information sent over the Internet has been an ongoing concern for companies and individuals alike. The chief technology officer for Bang Networks emphasizes that its object router system sets up "secure, reliable channels on top of the public Internet, so customers can run very high performance applications." In fact, he says, "You can have a level of security that is comparable if not better than what private networks can offer."[9]

Questions

1. Ten seconds is not very long. And yet Bang Networks has been successful because it can provide data in real time and eliminate this type of time lag. Why do you think a time lag of even ten seconds for market prices for stocks and bonds is so important to brokerage firms and securities traders?
2. Other than financial institutions, what types of businesses are likely to need Bang Networks' technology? Explain your answer.
3. Sometimes executives with no technical expertise must approve contracts for services such as those offered by Bang Networks. If you were a sales representative for Bang Networks, how would you explain to a bank's CEO the basic value and importance of your firm's services?

Building Skills for Career Success

1. Exploring the Internet

Computer technology is a fast-paced, highly competitive industry in which product life cycles are sometimes measured in months or even weeks. To keep up with changes and trends in hardware and software, MIS managers must routinely scan computer publications and websites that discuss new products.

A major topic of interest among MIS managers is groupware, software that facilitates the management of large projects among geographically dispersed employees as well as group activities such as problem solving and brainstorming.

Assignment

1. Use a search engine and enter the keyword *groupware* to locate companies that provide this type of software. Try the demonstration edition of the groupware if it is available.
2. Based on your research of this business application, why do you think groupware is growing in popularity?
3. Describe the structure of one of the groupware programs you examined as well as your impressions of its value to users.

2. Developing Critical Thinking Skills

To stay competitive in the marketplace, businesses must process data into information and make that information readily available to decision makers. For this, many businesses rely on a management information system (MIS). The purpose of an MIS is to provide managers with accurate, complete, and timely information so that they can perform their jobs as effectively as possible. Because an MIS must fit the needs of the firm it serves, these systems vary in the way they collect, store, update, and process data and present information to users.

Assignment

1. Select a local company large enough to have an MIS. Set up an interview with the person responsible for managing the flow of information within the company.
2. Prepare a list of questions you will ask during the interview. Structure the questions around the five basic functions of an MIS. Some sample questions follow.
   a. *Collecting data*: What type of data are needed? How often are data collected? What sources produce the data? How do you ensure that the data are accurate?
   b. *Storing data*: How are data stored?
   c. *Updating data*: What is the process for updating?
   d. *Processing data*: Can you show me some examples of the types of data that will be processed into information? How is the processing done?
   e. *Presenting information*: Would you show me some examples (reports, tables, graphs, charts) of how the information is presented to various decision makers and tell me why that particular format is used?
3. At the end of the interview, ask the interviewee to predict how the system will change in the next three years.
4. In a report, describe what you believe the strengths and weaknesses of this firm's MIS are and make recommendations for improving the system. Also describe the most important thing you learned from the interview.

3. Building Team Skills

To provide marketing managers with information about consumers' reactions to a particular product or service, business researchers often conduct focus groups. The participants in these groups are representative of the target market for the product or service under study. The leader poses questions and lets members of the group express their feelings and ideas about the product or service. The ideas are recorded, transcribed, and analyzed.

Assignment

1. Working in a small team, select a product or service to research—for example, your college's food service or bookstore or a new item you would like to see stocked in your local grocery store.
2. Form a focus group of five to seven people representative of the market for the product or service your team has selected. Try to find people who are representative of the target market for this product or service.
3. During the group sessions, record the input. Later, transcribe it into printed form, analyze it, and process it into information. On the basis of this information, make recommendations for improving the product or service.
4. In a report, describe your team's experiences in forming the focus groups and the value of focus groups in collecting data. Use the report as the basis for a five- to ten-minute class presentation.

4. Researching Different Careers

Firms today expect employees to be proficient in using computers and computer software. Typical business applications include e-mail, word processing, spreadsheets, and graphics. By improving your skills in these areas, you can increase your chances not only of being employed but also of being promoted once you are employed.

Assignment

1. Assess your computer skills by placing a check in the appropriate column in the following table:

	Skill Level			
Software	**None**	**Low**	**Average**	**High**
Database management				
Graphics				
Spreadsheet				
Word processing				
Desktop publishing				
Accounting				
Groupware				

2. Describe your self-assessment in a written report. Specify the software programs in which you need to become more proficient, and outline a plan for doing this.

5. Improving Communication Skills

Over the past decade, computers have changed the way we do business and conduct our daily lives. As computer technology continues to improve over the next decade, it will affect our lives in new and very different ways.

Assignment

1. Research articles that predict how computers will be used in the next decade and how their use will change the way we live.
2. Write a paper focusing on the future use of computers in two or more of the following areas: health care, genetics, travel, communications, manufacturing, transportation, management, farming, or meal preparation. Conclude your paper with a discussion of how you think computers will affect your life over the next ten years.

chapter

18 Using Accounting Information

learning objectives

1. Explain how new regulations affect the accounting industry and the way businesses report financial information.
2. Understand why accounting information is important and what accountants do.
3. Discuss the accounting process.
4. Read and interpret a balance sheet.
5. Read and interpret an income statement.
6. Describe business activities that affect a firm's cash flow.
7. Summarize how managers evaluate the financial health of a business.

Five SEC commissioners and more than 3,000 agency employees supervise the corporate reporting process.

inside business

The SEC Tackles Corporate Accountability

Question: Who polices the way publicly held corporations use accounting to report financial results?
Answer: The Securities and Exchange Commission (SEC) is the U.S. government agency charged with overseeing the accounting methods used to report sales, profits, and other data that stockholders use to evaluate a corporation's financial situation.

AFTER THE STOCK MARKET CRASH OF 1929, in which hundreds of thousands of people lost their investments in corporate stock, Congress passed laws to revive public confidence in the securities markets. It created the SEC in 1934 to enforce those laws and protect investors' interests. Today, five SEC commissioners and more than 3,000 agency employees supervise the corporate reporting process. They ensure that corporations release accurate financial information for investors every quarter and every year. They also require public disclosure of certain critical events, such as when a corporation is preparing to merge with or acquire another company. The goal is to help investors use accounting information to assess the true nature of the corporation's financial stability so that they can make informed decisions about buying, holding, and selling stock.

Over the years, the SEC has investigated the financial reporting practices of a number of major corporations, including Adelphia Communications, AOL/Time Warner, Cendant, Enron, Sunbeam, WorldCom, and Xerox. In the case of Xerox, the SEC was concerned about whether revenue was inflated by recording certain copier lease payments at the start of the leasing period rather than as the lease progressed. Xerox ultimately agreed to restate five years' worth of financial reports and pay a fine of $10 million, without admitting or denying wrongdoing. The fine was the largest ever imposed by the SEC in this type of case. Months later, the SEC also filed suit against KPMG—Xerox's accounting firm—and four of its accounting partners over their work on Xerox's financial statements. The accountants denied acting improperly and said they would fight the suit.

Other SEC investigations have led to charges against high-ranking executives for financial fraud. For example, the agency charged former CEO Al Dunlap and several other former managers of Sunbeam with defrauding company's stockholders on a massive scale. Stockholders also sued over company mismanagement and fraud. Ultimately, Sunbeam filed for bankruptcy protection, and Dunlap settled the stockholders' suit with a $15-million payout. In another major case, SEC and civil lawsuits charged Walter A. Forbes, the former chairman of the board of directors, and E. Kirk Shelton, the former vice chairman, of participating in a plan to inflate the corporate earnings of CUC International, which later became Cendant. As a result, Cendant had to restate three years' of financial reports to account for inflated earnings of about $500 million. Indeed, there are many more examples of corporations that have violated SEC financial and accounting standards.[1]

phony earnings! Inflated revenues! When does it stop? Well, according to the Securities and Exchange Commission (SEC), it stops now. As pointed out in the Inside Business feature for this chapter, the SEC is responsible for supervising corporate financial reporting. Today the SEC's job has never been more difficult. Stories about corporate executives at Xerox, Sunbeam, Enron, Tyco, WorldCom, and other public companies using questionable accounting methods to overstate profits and the financial condition of the company have never been more plentiful. To make matters worse, some of the largest accounting firms in the world were involved in efforts to "cook" their clients' books. And yet we begin this chapter with two assumptions. First, "creative" methods of reporting earnings and other financial information are not only unethical but also in many cases illegal. Second, a firm's accounting system should generate financial information that not only is easy to understand but also is accurate and above suspicion.

We begin this chapter by looking at the recent problems in the accounting industry and attempts to improve financial reporting. Then we look at the importance of accounting information both to a firm's managers and employees and to individuals and groups outside a firm. We also identify different types of accountants and career opportunities in the accounting industry. Next, we focus on the accounting process and the basics of an accounting system: the accounting equation, double-entry bookkeeping, and the process by which raw data are organized into financial statements. We also examine the three most important financial statements: the balance sheet, the income statement, and the statement of cash flows. Finally, we show how ratios are used to measure specific aspects of a firm's financial health.

Improved Accountability in the Accounting Industry

learning objective 1

Explain how new regulations affect the accounting industry and the way businesses report financial information.

Accounting is the process of systematically collecting, analyzing, and reporting financial information. Some people would even go so far as to say that accounting is the language of business. Today it is impossible to manage a business without accurate and up-to-date information supplied by the firm's accountants. And yet managers and other groups interested in a business firm's financial records must be able to "trust the numbers." Unfortunately, a large number of accounting scandals have caused people to doubt not only the numbers but also the accounting industry.

accounting the process of systematically collecting, analyzing, and reporting financial information

Recent Accounting Problems for Corporations and Their Auditors

Today much of the pressure on corporate executives to "cook" the books is driven by the desire to look good to Wall Street analysts and investors. Every three months companies report their revenues, expenses, profits, and projections for the future. If a company meets or exceeds "the street's" expectations, everything is usually fine. However, if a company reports financial numbers that are lower than expected, the company's stock value can drop dramatically. An earnings report that is lower by even a few pennies per share than what is expected can cause a company's stock value to drop immediately by as much as 30 to 40 percent. And as pointed out in the Examining Ethics boxed feature, greed is another factor that can lead some corporate executives to use questionable accounting methods to inflate a firm's financial performance.

In a perfect world, the accountants who inspect the corporate books would catch mistakes and disclose questionable accounting practices. Unfortunately, we do not live in a perfect world. Consider the part that auditors for the accounting firm of Arthur Andersen played in the Enron meltdown. When the SEC launched its inquiry into Enron's financial affairs, Andersen employees shredded the documents related to the audit. As a result, both the SEC and the Department of Justice began to investigate Andersen's role in the failure of Enron. Eventually, Andersen was convicted of obstruction of justice in June 2002 and was forced to cease auditing public companies.

examining ethics

Why "Cook" the Corporate Books?

WHY WOULD A CORPORATION or high-level executive "cook" the corporate books? While there are many reasons, greed is one of the strongest motivations behind manipulating corporate financial statements. Sometimes the manipulations involve inflating revenues or profits to qualify for higher performance bonuses or to boost the corporation's stock price. Sometimes they involve hiding questionable or unauthorized transactions for personal benefit. Regardless of the reasons, huge amounts of money are at stake.

For example, Dennis Kozlowski, the former CEO of Tyco International, and the firm's former chief financial officer Mark Swartz were charged with taking millions of dollars in stock gains, bonuses, and loans that were either illegal or unauthorized. The loans and bonuses were not disclosed in Tyco's financial statements despite SEC rules requiring such disclosure. At about the same time, Kozlowski also was indicted in New York City for evading $1 million in sales tax due for the purchase of expensive art. The controversy surrounding Tyco's executives and its financial statements drove the share price down more than 70 percent in 12 months, hurting large and small investors alike.

In the Enron scandal, former financial managers were charged with fraud, money laundering, and conspiracy for their part in accounting ruses that covered up the corporation's heavy debt and made earnings look better than they actually were. Some of the executives were paid millions of dollars in bonuses for managing special financial entities not adequately explained in Enron's financial statements. In fact, the situation created a conflict of interest because the managers could not ethically protect the corporation's interests as well as the interests of those who invested in the special entities.

Questions about conflict of interest also were raised about the relationship between auditor Arthur Andersen and its client Enron. Every year Enron paid Andersen millions of dollars for consulting projects on top of millions of dollars for auditing services. Could Andersen's auditors enforce strict standards for Enron's financial statements if the firm feared losing Enron's lucrative consulting business?

Finally, dubious accounting schemes designed by higher-level managers often depend on the cooperation of midlevel and lower-level employees. These employees may go along with questionable accounting practices because they will profit from their actions, because they fear the retaliation of high-level executives, or because they worry about losing their jobs—especially when new employment opportunities are scarce.

Issues to Consider

1. What are the potential risks of "cooking" the books? What are the potential rewards? In your opinion, are the rewards worth the risks?
2. Assume that a high-level corporate executive offers you money to "cook" the books by inflating the firm's sales revenues and profits. While you know the actions are both unethical and illegal, you are afraid that if you refuse, you will lose your job. What would you do in this situation? Explain your answer.

Andersen lost hundreds of corporate clients, and many employees defected to other accounting firms, started their own accounting firms, or joined the ranks of the unemployed. At the time of publication, Arthur Andersen—once known as one of the "Big Five" accounting firms with 28,000 employees and annual revenues of $9 billion—was in the process of selling buildings, office equipment, and its expensive art collection. Simply put, Andersen—the once proud accounting firm—was found guilty.[2] Less than a month after admitting accounting errors that inflated earnings by almost $600 million since 1994, Enron filed for bankruptcy. At the time, it was the largest bankruptcy case in U.S. history.[3] Unfortunately, Arthur Andersen is not the only major accounting firm to experience the hot seat. KPMG and PricewaterhouseCoopers also have been targeted by trial lawyers, government regulators, and in some cases the Internal Revenue Service (IRS) for providing questionable audit work for major corporations.[4]

Why Audited Financial Statements Are Important

So who cares if executives "cook" the books? Everyone! For example, assume that you are a bank officer responsible for evaluating loan applications. A business has applied for a loan. How do you make a decision to approve or reject the loan request? In this tuation, most bank officers rely on the information contained in the firm's balance ıeet, income statement, and statement of cash flows along with other information rovided by the prospective borrower. In fact, most lenders insist that these financial :atements be audited by a certified public accountant (CPA). An **audit** is an examina-on of a company's financial statements and the accounting practices that produced ıem. The purpose of an audit is to make sure that a firm's financial statements have een prepared in accordance with generally accepted accounting principles. Today, **enerally accepted accounting principles (GAAPs)** have been developed to pro-ide an accepted set of guidelines and practices for companies reporting financial in-ɔrmation and the accounting profession. Today, three organizations—the Financial ccounting Standards Board (FASB), the American Institute of Certified Public Ac-ountants (AICPA), and the International Accounting Standards Committee ASC)—have greatly influenced the methods used by the accounting profession.

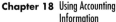

audit an examination of a company's financial statements and accounting practices that produced them

generally accepted accounting principles (GAAPs) an accepted set of guidelines and practices for companies reporting financial information and for the accounting profession

If an accountant determines that a firm's financial statements present financial in-ɔrmation fairly and conform to GAAPs, then he or she will issue the following state-ıent:

> In our opinion, the financial statements . . . present fairly, in all material respects . . . in conformity with generally accepted accounting principles.

While an audit and the resulting report do not *guarantee* that a company has not cooked" the books, it does imply that, on the whole, the company has followed GAAPs. Bankers, creditors, investors, and government agencies are willing to rely on n auditor's opinion when deciding to invest in a company or to make loans to a firm hat has been audited because of the historically ethical reputation and independence f auditors and accounting firms. Even with the recent scandals involving corpora-ions and their accountants that falsified or misled the general public, most of the na-ion's accountants still abide by the rules. And while it is easy to indict an entire rofession because of the actions of a few, there are many more accountants who ad-ıere to the rules and are honest, hard-working professionals. Finally, it should be ıoted that without the audit function and GAAPs, there would be very little oversight r supervision. The validity of a firm's financial statements and its accounting records vould drop quickly, and firms would find it difficult to obtain debt financing, acquire oods and services from suppliers, find investor financing, or prepare documents re-uested by government agencies.

Why is this man angry? If you were Roy Rinard, you would be angry too. His Enron stock dropped in value from almost $500,000 to less than $3,000 because of the accounting problems associated with Enron and its auditor Arthur Andersen. According to Rinard, he will have to work until the day he dies because he lost nearly all of the money he invested for retirement.

Reform: The Sarbanes-Oxley Act of 2002

How important is corporate accountability? According to John Bogle, founder o Vanguard Mutual Funds, "Investing is an act of faith. Without that faith—that re ported numbers reflect reality, that companies are being run honestly, that Wall Stree is playing it straight, and that investors aren't being hoodwinked—our capital market simply can't function."[5] In reality, what Mr. Bogle says is true. Integrity and faith ar important parts of our capitalistic system. People must have financial information tha they believe is accurate and not misleading. To help ensure that corporate financial in formation is accurate and in response to the many accounting scandals that surfaced i the last part of the 1990s and the first part of the twenty-first century, Congress en acted the Sarbanes-Oxley Act, which was signed by President Bush on July 30, 2002 According to Ann Yerger, spokeswoman for the Council of Institutional Investors "this is the most significant pro-investor legislation we've seen in many, many years." Some of the major provisions of the Sarbanes-Oxley Act designed to restore publi confidence are as follows:

- The SEC is required to establish a full-time five-member federal oversight boar that will police the accounting industry.
- Chief executive and financial officers are required to certify periodic financial reports and are subject to criminal penalties for violations of securities reporting requirements.
- Accounting firms are prohibited from providing many types of consulting services to the companies they audit.
- Auditors must maintain financial documents and audit work papers for 5 years.
- Auditors and accountants can be imprisoned for up to twenty years for destroying financial documents and willful violations of the securities laws.
- A public corporation must change its lead auditing firm every five years.
- There is added protection for whistle-blowers who report violations of the Sarbanes-Oxley Act.

While most people welcome the Sarbanes-Oxley Act, complex rules make compliance more expensive and time-consuming for corporate management and more difficult for accounting firms. And yet, when you consider the importance of having accurate financial information about public companies, most people agree that th cost is justified. As you read the next section, you will see just how important accurat accounting information is!

Why Accounting Information Is Important

learning objective

2 Understand why accounting information is important and what accountants do.

Managers and employees, lenders, suppliers, stockholders, and government agencie all rely on the information contained in three financial statements, each no more than one page in length. These three reports—the balance sheet, the income statement, and the statement of cash flows—are concise summaries of a firm's activities during a specific time period. Together they represent the results of perhaps tens of thousands of transactions that have occurred during the accounting period. Moreover, the form of the financial statements is pretty much the same for all businesses, from a neighborhood video store or small dry cleaner to giant conglomerates like the Home Depot, Boeing, and Bank of America. This information has a variety of uses both within the firm and outside it. However, first and foremost, accounting information is management information.

The People Who Use Accounting Information

The primary users of accounting information are *managers*. The firm's accounting system provides information that can be compiled for the entire firm—for each product; for each sales territory, store, or salesperson; for each division or department;

nd generally in any way that will help those who ıanage the organization. At a company such as ≤raft Foods, for example, financial information is athered for all its hundreds of food products: ⁄laxwell House Coffee, Tombstone Pizza, Post ∶ereals, Jell-O Desserts, Kool Aid, and so on. ∶he president of the company would be interested in total sales for all these products. The vice resident for marketing would be interested in ational sales for Tombstone Pizza and Jell-O)esserts. The northeastern sales manager might vant to look at sales figures for Kool Aid in New ∶ngland. For a large, complex organization like ≤raft, the accounting system must be complete nd yet flexible because managers at different levls must be able to get the information they need.

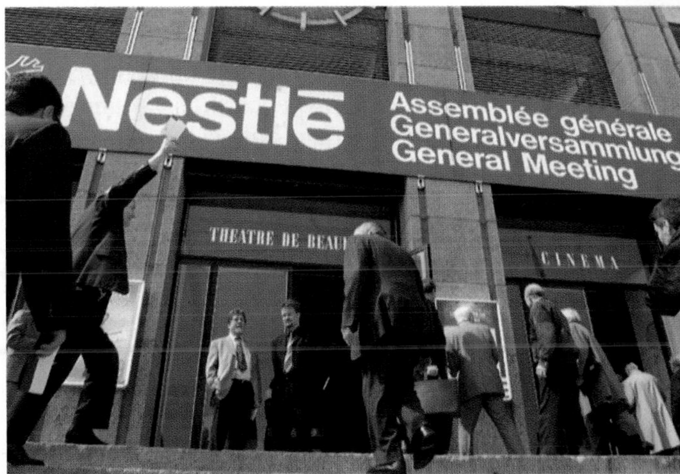

Happy stockholders? Not yet. At a recent shareholder's meeting in Lausanne, Switzerland, Nestlé—the world's largest food company—announced a 10 percent increase in sales. Although the sales increase was over $12 billion, the increase was short of Wall Street estimates causing shareholders to express concern about the firm's financial future.

Much of this accounting information is *proprietary*; it is not divulged to anyone utside the firm. This type of information is used by a firm's managers and employees o plan and set goals, organize, lead, motivate, and control—all the management funcions that were described in Chapter 7. To see how important accounting is, just think bout what happens when an employee or manager asks a supervisor for a new piece f equipment or a salary increase. Immediately, everyone involved in the decision beins discussing how much it will cost and what effect it will have on the firm's profits, ales, and expenses. It is the firm's accounting system that provides the answers to hese important questions. In addition to proprietary information used inside the irm, certain financial information must be supplied to individuals and organizations utside the firm (see Table 18.1).

- *Lenders* require information contained in the firm's financial statements before they will commit themselves to either short- or long-term loans. *Suppliers* who provide the raw materials, component parts, or finished goods a firm needs also generally ask for financial information before they will extend credit to a firm.
- *Stockholders* are provided with a summary of the firm's financial position, including how much profit or loss the company has earned over a specified period of time. In addition, *potential investors* must be provided with financial information about each new securities issue that the firm sells to the public.
- *Government agencies* require a variety of information about the firm's tax liabilities, payroll deductions for employees, and new issues of stocks and bonds.

An important function of accountants is to ensure that such information is accurate nd thorough enough to satisfy these outside groups.

table 18.1 Users of Accounting Information

The primary users of accounting information are a company's managers, but individuals and organizations outside the company also require information on its finances.

Management	Lenders and Suppliers	Stockholders and Potential Investors	Government Agencies
Plan and set goals Organize Lead and motivate Control	Evaluate credit risks before committing to short- or long-term financing	Evaluate the financial health of the firm before purchasing stocks or bonds	Confirm tax liabilities Confirm payroll deductions Approve new issues of stocks and bonds

Careers in Accounting

Wanted: An individual with at least two years of college accounting courses. Must be honest, dependable, and willing to complete all routine accounting activities for a manufacturing business. Salary dependent on experience.

Want a job? Positions such as the one described in this newspaper advertisement ar becoming increasingly available to those with the required training. According to th *Occupational Outlook Handbook*, published by the Department of Labor, job opportuni ties for accountants, auditors, and managers in the accounting area are expected to ex perience average growth between now and the year 2010.[7]

What is an average day in the life of an accountant like? Many people have th idea that accountants spend their day working with endless columns of numbers in small office locked away from other people. In fact, accountants do spend a lot of tim at their desks, but their job entails far more than just adding or subtracting number. Accountants are expected to share their ideas and the information they possess wit people who need the information. Accounting is serious business, but it also can be a exciting and rewarding career—one that offers higher than average starting salarie To be successful in the accounting industry, employees must

- Be responsible, honest, and ethical.
- Have a strong background in financial management.
- Know how to use a computer and software to process data into accounting information.
- Be able communicate with people who need accounting information.

private accountant an accountant employed by a specific organization

Today, accountants generally are classified as either private accountants or public ac countants. A **private accountant** is employed by a specific organization. A medium sized or large firm may employ one or more private accountants to design it accounting information system, manage its accounting department, and provide man agers with advice and assistance. Private accountants also perform the following serv ices for their employers:

1. *General accounting*—Recording business transactions and preparing financial statements
2. *Budgeting*—Helping managers develop budgets for sales and operating expenses
3. *Cost accounting*—Determining the cost of producing specific products or services
4. *Tax accounting*—Planning tax strategy and preparing tax returns for the firm
5. *Internal auditing*—Reviewing the company's finances and operations to determine whether goals and objectives are being achieved

public accountant an accountant who provides services to clients on a fee basis

certified public accountant (CPA) an individual who has met state requirements for accounting education and experience and has passed a rigorous two-day accounting examination prepared by the AICPA

Individuals, self-employed business owners, and smaller firms that do not require thei own full-time accountants can hire the services of public accountants. A **public ac countant** works on a fee basis for clients and may be self-employed or be the employe of an accounting firm. Accounting firms range in size from one-person operations t huge international firms with hundreds of accounting partners and thousands of em ployees. Today the largest accounting firms, sometimes referre to as the "Big Four," are PricewaterhouseCoopers, Ernst & Young, KPMG International, and Deloitte Touche Tohmatsu.

Typically, public accounting firms include on their staffs a least one **certified public accountant (CPA),** an individua who has met state requirements for accounting education an experience and has passed a rigorous two-day accounting exam ination prepared by the American Institute of Certified Publi Accountants (AICPA). The AICPA uniform CPA examinatio covers four areas: (1) business law and professional responsibili ties, (2) auditing, (3) accounting and reporting, and (4) financia accounting and reporting. More information about general re quirements and the CPA profession can be obtained by contact ing the AICPA at **www.aicpa.org.**[8] State requirements usuall include a college degree or a specified number of hours of col

Using the Internet

The American Institute of Certified Public Accountants (AICPA) is the preeminent professional body governing the profession. The organization's website **(www.aicpa.org)** provides users with a wide variety of information related to the accounting profession, including a host of online publications, articles, guidelines, career resources, employment opportunities, and links to other sites important to the field of accountancy.

ege coursework and from one to three years of on-the-job experience. Details regarding specific state requirements for practice as a CPA can be obtained by contacting the state's board of accountancy.

Once an individual becomes a CPA, he or she must participate in continuing-education programs to maintain state certification. These specialized programs are designed to provide the current training needed in today's changing business environment. CPAs also must take an ethics course to satisfy the continuing-education requirement.

Certification as a CPA brings both status and responsibility. Only an independent CPA can audit the financial statements contained in a corporation's annual report and express an opinion—as required by law—regarding the acceptability of the corporation's accounting practices. And because CPAs have a great deal of experience, they are often asked to help determine solutions for their client's financial problems. In addition to auditing a corporation's financial statements and performing routine accounting activities, typical services performed by CPAs include planning and preparing tax returns, determining the true cost of producing and marketing a firm's goods or services, and compiling the financial information needed to make major management decisions. Fees for the services provided by CPAs generally range from $50 to $300 an hour.

Spotlight

Salaries for accountants and auditors Median salaries paid to accountants and auditors in selected U.S. industries.

Computer and data processing $47,110

Accounting $45,890

Federal, state, and local government $42,133

Source: The Bureau of Labor Statistics website, **www.bls.gov**, March 21, 2003.

The Accounting Process

learning objective

3 Discuss the accounting process.

In Chapter 17, *information* was defined as data presented in a form that is useful for a specific purpose. In this section we examine accounting as the system for transforming raw financial *data* into useful financial *information*. Then, in the next sections we describe the three most important financial statements provided by the accounting process.

The Accounting Equation

The accounting equation is a simple statement that forms the basis for the accounting process. This important equation shows the relationship between the firm's assets, liabilities, and owners' equity.

- **Assets** are the resources a business owns—cash, inventory, equipment, and real estate.
- **Liabilities** are the firm's debts—what it owes to others.
- **Owners' equity** is the difference between total assets and total liabilities—what would be left for the owners if the firm's assets were sold and the money used to pay off its liabilities.

assets the resources that a business owns

liabilities a firm's debts and obligations

owners' equity the difference between a firm's assets and its liabilities—what would be left for the owners if assets were used to pay off its liabilities

The relationship between assets, liabilities, and owners' equity is shown by the following **accounting equation:**

Assets = liabilities + owners' equity

accounting equation the basis for the accounting process: *assets = liabilities + owners' equity*

Whether a business is a small corner grocery store or a giant corporation like General Motors, its assets must equal the sum of its liabilities and owners' equity. To use this equation, a firm's accountants must record raw data—that is, the firm's day-to-day financial transactions—using the double-entry system of bookkeeping.

double-entry bookkeeping a system in which each financial transaction is recorded as two separate accounting entries to maintain the balance shown in the accounting equation

The Double-Entry Bookkeeping System

Double-entry bookkeeping is a system in which each financial transaction i recorded as two separate accounting entries to maintain the balance shown in the accounting equation (assets = liabilities + owners' equity). By offsetting one side of th accounting equation with a change on the other side, the equation always remains i balance. For example, suppose that an entrepreneur named Maria Martin invest $50,000 in cash to start a new business called Maple Tree Software. Before she make this investment, both sides of the accounting equation equal zero. The firm has no assets, no liabilities, and no owners' equity. After Maria makes her original investmen the firm's cash account (an asset) would be increased by $50,000, and the owners' equity account would be increased by $50,000. The accounting equation would no look like this:

Assets	=	**liabilities**	+	**owners' equity**
$50,000	=	$0	+	$50,000

Thus the books are still balanced. Assets ($50,000) are equal to liabilities ($0) plu owners' equity ($50,000). Once established, the accounting system for Maple Tre Software must be able to process the accounting transactions that accurately reflec the financial decisions that are necessary to operate the business. For example, if Martin obtains a $10,000 bank loan to purchase computer equipment, two different accounts—liabilities and equipment (assets)—are affected. Liabilities are increased b the amount of the $10,000 loan. Equipment—an asset—is also increased by $10,00 After this transaction is recorded, the accounting equation would look like this:

Assets	=	**liabilities**	+	**owners' equity**
$60,000	=	$10,000	+	$50,000

After the first two transactions, assets total $60,000, and liabilities and owners' equit total $60,000. That is, assets are indeed equal to liabilities plus owners' equity. Additional transactions are recorded in much the same way using the five steps describe below.

The Accounting Cycle

In the typical accounting system, raw data are transformed into financial statements i five steps. The first three—analyzing, recording, and posting—are performed on regular basis throughout the accounting period. The last two—preparation of the tria balance and of the financial statements—are performed at the end of the accountin period.

Analyzing Source Documents Basic accounting data are contained in *source documents*, the receipts, invoices, sales slips, and other documents that show the dolla amounts for day-to-day business transactions. The accounting cycle begins with th analysis of each of these documents. The purpose of the analysis is to determine whic accounts are affected by the documents and how they are affected.

general journal a book of original entry in which typical transactions are recorded in order of their occurrence

Recording Transactions Every financial transaction is then recorded in a journal—a process called *journalizing*. Transactions must be recorded in the firm's general journal or in specialized journals. The **general journal** is a book of original entry in whic typical transactions are recorded in order of their occurrence. An accounting syster also may include *specialized journals* for specific types of transactions that occur frequently. Thus a retail store might have journals for cash receipts, cash disbursements purchases, and sales in addition to its general journal.

general ledger a book of accounts containing a separate sheet or section for each account

Posting Transactions After the information is recorded in the general journal an specialized journals, it is transferred to the general ledger. The **general ledger** is book of accounts containing a separate sheet or section for each account. Today, mos businesses use a computer and software to post accounting entries from the general journal or specialized journals to the general ledger.

Preparing the Trial Balance A **trial balance** is a summary of the balances of all general ledger accounts at the end of the accounting period. To prepare a trial balance, the accountant determines and lists the balances for all ledger accounts. If the trial balance totals are correct and the accounting equation is still in balance, the accountant can prepare the financial statements. If not, a mistake has occurred somewhere, and the accountant must find it and correct it before proceeding.

trial balance a summary of the balances of all general ledger accounts at the end of the accounting period

Preparing Financial Statements and Closing the Books The firm's financial statements are prepared from the information contained in the trial balance. This information is presented in a standardized format to make the statements as accessible as possible to the various people who may be interested in the firm's financial affairs—managers, employees, lenders, suppliers, stockholders, potential investors, and government agencies. A firm's financial statements are prepared at least once a year. Most firms also have financial statements prepared semiannually, quarterly, or monthly.

Once these statements have been prepared and checked, the firm's books are "closed" for the accounting period, and a *postclosing* trial balance is prepared. Although, like the trial balance just described, the postclosing trial balance generally is prepared after *all* accounting work is completed for one accounting period. If the postclosing trial balance totals agree, the accounting equation is still in balance at the end of the cycle. Only then can a new accounting cycle begin for the next accounting period.

With this brief information about the steps of the accounting cycle in mind, let's now examine the three most important financial statements generated by the accounting process: the balance sheet, the income statement, and the statement of cash flows.

The Balance Sheet

Question: Where could you find the total amount of assets, liabilities, or owners' equity for Hershey Foods Corporation?
Answer: The firm's balance sheet.

learning objective

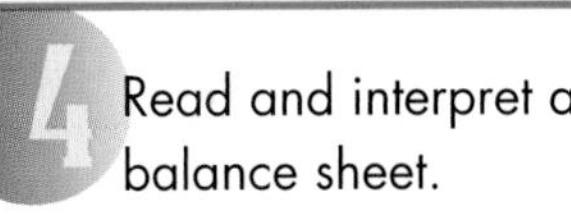

4 Read and interpret a balance sheet.

A **balance sheet** (sometimes referred to as a **statement of financial position**) is a summary of the dollar amounts of a firm's assets, liabilities, and owners' equity accounts at the end of a specific accounting period. The balance sheet must demonstrate that the accounting equation does indeed balance; that is, it must show that assets are equal to liabilities plus owners' equity. Most people think of a balance sheet as a statement that reports the financial condition of a business firm such as Hershey Foods Corporation, but balance sheets apply to individuals, too. Let's begin our discussion with an example of a personal balance sheet for a recent college graduate named Marty Campbell. Three years ago Marty graduated from college and obtained a full-time position as a sales representative for an office supply firm. After going to work, he established a checking and savings account and purchased an automobile, stereo, television, and a few pieces of furniture. Marty paid cash for some purchases, but he had to borrow money to pay for the larger ones. Figure 18.1 (on p. 542) shows Marty's current personal balance sheet.

balance sheet (sometimes referred to as a **statement of financial position**) a summary of the dollar amounts of a firm's assets, liabilities, and owners' equity accounts at the end of a specific accounting period

Marty Campbell's assets total \$26,500, and his liabilities amount to \$10,000. While the difference between total assets and total liabilities is referred to as *owners' equity* or *stockholders' equity* for a business, it is normally called *net worth* for an individual. As reported on Marty's personal balance sheet, net worth is \$16,500. The total assets (\$26,500) and the total liabilities *plus* net worth (\$26,500) are equal.

A balance sheet for a business reports the same type of financial information as a personal balance sheet. Figure 18.2 (on p. 543) shows the balance sheet for Northeast Art Supply, a small corporation that sells picture frames, paints, canvases, and other

figure 18.1

Personal Balance Sheet

Even individuals can determine their net worth, or owner's equity, by subtracting the value of their debts from the value of their assets.

Marty Campbell
Personal Balance Sheet
December 31, 20XX

ASSETS		
Cash	$ 2,500	
Savings account	5,000	
Automobile	15,000	
Stereo	1,000	
Television	500	
Furniture	2,500	
TOTAL ASSETS		$26,500
LIABILITIES		
Automobile loan	$ 9,500	
Credit card balance	500	
TOTAL LIABILITIES		$10,000
NET WORTH (Owner's Equity)		16,500
TOTAL LIABILITIES AND NET WORTH		$26,500

artists' supplies to retailers in New England. Note that assets are reported at the top of the statement, followed by liabilities and stockholders' equity. Let's work through the different accounts in Figure 18.2 from top to bottom.

Assets

liquidity the ease with which an asset can be converted into cash

current assets assets that can quickly be converted into cash or that will be used in one year or less

On a balance sheet, assets are listed in order, from the *most liquid* to the *least liquid*. The **liquidity** of an asset is the ease with which it can be converted into cash.

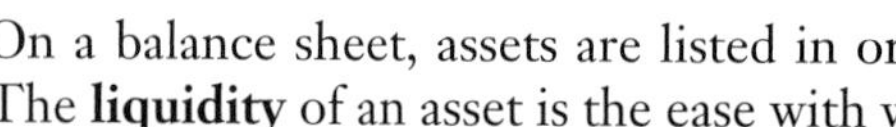

Current Assets **Current assets** are assets that can be converted quickly into cash or that will be used in one year or less. Because cash is the most liquid asset, it is listed first. Next are *marketable securities*—stocks, bonds, and other investments—that can be converted into cash in a matter of days. These are short-term investments of excess cash that Northeast Art Supply does not need immediately.

Next are the firm's receivables. Its *accounts receivables*, which result from allowing customers to make credit purchases, generally are paid within thirty to sixty days. However, the firm expects that some of these debts will not

A new type of asset? Not really. Regardless of where a business is located, accurate accounting is a must. Mohammad Koutcharov, head accountant for a cotton factory in Regar, Tajikistan, must account for all the firm's assets including raw cotton that will later be processed into cloth.

NORTHEAST ART SUPPLY, INC.		Balance Sheet December 31, 20XX	
ASSETS			
Current assets			
Cash		$ 59,000	
Marketable securities		10,000	
Accounts receivable	$ 40,000		
Less allowance for doubtful accounts	2,000	38,000	
Notes receivable		32,000	
Merchandise inventory		41,000	
Prepaid expenses		2,000	
Total current assets			$182,000
Fixed assets			
Delivery equipment	$110,000		
Less accumulated depreciation	20,000	$ 90,000	
Furniture and store equipment	62,000		
Less accumulated depreciation	15,000	47,000	
Total fixed assets			137,000
Intangible assets			
Patents		$ 6,000	
Goodwill		15,000	
Total intangible assets			21,000
TOTAL ASSETS			$340,000
LIABILITIES AND STOCKHOLDERS' EQUITY			
Current liabilities			
Accounts payable	$ 35,000		
Notes payable	25,675		
Salaries payable	4,000		
Taxes payable	5,325		
Total current liabilities		$ 70,000	
Long-term liabilities			
Mortgage payable on store equipment	$ 40,000		
Total long-term liabilities		$ 40,000	
TOTAL LIABILITIES			$110,00
Stockholders's equity			
Common stock		$150,000	
Retained earnings		80,000	
TOTAL OWNERS'S EQUITY			$230,000
TOTAL LIABILITIES AND OWNERS' EQUITY			$340,000

figure 18.2

Business Balance Sheet

A balance sheet summarizes a firm's accounts at the end of an accounting period, showing the various dollar amounts that enter into the accounting equation. Note that assets ($340,000) equal liabilities plus owners' equity ($340,000).

be collected. Thus it has reduced its accounts receivables by a 5 percent *allowance for doubtful accounts*. The firm's *notes receivables* are receivables for which customers have signed promissory notes. They are generally repaid over a longer period of time than the firm's accounts receivables.

Northeast's *merchandise inventory* represents the value of goods on hand for sale to customers. These goods are listed as current assets because they will be sold in one year or less. Since Northeast Art Supply is a wholesale operation, the inventory listed in Figure 18.2 represents finished goods ready for sale to retailers. For a manufacturing firm, merchandise inventory also may represent raw materials that will become

prepaid expenses assets that have been paid for in advance but have not yet been used

part of a finished product or work that has been partially completed but requires fur ther processing. For information on the methods used to determine the dollar value o inventory, read Exploring Business.

Northeast's last current asset is **prepaid expenses**, which are assets that have bee paid for in advance but have not yet been used. An example is insurance premiums They are usually paid at the beginning of the policy year. The unused portion (say, fo the last four months of the time period covered by the policy) is a prepaid expense For Northeast Art, all current assets total $182,000.

fixed assets assets that will be held or used for a period longer than one year

depreciation the process of apportioning the cost of a fixed asset over the period during which it will be used

Fixed Assets **Fixed assets** are assets that will be held or used for a period longe than one year. They generally include land, buildings, and equipment. Althoug Northeast owns no land or buildings because, like a lot of businesses, it rents or lease the space it needs to operate, it does own *delivery equipment* that originally cos $110,000. It also owns *furniture and store equipment* that originally cost $62,000.

Note that the values of both fixed assets are decreased by their *accumulated depre ciation*. **Depreciation** is the process of apportioning the cost of a fixed asset over it useful life. The depreciation amount allotted to each year is an expense for that year and the value of the asset must be reduced by the amount of depreciation expense. Al though the actual method used to calculate the dollar amounts for depreciation ex pense reported on a firm's financial statements are beyond the scope of this text, yo

exploring business

Evaluating Inventory

Question: What do Goodyear and J.C. Penney have in common?
Answer: Like many other large firms, both companies have millions of dollars invested in inventory.

AT THE END of the third quarter of 2002, Goodyear—an international manufacturer of tires and other rubber products for the transportation industry—reported inventory valued at $2.4 billion. J.C. Penney—a major retailer with department stores in all fifty states and Puerto Rico—reported inventory valued at $5.9 billion. Both corporations have invested vast sums of money in inventory for one simple reason: They must have merchandise to sell when their customers want it. For each firm, the dollar value of inventory represents a large part of its total assets. These dollar values must be reported accurately to investors, lenders, suppliers, and government regulatory agencies.

Methods Used to Evaluate Inventories

Reporting the dollar value of inventory on a firm's financial statement can be complicated because the prices a firm pays for the goods it sells or the materials it uses in manufacturing are likely to change during an accounting period. To determine the dollar value of inventory, one of four methods can be used. When the *specific identification method* is used, each inventory item is marked, tagged, or coded with its "specific" unit cost. The *average-cost method* assumes that each inventory item carries an equal, or average, cost. To arrive at the average cost, the total cost of all items available for sale is divided by the number of items. When the *first-in, first-out (FIFO) method* is used, the accountant assumes that the merchandise purchased at the beginning of the accounting period is sold first. With FIFO, the costs for the items purchased at the end of the accounting period are used to determine the value of the remaining inventory. Finally, the *last-in, first-out (LIFO) method* assumes that the merchandise purchased at the end of the accounting period is sold first. With LIFO, the costs for the items purchased at the beginning of the accounting period are used to determine the value of the remaining inventory.

Which Inventory Method Is Best?

Although none of these four methods of evaluating inventory is considered perfect, each method is acceptable for use when reporting the dollar value of inventory. When choosing an inventory method, a firm should consider the effect each method will have on its balance sheet, income statement, taxes, and management decisions.

should know that there are a number of different methods that can be used. You also should know that one method may increase or decrease the dollar amounts reported on a firm's financial statements when compared with another method of calculating depreciation expense. In the case of Northeast's delivery equipment, $20,000 of its value has been depreciated (or used up) since it was purchased. Its value at this time is thus $110,000 less $20,000, or $90,000. In a similar fashion, the original value of furniture and store equipment ($62,000) has been reduced by depreciation totaling $15,000. Furniture and store equipment now has a reported value of $47,000. For Northeast Art, all fixed assets total $137,000.

Intangible Assets **Intangible assets** are assets that do not exist physically but that have a value based on the rights or privileges they confer on a firm. They include patents, copyrights, trademarks, franchises, and goodwill. By their nature, intangible assets are long-term assets—they are of value to the firm for a number of years.

intangible assets assets that do not exist physically but that have a value based on the rights or privileges they confer on a firm

Northeast Art Supply lists two intangible assets. The first is a *patent* for an oil paint that the company has developed. The firm's accountants estimate that the patent has a current market value of $6,000. The second intangible asset, **goodwill,** is the value of a firm's reputation, location, earning capacity, and other intangibles that make the business a profitable concern. Goodwill is not normally listed on a balance sheet unless the firm has been purchased from previous owners. In such a case the new owners actually have paid an additional amount over and above the value of the firm's assets for goodwill. Goodwill exists because most businesses are worth more as going concerns than as a collection of assets. Northeast Art's accountants included a $15,000 amount for goodwill. The firm's intangible assets total $21,000. Now it is possible to total all three types of assets for Northeast Art. As calculated in Figure 18.2, total assets are $340,000.

goodwill the value of a firm's reputation, location, earning capacity, and other intangibles that make the business a profitable concern

Liabilities and Owners' Equity

The liabilities and the owners' equity accounts complete the balance sheet. The firm's liabilities are separated into two categories—current and long term.

Current Liabilities A firm's **current liabilities** are debts that will be repaid in one year or less. Northeast Art Supply purchased merchandise from its suppliers on credit. Thus its balance sheet includes an entry for accounts payable. **Accounts payable** are short-term obligations that arise as a result of a firm making credit purchases.

current liabilities debts that will be repaid in one year or less

accounts payable short-term obligations that arise as a result of making credit purchases

Notes payable are obligations that have been secured with promissory notes. They are usually short-term obligations, but they may extend beyond one year. Only those that must be paid within the year are listed under current liabilities.

notes payable obligations that have been secured with promissory notes

Northeast also lists *salaries payable* and *taxes payable* as current liabilities. These are both expenses that have been incurred during the current accounting period but will be paid in the next accounting period. For Northeast Art, current liabilities total $70,000.

Long-Term Liabilities **Long-term liabilities** are debts that need not be repaid for at least one year. Northeast lists only one long-term liability—a $40,000 *mortgage payable* for store equipment. Bonds and other long-term loans would be included here as well, if they existed. As you can see in Figure 18.2, Northeast's current and long-term liabilities total $110,000.

long-term liabilities debts that need not be repaid for at least one year

Owners' or Stockholders' Equity For a sole proprietorship or partnership, the owners' equity is shown as the difference between assets and liabilities. In a partnership, each partner's share of the ownership is reported separately in each owner's name. For a corporation, the owners' equity is usually referred to as *stockholders' equity.* The dollar amount reported on the balance sheet is the total value of stock plus retained earnings that have accumulated to date. **Retained earnings** are the portion of a business's profits not distributed to stockholders.

retained earnings the portion of a business's profits not distributed to stockholders

The original investment by the owners of Northeast Art Supply was $150,000. In addition, $80,000 of Northeast's earnings have been reinvested in the business since it was founded. Thus owners' equity totals $230,000.

As the two grand totals in Figure 18.2 show, Northeast's assets and the sum of its liabilities and owners' equity are equal—at $340,000. The accounting equation (assets = liabilities + owners' equity) is still in balance.

The Income Statement

learning objective

5 Read and interpret an income statement.

income statement
a summary of a firm's revenues and expenses during a specified accounting period

Question: Where can you find the profit or loss amount for The Gap, Inc.?
Answer: The firm's income statement

An **income statement** is a summary of a firm's revenues and expenses during a specified accounting period. The income statement is sometimes called the *earnings statement* or the *statement of income and expenses*. Let's begin our discussion by constructing a personal income statement for Marty Campbell. Having worked as a sales representative for an office supply firm for the past three years, Marty now earns $33,600 a year, or $2,800 a month. After income tax withholding and deductions for Social Security and Medicare, his take-home pay is $1,900 a month. As illustrated in Figure 18.3, Marty's typical monthly expenses include payments for an automobile loan, credit card purchases, apartment rent, utilities, food, clothing, and recreation and entertainment.

While the difference between income and expenses is referred to as *profit* or *loss* for a business, it is normally referred to as a *cash surplus* or *cash deficit* for an individual. Fortunately for Marty, he has a surplus of $250 at the end of each month. He can use this surplus for savings, investing, or paying off debts.

The typical income statement for a business reports the same type of information as Marty Campbell's personal income statement. Figure 18.4 shows the income statement for Northeast Art Supply. Generally, revenues *less* cost of goods sold *less* operating expenses equals net income.

figure 18.3

Personal Income Statement

By subtracting expenses from income, anyone can construct a personal income statement and determine if they have a surplus or deficit at the end of the month.

Marty Campbell
Personal Income Statement
For the month ended December 31, 20XX

INCOME (Take-home pay)		$1,900
LESS MONTHLY EXPENSES		
Automobile loan	$ 250	
Credit card payment	100	
Apartment rent	500	
Utilities	200	
Food	250	
Clothing	100	
Recreation & entertainment	250	
TOTAL MONTHLY EXPENSES		1,650
CASH SURPLUS (or profit)		$ 250

figure 18.4

Business Income Statement

An income statement summarizes a firm's revenues and expenses during a specified accounting period—one month, three months, six months, or a year. For Northeast Art, net income after taxes is $30,175.

NORTHEAST ART SUPPLY, INC.

Income Statement
For the Year Ended
December 31, 20XX

Revenues			
Gross sales		$465,000	
Less sales returns and allowances	$ 9,500		
Less sales discounts	4,500	14,000	
Net sales			$451,000
Cost of goods sold			
Beginning inventory, January 1, 20XX		$ 40,000	
Purchases	$346,000		
Less purchase discounts	11,000		
Net purchases		335,000	
Cost of goods available for sale		$375,000	
Less ending inventory December 31, 20XX		41,000	
Cost of goods sold			334,000
Gross profit			$117,000
Operating expenses			
Selling expenses			
Sales salaries	$ 22,000		
Advertising	4,000		
Sales promotion	2,500		
Depreciation—store equipment	3,000		
Depreciation—delivery equipment	4,000		
Miscellaneous selling expenses	1,500		
Total selling expenses		$ 37,000	
General expenses			
Office salaries	$ 28,500		
Rent	8,500		
Depreciation—office furniture	1,500		
Utilities expense	2,500		
Insurance expense	1,000		
Miscellaneous expense	500		
Total general expense		42,500	
Total operating expenses			$ 79,500
Net income from operations			$ 37,500
Less interest expense			2,000
NET INCOME BEFORE TAXES			$ 35,500
Less federal income taxes			5,325
NET INCOME AFTER TAXES			$ 30,175

Revenues

Revenues are the dollar amounts earned by a firm from selling goods, providing services, or performing business activities. For most businesses, sales are the primary source of revenues. However, some businesses have other sources of revenues that may include money from renting property or equipment, allowing other businesses to use the firm's patents and copyrights, and receiving interest and dividends on investments. Northeast obtains its revenues solely from the sale of its products to retailers in New England. The revenues section of its income statement begins with gross sales. **Gross sales** are the total dollar amount of all goods and services sold during the accounting period. From this amount are deducted the dollar amounts of

revenues the dollar amounts earned by a firm from selling goods, providing services, or performing business activities

gross sales the total dollar amount of all goods and services sold during the accounting period

- *Sales returns*—Merchandise returned to the firm by its customers
- *Sales allowances*—Price reductions offered to customers who accept slightly damaged or soiled merchandise

- *Sales discounts*—Price reductions offered to customers who pay their bills promptly

net sales the actual dollar amounts received by a firm for the goods and services it has sold, after adjustment for returns, allowances, and discounts

The remainder is the firm's net sales. **Net sales** are the actual dollar amounts receive[d] by the firm for the goods and services it has sold after adjustment for returns, allowances, and discounts. For Northeast Art, net sales are $451,000.

Cost of Goods Sold

cost of goods sold the dollar amount equal to beginning inventory *plus* net purchases *less* ending inventory

The standard method of determining the **cost of goods sold** by a retailing or wholesaling firm can be summarized as follows:

$$\textbf{Costs of goods sold} = \textbf{beginning inventory} + \textbf{net purchases} - \textbf{ending inventory}$$

A manufacturer must include raw materials inventories, work in progress, and direc[t] manufacturing costs in this computation.

According to Figure 18.4, Northeast began its accounting period on January [1] with a merchandise inventory that cost $40,000. During the next twelve months, th[e] firm purchased merchandise valued at $346,000. After taking advantage of *purchas[e] discounts*, however, it paid only $335,000 for this merchandise. Thus, during the year Northeast had total *goods available for sale* valued at $40,000 plus $335,000, o[r] $375,000.

gross profit a firm's net sales *less* the cost of goods sold

Twelve months later, at the end of the accounting period on December 31 Northeast had sold all but $41,000 worth of the available goods. The cost of good[s] sold by Northeast was therefore $375,000 less ending inventory of $41,000, o[r] $334,000. It is now possible to calculate gross profit. A firm's **gross profit** is its ne[t] sales *less* the cost of goods sold. For Northeast, gross profit was $117,000.

Operating Expenses

operating expenses all business costs other than the cost of goods sold

A firm's **operating expenses** are all business costs other than the cost of goods sold Total operating expenses generally are divided into two categories: selling expenses o[r] general expenses.

Selling expenses are costs related to the firm's marketing activities. For Northeas[t] Art, selling expenses total $37,000. *General expenses* are costs incurred in managing [a] business. For Northeast Art, general expenses total $42,500. Now it is possible to tota[l] both selling and general expenses. As Figure 18.4 shows, total operating expenses fo[r] the accounting period are $79,500.

A good cup of coffee perks up profits. Massachusetts-based Dunkin' Donuts is known for its mouth-watering donuts. And what goes with a donut better than a good cup of coffee? In addition to selling individual cups of coffee, the company started selling its own blend of coffee beans. The new product has boosted sales revenues and increased the firm's bottom-line profit amount on its income statement.

Net Income

When revenues exceed expenses, the difference is called **net income.** When expenses exceed revenues, the difference is called **net loss**. As Figure 18.4 shows, Northeast Art's *net income* is computed as gross profit ($117,000) *less* total operating expenses ($79,500). For Northeast Art, net income from operations is $37,500. From this amount, *interest expense* of $2,000 is deducted to obtain a *net income before taxes* of $35,500. The interest expense is deducted in this section of the income statement because it is not an operating expense. Rather, it is an expense that results from financing the business. Also note the difference between gross profit and net income before taxes. *Gross profit* is the amount that results from subtracting the cost of goods sold from net sales. A firm's gross profit amount *does not* include any operating expenses. *Net income before taxes*, on the other hand, is what remains after cost of goods sold *and* all expenses are deducted from net sales.

Northeast's *federal income taxes* are $5,325. Although these taxes may or may not be payable immediately, they are definitely an expense that must be deducted from income. This leaves Northeast Art with a *net income after taxes* of $30,175. This amount may be used to pay a dividend to stockholders, it may be retained or reinvested in the firm, it may be used to reduce the firm's debts, or all three.

Spotlight

Annual revenues for the big 4 accounting firms

Accounting firms, like all firms, generate revenues by satisfying the needs of their clients.

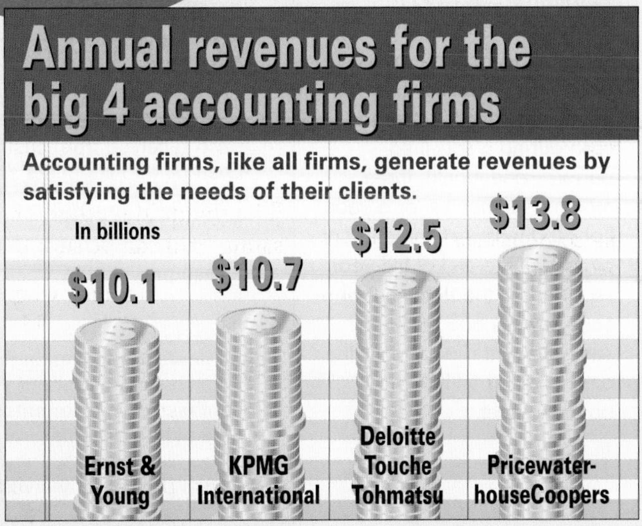

Source: Corporate websites and Hoover's Online, **www.hoovers.com**, March 21, 2003.

net income occurs when revenues exceed expenses

net loss occurs when expenses exceed revenues

The Statement of Cash Flows

learning objective

6 Describe business activities that affect a firm's cash flow.

Cash is the lifeblood of any business. In 1987, the Securities and Exchange Commission and the Financial Accounting Standards Board required all publicly traded companies to include a statement of cash flows, along with their balance sheet and income statement, in their annual report. The **statement of cash flows** illustrates how the operating, investing, and financing activities of a company affect cash during an accounting period. A statement of cash flows for Northeast Art Supply is illustrated in Figure 18.5 (on p. 550). It provides information concerning the company's cash receipts and cash payments and is organized around three different activities: operations, investing, and financing.

statement of cash flows a statement that illustrates how the operating, investing, and financing activities of a company affect cash during an accounting period

- *Cash flows from operating activities*. This is the first section of a statement of cash flows. It addresses the firm's primary revenue source—providing goods and services. The amounts paid to suppliers, employees, interest, taxes, and other expenses are deducted from the amount received from customers. Finally, the interest and dividends received by the firm are added to determine the total. After all adjustments are made, the total represents a true picture of cash flows from operating activities.
- *Cash flows from investing activities*. The second section of the statement is concerned with cash flow from investments. This includes the purchase and sale of land, equipment, and other long-term assets and investments.
- *Cash flows from financing activities*. The third and final section deals with the cash flow from all financing activities. It reports changes in debt obligation and owners' equity accounts. This includes loans and repayments, the sale and repurchase of the company's own stock, and cash dividends.

figure 18.5

Statement of Cash Flows

A statement of cash flows summarizes how a firm's operating, investing, and financing activities affect its cash during a specified period—one month, three months, six months, or a year. For Northeast Art, the amount of cash at the end of the year reported on the statement of cash flows is $59,000—the same amount reported for the cash account on the firm's balance sheet.

NORTHEAST ART SUPPLY, INC.

Statement of Cash Flows
For the Year Ended
December 31, 20XX

Cash flows from operating activities		
Cash received from customers	$ 451,000	
Cash paid to suppliers and employees	(385,500)	
Interest paid	(2,000)	
Income taxes paid	(5,325)	
Net cash provided by operating activities		$ 58,175
Cash flows from investing activities		
Purchase of equipment	$(2,000)	
Purchase of investments	(10,000)	
Sale of investments	10,000	
Net cash provided by investing activities		$(2,000)
Cash flows from financing activities		
Payment of short-term debt	$(9,000)	
Payment of long-term debt	(17,000)	
Payment of dividends	(15,000)	
Net cash provided by financing activities		$(41,000)
NET INCREASE (DECREASE) IN CASH		$ 15,175
Cash at beginning of year		43,825
CASH AT END OF YEAR		$ 59,000

The totals of all three activities are added to the beginning cash balance to determine the ending cash balance. For Northeast Art Supply, the ending cash balance is $59,000. Note that this is the same amount reported for the cash account on the firm's balance sheet. Together the cash flow statement, balance sheet, and income statement illustrate the results of past business decisions and reflect the firm's ability to pay debts and dividends and to finance new growth.

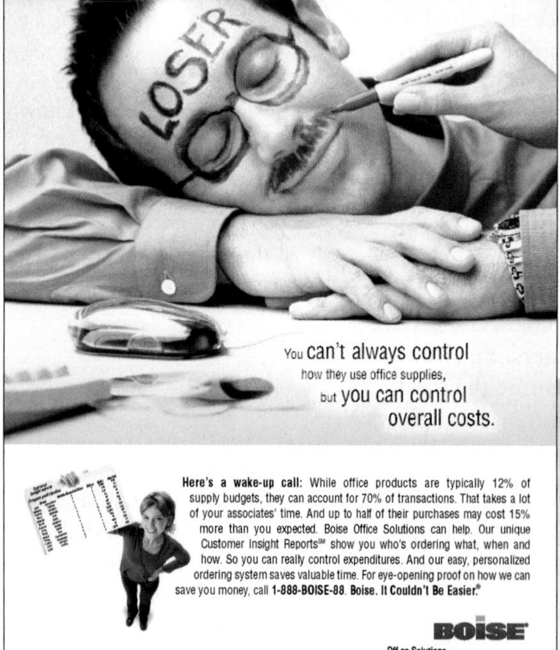

Asleep on the job! Today, many managers will tell you that if you're not wide awake, operating costs can get out of control. One firm—Boise Office Solutions—wants to help firms control not only the cost of office supplies, but also who orders the supplies, when supplies are ordered, and how they are ordered. By using Boise's unique Customer Insight ReportsSM, managers can reduce unnecessary expenses and increase profits.

Evaluating Financial Statements

learning objective

7 Summarize how managers evaluate the financial health of a business.

All three financial statements—the balance sheet, the income statement, and the statement of cash flows—can provide answers to a variety of questions about the firm's ability to do business and stay in business, its profitability, its value as an investment, and its ability to repay its debts. Even more information can be obtained by comparing present financial statements with those prepared for past accounting periods. Such comparisons permit managers, lenders, suppliers, and investors to (1) identify trends in sales, profits, borrowing, and other business variables and (2) determine whether the firm is on track in terms of meeting its long-term goals. To see how some firms enhance their net income to make it appear that they are meeting long-term goals, read Adapting to Change.

Comparing Data for Previous Accounting Periods

Most corporations include in their annual reports comparisons of the important elements of their financial statements for recent years. Figure 18.6 (on p. 552) shows such comparisons—of revenue, research and development (R&D), operating income, and cash and short-term investments—for Microsoft Corporation, a world leader in the computer software industry. By examining these data, an operating manager can tell whether R&D expenditures are increasing or decreasing over the past four years. The

adapting to change

Reality Accounting 101: Changes for the Better

CAN THE PUBLIC TRUST the accounting of American corporations? Scandals involving manipulations to inflate revenues, reduce expenses, or otherwise distort finances have left many investors wary. Enron's investors, for example, had no way of knowing that the company was deeper in debt and earning less than its financial reports indicated. When Enron's questionable accounting practices were revealed, the stock price plunged, and the company filed for bankruptcy reorganization. With companies from Adelphia to Xerox making headlines for dubious accounting, investors can't be blamed for losing confidence in the financial information provided by many major corporations.

How can the validity of accounting information be improved so that investors will regain their trust in U.S. corporations? Three suggestions under consideration are

- Banning the use of pro forma earnings, which typically exclude merger costs and one-time charges so that earnings will look better. The SEC requires corporations to report any differences between pro forma earnings and actual earnings calculated under GAAPs, but a ban would eliminate confusion. The rationale: Investors would have a more accurate picture of a corporation's earnings and be able to make a true comparison of earnings reported by different corporations.
- Preventing corporations from using pension income to inflate corporate income. The rationale: Corporations can get at income generated by pensions only by discontinuing the pension plan, an expensive and time-consuming process. At the very least, corporations should use realistic assumptions for pension fund returns, not overly optimistic assumptions that enhance income.
- Forcing corporations to account for the cost of closing facilities and laying off workers as an operating expense, not a one-time charge. The rationale: Such activities are integral to operations and should be reported accordingly.

No law or regulation governing accounting can cover every possible situation. However, if corporations want to rebuild trust, they will have to go beyond mere compliance. Hamid Moghadam, CEO of the real estate investment trust AMB Property, strives to meet the spirit of the law, not just the letter of the law. "We try to understand the principle behind the [accounting] guideline and live by it," he says. Why would a corporation go beyond the requirements? Moghadam's explanation is simple: "You want to make yourself attractive to the [investors] who supply you with capital."

figure 18.6

Comparisons of Present and Past Financial Statements for Microsoft Corporation

Most corporations include in their annual reports comparisons of the important elements of their financial statements for recent years.

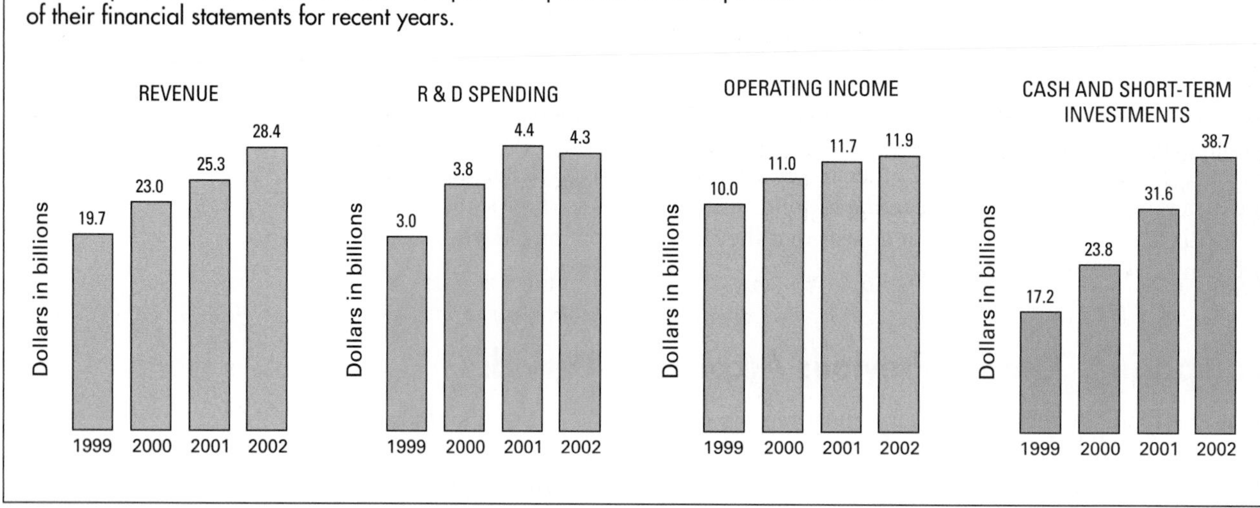

Source: Adapted from the Microsoft Corporation 2002 Annual Report, **www.microsoft.com**, February 24, 2003.

vice president of finance can determine if the amount of cash and short-term investments is changing. Stockholders and potential investors, on the other hand, may be more concerned with increases or decreases in Microsoft's revenues and operating income over the same time period.

Comparing Data with Other Firms' Data

Many firms also compare their financial results with those of competing firms and with industry averages. Comparisons are possible as long as accountants follow generally accepted accounting principles. Except for minor differences in format and terms, the balance sheet and income statement of Procter & Gamble, for example, will be similar to those of other large corporations, such as Alberto-Culver, Clorox, Colgate-Palmolive, and Unilever, in the consumer goods industry. Comparisons among firms give managers a general idea of a firm's relative effectiveness and its standing within the industry. Competitors' financial statements can be obtained from their annual reports—if they are public corporations. Industry averages are published by reporting services such as Dun & Bradstreet and Standard & Poor's, as well as by some industry trade associations.

financial ratio a number that shows the relationship between two elements of a firm's financial statements

Still another type of analysis of a firm's financial health involves computation of financial ratios. A **financial ratio** is a number that shows the relationship between two elements of a firm's financial statements. Among the most useful ratios are profitability ratios, short-term financial ratios, activity ratios, and the debt-to-owners' equity ratio. Like the individual elements in financial statements, these ratios can be compared with the firm's past ratios, with those of competitors, and with industry averages. The information required to form these ratios is found in a firm's balance sheet and income statement (in our examples, Figures 18.2 and 18.4).

Profitability Ratios

A firm's net income after taxes indicates whether the firm is profitable. It does not, however, indicate how effectively the firm's resources are being used. For this latter purpose, three ratios can be computed.

Return on Sales **Return on sales** is a financial ratio calculated by dividing net income after taxes by net sales. For Northeast Art Supply,

return on sales a financial ratio calculated by dividing net income after taxes by net sales

$$\textbf{Return on sales} = \frac{\textbf{net income after taxes}}{\textbf{net sales}} = \frac{\$30{,}175}{\$451{,}000}$$
$$= 0.067, \text{ or } 6.7 \text{ percent}$$

The return on sales indicates how effectively the firm is transforming sales into profits. A higher return on sales is better than a low one. Today, the average return on sales for all business firms is between 4 and 5 percent. With a return on sales of 6.7 percent, Northeast Art Supply is above average. A low return on sales can be increased by reducing expenses, by increasing sales, or both.

Return on Owners' Equity **Return on owners' equity** is a financial ratio calculated by dividing net income after taxes by owners' equity. For Northeast Art Supply,

return on owners' equity a financial ratio calculated by dividing net income after taxes by owners' equity

$$\textbf{Return on owners' equity} = \frac{\textbf{net income after taxes}}{\textbf{owners' equity}} = \frac{\$30{,}175}{\$230{,}000}$$
$$= 0.13, \text{ or } 13 \text{ percent}$$

Return on owners' equity indicates how much income is generated by each dollar of equity. Northeast is providing income of 13 cents per dollar invested in the business; the average for all businesses is between 12 and 15 cents. A higher return on owners' equity is better than a low one, and the only practical ways to increase return on owners' equity is to reduce expenses, increase sales, or both.

Earnings per Share From the point of view of stockholders, **earnings per share** is one of the best indicators of a corporation's success. It is calculated by dividing net income after taxes by the number of shares of common stock outstanding. If we assume that Northeast Art Supply has issued 25,000 shares of stock, then its earnings per share are

earnings per share a financial ratio calculated by dividing net income after taxes by the number of shares of common stock outstanding

$$\textbf{Earnings per share} = \frac{\textbf{net income after taxes}}{\textbf{common stock shares outstanding}} = \frac{\$30{,}175}{25{,}000}$$
$$= \$1.21 \text{ per share}$$

There is no meaningful average for this ratio mainly because the number of outstanding shares of a firm's stock is subject to change as a result of stock splits and stock dividends. As a general rule, however, an increase in earnings per share is a healthy sign for any corporation.

Short-Term Financial Ratios

Two short-term financial ratios permit managers (and lenders) to evaluate the ability of a firm to pay its current liabilities. Before we discuss these ratios, we should examine one other easily determined measure: working capital. Although it is not a ratio, it is an important indicator of a firm's ability to pay its short-term debts.

Working Capital **Working capital** is the difference between current assets and current liabilities. For Northeast Art,

working capital the difference between current assets and current liabilities

Current assets	$182,000
Less current liabilities	$ 70,000
Equals working capital	$112,000

Working capital indicates how much would remain if a firm paid off all current liabilities with cash and other current assets. The "proper" amount of working capital depends on the type of firm, its past experience, and its particular industry. A firm with too little working capital may have to borrow money to finance its operations.

Big Kmart emerges from big bankruptcy. In order to emerge from bankruptcy, Kmart closed 326 stores across the nation. At the same time, it eliminated 37,000 jobs. Hopefully, these actions along with other painful managerial decisions will help the firm return to profitability and improve its return on sales ratio and return on owners' equity ratio. If that happens, the firm's working capital, current ratio, and debt-to-owners' equity ratio will also improve.

current ratio a financial ratio computed by dividing current assets by current liabilities

Current Ratio A firm's **current ratio** is computed by dividing current assets by current liabilities. For Northeast Art Supply,

$$\textbf{Current ratio} = \frac{\textbf{current assets}}{\textbf{current liabilities}} = \frac{\$182{,}000}{\$70{,}000} = 2.6$$

This means that Northeast Art Supply has $2.60 of current assets for every $1 of current liabilities. The average current ratio for all industries is 2.0, but it varies greatly from industry to industry. Each firm should compare its current ratio with those of its own industry to determine whether it is high or low. A high current ratio indicates that a firm can pay its current liabilities. A low current ratio can be improved by repaying current liabilities, by reducing dividend payments to increase the firm's cash balance, or by obtaining additional cash from investors.

acid-test ratio a financial ratio calculated by subtracting the value of inventory from the current asset amount and dividing the total by current liabilities

Acid-Test Ratio This ratio, sometimes called the *quick ratio*, is a measure of the firm's ability to pay current liabilities *quickly*—with its cash, marketable securities, and receivables. The **acid-test ratio** is calculated by subtracting the value of inventory from the current asset amount and dividing the total by current liabilities. The value of inventory is "removed" from current assets because merchandise inventory is not converted into cash as easily as other current assets. For Northeast Art Supply,

$$\textbf{Acid-test ratio} = \frac{\textbf{current assets} - \textbf{inventory}}{\textbf{current liabilities}} = \frac{\$141{,}000}{\$70{,}000} = 2.01$$

For all businesses, the desired acid-test ratio is 1.0. Northeast Art Supply is above average with a ratio of 2.01, and the firm should be well able to pay its current liabilities. To increase a low ratio, a firm would have to repay current liabilities, reduce dividend payments to increase the firm's cash balance, or obtain additional cash from investors.

Activity Ratios

Two activity ratios permit managers to measure how many times each year a company collects its accounts receivables or sells its inventory. Both activity ratios are described below.

accounts receivable turnover a financial ratio calculated by dividing net sales by accounts receivable

Accounts Receivable Turnover A firm's **accounts receivable turnover** is the number of times the firm collects its accounts receivable in one year. If the data are available, this ratio should be calculated using a firm's net credit sales. Since data for

Northeast Art Supply's credit sales are unavailable, this ratio can be calculated by dividing net sales by accounts receivable. For Northeast Art,

$$\textbf{Accounts receivable turnover} = \frac{\textbf{net sales}}{\textbf{accounts receivable}} = \frac{\$451{,}000}{\$38{,}000}$$
$$= 11.9 \text{ times per year}$$

Northeast Art Supply collects its accounts receivables 11.9 times each year, or about every thirty days. If a firm's credit terms require customers to pay in twenty-five days, a collection period of thirty days is considered acceptable. There is no meaningful average for this measure mainly because credit terms differ among companies. A high accounts receivable turnover is better than a low one. As a general rule, a low accounts receivable turnover ratio can be improved by pressing for payment of past due accounts and by tightening requirements for prospective credit customers.

Inventory Turnover A firm's **inventory turnover** is the number of times the firm sells its merchandise inventory in one year. It is approximated by dividing the cost of goods sold in one year by the average value of the inventory.

inventory turnover a financial ratio calculated by dividing the cost of goods sold in one year by the average value of the inventory

The average value of the inventory can be found by adding the beginning inventory value and the ending inventory value (given on the income statement) and dividing the sum by 2. For Northeast Art Supply, this comes out to \$40,500. Thus

$$\textbf{Inventory turnover} = \frac{\textbf{cost of goods sold}}{\textbf{average inventory}} = \frac{\$334{,}000}{\$40{,}500}$$
$$= 8.2 \text{ times per year}$$

Northeast Art Supply sells its merchandise inventory 8.2 times each year, or about once every forty-five days. The average inventory turnover for all firms is about 9 times per year, but turnover rates vary widely from industry to industry. For example, supermarkets may have turnover rates of 20 or higher, whereas turnover rates for furniture stores are generally well below the national average. The quickest way to improve inventory turnover is to order merchandise in smaller quantities at more frequent intervals.

Debt-to-Owners' Equity Ratio

Our final category of financial ratios indicates the degree to which a firm's operations are financed through borrowing. Although other ratios can be calculated, the debt-to-owners' equity ratio is often used to determine whether a firm has too much debt. The **debt-to-owners' equity ratio** is calculated by dividing total liabilities by owners' equity. For Northeast Art Supply,

debt-to-owners' equity ratio a financial ratio calculated by dividing total liabilities by owners' equity

$$\textbf{Debt-to-owners' equity ratio} = \frac{\textbf{total liabilities}}{\textbf{owner's equity}} = \frac{\$110{,}000}{\$230{,}000} = 0.48, \text{ or } 48 \text{ percent}$$

A debt-to-owners' equity ratio of 48 percent means that creditors have provided about 48 cents of financing for every dollar provided by the owners. The average for the debt-to-owners'equity ratio varies greatly from one industry to the next, but the higher this ratio, the riskier the situation is for lenders. A high debt-to-owners' equity ratio may make borrowing additional money from lenders difficult. It can be reduced by paying off debts or by increasing the owners' investment in the firm.

Northeast's Financial Ratios: A Summary

Table 18.2 (on p. 556) compares the financial ratios of Northeast Art Supply with the average financial ratios for all businesses. It also lists the formulas we used to calculate Northeast's ratios. Northeast seems to be in good financial shape. Its return on sales, current ratio, and acid-test ratio are all above average. Its other ratios are about average, although its inventory turnover and debt-to-equity ratio could be improved.

table 18.2 Financial Ratios of Northeast Art Supply Compared with Average Ratios for All Businesses

Ratio	Formula	Northeast Ratio	Average Business Ratio	Direction for Improvement
Profitability Ratios				
Return on sales	$\frac{\text{net income after taxes}}{\text{net sales}}$	6.7%	4%–5%	Higher
Return on owners' equity	$\frac{\text{net income after taxes}}{\text{owners' equity}}$	13%	12%–15%	Higher
Earnings per share	$\frac{\text{net income after taxes}}{\text{common stock shares outstanding}}$	$1.21 per share	—	Higher
Short-Term Financial Ratios				
Working capital	current assets *less* current liabilities	$112,000	—	Higher
Current ratio	$\frac{\text{current assets}}{\text{current liabilities}}$	2.6	2.0	Higher
Acid-test ratio	$\frac{\text{current assets–inventory}}{\text{current liabilities}}$	2.01	1.0	Higher
Activity Ratios				
Accounts receivable turnover	$\frac{\text{net sales}}{\text{accounts receivable}}$	11.9	—	Higher
Inventory turnover	$\frac{\text{cost of goods sold}}{\text{average inventory}}$	8.2	9	Higher
Debt-to-owners' equity ratio	$\frac{\text{total liabilities}}{\text{owners' equity}}$	48 percent	—	Lower

This chapter ends our discussion of accounting information. In Chapter 19 we begin our examination of business finances by discussing money, banking, and credit.

Return To inside business

In the aftermath of the huge accounting scandals at WorldCom, Enron, and other corporations, Congress passed new laws to give the SEC more regulatory power over financial reporting. For example, under the Sarbanes-Oxley Act, CEOs and top financial executives must certify the accuracy of the quarterly and annual reports they file with the SEC. Also, the executives must affirm that they have disclosed to their auditors and to the board of directors' audit committee any changes or weaknesses in internal controls that could impair the corporation's ability to report its true financial situation.

Moreover, the SEC now requires corporations to disclose when their financial reports do not follow GAAPs. This is an issue for corporations that once publicized nontraditional *pro forma earnings* without including merger costs, one-time charges, and certain other elements. "This has been an area of much mischief in the past," commented one SEC commissioner. To be sure that investors get more complete information, corporations must now report any differences between pro forma earnings and financial results as calculated under GAAPs.

Questions

1. After a corporation such as Sunbeam files for bankruptcy protection, and if former executives are found guilty of securities fraud, should the corporation be forced to reimburse defrauded investors by giving them shares in the reorganized corporation? Explain your answer.
2. To identify and investigate questionable reporting practices, SEC employees need a solid understanding of securities law and corporate accounting. Would this type of work appeal to you?

Summary

Explain how new regulations affect the accounting industry and the way businesses report financial information.

Accounting is the process of systematically collecting, analyzing, and reporting financial information. Unfortunately, a large number of accounting scandals have caused people to doubt not only the financial information reported by a corporation but also the accounting industry. In a perfect world, accountants and auditors would catch mistakes and disclose questionable accounting practices in a firm's audit. The purpose of an audit is to make sure that a firm's financial statements have been prepared in accordance with generally accepted accounting principles (GAAPs). To help ensure that corporate financial information is accurate and in response to the many accounting scandals that surfaced in the last part of the 1990s and the first part of the twenty-first century, the Sarbanes-Oxley Act was signed into law on July 30, 2002. This law contains a number of provisions designed to restore public confidence in the accounting industry.

Understand why accounting information is important and what accountants do.

To be successful in the accounting industry, employees must be responsible, honest, and ethical; have a strong background in financial management; know how to use a computer and software to process data into accounting information; and be able communicate with people who need accounting information. Primarily management uses accounting information, but it is also demanded by lenders, suppliers, stockholders, potential investors, and government agencies. Typical services performed by accountants for their clients include general accounting, budgeting, cost accounting, tax accounting, and internal auditing. A private accountant is employed by a specific organization to operate its accounting system. A public accountant performs these functions for various individuals or firms on a fee basis. Most accounting firms include on their staffs at least one certified public accountant (CPA).

Discuss the accounting process.

The accounting process is based on the accounting equation: Assets = liabilities + owners' equity. Double-entry bookkeeping ensures that the balances shown by the accounting equation is maintained. The accounting process involves five steps: (1) Source documents are analyzed, (2) each transaction is recorded in a journal, (3) each journal entry is posted in the appropriate general ledger accounts, (4) at the end of each accounting period, a trial balance is prepared to make sure that the accounting equation is in balance, and (5) financial statements are prepared from the trial balance. Once statements are prepared, the books are closed. A new accounting cycle is then begun for the next accounting period.

Read and interpret a balance sheet.

A balance sheet is a summary of a firm's assets, liabilities, and owners' equity accounts at the end of an accounting period. This statement must demonstrate that the accounting equation is in balance. On the balance sheet, assets are categorized as current, fixed, or intangible. Similarly, liabilities can be divided into current liabilities and long-term ones. For a sole proprietorship or partnership, owners' equity is shown as the difference between assets and liabilities. For corporations, the owners' equity section reports the values of stock and retained earnings.

Read and interpret an income statement.

An income statement is a summary of a firm's financial operations during the specified accounting period. On the income statement, the company's gross profit is computed by subtracting the cost of goods sold from net sales. Operating expenses and interest expense are then deducted to compute net income before taxes. Finally, income taxes are deducted to obtain the firm's net income after taxes.

Describe business activities that affect a firm's cash flow.

Since 1987, the Securities and Exchange Commission (SEC) and the Financial Accounting Standards Board (FASB) have required all publicly traded companies to include a statement of cash flows in their annual reports. This statement illustrates how the operating, investing, and financing activities of a company affect cash during an accounting period. Together the cash flow statement, balance sheet, and income statement illustrate the results of past decisions and the business's ability to pay debts and dividends and to finance new growth.

Summarize how managers evaluate the financial health of a business.

The information in a firm's financial statements becomes more meaningful when compared with corresponding information for previous years, for competitors, and for the industry in which the firm operates. Such comparisons permit managers and other interested people to pick out trends in growth, borrowing, income, and other business variables and to determine whether the firm is on the way to accomplishing its long-term goals. A number of financial ratios can be computed from the information in a firm's financial statements. These ratios provide a picture of the firm's profitability, its short-term financial position, its activity in the area of accounts receivable and inventory, and its long-term debt financing. Like the information on the firm's financial statements, these ratios can and should be compared with those of past accounting periods, those of competitors, and those representing the average of the industry as a whole.

Key Terms

You should now be able to define and give an example relevant to each of the following terms:

accounting (533)
audit (535)
generally accepted accounting principles (GAAPs) (535)
private accountant (538)
public accountant (538)
certified public accountant (CPA) (538)
assets (539)
liabilities (539)
owners' equity (539)
accounting equation (539)
double-entry bookkeeping (540)
general journal (540)
general ledger (540)
trial balance (541)
balance sheet (or statement of financial position) (541)
liquidity (542)
current assets (542)
prepaid expenses (544)
fixed assets (544)
depreciation (544)
intangible assets (545)
goodwill (545)
current liabilities (545)
accounts payable (545)
notes payable (545)
long-term liabilities (545)
retained earnings (545)
income statement (546)
revenues (547)
gross sales (547)
net sales (548)
cost of goods sold (548)
gross profit (548)
operating expenses (548)
net income (549)
net loss (549)
statement of cash flows (549)
financial ratio (552)
return on sales (553)
return on owners' equity (553)
earnings per share (553)
working capital (553)
current ratio (554)
acid-test ratio (554)
accounts receivable turnover (554)
inventory turnover (555)
debt-to-owners' equity ratio (555)

Review Questions

1. What purpose do audits and generally accepted accounting principles (GAAPs) serve in today's business world?
2. How do the major provisions of the Sarbanes-Oxley Act of 2002 affect a public company's audit procedures?
3. List four groups that use accounting information, and briefly explain why each group has an interest in this information.
4. What is the difference between a private accountant and a public accountant? What are certified public accountants?
5. State the accounting equation, and list two specific examples of each term in the equation.
6. How is double-entry bookkeeping related to the accounting equation? Briefly, how does it work?
7. Briefly describe the five steps of the accounting cycle in order.
8. What is the principal difference between a balance sheet and an income statement?
9. How are current assets distinguished from fixed assets? Why are fixed assets depreciated on a balance sheet?
10. Explain how a retailing firm would determine the cost of goods sold during an accounting period.
11. How does a firm determine its net income after taxes?
12. What is the purpose of a statement of cash flows?
13. For each of the accounts listed below, indicate if the account should be included on a firm's balance sheet, income statement, or statement of cash flows.

Type of Account	Statement Where Reported
Assets	____________
Income	____________
Expenses	____________
Operating activities	____________
Liabilities	____________
Investing activities	____________
Owners' equity	____________

14. Explain the calculation procedure for and significance of each of the following:
    a. One of the profitability ratios
    b. A short-term financial ratio
    c. An activity ratio
    d. Debt-to-owners' equity ratio

Discussion Questions

1. Why do you think there have been so many accounting scandals involving public companies in the past two years?
2. Bankers usually insist that prospective borrowers submit audited financial statements along with a loan ap-

plication. Why should financial statements be audited by a CPA?

3. What can be said about a firm whose owners' equity is a negative amount? How could such a situation come about?
4. Do the balance sheet, the income statement, and the statement of cash flows contain all the information you might want as a potential lender or stockholder? What other information would you like to examine?
5. Why is it so important to compare a firm's current financial statements with those of previous years, those of competitors, and the average of all firms in the industry in which the firm operates?
6. Which do you think are the two or three most important financial ratios? Why?

video case

Best Software Helps Businesses Take Care of Business

Accounting and tax laws are so dynamic and complex that businesses are rarely able to keep up with every detail, let alone master all the nuances. This is where Best Software comes in. Based in Irvine, California, Best Software offers a variety of products and services to meet the demanding accounting and administrative needs of millions of business customers from national giants such as The Mills Real Estate Development Company to tiny family operations. Best Software stays on top of accounting and tax changes by maintaining a staff of fourteen CPAs to follow every twist and turn in legislation and regulation and keep all its software products up-to-date.

Imagine tracking all the buildings, land, equipment, furniture, and other fixed assets in dozens of shopping centers across America. This is the challenge for The Mills Real Estate Development Company, which manages Potomac Mills and many other major shopping malls. Best Software's systems help the real estate developer record and track every fixed asset it owns. With the software, management can close the books quickly at the end of each month and check on the company's financial health by calculating key ratios. The software also streamlines the process of computing depreciation and generating reports to comply with IRS regulations, saving The Mills additional time and money.

The market for accounting and administrative software is large and lucrative but increasingly competitive. Microsoft Business Solutions is a major rival. Intuit, which makes QuickBooks and other software products, is also a key competitor. Up against two well-known competitors, Best Software has carved out niches in four market subsegments: not-for-profit organizations, manufacturing firms, distribution companies, and accountants.

One of Best Software's most successful software packages is its Peachtree Accounting package. Small businesses can use Peachtree to manage accounting, inventory, and related functions. Not only is the software easy to use, but it also allows users to generate a wide variety of reports about the company's financial condition. This helps owners spot unusual figures or trends for further analysis and action while more efficiently managing vital financial data. One medium-sized company spent nearly $5,000 for a Best Software accounting package and cut its costs by $1 million through streamlined tax filings and other savings.

Knowing that accountants both use accounting software and recommend accounting software to their business customers, Best Software has established an accountants network to provide CPAs with specialized accounting and tax software plus the opportunity to share ideas. More than 40,000 accounting firms and bookkeeping experts already participate. "We are telling the accounting community that you are important to us and we are partnering with you to provide specific solutions to help you manage your own business more efficiently," explains a Best Software executive.

In addition, the company sells software designed to assist businesses with budgeting and planning tasks, human resources management and payroll duties, project accounting, time management, and customer relationship management. Having a large customer base for each software product puts Best Software in a good position to build revenues and profits by cross-selling other products in its line. Current customers are familiar with the company and its products, so they are more receptive to upgrading from their existing software as well as considering other products. Moreover, Best Software has higher-powered accounting packages for businesses to use as they expand and require software with additional capabilities.

As important as the software, however, is the knowledgeable customer service support that helps customers make the most of their software purchases. Users can attend training seminars in numerous U.S. locations, call toll-free numbers with any questions, and consult software specialists by e-mail if needed.

Through superior products and customer service, Best Software seeks to attract new customers and retain current customers "for life," as the executive vice president says. The focus on long-term customer satisfaction is a critical part of Best Software's competitive strategy. According to CEO Ron Verni,. "Our satisfaction rates are high. Our retention rates are high." That says a lot in the very competitive software industry.[9]

Questions

1. What kinds of accounting information would a firm like The Mills Real Estate Development Company track using Best Software's products?
2. Why would a fast-growing small business be especially interested in using software to generate reports about accounts receivable turnover?
3. If you were responsible for buying accounting software for a small business, what kinds of questions would you ask Best Software and its competitors before you make a decision?

Building Skills for Career Success

1. Exploring the Internet

To those unacquainted with current activities and practices in larger accounting firms, there is often some surprise at just how varied the accounting work involved actually is. Although setting up and maintaining accounting software for clients are standard, accounting firms also can provide a wide range of specialized services. For example, research into mergers or acquisitions of other firms, investment advice, and solutions to financial problems are now common strategies for revenue growth within accounting firms. Most websites for large accounting firms also will post information about current employment opportunities.

Assignment

1. Visit the website of a major accounting firm such as Deloitte Touche Tohmatsu (**www.deloitte.com**), KPMG (**www.kpmg.com**), PricewaterhouseCoopers (**www.pwc.com**), or Ernst & Young (**www.ey.com**). Describe in general terms how the website is used to communicate with clients and prospective clients. (Visit the text website for updates to this exercise.)
2. What are some of the content items presented on the site? What do these tell you about the firm and its clients?
3. Search the site for career information. Often the firm will post descriptions of employment opportunities along with educational and experience requirements. Describe what you find.

2. Developing Critical Thinking Skills

According to the experts, you must evaluate your existing financial condition before establishing an investment plan. As pointed out in this chapter, a personal balance sheet provides a picture of your assets, liabilities, and net worth. A personal income statement will tell you whether you have a cash surplus or cash deficit at the end of a specific period.

Assignment

1. Using your own financial information from last month, construct a personal balance sheet and personal income statement.
2. Based on the information contained in your personal financial statements, answer the following:
   a. What is your current net worth?
   b. Do you have a cash surplus or a cash deficit at the end of the month?
   c. What specific steps can you take to improve your financial condition?
3. Based on your findings, prepare a plan for improving your financial condition over the next six months.

3. Building Team Skills

This has been a bad year for Miami-based Park Avenue Furniture. The firm increased sales revenues to $1,400,000, but total expenses ballooned to $1,750,000. Although management realized that some of the firm's expenses were out of control, including cost of goods sold ($700,000), salaries ($450,000), and advertising costs ($140,000), it could not contain expenses. As a result, the furniture retailer lost $350,000. To make matters worse, the retailer applied for a $350,000 loan at Fidelity National Bank and was turned down. The bank officer, Mike Nettles, said that the firm already had too much debt. At that time, liabilities totaled $420,000; owners' equity was $600,000.

Assignment

1. In groups of three or four, analyze the financial condition of Park Avenue Furniture.
2. Discuss why you think the bank officer turned down Park Avenue's loan request.
3. Prepare a detailed plan of action to improve the financial health of Park Avenue Furniture over the next twelve months.

4. Researching Different Careers

As pointed out in this chapter, job opportunities for accountants and managers in the accounting area are expected to experience average growth between now and the year 2010. Employment opportunities range from entry-level positions for clerical workers and technicians to professional positions that require a college degree in accounting, management consulting, or computer technology. Typical job titles in the accounting field include bookkeeper, corporate accountant, public accountant, auditor, managerial accountant, and controller.

Assignment

1. Answer the following questions based on information obtained from interviews with people employed in accounting, from research in the library or by using the Internet, or from your college's career center:

a. What types of activities would a person employed in one of the accounting positions listed above perform on a daily basis?
b. Would you choose this career? Why or why not?

2. Summarize your findings in a report.

5. Improving Communication Skills

One of the best resources for determining the soundness of an investment opportunity is a corporation's annual report. An annual report will tell you about a company's management, its past performance, and its future goals. Most annual reports contain a letter from the chairman of the board, as well as photographs of smiling employees. While these are nice to look at, it is the financial statements and footnotes in an annual report that give the true picture of a corporation's financial health.

Assignment

1. Obtain a printed copy of an annual report or use the Internet to access a corporation's annual report for a company that you consider a "promising investment."
2. Use the report to answer the following questions:
   a. What does the CEO/president say about the company's past performance and future projections?
   b. Is the firm profitable? Are profits increasing or decreasing?
   c. Most annual reports contain graphs or illustrations that show trends for sales, profits, earnings per share, and other important financial measures over a five- or ten-year period. What significant trends for this company are illustrated in its annual report?
3. On the basis of your examination of its annual report, would you invest in this company? Prepare a brief report justifying your decision.

Information Systems and Accounting at Finagle A Bagel

Like the hole in a bagel, any hole in Finagle A Bagel's information and accounting systems means less dough for the company. Copresidents Alan Litchman and Laura Trust and their management team could not make timely, informed decisions to profitably build the business without reliable systems for collecting data, processing them, and presenting the results in a meaningful way.

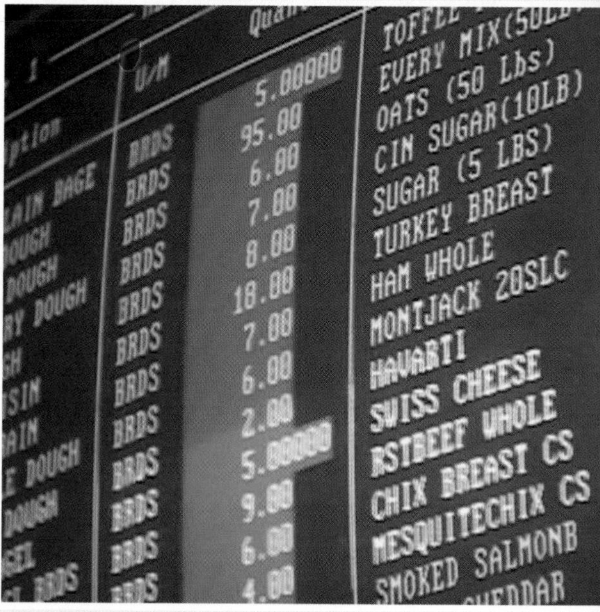

Putting Technology to Work

Regina Jerome is Finagle A Bagel's director of information systems. She and her assistant are responsible for running the computerized accounting system in the company support center as well as the management information and marketing information systems. As a small business, Finagle A Bagel can't afford to spend money for the sake of having the fastest computer equipment or the flashiest software. Having a limited budget means that "it's absolutely imperative that every piece of technology that we invest in directly supports our business," she says.

One of Jerome's biggest challenges has been implementing a point-of-sale system that supports the information needs of the stores as well as of the senior managers. Unlike restaurant chains that sell standard menu items, Finagle A Bagel customizes everything to the individual customer's taste. Thus store employees must be able to record, prepare, and serve complicated orders. "We designed our point-of-sale system so that when a customer orders, the system follows our menu and enables our cashiers to deliver exactly what the customer ordered," Jerome says. "At the same time, the system collects all the pertinent financial information. Every transaction is recorded and can be retrieved by minute, by day, by store, by cashier, and by terminal." With information from the point-of-sale system, general managers can analyze detailed sales patterns before making decisions about store staffing levels, food orders, and other day-to-day operational issues.

Tracking Cash, Calculating Profits

The copresidents use the financial data drawn from every cash register connected to this point-of-sale system to reconcile daily store sales with daily bank deposits. As a result, copresident Litchman knows by 7:30 each morning how much money was deposited on the previous day and the total amount the company has to cover payroll, food purchases, and other expenses. He also knows if a store's reported sales match its bank deposit. If not, a senior manager immediately looks into the discrepancy, which usually turns out to be some kind of error. Once in a while, however, the discrepancy is a sign of store-level theft that requires further investigation and—when warranted—legal action.

Finagle A Bagel's managers use the company's accounting system to make other important decisions. For every dollar of sales, a food service business makes only a few cents in profit. Finagle A Bagel makes about 8 cents in profit from every sales dollar, but Litchman is aiming to make a profit of 10 cents per dollar. He and his team need timely reports showing retailing and wholesaling revenues, the cost of goods sold, and operating expenses to calculate the company's pretax profit and measure progress toward this profit goal. Food and labor costs constitute more than two-thirds of Finagle A Bagel's costs—so the faster managers can see these numbers, the faster they can act if expenses are higher than expected.

Technology Drives the Frequent Finagler Card

Thanks to new software running on the point-of-sale system, Finagle A Bagel has been able to introduce a new and improved Frequent Finagler customer loyalty card. Customers pay $1 to buy this card, which is activated immediately at the store. From that point on, the cardholder receives one point for every dollar spent in any Finagle A Bagel store. Points can be redeemed for free food, such as a cup of coffee, a bagel sandwich, or—the top prize—a baker's dozen bagels.

From the company's perspective, the Frequent Finagler card is an excellent way to learn more about the buying habits of its most valuable customers. Managers can see which menu items loyal customers buy, in which store, and at what time of day. Going a step further, Finagle A Bagel is using the card to start a dialogue with loyal customers. The company's website (**www.finagleabagel.com**) plays a key role in this initiative. When cardholders log on and register personal data such as address, phone number, and e-mail address, they receive a coupon for six free bagels. Finagle A Bagel receives a wealth of customer data to analyze and use in more precisely targeting its marketing efforts.

Add a Product, Drop a Product

The technologies driving the Frequent Finagler card and the point-of-sale system help Finagle A Bagel gather sufficient data to support decisions about changing the product line. "We add products to categories that are doing well, we eliminate things that are not selling, and we bring back products that have done well," says Trust. "Being able to know that a product isn't selling so we can get it off the menu and try something new is a vital piece of information."

For example, says Trust, "We just introduced a new sausage bagel pizza based on the fact that our pepperoni pizza sells very well—better than our veggie pizza." When sales data confirmed the popularity of sausage, Finagle A Bagel began introducing it in a breakfast bagel sandwich. Now the company is looking at incorporating sausage into other menu items to delight customers' taste buds and boost sales. However, Trust and her management team won't make any product decisions without first consulting reports based on data collected by the Frequent Finagler card and the point-of-sale system.

Questions

1. Is Finagle A Bagel collecting data from internal sources, external sources, or both? What cautions apply to the sources of its data?
2. Finagle A Bagel uses information to track cash, sales revenues, and expenses on a daily basis. How does this type of accounting system encourage effective decision making and discourage store-level theft?
3. As a small business, which of the financial ratios might Finagle A Bagel want to track especially closely? Why?
4. Do you think the Frequent Finagler card has any effect on Finagle A Bagel's customer loyalty? For the firm, what are the benefits of the loyalty program?

Building a Business Plan   Part VI

INC.

Now that you have a marketing plan, the next big and important step is to prepare a financial plan. One of the biggest mistakes an entrepreneur makes when faced with a need for financing is not being prepared. Completing this section will show you that if you are prepared and you are creditworthy, the task may be easier than you think. Remember, most lenders and investors insist that you submit current financial statements that have been prepared by an independent certified public accountant (CPA). Chapter 18 in your textbook, "Using Accounting Information," should help you to answer the questions in this part of the business plan.

The Financial Plan Component

Your financial plan should answer at least the following questions about the investment needed, sales and cash-flow forecasts, breakeven analysis, and sources of funding:

6.1. What is the actual amount of money you need to open your business (start-up budget) and the amount needed to keep it open (operating budget)? Prepare a realistic budget.

6.2. How much money do you have and how much money will you need to start your business and stay in business?

6.3. Prepare an income statement by month for the first year of operation and by quarter for the second and third years.

6.4. Prepare balance sheets for each of the first three years of operation.

6.5. Prepare a breakeven analysis. How many units of your products or service will have to be sold to cover your costs?

6.6. Reinforce your final projections by comparing them with industry averages for your chosen industry.

Review of Business Plan Activities

Throughout this project you have been investigating what it takes to open and run a business, and now you are finally at the bottom line: What it is going to cost to open your business, and how much money you will need to keep it running for a year? Before tackling the last part of the business plan, review your answers to the questions in each part to make sure that all your answers are consistent throughout the entire business plan. Then write a brief statement that summarizes all the information for this part of the business plan.

part VII

Finance and Investment

In this part we look at another business resource—money. First we discuss the functions of money and the financial institutions that are part of our banking system. Then we examine the concept of financial management and investing for both firms and individuals.

chapter

19

Understanding Money, Banking, and Credit

Bank of America has the largest online banking customer base anywhere.

learning objectives

1. Identify the functions and characteristics of money.
2. Summarize how the Federal Reserve System regulates the money supply.
3. Describe the differences between commercial banks and other financial institutions in the banking industry.
4. Identify the services provided by financial institutions.
5. Understand how financial institutions are changing to meet the needs of domestic and international customers.
6. Explain why banks, savings and loan associations, and credit unions provide insurance for their customers
7. Discuss the importance of credit and credit management.

inside business

Bank of America Banks on Online Banking

MORE THAN FOUR MILLION Bank of America stomers bank at their keyboards rather than having to o to one of nearly 4,225 branches during "bankers' ours." In fact, these customers enjoy the convenience of aking their own banking hours—day or night, 365 days year. On average, they access the Bank of America ebsite (**www.bankofamerica.com**) sixteen million mes every month to look at account balances and complish other banking transactions.

Bank of America has a tradition of harnessing utting-edge technology to offer the latest in banking rvices. Decades ago its network of automated teller achines (ATMs) allowed customers to deposit or ithdraw money at any branch at any time. The next step as to link its ATM network to other banks' networks so at customers could withdraw money in other states and ountries. Today, the bank's online banking service lets stomers safely and securely bank from home, work, hool, or any location with a computer and an Internet onnection.

Bank of America has the largest online banking stomer base anywhere. Its extensive menu of online rvices makes the site convenient for time-pressed dividuals and business customers. In addition to erifying balances, customers can look at transactions in hecking and savings accounts, credit card accounts, curities portfolios, and other accounts. They also can ansfer money between different Bank of America accounts. Those who use financial management software such as Quicken or Microsoft Money can easily download transaction information to their personal computers and track their money more closely. Moreover, customers can order checks, stop payment on checks, request copies of statements, and submit changes of address or new phone numbers.

Bill Pay, an online bill-payment feature, is increasingly popular among Bank of America customers. This free service lets customers arrange for payments electronically rather than writing out individual checks, inserting them in envelopes, adding a stamp, and going to the mailbox. To start, they set up a list of payees (such as the electric utility, telephone company, department store charge accounts, and anyone else they want to pay). When they want to make a payment, they simply sign onto the bank's website and enter their individual passwords. Then they indicate who is to receive the payment, how much is to be paid, and when.

In any given month, nearly $2 billion in payments flow through the bank's Bill Pay system, saving customers both time and money. Customers can even sign up to have invoices delivered electronically to their Bill Pay accounts rather than receiving printed bills in the mail. And because some customers may be uneasy about paying bills over the Internet, Bank of America will pay any late fees if it does not pay a bill according to the customer's scheduled date.[1]

In Chapter 1 we defined a *business* as the organized effort of individuals to produce an sell, for a profit, the products and services that satisfy society's needs. Bank of Americ fulfills the last part of this definition by accepting deposits, making loans, and providing other financial services to its customers. But Bank of America does more than jus provide traditional banking services. It has developed a loyal base of customers wh want to bank online—twenty-four hours a day, seven days a week. Although onlin banking is a relative new method of meeting the needs of its customers, it shows ever sign of continuing to increase the bank's customer base and the amount of profit earns from its Internet banking services. But how does Bank of America—or for tha matter any bank—earn profits? To answer this question, you must understand th basic "bread and butter" operations of a bank or similar financial institution.

Most people regard a bank, savings and loan association, or similar financial institution as a place to deposit or borrow money. When you deposit money, you *receive* interest. When you borrow money, you must *pay* interest. You may borrow to buy home, a car, or some other high-cost item. In this case the resource that will be transformed into money to repay the loan is the salary you receive for your labor.

Businesses also transform resources into money. A business firm (even a new one may have a valuable asset in the form of an idea for a product or service. If the firm (o its founder) has a good credit history and the idea is a good one, a bank or other lende probably will lend it the money to develop, produce, and market the product or service. The loan—with interest—will be repaid out of future sales revenue. In this way both the firm and the lender will earn a reasonable profit.

In each of these situations, the borrower needs the money now and will have th ability to repay it later. But also, in each situation, the money will be used to *purchas something* and will be repaid through the use of *resources*. And while the decision to borrow money from a bank or other financial institution always should be made after careful deliberation, the fact is that responsible borrowing enables both individuals an business firms to meet specific needs. Responsible borrowing by both individuals an business firms also may help stabilize the nation's economy in uncertain times. Afte the downturn in the economy that began in 1999 and the tragic events of Septembe 11, both individuals and businesses used borrowed funds to purchase all kinds of products and services. The firms that sold those goods and services were able to generat sales revenues and, in turn, buy more raw materials, pay salaries, and continue to operate because at least some of their customers made purchases using borrowed money.

In this chapter we take a good look at money and the financial institutions tha create and handle it. We begin by outlining the functions and characteristics of mone that make it an acceptable means of payment for products, services, and resources Then we consider the role of the Federal Reserve System in maintaining a health economy. Next, we describe the banking industry—commercial banks, savings an loan associations, credit unions, and other institutions that offer banking services Then we turn our attention to how banking practices are changing to meet the need of customers. We also describe the safeguards established by the federal governmen to protect depositors against losses. In closing, we examine credit transactions, source of credit information, and effective collection procedures.

learning objective

1 Identify the functions and characteristics of money.

barter system a system of exchange in which goods or services are traded directly for other goods or services

What Is Money?

The members of some societies still exchange goods and services through barter without using money. A **barter system** is a system of exchange in which goods o services are traded directly for other goods or services. One family may raise vegetables and herbs, and another may weave cloth. To obtain food, the family of weaver trades cloth for vegetables, provided that the farming family is in need of cloth.

The trouble with the barter system is that the two parties in an exchange mus need each other's products at the same time, and the two products must be roughl equal in value. Thus even very isolated societies soon develop some sort of money t eliminate the inconvenience of trading by barter.

Money is anything a society uses to purchase products, services, or resources. Historically, different groups of people have used all sorts of objects as money—whales' teeth, stones, beads, copper crosses, clamshells, and gold and silver, for example. Today, the most commonly used objects are metal coins and paper bills, which together are called *currency*.

money anything a society uses to purchase products, services, or resources

The Functions of Money

Money aids in the exchange of goods and services. However, that is a rather general (and somewhat theoretical) way of stating money's function. Let's look instead at three *specific* functions money serves in any society.

Money as a Medium of Exchange A **medium of exchange** is anything accepted as payment for products, services, and resources. This definition looks very much like the definition of money. It is meant to, because the primary function of money is to serve as a medium of exchange. The key word here is *accepted*. As long as the owners of products, services, and resources accept money in an exchange, it is performing this function. For example, if you want to purchase a Hewlett Packard Desk Jet printer that is priced at $229 in a Circuit City store, you must give the store the correct amount of money. In return, the store gives you the product. Of course, the folks at Circuit City accept your money because they know that it is acceptable to the owners of other products, services, and resources that *they* may wish to purchase.

medium of exchange anything accepted as payment for products, services, and resources

Money as a Measure of Value A **measure of value** is a single standard or "yardstick" used to assign values to, and compare the values of, products, services, and resources. Money serves as a measure of value because the prices of all products, services, and resources are stated in terms of money. It is thus the "common denominator" we use to compare products and decide which we will buy. Imagine the difficulty you would have in deciding whether you could afford new Nike running shoes if they were priced in terms of yards of cloth or pounds of vegetables—especially if your employer happened to pay you in toothbrushes.

measure of value a single standard or "yardstick" used to assign values to, and compare the values of, products, services, and resources

Money as a Store of Value Money received by an individual or firm need not be used immediately. It may be held and spent later. Hence money serves as a **store of value,** or a means of retaining and accumulating wealth. This function of money comes into play whenever we hold onto money—in a pocket, a cookie jar, a savings account, or whatever.

store of value a means of retaining and accumulating wealth

Value that is stored as money is affected by *inflation*. Remember from Chapter 1 that *inflation* is a general rise in the level of prices. As prices go up in an inflationary period, money loses purchasing power. Suppose that you can buy a Sony home theater system for $1,000. Your $1,000 has a value equal to the value of that home theater system. But suppose that you

Which $20 bill is real? Actually, both are real and accepted as a medium of exchange. In an effort to make it more difficult to counterfeit the $20 bill—the most frequently counterfeited bill in the United States—the U.S. Treasury Department is redesigning it. Secretary of the Treasury John Snow says his department plans to redesign the nation's currency every 7 to 10 years to keep pace with counterfeiters as they develop new technology. The new bill, pictured in the top section of the photo, will have subtle green, peach, and blue tints added.

figure 19.1

The Consumer Price Index and the Purchasing Power of the Consumer Dollar (Base Period 1982–1984 = 100)
Inflation causes a loss of money's stored value. As the consumer price index goes up, the purchasing power of the consumer's dollar goes down.

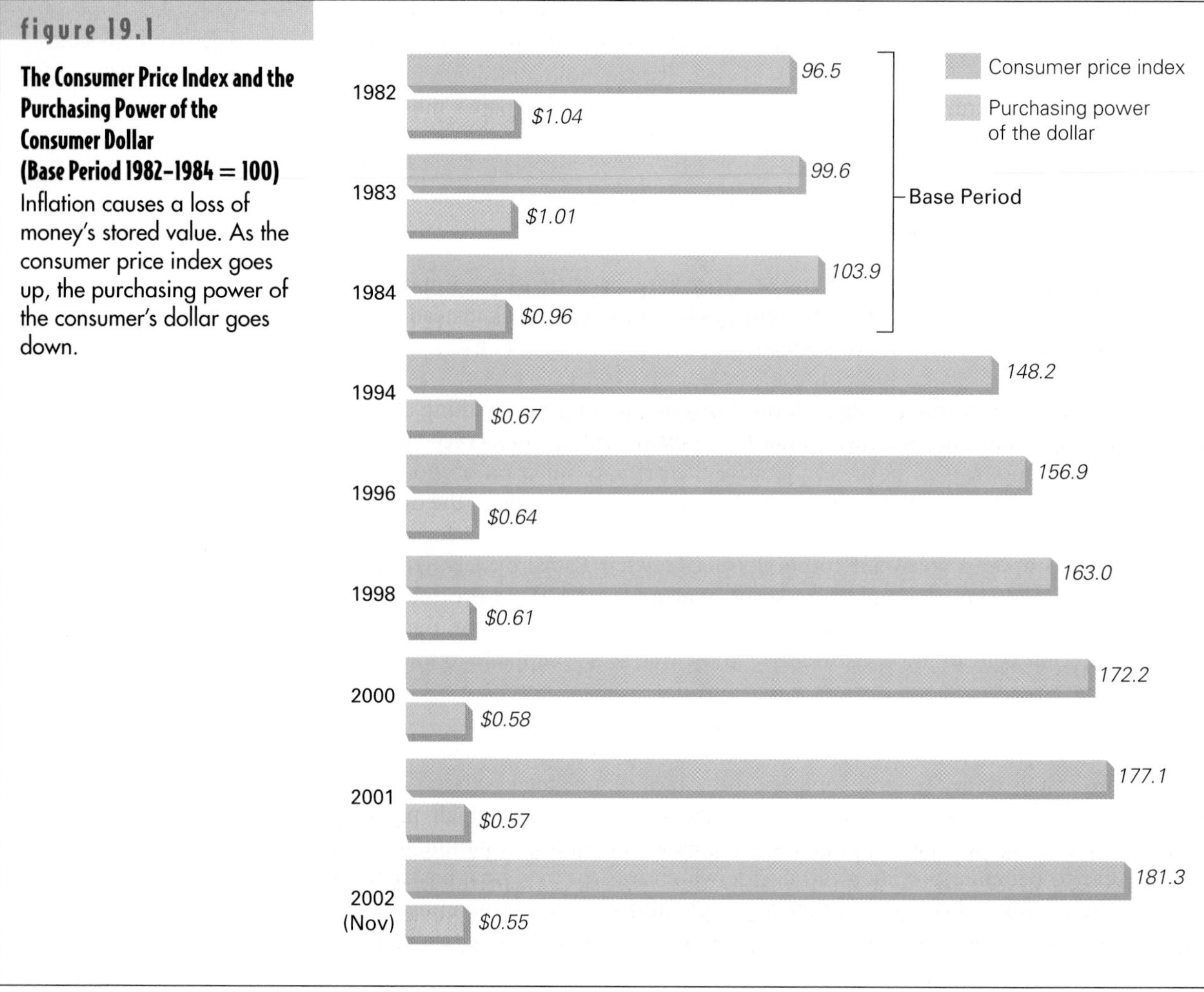

Source: The U.S. Bureau of Labor Statistics website, **www.bls.gov**, January 6, 2003.

wait and do not buy the home theater system immediately. If the price goes up t $1,050 in the meantime because of inflation, you can no longer buy the home theate system with your $1,000. Your money has *lost* purchasing power because it is no worth less than the home theater system. To determine the effect of inflation on th purchasing power of a dollar, economists often refer to a consumer price index such a the one illustrated in Figure 19.1. The consumer price index measures the changes i prices of a fixed basket of goods purchased by a typical consumer, including food transportation, shelter, utilities, clothing, medical care, entertainment, and othe items. The base amount for the consumer price index is 100 and was established by av eraging the cost of the items included in the consumer price index over the 1982–198 time period. In November 2002, it took approximately $181 to purchase the sam goods that could have been purchased for $100 in the base period 1982–1984.

Important Characteristics of Money

To be acceptable as a medium of exchange, money must be easy to use, trusted, an capable of performing the three functions just mentioned. To meet these require ments, money must possess the following five characteristics.

Divisibility The standard unit of money must be divisible into smaller units to ac commodate small purchases as well as large ones. In the United States, our standard i the dollar, and it is divided into pennies, nickels, dimes, quarters, and half-dollars hese coins allow us to make purchases of less than a dollar and of odd amounts eater than a dollar. Other nations have their own divisible currencies: the Euro in uropean nations, the rupee in India, and the yen in Japan, to mention a few.

ortability Money must be small enough and light enough to be carried easily. For is reason, paper currency is issued in larger *denominations*—multiples of the standard ollar unit. Five-, ten-, twenty-, fifty-, and hundred-dollar bills make our money con-nient for almost any purchase.

tability Money should retain its value over time. When it does not, people tend to se faith in their money. On October 27, 1997, when stock markets around the world ok a deep plunge, the New York Stock Exchange lost approximately 8 percent of its tal dollar value in one day. Although there were many reasons for the decline in ock values, one important reason heard time and again was the instability of foreign rrencies in Japan and other nations on the Pacific Rim. When money becomes ex-emely unstable, people may turn to other means of storing value, such as gold and wels, works of art, and real estate. They may even use such items as a medium of ex-ange in a barter system. During upheavals in eastern Europe including Russia in the 990s, farmers traded farm products for cigarettes because the value of cigarettes was ore stable than each nation's money.

urability The objects that serve as money should be strong enough to last through asonable usage. No one would appreciate (or use) dollar bills that disintegrated as ey were handled or coins that melted in the sun. To increase the life expectancy of aper currency, most nations use special paper with a high fiber content.

ifficulty of Counterfeiting If a nation's currency were easy to counterfeit—that is, imitate or fake—its citizens would be uneasy about accepting it as payment. Thus ountries do their best to ensure that it is very hard to reproduce their currency. In an tempt to make paper currency more difficult to counterfeit, the U.S. government designed hundred-, fifty-, twenty-, ten-, and five-dollar bills. Typically, countries se special paper and watermarks and print intricate designs on their currency to dis-ourage counterfeiting.

he Supply of Money: M_1, M_2, and M_3

ow much money is there in the United States? Before we can answer this question, e need to define a couple of concepts. A **demand deposit** is an amount on deposit in checking account. It is called a *demand* deposit because it can be claimed immedi-tely—on demand—by presenting a properly made out check, withdrawing cash from n automated teller machine (ATM), or transferring money between accounts.

demand deposit an amount on deposit in a checking account

A **time deposit** is an amount on deposit in an interest-bearing savings account. inancial institutions generally permit immediate withdrawal of money from savings ccounts. However, they can require written notice prior to withdrawal. The time be-ween notice and withdrawal is what leads to the name *time* deposits. Although time eposits are not available immediately to their owners, they can be converted to cash asily. For this reason, they are called *near-monies*. Other near-monies include short-rm government securities, government bonds, money-market mutual fund shares, nd the cash surrender values of insurance policies.

time deposit an amount on deposit in an interest-bearing savings account

Now we can discuss the question of how much money there is in the United tates. There are three main measures of the supply of money: M_1, M_2, and M_3.

The *M_1 supply of money* is a narrow definition and consists only of currency, de-and deposits, and travelers checks. By law, currency must be accepted as payment for roducts, services, and resources. Checks (demand deposits) are accepted as payment ecause they are convenient, convertible to cash, and generally safe.

The *M_2 supply of money* consists of M_1 (currency and demand deposits) plus certain oney-market securities and small-denomination time deposits or certificates of

figure 19.2

The Supply of Money
Three measures of the money supply are M_1, which includes currency and demand deposits; M_2, which includes M_1 plus certain securities and small-denomination time deposits, and M_3, which includes M_1, M_2, plus time deposits of $100,000 or more.

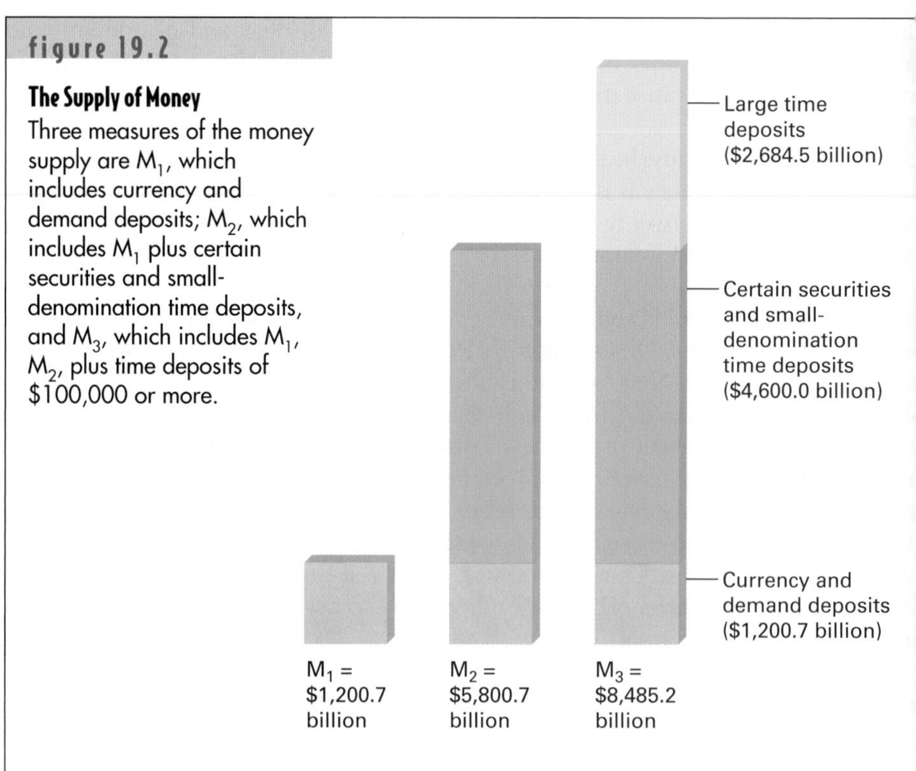

Source: The Federal Reserve website, **www.federalreserve.gov**, January 8, 2003.

deposit of less than $100,000. Another common definition of money—M_3—consis of M_1 and M_2 plus time deposits or certificates of deposit of $100,000 or more. Tl definitions of money that include the M_2 and M_3 supplies of money are based on tl assumption that time deposits can be converted to cash for spending. Figure 19 shows the elements of the M_1, M_2, and M_3 supplies. Take a closer look at M_3—abo 14 percent are coins, paper currency, and demand deposits; the remaining 86 perce are time deposits and certain securities.

We have, then, at least three measures of the supply of money. (Actually, there a other measures as well, which may be broader or narrower than M_1, M_2, and M Therefore, the answer to our original question is that the amount of money in tl United States depends very much on how we measure it. Generally, economist politicians, and bankers tend to focus on M_1 or some variation of M_1.

The Federal Reserve System

learning objective

2 Summarize how the Federal Reserve System regulates the money supply.

How do Federal Reserve actions affect me? What is the Federal Reserve Systen These are both good questions, and now for some answers. Lately, it seems like tl Federal Reserve Board, often referred to as the *Fed*, and its current chairman, Ala Greenspan, have been in the news more than usual. Part of the reason is that the Fe has lowered interest rates that banks pay to borrow money from the Fed in an effort shore up a sagging economy after an economic downturn that began in 1999 and tl terrorist attacks on September 11. A Fed rate change reverberates throughout tl economy. When the Fed lowers rates, banks pay less to borrow money from the Fe In turn, they often lower the interest rates they charge for business loans, home mor gages, car loans, and even credit cards. Lower rates often provide an incentive for bot business firms and individuals to buy goods and services, which, in turn, helps to r store the economic health of the nation. The effect on the economy is reversed whe

adapting to change

What's the Fed Up to Now?

THE OLD SAYING "MONEY TALKS" is particularly appropriate in the case of the Federal Reserve Bank. When Fed officials speak, markets pay close attention. And when Fed officials act, the U.S. public feels the results.

The chairman, vice chairman, and five members of the Fed board of governors have considerable influence because of their knowledge of and power over U.S. monetary policy. When the chairman expresses concern about the country's economic situation—which has happened more than once in recent years—stock prices often plunge. In turn, this lowers the value of investors' portfolios, so the stocks in your IRA or 401(k) retirement account are worth less. The reverse is also true: When Fed officials are optimistic about the economy, stock prices tend to rise. And investors in other countries may be affected because the gyrations of the U.S. stock market frequently prompt stock market fluctuations around the world.

The Fed's actions are especially critical during emergencies. For example, the Fed provided immediate low-cost loans to U.S. banks after terrorist attacks on the World Trade Center disrupted New York City's communications and transportation systems. Without these loans, the banks would have been reluctant to transfer funds out before they received incoming payments, which were delayed because of the disruptions. With the loans, however, the banks had sufficient liquidity to pay checks presented by customers or other financial institutions. In this way, the Fed avoided a crisis in the nation's banking system—which meant that you and other U.S. consumers and businesses had no problem getting money in or out of the bank.

When the Fed decides to manage the nation's economy by raising (or lowering) the discount rate, banks feel the immediate effect because they will pay more (or less) for borrowing funds from the Fed. Based on a higher discount rate, for example, banks raise the prime rate they charge their best loan customers. Prime rate hikes trigger higher interest rates for home equity loans and certain other loans. Thus, if you are applying for a loan, you will pay more interest to obtain the borrowed money you need. And you probably will face higher prices as businesses pass along the higher interests rates they are paying for borrowing as well.

the Fed raises rates. Banks must pay more to borrow money from the Fed. And the banks, in turn, charge higher rates for both consumer and business loans. For more information on how the Fed helps to maintain a healthy economy, read Adapting to Change.

Now let's answer to the second question. The **Federal Reserve System** is the central bank of the United States and is responsible for regulating the banking industry. Created by Congress on December 23, 1913, its mission is to maintain an economically healthy and financially sound business environment in which banks can operate. Even comments by its current board chairman, Alan Greenspan, about interest rates or inflation can send the stock and bond markets into a tailspin or provide support for sagging financial markets.

Federal Reserve System the central bank of the United States responsible for regulating the banking industry

The Federal Reserve System is controlled by its seven-member board of governors, who meet in Washington, D.C. Each governor is appointed by the president and confirmed by the Senate for a fourteen-year term. The president also selects the chairman and vice chairman of the board from among the board members for four-year terms.

The Federal Reserve System consists of twelve district banks located in major cities throughout the United States, as well as twenty-five branch banks (see Figure 19.3 on p. 574). Each of the twelve Federal Reserve District Banks is actually owned—but not controlled—by the commercial banks that are members of the Federal Reserve System in its district. All national (federally chartered) banks must be members of the Fed. State banks may join if they choose to and if they meet membership requirements. For more information about the Federal Reserve System, visit its website at **www.federalreserve.gov.**

The most important function of the Fed is to regulate the nation's supply of money in such a way as to maintain a healthy economy. It does so by controlling bank reserve requirements, regulating the discount rate, and running open-market operations.

figure 19.3

Federal Reserve System

The Federal Reserve System consists of twelve district banks and twenty-five branch banks.

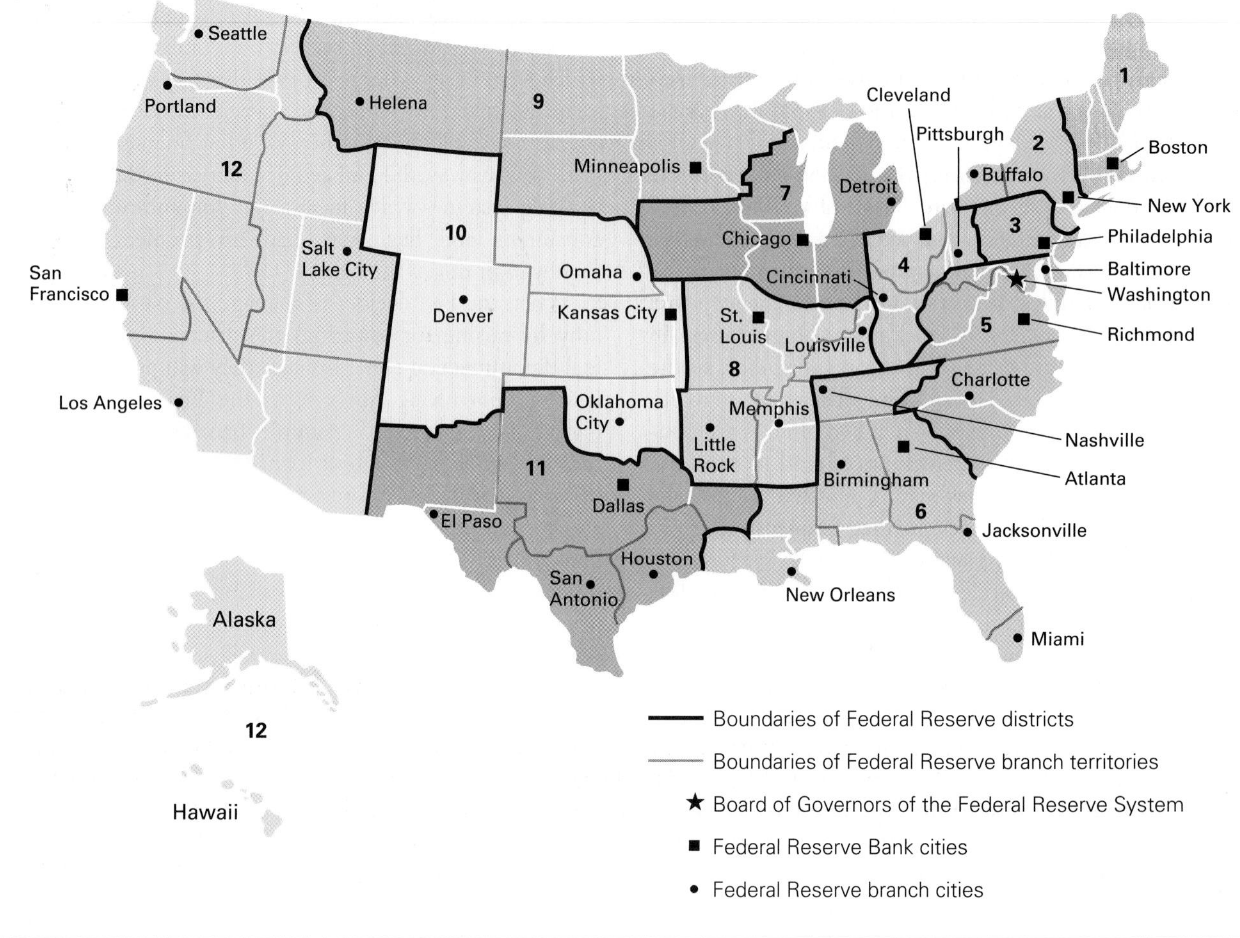

Source: *Federal Reserve Bulletin*, May 2002, pp. A84–86.

Regulation of Reserve Requirements

reserve requirement the percentage of its deposits a bank *must* retain, either in its own vault or on deposit with its Federal Reserve District Bank

When money is deposited in a bank, the bank must retain a portion of it to satisfy customers who may want to withdraw money from their accounts. The remainder i available to fund loans. The **reserve requirement** is the percentage of its deposits a bank *must* retain, either in its own vault or on deposit with its Federal Reserve Distric Bank. For example, if a bank has deposits of $20 million and the reserve requiremen is 10 percent, the bank must retain $2 million. The present reserve requirements range from 3 to 10 percent depending on such factors as the total amount individua banks have on deposit, average daily deposits, and the location of the particular member bank.[2]

Once reserve requirements are met, banks can use remaining funds to create more money and make more loans through a process called *deposit expansion*. Here's how deposit expansion works. In the preceding example, the bank must retain $2 million in a reserve account. It can use the remaining $18 million to fund consumer and business loans. Assume that the bank lends all $18 million to different borrowers. Also assume that before using any of the borrowed funds, all borrowers deposit the $18 million in their bank accounts at the lending institution. Now the bank's deposits have increased by an additional $18 million. Since these deposits are subject to the same reserve requirement described earlier, the bank must maintain $1.8 million in a reserve ccount, and the bank can lend the additional $16.2 million to ther bank customers. Of course, the bank's lending potential ecomes steadily smaller and smaller as it makes more loans. nd we should point out that since bankers are usually very onservative by nature, they will not use deposit expansion to aximize their lending activities; they will take a more midle-of-the-road approach.

A banker with economic power. Alan Greenspan, Chairman of the Federal Reserve System, and the Fed's other board members are responsible for maintaining a healthy economy. They do so by controlling bank reserve requirements (the percentage of deposits a bank must retain in its own vault or on deposit with its Federal Reserve District Bank), regulating the discount rate (the interest rate the Federal Reserve charges for loans to member banks), and open market operations (the buying and selling of U.S. government securities by the Federal Reserve).

The Fed's board of governors sets the reserve requireent. *When it increases the requirement, banks have less money vailable for lending.* Fewer loans are made, and the economy nds to slow. Thus, increasing the reserve requirement is a owerful anti-inflation weapon designed to hold prices that onsumers and businesses pay in check. *On the other hand, by ecreasing the reserve requirement, the Fed can make additional oney available for lending to stimulate a slow economy.* Because nis means of controlling the money supply is so very potent and has such far-reaching ffects on both consumers and financial institutions, the Fed seldom changes the reerve requirement.

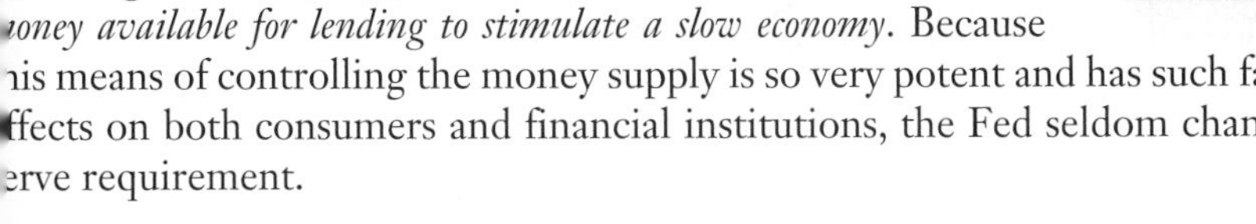

Regulation of the Discount Rate

Member banks may borrow money from the Fed to satisfy the reserve requirement nd to make additional loans to their customers. The interest rate the Federal Reserve harges for loans to member banks is called the **discount rate.** It is set by the Fed's oard of governors. In the past twenty-five years, the discount rate has been as low as .75 percent and as high as 14 percent.[3] At the beginning of 2003, the discount rate vas 0.75 percent, or the lowest it had been in twenty-five years.

When the Fed *lowers* the discount rate, it is easier and cheaper for banks to obtain noney. Member banks feel free to make more loans and to charge lower interest rates. This increases the amount of money available to both consumers and businesses and enerally stimulates the nation's economy. When the Fed *raises* the discount rate, anks begin to restrict loans. They increase the interest rates they charge and tighten neir own loan requirements. The overall effect is to slow the economy—to check inlation—by making money more difficult and more expensive to obtain. Although the iscount rate has declined slowly to the present rate of 0.75 percent over the past 3 ears, you should remember that the Fed can increase rates in an effort to maintain a ealthy economy.

discount rate the interest rate the Federal Reserve System charges for loans to member banks

Open-Market Operations

The federal government finances its activities partly by buying and selling securities ssued by the U.S. Treasury (Treasury bills and notes) and federal agency securities. These securities, which pay interest, may be purchased by any individual, firm, or oranization—including the Fed. **Open-market operations** are the buying and selling f U.S. government securities by the Federal Reserve System for the purpose of conrolling the supply of money. They are the Fed's most frequently used tool to control he nation's economy.

open-market operations the buying and selling of U.S. government securities by the Federal Reserve System for the purpose of controlling the supply of money

To reduce the nation's money supply, the Fed simply *sells* government securities n the open market. The money it receives from purchasers is taken out of circulation. Thus less money is available for investment, purchases, or lending. To increase the noney supply, the Fed *buys* government securities. The money the Fed pays for securities goes back into circulation, making more money available to individuals and irms.

Because the major purchasers of government securities are financial institutions, pen-market operations tend to have an immediate effect on lending and investment. Moreover, the Fed can control and adjust this effect by varying the amount of securities

table 19.1 Methods Used by the Federal Reserve System to Control the Money Supply and the Economy

Method Used	Immediate Result	End Result
Regulating reserve requirement		
1. Fed **increases** reserve requirement	Less money for banks to lend to customers—reduction in overall money supply	Economic slowdown
2. Fed **decreases** reserve requirement	More money for banks to lend to customers—increase in overall money supply	Increased economic activity
Regulating the discount rate		
1. Fed **increases** the discount rate	Less money for banks to lend to customers—reduction to overall money supply	Economic slowdown
2. Fed **decreases** the discount rate	More money for banks to lend to customers—increase in overall money supply	Increased economic activity
Open-market operations		
1. Fed **sells** government securities	Reduction in overall money supply	Economic slowdown
2. Fed **buys** government securities	Increase in overall money supply	Increased economic activity

it sells or buys at any given time and the amount of interest paid on these securitie Table 19.1 summarizes the effects of open-market operations and the other tools use by the Fed to regulate the money supply and control the economy.

Other Fed Responsibilities

In addition to its regulation of the money supply, the Fed is also responsible for ser ing as the government's bank, clearing checks and electronic transfers, inspecting cu rency, and applying selective credit controls.

Serving as Government Bank The Federal Reserve is the bank for the U.S. go ernment. As the government's bank, it processes a variety of financial transactions i volving trillions of dollars each year. For example, the U.S. Treasury keeps a checkin account with the Federal Reserve through which incoming tax deposits and outgoin government payments are handled.

Clearing Checks and Electronic Transfers Today, people use checks to pay fo nearly everything they buy. A check written by a customer of one bank and presente for payment to another bank in the same town may be processed through a local clea inghouse. The procedure becomes more complicated, however, when the banks ar not in the same town. This is where the Federal Reserve System comes in. The Fed responsible for the prompt and accurate collection of almost seventeen billion chec each year.[4]

The steps involved in clearing a check through the Federal Reserve System a outlined in Figure 19.4. About one-fourth of all the checks written in the Unite States are cleared in this way. Banks that use the Fed to clear checks are charged a fe for this service. The remainder are either presented directly to the paying bank processed through local clearinghouses. Through the use of electronic equipmen most checks can be cleared within two or three days.

Inspection of Currency As paper currency is handled, it becomes worn or dirt The typical one-dollar bill has a life expectancy of less than one year (larger denom nations usually last longer because they are handled less). When member banks d

figure 19.4

Clearing a Check Through the Federal Reserve System

Approximately one-fourth of all U.S. checks are cleared this way, a process that usually takes two to three days.

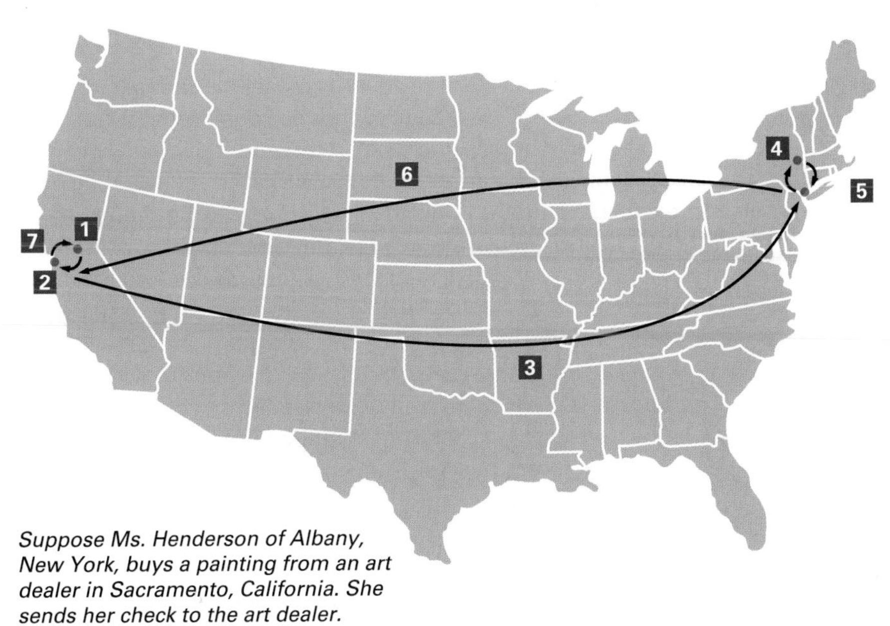

Suppose Ms. Henderson of Albany, New York, buys a painting from an art dealer in Sacramento, California. She sends her check to the art dealer.

1 The dealer deposits the check in his account at a Sacramento bank.

2 The Sacramento bank deposits the check for credit in its account with the Federal Reserve Bank of San Francisco.

3 The Federal Reserve Bank of San Francisco sends the check to the Federal Reserve Bank of New York for collection.

4 The Federal Reserve Bank of New York forwards the check to the Albany bank, which deducts the amount of the check from Ms. Henderson's account.

5 The Albany bank authorizes the Federal Reserve Bank of New York to deduct the amount of the check from its deposit account with the Federal Reserve Bank.

6 The Federal Reserve Bank of New York pays the Federal Reserve Bank of San Francisco.

7 The Federal Reserve Bank of San Francisco credits the Sacramento bank's deposit account, and the Sacramento bank credits the art dealer's account.

Source: Federal Reserve Bank of New York, *The Story of Checks*, 7th ed. New York, 1995, p. 11.

posit their surplus cash in a Federal Reserve Bank, the currency is inspected. Bills unfit for further use are separated and destroyed.

Selective Credit Controls The Federal Reserve System has the responsibility for enforcing the Truth-in-Lending Act, which Congress passed in 1968. This act requires lenders to state clearly the annual percentage rate and total finance charge for a consumer loan. The Federal Reserve System is also responsible for setting the margin requirements for stock transactions. The *margin* is the minimum amount (expressed as a percentage) of the purchase price that must be paid in cash or eligible securities. (The investor may borrow the remainder.) The current margin requirement is 50 percent. Thus, if an investor purchases $4,000 worth of stock, he or she must pay at least $2,000 in cash or its equivalent in securities. The remaining $2,000 may be borrowed from the brokerage firm. Although margin rules are regulated by the Federal Reserve, margin requirements and the interest charged on the loans used to fund margin transactions may vary among brokerage firms and different security exchanges. For example, the New York Stock Exchange does not allow an investor to open a margin account with a member firm without depositing at least $2,000. And investors may choose to use more of their money and to borrow less than the amount permitted by the Federal Reserve.

learning objective

3 Describe the differences between commercial banks and other financial institutions in the banking industry.

The American Banking Industry

Any banker you ask will tell you that for the American banking industry, the last few years have been exciting, to say the least. The economic problems that both individuals and business firms have encountered in the last three to four years have caused a ripple effect for banks, savings and loan associations, and other financial institutions. Simply put, unemployed consumers and businesses that are losing money often find that it is more difficult, if not impossible, to make payments on existing loans. To make matters worse, individuals worried about losing their jobs and businesses with reduced sales revenues are reluctant or unable to borrow more money. While bankers are in business to make loans, they also want to make sure that the loans will be repaid. As a result, lenders have begun to screen potential borrowers more carefully before approving loans. Fortunately, low interest rates have encouraged borrowers with the financial resources needed to pay back borrowed money to obtain loans to purchase all kinds of consumer products and to finance business needs.

@ Using the Internet

The American Bankers Association (**www.aba.com**), the long-established organization representing the banking industry's interests, provides a window into the world of banking through its website. Users can view articles on banking issues and concerns as well as statistics on the industry, personal financial advice, and links to related sites of interest.

In addition to the economic problems mentioned earlier, competition among banks, savings and loan associations, credit unions, and other business firms that want to perform banking activities has never been greater. In addition, banks from Japan, Canada, France, and other foreign nations have thrown their hat into U.S. banking circles. As a result, major banks such as Bank of America, Bank One, Chase Manhattan, and Wells Fargo have begun to provide innovative services for their customers. Even smaller banks have adopted the full-service banking philosophy and compete aggressively for customers, who expect more services than ever before. As you read the material in this section, keep in mind that banking will become even more competitive as bankers offer more services to attract new customers. Let's begin this section with some information about one of the major players in the banking industry—the commercial bank.

Commercial Banks

commercial bank a profit-making organization that accepts deposits, makes loans, and provides related services to its customers

A **commercial bank** is a profit-making organization that accepts deposits, makes loans, and provides related services to its customers. Like other businesses, the bank's primary goal—its mission—is to meet the needs of its customers while earning a profit. In a nutshell, here is how a bank earns its profit. It accepts money in the form of deposits, for which it pays interest. Once money is deposited in a bank, the bank lends it to qualified individuals and businesses that pay interest for the use of borrowed money. If the bank is successful, its income is greater than its expenses, and it will show a profit.

national bank a commercial bank chartered by the U.S. Comptroller of the Currency

state bank a commercial bank chartered by the banking authorities in the state in which it operates

Because they deal with money belonging to individuals and other business firms, banks are carefully regulated. They also must meet certain requirements before they receive a charter, or permission to operate, from either federal or state banking authorities. A **national bank** is a commercial bank chartered by the U.S. Comptroller of the Currency. There are approximately 2,200 national banks, accounting for about 46 percent of all bank deposits.[5] These banks must conform to federal banking regulations and are subject to unannounced inspections by federal auditors.

A **state bank** is a commercial bank chartered by the banking authorities in the state in which it operates. State banks outnumber national banks by about three to one, but they tend to be smaller than national banks. They are subject to unannounced inspections by both state and federal auditors.

Table 19.2 lists the seven largest banks in the United States. All are classified as national banks.

table 19.2 The Seven Largest U.S. Banks, Ranked by Total Revenues

Rank	Commercial Bank	Revenues (in millions)	Number of Employees
1	Bank of America Corp.	$52,641	142,670
2	J.P. Morgan Chase	50,429	95,812
3	Wells Fargo	26,891	119,714
4	Bank One Corp.	24,527	73,519
5	Wachovia Corp.	22,396	84,046
6	FleetBoston	19,190	55,909
7	U.S. Bancorp	16,443	49,955

Source: *Fortune,* April 15, 2002, p. F46.

Other Financial Institutions

In addition to commercial banks, at least eight other types of financial institutions perform either full or limited banking services for their customers. Included in this group are savings and loan associations, mutual savings banks, credit unions, insurance companies, pension funds, brokerage firms, finance companies, and investment banking firms.

Savings and Loan Associations A **savings and loan association (S&L)** is a financial institution that offers checking and savings accounts and certificates of deposit and that invests most of its assets in home mortgage loans and other consumer loans. Originally, S&Ls were permitted to offer their depositors *only* savings accounts. However, since Congress passed the Depository Institutions Deregulation and Monetary Control Act in 1980, they have been able to offer other services to attract depositors.

savings and loan association (S&L) a financial institution that offers checking and savings accounts and certificates of deposit and that invests most of its assets in home mortgage loans and other consumer loans

Today there are approximately 1,600 S&Ls in the United States.[6] Federal associations are chartered under provisions of the Home Owners' Loan Act of 1933 and are supervised by the Office of Thrift Supervision, a branch of the U.S. Treasury. S&Ls also can be chartered by state banking authorities in the state in which they operate. State-chartered S&Ls are subject to unannounced audits by state authorities.

During the 1980s and the first part of the 1990s, high interest rates, along with a reduced demand for homes and an increase in nonperforming loans and foreclosures, fraud and corruption, and mergers and acquisitions, led to a decrease in the number of S&Ls. In addition, over 1,000 S&Ls failed during the 1980s and early 1990s. However, the number of failed S&Ls had decreased dramatically by the end of the 1990s. On an annual basis, only one or two S&Ls have failed in recent years.[7] Reasons for the reduced number of failures include better regulation, much less corruption, and lower interest rates that led to an increased demand for loans to purchase homes, automobiles, and other major consumer items. Still, S&Ls, like their commercial bank competitors, have experienced some problems related to nonperforming loans due to a weak economy. According to the Office of Thrift Supervision (OTS), there were sixteen problem S&Ls that were being closely monitored by the OTS during 2002—the last year that complete results were available at the time of this publication.[8]

Credit Unions Today there are just over 10,000 credit unions in the United States.[9] A **credit union** is a financial institution that accepts deposits from and lends money to only those people who are its members. Usually the membership is composed of employees of a particular firm, people in a particular profession, or those who live in a community served by a local credit union. Some credit unions require that members purchase at least one share of ownership, at a cost of about $5 to $10. Credit unions

credit union a financial institution that accepts deposits from and lends money to only those people who are its members

generally pay higher interest on deposits than commercial banks and S&Ls, and they may provide loans at lower cost. The National Credit Union Administration regulates federally chartered credit unions and many state credit unions. State authorities may also regulate credit unions with state charters.

Organizations That Perform Banking Functions Six other types of financial institutions are involved in limited banking activities. Though not actually full-service banks, they offer customers limited banking services.

- *Mutual savings banks* are financial institutions that are owned by their depositors and offer many of the same services offered by banks, S&Ls, and credit unions, including checking accounts, savings accounts, and certificates of deposit. Like other financial institutions, they also fund home mortgages, commercial loans, and consumer loans. Unlike other types of financial institutions, the profits of a mutual savings bank go to the depositors, usually in the form of slightly higher interest rates on savings. Today there are approximately 400 mutual savings banks in operation, primarily in the Northeast.[10]
- *Insurance companies* provide long-term financing for office buildings, shopping centers, and other commercial real estate projects throughout the United States. The funds used for this type of financing are obtained from policyholders' insurance premiums.
- *Pension funds* are established by employers to guarantee their employees a regular monthly income on retirement. Contributions to the fund may come from the employer, the employee, or both. Pension funds earn additional income through generally conservative investments in corporate stocks, corporate bonds, and government securities, as well as through financing real estate developments.
- *Brokerage firms* offer combination savings and checking accounts that pay higher-than-usual interest rates (so-called money-market rates). Many people have switched to these accounts because they are convenient and to get the higher rates, but banks have instituted similar types of accounts, hoping to lure their depositors back.
- *Finance companies* provide financing to individuals and business firms that may not be able to get financing from banks, S&Ls, or credit unions. Firms such as Ford Motor Credit, GE Capital, and General Motors Acceptance Corporation provide loans to both individuals and business firms. Lenders such as Household Finance Corporation and Ace Cash Express, Inc., provide short-term loans to individuals. The interest rates charged by these lenders may be higher than the interest rates charged by other financial institutions.
- *Investment banking firms* are organizations that assist corporations in raising funds, usually by helping sell new issues of stocks, bonds, or other financial securities. Although these firms do not accept deposits or make loans like traditional banking firms, they do help companies raise millions of dollars that can be used to finance initial business start-ups, mergers and acquisitions, expansion, and new product development. More information about investment banking firms and the role they play in American business is provided in Chapters 20 and 21.

For a bank, how important is social responsibility?
Although the answer depends on the bank, Vermont-based Chittenden Bank believes that a bank should do more than just earn profits. In fact, Chittenden has developed a "Socially Responsible Banking" program that helps support affordable housing, education, agriculture, conservation, downtown revitalization, and economic growth. To obtain more information about Chittenden's Socially Responsible Banking program, visit their website at **www.chittenden.com.**

Socially Responsible Banking

Helps you put your money where your values are

Our **Socially Responsible Banking** program offers deposit accounts that support community development lending in:

Laura, Frankie the Beagle (adopted from NCAL), and Sarah enjoy some play time together.

- Affordable Housing
- Conservation
- Downtown Revitalization
- Education
- Economic Development

North Country Animal League benefited from a Socially Responsible Banking construction loan for a new animal shelter.

To find out how you can support local, community development lending:

Call: 800-545-2236 ext. 4069
E-mail: srb@chittenden.com
Web: sociallyresponsible.chittenden.com

Chittenden
Member FDIC

Careers in the Banking Industry

Take a second look at Table 19.2. The seven largest banks in the United States employ approximately 620,000 people. If you add to this amount the people employed by smaller banks not listed in Table 19.2 and those employed by S&Ls, credit unions, and other financial institutions, the number of employees grows dramatically. But be warned: According to the *Occupational Outlook Handbook*, published by the U.S. Department of Labor, the number of people employed in the banking industry is expected to decrease by about 2 percent between now and the year 2010. Even though employment within the industry is expected to decrease, there will be job growth for customer service representatives and for securities and financial services sales representatives. It also should be noted that job openings for tellers arising from replacement needs should be plentiful because turnover is high and the occupation is large.[11]

To be successful in the banking industry, you need a number of different skills. For starters, employees for a bank, S&L, credit union, or other financial institution must possess the following traits:

1. *You must be honest.* Because you are handling other people's money, many financial institutions go to great lengths to discover dishonest employees. In fact, some employees are warned when they are hired that they may be asked to take a polygraph test that detects employees who steal.
2. *You must be able to interact with people.* A number of positions in the banking industry require that you possess the interpersonal skills needed to interact not only with other employees but also with customers.
3. *You need a strong background in accounting.* Many of the routine tasks performed by employees in the banking industry are basic accounting functions. For example, a teller must post deposits or withdrawals to a customer's account and then balance out at the end of the day to ensure accuracy.
4. *You need to appreciate the relationship between banking and finance.* Bank officers must interview loan applicants and determine if their request for money is based on sound financial principles. Above all, loan officers must be able to evaluate applicants and their loan requests to determine if the borrower will be able to repay a loan.
5. *You should possess basic computer skills.* Almost all employees in the banking industry use a computer for some aspect of their work on a daily basis.

Typical job titles in the banking industry include teller, receptionist, computer specialist, supervisor, loan officer, and bank officer. Depending on qualifications, work experience, and education, starting salaries generally are between $15,000 and $30,000 a year, but it is not uncommon for college graduates to earn $35,000 a year or more.

If banking seems like an area you might be interested in, why not do more career exploration? You could take a banking course if your college or university offers one, or you could obtain a part-time job during the school year or a summer job in a bank, S&L, or credit union.

Traditional Services Provided by Financial Institutions

learning objective

4 Identify the services provided by financial institutions.

To determine how important banking services are to you, ask yourself the following questions:

- How many checks did you write last month?
- Do you have a major credit card? If so, how often do you use it?
- Do you have a savings account or a certificate of deposit?
- Have you ever financed the purchase of a new or used automobile?
- How many times did you visit an ATM last month?

If you are like most people and business firms, you would find it hard to live a normal life without the services provided by banks and other financial institutions. These services include the following:

- Checking accounts
- Savings accounts
- Loans
- Credit and debit cards
- Automatic teller machines (ATMs)
- Online banking
- Electronic transfer of funds
- Financial advice
- Payroll service
- Certified checks
- Trust services
- Safe-deposit boxes

The most important traditional banking services for both individuals and businesses are described in this section. Online banking, electronic transfer of funds, and other significant and future developments are discussed in the next section.

Checking Accounts

Imagine what it would be like living in today's world without a checking account. Although a few people do not have one, most of us like the convenience a checking account offers. Firms and individuals deposit money in checking accounts (demand deposits) so that they can write checks to pay for purchases. A **check** is a written order for a bank or other financial institution to pay a stated dollar amount to the business or person indicated on the face of the check. In order to attract new customers, many financial institutions offer free checking; others charge activity fees (or service charges) for checking accounts. Fees and charges generally range between $5 and $20 per month for individuals. For businesses, monthly charges are based on the average daily balance in the checking account and/or the number of checks written. Typically, charges for business checking accounts are higher than those for individual accounts.

check a written order for a bank or other financial institution to pay a stated dollar amount to the business or person indicated on the face of the check

Today most financial institutions offer interest-paying checking accounts, often called *NOW accounts*. A **NOW account** is an interest-bearing checking account. (*NOW* stands for *n*egotiable *o*rder of *w*ithdrawal.) For these accounts, the usual interest rate is between 0.50 and 1.5 percent. However, individual banks may impose certain restrictions on their NOW accounts, including the following:

NOW account an interest-bearing checking account; *NOW* stands for *n*egotiable *o*rder of *w*ithdrawal

- A minimum balance before any interest is paid
- Monthly fees for accounts whose balances fall below a set minimum amount
- Restrictions on the number of checks that may be written each month

When opening an interest-bearing checking account at a bank or financial institution, it pays to shop around for the highest interest rate and the fewest restrictions. Although banks and other financial institutions may pay low interest rates on checking accounts, even small earnings are better than no earnings. In addition to interest rates, be sure to compare monthly fees before opening a checking account.

Savings Accounts

Savings accounts (time deposits) provide a safe place to store money and a very conservative means of investing. The usual *passbook savings account* earns between 0.75 and 1.50 percent in commercial banks and S&Ls and slightly more in credit unions.

A depositor who is willing to leave money on deposit with a bank for a set period of time can earn a higher rate of interest. To do so, the depositor buys a certificate of deposit. A **certificate of deposit (CD)** is a document stating that the bank will pay the

certificate of deposit (CD) a document stating that the bank will pay the depositor a guaranteed interest rate for money left on deposit for a specified period of time.

depositor a guaranteed interest rate for money left on deposit for a specified period of time. The interest rates paid on CDs change weekly; they once briefly exceeded 11 percent in 1980. Recently, interest rates have ranged from 1.50 to 4 percent. The rate always depends on how much is invested and for how long. Generally, the rule is: The longer the period of time until maturity, the higher is the rate. Depositors are penalized for early withdrawal of funds invested in CDs.

Spotlight

Source: The Bureau of Economic Analysis website, **www.bea.gov**, March 23, 2003.

Short- and Long-Term Loans

Banks, S&Ls, credit unions, and other financial institutions provide short- and long-term loans to both individuals and businesses. *Short-term business loans* must be repaid within one year or less. Businesses generally use short-term loans to provide working capital that will be repaid with future sales revenues. Typical uses for the money obtained through short-term loans include solving cash-flow problems, purchasing inventory, financing promotional needs, and meeting unexpected emergencies.

To help ensure that short-term money will be available when needed, many firms establish a line of credit. A **line of credit** is a loan that is approved before the money is actually needed. Because all the necessary paperwork is already completed and the loan is preapproved, the business can later obtain the money without delay, as soon as it is required. Even with a line of credit, a firm may not be able to borrow money if the bank does not have sufficient funds available. For this reason, some firms prefer a **revolving credit agreement**, which is a guaranteed line of credit.

line of credit a loan that is approved before the money is actually needed

revolving credit agreement a guaranteed line of credit

Long-term business loans are repaid over a period of years. The average length of a long-term business loan is generally three to seven years but sometimes as long as fifteen years. Long-term loans are used most often to finance the expansion of buildings and retail facilities, mergers and acquisitions, replacement of equipment, or development of a firm's product mix.

Most lenders require some type of collateral for long-term loans. **Collateral** is real estate or property (stocks, bonds, land, equipment, or any other asset of value) pledged as security for a loan. For example, when an individual obtains a loan to pay for a new Chevrolet Camaro, the automobile is the collateral for the loan. If the borrower fails to repay the loan according to the terms specified in the loan agreement, the lender can repossess the car.

collateral real estate or property pledged as security for a loan

Repayment terms and interest rates for both short- and long-term loans are arranged between the lender and the borrower. For businesses, repayment terms may include monthly, quarterly, semiannual, or annual payments. Repayment terms (and interest rates) for personal loans vary depending on how the money will be used and what type of collateral, if any, is pledged. However, individuals typically make monthly payments to repay personal loans. Borrowers always should "shop" for a loan, comparing the repayment terms and interest rates offered by competing financial institutions. Helpful hints about obtaining financing from a lender are provided in the last major section of this chapter.

Credit Card and Debit Card Transactions

"Charge it!" If these two words sound familiar, it is no wonder. Over 159 million Americans use credit cards to pay for everything from tickets on American Airlines to Zebco fishing gear.[12] And the number of cardholders increases every month. In fact,

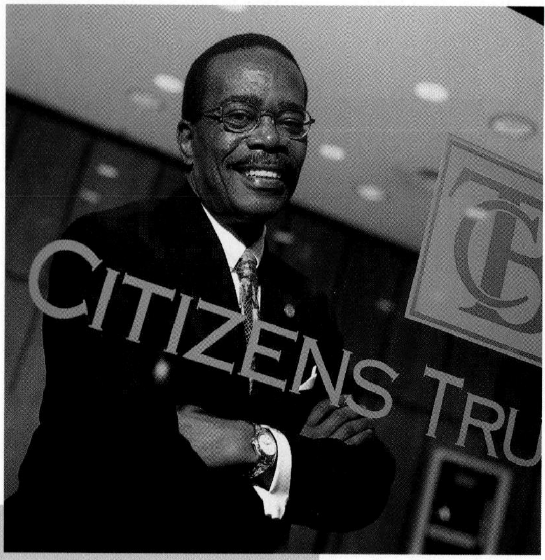

This banker wants $1,000,000,000. A billion dollars is a lot of money. But for James E. Young, president and CEO of Atlanta's Citizens Trust Bank, obtaining the money is a worthwhile goal. He wants Citizens Trust Bank to become the first black-owned bank with $1 billion in assets. In order to attract the people who will deposit the money to make his dream a reality, his bank stresses personal service to both consumers and business customers. According to Young, "Customers are always pleasantly surprised that they can talk directly to me, the president of the bank, when they have a complaint."

most Americans receive at least two or three credit card applications in the mail every month. Why have credit cards become so popular?

For a merchant, the answer is obvious. By depositing charge slips in a bank or other financial institution, the merchant can convert credit card sales into cash. In return for processing the merchant's credit card transactions, the bank charges a fee that ranges between 1.5 and 5 percent. Typically, small, independent businesses pay more than larger stores or chain stores. Let's assume that you use a Visa credit card to purchase a microwave oven for $300 from Richardson Appliance, a small retailer in Richardson, Texas. At the end of the day, the retailer deposits your charge slip, along with other charge slips, checks, and currency collected during the day, at its bank. If the bank charges Richardson Appliance 5 percent to process each credit card transaction, the bank deducts a processing fee of $15 ($300 × 0.05 = $15) for your credit card transaction and immediately deposits the remainder ($285) in Richardson Appliance's account. The number of credit card transactions, total dollar amount of credit sales, and how well the merchant can negotiate the fees the bank charges determine actual bank fees.

For the consumer, credit cards permit the purchase of goods and services even when funds are low. Today, most major credit cards are issued by banks or other financial institutions in cooperation with Visa International or MasterCard International. The unique feature of bank credit cards is that they extend a line of credit to the cardholder, much as a bank's consumer loan department does. Thus credit cards provide immediate access to short-term credit for the cardholder. Of course, the ability to obtain merchandise immediately and pay for it later can lead to credit card misuse. Today, the average American cardholder has a credit card balance of almost $4,300.[13] And with typical finance charges ranging from 1 to 1.5 percent a month (that's 12 to 18 percent a year), you can end up paying large finance charges. For example, if you carry a $4,000 balance on your credit card and your credit card company charges 1.5 percent a month, your monthly finance charge will be $60 ($4,000 × .015 = $60). And the monthly finance charges continue until you manage to pay off your credit card debt. If you find yourself getting deeper into debt, the first step for you to take is to *stop shopping!* Next, *cut up those credit cards!* Then contact your creditors and discuss options for repaying your debts with lower payments. If you do need assistance, organizations such as a local chapter of the Consumer Credit Counseling Service (**www.cccs.org**) or Myvesta (**www.myvesta.org**) or a local support group such as Debtors Anonymous is there to help you.

debit card a card that electronically subtracts the amount of your purchase from your bank account at the moment the purchase is made

Do not confuse debit cards with credit cards. Although they may look alike, there are important differences. A **debit card** electronically subtracts the amount of your purchase from your bank account at the moment the purchase is made. (By contrast, when you use your credit card, the credit card company extends short-term financing, and you do not make payment until you receive your next statement.) Debit cards are used most commonly to obtain cash at automatic teller machines and to purchase products and services from retailers. The use of debit cards is expected to increase because many people feel that they are more convenient than writing checks.

learning objective

5 Understand how financial institutions are changing to meet the needs of domestic and international customers.

Recent Innovations in Banking

Samantha Wood used an ATM three times this week. Why? She needed cash and did not have time to make a trip to the bank and wait in line. When Bart Jones, owner of Aquatic Pools, needed a short-term $50,000 loan to solve some of his firm's cash-flow problems, he turned to LendingTree.com (**www.lendingtree.com**), an online loan matching service. He answered some questions, and within an hour, three financial institutions had bid on his loan. He got approval (and the money he needed) without leaving his office. Like Samantha Wood and Bart Jones, many individuals, financial managers, and business owners are finding it convenient to do their banking electronically. By going online, many people can do most of the banking activities that used to require a trip to the bank. Let's begin by looking at how banking has changed over the last five years. Then we will discuss how those changes may provide a foundation for change in the future.

Recent Changes in the Banking Industry

In 1999, Congress enacted the Financial Services Modernization Banking Act of 1999. This act allowed banks to establish one-stop financial supermarkets where customers can bank, buy and sell securities, and purchase insurance coverage. Because of this act, competition among banks, brokerage firms, and insurance companies increased, and consumers have more choices on where to perform needed financial activities. This act also repealed the Glass Steagall Act of 1933, which prohibited banks from owning full-service brokerage firms and helping corporations sell stock issues. Now, as a result of this recent legislation and the increasing use of technology in the banking industry, even the experts are asking the question: How will banking change in the next five to ten years?

While the experts may not be able to predict with 100 percent accuracy the changes that will affect banking, they all agree that banking *will* change. The most obvious changes the experts do agree on are

- A reduction in the number of banks, S&Ls, credit unions, and financial institutions because of consolidation and mergers
- Fewer bank branch offices
- Globalization of the banking industry
- The importance of customer service as a way to keep customers from switching to competitors
- Increased use of credit and debit cards and a decrease in the number of written checks
- Increased competition from nonbank competitors that provide many of the same services as banks, S&Ls, credit unions, and other financial institutions
- Spectacular growth in online banking[14]

A most unusual ATM. Imagine visiting the Dusit zoo in Bangkok, Thailand, and running out of local currency. Not to worry, an ATM machine is available—one guarded by an elephant. Today, ATMs are located in bank parking lots, supermarkets, drugstores, gas stations, and even zoos around the world.

Online Banking and International Banking

As mentioned earlier, one of the fastest growing areas of banking is online banking. Online banking allows you to access your bank's computer system from home or even while you are traveling. For the customer, online banking offers a number of advantages, including the following:

- The convenience of electronic deposits
- The ability to obtain current account balances
- The convenience of transferring funds from one account to another
- The ability to pay bills
- The convenience of seeing which checks have cleared
- Easy access to current interest rates
- Simplified loan application procedures

Banks such as Bank One (**www.bankone.com**), Citibank (**www.citibank.com**), American Express (**www.americanexpress.com**), and Commerce Bank (**www.commerce-online.com**) are a few good examples for insight into this sector.

For people who bank online, the largest disadvantage is not being able to discuss financial matters with their "personal banker." With more and more people using online banking, the day may come when very few people will actually step inside a bank. To overcome this problem, many larger banks are investing huge amounts on electronic customer relationship management systems that will provide the type of service and financial advice that customers used to get when they walked through the doors of their financial institution.[15]

Online banking provides a number of advantages for the financial institution. Probably the most important advantage is the lower cost of processing large numbers of transactions. As you learned in Chapter 18, lower costs often lead to larger profits. In addition to lower costs and increased profits, financial institutions believe that online banking offers increased security because fewer people handle fewer paper documents.

electronic funds transfer (EFT) system a means of performing financial transactions through a computer terminal or telephone hookup

Electronic Funds Transfer (EFT) Although electronic funds transfer systems have been used for years, their use will increase dramatically as we continue through the twenty-first century. An **electronic funds transfer (EFT) system** is a means of performing financial transactions through a computer terminal or telephone hookup. The following three EFT applications are changing how banks do business:

1. *Automatic teller machines (ATMs)*. An ATM is an electronic bank teller—a machine that provides almost any service a human teller can provide. Once the customer is properly identified, the machine dispenses cash from the customer's checking or savings account or makes a cash advance charged to a credit card. ATMs are located in bank parking lots, supermarkets, drugstores, and even gas stations. Customers have access to them at all times of the day or night. Generally, there is a fee for each transaction.
2. *Automated clearinghouses (ACHs)*. Designed to reduce the number of paper checks, automated clearinghouses process checks, recurring bill payments, Social Security benefits, and employee salaries. For example, large companies use ACHs to transfer wages and salaries directly into their employees' bank accounts, thus eliminating the need to make out individual paychecks. The ACH system saves time and effort for both employers and employees and adds a measure of security to the transfer of these payments.
3. *Point-of-sale (POS) terminals*. A POS terminal is a computerized cash register located in a retail store and connected to a bank's computer. At the cash register, you pull your bank credit or debit card through a magnetic card reader. A central processing center notifies a computer at your bank that you want to make a purchase. The bank's computer immediately adds the amount to your account for a credit card transaction. In a similar process, the bank's computer deducts the amount of the purchase from your bank account if you use a debit card. Finally, the amount of your purchase is added to the store's account. The store is then notified that the transaction is complete, and the cash register prints out your receipt.

Bankers and business owners generally are pleased with online banking and EFT systems. Both online banking and EFT are fast, and they eliminate the costly processing of checks. However, many customers are reluctant to use online banking or EFT systems. Some simply do not like "the technology," whereas others fear that the computer will garble their accounts. Early on, in 1978, Congress responded to such fears by passing the Electronic Funds Transfer Act, which protects the customer in case the bank makes an error or the customer's personal identification number is stolen.

International Banking Services For international businesses, banking services are extremely important. Depending on the needs of an international firm, a bank can help by providing a letter of credit or a banker's acceptance. Although both a letter of credit and a banker's acceptance have been used for years, their use is expected to increase dramatically in the next five to ten years because of an increasing number of firms involved in international trade. To see how Citigroup is reaching both consumers and business customers around the world, read Going Global.

letter of credit a legal document issued by a bank or other financial institution guaranteeing to pay a seller a stated amount for a specified period of time

A **letter of credit** is a legal document issued by a bank or other financial institution guaranteeing to pay a seller a stated amount for a specified period of time—usually

30 to 60 days. (With a letter of credit, certain conditions, such as delivery of the merchandise, may be specified before payment is made.)

A **banker's acceptance** is a written order for the bank to pay a third party a stated amount of money on a specific date. (With a banker's acceptance, no conditions are specified. It is simply an order to pay without any strings attached.)

banker's acceptance a written order for the bank to pay a third party a stated amount of money on a specific date

Both a letter of credit and a banker's acceptance are popular methods of paying for import and export transactions. For example, imagine that you are a business owner in the United States who wants to purchase some leather products from a small business in Florence, Italy. You offer to pay for the merchandise with your company's check drawn on an American bank, but the Italian business owner is worried. After all, you have only talked over the phone and have never met this person. To solve the problem, your bank can issue either a letter of credit or a banker's acceptance to guarantee that payment will be made. In addition to a letter of credit and a banker's acceptance, banks also can use EFT technology to speed international banking transactions.

One other international banking service should be noted. Banks and other financial institutions provide for currency exchange. If you place an order for Japanese merchandise valued at $50,000, how do you pay for the order? Do you use U.S. dollars or Japanese yen? To solve this problem, you can use a bank's currency exchange service. To make payment, you can use either currency, and if necessary, the bank will exchange one currency for the other to complete your transaction.

going global

How Citigroup Meets Banking Needs Around the World

WITH A BANKING EMPIRE that spans more than 100 countries, Citigroup is experienced at meeting the diverse financial services needs of businesses, individual customers, and governments. The bank is headquartered in New York City but has offices in Africa, Asia, Central and South America, Europe, the Middle East, as well as throughout North America. Live or work in Japan? You can open a checking account at Citigroup's Citibank branch in downtown Tokyo. How about Mexico? Visit a Grupo Financiero Banamex-Accival branch, owned by Citigroup. Citigroup owns European American Bank and has even bought a stake in a Shanghai-based bank with an eye toward attracting more of China's $1 trillion in bank deposits. Between acquisitions and long-established branches, Citigroup covers the globe from the Atlantic to the Pacific and the Indian Oceans.

Many of Citigroup's banking services in other countries are geared toward business of all sizes. Small businesses (which the bank calls companies with up to $10 million in annual sales) not only can use Citigroup's checking and investment accounts, but they also can apply for loans. Retailers and other businesses can have Citigroup process their credit card transactions. The bank also provides more complex financial services for medium-sized and large businesses. For example, a corporation that needs capital can ask Citigroup to arrange for a public offering of its stock or have Citigroup sell bonds on its behalf. Businesses with sizable pension fund portfolios can contract with Citigroup to handle these investments.

Individuals can use Citigroup for all the usual banking services, but wealthy customers have additional options through the Citigroup Private Bank. Personalized service is the hallmark of this arm of the bank, which can help prepare customized financial plans for affluent customers, manage their securities trading activities, provide trust services, and much more. What's more, Citigroup is active in communities around the world through philanthropic contributions and grants, financial literacy seminars, volunteerism, and supplier diversity programs. This financial services giant strives for the best of both worlds, wielding its global presence and resources to meet banking needs locally, one customer at a time.

learning objective

6 Explain why banks, savings and loan associations, and credit unions provide deposit insurance for their customers.

The FDIC, SAIF, BIF, and NCUA

During the Depression, which began in 1929, a number of banks failed, and their depositors lost all their savings. To make sure that such a disaster does not happen again and to restore public confidence in the banking industry, Congress enacted legislation that created the *Federal Deposit Insurance Corporation (FDIC)* in 1933. The primary purpose of the FDIC is to insure deposits against bank failures. Then, in 1989, Congress passed legislation to bail out a large number of failed S&Ls and extend FDIC insurance coverage to deposits in S&Ls. As a result of the 1989 legislation, the FDIC was reorganized into two insurance units: the Bank Insurance Fund (BIF) and the Savings Association Insurance Fund (SAIF). BIF members are predominantly commercial and savings banks supervised by the FDIC, the Office of the Comptroller of the Currency, or the Federal Reserve System. SAIF members are predominantly S&Ls and are supervised by the Office of Thrift Supervision.

Today, the FDIC provides deposit insurance of $100,000 per account. Deposits maintained in different categories of legal ownership are insured separately. Thus you can have coverage for more than $100,000 in a single institution. The most common categories of ownership are single (or individual) ownership and joint ownership. Separate deposit insurance is also available for funds held for retirement purposes in individual retirement accounts (IRAs), Keogh retirement accounts, and pension or profit-sharing plans. A depositor also may obtain additional coverage by opening separate accounts in different banks or S&Ls.[16] To determine if your deposits are insured or if your bank or S&L is insured, visit the FDIC website at **www.fdic.gov.**

All banks that are members of the Federal Reserve System are required to belong to the FDIC. Nonmember banks and S&Ls are allowed to join if they qualify. To obtain coverage, banks and S&Ls must pay insurance premiums to the FDIC. In a similar manner, the National Credit Union Association (NCUA) insures deposits in member credit unions for up to $100,000 per account. Like the FDIC, the NCUA charges member credit unions for deposit insurance.

The FDIC and NCUA have improved banking in the United States. When either of these organizations insures a financial institution's deposits, they reserve the right to examine that institution's operations periodically. If a bank, S&L, savings bank, or credit union is found to be poorly managed, it is reported to the proper banking authority. In extreme cases, the FDIC or NCUA may cancel its insurance coverage. This is a particularly unwelcome action. It causes many depositors to withdraw their money from the institution and discourages most prospective depositors from opening an account.

Lending to individuals and firms is a vital function of banks. And deciding wisely to whom it will extend credit is one of the most important activities of any financial institution or business. The material in the next section explains the different factors used to evaluate credit applicants.

learning objective

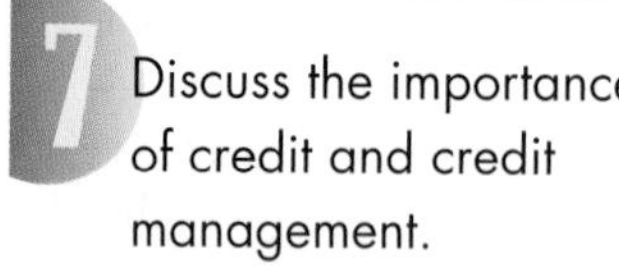

7 Discuss the importance of credit and credit management.

Effective Credit Management

credit immediate purchasing power that is exchanged for a promise to repay borrowed money, with or without interest, at a later date

Credit is immediate purchasing power that is exchanged for a promise to repay borrowed money, with or without interest, at a later date. A credit transaction is a two-sided business activity that involves both a borrower and a lender. The borrower is most often a person or business that wishes to make a purchase. The lender may be a bank, some other lending institution, or a business firm selling merchandise or services on credit.

For example, suppose that you obtain a bank loan to buy a $100,000 home. You, as the borrower, obtain immediate purchasing power. In return, you agree to certain terms imposed by the bank, S&L, or home mortgage company. The lender requires that you make a down payment, make monthly payments, pay interest, and purchase insurance to protect your home until the loan is paid in full.

Banks and other financial institutions lend money because they are in business for that purpose. The interest they charge is what provides their profit. Other businesses extend credit to their customers for at least three reasons. First, some customers simply cannot afford to pay the entire amount of their purchase immediately, but they *can* repay credit in a number of smaller payments, stretched out over some period of time. Second, some firms are forced to sell goods or services on credit to compete effectively when other firms offer credit to their customers. Finally, firms can realize a profit from interest charges that a borrower pays on some credit arrangements.

How Do You Get Money from a Bank or Lender?

Many individuals and business owners are nervous when applying for a loan. They are not sure what information they need. And what happens if they are turned down? Let's begin with the basics. Interest is what keeps a bank, S&L, or credit union in business. While lenders need interest from loans to help pay their business expenses and earn a profit, they also want to make sure that the loans they make will be repaid. Your job is to convince the lender that you are able and willing to repay the loan.

For individuals, the following suggestions may be helpful when applying for a loan:

- Although it may pay to shop around for lower interest rates, you usually have a better chance of obtaining a loan at a bank, S&L, or credit union where you already have an account.
- Obtain a loan application and complete it at home. At home, you have the information needed to answer *all* the questions on the loan application.
- Be prepared to describe how you will use the money and how the loan will be repaid.
- For most loans, an interview with a loan officer is required. Here again, preparation is the key. Think about how you would respond to questions a loan officer might ask.
- If your loan request is rejected, try to analyze what went wrong. Ask the loan officer why you were rejected. If the rejection is based on incorrect information, supply the correct information and reapply.

Business owners in need of financing may find the following additional tips helpful:

- It is usually best to develop a relationship with your banker before you need financing. Help the banker understand what your business is and how you may need future financing for expansion, cash-flow problems, or unexpected emergencies.
- Apply for a preapproved line of credit or revolving credit agreement even if you do not need the money. View the application as another way to showcase your company and its products or services.
- In addition to the application, supply certified public accountant (CPA)–prepared financial statements and business tax returns for the last three years and your own personal financial statements and tax returns for the same period.
- Write a cover letter describing how much experience you have, whether you are operating in an expanding market, or any other information that would help convince the banker to provide financing.

Source: *Statistical Abstract of the United States 2002*, Table 1165, p. 728.

Good credit can make the American dream a reality. For Lori Allen and her daughter D'neah, the dream of owning their own home almost turned into a nightmare. Like a lot of folks, Allen, a single parent whose husband died of a brain aneurysm 10 years ago, found that it was hard to stretch her salary to pay all of the bills and have anything left over to fund an investment program. To help solve her financial problems, she refinanced her home. According to Allen, lowering the interest rate on her mortgage by 2 points and opting for a shorter repayment period will save her over $165,000 over the life of the loan. According to the home mortgage experts, without an acceptable credit rating and a lender willing to work with her, it would have been impossible to refinance her home.

From the lender's viewpoint, the major pitfall in granting credit is the possibility of nonpayment. However, if a lender follows the five C's of credit management, it can minimize this possibility.

The Five C's of Credit Management

When a business extends credit to its customers, it must face the fact that some customers will be unable or unwilling to pay for their credit purchases. With this in mind, lenders must establish policies for determining who will receive credit and who will not. Most lenders build their credit policies around the five C's of credit: character, capacity, capital, collateral, and conditions.

Character *Character* means the borrower's attitude toward credit obligations. Experienced lenders often see this as the most important factor in predicting whether a borrower will make regular payments and ultimately repay a credit obligation. Typical questions to consider in judging a borrower's character include the following:

1. Is the borrower prompt in paying bills?
2. Have other lenders had to dun the borrower with overdue notices before receiving payment?
3. Have lenders been forced to take the borrower to court to obtain payment?
4. Has the customer ever filed for bankruptcy? If so, did the customer make an attempt to repay debts voluntarily?

Although it is illegal to discriminate, personal factors such as marital status and drinking or gambling habits may affect a lender's decision to loan money or extend credit to an individual.

Capacity *Capacity* means the borrower's financial ability to meet credit obligations—that is, to make regular loan payments as scheduled in the credit or loan agreement. If the customer is a business, the lender looks at the firm's income statement. For individuals, the lender checks salary statements and other sources of income, such as dividends and interest. The borrower's other financial obligations and monthly expenses are also taken into consideration before credit is approved. *Hint:* You may want to review the material on personal income statements presented in Chapter 18 before applying for a loan.

Capital The term *capital* as used here refers to the borrower's assets or net worth. In general, the greater the capital, the greater is the borrower's ability to repay a loan. The capital position of a business can be determined by examining its balance sheet. For individuals, information on net worth can be obtained by requiring that the borrower complete a credit application such as the one illustrated in Figure 19.5. The borrower also must authorize employers and financial institutions to release information to confirm the claims made in the credit application. *Hint:* You may want to review the material on personal balance sheets presented in Chapter 18 before applying for a loan.

Collateral For large amounts of credit—and especially for long-term loans—the lender may require some type of collateral. As mentioned earlier, collateral is real estate or property pledged as security for a loan. If the borrower fails to live up to the terms of the credit agreement, the lender can repossess the collateral and then sell it to satisfy the debt.

figure 19.5

Credit Application Form

Lenders use the information on credit application forms to help determine which customers should be granted credit.

Apply today! Just complete this application or call 1-800-438-9222.

Citizens Bank Customer Credit Card Application

Branch # ___________

This offer is for existing Citizens Bank Customers applying for a new credit card account

Existing Citizens Bank cardholders should call 1-800-438-9222 for special cardholder rate information.

Citizens Bank VISA® (Code: BVCFNU)

Please tell us about yourself

First Name   Middle Initial   Last Name

Address (street)

(City, state, zip)

Date of Birth   Social Security Number

❑ Own ❑ Rent ❑ Live with Parents

Years/Months at Present Address

$ (   )

Monthly Housing Payment   Home Telephone

Previous Address (*if less than 2 years at present address*)   Years/Months There

Mother's Maiden Name

Citizens Bank Account Information

❑ Checking ❑ Savings ❑ Loan ❑ Citizens Circle℠ Checking

account # ___________

Please tell us about your employment

Present Employer   Position

(   )

Years/Months Employed There   Business Telephone

Previous Employer (*if less than 2 years at present employer*)   Years/Months There

$ $

Gross Monthly Household Income   Other Monthly Income*

*Alimony, child support, or separate maintenance income need not be revealed if you do not wish it to be considered as a basis for repaying this obligation.

24-hour banking convenience

Your card(s) can be encoded with a four-digit personal identification number (PIN) to obtain cash advances at automated teller machines. This four-digit PIN will be known only to you. So that we may properly encode your card(s), please select the four digits of your choice and enter them in the spaces below:

____ ____ ____ ____

Please send a second card at no cost for

First Name   Middle Initial   Last Name

Please read and sign

Your Signature   Date

All information on this application is true and complete, and Citizens Bank of Rhode Island, the card issuer, is authorized to obtain further credit and employment information from any source. I understand that you will retain this application whether or not it is approved. You may share with others, only for valid business reasons, any information relating to me, this application, and any of my banking relationships with you. I request issuance of a Citizens credit card and agree to be bound by the terms and conditions of the Agreement received with the card(s). I understand that Citizens Bank of Rhode Island will assign a credit line based on information provided and information obtained from any other source; and the issuance of a Gold card is subject to a minimum annual income of $35,000 and qualification for a minimum $5,000 credit line.

Transfer balances and save

Citizens will transfer your high interest rate balances to your new Citizens Bank VISA Card at no extra charge. Use the form below to indicate the amount(s) to be transferred in order of priority. (Citizens Bank will not transfer balances from existing Citizens Bank accounts.) (see reverse side for balance transfer disclosure)

Creditor Name	Account Number	$ Amount
Creditor Name	Account Number	$ Amount
Creditor Name	Account Number	$ Amount

Bank Use Only   Bank Code: ❐ CBMA ❐ CBRI ❐ CBCT   Sales ID# ___________   Application code: 1122

Source: Courtesy of Citizens Financial Group, Inc., Providence, Rhode Island.

Conditions *Conditions* refers to the general economic conditions that can affect a borrower's ability to repay a loan or other credit obligation. How well a business firm can withstand an economic storm may depend on the particular industry the firm is in, its relative strength within that industry, the type of products it sells, its earnings history, and its earnings potential. For individuals, the basic question focuses on security—of both the applicant's job and the firm for which he or she works. For example, over the last two to three years, many employees lost their jobs when a large number of firms in the technology industry either closed or were forced to lay off workers. Even though these former employees lost their jobs, they still have mortgage payments, car payments, and credit card payments that must be paid.

Checking Credit Information

The five C's of credit are concerned mainly with information supplied by the applicant. But how can the lender determine whether this information is accurate? This depends on whether the potential borrower is a business or an individual consumer.

Credit information concerning businesses can be obtained from the following four sources:

- *Global credit-reporting agencies*. D&B (formerly Dun & Bradstreet) is the most widely used credit-reporting agency in the world. D&B Reports present detailed credit information about specific companies. The company's reference books include credit ratings for millions of businesses operating in countries around the globe. For more information on D&B services, visit the company's website at **www.dnb.com.**
- *Local credit-reporting agencies*, which may require a monthly or yearly fee for providing information on a continual basis.
- *Industry associations*, which may charge a service fee.
- *Other firms* that have given the applicant credit.

Various credit bureaus provide credit information concerning individuals. The following are the three major consumer credit bureaus:

- Experian—Allen, Texas, at **www.experian.com** or toll free at 888–397–3742
- Trans Union—Chester, Pennsylvania, at **www.transunion.com** or toll free at 800–888–4213
- Equifax Credit Information Services—Atlanta, Georgia, at **www.equifax.com** or toll free at 800–685–1111

With the recent rise in identity theft, experts recommend that you check your credit report at least once a year. For more information on how to prevent identity theft, read Exploring Business.

Consumer credit bureaus are subject to the provisions of the Fair Credit Reporting Act, which became effective in 1971. This act safeguards consumers' rights in two ways. First, every consumer has the right to know what information is contained in his or her credit bureau file. In most cases, a consumer who has been denied credit on the basis of information provided by a credit bureau can obtain a credit report without charge within 60 days after requesting a report from the credit bureau. In other situations, the consumer may obtain the information for a fee that is usually about $8.00 to $15.00.

Second, a consumer who feels that some information in the file is inaccurate, misleading, or vague has the right to request that the credit bureau verify it. If the disputed information is found to be correct, the consumer can provide a brief explanation, giving his or her side of the dispute. This explanation must become part of the consumer's credit file. If the disputed information is found to be inaccurate, it must be deleted or corrected. Furthermore, you may request that any lender that has been supplied an inaccurate credit report be sent a corrected credit report.

exploring business

Identity Theft: A Real Possibility

YOU COULD BE ONE IN A MILLION—the one million Americans who fall victim to the crime of identity theft every year. Crooks who steal your name, birth date, credit card numbers, bank account numbers, Social Security Number, and other aspects of your identity can profit from this information in several ways. They may withdraw money from your bank accounts, charge merchandise in your name, or contract for cell phone service. Some simply use your identity to obtain driver's licenses and other credentials as a stepping stone to more fraud.

Criminals use identity theft to steal nearly $1 billion every year. Who pays? "When you're a victim of identity theft, you're not liable for the money," stresses a consumer advocate, "but you are responsible for getting rid of the accounts and restoring your credit." That means contacting banks and retailers to close fraudulent accounts, alerting credit-reporting agencies, and filing crime reports. Straightening out the aftermath of identity theft can take hundreds of hours and cost victims, on average, about $800 in out-of-pocket expenses.

What can you do to guard against this fast-growing crime? Experts advise

- Pick up mail promptly so that thieves have less opportunity to steal credit card offers.
- Do not disclose your Social Security Number except when absolutely necessary for official purposes—and never to people who call to "verify" or "update" your personal data.
- Shred credit card and bank documents before discarding.
- Use caution when submitting personal data to web-based businesses.
- Order a copy of your credit record yearly from Experian (1–888–397–3742), TransUnion (1–800–888–4213), or Equifax (1–800–685–1111) to check that your identity has not been stolen.
- Safeguard your credit cards, ATM card, Social Security card, and other documents—as well as your PIN numbers.

If your identity has been stolen, you should

- Report the crime to the local police and the Federal Trade Commission.
- Contact the three credit bureaus to place a "fraud alert" warning on your account and check for unauthorized credit accounts.
- Contact creditors to close fraudulent accounts.
- Follow up until your credit history does not reflect accounts or activity that you did not authorize.

Sound Collection Procedures

The vast majority of borrowers follow the lender's repayment terms exactly. However, some accounts inevitably become overdue for a variety of reasons. Experience shows that such accounts should receive immediate attention.

Some firms handle their own delinquent accounts; others prefer to use a professional collection agency. (Charges for a collection agency's services are usually high—up to half the amount collected.) Both tend to use the following techniques, generally in the order in which they are listed:

1. Subtle reminders, such as duplicate statements marked "Past Due"
2. Telephone calls to urge prompt payment
3. Personal visits to business customers to stress the necessity of paying overdue amounts immediately
4. Legal action, although the time, expense, and uncertain outcome of a lawsuit make this action a last resort

Good collection procedures should be firm, but they also should allow for compromise. Harassment is both illegal and bad business. Ideally, the customer will be convinced to make up missed payments, and the firm will retain the customer's goodwill.

In the next chapter you will see why firms need financing, how they obtain the money they need, and how they ensure that funds are used efficiently, in keeping with their organizational objectives.

Return To inside business

Bank of America, the bank that loaned Walt Disney the money to create the original Disneyland and financed the construction of San Francisco's Golden Gate Bridge, offers financial services to customers in more than 150 nations. Its online banking system is easy to use yet boasts a variety of sophisticated features. For example, the bank knows that some customers—especially small business owners—can't wait to receive their monthly statements to see which checks have been paid or review their deposits. Therefore, it scans and stores digital images of all canceled checks and deposit slips so that online banking customers can view them within hours of being processed. That means scanning more than forty million checks and deposit slips every day.

But some customers may still wonder whether online banking is really safe and private. To reassure these customers, Bank of America guarantees that no one will be liable for any unauthorized online banking or bill-payment activity once a suspicious transaction has been reported. Going further, the bank uses the latest encryption technology and security systems to safeguard all its banking information, even e-mail messages to and from customers. It is small wonder that more customers sign up for Bank of America's online banking services every day.

Questions

1. ATMs are located nearly everywhere these days, from fast-food restaurants to gas stations. Why would a consumer prefer online banking to ATMs?
2. What additional services do you think Bank of America should offer its online banking customers? Explain.

chapter review

Summary

Identify the functions and characteristics of money.

Money is anything a society uses to purchase products, services, or resources. Money must serve as a medium of exchange, a measure of value, and a store of value. To perform its functions effectively, money must be divisible into units of convenient size, light and sturdy enough to be carried and used on a daily basis, stable in value, and difficult to counterfeit.

The M_1 supply of money is made up of coins and bills (currency) and deposits in checking accounts (demand deposits). The M_2 supply includes M_1 plus certain money market securities and small-denomination time deposits. Another common definition of the money supply—M_3—consists of M_1 and M_2 plus time deposits of $100,000 or more.

Summarize how the Federal Reserve System regulates the money supply.

The Federal Reserve System is responsible for regulating the U.S. banking industry and maintaining a sound economic environment. Banks with federal charters (national banks) must be members of the Fed. State banks may join if they choose to and if they can meet the requirements for membership. Twelve district banks and twenty-five branch banks compose the Federal Reserve System, whose seven-member board of governors is headquartered in Washington, D.C.

To control the supply of money, the Federal Reserve System regulates the reserve requirement, or the percentage of deposits a bank must keep on hand. It also regulates the discount rate, or the interest rate the Fed charges member banks for loans. And it engages in open-market operations, in which it buys and sells government securities. The Fed serves as the government's bank and is also responsible for clearing checks and electronic transfers, inspecting currency, enforcing the Truth-in-Lending Act, and setting margin requirements for stock transactions.

Describe the differences between commercial banks and other financial institutions in the banking industry.

A commercial bank is a profit-making organization that accepts deposits, makes loans, and provides related services to customers. Commercial banks are chartered by the federal government or state governments. Savings and loan associations and credit unions offer the same basic services that commercial banks provide. Mutual savings banks, insurance companies, pension funds, brokerage firms, finance companies, and investment banking firms provide some limited banking services. A large number of people work in the banking industry because of the number of banks and other financial institutions. To be successful in the banking industry, you must be honest, be able to interact with people, have a strong background in accounting, appreciate the elationship between banking and finance, and possess asic computer skills.

Identify the services provided by financial institutions.

anks and other financial institutions offer today's cusomers a tempting array of services. Among the most imortant and attractive banking services for both individuals nd businesses are checking accounts, savings accounts, hort- and long-term loans, and credit card and debit card ransactions. Other services include online banking, elecronic transfer of funds, financial advice, payroll services, ertified checks, trust services, and safe-deposit boxes.

Understand how financial institutions are changing to meet the needs of domestic and international customers.

mong the laws enacted during the last thirty years to eregulate the banking industry, probably the most imporant is the Financial Services Modernization Banking Act f 1999. This act allowed banks to establish one-stop fiancial supermarkets where customers can bank, buy and ell securities, and purchase insurance coverage. Because of his act, competition among banks, brokerage firms, and nsurance companies has increased. As we enter the wenty-first century, an increasing use of technology and he need for bankers to help American businesses compete n the global marketplace will change the way banks and ther financial institutions do business. The use of technology will increase as financial institutions continue to ffer online banking. Increased use of electronic funds ransfer systems (automated teller machines, automated learinghouses, and point-of-sale terminals) also will hange the way people bank. For firms in the global maretplace, a bank can provide letters of credit and banker's cceptances that will reduce the risk of nonpayment for ellers. Banks and financial institutions also can provide currency exchange to reduce payment problems for import or export transactions.

Explain why banks, savings and loan associations, and credit unions provide deposit insurance for their customers.

The Federal Deposit Insurance Corporation (FDIC), the Savings Association Insurance Fund (SAIF), the Bank Insurance Fund (BIF), and the National Credit Union Association (NCUA) insure accounts in member commercial banks, S&Ls, savings banks, and credit unions for up to $100,000 per individual account at one financial institution. The FDIC and NCUA have improved banking in the United States. When either of these organizations insures a financial institution's deposits, they reserve the right to examine that institution's operations periodically. If a bank, S&L, or credit union is found to be poorly managed, it is reported to the proper banking authority.

Discuss the importance of credit and credit management.

Credit is immediate purchasing power that is exchanged for a promise to repay borrowed money, with or without interest, at a later date. Banks lend money because they are in business for that purpose. Businesses sell goods and services on credit because some customers cannot afford to pay cash and because they must keep pace with competitors who offer credit. Businesses also may realize a profit from interest charges.

Decisions on whether to grant credit to businesses and individuals are usually based on the five C's of credit: character, capacity, capital, collateral, and conditions. Credit information can be obtained from various credit reporting agencies, credit bureaus, industry associations, and other firms. The techniques used to collect past-due accounts should be firm enough to prompt payment but flexible enough to maintain the borrower's goodwill.

Key Terms

You should now be able to define and give an example relevant to each of the following terms:

barter system (568)
money (569)
medium of exchange (569)
measure of value (569)
store of value (569)
demand deposit (571)
time deposit (571)
Federal Reserve System (573)
reserve requirement (574)
discount rate (575)
open-market operations (575)
commercial bank (578)
national bank (578)
state bank (578)
savings and loan association (S&L) (579)
credit union (579)
check (582)
NOW account (582)
certificate of deposit (CD) (582)
line of credit (583)
revolving credit agreement (583)
collateral (583)
debit card (584)
electronic funds transfer (EFT) system (586)
letter of credit (586)
banker's acceptance (587)
credit (588)

Review Questions

1. How does the use of money solve the problems associated with a barter system of exchange?
2. What are three functions money must perform in a sound monetary system?
3. Explain why money must have each of the following characteristics:
   a. Divisibility
   b. Portability
   c. Stability
   d. Durability
   e. Difficulty of counterfeiting
4. What is included in the definition of the M_1 supply of money? Of the M_2 supply? Of the M_3 supply?
5. What is the Federal Reserve System? How is it organized?
6. Explain how the Federal Reserve System uses each of the following to control the money supply:
   a. Reserve requirements
   b. The discount rate
   c. Open-market operations
7. The Federal Reserve is responsible for enforcing the Truth-in-Lending Act. How does this act affect you?
8. What is the difference between a national bank and a state bank? What other financial institutions compete with national and state banks?
9. Describe the major banking services provided by financial institutions today.
10. What are the major advantages of online banking? What is its major disadvantage?
11. How can a bank or other financial institution help American businesses compete in the global marketplace?
12. What is the basic function of the FDIC, SAIF, BIF, and NCUA? How do they perform this function?
13. List and explain the five C's of credit management.
14. How would you check the information provided by an applicant for credit at a department store? By a business applicant at a heavy-equipment manufacturer's sales office?

Discussion Questions

1. It is said that financial institutions "create" money when they make loans to firms and individuals. Explain what this means.
2. Is competition among financial institutions good or bad for the following:
   a. The institutions themselves
   b. Their customers
   c. The economy in general
3. Why does the Fed use indirect means of controlling the money supply instead of simply printing more money or removing money from circulation when necessary?
4. Why would banks pay higher interest on money left on deposit for longer periods of time (e.g., on CDs)?
5. How could an individual get in financial trouble by using a credit card?
6. Lenders generally are reluctant to extend credit to individuals with no previous credit history (and no outstanding debts). Yet they willingly extend credit to individuals who are in the process of repaying debts. Is this reasonable? Is it fair? Explain your answer.
7. Assume that you want to borrow $10,000. What can you do to convince the loan officer that you are a good credit risk?

video case

Financial Fusion Fuels Financial Services Transactions

Web-based and wireless banking is "really revolutionizing the way that banks process transactions," says Michon Schenck, former president of Financial Fusion. Based in Concord, Massachusetts, Financial Fusion's software is the firepower behind this revolution. Its technology drives online banking systems and securities trading systems for more than 200 banks and financial institutions around the world. California Federal Bank, eMarquette Holdings, and First Citizens Bank are just three of Financial Fusion's bank customers.

The company's Consumer e-Finance Suite provides the technology for offering a full range of banking services that individual customers can access from any web-enabled device, not just personal computers. Knowing that the needs of business customers differ from those of individuals, Financial Fusion also has developed a separate Business e-Finance Suite for banks to offer their small business customers. Financial institutions involved in securities trading can buy TradeForce Suite, a system for managing the communication of trade and payment transactions.

Financial Fusion customizes a system for each bank or institution, backing up the technology with personalized service through four regional offices in North America. Owned by high-tech Sybase, Inc., Financial Fusion implements customer systems through alliances with its parent company as well as with IBM and Sun Microsystems. The goal is not only to address each customer's current needs but also to allow for changes and future developments. The result is a system that grows as each financial services firm grows.

Consider how Financial Fusion helped First Citizens Bank. Headquartered in Raleigh, North Carolina, First Citizens is an $11-billion regional bank operating about 350 branches in North Carolina, Virginia, and West Virginia. The bank originally offered online banking through another technology supplier. When First Citizen's executives learned that its online banking technology was about to become obsolete, they decided to evaluate other suppliers and technologies. "We really distinguish ourselves by providing outstanding customer service in our branches and contact center," explains Executive Vice President Jeff Ward, "and we wanted to use this occasion to take our online service to the next level."

In particular, First Citizens was interested in making ne online banking system easier to use and in expanding s capabilities for consumers and small to medium-sized usinesses. At the same time, the bank wanted to ensure nat any system it chose would be able to keep pace with xpansion plans in Texas, Arizona, and other states. To :art, its executives sent a detailed listing of its criteria to x technology suppliers. They eliminated three suppli-rs and entered discussions with three finalists, including inancial Fusion. The First Citizens team carefully ooked at the ability of the finalists to provide a system nat was user friendly and customizable. Moreover, the ank wanted a system that would work well within its ex-ting security network. And, says Ward, "We wanted to nake sure there was a strong, long-term commitment or the online banking application on the part of the artner we selected."

Ultimately, First Citizens chose Financial Fusion's Consumer e-Finance Suite. Then Financial Fusion's tech-ical specialists went to work integrating the suite with ne bank's existing IBM system. They also tailored the ook and functionality to First Citizens specific require-nents. Once the system was operational, First Citizens nd its customers were so satisfied that top management ecided to expand into a new revenue-producing venture: ffering online services for other banks. As installed, the inancial Fusion system can easily accommodate many nore transactions, and it needs only minimal adaptation or each bank that First Citizens serves.

As the online banking revolution continues, Financial Fusion will have considerable opportunity to increase its customer base, product line, and profits. Today, about half the largest U.S. financial services firms use their own software to operate their online banking sites. However, experts foresee a trend away from "home grown" systems and toward systems provided by suppliers such as Financial Fusion and its competitors, including Corillian and S1 Corp. Watch for even more high-tech financial services innovations in the coming years—and more high-tech systems from Financial Fusion.[17]

Questions

1. From a management standpoint, describe the process that First Citizens Bank used to choose Financial Fusion to develop its current online banking system.
2. To establish an online banking system, a bank, S&L, or credit union must be willing to invest both time and money in technology. From a practical standpoint, what are the advantages and disadvantages of online banking for the financial institution? For the customer?
3. Although most online banking systems are seamless and a growing number of customers are using them, what fears might customers have about online banking? As a bank executive, how could you reduce those fears?

Building Skills for Career Success

1. Exploring the Internet

Internet-based banking is no longer a new concept. For many Americans, technology has changed the way they conduct their banking transactions. For example, most people no longer carry their paychecks to the bank to be deposited; instead, the money is deposited directly into their accounts. And an increasing number of individuals and businesses are using computers and the Internet to handle their finances, apply for loans, and pay their bills. Banking from a home computer is continually being made easier, giving bank customers access to their accounts 24 hours a day and seven days a week. As a result, you have more control over your money.

Assignment

1. Examine the websites for several major banks you are familiar with. Describe their online banking services. Are they worthwhile in your opinion?
2. In the past three years, how has technology changed the way you handle your money and conduct your banking transactions, such as depositing your paychecks, paying your monthly bills, obtaining cash, paying for purchases, and applying for loans?
3. In the next five to ten years, what will the banking industry be like? How will these changes affect you and the way you do your banking? How readily will you adapt to change? The Internet and the library can help you learn what is in the forefront of banking technology.
4. Prepare a report explaining your answers to these questions.

2. Developing Critical Thinking Skills

Every year your grandmother in Seattle, Washington, sends you a personal check for $100 for your birthday. You live in Monticello, Georgia, seventy-five miles southeast of Atlanta. You either cash the check or deposit it in your savings account at a local bank. Your banker does not return the canceled check directly to your grandmother, but somehow it ends up back in your grandmother's hands in Seattle. How does this happen?

Assignment

1. Research the process that your bank uses to collect a check that is from an individual located in another city and state.
2. Prepare a diagram showing the various steps in the process, and explain what happens in each step.

3. Summarize what you learned and how this information might be helpful to you in the future.

3. Building Team Skills

Three years ago, Ron and Ginger were happy to learn that on graduation, Ron would be teaching history in a large high school, making $30,000 a year, and Ginger would be working in a public accounting firm, starting at $34,000. They married immediately after graduation and bought a new home for $110,000. Since Ron had no personal savings, Ginger used her savings for the down payment. They soon began furnishing their home, charging their purchases to three separate credit cards, and that is when their debt began to mount. When the three credit cards reached their $10,000 limits, Ron and Ginger signed up for four additional credit cards with $10,000 limits that were offered through the mail, and they started using them. Soon their monthly payments were more than their combined take-home pay. To make their monthly payments, Ron and Ginger began to obtain cash advances on their credit cards. When they reached the credit ceilings on their seven credit cards, they could no longer get the cash advances they needed to cover their bills. Stress began to mount as creditors called and demanded payment. Ron and Ginger began to argue over money and just about everything else. Finally, things got so bad they considered filing for personal bankruptcy, but ironically, they could not afford the legal fees. What options are available to this couple?

Assignment

1. Working in teams of three or four, use your local library, the Internet, and personal interviews to investigate the following:
   a. Filling for personal bankruptcy.
   - What is involved in filing for personal bankruptcy?
   - How much does it cost?
   - How does bankruptcy affect individuals?

   b. The Consumer Credit Counseling Service at **www.cccs.org** or 888–577–2227 or Myvesta at **www.myvesta.org** or 800–698–3782.
   - What services do these organizations provide?
   - How could they help Ron and Ginger?
   - What will it cost?
2. Prepare a specific plan for repaying Ron and Ginger's debt.
3. Outline the advantages and disadvantages of credit cards, and make the appropriate recommendations for Ron and Ginger concerning their future use of credit cards.
4. Summarize what you have learned about credit card misuse.

4. Researching Different Careers

It has long been known that maintaining a good credit record is essential to obtaining loans from financial institutions, but did you know that employers often check credit records before offering an applicant a position? This is especially true of firms that handle financial accounts for others. Information contained in your credit report can tell an employer a lot about how responsible you are with money and how well you manage it. Individuals have the right to know what is in their credit bureau files and to have the credit bureau verify any inaccurate, misleading, or vague information. Before you apply for a job or a loan, you should check with a credit bureau to learn what is in your file.

Assignment

1. Using information in this chapter, call a credit bureau and ask for a copy of your credit report. A small fee may be required depending on the bureau and circumstances.
2. Review the information.
3. Have the bureau verify any information that you feel is inaccurate, misleading, or vague.
4. If the verification shows the information is correct, prepare a brief statement explaining your side of the dispute, and send it to the bureau.
5. Prepare a statement summarizing what the credit report says about you. Based on your credit report, would a firm hire you as its financial manager?

5. Improving Communication Skills

Often loan applicants—especially individuals—are afraid to talk with a loan officer about borrowing money. A number of suggestions were made in this chapter that could help you obtain money from a bank or lender. Assume that you are a business owner who has been operating a small manufacturing business. Also assume that your business is profitable and needs to expand and purchase new equipment to remain competitive in your region. Finally, assume that the equipment will cost $50,000.

Assignment

1. Describe the type of information that a loan officer at your bank would want to document this loan request.
2. Assume that for loans of this size, your bank requires an interview with a loan officer. Prepare a list of questions that you think the loan officer will ask.
3. How would you, as a business owner in need of financing, answer the questions that you just developed?
4. Based on the questions you prepared (as loan officer) and your answers to those questions (as a business owner in need of financing), describe your chances of getting approval and the money you need to expand your small manufacturing business in a one- to two-page report.

chapter

20 Mastering Financial Management

Outside investment should represent not just capital for capital's sake, but a true asset for the business.

learning objectives

1. Explain the need for financing and financial management in business.
2. Summarize the process of planning for financial management.
3. Describe the advantages and disadvantages of different methods of short-term debt financing.
4. Evaluate the advantages and disadvantages of equity financing.
5. Evaluate the advantages and disadvantages of long-term debt financing.

inside business

Money and More from the U.S. Business Exchange

When John E. Mack III went looking for financing, he was extremely particular about his investors. Mack previously had headed a security alarm manufacturer that was acquired by a large utility firm. Over the years, he supervised the acquisition of 200 smaller companies—and came to appreciate the need for informed guidance on such deals. With these experiences in mind, he founded the U.S. Business Exchange (USBX) in Santa Monica, California, to advise small and medium-sized companies on acquisitions, mergers, and financing.

As an entrepreneur, Mack received support from a business incubator during USBX's start-up stage. Within a short time, he needed additional funding for rapid growth. Mack was determined to raise capital only from investors whose background and expertise would help his company. Because he was reluctant to exchange equity in his company for money from *any* available source, he restricted his search to venture capitalists that offered services similar to his own. This is how he wound up with funding from The Carlyle Group, a major player in merger, acquisition, and equity transactions for smaller and midsized companies.

Carlyle's involvement opened the door to funding from other financing sources that were active or interested in USBX's type of operation. Just as important, these investors became valuable connections for Mack. "Not only were those people willing to invest in us because they understood our market," he notes, "but they've also provided us with access to customers and ideas that we can apply to our own situation."

Today, USBX gives its business customers what investors gave USBX: access to money, advice, and more. By focusing on selected industries—such as consumer products, technology, logistics, security, and telecommunications—Mack and his team can use their specialized knowledge to guide customers through decisions about debt and equity financing. They also provide research and guidance for companies that want to acquire or be acquired. In addition to helping determine the value of a company for merger or acquisition purposes, USBX can arrange funding for these types of transactions.

Over the years, USBX has handled more than 500 transactions for smaller businesses, middle-market companies, and giant corporations. Its customers have included Starbucks, Jack in the Box, the Sports Authority, Albertson's, AutoZone, Revlon, Dollar Tree, Quaker Oats, Continental Airlines, and many other large and small companies. Each customer has unique needs, so each deal is different. At the same time, each deal is about more than money. Mack's philosophy is that outside investment should represent "not just capital for capital's sake, but a true asset for the business."[1]

Before reading this chapter, consider the state of the economy. During the first part of the twenty-first century, there have been tremendous economic problems for firms and their employees. For example, a number of dot-com companies have gone out of business. At least two major airline carriers have filed for protection under the bankruptcy laws. And other firms have experienced lower sales revenues and profits or no profits at all. While all aspects of business have been affected by the downturn in the economy, the terrorists attacks of September 11, 2001, and an abnormally large number of business failures, the first part of this century has been especially difficult for financial managers because they must be able to raise the capital needed to weather the economic storm.

For companies such as Starbucks, Jack in the Box, the Sports Authority, Albertson's, AutoZone, Revlon, Dollar Tree, Quaker Oats, Continental Airlines, and many others large and small, typical business activities such as hiring employees, replacing outdated equipment, paying suppliers, and funding expansion all require financial resources. To raise the money needed to satisfy these needs and to obtain professional advice, they often turn to businesses like U.S. Business Exchange (USBX). In this chapter we focus on how firms like USBX help find the financing required to meet two needs of all business organizations: first, the need for money to start a business and keep it going, and second, the need to manage that money effectively. We also look at how firms develop financial plans and evaluate financial performance. Then we compare various methods of obtaining short-term financing—money that will be used one year or less. We also examine sources of long-term financing, which a firm may require for expansion, new product development, or replacement of equipment.

What Is Financial Management?

learning objective

1 Explain the need for financing and financial management in business.

Financial management consists of all the activities concerned with obtaining money and using it effectively. Within a business organization, the financial manager not only must determine the best way (or ways) to raise money, but he or she also must ensure that projected uses are in keeping with the organization's goals. Effective financial management thus involves careful planning. Such planning begins with a determination of the firm's financing needs.

financial management all the activities concerned with obtaining money and using it effectively

The Need for Financing

Money is needed both to start a business and to keep it going. The original investment of the owners, along with money they may have borrowed, should be enough to open the doors. After that, it would seem that sales revenues could be used to pay the firm's expenses and to provide a profit as well.

This is exactly what happens in a successful firm—over the long run. However, income and expenses may vary from month to month or from year to year. Temporary financing may be needed when expenses are high or sales are low. Then, too, situations such as the opportunity to purchase a new facility or expand an existing plant may require more money than is currently available within a firm. In either case, the firm must look for outside sources of financing.

Short-Term Financing **Short-term financing** is money that will be used for one year or less. Many financial managers define short-term financing as money that will be used for one year *or* one operating cycle of the business, whichever is longer. The *operating cycle of a business* may be longer than one year and is the amount of time between the purchase of raw materials and the sale of finished products to wholesalers, retailers, or consumers.

short-term financing money that will be used for one year or less

As illustrated in Table 20.1 (on p. 602), there are many short-term financing needs, but two deserve special attention. First, certain business practices may affect a

table 20.1 Comparison of Short- and Long-Term Financing

Whether a business seeks short- or long-term financing depends on what the money will be used for.

Corporate Cash Needs	
Short-Term Financing Needs	**Long-Term Financing Needs**
Cash-flow problems	Business start-up costs
Current inventory needs	Mergers and acquisitions
Monthly expenses	New product development
Speculative production	Long-term marketing activities
Short-term promotional needs	Replacement of equipment
Unexpected emergencies	Expansion of facilities

cash flow the movement of money into and out of an organization

firm's cash flow and create a need for short-term financing. **Cash flow** is the movement of money into and out of an organization. The ideal is to have sufficient money coming into the firm in any period to cover the firm's expenses during that period. The ideal, however, is not always achieved. For example, California-based Callaway Golf offers credit to retailers and wholesalers that carry the firm's golf clubs and balls. For Callaway, this extension of credit often creates cash-flow problems. Credit purchases made by Callaway's retailers generally are not paid until thirty to sixty days (or more) after the transaction. Callaway therefore may need short-term financing to pay its bills until its customers have paid theirs.

speculative production the time lag between the actual production of goods and when the goods are sold

A second major need for short-term financing that is related to a firm's cash-flow problem is inventory. For most manufacturers, wholesalers, and retailers, inventory requires considerable investment. Moreover, most goods are manufactured four to nine months before they are actually sold to the ultimate customer. This type of manufacturing is often referred to as *speculative production.* **Speculative production** refers to the time lag between the actual production of goods and when the goods are sold. Consider what happens when a firm such as Black & Decker begins to manufacture electric tools and small appliances for sale during the Christmas season. Manufacturing begins in February, March, and April, and Black & Decker negotiates short-term financing to buy materials and supplies, to pay wages and rent, and to cover inventory costs until its products eventually are sold to wholesalers and retailers later in the year. Take a look at Figure 20.1. Although Black & Decker manufactures and sells finished products all during the year, expenses peak during the first part of the year. During

figure 20.1

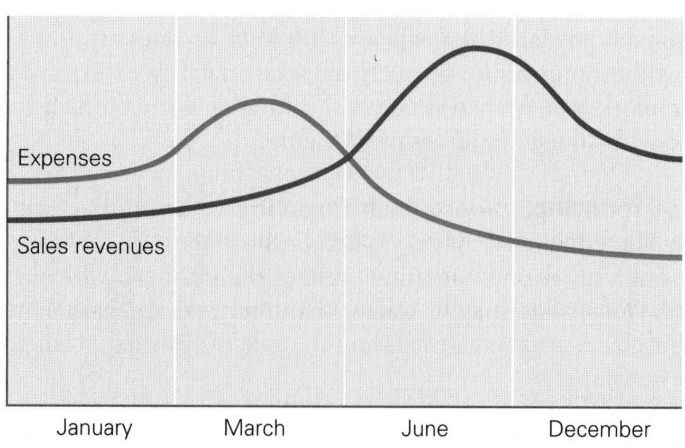

Cash Flow for a Manufacturing Business
Manufacturers such as Black & Decker often use short-term financing to pay expenses during the production process. Once goods are shipped to retailers and wholesalers and payment is received, sales revenues are used to repay short-term financing.

his same period, sales revenues are low. Once the firm's finished products are shipped ɔ retailers and wholesalers and payment is received (usually within thirty to sixty ays), sales revenues are used to repay short-term financing.

Retailers that range in size from Wal-Mart to the neighborhood drugstore also eed short-term financing to build up their inventories before peak selling periods. 'or example, Dallas-based Bruce Miller Nurseries must increase the amount of hrubs, trees, and flowering plants that it makes available for sale during the spring nd summer growing seasons. To obtain this merchandise from growers or wholealers, it uses short-term financing and repays the loans when the merchandise is sold.

ong-Term Financing **Long-term financing** is money that will be used for longer han one year. Long-term financing obviously is needed to start a new business. As 'able 20.1 shows, it is also needed for business mergers and acquisitions, new product evelopment, long-term marketing activities, replacement of equipment that has beome obsolete, and expansion of facilities.

long-term financing money that will be used for longer than one year

The amounts of long-term financing needed by large firms can seem almost uneal. Exxon spends about $10 million to drill an exploratory offshore oil well—without nowing for sure whether oil will be found. Toyota spent millions to develop, manufacure, and market the Lexus automobile. And Merck invested $2.9 billion in research nd development (R&D) to create new or improved prescription drugs in 2002—the ast year that complete dollar amounts are available at the time of this publication.[2]

'he Need for Financial Management

Vithout financing, there would be very little business. Financing gets a business tarted in the first place. Then it supports the firm's production and marketing activiies, pays its bills, and when carefully managed, produces a reasonable profit.

To some extent, financial management can be viewed as a two-sided problem. On ne side, the uses of funds often dictate the type or types of financing needed by a busiess. On the other side, the activities a business can undertake are determined by the ypes of financing available. Financial managers must ensure that funds are available vhen needed, that they are obtained at the lowest possible cost, and that they are used s efficiently as possible. And finally, financial mangers must ensure that funds are available for the epayment of debts in accordance with lenders' fiancing terms. Prompt repayment is essential to rotect the firm's credit rating and its ability to btain financing in the future.

Many firms have failed because their mangers did not pay enough attention to finances. n fact, poor financial management was one of he major reasons why over 39,000 businesses iled for bankruptcy in 2002—the most recent ear for which complete statistics are available.[3] n addition, many fairly successful firms could be ighly successful if they managed their finances nore carefully. However, many people often take inances for granted. Their first focus may be on roduction or marketing. As long as there is sufficient financing today, they don't worry about ow well it is used or whether it will be there tonorrow. Proper financial management can enure that

- Financing priorities are established in line with organizational goals and objectives.
- Spending is planned and controlled.

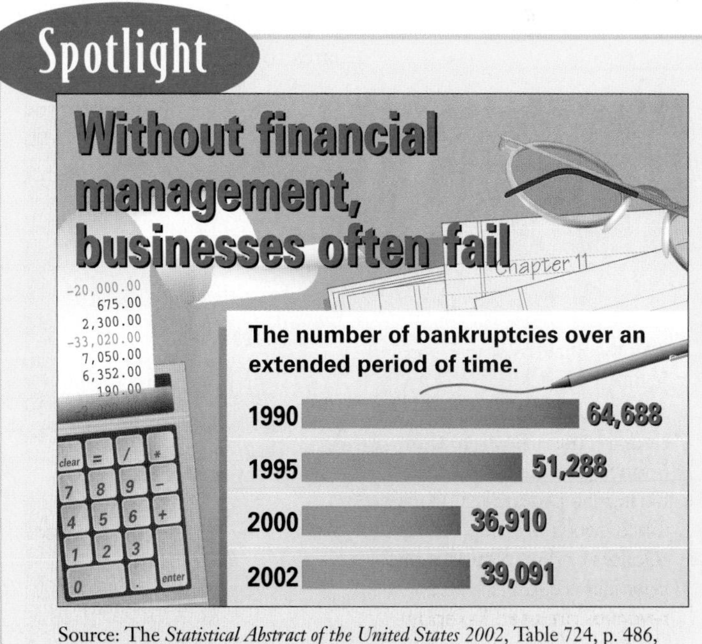
Spotlight
Without financial management, businesses often fail
The number of bankruptcies over an extended period of time.
1990 64,688
1995 51,288
2000 36,910
2002 39,091

Source: The *Statistical Abstract of the United States 2002*, Table 724, p. 486, and the Administrative Office of the U.S. Courts, *Statistical Tables for the Federal Judiciary*, March 23, 2003. Federal Judiciary website, **www.uscourts.gov**, March 23, 2003

- Sufficient financing is available when it is needed, both now and in the future.
- Excess cash is invested in certificates of deposit (CDs), government securities, o conservative, marketable securities.

These functions define effective management as applied to a particular resource– money. And like all effective management, financial management begins with peop who must set goals and plan for the future.

Careers in Finance

When you hear the word *finance*, you may think of highly paid executives who dete mine what a corporation can afford to do and what it can't. While some people in fi nance do make $300,000 a year or more, many entry-level and lower-level positior that pay quite a bit less are available. Banks, insurance companies, and investmer firms obviously have a need for workers who can manage and analyze financial dat So do businesses involved in manufacturing, services, and marketing. Colleges an universities, not-for-profit organizations, and government entities at all levels als need finance workers.

Whether they are high-level managers or entry-level employees, people in f nance must have certain traits and skills. After the scandals that have occurred in th last five years that involve accountants, auditors, and corporate executives, one of th most important priorities for someone interested in a finance career is honesty. B warned: Investors, lenders, and other corporate executives expect financial manage to be above reproach. And both federal and state government entities have enacte legislation to ensure that corporate financial statements reflect the "real" status of firm's financial position. In addition to honesty, managers and employees in the fi nance area must

1. Have a strong background in accounting or mathematics.
2. Know how to use a computer to analyze data.
3. Be an expert at both written and oral communication.

Typical job titles in finance include bank officer, consumer credit officer, financial an alyst, financial planner, loan officer, insurance analyst, and investment account execu tive. Depending on qualifications, work experience, and education, starting salarie generally begin at $25,000 to $30,000 a year, but it is not uncommon for college grad uates to earn $35,000 a year or more. In addition to salary, many employees have at tractive benefits and other perks that make a caree in financial management attractive. One very speci and often questionable perk is described in the Ex amining Ethics boxed feature.

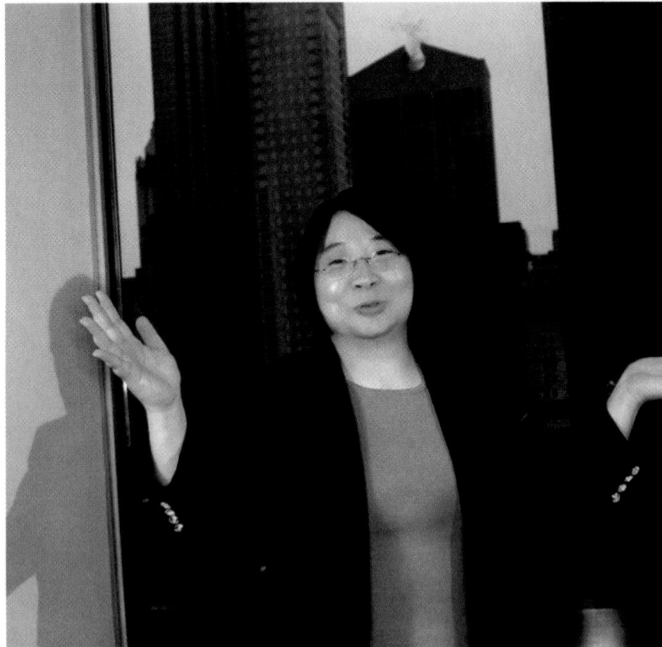

Careers in finance. Ping Zhao is an analyst for Sanford C. Bernstein—a well-respected investment firm in New York City that provides research information and manages portfolios for private and institutional investors. As an analyst, she must use accounting, mathematics, and computer skills to predict if an investment will increase or decrease in value. One of her recent investment picks was Corning—a company that specializes in glass products ranging from fiber optics to Steuben glassware. At the time, Corning stock was selling for $5 a share. Three months later, the same stock was selling for $8.00—a 60 percent return. Investors who followed her advice and purchased Corning stock at $5 a share are no doubt grateful for her expertise.

examining ethics

Should Executives Get Preferential IPO Treatment?

INITIAL PUBLIC OFFERINGS (IPOs) bring in funds for business use—and they also bring in fees for the investment banks that arrange these stock offerings. Now regulators and legislators are focusing on two controversial practices that give certain people preferential treatment in buying shares of particularly popular IPOs.

One controversy swirls around the practice of IPO *spinning*, in which investment banks earmark some shares in highly anticipated IPOs for executives of other corporations. Often the price of a coveted stock soars during the first days, which means the executives will reap hefty profits if they buy at the low initial price and sell at a higher market price. Government regulators are concerned about whether spinning reflects a conflict of interest because the executives who benefit are in a position to hire the investment banks for future financial deals.

A second controversy surrounds the practice of IPO *laddering*, in which investment banks allocate shares in "hot" IPOs to customers who commit to buying additional shares (presumably at higher prices) once the shares begin trading. Laddering can profit customers who buy at the low initial price while giving the share price a boost through additional purchases after trading starts.

Preferential allocation of IPO shares is not uncommon. When Bernie Ebbers was CEO of WorldCom (which later filed for bankruptcy), he was allocated more than 800,000 shares of high-demand IPOs at low initial prices through Citigroup's investment bank. Thanks to the bullish stock market of the period, prices skyrocketed during first-day trading, making those shares extremely valuable. The investment bank allocated IPO shares to other WorldCom executives and directors as well. Digging into the matter, the House Financial Services Committee looked at the possibility that the investment bank used the IPO allocations to gain favor with WorldCom's decision makers. "Insider allocation of initial public offering shares unfairly dilutes the value of the stock for the small investor," noted Representative Michael Oxley. "Free and fair markets—not favoritism or cronyism—are what have made America the premier place to invest." A Citigroup lawyer stated: "The IPO allocations to WorldCom officers and directors at issue here were reasonable since these were high net worth individuals and substantial retail clients."

Issues to Consider

1. Citigroup's lawyer notes that executives are wealthy and very good customers of the investment bank. On that basis, do you agree that they should be accorded preferential treatment for buying IPO shares?
2. Should any insiders—such as the management of the corporation going public—be allocated shares of an IPO before the general public is allowed to buy? Explain your answer.

Planning—The Basis of Sound Financial Management

learning objective

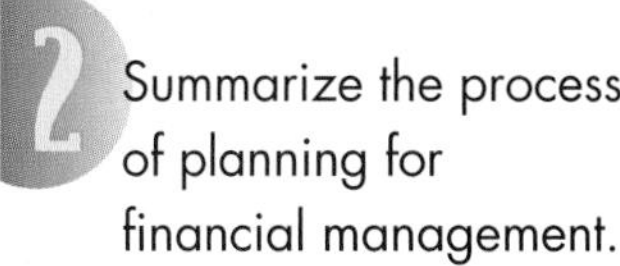

Summarize the process of planning for financial management.

financial plan a plan for obtaining and using the money needed to implement an organization's goals

In Chapter 7 we defined a *plan* as an outline of the actions by which an organization intends to accomplish its goals. A **financial plan**, then, is a plan for obtaining and using the money needed to implement an organization's goals.

Developing the Financial Plan

Financial planning (like all planning) begins with establishing a set of valid goals and objectives. Financial managers must next determine how much money is needed to accomplish each goal and objective. Finally, financial managers must identify available sources of financing and decide which to use. In the process, they must make sure that financing needs are realistic and that sufficient funding is available to meet those needs. The three steps involved in financial planning are illustrated in Figure 20.2 (on p. 606).

Establishing Organizational Goals and Objectives As pointed out in Chapter 7, a *goal* is an end state that an organization expects to achieve over a one- to ten-year period. *Objectives* are specific statements detailing what the organization intends to

20.2

...ee Steps of Financial Planning

After a financial plan has been developed, it must be monitored continually to ensure that it actually fulfills the firm's goals and objectives.

1 Establish organizational goals and objectives

2 Budget the money needed to accomplish the goals and objectives

3 Identify the sources of funds

Sales revenue	Equity capital	Debt capital	Sale of assets
• Revenue projections for this planning period	• Money from sole proprietor or partners • Common stock • Preferred stock	• Short-term borrowing • Long-term borrowing	• For profit • To raise cash

Monitor and evaluate

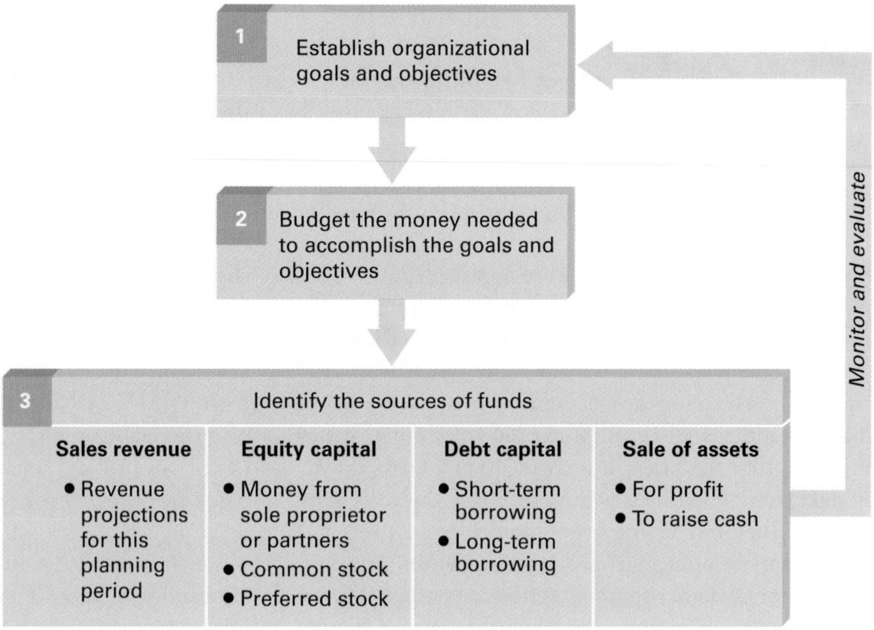

accomplish within a certain period of time. If goals and objectives are not specific an measurable, they cannot be translated into dollar costs, and financial planning cannc proceed. Goals and objectives also must be realistic. Otherwise, they may be impossi ble to finance or achieve. For large corporations, goals and objectives can be expen sive. For example, one objective for ChevronTexaco was to develop a "cohesiv worldwide marketing strategy." To fulfill this objective, management planned t spend an estimated $95 million on worldwide advertising in 2003.[4]

budget a financial statement that projects income and/or expenditures over a specified future period

cash budget a financial statement that projects cash receipts and expenditures over a specified period

zero-base budgeting a budgeting approach in which every expense in every budget must be justified

Budgeting for Financial Needs Once planners know what the firm's goals and ob jectives are for a specific period—say, the next calendar year—they can budget th costs the firm will incur and the sales revenues it will receive. Specifically, a **budget** i a financial statement that projects income and/or expenditures over a specified futur period. By combining these items into a company-wide budget, financial planners ca determine whether they must seek additional funding from sources outside the firm.

Usually the budgeting process begins with the construction of budgets for sales an various types of expenses. (A typical sales budget—for Stars and Stripes Clothing, a Cal ifornia-based retailer—is shown in Figure 20.3.) Budgeting accuracy is improved whe budgets are first constructed for separate departments and for shorter periods of time.

Financial managers can easily combine each department's budget for sales and ex penses into a company-wide cash budget. A **cash budget** estimates cash receipts an cash expenditures over a specified period. Notice in the cash budget for Stars an Stripes Clothing, shown in Figure 20.4, that cash sales and collections are listed at th top for each calendar quarter. Payments for purchases and routine expenses are liste in the middle section. Using this information, it is possible to calculate the anticipate cash gain or loss at the end of each quarter.

Most firms today use one of two approaches to budgeting. In the *traditional* ap proach, each new budget is based on the dollar amounts contained in the budget fo the preceding year. These amounts are modified to reflect any revised goals and ob jectives, and managers are required to justify only new expenditures. The probler with this approach is that it leaves room for padding budget items to protect th (sometimes selfish) interests of the manager or his or her department.

This problem is essentially eliminated through zero-base budgeting. **Zero-bas budgeting** is a budgeting approach in which every expense in every budget must b justified. It can dramatically reduce unnecessary spending because every budget iter

figure 20.3

Sales Budget for Stars and Stripes Clothing

Usually the budgeting process begins with the construction of departmental budgets for sales and various expenses.

STARS AND STRIPES CLOTHING

Sales Budget For January 1, 2005 to December 31, 2005

Department	First quarter	Second quarter	Third quarter	Fourth quarter	Totals
Infants'	$ 50,000	$ 55,000	$ 60,000	$ 70,000	$235,000
Children's	45,000	45,000	40,000	40,000	170,000
Women's	35,000	40,000	35,000	50,000	160,000
Men's	20,000	20,000	15,000	25,000	80,000
Totals	$150,000	$160,000	$150,000	$185,000	$645,000

must stand on its own merits. However, some managers oppose zero-base budgeting because it requires entirely too much time-consuming paperwork.

Because they focus on income and expenditures within a calendar year, departmental and cash budgets emphasize short-term financing needs. To develop a plan for long-term financing needs, managers often construct a capital budget. A **capital budget** estimates a firm's expenditures for major assets, including new product development, expansion of facilities, replacement of obsolete equipment, and mergers and acquisitions. For example, the Blackstone Group constructed a capital budget to determine the best way to finance the $4.73-billion purchase of a 58 percent stake in Michigan-based TRW Auto from Northrop Grumman Corporation.[5]

capital budget a financial statement that estimates a firm's expenditures for major assets and its long-term financing needs

figure 20.4

Cash Budget for Stars and Stripes Clothing

A company-wide cash budget projects sales, collections, purchases, and expenses over a specified period to anticipate cash surpluses and deficits.

STARS AND STRIPES CLOTHING

Cash Budget For January 1, 2005 to December 31, 2005

	First quarter	Second quarter	Third quarter	Fourth quarter	Totals
Cash sales and collections	$150,000	$160,000	$150,000	$185,000	$645,000
Less payments					
Purchases	$110,000	$ 80,000	$ 90,000	$ 60,000	$340,000
Wages/salaries	25,000	20,000	25,000	30,000	100,000
Rent	10,000	10,000	12,000	12,000	44,000
Other expenses	4,000	4,000	5,000	6,000	19,000
Taxes	8,000	8,000	10,000	10,000	36,000
Total payments	$157,000	$122,000	$142,000	$118,000	$539,000
Cash gain or (loss)	$ (7,000)	$ 38,000	$ 8,000	$ 67,000	$106,000

Financial planning worked for this entrepreneur. Lissa D'Aquanni, owner of The Chocolate Gecko, had to use her creative skills to raise the money she needed to make changes to her gourmet chocolate business in Albany, New York. When she wanted to move her business to an abandoned building, she needed $25,000 in owners' equity for the renovations. She mailed letters to area residents asking for financial help with her revitalization plan, and within a month she had raised the money. Then she obtained a $95,000 loan from the Albany Local Development Corporation to buy the building. Finally, she obtained a government-guaranteed loan for $100,000 from a local credit union to renovate the building. Sometimes, it pays to be creative.

Identifying Sources of Funds The four primary sources of funds, listed in Figure 20.2, are sales revenue, equity capital, debt capital, and proceeds from the sale of assets. Future sales revenu generally provides the greatest part of a firm's financing. Figur 20.4 shows that, for Stars and Stripes Clothing, sales for the ye are expected to cover all expenses and to provide a cash gain o $106,000, or about 16 percent of sales. However, Stars and Strip has a problem in the first quarter, when sales are expected to fa short of expenses by $7,000. In fact, one of the primary reasons for financial planning to provide management with adequate lead time to solve this type of cash-flow problem

equity capital money received from the owners or from the sale of shares of ownership in a business

A second type of funding is **equity capital.** For a sole proprietorship or partne ship, equity capital is provided by the owner or owners of the business. For a corpor tion, equity capital is money obtained from the sale of shares of ownership in th business. Equity capital is used almost exclusively for long-term financing. Thus might be used to start a business and to fund expansions or mergers. It would not b considered for short-term financing needs, such as Stars and Stripes Clothing's firs quarter $7,000 shortfall.

debt capital borrowed money obtained through loans of various types

A third type of funding is **debt capital**, which is borrowed money. Debt capit may be borrowed for either short- or long-term use—and a short-term loan seen made to order for Stars and Stripes Clothing's short-fall problem. The firm probab would borrow the needed $7,000 (or perhaps a bit more) at some point during the fir quarter and repay it from second-quarter sales revenue. Stars and Stripes Clothing a ready may have established a line of credit at a local bank to cover just such short-ter needs. As discussed in Chapter 19, a *line of credit* is a prearranged short-term loan.

Proceeds from the sale of assets are the fourth type of funding. A firm general acquires assets because it needs them for its business operations. Therefore, selling a sets is a drastic step. However, it may be a reasonable last resort when neither equi capital nor debt capital can be found. Assets also may be sold when they are no long needed or do not "fit" with the company's core business. To concentrate on its co defense business, Raytheon Company sold its D. C. Heath publishing unit t Houghton Mifflin for $455 million. To raise capital, Georgia Pacific Group sold i 60 percent interest in its Unisource Worldwide paper distribution subsidiary to Ba Capital for $850 million.[6] For the same reason Starwood Hotels and Resorts Worl wide sold its assets in Sardinia, Italy, to a consortium of Italian investors for Eur 350.0 million.[7]

Monitoring and Evaluating Financial Performance

It is important to ensure that financial plans are being properly implemented and t catch potential problems before they become major ones. For example, many Interne based businesses have reduced various expenses in order to become profitable. Even s nany of these high-tech companies have failed or will fail in the near future. Of par-icular concern are online retailers and content-oriented websites that need to spend uge amounts of money to generate brand awareness through costly advertising cam-aigns. Search engine AltaVista.com, which is 83 percent owned by CMGI, Inc., cut ack its marketing and advertising budget by one-third to $100 million and reduced he number of people employed in an attempt to improve the firm's bottom-line profit mount.[8] Pets.com is another example of a dot-com start-up that lost control of its fi-ances. Backed by Disney and Amazon, the firm spent $27 million on television and ther media advertising to generate awareness and sales. The funny advertisements resented by the famous talking dog sock-puppet could not create the critical mass of uyers quickly enough to offset the advertising and other operational costs. As a re-ult, the firm lost five dollars for every dollar of pet supplies revenue received. This uickly created a cash crisis and eventually led to failure. While tracking expenses is outine in most cases, there are unusual expenses associated with acquisitions, merg-rs, and stock options that also must be monitored. To see how accounting for ex-enses related to stock options can affect a firm's bottom-line profit amount, read xploring Business.

To prevent problems like those just described, financial managers should establish means of monitoring financial performance. Interim budgets (weekly, monthly, or uarterly) may be prepared for comparison purposes. These comparisons point up reas that require additional or revised planning—or at least those areas calling for a nore careful investigation. By comparing budgeted and actual sales and expenses for tars and Stripes Clothing, managers can determine if the firm is on track to meet its oals and objectives and can spot problem areas and take corrective action. Budget omparisons also can be used to improve the firm's future budgets.

exploring business

Expensing Stock Options: A New Reality?

STOCK OPTIONS may not make the world go around, but they often draw top talent to smaller corporations with limited payroll budgets. As the phrase implies, stock options give employees the opportunity to buy a certain number of shares at a preset price during a given time period. If the recipients buy after the share price moves higher than the option price, they can sell and take home the profits. If the share price plateaus or drops, however, recipients will not profit.

Corporations use stock options to reward executives and middle managers (and, in some cases, employees) for performance that makes the stock more attractive to investors—pushing the share price of the firm's stock higher. High-tech corporations in particular often use stock options instead of high salaries to lure executives from more established employers. Many of these companies reward rank-and-file employees with stock options as well. Today, about ten million U.S. managers and employees hold stock options, a tenfold increase in just a decade.

Do stock options actually encourage higher performance? One academic study found that options did, in fact, lead to decisions that increased productivity, boosted annual growth, and yielded a higher rate of return on the firm's assets. Yet the study failed to find any significant link, positive or negative, between options and shareholder returns.

Critics believe that corporations have been overly generous in granting options. In fact, some CEOs stand to make considerably more from exercising their options than from their salaries. Critics also argue that corporations have not properly accounted for options in their financial statements, acting as though options have no cost. "It is, without a doubt, the mother of all accounting abuses," according to a *Fortune* magazine writer.

Now Coca-Cola, Bank One, Wachovia Bank, and the Washington Post Company, among other corporations, are voluntarily "expensing" options by calculating the potential cost and deducting that dollar amount from the firm's earnings. While some investors applaud this development, others think corporations should focus on other rewards, such as cash bonuses or indexed options tied to a specific market index. If the boards governing U.S. and international accounting standards decide to mandate expensing of options, however, corporations will be forced to confront a new reality.

Sources of Short-Term Debt Financing

learning objective

3 Describe the advantages and disadvantages of different methods of short-term debt financing.

The decision to borrow money does not necessarily mean that a firm is in financi trouble. On the contrary, astute financial management often means regular, respons ble borrowing of many different kinds to meet different needs. In this section we ex amine the sources of *short-term debt financing* available to businesses. In the next tw sections we look at long-term financing options: equity capital and debt capital.

Sources of Unsecured Short-Term Financing

Short-term debt financing (money repaid in one year or less) is usually easier to obtai than long-term debt financing for three reasons:

1. For the lender, the shorter repayment period means less risk of nonpayment.
2. The dollar amounts of short-term loans usually are smaller than those of long-term loans.
3. A close working relationship normally exists between the short-term borrower and the lender.

Most lenders do not require collateral for short-term financing. When they do, it usually because they are concerned about the size of a particular loan, the borrowin firm's poor credit rating, or the general prospects of repayment.

unsecured financing financing that is not backed by collateral

Unsecured financing is financing that is not backed by collateral. A compan seeking unsecured short-term financing has several options. They include trad credit, promissory notes, bank loans, and commercial paper.

trade credit a type of short-term financing extended by a seller who does not require immediate payment after delivery of merchandise

Trade Credit Manufacturers and wholesalers often provide financial aid to retailer by allowing them thirty to sixty days (or more) in which to pay for merchandise. Thi delayed payment, known as **trade credit**, is a type of short-term financing extende by a seller who does not require immediate payment after delivery of merchandise. I is the most popular form of short-term financing; 80 to 90 percent of all transaction between businesses involve some trade credit.

When trade credit is used, the purchased goods are delivered along with an in voice that states the credit terms. Let's assume that a Barnes & Noble bookstore re ceives a shipment of books from a publisher. Along with the merchandise, th publisher sends an invoice that states the terms of payment. Barnes & Noble now ha two options for payment. First, the book retailer may pay the invoice promptly an take advantage of any cash discount the publisher offers. Cash discount terms ar specified on the invoice. For instance, "2/10, net 30" means that the customer— Barnes & Noble—may take a 2 percent discount if it pays the invoice within ten day of the invoice date. Cash discounts can generate substantial savings and lower the cos of purchasing merchandise for a retailer such as Barnes & Noble. Let's assume tha the dollar amount of the invoice is $140,000. In this case, the cash discount is $2,80 ($140,000 × 0.02 = $2,800). A second option is to wait until the end of the credit pe riod before making payment. If Barnes & Noble does not have the cash available t take advantage of the cash discount, payment within the first ten days is out of th question. If payment is made between eleven and thirty days after the date of the in voice, the customer must pay the entire (net) amount. As long as payment is made be fore the end of the credit period, the customer maintains the ability to purchas additional merchandise using the trade credit arrangement.

promissory note a written pledge by a borrower to pay a certain sum of money to a creditor at a specified future date

Promissory Notes Issued to Suppliers A **promissory note** is a written pledge b a borrower to pay a certain sum of money to a creditor at a specified future date. Sup pliers uneasy about extending trade credit may be less reluctant to offer credit to cus tomers who sign promissory notes. Unlike trade credit, however, promissory note usually require the borrower to pay interest. Although repayment periods may exten to one year, most short-term promissory notes are repaid in 60 to 180 days. A typica

figure 20.5

An Interest-Bearing Promissory Note

A promissory note is a borrower's written pledge to pay a certain sum of money to a creditor at a specified date.

$ 800.00 (1) Abilene, *Texas.* June 6 (4) *A.D. 20* 05

Ninety days (3) *after date, without grace, for value received, I, we, or either of us, promise to*

pay to the order of The Shelton Company (7)

(1) Eight hundred and no/100 --------------------- *Dollars*

at First Bank *with interest from* June 6 *to maturity at the rate of* 10 (2) *per cent, per annum.*

AND FROM MATURITY AT THE RATE OF TEN PER CENT PER ANNUM, WE THE MAKERS, SURETIES, ENDORSERS, AND GUARANTORS OF THIS NOTE HEREBY SEVERALLY WAIVE PRESENTATION FOR PAYMENT, NOTICE OF NONPAYMENT, PROTEST, AND NOTICE OF PROTEST AND DILIGENCE IN BRINGING SUIT AGAINST ANY PARTY HERETO AND CONSENT THAT THE TIME OF PAYMENT MAY BE EXTENDED BY RENEWAL NOTE OR OTHERWISE ONE OR MORE TIMES FOR PERIODS DISCRETIONARY WITH THE HOLDER WITHOUT NOTICE THEREOF TO ANY OF THE SURETIES, ENDORSERS, AND/OR GUARANTORS ON THIS NOTE. IT IS FURTHER EXPRESSLY AGREED THAT IF THIS NOTE IS PLACED IN THE HANDS OF AN ATTORNEY FOR COLLECTION OR IS COLLECTED THROUGH THE PROBATE OF BANKRUPTCY COURT, OR THROUGH OTHER LEGAL PROCEEDINGS, THEN IN ANY OF SAID EVENTS, A REASONABLE AMOUNT SHALL BE ADDED AND COLLECTED AS ATTORNEY AND COLLECTION FEES.

Due September 4, 2005 (5) — Paul Robertson (6)

Address 326 East Main Street — Financial Vice President

Phone (972) 555-1732 — The Richland Company

1. The principal ($800.00) is the original amount of the debt.
2. The rate (10 percent) expresses the annual interest rate paid for use of the borrowed money.
3. The time (90 days) is the period for which the money is borrowed.
4. The date (June 6) is the date the note was issued.
5. The maturity date (September 4) is the day the principal and interest are due ($800 principal + $20 interest = $820 maturity value).
6. The maker (The Richland Company) is the individual or company borrowing the money.
7. The payee (The Shelton Company) is the individual or company extending the credit.

romissory note is shown in Figure 20.5. Note that the customer buying on credit Richland Company) is called the *maker* and is the party that issues the note. The business selling the merchandise on credit (Shelton Company) is called the *payee*.

A promissory note offers two important advantages to the firm extending the redit. First, a promissory note is a legally binding and enforceable document that has een signed by the individual or business borrowing the money. Second, most promissory notes are negotiable instruments that can be sold when the money is needed immediately. The Shelton Company (the payee) may be able to discount, or sell, the note o its own bank. The maturity value is $820 ($800 principal + $20 interest = $820 naturity value). If the note is discounted, the dollar amount the Shelton Company vould receive is slightly less than the $820 maturity value because the bank charges a ee for the service. Shelton would recoup most of its money immediately, and the bank vould collect the $820 when the note matured.

Jnsecured Bank Loans Banks and other financial institutions offer unsecured hort-term loans to businesses at interest rates that vary with each borrower's credit ating. The **prime interest rate** (sometimes called the *reference rate*) is the lowest rate harged by a bank for a short-term loan. Figure 20.6 (on p. 612) traces the fluctuations n the average prime rate charged by U.S. banks from 1994 to 2002. This lowest rate enerally is reserved for large corporations with excellent credit ratings. Organizations with good to high credit ratings may pay the prime rate plus 2 percent. Firms vith questionable credit ratings may have to pay the prime rate plus 4 percent. Of ourse, if the banker believes that loan repayment may be a problem, the borrower's oan application may well be rejected.

prime interest rate the lowest rate charged by a bank for a short-term loan

figure 20.6

Average Prime Interest Rate Paid by U.S. Businesses, 1994–2002

The prime rate is the interest rate charged by U.S. banks when businesses with the "best" credit ratings borrow money. All other businesses pay interest rates higher than the prime rate.

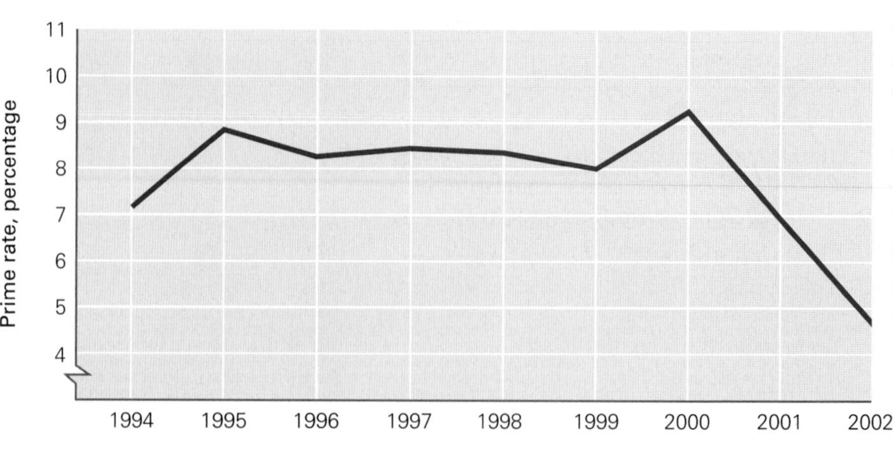

Source: Federal Reserve Bank website, **www.federalreserve.gov**, January 19, 2003.

Banks generally offer unsecured short-term loans through promissory notes, line of credit, or a revolving credit agreement. A bank promissory note is similar to th promissory note issued by suppliers described in the preceding section. For both typ of promissory notes, interest rates and repayment terms may be negotiated betwee the borrower and a bank or supplier. A bank that offers a promissory note or line credit may require that a *compensating balance* be kept on deposit at the bank. This ba ance may be as much as 20 percent of the borrowed funds. Assume that Bank of Ame ica requires a 20 percent compensating balance on a short-term promissory note or line of credit. If you borrow \$50,000, at least \$10,000 (\$50,000 × 0.20 = \$10,000) the loan amount must be kept on deposit at the bank. In this situation, the actual in terest rate you must pay on the original \$50,000 loan increases because you have th use of only \$40,000. The bank also may require that every commercial borrower *clea up* (pay off completely) its short-term promissory note or line of credit at least onc each year and not use it again for a period of thirty to sixty days. This second requir ment ensures that the money obtained through a short-term loan or a line of credit used only to meet short-term needs and that it does not gradually become a source long-term financing.

Even with a line of credit, a firm may not be able to borrow on short notice if th bank does not have sufficient funds available. For this reason, some firms prefer **revolving credit agreement**, which is a *guaranteed* line of credit. Under this type agreement, the bank guarantees that the money will be available when the borrowe needs it. In return for the guarantee, the bank charges a commitment fee ranging fro 0.25 to 1.0 percent of the *unused* portion of the revolving credit agreement. The usu interest is charged for the portion that *is* borrowed.

revolving credit agreement a guaranteed line of credit

commercial paper a short-term promissory note issued by a large corporation

Commercial Paper **Commercial paper** is a short-term promissory note issued b a large corporation. Commercial paper is secured only by the reputation of the issuin firm; no collateral is involved. It is usually issued in large denominations, rangin from \$5,000 to \$100,000. Corporations issuing commercial paper pay interest rat slightly below the interest rates charged by banks for short-term loans. Thus, issuin commercial paper is cheaper than getting short-term financing from a bank. The in terest rate a corporation pays when it issues commercial paper is tied to its credit ra ing and its ability to repay the commercial paper. For example, when the major U.S credit reporting agencies lowered the credit ratings of Lucent Technologies[9] and Di lard's Department Stores,[10] these firms had to pay higher interest rates to borro money.

Large firms with excellent credit reputations can raise large sums of mone quickly by issuing commercial paper. General Motors Acceptance Corporatio

(GMAC) and GE Capital, for example, may issue commercial paper totaling millions of dollars. However, commercial paper is not without risks. If a corporation has severe financial problems, it may not be able to repay commercial paper. Recently, California-based Pacific Gas & Electric Company defaulted on $726 million of short-term debt instruments, including a large amount of commercial paper.[11]

How hard is it to get short-term financing? For Mary Hall, assistant treasurer for Eastman Chemical in Kingsport, Tennessee, obtaining short-term financing has been pretty tough the last couple of years because of the weak economy, bankruptcy filings by well-known companies, and concern about credit risk. Fortunately, by the end of 2002, the credit squeeze for firms like Eastman Chemical was beginning to ease, and her job is getting easier. As an added bonus, short-term financing is also cheaper when compared to a year ago.

Sources of Secured Short-Term Financing

Financially secure firms prefer to reserve collateral for long-term borrowing needs. Yet, if a business cannot obtain enough capital through unsecured financing, it must put up collateral to obtain additional short-term financing. Almost any asset can serve as collateral. However, *inventories* and *accounts receivable* are the assets most commonly pledged for short-term financing. Even when it is willing to pledge collateral to back up a loan, a firm that is financially weak may have difficulty obtaining short-term financing.

Loans Secured by Inventory Normally, manufacturers, wholesalers, and retailers have large amounts of money invested in finished goods. In addition, manufacturers carry raw materials and work-in-process inventories. All three types of inventory may be pledged as collateral for short-term loans. However, lenders prefer the much more salable finished merchandise to raw materials or work-in-process inventories.

A lender may insist that inventory used as collateral be stored in a public warehouse. In such a case, the receipt issued by the warehouse is retained by the lender. Without this receipt, the public warehouse will not release the merchandise. The lender releases the warehouse receipt—and the merchandise—to the borrower when the borrowed money is repaid. In addition to paying the interest on the loan, the borrower must pay for storage in the public warehouse. As a result, this type of loan is more expensive than an unsecured short-term loan.

A special type of financing called *floor planning* is used by automobile, furniture, and appliance dealers. **Floor planning** is a method of financing in which title to merchandise is given to lenders in return for short-term financing. The major difference between floor planning and other types of secured short-term financing is that the borrower maintains control of the inventory. As merchandise is sold, the borrower repays the lender a portion of the loan, and the lender returns the title to the merchandise sold. When floor planning is used, it is quite common for the lender to check periodically to see whether the collateral is still in the borrower's possession.

floor planning method of financing in which title to merchandise is given to lenders in return for short-term financing

Loans Secured by Receivables As defined in Chapter 18, *accounts receivable* are amounts owed to a firm by its customers. They are created when trade credit is given to customers and usually are due within thirty to sixty days. A firm can pledge its accounts receivable as collateral to obtain short-term financing. A lender may advance 70 to 80 percent of the dollar amount of the receivables. First, however, it conducts a thorough investigation to determine the *quality* of the receivables. (The quality of the receivables is the credit standing of the firm's customers, coupled with the customers' ability to repay their credit obligations.) If a favorable determination is made, the loan is approved. When the borrowing firm collects from a customer whose account has been pledged as collateral, it must turn the money over to the lender as partial repayment of the loan. An alternative approach is to notify the borrower's credit customers to make their payments directly to the lender.

Factoring Accounts Receivable

factor a firm that specializes in buying other firms' accounts receivable

Accounts receivable may be used in one other way to help raise short-term financing: They can be sold to a factoring company (or factor). A **factor** is a firm that specializes in buying other firms' accounts receivable. The factor buys the accounts receivable for less than their face value, but it collects the full dollar amount when each account is due. The factor's profit is thus the difference between the face value of the accounts receivable and the amount the factor has paid for them. Generally, the amount of profit the factor receives is based on the risk the factor assumes. Risk, in this case, is the probability that the accounts receivable will not be repaid when they mature.

Even though the firm selling its accounts receivable gets less than face value, it does receive needed cash immediately. Moreover, it has shifted both the task of collecting and the risk of nonpayment to the factor, which now owns the accounts receivable. In many cases, the factor may purchase only selected accounts receivable—usually those with the highest potential of repayment. In other cases, the firm selling its accounts receivable must obtain approval from the factor *before* selling merchandise to a credit customer. Thus the firm receives instant feedback on whether the factor will purchase the credit customer's account. Generally, customers whose accounts receivable have been factored are given instructions to make their payments directly to the factor.

Cost Comparisons

Table 20.2 compares the various types of short-term financing. As you can see, trade credit is the least expensive. Generally, the less favorable a firm's credit rating, the more likely the firm will have to use a higher-cost means of financing. Factoring of accounts receivable is typically the highest-cost method shown.

For many purposes, short-term financing suits a firm's needs perfectly. At other times, however, long-term financing may be more appropriate. In this case, a business may try to raise equity capital or long-term debt capital.

table 20.2 Comparison of Short-Term Financing Methods

Type of Financing	Cost	Repayment Period	Businesses That May Use It	Comments
Trade credit	Low, if any	30–60 days	All businesses	Usually no finance charge
Promissory note issued to suppliers	Moderate	1 year or less	All businesses	Usually unsecured but requires legal document
Unsecured bank loan	Moderate	1 year or less	All businesses	Promissory note, a line of credit, or revolving credit agreement generally required
Commercial paper	Moderate	1 year or less	Large corporations with high credit ratings	Available only to large firms
Secured loan	High	1 year or less	Firms with questionable credit ratings	Inventory or accounts receivable often used as collateral
Factoring	High	None	Firms that have large numbers of credit customers	Accounts receivable sold to a factor

Sources of Equity Financing

learning objective

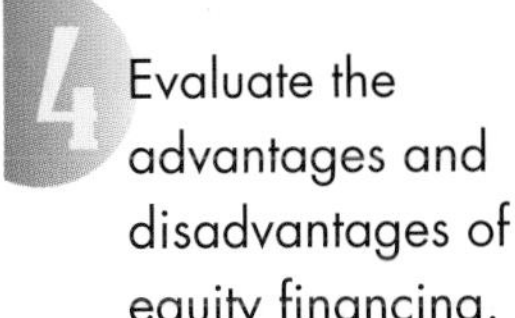

Evaluate the advantages and disadvantages of equity financing.

Sources of long-term financing vary with the size and type of business. As mentioned earlier, a sole proprietorship or partnership acquires equity capital (sometimes referred to as *owner's equity*) when the owner or owners invest money in the business. For corporations, equity-financing options include the sale of stock and the use of profits not distributed to owners. All three types of businesses also can obtain venture capital.

Selling Stock

Some equity capital is used to start every business—sole proprietorship, partnership, or corporation. In the case of corporations, stockholders who buy shares in the company provide equity capital.

Initial Public Offerings An **initial public offering (IPO)** occurs when a corporation sells common stock to the general public for the first time. To raise money, Seagate Technology used an IPO and raised over $870 million that it could use to fund expansion and other business activities. In a similar fashion, Wynn Resorts ($449 million), WellChoice ($346 million), and Dick's Sporting Goods ($87 million) used IPOs to raise capital.[12] Established companies that plan to raise capital by selling subsidiaries to the public also can use IPOs. For example, Nestlé SA raised $2.5 billion when it sold shares of stock in its Alcon eye-care subsidiary. And the proposed sale of Time Warner Cable by parent company Time Warner could raise anywhere from $2 billion to $6 billion once the deal is completed and new stock in the spinoff company is sold.[13] Generally, corporations sell off subsidiaries for two reasons. First, the sale of a subsidiary can boost the value of the firm's core business by shedding a unit that is growing more slowly. Second, the sale of a subsidiary also can bolster corporate finances and improve the parent company's balance sheet if the money is used to reduce corporate debt.

initial public offering (IPO) when a corporation sells common stock to the general public for the first time

A corporation selling stock often will use an **investment banking firm**—an organization that assists corporations in raising funds, usually by helping sell new issues of stocks, bonds, or other financial securities. The investment banking firm generally charges a fee of 2 to 20 percent of the proceeds received by the corporation issuing the securities. The size of the commission depends on the financial health of the corporation issuing the new securities and the size of the new security issue. To gain insight about the actual methods used to sell a new stock issue, read Adapting to Change (on p. 616).

investment banking firm an organization that assists corporations in raising funds, usually by helping sell new issues of stocks, bonds, or other financial securities

Although a corporation can have only one IPO, it can sell additional stock after the IPO, assuming that there is a market for the company's stock. In either case, selling stock is the most logical way for a corporation to raise capital. Even though the cost of selling stock (often referred to as *flotation costs*) is high, the *ongoing* costs associated with this type of equity financing are low for two reasons. First, the corporation does not have to repay money obtained from the sale of stock. While many investors assume that the corporation will repay the money it obtains from selling stock, the company is under no legal obligation to do so. If you purchase corporate stock and later decide to sell your stock, you may sell it to another investor—not the corporation.

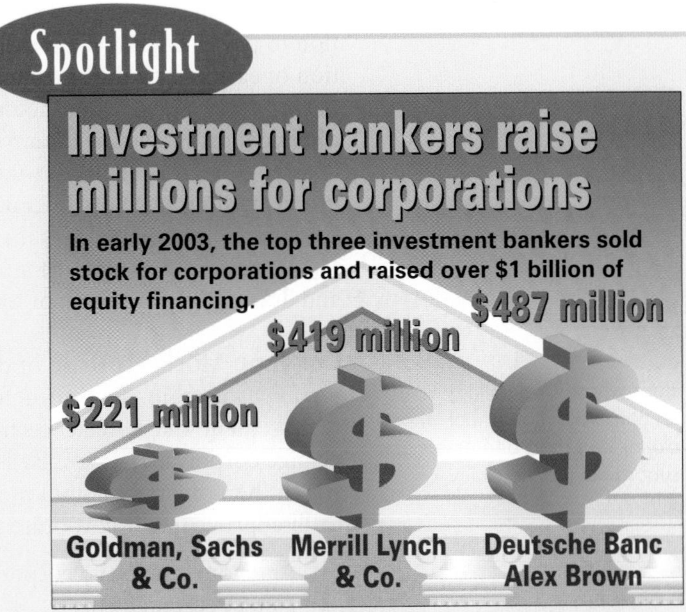

Spotlight
Investment bankers raise millions for corporations
In early 2003, the top three investment bankers sold stock for corporations and raised over $1 billion of equity financing.
$221 million
$419 million
$487 million
Goldman, Sachs & Co.
Merrill Lynch & Co.
Deutsche Banc Alex Brown

Source: **www.ipo.com**, March 21, 2003.

adapting to change

Separating Investment Banking Activities and Research

CAN WALL STREET FIRMS have investment banking activities and research activities under one roof without conflicts of interest? On the one hand, the investment bankers are hired to help corporate clients raise money through stock offerings called initial public offerings (IPOs). On the other, securities analysts are responsible for researching individual stocks to offer investors guidance about buying, holding, and selling those same stocks. The conflict arises when a firm's investment bankers pressure or expect the firm's research analysts to slant research and buy/sell recommendations in favor of the stocks issued by their corporate clients.

Investigators have found that some analysts who publicly urged investors to buy certain stocks were privately skeptical. For example, an internal Merrill Lynch e-mail uncovered by the New York Attorney General's office showed that an analyst was uneasy about giving a particular stock a "buy" recommendation: "I don't think it is the right thing to do," he wrote. "John and Mary Smith are losing their retirement because we don't want a client's CEO to be mad at us." Ultimately, Merrill Lynch paid a $100-million fine to settle charges of preparing misleading research to help its investment bankers obtain business in the lucrative IPO market.

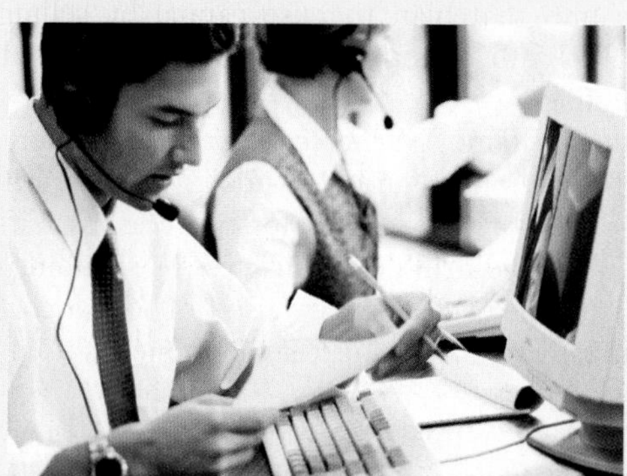

Not long afterward, ten other Wall Street firms paid a total of $1.43 billion to settle similar charges. "Investors know there is no guaranteed return in the market, but the one thing they deserve is honest advice," the New York Attorney General said in announcing the settlement. The firms agreed to keep analysts and investment bankers separate and to pay millions of dollars for investor education and independent research. In addition, an online database will allow investors to see how analysts' recommendations turned out.

Some regulators and industry observers want to further insulate analysts from any investment banking influence. One proposal calls for each firm to set up a separate research affiliate. Another calls for spinning the research department off as an independent company. A third calls for establishing a central research group to analyze stocks for the entire industry. However, money is the major stumbling block for any proposal. Analysts generate no revenues, whereas investment bankers bring in hefty revenues—so the debate over how to provide unbiased research goes on.

A second advantage of selling stock is that a corporation is under no legal obligation to pay dividends to stockholders. As noted in Chapter 5, a *dividend* is a distribution of earnings to the stockholders of a corporation. Recall from Chapter 5 that on of the basic rights of shareholders is the right to share in earnings through the receip of dividends. However, for any reason (if a company has a bad year, for example), th board of directors can vote to omit dividend payments. Earnings are then retained fo use in funding business operations. Of course, the corporate management may hea from unhappy stockholders if expected dividends are omitted too frequently.

There are two types of stock: common and preferred. Each type has advantage and drawbacks as a means of long-term financing.

common stock
stock whose owners may vote on corporate matters but whose claims on profits and assets are subordinate to the claims of others

Common Stock A share of **common stock** represents the most basic form of corporate ownership. In return for the financing provided by selling common stock management must make certain concessions to stockholders that may restrict o change corporate policies. By law, every corporation must hold an annual meeting, a which the holders of common stock may vote for the board of directors and approv or disapprove major corporate actions. Among such actions are

1. Amendments to the corporate charter or bylaws
2. Sale of certain assets
3. Mergers and acquisitions
4. New issues of preferred stock or bonds
5. Changes in the amount of common stock issued

ew investors will buy common stock unless they believe that their investment will increase in value. Information on the reasons why investors purchase stocks and how to valuate stock investments is provided in Chapter 21.

Preferred Stock As noted in Chapter 5, the owners of **preferred stock** must receive their dividends before holders of common stock receive theirs. And preferred stockholders have first claim (after creditors) on assets if the corporation is dissolved or declares bankruptcy. Even so, as with common stock, the board of directors must approve dividends on preferred stock, and this type of financing does not represent a debt that must be legally repaid. In return for preferential treatment, preferred stockholders generally give up the right to vote at a corporation's annual meeting and on corporate actions. (Remember from the preceding section that the right to vote usually is reserved for common stockholders.)

preferred stock stock whose owners usually do not have voting rights but whose claims on dividends and assets are paid before those of common-stock owners

Using the Internet

The New York Stock Exchange (**http://www.nyse.com**) and the Nasdaq (**http://www.nasdaq.com**) are the two most cited equity markets. Each provides financial information about the companies they list and news that might influence their stock values.

The dividend to be paid on a share of preferred stock is known before the stock is purchased. It is stated on the stock certificate either as a percent of the par value of the stock or as a specified dollar amount. The **par value** of a stock is an assigned (and often arbitrary) dollar value printed on the stock certificate. For example, Pitney Bowes—a U.S. manufacturer of office and business equipment—issued 4 percent preferred stock with a par value of \$50. The annual dividend amount is \$2 per share (\$50 par value × 0.04 = \$2 annual dividend).

Although a corporation usually issues only one type of common stock, it may issue many types of preferred stock with varying dividends or dividend rates. For example, New York–based Consolidated Edison has one common-stock issue but two preferred-stock issues with different dividend amounts for each type of preferred stock.

par value an assigned (and often arbitrary) dollar value printed on a stock certificate

When a corporation believes it can issue new preferred stock at a lower dividend rate (or common stock with no specified dividend), it may decide to "call in," or buy back, an earlier stock issue. In this case, management has two options. First, it can buy shares in the market—just like any other investor. Second, it can exercise a call provision because practically all preferred stock is "callable." When the corporation exercises a call provision, the investor *may* receive a call premium or dollar amount over the par value of the preferred stock that is being called. When considering the two options, management naturally will obtain the preferred stock in the less costly way.

convertible preferred stock preferred stock that the owner may exchange for a specified number of shares of common stock

To make preferred stock more attractive to investors, some corporations include a conversion feature. **Convertible preferred stock** is preferred stock that the owner may exchange for a specified number of shares of common stock. The Textron Corporation—a manufacturer of component parts for the automotive and aerospace industries—has issued convertible preferred stock. Each share of Textron preferred stock is convertible to 2.2 shares of the firm's common stock. This conversion feature provides the investor with the safety of preferred stock and the hope of greater speculative gain through conversion to common stock.

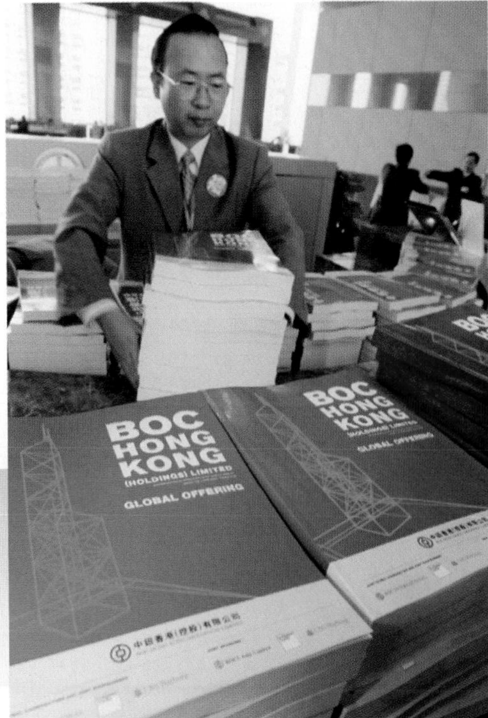

The story is in the IPO booklet. Corporations all over the world sell stock to raise equity financing. For example, the Bank of China (BOC) Hong Kong had hundreds of potential investors lined up to obtain IPO booklets detailing the firm's new stock offering. Expected to fetch an estimated \$3.17 billion, it is the largest initial public offering in the region in almost two years.

Retained Earnings

retained earnings the portion of a corporation's profits not distributed to stockholders

Most large corporations distribute only a portion of their after-tax earnings to stockholders. The portion of a corporation's profits not distributed to stockholders is called **retained earnings.** Because they are undistributed profits, retained earnings are considered a form of equity financing.

The amount of retained earnings in any year is determined by corporate management and approved by the board of directors. Most small and growing corporations pay no cash dividend—or a very small dividend—to their stockholders. All or most earnings are reinvested in the business for R&D, expansion, or the funding of major projects. Reinvestment tends to increase the value of the firm's stock while it provides essentially cost-free financing for the business. More mature corporations may distribute 40 to 60 percent of their after-tax profits as dividends. Utility companies and other corporations with very stable earnings often pay out as much as 80 to 90 percent of what they earn. For a large corporation, retained earnings can amount to a hefty bit of financing. For example, in 2001, the total amount of retained earnings for General Electric was almost $69 billion.[14] And for Exxon/Mobil Corporation in 2001, retained earnings totaled almost $96 billion.[15]

Venture Capital

To establish a new business or expand an existing one, an entrepreneur may try to obtain venture capital. In Chapter 6 we defined *venture capital* as money invested in small (and sometimes struggling) firms that have the potential to become very successful. The key word here is *successful*. Most venture capital firms do not invest in the typical small business—a neighborhood convenience store or a local dry cleaner—but in firms that have the potential to become extremely profitable. And while venture capital firms are willing to take chances, they are also more selective about where they invest their money after the high-tech bust that occurred in the last part of the 1990s and first part of the twenty-first century. What made high-tech firms attractive to venture capitalists was the race to develop new products and services. And yet, even in the heyday of high-tech investing, many financial analysts were concerned about the ability of these Internet firms to stay in business. Now, in the first part of the twenty-first century, a large number of these high-tech firms have failed, and many venture capital firms have lost large amounts of money. As a result of a large number of failures, most venture capital firms now take a more conservative approach.

A prescription for venture capital. Dr. Donald Ingber of Harvard Medical School believes that mapping the human genome was the first step in an important process. The next step combines the data from medical research with computer technology to produce drugs, medical equipment, and therapies for cancer, AIDS, and other dread diseases. This step is much more interesting and potentially profitable according to Dr. Ingber. The rush of activity in the biotech industry and the potential for large profits has many venture capitalists searching the biotech industry for firms that can turn potential scientific breakthroughs into reality.

Generally, a venture capital firm consists of a pool of investors, a traditional partnership established by a wealthy family, or a joint venture formed by corporations with money to invest. (Remember from Chapter 5 that a *joint venture* is two or more groups that form a business entity to achieve a specific goal or to operate for a specific period of time.) In return for financing, these investors generally receive an equity position in the business and share in its profits. Venture capital firms vary in size and scope of interest. Some offer financing for start-up businesses, whereas others finance only established businesses. Whether the firm requesting the money is a start-up or an established business, a business plan is essential. The majority of requests for venture capital are dropped after less than a day's study; most of these lack a business plan. Of the remaining requests, only a small fraction of total requests actually receive financial help from a venture capital firm.

Many factors are considered in the selection process. For example, the Denver-Boulder area is emerging as a telecommunications and high-tech hub, drawing on the region's roots in the telecom and cable-television industries, an educated labor pool, plenty of amenities, and a lifestyle that does not require the same outrageous sums demanded in California's Silicon Valley. As a result, venture capital is flowing into start-up and expansion projects that once were more likely to be found in traditional high-tech centers.[16]

Sources of Long-Term Debt Financing

learning objective

5 Evaluate the advantages and disadvantages of long-term debt financing.

Many people think that when a business borrows money, it signifies weakness. To be sure, borrowing may be a sign of financial weakness, but as we pointed out earlier in this chapter, businesses borrow money on a short-term basis for many valid reasons other than desperation. There are equally valid reasons for long-term borrowing. In addition to using borrowed money to meet the long-term needs listed in Table 20.1, successful businesses often use the financial leverage it creates to improve their financial performance. **Financial leverage** is the use of borrowed funds to increase the return on owners' equity. The principle of financial leverage works as long as a firm's earnings are larger than the interest charged for the borrowed money. Of course, if the firm's earnings should drop below the interest cost of borrowed money, the return on owners' equity will decrease.

financial leverage the use of borrowed funds to increase the return on owners' equity

To understand how financial leverage can increase a firm's return on owners' equity, study the information for Texas-based Cypress Springs Plastics presented in Table 20.3. Pete Johnston, the owner of the firm, is trying to decide how best to finance a $100,000 purchase of new high-tech manufacturing equipment. He could borrow the money and pay 9 percent annual interest. As a second option, Johnston could invest an additional $100,000 in the firm. Assuming that the firm earns $95,000 a year and that annual interest for this loan totals $9,000 ($100,000 × 0.09 = $9,000), the return on owners' equity for Cypress Springs Plastics would be higher if the firm borrowed the additional financing. Return on owners' equity—a topic covered in Chapter 18—is determined by dividing a firm's net income by the dollar amount of owners' equity. For Cypress Springs Plastics, return on owners' equity equals 17.2 percent ($86,000 ÷ $500,000 = 0.172, or 17.2 percent) if Johnston borrows the additional $100,000. The firm's return on owners' equity would decrease to 15.8 percent ($95,000 ÷ $600,000 = .158, or 15.8 percent) if Johnston invests an additional $100,000 in the business.

The most obvious danger when using financial leverage is that the firm's earnings may be less than expected. If this situation occurs, the fixed interest charge actually works to reduce or eliminate the return on owners' equity. Of course, borrowed

table 20.3 Analysis of the Effect of Additional Capital from Debt or Equity for Cypress Springs Plastics, Inc.

Additional Debt		**Additional Equity**	
Owners' equity	$500,000	Owners' equity	$500,000
Additional equity	+ 0	Additional equity	+100,000
Total equity	$500,000	Total equity	$600,000
Loan (@ 9 percent)	+100,000	No loan	+ 0
Total capital	$600,000	Total capital	$600,000
		Year-End Earnings	
Gross profit	$95,000	Gross profit	$95,000
Less loan interest	− 9,000	No interest	− 0
Operating profit	$86,000	Operating profit	$95,000
Return on owners' equity	17.2%	Return on owners' equity	15.8%
($86,000 ÷ $500,000 = 17.2%)		($95,000 ÷ $600,000 = 15.8%)	

money eventually must be repaid. Periodic payments for interest and debt reduction may be hard to manage for some businesses, especially if the firm has a bad year. Finally, because lenders always have the option to turn down a loan request, many managers are reluctant to rely on borrowed money.

lease an agreement by which the right to use real estate, equipment, or other assets is temporarily transferred from the owner to the user

term-loan agreement a promissory note that requires a borrower to repay a loan in monthly, quarterly, semiannual, or annual installments

A company that cannot obtain a long-term loan to acquire property, buildings, and equipment may be able to lease these assets. A **lease** is an agreement by which the right to use real estate, equipment, or other assets is transferred temporarily from the owner to the user. The owner of the leased item is called the *lessor*; the user is called the *lessee*. With the typical lease agreement, the lessee makes regular payments on a monthly, quarterly, or yearly basis. Even when a firm is able to obtain long-term debt financing, it may choose to lease assets because, under the right circumstances, a lease can have tax advantages.

For a small business, long-term debt financing generally is limited to loans. Large corporations have the additional option of issuing corporate bonds. Both types of long-term debt financing are discussed in the next two sections.

Long-Term Loans

Many businesses finance their long-range activities with loans from commercial banks, insurance companies, pension funds, and other financial institutions. Business start-up costs, mergers and acquisitions, new product development, long-term marketing activities, replacement of equipment, and expansion of facilities are likely to be partially or fully funded by long-term loans. Manufacturers and suppliers of heavy machinery also may provide long-term debt financing by granting extended credit to their customers.

Term-Loan Agreements When the loan repayment period is longer than one year, the borrower must sign a term-loan agreement. A **term-loan agreement** is a promissory note that requires a borrower to repay a loan in monthly, quarterly, semiannual, or annual installments. Long-term business loans normally are repaid in three to seven years.

Assume that Pete Johnson, the owner of Cypress Springs Plastics, decides to borrow $100,000 and take advantage of the principle of financial leverage illustrated in Table 20.3. Although the firm's return on owners' equity does increase, interest must be paid each year, and eventually, the loan must be repaid. Before accepting a loan, the owners or managers of a firm must determine if a company can pay interest and the payments required to pay off the loan as scheduled. To pay off a $100,000 loan over a three-year period with annual payments, Cypress Springs Plastics must pay $33,333 on the loan balance plus $9,000 annual interest, or a total of $42,333 the first year. While the amount of interest decreases each year because of the previous year's payment on the loan balance, annual payments of this amount are still a large commitment for a small firm like Cypress Springs Plastics.

The sweet sound of financing. Chris Martin, owner of Martin Guitar Co., based in Nazareth, Pennsylvania sells guitars big time! Bruce Springsteen, Bob Dylan, and Eric Clapton all own Martin guitars. A lot of ordinary folks own the firm's guitars too. As a result, the firm's revenues totaled $77 million last year. As you might guess, a firm selling this many guitars has big financing needs. That's why Martin Guitar arranged to borrow up to $20 million from its bank. According to David Kepler of First Union/Wachovia in Allentown, Pennsylvania, Martin Guitar has won his bank's esteem by proving that it is a well-managed, profitable company.

The interest rate and repayment terms for term loans often are based on such factors as the reasons for borrowing, the borrowing firm's credit rating, and the value of collateral. Although long-term loans occasionally may be unsecured, the lender usually requires some type of collateral. Acceptable collateral includes real estate, machinery, and equipment. Lenders also may require that borrowers maintain a minimum amount of working capital.

The Basics of Getting a Loan According to many financial experts, preparation is the key when applying for a ng-term business loan. In reality, preparation begins before you ever apply for the an. To begin the process, you should get to know potential lenders before requesting ebt financing. While there may be many potential lenders that can provide the money ou need, the logical place to borrow money is where your business does its banking. his fact underscores the importance of maintaining adequate balances in the firm's hecking account in order to pay the checks drawn on your account. Regardless of how ood an application looks or how well you answer the questions during an interview ith a bank officer, bounced checks or other problems at the bank can result in the ank rejecting your loan request. Before applying for a loan, you also may want to heck your firm's credit rating with a national credit bureau such as Dun & Bradstreet.

Typically, you will be asked to fill out a loan application. In addition to the loan pplication, the lender also will want to see your current business plan, including a ne- to two-page executive summary. Be sure to explain what your business is, how uch funding you require to accomplish your goals and objectives, and how the loan ill be repaid. Next, have your certified public accountant (CPA) prepare financial atements. Most lenders insist that you submit current financial statements that have een prepared by an independent CPA along with your business plan. Then compile a st of references that includes your suppliers, other lenders, or the professionals with hom you are associated. Once you submit your application, business plan, and supporting financial documents, a bank officer or a loan committee will examine the loan pplication. You may also be asked to discuss the loan request with a loan officer. Iopefully, your loan request will be approved. If not, try to determine why your loan equest was rejected. Think back over the loan process and determine what you could o to improve your chances of getting a loan the next time you apply.

Corporate Bonds

arge corporations issue bonds in denominations of $1,000 to $50,000; the total face alue of all the bonds in an issue usually amounts to millions of dollars. In fact, one of he reasons why corporations sell bonds is that they can borrow a lot of money from a ot of different bondholders and raise larger amounts of money than could be borowed from one lender. A **corporate bond** is a corporation's written pledge that it will epay a specified amount of money with interest. Figure 20.7 (on p. 622) shows a corporate bond for the American & Foreign Power Company. Note that it includes the nterest rate (5 percent) and the maturity date. The **maturity date** is the date on which the corporation is to repay the borrowed money. The bond also has spaces for he amount of its face value, the registration number, and the bond owner's name. Today, many corporations do not issue actual bonds like the one illustrated in Figure 0.7. Instead, the bonds are recorded electronically, and the specific details regarding he bond issue, along with the current owner's name and address, are maintained by omputer. While some people like to have physical possession of their corporate onds, computer entries are easier to transfer when a bond is sold. Computer entries lso are safer because they cannot be stolen, misplaced, or destroyed—all concerns hat you must worry about if you take physical possession of a corporate bond.

corporate bond a corporation's written pledge that it will repay a specified amount of money with interest

maturity date the date on which a corporation is to repay borrowed money

Until a bond's maturity, a corporation pays interest to the bond owner at the tated rate. Owners of the American & Foreign Power Company bond receive 5 perent per year for each bond. Because interest for corporate bonds is usually paid seminnually, bond owners receive a payment every six months for each bond they own.

Types of Bonds Today most corporate bonds are registered bonds. A **registered ond**—like the American & Foreign Power Company bond—is a bond registered in he owner's name by the issuing company. Until the maturity date, the registered wner receives periodic interest payments. On the maturity date, the owner returns a egistered bond to the corporation and receives cash equaling the face value.

registered bond a bond registered in the owner's name by the issuing company

Corporate bonds generally are classified as debentures, mortgage bonds, or convertible bonds. Most corporate bonds are debenture bonds. A **debenture bond** is a ond backed only by the reputation of the issuing corporation. To make its bonds

debenture bond a bond backed only by the reputation of the issuing corporation

figure 20.7

A Corporate Bond

A corporate bond is a corporation's written pledge that it will repay on the date of maturity a specified amount of money with interest.

mortgage bond a corporate bond secured by various assets of the issuing firm

convertible bond a bond that can be exchanged, at the owner's option, for a specified number of shares of the corporation's common stock

bond indenture a legal document that details all the conditions relating to a bond issue

more appealing to investors, a corporation may issue mortgage bonds. A **mortgag bond** is a corporate bond secured by various assets of the issuing firm. Typical corpo- rate assets that are used as collateral for a mortgage bond include real estate, machin- ery, and equipment that is not pledged as collateral for other debt obligations. Th corporation also can issue convertible bonds. A **convertible bond** can be exchanged at the owner's option, for a specified number of shares of the corporation's commo stock. Kerr McGee's bond that matures in 2010 is convertible: Each bond can be con- verted to 16.373 shares of Kerr McGee common stock. A corporation can gain i three ways by issuing convertible bonds. First, convertibles usually carry a lower in- terest rate than nonconvertible bonds. Second, the conversion feature attracts in- vestors who are interested in the speculative gain that conversion to common stoc may provide. Third, if the bondholder converts to common stock, the corporation nc longer has to redeem the bond at maturity.

Repayment Provisions for Corporate Bonds Maturity dates for bonds generall range from ten to thirty years after the date of issue. If the interest is not paid or th firm becomes insolvent, bond owners' claims on the assets of the corporation take precedence over the claims of both common and preferred stockholders. Some bonds are callable before the maturity date; that is, a corporation can buy back, or redeem them. For these bonds, the corporation may pay the bond owner a call premium. The amount of the call premium is specified, along with other provisions, in the bond in- denture. The **bond indenture** is a legal document that details all the conditions relat- ing to a bond issue.

Before deciding if bonds are the best way to obtain corporate financing, man- agers must determine if the company can afford to pay the interest on the corporate bonds. It should be obvious that the larger the bond issue, the higher the interest will be. For example, assume that AMR—the parent company of American Airlines—is- sues bonds with a face value of \$80 million. If the interest rate is 8.5 percent, the in- terest on this bond issue is \$6.8 million (\$80 million × 0.085 = \$6.8 million) each year until the bonds are repaid. In addition, corporate bonds must be redeemed for their face value at maturity. If the corporation defaults on (does not pay) either inter-st payments or repayment of the bond at maturity, owners of bonds can force the rm into bankruptcy.

A corporation may use one of three methods to ensure that it has sufficient funds vailable to redeem a bond issue. First, it can issue the bonds as **serial bonds**, which re bonds of a single issue that mature on different dates. For example, a company nay use a twenty-five-year $50-million bond issue to finance its expansion. None of ne bonds mature during the first fifteen years. Thereafter, 10 percent of the bonds nature each year until all the bonds are retired at the end of the twenty-fifth year. Second, the corporation can establish a sinking fund. A **sinking fund** is a sum of money) which deposits are made each year for the purpose of redeeming a bond issue. Vhen H. J. Heinz sold a $50-million bond issue, the company agreed to contribute 3 million to a sinking fund every year until the bond's maturity in the year 2007. 'hird, a corporation can pay off an old bond issue by selling new bonds. Although this nay appear to perpetuate the corporation's long-term debt, a number of utility companies and railroads use this repayment method.

serial bonds bonds of a single issue that mature on different dates

sinking fund a sum of money to which deposits are made each year for the purpose of redeeming a bond issue

A corporation that issues bonds also must appoint a **trustee**, an individual or an ndependent firm that acts as the bond owners' representative. A trustee's duties are andled most often by a commercial bank or other large financial institution. The orporation must report to the trustee periodically regarding its ability to make interest payments and eventually redeem the bonds. In turn, the trustee transmits this inormation to the bond owners, along with its own evaluation of the corporation's bility to pay.

trustee an individual or an independent firm that acts as a bond owners' representative

Cost Comparisons

'able 20.4 compares some of the methods that can be used to obtain long-term equity *nd* debt financing. Although the cost of issuing stock is high, selling common stock enerally is the first choice for most financial managers. Once the stock is sold and upront costs are paid, the *ongoing* costs of using stock to finance a business are low. The ype of long-term financing that generally has the highest *ongoing* costs is a long-term oan (debt).

table 20.4 Comparison of Long-Term Financing Methods

Type of Financing	Repayment	Repayment Period	Cost/Dividends Interest	Businesses That May Use It
Equity				
Common stock	No	None	High initial cost; low ongoing costs because dividends not required	All corporations that sell stock to investors
Preferred stock	No	None	Dividends not required but must be paid before common stockholders receive any dividends	Large corporations that have an established investor base of common stockholders
Debt				
Long-term loan	Yes	Usually 3–7 years	Interest rates between 4 and 12 percent, depending on economic conditions and the financial stability of the company requesting the loan	All firms that can meet the lender's repayment and collateral requirements
Corporate bond	Yes	Usually 10–30 years	Interest rates between 4 and 10 percent, depending on economic conditions and the financial stability of the company issuing the bonds	Large corporations that investors trust

To a great extent, firms are financed through the investments of individuals—money that people have deposited in banks or have used to purchase stocks, mutual funds, and bonds. In Chapter 21 we look at securities markets and how they help people invest their money in business.

Return To inside business

USBX is more than a money matchmaker. Yes, it helps companies arrange for IPOs, raise capital from private investors, arrange debt financing, and refinance debt. It also determines what a company is worth to potential buyers or the seller and advises owners and management about acquisitions and mergers. And when a certain niche looks especially promising, USBX is ready to step in with creative ideas for financing or acquisitions.

For example, after the Internet bubble burst and dot-com companies fell from favor, some investors saw opportunities in the increasing popularity of specialty foods. USBX and its competitors have helped a number of California-based ethnic food manufacturers obtain additional capital to expand or to acquire smaller rivals. USBX has worked with a number of food firms, so its experts can dish up knowledgeable advice along with viable financing alternatives. If the American public keeps its taste for specialty foods, these companies will prosper—and yield good returns for their investors as well.

Questions

1. When USBX—a company that specializes in helping other firms raise money—needed money, it turned to The Carlyle Group. Why would The Carlyle Group want to invest in a company that offers services much like its own? Why would USBX want to obtain an investor like The Carlyle Group?
2. For a small-business owner, what are the advantages and disadvantages of using a company such as USBX to help raise capital?

chapter review

Summary

Explain the need for financing and financial management in business.

Financial management consists of all activities concerned with obtaining money and using it effectively. Short-term financing is money that will be used for one year or less and then repaid. There are many short-term needs, but cash flow and inventory are two for which financing is often required. Long-term financing is money that will be used for more than one year. Such financing may be required for a business start-up, for a merger or acquisition, for new product development, for long-term marketing activities, for replacement of equipment, or for expansion of facilities. Financial management can be viewed as a two-sided problem. On one side, the uses of funds often dictate the type or types of financing needed by a business. On the other side, the activities a business can undertake are determined by the types of financing available. Financial managers must ensure that funds are available when needed, that they are obtained at the lowest possible cost, and that they are available for the repayment of debts.

Summarize the process of planning for financial management.

A financial plan begins with the organization's goals and objectives. Next, these goals and objectives are "translated" into departmental budgets that detail expected income and expenses. From these budgets, which may be combined into an overall cash budget, the financial manager determines what funding will be needed and where it may be obtained. Whereas departmental and cash budgets emphasize short-term financing needs, a capital budget can be used to estimate a firm's expenditures for major assets and its long-term financing needs. The four principal sources of financing are sales revenues, equity capital, debt capital, and proceeds from the sale of assets. Once the needed funds have been obtained, the financial manager is responsible for ensuring that they are used properly. This is accomplished through a system of monitoring and evaluating the firm's financial activities.

Describe the advantages and disadvantages of different methods of short-term debt financing.

Most short-term financing is unsecured; that is, no collateral is required. Sources of unsecured short-term financing include trade credit, promissory notes issued to suppliers, unsecured bank loans, and commercial paper. Sources of secured short-term financing include loans secured by inventory and accounts receivable. A firm also may sell its receivables to factors. Trade credit is the least expensive source of short-term financing. The cost of financing through other sources generally depends on the source and on the credit rating of the firm that requires the financing. Factoring is generally the most expensive approach.

Evaluate the advantages and disadvantages of equity financing.

A corporation can raise equity capital by selling either common or preferred stock. Common stock is voting stock; holders of common stock elect the corporation's directors and must approve changes to the corporate charter. Holders of preferred stock must be paid dividends before holders of common stock are paid any dividends. Another source of equity funding is retained earnings, which is the portion of a business's profits not distributed to stockholders. Venture capital—money invested in small (and sometimes struggling) firms that have the potential to become very successful—is yet another source of equity funding. Generally, the venture capital is provided by investors, partnerships established by wealthy families, or a joint venture formed by corporations with money to invest. In return, they share in the profits of the business.

Evaluate the advantages and disadvantages of long-term debt financing.

For a small business, debt financing generally is limited to loans. Large corporations have the additional option of issuing corporate bonds. Regardless of whether the business is small or large, it can take advantage of financial leverage. Financial leverage is the use of borrowed funds to increase the return on owners' equity. The rate of interest for long-term loans usually depends on the financial status of the borrower, the reason for borrowing, and the kind of collateral pledged to back up the loan. Long-term business loans normally are repaid in three to seven years. Money realized from the sale of corporate bonds must be repaid when the bonds mature. In addition, the corporation must pay interest on that money from the time the bonds are sold until maturity. Maturity dates for bonds generally range from ten to thirty years after the date of issue. When comparing the cost of equity and debt long-term financing, the ongoing costs of using stock (equity) to finance a business are low. The most expensive is a long-term loan (debt).

Key Terms

You should now be able to define and give an example relevant to each of the following terms:

financial management (601)
short-term financing (601)
cash flow (602)
speculative production (602)
long-term financing (603)
financial plan (605)
budget (606)
cash budget (606)
zero-base budgeting (606)
capital budget (607)
equity capital (608)
debt capital (608)
unsecured financing (610)
trade credit (610)
promissory note (610)
prime interest rate (611)
revolving credit agreement (612)
commercial paper (612)
floor planning (613)
factor (614)
initial public offering (IPO) (615)
investment banking firm (615)
common stock (616)
preferred stock (617)
par value (617)
convertible preferred stock (617)
retained earnings (618)
financial leverage (619)
lease (620)
term-loan agreement (620)
corporate bond (621)
maturity date (621)
registered bond (621)
debenture bond (621)
mortgage bond (622)
convertible bond (622)
bond indenture (622)
serial bonds (623)
sinking fund (623)
trustee (623)

Review Questions

1. How does short-term financing differ from long-term financing? Give two business uses for each type of financing.
2. What is the function of a cash budget? A capital budget?
3. What is zero-base budgeting? How does it differ from the traditional concept of budgeting?
4. What are four general sources of funds?
5. How does a financial manager monitor and evaluate a firm's financing?
6. How important is trade credit as a source of short-term financing?
7. What is the prime rate? Who gets the prime rate?
8. Why would a supplier require a customer to sign a promissory note?
9. What is the difference between a line of credit and a revolving credit agreement?
10. Explain how factoring works. Of what benefit is factoring to a firm that sells its receivables?
11. What are the advantages of financing through the sale of stock?
12. From a corporation's point of view, how does preferred stock differ from common stock?
13. Where do a corporation's retained earnings come from? What are the advantages of this type of financing?

14. What is venture capital?
15. Describe how financial leverage can increase return on owners' equity.
16. For the corporation, what are the advantages of corporate bonds over long-term loans?
17. Describe the three methods used to ensure that funds are available to redeem corporate bonds at maturity.

Discussion Questions

1. Describe the possible problems created by the downturn in the economy and the terrorist attacks of September 11, 2001, for managers and business owners in need of financing.
2. What does a financial manager do? How can he or she monitor a firm's financial success?
3. If you were the financial manager of Stars and Stripes Clothing, what would you do with the excess cash that the firm expects in the second and fourth quarters? (See Figure 20.4.)
4. Develop a *personal* cash budget for the next six months. Explain what you would do if there are budget shortfalls or excess cash amounts at the end of any month during the six-month period.
5. Why would a supplier offer both trade credit and cash discounts to its customers?
6. Why would a lender offer unsecured loans when it could demand collateral?
7. How can a small-business owner or corporate manager use financial leverage to improve a firm's profits and return on owners' equity?
8. In what circumstances might a large corporation sell stock rather than bonds to obtain long-term financing? In what circumstances would it sell bonds rather than stock?

video case

How Gilford Securities Serves as a Financial Matchmaker

Companies need money for operations and growth, and investors need good investments. This is where Gilford Securities comes in. Since 1979, employee-owned Gilford has served as an investment matchmaker, helping small and midsized companies raise money through IPOs and private debt placements. In addition to investment banking expertise, it has a full-service brokerage unit to buy and sell securities for individual and institutional investors. And to enhance its matchmaking capabilities, Gilford maintains a staff of expert research analysts who search out and study undervalued securities to identify good investment opportunities for the investors who use its brokerage services.

In a twenty-four-month period, matchmaker Gilford helped fifteen companies obtain capital. Its initial and secondary public offerings range in size from $5 million to $25 million; its private placements range from $5 million to $20 million. Although such numbers generally are too small to capture the attention of giant Wall Street investment banking firms, they are the right size for Gilford. Its specialists know that preparing for an IPO can be traumatic for a growing company and its management team. This is why they work closely with companies during every step in the process, from compiling and filing the necessary financial information to scheduling the offering, setting the initial share price, and arranging for the stock to begin and continue trading. After a transaction, Gilford tracks the performance of the companies it has taken public and issues regular research reports for current and prospective investors. Rather than hopping from deal to deal, Gilford carefully follows up after every transaction to be sure that each company's needs have been satisfied properly. This approach has earned the firm a reputation for building long-term relationships.

The first contact some companies have with Gilford is through its research analysts. For example, the CEO of Pennsylvania Enterprises was extremely impressed after a Gilford analyst researched his company and wrote a report demonstrating a thorough understanding of the company and the industry. Since that contact, Pennsylvania Enterprises has become an enthusiastic customer.

Casey Alexander, a senior vice president, explains that researching companies is challenging and time-consuming but essential if Gilford is to unearth potential investment opportunities for its institutional and individual brokerage customers. One clue he uses is whether managers and directors are buying their own company's stock and the level of their purchases. If insiders are buying heavily, he then digs deeper to find the catalyst prompting these investments so that he can alert Gilford's brokerage customers to the opportunity. Does the company have a new product, a new process, or a new patent? What special circumstances might induce insiders to make sizable investments that are clearly not guaranteed to pay off? Alexander and his team do not stop researching until they come up with answers.

By analyzing companies that few other firms research and recognizing stocks that seem poised to increase in value, Gilford helps its brokerage customers wring the most from their investment dollars. In some cases the firm can even arrange for large investors to meet with the management of companies whose stock its analysts are recommending for purchase. However, not every recommendation is a "buy." When they uncover emerging problems due to the environment, competition, or other factors that affect a corporation, Gilford's analysts will issue reports explaining their reasoning and suggesting that customers consider selling the stock.

Yet, having an investment banking group to advise companies and a research team to advise customers on the brokerage side of the business is a delicate balancing act these days. Gilford's Howard Perkins stresses that the company upholds the highest ethical standards as part of its commitment to professionalism and customer service. In fact, top brokers join Gilford because they know that they will have the freedom to do what's right for their customers. Over time, Gilford's customer orientation has helped Gilford to build a loyal customer base and to expand nationwide despite intense competition in the brokerage business. The firm now has 150 employees spread across offices in New York City, Pittsburgh, and other locations.[17]

Questions

1. In addition to significant insider buying, what other clues might Casey Alexander use in identifying companies that could be profitable investments for Gilford's brokerage customers?
2. Why do you think going public can be traumatic for a company's management team? How does Gilford make the process easier for a firm selling a new securities issue?
3. If you were the owner of a growing business in need of capital, what questions would you ask when choosing an investment bank to take your company public?

Building Skills for Career Success

1. Exploring the Internet

Finding capital for new business start-ups is never an easy task. Besides a good business plan, those seeking investor funds must be convincing and clear about how their business activities will provide sufficient revenue to pay back investors who help to get them going in the first place. To find out what others have done, it is useful to read histories of successful start-ups as well as failures in journals that specialize in this area. Visit the text website for updates to this exercise.

Assignment

1. Examine articles that profile successes and failures in the following publications and highlight the main points that led to either result.

   American Venture magazine (**http://www.avce.com**)

   Business 2.0 (**http://www.business2.com**)

   Red Herring (**http://www.redherring.com**)

   Fast Company (**http://www.fastcompany.com**)
2. What are the shared similarities?
3. What advice would you give to a start-up venture after reading these stories?

2. Developing Critical Thinking Skills

Financial management involves preparing a plan for obtaining and using the money needed to accomplish a firm's goals and objectives. After a financial plan has been developed, it must be monitored continually to ensure that it actually fulfills these goals and objectives. To accomplish your own goals, you should prepare a *personal* financial plan. Determine what is important in your life and what you want to accomplish, budget the amount of money required to get it, and identify sources for acquiring the funds. You should monitor and evaluate the results regularly and make changes when necessary.

Assignment

1. Using the three steps shown in Figure 20.2, prepare a personal financial plan.
2. Prepare a three-column table to display it.
   a. In column 1, list at least two objectives under each of the following areas:

      Financial (savings, investments, retirement)

      Education (training, degrees, certificates)

      Career (position, industry, location)

      Family (children, home, education, trips, entertainment)

   b. In column 2, list the amount of money it will take to accomplish your objectives.
   c. In column 3, identify the sources of funds for each objective.
3. Describe what you learned from doing this exercise in a comments section at the bottom of the table.

3. Building Team Skills

Suppose that for the past three years you have been repairing lawn mowers in your garage. Your business has grown steadily, and recently you hired two part-time workers. Your garage is no longer adequate for your business; it is also in violation of the city code, and you have been fined twice for noncompliance. You have decided that it is time to find another location for your shop and that it also would be a good time to expand your business. If the business continues to grow in the new location, you plan to hire a full-time employee to repair washing machines. You are concerned, however, about how you will get the money to move your shop and get it established in a new location.

Assignment

1. With all class members participating, use brainstorming to identify the following:
   a. The funds you will need to accomplish your business goals
   b. The sources of short-term financing available to you
   c. Problems that might prevent you from getting a short-term loan
   d. How you will repay the money if you get it
2. Have a classmate write the ideas on the board.
3. Discuss how you can overcome any problems that might hamper your current chances of getting a loan and how your business can improve its chances of securing short-term loans in the future.
4. Summarize what you learned from participating in this exercise.

4. Researching Different Careers

Financial managers are responsible for determining the best way to raise funds, for ensuring that the funds are used to accomplish their firm's goals and objectives, and for developing and implementing their firm's financial plan. Their decisions have a direct impact on the firm's level of success. When managers do not pay enough attention to finances, a firm is likely to fail.

Assignment

1. Investigate the job of financial manager by searching the library or Internet and/or by interviewing a financial manager.
2. Find answers to the following questions:
   a. What skills do financial managers need?
   b. How much education is required?
   c. What is the starting salary? Top salary?
   d. What will the job of financial manager be like in the future?
   e. What opportunities are available?
   f. What types of firms are most likely to hire financial managers? What is the employment potential?
3. Prepare a report on your findings.

5. Improving Communication Skills

Trade credit is a source of short-term financing extended by a seller who does not require immediate payment on delivery of merchandise. The bill, or invoice, states the credit terms, often offering a cash discount for prompt payment. Many managers and owners, however, fail to take advantage of these discounts, which can save a business hundreds and even thousands of dollars each year.

Assignment

1. Prepare an invoice that offers the buyer a 2 percent cash discount if the bill is paid within ten days.
2. Using the data in the following table, calculate how much a business would save per transaction and in the course of a year, based on six transactions, if it took advantage of trade credit that offered a 2 percent cash discount.

Invoice Amount	**Amount Saved per Transaction**	**Amount Saved Annually** (Based on Six Transactions)
$1,000		
$2,300		
$5,600		
$11,000		
$22,500		
TOTAL		

3. Discuss why you think businesses fail to take advantage of cash discounts.
4. Summarize what you have learned about trade credit from this exercise.

chapter

21

Understanding Securities Markets and Investments

learning objectives

1 Develop a personal investment plan.

2 Explain how the factors of safety, risk, income, growth, and liquidity affect your investment decisions.

3 Describe how securities are bought and sold.

4 Identify the advantages and disadvantages of savings accounts, bonds, stocks, mutual funds, and real estate.

5 Describe high-risk investment techniques.

6 Use financial information to evaluate investment alternatives.

Vanguard Mutual Funds is the only sizable mutual fund company owned by the people who invest in its funds.

inside business

Vanguard Stresses Long-Term, Low-Cost Investing

When most mutual funds zig, Vanguard zags. Why? Because Vanguard Mutual Funds is the only sizable mutual fund company owned by the people who invest in its funds. As a result, its managers have long been on a mission to boost its investors' (owners') returns by driving mutual fund costs lower and lower. Since Vanguard's start in 1975, the costs of administering its stock funds have dropped steadily and are now below 0.4 percent. By comparison, the costs of other stock mutual funds have risen to nearly 1.6 percent. As Vanguard's executives well know, even a slightly higher cost structure can eat up precious investment dollars and, over the years, keep people from getting the most out of their investments.

Founder John C. Bogle established Vanguard's unusual ownership structure so that the company could concentrate on serving its mutual fund investors rather than generating fees to pay an outside management firm and outside owners. Retired from the company he founded, Bogle remains an outspoken critic of the mutual fund industry. He believes that today's fund managers are too busy chasing short-term gains by constantly buying and selling stocks, which drives up trading costs and can hamper long-term performance. He also argues that the industry has launched too many new mutual funds, including specialized funds that may perform well—but only for a few years.

One of Bogle's biggest successes was creating the Vanguard 500 Index Fund with the goal of mirroring the stock mix and returns of the Standard & Poor's 500 Index. This fund's managers rarely have to buy and sell stocks because the 500 stocks in the Standard & Poor's index do not change very often. Less frequent trading keeps costs to a minimum and allows investors to reap returns that are similar to what they would receive if they owned shares in all 500 stocks contained in the index. Despite some significant dips during economic downturns, this index has provided investors with a respectable average annual return through the years. Not surprisingly, the Vanguard 500 Index fund has grown into the largest of Vanguard's 144 domestic and international mutual funds.

In addition to lowering the cost of investing, Vanguard also wants to educate investors so that they can make the best possible investment decisions. Consider the following recommendations that form the Vanguard investment philosophy:

- Focus on long-term investment goals and quality investments.
- If you are at the start of your career, you have many years to grow your retirement nest egg.
- Do not suddenly change your investment portfolio or jump in and out of the market.
- Be careful to diversify rather than putting too much money into a single security or type of security (not all stocks, not all mutual funds).
- Before you buy, investigate the cost of the security and the cost of the trade.
- Regardless of your age or the state of the market, it is time to start investing.[1]

Too often people try to build an investment program around risky investments to earn large returns over a short period of time. Certainly, the success stories that were common during the economic upturn of the mid 1990s made people think that long-term investment programs were old-fashioned. Why wait when you can make "big" returns so fast. Unfortunately, the bubble burst, and many people found that they could lose money just as fast as they made it. Now, four years since the economy took a nose-dive in the late 1990s, there are many investors who have adopted the Vanguard philosophy of long-term investing in quality investments. After reading this chapter, hopefully you will be prepared to embrace another Vanguard principle: Regardless of your age or the state of the market, it is time to start investing.

Today, a lot of people are actually "afraid" to invest money. Why? The answer is simple: Everyone has heard the horror stories of people who have lost 35 to 50 percent of the value of their investment portfolio over the past three or four years. To make matters worse, economic problems, the terrorist attacks of September 11, and record numbers of corporations reporting lower sales revenues and profits or no profits at all have convinced many would-be investors to sit on the sideline and wait for the investment world to settle down. Many people ask the question: Why begin an investment program now? Another simple answer: The sooner you start an investment program, the more time your investments have to work for you. As you will see later in this chapter, waiting just five or ten years before starting an investment program can *really* reduce your financial return—regardless of the investment you choose. And yet, choosing the right investment is only part of a successful investment program. It also takes discipline and the knowledge of where to find the information needed to evaluate an investment.

We begin this chapter by outlining the reasons for developing a personal investment plan and pointing out several factors that should be considered before investing any money. Next, we examine the process of buying and selling securities, noting the functions of securities exchanges, stock brokerage firms, and securities regulations. Then we discuss both traditional and high-risk (or speculative) investments. Finally, we explain how to obtain and interpret financial information from the Internet, newspapers, brokerage firms, corporate reports, and periodicals. It is time! Take the first step, and develop an investment plan.

Developing an Investment Plan

learning objective

1 Develop a personal investment plan.

Personal investment is the use of your personal funds to earn a financial return. Thus, in the most general sense, the goal of investing is to earn money with money. However, such a goal is completely useless for the individual because it is so vague and so easily attained. If you put $1000 in a savings account paying 2 percent annual interest, your money will earn $1.67 in one month. If your goal is simply to earn money with your $1000, you will have attained that goal at the end of the month. If your goals are somewhat more ambitious, you will find the material in the next section helpful.

personal investment the use of your personal funds to earn a financial return

Investment Goals

In reality, an investment goal must be specific and measurable. It must be tailored to you so that it takes into account your particular financial needs. It also must be oriented toward the future because investing is usually a long-term undertaking. Finally, an investment goal must be realistic in terms of current economic conditions and available investment opportunities.

Some financial planners suggest that investment goals should be stated in terms of money: "By January 1, 2010, I will have total assets of $80,000." Others believe that people are more motivated to work toward goals that are stated in terms of the particular things they desire: "By May 1, 2009, I will have accumulated enough money so that I can take a year off from work to travel around the world." Like the goals themselves, the way they are stated depends on you. The following questions can be helpful in establishing valid investment goals:

1. What financial goals do you want to achieve?
2. How much money will you need, and when?
3. What will you use the money for?
4. Is it reasonable to assume that you can obtain the amount of money you will need to meet your investment goals?
5. Do you expect your personal situation to change in a way that will affect your investment goals?
6. What economic conditions could alter your investment goals?
7. Are you willing to make the necessary sacrifices to ensure that your investment goals are met?
8. What are the consequences of not obtaining your investment goals?

A Personal Investment Plan

Once you have formulated specific goals, investment planning is similar to planning for a business. It begins with the evaluation of different investment opportunities—including the potential return and risk involved in each. At the very least, this process requires some careful study and maybe some expert advice. Investors should beware of people who call themselves "financial planners" but who are in reality nothing more than salespersons for various financial investments, tax shelters, or insurance plans.

financial planner
an individual who has had at least two years of training in investments, insurance, taxation, retirement planning, and estate planning and has passed a rigorous examination

A true **financial planner** has had at least two years of training in investments, insurance, taxation, retirement planning, and estate planning and has passed a rigorous examination. As evidence of training and successful completion of the qualifying examination, the Certified Financial Planners Board of Standards in Denver allows individuals to use the designation Certified Financial Planner (CFP). Similarly, the American College in Bryn Mawr, Pennsylvania, allows individuals who have completed the necessary requirements to use the designation Chartered Financial Consultant (ChFC). Most CFPs and ChFCs do not sell a particular investment product or charge commissions for their investment recommendations. Instead, they charge consulting fees that range from $100 to $250 an hour. If you are interested in a career in financial planning, visit the Certified Financial Planners Board of Standards website at **www.cfp-board.org** or the American College at **www.amercoll.edu** for more information.

Many financial planners suggest that you begin an investment program by accumulating an "emergency fund"—a certain amount of money that can be obtained

Investing doesn't have to be rocket science. While these NASA engineers know a lot about rocket science, they didn't know a lot about investing when they started an investment club called Fortune Builders back in 1995. Early on, they realized that to obtain their goal of picking high performing stocks, they would have to research different investment alternatives. They learned their lessons well—the club's annual return on investment has been stable at about 11 percent for the past eight years.

table 21.1 Suggestions to Help You Accumulate the Money Needed to Fund an Investment Plan

1. *Learn to balance your budget.* Many people regularly spend more than they make. It makes no sense to begin an investment program while you have large balances and high interest charges on credit card accounts.
2. *Make savings a higher priority.* Many financial experts recommend that you (1) pay your monthly bills, (2) save a reasonable amount of money, and (3) use whatever money is left over for personal expenses.
3. *Take advantage of employer-sponsored retirement programs.* Many employers will match part or all of the contributions you make to a 401(k) or 403(b) retirement account. (*Hint*: When looking for a new job, check out the retirement plan offered by the employer.)
4. *Participate in an elective savings program.* You can elect to have money withheld from your paycheck each payday and automatically deposited in a savings account.
5. *Make a special savings effort one or two months each year.* By cutting back to the basics, you can obtain money for investment purposes.
6. *Take advantage of gifts, inheritances, and windfalls.* During your lifetime, you likely will receive gifts, inheritances, salary increases, year-end bonuses, or federal income tax returns. Instead of spending these windfalls, invest these funds.

Source: Jack R. Kapoor, Les R. Dlabay, and Robert J. Hughes, *Personal Finance*, 7th ed. Burr Ridge, IL: Irwin–McGraw-Hill, 2004, p. 421.

quickly in case of immediate need. The amount of money that should be salted away in a savings account varies from person to person. However, most financial planners agree that an amount equal to at least three months' living expenses is reasonable.

After the emergency account is established, you may invest additional funds according to your investment plan. Some additional funds already may be available, or money for further investing may be saved out of earnings. For suggestions to help you obtain the money needed to fund your investment plan, see Table 21.1.

Once your plan has been put into operation, you must monitor it and, if necessary, modify it. Your circumstances and economic conditions are both subject to change. Hence all investment programs should be reevaluated regularly. To learn more about the value of a long-term investment program, read Adapting to Change (on p. 634).

Important Factors in Personal Investment

learning objective 2 Explain how the factors of safety, risk, income, growth, and liquidity affect your investment decisions.

How can you (or a financial planner) tell which investments are "right" for an investment plan and which are not? One way to start is to match potential investments with your investment goals in terms of safety, risk, income, growth, and liquidity.

Safety and Risk Safety and risk are two sides of the same coin. *Safety* in an investment means minimal risk of loss; *risk* in an investment means a measure of uncertainty about the outcome. If you want a steady increase in value over an extended period of time, choose safe investments, such as certificates of deposit (CDs), highly rated corporate and municipal bonds, and the stocks of highly regarded corporations—sometimes called *blue-chip stocks.* A **blue-chip stock** is a safe investment that generally attracts conservative investors. Corporations that often are industry leaders and have provided their stockholders with stable earnings and dividends over a number of years include Johnson & Johnson, General Electric, and Sara Lee Corporation. Selected mutual funds and real estate also may be very safe investments.

blue-chip stock a safe investment that generally attracts conservative investors

To implement goals that stress higher dollar returns on your investments, you generally must give up some safety. How much risk should you take in exchange for

adapting to change

What Is a 401(k) Retirement Account? What Is a Roth IRA?

IF YOU START AT AGE 25 and invest $150 per month in investments that earn an average 11 percent annually, you will be a millionaire by the time you reach age 65! But before you begin, consider two factors. First, you must be careful where you invest your money. To obtain an 11 percent return, you will need to invest in stocks or mutual funds. This is one of the major reasons for studying the material in this chapter. Second, you need to establish a retirement account. If you are ready to take the first step, read on.

The journey toward a comfortable retirement starts with a single step. When you work full time, your first step might be to set up a 401(k) retirement account through your employer. Using this account, you can set aside a certain percentage of your before-tax salary for retirement. This reduces your taxable salary by the amount you choose to set aside and at the same time reduces the amount paid to the Internal Revenue Service (IRS). For many people this is an immediate incentive to save for retirement.

Some employers match part or all of the funds their employees contribute to a 401(k), making the investment even more attractive. Suppose that your employer offers a 25 percent match. If you contribute $2,000 to your account the first year, your employer will add $500 ($2,000 × .25 = $500) to your account for that year. The more you contribute—usually through automatic payroll deductions—the more your employer contributes, and the more you will accumulate for retirement. Note that government rules cap the amount you can allocate to a 401(k) account in a single year.

Another advantage is that you do not pay tax on your 401(k) contributions (or what you earn by investing that money) until you begin to withdraw it at retirement. Year after year, your account will grow as you and your employer make contributions, your investments appreciate in value, and you receive interest and dividends.

The Roth IRA (*i*ndividual *r*etirement *a*ccount) works a little differently. First, to contribute to a Roth IRA, your annual income must be below certain guidelines. At the time of publication, you could contribute to a Roth IRA if you are a single taxpayer with income of less than $110,000 or less than $160,000 if you are married and filing a joint return. Second, contributions are not tax-deductible. There are no immediate tax benefits for contributing to a Roth IRA. Third, after five years, withdrawals and distributions are nontaxable if (1) you are 59½, (2) disabled, (3) or use the money to buy or build a first home (maximum $10,000). Although the cap on annual Roth IRA contributions ($3,000 for individuals 50 years of age or younger and $3,500 for individuals over the age of 50) is much lower than the cap on 401(k) contributions, remember that saving even a small amount regularly over a long period can add up to a comfortable retirement nest egg.

how much return? The answer depends very much on your investment goals and your age. In general, however, *the potential return should be directly related to the assumed risk*. That is, the greater the risk assumed by the investor, the greater the potential monetary reward should be. As you will see shortly, there are a number of risky—and potentially profitable—investments. They include some stocks, mutual funds, and bonds, commodities, and stock options. The securities issued by new and growing corporations usually fall in this category.

Investment Income CDs, corporate and government bonds, and certain stocks pay a predictable amount of interest or dividends each year. Some mutual funds and real estate also may offer steady income potential. Such investments generally are used to implement investment goals that stress income.

Investors in CDs and bonds know exactly how much income they will receive each year. The dividends paid to stockholders can and do vary, even for the largest and most stable corporations. However, a number of corporations have built their reputations on a policy of paying dividends every three months. As with dividends from stock, the income from mutual funds and real estate also may vary from one year to the next.

Investment Growth To investors, *growth* means that their investments will increase in value. For example, a growing corporation such as Wal-Mart usually pays a small ash dividend or no dividend at all. Instead, profits are reinvested in the business (as etained earnings) to finance additional expansion. In this case, the value of their stock ıcreases as the corporation expands.

For investors who choose their investments carefully, both mutual funds and real state may offer substantial growth possibilities. More speculative investments such as recious metals, gemstones, and collectibles (antiques and paintings) offer less preictable growth possibilities. Generally, corporate and government bonds are purhased for income, not growth. And investments in commodities and stock options sually stress immediate returns as opposed to continued growth.

nvestment Liquidity **Liquidity** is the ease with which an investment can be conerted into cash. Investments range from cash or cash equivalents (such as investments n government securities or money-market accounts) to the other extreme of frozen nvestments, which you cannot convert easily into cash.

liquidity the ease with which an investment can be converted into cash

Although you may be able to sell stock, mutual fund, and corporate bond investnents quickly, you may not regain the amount of money you originally invested beause of market conditions, economic conditions, or many other reasons. It also may e difficult to find buyers for real estate. For example, the owner of real estate may ave to lower the asking price to find a buyer for a property. And finding a buyer for nvestments in certain types of collectibles also may be difficult.

low Securities Are Bought and Sold

learning objective

3 Describe how securities are bought and sold.

To purchase a Geoffrey Beene sweater, you simply walk into a store that sells these weaters, choose one, and pay for it. To purchase stocks, bonds, mutual funds, and nany other investments, you often work through a representative—your account xecutive or stockbroker. In turn, your account executive must buy or sell for you in ither the primary or secondary market.

The Primary Market

The **primary market** is a market in which an investor purchases financial securities via an investment bank) directly from the issuer of those securities. As mentioned in Chapter 20, an *investment banking firm* is an organization that assists corporations in aising funds, usually by helping sell new issues of stocks, bonds, or other financial seurities. Typically, this type of stock or security offering is referred to as an *initial pubic offering* (IPO). An example of an IPO sold through the primary market is the ommon stock issue sold by United Parcel Service (UPS) that raised over $5 billion. n fact, UPS currently holds the record as the largest American IPO ever. Because this vas an IPO, the money investors paid for the stock went to UPS. (Although stock can e sold again and again in the secondary market—as you will see later in this section— he company only receives money from the IPO for the first time it is sold to the pubic.) Other highly visible companies that have sold stock to raise capital include Home Depot, Microsoft, Lucent Technologies, and E-bay. Because of the economic downurn, the number of IPOs has decreased in number in recent years. Still, companies uch as WellChoice, Inc., China Telecom, Dick's Sporting Goods, and Provident Financial Services are just a few of the corporations that have sold stock in the last part of 2002 and 2003. *Caution:* The promise of quick profits often lures investors to purhase an IPO. Investors should be aware, however, that an IPO is generally classified as a **high-risk investment**—one made in the uncertain hope of earning a relatively arge profit in a short time. Depending on the corporation selling the new security, IPOs may be too speculative for most people.

primary market a market in which an investor purchases financial securities (via an investment bank) directly from the issuer of those securities

high-risk investment an investment made in the uncertain hope of earning a relatively large profit in a short time

For a large corporation, the decision to sell securities is often complicated, timeconsuming, and expensive. Such companies usually choose one of two basic methods. Large firms that need a lot of financing often use an investment banking firm to sell and distribute the new security issue. Analysts for the investment bank examine th corporation's financial condition to determine whether the company is financial sound and how difficult it will be to sell the new security issue. If the analysts for th investment banking firm are satisfied that the new security issue is a good risk, th bank will buy the securities and then resell them to its customers—institutional in vestors or individuals. **Institutional investors** are pension funds, insurance comp nies, mutual funds, banks, and other organizations that trade large quantities o securities. As pointed out in Chapter 20, the investment banking firm generall charges a fee of 2 to 20 percent of the proceeds received by the corporation issuing th securities.

institutional investors pension funds, insurance companies, mutual funds, banks, and other organizations that trade large quantities of securities

The second method used by a corporation trying to obtain financing through th primary market is to sell directly to current stockholders. Usually, promotional mate rials describing the new security issue are mailed to current stockholders. Thes stockholders may then purchase securities directly from the corporation. Why woul a corporation try to sell securities on its own? The most obvious reason is to avoid th investment bank's commission.

The Secondary Market

secondary market a market for existing financial securities that are traded between investors

After securities are sold originally through the primary market, shares of open corpo rations are traded on a regular basis through the secondary market. The **secondar market** is a market for existing financial securities that are traded between investor Usually, secondary-market transactions are completed through a securities exchang or the over-the-counter market.

securities exchange a marketplace where member brokers meet to buy and sell securities

Securities Exchanges A **securities exchange** is a marketplace where member bro kers meet to buy and sell securities. Generally, securities issued by larger, nationwid corporations are traded at the New York Stock Exchange, the American Stock Ex change, or at *regional exchanges* located in Chicago, Philadelphia, Boston, and sever other cities. The securities of very large corporations may be traded at more than on of these exchanges. Securities of firms also may be listed on foreign securities ex changes—in Tokyo, London, or Paris, for example.

One of the largest and best known securities exchange in the world is the Ne York Stock Exchange (NYSE). The NYSE lists over 3,000 corporate stocks, with total market value of $15 trillion.[2] Before a corporation's stock is approved for listin on the NYSE, the firm usually must meet four criteria (see Figure 21.1). The Ameri can Stock Exchange, regional exchanges, and the over-the-counter market have dif ferent listing requirements and account for the remainder of securities traded in th United States.

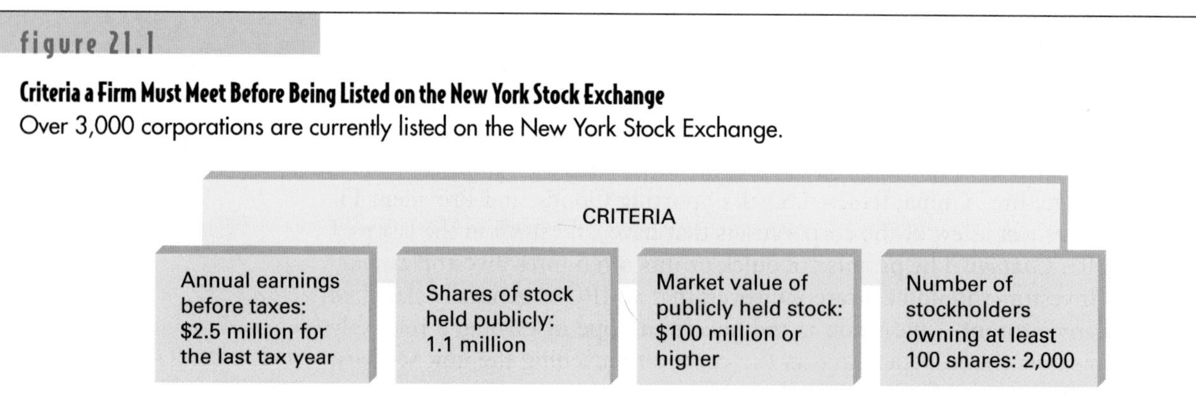

CRITERIA
Annual earnings before taxes: $2.5 million for the last tax year
Shares of stock held publicly: 1.1 million
Market value of publicly held stock: $100 million or higher
Number of stockholders owning at least 100 shares: 2,000

figure 21.1

Criteria a Firm Must Meet Before Being Listed on the New York Stock Exchange
Over 3,000 corporations are currently listed on the New York Stock Exchange.

Source: New York Stock Exchange, **www.nyse.com,** February 9, 2003.

The Over-the-Counter Market Stocks issued by several thousand companies are traded in the over-the-counter market. The **over-the-counter (OTC) market** is a network of dealers who buy and sell the stocks of corporations that are not listed on a securities exchange. The term *over-the-counter* was coined more than 100 years ago when securities were actually sold "over the counter" in stores and banks.

over-the-counter (OTC) market a network of dealers who buy and sell the stocks of corporations that are not listed on a securities exchange

Most OTC securities today are traded through an *electronic* exchange called the **Nasdaq** (pronounced "nazzdack"). The Nasdaq quotation system provides price information on over 5,000 different stocks. Begun in 1971 and regulated by the National Association of Securities Dealers, the Nasdaq is now one of the largest securities markets in the world. Today the Nasdaq is known for its forward-looking, innovative, growth companies. Although most companies that trade are small, the stock of some large firms, including Intel, Microsoft, Cisco Systems, and Dell Computer, is traded through the Nasdaq.

Nasdaq computerized electronic exchange system through which most over-the-counter securities are traded

When you want to sell shares of a company that trades on the Nasdaq—for example, Apple Computer—your account executive sends your order into the Nasdaq computer system, where it shows up on the screen, together with all the other orders from people who want to buy or sell Apple Computer. A Nasdaq dealer (sometimes referred to as a *marketmaker*) sits at a computer terminal putting together these buy and sell orders for Apple Computer. Once a match is found, your order is completed.

account executive an individual, sometimes called a *stockbroker* or *registered representative*, who buys and sells securities for clients

The Role of an Account Executive

An **account executive**—sometimes called a *stockbroker* or *registered representative*—is an individual who buys and sells securities for clients. Choosing an account executive can be difficult for at least two reasons. First, you must exercise a shrewd combination of trust and mistrust when you approach an account executive. Remember that you are interested in the broker's recommendations to increase your wealth, but the account executive is interested in your investment trading as a means to swell commissions. Unfortunately, some account executives are guilty of *churning*—a practice that generates commissions by excessive buying and selling of securities.

Second, you must decide whether you need a *full-service* broker or a *discount* broker. A full-service broker usually charges higher commissions but gives you personal investment advice and provides detailed research information. A discount broker simply executes buy and sell orders, usually over the phone or online. Most discount brokers offer no or very little free investment advice; you must make your own investment decisions. Some discount brokers will supply research reports for a nominal fee—usually $5 to $10.

Before deciding if you should use a full-service or a discount brokerage firm, you should consider how much help you need when making an investment decision. Many full-service brokerage firms argue that you need a professional to help you make important investment decisions. While this may be true for some investors, most account executives employed by full-service brokerage firms are too busy to spend unlimited time with you on a one-on-one basis, especially if you are investing a small amount. On the other side, many discount brokerage firms argue that you alone are responsible for making your investment decisions. And they argue that discount brokerage firms have both the personnel and research materials that can help you become a better investor.

At the New York Stock Exchange, people smile on a good day! Although individual stock prices can go up or down, the smiles on the faces of these people who work at the New York Stock Exchange (NYSE) indicate that stocks prices are climbing higher. Over 3000 corporate stocks are traded on the NYSE, which makes it one of the largest and best-known exchanges in the world.

The Mechanics of a Transaction Once investors have decided on a particular security, most

figure 21.2

Steps in a Typical Stock Transaction on the New York Stock Exchange
Although not quite a horse race, a typical stock transaction takes only about twenty minutes.

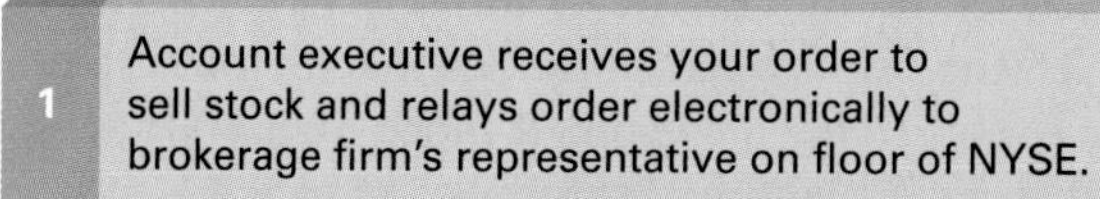

1
Account executive receives your order to
sell stock and relays order electronically to
brokerage firm's representative on floor of NYSE.

2 Firm's clerk signals transaction from booth to broker on stock-exchange floor.

3 Broker goes to trading post where stock is traded with a stock-exchange member who has an order to buy.

4 After the trade is executed, a notice is sent to the brokerage firm and the consolidated ticker tape.

5 Sale appears on the ticker tape, and confirmation is relayed to account executive, who notifies you of completed transaction.

market order a request that a security be purchased or sold at the current market price

limit order a request that a security be bought or sold at a price that is equal to or better than some specified price

discretionary order an order to buy or sell a security that lets the broker decide when to execute the transaction and at what price

simply telephone their account executive and place a market, limit, or discretionary order. A **market order** is a request that a security be purchased or sold at the current market price.

A **limit order** is a request that a security be bought or sold at a price equal to or better (lower for buying, higher for selling) than some specified price. Suppose that you place a limit order to *sell* Home Depot common stock at $21 per share. Your broker's representative sells the stock only if the price is $21 per share or *more*. If you place a limit order to *buy* Home Depot at $21, the representative buys it only if the price is $21 per share or *less*. Limit orders may or may not be transacted quickly depending on how close the limit price is to the current market price. Usually, a limit order is good for one day, one week, or one month or good until canceled (GTC).

Investors also can choose to place a discretionary order. A **discretionary order** is an order to buy or sell a security that lets the broker decide when to execute the transaction and at what price. *Caution:* Financial planners advise against using a discretionary order for two reasons. First, a discretionary order gives the account executive a great deal of authority. If the account executive makes a mistake, it is the investor who suffers the loss. Second, financial planners argue that only investors (with the help of their account executives) should make investment decisions.

Figure 21.2 illustrates one method of executing a market order to sell a stock listed on the NYSE at its current market value. The entire process, from receipt of the selling order to confirmation of the completed transaction, takes about twenty minutes. It is also possible for a brokerage firm to match a buy order for a security for one of its customers with a sell order for the same security from another of its customers. Let's say you want to purchase 100 shares of Johnson & Johnson at the market price. You call your account executive at Charles Schwab and place a buy order to purchase Johnson & Johnson. Your order is then "matched" with an order to sell 100 shares of Johnson & Johnson placed by another Charles Schwab customer. Matched orders are not completed through a security exchange or the over-the-counter market.

Regardless of how the security is bought or sold, payment for stocks, bonds, and other financial securities generally is required within three business days of the transaction.

Online Security Transactions A good investment software package can help you evaluate potential investments, manage your investments, monitor their value more closely, *and* place buy and sell orders online. While a computer and software can provide the information you need to make decisions about buying and selling stocks, bonds, and other financial securities, you are still the one who has to analyze the information and make the final decision. As a rule of thumb, the more active an investor is, the more it makes sense to use computers.

Although most people still prefer to talk with their account executive by telephone, a growing number of investors are using computers to complete security transactions. As you will see in the next section, one very good reason for trading securities online is the lower cost.

Another kind of computerized transaction is called *program trading*. **Program trading** is a computer-driven program to buy or sell selected stocks. When program trading is used, a computer monitors the market value of stocks and other securities. If security prices increase or decrease to a specified amount, the computer enters an order to buy or sell. Generally, institutional investors such as pension funds, mutual funds, banks, and insurance companies use program trading to monitor the value of their securities.

Using the Internet

Online brokerage firms such as American Express (**www.americanexpress.com/direct**), Ameritrade (**www.ameritrade.com**), E*Trade (**www.etrade.com**), Charles Schwab (**www.schwab.com**), and Harris*direct* (**www.harrisdirect.com**) are among the top online trading sites. These sites allow investors to open an account, get quotes, get investment advice, research investments, and more.

program trading a computer-driven program to buy or sell selected stocks

Commissions Most brokerage firms have a minimum commission ranging from $25 to $55 for buying and selling stock. Additional commission charges are based on the number of shares and the value of stock bought and sold. On the trading floor, stocks are traded in round lots. A **round lot** is a unit of 100 shares of a particular stock. An **odd lot** is fewer than 100 shares of a particular stock. Brokerage firms generally charge more for odd-lot transactions.

round lot a unit of 100 shares of a particular stock

odd lot fewer than 100 shares of a particular stock

Table 21.2 shows typical commission fees charged by online brokerage firms. Generally, online transactions are less expensive when compared with the costs of trading securities through a full-service or discount brokerage firm. As illustrated in Table 21.2, commissions for stock transactions can be as low as $10 per trade. As a rule of thumb, full-service brokerage firms charge as much as 1½ to 2 percent of the transaction amount. For example, if you use a full-service brokerage firm such as Morgan Stanley to purchase ExxonMobil stock valued at $10,000, and the brokerage firm charges 1½ percent, you will pay commissions totaling $150 ($\$10{,}000 \times 0.015 = \$150$). Discount brokerage firms, on the other hand, would charge commissions ranging between $55 to $85. Commissions for trading bonds, commodities, and options usually are lower than those for trading stocks. The charge for buying or selling a $1,000 corporate bond is typically $10 to $20. With the exception of most mutual funds, the investor generally pays a commission when buying *and* selling securities.

It should be apparent that vast sums of money are involved in securities trading. In an effort to protect investors from unfair treatment, both federal and state governments have acted to regulate securities trading.

table 21.2 Typical Commission Costs Charged by Online Brokerage Firms for a Transaction in Which 1,000 Shares Are Bought or Sold

	Internet	Interactive Voice Response Telephone System	Broker-Assisted
Ameritrade	$10.00	$14.99	$24.99
E*Trade	$14.99	$14.99	$59.99
HarrisDirect	$20.00	$20.00	$40.00
Schwab	$29.95	$49.95	$159.00
TD Waterhouse	$17.95	$35.00	$45.00

Source: The Ameritrade website, **www.ameritrade.com,** February 11, 2003.

Regulation of Securities Trading

Government regulation of securities began as a response to abusive and fraudulen practices in the sale of stocks, bonds, and other financial securities. The states wer the first to react, early in this century. Later, federal legislation was passed to regulat the interstate sale of securities.

State Regulation The first state law regulating the sale of securities was enacted i Kansas in 1911. Today, most states require that new issues be registered with a stat agency and that brokers and securities dealers operating within the state be licensed The states also provide for the prosecution of individuals accused of the fraudulen sale of stocks, bonds, and other securities.

Federal Regulation The *Securities Act of 1933*, sometimes referred to as the *Trut in Securities Act*, provides for full disclosure of important facts about corporations issu ing new securities. Such corporations are required to file a *registration statement* con taining specific information about the corporation's earnings, assets, and liabilities; it products or services; and the qualifications of its top management. Publication of a prospectus that can be given to prospective investors is also a requirement. A **prospectus** is a detailed, written description of a new security, the issuing corpora tion, and the corporation's top management.

prospectus a detailed written description of a new security, the issuing corporation, and the corporation's top management

Securities and Exchange Commission (SEC) the agency that enforces federal securities regulations

National Association of Securities Dealers (NASD) the organization responsible for the self-regulation of the over-the-counter securities market

The *Securities Exchange Act of 1934* created the **Securities and Exchange Commission (SEC)**, which is the agency that enforces federal securities regulations. The 1934 act gave the SEC the power to regulate trading on all national securities exchanges. It also requires that corporations' registration statements be brought up to date periodically. Finally, this act requires brokers and securities dealers to register with the SEC. Ten other federal acts have been passed primarily to protect investors:

- The *Maloney Act of 1938* made it possible to establish the **National Association of Securities Dealers (NASD)** to oversee self-regulation of the over-the-counter securities market.
- The *Investment Company Act of 1940* placed investment companies that sell mutual funds under the jurisdiction of the SEC.

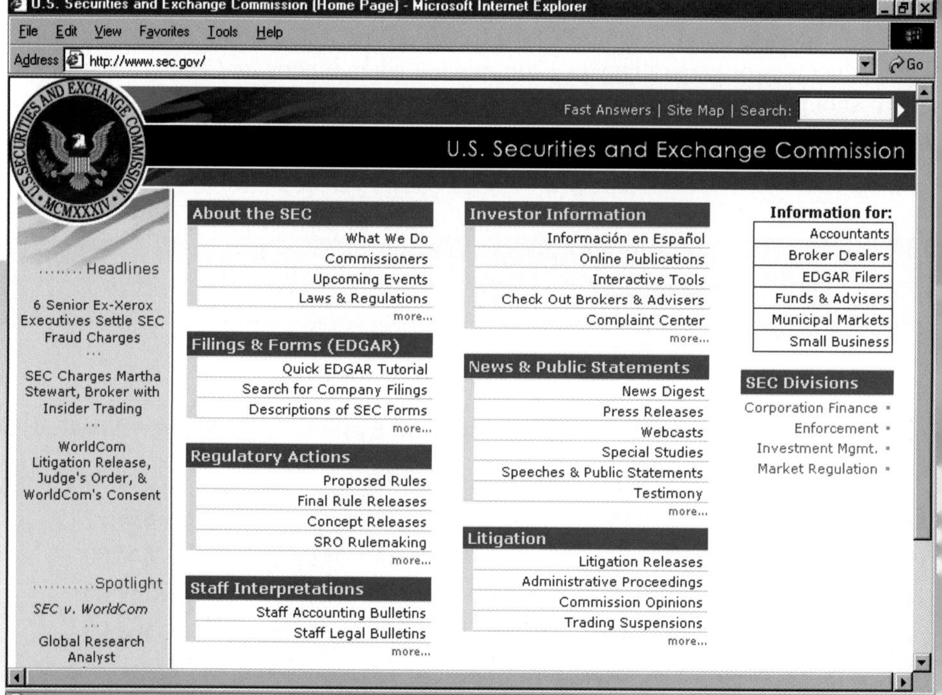

Don't mess with the SEC! Today, the SEC is cracking down on corporations that "cook" their books by enforcing stricter financial and accounting standards. But that's not all the SEC does. This federal agency also provides investors with a wealth of information about the corporations that issue stocks and other securities on its website at **www.sec.gov**.

- The *Investment Advisers Act of 1940* required financial advisers with more than fifteen clients to register with the SEC.
- The *Federal Securities Act of 1964* extended the SEC's jurisdiction to include companies whose stock is sold over the counter if they have total assets of at least $1 million or have more than 500 stockholders of any one class of stock.
- The *Securities Investor Protection Act of 1970* created the *Securities Investor Protection Corporation* (SIPC). The SIPC provides insurance of up to $500,000 per customer, including $100,000 for cash left on deposit with a brokerage firm that later fails.
- The *Securities Amendments Act of 1975* prohibited fixed commissions. As a result, commissions now vary from one brokerage firm to another.
- The *Insider Trading Sanctions Act of 1984* strengthened the penalty provisions of the Securities Exchange Act of 1934. This act applies not only to people who buy or sell using nonpublic information but also to anyone who gives such information or aids such individuals. This act also expanded the SEC's power to investigate such illegal behavior.
- The *Insider Trading and Securities Fraud Enforcement Act of 1988* made the top management of brokerage firms responsible for reporting to the SEC any transaction based on inside information. In addition, this act empowered the SEC to levy fines of up to $1 million for failure to report such trading violations.
- The *Financial Services Modernization Banking Act of 1999* repealed the Glass-Steagall Act of 1933 and portions of the Bank Holding Company Act of 1956. This act allows banks to establish one-stop financial supermarkets where customers can bank, buy and sell securities, and purchase insurance coverage.
- The Sarbanes-Oxley Act of 2002 required the CEOs of public corporations to swear to the accuracy of the financial reports they submit to the SEC. If they do not, they may be prosecuted and imprisoned or heavily fined. Also, the legislation outlaws destroying or altering company files to obstruct investigation of potential fraud, and it requires lawyers to bring questionable activities to the attention of senior management or the company's board of directors. Additional material on this act was presented in Chapter 18.

Traditional Investment Alternatives

learning objective

4 Identify the advantages and disadvantages of savings accounts, bonds, stocks, mutual funds, and real estate.

In this section we look at traditional investments; in the next section we explore high-risk investments. A number of the investments listed in Table 21.3 have been discussed. Others have only been mentioned and will be examined in more detail. We

table 21.3 Investment Alternatives

Traditional investments involve less risk than high-risk investments.

Traditional	High Risk
Bank accounts	Short transactions
Corporate and government bonds	Margin transactions
Common stock	Stock options
Preferred stock	Commodities
Mutual funds	Precious metals
Real estate	Gemstones
	Coins/antiques/collectibles

begin this section with an overview of how portfolio management can reduce invest ment risk. Then we describe how specific investments can help you to reach your in vestment goals.

Portfolio Management

By now you are probably thinking, "How can I choose the right investment?" Goo question! Unfortunately, there are no easy answers because your investment goal age, tolerance for risk, and financial resources available for investment purposes ar different than those of the next person. To help you decide what investment is righ for you, consider the following: Although the period from 1999 to 2003 has been "bummer" for the stock market, stocks still have outperformed other investment al ternatives over a long period of time. Since 1900, stocks have returned approxi mately 10 percent a year. During the same period, U.S. Treasury bills an government bonds have returned about 4 percent.[3] And projections by well-re spected Roger Ibbotson, chairman of Ibbotson Associates, an investment consulting software, and research firm, indicate that these same investments will perform a about the same pace between now and the year 2025.[4] Therefore, why not just in vest all your money in stocks or mutual funds that invest in stocks? After all, the offer the largest potential return? In reality, stocks have a place in every investmen portfolio, but there is more to investing than just picking a bunch of stocks or stoc mutual funds.

Asset Allocation, the Time Factor, and Your Age

asset allocation the process of spreading your money among several different types of investments to lessen risk

Asset allocation is the process of spreading your money among several different type of investments to lessen risk. While the term *asset allocation* is a fancy way of saying i simply put, it really means that you need to diversify and avoid the pitfall of putting a of your eggs in one basket—a common mistake made by investors. Asset allocation i often expressed in percentages. For example, what percentage of my assets do I wan to put in stocks and mutual funds? What percentage do I want to put in more conser vative investments such as CDs or government bonds? In reality, the answers to thes questions are often tied to your tolerance for risk.

Two other factors—the time your investments have to work for you and you age—also should be considered before deciding where to invest your money. Th amount of time you have before you need your investment money is crucial. If yo can leave your investments alone and let them work for five to ten years or more then you can invest in stocks, mutual funds, or real estate. On the other hand, if yo need your investment money in two years, you probably should invest in short-term government bonds, highly rated corporate bonds, or CDs. By taking a more conser vative approach for short-term investments, you reduce the possibility of having t sell your investments at a loss because of depressed market value or a staggerin economy.

You also should consider your age when developing an investment program Younger investors tend to invest a large percentage of their nest egg in growth-ori ented investments. If their investments take a nosedive, they have time to recover On the other hand, older investors tend to choose more conservative investments As a result, a smaller percentage of their nest egg is placed in growth-oriented invest ments. How much of your portfolio should be in growth-oriented investments Well-known personal financial expert Suze Orman suggests that you subtract you age from 110, and the difference is the percentage of your assets that should be in vested in growth investments. For example, if you are 30 years old, subtract 30 from 110, which gives you 80. Therefore, 80 percent of your assets should be invested in growth-oriented investments, whereas the remaining 30 percent should be kept in safer conservative investments.[5] Now it's time to take a closer look at specific invest ment alternatives.

Bank Accounts

Bank accounts that pay interest—and therefore are investments—include passbook savings accounts, CDs, and interest-bearing accounts. These were discussed in Chapter 19. The interest paid on bank accounts can be withdrawn to serve as income, or it can be left on deposit and increase the value of the bank account and provide for growth. At the time of this publication, one-year CDs were paying between 1.5 and 2.5 percent. While CDs and other bank accounts are risk-free for all practical purposes, many investors often choose other investments because of the potential for larger returns.

Corporate and Government Bonds

In Chapter 20 we discussed the issuing of bonds by corporations to obtain financing. The U.S. government and state and local governments also issue bonds for the same reason.

Corporate Bonds Because they are a form of long-term debt financing that must be repaid, bonds generally are considered a more conservative investment than either stocks or mutual funds. One of the principal advantages of corporate bonds is that they are primarily long-term, income-producing investments. Between the time of purchase and the maturity date, the bondholder will receive interest payments—usually semiannually, or every six months—at the stated interest rate. For example, assume that you purchase a \$1,000 bond issued by General Electric Capital Corporation and that the interest rate for this bond is 6.25 percent. In this situation, you receive interest of \$62.50 (\$1,000 × 0.0625 = \$62.50) a year from the corporation. General Electric Capital Corporation pays the interest every six months in \$31.25 installments.

Most beginning investors think that a \$1,000 bond is always worth \$1,000. In reality, the price of a bond may fluctuate until its maturity date. Changes in the overall interest rates in the economy are the primary cause of most bond price fluctuations. For example, when overall interest rates in the economy are rising, the market value of existing bonds with a fixed interest rate typically declines. They may then be purchased for less than their face value. By holding such bonds until maturity or until overall interest rates decline (causing the bond's market value to increase), bond owners can sell their bonds for more than they paid for them. In this case, the difference between the purchase price and the selling price is profit and is in addition to annual interest income.

A typical corporate bond transaction is illustrated in Table 21.4. Assume that on February 10, 1992, you purchased an 8.125 percent corporate bond issued by AT&T Corporation. Your cost for the bond was \$910 plus a \$10 commission, for a total investment of \$920. Also assume that you held the bond until February 10, 2003, and then sold it at its current market value of \$990. As illustrated in Table 21.4 (on p. 644), your total return for this bond transaction, including interest, is \$954. Also notice that most of your total return was the result of receiving interest on your AT&T bond investment over an eleven-year period. In fact, this example illustrates the fact that most investors choose bonds because of interest income and not necessarily for the growth potential that bond investments offer.

We should point out that everything in the bond investment illustrated in Table 21.4 went "as planned." However, remember that the price of a corporate bond can decrease and that interest payments and eventual repayment may be a problem for a corporation that encounters financial difficulty. When AMR, the parent company of American Airlines, encountered financial difficulties because of decreased passengers and mounting expenses after September 11, 2001, the firm's bond ratings were lowered by the major ratings agencies in the United States. As a result, AMR's bonds immediately dropped in value because of questions concerning the prospects of repayment.

table 21.4 Sample Corporate Bond Transaction for AT&T Corporation

Assumptions: Face value, $1,000; annual interest, 8.125 percent; maturity date, 2022; purchased February 10, 1992, for $910; sold February 10, 2003, for $990

Costs When Purchased		Return When Sold	
1 bond @ $910	$910	1 bond @ $990	$990
Plus commission	+ 10	Minus commission	− 10
Total investment	$920	Total return	$980

Transaction Summary

Total return when sold	$980
Minus total investment	− 920
Profit from bond sale	$ 60
Plus interest (11 years)	+ 894
Total return for this transaction	$954

Source: Price data and interest amounts were taken from the Yahoo Finance website, **http://finance.yahoo.com,** June 10, 2002, and the *Wall Street Journal*, February 11, 2003, p. C13.

Convertible Bonds Some corporations prefer to issue convertible bonds because they carry a lower interest rate than nonconvertible bonds—by about 1 to 2 percent. In return for accepting a lower interest rate, owners of convertible bonds have the opportunity for increased investment growth. For example, assume that you purchase a Kerr McGee $1,000 corporate bond that is convertible to 16.373 shares of the company's common stock. This means that you could convert the bond to common stock whenever the price of the company's stock is $61.08 (1,000 ÷ 16.373 = $61.08) or higher. However, owners may opt not to convert their bonds to common stock even if the market value of the common stock does increase to $61.08 or more. The reason for not exercising the conversion feature is quite simple. As the market value of the common stock increases, the price of the convertible bond also increases. By not converting to common stock, bondholders enjoy interest income from the bond in addition to the increased bond value caused by the price movement of the common stock.

Government Bonds The federal government sells bonds and securities to finance both the national debt and the government's ongoing activities. Generally, investors choose from four different types of U.S. government bonds:

1. *Treasury bills*—Treasury bills, sometimes called *T-bills*, are sold in minimum units of $1,000, with additional increments of $1,000 above the minimum. Although the maturities may be as long as one year, the Treasury Department currently only sells T-bills with four-, thirteen-, and twenty-six-week maturities.
2. *Treasury notes*—Treasury notes are issued in $1,000 units with a maturity of more than one year but not more than ten years. Typical maturities are two, five, and ten years.
3. *Treasury bonds*—A Treasury bond is issued in minimum units of $1,000 and has maturities ranging from ten to thirty years. (*Note:* The Treasury Department no longer issues Treasury bonds. However, many are still in existence and may be purchased in the secondary market.)
4. *Savings bonds*—Series EE bonds, often called *U.S. Savings Bonds*, are purchased for one-half their maturity value. Thus a $100 bond costs $50 when purchased. (*Note:* If the income derived from savings bonds is used to pay qualified college expenses, it is exempt from federal taxation.)

The main reason investors choose U.S. government bonds is that they consider them risk-free. The other side of the coin is that these bonds pay lower interest than most other investments.

Like the federal government, state and local governments sell bonds to obtain financing. A **municipal bond**, sometimes called a *muni*, is a debt security issued by a state or local government. One of the most important features of municipal bonds is that the interest on them may be exempt from federal taxes. Whether or not the interest on municipal bonds is tax exempt often depends on how the funds obtained from their sale are used. *Caution: It is your responsibility, as an investor, to determine whether or not the interest paid by municipal bonds is taxable. It is also your responsibility to evaluate municipal bonds.* Although most municipal bonds are relatively safe, defaults have occurred in recent years.

municipal bond sometimes called a *muni*, a debt security issued by a state or local government

Common Stock

How do you make money by buying common stock? Basically, there are three ways: through dividend payments, through an increase in the value of the stock, or through stock splits. Before reading the material on stocks presented below, read Exploring Business to see how Warren Buffett became the ultimate investor.

Dividend Payments One of the reasons why many stockholders invest in common stock is *dividend income*. Generally, dividends are paid on a quarterly basis. Although corporations are under no legal obligation to pay dividends, most corporate board members like to keep stockholders happy (and prosperous). Therefore, board members usually declare dividends if the corporation's after-tax profits are sufficient to do so. A corporation may pay stock dividends in place of—or in addition to—cash dividends. A **stock dividend** is a dividend in the form of additional stock. It is paid to shareholders just as cash dividends are paid: in proportion to the number of shares owned. An individual stockholder may sell the additional stock to obtain income or retain it to increase the total value of his or her stock holdings.

stock dividend a dividend in the form of additional stock

exploring business

Warren Buffett: The Ultimate Investor

WARREN BUFFETT is one of the world's most successful investors—and perhaps the best known as well. A native of Omaha, Nebraska, Buffett made his first investment at age 11, buying three shares of Cities Service and selling them for a net profit of $5. He started a series of small businesses to earn money during high school and college and then began building his fortune through smart investments after attending Columbia Business School. In just six years Buffett's smart stock picks swelled his account from $9,800 to $140,000.

Today his company, Berkshire Hathaway, owns shares in many corporate giants, including American Express and Coca-Cola. It is also the sole owner of an extremely diverse portfolio of companies, including GEICO (insurance), Mid-American Energy (electric and gas power), Dairy Queen (ice cream), and Jordan's Furniture (furniture retailer; see Chapter 16's Video Case). In total, Berkshire Hathaway's annual earnings top $3 billion, and a single share of its stock sells for more than $70,000. Over the years, the company has assembled a stock portfolio now worth roughly $26 billion.

How does Buffett do it? One of his key rules is to buy and hold for the long term. A second rule is to carefully analyze the company, not just the stock. For example, having been a young news carrier for the *Washington Post*, Buffett was well aware of the newspaper's quality. Recognizing the company's long-lasting value, he bought shares more than thirty years ago and has held them ever since.

A third rule is that a good investor does not simply follow the crowd. Many people scoffed when Buffett refused to get caught up in the brief, heady stampede to invest in Internet stocks. But looking back on the initial dot-com boom and the subsequent bust, he explains, "You can't do well in investments unless you think independently." Whether the market goes up or down, Buffett stresses: "Investors need to avoid the negatives of buying fads, crummy companies, and timing the market."

table 21.5 Sample Common-Stock Transaction for General Mills

Assumptions: 100 shares of common stock purchased on February 10, 2000, for $30 a share; 100 shares sold on February 10, 2003, for $45 a share; dividends for 3 years total $3.36 a share.

Costs When Purchased		Return When Sold	
100 shares @ $30	$3,000	100 shares @ $45	$4,500
Plus commission	+ 55	Minus commission	− 70
Total investment	$3,055	Total return	$4,430

Transaction Summary

Total return	$4,430
Minus total investment	− 3,055
Profit from stock sale	$1,375
Plus total dividends (3 years)	+ 336
Total return for this transaction	$1,711

Source: Price data and dividend amounts were taken from the Yahoo Finance website, **http://finance.yahoo.com,** February 11, 2003.

capital gain the difference between a security's purchase price and selling price

market value the price of one share of a stock at a particular time

Increase in Dollar Value Another way to make money on stock investments is through capital gains. A **capital gain** is the difference between a security's purchase price and its selling price. To earn a capital gain, you must sell when the market value of the stock is higher than the original purchase price. The **market value** is the price of one share of the stock at a particular time. Let's assume that on February 10, 2000, you purchase 100 shares of General Mills at a cost of $30 a share and that you paid $55 in commission charges, for a total investment of $3,055. Let's also assume that you held your 100 shares until February 10, 2003, and then sold the General Mills stock for $45 a share. Your total return on investment is shown in Table 21.5. You realized a profit of $1,711 because you received dividends totaling $3.36 a share and because the stock's market value increased by $15 a share. Of course, if the stock's market value had decreased, or if the firm's board of directors had voted to reduce or omit dividends, your return would have been less than the total dollar return illustrated in Table 21.5.

Stock Splits Directors of many corporations feel that there is an optimal price range within which their firm's stock is most attractive to investors. When the market value increases beyond that

E*TRADE makes it easy to invest online! Not only can you buy and sell stocks, mutual funds, bonds, and other securities online when you access the E*TRADE website, you can also obtain research information that will help you make better investment decisions. In addition to the website, E*TRADE also has physical locations such as this Financial Center in San Francisco.

range, they may declare a *stock split* to bring the price down. A **stock split** is the division of each outstanding share of a corporation's stock into a greater number of shares.

stock split the division of each outstanding share of a corporation's stock into a greater number of shares

The most common stock splits result in one, two, or three new shares for each original share. For example, in 2003, the board of directors of Microsoft Corporation approved a two-for-one stock split. After this split, a stockholder who originally owned 100 shares owned 200 shares. The value of an original share was proportionally reduced. In the case of Microsoft, the market value per share was reduced to half the stock's value before the two-for-one stock split. Every shareholder retained his or her proportional ownership of the firm. *Although there are no guarantees*, the stock is more attractive to the investing public because of the potential for a rapid increase in dollar value. This attraction is based on the belief that most corporations split their stock only when their financial future is improving and on the upswing.

Preferred Stock

As we noted in Chapter 20, a firm's preferred stockholders must receive their dividends before common stockholders are paid any dividend. Moreover, the terms of payment of a preferred-stock dividend are specified on the stock certificate. And the owners of preferred stock have first claim, after bond owners and general creditors, on corporate assets if the firm is dissolved or enters bankruptcy. These features make preferred stock a more conservative investment with an added degree of safety and a more predictable income when compared with common stock.

In addition, owners of preferred stock may gain through special features offered with certain preferred stock issues. Owners of *cumulative* preferred stocks are assured that omitted dividends will be paid to them before common stockholders receive any dividends. Owners of *convertible* preferred stock may profit through growth as well as dividends. When the value of a firm's common stock increases, the market value of its *convertible* preferred stock also grows. Convertible preferred stock thus combines the lower risk of preferred stock with the possibility of greater speculative gain through conversion to common stock.

Mutual Funds

In the 1990s, people loved their mutual funds. With a few exceptions, investors expected and got big returns each year until the end of the 1990s. Then the bubble burst. Since 1999, many people have firsthand knowledge that the value of mutual funds shares can decline. Still, they are the investment of choice for many investors, and there are plenty of funds from which to choose. In 1970 there were only about 400 mutual funds. In mid-2003 there were approximately 8,300 mutual funds.[6]

A **mutual fund** combines and invests the funds of many investors under the guidance of a professional manager. The major advantages of a mutual fund are its professional management and its diversification, or investment in a wide variety of securities. Diversification spells safety because an occasional loss incurred with one security usually is offset by gains from other investments.

mutual fund a professionally managed investment vehicle that combines and invests the funds of many individual investors

Mutual Fund Basics A *closed-end* mutual fund sells shares in the fund to investors only when the fund is originally organized. And only a specified number of shares are made available at that time. Once all the shares are sold, an investor must purchase shares from some other investor who is willing to sell them. The mutual fund itself is under no obligation to buy back shares from investors. Shares of closed-end mutual funds are traded on the floor of stock exchanges such as the NYSE or in the OTC market. The investment company sponsoring an *open-end* mutual fund issues and sells new shares to any investor who requests them. It also buys back shares from investors who wish to sell all or part of their holdings.

The share value for any mutual fund is determined by calculating its net asset value. **Net asset value (NAV)** per share is equal to the current market value of the mutual fund's portfolio minus the mutual fund's liabilities and divided by the number

net asset value (NAV) current market value of a mutual fund's portfolio minus the mutual fund's liabilities and divided by the number of outstanding shares

of outstanding shares. For most mutual funds, NAV is calculated at least once a day and is reported in newspapers, financial publications, and on the Internet.

With regard to costs, there are two types of mutual funds: load and no-load funds. An individual who invests in a *load fund* pays a sales charge every time he or she purchases shares. This charge may be as high as 8.5 percent. While many exceptions exist, the average load charge for mutual funds is between 3 and 5 percent. The purchaser of shares in a *no-load fund* pays no sales charges at all. Since no-load funds offer the same type of investment opportunities as load funds, you should investigate them further before deciding which type of mutual fund is best for you.

Mutual funds also collect a yearly management fee of about 0.25 to 2 percent of the total dollar amount of assets in the fund. While fees vary considerably, the average management fee is between 0.50 and 1.25 percent of the fund's assets. In addition, some funds charge a redemption fee (sometimes called a *contingent deferred sales fee*) of 1 to 5 percent of the total amount withdrawn from a mutual fund during the first five to seven years. Finally, some mutual funds charge a 12b-1 fee (sometimes referred to as a *distribution fee*) to defray the costs of advertising and marketing the mutual fund. Approved by the SEC in 1980, annual 12b-1 fees are calculated on the value of a fund's assets and are approximately 1 percent of the fund's assets. Unlike the one-time sales load fees that mutual funds charge to purchase *or* sell mutual fund shares, the management fee and the 12b-1 fee are ongoing fees charged each year.

Today, mutual funds also can be classified as A, B, or C shares. With A shares, investors pay commissions when they purchase shares in the mutual fund. With B shares, investors pay commissions when money is withdrawn or shares are sold during the first five to seven years. With C shares, investors pay no commissions to buy or sell shares but must pay higher ongoing management and 12b-1 fees.

Managed Funds versus Indexed Funds Most mutual funds are managed funds. In other words, there is a professional fund manager (or team of managers) who chooses the securities that are contained in the fund. The fund manager also decides when to buy and sell securities in the fund. Ultimately, the fund manager is responsible for the fund's success.

Instead of investing in a managed fund, some investors choose to invest in an index fund. Why? The answer to this question is simple: Over many years, index funds have outperformed almost 85 percent of all managed funds.[7] Simply put: It is hard to beat an index such as the Standard & Poor's 500. If the individual securities included in an index increase in value, the index goes up. Because an index mutual fund is a mirror image of a specific index, the dollar value of a share in an index fund also increases when the index increases. Unfortunately, the reverse is true. Index funds, sometimes called *passive funds*, have managers, but they simply buy the stocks or bonds contained in the index. A second reason why investors choose index funds is the lower expense ratio charged by these passively managed funds. (*Note:* Various indexes are discussed later in this chapter.)

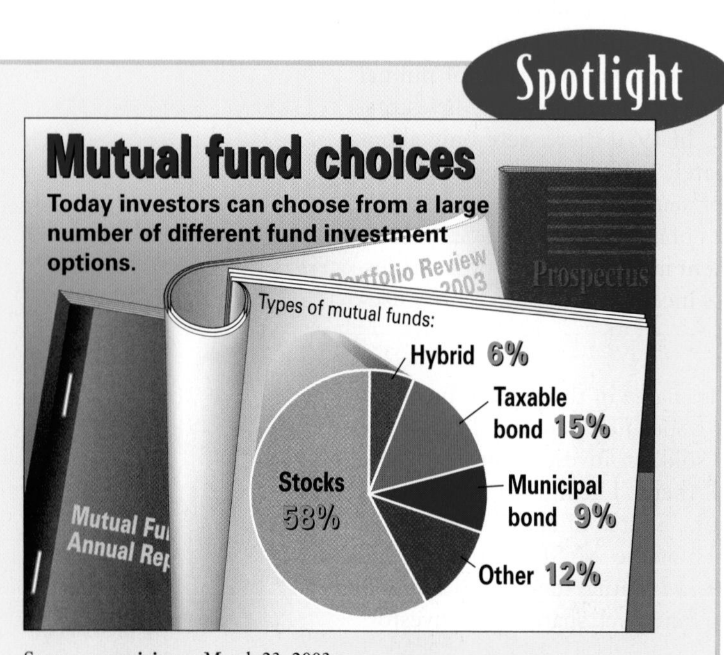

Source: **www.ici.org**, March 23, 2003.

Mutual Fund Investments It would take a whole book to describe all the mutual funds available today. In summary, however, mutual fund managers tailor their investment portfolios to provide growth, income, or a combination of both. The following list describes the major categories of mutual funds in terms of the types of securities they invest in:

- *Aggressive-growth funds* invest in stocks whose prices are expected to increase dramatically in a short period of time.
- *Asset-allocation funds* invest in various asset classes, including, but not limited to, stocks, bonds, and other fixed-income securities and money-market instruments.
- *Balanced funds* apportion their investments among common stocks, preferred stock, and bonds.
- *Bond funds* invest in federal, municipal, and/or corporate bonds that provide investors with interest income.
- *Global funds* invest in stocks, bonds, and other securities issued by firms throughout the world, including the United States.
- *Growth funds* invest in the common stock of well-managed, rapidly growing corporations.
- *Growth-income funds* invest in common and preferred stocks that pay good dividends *and* are expected to increase in market value.
- *Income funds* invest in stocks and bonds that pay high dividends and interest.
- *Index funds* invest in the same companies included in an index such as the Standard & Poor's 500 Stock Index.
- *International funds* invest in foreign stocks sold in securities markets throughout the world. Unlike global funds, which invest in stocks issued by companies in both foreign nations and the United States, a true international fund invests outside the United States.
- *Money-market funds* invest in CDs, government securities, and other safe and highly liquid investments.
- *Sector funds* invest in companies within the same industry. Examples of sectors include biotech, science, and technology and computers.
- *Small-cap funds* invest in smaller companies that offer higher growth potential and higher risk when compared with funds that invest in larger, more conservative companies.

Mutual funds designed to meet just about any conceivable investment objective are available. To help investors obtain their investment objectives, most investment companies now allow shareholders to switch from one fund to another fund within the same family of funds. A **family of funds** exists when one investment company manages a group of mutual funds. For example, shareholders, at their option, can change from the AIM Global Aggressive Growth fund to the AIM Value fund. Generally, investors may give instructions to switch from one fund to another fund within the same family either in writing, over the telephone, or via the Internet. Charges for exchanges, if any, are small for each transaction. For funds that do charge, the fee may be as low as $5 per transaction.

family of funds a group of mutual funds managed by one investment company

Real Estate

Real estate ownership represents one of the best hedges against inflation, but it—like all investments—has its risks. A piece of property in a poor location, for example, actually can decrease in value—as a number of people who bought land in the Florida Everglades from unscrupulous promoters learned to their dismay. Table 21.6 (on p. 650) cites some of the many factors you should consider before investing in real estate.

There are, of course, disadvantages to any investment, and real estate is no exception. If you want to sell your property, you must find an interested buyer with the ability to obtain enough money to complete the transaction. Finding such a buyer can be difficult if loan money is scarce, the real estate market is in a decline, or you overpaid for a piece of property. If you are forced to hold your investment longer than you originally planned, taxes, interest, and installment payments can be a heavy burden. As a rule, real estate increases in value and eventually sells at a profit, but there are no guarantees. The degree of your success depends on how well you evaluate different alternatives.

table 21.6 Real Estate Checklist

Although real estate offers one of the best hedges against inflation, not all property increases in value. Many factors should be considered before investing in real estate.

Evaluation of Property	Inspection of the Surrounding Neighborhood	Other Factors
Is the property priced competitively with similar property?	What are the present zoning requirements?	Why are the present owners selling the property?
What type of financing, if any, is available?	Is the neighborhood's population increasing or decreasing?	How long will you have to hold the property before selling it to someone else?
How much are the taxes?	What is the average income of people in the area?	How much profit can you reasonably expect to obtain?
	What is the state of repair of surrounding property? Do most of the buildings and homes need repair?	Is there a chance that the property value will decrease?

High-Risk Investment Techniques

learning objective 5 Describe high-risk investment techniques.

As defined earlier in this chapter, a high-risk investment is one made in the uncertain hope of earning a relatively large profit in a short time. (See the high-risk investment category in Table 21.3.) Most high-risk investments become so because of the methods used by investors to earn a quick profit. These methods can lead to large losses as well as to impressive gains. They should not be used by anyone who does not fully understand the risks involved. We begin this section with a discussion of selling short—an investment method that can be used when the stock market is in decline. Then we examine margin transactions and other high-risk investments.

Selling Short

buying long buying stock with the expectation that it will increase in value and can then be sold at a profit

selling short the process of selling stock that an investor does not actually own but has borrowed from a brokerage firm and will repay at a later date

Normally, you buy stocks expecting that they will increase in value and can then be sold at a profit. This procedure is referred to as **buying long.** However, many securities decrease in value for various reasons. Consider what happened to the values of many stocks between 1999 and 2003. Because of the nation's depressed economy and the terrorist attacks of September 11, 2001, many corporations also experienced a financial downturn. These same corporations experienced lower than expected sales revenues and profits. In some cases corporations actually posted losses during this same time period. While no industry was exempt from these financial problems, the high-tech industry was especially hard hit. As a result, a number of firms failed or merged with larger, more financially stable firms. For the firms that were able to weather the economic storm, their stock values were quite a bit lower than they were before the economic downturn began back in 1999. When this type of situation occurs, you can use a procedure called *selling short* to make a profit when the price of an individual stock is falling. **Selling short** is the process of selling stock that an investor does not actually own but has borrowed from a brokerage firm and will repay at a later date. The idea is to sell at today's higher price and then buy later at a lower price. To make a profit from a short transaction, you must proceed as follows:

1. Arrange to borrow a certain number of shares of a particular stock from a brokerage firm.
2. Sell the borrowed stock immediately, assuming that the price of the stock will drop in a reasonably short time.

3. After the price drops, buy the same number of shares that were sold in step 2.
4. Give the newly purchased stock to the brokerage firm in return for the stock borrowed in step 1.

Your profit is the difference between the amount received when the stock is sold in step 2 and the amount paid for the stock in step 3. For example, assume that you think that Home Depot stock is overvalued at $31 a share. You also believe the stock will decrease in value over the next three to four months. You call your broker and arrange to borrow 100 shares of Home Depot stock (step 1). The broker then sells your borrowed Home Depot stock for you at the current market price of $31 a share (step 2). Also assume that four months later the Home Depot stock has dropped to $21 a share. You instruct your broker to purchase 100 shares of Home Depot stock at the current lower price (step 3). The newly purchased Home Depot stock is given to the brokerage firm to repay the borrowed stock (step 4). In this example, you made $1,000 by selling short ($3,100 selling price − $2,100 purchase price = $1,000 profit).[8] Naturally, the $1,000 profit must be reduced by the commissions you paid to the broker for buying and selling the Home Depot stock.

People often ask where the broker obtains the stock for a short transaction. The broker probably borrows the stock from other investors who have purchased Home Depot stock and left stock certificates on deposit with the brokerage firm. As a result, the person who is selling short must pay any dividends declared on the borrowed stock. The most obvious danger when selling short, of course, is that a loss can result if the stock's market value increases instead of decreases. If the market value of the stock increases after the investor has sold it in step 2, he or she loses money.

Buying Stock on Margin

margin requirement the portion of the price of a stock that cannot be borrowed

An investor buys stock *on margin* by borrowing part of the purchase price, usually from a stock brokerage firm. The **margin requirement** is the portion of the price of a stock that cannot be borrowed. This requirement is set by the Federal Reserve Board.

Today, investors can borrow up to half the cost of a stock purchase. But why would they want to do so? Simply because they can buy twice as much stock by buying on margin. Suppose that an investor expects the market price of a share of common stock of TXU Corporation—a global energy company—to increase in the next three to four months. Let's say this investor has enough money to purchase 200 shares of the stock. However, if the investor buys on margin, he or she can purchase an additional 200 shares for a total of 400 shares. If the price of TXU's stock increases by $8 per share, the investor's profit will be $1,600 ($8 × 200 = $1,600) if he or she pays cash. But it will be $3,200 ($8 × 400 = $3,200) if he or she buys on margin.[9] That is, by buying more shares on margin, the investor will earn double the profit (less the interest he or she pays on the borrowed money and customary commission charges).

Financial leverage—a topic covered in Chapter 20—is the use of borrowed funds to increase the return on an investment. When margin is used as leverage, the investor's profit is earned by both the borrowed money and the investor's own money. The investor retains all the profit and pays interest only for the temporary use of the borrowed funds. Note that the stock purchased on margin serves as collateral for the borrowed funds. Before you become a margin investor, you should consider two factors. First, if the market price of the purchased stock does not increase as quickly as expected, interest costs mount and eventually drain your profit. Second, if the price of the margined stock falls, the leverage works against you. That is, because you have purchased twice as much stock, you lose twice as much money.

If the value of a stock you bought on margin decreases to approximately half its original price, you will receive a *margin call* from the brokerage firm. You must then provide additional cash or securities to serve as collateral for the borrowed money. If you cannot provide additional collateral, the stock is sold, and the proceeds are used to pay off the loan. Any funds remaining after the loan is paid off are returned to you.

Other High-Risk Investments

We have already discussed two high-risk investments—margin transactions and selling short. Other high-risk investments include the following:

- Stock options
- Commodities
- Precious metals
- Gemstones
- Coins
- Antiques and collectibles

Without exception, investments of this kind are normally referred to as high-risk investments for one reason or another. For example, the gold market has many unscrupulous dealers who sell worthless gold-plated lead coins to unsuspecting, uninformed investors. With each of the investments in this last category, it is extremely important that you deal with reputable dealers and recognized investment firms. It pays to be careful. *Although investments in this category can lead to large dollar gains, they should not be used by anyone who does not fully understand all the potential risks involved.*

Sources of Financial Information

learning objective

6 Use financial information to evaluate investment alternatives.

A wealth of information is available to investors. Sources include the Internet, newspapers, investors' services, brokerage firm reports, business periodicals, corporate reports, and securities averages.

The Internet

Today, more people have access to information provided by computers located in their homes or at libraries, universities, or businesses than ever before. And this number is growing. More important, a wealth of information is available on most investment and personal finance topics. For example, you can obtain interest rates for CDs; current price information for stocks, bonds, and mutual funds; and experts' recommendations to buy, hold, or sell an investment. You can even trade securities online just by pushing the right button on your computer keyboard.

Because the Internet makes so much information available, you need to use it selectively. One of the web search engines such as Yahoo! (**www.yahoo.com**), MSN (**www.msn.com**), Alta Vista (**www.altavista.com**), or Google (**www.google.com**) can help you locate the information you really need. These search engines allow you to do a word search for the personal finance or investment alternative you want to explore. Why not take a look? To access one of the above search engines, enter the Uniform Resource Locator (URL) address and then type in a key term such as *personal finance* and see the results. Additional information about using the Internet is presented in the Talking Technology boxed feature.

Corporations, investment companies that sponsor mutual funds, and federal, state, and local governments also have home pages where you can obtain valuable information. You may want to explore these websites for two reasons. First, they are easily accessible. All you have to do is type in the web address or use one of the above-mentioned search engines to locate the site. Second, the information on these sites may be more up to date than printed material obtained from published sources. Especially useful is the information provided on the SEC website (**www.sec.gov**).

In addition, you can access professional advisory services—a topic discussed later in this section—for information on stocks, bonds, mutual funds, and other investment alternatives. While some of the information provided by these services is free, there is

talking technology

To Pick a Winning Investment, Get Help Online

BUY AND HOLD, diversify, and control investment costs are traditional words of wisdom for investors. Yet how can you follow this advice by choosing a winning investment from a market filled with thousands of securities? The answer is to do your homework—with online help.

The finance section of Yahoo! (**http://finance.yahoo.com**) is among the best of the investment websites. On the main page you will find an overview of the news that moved the day's markets and where the main U.S. market indices stand. You also can check the latest quotes for individual stocks and list a number of securities to monitor online. You also will find an abundance of links to information about investing and personal finance. Novice investors will find the "Education" links useful, especially the "Investing 101" guide to the basics and the glossary defining typical investment terms.

When you are ready to narrow the field of potential investments, click on the "Screener" link under the "Stock Research," "Mutual Funds," or "Bonds" heading on the main Yahoo! Finance page. You can use the Yahoo! stock screener, for example, to investigate stocks by industry, share price, share volume, share performance, company sales and profits, analysts' estimates, and other criteria. Similarly, the mutual fund screener allows you to find funds by type of investment, fund family, ratings, performance, holdings, and other criteria.

Another source of investment information on selecting stocks or mutual funds, investing for retirement, short-term investing, financing college, and other topics is the *SmartMoney University* website (**http://university.smartmoney.com**). You also can take online quizzes to find out how much you *really* know about investing and then brush up by browsing the site's educational material.

Finally, check whether your employer provides online advice. Hallmark, General Motors, and a growing number of large companies are arranging access to specialized websites so that employees can make informed decisions about investments in their retirement accounts. Hallmark employees, for example, can use online tools to work through decisions about diversifying their holdings or choosing securities that meet their financial goals. Homework like this takes time, but savvy investors are willing to invest the time now for better investment returns later.

a charge for the more detailed information you may need to evaluate an investment. Although it is impossible to list all the Internet sites related to investments, those listed in Table 21.7 will get you started.

table 21.7 Internet Sites that Provide Useful Information for Evaluating Investments

The following five Internet sites provide information that you can use to establish a financial plan and begin an investment program.

Sponsor and Description	Web Address
1. The **Bloomberg** website provides information about stocks, mutual funds, and portfolio management. It also provides access to selected articles from the online version of *Bloomberg Personal Finance*.	**www.bloomberg.com**
2. The **CNNMoney** website provides current financial news and material that can help both beginning and experienced investors sharpen their investment skills. The Financial Tools section is especially useful for preparing for an investment program.	**http://money.cnn.com**
3. The **FinanCenter** website helps individuals calculate the cost of investments, homes, and autos. This site provides great education materials and also can help you establish an investment program.	**www.financecenter.com**
4. The **Motley Fool** website provides lighthearted but excellent investment advice. It also provides educational materials for beginning investors.	**www.fool.com**
5. The **Quicken** website provides information about investments, home mortgages, insurance, taxes, banking and credit, and different types of retirement programs.	**www.quicken.com**

Newspaper Coverage of Securities Transactions

Most local newspapers carry several pages of business news, including reports of securities transactions. The *Wall Street Journal* (published on weekdays) and *Barron's* (published once a week) are devoted almost entirely to financial and economic news. Both include complete coverage of transactions on all major securities exchanges.

Securities transactions are reported as long tables of figures that tend to look somewhat forbidding. However, they are easy to decipher when you know how to read them. Because transactions involving stocks, bonds, and mutual funds are reported differently, we shall examine each type of report separately.

Common and Preferred Stocks Stock transactions are reported in tables that usually look like the top section of Figure 21.3. Stocks are listed alphabetically. Your first task is to move down the table to find the stock you are interested in. To read the *stock quotation*, you read across the table. The highlighted line in Figure 21.3 gives detailed information about common stock issued by pharmaceutical giant Bristol-Myers Squibb.

figure 21.3

Reading Stock Quotations

Reproduced at the top of the figure is a portion of the stock quotations listed on the New York Stock Exchange. At the bottom is an enlargement of the same information. The numbers above each of the enlarged columns correspond to the numbered entries in the list of explanations that appears in the middle of the figure.

YLD % CHG	52 WEEKS HI	LO	STOCK (SYM)	DIV	YLD %	PE	VOL 100s	CLOSE	NET CHG
0.8	51.20	19.49	BrisMyrsSqb **BMY**	1.12	4.8	12	49365	23.33	- 0.27
−15.3	36.76	14.50	BritAir ADS **BAB**		...	...	677	18.95	0.28
7.7	13.55	0.27	BritEgy ADS **BGY**	.34e	81.0	...	7341	0.42	−0.07
−6.9	48.63	28.13	BritishSky **BSY** s		...	...	166	37.28	0.79
14.8	8.90	1.09	Broadwing **BRW**		...	dd	9109	4.04	−0.01

1. YTD % Chg reflects the stock price change for the calendar year to date: Bristol-Myers Squibb has increased 0.8 percent since January 1
2. Highest price paid for one share of Bristol-Myers Squibb during the past 52 weeks: $51.20
3. Lowest price paid for one share of Bristol-Myers Squibb during the past 52 weeks: $19.49
4. Name (often abbreviated) of the corporation: Bristol-Myers Squibb
5. Ticker symbol or letters that identify a stock for trading: BMY
6. Total dividends paid per share during the last 12 months: $1.12
7. Yield percentage, or the percentage of return based on the current dividend and current price of the stock: $1.12 ÷ $23.33 = 0.048 = 4.8%
8. Price earnings (PE) ratio—the price of a share of stock divided by the corporation's earnings per share of stock outstanding over the last 12 months: 12
9. Number of shares of Bristol-Myers Squibb traded during the day, expressed in hundreds of shares: 4,936,500
10. Price paid in the last transaction of the day: $23.33
11. Difference between the price paid for the last share sold today and the price paid for the last share sold on the previous day: −0.27 (in Wall Street terms, Bristol-Myers Squibb "closed down $0.27" on this day).

1	2	3	4 5	6	7	8	9	10	11
YTD % CHG	52 WEEKS HI	LO	STOCK (SYM)	DIV	YLD %	PE	VOL 100s	CLOSE	NET CHG
0.8	51.20	19.49	BrisMyrsSqb BMY	1.12	4.8	12	49365	23.33	- 0.27
−15.3	36.76	14.50	BritAir ADS BAB		...	...	677	18.95	0.28
7.7	13.55	0.27	BritEgy ADS BGY	.34e	81.0	...	7341	0.42	−0.07
−6.9	48.63	28.13	BritishSky BSY s		...	...	166	37.28	0.79
14.8	8.90	1.09	Broadwing BRW		...	dd	9109	4.04	−0.01

Source: *Wall Street Journal*, February 12, 2003, p. C3.

What kind of investment advice can you get from two Motley Fools? Well, if the two Motley Fools are David and Tom Gardner, you get very good advice. The two brothers established a website that helps the average person become an informed investor. Today, their website—**www.fool.com**—is recognized as one of the best investment educational sites on the Internet.

If a corporation has more than one stock ssue, the common stock is listed first. Then he preferred stock issue(s) are listed and inlicated with the letters *pf* behind the firm's name. (*Exception:* The *Wall Street Journal* has a separate section for preferred stock listings.)

Bonds Purchases and sales of bonds are reported in tables like that shown at the top of Figure 21.4. In bond quotations, prices are given as a percentage of the face value, which is usually $1,000. Thus, to find the actual price paid, you must multiply the face value ($1,000) by the quotation listed in the newspaper. For example, a price quoted as 84 translates to a selling price of $840 ($1,000 × 0.84 = $840). The fourth row of Figure 21.4 gives detailed information for the Household Finance Corporation $1,000 bond, which pays 6¾ percent interest and matures in 2011.

figure 21.4

Reading Bond Quotations

Reproduced at the top of the figure is a portion of the bond quotations as reported by the *Wall Street Journal*. At the bottom is an enlargement of the same information. The numbers above each of the enlarged columns correspond to numbered entries in the list of explanations that appears in the middle of the figure.

BONDS	CUR YLD	VOL	CLOSE	NET CHG
GoldmS 7.35s09	6.5	15	113	0.75
Henley 6cld	...	2	99.56	...
Hilton 5s06	cv	10	97	−0.25
HousF 6¾11	6.3	25	108	−0.75
IllPwr 7½25	8.3	10	90.13	−1.88

1. Abbreviated name of the corporation (Household Financial Corporation), the bond's interest rate (6¾% of its face value, or $1,000 x .0675 = $67.50, and the year of maturity (2011)
2. Current yield, determined by dividing the dollar amount of annual interest by the current price of the bond ($67.50 ÷ $1,080 = 6.3%)
3. Number (volume) of bonds traded during the day: 25
4. Price paid in the last transaction of the day: $1,000 x 108% = $1,080
5. Difference between the price paid for the last bond today and the price paid for the last bond on the previous day: −0.75 ($7.50 less than the day before). In Wall Street terms, the Household Financial Corporation bond "closed down 0.75" on this day.

1	2	3	4	5
BONDS	CUR YLD	VOL	CLOSE	NET CHG
GoldmS 7.35s09	6.5	15	113	0.75
Henley 6cld	...	2	99.56	...
Hilton 5s06	cv	10	97	−0.25
HousF 6¾11	6.3	25	108	−0.75
IllPwr 7½25	8.3	10	90.13	−1.88

Source: *Wall Street Journal*, February 11, 2003, p. C15.

figure 21.5

Reading Mutual Fund Quotations

Reproduced at the top of the figure is a portion of the mutual fund quotations as reported by the *Wall Street Journal*. At the bottom is an enlargement of the same information. The numbers above each of the enlarged columns correspond to numbered entries in the list of explanations that appears in the middle of the figure.

FUND	NAV	NET CHG	YTD %RET	3-YR %RET
Val&Inc p	17.17	−0.18	−4.7	−1.8
Dodge & Cox				
Balanced	58.65	−0.29	−3.5	7.9
Income	12.79	...	0.2	10.6
Intl Stk	14.93	...	−5.6	NS
Stock	83.20	−0.63	−5.5	5.6

1. The name of the mutual fund: Dodge & Cox Balanced Fund.
2. The net asset value (NAV) is the value of one share of the Dodge & Cox Balanced Fund: $58.65.
3. The difference between the net asset value today and the net asset value on the previous trading day: −0.29 (in Wall Street terms, the Dodge & Cox Balanced Fund closed down $0.29 on this day).
4. The YTD % RET gives the total return for Dodge & Cox Balanced Fund for the year to date: −3.5 percent.
5. The 3-YR % RET column gives the total return for the Dodge & Cox Balanced Fund for the past 3 years: 7.9 percent.

1	2	3	4	5
FUND	NAV	NET CHG	YTD %RET	3-YR %RET
Val&Inc p	17.17	−0.18	−4.7	−1.8
Dodge & Cox				
Balanced	58.65	−0.29	−3.5	7.9
Income	12.79	...	0.2	10.6
Intl Stk	14.93	...	−5.6	NS
Stock	83.20	−0.63	−5.5	5.6

Source: *Wall Street Journal*, February 12, 2003, p. D8.

Mutual Funds Purchases and sales of shares of mutual funds are reported in tables like the one shown in Figure 21.5. As in reading stock and bond quotations, your first task is to move down the table to find the mutual fund you are interested in. Then, to find the mutual fund price quotation, read across the table. Figure 21.5 gives detailed information for the Dodge & Cox Balanced mutual fund.

Other Sources of Financial Information

In addition to the Internet and newspaper coverage, other sources, which include investors' services, brokerage firm reports, business periodicals, and corporate reports, offer detailed and varied information about investment alternatives.

Investors' Services For a fee, various investors' services provide information about investments. Information from investors' services also may be available at university and public libraries.

Moody's and Standard & Poor's provide information that can be used to determine the quality and risk associated with bond issues. The bond ratings used by Moody's range from Aaa to C. Standard & Poor's ratings range from AAA to D. Investment-grade bonds are rated A or higher by both companies. Bonds with a B rating are considered speculative in nature and may not be suitable for all investors. Bonds with C and D ratings may be in default because of poor prospects of repayment or even continued payment of interest.

figure 21.6

Mergent's Research Report for the General Motors Corporation

A research report from Mergent is divided into six main parts that describe not only the financial condition of a company but also its history and the outlook for the future.

GENERAL MOTORS CORP.

EXCH.	SYM.	REC. PRICE	P/E RATIO	YLD.	MKT. CAP.	RANGE (52-WK.)	'01 Y/E PR.
NYSE	GM	33.25 (10/31/02)	15.3	6.0%	$47.77 bill.	68.17 - 30.80	48.60

MEDIUM GRADE. THE COMPANY ANTICIPATES FULL-YEAR 2002 EARNINGS OF APPROXIMATELY $6.75 PER SHARE, EXCLUDING HUGHES AND NON-RECURRING ITEMS.

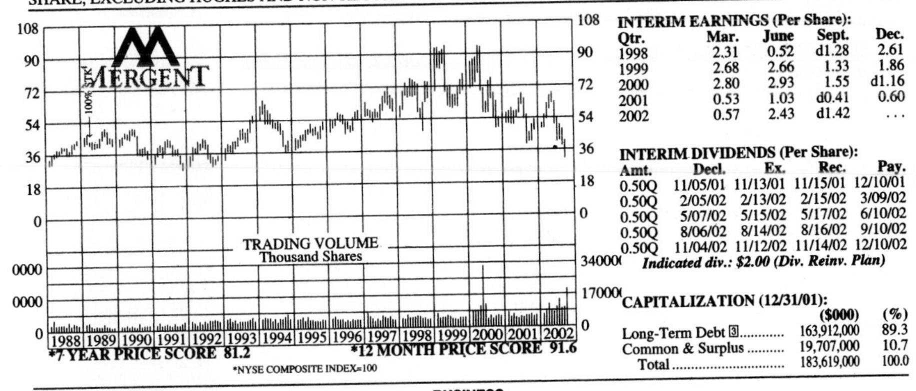

INTERIM EARNINGS (Per Share):

Qtr.	Mar.	June	Sept.	Dec.
1998	2.31	0.52	d1.28	2.61
1999	2.68	2.66	1.33	1.86
2000	2.80	2.93	1.55	d1.16
2001	0.53	1.03	d0.41	0.60
2002	0.57	2.43	d1.42	...

INTERIM DIVIDENDS (Per Share):

Amt.	Decl.	Ex.	Rec.	Pay.
0.50Q	11/05/01	11/13/01	11/15/01	12/10/01
0.50Q	2/05/02	2/13/02	2/15/02	3/09/02
0.50Q	5/07/02	5/15/02	5/17/02	6/10/02
0.50Q	8/06/02	8/14/02	8/16/02	9/10/02
0.50Q	11/04/02	11/12/02	11/14/02	12/10/02

Indicated div.: $2.00 (Div. Reinv. Plan)

CAPITALIZATION (12/31/01):

	($000)	(%)
Long-Term Debt [3]	163,912,000	89.3
Common & Surplus	19,707,000	10.7
Total	183,619,000	100.0

BUSINESS:

General Motors Corp. is the world's largest auto maker. The Automotive segment (79.4% of 2001 revenues) operates through Chevrolet, Pontiac, GMC, Oldsmobile, Buick, Cadillac, Saturn, Hummer, Opel, Vauxhall, Holden, Isuzu and Saab. General Motors Acceptance Corporation (GMAC) (14.5%) operates in the financial and insurance segment, which includes vehicle leasing, insurance and financing. Hughes Electronics Corporation (4.7%) is a telecommunications company. Other products (1.4%) include Allison Transmission division, which produces medium and heavy duty automatic transmissions for commercial-duty trucks and buses; and GM Locomotive Group, which produces diesel-electric locomotives, diesel engines and components. GM spun-off of Delphi Automotive Systems in May 1999.

RECENT DEVELOPMENTS:

For the quarter ended 9/30/02, GM reported a net loss of $804.0 million versus a net loss of $368.0 million in the corresponding prior-year quarter. Results for 2002 included an after-tax impairment charge of $1.37 billion for the write-down of GM's investment in Fiat Auto Holdings, B.V., an after-tax restructuring charge of $116.0 million and an after-tax net gain of $68.0 million at Hughes primarily from the sale of equity interests. Results for 2001 included non-recurring charges of $753.0 million. Total net sales and revenues increased 2.6% to $43.58 billion from $42.48 billion a year earlier. GM's global automotive operations earned $345.0 million, up 62.7% as a result of increased sales in North America and worldwide cost reductions. GMAC earnings advanced 8.9% to $476.0 million on improved mortgage operations.

PROSPECTS:

GM plans to revamp its entire car portfolio over the next three years, focusing on fewer, yet stronger nameplates, with new bodystyles, powertrains and performance packages. Meanwhile, GM expects total U.S. industry vehicle sales for 2002 to be approximately 17.0 million units. Separately, GM anticipates earnings, excluding Hughes and non-recurring charges, to be about $1.50 per share in the fourth quarter of 2002 and $6.75 per share for the full year.

ANNUAL FINANCIAL DATA:

FISCAL YEAR	TOT. REVS. ($mill.)	NET INC. ($mill.)	TOT. ASSETS ($mill.)	OPER. PROFIT %	NET PROFIT %	RET. ON EQUITY %	RET. ON ASSETS %	CURR. RATIO	EARN. PER SH. $	CASH FL. PER SH. $	TANG. BK. VAL. $	DIV. PER SH. $	PRICE RANGE	AVG. P/E RATIO	AVG. YIELD %
12/31/01	**177,260.0**	[8] **601.0**	**323,969.0**	**5.7**	**0.3**	**3.0**	**0.2**	**0.9**	[8] **1.77**	**24.12**	**10.71**	**2.00**	**67.80 - 39.17**	**30.2**	**3.7**
12/31/00	184,632.0	[7] 4,452.0	303,100.0	9.1	2.4	14.8	1.5	0.8	[7] 6.68	30.04	41.14	2.00	94.63 - 48.44	10.7	2.8
12/31/99	176,558.0	[4] [5] 5,576.0	274,730.0	10.5	3.2	27.0	2.0	0.9	[4] [5] 8.53	27.20	19.56	2.00	94.88 - 59.75	9.1	2.6
12/31/98	161,315.0	[6] 2,956.0	257,389.0	8.6	1.8	19.7	1.1	1.0	[6] 4.18	22.39	7.27	2.00	76.69 - 47.06	14.8	3.2
12/31/97	178,174.0	[5] 6,698.0	228,888.0	8.6	3.8	38.3	2.9	4.1	[5] 8.62	31.93	8.70	2.00	72.44 - 52.25	7.2	3.2
12/31/96	164,013.0	[2] [4] 4,953.0	222,142.0	8.8	3.0	21.2	2.2	4.1	[2] [4] 6.06	22.11	8.25	1.60	59.38 - 45.75	8.7	3.0
12/31/95	168,828.6	[1] 6,932.5	217,123.4	9.9	4.1	29.7	3.2	4.5	[1] 7.28	24.90	8.85	1.10	53.13 - 37.25	6.2	2.4
12/31/94	154,951.2	[1] 5,658.7	198,598.7	9.8	3.7	42.6	2.8	4.0	[1] 6.20	21.13	1.20	0.80	65.38 - 36.13	8.2	1.6
12/31/93	138,219.5	[2] 2,465.8	188,202.0	7.1	1.8	40.8	1.3	3.8	[2] 2.13	16.39	...	0.80	57.13 - 32.00	20.9	1.8
12/31/92	132,430.0	[1] [2] d2,621.0	191,014.0	4.2	...	...	...	3.5	[1] [2] d4.85	9.17	...	1.40	44.38 - 28.63	...	3.8

Statistics are as originally reported. [1] Bef. acctg. change chrg. $20.88 bill., 1992; $758.0 mill., 1994; $51.8 mill., 1995. [2] Incl non-recurr chrg. $749.0 mill., 1992; $478.0 mill., 1993; $938.0 mill., 1996. [3] Incl. long-term debt from GMAC. [4] Bef. disc. opers. gain $10.0 mill., 1996; $426.0 mill., 1999. [5] Incl. non-recurr. credit $30.0 mill., 1997; $597.0 mill., 1999. [6] Bef. disc. opers. chrg. $500.0 mill. [7] Incl. spec. chrgs. totaling $520.0 mill. [8] Bef. acctg. credit of $12.0 mill.; incl. after-tax net spec. chrgs. of $886.0 mill.

OFFICERS:
J. F. Smith Jr., Chmn.
J. M. Devine, Vice-Chmn., C.F.O.
G. R. Wagoner Jr., Pres., C.E.O.

INVESTOR CONTACT: Mark Tanner, (313) 665-3146

PRINCIPAL OFFICE: 300 Renaissance Center, Detroit, MI 48265-3000

TELEPHONE NUMBER: (313) 556-5000
FAX: (313) 556-5108
WEB: www.gm.com

NO. OF EMPLOYEES: 365,000 (avg.)

SHAREHOLDERS: 444,739 ($1 2/3 par common); 185,553 (class H common)

ANNUAL MEETING: In June

INCORPORATED: DE, Oct., 1916

INSTITUTIONAL HOLDINGS:
No. of Institutions: 655
Shares Held: 372,148,459
% Held: 66.4

INDUSTRY: Motor vehicles and car bodies (SIC: 3711)

TRANSFER AGENT(S): EquiServe, Providence, RI

Source: From *Mergent's Handbook of Common Stocks*, Winter 2002. (New York: Mergent, Inc., 2002). Used by permission.

Standard & Poor's, Mergent FIS, Inc., and Value Line also rate the companies that issue common and preferred stock. Each investor service provides detailed financial reports. Take a look at the Mergent's research report for General Motors illustrated in Figure 21.6. Notice that there are six main sections that provide financial

figure 21.7

Morningstar Research Report for the T. Rowe Price Equity-Income Mutual Fund

Morningstar research reports provide detailed financial information about a mutual fund's past financial performance, the investments in the fund's portfolio, the fund manager(s), and additional information that can be used to evaluate a mutual fund.

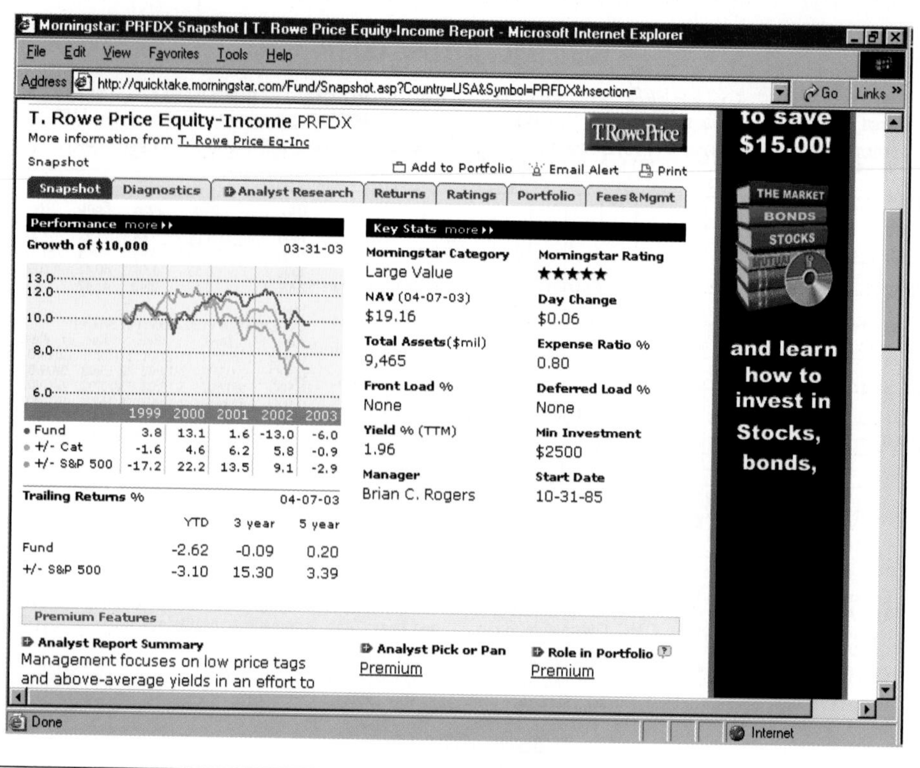

Source: "Morningstar Research Report for the T. Rowe Price Equity-Income Mutual Fund," **www.morningstar.com.** Chicago-based Morningstar, Inc., is a leading provider of investment information, research, and analysis. Its extensive line of Internet, software, and print products provides unbiased data and commentary on mutual funds, U.S. and international equities, closed-end funds, and variable annuities. Established in 1984, Morningstar continues to be the industry's most trusted source on key investment issues of the day. For more information about Morningstar, visit **www.morningstar.com** or call 800–735–0700.

data, information about the company's business operations, recent developments, prospects, and other valuable information. Research reports published by Standard & Poor's and Value Line are like Mergent's report and provide similar information.

A number of investors' services provide detailed information on mutual funds. Morningstar, Inc., Standard & Poor's, Lipper Analytical Services, and the Wiesenberger Investment Companies are four widely tapped sources of such information. Although some information may be free, a fee generally is charged for more detailed research reports. A portion of a Morningstar research report for the T. Rowe Price Equity-Income mutual fund is illustrated in Figure 21.7. In addition, various mutual fund newsletters supply financial information to subscribers for a fee.

Brokerage Firm Analysts' Reports Brokerage firms employ financial analysts to prepare detailed reports on individual corporations and their securities. Such reports are based on the corporation's sales, profits or losses, management, and planning, plus other information on the company, its industry, demand for its products, and its efforts to develop new products. The reports, which may include buy or sell recommendations, usually are provided free to the clients of full-service brokerage firms. Firms offering this service include UBS PaineWebber, Smith Barney, Merrill Lynch, and most other full-service brokerage firms. Brokerage firm reports also may be available from discount brokerage firms, but they may charge a fee.

Business Periodicals Business magazines such as *BusinessWeek*, *Fortune*, and *Forbes* provide not only general economic news but also detailed financial information about individual corporations. Trade or industry publications such as *Advertising Age* and *Business Insurance* include information about firms in a specific industry. News magazines such as *U.S. News & World Report*, *Time*, and *Newsweek* feature financial news egularly. *Money*, *Kiplinger's Personal Finance Magazine*, *Consumer Reports*, and similar nagazines provide information and advice designed to improve your investment skills. These periodicals are available at libraries and are sold at newsstands and by subscripion. Many of these same periodicals sponsor an online website that may contain all or elected articles that are contained in the print version. Why not check out the investng information available from *BusinessWeek Online* **at www.businessweek.com** or Kiplinger's *Personal Finance Magazine* at **www.kiplinger.com.**

Corporate Reports Publicly held corporations must send their stockholders annual reports. These reports include a description of the company's performance provided by the corporation's top management, information about the firm's products or services, and detailed financial statements that readers can use to evaluate the firm's actual performance. There also should be a letter from the accounting firm that audited the corporation. As mentioned in Chapter 18, an audit does not guarantee that a company hasn't "cooked" the books, but it does imply that the company has followed generally accepted accounting principles to report profits, assets, liabilities, and other financial information. While the audit process is not perfect, steps have been taken by the SEC and other government regulators to tighten the rules that apply to accountants and corporations.

In addition, a corporation issuing a new security must—by law—prepare a prospectus and ensure that copies are distributed to potential investors. A corporation's prospectus and its annual and quarterly reports are available to the general public.

Security Averages

Investors often gauge the stock market through the security averages reported in newspapers and on television news programs. A **security average** (or **security index**) is an average of the current market prices of selected securities. Over a period of time, these averages indicate price trends, but they cannot predict the performance of individual investments. At best, they can give the investor a "feel" for what is happening to investment prices generally.

security average (or **security index**) an average of the current market prices of selected securities

The *Dow Jones Industrial Average*, established in 1897, is the oldest security index in use today. This average is composed of the prices of the common stocks of thirty leading industrial corporations. In addition, Dow Jones publishes a transportation average, a utility average, and a composite average computed from the prices of sixty-five stocks included in the industrial, transportation, and utility averages.

In addition to the Dow Jones' averages, the Standard & Poor 500 Stock Index, the New York Stock Exchange Composite Index, the American Stock Exchange Index, and the Nasdaq Composite Index include more stocks when compared with the Dow averages. Thus they tend to reflect the stock market more fully. In addition to stock averages, there are averages for bonds, mutual funds, real estate, commodities, semiconductors, precious metals, fine art, most collectibles, and many other potential investments.

Before they can start investing, most people have to decide on a career and obtain a job that will provide the money needed to finance an investment program. In Appendix A, Careers in Business, we provide information that can help you explore different career options.

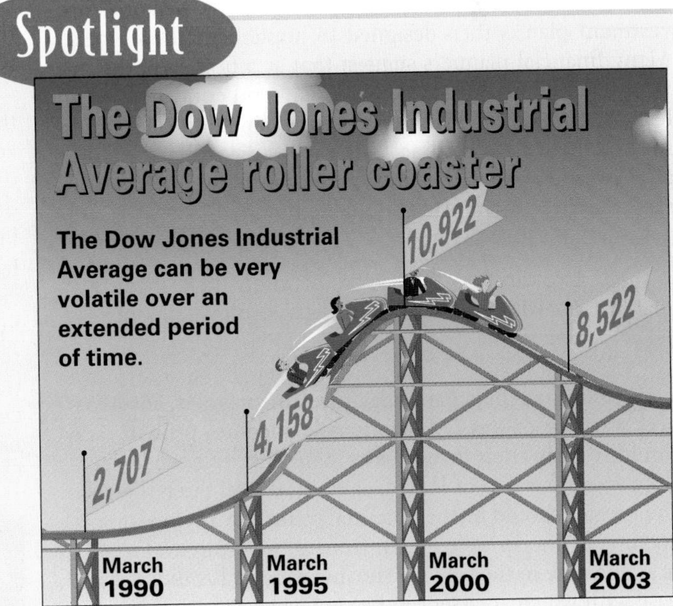
Spotlight
The Dow Jones Industrial Average roller coaster
The Dow Jones Industrial Average can be very volatile over an extended period of time.
2,707
4,158
10,922
8,522
March 1990
March 1995
March 2000
March 2003

Source: **http://finance.yahoo.com**, March 23, 2003.

Return To inside business

Based in Valley Forge, Pennsylvania, Vanguard Mutual Funds manages mutual fund investments for seventeen million investors. The company also offers brokerage services, financial planning advice, asset management, trust services, life insurance, and more. Being investor-owned allows Vanguard to take steps that other investment companies might not. During the heyday of dot-com stocks, Vanguard warned customers that those stock prices seemed overly high. During the economic downturn in which many investors switched to bond funds, Vanguard warned about a near-future drop in value because of imminent interest rate hikes.

Thanks to its long-standing tradition of acting in investors' best interests, Vanguard is now the number-two U.S. mutual fund company. With more than $500 billion in assets, the company is close behind the industry front-runner, Fidelity Investments. Current CEO John J. Brennan and his 10,500 employees continue to pursue lower costs and higher returns in true Vanguard tradition. "We were founded on the principle that our sole point of loyalty would be the clients who are our owners," Brennan states, "And today, that principle is even more strongly embedded in our culture."

Questions

1. Assume that Vanguard has warned its clients of overly high Internet stock prices and inflated values for mutual funds that contain Internet stocks. Would you act on Vanguard's advice or do your own evaluation? If Internet stocks (and mutual funds that contain Internet stocks) are overpriced, what action would you take?
2. As an investor, would you buy shares in the Vanguard 500 Index fund and hold them for a decade or more? Explain your answer.

chapter review

Summary

Develop a personal investment plan.

Personal investment planning begins with formulating measurable and realistic investment goals. A personal investment plan is then designed to implement those goals. Many financial planners suggest that as a first step, the investor should establish an emergency fund equivalent to at least three months' living expenses. Then additional funds may be invested according to the investment plan. Finally, all investments should be monitored carefully, and if necessary, the investment plan should be modified.

Explain how the factors of safety, risk, income, growth, and liquidity affect your investment decisions.

Depending on their particular investment goals, investors seek varying degrees of safety, risk, income, growth, and liquidity from their investments. Safety is, in essence, freedom from the risk of loss. Generally, the greater the risk, the greater should be the potential return on an investment. Income is the periodic return from an investment. Growth is an increase in the value of the investment. Liquidity is the ease with which an asset can be converted to cash.

Describe how securities are bought and sold.

Securities may be purchased in either the primary or the secondary market. The primary market is a market in which an investor purchases financial securities (via an investment bank) directly from the issuer of those securities. A corporation also can obtain financing by selling securities directly to current stockholders. The secondary market involves transactions for existing securities that are currently traded between investors and usually are bought and sold through a securities exchange or the over-the-counter (OTC) market.

If you invest in securities, chances are that you will use the services of an account executive who works for a brokerage firm. An investor should choose an account executive who is ethical, compatible, and able to provide the desired level of service. It is also possible to use a discount broker or trade securities online with a computer. State and federal regulations protect investors from unscrupulous securities trading practices. Federal laws, which are enforced by the Securities and Exchange Commission, require the registration of new securities, the publication and distribution of prospectuses, and the registration of brokers and securities dealers. These laws apply to securities listed on the national security exchanges, to mutual funds, and to some OTC stocks.

Identify the advantages and disadvantages of savings accounts, bonds, stocks, mutual funds, and real estate.

Asset allocation is the process of spreading your money among several different types of investments to lessen risk. Two other factors—the time your investments have to work for you and your age—also should be considered before eciding where to invest your money. Once the factors of sset allocation, time your investments have to work for ou, and your age are considered, it is time to examine diferent investment alternatives. In this section we examined raditional investments that include bank accounts, corpoate bonds, government bonds, common stock, preferred tock, mutual funds, and real estate. Although bank acounts and bonds can provide investment growth, they enerally are purchased by investors who seek a predictable ource of income. Both corporate and government bonds re a form of debt financing. As a result, bonds generally re considered a more conservative investment than stocks r most mutual funds. With stock investments, investors an make money through dividend payments, an increase in he value of the stock, or stock splits. The major advantages f mutual fund investments are professional management nd diversification. Today there are mutual funds to meet ust about any conceivable investment objective. The sucess of real estate investments is often tied to how well each nvestment alternative is evaluated.

Describe high-risk investment techniques.

High-risk investment techniques can provide greater returns, but they also entail greater risk of loss. You can make money by selling short when the market value of a financial security is decreasing. Selling short is the process of selling stock that an investor does not actually own but has borrowed from a brokerage firm and will repay at a later date. An investor also can buy stock on margin by borrowing part of the purchase price, usually from a stock brokerage firm. Because you can purchase up to twice as much stock by using margin, you can increase your return on investment as long as the stock's market value increases. Other high-risk investments include stock options, commodities, precious metals, gemstones, coins, and antiques and collectibles.

Use financial information to evaluate investment alternatives.

Today there is a wealth of information on securities and the firms that issue them. There is also a wealth of investment information on other types of investments, including mutual funds, real estate, and high-risk investment alternatives. Two popular sources—the Internet and the newspaper—report daily securities transactions. The Internet also can be used to obtain detailed financial information about different investment alternatives. Often the most detailed research information about securities—and the most expensive—is obtained from investors' services. In addition, brokerage firm reports, business periodicals, and corporate reports also can be used to evaluate different investment alternatives. Finally, there are a number of security indexes or averages that indicate price trends but reveal nothing about the performance of individual securities.

Key Terms

You should now be able to define and give an example relevant to each of the following terms:

personal investment (631)
financial planner (632)
blue-chip stock (633)
liquidity (635)
primary market (635)
high-risk investment (635)
institutional investors (636)
secondary market (636)
securities exchange (636)
over-the-counter (OTC) market (637)
Nasdaq (637)
account executive (637)
market order (638)
limit order (638)
discretionary order (638)
program trading (639)
round lot (639)
odd lot (639)
prospectus (640)
Securities and Exchange Commission (SEC) (640)
National Association of Securities Dealers (NASD) (640)
asset allocation (642)
municipal bond (645)
stock dividend (645)
capital gain (646)
market value (646)
stock split (647)
mutual fund (647)
net asset value (NAV) (647)
family of funds (649)
buying long (650)
selling short (650)
margin requirement (651)
security average (or security index) (659)

Review Questions

1. How would you go about developing a personal investment plan?
2. What is an "emergency fund," and why is it recommended?
3. What is meant by the safety of an investment? What is the tradeoff between safety and return on the investment?
4. In general, what kinds of investments provide income? What kinds provide growth?
5. What is the difference between the primary market and the secondary market?
6. When a corporation decides to sell stock, what is the role of an investment banking firm?
7. What is the difference between a securities exchange and the over-the-counter market?
8. In what ways could a computer help you invest?
9. What is the Securities and Exchange Commission? What are its principal functions?

10. How do you think that asset allocation, the time your investments have to work for you, and your age affect the choice of investments for someone who is 25 years old? For someone who is 59 years old?
11. Characterize the purchase of corporate bonds as an investment in terms of safety, risk, income, growth, and liquidity.
12. Describe the three methods by which investors can make money with stock investments.
13. An individual may invest in stocks either directly or through a mutual fund. How are the two investment methods different?
14. When would a speculator sell short?
15. What are the risks and rewards of purchasing stocks on margin?
16. How could the Internet help you research an investment?
17. In what ways are newspaper stock quotations useful to investors? In what ways are security averages useful?
18. In addition to the Internet and newspapers, what other sources of financial information could help you obtain your investment goals?

Discussion Questions

1. Many financial planners recommend that you begin an investment program by accumulating an emergency fund equal to at least three months' living expenses. How could you accumulate enough money to fund your emergency fund?
2. What personal circumstances might lead investors to emphasize income rather than growth in their investment planning? What might lead them to emphasize growth rather than income?
3. Federal laws prohibit corporate managers from making investments that are based on *inside information*—that is, special knowledge about their firms that is not available to the general public. Why are such laws needed?
4. Suppose that you have just inherited 500 shares of IBM common stock. What would you do with it, if anything?
5. In this chapter it was apparent that stocks have outperformed other investment alternatives over a long period of time. With this fact in mind, why would investors choose to use asset allocation to diversify their investments?
6. What type of individual would invest in government bonds? In global mutual funds? In real estate?
7. What kinds of information would you like to have before you invest in a particular common stock or mutual fund? From what sources can you get that information?
8. Take another look at Figure 21.6 (Mergent's Research Report for General Motors) and Figure 21.7 (Morningstar Research Report for the T. Rowe Price Equity-Income Mutual Fund). Based on the research provided by Mergent's and Morningstar, would you buy either of these two investments? Justify your decision by providing specific examples from Figures 21.6 and 21.7.

video case

Merrill Lynch Direct Offers Customers Its Direct Advantage

Merrill Lynch was a late-comer to online brokerage services. As Charles Schwab and other rivals rushed in during the mid-1990s to establish websites for customers to trade securities, Merrill Lynch watched and waited. When the company finally launched Merrill Lynch Direct (**www.mldirect.ml.com**), it built on the best of Internet technology and offered much more than online brokerage activities to satisfy its customers' needs.

Online brokerage has grown at a rapid pace, drawing millions of investors to buy and sell stocks, bonds, and mutual funds directly from their keyboards. The websites of discount brokerage firms such as E*Trade appeal to investors who can make their own investment decisions and want to save money by entering their own trades. In contrast, brokers for Merrill Lynch and other full-service brokerage firms traditionally have provided personalized service and advice about securities. Their customers initiated trades by calling or writing, not by clicking a mouse, and paid higher commissions to cover the one-to-one service and in-depth research they received.

Now, however, with online rivals charging lower commissions, adding services, and courting wealthier investors, Merrill Lynch is fighting back on the net. Its Merrill Lynch Direct site is both convenient and comprehensive, with lower commission fees for trades that do not involve broker contact. In addition to trading stocks, mutual funds, and bonds, customers can sign up for detailed research reports and recommendations from the brokerage firm's securities analysts. They also can read Standard & Poor's stock reports, check real-time stock prices when markets are open, buy shares in IPOs, and place more sophisticated orders. And those who want to invest a set amount every month can arrange to transfer money automatically from other accounts into their Merrill Lynch brokerage accounts.

Just as important as the transactional tools are the interactive tools Merrill Lynch Direct offers to help customers do their investment homework. For example, with a few clicks, customers can hunt for stocks, bonds, or mutual funds that meet specific criteria. With special calculators, customers can estimate how much money they will need for retirement, college, and family savings and then check their progress toward achieving these goals. Moreover, the online integrated account summary makes it easy for customers to see all their transactions and balances at a glance.

Although this site attracts numerous new accounts, it is also a smart way for Merrill Lynch to compete by strengthening relations between customers and brokers through enhanced personal service. Suppose that a Merrill Lynch broker wants to call attention to a particular stock during a phone call with a customer. The broker an ask the customer to log onto the Merrill Lynch Di-ect website, check out the research report, and continue he conversation without interruption or delay. This en-bles the customer to ask detailed questions, discuss the roker's recommendation, and make a more informed lecision about the stock. Customers are empowered be-ause they have more choices about contacting the bro-erage firm and more information about investments.

New customers can browse the Merrill Lynch Di-ect site and watch a demonstration of its features before pening an account. Once they sign up and fund their ccounts, they simply log on and enter a personal pass-word to begin trading, view account information, or use he site's interactive tools. Merrill Lynch ensures cus-omer privacy through state-of-the-art encryption and ecurity systems that safeguard personal financial data. As noted earlier, the company charges slightly higher commission fees for broker-assisted trades through Merrill Lynch Direct than for online trades entered by the customer. However, customers who value an ongo-ing relationship with brokers are willing to pay the difference for the personal touch.

Merrill Lynch was not the first or even the third brokerage firm to build a website for customer use. But because the company waited and watched while other firms experimented, its managers were able to take their time designing a top-notch site from scratch. Merrill Lynch Direct delivers its "Direct Advantage" through a sleek, user-friendly system that goes well beyond the basics to satisfy the diverse investment needs of customers throughout the United States.[10]

Questions

1. Why would Merrill Lynch Direct offer a demonstration of its site's main features?
2. How is an economic upturn likely to affect Merrill Lynch Direct's ability to attract new customers? Explain your answer.
3. As a Merrill Lynch Direct customer, would you enter trades using the company's online brokerage services or would you call your broker? Why?

Building Skills for Career Success

1. Exploring the Internet

For investors seeking information about individual companies and the industry to which they belong, the Internet is an excellent source. If you find the right website, it provides sales and revenue histories, graphs of recent trading on stock and bond markets, and discussions of anticipated changes within a firm or industry. The interested investor also can look at Internet business reports of stock and bond market activity. Among the many companies that issue these reports are Dow Jones, Standard & Poor's, Moody's, and Dun & Bradstreet—all firms that provide, for a fee, analysis and private research services. Visit the text website for updates to this exercise.

Assignment

1. Suppose that you are interested in investing within a particular industry, such as the semiconductor or computer industry. Explore some of the websites listed below, gathering information about the industry and a few related stocks that are of interest to the "experts."

   BusinessWeek: **www.businessweek.com**

   Dow Jones: **www.dowjones.com**

   Fortune: **www.fortune.com**

   Nasdaq: **www.nasdaq.com**

   Standard & Poor's: **www.standardpoor.com**

   New York Stock Exchange: **www.nyse.com**

   Wall Street Journal: **www.wsj.com**
2. List the stocks the experts recommend and their current trading value. You can use one of the web search engines such as Yahoo! Finance (**http://finance.yahoo.com**) to check the price. Also list several stocks the experts do not like and their current selling prices. Then list your own choices of "good" and "bad" stocks.
3. Explain why you and the experts believe these stocks are good or poor buys today. (You might want to monitor these same websites over the next six months to see how well your "good" stocks are performing.)

2. Developing Critical Thinking Skills

One way to achieve financial security is to invest a stated amount of money on a systematic basis. This investment strategy is called *dollar-cost averaging.* When the cost is lower, your investment buys more shares. When the cost is higher, your investment buys fewer shares. A good way to begin investing is to select a mutual fund that meets your financial objectives and to invest the same amount each month or each year.

Assignment

1. Select several mutual funds from the financial pages of the *Wall Street Journal* or a personal finance periodical such as *Money, Kiplinger's Personal Finance* Magazine, or *SmartMoney* that provides information about mutual funds. Call the toll-free number for each fund and ask about its objectives. Also request that the company send you a prospectus and an annual report.

2. Select one fund that meets your financial objectives.
3. Prepare a table that includes the following data:
   a. An initial investment of $2,000 in the mutual fund you have selected
   b. The NAV (net asset value)
   c. The number of shares purchased.
4. Record the investment information on a weekly basis. Look in the *Wall Street Journal* or on the Internet to find the NAV for each week.
5. Determine the value of your investments until the end of the semester.
6. Write a report describing the results. Include a summary of what you learned about investments. Be sure to indicate if you think that dollar-cost averaging (investing another $2,000 next year) would be a good idea.

3. Building Team Skills

Investing in stocks can be a way to beat inflation and accumulate money. Traditionally, stocks have returned on average approximately 10 percent per year. Fixed-rate investments, on the other hand, often earn little more than the inflation rate, making it very difficult to accumulate enough money for retirement. For a better understanding of how investing in stocks works, complete this exercise through the end of the semester.

Assignment

1. Form teams of three people. The teams will compete against each other, striving for the largest gain in investments.
2. Assume that you are buying stock in three companies; some should be listed on the NYSE, and some should be traded in the OTC market.
   a. Research different investments and narrow your choices to three different stocks.
   b. Divide your total investment of $25,000 into three amounts.
   c. Determine the number of shares of stock you can purchase in each company by dividing the budgeted amount by the price of the stock. Allow enough money to pay for the commission. To find the cost of the stock, multiply the number of shares you are going to purchase by the closing price of the stock.
   d. Assume that the commission is 2 percent. Calculate it by multiplying the cost of the stock by 0.02. Add the dollar amount of commission to the cost of the stock to determine the total purchase price.
3. Set up a table to reflect the following information:
   a. Name of the company
   b. Closing price per share
   c. Number of shares purchased
   d. Amount of the commission
   e. Cost of the stock
4. Record the closing price of the stock on a weekly basis. Prepare a chart to use for this step.
5. Before the end of the semester, assume that you sell the stock.
   a. Take the closing price and multiply it by the number of shares; then calculate the commission at 2 percent.
   b. Deduct the amount of commission from the selling price of the stock. This is the total return on your investment.
6. Calculate your profit or loss. Subtract the total purchase price of the stock from the total return. If the total return is less than the total purchase price, you have a loss
7. Prepare a report summarizing the results of the project. Include the table and individual stock charts, as well as a statement describing what you learned about investing in stocks.

4. Researching Different Careers

Account executives (sometimes referred to as *stockbrokers*) are agents who buy and sell securities for clients. After completing this exercise, you will have a better understanding of what account executives do on a daily basis.

Assignment

1. Look in the telephone directory for the names and numbers of financial companies or securities firms that sell stock.
2. Contact a stockbroker at one of these firms and explain that you would like to set up an interview so that you can learn firsthand about a stockbroker's job.
3. Summarize the results of your interview in a report. Include a statement about whether the job of stockbroker appeals to you, and explain your thoughts.

5. Improving Communication Skills

Assessment involves determining the amount of progress relative to a standard. It is a critical part of evaluating results in the workplace, as well as determining what you have learned in a course. In reality, learning often takes place in bits and pieces, and when you take the time for review and assessment as you complete a course, you may be surprised at how much you have learned. Since you are nearing the end of this course, it is time to assess what you have learned about business and business operations.

Assignment

If you have been writing in a journal as suggested in Exercise 5 in Chapter 1, you should refer to your journal notes to complete this exercise. Otherwise, use your class or study notes. Prepare a report reflecting your thoughts on the following questions:

1. What are three things you learned about business that impressed you the most? Or what was the greatest surprise to you?
2. How will you use the information you have learned? Give several examples applicable to your personal life, your career, and your job.
3. Has this course helped you make a decision on a career in business? If so, how did it make a difference?
4. What have you learned about systematically writing your thoughts in a journal? How important is this exercise for personal growth and development?

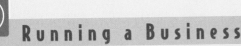

Managing Money at Finagle A Bagel

Like many other entrepreneurs, when Laura Trust and Alan Litchman decided to buy a business, they raised some money from friends and family. Unlike many entrepreneurs, however, they were so adamant about retaining full control of the business they bought—Finagle A Bagel—that they would not even consider venture capital financing or selling stock. Instead, Litchman says, "We made the decision to get banks to finance this company, which is a difficult thing."

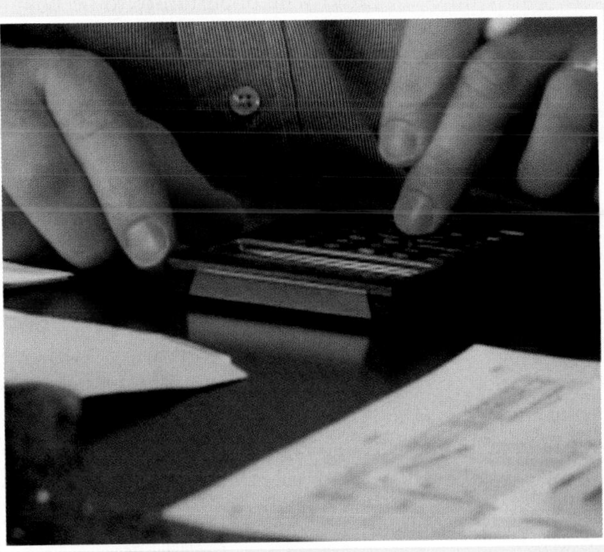

Bagels, Banking, and Borrowing

Ideally, banks prefer to make loans secured by assets such as inventory or accounts receivable. However, Finagle A Bagel has no inventory aside from each day's raw ingredients and fresh-baked bagels, which cannot be repossessed and resold if the company is unable to repay a loan. Nor does it have significant accounts receivable because most of its revenues come from cash transactions in the seventeen stores. The company has commercial ovens and other equipment in its central production facility, but, says copresident Litchman, banks do not consider such assets sufficient collateral for a secured loan. And not every bank is willing to offer an unsecured line of credit to a small, fast-growing company like Finagle A Bagel.

Fortunately, the copresidents bought Finagle A Bagel after the previous owner (who stayed on for a time after the purchase) had built the business into a highly successful six-store chain. To a bank, a company with a proven record of success and a detailed, practical business plan for continued growth looks less risky as a borrower than a newly established company without customers, assets, or cash flow. Thus Finagle A Bagel was able to negotiate an unsecured line of credit of nearly $4 million. As long as Trust and Litchman could show that the company was healthy and achieving certain financial ratios, they would be allowed to draw on the credit line to open new stores or for other business purposes.

Initially, the copresidents only paid the interest on borrowed money so that they would have more money available for growth. Within a few years, however, they began repaying the principal as well as the interest. This meant less money to fuel growth, but it also lightened the company's debt load.

Seventeen Stores, Three Banks, Two Checking Accounts

Even though Finagle A Bagel operates seventeen stores plus a wholesale division, it needs only two corporate checking accounts. Here's how the system works. For safety reasons, management does not want general managers or their assistants traveling too far to deposit each day's receipts. Yet no single bank has a branch near every Finagle A Bagel store because the stores are spread throughout downtown Boston and the outlying suburbs. Therefore, the company deals with three New England banks that maintain local branches near the stores. For each store, Finagle A Bagel opens an account in the closest branch of one of these three banks. After the day's deposits are made, money is transferred using an electronic funds transfer system to the company's main checking account.

Every morning, Litchman looks at the current balance in the main checking account and examines the report showing the previous day's sales and deposits. That tells him how much money he has to cover the bills to be paid that day. Given the slim profit margin in the food-service business—only pennies per sales dollar—Finagle A Bagel uses most of its cash to pay for food and labor. Clearly, cash flow is critical for a small, fast-growing business. Especially on slower sales days, Litchman observes, "You may be one check away from being cash-negative." If its main checking account balance is too low to cover checks that are presented for payment that day, the company may have to draw on its line of credit with the bank. Once this happens, the company must pay interest on any money it borrows, even for just a day.

Finagle A Bagel uses its second checking account only for payroll. This is a zero-balance account containing no money because its sole function is to clear payroll checks. Having two checking accounts allows the company to separate its payroll payments from its payments for supplies, rent, and other business expenses, a convenience for tax and accounting purposes. It also helps the copresidents maintain tight control over corporate finances: No check can be issued without either Litchman's or Trust's signature.

The Future of Finagle A Bagel

Looking ahead, the copresidents say they plan to continue growing the Finagle A Bagel brand and opening new stores. Within a few years, however, the firm's future course could take a very different turn. "The opportunity to be bought by, just for an example, a McDonald's or a Wendy's or one of the larger operators becomes more plausible as you start to prove to people that you can survive as a multiunit chain with twenty or more stores," says Trust. Because big companies are always on the lookout for innovative food-service concepts, Finagle A Bagel's owners might receive an acquisition offer that's too good to pass up if they keep up their expansion pace.

Even if the big companies have not yet noticed Finagle A Bagel's outstanding bagels and great performance, other people have. A few years ago the company was named Greater Boston's Small Business of the Year, and *Boston* magazine put it on the "Best of Boston" list for two consecutive years. As important and gratifying as such honors may be for a small business, money always must be—literally—the bottom line for Finagle A Bagel. "You have to make money," Trust emphasizes. "If you don't make money you're not in business."

Questions

1. If the copresidents of Finagle A Bagel had approached venture capitalists for funding, they probably would have been able to open more new stores in less time. Instead they opted to use bank financing that has to be repaid. Do you agree with their decision? Why?
2. Given their growth plans, why would the copresidents repay principal and interest on borrowed money rather than pay interest only? Which repayment plan would Finagle A Bagel's bank prefer?
3. Assuming that Finagle A Bagel decides to raise money through an IPO, what are the advantages and disadvantages of issuing stock to obtain the money needed to start or expand a business?
4. As an investor, would you be willing to buy shares in Finagle A Bagel? Explain why the company's stock would or would not be a good investment for you.

Building a Business Plan Part VII

In this last section, provide some information about your exit strategy, and discuss any potential trends, problems, or risks that you may encounter. These risks and assumptions could relate to your industry, markets, company, or personnel. Make sure to incorporate important information not included in other parts of the business plan in an appendix. Now is also the time to go back and prepare the executive summary, which should be placed at the beginning of the business plan.

The Exit Strategy Component

Your exit strategy component should at least include the answers to the following questions:

7.1. How do you intend to get yourself (and your money) out of the business?
7.2. Will your children take over the business, or do you intend to sell it later?
7.3. Do you intend to grow the business to the point of an initial public offering (IPO)?
7.4. How will investors get their money back?

The Critical Risks and Assumptions Component

Your critical risks and assumptions component should answer at least the following questions:

7.5. What will you do if your market does not develop as quickly as you predicted? What if your market develops too quickly?
7.6. What will you do if your competitors underprice or make your product obsolete?
7.7. What will you do if there is an unfavorable industry-wide trend?
7.8. What will happen if trained workers are not available as predicted?
7.9. What will you do if there is an erratic supply of products or raw materials?

The Appendix Component

Supplemental information and documents are often included in an appendix. Here are a few examples of some documents that can be included:

- Résumés of owners and principal managers
- Advertising samples and brochures
- An organization chart
- Floor plans

Review of Business Plan Activities

As you have discovered, writing a business plan involves a long series of interrelated steps. Like any project involving a number of complex steps and calculations, your business plan should be reviewed carefully and revised before you present it to potential investors.

Remember, there is one more component you need to prepare after your business plan is completed: The executive summary should be written last, but because of its importance, it appears after the introduction.

The Executive Summary Component

In the executive summary, give a one- to two-page overview of your entire business plan. This is the most important part of the business plan and is of special interest to busy bankers, investors, and other interested parties. Remember, this section is a summary; more detailed information is provided in the remainder of your business plan.

Make sure that the executive summary captures the reader's attention instantly in the first sentence by using a key selling point or benefit of the business.

Your executive summary should include answers to at least the following:

7.10. *Company information.* What product or service do you provide? What is your competitive advantage? When will the company be formed? What are your company objectives? What is the background of you and your management team?
7.11. *Market opportunity.* What is the expected size and growth rate of your market, your expected market share, and any relevant market trends?

Once again, review your answers to all the questions in the preceding parts to make sure that they are all consistent throughout the entire business plan.

Although many would-be entrepreneurs are excited about the prospects of opening their own business, remember that it takes a lot of hard work, time, and in most cases a substantial amount of money. While the business plan provides an enormous amount of information about your business, it is only the first step. Once it is completed, it is now your responsibility to implement the plan. Good luck in your business venture.

Careers in Business

APPENDIX A

Words such as *excited*, *challenged*, *scared*, and *frustrated* have been used to describe someone involved in a job search. The reality, however, is that everyone who is employed must have looked for a job at one time or another—and survived. Although first-time employees often think they will work for the same company for their entire career, most people change jobs and even careers during their lifetime. In fact, according to the Bureau of Labor Statistics, today's job applicants will change jobs over ten times. Therefore, the employment information that follows will be of lasting value. Let's begin our discussion with a look at the factors affecting an individual's career choices.

The Importance of Career Choices

Most people think that career planning begins with an up-to-date résumé and a job interview. In reality, it begins long before you prepare your résumé. It starts with you and what you want to become. In some ways you have been preparing for a career ever since you started first grade. Everything you have experienced during your lifetime you can now use as a resource to help define your career goals. Let's start with a basic assumption: It is likely that you will spend more time at work than at any other single place during your lifetime. It therefore makes sense to spend those hours doing something you enjoy. Unfortunately, some people just work at a *job* because they need money to survive. Other people choose a *career* because there is a commitment not only to a profession but also to their own interests and talents. Whether you are looking for a job or a career, you should examine your own priorities. Before reading the next section, you may want to evaluate your priorities by completing the exercise in Figure A.1.

Priorities Now	Job and Personal Variables	Priorities in 5–10 years
______	Salary	______
______	Family (children/spouse/parents)	______
______	Personal time	______
______	Job location	______
______	Work-related travel	______
______	Potential for advancement	______
______	Commuting time	______
______	Friendly coworkers/boss	______
______	Job responsibilities	______
______	Personal hobbies	______
______	Prestige	______
______	Benefits	______
______	Vacation time	______
______	Retirement plan	______
______	Security/stability	______
______	Personal growth/fulfillment	______
______	Exposure to new skills	______

figure A.1

Which Priorities Are Important to You?

Look over the list of job and personal variables. In the left-hand column, number them in order of current priority to you. Then renumber them in the right-hand column based on the priorities you anticipate having five or ten years down the road.

Source: Susan D. Greene and Melanie C. L Martel, *The Ultimate Job Hunter's Guidebook*, 4th ed., p. 17. Copyright © 2004 by Houghton Mifflin Company. Reprinted with permission.

Personal Factors Influencing Career Choices

Before you choose your career or job, you need to have a pretty good idea of what motivates you and what skills you can offer an employer. The following four questions may help you further refine what you consider important in life.

1. *What types of activities do you enjoy?* Although most people know what they enjoy in a general way, a number of interest inventories exist that can help you determine specific interests and activities that can help you land a job that will lead to a satisfying career. In some cases it may help just to list the interests or activities you enjoy, along with those you dislike. Watch for patterns that may influence your career choices.
2. *What do you do best?* All jobs in all careers require employees to be able to "do something." It is extremely important to assess what you do best. Be honest with yourself about your ability to succeed in a specific job. It may help to make a list of your strongest job-related skills. Also try looking at your skills from an employer's perspective. What can you do that an employer would be willing to pay for?
3. *What kind of education will you need?* The amount of education you need is determined by the type of career you choose. In some careers, it is impossible to get an entry-level position without at least a college degree. In other careers, technical or hands-on skills are more important than formal education. Generally, more education increases your potential earning power, as illustrated in Figure A.2.
4. *Where do you want to live?* When you enter the job market, you may want to move to a different part of the country. According to the *Occupational Outlook*

figure A.2

More Education Means Higher Earnings and Lower Unemployment
New data tell an old story: The more you learn, the more you earn—and the less likely you are to be unemployed. Earnings increase and unemployment decreases with additional years of education.

Education pays, in part, because employers believe educated workers learn tasks more easily and are better organized. However, the data here are averages; variations occur at all educational levels. The biggest reason for the variety in earnings is the different occupations people enter as a result of their education.

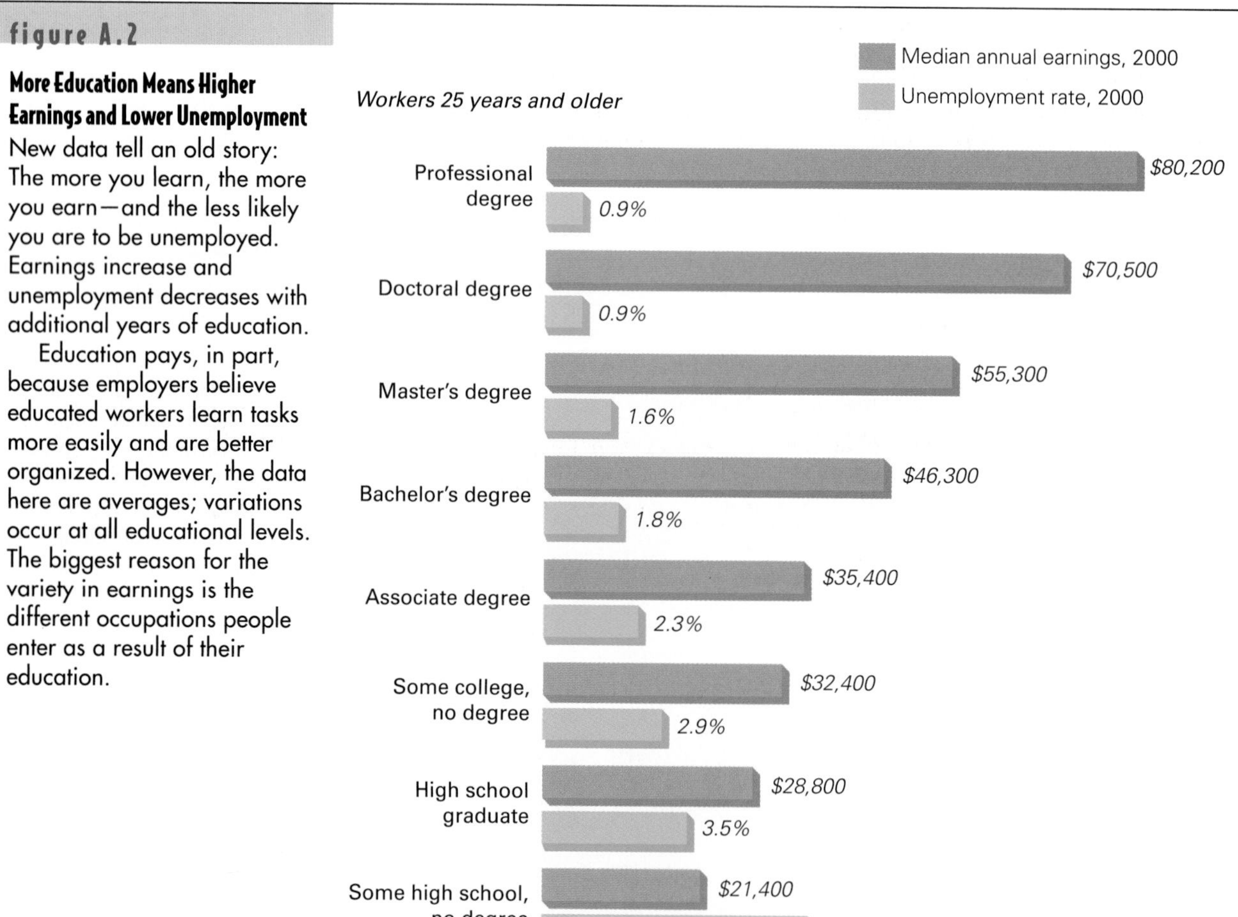

Source: U.S. Bureau of Labor Statistics.

Handbook, the western and southern sections of the United States will experience the greatest population increase between now and the year 2010. The population in the Midwest will stay about the same, whereas the Northeast will decrease slightly in population. These population changes will affect job prospects in each of those areas.

Before entering the job market, most people think that they are free to move any place they want. In reality, job applicants may be forced to move to a town, city, or metropolitan area that has jobs available.

Trends in Employment

The new millennium has brought change in employment opportunities to the U.S. labor market. Employment in 2010 is expected to reach 167.8 million, an increase of 22 million, or 15 percent, above the 2000 level. For the latest information, visit the Office of Occupational Statistics and Employment Projections website at **http://www.bls.gov/emp/.** (See Figure A.3.)

As you look ahead to your own career, you should consider the effects that the trends described below will have on employment and employment opportunities.

- Jobs in service industries will account for a larger proportion of total employment.
- Training—and retraining—will become increasingly important as firms require their employees to use the latest technology. Good jobs will require strong educational qualifications.
- Automation of factories and offices will create new types of jobs. Many of these will be computer-related.
- The number of women, Hispanics, Asians, two-income families, and older workers in the work force will increase.
- There will be a greater emphasis on job sharing, flexible hours, and other innovative work practices to accommodate employees. In some cases employees will be able to complete assignments at home on remote computer terminals.

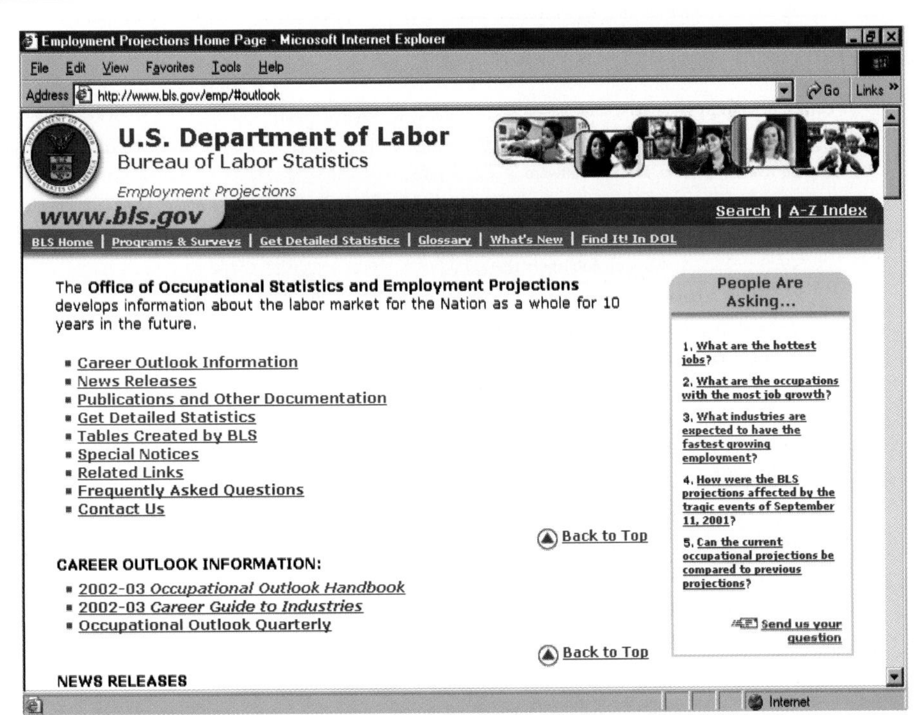

figure A.3

Easy Online Access to Job Outlook Information

The U.S. Bureau of Labor Statistics website offers a wealth of employment-related information. Even the full text of the *Occupational Outlook Handbook* is accessible on this website.

Source: U.S. Bureau of Labor Statistics.

College graduates with majors in business and management, computer science, education, engineering, and health professions will be in high demand according to human resources experts. There will be fewer manufacturing jobs, and those that remain will require high-tech skills.

Figure A.4 shows the twenty occupations that the Bureau of Labor Statistics projects will grow faster or much faster than average between now and the year 2010. And Figure A.5 shows the twenty occupations that are projected to add about eight million jobs, 39 percent of all projected growth. The jobs also have a great deal of variety with regard to the skills and aptitudes of workers, working conditions, and the nature of the work.

Occupational Search Activities

When most people begin to search for a job, they immediately think of the classified ads in the local newspaper. Those ads are an important source of information about jobs in your particular area, but they are only one source. Many other sources can lead to employment and a satisfying career. As illustrated in Figure A.6, a wealth of information about career planning is available. Therefore, you must be selective in both the type and the amount of information you use to guide your job search.

The library, a traditional job-hunting tool, has been joined in recent years by the Internet. Both the library and the Internet are sources of everything from classified newspaper ads and government job listings to detailed information on individual companies and industries. You can use either of them to research an area of employment that interests you or a particular company. In addition, the Internet allows you to check electronic bulletin boards for current job information, exchange ideas with other job seekers through online discussion groups or e-mail, and get career advice from professional counselors. You also can create your own web page to inform prospective employers of your qualifications. And you may even have a job interview online. Many prominent companies are now using their websites to post job openings, accept applications, and interview candidates. In fact, the Internet has been called the future of recruiting.

figure A.4

The Fastest Growing Occupations

The seven fastest growing occupations are computer-related: computer applications software engineer, computer support specialist, computer systems software engineer, network and computer systems administrator, network systems and data communications analyst, desktop publisher, and database administrator. Most of the other projected twenty fastest growing jobs are health care–related.

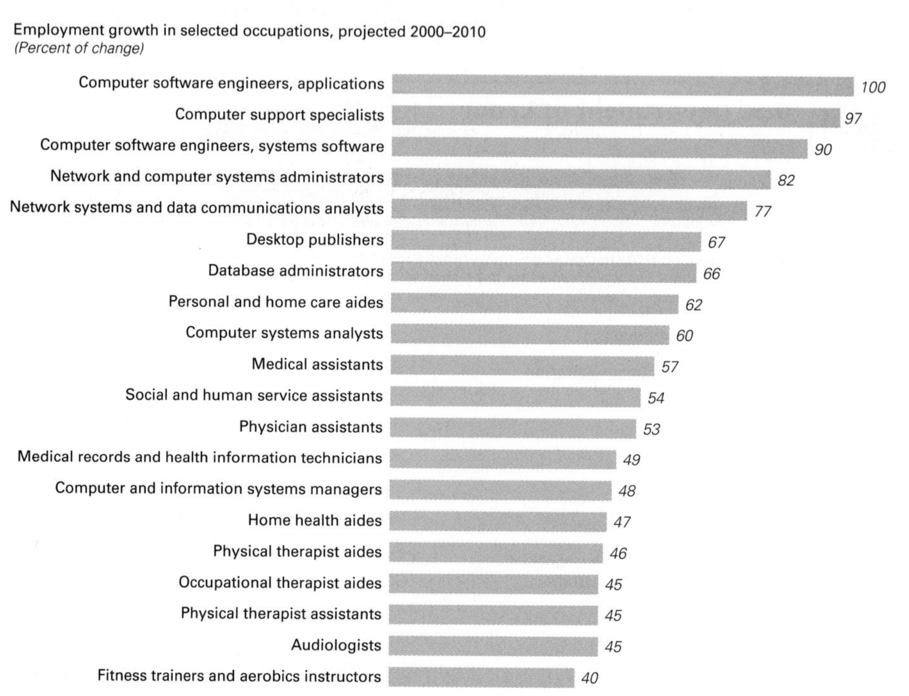

Source: U.S. Bureau of Labor Statistics, Occupational Outlook Quarterly, Winter 2001–2002, p. 21.

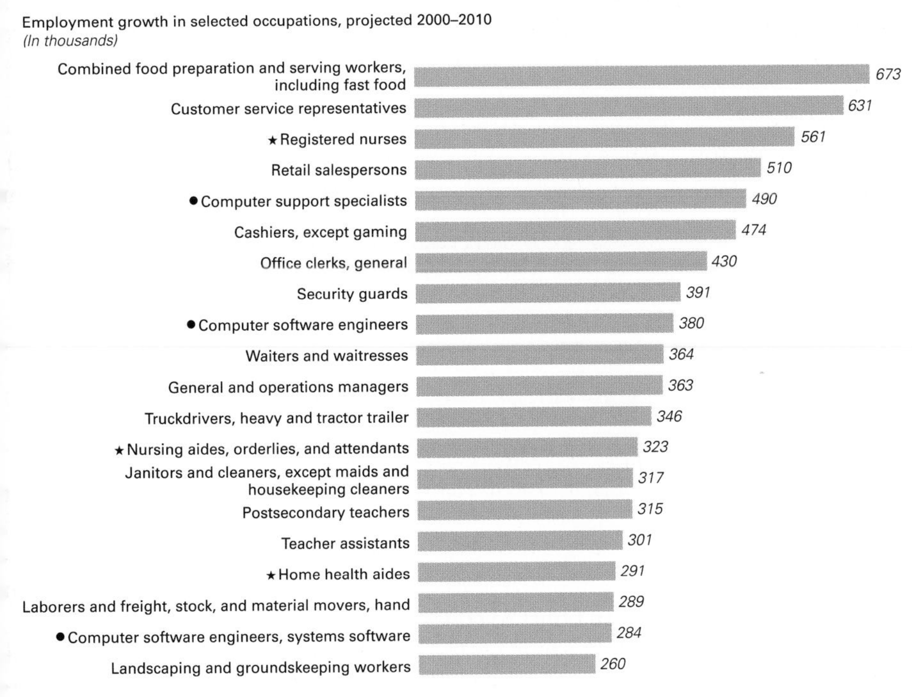

figure A.5

Occupations Gaining the Largest Number of Jobs

These 20 occupations—out of about 500—are projected to add about 8 million jobs, 39 percent of all projected growth. Three are health-related occupations (designated by ★), and three are computer related (designated by ●).

Four occupations also appear in the chart of fastest growing occupations: computer support specialists; home health aides; computer software engineers, applications; and computer software engineers, systems software.

ource: U.S. Bureau of Labor Statistics, Occupational Outlook Quarterly, Winter 2001-2002, p. 20.

As you start a job search, you may find websites helpful. In addition to the library nd the Internet, the following sources can be of great help when you are trying to ind the "perfect job":

1. *Campus placement offices.* Colleges and universities have placement offices staffed by trained personnel specialists. In most cases these offices serve as clearinghouses for career information. The staff also may be able to guide you in creating your résumé and preparing for a job interview.
2. *Professional sources and networks.* A network is a group of people—friends, relatives, and professionals—who are in a position to exchange information (including information about job openings) in your field of business. And according to many job applicants, networking is one of the best sources of career information and job leads. Start with as many people as you can think of to establish your initial network. (The Internet can be very useful in this regard.) Contact these individuals, and ask specific questions about job opportunities that they may be aware of. Also, ask each of these individuals to introduce or refer you to someone else who may be able to help you continue your job search. For networking to work, you must continue this process. Remember that you must follow all leads. Even if you have referrals and introductions, you must still "get" the job. Finally, remember to thank the people who have helped you.
3. *Private employment agencies.* Private employment agencies charge a fee for helping people find jobs. Typical fees can be as high as 15 to 20 percent of an employee's first-year salary. The fee may be paid by the employer or the employee. Like college placement offices, private employment agencies provide career counseling, help create résumés, and provide preparation for job interviews. Before you use a private employment agency, be sure you understand the terms of any contract or agreement you sign. Above all, make sure that you know who is responsible for paying the agency's fee.
4. *State employment agencies.* Another source of information about job openings in your immediate area is the local office of your state employment agency. Some job applicants are reluctant to use state agencies because the majority of jobs available through these agencies are for semiskilled or unskilled workers. From a

figure A.6

Career Information Sources

Career information is available from the library, campus placement offices, professional sources, and employment agencies.

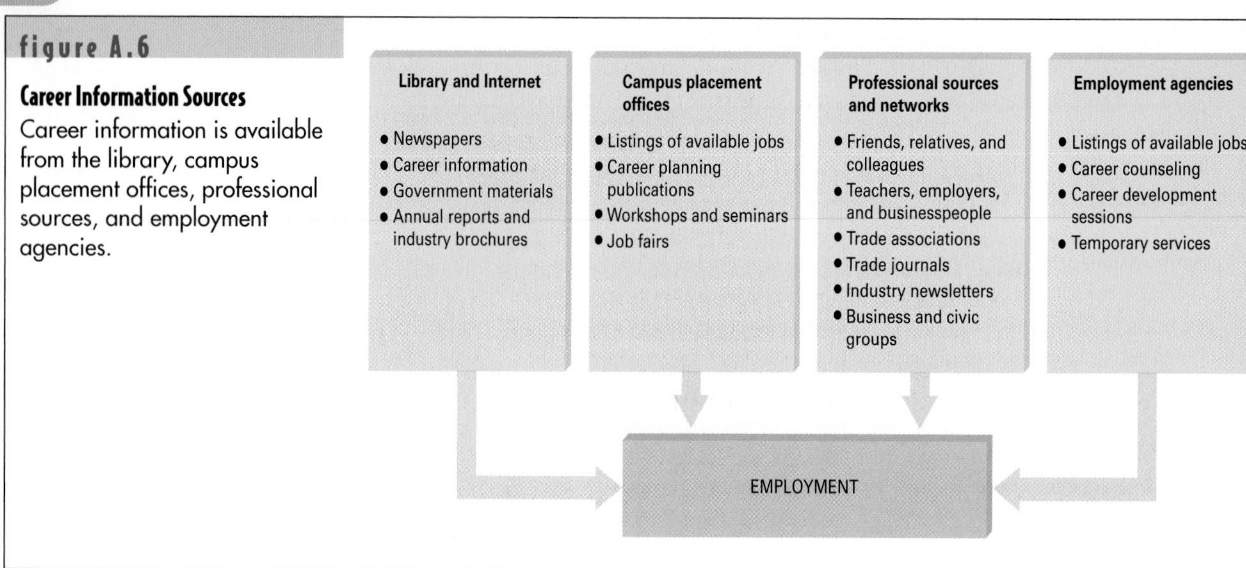

practical standpoint, it can't hurt to consult state employment agencies. They will have information about some professional and managerial positions availab in your area, and you will not be charged a fee if you obtain a job through a stat employment agency.

Many people want a job immediately and are discouraged at the thought of an occu pational search taking months. The fact is, though, that people seeking entry-lev jobs should expect their job search to take three to six months. Job applicants wh want higher-paying positions can expect to be looking for work for as long as a yea eighteen months, or more. Of course, the state of the economy and whether emplo ers are hiring or not can shorten or extend a job search for anyone.

Regardless of how long it takes, most people will tell you that a job search alwa takes too long. During a job search, you should use the same work habits that effecti employees use on the job. When searching for a job, resist the temptation to "take th day off." Instead, make a master list of activities that you want to accomplish each da If necessary, force yourself to make contacts, do job research, or schedule intervie that might lead to job opportunities. (Actually, many job applicants look at the jo hunt as their job and work from eight to five, five days a week until they find the jo they want.) Above all, realize that an occupational search requires patience and perse verance. And according to many individuals who have been through the process trying to find a job, perseverance may be the most important trait that successful jo hunters need.

Planning and Preparation

It is generally agreed that competition for the better jobs will get tougher and toughe The key to landing the job you want is planning and preparation—and planning be gins with goals. In particular, it is important to determine your *personal goals*, to decid on the role your career will play in reaching those goals, and then to develop your ca reer goals. Once you know where you are going, you can devise a reasonable plan fo getting there.

The time to begin planning is as early as possible. You must, of course, satisfy th educational requirements for the occupational area you wish to enter. Early plannin will give you the opportunity to do so. But those people with whom you will be com peting for the better jobs also will be fully prepared. Can you do more?

The answer is yes. Corporate recruiters say that the following factors give jo candidates a definite advantage:

- *Work experience*—You can get valuable work experience in cooperative work/school programs, during summer vacations, or in part-time jobs during the school year. Experience in your chosen occupational area carries the most weight, but even unrelated work experience is important.
- *The ability to communicate well*—Verbal and written communication skills are increasingly important in all aspects of business. Yours will be tested in your letters to recruiters, in your résumé, and in interviews. You will use these same communication skills throughout your career.
- *Clear and realistic job and career goals*—Recruiters feel most comfortable with candidates who know where they are headed and why they are applying for a specific job.

gain, early planning can make all the difference in defining your goals, in sharpening our communication skills (through elective courses, if necessary), and in obtaining olid work experience. See Table A.1 to learn about online career planning resources.

etter and Résumé

reparation is also important when it is time to apply for a position. Your college lacement office and various publications available in your library (including such diectories as *Standard & Poor's Register of Corporations* and the Thomas Register) can elp you find firms to apply to for jobs. As already mentioned, help-wanted ads, the nternet, networking, and employment agencies also may provide leads.

Your first contact with a prospective employer probably will be through the nail—in a letter in which you express your interest in working for that firm. This leter should be clear and straightforward, and it should follow proper business-letter

table A.1 Online Career Planning

Every day, more and more people are using the Internet for their career planning activities. Obtaining information about employers, picking up helpful résumé writing and interviewing tips, making contacts, and upgrading employment skills are just a few of the web-based career tasks growing in popularity. (Visit the text website for updates and additions to these URLs.)

American Marketing Association	**www.marketingpower.com**
America's Job Bank	**www.ajb.dni.us**
CareerBuilder.com	**www.careerbuilder.com**
CareerJournal	**www.careerjournal.com**
CollegeGrad.com	**www.collegegrad.com**
D&B's Million Dollar Databases	**http://mddi.dnb.com**
FedWorld	**www.fedworld.gov/jobs/jobsearch.html**
Hoover's Online	**www.hoovers.com**
HotJobs	**http://hotjobs.yahoo.com**
Industryview	**www.industryview.com**
job-interview.net	**www.job-interview.net**
JobStar	**www.jobstar.org**
JobWeb	**www.jobweb.com**
Monster	**www.monster.com**
The Riley Guide	**www.rileyguide.com**
Vault	**www.vault.com**
WetFeet	**www.wetfeet.com**

form (see Figure A.7). It (and any other letters you write to potential employers) wi be considered part of your employment credentials.

This first letter should be addressed to the personnel or human resources mar ager—by name if possible. You may include in this letter, very briefly, some informa tion regarding your qualifications and your reason for writing to that particular firn If your source of information (newspaper advertisement, employment agency, currer employee of the firm, and so on) indicates that this employer is looking for specific jo skills, you also may want to state and describe in the cover letter the skills you posses You should request an interview and, if the firm requires it, an employment applica tion.

You should include a copy of your résumé with your first letter (most applican do). In any case, you should already have prepared the résumé, which is a summary c all your attention-getting employment achievements and capabilities. Your goal i preparing both the cover letter and the résumé is to give the potential employer th impression that you are someone who deserves an interview.

A résumé should highlight and summarize your abilities and work achievement The résumé should fit on a single sheet of white high-quality bond letter paper. I should be carefully thought out—rework it as many times as necessary to get it righ and put your best foot forward. Make your résumé concise, but be sure to note every thing important. You need not include explanations or details; you will have an oppor tunity to discuss your qualifications during the interviews. It should be written to gra a potential employer's interest. The employer reading your résumé should want t meet you to find out more. Your résumé needs to show that despite your current jo title, you are qualified for the higher-level position you seek.

Remember that you are writing a résumé that will sell you to a potential em ployer. If necessary, ask former supervisors and colleagues to tell you what happene to projects or work that you produced. Then use action verbs to describe your majo contributions. Words such as *managed*, *created*, *developed*, and *coordinated* sound higl

figure A.7

Letter of Application

A letter of application should give your qualifications and your reasons for applying to a given company.

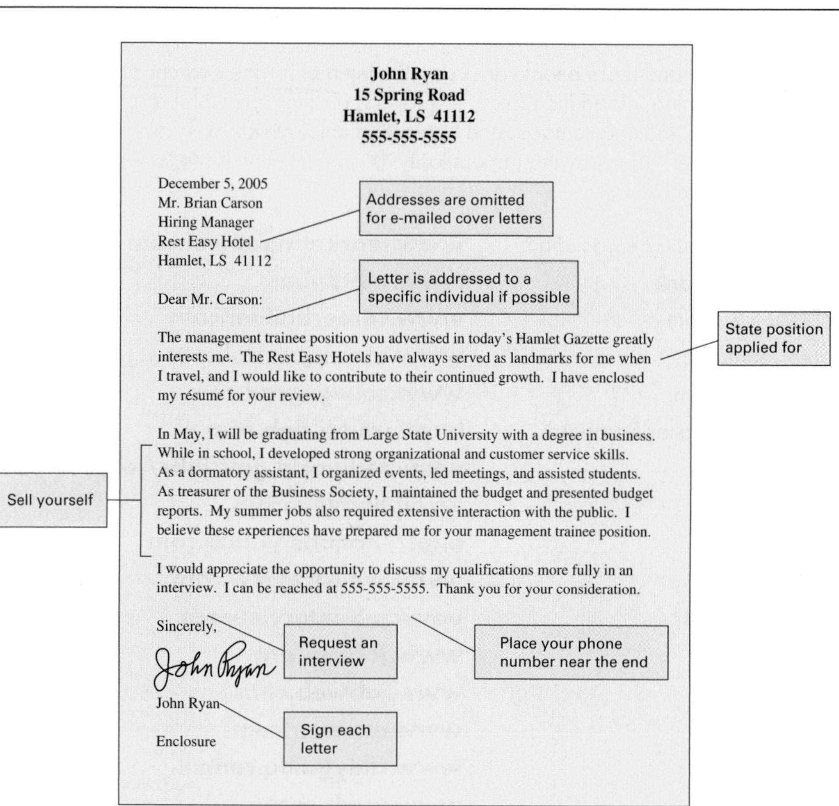

John Ryan
15 Spring Road
Hamlet, LS 41112
555-555-5555

December 5, 2005
Mr. Brian Carson
Hiring Manager
Rest Easy Hotel
Hamlet, LS 41112

Dear Mr. Carson:

The management trainee position you advertised in today's Hamlet Gazette greatly interests me. The Rest Easy Hotels have always served as landmarks for me when I travel, and I would like to contribute to their continued growth. I have enclosed my résumé for your review.

In May, I will be graduating from Large State University with a degree in business. While in school, I developed strong organizational and customer service skills. As a dormatory assistant, I organized events, led meetings, and assisted students. As treasurer of the Business Society, I maintained the budget and presented budget reports. My summer jobs also required extensive interaction with the public. I believe these experiences have prepared me for your management trainee position.

I would appreciate the opportunity to discuss my qualifications more fully in an interview. I can be reached at 555-555-5555. Thank you for your consideration.

Sincerely,

John Ryan

John Ryan

Enclosure

Source: U.S. Bureau of Labor Statistics website, **www.bls.gov.**

powered. Passive words or phrases such as *was responsible* for and *performed* are not attention-getting. Highlight your work achievements by using percentages, numbers, or dollar amounts. Such concrete details demonstrate just how important your contributions were. In some cases personal traits or the ability to "do something" may be more important than technical skills. Employers may be looking for someone who has the ability to

1. Prepare letters, memos, and other written communications
2. Answer the telephone and talk with customers
3. Analyze and solve problems related to a specific job
4. Work independently and make decisions
5. Be flexible and get the job done
6. Get along with others and be a team player

These traits may be extremely important to some employers. And a job applicant who does not have a lot of occupational experience can use these traits to "beef up" a slim résumé.

Figures A.8, A.9, and A.10 show a chronological résumé, a functional résumé, and a new database résumé. The chronological résumé presents your education, work experience, and other information in a reverse-time sequence (the most recent item first). The functional résumé emphasizes your abilities and skills in categories such as communication, supervision, project planning, human relations, and research. The database résumé, also called *plain text* or *e-mailed résumé*, includes the same basic information, except that the database résumé is written without columns, bullets, or bold or italic styles. Regardless of the form used, a résumé should include the following: your name, address, and telephone number; your work experience and major accomplishments on the job; your educational background; and any awards you have won. Avoid all extraneous information (such as weight, age, marital status, and the names and addresses of references) that could be supplied during an interview. Reserve

figure A.8

Sample Chronological Résumé

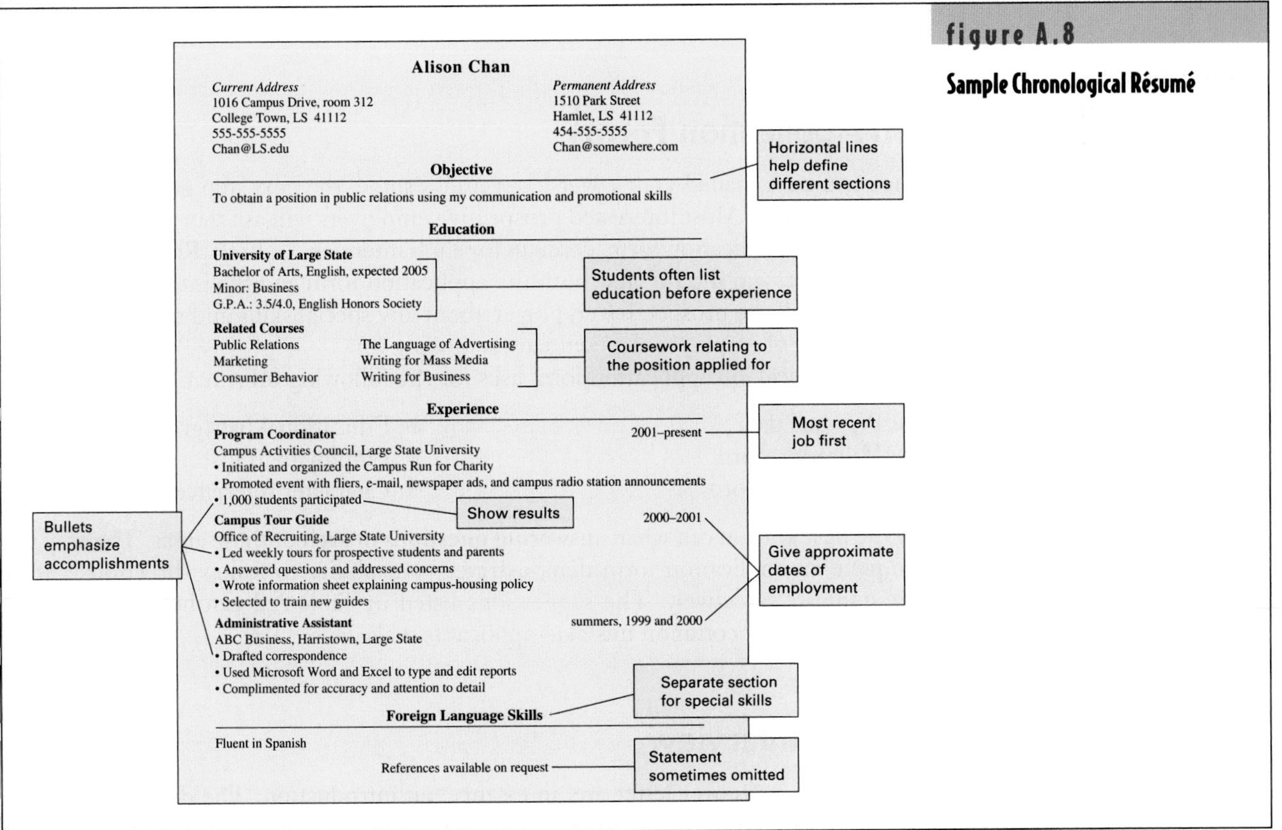
Alison Chan

Current Address
1016 Campus Drive, room 312
College Town, LS 41112
555-555-5555
Chan@LS.edu

Permanent Address
1510 Park Street
Hamlet, LS 41112
454-555-5555
Chan@somewhere.com

Objective

To obtain a position in public relations using my communication and promotional skills

Education

University of Large State
Bachelor of Arts, English, expected 2005
Minor: Business
G.P.A.: 3.5/4.0, English Honors Society

Related Courses
Public Relations | The Language of Advertising
Marketing | Writing for Mass Media
Consumer Behavior | Writing for Business

Experience

Program Coordinator 2001–present
Campus Activities Council, Large State University
• Initiated and organized the Campus Run for Charity
• Promoted event with fliers, e-mail, newspaper ads, and campus radio station announcements
• 1,000 students participated

Campus Tour Guide 2000–2001
Office of Recruiting, Large State University
• Led weekly tours for prospective students and parents
• Answered questions and addressed concerns
• Wrote information sheet explaining campus-housing policy
• Selected to train new guides

Administrative Assistant summers, 1999 and 2000
ABC Business, Harristown, Large State
• Drafted correspondence
• Used Microsoft Word and Excel to type and edit reports
• Complimented for accuracy and attention to detail

Foreign Language Skills

Fluent in Spanish

References available on request

Source: U.S. Bureau of Labor Statistics website, **www.bls.gov.**

figure A.9

Sample Functional Résumé

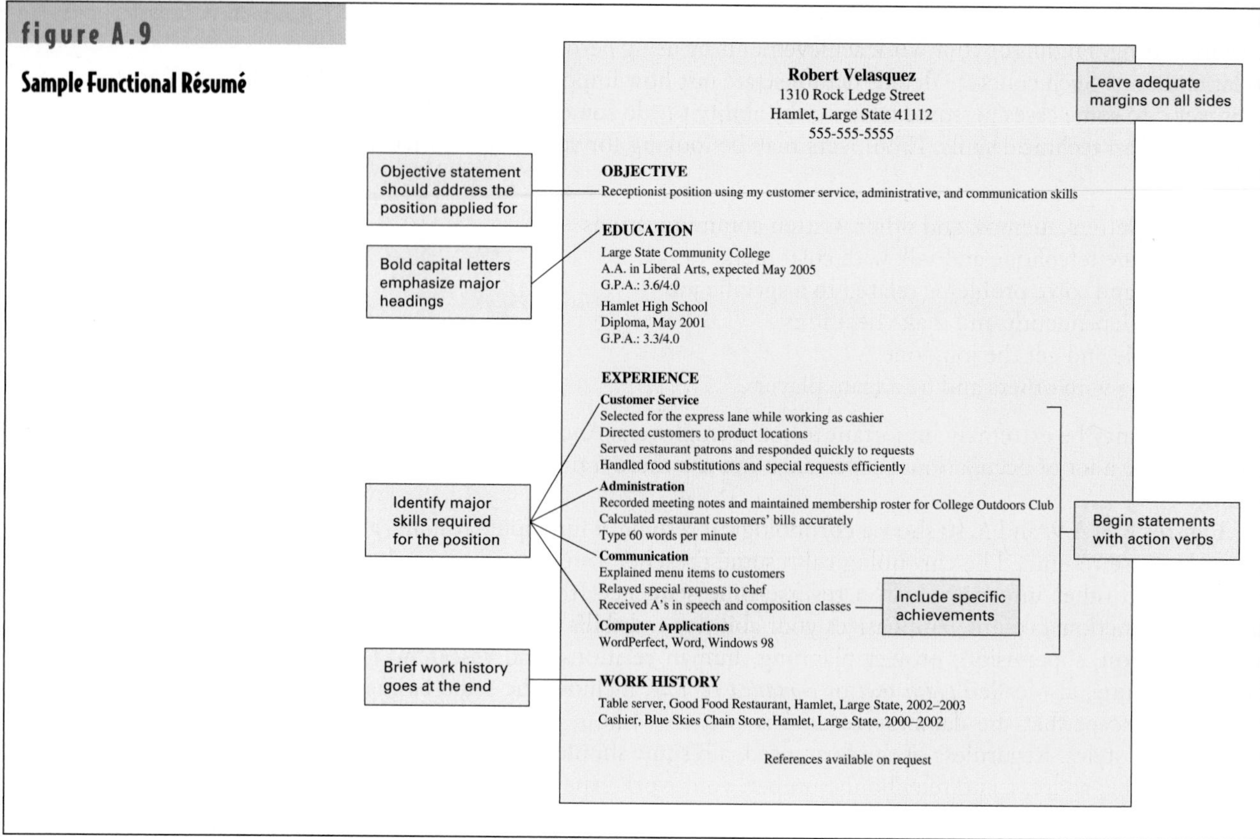

Source: U.S. Bureau of Labor Statistics website, **www.bls.gov.**

your employment and/or career objectives for mention in the one-page cover letters you send to potential employers with copies of your résumé.

Job Application Forms

Once you have mailed your cover letter and résumé, the next step generally depends on the employer. Most interested prospective employers will ask that you complete an employment application form, come in for a job interview, or both. Regardless of what happens next, you should view both the application form and the interview as opportunities to tell the prospective employer about any special skills and talents that make you the type of employee the company is looking for.

The typical job application form asks for the following information:

- Personal data
- Military record
- Criminal record
- Educational background
- Employment history
- Character references

Do the best job you can when answering questions in each of these areas. The way you complete an application form demonstrates your ability to follow directions and to communicate effectively. The suggestions listed in Table A.2 can help you to avoid some of the most common mistakes applicants make.

The Job Interview

Your résumé and cover letter are, in essence, an introduction. The deciding factor in the hiring process is the interview (or several interviews) with representatives of the firm. It is through the interview that the firm gets to know you and your qualifications. At the same time, the interview provides a chance for you to learn about the firm.

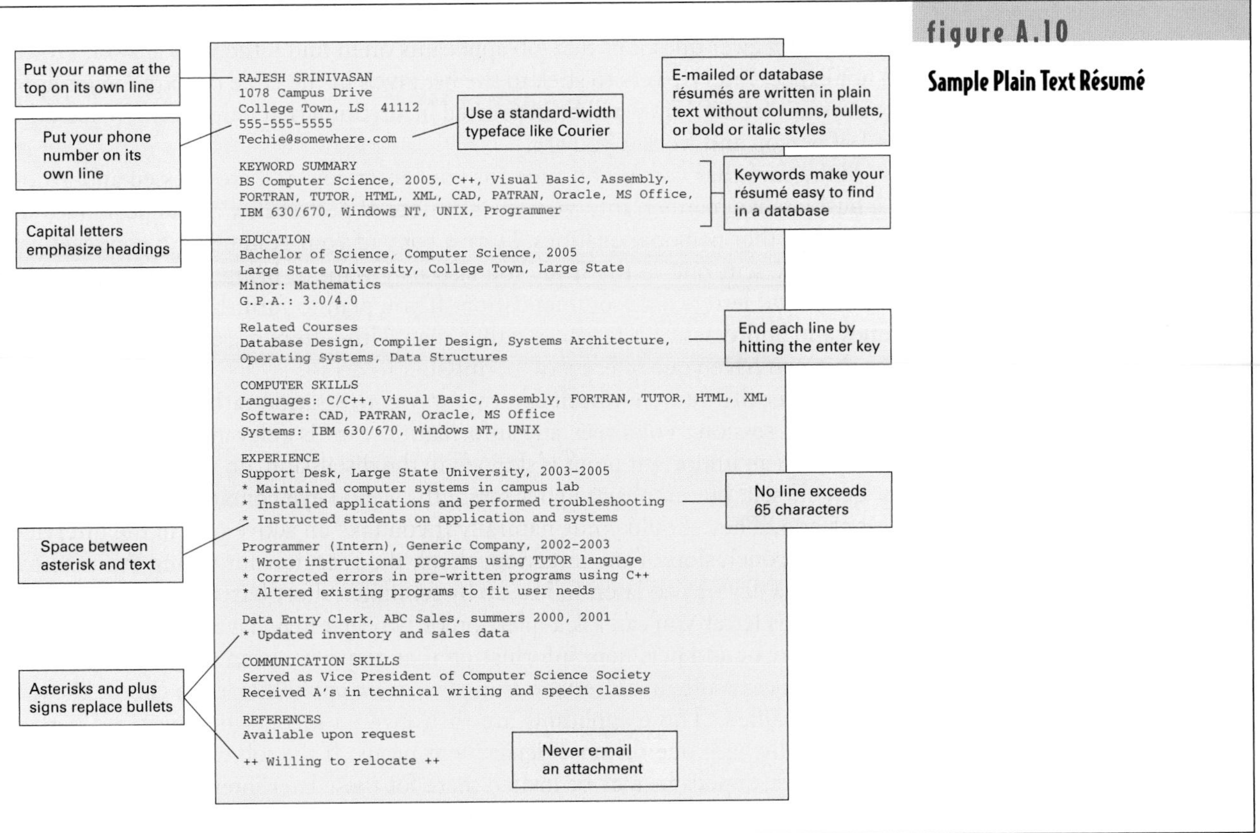


```
RAJESH SRINIVASAN
1078 Campus Drive
College Town, LS  41112
555-555-5555
Techie@somewhere.com

KEYWORD SUMMARY
BS Computer Science, 2005, C++, Visual Basic, Assembly,
FORTRAN, TUTOR, HTML, XML, CAD, PATRAN, Oracle, MS Office,
IBM 630/670, Windows NT, UNIX, Programmer

EDUCATION
Bachelor of Science, Computer Science, 2005
Large State University, College Town, Large State
Minor: Mathematics
G.P.A.: 3.0/4.0

Related Courses
Database Design, Compiler Design, Systems Architecture,
Operating Systems, Data Structures

COMPUTER SKILLS
Languages: C/C++, Visual Basic, Assembly, FORTRAN, TUTOR, HTML, XML
Software: CAD, PATRAN, Oracle, MS Office
Systems: IBM 630/670, Windows NT, UNIX

EXPERIENCE
Support Desk, Large State University, 2003-2005
* Maintained computer systems in campus lab
* Installed applications and performed troubleshooting
* Instructed students on application and systems

Programmer (Intern), Generic Company, 2002-2003
* Wrote instructional programs using TUTOR language
* Corrected errors in pre-written programs using C++
* Altered existing programs to fit user needs

Data Entry Clerk, ABC Sales, summers 2000, 2001
* Updated inventory and sales data

COMMUNICATION SKILLS
Served as Vice President of Computer Science Society
Received A's in technical writing and speech classes

REFERENCES
Available upon request

++ Willing to relocate ++
```

figure A.10

Sample Plain Text Résumé

Source: U.S. Bureau of Labor Statistics website, **www.bls.gov.**

Here, again, preparation is the key to success. Research the firm before your first interview. Learn all you can about its products, its subsidiaries, the markets it operates in, its history, the locations of its facilities, and so on. If possible, obtain and read the firm's most recent annual report. Be prepared to ask questions about the firm and the opportunities it offers. Interviewers welcome such questions. They expect you to be interested enough to spend some time thinking about your potential relationship with their firm.

table A.2 Tips for Completing Employment Application Forms

1. Do a "dry run" to practice answering the questions on a typical employment application.
2. If it is not possible to take the application home, complete the application in ink. Print clearly. Use one lettering style. Be neat.
3. Follow the directions on the employment application.
4. Read all questions before you begin answering them.
5. Judge the amount of space that you have to answer each question.
6. Fill in every blank even if you must write not applicable (N/A) or none.
7. Use only recognizable abbreviations.
8. Know your work history.
9. Answer all questions honestly.
10. Choose references carefully.
11. Be careful when writing salary requirements. Avoid committing yourself to a specific number, and know the going rate in your field.
12. Read over the completed application, and look for grammatical or spelling errors.

Source: Susan D. Greene and Melanie C. L. Martel, *The Ultimate Job Hunter's Guidebook*, 4th ed., pp. 155–156. Copyright © 2004 by Houghton Mifflin Company. Adapted with permission.

Prepare also to respond to questions the interviewer may ask. Table A.3 is a list typical interviewer questions that job applicants often find difficult to answer. Howeve do not expect interviewers to stick to the list given in the table or to the items appea ing in your résumé. They will be interested in anything that helps them to decide wh kind of person and worker you are.

Make sure that you are on time for your interview and are dressed and groome in a businesslike manner. Interviewers take note of punctuality and appearance, just they do of other personal qualities. Have a copy of your résumé with you, even if yo have already sent one to the firm. You also may want to bring a copy of your cour transcript and letters of recommendation. If you plan to furnish interviewers with th names and addresses of references rather than with letters of recommendation, mak sure that you have your references' permission to do so.

Consider the interview itself as a two-way conversation rather than as a questior and-answer session. Volunteer any information that is relevant to the interviewer questions. If an important point is skipped in the discussion, do not hesitate to bring up. Be yourself, but emphasize your strengths. Good eye contact and posture are im portant, too. They should come naturally if you take an active part in the interview.

At the conclusion of the interview, thank the recruiter for taking the time to se you. Then, a day or two later, follow up by sending a short letter of thanks (see Figur A.11). In this letter you can ask a question or two that may have occurred to you afte the interview or add pertinent information that may have been overlooked.

In most cases the first interview is used to *screen* applicants, or to choose those wh are best qualified. These applicants are then given a second interview and perhaps third—usually with one or more department heads. If the job requires relocation to different area, applicants may be invited there for these later interviews. After the inter viewing process is complete, applicants are told when to expect a hiring decision.

table A.3 **Interview Questions Job Applicants Often Find Difficult to Answer**

1. Tell me about yourself.
2. What do you know about our organization?
3. What can you do for us? Why should we hire you?
4. What qualifications do you have that make you feel you will be successful in your field?
5. What have you learned from the jobs that you have held?
6. If you could write your own ticket, what would be your ideal job?
7. What are your special skills, and how did you acquire them?
8. Have you had any special accomplishments in your lifetime that you are particularly proud of?
9. Why did you leave your most recent job?
10. How do you spend your spare time? What are your hobbies?
11. What are your strengths and weaknesses?
12. Discuss five major accomplishments.
13. What kind of boss would you like? Why?
14. If you could spend a day with someone you have known or known of, who would it be?
15. What personality characteristics rub you the wrong way?
16. How do you show your anger? What type of things make you angry?
17. With what type of person do you spend the majority of your time?
18. What activities have you ever quit?
19. Define cooperation.

Source: Adapted from Susan D. Greene and Melanie C. L. Martel, *The Ultimate Job Hunter's Guidebook*, 4th ed., pp. 176–177. Used by permission of The Houghton Mifflin Company.

figure A.11

Sample Thank You Letter

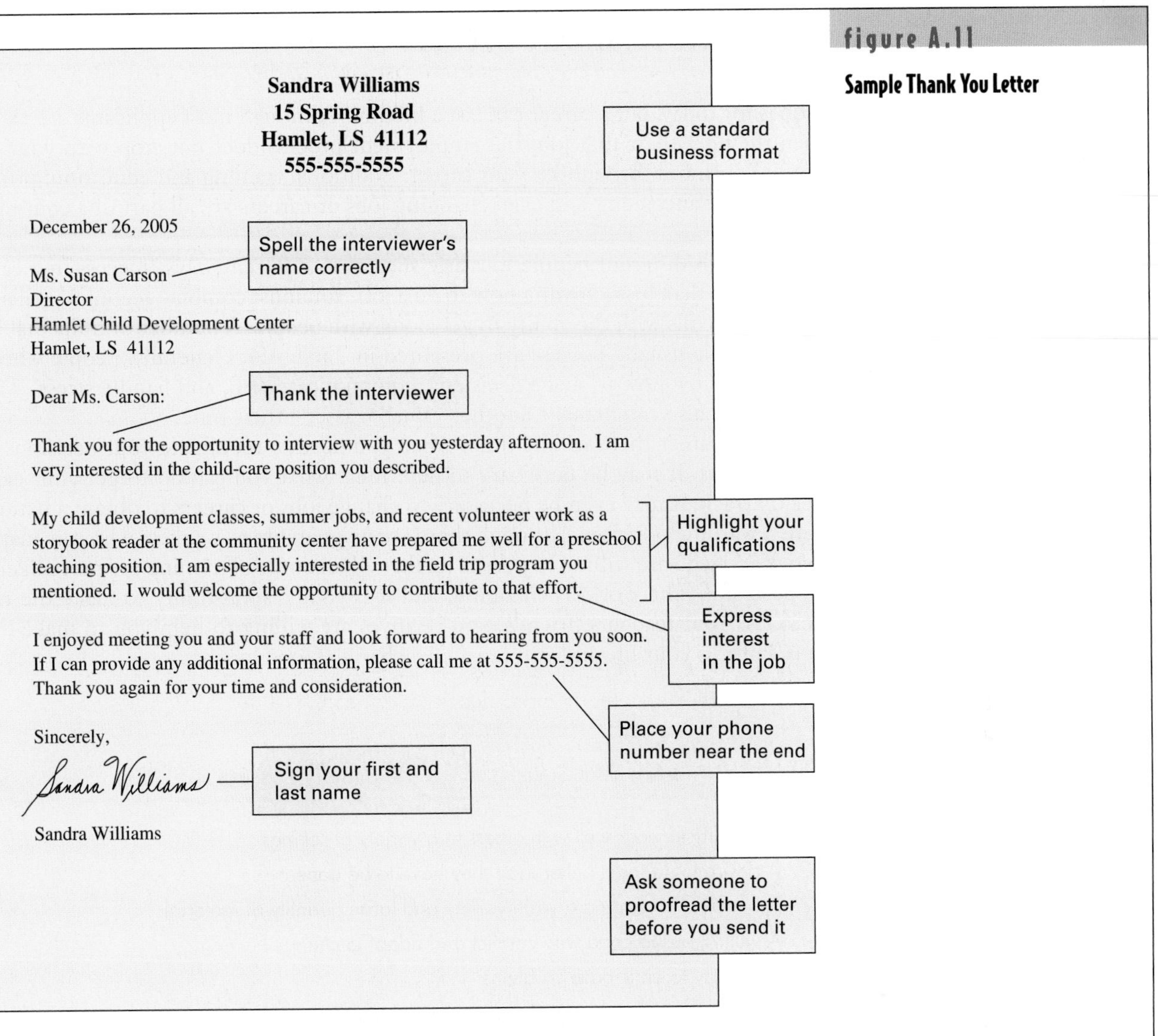

Sandra Williams
15 Spring Road
Hamlet, LS 41112
555-555-5555

December 26, 2005

Ms. Susan Carson
Director
Hamlet Child Development Center
Hamlet, LS 41112

Dear Ms. Carson:

Thank you for the opportunity to interview with you yesterday afternoon. I am very interested in the child-care position you described.

My child development classes, summer jobs, and recent volunteer work as a storybook reader at the community center have prepared me well for a preschool teaching position. I am especially interested in the field trip program you mentioned. I would welcome the opportunity to contribute to that effort.

I enjoyed meeting you and your staff and look forward to hearing from you soon. If I can provide any additional information, please call me at 555-555-5555. Thank you again for your time and consideration.

Sincerely,

Sandra Williams

Sandra Williams

Use a standard business format
Spell the interviewer's name correctly
Thank the interviewer
Highlight your qualifications
Express interest in the job
Place your phone number near the end
Sign your first and last name
Ask someone to proofread the letter before you send it

Source: U.S. Bureau of Labor Statistics website, **www.bls.gov.**

Accepting an Offer

"We'd like to offer you the job" may be the best news a job applicant can hear. To accept the job, you should send the firm a letter in which you express your appreciation, accept the offer, and restate the conditions of employment as you understand them. These conditions should include the starting salary, employee benefits, and a general description of the job (responsibilities, training, the immediate supervisor's name, and such). If you have any concerns regarding the job, make sure that they are cleared up before you send your letter of acceptance: The job offer and your acceptance constitute a contract between you and the firm.

Less exciting is the news that begins "We thank you for your interest in our firm, *but*. . . ." The fact is that there are many more applicants for jobs than there are jobs. (This is so because most people apply for several positions at the same time.) As a result, most people are turned down for some jobs during their careers. Do not be discouraged if you don't get the first position you apply for. Instead, think back over the application process, analyze it, and try to determine what you might improve. In other words, learn from your experience—and keep trying. Success will come if you persevere.

A Final Note about Careers

A job is for today, but a career can last a lifetime. Although most applicants are excited when they get their first job, the employment process does not stop with your first job—it continues throughout your career. Additional training and education, promotions and advancement, and even changing jobs or careers are all part of a continuing process.

Although different people measure success in different ways, success in a career means more than just knowing how to do a job. You must combine technical skills and managerial skills with the ability to get along with people. A number of traits that successful people usually possess are presented in Table A.4. Generally, people who are promoted know how to make decisions, communicate well, and handle stress. These same people also can manage another valuable asset—their time.

In any career there will be times when you need to reevaluate your decisions and opportunities. It may be necessary to determine what you can do to get your career back on track. It may even be necessary to change jobs or careers to obtain a better or more rewarding position. Although there are no guarantees, workers who can adapt to change and who are willing to pursue further education and training are more likely to be successful. The world is changing, and it is your responsibility to make the right decisions. Your teachers, friends, and relatives are willing to help you to make decisions, but it is your life and you must take charge. Good luck!

table A.4 Traits That Successful People Usually Possess

1. An ability to work well with others in a variety of settings
2. A desire to do tasks better than they have to be done
3. An interest in reading a wide variety and large quantity of material
4. A willingness to cope with conflict and adapt to change
5. An ability to anticipate problems
6. A knowledge of technology and computer software such as word processing, spreadsheet, and database programs
7. An ability to solve problems creatively
8. A knowledge of research techniques and library resources
9. Well-developed written and oral communication skills
10. An understanding of both their own motivations and the motivations of others

Source: Jack R. Kapoor, Les Diabay, and Robert J. Hughes, *Personal Finance,* 7th ed., pp. 38–39.

Risk Management and Insurance

APPENDIX B

We begin this appendix by defining two broad categories of risk: pure risk and speculative risk. We then examine several methods of risk management available to individuals and businesses and consider situations in which each method is appropriate. Next, we turn our attention to insurance companies—organizations that, for a fee, assume financial responsibility for losses resulting from certain kinds of risks. We see how insurance companies determine which risks they will cover and what prices they will charge for coverage. Then we list the major types of insurance against loss of property and loss due to accidents and discuss workers' compensation and health care insurance. We close the appendix with a comparison of several kinds of life insurance.

The Element of Risk

Risk is the possibility that a loss or injury will occur. It is impossible to escape all types of risk in today's world. For individuals, driving an automobile, investing in stocks or bonds, and even jogging along a country road are situations that involve some risk. For businesses, risk is a part of every decision. In fact, the essence of business decision making is weighing the potential risks and gains involved in various courses of action.

risk the possibility that a loss or injury will occur

There is obviously a difference between, say, the risk of losing money one has invested and the risk of being hit by a car while jogging. This difference leads to the classification of risks as either speculative or pure risks.

A **speculative risk** is a risk that accompanies the possibility of earning a profit. Most business decisions, such as the decision to market a new product, involve speculative risks. If the new product succeeds in the marketplace, there are profits; if it fails, there are losses. For example, PepsiCo repeatedly gambles on the introduction of new products to compete with Coca-Cola and reach the elusive top spot. But the gamble does not pay off when the product fizzles.

speculative risk a risk that accompanies the possibility of earning a profit

A **pure risk** is a risk that involves only the possibility of loss, with no potential for gain. The possibility of damage due to hurricane, fire, or automobile accident is a pure risk because there is no gain if such damage does not occur. Another pure risk is the risk of large medical bills resulting from a serious illness. Again, if there is no illness, there is no monetary gain.

pure risk a risk that involves only the possibility of loss, with no potential for gain

Let us now look at the various techniques available for managing risk.

Risk Management

Risk management is the process of evaluating the risks faced by a firm or an individual and then minimizing the costs involved with those risks. Any risk entails two types of costs. The first is the cost that will be incurred if a potential loss becomes an actual loss. An example is the cost of rebuilding and reequipping an assembly plant that burns to the ground. The second type consists of the costs of reducing or eliminating the risk of potential loss. Here we would include the cost of purchasing insurance against loss by fire or the cost of not building the plant at all (this cost is equal to the profit that the plant might have earned). These two types of costs must be balanced, one against the other, if risk management is to be effective.

risk management the process of evaluating the risks faced by a firm or an individual and then minimizing the costs involved with those risks

Most people think of risk management as simply buying insurance. However, insurance, although an important part of risk management, is not the only means of dealing with risk. Other methods may be less costly in specific situations. And some kinds of risks are uninsurable—not even an insurance company will issue a policy to protect against them. In this section we examine the four general risk-management techniques. Then, in the following sections, we look more closely at insurance.

Risk Avoidance

An individual can avoid the risk of an automobile accident by not riding in a car. A manufacturer can avoid the risk of product failure by refusing to introduce new products. Both would be practicing risk avoidance—but at a very high cost. The person who avoids automobile accidents by foregoing cars may have to give up his or her job to do so. The business that does not take a chance on new products probably will fail when the product life cycle, discussed in Chapter 14, catches up with existing products.

There are, however, situations in which risk avoidance is a practical technique. At the personal level, individuals who stop smoking or refuse to walk through a dark city park late at night are avoiding risks. Jewelry stores lock their merchandise in vaults at the end of the business day to avoid losses through robbery. And to avoid the risk of a holdup, many gasoline stations accept only credit cards or the exact amount of the purchase for sales made after dark.

Obviously, no person or business can eliminate all risks. By the same token, however, no one should assume that all risks are unavoidable.

Risk Reduction

If a risk cannot be avoided, perhaps it can be reduced. An automobile passenger can reduce the risk of injury in an automobile accident by wearing a seat belt. A manufacturer can reduce the risk of product failure through careful product planning and market testing. In both situations, the cost of reducing risk seems to be well worth the potential saving.

Businesses face risks as a result of their operating procedures and management decision making. An analysis of operating procedures—by company personnel or outside consultants—often can point out areas in which risk can be reduced. Among the techniques that can be used are

- The establishment of an employee safety program to encourage employees' awareness of safety
- The purchase *and* use of proper safety equipment, from hand guards on machinery to goggles and safety shoes for individuals
- Burglar alarms, security guards, and even guard dogs to protect warehouses from burglary
- Fire alarms, smoke alarms, and sprinkler systems to reduce the risk of fire and the losses due to fire
- Accurate and effective accounting and financial controls to protect a firm's inventories and cash from pilfering

The risks involved in management decisions can be reduced only through effective decision making. These risks increase when a decision is made hastily or is based on less than sufficient information. However, the cost of reducing these risks goes up when managers take too long to make decisions. Costs also increase when managers require an overabundance of information before they are willing to decide.

Risk Assumption

An individual or firm will—and probably must—take on certain risks as part of living or doing business. Individuals who drive to work assume the risk of having an accient, but they wear a seat belt to reduce the risk of injury in the event of an accident. The firm that markets a new product assumes the risk of product failure—after first reducing that risk through market testing.

Risk assumption, then, is the act of taking responsibility for the loss or injury that may result from a risk. Generally, it makes sense to assume a risk when one or more of the following conditions exist:

1. The potential loss is too small to worry about.
2. Effective risk management has reduced the risk.
3. Insurance coverage, if available, is too expensive.
4. There is no other way of protecting against the loss.

Large firms with many facilities often find a particular kind of risk assumption, called self-insurance, a practical way to avoid high insurance costs. **Self-insurance** is the process of establishing a monetary fund that can be used to cover the cost of a loss. For instance, suppose that approximately 16,000 7-Eleven convenience stores, each worth $400,000, are scattered around the country. A logical approach to self-insurance against fire losses would be to collect a certain sum—say, $600—from each store every year. The funds are placed in an interest-bearing reserve fund and used as necessary to repair any fire damage that occurs to 7-Eleven stores. Money not used remains the property of the firm. Eventually, if the fund grows, the yearly contribution from each store can be reduced.

self-insurance the process of establishing a monetary fund that can be used to cover the cost of a loss

Self-insurance does not eliminate risks; it merely provides a means for covering losses. And it is, itself, a risky practice—at least in the beginning. For example, 7-Eleven would suffer a considerable financial loss if more than twenty-four stores were destroyed by fire in the first year the self-insurance program was in effect.

Shifting Risks

Perhaps the most common method of dealing with risk is to shift, or transfer, the risk to an insurance company. An **insurer** (or **insurance company**) is a firm that agrees, for a fee, to assume financial responsibility for losses that may result from a specific risk. The fee charged by an insurance company is called a **premium**. A contract between an insurer and the person or firm whose risk is assumed is known as an **insurance policy**. Generally, an insurance policy is written for a period of one year. Then, if both parties are willing, it is renewed each year. It specifies exactly which risks are covered by the agreement, the dollar amounts the insurer will pay in case of a loss, and the amount of the premium.

insurer (or insurance company) a firm that agrees, for a fee, to assume financial responsibility for losses that may result from a specific risk

premium the fee charged by an insurance company

insurance policy the contract between an insurer and the person or firm whose risk is assumed

Insurance is thus the protection against loss that the purchase of an insurance policy affords. Insurance companies will not, however, assume every kind of risk. A risk that insurance companies will assume is called an **insurable risk**. Insurable risks include the risk of loss by fire and theft, the risk of loss by automobile accident, and the risks of sickness and death. A risk that insurance companies will not assume is called an **uninsurable risk**.

insurance the protection against loss that the purchase of an insurance policy affords

insurable risk a risk that insurance companies will assume

uninsurable risk a risk that insurance companies will not assume

In general, pure risks are insurable, whereas speculative risks are uninsurable (see Figure B.1). An insurance company will protect a Ford Motor Company assembly plant against losses due to fire or tornadoes. It will not, however, protect Ford against losses resulting from a lack of sales orders for automobiles.

The next section provides an overview of the basic principles of insurance and the kinds of companies that provide insurance.

Insurance and Insurance Companies

An insurance company is a business. Like other businesses, an insurer provides a product—protection from loss—in return for a reasonable fee. Its sales revenues are the premiums it collects from the individuals and firms it insures. (Insurance companies

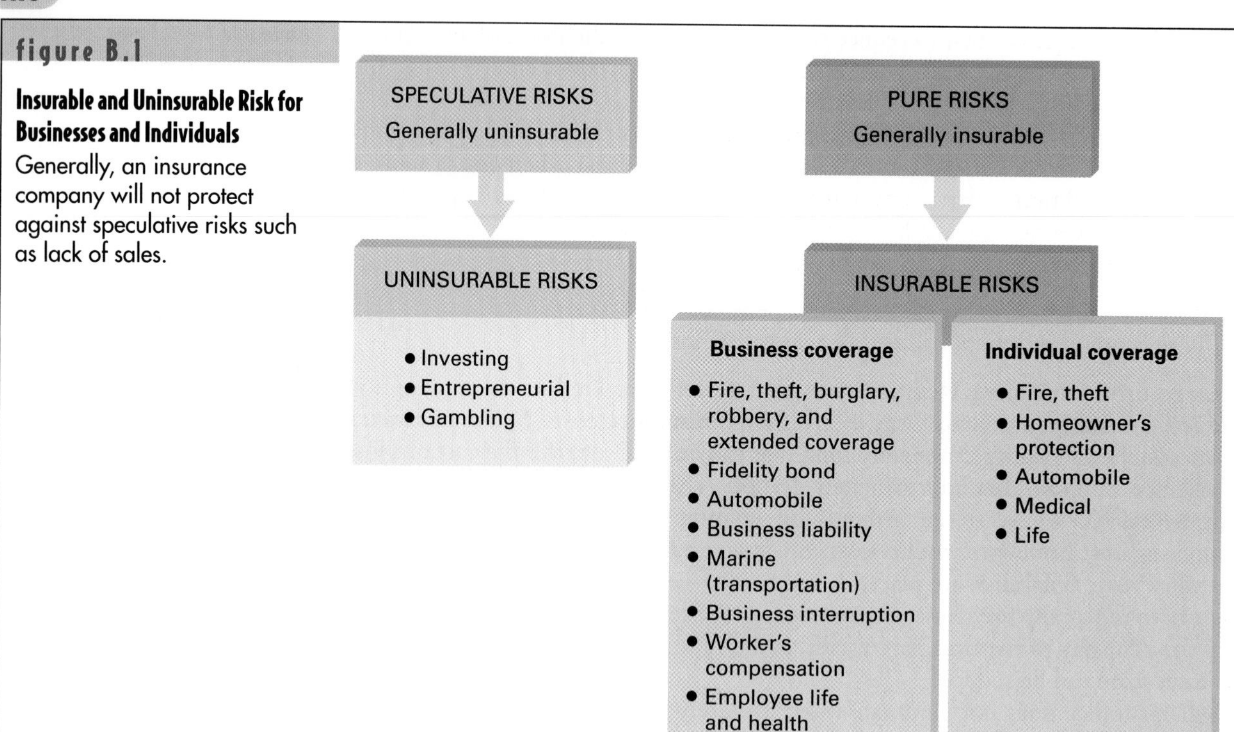

figure B.1

Insurable and Uninsurable Risk for Businesses and Individuals
Generally, an insurance company will not protect against speculative risks such as lack of sales.

typically invest the money they have on hand; thus we should include interest and dividend income as part of their revenues.) Its expenses are the costs of the various resources—salaries, rent, utilities, and so on—plus the amounts the insurance company pays out to cover its clients' losses.

The year 2001 was a difficult one for the insurance industry. An unprecedented surge of catastrophic claims after the September 11 terrorist attacks left the industry reeling. The terrorist attack was the largest single event in all segments of the insurance industry, including health, workers' compensation, property, and airline liability insurance. In fact, catastrophic losses were the highest in the insurance industry's history, amounting to approximately $50 billion in 2001. For the first time ever, insurance companies paid more for claims than they collected from premiums plus investment earnings.

In response to the unexpected rise in claims and weaker investment returns in the 2001–2002 bear market, the insurance companies cut back coverage and sharply increased premium rates. The risks that previously seemed remote are more probable now than they were only a year ago. Thus terrorism coverage has become particularly difficult for both insurance companies and businesses. Insurance companies generally are reluctant to issue policies for risks they believe are unpredictable and undiversifiable. Therefore, while limited coverage is available at higher premiums, most insurance companies no longer offer terrorism coverage. Reason? Insurance companies are unable to predict the frequency and magnitude of potential losses. Indeed, recent surveys by the National Federation of Independent Business report that the cost and affordability of insurance are among the important problems facing small businesses.

Pricing and product are very important and exacting issues to an insurance company primarily because it must set its price (its premiums) before knowing the specific cost of its product (the amount of money it will have to pay out in claims). For this reason, insurance companies employ mathematicians called actuaries to predict the likelihood of losses and to determine the premiums that should be charged. Let us look at some of the more important concepts on which insurance (and the work of actuaries) is based.

asic Insurance Concepts

ısurance is based on several principles, including the principle of indemnity, insura-lity of the risk, and low-cost, affordable coverage.

he Principle of Indemnity The purpose of insurance is to provide protection gainst loss; it is neither speculation nor gambling. This concept is expressed in the **rinciple of indemnity**: In the event of a loss, an insured firm or individual cannot ollect from the insurer an amount greater than the actual dollar amount of the loss. uppose that you own a home valued at $150,000. However, you purchase $200,000 orth of fire insurance on your home. Even if it is destroyed by fire, the insurer will ay you only $150,000, the actual amount of your loss.

principle of indemnity in the event of a loss, an insured firm or individual cannot collect from the insurer an amount greater than the actual dollar amount of the loss

The premiums set by actuaries are based on the amount of risk involved and the mount to be paid in case of a loss. Generally, the greater the risk and the amount to e paid, the higher is the premium.

ısurability of the Risk Insurers will accept responsibility for risks that meet at ast the following conditions:

1. *Losses must not be under the control of the insured.* Losses caused by fire, wind, or accident generally are insurable, but gambling losses are not. Nor will an insurer pay a claim for damage intentionally caused by the insured person. For example, a person who sets fire to an insured building cannot collect on a fire insurance policy.
2. *The insured hazard must be geographically widespread.* That is, the insurance company must be able to write many policies covering the same specific hazard throughout a wide geographic area. This condition allows the insurer to minimize its own risk: the risk that it will have to pay huge sums of money to clients within a particular geographic area in the event of a catastrophe caused, for example, by a tornado or an earthquake.
3. *The probability of a loss should be predictable.* Insurance companies cannot tell which particular clients will suffer losses. However, their actuaries must be able to determine, statistically, what fraction of their clients will suffer each type of loss. They can do so, for insurable risks, by examining records of losses for past years. They can then base their premiums, at least in part, on the number and value of the losses that are expected to occur.
4. *Losses must be measurable.* Insured property must have a value that is measurable in dollars because insurance firms reimburse losses with money. Moreover, premiums are based partly on the measured value of the insured property. As a result of this condition, insurers will not insure an item for its emotional or sentimental value but only for its actual monetary value.
5. *The policyholder must have an insurable interest.* That is, the individual or firm that purchases an insurance policy must be the one that would suffer from a loss. You can purchase insurance on your own home, but you cannot insure your neighbor's home in the hope of making a profit if it should burn down! Generally, individuals are considered to have an insurable interest in their family members. Therefore, a person can insure the life of a spouse, a child, or a parent. Corporations may purchase "key executive" insurance covering certain corporate officers. The proceeds from this insurance help offset the loss of the services of these key people if they die or become incapacitated.

Using the Internet

There is a wide variety of websites that provide useful information about insurance, including the sites of insurance companies themselves. For authoritative quick tips and links to other relevant sites, visit CNNmoney's Personal Finance/Insurance site at **http://money.cnn.com/pf/insurance.**

Low-Cost, Affordable Coverage Price is usually a marketing issue rather than a technical concept. However, the price of insurance is intimately tied to the risks and potential losses involved in a particular type of coverage. Insurers would like to "produce" insurance at a very low cost to their policyholders, but they must charge enough in premiums to cover their expected payouts.

Customers purchase insurance when they believe premiums are low in relation t the possible dollar loss. For certain risks, premiums can soar so high that insurance simply not cost-effective. A $1,000 life insurance policy for a 99-year-old man woul cost about $950 per year. Clearly, a man of that age would be better off if he investe the premium amount in a bank. He would thus be using self-insurance rather tha shifting the risk. Although this is an extreme example, it illustrates that insurers mus compete, through their prices, with alternative methods of managing risk.

Ownership of Insurance Companies

stock insurance company an insurance company owned by stockholders and operated to earn a profit

mutual insurance company an insurance company that is owned collectively by its policyholders and is thus a cooperative

Insurance companies are owned either by stockholders or by policyholders. A **stock insurance company** is owned by stockholders and is operated to earn a profit. Lik other profit-making corporations, stock insurance companies pay dividends to stockholders from surplus of income (left over after benefit payments, operating expenses and taxes have been paid). Most of the approximately 6,000 insurance companies in the United States are stock insurance companies.

A **mutual insurance company** is owned collectively by its policyholders and i thus a cooperative. Because a mutual insurance company has no stockholders, its policyholders elect the board of directors. The members of the board, in turn, choose the executives who manage the firm. Any surplus of income over expenses is distributed to policyholders as a return of part of their premiums. (This return may take the form of a reduced premium at the start of the policy year or of a "dividend" at the end of the policy year.)

Both stock and mutual insurance companies must maintain cash reserves to cove future obligations and policyholders' claims. Cash reserves typically are invested in certificates of deposit, stocks, bonds, and real estate.

Careers in Insurance

Insurance companies form one of the largest industries in the United States. The industry ranks in importance with banking and finance, manufacturing, building, and electronics. Careers in insurance generally fall into two categories: sales and administration.

In the sales category, individuals can work as employees of insurance companies or as independent agents representing more than one insurance company. Recently, the insurance industry has placed more emphasis on advanced training for sales personnel. Life insurance salespeople who pass examinations and meet other requirements are awarded the Chartered Life Underwriter (CLU) designation. The Chartered Property Casualty Underwriter (CPCU) designation is awarded to individuals who pass examinations and meet the requirements in all areas except life insurance.

Administrative employees work to meet the needs of the firm's customers. They must process policies and claims and handle an amazing amount of paperwork. Jobs in this category include actuary, claims adjuster, claims clerk, underwriter, and a number of other essential positions. In addition to meeting the needs of customers, administrative employees are responsible for investing funds for an insurance company.

Property and Casualty Insurance

Businesses and individuals insure their property, such as buildings, against losses and purchase casualty insurance to cover financial losses resulting from injuries or damage caused by automobile accidents.

Insurance is available to cover most pure risks, but specialized or customized policies can be expensive. A part of effective risk management is to ensure that when insurance is purchased, the coverage is proper for the individual situation. Three questions can be used as guidelines in this regard:

- What hazards must be insured against?
- Is the cost of insurance coverage reasonable in this situation?
- What other risk-management techniques can be used to reduce insurance costs?

Fire Insurance

Fire insurance covers losses due to fire. The standard fire insurance policy provides protection against partial or complete loss of a building and/or its contents when that loss is caused by fire or lightening. Premiums depend on the construction of the building, its use and contents, whether risk-reduction devices (such as smoke and fire alarms) are installed in the building, and other factors. If a fire occurs, the insurance company reimburses the policyholder for either the actual dollar loss or the maximum amount stated in the policy, whichever is lower.

fire insurance insurance that covers losses due to fire

Coinsurance Clause To reduce their insurance premiums, individuals and businesses sometimes insure property for less than its actual cash value. Their theory is that fire rarely destroys a building completely—thus they need not buy full insurance. However, if the building is partially destroyed, they expect their insurance to cover all the damage. This places an unfair burden on the insurance company, which receives less than the full premium but must cover the full loss. To avoid this problem, insurance companies include a coinsurance clause in most fire insurance policies.

A **coinsurance clause** is a part of a fire insurance policy that requires the policyholder to purchase coverage at least equal to a specified percentage of the replacement cost of the property to obtain full reimbursement for losses. In most cases, the requirement is 80 percent of the replacement cost. Suppose that the owners of a $600,000 building decide to purchase only $300,000 worth of fire insurance. If the building is totally destroyed, the insurance company must pay the policy's face value of $300,000. However, if the building is only partially destroyed, and the damage amounts to $200,000, the insurance company will pay only $125,000. This dollar amount is calculated in the following manner:

coinsurance clause a part of a fire insurance policy that requires the policyholder to purchase coverage at least equal to a specified percentage of the replacement cost of the property to obtain full reimbursement for losses

1. The coinsurance clause requires coverage of at least 80 percent of $600,000, or $480,000.
2. The owners have purchased only $300,000 of insurance. Thus they have insured themselves for only a portion of any loss. That portion is $300,000 ÷ $480,000 = 0.625, or 62.5 percent.
3. The insurance company therefore will reimburse the owner for only 62.5 percent of any loss. In the case of a $200,000 loss, the insurance company will pay 62.5 percent of $200,000, or $125,000.

If the owners of the building had insured it for $480,000, the insurance company would have covered the entire $200,000 loss.

Extended Coverage **Extended coverage** is insurance protection against damage caused by wind, hail, explosion, vandalism, riots or civil commotion, falling aircraft, and smoke. Extended coverage is available as an endorsement, or addition, to some other insurance policy—usually a fire insurance policy. The premium for extended coverage is generally quite low (much lower than the total cost of separate policies covering each individual hazard). Normally, losses caused by war, nuclear radiation or contamination, and water (other than in storms and floods) are excluded from extended-coverage endorsements.

extended coverage insurance protection against damage caused by wind, hail, explosion, vandalism, riots or civil commotion, falling aircraft, and smoke

Burglary, Robbery, and Theft Insurance

Burglary is the illegal taking of property through forcible entry. A kicked-in door, a broken window pane, or pry marks on a windowsill are evidence of a burglary or attempted burglary. *Robbery* is the unlawful taking of property from an individual by force or threat of violence. A thief who uses a gun to rob a gas station is committing robbery. Theft (or larceny) is a general term that means the wrongful taking of property that belongs to another. Insurance policies are available to cover burglary only, robbery only, theft only, or all three. Premiums vary with the type and value of the property covered by the policy.

fidelity bond an insurance policy that protects a business from theft, forgery, or embezzlement by its employees

Business owners also must be concerned about crimes that employees may commit. A **fidelity bond** is an insurance policy that protects a business from theft, forgery, or embezzlement by its employees. If such a crime does occur, the insurance company reimburses the business for financial losses up to the dollar amount specified in the policy. Individual employees or specific positions within an organization may be bonded. It is also possible to purchase a "blanket" policy that covers the entire work force. Fidelity bonds are purchased most commonly by banks, savings and loan associations, finance companies, and other firms whose employees handle cash on a regular basis.

Although business owners are concerned about shoplifting, they often find that insurance coverage, if available, is too expensive. And it is often difficult to collect on losses resulting from shoplifting because such losses are difficult to prove.

Motor Vehicle Insurance

Individuals and businesses purchase automobile insurance because it is required by state law, because it is required by the firm financing the purchase of the vehicle, and/or because they want to protect their investment. Most types of automobile coverage can be broadly classified as either liability or physical damage insurance. Table B.1 shows the distinction.

automobile liability insurance insurance that covers financial losses resulting from injuries or damage caused by the insured vehicle

Automobile Liability Insurance

Automobile liability insurance is insurance that covers financial losses resulting from injuries or damage caused by the insured vehicle. Most automobile policies have a liability limit that contains three numbers. For example, the liability limits stated on a policy might be 100/300/50. The first two numbers indicate the maximum amounts, in thousands of dollars, the insurance company will pay for bodily injury. *Bodily injury liability coverage* pays medical bills and other costs in the event that an injury or death results from an automobile accident in which the policyholder is at fault. Bodily injury liability coverage protects the person in the other car and usually is specified as a pair of dollar amounts. In the preceding example, the policy limits are \$100,000 for each person and \$300,000 for each occurrence. This means that the insurance company will pay up to \$100,000 to each person injured in an accident and up to a total of \$300,000 to all those injured in a single accident. Coverage limits can be as low as the state requires and as high as \$500,000 per person and \$1 million per accident. Payment for additional damage above the policy limits is the responsibility of the insured. In view of the cost of medical care today, and considering the size of legal settlements resulting from automobile accidents, insurance companies recommend coverage of at least \$100,000 per person and \$300,000 per occurrence.

table B.1 Automobile Insurance Coverage

Liability insurance covers financial losses resulting from injuries or damage caused by the insured vehicle; physical damage insurance covers damage to the insured vehicle.

Liability Insurance	Physical Damage Insurance
Bodily injury	Collision
Property damage	Comprehensive
Medical payments	Uninsured motorists

Property damage liability coverage pays for the repair of damage that the insured vehicle does to the property of another person. Such damage is covered up to the amount specified in the policy. In the preceding example, the third number (50) indicates that the insurance company will pay up to $50,000 to repair property damage. Insurance companies generally recommend at least $100,000 worth of property damage liability.

Along with other automobile liability insurance, most car owners also purchase protection for the passengers in their own cars. A *medical payments endorsement* can be included in automobile coverage for a small additional premium. This endorsement provides for the payment of medical bills, up to a specified amount, for passengers (including the policyholder) injured in the policyholder's vehicle. Most insurers sell this coverage in increments of $1,000 or $5,000, up to $25,000. There is no deductible.

Automobile Physical Damage Insurance Liability insurance does not pay for the repair of the insured vehicle. **Automobile physical damage insurance** is insurance that covers damage to the insured vehicle. Collision insurance pays for the repair of damage to the insured vehicle as a result of an accident. Most collision coverages include a deductible amount—anywhere from $100 up—that the policyholder must pay. The insurance company then pays either the remaining cost of the repairs or the actual cash value of the vehicle (when the vehicle is "totaled"), whichever is less. For most automobiles, collision insurance is the most costly coverage. Premiums can be reduced, however, by increasing the deductible amount.

automobile physical damage insurance insurance that covers damage to an insured vehicle

Comprehensive insurance covers damage to the insured vehicle caused by fire, theft, hail, dust storm, vandalism, and almost anything else that could damage a car, except collision and normal wear and tear. With the possible exception of CB radios and tape decks that are installed by the owner of the car, even the contents of the car are insured. For example, comprehensive coverage will pay for a broken windshield, stolen hubcaps, or small dents caused by a hailstorm. Like collision coverage, comprehensive coverage includes a deductible amount, usually up to $1,000.

Uninsured motorists insurance covers the insured driver and passengers from bodily injury losses (and in some states, property damage losses) resulting from an accident caused by a driver with no liability insurance. It also covers damage caused by a hit-and-run driver. In some states and with some insurance companies, uninsured motorists coverage is not automatically included in a typical policy. And yet it is important coverage that is quite reasonable. Often, annual premiums are about $100.

No-Fault Auto Insurance **No-fault auto insurance** is a method of paying for losses suffered in an automobile accident. It is enacted by state law and requires that those suffering injury or loss be reimbursed by their own insurance companies, without regard to who was at fault in the accident. Although there are numerous exceptions, most no-fault laws also limit the rights of involved parties to sue each other.

no-fault auto insurance a method of paying for losses suffered in an automobile accident; enacted by state law, that requires that those suffering injury or loss be reimbursed by their own insurance companies, without regard to who was at fault in the accident

Massachusetts enacted the first no-fault law in 1971 in an effort to reduce both auto insurance premiums and the crushing caseload in its court system. Since then, at least twelve states have followed suit. Every state with a no-fault law requires coverage for all vehicles registered in the state.

Business Liability Insurance

Business liability coverage protects the policyholder from financial losses resulting from an injury to another person or damage to another person's property. During the past fifteen years or so, both the number of liability claims and the size of settlements have increased dramatically. The result has been heightened awareness of the need for liability coverage—along with quickly rising premiums for this coverage.

Public liability insurance protects the policyholder from financial losses due to injuries suffered by others as a result of negligence on the part of a business owner or employee. It covers injury or death resulting from hazards at the place of business or from the actions of employees. For example, liability claims totaling more than $2 billion

public liability insurance insurance that protects the policyholder from financial losses due to injuries suffered by others as a result of negligence on the part of a business owner or employee were filed on behalf of the victims of the 1981 skybridge collapse at the Hyatt Regency Hotel in Kansas City, Missouri. More recent examples in which damage claims totaled more than a billion dollars include the chemical accident at Union Carbide's plant in Bhopal, India; the 1987 Du Pont Hotel fire in San Juan, Puerto Rico; and the $368-billion tobacco industry settlement in 1997. Malpractice insurance, which is purchased by physicians, lawyers, accountants, engineers, and other professionals, is a form of public liability insurance.

product liability insurance insurance that protects the policyholder from financial losses due to injuries suffered by others as a result of using the policyholder's products

Product liability insurance protects the policyholder from financial losses due to injuries suffered by others as a result of using the policyholder's products. Recent court settlements for individuals injured by defective products have been extremely large. A classic product liability case involved the Ford Motor Company and Richard Grimshaw. Grimshaw was injured when he was a passenger in a Ford compact automobile that was hit from behind and burst into flames. He was so severely burned that more than fifty operations were required to treat him. He sued Ford and was awarded $128.5 million by a jury, which decided that his injuries resulted from poor design on the part of Ford. (Later, on appeal, the award was reduced to $6 million.)

Some juries have found manufacturers and retailers guilty of negligence even when the consumer used the product incorrectly. This development and the very large awards given to injured consumers have caused management to take a hard look at potential product hazards. As part of their risk-management efforts, most manufacturers now take the following precautions:

1. They include thorough and explicit directions with products.
2. They warn customers about the hazards of using products incorrectly.
3. They remove from the market those products that are considered hazardous.
4. They test products in-house to determine whether safety problems can arise from either proper *or* improper use.

Such precautions can reduce both the risk of product liability losses and the cost of liability insurance. When the risk of death, injury, or lawsuits cannot be eliminated or at least reduced, some manufacturers simply have discontinued the product.

Marine (Transportation) Insurance

Marine, or transportation, insurance provides protection against the loss of goods that are being shipped from one place to another. It is the oldest type of insurance, having originated with the ancient Greeks and Romans. The term *marine insurance* was coined at a time when only goods transported by ship were insured.

ocean marine insurance insurance that protects the policyholder against loss or damage to a ship or its cargo on the high seas

inland marine insurance insurance that protects against loss or damage to goods shipped by rail, truck, airplane, or inland barge

Today marine insurance is available for goods shipped over water or land. **Ocean marine insurance** protects the policyholder against loss or damage to a ship or its cargo on the high seas. **Inland marine insurance** protects against loss or damage to goods shipped by rail, truck, airplane, or inland barge. Both types cover losses from fire, theft, and most other hazards.

Business Interruption Insurance

business interruption insurance insurance protection for a business whose operations are interrupted because of a fire, storm, or other natural disaster

Business interruption insurance provides protection for a business whose operations are interrupted because of a fire, storm, or other natural disaster. It is even possible to purchase coverage to protect a firm if its employees should go out on strike. For most businesses, interruption coverage is available as an endorsement to a fire insurance policy. Premiums are determined by the amount of coverage and the risks that are covered.

The standard business interruption policy reimburses the policyholder for both loss of profit and fixed costs in the event that it cannot operate. Profit payments are based on profits earned by the firm during some specified period. Fixed-cost payments cover expenses the firm incurs even when it is not operating. Employee salaries normally are not covered by the standard policy. However, they may be included for an increased premium.

Public and Employer-Sponsored Insurance for Individuals

Both the government and private insurance companies offer a number of different types of coverage for individuals in the United States. In this section we discuss Social Security, unemployment insurance, workers' compensation, and medical insurance.

Public Insurance

Federal and state governments offer insurance programs to meet the specific needs of individuals who are eligible for coverage. The Social Security program, established by the Social Security Act of 1935, today provides benefits for more than forty-five million people, almost one out of every six Americans. The Social Security program—financed by taxes paid by both employees and employers—actually consists of four programs. First, *retirement* benefits are paid to eligible employees and self-employed individuals when they reach age 65. They can obtain reduced benefits at age 62. Second, *survivor* benefits are paid to a worker's spouse, dependent children, or in some cases dependent parents when a covered worker dies before retirement. Third, *disability* benefits are paid to workers who are severely disabled and unable to work. Benefits continue until it is determined that the individual is no longer disabled. When a disabled worker reaches age 65, the worker is then eligible for retirement benefits. Fourth, the *Medicare* program provides both hospital and medical coverage. Workers are eligible for coverage when they reach age 65. Persons who have received disability benefits for a period of at least twenty-four months are also eligible for Medicare coverage.

Unlike the federal Social Security program, *unemployment insurance* is a joint program between the federal and state governments. The purpose of the program is to provide benefits (employment services and money) to unemployed workers. The dollar amount and the duration of benefits are determined by state laws. The program is funded by a tax paid by employers.

Workers' Compensation

workers' compensation insurance insurance that covers medical expenses and provides salary continuation for employees who are injured while at work

Workers' compensation insurance covers medical expenses and provides salary continuation for employees who are injured while at work. This insurance also pays benefits to the dependents of workers killed on the job. Every state now requires employers to provide some form of workers' compensation insurance; specific benefits are established by the state. Employers may purchase this type of insurance from insurance companies or, in some cases, from the state. Self-insurance also can be used to meet requirements in a few states. State laws do vary; some are more stringent than others. In fact, the low cost of workers' compensation in some states is one of many reasons businesses might choose to locate or move there.

Salary continuation payments to employees unable to work because of injuries sustained on the job normally range from 60 to 75 percent of an employee's usual wage. They may, however, be limited to a specified number of payments. In all cases, they stop when the employee is able to return to work.

Workers' compensation premiums, paid by the employer, generally are computed as a small percentage of each employee's wages. The percentage varies with the type of job and is, in general, higher for jobs that involve greater risk of injury.

Health Care Insurance

Today, most employers pay, as an employee benefit, part or all of the cost of health care insurance for employees. When the employer does not pay for coverage, most individuals purchase their own health care insurance—when they can afford the coverage.

health care insurance insurance that covers the cost of medical attention, including hospital care, physicians' and surgeons' fees, prescription medicines, and related services

Health care insurance covers the cost of medical attention, including hospital care, physicians' and surgeons' fees, prescription medicines, and related services. In addition, some firms also provide employees with dental and life insurance. *Major medical insurance* also can be purchased to extend medical coverage beyond the dollar limits of the standard health care insurance policy. In all cases, the types of coverage and the premiums vary according to the provisions of the specific health care policy, whether it is paid for by the employer or the individual.

The cost of medical care has been increasing over the last forty years. National expenditures for health care in 2002 were more than $1.54 trillion, or over $5,800 per individual, according to the Centers for Medicare and Medical Services. Thus about 14 percent of our gross domestic product is spent on health care.[1] In an attempt to keep medical insurance premiums down, insurers have developed a variety of insurance plans that are less expensive than full-coverage plans. Some plans have deductibles of $500 to $1,000. Some require that the policyholder pay 20 to 30 percent of the first $1,000 to $3,000 in medical bills. And some pay the entire hospital bill but only a percentage of other medical expenses. One additional method that can reduce the cost of health care coverage is the use of a health maintenance organization. A **health maintenance organization (HMO)** is an insurance plan that directly employs or contracts with selected physicians and hospitals to provide health care services in exchange for a fixed, prepaid monthly premium. Although there have been concerns about the quality of care provided by some HMOs, they are expected to grow because they offer a lower-cost alternative to traditional health care plans.

health maintenance organization (HMO) an insurance plan that directly employs or contracts with selected physicians and hospitals to provide health care services in exchange for a fixed, prepaid monthly premium

preferred provider organization (PPO) an insurance plan that offers the services of doctors and hospitals at discount rates or gives breaks in copayments and deductibles

Preferred provider organizations (PPOs) offer the services of doctors and hospitals at discount rates or give breaks in copayments (the portion of the bill the insured must pay each time services are used) and deductibles. An insurance company or an employer contracts with a PPO to provide specified services at predetermined fees to PPO members.

Life Insurance

life insurance insurance that pays a stated amount of money on the death of the insured individual

beneficiary person or organization named in a life insurance policy as a recipient of the proceeds of that policy on the death of the insured

Life insurance pays a stated amount of money on the death of the insured individual. The money is paid to one or more beneficiaries. A **beneficiary** is a person or organization named in a life insurance policy as a recipient of the proceeds of that policy on the death of the insured.

Life insurance thus provides protection for the beneficiaries of the insured. The amount of insurance needed depends very much on *their* situation. A wage earner with three small children generally needs more life insurance than someone who is single. Moreover, the need for life insurance changes as a person's situation changes. When the wage earner's children are grown and on their own, they need less protection (through their parent's life insurance) than they did when they were young.

For a particular dollar amount of life insurance, premiums depend primarily on the age of the insured and on the type of insurance. The older a person is, the higher is the premium. (On average, older people are less likely to survive each year than younger people.) Finally, insurers offer several types of life insurance for customers with varying insurance needs. The price of each type depends on the benefits it provides.

Term Life Insurance

term life insurance life insurance that provides protection to beneficiaries for a stated period of time

Term life insurance provides protection to beneficiaries for a stated period of time. Because term life insurance includes no other benefits, it is the least expensive form of life insurance. It is especially attractive to young married couples who want as much protection as possible but cannot afford the higher premiums charged for other types of life insurance.

Most term life policies are in force for a period of one year. At the end of each policy year, a term life policy can be renewed at a slightly higher cost—to take into account the fact that the insured individual has aged one year. In addition, some term policies can be converted into other forms of life insurance at the option of the policyholder. This feature permits policyholders to modify their insurance protection to keep pace with changes in their personal circumstances.

Whole Life Insurance

Whole life insurance, also called *ordinary life insurance*, provides both protection and savings. In the beginning, premiums generally are higher than those for term life insurance. However, premiums for whole life insurance remain constant for as long as the policy is in force.

whole life insurance life insurance that provides both protection and savings

A whole life policy builds up savings over the years. These savings are in the form of a **cash surrender value**, which is the amount payable to the holder of a whole life insurance policy if the policy is canceled. In addition, the policyholder may borrow from the insurance company, at a relatively low interest rate, amounts up to the policy's cash surrender value.

cash surrender value the amount payable to the holder of a whole life insurance policy if the policy is canceled

Whole life insurance policies are sold in these three forms:

- *Straight life insurance*, for which the policyholder must pay premiums as long as the insured is alive
- *Limited-payment life insurance*, for which premiums are paid for only a stated number of years
- *Single-payment life insurance*, for which one lump-sum premium is paid at the time the insurance is purchased

Which of these is best for a given individual depends, as usual, on that individual's particular situation and insurance needs.

Endowment Life Insurance

Endowment life insurance provides protection and guarantees the payment of a stated amount to the policyholder after a specified number of years. Endowment policies generally are in force for twenty years or until the insured person reaches age 65. If the insured dies while the policy is in force, the beneficiaries are paid the face amount of the policy. However, if the insured survives through the policy period, the stated amount is paid to the policyholder.

endowment life insurance life insurance that provides protection and guarantees the payment of a stated amount to the policyholder after a specified number of years

The premiums for endowment policies generally are higher than those for whole life policies. In return, the policyholder is guaranteed a future payment. Thus the endowment policy includes a sort of "enforced savings" feature. In addition, the cash surrender values of endowment policies usually are higher than those of whole life policies.

Universal Life Insurance

Universal life insurance combines insurance protection with an investment plan that offers a potentially greater return than that guaranteed by a whole life insurance policy. Universal life insurance is the newest product available from life insurance companies. It offers policyholders several options unavailable with other types of policies. For example, policyholders may choose to make larger or smaller premium payments, to increase or decrease their insurance coverage, or even to withdraw the policy's cash value without canceling the policy. Essentially, the purchase of universal life insurance combines the purchase of annual term insurance with the buying and selling of investments.

universal life insurance life insurance that combines insurance protection with an investment plan that offers a potentially greater return than that guaranteed by a whole life insurance policy

Universal life insurance generally offers lower premiums than whole life insurance. In fact, the premium is often called a *contribution*. However, companies that offer universal life insurance may charge a fee when the policy is first purchased, each time an annual premium is paid, and when funds are withdrawn from the policy's cash value. Such fees tend to decrease the return on the savings account part of the policy.

Business Law, Regulation, and Taxation

Our initial task in this appendix is to examine the sources of laws and the functions of federal and state court systems. Next, we discuss the major categories of laws that apply to business activities: contract law, property law, and laws relating to negotiable instruments, the agent-principal relationship, and bankruptcy. Then we describe federal laws that encourage competition, and we look at the issue of deregulation of business. We conclude with a discussion of federal, state, and local taxes—the primary means by which all governments finance their activities.

Laws and the Courts

A **law** is a rule developed by a society to govern the conduct of and relationships among its members. Laws set standards of behavior for both businesses and individuals. They establish the rights of parties in exchanges and various types of agreements. Laws provide remedies in the event that one business (or individual) believes that it has been injured by another. In the United States, the supreme law of the land is the U.S. Constitution. The federal, state, and local governments enact and administer laws, but no law is valid if it violates the Constitution.

law a rule developed by a society to govern the conduct of and relationships among its members

Sources of Laws

Each level of government derives its laws from two major sources: (1) judges' decisions, which make up common law, and (2) legislative bodies, which enact statutory laws.

Common Law **Common law**, also known as *case law* or *judicial law*, is the body of law created by court decisions rendered by judges. Common law began as custom and tradition in England. It was then transported to America during the colonial period and, since then, has been further enlarged by the decisions of American judges.

common law the body of law created by court decisions rendered by judges; also known as case law or judicial law

The growth of common law is founded on the doctrine of *stare decisis*, a Latin term meaning "to stand by a previous decision." The doctrine of *stare decisis* is a practical source of law for two reasons. First, a judge's decision in a case may be used by other judges as the basis for later decisions. The earlier decision thus has the strength of law and is, in effect, a source of law. Second, the doctrine of *stare decisis* makes law more stable and predictable. If someone brings a case to court *and* the facts are the same as those in a case that has already been decided, the court will make a decision based on the previous legal decision. The court may depart from the doctrine of *stare decisis* if the facts in the current case differ from those in an earlier case or if business practices, technology, or the attitudes of society have changed.

statute a law passed by the U.S. Congress, a state legislature, or a local government

Statutory Law A **statute** is a law passed by the U.S. Congress, a state legislature, or a local government. **Statutory law**, then, consists of all the laws that have been enacted by legislative bodies. For businesses, one very important part of statutory law is the Uniform Commercial Code. The **Uniform Commercial Code (UCC)** is a set of laws designed to eliminate differences among state regulations affecting business and to simplify interstate commerce. The UCC consists of eleven articles, or chapters, that cover sales, commercial paper, bank deposits and collections, letters of credit, transfers of title, securities, and transactions that involve collateral. It has been adopted with variations in all fifty states. The state statutes that the UCC replaced varied from state to state and caused problems for firms that did business in more than one state.

statutory law all the laws that have been enacted by legislative bodies

Uniform Commercial Code (UCC) a set of laws designed to eliminate differences among state regulations affecting business and to simplify interstate commerce

administrative law the regulations created by government agencies established by legislative bodies

Today, most legal experts have expanded the concept of statutory law to include administrative law. **Administrative law** consists entirely of the regulations created by government agencies established by legislative bodies. The Nuclear Regulatory Commission, for example, has the power to set specific requirements for nuclear power plants. It can even halt the construction or operation of plants that do not meet such requirements. These requirements thus have the force and effect of law.

Most regulatory agencies hold hearings that are similar to court trials. Evidence is introduced, and the parties are represented by legal counsel. Moreover, the decisions of these agencies may be appealed in state or federal courts.

Public Law and Private Law: Crimes and Torts

public law the body of law that deals with the relationships between individuals or businesses and society

crime a violation of a public law

Public law is the body of law that deals with the relationships between individuals or businesses and society. A violation of a public law is called a **crime**. Among the crimes that can affect a business are the following:

- Burglary, robbery, and theft
- Embezzlement, or the unauthorized taking of money or property by an employee, agent, or trustee
- Forgery, or the false signing or changing of a legal document with the intent to alter the liability of another person
- The use of inaccurate weights, measures, or labels
- The use of the mails to defraud, or cheat, an individual or business
- The receipt of stolen property
- The filing of a false and fraudulent income tax return

Those accused of violating public laws—or committing crimes—are prosecuted by a federal, state, or local government.

private law the body of law that governs the relationships between two or more individuals or businesses

tort a violation of a private law

negligence a failure to exercise reasonable care, resulting in injury to another

Private law is the body of law that governs the relationships between two or more individuals or businesses. A violation of a private law is called a **tort**. In some cases a single illegal act—such as embezzlement—can be both a crime and a tort.

Torts may result either from intentional acts or from negligence. Such acts as shoplifting and embezzlement are intentional torts. **Negligence**, on the other hand, is a failure to exercise reasonable care, resulting in injury to another. Suppose that the driver of a delivery truck loses control at the wheel and rams into a building. A tort has been committed, and the owner of the building may sue both the driver and the driver's employer to recover the cost of repairing the damage. Among the torts that can affect a business are the following:

- *Slander*—A false oral statement that injures a person's or business's reputation
- *Libel*—A false written statement that injures a person's or business's reputation
- *Fraud*—A misrepresentation of facts designed to take advantage of another individual or business
- *Product liability*—A manufacturer's responsibility for negligence in designing, manufacturing, or providing operating instructions for its products
- *Personal injury*—Damage caused by accidents, intentional acts, or defective products
- *Unfair competitive practices*—Behavior of an entity that unfairly lessens another organization's ability to compete

The purpose of private law is to provide a remedy for the party injured by a tort. In most cases the injured party must bring a legal action and present the facts in a court of law. Either a judge or jury will then render a decision. In most cases the remedy consists of monetary damages to compensate the injured party and punish the person committing the tort. For example, the courts ruled that Eastman Kodak committed a tort by infringing on certain patent rights owned by Polaroid. Eastman Kodak was forced to pay Polaroid almost $900 million in damages. Because large dollar settlements have become commonplace, many business owners and politicians insist that there is a need for tort reform.

The Court System

The United States has two separate and distinct court systems. The federal court system consists of the Supreme Court of the United States, which was established by the Constitution, and other federal courts that were created by Congress. In addition, each of the fifty states has established its own court system. Figure C.1 shows both the federal court system and a typical state court system.

The Federal Court System Federal courts generally hear cases that involve

- Questions of constitutional law
- Federal crimes or violations of federal statutes
- Property valued at $50,000 or more in dispute between citizens of different states or between a U.S. citizen and a foreign nation
- Bankruptcy; the Internal Revenue Service (IRS); the postal laws; or copyright, patent, and trademark laws
- Admiralty and maritime cases

The United States is divided into federal judicial districts. Each state includes at least one district court, and more populous states have two or more. A district court is a **court of original jurisdiction**, which is the first court to recognize and hear testimony in a legal action. In many cases the decision reached in the district court may be appealed to a higher court. A court that hears cases appealed from lower courts is called an **appellate court**. If the appellate court finds the lower court's ruling to be in error, it may reverse that ruling, modify the decision, or return the case to the lower court for a new trial. Currently, there are thirteen U.S. courts of appeal.

court of original jurisdiction the first court to recognize and hear testimony in a legal action

appellate court a court that hears cases appealed from lower courts

The U.S. Supreme Court—the highest court in the land—consists of nine justices (the chief justice and eight associate justices). The Supreme Court has original jurisdiction in cases that involve ambassadors and consuls and in certain cases involving one or more states. However, its main function is to review decisions made by the U.S. courts of appeal and, in some cases, by state supreme courts.

The State Court Systems The state court systems are quite similar to the federal system in structure. All have courts of original jurisdiction and supreme courts, and most have intermediate appellate courts as well. The decision of a state supreme court may be appealed to the U.S. Supreme Court if it involves a question of constitutional or federal law.

Other Types of Courts Other courts have been created to meet special needs at both the federal and state levels. A **court of limited jurisdiction** hears only specific types of cases. At the federal level, for example, Congress has created courts to hear cases that involve international trade, taxes and disputes with the IRS, and bankruptcy. At the state level, there are small-claims courts, which hear cases involving claims for less than a specified dollar amount (usually $500 or $5,000, depending on the state), traffic courts, divorce courts, juvenile courts, and probate courts.

court of limited jurisdiction a court that hears only specific types of cases

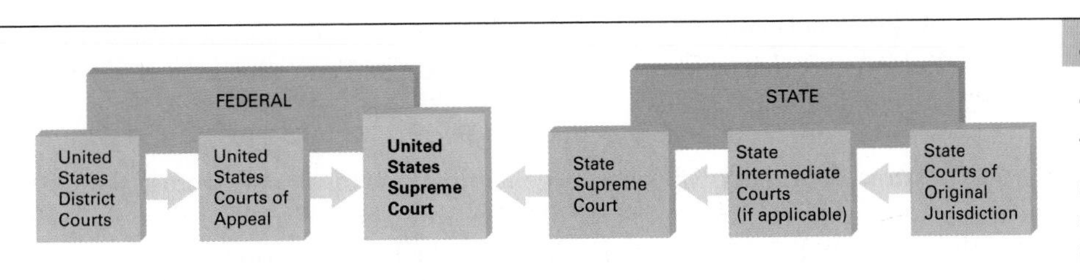

figure C.1

The Court System

The United States has two separate and distinct court systems, as illustrated here by the federal court system and a typical state court system.

Contract Law

Contract law is perhaps the most important area of business law because contracts are so much a part of doing business. Every business person should understand what a valid contract is and how a contract is fulfilled or violated.

contract a legally enforceable agreement between two or more competent parties who promise to do or not to do a particular thing

A **contract** is a legally enforceable agreement between two or more competent parties who promise to do or not to do a particular thing. An *implied contract* is an agreement that results from the actions of the parties. For example, a person who orders dinner at a local Chili's restaurant assumes that the food will be served within a reasonable time and will be fit to eat. The restaurant owner, for his or her part, assumes that the customer will pay for the meal.

Most contracts are more explicit and formal than that between a restaurant and its customers. An *expressed contract* is one in which the parties involved have made oral or written promises about the terms of their agreement.

Requirements for a Valid Contract

To be valid and legally enforceable, a contract must meet five specific requirements as follows: (1) voluntary agreement, (2) consideration, (3) legal competence of all parties, (4) lawful subject matter, and (5) proper form.

voluntary agreement a contract requirement consisting of an offer by one party to enter into a contract with a second party and acceptance by the second party of all the terms and conditions of the offer

Voluntary Agreement **Voluntary agreement** consists of both an *offer* by one party to enter into a contract with a second party and *acceptance* by the second party of all the terms and conditions of the offer. If any part of the offer is not accepted, there is no contract. And if it can be proved that coercion, undue pressure, or fraud was used to obtain a contract, it may be voided by the injured party.

consideration the value or benefit that one party to a contract furnishes to the other party

Consideration A contract is a binding agreement only when each party provides something of value to the other party. The value or benefit that one party furnishes to the other party is called **consideration**. This consideration may be money, property, a service, or the promise not to exercise a legal right. However, the consideration given by one party need not be equal in dollar value to the consideration given by the other party. As a general rule, the courts will not void a contract just because one party got a bargain.

Legal Competence All parties to a contract must be legally competent to manage their own affairs and must have the authority to enter into binding agreements. The intent of the legal competence requirement is to protect individuals who may not have been able to protect themselves. The courts generally will not require minors, persons of unsound mind, or those who entered into contracts while they were intoxicated to comply with the terms of their contracts.

usury the practice of charging interest in excess of the maximum legal rate

Lawful Subject Matter A contract is not legally enforceable if it involves an unlawful act. Certainly, a person who contracts with an arsonist to burn down a building cannot go to court to obtain enforcement of the contract. Equally unenforceable is a contract that involves **usury**, which is the practice of charging interest in excess of the maximum legal rate. Other contracts that may be unlawful include promissory notes resulting from illegal gambling activities, contracts to bribe public officials, agreements to perform services without required licenses, and contracts that restrain trade or eliminate competition.

Proper Form of Contract Businesses generally draw up all contractual agreements in writing so that differences can be resolved readily if a dispute develops. Figure C.2 shows that a contract need not be complicated to be legally enforceable.

A written contract must contain the names of the parties involved, their signatures, the purpose of the contract, and all terms and conditions to which the parties

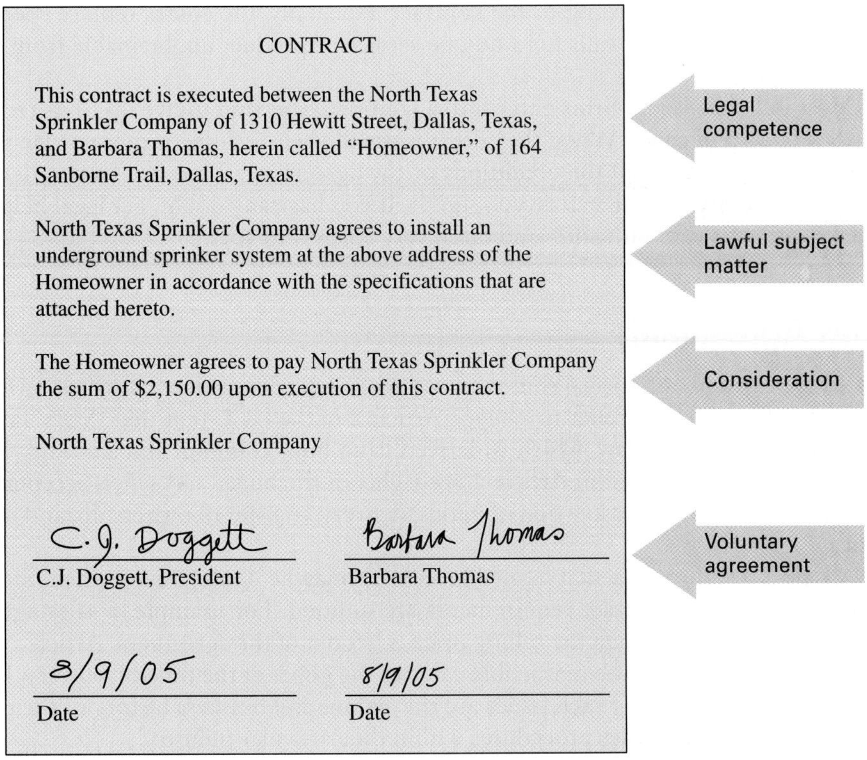

CONTRACT

This contract is executed between the North Texas Sprinkler Company of 1310 Hewitt Street, Dallas, Texas, and Barbara Thomas, herein called "Homeowner," of 164 Sanborne Trail, Dallas, Texas.

North Texas Sprinkler Company agrees to install an underground sprinker system at the above address of the Homeowner in accordance with the specifications that are attached hereto.

The Homeowner agrees to pay North Texas Sprinkler Company the sum of $2,150.00 upon execution of this contract.

North Texas Sprinkler Company

C.J. Doggett — C.J. Doggett, President

Barbara Thomas — Barbara Thomas

8/9/05 — Date

8/9/05 — Date

figure C.2

Contract Between a Business and a Customer
Notice that the requirements for a valid contract are satisfied and that the contract takes the proper form by containing the names of the parties involved, their signatures, the purpose of the contract, and all terms and conditions.

have agreed. Any changes to a written contract should be made in writing, initialed by all parties, and attached to the original contract.

The *Statute of Frauds*, which has been passed in some form by all states, requires that certain types of contracts be in writing to be enforceable. These include contracts dealing with

- The exchange of land or real estate
- The sale of goods, merchandise, or personal property valued at $500 or more
- The sale of securities, regardless of the dollar amount
- Acts that will not be completed within one year after the agreement is made
- A promise to assume someone else's financial obligation
- A promise made in contemplation of marriage

Performance and Nonperformance

Ordinarily, a contract is terminated by **performance**, which is the fulfillment of all obligations by all parties to the contract. Occasionally, however, performance may become impossible. Death, disability, or bankruptcy, for example, may legally excuse one party from a contractual obligation. However, what happens when one party simply does not perform according to a legal contract? A **breach of contract** is the failure of one party to fulfill the terms of a contract when there is no legal reason for that failure. In such a case it may be necessary for the other parties to the contract to bring legal action to discharge the contract, obtain monetary damages, or require specific performance.

Discharge by mutual assent is the termination of a contract when all parties agree to void a contract. Any consideration received by the parties must be returned when a contract is discharged by mutual assent.

Damages are a monetary settlement awarded to a party injured through a breach of contract. When damages are awarded, an attempt is made to place the injured party in the position it would be in if the contract had been performed.

performance the fulfillment of all obligations by all parties to the contract

breach of contract the failure of one party to fulfill the terms of a contract when there is no legal reason for that failure

discharge by mutual assent termination of a contract by mutual agreement of all parties

damages a monetary settlement awarded to a party injured through a breach of contract

specific performance the legal requirement that the parties to a contract fulfill their obligations according to the contract

Specific performance is the legal requirement that the parties to a contract fulfill their obligations according to the contract. Generally, the courts require specific performance if a contract calls for a unique service or product unobtainable from another source.

Most individuals and firms enter into a contract expecting to live up to its terms. Very few end up in court. When they do, it is usually because one or more of the parties did not understand all the conditions of the agreement. Thus it is imperative to know what you are signing before you sign it. If you have any doubt, get legal help! A signed contract is very difficult—and often very costly—to void.

Sales Agreements

sales agreement a type of contract by which ownership is transferred from a seller to a buyer

A **sales agreement** is a special (but very common) type of contract by which ownership is transferred from a seller to a buyer. Article 2 of the UCC (entitled "Sales") provides much of our sales law, which is derived from both common and statutory law. Among the topics included in Article 2 are rights of the buyer and seller, acceptance and rejection of an offer, inspection of goods, delivery, transfer of ownership, and warranties.

Article 2 also provides that a sales agreement may be binding even when one or more of the general contract requirements are omitted. For example, a sales agreement is legally binding when the selling price is left out of the agreement. Article 2 requires that the buyer pay the reasonable value of the goods at the time of delivery. Key considerations in resolving such issues are the actions and business history of the parties and any customary sales procedures within the particular industry.

express warranty a written explanation of the responsibilities of the producer (or seller) in the event that a product is found to be defective or otherwise unsatisfactory

implied warranty a guarantee imposed or required by law

Finally, Article 2 deals with warranties—both express and implied. As we saw in Chapter 14, an **express warranty** is a written explanation of the responsibilities of the producer (or seller) in the event that a product is found to be defective or otherwise unsatisfactory. An **implied warranty** is a guarantee imposed or required by law. In general, the buyer is entitled to assume that

1. The merchandise offered for sale has a clear title and is not stolen.
2. The merchandise is as advertised.
3. The merchandise will serve the purpose for which it was manufactured and sold.

Any limitation to an express or implied warranty must be clearly stated so that the buyer can understand any exceptions or disclaimers.

Other Laws That Affect Business

In addition to contract law, many other kinds of law affect the way a firm does business. In this section we describe the impact of laws relating to property, negotiable instruments, the agent-principal relationship, and bankruptcy on the day-to-day operations of a business firm.

Property Law

property anything that can be owned

Property is anything that can be owned. The concept of private ownership of property is fundamental to the free-enterprise system. Our Constitution guarantees to individuals and businesses the right to own property and to use it in their own best interests.

real property land and anything permanently attached to it

Kinds of Property Property is legally classified as either real property or personal property. **Real property** is land and anything permanently attached to it. The term also applies to water on the ground and minerals and natural resources beneath the surface. Thus a house, a factory, a garage, and a well are all considered real property.

The degree to which a business is concerned with real property law depends on its size and the kind of business it is. The owner of a small convenience store needs only a limited knowledge of real property law. However, a national grocery-store chain such as Albertson's might employ several real estate experts with extensive knowledge of real property law, property values, and real estate zoning ordinances throughout the country.

Personal property is all property other than real property. Personal property that has physical or material value—such as inventories, equipment, store fixtures, an automobile, or a book—is referred to as *tangible personal property* because it is movable and can be felt, tasted, or seen. Property that derives its value from a legal right or claim is called *intangible personal property*. Examples include stocks and bonds, receivables, trademarks, patents, and copyrights.

personal property all property other than real property

A *trademark* is a brand that is registered with the U.S. Patent and Trademark Office. Registration guarantees the owner the exclusive use of the trademark for ten years. At the end of that time, the registration can be renewed for additional ten-year periods. The owner may at times have to defend the trademark from unauthorized use—usually through legal action. McDonald's was forced to do exactly that when the trademark "Big Mac" was used by another fast-food outlet in a foreign country.

A **patent** is the exclusive right to make, use, or sell or to license others to make and sell a newly invented product or process. Patents are granted by the U.S. Patent and Trademark Office for a period of twenty years. After that period has elapsed, the invention becomes available for general use.

patent the exclusive right to make, use, or sell a newly invented product or process

A **copyright** is the exclusive right to publish, perform, copy, or sell an original work. Copyright laws cover fiction and nonfiction, plays, poetry, musical works, photographs, films, and computer programs. For example, the copyright on this textbook is held by the publisher, Houghton Mifflin Company. The copyright on the movie The Lion King is held by Walt Disney. A copyright is usually held by the creator or the owner of the work and is generally in effect for the lifetime of the creator or owner plus seventy years. The copyright for certain works, including those created for an employer, lasts 120 years from creation or 95 years from publication, whichever occurs first.

copyright the exclusive right to publish, perform, copy, or sell an original work

Transfer of Ownership The transfer of ownership for both real property and personal property usually involves either a purchase, a gift, or an inheritance. As we noted earlier, the Statute of Frauds requires that exchanges of real estate be in writing. A **deed** is a written document by which the ownership of real property is transferred from one person or organization to another. The deed must contain the names of the previous owner and the new owner, as well as a legally acceptable description of the property being transferred. A **lease** is an agreement by which the right to use real property is temporarily transferred from its owner, the landlord, to a tenant. In return for use of the property, the tenant generally pays rent on a weekly, monthly, or yearly basis. A lease is granted for a specific period of time, after which a new lease may be negotiated. If the lease is terminated, the right to use the real property reverts to the landlord.

deed a written document by which the ownership of real property is transferred from one person or organization to another

lease an agreement by which the right to use real estate, equipment, or other assets is temporarily transferred from its owner to the user

Transfer of ownership for personal property depends on how payment is made. When the buyer pays the *full cash price* at the time of purchase, the title to personal property passes to the buyer immediately. When the buyer purchases goods on an *installment plan*, the title passes to the buyer when he or she takes possession of the goods. Although the full cash price has not been paid, the buyer has made a legally enforceable promise to pay it. This is sufficient consideration for the transfer of ownership. Moreover, if the purchased goods are stolen from the buyer, the buyer still must pay the full purchase price.

Laws Relating to Negotiable Instruments

negotiable instrument a written document that (1) is a promise to pay a stated sum of money and (2) can be transferred from one person or firm to another

A **negotiable instrument** is a written document that (1) is a promise to pay a stated sum of money and (2) can be transferred from one person or firm to another. In effect, a negotiable instrument is a substitute for money. Checks are the most familiar form of negotiable instruments. However, promissory notes, drafts, certificates of deposit, and commercial paper are also negotiable. Even a warehouse receipt can qualify as a negotiable instrument if certain conditions are met.

Requirements for Negotiability The UCC establishes the following conditions for negotiability:

- The credit instrument must be in writing and signed.
- The instrument must contain an unconditional promise or order to pay a stated sum of money.
- The instrument must be payable on demand or at a definite future date.
- The instrument must be payable to a specified person or firm or to the bearer.

A financial document that does not meet all these requirements is not negotiable. It may still be valid and legally enforceable, but it cannot be transferred to another business or individual.

endorsement the payee's signature on the back of a negotiable instrument

Endorsements To transfer a negotiable instrument, the payee (the person named on the face of the document) must sign it on the back. The payee's signature on the back of a negotiable instrument is called an **endorsement**. There are three types of endorsements, as shown at the bottom of Figure C.3.

A *blank endorsement* consists only of the payee's signature. It is quick, easy, and dangerous because it makes the instrument payable to anyone who gets possession of it—legally or otherwise. A *restrictive endorsement* states the purpose for which the instrument is to be used. For example, the words *for deposit only* mean that this check *must* be deposited in the specified account.

A *special endorsement* identifies the person or firm to whom the instrument is payable. The words *Pay to the order of Robert Jones* mean that the only person who can cash, deposit, or negotiate this check is Robert Jones.

figure C.3

Endorsements

The names of both the payee (Charles Hall) and the payor (Maria Martinez) are included on the front of the check. The payee's signature on the back of a negotiable instrument is called an endorsement. There are three types of endorsements.

PERSONAL CHECK

Maria Martinez
2497 Kennedy Drive
Atlanta, GA 30303

2000

June 8 20 05

Pay to the order of Charles Hall $ 25.00

Twenty five dollars only Dollars

National Bank

Memo Tutoring

Maria Martinez

⑆2112001101⑆ 002221112 ⑈ 2000

ENDORSEMENTS

Blank endorsement	Restrictive endorsement	Special endorsement
Charles Hall	For Deposit Only Acct#434-422-01 Charles Hall	Pay to the order of Robert Jones Charles Hall

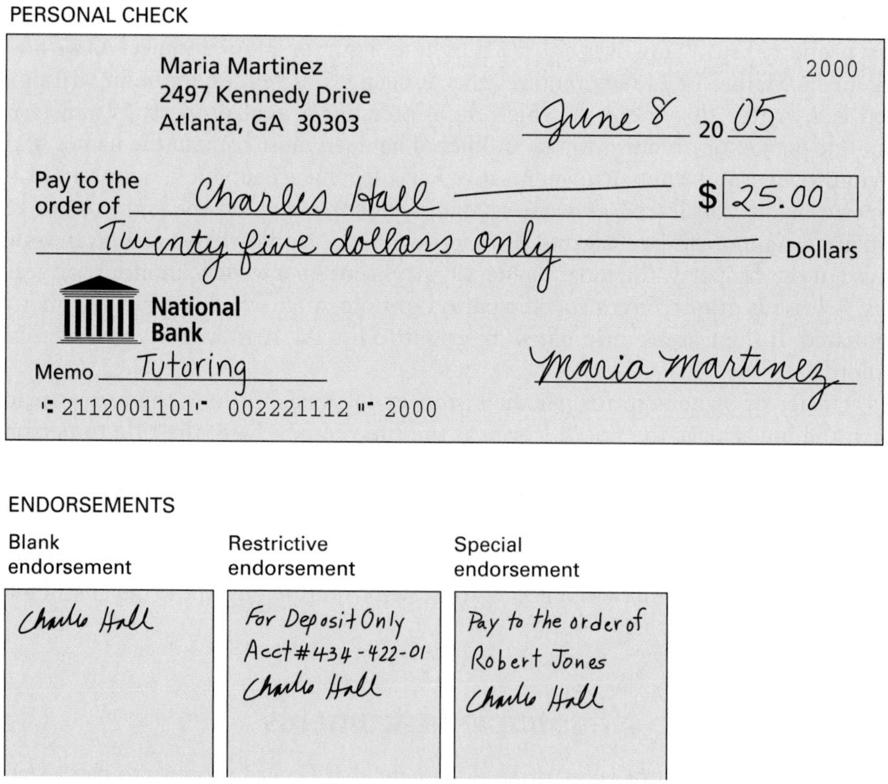

Agency Law

An **agency** is a business relationship in which one party, called the *principal*, appoints a second party, called the *agent*, to act on its behalf. Most agents are independent business people or firms and are paid for their services with either set fees or commissions. They are hired to use their special knowledge for a specific purpose. For example, real estate agents are hired to sell or buy real property, insurance agents are hired to sell insurance, and theatrical agents are hired to obtain engagements for entertainers. The officers of a corporation, lawyers, accountants, and stockbrokers also act as agents.

agency a business relationship in which one party, called the principal, appoints a second party, called the agent, to act on its behalf

Almost any legal activity that can be accomplished by an individual also can be accomplished through an agent. (The exceptions are voting, giving sworn testimony in court, and making a will.) Moreover, under the law, the principal is bound by the actions of the agent. However, the principal may sue an agent who performs an unauthorized act and may collect damages. For this reason, a written contract describing the conditions and limits of the agency relationship is extremely important to both parties.

A **power of attorney** is a legal document that serves as evidence that an agent has been appointed to act on behalf of a principal. In most states in the United States, a power of attorney is required in agency relationships involving the transfer of real estate, as well as in other specific situations.

power of attorney a legal document that serves as evidence that an agent has been appointed to act on behalf of a principal

An agent is responsible for carrying out the principal's instructions in a professional manner, for acting reasonably and with good judgment, and for keeping the principal informed of progress according to their agreement. The agent also must be careful to avoid a conflict involving the interests of two or more principals. The agency relationship is terminated when its objective is accomplished, at the end of a specified time period, or in some cases when either party renounces the agency relationship.

Bankruptcy Law

Bankruptcy is a legal procedure designed both to protect an individual or business that cannot meet its financial obligations and to protect the creditors involved. The Bankruptcy Reform Act was enacted in 1978 and was amended subsequently in July 1984. Under the act, bankruptcy proceedings may be initiated by either the person or the business in financial difficulty or by the creditors.

bankruptcy a legal procedure designed both to protect an individual or business that cannot meet its financial obligations and to protect the creditors involved

Initiating Bankruptcy Proceedings **Voluntary bankruptcy** is a bankruptcy procedure initiated by an individual or business that can no longer meet its financial obligations. Individuals, partnerships, and most corporations may file for voluntary bankruptcy. **Involuntary bankruptcy** is a bankruptcy procedure initiated by creditors. The creditors must be able to prove that the individual or business has debts in excess of $10,000 and cannot pay its debts as they come due.

voluntary bankruptcy a bankruptcy procedure initiated by an individual or business that can no longer meet its financial obligations

involuntary bankruptcy a bankruptcy procedure initiated by creditors

Today, most bankruptcies are voluntary. Creditors are wary of initiating bankruptcy proceedings because they usually end up losing most of the money they are owed. They usually prefer to wait and to hope that the debtor eventually will be able to pay.

Resolving a Bankruptcy Case A petition for bankruptcy is filed in a bankruptcy court. If the court declares the individual or business bankrupt, three means of resolution are available: liquidation, reorganization, and repayment.

Chapter 7 of the Bankruptcy Reform Act concerns *liquidation*, the sale of assets of a bankrupt individual or business to pay its debts (see Figure C.4). In principle, the assets of the individual or business are sold to satisfy the claims of creditors. The debtor is then relieved of all remaining debts. Liquidation pursuant to Chapter 7 does not apply to railroads, banks, savings and loan associations, insurance companies, or government units. Chapter 7 also specifies the order in which claims are to be paid. First, creditors with secured claims are allowed to repossess (or assume ownership of) the collateral for their claims. Then the remaining cash and assets—if any—are paid to unsecured creditors in the order prescribed by the bankruptcy act.

figure C.4

Steps Involved in Chapter 7 (Liquidation) of the Bankruptcy Reform Act

Chapter 7 of the Bankruptcy Reform Act concerns liquidation of assets.

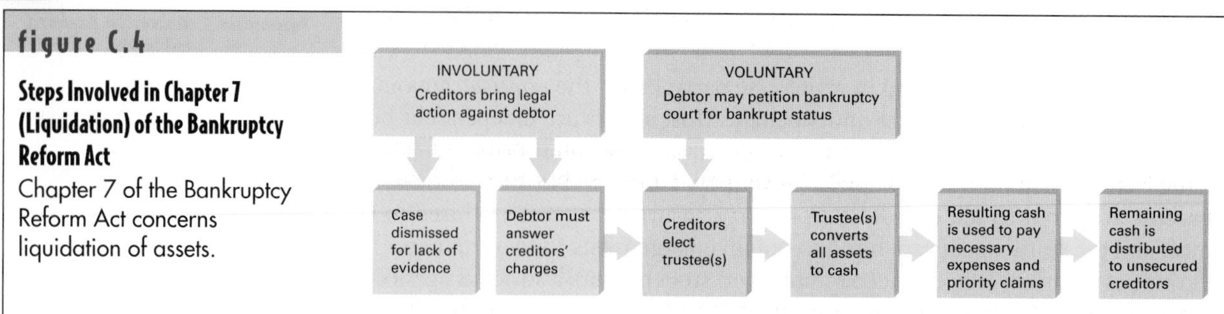

Chapter 11 of the Bankruptcy Reform Act outlines the procedure for *reorganizin* a bankrupt business. The idea is simple. The distressed business will be preserved b correcting or eliminating the factors that got the firm into financial trouble. To im plement this idea, a plan to reorganize the business is developed. Only a debtor ma file a reorganization plan for the first 120 days, unless a trustee has been appointed b the court. After 120 days, any interested party may file a reorganization plan. After th plan has been filed with the court, both the plan and a written disclosure statement ar distributed to all individuals and businesses with claims against the bankrupt firm These people and firms may testify at a hearing held for the purpose of confirming th plan. If the plan is confirmed by the court, the reorganized business emerges fron bankruptcy with only the financial obligations imposed on it by the plan. This is ex actly what occurred when United Air Lines, Federated Department Stores, U.S. Air and Texaco filed for protection under Chapter 11.

Chapter 13 of the Bankruptcy Reform Act permits a bankrupt individual to file with the courts, a plan for *repaying* specific debts. (Only individuals with a regular in come, less than $250,000 in unsecured debts, and less than $750,000 in secured debt are eligible to file for repayment under Chapter 13.) The plan must provide for the re payment of specified amounts in up to three years. (In unusual circumstances, th court may extend the repayment period to five years.) If the plan is approved by th court, the individual usually pays the money to a court-appointed trustee in monthl installments. The trustee, in turn, pays the individual's creditors.

Government Regulation of Business

Government helps to ensure that there is an even playing field for businesses and con sumers. In this section we examine laws designed to promote competition and othe areas of regulation in which government oversight is needed to reduce or eliminat abuses.

Federal Regulations to Encourage Competition

Most states have laws to encourage competition, but for the most part these laws du plicate federal laws. Therefore, we discuss only federal legislation designed to encour age competition. Federal laws protect consumers by ensuring that they have a choice in the marketplace. The same laws protect businesses by ensuring that they are free to compete.

The need for such laws became apparent in the late 1800s, when trusts, or mo nopolies, developed in the sugar, whiskey, tobacco, shoe, and oil industries, among others. A **trust** is created when one firm gains control of an entire industry and can set prices and manipulate trade to suit its own interests.

trust a business combination created when one firm obtains control of an entire industry and can set prices and manipulate trade to suit its own interest

One of the most successful trusts was the Standard Oil Trust, created by John D. Rockefeller in 1882. Until 1911, the Standard Oil Trust controlled between 80 and 90 percent of the petroleum industry. The firm earned extremely high profits primarily because it had obtained secret price concessions from the railroads that shipped its products. Very low shipping costs, in turn, enabled the firm systematically to eliminate most of its competition by deliberately holding prices down. Once this was accomplished, Standard Oil quickly raised its prices.

In response to public outcry against such practices—and high prices—Congress passed the Sherman Antitrust Act in 1890. Since then, Congress has enacted a number of other laws designed to protect American businesses and consumers from monopolies.

The Sherman Antitrust Act (1890) The objectives of the *Sherman Antitrust Act* are to encourage competition and to prevent monopolies. The act specifically prohibits any contract or agreement entered into for the purpose of restraining trade. Specific business practices prohibited by the Sherman Antitrust Act include price fixing, allocation of markets among competitors, and boycotts in restraint of trade. **Price fixing** is an agreement between two businesses about the prices to be charged for goods. A **market allocation** is an agreement to divide a market among potential competitors. A **boycott in restraint of trade** is an agreement between businesses not to sell to or buy from a particular entity. Power to enforce the Sherman Antitrust Act was given to the Department of Justice.

price fixing an agreement between two businesses about the prices to be charged for goods

market allocation an agreement to divide a market among potential competitors

boycott in restraint of trade an agreement between businesses not to sell or buy from a particular entity

Today the Sherman Act is still the cornerstone of the federal government's commitment to encourage competition and to break up large businesses that monopolize trade. An amendment to the Sherman Antitrust Act, the *Antitrust Procedures and Penalties Act of 1974*, made violation of the Sherman Act a felony rather than a misdemeanor. It provides for fines of up to $100,000 and prison terms of up to three years for individuals convicted of antitrust violations. The act also provides that a guilty corporation may be fined up to $1 million and may be sued by competitors or customers for treble monetary damages plus attorneys' fees.

The Clayton Act (1914) Because the wording of the Sherman Antitrust Act is somewhat vague, it could not be used to halt specific monopolistic tactics. Congress therefore enacted the *Clayton Act* in 1914. This legislation identifies and prohibits five distinct practices that had been used to weaken trade competition:

- **Price discrimination**—The practice in which producers and wholesalers charge larger firms a lower price for goods than they charge smaller firms. The Clayton Act does, however, allow quantity discounts.
- **Tying agreement**—A contract that forces an intermediary to purchase unwanted products along with the products it actually wants to buy. This practice was used to "move" a producer's slow-selling merchandise along with its more desirable merchandise.
- **Binding contract**—An agreement that requires an intermediary to purchase products from a particular supplier, not from the supplier's competitors. In return for signing a binding contract, the intermediary was generally given a price discount.
- **Interlocking directorate**—An arrangement in which members of the board of directors of one firm are also directors of a competing firm. Thus, for example, a person may not sit on the board of American Airlines and Delta Air Lines at the same time.
- **Community of interests**—A situation in which one firm buys the stock of a competing firm. If this type of merger substantially lessens competition or tends to create a monopoly, it is unlawful.

price discrimination the practice in which producers and wholesalers charge larger firms a lower price for goods than they charge smaller firms

tying agreement a contract that forces an intermediary to purchase unwanted products along with the products it actually wants to buy

binding contract an agreement that requires an intermediary to purchase products from a particular supplier, not from the supplier's competitors

interlocking directorate an arrangement in which members of the board of directors of one firm are also directors of a competing firm

community of interests a situation in which one firm buys the stock of a competing firm to reduce competition between the two.

The Federal Trade Commission Act (1914) In 1914, Congress also passed the *Federal Trade Commission Act*, which states, "Unfair methods of competition in commerce are hereby declared unlawful." This act also created the **Federal Trade Commission (FTC)**, a five-member committee charged with the responsibility of investigating illegal trade practices and enforcing antitrust laws.

Federal Trade Commission (FTC) a five-member committee charged with the responsibility of investigating illegal trade practices and enforcing antitrust laws

At first, the FTC was limited to enforcement of the Sherman Antitrust, Clayton, and FTC Acts. However, in the 1938 *Wheeler-Lea Amendment* to the FTC Act,

Congress gave the FTC the power to eliminate deceptive business practices—includ ing those aimed at consumers rather than competitors. This early "consumer legisla tion" empowered the FTC to deal with a variety of unfair business tactics withou having to prove that they endangered competition.

The Robinson-Patman Act (1936) Although the Clayton Act prohibits price dis crimination, it does permit quantity discounts. This provision turned out to be major loophole in the law. It was used by large chain retailers to obtain sizable pric concessions that gave them a strong competitive edge over independent stores. T correct this imbalance, Congress passed the *Robinson-Patman Act* in 1936. This la specifically prohibits

- Price differentials that "substantially" weaken competition, unless they can be justified by the actual lower selling costs associated with larger orders
- Advertising and promotional allowances, unless they are offered to small retailers as well as large retailers

The Robinson-Patman Act is more controversial than most antitrust legislation Many economists believe the act tends to discourage price competition rather than t eliminate monopolies.

The Celler-Kefauver Act (1950) The Clayton Act prohibited building a trust b purchasing the stock of competing firms. To get around that prohibition, however, firm could still purchase the assets of its competitors. The result was the same: th elimination of competition. This gigantic loophole was closed by the *Celler-Kefauve Act*, which prohibits mergers through the purchase of assets if these mergers will ten to reduce competition. The act also requires all proposed mergers to be approved b both the FTC and the Justice Department.

The Antitrust Improvements Act (1976) In 1976, Congress passed the *Antitrus Improvements Act* to strengthen previous legislation. This law provided additional tim for the FTC and the Justice Department to evaluate proposed mergers, and it ex panded the investigative powers of the Justice Department. It also authorized the at torneys general of individual states to prosecute firms accused of price fixing and t recover monetary damages for *consumers*.

The Present Antitrust Environment The problem with antitrust legislation and it enforcement is that it is hard to define exactly what an appropriate level of competi tion is. For example, a particular merger may be in the public interest because it in creases the efficiency of an industry. At the same time, however, it may be harmfu because it reduces competition. There is really no rule of law (or of economics) tha can be used to determine which of these two considerations is more important in given case.

Three factors tend to influence the enforcement and effectiveness of antitrust leg islation at the present time. The first is the growing presence of foreign firms i American markets. Foreign firms have increased competition in America and thu have made it more difficult for any firm to monopolize an industry. Second, most an titrust legislation must be interpreted by the courts because the laws are often vagu and open-ended. Thus the attitude of the courts has a lot to do with the effectivenes of these laws. And third, political considerations often determine how actively th FTC and the Justice Department pursue antitrust cases.

Other Areas of Regulation

It is impossible to manage even a small business without being affected by local, state, and federal regulations. And it is just as impossible to describe all the government regulations that affect business. In addition to the regulations that affect competition just discussed, we have examined a variety of regulations in this text. Chapter 2 discussed laws and regulations dealing with the environment, consumerism, and discrimination; Chapter 3, international trade; Chapter 5, organization of business entities; Chapter 10, human resources and employee relations; Chapter 12 union-management relations; and Chapter 21, securities.

By now you may think that there must be a government regulation to govern any possible situation. Actually, government regulations increased from the 1930s through the 1970s, but the country then entered a deregulation period that lasted over twenty years. Today the deregulation drive continues, but there is a question as to how far it should go. Many experts now suggest that any evaluation of government regulations should determine which regulations make sense, which should be modified, and which should be eliminated. Above all, they believe, any reworking of the regulatory environment should create a "livable" environment for consumers, workers, and businesses. We look at the current status of the deregulation movement in the next section.

The Deregulation Movement

deregulation the process of removing existing government regulations, forgoing proposed regulations,or reducing the rate at which new regulations are enacted

Deregulation is the process of removing existing government regulations, forgoing proposed regulations, or reducing the rate at which new regulations are enacted. The primary aim of the deregulation movement is to minimize the complexity of regulations that affect business and the cost of compliance.

Today many Americans believe that the federal government is out of control and out of touch with the needs of average citizens. These same people often complain that the federal government has too many employees and spends too much money. At the time of this publication, the U.S. government

- Employed over 2.2 million civilian workers (in addition to over 1 million military personnel).
- Spent more than $1.9 trillion a year, which is approximately $6,400 for every person in the United States.

Critics also complain that too many government agencies regulate business activities. More than one hundred federal agencies are currently responsible for enforcing a staggering array of regulations. And at least fifteen federal agencies now have a direct impact on business firms. These agencies and the activities they regulate are listed in Table C.1.

Advocates of deregulation are quick to point out that every business—both large and small—must obey a large number of government restrictions and directives and that doing so is costly. Large corporations can cope with government regulation. They have been doing so for some time. In essence, coping means passing the cost of regulation along to stockholders in the form of lower dividends and to consumers in the form of higher prices. Smaller firms bear a smaller regulatory burden, but they may find it harder to cope with that burden. Some may not have the staff necessary to comply with the various documentation requirements. And for many small businesses, stiff competition for customers requires that they pass the cost of compliance directly to their owners.

In every presidential election since the 1970s, the candidates elected to office were sincere when they promised the American people that they were prepared to declare war on the bureaucracy in Washington and cut unnecessary government spending from the federal budget. Presidents Nixon, Carter, Reagan, Bush, Clinton, and George W. Bush all had their own ideas on how government should be reorganized. But each president found that government reform is often stymied by overwhelming red tape in federal regulations, duplication of services, rigid civil service rules, and opposition from senators and representatives who seek to protect their favorite agencies or "pork barrel." Each president found that decades of growth and power in government cannot be swept away overnight.

table C.1 Government Agencies and What They Regulate

Government Agency or Commission	Regulates
Consumer Product Safety Commission	Consumer protection
Environmental Protection Agency	Pollution control
Equal Employment Opportunity Commission	Discrimination in employment practices
Federal Aviation Administration	Airline industry
Federal Communications Commission	Radio, television, telephone, and telegraph communications
Federal Energy Regulatory Commission	Electric power and natural gas
Federal Highway Administration	Vehicle safety
Federal Maritime Commission	Ocean shipping
Federal Mine Safety and Health Review Commission	Worker safety and health in the mining industry
Federal Trade Commission	Antitrust, consumer protection
Food and Drug Administration	Consumer protection
Interstate Commerce Commission	Railroads, bus lines, trucking, pipelines, and waterways
Nuclear Regulatory Commission	Nuclear power and nuclear industry
Occupational Safety and Health Review Commission	Worker safety and health
Securities and Exchange Commission	Corporate securities

Government Taxation

Whether you believe that there is too much government or too little, you are required to help pay for it. In one way or another, each of us pays for everything government does—from regulating business to funding research into the causes and cures of cancer. We pay taxes to our local, state, and federal governments on the basis of what we earn, what we own, and even what we purchase.

Federal Taxes

It takes a lot of money to run something as big as the U.S. government. Each year vast sums are spent for human services, national defense, and interest on the national debt. In addition, the federal government must pay the salaries of its employees, cover its operating expenses, and purchase equipment and supplies that range from typewriter ribbons to aircraft carriers. Most of the money comes from taxes. In 2001, the federal government had revenues of nearly $2 trillion. About 95 percent of that sum was obtained through taxation. As Figure C.5 shows, by 2005, revenues are projected to be over $2 trillion, with just over 95 percent coming from taxation.

Individual Income Taxes An individual's income tax liability is computed from his or her taxable income, which is gross income less various authorized deductions from income. In 1914, the federal government collected an average of 28 cents per taxpayer. Today that average is more than $2,200 per person.

progressive tax a tax that requires the payment of an increasing proportion of income as the individual's income increases

The federal income tax is a progressive tax. A **progressive tax** requires the payment of an increasing proportion of income as the individual's income increases. For example, a single individual with a taxable income of $20,000 must currently pay a

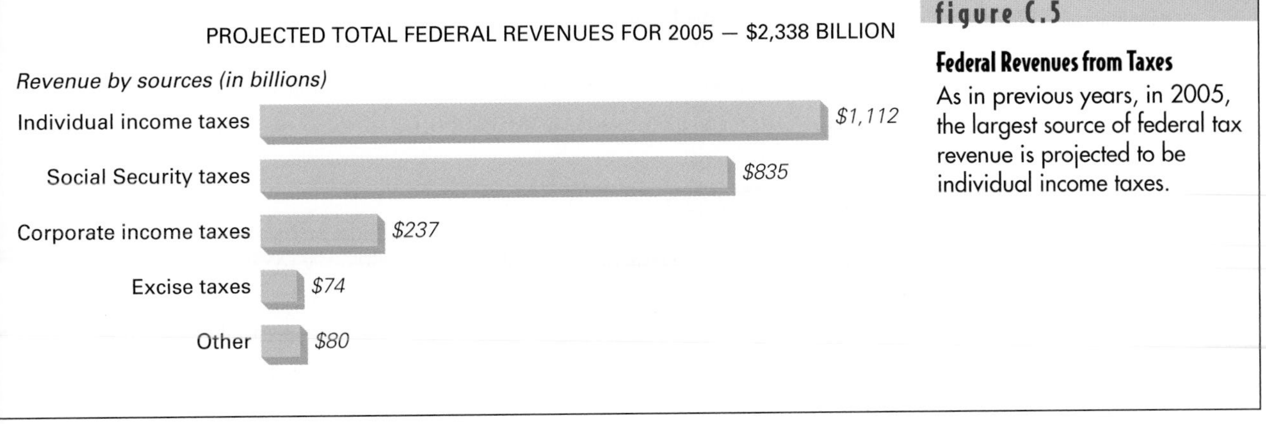

figure C.5

Federal Revenues from Taxes

As in previous years, in 2005, the largest source of federal tax revenue is projected to be individual income taxes.

Source: **www.taxpolicycenter.org/taxfacts/overview/service.cfm.**

federal income tax of $2,696, or about 13 percent of that taxable income. A single taxpayer with a taxable income of $40,000 must pay $7,139, or about 18 percent of that income.

Taxpayers must file an annual tax return by April 15 of each year for the previous calendar year. The return shows the income, deductions, and computations on which the taxpayer's tax liability is based. As shown in Figure C.5, individual income taxes provide nearly half the total federal revenues.

Corporate Income Taxes Corporate income taxes provide approximately 7 percent of total federal revenues. Corporations pay federal income tax only on their taxable income, which is what remains after deducting all legal business expenses from net sales. Currently, the federal corporate tax rate is

Taxable Income	Tax
Not over $50,000	15%
Over $50,000 but not over $75,000	$7,500 + 25% of excess over $50,000
$75,000 but not over $100,000	$13,750 + 34% of excess over $75,000
$100,000 but not over $330,000	$22,250 + 39% of excess over $100,000
$330,000 but not over $10,000,000	$113,900 + 34% of excess over $330,000
$10,000,000 but not over $15,000,000	$3,400,000 + 35% of excess over $10,000,000
$15,000,000 but not over $18,333,333	$5,150,000 + 38% of excess over $15,000,000
$18,333,333 and over	35%

As Table C.2 shows, a corporation with a taxable income of $330,000 must pay a total of $111,950 to the federal government.

Other Federal Taxes Additional sources of federal revenue include Social Security, unemployment, and excise taxes, as well as customs duties. An objective of all taxes is to raise money, but excise taxes and customs duties are also designed to regulate the use of specific goods and services.

As Figure C.5 shows, the second largest source of federal revenue is the *Social Security tax*, which is collected under the Federal Insurance Contributions Act (FICA). This tax provides funding for retirement, disability, and death benefits for contributing employees. FICA taxes are paid by both the employer and the employee. The employee's share is withheld from his or her salary by the employer and sent to the federal government with the employer's share. The Social Security tax is broken into two components: (1) old age, survivors, and disability insurance and (2) Medicare. For old age, survivors, and disability insurance, the annual tax in 2002 was 12.4 percent of the first $84,900 earned. For Medicare, the annual tax was 2.9 percent of all wages.

table C.2 Federal Corporate Income Tax on an Income of $330,000

According to the tax rate table, the tax is $22,250 + 39% of the excess over $100,000.

Step 1 Determine the excess over $100,000.

$$\begin{array}{r} \$330{,}000 \\ -\ 100{,}000 \\ \hline \$230{,}000 \end{array}$$

Step 2 Multiply the excess amount (step 1) by the tax rate (39%).
$230,000 × 0.39 = $89,700

Step 3 To determine the total tax, add the base amount to the additional tax determined in step 2.

$$\begin{array}{r} \$\ 22{,}250 \\ +\ \ 89{,}700 \\ \hline 111{,}950 \end{array}$$

Under the provisions of the Federal Unemployment Tax Act (FUTA), employers must pay an *unemployment tax* equal to 6.2 percent of the first $7,000 of each employee's annual wages. Because employers are allowed credits against the 6.2 percent through participation in state unemployment programs, the actual unemployment rate paid by most employers is 0.8 percent. The tax is paid to the federal government to fund benefits for unemployed workers. Unlike the Social Security tax, the FUTA tax is levied only on employers.

excise tax a tax on the manufacture or sale of a particular domestic product

An **excise tax** is a tax on the manufacture or sale of a particular domestic product. Excise taxes are used to help pay for government services directed toward the users of these products and, in some cases, to limit the use of potentially harmful products. Alcohol and tobacco products are potentially harmful to consumers. They are taxed to raise the prices of these goods and thus discourage consumption. The federal excise tax on gasoline is a source of income that can be used to build and repair highways. Although manufacturers and retailers are responsible for paying excise taxes, these taxes usually are passed on to the consumer in the form of higher retail prices.

customs (or import) duty a tax on a foreign product entering a country

A **customs** (or **import**) **duty** is a tax on a foreign product entering a country. Import duties are designed to protect specific domestic industries by raising the prices of competing imported products. They are first paid by the importer, but the added costs are passed on to consumers through higher—and less competitive—prices.

State and Local Taxes

Like the federal government, state and local governments are financed primarily through taxes. Sales taxes provide about 35 percent of state and local tax revenues. Most states and some cities also levy taxes on the incomes of individuals and businesses. Finally, many local and county governments also tax consumer sales, real estate, and some forms of personal property.

regressive tax a tax that takes a greater percentage of a lower income than of a higher income

Sales Taxes Sales taxes are levied by both states and cities and are paid by the purchasers of consumer products. Retailers collect sales taxes as a specified percentage of the price of each taxed product and then forward them to the taxing authority. A sales tax is a regressive tax. A **regressive tax** is one that takes a greater percentage of a lower income than of a higher income. The regressiveness of the sales tax stems from the fact that lower-income households generally spend a greater proportion of their income on taxable products such as food, clothing, and other essentials. Consider the impact of a 5 percent sales tax on food items purchased by a low-income family. A family that earns $10,000 a year and spends $3,000 on food will pay sales taxes of $150, or 1.5 percent of their total earnings. By comparison, a family that earns $40,000 a year and spends $3,000 on food will pay the same amount of sales tax, but the amount represents only 0.38 percent of their total earnings. Not all states collect a sales tax on all items. In fact, many states exempt food from their sales tax.

roperty Taxes Many local governments rely on the property taxes they levy on eal estate and personal property owned by businesses and individuals to finance their ngoing activities. *Real estate taxes* usually are computed as a percentage of the assessed alue of the real property. (The assessed value is determined by the local tax assessor s the fair market value of the property, a portion of its fair market value, or its relacement cost.) For example, suppose that the city council has established a real estate tax rate of $2.10 per $100 of assessed valuation. Then the property tax bill for an ffice building with an assessed value of $200,000 will be $4,200 ($200,000 × $2.10 ÷ 100 = $4,200). This type of tax is called a *proportional tax*. A **proportional tax** is one hose percentage rate remains constant as the tax base increases. Therefore, if the tax ate remains constant at $2.10 per $100, a taxpayer who owns real estate valued at 10,000 pays $210 in taxes; a taxpayer who owns real estate valued at $100,000 pays 2,100 in taxes.

proportional tax a tax whose percentage rate remains constant as the tax base increases

Certain personal property owned by businesses and individuals is also subject to ocal taxation. For businesses, taxable personal property normally includes machinery, quipment, raw materials, and finished inventory. In some cases local authorities also ax the value of stocks, bonds, mortgages, and promissory notes held by businesses. or individuals, such items as trucks, automobiles, and boats may be classified as personal property and taxed by local authorities.

Glossary

A

absolute advantage the ability to produce a specific product more efficiently than any other nation (3)
accessory equipment standardized equipment used in a firm's production or office activities (14)
account executive an individual, sometimes called a *stock-broker* or *registered representative*, who buys and sells securities for clients (21)
accountability the obligation of a worker to accomplish an assigned job or task (8)
accounting the process of systematically collecting, analyzing, and reporting financial information (18)
accounting equation the basis for the accounting process: assets = liabilities + owners' equity (18)
accounting program a software package that enables users to record and report financial information (17)
accounts payable short-term obligations that arise as a result of making credit purchases (18)
accounts receivable turnover a financial ratio calculated by dividing net sales by accounts receivable (18)
acid-test ratio a financial ratio calculated by subtracting the value of inventory from the current asset amount and dividing the total by current liabilities (18)
ad hoc committee a committee created for a specific short-term purpose (8)
administrative law the regulations created by government agencies established by legislative bodies (Appendix C)
administrative manager a manager who is not associated with any specific functional area but who provides overall administrative guidance and leadership (7)
advertising a paid nonpersonal message communicated to a select audience through a mass medium (16)
advertising agency an independent firm that plans, produces, and places advertising for its clients (16)
advertising media the various forms of communication through which advertising reaches its audience (16)
affirmative action program a plan designed to increase the number of minority employees at all levels within an organization (2)
agency a business relationship in which one party, called the principal, appoints a second party, called the agent, to act on its behalf (Appendix C)
agency shop a workplace in which employees can choose not to join the union but must pay dues to the union anyway (12)
agent a middleman that expedites exchanges, represents a buyer or a seller, and often is hired permanently on a commission basis (15)
alien corporation a corporation chartered by a foreign government and conducting business in the United States (5)
analytical process a process in operations management in which raw materials are broken into different component parts (9)
appellate court a court that hears cases appealed from lower courts (Appendix C)
arbitration the step in a grievance procedure in which a neutral third party hears the two sides of a dispute and renders a decision (12)
arithmetic mean the sum of all the values of a set of data divided by the number of items in the set (17)
asset allocation the process of spreading your money among several different types of investments to lessen risk (21)
assets the resources that a business owns (18)
audit an examination of a company's financial statements and accounting practices that produced them (18)
authoritarian leader one who holds all authority and responsibility, with communication usually moving from top to bottom (7)
authority the power, within an organization, to accomplish an assigned job or task (8)
automatic vending the use of machines to dispense products (15)
automation the total or near-total use of machines to do work (9)
automobile liability insurance insurance that covers financial losses resulting from injuries or damage caused by the insured vehicle (Appendix B)
automobile physical damage insurance insurance that covers damage to an insured vehicle (Appendix B)

B

balance of payments the total flow of money into the country minus the total flow of money out of the country over some period of time (3)
balance of trade the total value of a nation's exports minus the total value of its imports over some period of time (3)
balance sheet a summary of the dollar amounts of a firm's assets, liabilities, and owners' equity accounts at a particular time; same as *statement of financial position* (18)
banker's acceptance a written order for the bank to pay a third party a stated amount of money on a specific date (19)
bankruptcy a legal procedure designed both to protect an individual or business that cannot meet its financial obligations and to protect the creditors involved (Appendix C)
bargaining unit the specific group of employees represented by a union (12)
barter a system of exchange in which goods or services are traded directly for other goods and/or services without using money (1)
barter system a system of exchange in which goods or services are traded directly for other goods or services (19)
behavior modification a systematic program of reinforcement to encourage desirable behavior (11)
beneficiary person or organization named in a life insurance policy as a recipient of the proceeds of that policy on the death of the insured (Appendix B)
bill of lading issued by a transport carrier to an exporter to prove merchandise has been shipped (3)
binding contract an agreement that requires an intermediary to purchase products from a particular supplier, not from the supplier's competitors (Appendix C)
blue-chip stock a safe investment that generally attracts conservative investors (21)
board of directors the top governing body of a corporation, the members of which are elected by the stockholders (5)
bond indenture a legal document that details all the conditions relating to a bond issue (20)
boycott a refusal to do business with a particular firm (12)
boycott in restraint of trade an agreement between businesses not to sell or buy from a particular entity (Appendix C)

brand a name, term, symbol, design, or any combination of these that identifies a seller's products as distinct from those of other sellers (14)
brand equity marketing and financial value associated with a brand's strength in a market (14)
brand loyalty extent to which a customer is favorable toward buying a specific brand (14)
brand mark the part of a brand that is a symbol or distinctive design (14)
brand name the part of a brand that can be spoken (14)
breach of contract the failure of one party to fulfill the terms of a contract when there is no legal reason for that failure (Appendix C)
breakeven quantity the number of units that must be sold for the total revenue (from all units sold) to equal the total cost (of all units sold) (14)
broker a middleman that specializes in a particular commodity, represents either a buyer or a seller, and is likely to be hired on a temporary basis (15)
budget a financial statement that projects income and/or expenditures over a specified future period (20)
bundle pricing packaging together two or more complementary products and selling them for a single price (14)
bureaucratic structure a management system based on a formal framework of authority that is outlined carefully and followed precisely (8)
business the organized effort of individuals to produce and sell, for a profit, the products and services that satisfy society's needs (1)
business buying behavior the purchasing of products by producers, resellers, governmental units, and institutions (13)
business cycle the recurrence of periods of growth and recession in a nation's economic activity (1)
business ethics the application of moral standards to business situations (2)
business interruption insurance insurance protection for a business whose operations are interrupted because of a fire, storm, or other natural disaster (Appendix B)
business model represents a group of common characteristics and methods of doing business to generate sales revenues and reduce expenses (4)
business plan a carefully constructed guide for the person starting a business (6)
business product a product bought for resale, for making other products, or for use in a firm's operations (14)
business service an intangible product that an organization uses in its operations (14)
business-to-business (B2B) model firms that conduct business with other businesses (4)
business-to-consumer (B2C) model firms that focus on conducting business with individual buyers (4)
buying allowance a temporary price reduction to resellers for purchasing specified quantities of a product (16)
buying behavior the decisions and actions of people involved in buying and using products (13)
buying long buying stock with the expectation that it will increase in value and can then be sold at a profit (21)

C

capacity the amount of products or services that an organization can produce in a given time (9)
capital budget a financial statement that estimates a firm's expenditures for major assets and its long-term financing needs (20)
capital gain the difference between a security's purchase price and selling price (21)
capital-intensive technology a process in which machines and equipment do most of the work (9)
capitalism an economic system in which individuals own and operate the majority of businesses that provide goods and services (1)
captioned photograph a picture accompanied by a brief explanation (16)
captive pricing pricing the basic product in a product line low, but pricing related items at a higher level (14)
carrier a firm that offers transportation services (15)
cash budget a financial statement that projects cash receipts and expenditures over a specified period (20)
cash flow the movement of money into and out of an organization (20)
cash surrender value the amount payable to the holder of a whole life insurance policy if the policy is canceled (Appendix B)
catalog marketing marketing in which an organization provides a catalog from which customers make selections and place orders by mail or telephone (15)
catalog showroom a retail outlet that displays well-known brands and sells them at discount prices through catalogs within the store (15)
category killer a very large specialty store that concentrates on a single product line and competes on the basis of low prices and product availability (15)
caveat emptor a Latin phrase meaning "let the buyer beware" (2)
centralized organization an organization that systematically works to concentrate authority at the upper levels of the organization (8)
certificate of deposit (CD) a document stating that the bank will pay the depositor a guaranteed interest rate for money left on deposit for a specified period of time. (19)
certified public accountant (CPA) an individual who has met state requirements for accounting education and experience and has passed a rigorous two-day accounting examination prepared by the AICPA (18)
chain of command the line of authority that extends from the highest to the lowest levels of an organization (8)
chain retailer a company that operates more than one retail outlet (15)
channel of distribution a sequence of marketing organizations that directs a product from the producer to the ultimate user; same as *marketing channel* (15)
check a written order for a bank or other financial institution to pay a stated dollar amount to the business or person indicated on the face of the check (19)
closed corporation a corporation whose stock is owned by relatively few people and is not sold to the general public (5)
closed shop a workplace in which workers must join the union before they are hired; outlawed by the Taft-Hartley Act (12)
cluster structure an organization that consists primarily of teams with no or very few underlying departments (8)
code of ethics a guide to acceptable and ethical behavior as defined by the organization (2)
coinsurance clause a part of a fire insurance policy that requires the policyholder to purchase coverage at least equal to a specified percentage of the replacement cost of the property to obtain full reimbursement for losses (Appendix B)

ollaborative learning system a work environment that allows problem-solving participation by all team members (17)
ollateral real estate or property pledged as security for a loan (19)
ollective bargaining the process of negotiating a labor contract with management (12)
ommand economy an economic system in which the government decides what will be produced, how it will be produced, who gets what is produced, and who owns and controls the major factors of production (1)
ommercial bank a profit-making organization that accepts deposits, makes loans, and provides related services to its customers (19)
ommercial paper a short-term promissory note issued by a large corporation (20)
ommission a payment that is a percentage of sales revenue (10)
ommission merchant a middleman that carries merchandise and negotiates sales for manufacturers (15)
common law the body of law created by court decisions rendered by judges; also known as case law or judicial law (Appendix C)
common stock stock whose owners may vote on corporate matters but whose claims on profits and assets are subordinate to the claims of others (5, 20)
community of interests a situation in which one firm buys the stock of a competing firm to reduce competition between the two (Appendix C)
community shopping center a planned shopping center that includes one or two department stores and some specialty stores, along with convenience stores (15)
comparable worth a concept that seeks equal compensation for jobs requiring about the same level of education, training, and skills (10)
comparative advantage the ability to produce a specific product more efficiently than any other product (3)
comparison discounting setting a price at a specific level and comparing it with a higher price (14)
compensation the payment employees receive in return for their labor (10)
compensation system the policies and strategies that determine employee compensation (10)
competition rivalry among businesses for sales to potential customers (1)
component part an item that becomes part of a physical product and is either a finished item ready for assembly or a product that needs little processing before assembly (14)
computer viruses software codes that are designed to disrupt normal computer operations (4)
computer-aided design (CAD) the use of computers to aid in the development of products (9)
computer-aided manufacturing (CAM) the use of computers to plan and control manufacturing processes (9)
computer-integrated manufacturing (CIM) a computer system that not only helps to design products but also controls the machinery needed to produce the finished product (9)
conceptual skill the ability to think in abstract terms (7)
consideration the value or benefit that one party to a contract furnishes to the other party (Appendix C)
consumer buying behavior the purchasing of products for personal or household use, not for business purposes (13)
consumer product goods and services purchased by individuals for personal consumption (1, 14)
consumer sales promotion method a sales promotion method designed to attract consumers to particular retail stores and to motivate them to purchase certain new or established products (16)
consumerism all activities undertaken to protect the rights of consumers (2)
contingency plan a plan that outlines alternative courses of action that may be taken if an organization's other plans are disrupted or become ineffective (7)
contract a legally enforceable agreement between two or more competent parties who promise to do or not to do a particular thing (Appendix C)
controlling the process of evaluating and regulating ongoing activities to ensure that goals are achieved (7)
convenience product a relatively inexpensive, frequently purchased item for which buyers want to exert only minimal effort (14)
convenience store a small food store that sells a limited variety of products but remains open well beyond normal business hours (15)
convergence of technologies the overlapping capabilities and the merging of products and services into one fully integrated interactive system (4)
convertible bond a bond that can be exchanged, at the owner's option, for a specified number of shares of the corporation's common stock (20)
convertible preferred stock preferred stock that the owner may exchange for a specified number of shares of common stock (20)
cookie a small piece of software sent by a website that tracks an individual's Internet use (4)
cooperative an association of individuals or firms whose purpose is to perform some business function for its members (5)
cooperative advertising an arrangement whereby a manufacturer agrees to pay a certain amount of the retailer's media cost for advertising the manufacturer's product (16)
copyright legal right to control content ownership (4, Appendix C)
corporate bond a corporation's written pledge that it will repay a specified amount of money with interest (20)
corporate charter a contract between the corporation and the state in which the state recognizes the formation of the artificial person that is the corporation (5)
corporate culture the inner rites, rituals, heroes, and values of a firm (8)
corporate officers the chairman of the board, president, executive vice presidents, corporate secretary, treasurer, or any other top executive appointed by the board of directors (5)
corporation an artificial person created by law with most of the legal rights of a real person, including the rights to start and operate a business, to buy or sell property, to borrow money, to sue or be sued, and to enter into binding contracts (5)
cost of goods sold the dollar amount equal to beginning inventory plus net purchases less ending inventory (18)
countertrade an international barter transaction (3)
coupon reduces the retail price of a particular item by a stated amount at the time of purchase (16)
court of limited jurisdiction a court that hears only specific types of cases (Appendix C)
court of original jurisdiction the first court to recognize and hear testimony in a legal action (Appendix C)
craft union an organization of skilled workers in a single craft or trade (12)
creative selling selling products to new customers and increasing sales to present customers (16)

credit immediate purchasing power that is exchanged for a promise to repay borrowed money, with or without interest, at a later date (19)

credit union a financial institution that accepts deposits from and lends money to only those people who are its members (19)

crime a violation of a public law (Appendix C)

critical path the sequence of production activities that takes the longest time from start to finish (9)

cross-functional team a group of employees from different departments who work together on a specific project (8)

cultural (workplace) diversity differences among people in a work force due to race, ethnicity, and gender (10)

currency devaluation the reduction of the value of a nation's currency relative to the currencies of other countries (3)

current assets assets that can quickly be converted into cash or that will be used in one year or less (18)

current liabilities debts that will be repaid in one year or less (18)

current ratio a financial ratio computed by dividing current assets by current liabilities (18)

customary pricing pricing on the basis of tradition (14)

customer relationship management (CRM) software software solutions that incorporate a variety of methods that can be used to manage communication with customers and share important information with all of the firm's employees (4)

customs duty a tax on a foreign product entering a country; same as *import duty* (Appendix C)

D

damages a monetary settlement awarded to a party injured through a breach of contract (Appendix C)

data numerical or verbal descriptions that usually result from some sort of measurement (17)

data mining the practice of searching through data records looking for useful information (4)

data processing the transformation of data into a form that is useful for a specific purpose (17)

database a single collection of data stored in one place that can be used by people throughout an organization to make decisions (17)

database management program software that allows users to electronically store large amounts of data and to transform the data into information (17)

debenture bond a bond backed only by the reputation of the issuing corporation (20)

debit card a card that electronically subtracts the amount of your purchase from your bank account at the moment the purchase is made (19)

debt capital borrowed money obtained through loans of various types (20)

debt-to-owners' equity ratio a financial ratio calculated by dividing total liabilities by owners' equity (18)

decentralized organization an organization in which management consciously attempts to spread authority widely in the lower levels of the organization (8)

decision making the act of choosing one alternative from among a set of alternatives (7)

decisional role a role that involves various aspects of management decision making (7)

deed a written document by which the ownership of real property is transferred from one person or organization to another (Appendix C)

delegation assigning part of a manager's work and power to other workers (8)

demand the quantity of a product that buyers are willing to purchase at each of various prices (1, 14)

demand deposit an amount on deposit in a checking account (19)

democratic leader one who holds final responsibility but also delegates authority to others, who help determine work assignments; communication is active upward and downward (7)

department store a retail store that (1) employs twenty-five or more persons and (2) sells at least home furnishings, appliances, family apparel, and household linens and dry goods, each in a different part of the store (15)

departmentalization the process of grouping jobs into manageable units (8)

departmentalization by customer grouping activities according to the needs of various customer populations (8)

departmentalization by function grouping jobs that relate to the same organizational activity (8)

departmentalization by location grouping activities according to the defined geographic area in which they are performed (8)

departmentalization by product grouping activities related to a particular product or service (8)

depreciation the process of apportioning the cost of a fixed asset over the period during which it will be used (18)

depression a severe recession that lasts longer than a recession (1)

deregulation the process of removing existing government regulations, forgoing proposed regulations, or reducing the rate at which new regulations are enacted (Appendix C)

design planning the development of a plan for converting a product idea into an actual product (9)

desktop publishing program a software package that enables users to combine text and graphics in reports, newsletters, and pamphlets (17)

digitized data that have been converted to a type of signal that computers and telecommunications equipment that make up the Internet can understand (4)

direct marketing the use of computers, telephones, and nonpersonal media to show products to customers, who can then purchase them by mail, telephone, or online (15)

direct selling the marketing of products to ultimate consumers through face-to-face sales presentations at home or in the workplace (15)

directing the combined processes of leading and motivating (7)

direct-mail advertising promotional material mailed directly to individuals (16)

direct-response marketing marketing that occurs when a retailer advertises a product and makes it available through mail or telephone orders (15)

discharge by mutual assent termination of a contract by mutual agreement of all parties (Appendix C)

discount a deduction from the price of an item (14)

discount rate the interest rate the Federal Reserve System charges for loans to member banks (19)

discount store a self-service general merchandise outlet that sells products at lower-than-usual prices (15)

discretionary income disposable income less savings and expenditures on food, clothing, and housing (13)

discretionary order an order to buy or sell a security that lets the broker decide when to execute the transaction and at what price (21)

isposable income personal income less all additional personal taxes (13)

ivestiture the process of dismantling a company and selling off different parts (5)

ividend a distribution of earnings to the stockholders of a corporation (5)

omestic corporation a corporation in the state in which it is incorporated (5)

omestic system a method of manufacturing in which an entrepreneur distributes raw materials to various homes, where families would process them into finished goods to be offered for sale by the merchant entrepreneur (1)

ouble-entry bookkeeping a system in which each financial transaction is recorded as two separate accounting entries to maintain the balance shown in the accounting equation (18)

raft issued by the exporter's bank, ordering the importer's bank to pay for the merchandise, thus guaranteeing payment once accepted by the importer's bank (3)

umping exportation of large quantities of a product at a price lower than that of the same product in the home market (3)

E

earnings per share a financial ratio calculated by dividing net income after taxes by the number of shares of common stock outstanding (18)

e-business the organized effort of individuals to produce and sell, for a profit, the products and services that satisfy society's needs through the Internet. (1, 4)

e-commerce buying and selling activities conducted online (4)

economic community an organization of nations formed to promote the free movement of resources and products among its members and to create common economic policies (3)

economic model of social responsibility the view that society will benefit most when business is left alone to produce and market profitable products that society needs (2)

economics the study of how wealth is created and distributed (1)

economy the way in which people deal with the creation and distribution of wealth. (1)

electronic funds transfer (EFT) system a means of performing financial transactions through a computer terminal or telephone hookup (19)

embargo a complete halt to trading with a particular nation or in a particular product (3)

employee benefit a reward in addition to regular compensation that is provided indirectly to employees (10)

employee ownership a situation in which employees own the company they work for by virtue of being stockholders (11)

employee training the process of teaching operations and technical employees how to do their present jobs more effectively and efficiently (10)

empowerment making employees more involved in their jobs by increasing their participation in decision making (11)

endorsement the payee's signature on the back of a negotiable instrument (Appendix C)

endowment life insurance life insurance that provides protection and guarantees the payment of a stated amount to the policyholder after a specified number of years (Appendix B)

entrepreneur a person who risks time, effort, and money to start and operate a business (1)

Equal Employment Opportunity Commission (EEOC) a government agency with power to investigate complaints of employment discrimination and power to sue firms that practice it (2)

equity capital money received from the owners or from the sale of shares of ownership in a business (20)

equity theory a theory of motivation based on the premise that people are motivated to obtain and preserve equitable treatment for themselves (11)

esteem needs our need for respect, recognition, and a sense of our own accomplishment and worth (11)

ethics the study or right and wrong and of the morality of the choices individuals make (2)

everyday low prices (EDLPs) setting a low price for products on a consistent basis (14)

excise tax a tax on the manufacture or sale of a particular domestic product (Appendix C)

exclusive distribution the use of only a single retail outlet for a product in a large geographic area (15)

expectancy theory a model of motivation based on the assumption that motivation depends on how much we want something and on how likely we think we are to get it (11)

Export-Import Bank of the United States an independent agency of the U.S. government whose function it is to assist in financing the exports of American firms (3)

exporting selling and shipping raw materials or products to other nations (3)

express warranty a written explanation of the responsibilities of the producer in the event that the product is found to be defective or otherwise unsatisfactory (14, Appendix C)

extended coverage insurance protection against damage caused by wind, hail, explosion, vandalism, riots or civil commotion, falling aircraft, and smoke (Appendix B)

external recruiting the attempt to attract job applicants from outside the organization (10)

e-zines small online magazines (4)

F

factor a firm that specializes in buying other firms' accounts receivable (20)

factors of production land and natural resources, labor, capital, and entrepreneurship (1)

factory system a system of manufacturing in which all the materials, machinery, and workers required to manufacture a product are assembled in one place (1)

family branding the strategy in which a firm uses the same brand for all or most of its products (14)

family of funds a group of mutual funds managed by one investment company (21)

feature article a piece (of up to 3,000 words) prepared by an organization for inclusion in a particular publication (16)

federal deficit a shortfall created when the federal government spends more in a fiscal year than it receives (1)

Federal Reserve System the central bank of the United States responsible for regulating the banking industry (19)

Federal Trade Commission (FTC) a five-member committee charged with the responsibility of investigating illegal trade practices and enforcing antitrust laws (Appendix C)

fidelity bond an insurance policy that protects a business from theft, forgery, or embezzlement by its employees (Appendix B)

financial leverage the use of borrowed funds to increase the return on owners' equity (20)

financial management all the activities concerned with obtaining money and using it effectively (20)

financial manager a manager who is primarily responsible for an organization's financial resources (7)

financial plan a plan for obtaining and using the money needed to implement an organization's goals (20)

financial planner an individual who has had at least two years of training in investments, insurance, taxation, retirement planning, and estate planning and has passed a rigorous examination (21)

financial ratio a number that shows the relationship between two elements of a firm's financial statements (18)

fire insurance insurance that covers losses due to fire (Appendix B)

first-line manager a manager who coordinates and supervises the activities of operating employees (7)

fiscal policy government influence on the amount of savings and expenditures; accomplished by altering the tax structure and by changing the levels of government spending (1)

fixed assets assets that will be held or used for a period longer than one year (18)

fixed cost a cost incurred no matter how many units of a product are produced or sold (14)

flexible benefit plan compensation plan whereby an employee receives a predetermined amount of benefit dollars to spend on a package of benefits he or she has selected to meet individual needs (10)

flexible manufacturing system (FMS) a single production system that combines robotics and computer-integrated manufacturing (9)

flextime a system in which employees set their own work hours within employer-determined limits (11)

floor planning method of financing in which title to merchandise is given to lenders in return for short-term financing (20)

foreign corporation a corporation in any state in which it does business except the one in which it is incorporated (5)

foreign-exchange control a restriction on the amount of a particular foreign currency that can be purchased or sold (3)

form utility utility created by converting raw materials, people, finances, and information, into finished products (9, 13)

franchise a license to operate an individually owned business as though it were part of a chain of outlets or stores (6)

franchisee a person or organization purchasing a franchise (6)

franchising the actual granting of a franchise (6)

franchisor an individual or organization granting a franchise (6)

free enterprise the system of business in which individuals are free to decide what to produce, how to produce it, and at what price to sell it. (1)

frequency distribution a listing of the number of times each value appears in a set of data (17)

frequent-user incentive a program developed to reward customers who engage in repeat (frequent) purchases (16)

full-service wholesaler a middleman that performs the entire range of wholesaler functions (15)

functional middleman a middleman that helps in the transfer of ownership of products but does not take title to the products (15)

G

Gantt chart a graphic scheduling device that displays the tasks to be performed on the vertical axis and the time required for each task on the horizontal axis (9)

General Agreement on Tariffs and Trade (GATT) an international organization of 132 nations dedicated to reducing or eliminating tariffs and other barriers to world trade (3)

general journal a book of original entry in which typical transactions are recorded in order of their occurrence (18)

general ledger a book of accounts containing a separate sheet or section for each account (18)

general merchandise wholesaler a middleman that deals in a wide variety of products (15)

general partner a person who assumes full or shared responsibility for operating a business (5)

general partnership a business co-owned by two or more general partners who are liable for everything the business does (5)

generally accepted accounting principles (GAAPs) an accepted set of guidelines and practices for companies reporting financial information and for the accounting profession (18)

generic product (or brand) a product with no brand at all (14)

goal an end result that an organization is expected to achieve over a one- to ten-year period (7)

goal-setting theory a theory of motivation suggesting that employees are motivated to achieve goals they and their managers establish together (11)

goodwill the value of a firm's reputation, location, earning capacity, and other intangibles that make the business a profitable concern (18)

government-owned corporation a corporation owned and operated by a local, state, or federal government (5)

grapevine the informal communications network within an organization (8)

graphics program software that enables users to display and print pictures, drawings, charts, and diagrams (17)

grievance procedure a formally established course of action for resolving employee complaints against management (12)

gross domestic product (GDP) the total dollar value of all goods and services produced by all people within the boundaries of a country during a one-year period (1)

gross profit a firm's net sales less the cost of goods sold (18)

gross sales the total dollar amount of all goods and services sold during the accounting period (18)

groupware one of the latest types of software that facilitates the management of large projects among geographically dispersed employees as well as such group activities as problem solving and brainstorming (17)

H

hard-core unemployed workers with little education or vocational training and a long history of unemployment (2)

health care insurance insurance that covers the cost of medical attention, including hospital care, physicians' and surgeons' fees, prescription medicines, and related services (Appendix B)

health maintenance organization (HMO) an insurance plan that directly employs or contracts with selected physicians and hospitals to provide health care services in exchange for a fixed, prepaid monthly premium (Appendix B)

high-risk investment an investment made in the uncertain hope of earning a relatively large profit in a short time (21)

hostile takeover a situation in which the management and board of directors of the firm targeted for acquisition disapprove of the merger (5)

hourly wage a specific amount of money paid for each hour of work (10)

human resources management (HRM) all the activities involved in acquiring, maintaining, and developing an organization's human resources (10)

human resources manager a person charged with managing an organization's human resources programs (7)

human resources planning the development of strategies to meet a firm's future human resources needs (10)

hygiene factors job factors that reduce dissatisfaction when present to an acceptable degree but that do not necessarily result in high levels of motivation (11)

I

implied warranty a guarantee imposed or required by law (Appendix C)

import duty (or tariff) a tax on a foreign product entering a country; same as *customs duty* (3, Appendix C)

import quota a limit on the amount of a particular good that may be imported into a country during a given period of time (3)

importing purchasing raw materials or products in other nations and bringing them into one's own country (3)

incentive payment a payment in addition to wages, salary, or commissions (10)

income statement a summary of a firm's revenues and expenses during a specified accounting period (18)

incorporation the process of forming a corporation (5)

independent retailer a firm that operation only one retail outlet (15)

individual branding the strategy in which a firm uses a different brand for each of its products (14)

industrial union an organization of both skilled and unskilled workers in a single industry (12)

inflation a general rise in the level of prices (1)

infomercial a program-length televised commercial message resembling an entertainment or consumer affairs program (16)

informal group a group created by the members themselves to accomplish goals that may or may not be relevant to an organization (8)

informal organization the pattern of behavior and interaction that stems from personal rather than official relationships (8)

information data presented in a form that is useful for a specific purpose (17)

information society a society in which large groups of employees generate or depend on information to perform their jobs (17)

information technology officer a manager at the executive level who is responsible for ensuring that a firm has the equipment necessary to provide the information the firm's employees and managers need to make effective decisions (17)

informational role a role in which the manager either gathers or provides information (7)

initial public offering (IPO) when a corporation sells common stock to the general public for the first time (20)

injunction a court order requiring a person or group either to perform some act or to refrain from performing some act (12)

inland marine insurance insurance that protects against loss or damage to goods shipped by rail, truck, airplane, or inland barge (Appendix B)

inspection the examination of the quality of work in process (9)

institutional advertising advertising designed to enhance a firm's image or reputation (16)

institutional investors pension funds, insurance companies, mutual funds, banks, and other organizations that trade large quantities of securities (21)

insurable risk a risk that insurance companies will assume (Appendix B)

insurance the protection against loss that the purchase of an insurance policy affords (Appendix B)

insurance company a firm that agrees, for a fee, to assume financial responsibility for losses that may result from a specific risk; same as *insurer* (Appendix B)

insurance policy the contract between an insurer and the person or firm whose risk is assumed (Appendix B)

insurer a firm that agrees, for a fee, to assume financial responsibility for losses that may result from a specific risk; same as *insurance company* (Appendix B)

intangible assets assets that do not exist physically but that have a value based on the rights or privileges they confer on a firm (18)

integrated marketing communications coordination of promotion efforts for maximum informational and persuasive impact on customers (16)

intensive distribution the use of all available outlets for a product (15)

interlocking directorate an arrangement in which members of the board of directors of one firm are also directors of a competing firm (Appendix C)

internal recruiting considering present employees as applicants for available positions (10)

international business all business activities that involve exchanges across national boundaries (3)

International Monetary Fund (IMF) an international bank with more than 183 member nations that makes short-term loans to developing countries experiencing balance-of-payment deficits (3)

Internet a worldwide network of computers linked through telecommunications (17)

Internet service providers (ISPs) provide customers with a connection to the Internet through various phone plugs and cables (4)

interpersonal role a role in which the manager deals with people (7)

interpersonal skill the ability to deal effectively with other people (7)

intranet a smaller version of the Internet for use only within a firm (17)

intrapreneur an employee who pushes an innovative idea, product, or process through an organization (8)

inventory control the process of managing inventories in such a way as to minimize inventory costs, including both holding costs and potential stock-out costs (9)

inventory management the process of managing inventories in such a way as to minimize inventory costs, including both holding costs and potential stock-out costs (15)

inventory turnover a financial ratio calculated by dividing the cost of goods sold in one year by the average value of the inventory (18)

investment banking firm an organization that assists corporations in raising funds, usually by helping sell new issues of stocks, bonds, or other financial securities (20)

involuntary bankruptcy a bankruptcy procedure initiated by creditors (Appendix C)

J

job analysis a systematic procedure for studying jobs to determine their various elements and requirements (10)

job description a list of the elements that make up a particular job (10)

job enlargement expanding a worker's assignments to include additional but similar tasks (11)

job enrichment a motivation technique that provides employees with more variety and responsibility in their jobs (11)

job evaluation the process of determining the relative worth of the various jobs within a firm (10)

job redesign a type of job enrichment in which work is restructured to cultivate the worker-job match (11)

job rotation the systematic shifting of employees from one job to another (8)

job security protection against the loss of employment (12)

job sharing an arrangement whereby two people share one full-time position (11)

job specialization the separation of all organizational activities into distinct tasks and the assignment of different tasks to different people (8)

job specification a list of the qualifications required to perform a particular job (10)

joint venture an agreement between two or more groups to form a business entity in order to achieve a specific goal or to operate for a specific period of time (5)

jurisdiction the right of a particular union to organize particular workers (12)

just-in-time inventory system a system designed to ensure that materials or supplies arrive at a facility just when they are needed so that storage and holding costs are minimized (9)

L

labeling the presentation of information on a product or its package (14)

labor union an organization of workers acting together to negotiate their wages and working conditions with employers (12)

labor-intensive technology a process in which people must do most of the work (9)

laissez-faire leader one who gives authority to employees and allows subordinates to work as they choose with a minimum of interference; communication flows horizontally among group members (7)

law a rule developed by a society to govern the conduct of and relationships among its members (Appendix C)

leadership the ability to influence others (7)

leading the process of influencing people to work toward a common goal (7)

lease an agreement by which the right to use real estate, equipment, or other assets is temporarily transferred from the owner to the user (20, Appendix C)

letter of credit a legal document issued by a financial institution guaranteeing to pay a seller a stated amount for a specified period of time (3, 19)

leveraged buyout (LBO) a purchase arrangement that allows a firm's managers and employees or a group of investors to purchase the company (5)

liabilities a firm's debts and obligations (18)

licensing a contractual agreement in which one firm permits another to produce and market its product and use its brand name in return for a royalty or other compensation (3)

life insurance insurance that pays a stated amount of money on the death of the insured individual (Appendix B)

limit order a request that a security be bought or sold at a price that is equal to or better than some specified price (21)

limited liability a feature of corporate ownership that limits each owner's financial liability to the amount of money that he or she has paid for the corporation's stock (5)

limited partner a person who contributes capital to a business but has no management responsibility or liability for losses beyond the amount he or she invested in the partnership (5)

limited partnership a business co-owned by one or more general partners who manage the business and limited partners who invest money in it (5)

limited-liability company (LLC) a form of business ownership that provides limited-liability protection and is taxed like a partnership (5)

limited-line wholesaler a middleman that stocks only a few product lines but carries numerous product items within each line (15)

limited-service wholesaler a middleman that assumes responsibility for a few wholesale services only (15)

line management position a position that is part of the chain of command and that includes direct responsibility for achieving the goals of the organization (8)

line of credit a loan that is approved before the money is actually needed (19)

liquidity the ease with which an asset or investment can be converted into cash (18, 21)

lockout a firm's refusal to allow employees to enter the workplace (12)

log-file records files that store a record of the websites visited (4)

long-term financing money that will be used for longer than one year (20)

long-term liabilities debts that need not be repaid for at least one year (18)

lump-sum salary increase an entire pay raise taken in one lump sum (10)

M

maintenance shop a workplace in which an employee who joins the union must remain a union member as long as he or she is employed by the firm (12)

major equipment large tools and machines used for production purposes (14)

management the process of coordinating people and other resources to achieve the goals of the organization (7)

management by objectives (MBO) a motivation technique in which managers and employees collaborate in setting goals (11)

management development the process of preparing managers and other professionals to assume increased responsibility in both present and future positions (10)

management information system (MIS) a system that provides managers and employees with the information they need to perform their jobs as effectively as possible (17)

managerial hierarchy the arrangement that provides increasing authority at higher levels of management (8)

manufacturer brand a brand that is owned by a manufacturer; same as *producer brand* (14)

manufacturer's sales branch essentially a merchant wholesaler that is owned by a manufacturer (15)

manufacturer's sales office essentially a sales agent owned by a manufacturer (15)

margin requirement the portion of the price of a stock that cannot be borrowed (21)

market a group of individuals or organizations, or both, that need products in a given category and that have the ability, willingness, and authority to purchase such products (13)

market allocation an agreement to divide a market among potential competitors (Appendix C)

market economy an economic system in which businesses and individuals decide what to produce and buy, and the market determines quantities sold and prices (1)

market order a request that a security be purchased or sold at the current market price (21)

market price the price at which the quantity demanded is exactly equal to the quantity supplied (1)

market segment a group of individuals or organizations within a market that share one or more common characteristics (13)

market segmentation the process of dividing a market into segments and directing a marketing mix at a particular segment or segments rather than at the total market (13)

market value the price of one share of a stock at a particular time (21)

marketing the process of planning and executing the conception, pricing, promotion, and distribution of ideas, goods, and services to create exchanges that satisfy individual and organizational objectives (13)

marketing concept a business philosophy that involves the entire organization in the process of satisfying customers' needs while achieving the organization's goals (13)

marketing information system a system for managing marketing information that is gathered continually from internal and external sources (13)

marketing manager a manager who is responsible for facilitating the exchange of products between an organization and its customers or clients (7)

marketing mix a combination of product, price, distribution, and promotion developed to satisfy a particular target market (13)

marketing plan a written document that specifies an organization's resources, objectives, strategy, and implementation and control efforts to be used in marketing a specific product or product group (13)

marketing research the process of systematically gathering, recording, and analyzing data concerning a particular marketing problem (13)

marketing strategy a plan that will enable an organization to make the best use of its resources and advantages to meet its objectives (13)

markup the amount a seller adds to the cost of a product to determine its basic selling price (14)

Maslow's hierarchy of needs a sequence of human needs in the order of their importance (11)

master limited partnership (MLP) a business partnership that is owned and managed like a corporation but taxed like a partnership (5)

materials handling the actual physical handling of goods, in warehousing as well as during transportation (15)

materials requirements planning (MRP) a computerized system that integrates production planning and inventory control (9)

matrix structure an organizational structure that combines vertical and horizontal lines of authority, usually by superimposing product departmentalization on a functionally departmentalized organization (8)

maturity date the date on which a corporation is to repay borrowed money (20)

measure of value a single standard or "yardstick" used to assign values to, and compare the values of, products, services, and resources (19)

median the value at the exact middle of a set of data when the data are arranged in order (17)

mediation the use of a neutral third party to assist management and the union during their negotiations (12)

medium of exchange anything accepted as payment for products, services, and resources (19)

merchant middleman a middleman that actually takes title to products by buying them (15)

merchant wholesaler a middleman that purchases goods in large quantities and then sells them to other wholesalers or retailers and to institutional, farm, government, professional, or industrial users (15)

merger the purchase of one corporation by another (5)

middle manager a manager who implements the strategy and major policies developed by top management (7)

middleman a marketing organization that links a producer and user within a marketing channel; same as *marketing intermediary* (15)

minority a racial, religious, political, national, or other group regarded as different from the larger group of which it is a part and that is often singled out for unfavorable treatment (2)

mission a statement of the basic purpose that makes an organization different from others (7)

missionary salesperson a salesperson—generally employed by a manufacturer—who visits retailers to persuade them to buy the manufacturer's products (16)

mixed economy an economy that exhibits elements of both capitalism and socialism (1)

mode the value that appears most frequently in a set of data (17)

monetary policies Federal Reserve decisions that determine the size of the supply of money in the nation and the level of interest rates (1)

money anything a society uses to purchase products, services, or resources (19)

monopolistic competition a market situation in which there are many buyers along with a relatively large number of sellers who differentiate their products from the products of competitors (1)

monopoly a market (or industry) with only one seller (1)

morale an employee's feelings about his or her job and superiors and about the firm itself (11)

mortgage bond a corporate bond secured by various assets of the issuing firm (20)

motivating the process of providing reasons for people to work in the best interests of an organization (7)

motivation the individual internal process that energizes, directs, and sustains behavior; the personal "force" that causes us to behave in a particular way (11)

motivation factor job factors that increase motivation but whose absence does not necessarily result in dissatisfaction (11)

motivation-hygiene theory the idea that satisfaction and dissatisfaction are separate and distinct dimensions (11)

multilateral development bank (MDB) an internationally supported bank that provides loans to developing countries to help them grow (3)

multinational enterprise a firm that operates on a worldwide scale without ties to any specific nation or region (3)

multiple-unit pricing the strategy of setting a single price for two or more units (14)

municipal bond sometimes called a muni, a debt security issued by a state or local government (21)

mutual fund a professionally managed investment vehicle that combines and invests the funds of many individual investors (21)

mutual insurance company an insurance company that is owned collectively by its policyholders and is thus a cooperative (Appendix B)

N

Nasdaq computerized electronic exchange system through which most over-the-counter securities are traded (21)

National Alliance of Business (NAB) a joint business-government program to train the hard-core unemployed (2)

National Association of Securities Dealers (NASD) the organization responsible for the self-regulation of the over-the-counter securities market (21)

national bank a commercial bank chartered by the U.S. Comptroller of the Currency (19)

national debt the total of all federal deficits (1)

National Labor Relations Board (NLRB) the federal agency that enforces the provisions of the Wagner Act (12)

natural monopoly an industry requiring huge investments in capital and within which duplication of facilities would be wasteful and thus not in the public interest (1)

need a personal requirement (11)

negligence a failure to exercise reasonable care, resulting in injury to another (Appendix C)

negotiable instrument a written document that (1) is a promise to pay a stated sum of money and (2) can be transferred from one person or firm to another (Appendix C)

negotiated pricing establishing a final price through bargaining (14)

neighborhood shopping center a planned shopping center consisting of several small convenience and specialty stores (15)

net asset value (NAV) current market value of a mutual fund's portfolio minus the mutual fund's liabilities and divided by the number of outstanding shares (21)

net income occurs when revenues exceed expenses (18)

net loss occurs when expenses exceed revenues (18)

net sales the actual dollar amounts received by a firm for the goods and services it has sold, after adjustment for returns, allowances, and discounts (18)

network structure an organization in which administration is the primary function and most other functions are contracted out to other firms (8)

news release a typed page of about 300 words provided by an organization to the media as a form of publicity (16)

no-fault auto insurance a method of paying for losses suffered in an automobile accident; enacted by state law, that requires that those suffering injury or loss be reimbursed by their own insurance companies, without regard to who was at fault in the accident (Appendix B)

nonprice competition competition based on factors other than price (14)

nonstore retailing a type of retailing whereby consumers purchase products without visiting a store (15)

nontariff barrier a nontax measure imposed by a government to favor domestic over foreign suppliers (3)

notes payable obligations that have been secured with promissory notes (18)

not-for-profit corporation a corporation organized to provide a social, educational, religious, or other service rather than to earn a profit (5)

NOW account an interest-bearing checking account; NOW stands for negotiable order of withdrawal (19)

O

objective a specific statement detailing what an organization intends to accomplish over a shorter period of time (7)

ocean marine insurance insurance that protects the policy holder against loss or damage to a ship or its cargo on the high seas (Appendix B)

odd lot fewer than 100 shares of a particular stock (21)

odd-number pricing the strategy of setting prices using odd numbers that are slightly below whole-dollar amounts (14)

off-price retailer a store that buys manufacturers' seconds, overruns, returns, and off-season merchandise for resale to consumers at deep discounts (15)

oligopoly a market (or industry) in which there are few sellers (1)

online communities groups of individuals or firms that want to exchange information, products, or services over the Internet (4)

online retailing presenting and selling products through computer connections (15)

open corporation a corporation whose stock is bought and sold on security exchanges and can be purchased by any individual (5)

open-market operations the buying and selling of U.S. government securities by the Federal Reserve System for the purpose of controlling the supply of money (19)

operating expenses all business costs other than the cost of goods sold (18)

operational plan a type of plan designed to implement tactical plans (7)

operations management all activities managers engage in to produce goods and services (9)

operations manager a manager who manages the systems that convert resources into goods and services (7)

order getter a salesperson who is responsible for selling a firm's products to new customers and increasing sales to present customers (16)

order processing activities involved in receiving and filling customers' purchase orders (15)

order taker a salesperson who handles repeat sales in ways that maintain positive relationships with customers (16)

organization a group of two or more people working together to achieve a common set of goals (8)

organization chart a diagram that represents the positions and relationships within an organization (8)

organizational height the number of layers, or levels, of management in a firm (8)

organizing the grouping of resources and activities to accomplish some end result in an efficient and effective manner (7)

orientation the process of acquainting new employees with an organization (10)

out-of-home advertising short promotional messages on billboards, posters, signs, and transportation vehicles (16)

over-the-counter (OTC) market a network of dealers who buy and sell the stocks of corporations that are not listed on a securities exchange (21)

overtime time worked in excess of forty hours in one week; under some union contracts, time worked in excess of eight hours in a single day (12)

owners' equity the difference between a firm's assets and its liabilities—what would be left for the owners if assets were used to pay off its liabilities (18)

P

packaging all the activities involved in developing and providing a container with graphics for a product (14)

par value an assigned (and often arbitrary) dollar value printed on a stock certificate (20)

artnership a voluntary association of two or more persons to act as co-owners of a business for profit (5)

art-time work permanent employment in which individuals work less than a standard work week (11)

atent the exclusive right to make, use, or sell a newly invented product or process (Appendix C)

enetration pricing the strategy of setting a low price for a new product (14)

erformance the fulfillment of all obligations by all parties to the contract (Appendix C)

erformance appraisal the evaluation of employees' current and potential levels of performance to allow managers to make objective human resources decisions (10)

eriodic discounting temporary reduction of prices on a patterned or systematic basis (14)

ersonal income the income an individual receives from all sources less the Social Security taxes the individual must pay (13)

ersonal investment the use of your personal funds to earn a financial return (21)

ersonal property all property other than real property (Appendix C)

ersonal selling personal communication aimed at informing customers and persuading them to buy a firm's products (16)

ERT (Program Evaluation and Review Technique) a scheduling technique that identifies the major activities necessary to complete a project and sequences them based on the time required to perform each one (9)

hysical distribution all those activities concerned with the efficient movement of products from the producer to the ultimate user (15)

physiological needs the things we require for survival (11)

picketing marching back and forth in front of a place of employment with signs informing the public that a strike is in progress (12)

piece-rate system a compensation system under which employees are paid a certain amount for each unit of output they produce (11)

place utility utility created by making a product available at a location where customers wish to purchase it (13)

plan an outline of the actions by which an organization intends to accomplish its goals and objectives (7)

planning establishing organizational goals and deciding how to accomplish them (7)

planning horizon the period during which a plan will be in effect (9)

plant layout the arrangement of machinery, equipment, and personnel within a production facility (9)

point-of-purchase display promotional material placed within a retail store (16)

pollution the contamination of water, air, or land through the actions of people in an industrialized society (2)

positioning the development of a product image in buyers' minds relative to the images they have of competing products (16)

possession utility utility created by transferring title (or ownership) of a product to the buyer (13)

power of attorney a legal document that serves as evidence that an agent has been appointed to act on behalf of a principal (Appendix C)

preferred provider organization (PPO) an insurance plan that offers the services of doctors and hospitals at discount rates or gives breaks in copayments and deductibles (Appendix B)

preferred stock stock whose owners usually do not have voting rights but whose claims on dividends and assets are paid before those of common-stock owners (5, 20)

premium (promotion) a gift that a producer offers the customer in return for buying its product (16)

premium the fee charged by an insurance company (Appendix B)

premium pricing pricing the highest quality or most versatile products higher than other models in the product line (14)

prepaid expenses assets that have been paid for in advance but have not yet been used (18)

press conference a meeting at which invited media personnel hear important news announcements and receive supplementary textual materials and photographs (16)

price the amount of money a seller is willing to accept in exchange for a product at a given time and under given circumstances (14)

price competition an emphasis on setting a price equal to or lower than competitors' prices to gain sales or market share (14)

price discrimination the practice in which producers and wholesalers charge larger firms a lower price for goods than they charge smaller firms (Appendix C)

price fixing an agreement between two businesses about the prices to be charged for goods (Appendix C)

price leaders products priced below the usual markup, near cost, or below cost (14)

price lining setting a limited number of prices for selected groups or lines of merchandise (14)

price skimming the strategy of charging the highest possible price for a product during the introduction stage of its life cycle (14)

primary market a market in which an investor purchases financial securities (via an investment bank) directly from the issuer of those securities (21)

primary-demand advertising advertising whose purpose is to increase the demand for all brands of a product within a specific industry (16)

prime interest rate the lowest rate charged by a bank for a short-term loan (20)

principle of indemnity in the event of a loss, an insured firm or individual cannot collect from the insurer an amount greater than the actual dollar amount of the loss (Appendix B)

private accountant an accountant employed by a specific organization (18)

private law the body of law that governs the relationships between two or more individuals or businesses (Appendix C)

problem the discrepancy between an actual condition and a desired condition (7)

process material a material that is used directly in the production of another product but is not readily identifiable in the finished product (14)

producer brand a brand that is owned by a manufacturer; same as *manufacturer brand* (14)

product everything one receives in an exchange, including all tangible and intangible attributes and expected benefits; it may be a good, service, or idea (14)

product deletion the elimination of one or more products from a product line (14)

product design the process of creating a set of specifications from which a product can be produced (9)

product differentiation the process of developing and promoting differences between one's products and all similar products (1, 14)

product liability insurance insurance that protects the policyholder from financial losses due to injuries suffered by others as a result of using the policyholder's products (Appendix B)

product life cycle a series of stages in which a product's sales revenue and profit increase, reach a peak, and then decline (14)

product line a group of similar products that differ only in relatively minor characteristics (9, 14)
product mix all the products a firm offers for sale (14)
product modification the process of changing one or more of a product's characteristics (14)
productivity the average level of output per worker per hour (1, 9)
profit what remains after all business expenses have been deducted from sales revenue (1)
profit sharing the distribution of a percentage of the firm's profit among its employees (10)
program trading a computer-driven program to buy or sell selected stocks (21)
progressive tax a tax that requires the payment of an increasing proportion of income as the individual's income increases (Appendix C)
promissory note a written pledge by a borrower to pay a certain sum of money to a creditor at a specified future date (20)
promotion communication about an organization and its products that is intended to inform, persuade, or remind target market members (16)
promotion mix the particular combination of promotion methods a firm uses to reach a target market (16)
promotional campaign a plan for combining and using the four promotional methods—advertising, personal selling, sales promotion, and publicity—in a particular promotion mix to achieve one or more marketing goals (16)
property anything that can be owned (Appendix C)
proportional tax a tax whose percentage rate remains constant as the tax base increases (Appendix C)
prospectus a detailed written description of a new security, the issuing corporation, and the corporation's top management (21)
proxy a legal form listing issues to be decided at a stockholders' meeting and enabling stockholders to transfer their voting rights to some other individual or individuals (5)
proxy fight a technique used to gather enough stockholder votes to control the targeted company (5)
public accountant an accountant who provides services to clients on a fee basis (18)
public law the body of law that deals with the relationships between individuals or businesses and society (Appendix C)
public liability insurance insurance that protects the policyholder from financial losses due to injuries suffered by others as a result of negligence on the part of a business owner or employee (Appendix B)
public relations communication activities used to create and maintain favorable relations between an organization and various public groups, both internal and external (16)
publicity communication in news-story form about an organization, its products, or both (16)
purchasing all the activities involved in obtaining required materials, supplies, and parts from other firms (9)
pure competition the market situation in which there are many buyers and sellers of a product, and no single buyer or seller is powerful enough to affect the price of that product (1)
pure risk a risk that involves only the possibility of loss, with no potential for gain (Appendix B)

Q

qualitative research a process that involves the descriptive or subjective reporting of information discovered by a researcher (17)
quality circle a group of employees who meet on company tin to solve problems of product quality (9)
quality control the process of ensuring that goods and servic are produced in accordance with design specifications (9)
quantitative research a process that involves the collection numerical data for analysis through a survey, experiment, content analysis (17)
quasi-government corporation a business owned partly by th government and partly by private citizens or firms (5)

R

random discounting temporary reduction of prices on a unsystematic basis (14)
range the difference between the highest value and the lowes value in a set of data (17)
ratification approval of a labor contract by a vote of the unio membership (12)
raw material a basic material that actually becomes part of physical product; usually comes from mines, forests, oceans, o recycled solid wastes (14)
real property land and anything permanently attached to i (Appendix C)
rebate a return of part of the purchase price of a product (16)
recession two or more consecutive three-month periods of decline in a country's gross domestic product (1)
recruiting the process of attracting qualified job applicants (10)
reference pricing pricing a product at a moderate level and positioning it next to a more expensive model or brand (14)
regional shopping center a planned shopping center containing large department stores, numerous specialty stores, restaurants, movie theaters, and sometimes even hotels (15)
registered bond a bond registered in the owner's name by the issuing company (20)
registered representative an individual who buys and sells securities for clients, also called an *account executive* or *stockbroker* (21)
regressive tax a tax that takes a greater percentage of a lower income than of a higher income (Appendix C)
reinforcement theory a theory of motivation based on the premise that behavior that is rewarded is likely to be repeated, whereas behavior that is punished is less likely to recur (11)
relationship marketing developing mutually beneficial long-term partnerships with customers to enhance customer satisfaction and to stimulate long-term customer loyalty (13)
replacement chart a list of key personnel and their possible replacements within a firm (10)
research and development (R&D) a set of activities intended to identify new ideas that have the potential to result in new goods and services (9)
reserve requirement the percentage of its deposits a bank must retain, either in its own vault or on deposit with its Federal Reserve District Bank (19)
responsibility the duty to do a job or perform a task (8)
retailer a middleman that buys from producers or other middlemen and sells to consumers (15)
retained earnings the portion of a business's profits not distributed to stockholders (18, 20)
return on owners' equity a financial ratio calculated by dividing net income after taxes by owners' equity (18)
return on sales a financial ratio calculated by dividing net income after taxes by net sales (18)

evenue stream a source of revenue flowing into a firm (4)
evenues the dollar amounts earned by a firm from selling goods, providing services, or performing business activities (18)
evolving credit agreement a guaranteed line of credit (19, 20)
isk the possibility that a loss or injury will occur (Appendix B)
isk management the process of evaluating the risks faced by a firm or an individual and then minimizing the costs involved with those risks (Appendix B)
obotics the use of programmable machines to perform a variety of tasks by manipulating materials and tools (9)
ound lot a unit of 100 shares of a particular stock (21)

S

safety needs the things we require for physical and emotional security (11)
salary a specific amount of money paid for an employee's work during a set calendar period, regardless of the actual number of hours worked (10)
sales agreement a type of contract by which ownership is transferred from a seller to a buyer (Appendix C)
sales forecast an estimate of the amount of a product that an organization expects to sell during a certain period of time based on a specified level of marketing effort (13)
sales promotion the use of activities or materials as direct inducements to customers or salespersons (16)
sales support personnel employees who aid in selling but are more involved in locating prospects, educating customers, building goodwill for the firm, and providing follow-up service (16)
sample a free product given to customers to encourage trial (16)
savings and loan association (S&L) a financial institution that offers checking and savings accounts and certificates of deposit and that invests most of its assets in home mortgage loans and other consumer loans (19)
scheduling the process of ensuring that materials and other resources are at the right place at the right time (9)
scientific management the application of scientific principles to management of work and workers (11)
S-corporation a corporation that is taxed as though it were a partnership (5)
secondary market a market for existing financial securities that are traded between investors (21)
secondary-market pricing setting one price for the primary target market and a different price for another market (14)
secure electronic transaction (SET) an encryption process developed by MasterCard, Visa, IBM, Microsoft, and Netscape that prevents merchants from ever actually seeing any transaction data, including the customer's credit card number (4)
Securities and Exchange Commission (SEC) the agency that enforces federal securities regulations (21)
securities exchange a marketplace where member brokers meet to buy and sell securities (21)
security average (or security index) an average of the current market prices of selected securities (21)
selection the process of gathering information about applicants for a position and then using that information to choose the most appropriate applicant (10)
selective distribution the use of only a portion of the available outlets for a product in each geographic area (15)
selective-demand advertising advertising that is used to sell a particular brand of product; same as *brand advertising* (16)
self-actualization needs the need to grow and develop and to become all that we are capable of being (11)
self-insurance the process of establishing a monetary fund that can be used to cover the cost of a loss (Appendix B)
self-managed work teams groups of employees with the authority and skills to manage themselves (11)
selling short the process of selling stock that an investor does not actually own but has borrowed from a brokerage firm and will repay at a later date (21)
seniority the length of time an employee has worked for an organization (12)
serial bonds bonds of a single issue that mature on different dates (20)
Service Corps of Retired Executives (SCORE) a group of retired business people who volunteer their services to small businesses through SBA (6)
service economy an economy in which more effort is devoted to the production of services than to the production of goods (9)
shop steward an employee elected by union members to serve as their representative (12)
shopping product an item for which buyers are willing to expend considerable effort on planning and making the purchase (14)
short-term financing money that will be used for one year or less (20)
sinking fund a sum of money to which deposits are made each year for the purpose of redeeming a bond issue (20)
skills inventory a computerized data bank containing information on the skills and experience of all present employees (10)
slowdown technique whereby workers report to their jobs but work at a slower pace than normal (12)
small business one that is independently owned and operated for profit and is not dominant in its field (6)
Small Business Administration (SBA) a governmental agency that assists, counsels, and protects the interests of small businesses in the United States (6)
Small Business Development Center (SBDC) a university-based group that provides individual counseling and practical training to owners of small businesses (6)
Small Business Institute (SBI) a group of senior and graduate students in business administration who provide management counseling to small businesses (6)
small business investment companies (SBICs) privately owned firms that provide venture capital to small enterprises that meet their investment standards (6)
social audit a comprehensive report of what an organization has done and is doing with regard to social issues that affect it (2)
social needs our requirements for love and affection and a sense of belonging (11)
social responsibility the recognition that business activities have an impact on society and the consideration of that impact in business decision making (2)
socioeconomic model of social responsibility the concept that business should emphasize not only profits but also the impact of its decisions on society (2)
sole proprietorship a business that is owned (and usually operated) by one person (5)
span of control the number of workers who report directly to one manager; same as *span of management* (8)
span of management the number of workers who report directly to one manager (8)

special-event pricing advertised sales or price cutting linked to a holiday, season, or event (14)

specialization the separation of a manufacturing process into distinct tasks and the assignment of different tasks to different individuals (1)

specialty product an item that possesses one or more unique characteristics for which a significant group of buyers is willing to expend considerable purchasing effort (14)

specialty-line wholesaler a middleman that carries a select group of products within a single line (15)

specific performance the legal requirement that the parties to a contract fulfill their obligations according to the contract (Appendix C)

speculative production the time lag between the actual production of goods and when the goods are sold (20)

speculative risk a risk that accompanies the possibility of earning a profit (Appendix B)

spreadsheet program a software package that allows users to organize numerical data into a grid of rows and columns (17)

staff management position a position created to provide support, advice, and expertise within an organization (8)

standard of living a loose, subjective measure of how well off an individual or a society is mainly in terms of want satisfaction through goods and services (1)

standardization the guidelines that let products, services, materials, and processes achieve their purposes (17)

standing committee a relatively permanent committee charged with performing some recurring task (8)

state bank a commercial bank chartered by the banking authorities in the state in which it operates (19)

statement of cash flows a statement that illustrates how the operating, investing, and financing activities of a company affect cash during an accounting period (18)

statistic a measure that summarizes a particular characteristic of an entire group of numbers (17)

statistical process control (SPC) a system that uses random sampling to obtain data that are plotted on control charts and graphs to see if the production process is operating as it should and to pinpoint problem areas (9)

statistical quality control (SQC) a set of specific statistical techniques used to monitor all aspects of the production process to ensure that both work in progress and finished products meet the firm's quality standards (9)

statute a law passed by the U.S. Congress, a state legislature, or a local government (Appendix C)

statutory law all the laws that have been enacted by legislative bodies (Appendix C)

stock the shares of ownership of a corporation (5)

stock dividend a dividend in the form of additional stock (21)

stock insurance company an insurance company owned by stockholders and operated to earn a profit (Appendix B)

stock split the division of each outstanding share of a corporation's stock into a greater number of shares (21)

stockbroker an individual who buys and sells securities for clients, also called an *account executive* or *registered representative* (21)

stockholder a person who owns a corporation's stock (5)

store brand a brand that is owned by an individual wholesaler or retailer; same as *private brand* (14)

store of value a means of retaining and accumulating wealth (19)

strategic alliance a partnership formed to create competitive advantage on a worldwide basis (3)

strategic planning the process of establishing an organization's major goals and objectives and allocating the resources to achieve them (7)

strategy an organization's broadest set of plans, developed as a guide for major policy setting and decision making (7)

strike a temporary work stoppage by employees, calculated to add force to their demands (12)

strikebreaker a nonunion employee who performs the job of a striking union member (12)

supermarket a large self-service store that sells primarily food and household products (15)

superstore a large retail store that carries not only food and nonfood products ordinarily found in supermarkets but also additional product lines (15)

supply (economics) the quantity of a product that producers are willing to sell at each of various prices (1, 14)

supply (product) an item that facilitates production and operations but does not become part of the finished product (14)

supply-chain management long-term partnership among channel members working together to create a distribution system that reduces inefficiencies, costs, and redundancies while creating a competitive advantage and satisfying customers (15)

supply-chain management (SCM) software software solutions that focus on ways to improve communication between the suppliers and users of materials and components (4)

syndicate a temporary association of individuals or firms organized to perform a specific task that requires a large amount of capital (5)

synthetic process a process in operations management in which raw materials or components are combined to create a finished product (9)

T

tactical plan a smaller-scale plan developed to implement a strategy (7)

target market a group of individuals or organizations, or both, for which a firm develops and maintains a marketing mix suitable for the specific needs and preferences of that group (13)

task force a committee established to investigate a major problem or pending decision (8)

technical salesperson a salesperson who assists a company's current customers in technical matters (16)

technical skill a specific skill needed to accomplish a specialized activity (7)

telecommuting working at home all the time or for a portion of the work week (11)

telemarketing the performance of marketing-related activities by telephone (15)

television home shopping selling in which products are displayed to television viewers, who can then order them by calling a toll-free number and paying by credit card (15)

tender offer an offer to purchase the stock of a firm targeted for acquisition at a price just high enough to tempt stockholders to sell their shares (5)

term life insurance life insurance that provides protection to beneficiaries for a stated period of time (Appendix B)

term-loan agreement a promissory note that requires a borrower to repay a loan in monthly, quarterly, semiannual, or annual installments (20)

Theory X a concept of employee motivation generally consistent with Taylor's scientific management; assumes that employees dislike work and will function only in a highly controlled work environment (11)

Theory Y a concept of employee motivation generally consistent with the ideas of the human relations movement; assumes that employees accept responsibility and work toward organizational goals if by so doing they also achieve personal rewards (11)

Theory Z the belief that some middle ground between Ouchi's type A and type J practices is best for American business (11)

time deposit an amount on deposit in an interest-bearing savings account (19)

time utility utility created by making a product available when customers wish to purchase it (13)

top manager an upper-level executive who guides and controls the overall fortunes of an organization (7)

tort a violation of a private law (Appendix C)

total cost the sum of the fixed costs and the variable costs attributed to a product (14)

total quality management (TQM) the coordination of efforts directed at improving customer satisfaction, increasing employee participation, strengthening supplier partnerships, and facilitating an organizational atmosphere of continuous quality improvement (7)

total revenue the total amount received from sales of a product (14)

trade credit a type of short-term financing extended by a seller who does not require immediate payment after delivery of merchandise (20)

trade deficit a negative balance of trade (3)

trade name the complete and legal name of an organization (14)

trade sales promotion method a sales promotion method designed to encourage wholesalers and retailers to stock and actively promote a manufacturer's product (16)

trade salesperson a salesperson—generally employed by a food producer or processor—who assists customers in promoting products, especially in retail stores (16)

trade show an industry-wide exhibit at which many sellers display their products (16)

trademark a brand name or brand mark that is registered with the U.S. Patent and Trademark Office and is thus legally protected from use by anyone except its owner (14)

trading company provides a link between buyers and sellers in different countries (3)

traditional specialty store a store that carries a narrow product mix with deep product lines (15)

transfer pricing prices charged in sales between an organization's units (14)

transportation the shipment of products to customers (15)

trial balance a summary of the balances of all general ledger accounts at the end of the accounting period (18)

trust a business combination created when one firm obtains control of an entire industry and can set prices and manipulate trade to suit its own interest (Appendix C)

trustee an individual or an independent firm that acts as a bond owner's representative (20)

tying agreement a contract that forces an intermediary to purchase unwanted products along with the products it actually wants to buy (Appendix C)

U

undifferentiated approach directing a single marketing mix at the entire market for a particular product (13)

Uniform Commercial Code (UCC) a set of laws designed to eliminate differences among state regulations affecting business and to simplify interstate commerce (Appendix C)

uninsurable risk a risk that insurance companies will not assume (Appendix B)

union security protection of the union's position as the employees' bargaining agent (12)

union shop a workplace in which new employees must join the union after a specified probationary period (12)

union-management (labor) relations the dealings between labor unions and business management, both in the bargaining process and beyond it (12)

universal life insurance life insurance that combines insurance protection with an investment plan that offers a potentially greater return than that guaranteed by a whole life insurance policy (Appendix B)

unlimited liability a legal concept that holds a business owner personally responsible for all the debts of the business (5)

unsecured financing financing that is not backed by collateral (20)

usury the practice of charging interest in excess of the maximum legal rate (Appendix C)

utility the ability of a good or service to satisfy a human need (9, 13)

V

variable cost a cost that depends on the number of units produced (14)

venture capital money that is invested in small (and sometimes struggling) firms that have the potential to become very successful (6)

vertical channel integration the combining of two or more stages of a distribution channel under a single firm's management (15)

vertical marketing system (VMS) a centrally managed distribution channel resulting from vertical channel integration (15)

voluntary agreement a contract requirement consisting of an offer by one party to enter into a contract with a second party and acceptance by the second party of all the terms and conditions of the offer (Appendix C)

voluntary bankruptcy a bankruptcy procedure initiated by an individual or business that can no longer meet its financial obligations (Appendix C)

W

wage survey a collection of data on prevailing wage rates within an industry or a geographic area (10)

warehouse club a large-scale members-only establishment that combines features of cash-and-carry wholesaling with discount retailing (15)

warehouse showroom a retail facility in a large, low-cost building with large on-premises inventories and minimal service (15)

warehousing the set of activities involved in receiving and storing goods and preparing them for reshipment (15)

wheel of retailing a hypothesis that suggests that new retail operations usually begin at the bottom—in price, profits, and prestige—and gradually move up the cost/price scale, competing with newer businesses that are evolving in the same way (15)

whistle-blowing informing the press or government officials about unethical practices within one's organization (2)

whole life insurance life insurance that provides both protection and savings (Appendix B)

wholesaler a middleman that sells products to other firms (15)

wildcat strike a strike not approved by the strikers' union (12)

word-processing program software that allows a user to prepare and edit written documents and to store them in the computer or on a disk (17)

workers' compensation insurance insurance that covers medical expenses and provides salary continuation for employees who are injured while at work (Appendix B)

working capital the difference between current assets and current liabilities (18)

World Trade Organization (WTO) powerful successor to GATT that incorporates trade in goods, services, and ideas (3)

World Wide Web (the web) the Internet's multimedia environment of audio, visual, and text data (4)

Y

yellow pages advertising simple listings or display advertisements presented under specific product categories appearing in print and online telephone directories (16)

Z

zero-base budgeting a budgeting approach in which every expense in every budget must be justified (20)

Notes

CHAPTER 1

1. Based on information from Robert Levering and Milton Moskowitz, "100 Best Companies to Work For," Fortune, January 20, 2003, p. 128; Verne Harnish, "Managing: The X Factor," *Fortune Small Business*, December 1, 2002, **www.fortune.com/fortune/smallbusiness/managing/articles/0,15114,400692,00.html;** Debby Garbato Stankevich, "Three Is Never a Crowd," *Retail Merchandiser*, August 2002, pp. 37ff; Lorrie Grant, "Container Store's Workers Huddle Up to Help You Out," *USA Today*, April 29, 2002, **www.usatoday.com/money/covers/2002-04-30-container-store.html; www.containerstore.com.**
2. The Dudley Products, Inc., website at **www.dudleyq.com,** January 28, 2003.
3. Dave Ellis, *Becoming a Master Student*, 10th ed. (Boston: Houghton Mifflin, 2003), p. 30.
4. Alan Goldstein, "Most Dot.Coms Doomed to Fail, Cuban Tells Entrepreneurs," *Dallas Morning News*, April 7, 2000, p. 1D.
5. Karen Klein, "The Bottom Line on Startup Failures," *BusinessWeek Online* at **www.businessweek.com,** March 4, 2002.
6. The Wal-Mart website at **www.walmart.com,** January 30, 2003.
7. *Ibid.*
8. Amey Stone, "Internet Meltdown, Phase Two," *BusinessWeek Online* at **www.businessweek.com,** April 23, 2001.
9. The Yahoo Finance website at **http://finance.yahoo.com,** January 30, 2003.
10. U.S. Census Bureau, *Statistical Abstract of the United States*, 2001, 121st ed. (Washington: U.S. Government Printing Office, 2002), p. 417.
11. The Bureau of Labor Statistics website at **www.bls.gov,** January 3, 2003.
12. The Bureau of Economic Analysis website at **www.bea.gov,** February 1, 2003.
13. The Bureau of Labor Statistics website at **www.bls.gov,** February 1, 2003.
14. The Bureau of Economic Analysis website at **www.bea.gov,** February 1, 2003.
15. U.S. Census Bureau, *Statistical Abstract of the United States, 2001*, 121st ed. (Washington: U.S. Government Printing Office, 2002), p. 303.
16. Bureau of Labor Statistics, *Monthly Labor Review*, August, 2002, p. 72.
17. Based on information from David Goodman, "Culture Change," *Mother Jones*, January–February 2003, pp. 52–78; and the Stonyfield Farms website at **www.stonyfield.com,** February 4, 2003.

CHAPTER 2

1. Based on information from Stanley Holmes and Geri Smith, "For Coffee Growers, Not Even a Whiff of Profits," *BusinessWeek*, September 9, 2002, p. 110; Stanley Holmes, "Planet Starbucks," *BusinessWeek*, September 9, 2002, pp. 100ff; "Bean Bonanza," *Restaurants and Institutions*, April 15, 2001, p.18; Robert Levering and Milton Moskowitz, "The 100 Best Companies to Work For," *Fortune*, February 4, 2002, pp. 72ff; **www.starbucks.com.**
2. Lynna Goch, "Lawyers, Guns and Money," *Best Reviews*, January 2000, p. 55.
3. Charles Haddad and Amy Barrett, "A Whistle-Blower Rocks an Industry," *BusinessWeek*, June 24, 2002, pp. 126–130.
4. Gary Weiss et al., "Revenge of the Investor," *BusinessWeek*, December 16, 2002, p. 122.
5. Consumer Protection Laws, **http://nolo.com/lawcenter/ency/article,** January 6, 2003.
6. Anthony Bianco, William Symonds, and Nanette Byrnes, "The Rise and Fall of Dennis Kozlowski," *BusinessWeek*, December 23, 2002, pp. 64–77.
7. James Underwood, "Should You Watch Them on the Web," CIO, **http://www.cio.com/archive/051500_face.html,** May 15, 2000.
8. Paula Dwyer et al., "Year of the Whistleblower," *BusinessWeek*, December 16, 2002, pp. 107–110.
9. ExxonMobil, 2001 *Summary Annual Report;* and **www.exxonmobil.com,** December 16, 2002.
10. Microsoft, *2002 Annual Report*, pp. 6–7.
11. Cisco Systems, *2001 Annual Report*, p. 4.
12. General Mills, *2002 Corporate Citizenship Report*, pp. 1–4.
13. Foot Locker, Inc., *2001 Annual Report*, p. 5.
14. "AT&T Foundation," **http://www.att.com/foundation/programs,** January 2, 2003.
15. Dell Computer Corporation, *Fiscal 2002 in Review*, p. 25; and "About Dell," **www.dell.com,** January 4, 2003.
16. "GE in the Community," **www.ge.com,** January 5, 2003; and General Electric, *Annual Report 2001*, p. 1.
17. Ilan Greenberg, "The PC Crowd," *Red Herring*, **http://www.redherring.com/mag/issue51/rd.html,** May 18, 2000.
18. Paul Kapustka, "Big Fish: Clinton Pushes to Close Digital Divide," *Red Herring*, **http://www.redherring.com/companies/2000/0419/com-big-fish041900.html,** April 19, 2000.
19. General Mills, *2002 Corporate Citizenship Report*, p. 6.
20. *Month in Review: February 1999*, "Aviation and the Environment: Aviation's Effects on Global Atmosphere Are Potentially Significant and Expected to Grow" (Washington: General Accounting Office, February 18, 2000).
21. *ExxonMobil Corporation, The Lamp*, Spring 2002, p. 28.
22. *Month in Review: February 2000*, "Superfund: Analysis of Costs at Five Superfund Sites," GAO/RCED-00-22 (Washington: General Accounting Office, February 2000), pp 13–14.
23. Based on information from "New Belgium Brewing Wins Ethics Award," *Denver Business Journal*, January 2, 2003, **denver.bizjournals.com/denver/stories/2002/12/30/daily21.html;** Richard Brandes, "Beer Growth Brands," *Beverage Dynamics*, September–October 2002, pp. 37ff; **www.newbelgium.com.**

CHAPTER 3

1. Based on information from Cait Murphy, "The Hunt for Globalization That Works," *Fortune*, October 28, 2002, pp. 163–176; Betsy McKay, "Coke's Heyer Finds Test in Fixing Latin America," *Wall Street Journal*, October 15, 2002, **www.wsj.com;** Manjeet Kripalani, "Battling for Pennies in India's Villages," *BusinessWeek*, June 10, 2002, p. 22E7; Betsy McKay, "Coca-Cola's Profit Rises 8.1% on Strong Sales in the U.S.," *Wall Street Journal*, October 17, 2002, **www.wsj.com.**
2. The White House, Office of the Press Secretary. Press Release, April 19, 2000.
3. The White House, Office of the Press Secretary. Press Release, August 6, 2002.
4. Clay Shirky, "Go Global or Bust," *Business2.0*, **http://www.business2.com/content/magazine/breakthrough/2000/03/01/11018,** March 2000.
5. U.S. Department of Commerce, International Trade Administration, **http://www.ita.doc.gov/td/industry/ostea,** January 2, 2003.

6. Matthew R. Sanders and Bruce D. Temkin, "Global E-Commerce Approaches Hypergrowth," *The Forrester Brief,* **http://www.forrester.com/,** April 18, 2000.
7. **www.wto.org,** January 3, 2003.
8. Paul Magnusson, "A U.S. Trade Policy That Is Starting to Boomerang," *BusinessWeek,* July 29, 2002, p. 64.
9. Mohanbir Sawhney and Sumant Mandal, "Go Global," *Business 2.0,* **http://www.business2.com/content/magazine/indepth/2000/05/01/11057,** May 2000.
10. David Gould, "The Benefits of GATT for the U.S. and World Economies," *Southwest Economy,* Federal Reserve Bank of Dallas, May 1994, p. 2.
11. Aaron Steelman, "Steelmakers Receive Protection," *Region Focus,* Federal Reserve Bank of Richmond, Spring 2002, pp. 28–29.
12. All trade and growth statistics from the "World Economic Outlook," International Monetary Fund, September 2002; and "Global Economic Outlook," United Nations, Department of Economic and Social Affairs, New York, April 24–26, 2002.
13. "The Global 500," *Fortune,* July 22, 2002, p. 146.
14. Stephen Jacobs, "The New Doha Development Agenda," *Export America,* January 2002, pp. 21–22.
15. William M. Pride and O. C. Ferrell, *Marketing,* 12th ed. (Boston: Houghton Mifflin, 2003), p. 122.
16. *Ibid.,* p. 127.
17. Kim Cross, "The Ultimate Enablers: Business Partners," *Business 2.0,* **http://www.business2.com/content/magazine/indepth/2000/02/01/10441,** February 2000.
18. Pride and Ferrell, *Marketing,* p. 128.
19. *Ibid.,* p. 127.
20. "ADB Operations," **www.adb.org,** January 4, 2003.
21. Based on information from "Subway Sandwich Chain Hopes for Consistency in Expansion," *Reading (PA) Eagle,* August 4, 2002, **www.readingeagle.com;** Michelle Prather, "No. 1 with Everything," *Entrepreneur,* January 2002, pp. 134ff; **www.subway.com.**

CHAPTER 4

1. Based on information from Jim Krane, "Microsoft and Disney Release Combined Internet Service," *InformationWeek,* October 25, 2002, **www.informationweek.com;** Anita Hamilton, "The Giant Plays the Underdog," *Time,* October 21, 2002, pp. 85ff; Heather Green, "Can MSN Play David to AOL's Goliath?" *BusinessWeek,* August 5, 2002, p. 76; Chris Dillabough, "Developing Digital Content for Next-Generation Users," *New Media Age,* July 25, 2002, pp. 22ff; Catharine P. Taylor, "Slow and Steady Can't Win This Race," *Mediaweek,* June 24, 2002, pp. 26ff; MSN home page, **www.msn.com; Microsoft PressPass, www.microsoft.com/presspass.**
2. Forrester Research, Inc., online glossary, **www.forrester.com,** March 3, 2003.
3. Stacy Perman, "Automate or Die," *eCompany Now,* July 2001, pp. 60–67.
4. "U.S. Q4 E-commerce Sales at $5.3B," **www.usatoday.com/money,** March 2, 2000.
5. "Small Businesses Buy, but Shy to Sell, Online," **http://cyberatlas.internet.com/markets/professional/article/0,1323,5971_365281,00.html,** May 17, 2000.
6. Robyn Greenspan, "Small Biz Benefits from Internet Tools," **http://cyberatlas.internet.com/markets/smallbiz/article/0,,10098_1000171,00.html,** March 28, 2002.
7. *BusinessWeek,* special supplement, February 28, 2000, p. 74.
8. Don Tapscott, "Online Parts Exchange Heralds New Era," *Financial Post,* May 5, 2000, p. C7.
9. Anne Marie Owens, "Mad About Harry," *National Post,* July 10, 2000, p. D1.
10. Associated Press, "Bosses Say They Know Who's Surfing," *Montreal Gazette,* July 16, 2001, p. E2.
11. *Ibid.*
12. Paul Lima, "Internet Fights the Fear Factor," *Financial Post,* August 20, 2001, p. E1.
13. "Online Music Sales Will Grow 520% to $6.2 Billion in 2006," Jupiter Media Metrix Press Release, New York, **www.jmm.com/xp/press/2001/pr_072301.xml,** July 23, 2001.
14. "Global E-Commerce Approaches Hypergrowth," Forrester Research, Inc., website at **www.forrester.com,** April 18, 2000.
15. Cyberatlas Staff, "B2B E-Commerce Headed for Billions," **http://cyberatlas.internet.com/markets/b2b/article/0,,10091_986661,00.html,** March 6, 2002.
16. Michael Pastore, "Why the Offline Are Offline," Cyberatlas website, **http://cyberatlas.internet.com/big_picture/demographics/article/0,,5901_784691,00.html#table,** July 14, 2001.
17. "Industry Projections for 2000 to 2006," Jupiter Media Metrix website at **http://www.jmm.com/xp/jmm/press/industryProjections.xml,** June 16, 2002.
18. "Media Metrix Releases Worldwide Internet Measurement Results for Australia, Canada, France, Germany & United Kingdom," Jupiter Media Metrix website at **www.mediametrix.com/usa/press/releases/20000510a.jsp,** May 10, 2000.
19. Data available from Nielsen/NetRatings website at **http://pm.netratings.com/nnpm/owa/Nrpublicreports.usagemonthly,** March 10, 2003.
20. "Media Metrix Releases Worldwide Internet Measurement Results" and "Media Metrix Releases U.S. Top 50 Web and Digital Media Properties for March 2000," Jupiter Media Metrix website at **www.mediametrix.com/usa/press/releases/20000424.jsp,** April 24, 2000.
21. Based on information from Roger Hughlett, "Putting Technology to the Test," *Baltimore Business Journal,* August 10, 2001, **baltimore.bizjournals.com/baltimore/stories/2001/08/13/story7.html; www.absolutequality.com.**

CHAPTER 5

1. Based on information from Procter & Gamble website at **www.pg.com;** "Clorox and P&G in Joint Venture," *United Press International,* November 14, 2002, **www.comtexnews.com;** Daniel Eisenberg, "A Healthy Gamble: How Did A. G. Lafley Turn Procter & Gamble's Old Brands into Hot Items? Here's the Beauty of It," *Time,* September 16, 2002, pp. 46ff.
2. Phone interview on January 4, 2003, 15204 Omega Drive, Suite 110, Rockville, MD 20850, (301) 963-1669.
3. The Yahoo Small Business website at **http://smallbusiness.yahoo.com/resources/business_incorporation/learn_about_delaware.html,** January 2, 2003; Yahoo, Inc., 701 First Avenue, Sunnyvale, CA 94089.
4. The HispanicBusiness.com website at **www.hispanicbusiness.com,** January 5, 2003.
5. Bruce Einhorn, "Shenzhen: The New Bangalore? *BusinessWeek Online,* **www.businessweek.com,** December 16, 2002.
6. The Oracle Website at **www.oracle.com,** January 3, 2003; Oracle Corporation, 500 Oracle Parkway, Redwood, City, CA 94065.
7. Based on information from Matt Marshall, "Start-Ups Getting Venture Funding; 'Healthy' Pace Resumes," *San Jose Mercury News,* February 4, 2003, **http://www.bayarea.com/mld/mercurynews/business/5100882.htm; www.baypartners.com** and **www.sportvision.com.**

CHAPTER 6

1. Based on information from Julie Rose, "Me Inc.," *Fortune,* October 28, 2002, pp. 192[B]–192[H]; Brook S. Mason, "An Empire, Yes, But More Serene Than Martha's," *New York Times,* April 28, 2002, Sec. 3, p. 4.
2. U.S. Small Business Administration, **www.sba.gov/size/13cfr121,** January 11, 2003.
3. *Ibid.*
4. *Ibid.*
5. Online Women Business Center, SBA Success Stories, "Business Was Always Her Passion," **http://www.onlinewbc.org/docs/success_stories/ss_innovativetech. html, June 3, 2000.**
6. U.S. Small Business Administration, *Small Business's Vital Statistics.*
7. Based on information from Rochelle Sharpe, "Teen Moguls," *BusinessWeek,* May 29, 2000, pp. 108–118; "High-Tech Teens," *McLean's,* June 7, 1999, p. 9.

8. The National Foundation for Women Business Owners, **www.franchise.org,** January 12, 2003.
9. Kim Girard and Sean Donahue, "Crash and Learn: A Field Manual for e-Business Survival," *Business2.0,* **http://www.business2.com/content/magazine/indepth/2000/06/28/13700,** June 11, 2000.
10. Office of Advocacy, U.S. *Small Business Administration, Small Business Economic Indicators for 2001,* February 2003, p. 3.
11. U. S. Small Business Administration, "Small Business by the Numbers," **www.sba.gov,** January 11, 2003.
12. Alan Joch, "E-Business Without the E-Cost," *Fortunes Small Business Online,* **http://www.fsb.com/fortunesb/articles/0,2227,320,00.html,** July 16, 1999.
13. "Challenges to Small Businesses on the Net" *Business 2.0,* **http://www.business2.com/content/research/numbers/2000/06/26/13389,** June 26, 2000.
14. U.S. Small Business Administration, "The Digital Divide," **www.sba.gov/classroom/digitaldivide.html,** January 6, 2003.
15. *Ibid.*
16. William M. Pride and O.C. Ferrell, *Marketing,* 12th ed. (Boston: Houghton Mifflin, 2003), p. 414.
17. McDonald's Corporation, **www.mcdonalds.com,** January 14, 2003.
18. Rick Romell, "Dunkin' Donuts Sues Three Milwaukee Franchisees," *Milwaukee Journal Sentinel,* March 24, 1997, p. 324B.
19. Zarco Einhorn & Salkowski, "Recent Decisions," **http://www.zarcolaw.com/FSL5CS/Custom,** January 12, 2003.
20. "Challenges to Small Businesses on the Net," *Business 2.0,* **http://www.business2.com/content/research/numbers/2000/06/26/13389,** June 26, 2000.
21. The U.S. Small Business Administration, **http://www.sba.gov/advo/stats,** January 16, 2003.
22. Based on information from Sacha Cohen, "Bed and Breakfasts Mix Business with Pleasure," *USA Today.com,* June 6, 2002, **www.usatoday.com;** and **www.percyinn.com.**

CHAPTER 7

1. Based on information from "Yahoo Inks Portal Pact with Sun," *Investor's Business Daily,* May 21, 2002, pp. A6ff; Ben Elgin, "Can Yahoo Make 'Em Pay?" BusinessWeek, September 9, 2002, pp. 92ff; Saul Hansell, "Yahoo's Profits and Sales Are Better Than Expected," *New York Times,* October 10, 2002, **www.nytimes.com;** Daniel Roth, "Terry Semel Thinks Yahoo Should Grow Up Already," *Fortune,* September 30, 2002, pp. 107ff; Kristi Heim, "Yahoo! Inc. Succeeds on Internet with Unique Business Methods, Philosophy," *San Jose Mercury News,* April 3, 2000, **www.lexis-nexis.com.**
2. Geoff Armstrong, "People Strategies Are Key to Future Success," *Personnel Today,* January 7, 2003, p. 2.
3. **www.flycontinental.com/corporate,** January 2, 2003.
4. Dana James, "Don't Forget Staff in Marketing Plan," *Marketing News,* March 13, 2000, pp. 10–11.
5. Fara Warner, "GM Goes Off-Road," *Fast Company,* February 2003, p. 40.
6. Bill Saporito, "Can Wal-Mart Get Any Bigger? (Yes, a lot Bigger . . . Here's How)," *Time,* January 13, 2003, p. 38.
7. Melanie Shanley, "Phillips–Van Heusen Gets Dressed Up," *Fortune.com,* **http://www.fortune.com/fortune/print/0.15935,405415,00.html,** January 7, 2003.
8. Fara Warner, "GM Goes Off-Road," *Fast Company,* February 2003, p. 40.
9. William Diem, "Competitors Look at Nissan's Leadership," *Detroit Free Press Knight Ridder/Tribune Business News,* January 6, 2003, p. 9.
10. Scott Morrison, "From Tactics to Strategy," *Financial Times,* January 24, 2003, p. 8.
11. **www.monster.com.**
12. Davide Dukcevich, "Best Fraternities For Future CEOs," *Forbes.com,* **http://www.forbes.com/2003/01/31/cx_dd_0131frat_print.html,** January 31, 2003.
13. Henry Mintzberg, "The Manager's Job: Folklore and Fact," *Harvard Business Review,* July–August 1975, pp. 49–61.
14. Chana R. Schoenberger, "The Greenhouse Effect," *Forbes.com,* **http://www.forbes.com/global/2003/0203/030_print.html,** February 3, 2003.
15. Robert Kreitner, *Management,* 9th ed. (Boston: Houghton Mifflin, 2004), p. 505.
16. Ricky W. Griffin, *Fundamentals of Management,* 3d ed. (Boston: Houghton Mifflin, 2003), p. 96.
17. "Sega Chooses a New Chief at Its U.S. Unit," *New York Times,* January 20, 2003, p. C10.
18. William Bulkeley, "IBM Sets Sanmina Outsource Pact," *Wall Street Journal,* January 8, 2003, p. B11.
19. "Today Show," NBC News Transcript. December 24, 2002.
20. Based on information from Toddi Gutner, "A Dot-Com's Survival Story," *BusinessWeek,* May 2, 2002, **www.businessweek.com;** E. Sandra Simpson, "Get with the Program," *Customer Support Management,* November 1, 2001, **industryclick.com; www.vipdesk.com.**

CHAPTER 8

1. Based on information from Seth Stevenson, "How to Beat Nike," *New York Times Magazine,* January 5, 2003, pp. 28–33; Stanley Holmes, "How Nike Got Its Game Back," *BusinessWeek,* November 4, 2002, pp. 129ff; Fara Warner, "Nike's Women's Movement," *Fast Company,* August 2002, pp. 70ff; Eric Ransdell, "The Nike Story? Just Tell It!" *Fast Company,* January–February 2000, pp. 44ff; "Can Nike Still Do It?" *BusinessWeek,* February 21, 2000, pp. 120ff.
2. Mark Tatge, "Prescription for Growth," *Forbes,* February 17, 2003, p. 64.
3. "Canada Life Financial Corporation Press Release," *Canadian Corporate Newswire,* January 27, 2000.
4. Kim Peterson, "Microsoft Realigns Windows Operations," *The Seattle Times,* January 23, 2003, p. 36.
5. George Anders, "The Carly Chronicles," *Fast Company,* February 2003, p. 66.
6. Henry Unger, "Draft Outlines Decentralized Coke," *Atlanta Journal and Constitution,* January 29, 2000, p. 1B.
7. Bill Saporito, "Can Wal-Mart Get Any Bigger? (Yes, a lot Bigger . . . Here's How)," *Time,* January 13, 2003, p. 38.
8. Robert Kreitner, *Management,* 9th ed. (Boston: Houghton Mifflin, 2004), pp. 330–331.
9. Paul Kaihla, "Raytheon on Target," *Business 2.0,* **http://www.business2.com/articles/mag/0,1640,46335,00.html,** February 4, 2003.
10. Peter Burrows, "The Second Coming of Software," *BusinessWeek,* June 19,2000, p. 88.
11. Stephanie Thompson, "'God Is in the Details': Campbell Soup Chief Energizes Marketing; Fingerman Pushes Innovation Agenda to Stimulate Sleepy Sales," *Advertising Age,* January 27, 2003, p. 3.
12. Robert Kreitner, *Management,* 9th ed. (Boston: Houghton Mifflin, 2004), p. 343.
13. Ricky Griffin, *Fundamentals of Management* (Boston: Houghton Mifflin, 2003), p. 175.
14. **http://careers.marriott.com.**
15. Rob Goffee and Gareth Jones, "The Character of a Corporation: How Your Company's Culture Can Make or Break Your Business," *Jones Harper Business,* p. 182.
16. Paul Sloan, "Dells Man on Deck," *Business 2.0,* February 2003.
17. "Mergers' Missing Link: Cultural Integration," *PR Newswire,* January 23, 2003.
18. Kreitner, *Management,* p. 99.
19. Jeffrey H. Birnbaum et al., "People to Watch 2003: Moguls! Scapegoats! Insiders! Our Bet? If You Don't Know All These Names Now, You Will Soon," *Fortune,* February 3, 2003, p. 86.
20. Based on information from interview with Michael Baker, February 7, 2003; **www.bakersbestcatering.com.**

CHAPTER 9

1. Based on information from "The Forging of a Steel Magnate," *BusinessWeek Online,* November 22, 2002, **www.businessweek.com/bwdaily/dnflash/nov2002/nf20021122_2221.htm;** Nelson D. Schwartz, "Bent but Unbowed," *Fortune,* July 22, 2002, pp. 118–126.

2. U.S. Department of Labor, Bureau of Labor Statistics, *Monthly Labor Review*, August 2002, p.72.
3. Robert Kreitner, *Management*, 9th ed. (Boston: Houghton Mifflin, 2004), pp. 577–578.
4. The IBM website at **www.ibm.com,** January 5, 2003.
5. The 3M Company website at **www.3M.com,** January 5, 2003.
6. The Campbell Soup website at **www.campbellsoup.com,** January 6, 2003.
7. The Kraft Foods website at **www.kraft.com,** January 4, 2003.
8. Dale Buss, "Not So Magical Kingdom," *Business 2.0,* **www.business2.com,** June 1, 2000.
9. The Berry Plastics website at **www.berryplastics.com,** January 3, 2003.
10. Steve Bennett, "Wings and a Prayer," *Business 2.0,* **www.business2.com,** June 1, 2000.
11. The Harvard Technologies website at **www.harvardtechnologies.com,** January 4, 2003.
12. David Shook, "A Tool-and-Die Maker for Genesmiths," *Business-Week Online* at **www.businessweek.com,** October 15, 2002.
13. The Maxager Technology website at **www.maxager.com,** January 7, 2003.
14. The Dell website at **www.dell.com,** January 6, 2003.
15. Tyler Maroney, "An Air Battle Comes to the Web," *Fortune,* June 26, 2000, p. 315.
16. Bureau of Labor Statistics website at **www.bls.gov,** January 3, 2003.
17. Based on information from "Remington Seeks Sexy Image After Court Win," *Marketing,* June 27, 2002, p. 1; "Analysis: What Remington's Ruling Means For Brands," *Marketing,* June 27, 2002, p. 15; and **www.remington-products.com.**

CHAPTER 10

1. Based on information from Steven Levy, "The World According to Google," *Newsweek,* December 16, 2002, pp. 46–51; Peter Hum, "Inside the Googleplex," *Ottawa Citizen,* July 18, 2002, pp. F2ff.
2. Margaret Steen, "Nationwide Boom in Tech Hiring Predicted This Year," *Mercury News,* May 5, 2002.
3. Joseph Mann, "Fort Lauderdale, Florida-Based AutoNation Reports Earnings Increase," *South Florida Sun-Sentinel,* February 7, 2003.
4. Bureau of Labor Statistics website at **www.bls.gov.**
5. Travis E. Poling, "Toyota to Build Truck Factory in San Antonio," *San Antonio Express-News,* February 5, 2003.
6. Vicki Lee Parker, "Workers at North Carolina Companies Undergo Diversity Training," *News and Observer,* Raleigh, January 13, 2003, p. 03013039.
7. **www.ti.com/diversity,** January 17, 2003.
8. **www.bankofamerica.com/careers/index,** January 17, 2003.
9. Harry Wessel, "Jobs Column," *The Orlando Sentinel,* January 15, 2003, p. 03015055.
10. "100 Best Companies to Work For," *Fortune,* January 20, 2003, p. 129.
11. U.S. Department of Labor, Bureau of Labor Statistics, News Release, June 18, 2002.
12. "Employees, HR Out of Sync," *Employee Benefit News,* January 1, 2003, p. 5.
13. Douglas Harbrecht, "When Active Duty Calls IBM'ers," *Business-Week Online,* **http://www.businessweek.com:/print/careers/content/feb2003/ca/20030210_9434_ca030.html,** February 10, 2003.
14. **www.readingeagle.com/KRT/business,** January 17, 2003.
15. Kip Tindel, "Who Said the Trash Can Can Make You Smile? Transcending Value at the Container Store." Arthur Andersen Retailing Issues Letter, Center for Retailing Studies, Texas A&M University, January 2000, p. 3.
16. Robert Levering, Milton Moskowitz, Ann Harrington, and Christopher Tkaczyk, "100 Best Companies to Work For," *Fortune,* January 20, 2003, p. 127.
17. Sandra Dillich, "Training or Learning," *Computing Canada,* June 23, 2000, p. 25.
18. Cynthia D. Fisher, Lyle F. Schoenfeldt, and James B. Shaw *Human Resource Management* (Boston: Houghton Mifflin, 2003 p. 527.
19. *Ibid.,* pp. 521–523.
20. "Foot Locker to Pay $3.5 Million to Former Woolworth Employees," *Fair Employment Practices Guidelines,* January 15, 2003, p. 8.
21. David Barstow and Lowell Bergman, "Deaths of the Job, Slaps o the Wrist," *New York Times,* January 10, 2003, p. A1.
22. "Study Reveals Increase in Federal Court Cases," LRP Publications, February 11, 2000.
23. Based on information from Jeffrey Krasner, "New England Aquarium Plunges into Financial Turmoil," *Boston Globe,* December 13, 2002, **www.boston.com/global; www.neaq.org.**

CHAPTER 11

1. Based on information from David Kiley, "Workplace Woes Almost Eclipse Mitsubishi Plant," *USA Today,* October 21, 2002 pp. 1B, 2B; "Mitsubishi Launches Quality-Enhancement Drive," *Automotive News,* March 25, 2002, pp. 16Nff.
2. David Greising, "Sun's Gosling Defiant: But Staff Morale Down," *America's Intelligence Wire,* January 8, 3003.
3. Cora Daniels, "This Man Wants to Help You. Seriously," *Fortune* June 26, 2000, pp. 327–330.
4. Christopher Bowe and Andrew Hill, "This Month's Strike at General Electric Highlights the Growing Tensions Between Management and Workers Over Healthcare and Retirement Benefits," *Financial Times,* January 30, 2003, p. 11.
5. "Isle of Capri Casinos, Inc. Creates Real-Life Employee 'Survivor' Event," *PR Newswire,* January 20, 2003 p. CGM00520012003.
6. Michael Petrou, "Striking a Nerve," *Financial Post,* July 8, 2000 p. D7.
7. Douglas McGregor, *The Human Side of the Enterprise* (New York McGraw-Hill, 1960).
8. William Ouchi, *Theory Z* (Reading, MA:Addison-Wesley, 1981).
9. Ricky W. Griffin, *Fundamentals of Management,* 2d ed. (Boston Houghton Mifflin, 2003), p. 285.
10. Ricky W. Griffin, *Management,* 6th ed. (Boston: Houghton Mifflin, 2002), p. 219.
11. Alison Overholt, "Power up the People: Economy Stuck in the Doldrums? Morale Stuck There Too? Here are a Few Things That You Can Do to Jazz Things up in 2003," *Fast Company,* January 2003, p. 50.
12. "Is Job Stress Taking Its Toll in Your Facility," *Safety Management,* February 2003, p. 3.
13. J. K. Wall, "Smaller Firms That Can't Pay as Much Use Other Lures," *Indianapolis Star,* January 22, 2003, p. 2.
14. Leigh Strope, "More Workers Have Option of Growing Flex-Time Trend," Associated Press, January 6, 2003.
15. **www.starbucks.com/job center.**
16. Alison Maitland, "Two for the Price of One." *Financial Times Limited,* January 24, 2001, p. 17.
17. "World News This Morning," Transcript, ABC News, January 10, 2003.
18. "Telework Succeeds for U.S. Agencies," *Work & Family Newsbrief,* January 2003, p. 7.
19. "Boston College Report Presents Challenges and Advantages of Telework," *Work & Family Newsbrief,* January 2003, p. 8.
20. L. A. Lorek, "Telecommuting Is a Growing Trend," *San Antonio Express News,* October 27, 2002.
21. Jill Elswick, "Puttin' on the Ritz: Hotel Chain Touts Training to Benefit Its Recruiting and Retention," *Employee Benefit News,* February 2000, pp.1, 34–35.
22. Milton Moskowitz and Robert Levering, "10 Great Companies to Work For," *Fortune International,* January 20, 2003, p. 26.
23. Bob Parks, "The Garage That Saved Whirlpool's Soul," *Business 2.0,* **http://www.business2.com/articles/mag/print/0,1643,46305,00.html,** February 6, 2003.
24. "A Short History of ESOP," **www.nceo.org.**
25. Bruce Upbin, "Work and Buy and Hold," *Forbes,* January 20, 2003, p. 56.

6. Based on information from Tim Heffernan, "Making Bike Lovers Swoon, Employee-Owned Company Seeks the Perfect Ride," *Boston Globe*, April 28, 2002, p. 11; interview with Deborah Bernard of Wheelworks, August 22, 2001; "Wheelworks Spotlights Its Employees," *Bicycle Retailer and Industry News*, July 15, 2001, p. 19; **www.wheelworks.com.**

CHAPTER 12

1. Based on information from Edward Wong, "Judge Orders Pay Cut for Machinists at United," *New York Times*, January 11, 2003, pp. C1ff; Francine Knowles, "UAL Now Seeks Savings from Machinists Union," *Chicago Sun-Times*, November 4, 2002, p. 14; Marilyn Adams, "United, Unions Dig in for Deal to Dodge Chapter 11," *USA Today*, September 16, 2002, **www.usatoday.com.**
2. "Union and Management Look for New Ways of Doing Business," *Canadian Corporate News*, February 15, 2000.
3. Martha Lynn Craver and Nikki Eyman, "Workers Grow Grumpy Over Health Care Costs," *Kiplinger's Business Forecasts*, January 31, 2003.
4. Saul A. Rubenstein, "The Impact of Co-Management on Quality Performance: The Case of the Saturn Corporations," *Industrial and Labor Relations Review*, January 2000, pp. 197–218.
5. Patrick Danner, "Point Blank Body Armor Must Rehire Strikers, Judge Rules," *Miami Herald*, January 31, 2003.
6. "NLRB: No Unionization for Allstate Contractors," *HR Briefing*, January 1, 2003, p. 1.
7. Ari Weinberg, "America's Most Dangerous Unions," *Forbes.com*, **http://www.forbes.com/2003/01/13/cz_aw_0113union.html,** January 13, 2003.
8. Greg Hernandez, "Two Actors Unions Consider Plans to Merge," *Daily News*, Los Angeles, February 7, 2003.
9. Christopher Bowe and Andrew Hill, "Workers Feeling Sick over Rising Healthcare Costs," *Financial Times*, January 14, 2003, p. 21.
10. David Welch and Kathleen Kerwin, "Rick Wagoner's Game Plan," *BusinessWeek*, February 10, 2003.
11. Bureau of Labor Statistics website at **www.bls.gov,** January 23, 2003.
12. "ALPA American Eagle Pilots to Conduct Infromation Picketing in San Juan and Miami," *PR Newswire*, January 8, 2003, p. DCW02208012003.
13. "AFL-CIO and PACE Union Announces Boycott Against Graphic Packaging Corp., Coors Beer to be Targeted," *PR Newswire*, January 2, 2003.
14. Dave Hirschman, "UPS, Pilots Gear Up for New Bargaining Approach," *Atlanta Journal-Constitution*, February 9, 2003.
15. Based on information from Stephanie Armour, "Wal-Mart Takes Hits on Worker Treatment," *USA Today*, February 10, 2003, **www.usatoday.com;** Karen Olsson, "Up Against Wal-Mart," *Mother Jones*, March-April 2003, **www.motherjones.com;** Wendy Zellner, "How Wal-Martt Keeps Unions at Bay," *Business Week*, October 28, 2002, pp.94+; Jef Feeley, "Wal-Mart Found Guilty in Oregon Pay Case," *Seattle Times*, December 20, 2002, **www.seattletimes.com;** Wal-Mart web site, **www.walmartstores.com.**

CHAPTER 13

1. Based on information from Heather Johnson, "Business War Games," *Training*, December 2002, p. 18; John Helyar, "Harley-Davidson: It Redefined the Motorcycle Industry as It Roared Through 16 Years of Growth," *Fortune*, August 12, 2002, **www.fortune.com;** Thomas Content, "Harley Shifts Gears in Effort to Sustain Success," *Milwaukee Journal Sentinel*, July 8, 2002, pp. 1Aff.
2. Jathon Sapsford, "New Jersey's Commerce Bancorp Stretches Hours, Cuts Service Fees," *Wall Street Journal*, Interactive Edition, p.1
3. "Marriott Revamped Mileage Awards," Colloquy, **www.colloquy.org/news,** March 22, 2000.
4. **www.pikeplacefish.com,** January 24, 2003.
5. Dale Buss, "Up with Brown," *Brandweek*, January 27, 2003, p. 16.
6. Kenneth Hein, "Lego Building Arts and Crafts Line to Click with Female Customers," *Brandweek*, February 3, 2003, p. 9.
7. Megan E. Mulligan, "Wireless for the Well Off," *Forbes.com*, **http://forbes.com/2003/01/21/cz_mm_0121tentech_print.html,** January 21, 2003.
8. Chester Dawson, "No Kidding—A New Market for Baby Food," *BusinessWeek Online*, **http://www.buisnessweek.com:/print/magazine/content/03_04/b381761.html,** January 27, 2003.
9. Peter Kafka, "Sony Music's New Boss Lacks Experience," *Forbes.com*, **http://www.forbes.com/2003/01/10/cz_pk_0110lack_print.html,** January 10, 2003.
10. Kenneth Hein, "Disney Puts Pooh, Power Rangers, Princess under Wing With $500M," *Brandweek*, January 27, 2003, p. 6.
11. Don Clark, "The Affluent Avatar," *Wall Street Journal*, January 8, 2003, pp. B1, B4.
12. William M. Pride and O. C. Ferrell, *Marketing: Concepts and Strategies* (Boston: Houghton Mifflin Company, 2003), p. 197.
13. Chad Kaydo, "A Position of Power," *Sales and Marketing Management*, June 2000, p. 106.
14. Del Jones, "Some Schools to Surf Net to Cut Costs of Supplies," *USA Today*, March 20, 2000, p. B1.
15. "Consumer Expenditures in 2000," U.S. Department of Labor, Bureau of Labor Statistics, April 2002.
16. Ira P. Schneiderman, "Rich Boomers Prove to be Savers, Not Spenders," *DNR*, January 2000, p. 11.
17. Alex Frew McMillan, "Net Shopping Differs by Sex," CNN FN, April 19, 2000.
18. Melanie Warner, "Cool Companies 2000," *Fortune*, June 26, 2000, p.108.
19. Based on information from Thomas K. Grose, "Teddy Bear Tussle," *U.S. News & World Report*, November 11, 2002, p. 46; Janine E. Gilbertson, "Build-a-Bear Approach to Holiday Fun," *Union Leader* (Manchester, NH), November 17, 2002, p. D1; "Build-a-Bear Workshop Offers Build-a-Sound Online," *St. Louis Business Journal*, January 31, 2002; Sharon Nelton, "Building an Empire One Smile at a Time," *Success*, September 2000, pp. 34ff; Brad Patten, "Teddy Bear Bonanza Run by Sweetheart of a System," *Washington Business Journal*, February 4, 2000, p. 53.
20. Kay Parker, "Old - Line Goes Online," *Business 2.0*, **http://www.business2.com/content/magazine/marketing/2000/06/01/1270,** June 1, 2000.

CHAPTER 14

1. Based on information from Barry Shlachter, "Blockbuster to Convert 1,000 Stores to Hispanic Theme," *Fort Worth Star-Telegram*, November 14, 2002, **www.star-telegram.com;** Stephanie Anderson Forest and Tom Lowry, "Blockbuster: The Sequel," *BusinessWeek*, September 16, 2002, pp. 52ff; Steve Traiman, "Blockbuster Rethinks Videogame Strategies," *Billboard*, July 6, 2002, p. 56.
2. Phil Davies, "Digital Photography Hits the Mainstream," **ComputerUser.com,** May 2002.
3. William Hall, "Logitech Proves No Mouse Among Men," *Financial Times*, January 6, 2003, p. 15.
4. **www.gefn.com/search/index,** January 24, 2003.
5. Melanie Wells, "Happier Meals," *Forbes*, January 20, 2003, p. 76.
6. Joseph B. White and Norihiko Shirouzu, "Ford Gambles in Rolling Out New F-150," *Wall Street Journal*, January 6, 2003, p. A15.
7. Lisa Campbell, "Why Unilever B-Brands Must Be Cast Aside," *Marketing*, June 10, 1999, p. 13.
8. Keith Naughton, "Crunch Time at Kellogg," *Newsweek*, February 14, 2000, pp. 52–53.
9. Mike Beirne, "Hershey Gets Sweet with Sugarfree," *Brandweek*, January 20, 2003, p. 4.
10. Elana Harris, "Digital Face Off," *Sales and Marketing Management*, July 2000, p. 17.
11. Peter D. Bennett (ed.), *Dictionary of Marketing Terms* (Chicago: American Marketing Association and NTC Publishing Group, 1995), p. 27.
12. Tom Prendergast, Manager of Research Services, Private Label Manufacturers Association, Telephone Interview, May 3, 2000.
13. Deborah Ball and Sarah Ellison. "Two Shampoos Lather Up for Duel," *Wall Street Journal*, January 28, 2003, p. B7.
14. "World's Most Valuable Brands," Interbrand, **www.interbrand.com,** July 2002.
15. Gabriel Kahn, "Still Going for the Gold," *Wall Street Journal*, January 28, 2003, pp. B1 and B4.

16. Kay Parker, "Old-Line Goes Online," *Business 2.0,* **http://www.business2.com/content/magazine/marketing/2000/06/01/12979.** June 1, 2000.
17. Emily Lambert, "The Buck Stops Here," *Forbes.com,* **http://www.forbes.com/forbes/2003/0106/052.html,** January 6, 2003.
18. Leonard L. Berry, "Retailers with a Future," *Marketing Management,* Spring 1996, pp. 38–46.
19. Alex Taylor III, "Porsche's Risky Recipe," *Fortune,* **http://www.fortune.com/fortune/print/0,15935,418670,00.html,** February 3, 2003.
20. "AOL Anywhere," **www.aol.com/info/pricing,** January 24, 2003.
21. Joann Muller, "Outpsyching the Car Buyer," *Forbes,* February 17, 2003, p. 52.
22. Jane Black, "Here Comes the Real Fun for Telecom," *BusinessWeek Online,* **http://www.businessweek.com:/print/technology/content/feb2003/tc2003024_7152_tc103.html,** February 4, 2003.
23. Based on information from Melanie Wells, "Lord of the Skies," *Forbes,* October 14, 2002, pp. 130ff; Stephanie Overby, "JetBlue Skies Ahead," *CIO Magazine,* July 1, 2002, **www.cio.com/archive/070102/jetblue_content.html; www.jetblue.com.**

CHAPTER 15

1. Based on information from "Special Items Lift Dollar General Net," *MMR,* January 13, 2002, pp. 31ff; "Dollar General Names Acting CEO," *Associated Press,* November 11, 2002; "Dollar Store Channel Positions for Further Expansion," *DSN Retailing Today,* June 10, 2002, p. 10; Elizabeth Kelleher, "Focused on Basics, Dollar Stores May Show Strength," *New York Times,* September 30, 2002, Sec. 3, p. 9.
2. Melanie Wells, "Pepsi's New Challenge," *Forbes,* January 20, 2003.
3. Sally Beatty, "Levi's Strives to Keep a Hip Image," *Wall Street Journal,* January 23, 2003, p. B12.
4. Andrew Raskin, "Who's Minding the Store?" *Business 2.0,* **http://www.business2.com/articles/mag/0,1640,46334,00.html,** February 2003.
5. William M. Pride and O. C. Ferrell, *Marketing: Concepts and Strategies* (Boston: Houghton Mifflin, 2003) p. 406.
6. Steve Bullock, "Transactions in Transition," *Promo,* January 1, 2003.
7. *Chain Store Age/Supermarkets,* July 1983, p. 11.
8. Sandra O'Loughlin and Barry Janoff, "Retailers Seek New Ways to Sell Wares," *Brandweek,* January 6, 2003, p. 12.
9. Jonathan Fuerbringer, "A Miffed Moscow Means Headaches for IKEA," *New York Times,* April 9, 2000, Sec. 3, p. 4.
10. **www.dsa.org,** February 7, 2003.
11. Ken Ibold, "Take This Job and Love It," *Florida Trend,* February 2000, p. 40.
12. Ira Teinowitz, "FTC 'Do Not Call' List Hits Setback in Congress," *AdAge.com,* **http://www.adage.com/news.cms?newsId=37125,** February 12, 2003.
13. Leigh Gallagher, "Drugstore.com Turns to Sex," *Forbes.com,* **http://www.forbes.com/2003/01/30/cz_lg_0130dscm_print.html,** January 30, 2003.
14. Susan Kuchinskas, "By Invitation Only," *Business 2.0,* **http://www.business2.com/content/magazine/indepth/2000/06/01/12927?page=1,** June 1, 2000.
15. Stanley C. Hollander, "The Wheel of Retailing," *Journal of Marketing,* July 1960, p. 37.
16. "Retek and Best Buy Develop Retail Inventory System," *InternetWeek,* January 14, 2003.
17. Todd Murphy, "Developers Rush to Meet Demands of E-Commerce," *New York Times,* January 23, 2000, Sec. 3, p. 3.
18. Based on information from Nichole Cipriani, "Testing Your Child—Online," *Parenting,* May 2001, p. 21; Susan Holly, "Get Smarter," *PC Magazine,* October 17, 2000, pp. 19ff; **www.smarterkids.com.**

CHAPTER 16

1. Based on information from Scott Leith, "AutoTrader.com to Start Auction/Online Sales to Allow Inspections," *Atlanta Journal-Constitution,* December 17, 2002, p. F3; "AutoTrader.com Uses Game for Push," *New Media Age,* October 31, 2002, p. 12; Steve Jarvis, "Pedal to the Cyber-Metal," *Marketing News,* January 21, 2002 pp. 6–7; Andrew Gordon, "AutoTrader.com Gets Game," *Brandweek* August 9, 2001, **www.brandweek.com; www.autotrader.com.**
2. Terence A. Shimp, *Advertising, Promotion, and Supplemental Aspect of Integrated Marketing Communications* (Mason, OH: South-Western, 2003), pp. 15–16.
3. "Taco Bell, Match.com Cooking Up Quesadilla Campaign," *Brandweek,* February 3, 2003, p. 5.
4. "Coen's Spending Totals for 2001," **www.adage.com/datacenter cms,** May 13, 2002.
5. "Direct E-Mail Keeps Them Coming Back," **www.pccomputing com,** February 2000, p. 163.
6. Wayne Friedman, "Spot-Free Show Nears Deal with WB," *AdAge.com,* **http://www.adage.com/news.cms?newsId=36855** January 8, 2003.
7. Scott Hovanyetz, "Aero Aims to Duplicate Crouching Tiger Success," *DM News,* February 11, 2002.
8. Michael McCarthy, "Some Corporate Giants Back Away from Super Bowl Ads," *USA Today,* January 20, 2003, p. 1B.
9. Lisa Sanders, "Coke Ads to Showcase Celebrities," *AdAge.com,* **http://www.adage.com/news.cms?newsId=36868,** January 9 2003.
10. Rich Thomaselli, "47 Percent of Doctors Felt Pressured by DTC Drug Advertising," *AdAge.com,* **http://www.adage.com/news cms?newsId=36897,** January 14, 2003.
11. "Sales Forces in America," *Selling Power,* October 2002, p. 57.
12. Shimp, *Advertising, Promotion, and Supplemental Aspects of Integrated Marketing Communications,* p. 476.
13. William Baldwin, "A Nation of Hagglers," *Forbes,* February 17, 2003, p. 18.
14. Janet Singleton, "Mail-in Rebates Aren't Worth the Trouble for Most Customers," *Denver Post,* May 6, 2001, p. D08.
15. Rafe Needleman, "Better Nutrition Through Database Mining," *Business 2.0,* **http://www.business2.com/articles/web/print/0,1650,46236,00.html,** January 6, 2003.
16. Christine Bittar, "Revlon, Conde Nast Partner on "How to Lose a Guy," *Brandweek,* February 3, 2003, p. 34.
17. Karen J. Bannan, "Freebies in Cyberspace: Online Companies Let Consumers Pick the Samples They Want Mailed to Them," *Wall Street Journal,* November 27, 2000, p. 10.
18. Jason Compton, "Reward Your Customers," *Smartbusiness.com,* May 2000, pp. 196–199.
19. Jane Applegate, "Size Doesn't Matter If You Have a Trade Show Booth," *Arizona Republic,* February 22, 2000, p. D2.
20. Ben & Jerry's News Release, March 30, 2001.
21. Todd Wasserman, "H&R Block Takes Diversified Services into Account in Branding Makeover," *Brandweek,* January 13, 2003, p. 9.
22. Kate MacArthur, "Hardee's Shifts to a Big-Beef Menu," *Ad Age.com,* **http://www.adage.com/news.cms?newsId=37048,** February 3, 2003.
23. Based on information from David Gianatasio, "Rooms to Grow," *Adweek,* January 14, 2003, p. 3; Jon Chesto, "Buffet Helps Jordan's Flip Switch," *Boston Herald,* August 22, 2002, p. 37; "At the Movies with Buffet," *Financial Express,* October 28, 2002; Barry Tatelman, "You Can't Take That Away from Us," *Operations Management* (n.d.), **www.furninfo.com/operations/jordans0402.html; www.jordansfurniture.com.**

CHAPTER 17

1. Based on information from "Built-In Analytics," *Information Week,* December 7, 2002, **www.informationweek.com;** Heather Harreld, "PeopleSoft, IBM Announce Partnership," *InfoWorld,* October 22, 2002, **www.inforworld.com/articles/hn/xml/02/10/22/021022hnpeoplesoft.xml;** Rick Whiting, "'Meaningful Data Objects' on the Horizon," *Information Week,* August 29, 2002, **www.informationweek.com;** Ian Mount, "Attention Underlings: That's Mister Conway to you. And I Am Not a PeoplePerson!" *Business 2.0,* February 2002, pp. 52–58; PeopleSoft website at **www.peoplesoft.com.**
2. Fred Moore, "Storage Changing So Fast It Even Obsoletes the Future," *Computer Technology Review,* January 2001, p. 1.

3. Steve Hamm, "B2B Isn't Dead. It's Learning," *BusinessWeek Online*, **www.businessweek.com,** December 23, 2002.
4. Christine Winter, "South Florida Sun-Sentinel Christine Winter Column," *Sun-Sentinel* website at **www.sun-sentiel.com,** January 5, 2003.
5. Fred Moore, "Storage Changing So Fast It Even Obsoletes the Future," *Computer Technology Review*, January 2001, p. 1.
6. "The Web at Your Service," *BusinessWeek Online*, **www.businessweek.com,** March 18, 2002.
7. *Guardian Newspaper* website at **www.guardian.co.uk,** October 5, 2002.
8. The Necho Systems Corporation website at **www.necho.com,** February 16, 2003.
9. Based on information from Cristina McEachern, "GovPX Turns to Bang Networks for Business Continuity Needs," *Wall Street & Technology*, January 2002, pp. 29ff; Evan Koblentz, "Getting Key Info Right Away," *eWeek*, April 23, 2001, p. 37; **www.bangnetworks.com.**

CHAPTER 18

1. Based on information from Judith Burns, "SEC's Top Cop Again Says Audit Firms May Face Suits," *Wall Street Journal*, January 31, 2003, **www.wsj.com;** Michael Schroeder, "SEC Orders New Disclosures in Companies' Profit Reports," *Wall Street Journal*, January 16, 2003, **www.wsj.com;** Cassell Bryan-Low, "SEC May Take Tougher Tone on Accountants in Bad Audits," *Wall Street Journal*, December 13, 2003, **www.wsj.com;** Penelope Patsuris, "The Corporate Scandal Sheet," *Forbes.com*, **www.forbes.com2002/07/25/accountingtracker.html,** August 26, 2002; SEC website at **www.sec.gov;** Thomas S. Mulligan, "Xerox Agrees to Record SEC Fine," *Los Angeles Times*, April 2, 2002, pp. C1ff.
2. Jeremy Kahn, "Do Accountants Have a Future," *Fortune*, February 18, 2003, **www.fortune.com.**
3. American Institute of Certified Public Accountants (AICPA) website at **www.aicpa.org,** February 25, 2003.
4. Nanette Byrnes and William Symonds, "Is the Avalanche Headed for Pricewaterhouse?" *BusinessWeek*, October 14, 2002, pp. 45–46.
5. "System Failure," *Fortune*, June 24, 2002, p. 64.
6. Jeffrey H. Birnbaum, "Congress Scores One for Your Portfolio," *Fortune.com*, **www.fortune.com,** August 12, 2002.
7. Bureau of Labor Statistics website at **www.bls.gov,** February 23, 2003.
8. American Institute of Certified Public Accountants (AICPA) website at **www.aicpa.org,** February 18, 2003.
9. Based on information from Robert Scott, "Battle for the Mid-Market," *Accounting Technology*, December 2002, pp. 16ff; "Best's Dedicated Units Offer Accounting Solutions," *Accounting Today*, December 16, 2002, p. S14; **www.bestsoftware.com.**

CHAPTER 19

1. Based on information from Steven Marlin, "BofA to Install Secure Messaging System," *Bank Systems & Technology*, January 2003, p. 34; "BofA to Provide Images of Checks, Deposit Slips to Online Customers," *InternetWeek*, December 2, 2002, **www.internetweek.com;** and **www.bankofamerica.com.**
2. Federal Reserve website at **www.federalreserve.gov,** January 8, 2003.
3. *Ibid.*
4. *Ibid.*
5. William A. McGeveran, *The World Almanac and Book of Facts 2002* (New York: World Almanac Books, 2002), p. 108.
6. U.S. Department of Commerce, Economics and Statistics Administration, and U.S. Census Bureau, *Statistical Abstract of the United States 2001*, 121st ed. (Washington: U.S. Government Printing Office, 2002), p. 732.
7. Office of Thrift Supervision website at **www.ots.treas.gov,** January 10, 2003.
8. *Ibid.*
9. U.S. Department of Commerce, Economics and Statistics Administration, and U.S. Census Bureau, *Statistical Abstract of the United States 2001*, 121st ed. (Washington: U.S. Government Printing Office, 2002), p. 732.
10. Office of Thrift Supervision website at **www.ots.treas.gov,** January 10, 2003.
11. U.S. Department of Labor website at **www.bls.gov,** January 10, 2003.
12. U.S. Department of Commerce, Economics and Statistics Administration, and U.S. Census Bureau, *Statistical Abstract of the United States 2001*, 121st ed. (Washington: U.S. Government Printing Office, 2002), p. 735.
13. *Ibid.*
14. Dr. Patrick Dixon, Global Change, Ltd., website at **www.globalchange.com,** January 14, 2003.
15. *Ibid.*
16. Federal Deposit Insurance Corporation website at **www.fdic.gov,** January 11, 2003.
17. Based on information from Steve Bills, "Online Banking," *American Banker*, March 11, 2002, p. 23; **www.financialfusion.com.**

CHAPTER 20

1. Based on information from Bridget McCrea, "Creative Financing: The Perfect Match," *Fortune Small Business*, November 20, 2002, **www.fortune.com/fortune/smallbusiness/creative/0,15704,392625,00.html;** Melinda Fulmer, "Investors Nibbling at the Mexican Food Industry," *Los Angeles Times*, November 22, 2002, **http://www.latimes.com/business/la-fi-mexfood22nov22.story;** and **www.usbxadvisory.com.**
2. Merck Corporation website at **www.merck.com,** January 18, 2003.
3. U.S. Census Bureau, *Statistical Abstract of the United States*, **www.census.gov,** January 23, 2003.
4. *AdAge.com*, **www.adage.com,** January 19, 2003.
5. Yahoo! Finance website at **http://biz.yahoo.com/rf/030116/autos_trw_bonds_5.html,** January 19, 2003.
6. *Mergent's Handbook of Common Stocks*, Fall 2002, (New York: Mergent, Inc, 2002).
7. *Ibid.*
8. Nelson D. Schwartz, "Trial by Fire," *Fortune*, June 26, 2000, pp. 141–146.
9. Paul M. Sherer, "Commercial Paper Market Faces Problems as Lenders Grow Cautious," *Wall Street Jounal*, **www.wsj.com,** January 25, 2001.
10. Lee Barney, "The Daily Interview: What the Fed Rate Cuts Mean for Corporations," *The Street.com*, **www.thestreet.com,** June 15, 2001.
11. Stephen Taub, "Unemployment Rate Jumps to 4.2 Percent," *CFO.com*, **www.cfo.com,** February 2, 2001.
12. *Hoover's Online*, **www.hoovers.com/ipo/pricings/aftermkt/0,2263,201,00.html,** January 20, 2003.
13. Yahoo! Finance website at **http://biz.yahoo.com/rf/030119/markets_stocks_ipo_1.html,** January 20, 2003.
14. General Electric, *2001 Annual Report*, **www.ge.com,** January 23, 2003.
15. ExxonMobil, *2001 Annual Report*, **www.exxonmobil.com,** January 23, 2003.
16. Roger Fillion, "Rocky Mountain High Tech," *Business 2.0*, **http://www.business2.com/content/magazine/ebusiness/2000/06001/12934,** June 1, 2000.
17. Based on information from **www.gilfordsecurities.com.**

CHAPTER 21

1. Based on information from Justin Fox, "Saint Jack on the Attack," *Fortune*, January 20, 2003, pp. 112–116; Riva D. Atlas, "Vanguard Tinkers with Its Success Formula," *New York Times*, January 5, 2003, sec. 3, pp. 27, 32; and **www.vanguard.com.**
2. New York Stock Exchange website at **www.nyse.com,** February 9, 2003.
3. Motley Fool website at **www.fool.com,** February 10, 2003.
4. Roger G. Ibbotson, "Predictions of the Past and Forecasts for the Future: 1976–2025," Ibbotson Associates website, **www.ibbotson.com,** February 10, 2003.
5. Suze Orman, *The Road to Wealth* (New York: Riverbend Books, 2001), p. 371.

6. Investment Company Institute website at **www.ici.org**, February 11, 2003.
7. Orman, *The Road to Wealth*, p. 393.
8. Market values for Home Depot were obtained from the Yahoo! Finance website at **hpp://finance.yahoo.com,** February 12, 2003.
9. Market values for TXU Corporation were obtained from the Yahoo! Finance website at **hpp://finance.yahoo.com,** February 12, 2003.
10. Based on information from "Firms Retreat from Online Broke age," *Securities Industry News*, July 15, 2002; **www.mldirect.com**

APPENDIX B

1. Jack R. Kapoor, Les R. Dlabay, and Robert J. Hughes, *Personal Finance*, 7th ed. (New York: McGraw-Hill, 2004), pp. 344–345.

Credits

BOX CREDITS

Chapter 1 **p. 7** Based on information from Karen Alexander, "Ways to Move Up When the Economy Moves Down," *New York Times,* August 18, 2002, pp. 9ff; Peter Vogt, "We Are All Self-Employed," *Monster,* n.d., **featuredreports.monster.com/independents/selfemployed.** **p. 12** Based on information from Mike France, "What About the Lawyers?" *Business Week,* December 23, 2002, pp. 58–62; Christopher Farrell, "Biting the Invisible Hand," *Business Week Online,* November 27, 2002, **www.businessweek.com/bwdaily/dnflash/nov2002/nf20021127_9555.htm;** Penelope Patsuris, "The Corporate Scandal Sheet," *Forbes.com,* August 26, 2002,**www.forbes.com2002/07/25/accountingtracker.html.** **p. 25** Based on information from Andy Reinhardt, "E-Commerce Starts to Click," *Business Week,* August 6, 2002, p. 56; Steve Bodow, "The Care and Feeding of a Killer App," *Business 2.0,* August 2002, pp. 76–78; Keith Regan, "New Rule of E-Commerce: Go Back to the Old Rules," *E-Commerce Times,* August 1, 2002, **www.ecommercetimes.com.**

Chapter 2 **p. 36** Based on information from Eric Goldman, "On My Mind: The Privacy Hoax," *Forbes,* October 14, 2002, p. 42; "Opinion: Laxity May Lead to New Laws on Internet Privacy," *Marketing,* June 13, 2002, p. 18; Saul Hansell, "Seeking Profits, Internet Companies Alter Privacy Policy," *New York Times,* April 11, 2002, **www.nytimes.com.** **p. 48** Based on information from "MGM Mirage Launches Online Casino," *Associated Press,* October 3, 2002, **www.smartmoney.com/bn/ON/index.cfm?story=ON-20021003-000189-0603;** Ira Sager, Ben Elgin, Peter Elstrom, Faith Keenan, and Pallavi Gogoi, "The Underground Web," *BusinessWeek,* September 2, 2002, pp. 67–74. **p. 51** Based on information from Khanh T. L. Tran, "Biking Videogame to Feature Scenes of Prostitutes, Strippers," *Wall Street Journal,* October 14, 2002, **www.wsj.com;** Jon M. Gibson, 'Games Gone Bad: Developers Follow in the M-Rated Wake of GTA III," *Video Business,* June 17, 2002, pp. 4ff.

Chapter 3 **p. 75** Based on information from Colin Baker, "SAA Lays Groundwork for Key Strategic Decisions," *Airline Business,* September 1, 2002, p. 30; Henri E. Cauvin, "Wanted: An Airline for All of Africa," *New York Times,* August 4, 2002, sec. 3, p. 5; Murdo Morrison, "Falling Rand Hits South African Carriers," *Airline Business,* January 1, 2002, p. 22. **p. 79** Based on information from Andrew Raskin, "Lost in Translation," *Business 2.0,* November 2002, p. 26; Ken Belson, "Rival to Pokémon Keeps Market Hot," *New York Times,* October 6, 2002, sec. 3, p. 5. **p. 84** Based on information from Dexter Roberts, "The Tricks of the Trade," *BusinessWeek,* July 15, 2002, pp. 52–53; Dexter Roberts, "Clear Sailing for Pirates," *BusinessWeek,* July 15, 2002, p. 53; John McKeon, "A Flood of Fakes," *Entertainment Design,* August 2001, pp. 10ff. **p. 100** Based on information from Donna Hood Crecca, "Higher Calling," *Chain Leader,* December 2002, p. 14; "State Fare: Finagle A Bagel, Boston," *Restaurants and Institutions,* October 1, 2002, **www.rimag.com/1902/sr.htm;** "Finagle Sees a Return to More Normal Business Mode," *Foodservice East,* Fall 2002, pp. 1, 17; "Sloan Grads Bet Their Money on Bagels," *Providence Business News,* October 25, 1999, p. 14; interview with Laura B. Trust and Alan Litchman, February 25, 2003.

Chapter 4 **p. 111** Based on information from Ken Belson, "How Dell Is Defying an Industry's Gravity in Japan," *New York Times,* December 8, 2002, sec. 3, p. 4; "How to Thrive in a Sick Economy: Michael Dell," *Business 2.0,* December 2002, p. 88; and **www.dell.com.** **p. 114** Based on information from "Semtech Announces Third Quarter Results," Semtech news release, November 25, 2002, **www.businesswire.com; www.semtech.com;** "Semtech Corporation," *Yahoo! Finance* (n.d.), **http://yahoo.marketguide.com.** **p. 129** Based on information from Antony Adshead, "Shell Sets Up 85,000 Seat Portal," *Computer Weekly,* September 26, 2002, p. 4; Chaz Osburn, "SAP Shows That Being Big Has Its Advantages," *Automotive News,* September 23, 2002, p. 20T; "Restaurant Chain Plans Whopper of a MySAP Implementation," *InternetWeek,* June 25, 2002, **www.internet.com;** and **www.sap.com.**

Chapter 5 **p. 149** Based on information from "A Bluedot Happy Meal," *Asia Africa Intelligence Wire,* December 8, 2002; Stephanie Basalyga, "Volunteers Light Way for McDonald House Fundraiser," *Daily Journal of Commerce, Portland,* December 3, 2002; "United Way, Target." **p. 155** Based on information from Amy Tsao, "Will Wal-Mart Take Over the World?" *BusinessWeek,* November 27, 2002, *BusinessWeek Online,* **www.businessweek.com/bwdaily/dnflash/nov2002/nf20021127_4108.htm;** Richard Ernsberger, Jr., Stefan Theil, Bianca Toness, Alexandra A. Seno, William Underhill, and Amy L. Webb, "Wal-Mart World," *Newsweek International,* May 20, 2002, pp. 50ff; Wal-Mart Stores Company Profile, *S&P Business Summary,* **http://research.businessweek.com;** Wal-Mart Stores website, **www.walmartstores.com.** **p. 158** Based on information from Adam Lashinsky, "Now for the Hard Part," *Fortune,* November 18, 2002, pp. 94–106; David Henry and Frederick F. Jespersen, "Mergers: Why Most Big Deals Don't Pay Off," *BusinessWeek,* October 14, 2002, pp. 60ff; Karen Lowry Miller, "The Giants Stumble," *Newsweek International,* July 8, 2002, pp. 14ff.

Chapter 6 **p. 172** Based on information from Pete Engardio, "Small Loan, Big Dream," *BusinessWeek,* October 14, 2002, p. 118; "African's Women Go to Work," *Economist,* January 13, 2001, pp. 1ff; Pete Engardio, "Special Report: Global Poverty," *BusinessWeek,* October 14, 2002, pp. 108ff. **p. 175** Based on information from Jeff Bailey, "Co-ops Gain as Companies Seek Competitive Power," *Wall Street Journal,* October 15, 2002, **www.wsj.com;** Susan Greco and Kate O'-Sullivan, "Independents' Day," *Inc.,* August 2001, pp. 76–83. **p. 177** Based on information from Tricia A. Holly, "A Common Thread: Agencies Large and Small Are Developing Homegrown Methods to Reel in New Business," *Travel Agent,* October 21, 2002, pp. 30ff; "Fit for DIY? Travel Agents," *Economist,* June 1, 2002, **www.economist.com;** Paulette Thomas, "Case Study: Travel Agency Meets Technology's Threat," *Wall Street Journal,* May 21, 2002, p. B4; Bonnie Harris, "For Storefront Agencies, More Cuts on the Horizon," *Los Angeles Times,* October 15, 2002, pp. C1ff. **p. 192** Based on information from Donna Hood Crecca, "Higher Calling," *Chain Leader,* December 2002, p. 14; "State Fare: Finagle A Bagel, Boston," *Restaurants and Institutions,* October 1, 2002, **www.rimag.com/1902/sr.htm;** "Sloan Grads Bet Their Money on Bagels," *Providence Business News,* October 25, 1999, p. 14; interview with Laura B. Trust and Alan Litchman, February 25, 2003.

Chapter 7 **p. 208** Based on information from Joshua Macht, "What Makes a Great Leader?" *Business 2.0,* August 2002, pp. 72ff; Lori Ioannou, "The Era of the Demagogue Is Dead," *Fortune Small*

Business, July 11, 2002, **www.fortune.com;** Tom Peters, "Rule #3: Leadership Is Confusing as Hell," *Fast Company*, March 2001, **www.fastcompany.com;** Carole Matthews, "Core Competencies of a CEO," *Inc.*, October 17, 2001, **www.inc.com;** Jerry Useem, "Rudy Giuliani Has It. Gustavus Smith Didn't. Do You Have the Chops to Lead in a Crisis?" *Fortune*, November 12, 2001, **www.fortune.com. p. 210** Based on information from Thomas A. Stewart, "How to Think with Your Gut," *Business 2.0*, November 2002, pp. 98ff; Bill Breen, "What's Your Intuition?" *Fast Company*, September 2000, pp. 290ff. **p. 213** Based on information from "Novell Homes in on Secure ID Management," *eWeek*, October 16, 2002, **www.eweek.com;** Owen Thomas, "Seven Secrets of Success," *Business 2.0*, October 2002, p. 87; Russ Mitchell, "How to Manage Geeks," *Fast Company*, June 1999, pp. 174ff.

Chapter 8 **p. 231** Based on information from Ellyn Spragins, "Is This the Best Company to Work for Anywhere?" *Fortune Small Business*, October 21, 2002, **www.fortune.com;** "Motek Honored as Ernst & Young's Entrepreneur of the Year Finalist," June 24, 2002, **www.motek.com/news/press29.html;** P. Schneider, "Debunking the Sweatshop," *CIO Magazine* (n.d.), **www.motek.com/news/press10.html. p. 234** Based on information from Daniel Altman, "Downsizing Could Have a Downside," *New York Times*, December 26, 2002, pp. C1ff; Louis Uchitelle, "Data Show Growing Trend Toward Permanent Layoffs," *New York Times*, August 22, 2002, p. C9; Reylito A. H. Elbo, "In the Workplace: Rightsizing Pressure of Survivors," *BusinessWorld*, August 28, 2002, p. 23; Barbara Davison, "The Difference Between Rightsizing and Wrongsizing," *Journal of Business Strategy*, July–August 2002, pp. 31ff. **p. 240** Based on information from Ron Insana, "Rakesh Khurana of Harvard, Author Emmett Murphy, and Columnist James Surowiecki Discuss Executive Perks and Compensation," *CNBC Business Center*, September 9, 2002; Rachel Beck, "CEOs Need to Return Focus to Running Firms," *Chicago Sun-Times*, July 21, 2002, p. 42; Erin Strout, "Crafty or Crazy?" *Sales and Marketing Management*, April 2002, pp. 28–33.

Chapter 9 **p. 251** Based on information from Ron Harbour, "The Best Is Never Good Enough," *Automotive Industries*, October 2002, pp. 12ff; "Pushing Carmakers to Rev Up Factories," *BusinessWeek*, February 18, 2002, pp. 28Bff. **p. 256** Based on information from "Accelerated Approval Granted for Iressa (ZD1839)," *Cancer Weekly*, December 17, 2002, p. 39; Robert Langreth, "Conquering Cancer," *Forbes*, November 11, 2002, **www.forbes.com/forbes/2002/1111/118.html;** "Another Blow to AstraZeneca Pipeline," *Chemistry and Industry*, July 1, 2002, p. 6; "AstraZeneca Drug Test Flow," *Chemistry and Industry*, September 2, 2002, p. 5; **www.astrazeneca.com;** "FDA Approval Granted for Arimidex," *Cancer Weekly*, October 29, 2002, p. 13; "New Medicine Approved Specifically for Localized Disease," *Cancer Weekly*, October 9, 2002; "Casodex Reduces Disease, Tumor Progression," *Cancer Weekly*, September 17, 2002, p. 22; "New Analysis of Casodex Trial Reveals Positive Results," *Cancer Weekly*, July 30, 2002, p. 21. **p. 259** Based on information from Jennifer Bjorhus, "3M to Seek Even Better Business in 2003," *St. Paul Press*, December 22, 2002, **www.twincities.com/mld/pioneerpress;** 3M website at **www.3m.com;** Michael Arndt, "3M: A Lab for Growth?" *BusinessWeek*, January 21, 2002, pp. 50–51. **p. 276** Based on information from Donna Hood Crecca, "Higher Calling," *Chain Leader*, December 2002, p. 14; "While Finagle Flaunts a Breakfast Bagel Pizza," *Restaurant Business Menu Strategies*, November 12, 2002, **www.restaurantbusiness.com;** Finagle A Bagel website at **www.finagleabagle.com;** interview with Laura B. Trust and Alan Litchman, February 25, 2003.

Chapter 10 **p. 292** Based on information from Amy Tsao, "Will Wal-Mart Take Over the World?" *BusinessWeek*, November 27, 2002, *BusinessWeek Online*, **www.businessweek.com/bwdaily/dnflash/nov2002/nf20021127_4108.htm;** Stephanie Armour, "While Hiring at Most Firms Chills, Wal-Mart's Heats Up," *USA Today*, August 26, 2002, p. 3B; Maria Bartiromo, "Culture and Great Success of Wal-Mart Stores," *CNBC*, March 18, 2002. **p. 294** Based on information from Robert Levering and Milton Moskowitz, "Fortune 100 Best Companies to Work For," *Fortune*, January 20, 2003, pp. 127ff; Car[e] Lachnit, "Ready for the Résumé Deluge," *Workforce*, July 2002, p. 1[…] John Engen, "Profiting from Conventional Wisdom," *Future Bank[…]* January–February 2002, pp. 22ff; "Edward Jones Tops Fortune List [of] 100 Best Companies to Work For," Fortune news release, January 2[…] 2002, **www.businesswire.com;** "Best Companies to Work For: E[d]ward Jones," *Fortune*, February 4, 2002, **www.fortune.com;** Jim Ga[l]lagher, "Edward Jones Gets Survey's Top Spot," *St. Louis Post-Dispatc[h]* January 22, 2002, p. A1. **p. 301** Based on information from Brad Dav[i]son, "Failing Grade," *Rubber & Plastics News*, September 16, 2002, p[p.] 1ff; Carol Hazard, "Forced Rankings in Legal Tangle," *Richmo[nd] Times-Dispatch*, June 4, 2002, pp. A1ff.

Chapter 11 **p. 314** Based on information from Stephanie A[r]mour, "Job Seekers Take Creativity to New Level," *USA Today*, Se[p]tember 13, 2002, p. 1B; Fredricka Whitfield and Carolyn Mung[e] "Recent College Grad Gets Creative Searching for a Job," *CNN*, Ju[ly] 13, 2002; Davis Bushnell, "Job Hunters Up Antics to Get Noticed[,]" *Boston Globe*, June 9, 2002, p. G1; "No Need for a Résumé—My Sock[s] Speak for Themselves," Creative Group news release, August 2[…] 2002, **www.prnewswire.com. p. 317** Based on information fro[m] Betsy Cummings, "Target for Terror," *Sales and Marketing Manag[e]ment*, August 2002, pp. 30–35; Kevin Sullivan, "Kidnapping Is Growt[h] Industry in Mexico," *Washington Post*, September 17, 2002, pp. A1f[f;] Joseph B. Treaster, "Among Executives, Fear of Kidnapping Rises," *New York Times*, July 2, 2002, pp. C10ff. **p. 325** Based on informatio[n] from Glenn Baker, "Power Napping," *New Zealand Management*, Oc[…]tober 2002, p. 17; Catherine Callaway and Bill Delaney, "Study Show[s] Naps Keep Employees Alert," *CNN*, May 26, 2002; "Sleep on the Jo[b:] It Improves Performance," *The Straits Times*, August 14, 2002; Micha[e]l Miller, "The Benefits of Napping at Work," *South Florida Busine[ss] Journal*, March 1, 2002, **www.bizjournals.com.**

Chapter 12 **p. 344** Based on information from Gary Weiss, "Revenge of the Investor," *BusinessWeek*, December 16, 2002, pp. 116–12[2;] Amy Borrus, "Getting the Boss to Behave," *BusinessWeek*, July 15[,] 2002, p. 110. **p. 348** Based on information from "UAW Must Help Not Hurt, Supplier Plants It Organizes," *Automotive News*, Decembe[r] 9, 2002, p. 12; Robert Sherefkin, "Metaldyne Won't Fight UAW Organizing Effort," *Automotive News*, December 2, 2002, p. 1; Davi[d] Sedgwick, "Intier Talks With UAW," *Automotive News*, July 29, 2002[,] pp. 1ff; Joann Muller, "Has the UAW Found a Better Road?" *BusinessWeek*, July 15, 2002, pp. 108ff. **p. 354** Based on information from Stefan Fatsis, "Baseball Stars Find Owners Now Have the Upper Hand," *Wall Street Journal*, December 23, 2002, **www.wsj.com;** Helene Elliott, "Inside the NHL: Bettman Sings Owners' Song on Road Show," *Los Angeles Times*, November 26, 2002, pp. D-5ff; Dan Haar, "Unwitting Non-Fans Contributed to Baseball's Labor Strife," *Hartfor[d] Courant*, August 31, 2002, p. E1; "Like Baseball, WNBA Labor Problems Loom," *USA Today*, August 24, 2002, **www.usatoday.com;** Stuart Elliott, "Marketers and Agencies Make Contingency Plans for a Baseball Strike and Worry About Fan Loyalty," *New York Times*, August 29, 2002, p. C8; David Shook, "One More Strike—and They're Out," *BusinessWeek*, July 22, 2002, **www.businessweek.com. p. 361** Based on information from Stephanie Armour, "Wall-Mart Takes Hits on Worker Treatment.", *USA Today*, February 10, 2003, **www.usatoday.com;** Karen Olsson, "Up Against Wal-Mart," *Mother Jones*, March–April 2003, **www.motherjones.com;** Wendy Zellner, "How Wal-Mart Keeps Unions at Bay," *BusinessWeek*, October 28, 2002, pp. 94ff; Jef Feeley, "Wal-Mart Found Guilty in Oregon Pay Case," *Seattle Times*, December 20, 2002, **www.seattletimes.com;** Wal-Mart website at **www.walmartstores.com. p. 364** Based on information from Donna Hood Crecca, "High Calling," *Chain Leader*, December 2002, p. 14; Finagle A Bagel website at **www.finagleabagle.com;** interview with Laura B. Trust and Alan Litchman, February 25, 2003.

Chapter 13 **p. 373** Based on information from Russell Mokhiber, "Household's Predatory Plea," *Multinational Monitor*, October–November 2002, pp. 6ff; Erin Strout, "To Tell the Truth," *Sales and*

Marketing Management, July 2002, pp. 40–47; Philip Reed, "Low Down, Low Payments!" *Edmunds.com*, **www.edmunds.com,** April 25, 2002. **p. 384** Based on information from Leigh Dyer, "Retail Spies Watch What Customers Buy and Why They Don't," *Charlotte Observer*, July 26, 2002, **www.charlotte.com;** Bruce Horovitz, "Shop, You're on Candid Camera," *USA Today*, November 6, 2002, pp. 1Bff; David Humphries and Helen Perks, "Case History: Clarks U.K. Ethnography and Co-Development Help Clarks UK Create a New Line of Active Footwear," *Visions* (n.d.), **www.pdma.org.uk. p. 390** Based on information from Russ Mitchell, "Harlem Globetrotters," *CBS Sunday Morning*, September 29, 2002; Elena Romero, "Hoop Dreams: Fubu Adds Harlem Globetrotters to Its Platinum Collection," *Daily News Record*, July 22, 2002, p. 29; "Burger King Corporation and the Harlem Globetrotters Renew Strong Relationship," Burger King news release, July 10, 2002, **www.prnewswire.com;** Harlem Globetrotters website at **http://harlemglobetrotters.com.**

Chapter 14 **p. 404** Based on information from David Pogue, "TiVo Rivals Add DVD to the Mix," *New York Times*, November 14, 2002, pp. G2ff; "Is TiVo Bad for Business?" *Business 2.0*, **www.business2.com,** September 2002; Jimmy Guterman and Matthew Maier, "Nowhere to Hide: Ads Arrive on TiVo," *Business 2.0*, **www.business2.com,** May 23, 2002; Scott Kirsner, "Can TiVo Go Prime Time?" *Fast Company*, August 2002, pp. 82ff. **p. 406** Based on information from Ken Hoffman, "Ultra Is Low in Carbs, Calories, and Taste, But It Is a Beer," *Houston Chronicle*, November 15, 2002, p. 5; Brent Hopkins, "Could This Be the New Beer Belly?" *Daily News of Los Angeles*, May 17, 2002, p. B1; Leon Harris, Rhonda Rowland, and Daryn Kagan, "New Low-Carb Beer Unveiled," *CNN Live Today*, May 15, 2002; Rob Turner, "Battling the Bulge with Beer and Sugar," *Fortune*, October 28, 2002, p. 42. **p. 410** Based on information from Rebecca Beer, "Agencies Aren't Worried By Kellogg's Deal with Cartoon Network," *Campaign*, August 9, 2002, p. 18; Theresa Howard, "Ad Icons Star in Other Brands' Commercials," *USA Today*, May 20, 2002, p. 3B; Mark McMaster, "Lessons from the Marlboro Man," *Sales and Marketing Management*, February 2002, pp. 44–45.

Chapter 15 **p. 439** Based on information from Julia Chang, "Grab Your Partner," *Sales and Marketing Management*, July 2002, p. 59; Paula Rooney and Barbara Darrow, "Microsoft Gets Serious," *Computer Reseller News*, July 8, 2002, pp. 14ff; Diane Krakora, "Strategic Maneuvers—Courting the Channel," *VAR Business*, June 10, 2002, pp. 40. **p. 442** Based on information from Graham J. Sharman, "Lead Role for Multinational Distributors?" *Supply Chain Management Review*, November–December 2002, pp. 12ff; David Arnold, "Seven Rules of International Distribution," *Harvard Business Review*, November–December 2000, pp. 131–137. **p. 450** Based on information from Bob Tedeschi, "E-Commerce Report," *New York Times*, October 28, 2002, p. C7ff; Peter Barlas, "Well, Doggone! Pet Suppliers Survived the Dot-Bombs," *Investors Business Daily*, September 9, 2002; Robert Barker, "The Money in Creature Comforts," *BusinessWeek Online*, **www.businessweek.com,** September 23, 2002; "Petsmart, Inc.," *Hoover's Handbook of American Business 2002* (Austin, TX: Hoover's, 2002), pp. 1116–1117.

Chapter 16 **p. 474** Based on information from Michael Snider, "Hey, Kids! Let's Play Adver-Games!" *Maclean's*, December 23, 2002, pp. 36ff; Anni Layne Rodgers, "More Than a Game," *Fast Company*, May 2002, pp. 46ff; Marc Weingarten, "It's an Ad! It's a Game! It's . . . Both!" *Business 2.0*, **www.business2.com,** March 2002. **p. 479** Based on information from Grant Robinson, "Hiring for Retention, Productivity, and Revenues," *Supply House Times*, September 2002, pp. 78ff; Betsy Cummings, "Roll with the Punches," *Sales and Marketing Management*, June 2002, pp. 59ff; Becky Meiser, "School's Out," *Sales and Marketing Management*, May 2002, p. 60. **p. 481** Based on information from Tim Bonfield, "Drug Firms' Gifts to Docs Draw Scrutiny," *Cincinnati Enquirer*, October 3, 2002, **www.enquirer.com;** Julie Appleby, "Feds Warn Drugmakers: Gifts to Doctors May Be Illegal," *USA Today*, October 2, 2002, **www.usatoday.com;** Helen Jung, "Some Doctors Are Getting Awful Tired of Visits from Drug-Industry Sales Reps," *Associated Press*, June 14, 2002, Lexis-Nexis; Melinda Ligos, "Gimme! Gimme!" *Sales and Marketing Management*, March 2002, pp. 33–40. **p. 494** Based on information from Donna Hood Crecca, "Higher Calling," *Chain Leader*, December 2002, p. 14; Finagle A Bagel web site at **www.finagleabagle.com** and company profile; interview with Laura B. Trust and Alan Litchman, February 25, 2003.

Chapter 17 **p. 508** Based on information from Victor Homola, "Chinese and German Chip Makers Sign Deal," *New York Times*, December 10, 2002, p. C12; Bruce Einhorn, "High Tech in China," *BusinessWeek*, October 28, 2002, pp. 80–88; Bruce Einhorn, "The Well-Heeled Upstart on Cisco's Tail," *BusinessWeek*, October 28, 2002, p. 91. **p. 515** Based on information from Scott Kessler, "Intuit's Shining Star," *BusinessWeek Online*, **www.businessweek.com,** January 21, 2003; Timothy J. Mullaney, "The Wizard of Intuit," *BusinessWeek*, October 28, 2002, pp. 60–63; "Intuit to Buy Eclipse for $85 Million," *New York Times*, June 28, 2002, p. C7. **p. 519** Based on information from Peter Loftus, "Computer Services Firms Signed Big Pacts but Results Were Mixed," *Dow Jones Newswires*, January 8, 2003, **www.wsj.com;** Marie Lingblom, "EDS Dashboard to Aid Customers," *Computer Reseller News*, December 9, 2003, p. 126; Bill Breen, "How EDS Got Its Groove Back," *Fast Company*, October 2001, pp. 106ff.

Chapter 18 **p. 534** Based on information from Andrew Ross Sorkin, "Court Is Told Tyco Deals Had Backing of Auditors," *New York Times*, February 8, 2003, pp. C2ff; "Tyco Gimmicks Inflated Profit, Audit Shows," *Los Angeles Times*, December 31, 2002, p. C3; Paula Dwyer, "Nowhere to Run, Nowhere to Hide," *BusinessWeek*, October 14, 2002, pp. 44–45. **p. 544** The values for inventory for Goodyear Tire and Rubber Company and the J.C. Penney Corporation were obtained from the Yahoo! Finance website at **http://finance.yahoo.com,** February 23, 2003. p. 551 Based on information from Jerry Useem, "In Corporate America, It's Cleanup Time," *Fortune*, September 16, 2002, pp. 62–70; Joseph Nocera, "System Failure," *Fortune*, June 24, 2002, pp. 62–74; Alfred Rappaport, "Show Me the Cash Flow!" *Fortune*, September 16, 2002, pp. 192–194. **p. 562** Based on information from Donna Hood Crecca, "Higher Calling," *Chain Leader*, December 2002, p. 14; "State Fare: Finagle A Bagel, Boston," *Restaurants and Institutions*, October 1, 2002, **www.rimag.com/1902/sr.htm;** Finagle A Bagel website at **www.finagleabagle.com** and company profile; interview with Laura B. Trust and Alan Litchman, February 25, 2003.

Chapter 19 **p. 573** Based on information from Marilyn Geewax, "Greenspan Questions Tax Cuts," *Atlanta Journal-Constitution*, February 12, 2003, pp. D1ff; "Markets: Fed Underscores Role as Lender of Last Resort," *Los Angeles Times*, February 6, 2003, p. C4; Rich Miller, "The Future of the Fed," *BusinessWeek*, December 16, 2002, pp. 94–104. **p. 587** Based on information from Riva D. Atlas, "Bank Deals May Be Ahead at Citigroup," *New York Times*, February 18, 2003, p. C1; "Citigroup to Buy Stake in Big Chinese Bank," *New York Times*, January 1, 2003, p. W1; **www.citigroup.com. p. 593** Based on information from "Identity Theft Ring Broken Up, 22 Arrested," *United Press International*, February 4, 2003, **www.comtexnews.com;** Annelena Lobb, "Identity Theft Survival Guide," *CNN Money*, November 26, 2002, **money.cnn.com/2002/11/26/pf/saving/q_identity/index.htm.**

Chapter 20 **p. 605** Based on information from Charles Gasparino and Randall Smith, "Wall Street Deal May End IPO Suits," *Wall Street Journal*, November 4, 2002, **www.wsj.com;** Brock N. Meeks, "House Panel Digs Deeper into IPOs," *MSNBC*, September 4, 2002, **www.msnbc.com/news/803612.asp;** Brock N. Meeks, "WorldCom Execs Got IPO Windfall," *MSNBC*, August 27, 2002, **www.msnbc.com/news/799919.asp. p. 609** Based on information from David Henry and Louis Lavelle, "Exploring Options," *BusinessWeek*, February 3, 2003, pp. 78–79; Justin Fox, "Reform Is the Only Option (for Stock Options, That Is)," *Fortune*, August 12, 2002, **www.fortune.com/fortune/investing/articles/0,15114,369130,00.html;** Cait Murphy, "Stop Trashing Stock Options," *Fortune Small Business*, November 1, 2002, **www.fortune.com/fortune/**

print/0,15935,389901,00.html. p. 616 Based on information from Shelley Emling, "Wall Street Firms Settle Conflict Case," Atlanta Journal-Constitution, December 21, 2002, p. F1; Jeremy Kahn, "Splitting Up the Street," *Fortune*, October 28, 2002, pp. 30–31; Mike McNamee, "A Clean Break for the Street?" *BusinessWeek*, October 14, 2002, pp. 42–43.

Chapter 21 **p. 634** Based on information from Donna Rosato, "New 401(k) Tool, But Who Needs It?" *New York Times*, February 2, 2003, sec. 3, p. 9; "Is It Time to Switch to a Roth IRA?" *CPA Client Bulletin*, November 2002, p. 5; "Where Should You Turn?" *BusinessWeek Online*, **www.businessweek.com/magazine/content/02_30/b3793606.html,** July 29, 2002; **www.wellsfargo.com. p. 645** Based on information from Andy Serwer, "The Oracle of Everything," *Fortune*, November 11, 2002, pp. 68–82; Yi-Hsin Chang, "Getting to Know Warren," *The Motley Fool*, April 29, 1999, **www.fool.com specials/1999/sp990429Bershire002.htm. p. 653** Based on information from Virginia Munger Kahn, "Online Advice Finds Few Takers," *New York Times*, March 2, 2003, sec. 3, p. 6; Justin Fox, "Investor's Guide 2003," *Fortune*, December 3, 2002, **www.fortune.com http://finance.yahoo.com;** and **http://university.smartmoney.com p. 665** Based on information from Donna Hood Crecca, "Higher Calling," *Chain Leader*, December 2002, p. 14; Finagle A Bagel website at **www.finagleabagle.com** and company profile; *Boston* magazine website at **www.bostonmagazine.com;** interview with Laura B. Trust and Alan Litchman, February 25, 2003.

PHOTO CREDITS

Part I: AP/Wide World Photos.

Chapter 1: p. 3, © CORBIS; p. 8, Reprinted with permission of Deluna by Design, Inc./Photo by Mathew Wilson; p. 10, Brad Stringer; p. 12, PhotoDisc Collection/Getty Images; p. 13, Mark Leong; p. 20, David Young-Wolff/PhotoEdit, Inc.; p. 24, Bettmann/CORBIS; p. 26, Douglas Woods; p. 30, Mitch Hrdlicka/Getty Images.

Chapter 2: p. 34, PhotoDisc Collection/Getty Images; p. 36, PhotoDisc Collection/Getty Images; p. 37, Image Courtesy of **www.adbusters.org;** p. 41, Mark Wilson/Getty Images; p. 43, AP/Wide World Photos; p. 55, Jim West/The Image Works; p. 57, Sam Kittner; p. 59, Reprinted with permission of the Virginia Department of Environmental Quality 2003.

Chapter 3: p. 68, AP/Wide World Photos; p. 72, Christopher Anderson/VII; p. 75, © CORBIS; p. 76, Kelly Guenther; p. 80, AP/Wide World Photos; p. 85, AP/Wide World Photos; p. 89 (top), Toru Yamanaka/AFP/CORBIS; p. 89 (bottom), Mark Leong; p. 97, © Artville; p. 100, Copyright © 2003 by Houghton Mifflin Company. All rights reserved.

Part II: Tim Boyle/Getty Images.

Chapter 4: p. 107, AP/Wide World Photos; p. 114, Ryan McVay/Getty Images; p. 115, Roger Jerkovich; p. 117, © 2003 Dell Computer Corp. All rights reserved.; p. 118, Marvin Christian; p. 124, Cary Herz for the *New York Times;* p. 128, AP/Wide World Photos.

Chapter 5: p. 136, Ryan McVay/Getty Images; p. 139, Sammy Davis; p. 141, Reprinted with permission of 8minutedating.com/Photography by Kathy Tarantola; p. 146, Courtesy of The Company Corporation®; p. 148, AP/Wide World Photos; p. 149, Jeff Greenberg/PhotoEdit; p. 153, Essdras M. Suarez/Republished with permission of Globe Newspaper Company, Inc. from February 18th issue of *The Boston Globe*, © 2002; p. 156, AP/Wide World Photos; p. 161, Don Farrall/Getty Images.

Chapter 6: p. 166, AP/Wide World Photos; p. 168, Norbert Schwerin/The Image Works; p. 171, Sammy Davis; p. 172, PhotoDisc Collection/Getty Images; p. 173, Larry Ford; p. 175, Courtesy of BitFlip Interactive Group, Inc.; p. 181, Courtesy of Intelliseek, Inc. & PlanetFeedback; p. 183, Reprinted with permission of Learning Express, Inc. © 2003; p.192, Copyright © 2003 by Houghton Mifflin Company. All rights reserved.

Part III: Frank Schwere.

Chapter 7: p. 197, Francis Dean/The Image Works; p. 200, David Deal; p. 202, Brian Warling; p. 204, Peter DaSilva/Corbis Sygma; p. 205, Simon Griffiths; p. 209, Nathaniel Welch; p. 210, Concept Icons Comstock Images; p. 215, AP/Wide World Photos; p. 218, PhotoDisc Collection/Getty Images.

Chapter 8: p. 222, Steve Raymer/CORBIS; p. 223 (left), Courtesy of Xerox Corporation; p. 223 (right), Courtesy of Michael Colca; p. 226, Keith Dannemiller/Corbis SABA; p. 230, Stuart Isett/Polaris Images Corporation; p. 234, Chris Windsor/Getty Images; p. 235, Charlie Archambault for *U. S. New & World Report;* p. 238, Bill Cramer; p. 244, PhotoDisc Collection/Getty Images.

Chapter 9: p. 248, AP/Wide World Photos; p. 250, Lester Lefkowitz/CORBIS; p. 253, Amy Etra/PhotoEdit, Inc.; p. 255, Steven Ahlgren; p. 256, PhotoDisc Collection/Getty Images; p. 257, PAXTON; p. 267, Josef Polleross/The Image Works; p. 271, Munshi Ahmed; p. 276, Copyright © 2003 by Houghton Mifflin Company. All rights reserved.

Part IV: AP/Wide World Photos.

Chapter 10: p. 281, Norbert Schwerin/The Image Works; p. 283, Pablo Bartholomew/NetPhotograph.com; p. 284, Courtesy of IfulFill.com; p. 286, Reprinted with permission of Newton Wellesley Hospital; p. 289 (top), Reprinted with permission of Monster.com; p. 289 (bottom), AP/Wide World Photo; p. 296, Reprinted with permission of CIGNA and CIPI. All rights reserved.; p. 299, AP/Wide World Photos; p. 301, Steve Cole/Getty Images; p. 304, Spencer Grant/PhotoEdit, Inc.; p. 308, PhotoDisc Collection/Getty Images.

Chapter 11: p. 312, David Young-Wolff/PhotoEdit, Inc.; p. 313, Nancy Newberry; p. 322, Stuart Isett/Polaris Images Corporation; p. 325, PhotoDisc Collection/Getty Images; p. 328, Brad Norton; p. 329, Bridget Barrett; p. 330, AP/Wide World Photos; p. 334, PhotoDisc Collection/Getty Images.

Chapter 12: p. 338, EyeWire/Getty Images; p. 340, © CORBIS; p. 342, AP/Wide World Photos; p. 347, Bettmann/CORBIS; p. 351, Ann States; p. 354, Ryan McVay/Getty Images; p. 357, AP/Wide World Photos; p. 365, Copyright © 2003 by Houghton Mifflin Company. All rights reserved.

Part V: David McNew/Getty Images.

Chapter 13: p. 369, Photo Courtesy of Harley Davidson/Getty Images; p. 372, Reprinted with permission of First Banks, Inc.; p. 374, Reprinted with permission of YMCA of the USA.; p. 378, Reproduced with permission of Planet Propaganda; p. 382, Reprinted with permission of DoubleClick, Inc.; p. 386, Michael Newman/PhotoEdit, Inc.; p. 388, Reprinted with permission of Neutrogena Corp.; p. 389, Tim Boyle/Getty Images; p. 390, © Squared Studios/Getty Images; p. 394, PhotoDisc Collection/Getty Images.

Chapter 14: p. 398, Spencer Grant/PhotoEdit, Inc.; p. 400 (left), Courtesy of A. T. Cross Company; p. 400 (right), Reprinted with permission of Golden Grain Company; p. 401, Courtesy of Xerox Corporation; p. 403, Reuters NewMedia Inc./CORBIS; p. 404, PhotoDisc Collection/Getty Images; p. 406, Bonnie Kamin/PhotoEdit, Inc.; p. 411, The Tabasco® print ad illustration on page 411 is copyrighted © (1992) by Mcllhenny Company, Avery Island, Louisiana 70513 and is used with permission of Mcllhenny Company. The TABASCO® marks, bottle, and label designs are registered trademarks and service marks exclusively of Mcllhenny Company, Avery Island, LA 70513; p.414, Felicia Martinez/PhotoEdit, Inc.; p. 417, Courtesy of JetBlue Airways; p. 418, Reprinted with permission of Hacienda Mexican Restaurants and Riley & Co.; p. 424, Dennis MacDonald/PhotoEdit, Inc.

Chapter 15: p. 434, PhotoDisc Collection/Getty Images; p. 438 (left), David Young-Wolff/PhotoEdit, Inc.; p. 438 (right), Bonn Sequenz/Imapress/The Image Works; p. 439, Courtesy of Menlo WorldWide; p. 448, Sonda Dawes/The Image Works; p. 449 (left), Dion Ogust/The Image Works; p. 449 (right), Maya Barnes/The Image Works; p. 450, PhotoDisc Collection/Getty Images; p. 454, Tony Freeman/PhotoEdit, Inc.; p. 456, Roger Ball/CORBIS; p. 457, Reprinted with permission of Bax Global/Photography by Bill Frymire/Masterfile; p. 462, PhotoDisc Collection/Getty Images.

Chapter 16: p. 466, David Young-Wolff/PhotoEdit, Inc.; p. 467, John Maier, Jr./The Image Works; p. 470, Reproduced with permission by Bozell Worldwide, Inc. As Agent for National Fluid Milk Processor Promotion Board. All Rights Reserved.; p. 473, Courtesy of American Advertising Federation; p. 475, Reprinted with permission of Jersey Gardens; p. 481, © Squared Studios/Getty Images; p. 483, Jonathan Nourok/PhotoEdit, Inc.; p. 484, The Detroit News/Gamma Press; p. 494, Copyright © 2003 by Houghton Mifflin Company. All rights reserved.

Part VI: Frank Schwere.

Chapter 17: p. 499, Norbert Schwerin/The Image Works; p. 501, Amanda Friedman; p. 505, © Hoovers Online; p. 507, PAXTON; p. 509, Reprinted with permission of Reference USA; p. 515, Bryan Mullennix/Getty Images; p. 516, Susan Plannmuller; p. 521, Reprinted with permission of Monster.com; p. 527, PhotoDisc Collection/Getty Images.

Chapter 18: p. 532, PhotoDisc Collection/Getty Images; p. 535, John Gress/Corbis Sygma; p. 537, AFP/CORBIS; p. 542, Stephane Herbert/Corbis Sygma; p. 544, Steve Cole/Getty Images; p. 548, Sulley/WirePix/The Image Works; p. 550, Reprinted with permission by Boise® Office Solutions; p. 554, Najlah Feanny/Corbis SABA; p. 562, Copyright © 2003 by Houghton Mifflin Company. All rights reserved.

Part VII: Mario Tama/Getty Images.

Chapter 19: p. 567, David Young-Wolff/PhotoEdit, Inc.; p. 569, Paul J. Richards/AFP/Getty Images; p. 575, AP/Wide World Photos; p. 580, Courtesy of Chittenden Bank; p. 584, Ann States; p. 585, AP/Wide World Photos; p. 587, AP/Wide World Photos; p. 590, Jennifer Pottheiser.

Chapter 20: p. 600, Chad Baker/Ryan McVay/Getty Images; p. 604, PAXTON; p. 608, Larry Ford; p. 613, Wade Alexander Payne; p. 616, PhotoDisc Collection/Getty Images; p. 617, Reuters NewMedia Inc./CORBIS; p. 618, David L. Ryan/Republished with permission of Globe Newspaper Company, Inc., from May 8th issue of *The Boston Globe*, © 2002; p. 620, Andrea Artz; p. 622, © David R. Frazier Photolibrary, Inc.; p. 626, Steve Cole/Getty Images.

Chapter 21: p. 630, PhotoDisc Collection/Getty Images; p. 632, Jim Caldwell; p. 637, AP/Wide World Photos; p. 645, AP/Wide World Photos; p. 646, Mark Richards/PhotoEdit, Inc.; p. 655, David Young-Wolff/PhotoEdit, Inc.; p. 665, Copyright © 2003 by Houghton Mifflin Company. All rights reserved.

ame Index

Subject Index